ESSENTIAL READINGS IN WORLD POLITICS

WORLD POLITICS

THIRD EDITION

i

The Norton Series in World Politics
Jack Snyder, General Editor

ESSENTIAL READINGS IN WORLD POLITICS

THIRD EDITION

EDITED BY

KAREN A. MINGST AND JACK L. SNYDER

W.W. NORTON & COMPANY
New York · London

Copyright © 2008, 2004, 2001 by W. W. Norton & Company, Inc.

All rights reserved
Printed in the United States of America

Library of Congress Cataloging-in-Publication Data

Essential readings in world politics / edited by Karen A. Mingst and Jack L.
Snyder. — 3rd ed.
p. cm. — (The Norton series in world politics)
Includes bibliographical references.
ISBN 978-0-393-93114-3 (pbk.)
1. International relations.   2. World politics.   I. Mingst, Karen A., 1947–
II. Snyder, Jack L.
JZ1305.E85   2008
327—dc22
2007049147

W. W. Norton & Company, Inc., 500 Fifth Avenue, New York, N.Y. 10110
www.wwnorton.com
W. W. Norton & Company Ltd., Castle House, 75/76 Wells Street, London W1T 3QT

4   5   6   7   8   9   0

CONTENTS

v

4 THE INTERNATIONAL SYSTEM 126

5 THE STATE 175

6 THE INDIVIDUAL 227

7 IGOS, NGOS, AND INTERNATIONAL LAW 250

8 WAR AND STRIFE 332

9 INTERNATIONAL POLITICAL ECONOMY 478

10 GLOBALIZATION AND GLOBALIZING ISSUES

PREFACE

This reader is a quintessential collaborative effort between the two co-editors. For the first and second editions, the co-editors suggested articles for inclusion, traced the sources, and rejected or accepted them, defending choices to skeptical colleagues. In a flurry of e-mails in 2006, they repeated the process for this new edition. It became apparent early in the process that the co-editors, while both international relations scholars, read very different literatures. This book represents a product of that collaborative process and is all the better for the differences.

The articles have been selected to meet several criteria. First, the collection is designed to augment and amplify the core text, *Essentials of International Relations*, Fourth Edition, by Karen Mingst. The chapters in this book follow those in the text. Second, the selections are purposefully eclectic; that is, key theoretical articles are paired with contemporary pieces found in the popular literature. When possible, articles have been chosen to reflect diverse theoretical perspectives and policy viewpoints. The articles are also both readable and engaging to undergraduates. The co-editors struggled to maintain the integrity of the challenging pieces while making them accessible to undergraduates at a variety of colleges and universities.

Special thanks go to those individuals who provided reviews of this book and offered suggestions and reflections based on teaching experience. Our product benefited greatly from these evaluations, although had we included all the suggestions, the book would have been thousands of pages! Our W. W. Norton editor, Ann Shin, orchestrated the process, reacting to our suggestions, mediating our differences, and keeping us "on task." To her, we owe a special thanks. Mollie Eisenberg guided the manuscript through the editing and production process, a very labor-intensive task. We also thank W. W. Norton's copyediting and production staff for their careful work on this book.

ESSENTIAL READINGS IN
WORLD POLITICS

THIRD EDITION

1 APPROACHES

In Essentials of International Relations, *Karen Mingst introduces theories and approaches used to study international relations. The readings in this section complement that introduction.*

Both historical analysis and philosophical discourse contribute to the study of international relations. In his history of the Peloponnesian War, Thucydides (c. 460 BCE–c. 395 BCE) presents a classic realist/idealist dilemma in the Melian dialogue. The leaders of Melos ponder the fate of the island, deciding whether to fight their antagonists, the Athenians, or to rely on the gods and the enemy of Athens, the Lacedaemonians (also known as Spartans), for their safety. In a key work from philosophical discourse, the philosopher Immanuel Kant (1724–1804) posited that a group of republican states with representative forms of government that were accountable to their citizens would be able to form an effective league of peace. That observation has generated a plethora of theoretical and empirical research known as the democratic peace debate, discussed in more detail in Essentials of International Relations, *Chapter 5.*

Among the persistent debates in international relations is the controversy over empire—whether an empire exists and why a state would seek to be an empire. The collapse of the Soviet Union and the assertive response of the George W. Bush administration to the September 11, 2001, terrorist attacks have spurred a lively debate on what some have called the new American empire. By far the most influential theory of imperialism has been that of V. I. Lenin (1870–1924), leader of the Russian Bolshevik Revolution and the Soviet Union. Marxist theories have declined in popularity since the Soviet collapse, but some readers may find that Lenin's 1916 analysis of the relationship between the global spread of capital and imperial war retains some contemporary resonance. (See Mingst, Essentials, *Chapter 3.)*

JACK SNYDER

ONE WORLD, RIVAL THEORIES

The U.S. government has endured several painful rounds of scrutiny as it tries to figure out what went wrong on Sept. 11, 2001. The intelligence community faces radical restructuring; the military has made a sharp pivot to face a new enemy; and a vast new federal agency has blossomed to coordinate homeland security. But did September 11 signal a failure of theory on par with the failures of intelligence and policy? Familiar theories about how the world works still dominate academic debate. Instead of radical change, academia has adjusted existing theories to meet new realities. Has this approach succeeded? Does international relations theory still have something to tell policymakers?

Six years ago, political scientist Stephen M. Walt published a much-cited survey of the field in these pages ("One World, Many Theories," Spring 1998). He sketched out three dominant approaches: realism, liberalism, and an updated form of idealism called "constructivism." Walt argued that these theories shape both public discourse and policy analysis. Realism focuses on the shifting distribution of power among states. Liberalism highlights the rising number of democracies and the turbulence of democratic transitions. Idealism illuminates the changing norms of sovereignty, human rights, and international justice, as well as the increased potency of religious ideas in politics.

The influence of these intellectual constructs extends far beyond university classrooms and tenure committees. Policymakers and public commentators invoke elements of all these theories when articulating solutions to global security dilemmas. President George W. Bush promises to fight terror by spreading liberal democracy to the Middle East and claims that

From *Foreign Policy* (Nov. / Dec. 2004): 53–62.

skeptics "who call themselves 'realists' . . . have lost contact with a fundamental reality" that "America is always more secure when freedom is on the march." Striking a more eclectic tone, National Security Advisor Condoleezza Rice, a former Stanford University political science professor, explains that the new Bush doctrine is an amalgam of pragmatic realism and Wilsonian liberal theory. During the recent presidential campaign, Sen. John Kerry sounded remarkably similar: "Our foreign policy has achieved greatness," he said, "only when it has combined realism and idealism."

International relations theory also shapes and informs the thinking of the public intellectuals who translate and disseminate academic ideas. During the summer of 2004, for example, two influential framers of neoconservative thought, columnist Charles Krauthammer and political scientist Francis Fukuyama, collided over the implications of these conceptual paradigms for U.S. policy in Iraq. Backing the Bush administration's Middle East policy, Krauthammer argued for an assertive amalgam of liberalism and realism, which he called "democratic realism." Fukuyama claimed that Krauthammer's faith in the use of force and the feasibility of democratic change in Iraq blinds him to the war's lack of legitimacy, a failing that "hurts both the realist part of our agenda, by diminishing our actual power, and the idealist portion of it, by undercutting our appeal as the embodiment of certain ideas and values."

Indeed, when realism, liberalism, and idealism enter the policymaking arena and public debate, they can sometimes become intellectual window dressing for simplistic worldviews. Properly understood, however, their policy implications are subtle and multifaceted. Realism instills a pragmatic appreciation of the role of

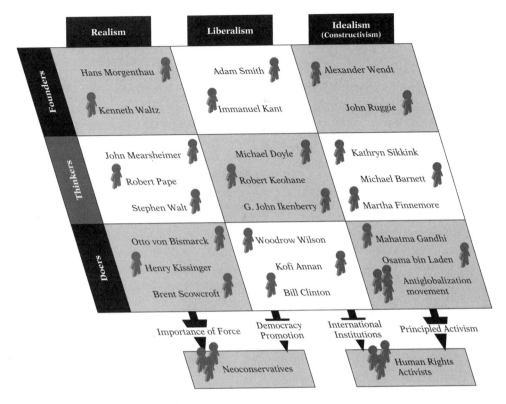

Figure 1.1. From Theory to Practice

power but also warns that states will suffer if they overreach. Liberalism highlights the cooperative potential of mature democracies, especially when working together through effective institutions, but it also notes democracies' tendency to crusade against tyrannies and the propensity of emerging democracies to collapse into violent ethnic turmoil. Idealism stresses that a consensus on values must underpin any stable political order, yet it also recognizes that forging such a consensus often requires an ideological struggle with the potential for conflict.

Each theory offers a filter for looking at a complicated picture. As such, they help explain the assumptions behind political rhetoric about foreign policy. Even more important, the theories act as a powerful check on each other.

Deployed effectively, they reveal the weaknesses in arguments that can lead to misguided policies.

Is Realism Still Realistic?

At realism's core is the belief that international affairs is a struggle for power among self-interested states. Although some of realism's leading lights, notably the late University of Chicago political scientist Hans J. Morgenthau, are deeply pessimistic about human nature, it is not a theory of despair. Clearsighted states can mitigate the causes of war by finding ways to reduce the danger they pose to each other. Nor is realism necessarily amoral; its advocates emphasize that a ruthless pragmatism about power can actually yield a more peaceful world, if not an ideal one.

In liberal democracies, realism is the theory that everyone loves to hate. Developed largely by European émigrés at the end of World War II, realism claimed to be an antidote to the naive belief that international institutions and law alone can preserve peace, a misconception that this new generation of scholars believed had paved the way to war. In recent decades, the realist approach has been most fully articulated by U.S. theorists, but it still has broad appeal outside the United States as well. The influential writer and editor Josef Joffe articulately comments on Germany's strong realist traditions. (Mindful of the overwhelming importance of U.S. power to Europe's development, Joffe once called the United States "Europe's pacifier.") China's current foreign policy is grounded in realist ideas that date back millennia. As China modernizes its economy and enters international institutions such as the World Trade Organization, it behaves in a way that realists understand well: developing its military slowly but surely as its economic power grows, and avoiding a confrontation with superior U.S. forces.

Realism gets some things right about the post-9/11 world. The continued centrality of military strength and the persistence of conflict, even in this age of global economic interdependence, does not surprise realists. The theory's most obvious success is its ability to explain the United States' forceful military response to the September 11 terrorist attacks. When a state grows vastly more powerful than any opponent, realists expect that it will eventually use that power to expand its sphere of domination, whether for security, wealth, or other motives. The United States employed its military power in what some deemed an imperial fashion in large part because it could.

It is harder for the normally state-centric realists to explain why the world's only superpower announced a war against al Qaeda, a nonstate terrorist organization. How can realist theory account for the importance of powerful and violent individuals in a world of states? Realists point out that the central battles in the "war on terror" have been fought against two states (Afghanistan and Iraq), and that states, not the United Nations or Human Rights Watch, have led the fight against terrorism.

Even if realists acknowledge the importance of nonstate actors as a challenge to their assumptions, the theory still has important things to say about the behavior and motivations of these groups. The realist scholar Robert A. Pape, for example, has argued that suicide terrorism can be a rational, realistic strategy for the leadership of national liberation movements seeking to expel democratic powers that occupy their homelands. Other scholars apply standard theories of conflict in anarchy to explain ethnic conflict in collapsed states. Insights from political realism—a profound and wide-ranging intellectual tradition rooted in the enduring philosophy of Thucydides, Niccolò Machiavelli, and Thomas Hobbes—are hardly rendered obsolete because some nonstate groups are now able to resort to violence.

Post-9/11 developments seem to undercut one of realism's core concepts: the balance of power. Standard realist doctrine predicts that weaker states will ally to protect themselves from stronger ones and thereby form and reform a balance of power. So, when Germany unified in the late 19th century and became Europe's leading military and industrial power, Russia and France (and later, Britain) soon aligned to counter its power. Yet no combination of states or other powers can challenge the United States militarily, and no balancing coalition is imminent. Realists are scrambling to find a way to fill this hole in the center of their theory. Some theorists speculate that the United States' geographic distance and its relatively benign intentions have tempered the balancing instinct. Second-tier powers tend to worry more about their immediate neighbors and even see the United States as a helpful source of stability in regions such as East Asia. Other scholars insist that armed resistance by U.S. foes in Iraq, Afghanistan, and elsewhere, and foot-dragging by its formal allies actually constitute the beginnings of balancing against U.S. hegemony. The United States' strained relations with Europe offer ambiguous evidence: French and German opposition to recent U.S. policies could be seen as classic balancing, but they do not resist U.S. dominance militarily. Instead, these states have tried to undermine U.S. moral legitimacy and constrain the superpower in a web of multilateral institutions and treaty regimes—not what standard realist theory predicts.

These conceptual difficulties notwithstanding, realism is alive, well, and creatively reassessing how its root principles relate to the post-9/11 world. Despite changing configurations of power, realists remain steadfast in stressing that policy must be based on positions of real strength, not on either empty bravado or hopeful illusions about a world without conflict. In the run-up to the recent Iraq war, several prominent realists signed a public letter criticizing what they perceived as an exercise in American hubris. And in the continuing aftermath of that war, many prominent thinkers called for a return to realism. A group of scholars and public intellectuals (myself included) even formed the Coalition for a Realistic Foreign Policy, which calls for a more modest and prudent approach. Its statement of principles argues that "the move toward empire must be halted immediately." The coalition, though politically diverse, is largely inspired by realist theory. Its membership of seemingly odd bedfellows—including former Democratic Sen. Gary Hart and Scott McConnell, the executive editor of the *American Conservative* magazine—illustrates the power of international relations theory to cut through often ephemeral political labels and carry debate to the underlying assumptions.

The Divided House of Liberalism

The liberal school of international relations theory, whose most famous proponents were German philosopher Immanuel Kant and U.S. President Woodrow Wilson, contends that realism has a stunted vision that cannot account for progress in relations between nations. Liberals foresee a slow but inexorable journey away from the anarchic world the realists envision, as trade and finance forge ties between nations, and democratic norms spread. Because elected leaders are accountable to the people (who bear the burdens of war), liberals expect that democracies will not attack each other and will regard each other's regimes as legitimate and nonthreatening. Many liberals also believe that the rule of law and transparency of democratic processes make it easier to sustain international cooperation, especially when these practices are enshrined in multilateral institutions.

Liberalism has such a powerful presence that the entire U.S. political spectrum, from neoconservatives to human rights advocates, assumes it as largely self-evident. Outside the United States, as well, the liberal view that only elected governments are legitimate and politically reliable has taken hold. So it is no surprise that liberal themes are constantly invoked as a response to today's security dilemmas. But the last several years have also produced a fierce tug-of-war between disparate strains of liberal thought. Supporters and critics of the Bush administration, in particular, have emphasized very different elements of the liberal canon.

For its part, the Bush administration highlights democracy promotion while largely turning its back on the international institutions that most liberal theorists champion. The U.S. National Security Strategy of September 2002, famous for its support of preventive war, also dwells on the need to promote democracy as a means of fighting terrorism and promoting peace. The Millennium Challenge program allocates part of U.S. foreign aid according to how well countries improve their performance on several measures of democratization and the rule of law. The White House's steadfast support for promoting democracy in the Middle East—even with turmoil in Iraq and rising anti-Americanism in the Arab world—demonstrates liberalism's emotional and rhetorical power.

In many respects, liberalism's claim to be a wise policy guide has plenty of hard data behind it. During the last two decades, the proposition that democratic institutions and values help states cooperate with each other is among the most intensively studied in all of international relations, and it has held up reasonably well. Indeed, the belief that democracies never fight wars against each other is the closest thing we have to an iron law in social science.

But the theory has some very important corollaries, which the Bush administration glosses over as it draws upon the democracy-promotion element of liberal thought. Columbia University political scientist Michael W. Doyle's articles on democratic peace warned that, though democracies never fight each other, they are prone to launch messianic struggles against warlike authoritarian regimes to "make the world safe for democracy." It was precisely American democracy's tendency to oscillate between self-righteous crusading and jaded isolationism that prompted early Cold War realists' call for a more calculated, prudent foreign policy.

Countries transitioning to democracy, with weak political institutions, are more likely than other states to get into international and civil wars. In the last 15 years, wars or large-scale civil violence followed experiments with mass electoral democracy in countries including Armenia, Burundi, Ethiopia, Indonesia, Russia, and the former Yugoslavia. In part, this violence is caused by ethnic groups' competing demands for national self-determination, often a problem in new, multiethnic democracies. More fundamental, emerging democracies often have nascent political institutions that cannot channel popular demands in constructive directions or credibly enforce compromises among rival groups. In this setting, democratic accountability works imperfectly, and nationalist politicians can hijack public debate. The violence that is vexing the experiment with democracy in Iraq is just the latest chapter in a turbulent story that began with the French Revolution.

Contemporary liberal theory also points out that the rising democratic tide creates the presumption that all nations ought to enjoy the benefits of self-determination. Those left out may undertake violent campaigns to secure democratic rights. Some of these movements direct their struggles against democratic or semidemocratic states that they consider occupying powers—such as in Algeria in the 1950s, or Chechnya, Palestine, and the Tamil region of Sri Lanka today. Violence may also be directed at democratic supporters of oppressive regimes, much like the U.S. backing of the governments of Saudi Arabia and Egypt. Democratic regimes make attractive targets for terrorist violence by national liberation movements precisely because they are accountable to a cost-conscious electorate.

Nor is it clear to contemporary liberal scholars that nascent democracy and economic liberalism can always cohabitate. Free trade and the multifaceted globalization that advanced democracies promote often buffet transitional societies. World markets' penetration of societies that run on patronage and protectionism can disrupt social relations and spur strife between potential winners and losers. In other cases, universal free trade can make separatism look attractive, as small regions such as Aceh in Indonesia can lay claim to lucrative natural resources. So far, the trade-fueled boom in China has created incentives for improved relations with the advanced democracies, but it has also set the stage for a possible showdown between the relatively wealthy coastal entrepreneurs and the still impoverished rural masses.

While aggressively advocating the virtues of democracy, the Bush administration has shown little patience for these complexities in liberal thought—or for liberalism's emphasis on the importance of international institutions. Far from trying to assure other powers that the United States would adhere to a constitutional order, Bush "unsigned" the International Criminal Court statute, rejected the Kyoto environmental agreement, dictated take-it-or-leave-it arms control changes to Russia, and invaded Iraq despite opposition at the United Nations and among close allies.

Recent liberal theory offers a thoughtful challenge to the administration's policy choices. Shortly

Theories:	Realism	Liberalism	Idealism (Constructivism)
Core Beliefs	Self-interested states compete for power and security	Spread of democracy, global economic ties, and international organizations will strengthen peace	International politics is shaped by persuasive ideas, collective values, culture, and social identities
Key Actors in International Relations	States, which behave similarly regardless of their type of government	States, international institutions, and commercial interests	Promoters of new ideas, transnational activist networks, and nongovernmental organizations
Main Instruments	Military power and state diplomacy	International institutions and global commerce	Ideas and values
Theory's Intellectual Blind Spots	Doesn't account for progress and change in international relations or understanding that legitimacy can be a source of military power	Fails to understand that democratic regimes survive only if they safeguard military power and security; some liberals forget that transitions to democracy are sometimes violent	Does not explain which power structures and social conditions allow for changes in values
What the Theory Explains About the Post-9/11 World	Why the United States responded aggressively to terrorist attacks; the inability of international institutions to restrain military superiority	Why spreading democracy has become such an integral part of current U.S. international security strategy	The increasing role of polemics about values; the importance of transnational political networks (whether terrorists or human rights advocates)
What the Theory Fails to Explain About the Post-9/11 World	The failure of smaller powers to militarily balance the United States; the importance of non-state actors such as al Qaeda; the intense U.S. focus on democratization	Why the United States has failed to work with other democracies through international organizations	Why human rights abuses continue, despite intense activism for humanitarian norms and efforts for international justice

Figure 1.2. The Leading Brands

before September 11, political scientist G. John Ikenberry studied attempts to establish international order by the victors of hegemonic struggles in 1815, 1919, 1945, and 1989. He argued that even the most powerful victor needed to gain the willing cooperation of the vanquished and other weak states by offering a mutually attractive bargain, codified in an international constitutional order. Democratic victors, he found, have the best chance of creating a working constitutional order, such as the Bretton Woods system after World War II, because their transparency and legalism make their promises credible.

Does the Bush administration's resistance to institution building refute Ikenberry's version of liberal theory? Some realists say it does, and that recent events demonstrate that interna-

tional institutions cannot constrain a hegemonic power if its preferences change. But international institutions can nonetheless help coordinate outcomes that are in the long-term mutual interest of both the hegemon and the weaker states. Ikenberry did not contend that hegemonic democracies are immune from mistakes. States can act in defiance of the incentives established by their position in the international system, but they will suffer the consequences and probably learn to correct course. In response to Bush's unilateralist stance, Ikenberry wrote that the incentives for the United States to take the lead in establishing a multilateral constitutional order remain powerful. Sooner or later, the pendulum will swing back.

Idealism's New Clothing

Idealism, the belief that foreign policy is and should be guided by ethical and legal standards, also has a long pedigree. Before World War II forced the United States to acknowledge a less pristine reality, Secretary of State Henry Stimson denigrated espionage on the grounds that "gentlemen do not read each other's mail." During the Cold War, such naive idealism acquired a bad name in the Kissingerian corridors of power and among hardheaded academics. Recently, a new version of idealism—called constructivism by its scholarly adherents—returned to a prominent place in debates on international relations theory. Constructivism, which holds that social reality is created through debate about values, often echoes the themes that human rights and international justice activists sound. Recent events seem to vindicate the theory's resurgence; a theory that emphasizes the role of ideologies, identities, persuasion, and transnational networks is highly relevant to understanding the post-9/11 world.

The most prominent voices in the development of constructivist theory have been American, but Europe's role is significant. European philosophical currents helped establish constructivist theory, and the *European Journal of International Relations* is one of the principal outlets for constructivist work. Perhaps most important, Europe's increasingly legalistic approach to international relations, reflected in the process of forming the European Union out of a collection of sovereign states, provides fertile soil for idealist and constructivist conceptions of international politics.

Whereas realists dwell on the balance of power and liberals on the power of international trade and democracy, constructivists believe that debates about ideas are the fundamental building blocks of international life. Individuals and groups become powerful if they can convince others to adopt their ideas. People's understanding of their interests depends on the ideas they hold. Constructivists find absurd the idea of some identifiable and immutable "national interest," which

some realists cherish. Especially in liberal societies, there is overlap between constructivist and liberal approaches, but the two are distinct. Constructivists contend that their theory is deeper than realism and liberalism because it explains the origins of the forces that drive those competing theories.

For constructivists, international change results from the work of intellectual entrepreneurs who proselytize new ideas and "name and shame" actors whose behavior deviates from accepted standards. Consequently, constructivists often study the role of transnational activist networks—such as Human Rights Watch or the International Campaign to Ban Landmines—in promoting change. Such groups typically uncover and publicize information about violations of legal or moral standards at least rhetorically supported by powerful democracies, including "disappearances" during the Argentine military's rule in the late 1970s, concentration camps in Bosnia, and the huge number of civilian deaths from land mines. This publicity is then used to press governments to adopt specific remedies, such as the establishment of a war crimes tribunal or the adoption of a landmine treaty. These movements often make pragmatic arguments as well as idealistic ones, but their distinctive power comes from the ability to highlight deviations from deeply held norms of appropriate behavior.

Progressive causes receive the most attention from constructivist scholars, but the theory also helps explain the dynamics of illiberal transnational forces, such as Arab nationalism or Islamist extremism. Professor Michael N. Barnett's 1998 book *Dialogues in Arab Politics: Negotiations in Regional Order* examines how the divergence between state borders and transnational Arab political identities requires vulnerable leaders to contend for legitimacy with radicals throughout the Arab world—a dynamic that often holds moderates hostage to opportunists who take extreme stances.

Constructivist thought can also yield broader insights about the ideas and values in the current international order. In his 2001 book, *Revolu-*

tions in Sovereignty: How Ideas Shaped Modern International Relations, political scientist Daniel Philpott demonstrates how the religious ideas of the Protestant Reformation helped break down the medieval political order and provided a conceptual basis for the modern system of secular sovereign states. After September 11, Philpott focused on the challenge to the secular international order posed by political Islam. "The attacks and the broader resurgence of public religion," he says, ought to lead international relations scholars to "direct far more energy to understanding the impetuses behind movements across the globe that are reorienting purposes and policies." He notes that both liberal human rights movements and radical Islamic movements have transnational structures and principled motivations that challenge the traditional supremacy of self-interested states in international politics. Because constructivists believe that ideas and values helped shape the modern state system, they expect intellectual constructs to be decisive in transforming it—for good or ill.

When it comes to offering advice, however, constructivism points in two seemingly incompatible directions. The insight that political orders arise from shared understanding highlights the need for dialogue across cultures about the appropriate rules of the game. This prescription dovetails with liberalism's emphasis on establishing an agreed international constitutional order. And, yet, the notion of cross-cultural dialogue sits awkwardly with many idealists' view that they already know right and wrong. For these idealists, the essential task is to shame rights abusers and cajole powerful actors into promoting proper values and holding perpetrators accountable to international (generally Western) standards. As with realism and liberalism, constructivism can be many things to many people.

Stumped by Change

None of the three theoretical traditions has a strong ability to explain change—a significant weakness in such turbulent times. Realists failed to predict the end of the Cold War, for example. Even after it happened, they tended to assume that the new system would become multipolar ("back to the future," as the scholar John J. Mearsheimer put it). Likewise, the liberal theory of democratic peace is stronger on what happens after states become democratic than in predicting the timing of democratic transitions, let alone prescribing how to make transitions happen peacefully. Constructivists are good at describing changes in norms and ideas, but they are weak on the material and institutional circumstances necessary to support the emergence of consensus about new values and ideas.

With such uncertain guidance from the theoretical realm, it is no wonder that policymakers, activists, and public commentators fall prey to simplistic or wishful thinking about how to effect change by, say, invading Iraq or setting up an International Criminal Court. In lieu of a good theory of change, the most prudent course is to use the insights of each of the three theoretical traditions as a check on the irrational exuberance of the others. Realists should have to explain whether policies based on calculations of power have sufficient legitimacy to last. Liberals should consider whether nascent democratic institutions can fend off powerful interests that oppose them, or how international institutions can bind a hegemonic power inclined to go its own way. Idealists should be asked about the strategic, institutional, or material conditions in which a set of ideas is likely to take hold.

Theories of international relations claim to explain the way international politics works, but each of the currently prevailing theories falls well short of that goal. One of the principal contributions that international relations theory can make is not predicting the future but providing the vocabulary and conceptual framework to ask hard questions of those who think that changing the world is easy.

THUCYDIDES

MELIAN DIALOGUE

adapted by Suresht Bald

It was the sixteenth year of the Peloponnesian War, but for the last six years the two great feuding empires headed by Athens and Sparta (Lacedaemon) had avoided open hostile action against each other. Ten years into the war they had signed a treaty of peace and friendship; however, this treaty did not dissipate the distrust that existed between them. Each feared the other's hegemonic designs on the Peloponnese and sought to increase its power to thwart the other's ambitions. Without openly attacking the other, each used persuasion, coercion, and subversion to strengthen itself and weaken its rival. This struggle for hegemony by Athens and Sparta was felt most acutely by small, hitherto "independent" states who were now being forced to take sides in the bipolar Greek world of the fifth century B.C. One such state was Melos.

Despite being one of the few island colonies of Sparta, Melos had remained neutral in the struggle between Sparta and Athens. Its neutrality, however, was unacceptable to the Athenians, who, accompanied by overwhelming military and naval power, arrived in Melos to pressure it into submission. After strategically positioning their powerful fleet, the Athenian generals sent envoys to Melos to negotiate the island's surrender.

The commissioners of Melos agreed to meet the envoys in private. They were afraid the Athenians, known for their rhetorical skills, might sway the people if allowed a public forum. The envoys came with an offer that if the Melians submitted and became part of the Athenian em-

From Thucydides, *Complete Writings: The Peloponnesian War*, trans. Richard Crawley (New York: Modern Library, 1951), adapted by Suresht Bald, Williamette University.

pire, their people and their possessions would not be harmed. The Melians argued that by the law of nations they had the right to remain neutral, and no nation had the right to attack without provocation. Having been a free state for seven hundred years they were not ready to give up that freedom. Thucydides captures the exchange between the Melian commissioners and the Athenian envoys:

> MELIANS: . . . All we can reasonably expect from this negotiation is war, if we prove to have right on our side and refuse to submit, and in the contrary case, slavery.

> ATHENIANS: . . . We shall not trouble you with specious pretenses—either of how we have a right to our empire because we overthrew the Mede, or are now attacking you because of the wrong that you have done us—and make a long speech that would not be believed; and in return we hope that you, instead of thinking to influence us by saying that you did not join the Lacedaemonians, although their colonists, or that you have done us no wrong, will aim at what is feasible, . . . since you know as well as we do that right, as the world goes, is only in question between equals in power, while the strong do what they can and the weak suffer what they want. (331)

The Melians pointed out that it was in the interest of all states to respect the laws of nations: "you should not destroy what is our common protection, the privilege of being allowed in danger to invoke what is fair and right. . . ." (331) They reminded the Athenians that a day might come when the Athenians themselves would need such protection.

But the Athenians were not persuaded. To them, Melos' submission was in the interest of their empire, and Melos.

MELIANS: And how pray, could it turn out as good for us to serve as for you to rule?

ATHENIANS: Because you would have the advantage of submitting before suffering the worst, and we should gain by not destroying you.

MELIANS: So you would not consent to our being neutral, friends instead of enemies, but allies of neither side.

ATHENIANS: No; for your hostility cannot so much hurt us as your friendship will be an argument to our subjects of our weakness, and your enmity of our power. (332)

When the Melians asked if that was their "idea of equity," the Athenians responded,

As far as right goes . . . one has as much of it as the other, and if any maintain their independence it is because they are strong, and that if we do not molest them it is because we are afraid. . . . (332)

By subjugating the Melians the Athenians hoped not only to extend their empire but also to improve their image and thus their security. To allow the weaker Melians to remain free, according to the Athenians, would reflect negatively on Athenian power.

Aware of their weak position the Melians hoped that the justice of their cause would gain them the support of the gods, "and what we want in power will be made up by the alliance with the Lacedaemonians, who are bound, if only for very shame, to come to the aid of their kindred."

ATHENIANS: . . . Of the gods we believe, and of men we know, that by a necessary law of their nature they rule wherever they can. And it is not as if we were the first to make this law, or to act upon it when made: we found it existing before us, and will leave it to exist for ever after us; all we do is to make use of it, knowing that you and everybody else having the same power as we have, would do the same as we do. Thus, as far as the gods are concerned we have no fear and no reason to fear that we shall be at a disadvantage. But . . . your notion about the Lacedaemonians, which leads you to believe that shame will make them help you, here we bless your simplicity but do not envy your folly. The Lacedaemonians . . . are conspicuous in considering what is agreeable honourable, and what is expedient just. . . . Your strongest arguments depend upon hope and the future, and your actual resources are too scanty as compared to those arrayed against you, for you to come out victorious. You will therefore show great blindness of judgment, unless, after allowing us to retire you can find some counsel more prudent than this. (334–36)

The envoys then left the conference, giving the Melians the opportunity to deliberate on the Athenian offer and decide the best course for them to follow.

The Melians decided to stand by the position they had taken at the conference with the Athenian envoys. They refused to submit, placing their faith in the gods and the Lacedaemonians. Though they asked the Athenians to accept their neutrality and leave Melos, the Athenians started preparations for war.

In the war that ensued the Melians were soundly defeated. The Athenians showed no mercy, killing all the adult males and selling the women and children as slaves. Subsequently, they sent out five hundred colonists to settle in Melos, which became an Athenian colony.

*   *   *

IMMANUEL KANT

TO PERPETUAL PEACE:
A PHILOSOPHICAL SKETCH

*   *   *

The state of peace among men living in close proximity is not the natural state * * * ; instead, the natural state is a one of war, which does not just consist in open hostilities, but also in the constant and enduring threat of them. The state of peace must therefore be *established*, for the suspension of hostilities does not provide the security of peace, and unless this security is pledged by one neighbor to another (which can happen only in a state of *lawfulness*), the latter, from whom such security has been requested, can treat the former as an enemy.

First Definitive Article of Perpetual Peace: The Civil Constitution of Every Nation Should Be Republican

The sole established constitution that follows from the idea of an original contract, the one on which all of a nation's just legislation must be based, is republican. For, first, it accords with the principles of the *freedom* of the members of a society (as men), second, it accords with the principles of the *dependence* of everyone on a single, common [source of] legislation (as subjects), and

From Immanuel Kant, *Perpetual Peace, and Other Essays on Politics, History, and Morals*, trans. Ted Humphrey (Indianapolis: Hackett Publishing, 1983), 110–18. Both the author's and the translator's notes have been omitted. Bracketed editorial insertions are the translator's.

third, it accords with the law of the equality of them all (as citizens). Thus, so far as [the matter of] right is concerned, republicanism is the original foundation of all forms of civil constitution. Thus, the only question remaining is this, does it also provide the only foundation for perpetual peace?

Now in addition to the purity of its origin, a purity whose source is the pure concept of right, the republican constitution also provides for this desirable result, namely, perpetual peace, and the reason for this is as follows: If (as must inevitably be the case, given this form of constitution) the consent of the citizenry is required in order to determine whether or not there will be war, it is natural that they consider all its calamities before committing themselves to so risky a game. (Among these are doing the fighting themselves, paying the costs of war from their own resources, having to repair at great sacrifice the war's devastation, and, finally, the ultimate evil that would make peace itself better, never being able—because of new and constant wars—to expunge the burden of debt.) By contrast, under a nonrepublican constitution, where subjects are not citizens, the easiest thing in the world to do is to declare war. Here the ruler is not a fellow citizen, but the nation's owner, and war does not affect his table, his hunt, his places of pleasure, his court festivals, and so on. Thus, he can decide to go to war for the most meaningless of reasons, as if it were a kind of pleasure party, and he can blithely leave its justification (which decency requires) to his diplomatic corps, who are always prepared for such exercises.

The following comments are necessary to prevent confusing (as so often happens) the republican form of constitution with the democratic one: The forms of a nation (*civitas*) can be analyzed either on the basis of the persons who possess the highest political authority or on the basis of the way the people are *governed* by their ruler, whoever he may be. The first is called the form of sovereignty * * *, of which only three kinds are possible, specifically, where either *one*, or *several* in association, or *all* those together who make up civil society possess the sovereign power (Autocracy, Aristocracy and Democracy, the power of a monarch, the power of a nobility, the power of a people). The second is the form of government (*forma regiminis*) and concerns the way in which a nation, based on its constitution (the act of the general will whereby a group becomes a people), exercises its authority. In this regard, government is either *republican* or *despotic*. *Republicanism* is that political principle whereby executive power (the government) is separated from legislative power. In a despotism the ruler independently executes laws that it has itself made; here rulers have taken hold of the public will and treated it as their own private will. Among the three forms of government, *democracy*, in the proper sense of the term, is necessarily a *despotism*, because it sets up an executive power in which all citizens make decisions about and, if need be, against one (who therefore does not agree); consequently, all, who are not quite all, decide, so that the general will contradicts both itself and freedom.

Every form of government that is not *representative* is properly speaking *without form*, because one and the same person can no more be at one and the same time the legislator and executor of his will (than the universal proposition can serve as the major premise in a syllogism and at the same time be the subsumption of the particular under it in the minor premise). And although the other two forms of political constitution are defective inasmuch as they always leave room for a democratic form of government, it is nonetheless possible that they assume a form of government that accords with the *spirit* of a representative system: As Friederick II at least *said*, "I am merely the nation's highest servant."

The democratic system makes this impossible, for everyone wants to rule. One can therefore say, the smaller the number of persons who exercise the power of the nation (the number of rulers), the more they represent and the closer the political constitution approximates the possibility of republicanism, and thus, the constitution can hope through gradual reforms finally to become republican. For this reason, attaining this state that embodies a completely just constitution is more difficult in an aristocracy than in a monarchy, and, except by violent revolution, there is no possibility of attaining it in a democracy. Nonetheless, the people are incomparably more concerned with the form of government than with the form of constitution (although a great deal depends on the degree to which the latter is suited to the goals of the former). But if the form of government is to cohere with the concept of right, it must include the representative system, which is possible only in a republican form of government and without which (no matter what the constitution may be) government is despotic and brutish. None of the ancient so-called republics were aware of this, and consequently they inevitably degenerated into despotism; still, this is more bearable under a single person's rulership than other forms of government are.

Second Definitive Article for a Perpetual Peace: The Right of Nations Shall Be Based on a Federation of Free States

As nations, peoples can be regarded as single individuals who injure one another through their close proximity while living in the state of nature (i.e., independently of external laws). For the sake of its own security, each nation can and should demand that the others enter into a contract resembling the civil one and guaranteeing the rights of each. This would be a federation *of nations*, but it must not be a nation consisting of nations. The latter would be contradictory, for in every nation there exists the relation of *ruler* (legislator) to *subject* (those who obey, the people); however, many nations in a single nation would constitute only a single nation, which contradicts our assumption (since we are here weighing the rights of *nations* in relation to one another, rather than fusing them into a single nation).

Just as we view with deep disdain the attachment of savages to their lawless freedom—preferring to scuffle without end rather than to place themselves under lawful restraints that they themselves constitute, consequently preferring a mad freedom to a rational one—and consider it barbarous, rude, and brutishly degrading of humanity, so also should we think that civilized peoples (each one united into a nation) would hasten as quickly as possible to escape so similar a state of abandonment. Instead, however, each *nation* sees its majesty (for it is absurd to speak of the majesty of a people) to consist in not being subject to any external legal constraint, and the glory of its ruler consists in being able, without endangering himself, to command many thousands to sacrifice themselves for a matter that does not concern them. The primary difference between European and American savages is this, that while many of the latter tribes have been completely eaten by their enemies, the former know how to make better use of those they have conquered than to consume them: they increase the number of their subjects and thus also the quantity of instruments they have to wage even more extensive wars.

Given the depravity of human nature, which is revealed and can be glimpsed in the free relations among nations (though deeply concealed by governmental restraints in law governed civilsociety), one must wonder why the word *right* has not been completely discarded from the politics of war as pedantic, or why no nation has openly ventured to declare that it should be. For while Hugo Grotius, Pufendorf, Vattel, and others whose philosophically and diplomatically formulated codes do not and cannot have the slightest legal force (since nations do not stand under any common external constraints), are always piously cited in justification of a war of aggression (and who therefore provide only cold comfort), no example can be given of a nation having foregone its intention [of going to war] based on the arguments provided by such important men. The homage that every nation pays (at least in words) to the concept of right proves, nonetheless, that there is in man a still greater, though presently dormant, moral aptitude to master the evil principle in himself (a principle he cannot deny) and to hope that others will also overcome it. For otherwise the word *right* would never leave the mouths of those nations that want to make war on one another, unless it were used mockingly, as when that Gallic prince declared, "Nature has given the strong the prerogative of making the weak obey them."

Nations can press for their rights only by waging war and never in a trial before an independent tribunal, but war and its favorable consequence, victory, cannot determine the right. And although a *treaty of peace* can put an end to some particular war, it cannot end the state of war (the tendency always to find a new pretext for war). (And this situation cannot straightforwardly be declared unjust, since in this circumstance each nation is judge of its own case.) Nor can one say of nations as regards their rights what one can say concerning the natural rights of men in a state of lawlessness, to wit, that "they should abandon this state." (For as nations they already have an internal, legal constitution and therefore have outgrown the compulsion to subject themselves to another legal constitution that is subject to someone else's concept of right.) Nonetheless, from the throne of its moral legislative power, reason absolutely condemns war as a means of determining the right and makes seeking the state of peace a matter of unmitigated duty. But without a contract among nations peace can be neither inaugurated nor guaranteed. A league of a special sort must therefore be established, one that we can call a *league of peace* (*foedus pacificum*), which will be distinguished from a *treaty of peace* (*pactum pacis*) because the latter seeks merely to stop *one* war, while the former seeks to end *all* wars forever. This league does not seek any power of the sort possessed by nations, but only the maintenance and security of each nation's own freedom, as well as that of the other nations leagued with it, without their having thereby to subject themselves to civil laws and their constraints (as men in the state of nature must do). It can be shown that this *idea of federalism* should eventually include all nations and thus lead to perpetual peace. For if good fortune should so dispose matters that a powerful and enlightened people should form a republic (which by its nature must be inclined to seek perpetual peace), it will provide a focal point for a federal association among other nations that will join it in order to guarantee a state of peace among nations that is in accord with the idea of the right of nations, and through several associations of this sort such a federation can extend further and further.

That a people might say, "There should be no war among us, for we want to form ourselves into a nation, i.e., place ourselves under a supreme legislative, executive, and judicial power to resolve our conflicts peacefully," is understandable. But when a nation says, "There should be no war between me and other nations, though I recognize no supreme legislative power to guarantee me my rights and him his," then if there does not exist a surrogate of the union in a civil society, which is a free federation, it is impossible to understand what the basis for so entrusting my rights is. Such a federation is necessarily tied rationally to the concept of the right of nations, at least if this latter notion has any meaning.

The concept of the right of nations as a right to go to war is meaningless (for it would then be the right to determine the right not by independent, universally valid laws that restrict the freedom of everyone, but by one-sided maxims backed by force). Consequently, the concept of the right of nations must be understood as follows: that it serves justly those men who are disposed to seek one another's destruction and thus to find perpetual peace in the grave that covers all the horrors of violence and its perpetrators. Reason can provide related nations with no other means for emerging from the state of lawlessness, which consists solely of war, than that they give up their savage (lawless) freedom, just as individual persons do, and, by accommodating themselves to the constraints of common law, establish a *nation of peoples* (*civitas gentium*) that (continually growing) will finally include all the people of the earth. But they do not will to do this because it does not conform to their idea of the right of nations, and consequently they discard in *hypothesis* what is true in *thesis*. So (if everything is not to be lost) in place of the positive idea of *a world republic* they put only the *negative* surrogate of an enduring, ever expanding *federation* that prevents war and curbs the tendency of that hostile inclination to defy the law, though there will always be constant danger of their breaking loose. * * *

*   *   *

V. I. LENIN

FROM *IMPERIALISM, THE HIGHEST STAGE OF CAPITALISM: A POPULAR OUTLINE*

*   *   *

Chapter V

The Division of the World among Capitalist Combines

Monopolist capitalist combines—cartels, syndicates, trusts—divide among themselves, first of all, the whole internal market of a country, and impose their control, more or less completely, upon the industry of that country. But under capitalism the home market is inevitably bound up with the foreign market. Capitalism long ago created a world market. As the export of capital increased, and as the foreign and colonial relations and the "spheres of influence" of the big monopolist combines expanded, things "naturally" gravitated towards an international agreement among these combines, and towards the formation of international cartels.

This is a new stage of world concentration of capital and production, incomparably higher than the preceding stages. Let us see how this super-monopoly develops.

*   *   *

Chapter X

The Place of Imperialism in History

We have seen that the economic quintessence of imperialism is monopoly capitalism. This very

From V. I. Lenin, *Imperialism, The Highest Stage of Capitalism: A Popular Outline* (New York: International Publishers, 1939). The order of some passages has been changed. The author's notes have been omitted.

fact determines its place in history, for monopoly that grew up on the basis of free competition, and precisely out of free competition, is the transition from the capitalist system to a higher social-economic order. We must take special note of the four principal forms of monopoly, or the four principal manifestations of monopoly capitalism, which are characteristic of the epoch under review.

Firstly, monopoly arose out of the concentration of production at a very advanced stage of development. This refers to the monopolist capitalist combines, cartels, syndicates and trusts. We have seen the important part that these play in modern economic life. At the beginning of the twentieth century, monopolies acquired complete supremacy in the advanced countries. And although the first steps towards the formation of the cartels were first taken by countries enjoying the protection of high tariffs (Germany, America), Great Britain, with her system of free trade, was not far behind in revealing the same basic phenomenon, namely, the birth of monopoly out of the concentration of production.

Secondly, monopolies have accelerated the capture of the most important sources of raw materials, especially for the coal and iron industries, which are the basic and most highly cartelised industries in capitalist society. The monopoly of the most important sources of raw materials has enormously increased the power of big capital, and has sharpened the antagonism between cartelised and non-cartelised industry.

Thirdly, monopoly has sprung from the banks. The banks have developed from modest intermediary enterprises into the monopolists of finance capital. Some three or five of the biggest banks in each of the foremost capitalist countries have achieved the "personal union" of industrial and bank capital, and have concentrated in their hands the disposal of thousands upon thousands of millions which form the greater part of the capital and income of entire countries. A financial oligarchy, which throws a close net of relations of dependence over all the economic and political institutions of contemporary bourgeois society without exception—such is the most striking manifestation of this monopoly.

Fourthly, monopoly has grown out of colonial policy. To the numerous "old" motives of colonial policy, finance capital has added the struggle for the sources of raw materials, for the export of capital, for "spheres of influence," *i.e.*, for spheres for profitable deals, concessions, monopolist profits and so on; in fine, for economic territory in general. When the colonies of the European powers in Africa, for instance, comprised only one-tenth of that territory (as was the case in 1876), colonial policy was able to develop by methods other than those of monopoly—by the "free grabbing" of territories, so to speak. But when nine-tenths of Africa had been seized (approximately by 1900), when the whole world had been divided up, there was inevitably ushered in a period of colonial monopoly and, consequently, a period of particularly intense struggle for the division and the redivision of the world.

The extent to which monopolist capital has intensified all the contradictions of capitalism is generally known. It is sufficient to mention the high cost of living and the oppression of the cartels. This intensification of contradictions constitutes the most powerful driving force of the transitional period of history, which began from the time of the definite victory of world finance capital.

Monopolies, oligarchy, the striving for domination instead of the striving for liberty, the exploitation of an increasing number of small or weak nations by an extremely small group of the richest or most powerful nations—all these have given birth to those distinctive characteristics of imperialism which compel us to define it as parasitic or decaying capitalism. More and more

prominently there emerges, as one of the tendencies of imperialism, the creation of the "bond-holding" (rentier) state, the usurer state, in which the bourgeoisie lives on the proceeds of capital exports and by clipping coupons." It would be a mistake to believe that this tendency to decay precludes the possibility of the rapid growth of capitalism. It does not. In the epoch of imperialism, certain branches of industry, certain strata of the bourgeoisie and certain countries betray, to a more or less degree, one or other of these tendencies. On the whole, capitalism is growing far more rapidly than before. But this growth is not only becoming more and more uneven in general; its unevenness also manifests itself, in particular, in the decay of the countries which are richest in capital (such as England).

*   *   *

When free competition in Great Britain was at its zenith, *i.e.*, between 1840 and 1860, the leading British bourgeois politicians were opposed to colonial policy and were of the opinion that the liberation of the colonies and their complete separation from Britain was inevitable and desirable. M. Beer, in an article, "Modern British Imperialism," published in 1898, shows that in 1852, Disraeli, a statesman generally inclined towards imperialism, declared: "The colonies are millstones round our necks." But at the end of the nineteenth century the heroes of the hour in England were Cecil Rhodes and Joseph Chamberlain, open advocates of imperialism, who applied the imperialist policy in the most cynical manner.

It is not without interest to observe that even at that time these leading British bourgeois politicians fully appreciated the connection between what might be called the purely economic and the politico-social roots of modern imperialism. Chamberlain advocated imperialism by calling it a "true, wise and economical policy," and he pointed particularly to the German, American and Belgian competition which Great Britain was encountering in the world market. Salvation lies in monopolies, said the capitalists as they formed cartels, syndicates and trusts. Salvation lies in monopolies, echoed the political leaders of the bourgeoisie, hastening to appropriate the parts of the world not yet shared out. The journalist, Stead, relates the following remarks uttered by his close friend Cecil Rhodes, in 1895, regarding his imperialist ideas:

> "I was in the East End of London yesterday and attended a meeting of the unemployed. I listened to the wild speeches, which were just a cry for 'bread,' 'bread,' 'bread,' and on my way home I pondered over the scene and I became more than ever convinced of the importance of imperialism. . . . My cherished idea is a solution for the social problem, *i.e.*, in order to save the 40,000,000 inhabitants of the United Kingdom from a bloody civil war, we colonial statesmen must acquire new lands to settle the surplus population, to provide new markets for the goods produced by them in the factories and mines. The Empire, as I have always said, is a bread and butter question. If you want to avoid civil war, you must become imperialists."

This is what Cecil Rhodes, millionaire, king of finance, the man who was mainly responsible for the Boer War, said in 1895. * * *

*   *   *

* * * The unevenness in the rate of expansion of colonial possessions is very marked. If, for instance, we compare France, Germany and Japan, which do not differ very much in area and population, we will see that the first has annexed almost three times as much colonial territory as the other two combined. In regard to finance capital, also, France, at the beginning of the period we are considering, was perhaps several times richer than Germany and Japan put together. In addition to, and on the basis of, purely economic causes, geographical conditions and other factors also affect the dimensions of colonial possessions. However strong the process of levelling the world, of levelling the economic and living conditions in different countries, may have been in the past decades as a result of the pressure of large-scale industry, exchange and finance capital, great differences still remain; and among the six powers, we see, firstly, young capitalist powers

(America, Germany, Japan) which progressed very rapidly; secondly, countries with an old capitalist development (France and Great Britain), which, of late, have made much slower progress than the previously mentioned countries, and, thirdly, a country (Russia) which is economically most backward, in which modern capitalist imperialism is enmeshed, so to speak, in a particularly close network of pre-capitalist relations.

*   *   *

Colonial policy and imperialism existed before this latest stage of capitalism, and even before capitalism. Rome, founded on slavery, pursued a colonial policy and achieved imperialism. But "general" arguments about imperialism, which ignore, or put into the background the fundamental difference of social-economic systems, inevitably degenerate into absolutely empty banalities, or into grandiloquent comparisons like "Greater Rome and Greater Britain." Even the colonial policy of capitalism in its *previous* stages is essentially different from the colonial policy of finance capital.

The principal feature of modern capitalism is the domination of monopolist combines of the big capitalists. These monopolies are most firmly established when *all* the sources of raw materials are controlled by the one group. And we have seen with what zeal the international capitalist combines exert every effort to make it impossible for their rivals to compete with them; for example, by buying up mineral lands, oil fields, etc. Colonial possession alone gives complete guarantee of success to the monopolies against all the risks of the struggle with competitors, including the risk that the latter will defend themselves by means of a law establishing a state monopoly. The more capitalism is developed, the more the need for raw materials is felt, the more bitter competition becomes, and the more feverishly the hunt for raw materials proceeds throughout the whole world, the more desperate becomes the struggle for the acquisition of colonies.

*   *   *

The bourgeois reformists, and among them particularly the present-day adherents of Kautsky, of course, try to belittle the importance of facts of this kind by arguing that it "would be possible" to obtain raw materials in the open market without a "costly and dangerous" colonial policy; and that it would be "possible" to increase the supply of raw materials to an enormous extent "simply" by improving agriculture. But these arguments are merely an apology for imperialism, an attempt to embellish it, because they ignore the principal feature of modern capitalism: monopoly. Free markets are becoming more and more a thing of the past; monopolist syndicates and trusts are restricting them more and more every day, and "simply" improving agriculture reduces itself to improving the conditions of the masses, to raising wages and reducing profits. Where, except in the imagination of the sentimental reformists, are there any trusts capable of interesting themselves in the condition of the masses instead of the conquest of colonies?

Finance capital is not only interested in the already known sources of raw materials; it is also interested in potential sources of raw materials, because present-day technical development is extremely rapid, and because land which is useless today may be made fertile tomorrow if new methods are applied (to devise these new methods a big bank can equip a whole expedition of engineers, agricultural experts, etc.), and large amounts of capital are invested. This also applies to prospecting for minerals, to new methods of working up and utilising raw materials, etc., etc. Hence, the inevitable striving of finance capital to extend its economic territory and even its territory in general. In the same way that the trusts capitalise their property by estimating it at two or three times its value, taking into account its "potential" (and not present) returns, and the further results of monopoly, so finance capital strives to seize the largest possible amount of land of all kinds and in any place it can, and by any means, counting on the possibilities of finding raw materials there, and fearing to be left

behind in the insensate struggle for the last available scraps of undivided territory, or for the repartition of that which has been already divided.

*   *   *

The necessity of exporting capital also gives an impetus to the conquest of colonies, for in the colonial market it is easier to eliminate competition, to make sure of orders, to strengthen the necessary "connections," etc., by monoplist methods (and sometimes it is the only possible way).

The non-economic superstructure which grows up on the basis of finance capital, its politics and its ideology, stimulates the striving for colonial conquest. "Finance capital does not want liberty, it wants domination," as Hilferding very truly says. * * *

*   *   *

Since we are speaking of colonial policy in the period of capitalist imperialism, it must be observed that finance capital and its corresponding foreign policy, which reduces itself to the struggle of the Great Powers for the economic and political division of the world, give rise to a number of *transitional* forms of national dependence. The division of the world into two main groups—of colony-owning countries on the one hand and colonies on the other—is not the only typical feature of this period; there is also a variety of forms of dependent countries; countries which, officially, are politically independent, but which are, in fact, enmeshed in the net of financial and diplomatic dependence. We have already referred to one form of dependence— the semi-colony. Another example is provided by Argentina.

"South America, and especially Argentina," writes Schulze-Gaevernitz in his work on British imperialism, "is so dependent financially on London that it ought to be described as almost a British commercial colony."

*   *   *

Chapter VII

Imperialism as a Special Stage of Capitalism

We must now try to sum up and put together what has been said above on the subject of imperialism. Imperialism emerged as the development and direct continuation of the fundamental attributes of capitalism in general. But capitalism only became capitalist imperialism at a definite and very high stage of its development, when certain of its fundamental attributes began to be transformed into their opposites, when the features of a period of transition from capitalism to a higher social and economic system began to take shape and reveal themselves all along the line. Economically, the main thing in this process is the substitution of capitalist monopolies for capitalist free competition. Free competition is the fundamental attribute of capitalism, and of commodity production generally. Monopoly is exactly the opposite of free competition; but we have seen the latter being transformed into monopoly before our very eyes, creating large-scale industry and eliminating small industry, replacing large-scale industry by still larger-scale industry, finally leading to such a concentration of production and capital that monopoly has been and is the result: cartels, syndicates and trusts, and merging with them, the capital of a dozen or so banks manipulating thousands of millions. At the same time monopoly, which has grown out of free competition, does not abolish the latter, but exists over it and alongside of it, and thereby gives rise to a number of very acute, intense antagonisms, friction and conflicts. Monopoly is the transition from capitalism to a higher system.

If it were necessary to give the briefest possible definition of imperialism we should have to say that imperialism is the monopoly stage of capitalism. Such a definition would include what is most important, for, on the one hand, finance capital is the bank capital of a few big monopolist banks, merged with the capital of the monopolist combines of manufacturers; and, on the other hand, the division of the world is the transition from a colonial policy which has extended without hindrance to territories unoccupied by any capitalist power, to a colonial policy of monopolistic possession of the territory of the world which has been completely divided up.

But very brief definitions, although convenient, for they sum up the main points, are nevertheless inadequate, because very important features of the phenomenon that has to be defined have to be especially deduced. And so, without forgetting the conditional and relative value of all definitions, which can never include all the concatenations of a phenomenon in its complete development, we must give a definition of imperialism that will embrace the following five essential features:

1. The concentration of production and capital developed to such a high stage that it created monopolies which play a decisive role in economic life.
2. The merging of bank capital with industrial capital, and the creation, on the basis of this "finance capital," of a "financial oligarchy."
3. The export of capital, which has become extremely important, as distinguished from the export of commodities.
4. The formation of international capitalist monopolies which share the world among themselves.
5. The territorial division of the whole world among the greatest capitalist powers is completed.

Imperialism is capitalism in that stage of development in which the dominance of monopolies and finance capital has established itself; in which the export of capital has acquired pronounced importance; in which the division of the world among the international trusts has begun; in which the division of all territories of the globe among the great capitalist powers has been completed.

*   *   *

Another special feature of imperialism, which is connected with the facts we are describing, is the decline in emigration from imperialist countries, and the increase in immigration into these countries from the backward countries where lower wages are paid. As Hobson observes, emigration from Great Britain has been declining since 1884. In that year the number of emigrants was 242,000, while in 1900, the number was only 169,000. German emigration reached the highest point between 1880 and 1890, with a total of 1,453,000 emigrants. In the course of the following two decades, it fell to 544,000 and even to 341,000. On the other hand, there was an increase in the number of workers entering Germany from Austria, Italy, Russia and other countries. According to the 1907 census, there were 1,342,294 foreigners in Germany, of whom 440,800 were industrial workers and 257,329 were agricultural workers. In France, the workers employed in the mining industry are, "in great part," foreigners: Polish, Italian and Spanish. In the United States, immigrants from Eastern and Southern Europe are engaged in the most poorly paid occupations, while American workers provide the highest percentage of overseers or of the better paid workers. Imperialism has the tendency to create privileged sections even among the workers, and to detach them from the main proletarian masses.

It must be observed that in Great Britain the tendency of imperialism to divide the workers, to encourage opportunism among them and to cause temporary decay in the working class movement, revealed itself much earlier than the end of the nineteenth and the beginning of the twentieth centuries; for two important distinguishing features of imperialism were observed in Great Britain in the middle of the nineteenth century, *viz.*, vast colonial possessions and a monopolist position in the world market. Marx and Engels systematically traced this relation between opportunism in the labour movement and the imperialist features of British capitalism for several decades. For example, on October 7, 1858, Engels wrote to Marx:

"The English proletariat is becoming more and more bourgeois, so that this most bourgeois of all nations is apparently aiming ultimately at the possession of a bourgeois aristocracy, and a bourgeois proletariat *as well as* a bourgeoisie. For a nation which exploits the whole world—this is, of course, to a certain extent justifiable."

Almost a quarter of a century later, in a letter dated August 11, 1881, Engels speaks of ". . . the worst type of English trade unions which allow themselves to be led by men sold to, or at least, paid by the bourgeoisie." In a letter to Kautsky, dated September 12, 1882, Engels wrote:

"You ask me what the English workers think about colonial policy? Well, exactly the same as they think about politics in general. There is no workers' party here, there are only Conservatives and Liberal-Radicals, and the workers merrily share the feast of England's monopoly of the colonies and the world market. . . ." (Engels expressed similar ideas in the press in his preface to the second edition of *The Condition of the Working Class in England,* which appeared in 1892.)

We thus see clearly the causes and effects. The causes are: 1) Exploitation of the whole world by this country. 2) Its monopolistic position in the world market. 3) Its colonial monopoly. The effects are: 1) A section of the British proletariat becomes bourgeois. 2) A section of the proletariat permits itself to be led by men sold to, or at least, paid by the bourgeoisie. The imperialism of the beginning of the twentieth century completed the division of the world among a handful of states, each of which today exploits (*i.e.,* draws super-profits from) a part of the world only a little smaller than that which England exploited in 1858. * * *

The distinctive feature of the present situation is the prevalence of economic and political conditions which could not but increase the irreconcilability between opportunism and the general and vital interests of the working class movement. Embryonic imperialism has grown into a dominant system; capitalist monopolies occupy first place in economics and politics; the division of the world has been completed. On the other hand, instead of an undisputed monopoly by Great Britain, we see a few imperialist powers contending for the right to share in this monopoly, and this struggle is characteristic of the whole period of the beginning of the twentieth century. Opportunism, therefore, cannot now triumph in the working class movement of any country for decades as it did in England in the second half of the nineteenth century. But, in a number of countries it has grown ripe, over-ripe, and rotten, and has become completely merged with bourgeois policy in the form of "social-chauvinism."

*   *   *

Chapter IX

The Critique of Imperialism

By the critique of imperialism, in the broad sense of the term, we mean the attiude towards imperialist policy of the different classes of society as part of their general ideology.

The enormous dimensions of finance capital concentrated in a few hands and creating an extremely extensive and close network of ties and relationships which subordinate not only the small and medium, but also even the very small capitalists and small masters, on the one hand, and the intense struggle waged against other national state groups of financiers for the division of the world and domination over other countries, on the other hand, cause the wholesale transition of the possessing classes to the side of imperialism. The signs of the times are a "general" enthusiasm regarding its prospects, a passionate defence of imperialism, and every possible embellishment of its real nature. The imperialist ideology also penetrates the working class. There is no Chinese Wall between it and the other classes. The leaders of the so-called "Social-Democratic" Party of Germany are today justly called "social-imperialists," that is, socialists in words and imperialists in deeds; but as early as 1902, Hobson noted the existence of "Fabian imperialists" who belonged to the opportunist Fabian Society in England.

Bourgeois scholars and publicists usually come out in defence of imperialism in a somewhat veiled form, and obscure its complete domination and its profound roots; they strive to concentrate attention on partial and secondary details and do their very best to distract attention from the main issue by means of ridiculous schemes for "reform," such as police supervision of the trusts and banks, etc. Less frequently, cynical and frank imperialists speak out and are bold enough to admit the absurdity of the idea of reforming the fundamental features of imperialism.

*   *   *

2 HISTORY

Core ideas about international relations, introduced in Chapter 1 and elabo-rated in Chapter 3 of Essentials of International Relations, *have emerged as responses to historic diplomatic challenges. The four selections in this chapter provide insight into key events and trends that spawned many of the ideas that still shape debates about contemporary international politics.*

The post–World War I peace process led to a clear statement of the liberal perspective. U.S. President Woodrow Wilson's "Fourteen Points," in an address to Congress in January 1918, summarizes some of the key ideas emerging from liberal theory. Wilson blames power politics, secret diplomacy, and auto-cratic leaders for the devastating world war. He suggests that with the spread of democracy and the creation of a "league of nations" aggression would be stopped.

The Cold War also provides the historical setting for the realist/liberal per-spective. George F. Kennan, then director of the State Department's Policy Planning Staff, published his famous "X" article in Foreign Affairs *in 1947. He assesses Soviet conduct and provides the intellectual justification for Cold War containment policy. Using realist logic, he suggests that counterforce must be applied to prevent Soviet expansion.*

The end of the Cold War in the late 1980s was believed by many to have ushered in a new historical era. In 1989, the writer Francis Fukuyama pro-nounced the end of history and ideology and the triumph of Western liberal-ism, but his predictions turned out to be premature. History roared back with a vengeance in the forms of ethnic conflict, genocide, and terrorism. The Bush Administration's 2001 National Security Strategy of the United States laid out a justification for preventive war against terrorists and dangerous dictators like Iraq's Saddam Hussein. In an ironic twist on Fukuyama's thesis, the Bush Administration held that U.S. military power should bring democracy and peace to lands that harbor these threats.

WOODROW WILSON

THE FOURTEEN POINTS

It will be our wish and purpose that the processes of peace, when they are begun, shall be absolutely open and that they shall involve and permit henceforth no secret understandings of any kind. The day of conquest and aggrandizement is gone by; so is also the day of secret covenants entered into in the interest of particular governments and likely at some unlooked-for moment to upset the peace of the world. It is this happy fact, now clear to the view of every public man whose thoughts do not still linger in an age that is dead and gone, which makes it possible for every nation whose purposes are consistent with justice and the peace of the world to avow now or at any other time the objects it has in view.

We entered this war because violations of right had occurred which touched us to the quick and made the life of our own people impossible unless they were corrected and the world secured once and for all against their recurrence. What we demand in this war, therefore, is nothing peculiar to ourselves. It is that the world be made fit and safe to live in; and particularly that it be made safe for every peace-loving nation which, like our own, wishes to live its own life, determine its own institutions, be assured of justice and fair dealing by the other people of the world as against force and selfish aggression. All the peoples of the world are in effect partners in this interest, and for our own part we see very clearly that unless justice be done to others it will not be done to us. The program of the world's peace, therefore, is our program; and that program, the only possible program, as we see it, is this:

I. Open covenants of peace, openly arrived at, after which there shall be no private interna-

From Woodrow Wilson's address to the U.S. Congress, 8 January, 1918.

tional understandings of any kind but diplomacy shall proceed always frankly and in the public view.

II. Absolute freedom of navigation upon the seas, outside territorial waters, alike in peace and in war, except as the seas may be closed in whole or in part by international action for the enforcement of international covenants.

III. The removal, so far as possible, of all economic barriers and the establishment of an equality of trade conditions among all the nations consenting to the peace and associating themselves for its maintenance.

IV. Adequate guarantees given and taken that national armaments will be reduced to the lowest point consistent with domestic safety.

V. A free, open-minded, and absolutely impartial adjustment of all colonial claims, based upon a strict observance of the principle that in determining all such questions of sovereignty the interests of the populations concerned must have equal weight with the equitable claims of the government whose title is to be determined.

VI. The evacuation of all Russian territory and such a settlement of all questions affecting Russia as will secure the best and freest cooperation of the other nations of the world in obtaining for her an unhampered and unembarrassed opportunity for the independent determination of her own political development and national policy and assure her of a sincere welcome into the society of free nations under institutions of her own choosing; and, more than a welcome, assistance also of every kind that she may need and may herself desire. The treatment accorded Russia by her sister nations in the months to come will be the acid test of their good will, of their comprehension of her needs as distinguished from their own interests, and of their intelligent and unselfish sympathy.

VII. Belgium, the whole world will agree, must be evacuated and restored, without any attempt to limit the sovereignty which she enjoys in common with all other free nations. No other single act will serve as this will serve to restore confidence among the nations in the laws which they have themselves set and determined for the government of their relations with one another. Without this healing act the whole structure and validity of international law is forever impaired.

VIII. All French territory should be freed and the invaded portions restored, and the wrong done to France by Prussia in 1871 in the matter of Alsace-Lorraine, which has unsettled the peace of the world for nearly fifty years, should be righted, in order that peace may once more be made secure in the interest of all.

IX. A readjustment of the frontiers of Italy should be effected along clearly recognizable lines of nationality.

X. The peoples of Austria-Hungary, whose place among the nations we wish to see safeguarded and assured, should be accorded the freest opportunity of autonomous development.

XI. Rumania, Serbia, and Montenegro should be evacuated; occupied territories restored; Serbia accorded free and secure access to the sea; and the relations of the several Balkan states to one another determined by friendly counsel along historically established lines of allegiance and nationality; and international guarantees of the political and economic independence and territorial integrity of the several Balkan states should be entered into.

XII. The Turkish portions of the present Ottoman Empire should be assured a secure sovereignty, but the other nationalities which are now under Turkish rule should be assured an undoubted security of life and an absolutely unmolested opportunity of autonomous development, and the Dardanelles should be permanently opened as a free passage to the ships and commerce of all nations under international guarantees.

XIII. An independent Polish state should be erected which should include the territories inhabited by indisputably Polish populations, which should be assured a free and secure access to the sea, and whose political and economic independence and territorial integrity should be guaranteed by international covenant.

XIV. A general association of nations must be formed under specific covenants for the purpose of affording mutual guarantees of political independence and territorial integrity to great and small states alike.

In regard to these essential rectifications of wrong and assertions of right we feel ourselves to be intimate partners of all the governments and peoples associated together against the imperialists. We cannot be separated in interest or divided in purpose. We stand together until the end.

For such arrangements and covenants we are willing to fight and to continue to fight until they are achieved; but only because we wish the right to prevail and desire a just and stable peace such as can be secured only by removing the chief provocations to war, which this program does remove. We have no jealousy of German greatness, and there is nothing in this program that impairs it. We grudge her no achievement or distinction of learning or of pacific enterprise such as have made her record very bright and very enviable. We do not wish to injure her or to block in any way her legitimate influence or power. We do not wish to fight her either with arms or with hostile arrangements of trade if she is willing to associate herself with us and the other peace-loving nations of the world in covenants of justice and law and fair dealing. We wish her only to accept a place of equality among the peoples of the world—the new world in which we now live—instead of a place of mastery.

Neither do we presume to suggest to her any alteration or modification of her institutions. But it is necessary, we must frankly say, and necessary as a preliminary to any intelligent dealings with her on our part, that we should know whom her spokesmen speak for when they speak to us, whether for the Reichstag majority or for the military party and the men whose creed is imperial domination.

We have spoken now, surely, in terms too concrete to admit of any further doubt or question. An evident principle runs through the whole program I have outlined. It is the principle of justice to all peoples and nationalities, and their right to live on equal terms of liberty and safety with one another, whether they be strong or weak. Unless this principle be made its foundation no part of the structure of international justice can stand. The people of the United States could act upon no other principle; and to the vindication of this principle they are ready to devote their lives, their honor, and everything that they possess. The moral climax of this the culminating and final war for human liberty has come, and they are ready to put their own strength, their own highest purpose, their own integrity and devotion to the test.

GEORGE F. KENNAN ("X")

THE SOURCES OF SOVIET CONDUCT

I

The political personality of Soviet power as we know it today is the product of ideology and circumstances: ideology inherited by the present Soviet leaders from the movement in which they had their political origin, and circumstances of the power which they now have exercised for nearly three decades in Russia. There can be few tasks of psychological analysis more difficult than to try to trace the interaction of these two forces and the relative role of each in the determination of official Soviet conduct. Yet the attempt must be made if that conduct is to be understood and effectively countered.

It is difficult to summarize the set of ideological concepts with which the Soviet leaders came into power. Marxian ideology, in its Russian-Communist projection, has always been in process of subtle evolution. The materials on which it bases itself are extensive and complex. But the outstanding features of Communist thought as it existed in 1916 may perhaps be summarized as follows: (*a*) that the central factor in the life of man, the fact which determines the character of public life and the "physiognomy of society," is the system by which material goods are produced and exchanged; (*b*) that the capitalist system of production is a nefarious one which inevitably leads to the exploitation of the working class by the capital-owning class and is incapable of developing adequately the economic resources of society or of distributing fairly the material goods produced by human labor; (*c*) that capitalism contains the seeds of its own destruction and must, in view of the inability of the capital-owning class to adjust itself to economic change, result eventually and inescapably in a revolutionary transfer of power to the working class; and (*d*) that imperialism, the final phase of capitalism, leads directly to war and revolution.

*   *   *

Now it must be noted that through all the years of preparation for revolution, the attention of these men, as indeed of Marx himself, had been centered less on the future form which Socialism[1] would take than on the necessary overthrow of rival power which, in their view, had to precede the introduction of Socialism. Their views, therefore, on the positive program to be put into effect, once power was attained, were for the most part nebulous, visionary and impractical. Beyond the nationalization of industry and the expropriation of large private capital holdings there was no agreed program. The treatment of the peasantry, which according to the Marxist formulation was not of the proletariat, had always been a vague spot in

From *Foreign Affairs* 25, no. 4 (July 1947): 566–82.

the pattern of Communist thought; and it remained an object of controversy and vacillation for the first ten years of Communist power.

The circumstances of the immediate post-Revolution period—the existence in Russia of civil war and foreign intervention, together with the obvious fact that the Communists represented only a tiny minority of the Russian people—made the establishment of dictatorial power a necessity. The experiment with "war Communism" and the abrupt attempt to eliminate private production and trade had unfortunate economic consequences and caused further bitterness against the new revolutionary regime. While the temporary relaxation of the effort to communize Russia, represented by the New Economic Policy, alleviated some of this economic distress and thereby served its purpose, it also made it evident that the "capitalistic sector of society" was still prepared to profit at once from any relaxation of governmental pressure, and would, if permitted to continue to exist, always constitute a powerful opposing element to the Soviet regime and a serious rival for influence in the country. Somewhat the same situation prevailed with respect to the individual peasant who, in his own small way, was also a private producer.

Lenin, had he lived, might have proved a great enough man to reconcile these conflicting forces to the ultimate benefit of Russian society, though this is questionable. But be that as it may, Stalin, and those whom he led in the struggle for succession to Lenin's position of leadership, were not the men to tolerate rival political forces in the sphere of power which they coveted. Their sense of insecurity was too great. Their particular brand of fanaticism, unmodified by any of the Anglo-Saxon traditions of compromise, was too fierce and too jealous to envisage any permanent sharing of power. From the Russian-Asiatic world out of which they had emerged they carried with them a skepticism as to the possibilities of permanent and peaceful coexistence of rival forces. Easily persuaded of their own doctrinaire "rightness," they insisted on the submission or destruction of all competing power. Outside of the Communist Party, Russian society was to have no rigidity. There were to be no forms of collective human activity or association which would not be dominated by the Party. No other force in Russian society was to be permitted to achieve vitality or integrity. Only the Party was to have structure. All else was to be an amorphous mass.

And within the Party the same principle was to apply. The mass of Party members might go through the motions of election, deliberation, decision and action; but in these motions they were to be animated not by their own individual wills but by the awesome breath of the Party leadership and the overbrooding presence of "the world."

Let it be stressed again that subjectively these men probably did not seek absolutism for its own sake. They doubtless believed—and found it easy to believe—that they alone knew what was good for society and that they would accomplish that good once their power was secure and unchallengeable. But in seeking that security of their own rule they were prepared to recognize no restrictions, either of God or man, on the character of their methods. And until such time as that security might be achieved, they placed far down on their scale of operational priorities the comforts and happiness of the peoples entrusted to their care.

Now the outstanding circumstance concerning the Soviet regime is that down to the present day this process of political consolidation has never been completed and the men in the Kremlin have continued to be predominantly absorbed with the struggle to secure and make absolute the power which they seized in November 1917. They have endeavored to secure it primarily against forces at home, within Soviet society itself. But they have also endeavored to secure it against the outside world. For ideology, as we have seen, taught them that the outside world was hostile and that it was their duty eventually to overthrow the political forces beyond their borders. The powerful hands of Russian history and tradition reached up to sustain them in this feeling. Finally, their own aggressive intransigence with respect to the outside world began to find its own reaction; and they were soon forced, to use another Gibbonesque phrase [from Edward Gibbon, *The Decline and Fall of the Roman Empire*], "to chastise the contumacy" which they themselves had provoked. It is an undeniable privilege of every man to prove himself right in the thesis that the world is his enemy; for if he reiterates it frequently enough and makes it the background of his conduct he is bound eventually to be right.

Now it lies in the nature of the mental world of the Soviet leaders, as well as in the character of their ideology, that no opposition to them can be officially recognized as having any merit or justification whatsoever. Such opposition can flow, in theory, only from the hostile and incorrigible forces of dying capitalism. As long as remnants of capitalism were officially recognized as existing in Russia, it was possible to place on them, as an internal element, part of the blame for the maintenance of a dictatorial form of society. But as these remnants were liquidated, little by little, this justification fell away; and when it was indicated officially that they had been finally destroyed, it disappeared altogether. And this fact created one of the most basic of the compulsions which came to act upon the Soviet regime: since capitalism no longer existed in Russia and since it could not be admitted that there could be serious or widespread opposition to the Kremlin springing spontaneously from the liberated masses under its authority, it became necessary to justify the retention of the dictatorship by stressing the menace of capitalism abroad.

*   *   *

Now the maintenance of this pattern of Soviet power, namely, the pursuit of unlimited authority domestically, accompanied by the cultivation of the semi-myth of implacable foreign hostility, has gone far to shape the actual machinery of Soviet power as we know it today. Internal organs of administration which did not serve this purpose withered on the vine. Organs which did serve this purpose became vastly swollen. The security of Soviet power came to rest on the iron discipline of the Party, on the severity and ubiquity of the secret police, and on the uncompromising economic monopolism of the state. The "organs of suppression," in which the Soviet leaders had sought security from rival forces, became in large measure the masters of those whom they were designed to serve. Today the major part of the structure of Soviet power is committed to the perfection of the dictatorship and to the maintenance of the concept of Russia as in a state of siege, with the enemy lowering beyond the walls. And the millions of human beings who form that part of the structure of power must defend at all costs this concept of Russia's position, for without it they are themselves superfluous.

As things stand today, the rulers can no longer dream of parting with these organs of suppression. The quest for absolute power, pursued now for nearly three decades with a ruthlessness unparalleled (in scope at least) in modern times, has again produced internally, as it did externally, its own reaction. The excesses of the police apparatus have fanned the potential opposition to the regime into something far greater and more dangerous than it could have been before those excesses began.

But least of all can the rulers dispense with the fiction by which the maintenance of dictatorial power has been defended. For this fiction has been canonized in Soviet philosophy by the excesses already committed in its name; and it is now anchored in the Soviet structure of thought by bonds far greater than those of mere ideology.

II

So much for the historical background. What does it spell in terms of the political personality of Soviet power as we know it today?

Of the original ideology, nothing has been officially junked. Belief is maintained in the basic badness of capitalism, in the inevitability of its destruction, in the obligation of the proletariat to assist in that destruction and to take power into its own hands. But stress has come to be laid primarily on those concepts which relate most specifically to the Soviet regime itself: to its position as the sole truly Socialist regime in a dark and misguided world, and to the relationships of power within it.

The first of these concepts is that of the innate antagonism between capitalism and Socialism. We have seen how deeply that concept has become imbedded in foundations of Soviet power. It has profound implications for Russia's conduct as a member of international society. It means that there can never be on Moscow's side any sincere assumption of a community of aims between the Soviet Union and powers which are regarded as capitalism. It must invariably be assumed in Moscow that the aims of the capitalist world are antagonistic to the Soviet regime and, therefore, to the interests of the peoples it controls. If the Soviet Government occasionally sets its signature to documents which would indicate the contrary, this is to be regarded as a tactical maneuver permissible in dealing with the enemy (who is without honor) and should be taken in the spirit of *caveat emptor* [let the buyer beware]. Basically, the antagonism remains. It is postulated. And from it flow many of the phenomena which we find disturbing in the Kremlin's conduct of foreign policy: the secretiveness, the lack of frankness, the duplicity, the war suspiciousness, and the basic unfriendliness of purpose. These phenomena are there to stay, for the foreseeable future. There can be variations of degree and of emphasis. When there is something the Russians want from us, one or the other of these features of their policy may be thrust temporarily into the background; and when that happens there will always be Americans who will leap forward with gleeful announcements that "the Russians have changed," and some who will even try to take credit for having brought about such "changes." But we should not be misled by tactical maneuvers. These characteristics of Soviet policy, like the postulate from which they flow, are basic to the internal nature of Soviet power, and will be with us, whether in the foreground or the background, until the internal nature of Soviet power is changed.

This means that we are going to continue for a long time to find the Russians difficult to deal with. It does not mean that they should be considered as embarked upon a do-or-die program to overthrow our society by a given date. The theory of the inevitability of the eventual fall of capitalism has the fortunate connotation that there is no hurry about it. * * *

*   *   *

* * * [T]he Kremlin is under no ideological compulsion to accomplish its purposes in a hurry. Like the Church, it is dealing in ideological concepts which are of long-term validity, and it can afford to be patient. It has no right to risk the existing achievements of the revolution for the sake of vain baubles of the future. The very teachings of Lenin himself require great caution and flexibility in the pursuit of Communist purposes. Again, these precepts are fortified by the lessons of Russian history: of centuries of obscure battles between nomadic forces over the stretches of a vast unfortified plain. Here caution, circumspection, flexibility and deception are the valuable qualities; and their value finds natural appreciation in the Russian or the oriental mind. Thus the Kremlin has no compunction about retreating in the face of superior force. And being under the compulsion of no timetable, it does not get panicky under the necessity for such retreat. Its political action is a fluid stream which moves constantly, wherever it is permitted to move, toward a given goal. Its main concern is to make sure that it has filled every nook and cranny available to it in the basin of world power. But if it finds unassailable barriers in its path, it accepts these philosophically and accommodates itself to them. The main thing is that there should always be pressure, increasing constant pressure, toward the desired goal. There is no trace of any feeling in Soviet psychology that that goal must be reached at any given time.

These considerations make Soviet diplomacy at once easier and more difficult to deal with than the diplomacy of individual aggressive leaders like Napoleon and Hitler. On the one hand it is more sensitive to contrary force, more ready to yield on individual sectors of the diplomatic front when that force is felt to be too strong, and thus more rational in the logic and rhetoric of power. On the other hand it cannot be easily defeated or discouraged by a single victory on the part of its opponents. And the patient persistence by which it is animated means that it can be effectively countered not by sporadic acts which represent the momentary whims of democratic opinion but only by intelligent long-range policies on the part of Russia's adversaries—policies no less steady in their purpose, and no less variegated and resourceful in their application, than those of the Soviet Union itself.

In these circumstances it is clear that the main element of any United States policy toward the Soviet Union must be that of a long-term, patient but firm and vigilant containment of Russian expansive tendencies. It is important to note, however, that such a policy has nothing to do with outward histrionics: with threats or blustering or superfluous gestures of outward "toughness." While the Kremlin is basically flexible in its reaction to political realities, it is by no means unamenable to considerations of prestige. Like almost any other government, it can be placed by tactless and threatening gestures in a position where it cannot afford to yield even though this might be dictated by its sense of realism. The Russian leaders are keen judges of human psychology, and as such they are highly conscious that loss of temper and of self-control is never a source of strength in political affairs. They are quick to exploit such evidences of weakness. For these reasons, it is a *sine qua non* of successful dealing with Russia that the foreign government in question should remain at all times cool and collected and that its demands on Russian policy should be put forward in such a manner as to leave the way open for a compliance not too detrimental to Russian prestige.

III

In the light of the above, it will be clearly seen that the Soviet pressure against the free institutions of the Western world is something that can be contained by the adroit and vigilant application of counter-force at a series of constantly shifting geographical and political points, corresponding to the shifts and maneuvers of Soviet policy, but which cannot be charmed or talked out of existence. * * *

*   *   *

IV

*   *   *

But in actuality the possibilities for American policy are by no means limited to holding the line and hoping for the best. It is entirely possible for the United States to influence by its actions the internal developments, both within Russia and throughout the international Communist movement, by which Russian policy is largely determined. This is not only a question of the modest measure of informational activity which this government can conduct in the Soviet Union and elsewhere, although that, too, is important. It is rather a question of the degree to which the United States can create among the peoples of the world generally the impression of a country which knows what it wants, which is coping successfully with the problems of its internal life and with the responsibilities of a World Power, and which has a spiritual vitality capable of holding its own among the major ideological currents of the time. To the extent that such an impression can be created and maintained, the aims of Russian Communism must appear sterile and quixotic, the hopes and enthusiasm of Moscow's supporters must wane, and added strain must be imposed on the Kremlin's foreign policies. For the palsied decrepitude of the capitalist world is the keystone of Communist philosophy. Even the failure of the United States to experience the early economic depression which the ravens of the Red Square have been predicting with such complacent confidence since hostilities ceased would have deep and important repercussions throughout the Communist world.

By the same token, exhibitions of indecision, disunity and internal disintegration within this country have an exhilarating effect on the whole Communist movement. * * *

* * * [T]he United States has it in its power to increase enormously the strains under which Soviet policy must operate, to force upon the Kremlin a far greater degree of moderation and circumspection than it has had to observe in recent years, and in this way to promote tendencies which must eventually find their outlet in either the break-up or the gradual mellowing of Soviet power. For no mystical, Messianic movement—and particularly not that of the Kremlin—can face frustration indefinitely without eventually adjusting itself in one way or another to the logic of that state of affairs.

*   *   *

NOTES

1. Here and elsewhere in this paper "Socialism" refers to Marxist or Leninist Communism. * * *

FRANCIS FUKUYAMA

THE END OF HISTORY?

In watching the flow of events over the past decade or so, it is hard to avoid the feeling that something very fundamental has happened in world history. The past year has seen a flood of articles commemorating the end of the Cold War, and the fact that "peace" seems to be breaking out in many regions of the world. Most of these analyses lack any larger conceptual framework for distinguishing between what is essential and what is contingent or accidental in world history, and are predictably superficial. If Mr. Gorbachev were ousted from the Kremlin or a new Ayatollah proclaimed the millennium from a desolate Middle Eastern capital, these same commentators would scramble to announce the rebirth of a new era of conflict.

And yet, all of these people sense dimly that there is some larger process at work, a process that gives coherence and order to the daily headlines. The twentieth century saw the developed world descend into a paroxysm of ideological violence, as liberalism contended first with the remnants of absolutism, then bolshevism and fascism, and finally an updated Marxism that threatened to lead to the ultimate apocalypse of nuclear war. But the century that began full of self-confidence in the ultimate triumph of Western liberal democracy seems at its close to be returning full circle to where it started: not to an "end of ideology" or a convergence between capitalism and socialism, as earlier predicted, but to an unabashed victory of economic and political liberalism.

The triumph of the West, of the Western *idea*, is evident first of all in the total exhaustion of viable systematic alternatives to Western liberalism. In the past decade, there have been unmistakable changes in the intellectual climate of the world's two largest communist countries, and the beginnings of significant reform movements in both. But this phenomenon extends beyond high politics and it can be seen also in the ineluctable spread of consumerist Western culture in such diverse contexts as the peasants' markets and color television sets now omnipresent throughout China, the cooperative restaurants and clothing

From *The National Interest* no. 16 (summer 1989): 3–18. Some of the author's notes have been omitted.

stores opened in the past year in Moscow, the Beethoven piped into Japanese department stores, and the rock music enjoyed alike in Prague, Rangoon, and Tehran.

What we may be witnessing is not just the end of the Cold War, or the passing of a particular period of postwar history, but the end of history as such: that is, the end point of mankind's ideological evolution and the universalization of Western liberal democracy as the final form of human government. This is not to say that there will no longer be events to fill the pages of *Foreign Affairs*'s yearly summaries of international relations, for the victory of liberalism has occurred primarily in the realm of ideas or consciousness and is as yet incomplete in the real or material world. But there are powerful reasons for believing that it is the ideal that will govern the material world *in the long run*. To understand how this is so, we must first consider some theoretical issues concerning the nature of historical change.

I

The notion of the end of history is not an original one. Its best known propagator was Karl Marx, who believed that the direction of historical development was a purposeful one determined by the interplay of material forces, and would come to an end only with the achievement of a communist utopia that would finally resolve all prior contradictions. But the concept of history as a dialectical process with a beginning, a middle, and an end was borrowed by Marx from his great German predecessor, Georg Wilhelm Friedrich Hegel.

For better or worse, much of Hegel's historicism has become part of our contemporary intellectual baggage. The notion that mankind has progressed through a series of primitive stages of consciousness on his path to the present, and that these stages corresponded to concrete forms of social organization, such as tribal, slave-owning, theocratic, and finally democratic-egalitarian societies, has become inseparable from the modern

understanding of man. Hegel was the first philosopher to speak the language of modern social science, insofar as man for him was the product of his concrete historical and social environment and not, as earlier natural right theorists would have it, a collection of more or less fixed "natural" attributes. The mastery and transformation of man's natural environment through the application of science and technology was originally not a Marxist concept, but a Hegelian one. Unlike later historicists whose historical relativism degenerated into relativism *tout court*, however, Hegel believed that history culminated in an absolute moment—a moment in which a final, rational form of society and state became victorious.

It is Hegel's misfortune to be known now primarily as Marx's precursor, and it is our misfortune that few of us are familiar with Hegel's work from direct study, but only as it has been filtered through the distorting lens of Marxism. In France, however, there has been an effort to save Hegel from his Marxist interpreters and to resurrect him as the philosopher who most correctly speaks to our time. Among those modern French interpreters of Hegel, the greatest was certainly Alexandre Kojève, a brilliant Russian emigre who taught a highly influential series of seminars in Paris in the 1930s at the *Ecole Practique des Hautes Etudes*.[1] While largely unknown in the United States, Kojève had a major impact on the intellectual life of the continent. Among his students ranged such future luminaries as Jean-Paul Sartre on the Left and Raymond Aron on the Right; postwar existentialism borrowed many of its basic categories from Hegel via Kojève.

Kojève sought to resurrect the Hegel of the *Phenomenology of Mind,* the Hegel who proclaimed history to be at an end in 1806. For as early as this Hegel saw in Napoleon's defeat of the Prussian monarchy at the Battle of Jena the victory of the ideals of the French Revolution, and the imminent universalization of the state incorporating the principles of liberty and equality. Kojève, far from rejecting Hegel in light of the turbulent events of the next century and a half, insisted that the latter had been essentially correct. The Battle of Jena marked the end of history because it was at that point that the *vanguard* of humanity (a term quite familiar to Marxists) actualized the principles of the French Revolution. While there was considerable work to be done after 1806—abolishing slavery and the slave trade, extending the franchise to workers, women, blacks, and other racial minorities, etc.— the basic *principles* of the liberal democratic state could not be improved upon. The two world wars in this century and their attendant revolutions and upheavals simply had the effect of extending those principles spatially, such that the various provinces of human civilization were brought up to the level of its most advanced outposts, and of forcing those societies in Europe and North America at the vanguard of civilization to implement their liberalism more fully.

The state that emerges at the end of history is liberal insofar as it recognizes and protects through a system of law man's universal right to freedom, and democratic insofar as it exists only with the consent of the governed. For Kojève, this so-called "universal homogenous state" found real-life embodiment in the countries of postwar Western Europe—precisely those flabby, prosperous, self-satisfied, inward-looking, weak-willed states whose grandest project was nothing more heroic than the creation of the Common Market. But this was only to be expected. For human history and the conflict that characterized it was based on the existence of "contradictions": primitive man's quest for mutual recognition, the dialectic of the master and slave, the transformation and mastery of nature, the struggle for the universal recognition of rights, and the dichotomy between proletarian and capitalist. But in the universal homogenous state, all prior contradictions are resolved and all human needs are satisfied. There is no struggle or conflict over "large" issues, and consequently no need for generals or statesmen; what remains is primarily economic activity. And indeed, Kojève's life was consistent with his teaching. Believing that there was no more work for philosophers as well, since Hegel (correctly understood) had already achieved absolute knowledge, Kojève left teaching after the war and spent the remainder of his life working as a bureaucrat in the European Economic Community, until his death in 1968.

To his contemporaries at mid-century, Kojève's proclamation of the end of history must have seemed like the typical eccentric solipsism of a French intellectual, coming as it did on the heels of World War II and at the very height of the Cold War. To comprehend how Kojève could have been so audacious as to assert that history has ended, we must first of all understand the meaning of Hegelian idealism.

II

For Hegel, the contradictions that drive history exist first of all in the realm of human consciousness, i.e. on the level of ideas—not the trivial election year proposals of American politicians, but ideas in the sense of large unifying world views that might best be understood under the rubric of ideology. Ideology in this sense is not restricted to the secular and explicit political doctrines we usually associate with the term, but can include religion, culture, and the complex of moral values underlying any society as well.

Hegel's view of the relationship between the ideal and the real or material worlds was an extremely complicated one, beginning with the fact that for him the distinction between the two was only apparent. He did not believe that the real world conformed or could be made to conform to ideological preconceptions of philosophy professors in any simple-minded way, or that the "material" world could not impinge on the ideal. Indeed, Hegel the professor was temporarily thrown out of work as a result of a very material event, the Battle of Jena. But while Hegel's writing and thinking could be stopped by a bullet from the material world, the hand on the trigger of the gun was motivated in turn by the ideas of liberty and equality that had driven the French Revolution.

For Hegel, all human behavior in the material world, and hence all human history, is rooted in a prior state of consciousness—an idea similar to the one expressed by John Maynard Keynes when he said that the views of men of affairs were usually derived from defunct economists and academic scribblers of earlier generations. This consciousness may not be explicit and self-aware, as are modern political doctrines, but may rather take the form of religion or simple cultural or moral habits. And yet this realm of consciousness *in the long run* necessarily becomes manifest in the material world, indeed creates the material world in its own image. Consciousness is cause and not effect, and can develop autonomously from the material world; hence the real subtext underlying the apparent jumble of current events is the history of ideology.

Hegel's idealism has fared poorly at the hands of later thinkers. Marx reversed the priority of the real and the ideal completely, relegating the entire realm of consciousness—religion, art, culture, philosophy itself—to a "superstructure" that was determined entirely by the prevailing material mode of production. Yet another unfortunate legacy of Marxism is our tendency to retreat into materialist or utilitarian explanations of political or historical phenomena, and our disinclination to believe in the autonomous power of ideas. A recent example of this is Paul Kennedy's hugely successful *The Rise and Fall of the Great Powers*, which ascribes the decline of great powers to simple economic overextension. Obviously, this is true on some level: an empire whose economy is barely above the level of subsistence cannot bankrupt its treasury indefinitely. But whether a highly productive modern industrial society chooses to spend 3 or 7 percent of its GNP on defense rather than consumption is entirely a matter of that society's political priorities, which are in turn determined in the realm of consciousness.

The materialist bias of modern thought is characteristic not only of people on the Left who may be sympathetic to Marxism, but of many passionate anti-Marxists as well. Indeed, there is on the Right what one might label the *Wall Street Journal* school of deterministic materialism that discounts the importance of ideology and culture and sees man as essentially a rational, profit-maximizing individual. It is precisely this kind of individual and his pursuit of material incentives that is posited as the basis for economic life as such in economic textbooks. One small example will illustrate the problematic character of such materialist views.

Max Weber begins his famous book, *The Protestant Ethic and the Spirit of Capitalism*, by noting the different economic performance of Protestant and Catholic communities throughout Europe and America, summed up in the proverb that Protestants eat well while Catholics sleep well. Weber notes that according to any economic theory that posited man as a rational profit-maximizer, raising the piece-work rate should increase labor productivity. But in fact, in many traditional peasant communities, raising the piece-work rate actually had the opposite effect of *lowering* labor productivity: at the higher rate, a peasant accustomed to earning two and one-half marks per day found he could earn the same amount by working less, and did so because he valued leisure more than income. The choices of leisure over income, or of the militaristic life of the Spartan hoplite over the wealth of the Athenian trader, or even the ascetic life of the early capitalist entrepreneur over that of a traditional leisured aristocrat, cannot possibly be explained by the impersonal working of material forces, but come preeminently out of the sphere of consciousness—what we have labeled here broadly as ideology. And indeed, a central theme of Weber's work was to prove that contrary to Marx, the material mode of production, far from being the "base," was itself a "superstructure" with roots in religion and culture, and that to understand the emergence of modern capitalism and the profit motive one had to study their antecedents in the realm of the spirit.

As we look around the contemporary world, the poverty of materialist theories of economic development is all too apparent The *Wall Street Journal* school of deterministic materialism habitually points to the stunning economic success of Asia in the past few decades as evidence of the viability of free market economics, with the implication that all societies would see similar development were they simply to allow their populations to pursue their material self-interest freely. Surely free markets and stable political systems are a necessary precondition to capitalist economic growth. But just as surely the cultural heritage of those Far Eastern societies, the ethic of work and saving and family, a religious heritage that does not, like Islam, place restrictions on certain forms of economic behavior, and other deeply ingrained moral qualities, are equally important in explaining their economic performance. And yet the intellectual weight of materialism is such that not a single respectable contemporary theory of economic development addresses consciousness and culture seriously as the matrix within which economic behavior is formed.

Failure to understand that the roots of economic behavior lie in the realm of consciousness and culture leads to the common mistake of attributing material causes to phenomena that are essentially ideal in nature. For example, it is commonplace in the West to interpret the reform movements first in China and most recently in the Soviet Union as the victory of the material over the ideal—that is, a recognition that ideological incentives could not replace material ones in stimulating a highly productive modern economy, and that if one wanted to prosper one had to appeal to baser forms of self-interest. But the deep defects of socialist economies were evident thirty or forty years ago to anyone who chose to look. Why was it that these countries moved away from central planning only in the 1980s? The answer must be found in the consciousness of the elites and leaders ruling them, who decided to opt for the "Protestant" life of wealth and risk over the "Catholic" path of poverty and security. That change was in no way made inevitable by the material conditions in which either country found itself on the eve of the reform, but instead came about as the result of the victory of one idea over another.[2]

For Kojève, as for all good Hegelians, understanding the underlying processes of history requires understanding developments in the realm of consciousness or ideas, since consciousness will ultimately remake the material world in its own image. To say that history ended in 1806 meant that mankind's ideological evolution ended in the ideals of the French or American Revolutions: while particular regimes in the real world might not implement these ideals fully, their theoretical truth is absolute and could not be improved upon. Hence it did not matter to Kojève that the consciousness of the postwar generation of Europeans had not been universalized throughout the world; if ideological development had in fact ended, the homogenous state would eventually become victorious throughout the material world.

I have neither the space nor, frankly, the ability to defend in depth Hegel's radical idealist perspective. The issue is not whether Hegel's system was right, but whether his perspective might uncover the problematic nature of many materialist explanations we often take for granted. This is not to deny the role of material factors as such. To a literal-minded idealist, human society can be built around any arbitrary set of principles regardless of their relationship to the material world. And in fact men have proven themselves able to endure the most extreme material hardships in the name of ideas that exist in the realm of the spirit alone, be it the divinity of cows or the nature of the Holy Trinity.[3]

But while man's very perception of the material world is shaped by his historical consciousness of it, the material world can clearly affect in return the viability of a particular state of consciousness. In particular, the spectacular abundance of advanced liberal economies and the infinitely diverse consumer culture made possible by them seem to both foster and preserve liberalism in the political sphere. I want to avoid the materialist determinism that says that liberal economics inevitably produces liberal politics, because I believe that both economics and politics presuppose an autonomous prior state of consciousness that makes them possible. But that state of consciousness that permits the growth of liberalism seems to stabilize in the way one would expect at the end of history if it is underwritten by the abundance of a modern free market economy. We might summarize the content of the universal homogenous state as liberal democracy in the political sphere combined with easy access to VCRs and stereos in the economic.

III

Have we in fact reached the end of history? Are there, in other words, any fundamental "contradictions" in human life that cannot be resolved in the context of modern liberalism, that would be resolvable by an alternative political-economic structure? If we accept the idealist premises laid out above, we must seek an answer to this question in the realm of ideology and consciousness. Our task is not to answer exhaustively the challenges to liberalism promoted by every crackpot messiah around the world, but only those that are embodied in important social or political forces and movements, and which are therefore part of world history. For our purposes, it matters very little what strange thoughts occur to people in Albania or Burkina Faso, for we are interested in what one could in some sense call the common ideological heritage of mankind.

In the past century, there have been two major challenges to liberalism, those of fascism and of communism. The former saw the political weakness, materialism, anomie, and lack of community of the West as fundamental contradictions in liberal societies that could only be resolved by a strong state that forged a new "people" on the basis of national exclusiveness. Fascism was destroyed as a living ideology by World War II. This was a defeat, of course, on a very material level, but it amounted to a defeat of the idea as well. What destroyed fascism as an idea was not universal moral revulsion against it, since plenty of people were willing to endorse the idea as long as it seemed the wave of the future, but its lack of

success. After the war, it seemed to most people that German fascism as well as its other European and Asian variants were bound to self-destruct. There was no material reason why new fascist movements could not have sprung up again after the war in other locales, but for the fact that expansionist ultranationalism, with its promise of unending conflict leading to disastrous military defeat, had completely lost its appeal. The ruins of the Reich chancellory as well as the atomic bombs dropped on Hiroshima and Nagasaki killed this ideology on the level of consciousness as well as materially, and all of the proto-fascist movements spawned by the German and Japanese examples like the Peronist movement in Argentina or Subhas Chandra Bose's Indian National Army withered after the war.

The ideological challenge mounted by the other great alternative to liberalism, communism, was far more serious. Marx, speaking Hegel's language, asserted that liberal society contained a fundamental contradiction that could not be resolved within its context, that between capital and labor, and this contradiction has constituted the chief accusation against liberalism ever since. But surely, the class issue has actually been successfully resolved in the West. As Kojève (among others) noted, the egalitarianism of modern America represents the essential achievement of the classless society envisioned by Marx. This is not to say that there are not rich people and poor people in the United States, or that the gap between them has not grown in recent years. But the root causes of economic inequality do not have to do with the underlying legal and social structure of our society, which remains fundamentally egalitarian and moderately redistributionist, so much as with the cultural and social characteristics of the groups that make it up, which are in turn the historical legacy of premodern conditions. Thus black poverty in the United States is not the inherent product of liberalism, but is rather the "legacy of slavery and racism" which persisted long after the formal abolition of slavery.

As a result of the receding of the class issue, the appeal of communism in the developed Western world, it is safe to say, is lower today than any time since the end of the First World War. This can be measured in any number of ways: in the declining membership and electoral pull of the major European communist parties, and their overtly revisionist programs; in the corresponding electoral success of conservative parties from Britain and Germany to the United States and Japan, which are unabashedly pro-market and anti-statist; and in an intellectual climate whose most "advanced" members no longer believe that bourgeois society is something that ultimately needs to be overcome. This is not to say that the opinions of progressive intellectuals in Western countries are not deeply pathological in any number of ways. But those who believe that the future must inevitably be socialist tend to be very old, or very marginal to the real political discourse of their societies.

One may argue that the socialist alternative was never terribly plausible for the North Atlantic world, and was sustained for the last several decades primarily by its success outside of this region. But it is precisely in the non-European world that one is most struck by the occurrence of major ideological transformations. Surely the most remarkable changes have occurred in Asia. Due to the strength and adaptability of the indigenous cultures there, Asia became a battleground for a variety of imported Western ideologies early in this century. Liberalism in Asia was a very weak reed in the period after World War I; it is easy today to forget how gloomy Asia's political future looked as recently as ten or fifteen years ago. It is easy to forget as well how momentous the outcome of Asian ideological struggles seemed for world political development as a whole.

The first Asian alternative to liberalism to be decisively defeated was the fascist one represented by Imperial Japan. Japanese fascism (like its German version) was defeated by the force of American arms in the Pacific war, and liberal democracy was imposed on Japan by a victorious United States. Western capitalism and political liberalism when transplanted to Japan were adapted and transformed by the Japanese in such a way as to

be scarcely recognizable. Many Americans are now aware that Japanese industrial organization is very different from that prevailing in the United States or Europe, and it is questionable what relationship the factional maneuvering that takes place with the governing Liberal Democratic Party bears to democracy. Nonetheless, the very fact that the essential elements of economic and political liberalism have been so successfully grafted onto uniquely Japanese traditions and institutions guarantees their survival in the long run. More important is the contribution that Japan has made in turn to world history by following in the footsteps of the United States to create a truly universal consumer culture that has become both a symbol and an underpinning of the universal homogenous state. V.S. Naipaul travelling in Khomeini's Iran shortly after the revolution noted the omnipresent signs advertising the products of Sony, Hitachi, and JVC, whose appeal remained virtually irresistible and gave the lie to the regime's pretensions of restoring a state based on the rule of the *Shariah*. Desire for access to the consumer culture, created in large measure by Japan, has played a crucial role in fostering the spread of economic liberalism throughout Asia, and hence in promoting political liberalism as well.

The economic success of the other newly industrializing countries (NICs) in Asia following on the example of Japan is by now a familiar story. What is important from a Hegelian standpoint is that political liberalism has been following economic liberalism, more slowly than many had hoped but with seeming inevitability. Here again we see the victory of the idea of the universal homogenous state. South Korea had developed into a modern, urbanized society with an increasingly large and well-educated middle class that could not possibly be isolated from the larger democratic trends around them. Under these circumstances it seemed intolerable to a large part of this population that it should be ruled by an anachronistic military regime while Japan, only a decade or so ahead in economic terms, had parliamentary institutions for over forty years. Even the former socialist regime in Burma, which for so many decades existed in dismal isolation from the larger trends dominating Asia, was buffeted in the past year by pressures to liberalize both its economy and political system. It is said that unhappiness with strongman Ne Win began when a senior Burmese officer went to Singapore for medical treatment and broke down crying when he saw how far socialist Burma had been left behind by its ASEAN neighbors.

But the power of the liberal idea would seem much less impressive if it had not infected the largest and oldest culture in Asia, China. The simple existence of communist China created an alternative pole of ideological attraction, and as such constituted a threat to liberalism. But the past fifteen years have seen an almost total discrediting of Marxism-Leninism as an economic system. Beginning with the famous third plenum of the Tenth Central Committee in 1978, the Chinese Communist party set about decollectivizing agriculture for the 800 million Chinese who still lived in the countryside. The role of the state in agriculture was reduced to that of a tax collector, while production of consumer goods was sharply increased in order to give peasants a taste of the universal homogenous state and thereby an incentive to work. The reform doubled Chinese grain output in only five years, and in the process created for Deng Xiao-ping a solid political base from which he was able to extend the reform to other parts of the economy. Economic statistics do not begin to describe the dynamism, initiative, and openness evident in China since the reform began.

China could not now be described in any way as a liberal democracy. At present, no more than 20 percent of its economy has been marketized, and most importantly it continues to be ruled by a self-appointed Communist party which has given no hint of wanting to devolve power. Deng has made none of Gorbachev's promises regarding democratization of the political system and there is no Chinese equivalent of *glasnost*. The Chinese leadership has in fact been much more

circumspect in criticizing Mao and Maoism than Gorbachev with respect to Brezhnev and Stalin, and the regime continues to pay lip service to Marxism-Leninism as its ideological underpinning. But anyone familiar with the outlook and behavior of the new technocratic elite now governing China knows that Marxism and ideological principle have become virtually irrelevant as guides to policy, and that bourgeois consumerism has a real meaning in that country for the first time since the revolution. The various slowdowns in the pace of reform, the campaigns against "spiritual pollution" and crackdowns on political dissent are more properly seen as tactical adjustments made in the process of managing what is an extraordinarily difficult political transition. By ducking the question of political reform while putting the economy on a new footing, Deng has managed to avoid the breakdown of authority that has accompanied Gorbachev's *perestroika*. Yet the pull of the liberal idea continues to be very strong as economic power devolves and the economy becomes more open to the outside world. There are currently over 20,000 Chinese students studying in the U.S. and other Western countries, almost all of them the children of the Chinese elite. It is hard to believe that when they return home to run the country they will be content for China to be the only country in Asia unaffected by the larger democratizing trend. The student demonstrations in Beijing that broke out first in December 1986 and recurred recently on the occasion of Hu Yao-bang's death were only the beginning of what will inevitably be mounting pressure for change in the political system as well.

What is important about China from the standpoint of world history is not the present state of the reform or even its future prospects. The central issue is the fact that the People's Republic of China can no longer act as a beacon for illiberal forces around the world, whether they be guerrillas in some Asian jungle or middle class students in Paris. Maoism, rather than being the pattern for Asia's future, became an anachronism, and it was the mainland Chinese who in fact were decisively influenced by the prosperity and dynamism of their overseas co-ethnics—the ironic ultimate victory of Taiwan.

Important as these changes in China have been, however, it is developments in the Soviet Union—the original "homeland of the world proletariat"—that have put the final nail in the coffin of the Marxist-Leninist alternative to liberal democracy. It should be clear that in terms of formal institutions, not much has changed in the four years since Gorbachev has come to power: free markets and the cooperative movement represent only a small part of the Soviet economy, which remains centrally planned; the political system is still dominated by the Communist party, which has only begun to democratize internally and to share power with other groups; the regime continues to assert that it is seeking only to modernize socialism and that its ideological basis remains Marxism-Leninism; and, finally, Gorbachev faces a potentially powerful conservative opposition that could undo many of the changes that have taken place to date. Moreover, it is hard to be too sanguine about the chances for success of Gorbachev's proposed reforms, either in the sphere of economics or politics. But my purpose here is not to analyze events in the short-term, or to make predictions for policy purposes, but to look at underlying trends in the sphere of ideology and consciousness. And in that respect, it is clear that an astounding transformation has occurred.

Emigres from the Soviet Union have been reporting for at least the last generation now that virtually nobody in that country truly believed in Marxism-Leninism any longer, and that this was nowhere more true than in the Soviet elite, which continued to mouth Marxist slogans out of sheer cynicism. The corruption and decadence of the late Brezhnev-era Soviet state seemed to matter little, however, for as long as the state itself refused to throw into question any of the fundamental principles underlying Soviet society, the system was capable of functioning adequately out of sheer inertia and could even muster some dynamism in the realm of foreign and defense policy. Marxism-Leninism was like a magical incantation which, however absurd and devoid of meaning, was the only common basis on which the elite could agree to rule Soviet society.

What has happened in the four years since Gorbachev's coming to power is a revolutionary assault on the most fundamental institutions and principles of Stalinism, and their replacement by other principles which do not amount to liberalism *per se* but whose only connecting thread is liberalism. This is most evident in the economic sphere, where the reform economists around Gorbachev have become steadily more radical in their support for free markets, to the point where some like Nikolai Shmelev do not mind being compared in public to Milton Friedman. There is a virtual consensus among the currently dominant school of Soviet economists now that central planning and the command system of allocation are the root cause of economic inefficiency, and that if the Soviet system is ever to heal itself, it must permit free and decentralized decision-making with respect to investment, labor, and prices. After a couple of initial years of ideological confusion, these principles have finally been incorporated into policy with the promulgation of new laws on enterprise autonomy, cooperatives, and finally in 1988 on lease arrangements and family farming. There are, of course, a number of fatal flaws in the current implementation of the reform, most notably the absence of a thoroughgoing price reform. But the problem is no longer a *conceptual* one: Gorbachev and his lieutenants seem to understand the economic logic of marketization well enough, but like the leaders of a Third World country facing the IMF, are afraid of the social consequences of ending consumer subsidies and other forms of dependence on the state sector.

In the political sphere, the proposed changes to the Soviet constitution, legal system, and party rules amount to much less than the establishment of a liberal state. Gorbachev has spoken of democratization primarily in the sphere of internal party affairs, and has shown little intention of ending the Communist party's monopoly of power; indeed, the political reform seeks to legitimize and therefore strengthen the CPSU's rule.[4] Nonetheless, the general principles underlying many of the reforms—that the "people" should be truly responsible for their own affairs, that higher political bodies should be answerable to lower ones, and not vice versa, that the rule of law should prevail over arbitrary police actions, with separation of powers and an independent judiciary, that there should be legal protection for property rights, the need for open discussion of public issues and the right of public dissent, the empowering of the Soviets as a forum in which the whole Soviet people can participate, and of a political culture that is more tolerant and pluralistic—come from a source fundamentally alien to the USSR's Marxist-Leninist tradition, even if they are incompletely articulated and poorly implemented in practice.

Gorbachev's repeated assertions that he is doing no more than trying to restore the original meaning of Leninism are themselves a kind of Orwellian doublespeak. Gorbachev and his allies have consistently maintained that intraparty democracy was somehow the essence of Leninism, and that the various liberal practices of open debate, secret ballot elections, and rule of law were all part of the Leninist heritage, corrupted only later by Stalin. While almost anyone would look good compared to Stalin, drawing so sharp a line between Lenin and his successor is questionable. The essence of Lenin's democratic centralism was centralism, not democracy; that is, the absolutely rigid, monolithic, and disciplined dictatorship of a hierarchically organized vanguard Communist party, speaking in the name of the *demos*. All of Lenin's vicious polemics against Karl Kautsky, Rosa Luxemburg, and various other Menshevik and Social Democratic rivals, not to mention his contempt for "bourgeois legality" and freedoms, centered around his profound conviction that a revolution could not be successfully made by a democratically run organization.

Gorbachev's claim that he is seeking to return to the true Lenin is perfectly easy to understand:

having fostered a thorough denunciation of Stalinism and Brezhnevism as the root of the USSR's present predicament, he needs some point in Soviet history on which to anchor the legitimacy of the CPSU's continued rule. But Gorbachev's tactical requirements should not blind us to the fact that the democratizing and decentralizing principles which he has enunciated in both the economic and political spheres are highly subversive of some of the most fundamental precepts of both Marxism and Leninism. Indeed, if the bulk of the present economic reform proposals were put into effect, it is hard to know how the Soviet economy would be more socialist than those of other Western countries with large public sectors.

The Soviet Union could in no way be described as a liberal or democratic country now, nor do I think that it is terribly likely that *perestroika* will succeed such that the label will be thinkable any time in the near future. But at the end of history it is not necessary that all societies become successful liberal societies, merely that they end their ideological pretensions of representing different and higher forms of human society. And in this respect I believe that something very important has happened in the Soviet Union in the past few years: the criticisms of the Soviet system sanctioned by Gorbachev have been so thorough and devastating that there is very little chance of going back to either Stalinism or Brezhnevism in any simple way. Gorbachev has finally permitted people to say what they had privately understood for many years, namely, that the magical incantations of Marxism-Leninism were nonsense, that Soviet socialism was not superior to the West in any respect but was in fact a monumental failure. The conservative opposition in the USSR, consisting both of simple workers afraid of unemployment and inflation and of party officials fearful of losing their jobs and privileges, is outspoken and may be strong enough to force Gorbachev's ouster in the next few years. But what both groups desire is tradition, order, and authority; they manifest no deep commitment to Marxism-Leninism, except insofar as they have invested much of their own lives in it. For authority to be restored in the Soviet Union after Gorbachev's demolition work, it must be on the basis of some new and vigorous ideology which has not yet appeared on the horizon.

If we admit for the moment that the fascist and communist challenges to liberalism are dead, are there any other ideological competitors left? Or put another way, are there contradictions in liberal society beyond that of class that are not resolvable? Two possibilities suggest themselves, those of religion and nationalism.

The rise of religious fundamentalism in recent years within the Christian, Jewish, and Muslim traditions has been widely noted. One is inclined to say that the revival of religion in some way attests to a broad unhappiness with the impersonality and spiritual vacuity of liberal consumerist societies. Yet while the emptiness at the core of liberalism is most certainly a defect in the ideology—indeed, a flaw that one does not need the perspective of religion to recognize—it is not at all clear that it is remediable through politics. Modern liberalism itself was historically a consequence of the weakness of religiously-based societies which, failing to agree on the nature of the good life, could not provide even the minimal preconditions of peace and stability. In the contemporary world only Islam has offered a theocratic state as a political alternative to both liberalism and communism. But the doctrine has little appeal for non-Muslims, and it is hard to believe that the movement will take on any universal significance. Other less organized religious impulses have been successfully satisfied within the sphere of personal life that is permitted in liberal societies.

The other major "contradiction" potentially unresolvable by liberalism is the one posed by nationalism and other forms of racial and ethnic consciousness. It is certainly true that a very large degree of conflict since the Battle of Jena has had its roots in nationalism. Two cataclysmic world wars in this century have been spawned by the nationalism of the developed world in various guises, and if those passions have been muted to a certain extent in postwar Europe, they are still extremely powerful in the Third World. Nationalism has been a threat to liberalism historically in Germany, and continues to be one in isolated parts of "post-historical" Europe like Northern Ireland.

But it is not clear that nationalism represents an irreconcilable contradiction in the heart of liberalism. In the first place, nationalism is not one single phenomenon but several, ranging from mild cultural nostalgia to the highly organized and elaborately articulated doctrine of National Socialism. Only systematic nationalisms of the latter sort can qualify as a formal ideology on the level of liberalism or communism. The vast majority of the world's nationalist movements do not have a political program beyond the negative desire of independence *from* some other group or people, and do not offer anything like a comprehensive agenda for socio-economic organization. As such, they are compatible with doctrines and ideologies that do offer such agendas. While they may constitute a source of conflict for liberal societies, this conflict does not arise from liberalism itself so much as from the fact that the liberalism in question is incomplete. Certainly a great deal of the world's ethnic and nationalist tension can be explained in terms of peoples who are forced to live in unrepresentative political systems that they have not chosen.

While it is impossible to rule out the sudden appearance of new ideologies or previously unrecognized contradictions in liberal societies, then, the present world seems to confirm that the fundamental principles of socio-political organization have not advanced terribly far since 1806. Many of the wars and revolutions fought since that time have been undertaken in the name of ideologies which claimed to be more advanced than liberalism, but whose pretensions were ultimately unmasked by history. In the meantime, they have helped to spread the universal homogenous state to the point where it could have a significant effect on the overall character of international relations.

IV

What are the implications of the end of history for international relations? Clearly, the vast bulk of the Third World remains very much mired in history, and will be a terrain of conflict for many years to come. But let us focus for the time being on the larger and more developed states of the world who after all account for the greater part of world politics. Russia and China are not likely to join the developed nations of the West as liberal societies any time in the foreseeable future, but suppose for a moment that Marxism-Leninism ceases to be a factor driving the foreign policies of these states—a prospect which, if not yet here, the last few years have made a real possibility. How will the overall characteristics of a de-ideologized world differ from those of the one with which we are familiar at such a hypothetical juncture?

The most common answer is—not very much. For there is a very widespread belief among many observers of international relations that underneath the skin of ideology is a hard core of great power national interest that guarantees a fairly high level of competition and conflict between nations. Indeed, according to one academically popular school of international relations theory, conflict inheres in the international system as such, and to understand the prospects for conflict one must look at the shape of the system—for example, whether it is bipolar or multipolar—rather than at the specific character of the nations and regimes that constitute it. This school in effect applies a Hobbesian view of politics to international relations, and assumes that aggression and insecurity are universal characteristics of human societies rather than the product of specific historical circumstances.

Believers in this line of thought take the relations that existed between the participants in the classical nineteenth century European balance of power as a model for what a de-ideologized contemporary world would look like. Charles Krauthammer, for example, recently explained that if as a result of Gorbachev's reforms the USSR is shorn of Marxist-Leninist ideology, its behavior will revert to that of nineteenth century imperial Russia. While he finds this more reassuring than the threat posed by a communist Russia, he implies that there will still be a substantial degree of competition and conflict in the international system, just as there was say between Russia and Britain or Wilhelmine Germany in the last century. This is, of course, a convenient point of view for people who want to admit that something major is changing in the Soviet Union, but do not want to accept responsibility for recommending the radical policy redirection implicit in such a view. But is it true?

In fact, the notion that ideology is a superstructure imposed on a substratum of permanent great power interest is a highly questionable proposition. For the way in which any state defines its national interest is not universal but rests on some kind of prior ideological basis, just as we saw that economic behavior is determined by a prior state of consciousness. In this century, states have adopted highly articulated doctrines with explicit foreign policy agendas legitimizing expansionism, like Marxism-Leninism or National Socialism.

The expansionist and competitive behavior of nineteenth-century European states rested on no less ideal a basis; it just so happened that the ideology driving it was less explicit than the doctrines of the twentieth century. For one thing, most "liberal" European societies were illiberal insofar as they believed in the legitimacy of imperialism, that is, the right of one nation to rule over other nations without regard for the wishes of the ruled. The justifications for imperialism varied from nation to nation, from a crude belief in the legitimacy of force, particularly when applied to non-Europeans, to the White Man's Burden and Europe's Christianizing mission, to the desire to give people of color access to the culture of Rabelais and Molière. But whatever the particular ideological basis, every "developed" country believed in the acceptability of higher civilizations ruling lower ones—including, incidentally, the United States with regard to the Philippines. This led to a drive for pure territorial aggrandizement in the latter half of the century and played no small role in causing the Great War.

The radical and deformed outgrowth of nineteenth-century imperialism was German fascism, an ideology which justified Germany's right not only to rule over non-European peoples, but over *all* non-German ones. But in retrospect it seems that Hitler represented a diseased bypath in the general course of European development, and since his fiery defeat, the legitimacy of any kind of territorial aggrandizement has been thoroughly discredited. Since the Second World War, European nationalism has been defanged and shorn of any real relevance to foreign policy, with the consequence that the nineteenth-century model of great power behavior has become a serious anachronism. The most extreme form of nationalism that any Western European state has mustered since 1945 has been Gaullism, whose self-assertion has been confined largely to the realm of nuisance politics and culture. International life for the part of the world that has reached the end of history is far more preoccupied with economics than with politics or strategy.

The developed states of the West do maintain defense establishments and in the postwar period have competed vigorously for influence to meet a worldwide communist threat. This behavior has been driven, however, by an external threat from states that possess overtly expansionist ideologies, and would not exist in their absence. To take the "neo-realist" theory seriously, one would have to believe that "natural" competitive behavior would reassert itself among the OECD states were Russia and China to disappear from the face of the earth. That is, West Germany and France would arm themselves against each other as they did in the 1930s, Australia and New Zealand would send military advisers to block each others' advances in Africa, and the U.S.-Canadian border would become fortified. Such a prospect is, of course, ludicrous: minus Marxist-Leninist ideology, we are far more likely to see the "Common Marketization" of world politics than the disintegration of the EEC into nineteenth-century competitiveness. Indeed, as our experience in dealing

with Europe on matters such as terrorism or Libya prove, they are much further gone than we down the road that denies the legitimacy of the use of force in international politics, even in self-defense.

The automatic assumption that Russia shorn of its expansionist communist ideology should pick up where the czars left off just prior to the Bolshevik Revolution is therefore a curious one. It assumes that the evolution of human consciousness has stood still in the meantime, and that the Soviets, while picking up currently fashionable ideas in the realm of economics, will return to foreign policy views a century out of date in the rest of Europe. This is certainly not what happened to China after it began its reform process. Chinese competitiveness and expansionism on the world scene have virtually disappeared: Beijing no longer sponsors Maoist insurgencies or tries to cultivate influence in distant African countries as it did in the 1960s. This is not to say that there are not troublesome aspects to contemporary Chinese foreign policy, such as the reckless sale of ballistic missile technology in the Middle East; and the PRC continues to manifest traditional great power behavior in its sponsorship of the Khmer Rouge against Vietnam. But the former is explained by commercial motives and the latter is a vestige of earlier ideologically-based rivalries. The new China far more resembles Gaullist France than pre-World War I Germany.

The real question for the future, however, is the degree to which Soviet elites have assimilated the consciousness of the universal homogenous state that is post-Hitler Europe. From their writings and from my own personal contacts with them, there is no question in my mind that the liberal Soviet intelligentsia rallying around Gorbachev has arrived at the end-of-history view in a remarkably short time, due in no small measure to the contacts they have had since the Brezhnev era with the larger European civilization around them. "New political thinking," the general rubric for their views, describes a world dominated by economic concerns, in which there are no ideological grounds for major conflict between nations, and in which, consequently, the use of military force becomes less legitimate. As Foreign Minister She-vardnadze put it in mid-1988:

> The struggle between two opposing systems is no longer a determining tendency of the present-day era. At the modern stage, the ability to build up material wealth at an accelerated rate on the basis of front-ranking science and high-level techniques and technology, and to distribute it fairly, and through joint efforts to restore and protect the resources necessary for mankind's survival acquires decisive importance.

The post-historical consciousness represented by "new thinking" is only one possible future for the Soviet Union, however. There has always been a very strong current of great Russian chauvinism in the Soviet Union, which has found freer expression since the advent of *glasnost*. It may be possible to return to traditional Marxism-Leninism for a while as a simple rallying point for those who want to restore the authority that Gorbachev has dissipated. But as in Poland, Marxism-Leninism is dead as a mobilizing ideology: under its banner people cannot be made to work harder, and its adherents have lost confidence in themselves. Unlike the propagators of traditional Marxism-Leninism, however, ultra-nationalists in the USSR believe in their Slavophile cause passionately, and one gets the sense that the fascist alternative is not one that has played itself out entirely there.

The Soviet Union, then, is at a fork in the road: it can start down the path that was staked out by Western Europe forty-five years ago, a path that most of Asia has followed, or it can realize its own uniqueness and remain stuck in history. The choice it makes will be highly important for us, given the Soviet Union's size and military strength, for that power will continue to preoccupy us and slow our realization that we have already emerged on the other side of history.

V

The passing of Marxism-Leninism first from China and then from the Soviet Union will mean its death as a living ideology of world historical significance. For while there may be some isolated true believers left in places like Managua, Pyongyang, or Cambridge, Massachusetts, the fact that there is not a single large state in which it is a going concern undermines completely its pretensions to being in the vanguard of human history. And the death of this ideology means the growing "Common Marketization" of international relations, and the diminution of the likelihood of large-scale conflict between states.

This does not by any means imply the end of international conflict *per se*. For the world at that point would be divided between a part that was historical and a part that was post-historical. Conflict between states still in history, and between those states and those at the end of history, would still be possible. There would still be a high and perhaps rising level of ethnic and nationalist violence, since those are impulses incompletely played out, even in parts of the post-historical world. Palestinians and Kurds, Sikhs and Tamils, Irish Catholics and Walloons, Armenians and Azeris, will continue to have their unresolved grievances. This implies that terrorism and wars of national liberation will continue to be an important item on the international agenda. But large-scale conflict must involve large states still caught in the grip of history, and they are what appear to be passing from the scene.

The end of history will be a very sad time. The struggle for recognition, the willingness to risk one's life for a purely abstract goal, the worldwide ideological struggle that called forth daring, courage, imagination, and idealism, will be replaced by economic calculation, the endless solving of technical problems, environmental concerns, and the satisfaction of sophisticated consumer demands. In the post-historical period there will be neither art nor philosophy, just the perpetual caretaking of the museum of human history. I can feel in myself, and see in others around me, a powerful nostalgia for the time when history existed. Such nostalgia, in fact, will continue to fuel competition and conflict even in the post-historical world for some time to come. Even though I recognize its inevitability, I have the most ambivalent feelings for the civilization that has been created in Europe since 1945, with its north Atlantic and Asian off-shoots. Perhaps this very prospect of centuries of boredom at the end of history will serve to get history started once again.

NOTES

1. Kojève's best-known work is his *Introduction à la lecture de Hegel* (Paris: Editions Gallimard, 1947), which is a transcript of the *Ecole Pratique* lectures from the 1930s. This book is available in English entitled *Introduction to the Reading of Hegel* arranged by Raymond Queneau, edited by Allan Bloom, and translated by James Nichols (New York: Basic Books, 1969).
2. It is still not clear whether the Soviet peoples are as "Protestant" as Gorbachev and will follow him down that path.
3. The internal politics of the Byzantine Empire at the time of Justinian revolved around a conflict between the so-called monophysites and monothelites, who believed that the unity of the Holy Trinity was alternatively one of nature or of will. This conflict corresponded to some extent to one between proponents of different racing teams in the Hippodrome in Byzantium and led to a not insignificant level of political violence. Modern historians would tend to seek the roots of such conflicts in antagonisms between social classes or some other modern economic category, being unwilling to believe that men would kill each other over the nature of the Trinity.
4. This is not true in Poland and Hungary, however, whose Communist parties have taken moves toward true power-sharing and pluralism.

GEORGE W. BUSH

THE NATIONAL SECURITY STRATEGY OF THE UNITED STATES OF AMERICA

I. Overview of America's International Strategy

The United States possesses unprecedented—and unequaled—strength and influence in the world. Sustained by faith in the principles of liberty, and the value of a free society, this position comes with unparalleled responsibilities, obligations, and opportunity. The great strength of this nation must be used to promote a balance of power that favors freedom.

From "The National Security Strategy of the United States," September 2002.

For most of the twentieth century, the world was divided by a great struggle over ideas: destructive totalitarian visions versus freedom and equality.

That great struggle is over. The militant visions of class, nation, and race which promised utopia and delivered misery have been defeated and discredited. America is now threatened less by conquering states than we are by failing ones. We are menaced less by fleets and armies than by catastrophic technologies in the hands of the embittered few. We must defeat these threats to our Nation, allies, and friends.

This is also a time of opportunity for America. We will work to translate this moment of influence into decades of peace, prosperity, and liberty. The U.S. national security strategy will be based on a distinctly American internationalism that reflects the union of our values and our national interests. The aim of this strategy is to help make the world not just safer but better. Our goals on the path to progress are clear: political and economic freedom, peaceful relations with other states, and respect for human dignity.

And this path is not America's alone. It is open to all.

To achieve these goals, the United States will:

- champion aspirations for human dignity;
- strengthen alliances to defeat global terrorism and work to prevent attacks against us and our friends;
- work with others to defuse regional conflicts;
- prevent our enemies from threatening us, our allies, and our friends, with weapons of mass destruction;
- ignite a new era of global economic growth through free markets and free trade;
- expand the circle of development by opening societies and building the infrastructure of democracy;
- develop agendas for cooperative action with other main centers of global power; and
- transform America's national security institutions to meet the challenges and opportunities of the twenty-first century.

II. Champion Aspirations for Human Dignity

In pursuit of our goals, our first imperative is to clarify what we stand for: the United States must defend liberty and justice because these principles are right and true for all people everywhere. No nation owns these aspirations, and no nation is exempt from them. Fathers and mothers in all societies want their children to be educated and to live free from poverty and violence. No people on earth yearn to be oppressed, aspire to servitude, or eagerly await the midnight knock of the secret police.

America must stand firmly for the nonnegotiable demands of human disgnity: the rule of law; limits on the absolute power of the state; free speech; freedom of worship; equal justice; respect for women; religious and ethnic tolerance; and respect for private property.

These demands can be met in many ways. America's constitution has served us well. Many other nations, with different histories and cultures, facing different circumstances, have successfully incorporated these core principles into their own systems of governance. History has not been kind to those nations which ignored or flouted the rights and aspirations of their people.

America's experience as a great multi-ethnic democracy affirms our conviction that people of many heritages and faiths can live and prosper in peace. Our own history is a long struggle to live up to our ideals. But even in our worst moments, the principles enshrined in the Declaration of Independence were there to guide us. As a result, America is not just a stronger, but is a freer and more just society.

Today, these ideals are a lifeline to lonely defenders of liberty. And when openings arrive, we can encourage change—as we did in central and eastern Europe between 1989 and 1991, or in Belgrade in 2000. When we see democratic processes take hold among our friends in Taiwan or in the Republic of Korea, and see elected leaders replace generals in Latin America and Africa, we see examples of how authoritarian systems can evolve, marrying local history and traditions with the principles we all cherish.

Embodying lessons from our past and using the opportunity we have today, the national security strategy of the United States must start from these core beliefs and look outward for possibilities to expand liberty.

Our principles will guide our government's decisions about international cooperation, the character of our foreign assistance, and the allocation of resources. They will guide our actions and our words in international bodies.

We will:

- speak out honestly about violations of the nonnegotiable demands of human dignity using our voice and vote in international institutions to advance freedom;
- use our foreign aid to promote freedom and support those who struggle non-violently for it, ensuring that nations moving toward democracy are rewarded for the steps they take;
- make freedom and the development of democratic institutions key themes in our bilateral relations, seeking solidarity and cooperation from other democracies while we press governments that deny human rights to move toward a better future; and
- take special efforts to promote freedom of religion and conscience and defend it from encroachment by repressive governments.

We will champion the cause of human dignity and oppose those who resist it.

III. Strengthen Alliances to Defeat Global Terrorism and Work to Prevent Attacks against Us and Our Friends

The United States of America is fighting a war against terrorists of global reach. The enemy is not a single political regime or person or religion or ideology. The enemy is terrorism—premeditated, politically motivated violence perpetrated against innocents.

In many regions, legitimate grievances prevent the emergence of a lasting peace. Such grievances deserve to be, and must be, addressed within a political process. But no cause justifies terror. The United States will make no concessions to terrorist demands and strike no deals with them. We make no distinction between terrorists and those who knowingly harbor or provide aid to them.

The struggle against global terrorism is different from any other war in our history. It will be fought on many fronts against a particu-

larly elusive enemy over an extended period of time. Progress will come through the persistent accumulation of successes—some seen, some unseen.

Today our enemies have seen the results of what civilized nations can, and will, do against regimes that harbor, support, and use terrorism to achieve their political goals. Afghanistan has been liberated; coalition forces continue to hunt down the Taliban and al-Qaida. But it is not only this battlefield on which we will engage terrorists. Thousands of trained terrorists remain at large with cells in North America, South America, Europe, Africa, the Middle East, and across Asia.

Our priority will be first to disrupt and destroy terrorist organizations of global reach and attack their leadership; command, control, and communications; material support; and finances. This will have a disabling effect upon the terrorists' ability to plan and operate.

We will continue to encourage our regional partners to take up a coordinated effort that isolates the terrorists. Once the regional campaign localizes the threat to a particular state, we will help ensure the state has the military, law enforcement, political, and financial tools necessary to finish the task.

The United States will continue to work with our allies to disrupt the financing of terrorism. We will identify and block the sources of funding for terrorism, freeze the assets of terrorists and those who support them, deny terrorists access to the international financial system, protect legitimate charities from being abused by terrorists, and prevent the movement of terrorists' assets through alternative financial networks.

However, this campaign need not be sequential to be effective, the cumulative effect across all regions will help achieve the results we seek.

We will disrupt and destroy terrorist organizations by:

- direct and continuous action using all the elements of national and international power. Our immediate focus will be those terrorist organizations of global reach and any terrorist or state sponsor of terrorism which attempts to gain or use weapons of mass destruction (WMD) or their precursors;

- defending the United States, the American people, and our interests at home and abroad by identifying and destroying the threat before it reaches our borders. While the United States will constantly strive to enlist the support of the international community, we will not hesitate to act alone, if necessary, to exercise our right of self-defense by acting pre-emptively against such terrorists, to prevent them from doing harm against our people and our country; and

- denying further sponsorship, support, and sanctuary to terrorists by convincing or compelling states to accept their sovereign responsibilities.

We will also wage a war of ideas to win the battle against international terrorism. This includes:

- using the full influence of the United States, and working closely with allies and friends, to make clear that all acts of terrorism are illegitimate so that terrorism will be viewed in the same light as slavery, piracy, or genocide: behavior that no respectable government can condone or support and all must oppose;

- supporting moderate and modern government, especially in the Muslim world, to ensure that the conditions and ideologies that promote terrorism do not find fertile ground in any nation;

- diminishing the underlying conditions that spawn terrorism by enlisting the international community to focus its efforts and resources on areas most at risk; and

- using effective public diplomacy to promote the free flow of information and ideas to kindle the hopes and aspirations of freedom of those in societies ruled by the sponsors of global terrorism.

While we recognize that our best defense is a good offense, we are also strengthening America's homeland security to protect against and deter attack.

This Administration has proposed the largest government reorganization since the Truman Administration created the National Security Council and the Department of Defense. Centered on a new Department of Homeland Security and including a new unified military command and a fundamental reordering of the FBI, our comprehensive plan to secure the homeland encompasses every level of government and the cooperation of the public and the private sector.

This strategy will turn adversity into opportunity. For example, emergency management systems will be better able to cope not just with terrorism but with all hazards. Our medical system will be strengthened to manage not just bioterror, but all infectious diseases and mass-casualty dangers. Our border controls will not just stop terrorists, but improve the efficient movement of legitimate traffic.

While our focus is protecting America, we know that to defeat terrorism in today's globalized world we need support from our allies and friends. Wherever possible, the United States will rely on regional organizations and state powers to meet their obligations to fight terrorism. Where governments find the fight against terrorism beyond their capacities, we will match their willpower and their resources with whatever help we and our allies can provide.

As we pursue the terrorists in Afghanistan, we will continue to work with international organizations such as the United Nations, as well as non-governmental organizations, and other countries to provide the humanitarian, political, economic, and security assistance necessary to rebuild Afghanistan so that it will never again abuse its people, threaten its neighbors, and provide a haven for terrorists.

In the war against global terrorism, we will never forget that we are ultimately fighting for our democratic values and way of life. Freedom and fear are at war, and there will be no quick or easy end to this conflict. In leading the campaign against terrorism, we are forging new, productive international relationships and redefining existing ones in ways that meet the challenges of the twenty-first century.

IV. Work with Others to Defuse Regional Conflicts

Concerned nations must remain actively engaged in critical regional disputes to avoid explosive escalation and minimize human suffering. In an increasingly interconnected world, regional crisis can strain our alliances, rekindle rivalries among the major powers, and create horrifying affronts to human dignity. When violence erupts and states falter, the United States will work with friends and partners to alleviate suffering and restore stability.

No doctrine can anticipate every circumstance in which U.S. action—direct or indirect—is warranted. We have finite political, economic, and military resources to meet our global priorities. The United States will approach each case with these strategic principles in mind:

- The United States should invest time and resources into building international relationships and institutions that can help manage local crises when they emerge.
- The United States should be realistic about its ability to help those who are unwilling or unready to help themselves. Where and when people are ready to do their part, we will be willing to move decisively.

The Israeli-Palestinian conflict is critical because of the toll of human suffering, because of America's close relationship with the state of Israel and key Arab states, and because of that region's importance to other global priorities of the United States. There can be no peace for either side without freedom for both sides. America stands committed to an independent and democratic Palestine, living beside Israel in peace and security. Like all other people, Palestinians deserve a government that serves their interests and listens to their voices. The United States will con-

tinue to encourage all parties to step up to their responsibilities as we seek a just and comprehensive settlement to the conflict.

The United States, the international donor community, and the World Bank stand ready to work with a reformed Palestinian government on economic development, increased humanitarian assistance, and a program to establish, finance, and monitor a truly independent judiciary. If Palestinians embrace democracy, and the rule of law, confront corruption, and firmly reject terror, they can count on American support for the creation of a Palestinian state.

V. Prevent Our Enemies from Threatening Us, Our Allies, and Our Friends with Weapons of Mass Destruction

The nature of the Cold War threat required the United States—with our allies and friends—to emphasize deterrence of the enemy's use of force, producing a grim strategy of mutual assured destruction. With the collapse of the Soviet Union and the end of the Cold War, our security environment has undergone profound transformation.

Having moved from confrontation to cooperation as the hallmark of our relationship with Russia, the dividends are evident: an end to the balance of terror that divided us; an historic reduction in the nuclear arsenals on both sides; and cooperation in areas such as counterterrorism and missile defense that until recently were inconceivable.

But new deadly challenges have emerged from rogue states and terrorists. None of these contemporary threats rival the sheer destructive power that was arrayed against us by the Soviet Union. However, the nature and motivations of these new adversaries, their determination to obtain destructive powers hitherto available only to the world's strongest states, and the greater likelihood that they will use weapons of mass destruction against us, make today's security environment more complex and dangerous.

In the 1990s we witnessed the emergence of a small number of rogue states that, while different in important ways, share a number of attributes. These states:

- brutalize their own people and squander their national resources for the personal gain of the rulers;
- display no regard for international law, threaten their neighbors, and callously violate international treaties to which they are party;
- are determined to acquire weapons of mass destruction, along with other advanced military technology, to be used as threats or offensively to achieve the aggressive designs of these regimes;
- sponsor terrorism around the globe; and
- reject basic human values and hate the United States and everything for which it stands.

At the time of the Gulf War, we acquired irrefutable proof that Iraq's designs were not limited to the chemical weapons it had used against Iran and its own people, but also extended to the acquisition of nuclear weapons and biological agents. In the past decade North Korea has become the world's principal purveyor of ballistic missiles, and has tested increasingly capable missiles while developing its own WMD arsenal. Other rogue regimes seek nuclear, biological, and chemical weapons as well. These states' pursuit of, and global trade in, such weapons has become a looming threat to all nations.

We must be prepared to stop rogue states and their terrorist clients before they are able to threaten or use weapons of mass destruction against the United States and our allies and friends. Our response must take full advantage of strengthened alliances, the establishment of new partnerships with former adversaries, innovation in the use of military forces, modern technologies, including the development of an effective missile defense system, and increased emphasis on intelligence collection and analysis.

Our comprehensive strategy to combat WMD includes:

- *Proactive counterproliferation efforts.* We must deter and defend against the threat before it is unleashed. We must ensure that key capabilities—detection, active and passive defenses, and counterforce capabilities—are integrated into our defense transformation and our homeland security systems. Counterproliferation must also be integrated into the doctrine, training, and equipping of our forces and those of our allies to ensure that we can prevail in any conflict with WMD-armed adversaries.
- *Strengthened nonproliferation efforts to prevent rogue states and terrorists from acquiring the materials, technologies, and expertise necessary for weapons of mass destruction.* We will enhance diplomacy, arms control, multilateral export controls, and threat reduction assistance that impede states and terrorists seeking WMD, and when necessary, interdict enabling technologies and materials. We will continue to build coalitions to support these efforts, encouraging their increased political and financial support for nonproliferation and threat reduction programs. The recent G-8 agreement to commit up to $20 billion to a global partnership against proliferation marks a major step forward.
- *Effective consequence management to respond to the effects of WMD use, whether by terrorists or hostile states.* Minimizing the effects of WMD use against our people will help deter those who possess such weapons and dissuade those who seek to acquire them by persuading enemies that they cannot attain their desired ends. The United States must also be prepared to respond to the effects of WMD use against our forces abroad, and to help friends and allies if they are attacked.

It has taken almost a decade for us to comprehend the true nature of this new threat. Given the goals of rogue states and terrorists, the United States can no longer solely rely on a reactive posture as we have in the past. The inability to deter a potential attacker, the immediacy of today's threats, and the magnitude of potential harm that could be caused by our adversaries' choice of weapons, do not permit that option. We cannot let our enemies strike first.

- In the Cold War, especially following the Cuban missile crisis, we faced a generally status quo, risk-averse adversary. Deterrence was an effective defense. But deterrence based only upon the threat of retaliation is less likely to work against leaders of rogue states more willing to take risks, gambling with the lives of their people, and the wealth of their nations.
- In the Cold War, weapons of mass destruction were considered weapons of last resort whose use risked the destruction of those who used them. Today, our enemies see weapons of mass destruction as weapons of choice. For rogue states these weapons are tools of intimidation and military aggression against their neighbors. These weapons may also allow these states to attempt to blackmail the United States and our allies to prevent us from deterring or repelling the aggressive behavior of rogue states. Such states also see these weapons as their best means of overcoming the conventional superiority of the United States.
- Traditional concepts of deterrence will not work against a terrorist enemy whose avowed tactics are wanton destruction and the targeting of innocents; whose so-called soldiers seek martyrdom in death and whose most potent protection is statelessness. The overlap between states that sponsor terror and those that pursue WMD compels us to action.

For centuries, international law recognized that nations need not suffer an attack before they can lawfully take action to defend themselves against forces that present an imminent danger of attack. Legal scholars and international jurists often conditioned the legitimacy of preemption on the existence of an imminent threat—most often a visible mobilization of armies, navies, and air forces preparing to attack.

We must adapt the concept of imminent threat to the capabilities and objectives of today's adversaries. Rogue states and terrorists do not seek to attack us using conventional means. They know such attacks would fail. Instead, they rely on acts of terror and, potentially, the use of weapons of mass destruction—weapons that can be easily concealed, delivered covertly, and used without warning.

The targets of these attacks are our military forces and our civilian population, in direct violation of one of the principal norms of the law of warfare. As was demonstrated by the losses on September 11, 2001, mass civilian casualties is the specific objective of terrorists and these losses would be exponentially more severe if terrorists acquired and used weapons of mass destruction.

The United States has long maintained the option of preemptive actions to counter a sufficient threat to our national security. The greater the threat, the greater is the risk of inaction—and the more compelling the case for taking anticipatory action to defend ourselves, even if uncertainty remains as to the time and place of the enemy's attack. To forestall or prevent such hostile acts by our adversaries, the United States will, if necessary, act preemptively.

The United States will not use force in all cases to preempt emerging threats, nor should nations use preemption as a pretext for aggression. Yet in an age where the enemies of civilization openly and actively seek the world's most destructive technologies, the United States cannot remain idle while dangers gather.

We will always proceed deliberately, weighing the consequences of our actions. To support preemptive options, we will:

- build better, more integrated intelligence capabilities to provide timely, accurate information on threats, wherever they may emerge;
- coordinate closely with allies to form a common assessment of the most dangerous threats; and
- continue to transform our military forces to ensure our ability to conduct rapid and precise operations to achieve decisive results.

The purpose of our actions will always be to eliminate a specific threat to the United States or our allies and friends. The reasons for our actions will be clear, the force measured, and the cause just.

*   *   *

VIII. Develop Agendas for Cooperative Action with the Other Main Centers of Global Power

The United States relationship with China is an important part of our strategy to promote a stable, peaceful, and prosperous Asia-Pacific region. We welcome the emergence of a strong, peaceful, and prosperous China. The democratic development of China is crucial to that future. Yet, a quarter century after beginning the process of shedding the worst features of the Communist legacy, China's leaders have not yet made the next series of fundamental choices about the character of their state. In pursuing advanced military capabilities that can threaten its neighbors in the Asia-Pacific region, China is following an outdated path that, in the end, will hamper its own pursuit of national greatness. In time, China will find that social and political freedom is the only source of that greatness.

The United States seeks a constructive relationship with a changing China. We already cooperate well where our interests overlap, including the current war on terrorism and in promoting stability on the Korean peninsula. Likewise, we have coordinated on the future of Afghanistan and have initiated a comprehensive dialogue on counterterrorism and similar transitional concerns. Shared health and environmental threats, such as the spread of HIV/AIDS, challenge us to promote jointly the welfare of our citizens.

Addressing these transnational threats will challenge China to become more open with information, promote the development of civil society, and enhance individual human rights. China has begun to take the road to political openness, permitting many personal freedoms and conducting village-level elections, yet remains strongly committed to national one-party rule by the Communist Party. To make that nation truly accountable to its citizen's needs and aspirations, however, much work remains to be done. Only by allowing the Chinese people to think, assemble, and worship freely can China reach its full potential.

Our important trade relationship will benefit from China's entry into the World Trade Organization, which will create more export opportunities and ultimately more jobs for American farmers, workers, and companies. China is our fourth largest trading partner, with over $100 billion in annual two-way trade. The power of market principles and the WTO's requirements for transparency and accountability will advance openness and the rule of law in China to help establish basic protections for commerce and for citizens. There are, however, other areas in which we have profound disagreements. Our commitment to the self-defense of Taiwan under the Taiwan Relations Act is one. Human rights is another. We expect China to adhere to its nonproliferation commitments. We will work to narrow differences where they exist, but not allow them to preclude cooperation where we agree.

3 CONTENDING PERSPECTIVES

Over the past century, the most prominent perspectives for understanding the basic nature of international politics have been realism, liberalism, and radicalism. These viewpoints have vied for influence both in public debates and in academic arguments.

The readings in this chapter constitute some of the most concise and important statements of each theoretical tradition. Hans Morgenthau, the leading figure in the field of international relations in the period after World War II and at that time a professor at the University of Chicago, presents a realist view of power politics. His influential book, Politics among Nations *(1948), excerpted below, played a central role in intellectually preparing Americans to exercise global power in the Cold War period and to reconcile power politics with the idealistic ethics that had often dominated American discussions about foreign relations.*

In The Tragedy of Great Power Politics *(2001), John Mearsheimer offers a contemporary interpretation of international politics that he calls "offensive realism." The chapter reprinted here describes clearly and concisely international anarchy and its implications. States operate in a self-help system; to ensure their survival in that system, states must strive to become as powerful as possible. This competitive striving for security makes conflict the enduring and dominant feature of international relations, in Mearsheimer's view.*

Michael Doyle, a professor at Columbia University, advances the liberal theory of the democratic peace. His 1986 article in the American Political Science Review *points out that no two democracies had ever fought a war against each other. This sparked a huge ongoing debate among academics and public commentators on why this was the case, and whether it meant that the U.S. and other democracies should place efforts to promote the further spreading of democracy at the head of their foreign policy agendas.*

Whereas realists like Mearsheimer argued that the situation of anarchy necessarily causes insecurity and fear among states, "social constructivists" such as Alexander Wendt insisted that behavior in anarchy depends on the ideas, cultures, and identities that people and their states bring to the anarchical situation. The excerpt below is drawn from the seminal piece in that debate, which has spawned influential research on such topics as the taboo against using nuclear weapons, changing norms of humanitarian military intervention, and the rise of powerful transnational human rights networks (see also the excerpt by Margaret Keck and Kathryn Sikkink in Chapter 7).

The final selection illustrates currents in the study of international politics that fundamentally challenge the realist, liberal, and radical perspectives. Arguing from a feminist perspective, J. Ann Tickner of the University of Southern California, in an excerpt from Gender and International Relations, *suggests that much of the warlike behavior realists attribute to the situation of international anarchy is better understood as a consequence of the way male identity has been constructed.*

HANS MORGENTHAU

A REALIST THEORY OF INTERNATIONAL POLITICS

This book purports to present a theory of international politics. The test by which such a theory must be judged is not *a priori* and abstract but empirical and pragmatic. The theory, in other words, must be judged not by some preconceived abstract principle or concept unrelated to reality, but by its purpose: to bring order and meaning to a mass of phenomena which without it would remain disconnected and unintelligible. It must meet a dual test, an empirical and a logical one: Do the facts as they actually are lend themselves to the interpretation the theory has put upon them, and do the conclusions at which the theory arrives follow with logical necessity from its premises? In short, is the theory consistent with the facts and within itself?

The issue this theory raises concerns the nature of all politics. The history of modern political thought is the story of a contest between two schools that differ fundamentally in their con-

From Hans Morganthau, *Politics among Nations: The Struggle for Power and Peace* (1948; reprint, New York: Knopf, 1960), Chaps. 1, 3. Some of the author's notes have been omitted.

ceptions of the nature of man, society, and politics. One believes that a rational and moral political order, derived from universally valid abstract principles, can be achieved here and now. It assumes the essential goodness and infinite malleability of human nature, and blames the failure of the social order to measure up to the rational standards on lack of knowledge and understanding, obsolescent social institutions, or the depravity of certain isolated individuals or groups. It trusts in education, reform, and the sporadic use of force to remedy these defects.

The other school believes that the world, imperfect as it is from the rational point of view, is the result of forces inherent in human nature. To improve the world one must work with those forces, not against them. This being inherently a world of opposing interests and of conflict among them, moral principles can never be fully realized, but must at best be approximated through the ever temporary balancing of interests and the ever precarious settlement of conflicts. This school, then, sees in a system of checks and balances a universal principle for all pluralist societies. It appeals to historic precedent rather than to abstract principles, and aims at the realization of the lesser evil rather than of the absolute good.

*   *   *

*** Principles of Political Realism

Political realism believes that politics, like society in general, is governed by objective laws that have their roots in human nature. In order to improve society it is first necessary to understand the laws by which society lives. The operation of these laws being impervious to our preferences, men will challenge them only at the risk of failure.

Realism, believing as it does in the objectivity of the laws of politics, must also believe in the possibility of developing a rational theory that reflects, however imperfectly and one-sidedly, these objective laws. It believes also, then, in the possibility of distinguishing in politics between truth and opinion—between what is true objectively and rationally, supported by evidence and illuminated by reason, and what is only a subjective judgment, divorced from the facts as they are and informed by prejudice and wishful thinking.

*   *   *

For realism, theory consists in ascertaining facts and giving them meaning through reason. It assumes that the character of a foreign policy can be ascertained only through the examination of the political acts performed and of the foreseeable consequences of these acts. Thus, we can find out what statesmen have actually done, and from the foreseeable consequences of their acts we can surmise what their objectives might have been.

Yet examination of the facts is not enough. To give meaning to the factual raw material of foreign policy, we must approach political reality with a kind of rational outline, a map that suggests to us the possible meanings of foreign policy. In other words, we put ourselves in the position of a statesman who must meet a certain problem of foreign policy under certain circumstances, and we ask ourselves what the rational alternatives are from which a statesman may choose who must meet this problem under these circumstances (presuming always that he acts in a rational manner), and which of these rational alternatives this particular statesman, acting under these circumstances, is likely to choose. It is the testing of this rational hypothesis against the actual facts and their consequences that gives meaning to the facts of international politics and makes a theory of politics possible.

The main signpost that helps political realism to find its way through the landscape of international politics is the concept of interest defined in terms of power. This concept provides the link between reason trying to understand international politics and the facts to be understood. *   *   *

We assume that statesmen think and act in terms of interest defined as power, and the evidence of history bears that assumption out. That assumption allows us to retrace and anticipate, as it were, the steps a statesman—past, present, or future—has taken or will take on the political scene. We look over his shoulder when he writes his dispatches; we listen in on his conversation with other statesmen; we read and anticipate his very thoughts. Thinking in terms of interest defined as power, we think as he does, and as disinterested observers we understand his thoughts and actions perhaps better than he, the actor on the political scene, does himself.

*   *   *

Political realism is aware of the moral significance of political action. It is also aware of the ineluctable tension between the moral command and the requirements of successful political action. And it is unwilling to gloss over and obliterate that tension and thus to obfuscate both the moral and the political issue by making it appear as though the stark facts of politics were morally more satisfying than they actually are, and the moral law less exacting than it actually is.

Realism maintains that universal moral principles cannot be applied to the actions of states in their abstract universal formulation, but that they must be filtered through the concrete circumstances of time and place. The individual may say for himself: *"Fiat justitia, pereat mundus* (Let justice be done, even if the world perish)," but the state has no right to say so in the name of those who are in its care. Both individual and state must judge political action by universal moral principles, such as that of liberty. Yet while the individual has a moral right to sacrifice himself in defense of such a moral principle, the state has no right to let its moral disapprobation of the infringement of liberty get in the way of success-ful political action, itself inspired by the moral principle of national survival. There can be no political morality without prudence; that is, without consideration of the political consequences of seemingly moral action. Realism, then, considers prudence—the weighing of the consequences of alternative political actions—to be the supreme virtue in politics. Ethics in the abstract judges action by its conformity with the moral law; political ethics judges action by its political consequences. * * *

POLITICAL POWER

What Is Political Power?

*   *   *

International politics, like all politics, is a struggle for power. Whatever the ultimate aims of international politics, power is always the immediate aim. Statesmen and peoples may ultimately seek freedom, security, prosperity, or power itself. They may define their goals in terms of a religious, philosophic, economic, or social ideal. They may hope that this ideal will materialize through its own inner force, through divine intervention, or through the natural development of human affairs. They may also try to further its realization through nonpolitical means, such as technical co-operation with other nations or international organizations. But whenever they strive to realize their goal by means of international politics, they do so by striving for power. The Crusaders wanted to free the holy places from domination by the Infidels; Woodrow Wilson wanted to make the world safe for democracy; the Nazis wanted to open Eastern Europe to German colonization, to dominate Europe, and to conquer the world. Since they all chose power to achieve these ends, they were actors on the scene of international politics.

*   *   *

* * * When we speak of power, we mean man's control over the minds and actions of other men. By political power we refer to the mutual relations of control among the holders of public authority and between the latter and the people at large.

Political power, however, must be distinguished from force in the sense of the actual exercise of physical violence. The threat of physical violence in the form of police action, imprisonment, capital punishment, or war is an intrinsic element of politics. When violence becomes an actuality, it signifies the abdication of political power in favor of military or pseudo-military power. In international politics in particular, armed strength as a threat or a potentiality is the most important material factor making for the political power of a nation. If it becomes an actuality in war, it signifies the substitution of military for political power. The actual exercise of physical violence substitutes for the psychological relation between two minds, which is of the essence of political power, the physical relation between two bodies, one of which is strong enough to dominate the other's movements. It is for this reason that in the exercise of physical violence the psychological element of the political relationship is lost, and that we must distinguish between military and political power.

Political power is a psychological relation between those who exercise it and those over whom it is exercised. It gives the former control over certain actions of the latter through the influence which the former exert over the latter's minds. That influence derives from three sources: the expectation of benefits, the fear of disadvantages, the respect or love for men or institutions. It may be exerted through orders, threats, persuasion, the authority or charisma of a man or of an office, or a combination of any of these.

While it is generally recognized that the interplay of these factors, in ever changing combinations, forms the basis of all domestic politics, the importance of these factors for international politics is less obvious, but no less real. There has been a tendency to reduce political power to the actual application of force or at least to equate it with successful threats of force and with persuasion, to the neglect of charisma. That neglect * * * accounts in good measure for the neglect of prestige as an independent element in international politics. * * *

*   *   *

An economic, financial, territorial, or military policy undertaken for its own sake is subject to evaluation in its own terms. Is it economically or financially advantageous? * * *

When, however, the objectives of these policies serve to increase the power of the nation pursuing them with regard to other nations, these policies and their objectives must be judged primarily from the point of view of their contribution to national power. An economic policy that cannot be justified in purely economic terms might nevertheless be undertaken in view of the political policy pursued. The insecure and unprofitable character of a loan to a foreign nation may be a valid argument against it on purely financial grounds. But the argument is irrelevant if the loan, however unwise it may be from a banker's point of view, serves the political policies of the nation. It may of course be that the economic or financial losses involved in such policies will weaken the nation in its international position to such an extent as to outweigh the political advantages to be expected. On these grounds such policies might be rejected. In such a case, what decides the issue is not purely economic and financial considerations but a comparison of the political changes and risks involved; that is, the probable effect of these policies upon the power of the nation.

The Depreciation of Political Power

The aspiration for power being the distinguishing element of international politics, as of all politics, international politics is of necessity power politics. While this fact is generally recognized in the practice of international affairs, it is frequently denied in the pronouncements of scholars, publicists, and even statesmen. Since the end of the Napoleonic Wars, ever larger groups in the Western world have been persuaded that the struggle for power on the international scene is a temporary phenomenon, a historical accident that is bound to disappear once the peculiar historic conditions that have given rise to it have been eliminated. * * * During the nineteenth century, liberals everywhere shared the conviction that power politics and war were residues of an obsolete system of government, and that with the victory of democracy and constitutional government over absolutism and autocracy international harmony and permanent peace would win out over power politics and war. Of this liberal school of thought, Woodrow Wilson was the most eloquent and most influential spokesman.

In recent times, the conviction that the struggle for power can be eliminated from the international scene has been connected with the great attempts at organizing the world, such as the League of Nations and the United Nations. * * *

* * * [In fact,] the struggle for power is universal in time and space and is an undeniable fact of experience. It cannot be denied that throughout

historic time, regardless of social, economic, and political conditions, states have met each other in contests for power. Even though anthropologists have shown that certain primitive peoples seem to be free from the desire for power, nobody has yet shown how their state of mind and the conditions under which they live can be recreated on a worldwide scale so as to eliminate the struggle for power from the international scene[1] It would be useless and even self-destructive to free one or the other of the peoples of the earth from the desire for power while leaving it extant in others. If the desire for power cannot be abolished everywhere in the world, those who might be cured would simply fall victims to the power of others.

The position taken here might be criticized on the ground that conclusions drawn from the past are unconvincing, and that to draw such conclusions has always been the main stock in trade of the enemies of progress and reform. Though it is true that certain social arrangements and institutions have always existed in the past, it does not necessarily follow that they must always exist in the future. The situation is, however, different when we deal not with social arrangements and institutions created by man, but with those elemental biopsychological drives by which in turn society is created. The drives to live, to propagate, and to dominate are common to all men.[2] Their relative strength is dependent upon social conditions that may favor one drive and tend to repress another, or that may withhold social approval from certain manifestations of these drives while they encourage others. Thus, to take examples only from the sphere of power, most societies condemn killing as a means of attaining power within society, but all societies encourage the killing of enemies in that struggle for power which is called war. * * *

NOTES

1. For an illuminating discussion of this problem, see Malcolm Sharp, "Aggression: A Study of Values and Law," *Ethics*, Vol. 57, No. 4, Part II (July 1947).

2. Zoologists have tried to show that the drive to dominate is found even in animals, such as chickens and monkeys, who create social hierarchies on the basis of the will and the ability to dominate. See e.g., Warder Allee, *Animal Life and Social Growth* (Baltimore: The Williams and Wilkins Company, 1932), and *The Social Life of Animals* (New York: W. W. Norton and Company, Inc., 1938).

JOHN MEARSHEIMER

ANARCHY AND THE STRUGGLE FOR POWER

Great powers, I argue, are always searching for opportunities to gain power over their rivals, with hegemony as their final goal. This perspective does not allow for status quo powers, except for the unusual state that achieves

From *The Tragedy of Great Power Politics* (New York: Norton, 2001): 29–54. Some of the author's notes have been edited.

preponderance. Instead, the system is populated with great powers that have revisionist intentions at their core.[1] This chapter presents a theory that explains this competition for power. Specifically, I attempt to show that there is a compelling logic behind my claim that great powers seek to maximize their share of world power. I do not, however, test offensive realism against the historical record in this chapter. That important task is reserved for later chapters.

Why States Pursue Power

My explanation for why great powers vie with each other for power and strive for hegemony is derived from five assumptions about the international system. None of these assumptions alone mandates that states behave competitively. Taken together, however, they depict a world in which states have considerable reason to think and sometimes behave aggressively. In particular, the system encourages states to look for opportunities to maximize their power vis-à-vis other states.

How important is it that these assumptions be realistic? Some social scientists argue that the assumptions that underpin a theory need not conform to reality. Indeed, the economist Milton Friedman maintains that the best theories "will be found to have assumptions that are wildly inaccurate descriptive representations of reality, and, in general, the more significant the theory, the more unrealistic the assumptions."[2] According to this view, the explanatory power of a theory is all that matters. If unrealistic assumptions lead to a theory that tells us a lot about how the world works, it is of no importance whether the underlying assumptions are realistic or not.

I reject this view. Although I agree that explanatory power is the ultimate criterion for assessing theories, I also believe that a theory based on unrealistic or false assumptions will not explain much about how the world works.[3] Sound theories are based on sound assumptions. Accordingly, each of these five assumptions is a reasonably accurate representation of an important aspect of life in the international system.

Bedrock Assumptions

The first assumption is that the international system is anarchic, which does not mean that it is chaotic or riven by disorder. It is easy to draw that conclusion, since realism depicts a world characterized by security competition and war. By itself, however, the realist notion of anarchy has nothing to do with conflict; it is an ordering principle, which says that the system comprises independent states that have no central authority above them.[4] Sovereignty, in other words, inheres in states because there is no higher ruling body in the international system.[5] There is no "government over governments."[6]

The second assumption is that great powers inherently possess some offensive military capability, which gives them the wherewithal to hurt and possibly destroy each other. States are potentially dangerous to each other, although some states have more military might than others and are therefore more dangerous. A state's military power is usually identified with the particular weaponry at its disposal, although even if there were no weapons, the individuals in those states could still use their feet and hands to attack the population of another state. After all, for every neck, there are two hands to choke it.

The third assumption is that states can never be certain about other states' intentions. Specifically, no state can be sure that another state will not use its offensive military capability to attack the first state. This is not to say that states necessarily have hostile intentions. Indeed, all of the states in the system may be reliably benign, but it is impossible to be sure of that judgment because intentions are impossible to divine with 100 percent certainty.[7] There are many possible causes of aggression, and no state can be sure that another state is not motivated by one of them.[8] Furthermore, intentions can change quickly, so a state's intentions can be benign one day and hostile the next. Uncertainty about intentions is unavoidable, which means that states can never be sure that other states do not have offensive intentions to go along with their offensive capabilities.

The fourth assumption is that survival is the primary goal of great powers. Specifically, states seek to maintain their territorial integrity and the autonomy of their domestic political order. Survival dominates other motives because, once a state is conquered, it is unlikely to be in a position to pursue other aims. Soviet leader Josef Stalin put the point well during a war scare in 1927: "We can and must build socialism in the [Soviet Union]. But in order to do so we first of all have to exist."[9] States can and do pursue other goals, of course, but security is their most important objective.

The fifth assumption is that great powers are rational actors. They are aware of their external environment and they think strategically about how to survive in it. In particular, they consider the preferences of other states and how their own behavior is likely to affect the behavior of those other states, and how the behavior of those other states is likely to affect their own strategy for survival. Moreover, states pay attention to the long term as well as the immediate consequences of their actions.

As emphasized, none of these assumptions alone dictates that great powers as a general rule *should* behave aggressively toward each other. There is surely the possibility that some state might have hostile intentions, but the only assumption dealing with a specific motive that is common to all states says that their principal objective is to survive, which by itself is a rather harmless goal. Nevertheless, when the five assumptions are married together, they create powerful incentives for great powers to think and act offensively with regard to each other. In particular, three general patterns of behavior result: fear, self-help, and power maximization.

State Behavior

Great powers fear each other. They regard each other with suspicion, and they worry that war might be in the offing. They anticipate danger. There is little room for trust among states. For sure, the level of fear varies across time and space, but it cannot be reduced to a trivial level. From the perspective of any one great power, all other great powers are potential enemies. This point is illustrated by the reaction of the United Kingdom and France to German reunification at the end of the Cold War. Despite the fact that these three states had been close allies for almost forty-five years, both the United Kingdom and France immediately began worrying about the potential dangers of a united Germany.[10]

The basis of this fear is that in a world where great powers have the capability to attack each other and might have the motive to do so, any state bent on survival must be at least suspicious of other states and reluctant to trust them. Add to this the "911" problem—the absence of a central authority to which a threatened state can turn for help—and states have even greater incentive to fear each other. Moreover, there is no mechanism, other than the possible self-interest of third parties, for punishing an aggressor. Because it is sometimes difficult to deter potential aggressors, states have ample reason not to trust other states and to be prepared for war with them.

The possible consequences of falling victim to aggression further amplify the importance of fear as a motivating force in world politics. Great powers do not compete with each other as if international politics were merely an economic marketplace. Political competition among states is a much more dangerous business than mere economic intercourse; the former can lead to war, and war often means mass killing on the battlefield as well as mass murder of civilians. In extreme cases, war can even lead to the destruction of states. The horrible consequences of war sometimes cause states to view each other not just as competitors, but as potentially deadly enemies. Political antagonism, in short, tends to be intense, because the stakes are great.

States in the international system also aim to guarantee their own survival. Because other states are potential threats, and because there is no higher authority to come to their rescue when they dial 911, states cannot depend on others for their own security. Each state tends to see itself as vulnerable and alone, and therefore it aims to provide for its own survival. In international politics, God helps those who help themselves. This emphasis on self-help does not preclude states from forming alliances.[11] But alliances are only temporary marriages of convenience: today's alliance partner might be tomorrow's enemy, and today's enemy might be tomorrow's alliance partner. For example, the United States fought with China and the Soviet Union against Germany and Japan in World War II, but soon thereafter flip-flopped enemies and partners and allied with West Germany and Japan against China and the Soviet Union during the Cold War.

States operating in a self-help world almost always act according to their own self-interest and do not subordinate their interests to the interests of other states, or to the interests of the so-called international community. The reason is simple: it pays to be selfish in a self-help world. This is true in the short term as well as in the long term, because if a state loses in the short run, it might not be around for the long haul.

Apprehensive about the ultimate intentions of other states, and aware that they operate in a self-help system, states quickly understand that the best way to ensure their survival is to be the most powerful state in the system. The stronger a state is relative to its potential rivals, the less likely it is that any of those rivals will attack it and threaten its survival. Weaker states will be reluctant to pick fights with more powerful states because the weaker states are likely to suffer military defeat. Indeed, the bigger the gap in power between any two states, the less likely it is that the weaker will attack the stronger. Neither Canada nor Mexico, for example, would countenance attacking the United States, which is far more powerful than its neighbors. The ideal situation is to be the hegemon in the system. As Immanuel Kant said, "It is the desire of every state, or of its ruler, to arrive at a condition of perpetual peace by conquering the whole world, if that were possible."[12] Survival would then be almost guaranteed.[13]

Consequently, states pay close attention to how power is distributed among them, and they make a special effort to maximize their share of world power. Specifically, they look for opportunities to alter the balance of power by acquiring additional increments of power at the expense of potential rivals. States employ a variety of means—economic, diplomatic, and military—to shift the balance of power in their favor, even if doing so makes other states suspicious or even hostile. Because one state's gain in power is another state's loss, great powers tend to have a zero-sum mentality when dealing with each other. The trick, of course, is to be the winner in this competition and to dominate the other states in the system. Thus, the claim that states maximize relative power is tantamount to arguing that states are disposed to think offensively toward other states, even though their ultimate motive is simply to survive. In short, great powers have aggressive intentions.[14]

Even when a great power achieves a distinct military advantage over its rivals, it continues looking for chances to gain more power. The pursuit of power stops only when hegemony is achieved. The idea that a great power might feel secure without dominating the system, provided it has an "appropriate amount" of power, is not persuasive, for two reasons.[15] First, it is difficult to assess how much relative power one state must have over its rivals before it is secure. Is twice as much power an appropriate threshold? Or is three times as much power the magic number? The root of the problem is that power calculations alone do not determine which side wins a war. Clever strategies, for example, sometimes allow less powerful states to defeat more powerful foes.

Second, determining how much power is enough becomes even more complicated when great powers contemplate how power will be distributed among them ten or twenty years down the road. The capabilities of individual states vary over time, sometimes markedly, and it is often difficult to predict the direction and scope of change in the balance of power. Remember, few in the West anticipated the collapse of the Soviet Union before it happened. In fact, during the first half of the Cold War, many in the West feared that the Soviet economy would eventually generate greater wealth than the American economy, which would cause a marked power shift against the United States and its allies. What the future holds for China and Russia and what the balance of power will look like in 2020 is difficult to foresee.

Given the difficulty of determining how much power is enough for today and tomorrow, great powers recognize that the best way to ensure their security is to achieve hegemony now, thus eliminating any possibility of a challenge by another great power. Only a misguided state would pass up an opportunity to be the hegemon in the system because it thought it already had sufficient power to survive.[16] But even if a great power does not have the wherewithal to achieve hegemony (and that is usually the case), it will still act offensively to amass as much power as it can, because states are almost always better off with more rather than less power. In short, states do not become status quo powers until they completely dominate the system.

All states are influenced by this logic, which means that not only do they look for opportunities to take advantage of one another, they also work to ensure that other states do not take advantage of them. After all, rival states are driven by the same logic, and most states are likely to recognize their own motives at play in the actions of other states. In short, states ultimately pay attention to defense as well as offense. They think about conquest themselves, and they work to check aggressor states from gaining power at their expense. This inexorably leads to a world of constant security competition, where states are willing to lie, cheat, and use brute force if it helps them gain advantage over their rivals. Peace, if one defines that concept as a state of tranquility or mutual concord, is not likely to break out in this world.

The "security dilemma," which is one of the most well-known concepts in the international relations literature, reflects the basic logic of offensive realism. The essence of the dilemma is that the measures a state takes to increase its own security usually decrease the security of other states. Thus, it is difficult for a state to increase its own chances of survival without threatening the survival of other states. John Herz first introduced the security dilemma in a 1950 article in the journal *World Politics*.[17] After discussing the anarchic nature of international politics, he writes, "Striving to attain security from . . . attack, [states] are driven to acquire more and more power in order to escape the impact of the power of others. This, in turn, renders the others more insecure and compels them to prepare for the worst. Since none can ever feel entirely secure in such a world of competing units, power competition ensues, and the vicious circle of security and power accumulation is on."[18] The implication of Herz's analysis is clear: the best way for a state to survive in anarchy is to take advantage of other states and gain power at their expense. The best defense is a good offense. Since this message is widely understood, ceaseless security competition ensues. Unfortunately, little can be done to ameliorate the security dilemma as long as states operate in anarchy.

It should be apparent from this discussion that saying that states are power maximizers is tantamount to saying that they care about relative power, not absolute power. There is an important distinction here, because states concerned about relative power behave differently than do states interested in absolute power.[19] States that maximize relative power are concerned primarily with the distribution of material capabilities. In particular, they try to gain as large a power advantage as possible over potential rivals, because power is the best means to survival in a dangerous world. Thus, states motivated by relative power concerns are likely to forgo large gains in their own power, if such gains give rival states even greater power, for smaller national gains that nevertheless provide them with a power advantage over their rivals.[20] States that maximize absolute power, on the other hand, care only about the size of their own gains, not those of other states. They are not motivated by balance-of-power logic but instead are concerned with amassing power without regard to how much power other states control. They would jump at the opportunity for large gains, even if a rival gained more in the deal. Power, according to this logic, is not a means to an end (survival), but an end in itself.[21]

Calculated Aggression

There is obviously little room for status quo powers in a world where states are inclined to look for opportunities to gain more power. Nevertheless, great powers cannot always act on their offensive intentions, because behavior is influenced not only by what states want, but also by their capacity to realize these desires. Every state might want to be king of the hill, but not every state has the wherewithal to compete for that lofty position, much less achieve it. Much depends on how military might is distributed among the great powers. A great power that has a marked power advantage over its rivals is likely to behave more aggressively, because it has the capability as well as the incentive to do so.

By contrast, great powers facing powerful opponents will be less inclined to consider offensive action and more concerned with defending the existing balance of power from threats by their more powerful opponents. Let there be an opportunity for those weaker states to revise the balance in their own favor, however, and they will take advantage of it. Stalin put the point well at the end of World War II: "Everyone imposes his own system as far as his army can reach. It cannot be otherwise."[22] States might also have the capability to gain advantage over a rival power but nevertheless decide that the perceived costs of offense are too high and do not justify the expected benefits.

In short, great powers are not mindless aggressors so bent on gaining power that they charge headlong into losing wars or pursue Pyrrhic victories. On the contrary, before great powers take offensive actions, they think carefully about the balance of power and about how other states will react to their moves. They weigh the costs and risks of offense against the likely benefits. If the benefits do not outweigh the risks, they sit tight and wait for a more propitious moment. Nor do states start arms races that are unlikely to improve their overall position. As discussed at greater length in Chapter 3, states sometimes limit defense spending either because spending more would bring no strategic advantage or because spending more would weaken the economy and undermine the state's power in the long run.[23] To paraphrase Clint Eastwood, a state has to know its limitations to survive in the international system.

Nevertheless, great powers miscalculate from time to time because they invariably make important decisions on the basis of imperfect information. States hardly ever have complete information about any situation they confront. There are two dimensions to this problem. Potential adversaries have incentives to misrepresent their own strength or weakness, and to conceal their true aims.[24] For example, a weaker state trying to deter a stronger state is likely to exaggerate its own power to discourage the potential aggressor from attacking. On the other hand, a state bent on aggression is likely to emphasize its peaceful goals while exaggerating its military weakness, so that the potential victim does not build up its own arms and thus leaves itself vulnerable to attack. Probably no national leader was better at practicing this kind of deception than Adolf Hitler.

But even if disinformation was not a problem, great powers are often unsure about how their own military forces, as well as the adversary's, will perform on the battlefield. For example, it is sometimes difficult to determine in advance how new weapons and untested combat units will perform in the face of enemy fire. Peacetime maneuvers and war games are helpful but imperfect indicators of what is likely to happen in actual combat. Fighting wars is a complicated business in which it is often difficult to predict outcomes. Remember that although the United States and its allies scored a stunning and remarkably easy victory against Iraq in early 1991, most experts at the time believed that Iraq's military would be a formidable foe and put up stubborn resistance before finally succumbing to American military might.[25]

Great powers are also sometimes unsure about the resolve of opposing states as well as allies. For example, Germany believed that if it went to war against France and Russia in the summer of 1914, the United Kingdom would probably stay out of the fight. Saddam Hussein expected the United States to stand aside when he invaded Kuwait in August 1990. Both aggressors guessed wrong, but each had good reason to think that its initial judgment was correct. In the 1930s, Adolf Hitler believed that his great-power rivals would be easy to exploit and isolate because each had little interest in fighting Germany and instead was determined to get someone else to assume that burden. He guessed right. In short, great powers constantly find themselves confronting situations in which they have to make important decisions with incomplete information. Not surprisingly, they sometimes make faulty judgments and end up doing themselves serious harm.

Some defensive realists go so far as to suggest that the constraints of the international system are so powerful that offense rarely succeeds, and that aggressive great powers invariably end up being punished.[26] As noted, they emphasize that 1) threatened states balance against aggressors and ultimately crush them, and 2) there is an offense-defense balance that is usually heavily tilted toward the defense, thus making conquest especially difficult. Great powers, therefore, should be content with the existing, balance of power and not try to change it by force. After all, it makes little sense for a state to initiate a war that it is likely to lose; that would be self-defeating behavior. It is better to concentrate instead on preserving the balance of power.[27] Moreover, because aggressors seldom succeed, states should understand that security is abundant, and thus there is no good strategic reason for wanting more power in the first place. In a world where conquest seldom pays, states should have relatively benign intentions toward each other. If they do not, these defensive realists argue, the reason is probably poisonous domestic politics, not smart calculations about how to guarantee one's security in an anarchic world.

There is no question that systemic factors constrain aggression, especially balancing by threatened states. But defensive realists exaggerate those restraining forces.[28] Indeed, the historical record provides little support for their claim that offense rarely succeeds. One study estimates that there were 63 wars between 1815 and 1980, and the initiator won 39 times, which translates into about a 60 percent success rate.[29] Turning to specific cases, Otto von Bismarck unified Germany by winning military victories against Denmark in 1864, Austria in 1866, and France in 1870, and the United States as we know it today was created in good part by conquest in the nineteenth century. Conquest certainly paid big dividends in these cases. Nazi Germany won wars against Poland in 1939 and France in 1940, but lost to the Soviet Union between 1941 and 1945. Conquest ultimately did not pay for the Third Reich, but if Hitler had restrained himself after the fall of France and had not invaded the Soviet Union, conquest probably would have paid handsomely for the Nazis. In short, the historical record shows that offense sometimes succeeds and sometimes does not. The trick for a sophisticated power maximizer is to figure out when to raise and when to fold.[30]

Hegemony's Limits

Great powers, as I have emphasized, strive to gain power over their rivals and hopefully become hegemons. Once a state achieves that exalted position, it becomes a status quo power. More needs to be said, however, about the meaning of hegemony.

A hegemon is a state that is so powerful that it dominates all the other states in the system.[31] No other state has the military wherewithal to put up a serious fight against it. In essence, a hegemon is the only great power in the system. A state that is substantially more powerful than the other great powers in the system is not a hegemon, because it faces, by definition, other great powers. The United Kingdom in the mid-nineteenth century, for example, is sometimes called a hegemon. But it was not a hegemon, because there were four other great powers in Europe at the time—Austria, France, Prussia, and Russia—and the United Kingdom did not dominate them in any meaningful way. In fact, during that period, the United Kingdom considered France to be a serious threat to the balance of power. Europe in the nineteenth century was multipolar, not unipolar.

Hegemony means domination of the system, which is usually interpreted to mean the entire world. It is possible, however, to apply the concept of a system more narrowly and use it to describe particular regions, such as Europe, Northeast Asia, and the Western Hemisphere. Thus, one can distinguish between *global hegemons*, which dominate the world, and *regional hegemons*, which dominate distinct geographical areas. The United States has been a regional hegemon in the Western Hemisphere for at least the past one hundred years. No other state in the Americas has sufficient military might to challenge it, which is why the United States is widely recognized as the only great power in its region.

My argument, which I develop at length in subsequent chapters, is that except for the unlikely event wherein one state achieves clear-cut nuclear superiority, it is virtually impossible for any state to achieve global hegemony. The principal impediment to world domination is the difficulty of projecting power across the world's oceans onto the territory of a rival great power. The United States, for example, is the most powerful state on the planet today. But it does not dominate Europe and Northeast Asia the way it does the Western Hemisphere, and it has no intention of trying to conquer and control those distant regions, mainly because of the stopping power of water. Indeed, there is reason to think that the American military commitment to Europe and Northeast Asia might wither away over the next decade. In short, there has never been a global hegemon, and there is not likely to be one anytime soon.

The best outcome a great power can hope for is to be a regional hegemon and possibly control another region that is nearby and accessible over land. The United States is the only regional hegemon in modern history, although other states have fought major wars in pursuit of regional hegemony: imperial Japan in Northeast Asia, and Napoleonic France, Wilhelmine Germany, and Nazi Germany in Europe. But none succeeded. The Soviet Union, which is located in Europe and Northeast Asia, threatened to dominate both of those regions during the Cold War. The Soviet Union might also have attempted to conquer the oil-rich Persian Gulf region, with which it shared a border. But even if Moscow had been able to dominate Europe, Northeast Asia, and the Persian Gulf, which it never came close to doing, it still would have been unable to conquer the Western Hemisphere and become a true global hegemon.

States that achieve regional hegemony seek to prevent great powers in other regions from duplicating their feat. Regional hegemons, in other words, do not want peers. Thus the United States, for example, played a key role in preventing imperial Japan, Wilhelmine Germany, Nazi Germany, and the Soviet Union from gaining regional supremacy. Regional hegemons attempt to check aspiring hegemons in other regions because they fear that a rival great power that dominates its own region will be an especially powerful foe that is essentially free to cause trouble in the fearful great power's backyard. Regional hegemons prefer that there be at least two great powers located together in other regions, because their proximity will force them to concentrate their attention on each other rather than on the distant hegemon.

Furthermore, if a potential hegemon emerges among them, the other great powers in that region might be able to contain it by themselves, allowing the distant hegemon to remain safely on the sidelines. Of course, if the local great powers were unable to do the job, the distant hegemon would take the appropriate measures to deal with the threatening state. The United States, as noted, has assumed that burden on four separate occasions in the twentieth century, which is why it is commonly referred to as an "offshore balancer."

In sum, the ideal situation for any great power is to be the only regional hegemon in the world. That state would be a status quo power, and it would go to considerable lengths to preserve the existing distribution of power. The United States is in that enviable position today; it dominates the Western Hemisphere and there is no hegemon in any other area of the world. But if a regional hegemon is confronted with a peer competitor, it would no longer be a status quo power. Indeed, it would go to considerable lengths to weaken and maybe even destroy its distant rival. Of course, both regional hegemons would be motivated by that logic, which would make for a fierce security competition between them.

Power and Fear

That great powers fear each other is a central aspect of life in the international system. But as noted, the level of fear varies from case to case. For example, the Soviet Union worried much less about Germany in 1930 than it did in 1939. How much states fear each other matters greatly, because the amount of fear between them largely determines the severity of their security competition, as well as the probability that they will fight a war. The more profound the fear is, the more intense is the security competition, and the more likely is war. The logic is straightforward: a scared state will look especially hard for ways to enhance its security, and it will be disposed to pursue risky policies to achieve that end. Therefore, it is important to understand what causes states to fear each other more or less intensely.

Fear among great powers derives from the fact that they invariably have some offensive military capability that they can use against each other, and the fact that one can never be certain that other states do not intend to use that power against oneself. Moreover, because states operate in an anarchic system, there is no night watchman to whom they can turn for help if another great power attacks them. Although anarchy and uncertainty about other states' intentions create an irreducible level of fear among states that leads to power-maximizing behavior, they cannot account for why sometimes that level of fear is greater than at other times. The reason is that anarchy and the difficulty of discerning state intentions are constant facts of life, and constants cannot explain variation. The capability that states have to threaten each other, however, varies from case to case, and it is the key factor that drives fear levels up and down. Specifically, the more power a state possesses, the more fear it generates among its rivals. Germany, for example, was much more powerful at the end of the 1930s than it was at the decade's beginning, which is why the Soviets became increasingly fearful of Germany over the course of that decade.

This discussion of how power affects fear prompts the question, What is power? It is important to distinguish between potential and actual power. A state's potential power is based on the size of its population and the level of its wealth. These two assets are the main building blocks of military power. Wealthy rivals with large populations can usually build formidable military forces. A state's actual power is embedded mainly in its army and the air and naval forces that directly support it. Armies are the central ingredient of military power, because they are the principal instrument for conquering and controlling territory—the paramount political objective in a world of territorial states. In short, the key component of military might, even in the nuclear age, is land power.

Power considerations affect the intensity of fear among states in three main ways. First, rival states that possess nuclear forces that can survive a nuclear attack and retaliate against it are likely to fear each other less than if these same states had no nuclear weapons. During the Cold War, for example, the level of fear between the superpowers probably would have been substantially greater if nuclear weapons had not been invented. The logic here is simple: because nuclear weapons can inflict devastating destruction on a rival state in a short period of time, nuclear-armed rivals are going to be reluctant to fight with each other, which means that each side will have less reason to fear the other than would otherwise be the case. But as the Cold War demonstrates, this does not mean that war between nuclear powers is no longer thinkable; they still have reason to fear each other.

Second, when great powers are separated by large bodies of water, they usually do not have much offensive capability against each other, regardless of the relative size of their armies. Large bodies of water are formidable obstacles that cause significant power-projection problems for attacking armies. For example, the stopping power of water explains in good part why the United Kingdom and the United States (since becoming a great power in 1898) have never been invaded by another great power. It also explains why the United States has never tried to conquer territory in Europe or Northeast Asia, and why the United Kingdom has never attempted to dominate the European continent. Great powers located on the same landmass are in a much better position to attack and conquer each other. That is especially true of states that share a common border. Therefore, great powers separated by water are likely to fear each other less than great powers that can get at each other over land.

Third, the distribution of power among the states in the system also markedly affects the levels of fear.[32] The key issue is whether power is distributed more or less evenly among the great powers or whether there are sharp power asymmetries. The configuration of power that generates the most fear is a multipolar system that contains a potential hegemon—what I call "unbalanced multipolarity."

A potential hegemon is more than just the most powerful state in the system. It is a great power with so much actual military capability and so much potential power that it stands a good chance of dominating and controlling all of the other great powers in its region of the world. A potential hegemon need not have the wherewithal to fight all of its rivals at once, but it must have excellent prospects of defeating each opponent alone, and good prospects of defeating some of

them in tandem. The key relationship, however, is the power gap between the potential hegemon and the second most powerful state in the system: there must be a marked gap between them. To qualify as a potential hegemon, a state must have—by some reasonably large margin—the most formidable army as well as the most latent power among all the states located in its region.

Bipolarity is the power configuration that produces the least amount of fear among the great powers, although not a negligible amount by any means. Fear tends to be less acute in bipolarity, because there is usually a rough balance of power between the two major states in the system. Multipolar systems without a potential hegemon, what I call "balanced multipolarity," are still likely to have power asymmetries among their members, although these asymmetries will not be as pronounced as the gaps created by the presence of an aspiring hegemon. Therefore, balanced multipolarity is likely to generate less fear than unbalanced multipolarity, but more fear than bipolarity.

This discussion of how the level of fear between great powers varies with changes in the distribution of power, not with assessments about each other's intentions, raises a related point. When a state surveys its environment to determine which states pose a threat to its survival, it focuses mainly on the offensive *capabilities* of potential rivals, not their intentions. As emphasized earlier, intentions are ultimately unknowable, so states worried about their survival must make worst-case assumptions about their rivals' intentions. Capabilities, however, not only can be measured but also determine whether or not a rival state is a serious threat. In short, great powers balance against capabilities, not intentions.[33]

Great powers obviously balance against states with formidable military forces, because that offensive military capability is the tangible threat to their survival. But great powers also pay careful attention to how much latent power rival states control, because rich and populous states usually can and do build powerful armies. Thus, great powers tend to fear states with large populations and rapidly expanding economies, even if these states have not yet translated their wealth into military might.

The Hierarchy of State Goals

Survival is the number one goal of great powers, according to my theory. In practice, however, states pursue non-security goals as well. For example, great powers invariably seek greater economic prosperity to enhance the welfare of their citizenry. They sometimes seek to promote a particular ideology abroad, as happened during the Cold War when the United States tried to spread democracy around the world and the Soviet Union tried to sell communism. National unification is another goal that sometimes motivates states, as it did with Prussia and Italy in the nineteenth century and Germany after the Cold War. Great powers also occasionally try to foster human rights around the globe. States might pursue any of these, as well as a number of other non-security goals.

Offensive realism certainly recognizes that great powers might pursue these non-security goals, but it has little to say about them, save for one important point: states can pursue them as long as the requisite behavior does not conflict with balance-of-power logic, which is often the case.[34] Indeed, the pursuit of these non-security goals sometimes complements the hunt for relative power. For example, Nazi Germany expanded into eastern Europe for both ideological and realist reasons, and the superpowers competed with each other during the Cold War for similar reasons. Furthermore, greater economic prosperity invariably means greater wealth, which has significant implications for security, because wealth is the foundation of military power. Wealthy states can afford powerful military forces, which enhance a state's prospects for survival. As the political economist Jacob Viner noted more than fifty years ago, "there is a long-run harmony" between wealth and power.[35] National unification is another goal that usually complements the pursuit of power. For example, the unified German state that emerged in 1871 was more powerful than the Prussian state it replaced.

Sometimes the pursuit of non-security goals has hardly any effect on the balance of power, one way or the other. Human rights interventions usually fit this description, because they tend to be small-scale operations that cost little and do not detract from a great power's prospects for survival. For better or for worse, states are rarely willing to expend blood and treasure to protect foreign populations from gross abuses, including genocide. For instance, despite claims that American foreign policy is infused with moralism, Somalia (1992–93) is the only instance during the past one hundred years in which U.S. soldiers were killed in action on a humanitarian mission. And in that case, the loss of a mere eighteen soldiers in an infamous firefight in October 1993 so traumatized American policymakers that they immediately pulled all U.S. troops out of Somalia and then refused to intervene in Rwanda in the spring of 1994, when ethnic Hutu went on a genocidal rampage against their Tutsi neighbors.[36] Stopping that genocide would have been relatively easy and it would have had virtually no effect on the position of the United States in the balance of power.[37] Yet nothing was done. In short, although realism does not prescribe human rights interventions, it does not necessarily proscribe them.

But sometimes the pursuit of non-security goals conflicts with balance-of-power logic, in which case states usually act according to the dictates of realism. For example, despite the U.S. commitment to spreading democracy across the globe, it helped overthrow democratically elected governments and embraced a number of authoritarian regimes during the Cold War, when American policymakers felt that these actions would help contain the Soviet Union.[38] In World War II, the liberal democracies put aside their antipathy for communism and formed an alliance with the Soviet Union against Nazi Germany. "I can't take communism," Franklin Roosevelt emphasized, but to defeat Hitler "I would hold hands with the Devil."[39] In the same way, Stalin repeatedly demonstrated that when his ideological preferences clashed with power considerations, the latter won out. To take the most blatant example of his realism, the Soviet Union formed a non-aggression pact with Nazi Germany in August 1939—the infamous Molotov-Ribbentrop Pact—in hopes that the agreement would at least temporarily satisfy Hitler's territorial ambitions in eastern Europe and turn the Wehrmacht toward France and the United Kingdom.[40] When great powers confront a serious threat, in short, they pay little attention to ideology as they search for alliance partners.[41]

Security also trumps wealth when those two goals conflict, because "defence," as Adam Smith wrote in *The Wealth of Nations*, "is of much more importance than opulence."[42] Smith provides a good illustration of how states behave when forced to choose between wealth and relative power. In 1651, England put into effect the famous Navigation Act, protectionist legislation designed to damage Holland's commerce and ultimately cripple the Dutch economy. The legislation mandated that all goods imported into England be carried either in English ships or ships owned by the country that originally produced the goods. Since the Dutch produced few goods themselves, this measure would badly damage their shipping, the central ingredient in their economic success. Of course, the Navigation Act would hurt England's economy as well, mainly because it would rob England of the benefits of free trade. "The act of navigation," Smith wrote, "is not favorable to foreign commerce, or to the growth of that opulence that can arise from it." Nevertheless, Smith considered the legislation "the wisest of all the commercial regulations of England" because it did more damage to the Dutch economy than to the English economy, and in the mid-seventeenth century Holland was "the only naval power which could endanger the security of England."[43]

Creating World Order

The claim is sometimes made that great powers can transcend realist logic by working together to build an international order that fosters peace and justice. World peace, it would appear, can only enhance a state's prosperity and security. America's political leaders paid considerable lip service to this line of argument over the course of the twentieth century. President Clinton, for example, told an audience at the United Nations in September 1993 that "at the birth of this organization 48 years ago . . . a generation of gifted leaders from many nations stepped forward to organize the world's efforts on behalf of security and prosperity. . . . Now history has granted to us a moment of even greater opportunity. . . . Let us resolve that we will dream larger. . . . Let us ensure that the world we pass to our children is healthier, safer and more abundant than the one we inhabit today."[44]

This rhetoric notwithstanding, great powers do not work together to promote world order for its own sake. Instead, each seeks to maximize its own share of world power, which is likely to clash with the goal of creating and sustaining stable international orders.[45] This is not to say that great powers never aim to prevent wars and keep the peace. On the contrary, they work hard to deter wars in which they would be the likely victim. In such cases, however, state behavior is driven largely by narrow calculations about relative power, not by a commitment to build a world order independent of a state's own interests. The United States, for example, devoted enormous resources to deterring the Soviet Union from starting a war in Europe during the Cold War, not because of some deep-seated commitment to promoting peace around the world, but because American leaders feared that a Soviet victory would lead to a dangerous shift in the balance of power.[46]

The particular international order that obtains at any time is mainly a by-product of the self-interested behavior of the system's great powers. The configuration of the system, in other words, is the unintended consequence of great-power security competition, not the result of states acting together to organize peace. The establishment of the Cold War order in Europe illustrates this point. Neither the Soviet Union nor the United States intended to establish it, nor did they work together to create it. In fact, each superpower worked hard in the early years of the Cold War to gain power at the expense of the other, while preventing the other from doing likewise.[47] The system that emerged in Europe in the aftermath of World War II was the unplanned consequence of intense security competition between the superpowers.

Although that intense superpower rivalry ended along with the Cold War in 1990, Russia and the United States have not worked together to create the present order in Europe. The United States, for example, has rejected out of hand various Russian proposals to make the Organization for Security and Cooperation in Europe the central organizing pillar of European security (replacing the U.S.-dominated NATO). Furthermore, Russia was deeply opposed to NATO expansion, which it viewed as a serious threat to Russian security. Recognizing that Russia's weakness would preclude any retaliation, however, the United States ignored Russia's concerns and pushed NATO to accept the Czech Republic, Hungary, and Poland as new members. Russia has also opposed U.S. policy in the Balkans over the past decade, especially NATO's 1999 war against Yugoslavia. Again, the United States has paid little attention to Russia's concerns and has taken the steps it deems necessary to bring peace to that volatile region. Finally, it is worth noting that although Russia is dead set against allowing the United States to deploy ballistic missile defenses, it is highly likely that Washington will deploy such a system if it is judged to be technologically feasible.

For sure, great-power rivalry will sometimes produce a stable international order, as happened during the Cold War. Nevertheless, the great powers will continue looking for opportunities to increase their share of world power, and if a favorable situation arises, they will move to undermine that stable order. Consider how hard the United States worked during the late 1980s to weaken the Soviet Union and bring down the sta-

ble order that had emerged in Europe during the latter part of the Cold War.[48] Of course, the states that stand to lose power will work to deter aggression and preserve the existing order. But their motives will be selfish, revolving around balance-of-power logic, not some commitment to world peace.

Great powers cannot commit themselves to the pursuit of a peaceful world order for two reasons. First, states are unlikely to agree on a general formula for bolstering peace. Certainly, international relations scholars have never reached a consensus on what the blueprint should look like. In fact, it seems there are about as many theories on the causes of war and peace as there are scholars studying the subject. But more important, policymakers are unable to agree on how to create a stable world. For example, at the Paris Peace Conference after World War I, important differences over how to create stability in Europe divided Georges Clemenceau, David Lloyd George, and Woodrow Wilson.[49] In particular, Clemenceau was determined to impose harsher terms on Germany over the Rhineland than was either Lloyd George or Wilson, while Lloyd George stood out as the hard-liner on German reparations. The Treaty of Versailles, not surprisingly, did little to promote European stability.

Furthermore, consider American thinking on how to achieve stability in Europe in the early days of the Cold War.[50] The key elements for a stable and durable system were in place by the early 1950s. They included the division of Germany, the positioning of American ground forces in Western Europe to deter a Soviet attack, and ensuring that West Germany would not seek to develop nuclear weapons. Officials in the Truman administration, however, disagreed about whether a divided Germany would be a source of peace of war. For example, George Kennan and Paul Nitze, who held important positions in the State Department, believed that a divided Germany would be a source of instability, whereas Secretary of State Dean Acheson disagreed with them. In the 1950s, President Eisenhower sought to end the American commitment to defend Western

Europe and to provide West Germany with its own nuclear deterrent. This policy, which was never fully adopted, nevertheless caused significant instability in Europe, as it led directly to the Berlin crises of 1958–59 and 1961.[51]

Second, great powers cannot put aside power considerations and work to promote international peace because they cannot be sure that their efforts will succeed. If their attempt fails, they are likely to pay a steep price for having neglected the balance of power, because if an aggressor appears at the door there will be no answer when they dial 911. That is a risk few states are willing to run. Therefore, prudence dictates that they behave according to realist logic. This line of reasoning accounts for why collective security schemes, which call for states to put aside narrow concerns about the balance of power and instead act in accordance with the broader interests of the international community, invariably die at birth.[52]

Cooperation Among States

One might conclude from the preceding discussion that my theory does not allow for any cooperation among the great powers. But this conclusion would be wrong. States can cooperate, although cooperation is sometimes difficult to achieve and always difficult to sustain. Two factors inhibit cooperation: considerations about relative gains and concern about cheating.[53] Ultimately, great powers live in a fundamentally competitive world where they view each other as real, or at least potential, enemies, and they therefore look to gain power at each other's expense.

Any two states contemplating cooperation must consider how profits or gains will be distributed between them. They can think about the division in terms of either absolute or relative gains (recall the distinction made earlier between pursuing either absolute power or relative power; the concept here is the same). With absolute gains, each side is concerned with maximizing its own profits and cares little about how much the other side gains or loses in the deal. Each side

cares about the other only to the extent that the other side's behavior affects its own prospects for achieving maximum profits. With relative gains, on the other hand, each side considers not only its own individual gain, but also how well it fares compared to the other side.

Because great powers care deeply about the balance of power, their thinking focuses on relative gains when they consider cooperating with other states. For sure, each state tries to maximize its absolute gains; still, it is more important for a state to make sure that it does no worse, and perhaps better, than the other state in any agreement. Cooperation is more difficult to achieve, however, when states are attuned to relative gains rather than absolute gains.[54] This is because states concerned about absolute gains have to make sure that if the pie is expanding, they are getting at least some portion of the increase, whereas states that worry about relative gains must pay careful attention to how the pie is divided, which complicates cooperative efforts.

Concerns about cheating also hinder cooperation. Great powers are often reluctant to enter into cooperative agreements for fear that the other side will cheat on the agreement and gain a significant advantage. This concern is especially acute in the military realm, causing a "special peril of defection," because the nature of military weaponry allows for rapid shifts in the balance of power.[55] Such a development could create a window of opportunity for the state that cheats to inflict a decisive defeat on its victim.

These barriers to cooperation notwithstanding, great powers do cooperate in a realist world. Balance-of-power logic often causes great powers to form alliances and cooperate against common enemies. The United Kingdom, France, and Russia, for example, were allies against Germany before and during World War I. States sometimes cooperate to gang up on a third state, as Germany and the Soviet Union did against Poland in 1939.[56] More recently, Serbia and Croatia agreed to conquer and divide Bosnia between them, although the United States and its European allies prevented them from executing their agreement.[57]

Rivals as well as allies cooperate. After all, deals can be struck that roughly reflect the distribution of power and satisfy concerns about cheating. The various arms control agreements signed by the superpowers during the Cold War illustrate this point.

The bottom line, however, is that cooperation takes place in a world that is competitive at its core—one where states have powerful incentives to take advantage of other states. This point is graphically highlighted by the state of European politics in the forty years before World War I. The great powers cooperated frequently during this period, but that did not stop them from going to war on August 1, 1914.[58] The United States and the Soviet Union also cooperated considerably during World War II, but that cooperation did not prevent the outbreak of the Cold War shortly after Germany and Japan were defeated. Perhaps most amazingly, there was significant economic and military cooperation between Nazi Germany and the Soviet Union during the two years before the Wehrmacht attacked the Red Army.[59] No amount of cooperation can eliminate the dominating logic of security competition. Genuine peace, or a world in which states do not compete for power, is not likely as long as the state system remains anarchic.

Conclusion

In sum, my argument is that the structure of the international system, not the particular characteristics of individual great powers, causes them to think and act offensively and to seek hegemony.[60] I do not adopt Morgenthau's claim that states invariably behave aggressively because they have a will to power hardwired into them. Instead, I assume that the principal motive behind great-power behavior is survival. In anarchy, however, the desire to survive encourages states to behave aggressively. Nor does my theory classify states as more or less aggressive on the basis of their economic or political systems. Offensive realism makes only a handful of assumptions about great powers, and these assumptions

apply equally to all great powers. Except for differences in how much power each state controls, the theory treats all states alike.

I have now laid out the logic explaining why states seek to gain as much power as possible over their rivals. * * *

NOTES

1. Most realist scholars allow in their theories for status quo powers that are not hegemons. At least some states, they argue, are likely to be satisfied with the balance of power and thus have no incentive to change it. See Randall L. Schweller, "Neorealism's Status-Quo Bias: What Security Dilemma?" *Security Studies* 5, No. 3 (Spring 1996, special issue on "Realism: Restatements and Renewal," ed. Benjamin Frankel), pp. 98–101; and Arnold Wolfers, *Discord and Collaboration: Essays on International Politics* (Baltimore, MD: Johns Hopkins University Press, 1962), pp. 84–86, 91–92, 125–26.

2. Milton Friedman, *Essays in Positive Economics* (Chicago: University of Chicago Press, 1953), p. 14. Also see Kenneth N. Waltz, *Theory of International Politics* (Reading, MA: Addison-Wesley, 1979), pp. 5–6, 91, 119.

3. Terry Moe makes a helpful distinction between assumptions that are simply useful simplifications of reality (i.e., realistic in themselves but with unnecessary details omitted), and assumptions that are clearly contrary to reality (i.e., that directly violate well-established truths). See Moe, "On the Scientific Status of Rational Models," *American Journal of Political Science* 23, No. 1 (February 1979), pp. 215–43.

4. The concept of anarchy and its consequences for international politics was first articulated by G. Lowes Dickinson, *The European Anarchy* (New York: Macmillan, 1916). For a more recent and more elaborate discussion of anarchy, see Waltz, *Theory of International Politics*, pp. 88–93. Also see Robert J. Art and Robert

Jervis, eds., *International Politics: Anarchy, Force, Imperialism* (Boston: Little, Brown, 1973), pt. 1; and Helen Milner, "The Assumption of Anarchy in International Relations Theory: A Critique," *Review of International Studies* 17, No. 1 (January 1991), pp. 67–85.

5. Although the focus in this study is on the state system, realist logic can be applied to other kinds of anarchic systems. After all, it is the absence of central authority, not any special characteristic of states, that causes them to compete for power.

6. Inis L. Claude, Jr., *Swords into Plowshares: The Problems and Progress of International Organization*, 4th ed. (New York: Random House, 1971), p. 14.

7. The claim that states might have benign intentions is simply a starting assumption. I argue subsequently that when you combine the theory's five assumptions, states are put in a position in which they are strongly disposed to having hostile intentions toward each other.

8. My theory ultimately argues that great powers behave offensively toward each other because that is the best way for them to guarantee their security in an anarchic world. The assumption here, however, is that there are many reasons besides security for why a state might behave aggressively toward another state. In fact, it is uncertainty about whether those non-security causes of war are at play, or might come into play, that pushes great powers to worry about their survival and thus act offensively. Security concerns alone cannot cause great powers to act aggressively. The possibility that at least one state might be motivated by non-security calculations is a necessary condition for offensive realism, as well as for any other structural theory of international politics that predicts security competition.

9. Quoted in Jon Jacobson, *When the Soviet Union Entered World Politics* (Berkeley: University of California Press, 1994), p. 271.

10. See Elizabeth Pond, *Beyond the Wall: Germany's Road to Unification* (Washington, DC: Brookings Institution Press, 1993), chap. 12; Margaret Thatcher, *The Downing Street Years* (New York: HarperCollins, 1993), chaps. 25–26; and Philip Zelikow and Condoleezza Rice, *Germany Unified and Europe Transformed: A Study in Statecraft* (Cambridge, MA: Harvard University Press, 1995), chap. 4.

11. Frederick Schuman introduced the concept of self-help in *International Politics: An Introduction to the Western State System* (New York: McGraw-Hill, 1933), pp. 199–202, 514, although Waltz made the concept famous in *Theory of International Politics*, chap. 6. On realism and alliances, see Stephen M. Walt, *The Origins of Alliances* (Ithaca, NY: Cornell University Press, 1987).

12. Quoted in Martin Wight, *Power Politics* (London: Royal Institute of International Affairs, 1946), p. 40.

13. If one state achieves hegemony, the system ceases to be anarchic and becomes hierarchic. Offensive realism, which assumes international anarchy, has little to say about politics under hierarchy. But as discussed later, it is highly unlikely that any state will become a global hegemon, although regional hegemony is feasible. Thus, realism is likely to provide important insights about world politics for the foreseeable future, save for what goes on inside in a region that is dominated by a hegemon.

14. Although great powers always have aggressive intentions, they are not always *aggressors*, mainly because sometimes they do not have the capability to behave aggressively. I use the term "aggressor" throughout this book to denote great powers that have the material wherewithal to act on their aggressive intentions.

15. Kenneth Waltz maintains that great powers should not pursue hegemony but instead should aim to control an "appropriate" amount of world power. See Waltz, "The Origins of War in Neorealist Theory," in Robert I. Rotberg and Theodore K. Rabb, eds., *The Origin and Prevention of Major Wars* (Cambridge: Cambridge University Press, 1989), p. 40.

16. The following hypothetical example illustrates this point. Assume that American policy-makers were forced to choose between two different power balances in the Western Hemisphere. The first is the present distribution of power, whereby the United States is a hegemon that no state in the region would dare challenge militarily. In the second scenario, China replaces Canada and Germany takes the place of Mexico. Even though the United States would have a significant military advantage over both China and Germany, it is difficult to imagine any American strategist opting for this scenario over U.S. hegemony in the Western Hemisphere.

17. John H. Herz, "Idealist Internationalism and the Security Dilemma," *World Politics* 2, No. 2 (January 1950), pp. 157–80. Although Dickinson did not use the term "security dilemma," its logic is clearly articulated in *European Anarchy*, pp. 20, 88.

18. Herz, "Idealist Internationalism," p. 157.

19. See Joseph M. Grieco, "Anarchy and the Limits of Cooperation: A Realist Critique of the Newest Liberal Institutionalism," *International Organization* 42, No. 3 (Summer 1988), pp. 485–507; Stephen D. Krasner, "Global Communications and National Power: Life on the Pareto Frontier," *World Politics* 43, No. 3 (April 1991), pp. 336–66; and Robert Powell, "Absolute and Relative Gains in International Relations Theory," *American Political Science Review* 85, No. 4 (December 1991), pp. 1303–20.

20. See Michael Mastanduno, "Do Relative Gains Matter? America's Response to Japanese Industrial Policy," *International Security* 16, No. 1 (Summer 1991), pp. 73–113.

21. Waltz maintains that in Hans Morgenthau's theory, states seek power as an end in itself; thus, they are concerned with absolute power, not relative power. See Waltz, "Origins of War," pp. 40–41; and Waltz, *Theory of International Politics*, pp. 126–27.

22. Quoted in Marc Trachtenberg, *A Constructed Peace: The Making of the European Settlement, 1945–1963* (Princeton, NJ: Princeton University Press, 1999), p. 36.

23. In short, the key issue for evaluating offensive realism is not whether a state is constantly trying to conquer other countries or going all out in terms of defense spending, but whether or not great powers routinely pass up promising opportunities to gain power over rivals.

24. See Richard K. Betts, *Surprise Attack: Lessons for Defense Planning* (Washington, DC: Brookings Institution Press, 1982); James D. Fearon, "Rationalist Explanations for War," *International Organization* 49, No. 3 (Summer 1995), pp. 390–401; Robert Jervis, *The Logic of Images in International Relations* (Princeton, NJ: Princeton University Press, 1970); and Stephen Van Evera, *Causes of War: Power and the Roots of Conflict* (Ithaca, NY: Cornell University Press, 1999), pp. 45–51, 83, 137–42.

25. See Joel Achenbach, "The Experts in Retreat: After-the-Fact Explanations for the Gloomy Predictions," *Washington Post*, February 28, 1991; and Jacob Weisberg, "Gulfballs: How the Experts Blew It, Big-Time," *New Republic*, March 25, 1991.

26. Jack Snyder and Stephen Van Evera make this argument in its boldest form. See Jack Snyder, *Myths of Empire: Domestic Politics and International Ambition* (Ithaca, NY: Cornell University Press, 1991), esp. pp. 1, 307–8; and Van Evera, *Causes of War*, esp. pp. 6, 9.

27. Relatedly, some defensive realists interpret the security dilemma to say that the offensive measures a state takes to enhance its own security force rival states to respond in kind, leaving all states no better off than if they had done nothing, and possibly even worse off. See Charles L. Glaser, "The Security Dilemma Revisited," *World Politics* 50, No. 1 (October 1997), pp. 171–201.

28. Although threatened states sometimes balance efficiently against aggressors, they often do not, thereby creating opportunities for successful offense. Snyder appears to be aware of

this problem, as he adds the important qualifier "at least in the long run" to his claim that "states typically form balancing alliances to resist aggressors." *Myths of Empire*, p. 11.

29. John Arquilla, *Dubious Battles: Aggression, Defeat, and the International System* (Washington, DC: Crane Russak, 1992), p. 2. Also see Bruce Bueno de Mesquita, *The War Trap* (New Haven, CT: Yale University Press, 1981), pp. 21–22; and Kevin Wang and James Ray, "Beginners and Winners: The Fate of Initiators of Interstate Wars Involving Great Powers since 1495," *International Studies Quarterly* 38, No. 1 (March 1994), pp. 139–54.

30. Although Snyder and Van Evera maintain that conquest rarely pays, both concede in subtle but important ways that aggression sometimes succeeds. Snyder, for example, distinguishes between expansion (successful offense) and overexpansion (unsuccessful offense), which is the behavior that he wants to explain. See, for example, his discussion of Japanese expansion between 1868 and 1945 in *Myths of Empire*, pp. 114–16. Van Evera allows for variation in the offense-defense balance, to include a few periods where conquest is feasible. See *Causes of War*, chap. 6. Of course, allowing for successful aggression contradicts their central claim that offense hardly ever succeeds.

31. See Robert Gilpin, *War and Change in World Politics* (Cambridge: Cambridge University Press, 1981), p. 29; and William C. Wohlforth, *The Elusive Balance: Power and Perceptions during the Cold War* (Ithaca, NY: Cornell University Press, 1993), pp. 12–14.

32. In subsequent chapters, the power-projection problems associated with large bodies of water are taken into account when measuring the distribution of power (see Chapter 4). Those two factors are treated separately here, however, simply to highlight the profound influence that oceans have on the behavior of great powers.

33. For an opposing view, see David M. Edelstein, "Choosing Friends and Enemies: Perceptions of Intentions in International Relations," Ph.D. diss., University of Chicago, August 2000; Andrew Kydd, "Why Security Seekers Do Not Fight Each Other," *Security Studies* 7, No. 1 (Autumn 1997), pp. 114–54; and Walt, *Origins of Alliances*.

34. See note 8 in this chapter.

35. Jacob Viner, "Power versus Plenty as Objectives of Foreign Policy in the Seventeenth and Eighteenth Centuries," *World Politics* I, No. 1 (October 1948), p. 10.

36. See Mark Bowden, *Black Hawk Down: A Story of Modern War* (London: Penguin, 1999); Alison Des Forges, *"Leave None to Tell the Story": Genocide in Rwanda* (New York: Human Rights Watch, 1999), pp. 623–25; and Gerard Prunier, *The Rwanda Crisis: History of a Genocide* (New York: Columbia University Press, 1995), pp. 274–75.

37. See Scott R. Feil, *Preventing Genocide: How the Early Use of Force Might Have Succeeded in Rwanda* (New York: Carnegie Corporation, 1998); and John Mueller, "The Banality of 'Ethnic War,'" *International Security* 25, No. 1 (Summer 2000), pp. 58–62. For a less sanguine view of how many lives would have been saved had the United States intervened in Rwanda, see Alan J. Kuperman, "Rwanda in Retrospect," *Foreign Affairs* 79, No. 1 (January–February 2000), pp. 94–118.

38. See David F. Schmitz, *Thank God They're on Our Side: The United States and Right-Wing Dictatorships, 1921–1965* (Chapel Hill: University of North Carolina Press, 1999), chaps. 4–6; Gaddis Smith, *The Last Years of the Monroe Doctrine, 1945–1993* (New York: Hill and Wang, 1994); Tony Smith, *America's Mission: The United States and the Worldwide Struggle for Democracy in the Twentieth Century* (Princeton, NJ: Princeton University Press, 1994); and Stephen Van Evera, "Why Europe Matters, Why the Third World Doesn't: American Grand Strategy after the Cold War," *Journal of Strategic Studies* 13, No. 2 (June 1990), pp. 25–30.

39. Quoted in John M. Carroll and George C. Herring, eds., *Modern American Diplomacy*,

rev. ed. (Wilmington, DE: Scholarly Resources, 1996), p. 122.

40. Nikita Khrushchev makes a similar point about Stalin's policy toward Chinese nationalist leader Chiang Kai-shek during World War II.

41. See Walt, *Origins of Alliances*, pp. 5, 266–68.

42. Adam Smith, *An Inquiry into the Nature and Causes of the Wealth of Nations*, ed. Edwin Cannan (Chicago: University of Chicago Press, 1976), Vol. 1, p. 487. All the quotes in this paragraph are from pp. 484–87 of that book.

43. For an overview of the Anglo-Dutch rivalry, see Jack S. Levy, "The Rise and Decline of the Anglo-Dutch Rivalry, 1609–1689," in William R. Thompson, ed., *Great Power Rivalries* (Columbia: University of South Carolina Press, 1999), pp. 172–200; and Paul M. Kennedy, *The Rise and Fall of British Naval Mastery* (London: Allen Lane, 1976), chap. 2.

44. William J. Clinton, "Address by the President to the 48th Session of the United Nations General Assembly," United Nations, New York, September 27, 1993. Also see George Bush, "Toward a New World Order: Address by the President to a Joint Session of Congress," September 11, 1990.

45. Bradley Thayer examined whether the victorious powers were able to create and maintain stable security orders in the aftermath of the Napoleonic Wars, World War I, and World War II, or whether they competed among themselves for power, as realism would predict. Thayer concludes that the rhetoric of the triumphant powers notwithstanding, they remained firmly committed to gaining power at each other's expense. See Bradley A. Thayer, "Creating Stability in New World Orders," Ph.D. diss., University of Chicago, August 1996.

46. See Melvyn P. Leffler, *A Preponderance of Power: National Security, the Truman Administration, and the Cold War* (Stanford, CA: Stanford University Press, 1992).

47. For a discussion of American efforts to undermine Soviet control of Eastern Europe,
see Peter Grose, *Operation Rollback: America's Secret War behind the Iron Curtain* (Boston: Houghton Mifflin, 2000); Walter L. Hixson, *Parting the Curtain: Propaganda, Culture, and the Cold War, 1945–1961* (New York: St. Martin's, 1997); and Gregory Mitrovich, *Undermining the Kremlin: America's Strategy to Subvert the Soviet Bloc, 1947–1956* (Ithaca, NY: Cornell University Press, 2000).

48. For a synoptic discussion of U.S. policy toward the Soviet Union in the late 1980s that cites most of the key sources on the subject, see Randall L. Schweller and William C. Wohlforth, "Power Test: Evaluating Realism in Response to the End of the Cold War," *Security Studies* 9, No. 3 (Spring 2000), pp. 91–97.

49. The editors of a major book on the Treaty of Versailles write, "The resulting reappraisal, as documented in this book, constitutes a new synthesis of peace conference scholarship. The findings call attention to divergent peace aims within the American and Allied camps and underscore the degree to which the negotiators themselves considered the Versailles Treaty a work in progress." Manfred F. Boemeke, Gerald D. Feldman, and Elisabeth Glaser, eds., *The Treaty of Versailles: A Reassessment after 75 Years* (Cambridge: Cambridge University Press, 1998), p. 1.

50. This paragraph draws heavily on Trachtenberg, *Constructed Peace*; and Marc Trachtenberg, *History and Strategy* (Princeton, NJ: Princeton University Press, 1991), chaps. 4–5. Also see G. John Ikenberry, "Rethinking the Origins of American Hegemony," *Political Science Quarterly* 104, No. 3 (Autumn 1989), pp. 375–400.

51. The failure of American policymakers during the early Cold War to understand where the security competition in Europe was leading is summarized by Trachtenberg, "The predictions that were made pointed as a rule in the opposite direction: that Germany could not be kept down forever; that the Federal Republic would ultimately . . . want nuclear forces of her own; that U.S. troops could not

be expected to remain in . . . Europe. . . . Yet all these predictions—every single one—turned out to be wrong." Trachtenberg, *History and Strategy*, pp. 231–32. Also see Trachtenberg, *Constructed Peace*, pp. vii–viii.

52. For more discussion of the pitfalls of collective security, see John J. Mearsheimer, "The False Promise of International Institutions," *International Security* 19, No. 3 (Winter 1994–95), pp. 26–37.

53. See Grieco, "Anarchy and the Limits of Cooperation," pp. 498, 500.

54. For evidence of relative gains considerations thwarting cooperation among states, see Paul W. Schroeder, *The Transformation of European Politics, 1763–1848* (Oxford: Clarendon, 1994), chap. 3.

55. Charles Lipson, "International Cooperation in Economic and Security Affairs," *World Politics* 37, No. 1 (October 1984), p. 14.

56. See Randall L. Schweller, "Bandwagoning for Profit: Bringing the Revisionist State Back In," *International Security* 19, No. 1 (Summer 1994), pp. 72–107. See also the works cited in note 59 in this chapter.

57. See Misha Glenny, *The Fall of Yugoslavia: The Third Balkan War*, 3d rev. ed. (New York: Penguin, 1996), p. 149; Philip Sherwell and Alina Petric, "Tudjman Tapes Reveal Plans to Divide Bosnia and Hide War Crimes," *Sunday Telegraph* (London), June 18, 2000; Laura Silber and Allan Little, *Yugoslavia: Death of a Nation*, rev. ed. (New York: Penguin, 1997), pp. 131–32, 213; and Warren Zimmerman,

Origins of a Catastrophe: Yugoslavia and Its Destroyers—America's Last Ambassador Tells What Happened and Why (New York: Times Books, 1996), pp. 116–17.

58. See John Maynard Keynes, *The Economic Consequences of the Peace* (New York: Penguin, 1988), chap. 2; and J. M. Roberts, *Europe, 1880–1945* (London: Longman, 1970), pp. 239–41.

59. For information on the Molotov-Ribbentrop Pact of August 1939 and the ensuing cooperation between those states, see Alan Bullock, *Hitler and Stalin: Parallel Lives* (London: HarperCollins, 1991), chaps. 14–15; I.C.B. Dear, ed., *The Oxford Companion to World War II* (Oxford: Oxford University Press, 1995), pp. 780–82; Anthony Read and David Fisher, *The Deadly Embrace: Hitler, Stalin, and the Nazi-Soviet Pact, 1939–1941* (New York: Norton, 1988); Geoffrey Roberts, *The Unholy Alliance: Stalin's Pact with Hitler* (Bloomington: Indiana University Press, 1989), chaps. 8–10; and Adam B. Ulam, *Expansion and Coexistence: Soviet Foreign Policy, 1917–1973*, 2d ed. (New York: Holt, Rinehart, and Winston, 1974), chap. 6.

60. Waltz maintains that structural theories can explain international outcomes—i.e., whether war is more likely in bipolar or multipolar systems—but that they cannot explain the foreign policy behavior of particular states. A separate theory of foreign policy, he argues, is needed for that task. See *Theory of International Politics*, pp. 71–72, 121–23.

MICHAEL W. DOYLE

LIBERALISM AND WORLD POLITICS

Promoting freedom will produce peace, we have often been told. In a speech before the British Parliament in June of 1982, President Reagan proclaimed that governments founded on a respect for individual liberty exercise "restraint" and "peaceful intentions" in their foreign policy. He then announced a "crusade for freedom" and a "campaign for democratic development" (Reagan, June 9, 1982).

In making these claims the president joined a long list of liberal theorists (and propagandists) and echoed an old argument: the aggressive instincts of authoritarian leaders and totalitarian ruling parties make for war. Liberal states, founded on such individual rights as equality before the law, free speech and other civil liberties, private property, and elected representation are fundamentally against war this argument asserts. When the citizens who bear the burdens of war elect their governments, wars become impossible. Furthermore, citizens appreciate that the benefits of trade can be enjoyed only under conditions of peace. Thus the very existence of liberal states, such as the U.S., Japan, and our European allies, makes for peace.

Building on a growing literature in international political science, I reexamine the liberal claim President Reagan reiterated for us. I look at three distinct theoretical traditions of liberalism, attributable to three theorists: Schumpeter, a brilliant explicator of the liberal pacifism the president invoked; Machiavelli, a classical republican whose glory is an imperialism we often practice; and Kant.

Despite the contradictions of liberal pacifism and liberal imperialism, I find, with Kant and other liberal republicans, that liberalism does leave a coherent legacy on foreign affairs. Liberal states are different. They are indeed peaceful, yet they are also prone to make war, as the U.S. and our "freedom fighters" are now doing, not so covertly, against Nicaragua. Liberal states have created a separate peace, as Kant argued they would, and have also discovered liberal reasons for aggression, as he feared they might. I conclude by arguing that the differences among liberal pacifism, liberal imperialism, and Kant's liberal internationalism are not arbitrary but rooted in differing conceptions of the citizen and the state.

Liberal Pacifism

There is no canonical description of liberalism. What we tend to call *liberal* resembles a family portrait of principles and institutions, recognizable by certain characteristics—for example, individual freedom, political participation, private property, and equality of opportunity—that most liberal states share, although none has perfected them all. Joseph Schumpeter clearly fits within this family when he considers the international effects of capitalism and democracy.

Schumpeter's "Sociology of Imperialisms," published in 1919, made a coherent and sustained argument concerning the pacifying (in the sense of nonaggressive) effects of liberal institutions and principles (Schumpeter, 1955; see also Doyle, 1986, pp. 155–59). Unlike some of the earlier liberal theorists who focused on a single feature such as trade (Montesquieu, 1949, vol. I, bk. 20, chap. 1) or failed to examine critically the arguments they were advancing, Schumpeter saw the interaction of capitalism and democracy as the foundation of liberal pacifism, and he tested his arguments in a sociology of historical imperialisms.

From *American Political Science Review* 80, no. 4 (December 1986): 1151–69. The author's notes have been omitted.

He defines *imperialism* as "an objectless disposition on the part of a state to unlimited forcible expansion" (Schumpeter, 1955, p. 6). Excluding imperialisms that were mere "catchwords" and those that were "object-ful" (e.g., defensive imperialism), he traces the roots of objectless imperialism to three sources, each an atavism. Modern imperialism, according to Schumpeter, resulted from the combined impact of a "war machine," warlike instincts, and export monopolism.

Once necessary, the war machine later developed a life of its own and took control of a state's foreign policy: "Created by the wars that required it, the machine now created the wars it required" (Schumpeter, 1955, p. 25). Thus, Schumpeter tells us that the army of ancient Egypt, created to drive the Hyksos out of Egypt, took over the state and pursued militaristic imperialism. Like the later armies of the courts of absolutist Europe, it fought wars for the sake of glory and booty, for the sake of warriors and monarchs—wars *gratia* warriors.

A warlike disposition, elsewhere called "instinctual elements of bloody primitivism," is the natural ideology of a war machine. It also exists independently; the Persians, says Schumpeter (1955, pp. 25–32), were a warrior nation from the outset.

Under modern capitalism, export monopolists, the third source of modern imperialism, push for imperialist expansion as a way to expand their closed markets. The absolute monarchies were the last clear-cut imperialisms. Nineteenth-century imperialisms merely represent the vestiges of the imperialisms created by Louis XIV and Catherine the Great. Thus, the export monopolists are an atavism of the absolute monarchies, for they depend completely on the tariffs imposed by the monarchs and their militaristic successors for revenue (Schumpeter, 1955, p. 82–83). Without tariffs, monopolies would be eliminated by foreign competition.

Modern (nineteenth century) imperialism, therefore, rests on an atavistic war machine, militaristic attitudes left over from the days of monarchical wars, and export monopolism, which is nothing more than the economic residue of monarchical finance. In the modern era, imperialists gratify their private interests. From the national perspective, their imperialistic wars are objectless.

Schumpeter's theme now emerges. Capitalism and democracy are forces for peace. Indeed, they are antithetical to imperialism. For Schumpeter, the further development of capitalism and democracy means that imperialism will inevitably disappear. He maintains that capitalism produces an unwarlike disposition; its populace is "democratized, individualized, rationalized" (Schumpeter, 1955, p. 68). The people's energies are daily absorbed in production. The disciplines of industry and the market train people in "economic rationalism"; the instability of industrial life necessitates calculation. Capitalism also "individualizes"; "subjective opportunities" replace the "immutable factors" of traditional, hierarchical society. Rational individuals demand democratic governance.

Democratic capitalism leads to peace. As evidence, Schumpeter claims that throughout the capitalist world an opposition has arisen to "war, expansion, cabinet diplomacy"; that contemporary capitalism is associated with peace parties; and that the industrial worker of capitalism is "vigorously anti-imperialist." In addition, he points out that the capitalist world has developed means of preventing war, such as the Hague Court and that the least feudal, most capitalist society—the United States—has demonstrated the least imperialistic tendencies (Schumpeter, 1955, pp. 95–96). An example of the lack of imperialistic tendencies in the U.S., Schumpeter thought, was our leaving over half of Mexico unconquered in the war of 1846–48.

Schumpeter's explanation for liberal pacifism is quite simple: Only war profiteers and military aristocrats gain from wars. No democracy would pursue a minority interest and tolerate the high costs of imperialism. When free trade prevails, "no class" gains from forcible expansion because

foreign raw materials and food stuffs are as accessible to each nation as though they were in its own territory. Where the cultural backwardness of a region makes normal economic intercourse dependent on colonization it does not matter, assuming free trade, which of the "civilized" nations undertakes the task of colonization. (Schumpeter, 1955, pp. 75–76)

Schumpeter's arguments are difficult to evaluate. In partial tests of quasi-Schumpeterian propositions, Michael Haas (1974, pp. 464–65) discovered a cluster that associates democracy, development, and sustained modernization with peaceful conditions. However, M. Small and J. D. Singer (1976) have discovered that there is no clearly negative correlation between democracy and war in the period 1816–1965—the period that would be central to Schumpeter's argument (see also Wilkenfeld, 1968, Wright, 1942, p. 841).

* * * A recent study by R. J. Rummel (1983) of "libertarianism" and international violence is the closest test Schumpeterian pacifism has received. "Free" states (those enjoying political and economic freedom) were shown to have considerably less conflict at or above the level of economic sanctions than "nonfree" states. The free states, the partly free states (including the democratic socialist countries such as Sweden), and the nonfree states accounted for 24%, 26%, and 61%, respectively, of the international violence during the period examined.

These effects are impressive but not conclusive for the Schumpeterian thesis. The data are limited, in this test, to the period 1976 to 1980. It includes, for example, the Russo-Afghan War, the Vietnamese invasion of Cambodia, China's invasion of Vietnam, and Tanzania's invasion of Uganda but just misses the U.S., quasi-covert intervention in Angola (1975) and our not so covert war against Nicaragua (1981–). More importantly, it excludes the cold war period, with its numerous interventions, and the long history of colonial wars (the Boer War, the Spanish-American War, the Mexican Intervention, etc.) that marked the history of liberal, including democratic capitalist, states (Doyle, 1983b; Chan, 1984; Weede, 1984).

The discrepancy between the warlike history of liberal states and Schumpeter's pacifistic expectations highlights three extreme assumptions. First, his "materialistic monism" leaves little room for noneconomic objectives, whether espoused by states or individuals. Neither glory, nor prestige, nor ideological justification, nor the pure power of ruling shapes policy. These nonmaterial goals leave little room for positive-sum gains, such as the comparative advantages of trade. Second, and relatedly, the same is true for his states. The political life of individuals seems to have been homogenized at the same time as the individuals were "rationalized, individualized, and democratized." Citizens—capitalists and workers, rural and urban—seek material welfare. Schumpeter seems to presume that ruling makes no difference. He also presumes that no one is prepared to take those measures (such as stirring up foreign quarrels to preserve a domestic ruling coalition) that enhance one's political power, despite deterimental effects on mass welfare. Third, like domestic politics, world politics are homogenized. Materially monistic and democratically capitalist, all states evolve toward free trade and liberty together. Countries differently constituted seem to disappear from Schumpeter's analysis. "Civilized" nations govern "culturally backward" *regions*. These assumptions are not shared by Machiavelli's theory of liberalism.

Liberal Imperialism

Machiavelli argues, not only that republics are not pacifistic, but that they are the best form of state for imperial expansion. Establishing a republic fit for imperial expansion is, moreover, the best way to guarantee the survival of a state.

Machiavelli's republic is a classical mixed republic. It is not a democracy—which he thought would quickly degenerate into a tyranny—but is characterized by social equality, popular liberty, and political participation (Machiavelli, 1950, bk. 1, chap. 2, p. 112; see also Huliung, 1983, chap. 2; Mansfield, 1970; Pocock, 1975, pp. 198–99; Skinner, 1981, chap. 3). The consuls serve as "kings," the senate as an aristocracy managing the state, and the people in the assembly as the source of strength.

Liberty results from "disunion"—the competition and necessity for compromise required by the division of powers among senate, consuls, and tribunes (the last representing the common people). Liberty also results from the popular veto. The powerful few threaten the rest with tyranny, Machiavelli says, because they seek to dominate. The mass demands not to be dominated, and their veto thus preserves the liberties of the state (Machiavelli, 1950, bk. 1, chap. 5, p. 122). However, since the people and the rulers have different social characters, the people need to be "managed" by the few to avoid having their recklessness overturn or their fecklessness undermine the ability of the state to expand (Machiavelli, 1950, bk. 1, chap. 53, pp. 249–50). Thus the senate and the consuls plan expansion, consult oracles, and employ religion to manage the resources that the energy of the people supplies.

Strength, and then imperial expansion, results from the way liberty encourages increased population and property, which grow when the citizens know their lives and goods are secure from arbitrary seizure. Free citizens equip large armies and provide soldiers who fight for public glory and the common good because these are, in fact, their own (Machiavelli, 1950, bk. 2, chap. 2, pp. 287–90). If you seek the honor of having your state expand, Machiavelli advises, you should organize it as a free and popular republic like Rome, rather than as an aristocratic republic like Sparta or Venice. Expansion thus calls for a free republic.

"Necessity"—political survival—calls for expansion. If a stable aristocratic republic is forced by foreign conflict "to extend her territory, in such a case we shall see her foundations give way and herself quickly brought to ruin"; if, on the other hand, domestic security prevails, "the continued tranquility would enervate her, or provoke internal disensions, which together, or either of them separately, will apt to prove her ruin" (Machiavelli, 1950, bk. 1, chap. 6, p. 129). Machiavelli therefore believes it is necessary to take the

constitution of Rome, rather than that of Sparta or Venice, as our model.

Hence, this belief leads to liberal imperialism. We are lovers of glory, Machiavelli announces. We seek to rule or, at least, to avoid being oppressed. In either case, we want more for ourselves and our states than just material welfare (materialistic monism). Because other states with similar aims thereby threaten us, we prepare ourselves for expansion. Because our fellow citizens threaten us if we do not allow them either to satisfy their ambition or to release their political energies through imperial expansion, we expand.

There is considerable historical evidence for liberal imperialism. Machiavelli's (Polybius's) Rome and Thucydides' Athens both were imperial republics in the Machiavellian sense (Thucydides, 1954, bk. 6). The historical record of numerous U.S. interventions in the postwar period supports Machiavelli's argument (* * * Barnet, 1968, chap. 11), but the current record of liberal pacifism, weak as it is, calls some of his insights into question. To the extent that the modern populace actually controls (and thus unbalances) the mixed republic, its diffidence may outweigh elite ("senatorial") aggressiveness.

We can conclude either that (1) liberal pacifism has at least taken over with the further development of capitalist democracy, as Schumpeter predicted it would or that (2) the mixed record of liberalism—pacifism and imperialism—indicates that some liberal states are Schumpeterian democracies while others are Machiavellian republics. Before we accept either conclusion, however, we must consider a third apparent regularity of modern world politics.

Liberal Internationalism

Modern liberalism carries with it two legacies. They do not affect liberal states separately, according to whether they are pacifistic or imperialistic, but simultaneously.

The first of these legacies is the pacification of foreign relations among liberal states. * * *

Beginning in the eighteenth century and slowly growing since then, a zone of peace, which Kant called the "pacific federation" or "pacific union," has begun to be established among liberal societies. More than 40 liberal states currently make up the union. Most are in Europe and North America, but they can be found on every continent, as Appendix 1 indicates.

Here the predictions of liberal pacifists (and President Reagan) are borne out: liberal states do exercise peaceful restraint, and a separate peace exists among them. This separate peace provides a solid foundation for the United States' crucial alliances with the liberal powers, e.g., the North Atlantic Treaty Organization and our Japanese alliance. This foundation appears to be impervious to the quarrels with our allies that bedeviled the Carter and Reagan administrations. It also offers the promise of a continuing peace among liberal states, and as the number of liberal states increases, it announces the possibility of global peace this side of the grave or world conquest.

Of course, the probability of the outbreak of war in any given year between any two given states is low. The occurrence of a war between any two adjacent states, considered over a long period of time, would be more probable. The apparent absence of war between liberal states, whether adjacent or not, for almost 200 years thus may have significance. Similar claims cannot be made for feudal, fascist, communist, authoritarian, or totalitarian forms of rule (Doyle, 1983a, pp. 222), nor for pluralistic or merely similar societies. More significant perhaps is that when states are forced to decide on which side of an impending world war they will fight, liberal states all wind up on the same side despite the complexity of the paths that take them there. These characteristics do not prove that the peace among liberals is statistically significant nor that liberalism is the sole valid explanation for the peace. They do suggest that we consider the possibility that liberals have indeed established a separate peace—but only among themselves.

Liberalism also carries with it a second legacy: international "imprudence" (Hume, 1963, pp. 346–47). Peaceful restraint only seems to work in liberals' relations with other liberals. Liberal states have fought numerous wars with nonliberal states. (For a list of international wars since 1816 see Appendix 2.)

Many of these wars have been defensive and thus prudent by necessity. Liberal states have been attacked and threatened by nonliberal states that do not exercise any special restraint in their dealings with the liberal states. Authoritarian rulers both stimulate and respond to an international political environment in which conflicts of prestige, interest, and pure fear of what other states might do all lead states toward war. War and conquest have thus characterized the careers of many authoritarian rulers and ruling parties, from Louis XIV and Napoleon to Mussolini's fascists, Hitler's Nazis, and Stalin's communists.

Yet we cannot simply blame warfare on the authoritarians or totalitarians, as many of our more enthusiastic politicians would have us do. Most wars arise out of calculations and miscalculations of interest, misunderstandings, and mutual suspicions, such as those that characterized the origins of World War I. However, aggression by the liberal state has also characterized a large number of wars. Both France and Britain fought expansionist colonial wars throughout the nineteenth century. The United States fought a similar war with Mexico from 1846 to 1848, waged a war of annihilation against the American Indians, and intervened militarily against sovereign states many times before and after World War II. Liberal states invade weak nonliberal states and display striking distrust in dealings with powerful nonliberal states (Doyle, 1983b).

Neither realist (statist) nor Marxist theory accounts well for these two legacies. While they can account for aspects of certain periods of international stability (* * * Russett, 1985), neither the logic of the balance of power nor the logic of international hegemony explains the separate peace maintained for more than 150 years among states sharing one particular form of governance—

liberal principles and institutions. Balance-of-power theory expects—indeed is premised upon—flexible arrangements of geostrategic rivalry that include preventive war. Hegemonies wax and wane, but the liberal peace holds. Marxist "ultra-imperialists" expect a form of peaceful rivalry among capitalists, but only liberal capitalists maintain peace. Leninists expect liberal capitalists to be aggressive toward nonliberal states, but they also (and especially) expect them to be imperialistic toward fellow liberal capitalists.

Kant's theory of liberal internationalism helps us understand these two legacies. * * * *Perpetual Peace*, written in 1795 (Kant, 1970, pp. 93–130), helps us understand the interactive nature of international relations. Kant tries to teach us methodologically that we can study neither the systemic relations of states nor the varieties of state behavior in isolation from each other. Substantively, he anticipates for us the ever-widening pacification of a liberal pacific union, explains this pacification, and at the same time suggests why liberal states are not pacific in their relations with nonliberal states. Kant argues that perpetual peace will be guaranteed by the ever-widening acceptance of three "definitive articles" of peace. When all nations have accepted the definitive articles in a metaphorical "treaty" of perpetual peace he asks them to sign, perpetual peace will have been established.

The First Definitive Article requires the civil constitution of the state to be republican. By *republican* Kant means a political society that has solved the problem of combining moral autonomy, individualism, and social order. A private property and market-oriented economy partially addressed that dilemma in the private sphere. The public, or political, sphere was more troubling. His answer was a republic that preserved juridical freedom—the legal equality of citizens as subjects—on the basis of a representative government with a separation of powers. Juridical freedom is preserved because the morally autonomous individual is by means of representation a self-legislator making laws that apply to all citizens equally, including himself or

herself. Tyranny is avoided because the individual is subject to laws he or she does not also administer (Kant, *PP* [*Perpetual Peace*], pp. 99–102 * * *).

Liberal republics will progressively establish peace among themselves by means of the pacific federation, or union (*foedus pacificum*), described in Kant's Second Definitive Article. The pacific union will establish peace within a federation of free states and securely maintain the rights of each state. The world will not have achieved the "perpetual peace" that provides the ultimate guarantor of republican freedom until "a late stage and after many unsuccessful attempts" (Kant, *UH* [*The Idea for a Universal History with a Cosmopolitan Purpose*], p. 47). At that time, all nations will have learned the lessons of peace through right conceptions of the appropriate constitution, great and sad experience, and good will. Only then will individuals enjoy perfect republican rights or the full guarantee of a global and just peace. In the meantime, the "pacific federation" of liberal republics—"an enduring and gradually expanding federation likely to prevent war"—brings within it more and more republics—despite republican collapses, backsliding, and disastrous wars—creating an ever-expanding separate peace (Kant, *PP*, p. 105). Kant emphasizes that

> it can be shown that this idea of federalism, extending gradually to encompass all states and thus leading to perpetual peace, is practicable and has objective reality. For if by good fortune one powerful and enlightened nation can form a republic (which is by nature inclined to seek peace), this will provide a focal point for federal association among other states. These will join up with the first one, thus securing the freedom of each state in accordance with the idea of international right, and the whole will gradually spread further and further by a series of alliances of this kind. (Kant, *PP*, p. 104)

The pacific union is not a single peace treaty ending one war, a world state, nor a state of nations. Kant finds the first insufficient. The second and third are impossible or potentially tyrannical. National sovereignty precludes reliable subservience to a state of nations; a world state destroys the civic freedom on which the development of human capacities rests (Kant, *UH*, p. 50). Although Kant obliquely refers to various classical interstate confederations and modern diplomatic congresses, he develops no systematic organizational embodiment of this treaty and presumably does not find institutionalization necessary (Riley, 1983, chap. 5; Schwarz, 1962, p. 77). He appears to have in mind a mutual nonaggression pact, perhaps a collective security agreement, and the cosmopolitan law set forth in the Third Definitive Article.

The Third Definitive Article establishes a cosmopolitan law to operate in conjunction with the pacific union. The cosmopolitan law "shall be limited to conditions of universal hospitality." In this Kant calls for the recognition of the "right of a foreigner not to be treated with hostility when he arrives on someone else's territory." This "does not extend beyond those conditions which make it possible for them [foreigners] to attempt to enter into relations [commerce] with the native inhabitants" (Kant, *PP*, p. 106). Hospitality does not require extending to foreigners either the right to citizenship or the right to settlement, unless the foreign visitors would perish if they were expelled. Foreign conquest and plunder also find no justification under this right. Hospitality does appear to include the right of access and the obligation of maintaining the opportunity for citizens to exchange goods and ideas without imposing the obligation to trade (a voluntary act in all cases under liberal constitutions).

Perpetual peace, for Kant, is an epistemology, a condition for ethical action, and, most importantly, an explanation of how the "mechanical process of nature visibly exhibits the purposive plan of producing concord among men, even against their will and indeed by means of their very discord" (Kant, *PP*, p. 108; *UH*, pp. 44–45). Understanding history requires an epistemological foundation, for without a teleology, such as the promise of perpetual peace, the complexity of history would overwhelm human understanding (Kant, *UH*, pp. 51–53). Perpetual peace, however,

is not merely a heuristic device with which to interpret history. It is guaranteed, Kant explains in the "First Addition" to *Perpetual Peace* ("On the Guarantee of Perpetual Peace"), to result from men fulfilling their ethical duty or, failing that, from a hidden plan. Peace is an ethical duty because it is only under conditions of peace that all men can treat each other as ends, rather than means to an end (Kant, *UH*, p. 50; Murphy, 1970, chap. 3). * * *

In the end, however, our guarantee of perpetual peace does not rest on ethical conduct. * * * The guarantee thus rests, Kant argues, not on the probable behavior of moral angels, but on that of "devils, so long as they possess understanding" (*PP*, p. 112). In explaining the sources of each of the three definitive articles of the perpetual peace, Kant then tells us how we (as free and intelligent devils) could be motivated by fear, force, and calculated advantage to undertake a course of action whose outcome we could reasonably anticipate to be perpetual peace. Yet while it is possible to conceive of the Kantian road to peace in these terms, Kant himself recognizes and argues that social evolution also makes the conditions of moral behavior less onerous and hence more likely (*CF* [*The Contest of Faculties*], pp. 187–89; Kelly, 1969, pp. 106–13). In tracing the effects of both political and moral development, he builds an account of why liberal states do maintain peace among themselves and of how it will (by implication, has) come about that the pacific union will expand. He also explains how these republics would engage in wars with nonrepublics and therefore suffer the "sad experience" of wars that an ethical policy might have avoided.

*   *   *

Kant shows how republics, once established, lead to peaceful relations. He argues that once the aggressive interests of absolutist monarchies are tamed and the habit of respect for individual rights engrained by republican government, wars would appear as the disaster to the people's welfare that he and the other liberals thought them to be. The fundamental reason is this:

If, as is inevitability the case under this constitution, the consent of the citizens is required to decide whether or not war should be declared, it is very natural that they will have a great hesitation in embarking on so dangerous an enterprise. For this would mean calling down on themselves all the miseries of war, such as doing the fighting themselves, supplying the costs of the war from their own resources, painfully making good the ensuing devastation, and, as the crowning evil, having to take upon themselves a burden of debts which will embitter peace itself and which can never be paid off on account of the constant threat of new wars. But under a constitution where the subject is not a citizen, and which is therefore not republican, it is the simplest thing in the world to go to war. For the head of state is not a fellow citizen, but the owner of the state, and war will not force him to make the slightest sacrifice so far as his banquets, hunts, pleasure palaces and court festivals are concerned. He can thus decide on war, without any significant reason, as a kind of amusement, and unconcernedly leave it to the diplomatic corps (who are always ready for such proposes) to justify the war for the sake of propriety. (Kant, *PP*, p. 100).

Yet these domestic republican restraints do not end war. If they did, liberal states would not be warlike, which is far from the case. They do introduce republican caution—Kant's "hesitation"—in place of monarchical caprice. Liberal wars are only fought for popular, liberal purposes. The historical liberal legacy is laden with popular wars fought to promote freedom, to protect private property, or to support liberal allies against nonliberal enemies. Kant's position is ambiguous. He regards these wars as unjust and warns liberals of their susceptibility to them (Kant, *PP*, p. 106). At the same time, Kant argues that each nation "can and ought to" demand that its neighboring nations enter into the pacific union of liberal states (*PP*, p. 102). * * *

*   *   *

* * * As republics emerge (the first source) and as culture progresses, an understanding of the legitimate rights of all citizens and of all republics comes into play; and this, now that caution characterizes policy, sets up the moral foundations for the liberal peace. Correspondingly, international law highlights the importance of Kantian publicity. Domestically, publicity helps ensure that the officials of republics act according to the principles they profess to hold just and according to the interests of the electors they claim to represent. Internationally, free speech and the effective communication of accurate conceptions of the political life of foreign peoples is essential to establishing and preserving the understanding on which the guarantee of respect depends. Domestically just republics, which rest on consent, then presume foreign republics also to be consensual, just, and therefore deserving of accommodation. * * * Because nonliberal governments are in a state of aggression with their own people, their foreign relations become for liberal governments deeply suspect. In short, fellow liberals benefit from a presumption of amity; nonliberals suffer from a presumption of enmity. Both presumptions may be accurate; each, however, may also be self-confirming.

Lastly, cosmopolitan law adds material incentives to moral commitments. The cosmopolitan right to hospitality permits the "spirit of commerce" sooner or later to take hold of every nation, thus impelling states to promote peace and to try to avert war. Liberal economic theory holds that these cosmopolitan ties derive from a cooperative international division of labor and free trade according to comparative advantage. Each economy is said to be better off than it would have been under autarky; each thus acquires an incentive to avoid policies that would lead the other to break these economic ties. Because keeping open markets rests upon the assumption that the next set of transactions will also be determined by prices rather than coercion, a sense of mutual security is vital to avoid security-motivated searches for economic autarky. Thus, avoiding a challenge to another liberal state's security or even enhancing each other's security by means of alliance naturally follows economic interdependence.

A further cosmopolitan source of liberal peace is the international market's removal of difficult decisions of production and distribution from the direct sphere of state policy. A foreign state thus does not appear directly responsible for these outcomes, and states can stand aside from, and to some degree above, these contentious market rivalries and be ready to step in to resolve crises. The interdependence of commerce and the international contacts of state officials help create crosscutting transnational ties that serve as lobbies for mutual accommodation. According to modern liberal scholars, international financiers and transnational and transgovernmental organizations create interests in favor of accommodation. Moreover, their variety has ensured that no single conflict sours an entire relationship by setting off a spiral of reciprocated retaliation * * *. Conversely, a sense of suspicion, such as that characterizing relations between liberal and nonliberal governments, can lead to restrictions on the range of contacts between societies, and this can increase the prospect that a single conflict will determine an entire relationship.

No single constitutional, international, or cosmopolitan source is alone sufficient, but together (and only together) they plausibly connect the characteristics of liberal polities and economies with sustained liberal peace. Alliances founded on mutual strategic interest among liberal and nonliberal states have been broken; economic ties between liberal and nonliberal states have proven fragile; but the political bonds of liberal rights and interests have proven a remarkably firm foundation for mutual nonaggression. A separate peace exists among liberal states.

In their relations with nonliberal states, however, liberal states have not escaped from the insecurity caused by anarchy in the world political system considered as a whole. Moreover, the very constitutional restraint, international respect for individual rights, and shared commercial interests that establish grounds for peace among liberal states establish grounds for additional conflict in relations between liberal and nonliberal societies.

Conclusion

Kant's liberal internationalism, Machiavelli's liberal imperialism, and Schumpeter's liberal pacifism rest on fundamentally different views of the nature of the human being, the state, and international relations. Schumpeter's humans are rationalized, individualized, and democratized. They are also homogenized, pursuing material interests "monistically." Because their material interests lie in peaceful trade, they and the democratic state that these fellow citizens control are pacifistic. Machiavelli's citizens are splendidly diverse in their goals but fundamentally unequal in them as well, seeking to rule or fearing being dominated. Extending the rule of the dominant elite or avoiding the political collapse of their state, each calls for imperial expansion.

Kant's citizens, too, are diverse in their goals and individualized and rationalized, but most importantly, they are capable of appreciating the moral equality of all individuals and of treating other individuals as ends rather than as means. The Kantian state thus is governed publicly according to law, as a republic. Kant's is the state that solves the problem of governing individualized equals, whether they are the "rational devils" he says we often find ourselves to be or the ethical agents we can and should become. Republics tell us that

> in order to organize a group of rational beings who together require universal laws for their survival, but of whom each separate individual is secretly inclined to exempt himself from them, the constitution must be so designed so that, although the citizens are opposed to one another in their private attitudes, these opposing views may inhibit one another in such a way that the public conduct of the citizens will be the same as if they did not have such evil attitudes. (Kant, *PP*, p. 113)

Unlike Machiavelli's republics, Kant's republics are capable of achieving peace among themselves because they exercise democratic caution and are capable of appreciating the international rights of foreign republics. These international rights of republics derive from the representation of foreign individuals, who are our moral equals. Unlike Schumpeter's capitalist democracies, Kant's republics—including our own—remain in a state of war with nonrepublics. Liberal republics see themselves as threatened by aggression from nonrepublics that are not constrained by representation. Even though wars often cost more than the economic return they generate, liberal republics also are prepared to protect and promote—sometimes forcibly—democracy, private property, and the rights of individuals overseas against nonrepublics, which, because they do not authentically represent the rights of individuals, have no rights to noninterference. These wars may liberate oppressed individuals overseas; they also can generate enormous suffering.

*   *   *

Perpetual peace, Kant says, is the end point of the hard journey his republics will take. The promise of perpetual peace, the violent lessons of war, and the experience of a partial peace are proof of the need for and the possibility of world peace. They are also the grounds for moral citizens and statesmen to assume the duty of striving for peace.

Appendix 1. Liberal Regimes and the Pacific Union, 1700–1982

Period	Period	Period
18th Century	1850–1900 (cont.)	1900–1945 (cont.)
Swiss Cantons[a]	Canada, 1867–	Austria, 1918–1934
French Republie, 1790–1795	France, 1871–	Estonia, 1919–1934
United States,[a] 1776–	Argentina, 1880–	Finland, 1919–
Total = 3	Chile, 1891–	Uruguay, 1919–
	Total = 13	Costa Rica, 1919–
1800–1850		Czechosovakia, 1920–1939
Swiss Confederation	1900–1945	Ireland, 1920–
United States	Switzerland	Mexico, 1928–
France, 1830–1849	United States	Lebenon, 1944–
Belgium, 1830–	Great Britain	Total = 29
Great Britain, 1832–	Sweden	
Netherlands, 1848–	Canada	1945–[b]
Piedmont, 1848–	Greece, –1911; 1928–1936	Switzerland
Denmark, 1849–	Italy, –1922	United States
Total = 8	Belgium, –1940	Great Britain
	Netherlands, –1940	Sweden
1850–1900	Argentina, –1943	Canada
Switzerland	France, –1940	Australia
United States	Chile, –1924; 1932–	New Zealand
Belgium	Australia, 1901	Finland
Great Britain	Norway, 1905–1940	Ireland
Netherlands	New Zealand, 1907–	Mexico
Piedmont, –1861	Colombia, 1910–1949	Uruguay, –1973
Italy, 1861–	Denmark, 1914–1940	Chile, –1973
Denmark, –1866	Poland, 1917–1935	Lebanon, –1975
Sweden, 1864–	Latvia, 1922–1934	Costa Rica, –1948; 1953–
Greece, 1864–	Germany, 1918–1932	Iceland, 1944–

(continued)

Appendix 1. *Continued*

Period	*Period*	*Period*
1945 (cont.)	Ecuador, 1948–1963;	Nigeria, 1961–1964;
France, 1945–	1979–	1979–1984
Denmark, 1945	Israel, 1949–	Jamaica, 1962–
Norway, 1945	West Germany, 1949–	Trinidad and Tobago, 1962–
Austria, 1945–	Greece, 1950–1967; 1975–	Senegal, 1963–
Brazil, 1945–1954; 1955–1964	Peru, 1950–1962; 1963–1968;	Malaysia, 1963–
Belgium, 1946–	1980–	Botswana, 1966–
Luxembourg, 1946–	El Salvador, 1950–1961	Singapore, 1965–
Netherlands, 1946–	Turkey, 1950–1960;	Portugal, 1976–
Italy, 1946–	1966–1971	Spain, 1978–
Philippines, 1946–1972	Japan, 1951–	Dominican Republic, 1978–
India, 1947–1975; 1977–	Bolivia, 1956–1969; 1982–	Honduras, 1981–
Sri Lanka, 1948–1961;	Colombia, 1958–	Papua New Guinea, 1982–
1963–1971; 1978–	Venezuela, 1959–	Total = 50

Note: I have drawn up this approximate list of "Liberal Regimes" according to the four institutions Kant described as essential: market and private property economies; politics that are externally sovereign; citizens who possess juridical rights; and "republican" (whether republican or parliamentary monarchy), representative government. This latter includes the requirement that the legislative branch have an effective role in public policy and be formally and competitively (either inter- or intra-party) elected. Furthermore, I have taken into account whether male suffrage is wide (i.e., 30%) or, as Kant (*MM* [*The Metaphysics of Morals*], p. 139) would have had it, open by "achievement" to inhabitants of the national or metropolitan territory (e.g., to poll-tax payers or householders). This list of liberal regimes is thus more inclusive than a list of democratic regimes, or polyarchies (Powell, 1982, p. 5). Other conditions taken into account here are that female suffrage is granted within a generation of its being demanded by an extensive female suffrage movement and that representative government is internally sovereign (e.g., including, and especially over military and foreign affairs) as well as stable (in existence for at least three years). Sources for these data are Banks and Overstreet (1983), Gastil (1985), *The Europa Yearbook, 1985* (1985), Langer (1968), U.K. Foreign and Commonwealth Office (1980), and U.S. Department of State (1981). Finally, these lists exclude ancient and medieval "republics," since none appears to fit Kant's commitment to liberal individualism (Holmes, 1979).

[a]There are domestic variations within these liberal regimes: Switzerland was liberal only in certain cantons; the United States was liberal only north of the Mason-Dixon line until 1865, when it became liberal throughout.

[b]Selected list, excludes liberal regimes with populations less than one million. These include all states categorized as "free" by Gastil and those "partly free" (four-fifths or more free) states with a more pronounced capitalist orientation.

Appendix 2. *International Wars Listed Chronologically*

British-Maharattan (1817–1818)
Greek (1821–1828)
Franco-Spanish (1823)
First Anglo-Burmese (1823–1826)
Javanese (1825–1830)
Russo-Persian (1826–1828)
Russo-Turkish (1828–1829)
First Polish (1831)
First Syrian (1831–1832)

Texas (1835–1836)
First British-Afghan (1838–1842)
Second Syrian (1839–1940)
Franco-Algerian (1839–1847)
Peruvian-Bolivian (1841)
First British-Sikh (1845–1846)
Mexican-American (1846–1848)
Austro-Sardinian (1848–1849)
First Schleswig-Holstein (1848–1849)

Appendix 2. *Continued*

Hungarian (1848–1849)
Second British-Sikh (1848–1849)
Roman Republic (1849)
La Plata (1851–1852)
First Turco-Montenegran (1852–1853)
Crimean (1853–1856)
Anglo-Persian (1856–1857)
Sepoy (1857–1859)
Second Turco-Montenegran (1858–1859)
Italian Unification (1859)
Spanish-Moroccan (1859–1860)
Italo-Roman (1860)
Italo-Sicilian (1860–1861)
Franco-Mexican (1862–1867)
Ecuadorian-Colombian (1863)
Second Polish (1863–1864)
Spanish-Santo Dominican (1863–1865)
Second Schleswig-Holstein (1864)
Lopez (1864–1870)
Spanish-Chilean (1865–1866)
Seven Weeks (1866)
Ten Years (1868–1878)
Franco-Prussian (1870–1871)
Dutch-Achinese (1873–1878)
Balkan (1875–1877)
Russo-Turkish (1877–1878)
Bosnian (1878)
Second British-Afghan (1878–1880)
Pacific (1879–1883)
British-Zulu (1879)
Franco-Indochinese (1882–1884)
Mahdist (1882–1885)
Sino-French (1884–1885)
Central American (1885)
Serbo-Bulgarian (1885)
Sino-Japanese (1894–1895)
Franco-Madagascan (1894–1895)
Cuban (1895–1898)
Italo-Ethiopian (1895–1896)
First Philippine (1896–1898)
Greco-Turkish (1897)
Spanish-American (1898)
Second Philippine (1899–1902)
Boer (1899–1902)
Boxer Rebellion (1900)
Ilinden (1903)

Russo-Japanese (1904–1905)
Central American (1906)
Central American (1907)
Spanish-Moroccan (1909–1910)
Italo-Turkish (1911–1912)
First Balkan (1912–1913)
Second Balkan (1913)
World War I (1914–1918)
Russian Nationalities (1917–1921)
Russo-Polish (1919–1920)
Hungarian-Allies (1919)
Greco-Turkish (1919–1922)
Riffian (1921–1926)
Druze (1925–1927)
Sino-Soviet (1929)
Manchurian (1931–1933)
Chaco (1932–1935)
Italo-Ethiopian (1935–1936)
Sino-Japanese (1937–1941)
Changkufeng (1938)
Nomohan (1939)
World War II (1939–1945)
Russo-Finnish (1939–1940)
Franco-Thai (1940–1941)
Indonesian (1945–1946)
Indochinese (1945–1954)
Madagascan (1947–1948)
First Kashmir (1947–1949)
Palestine (1948–1949)
Hyderabad (1948)
Korean (1950–1953)
Algerian (1954–1962)
Russo-Hungarian (1956)
Sinai (1956)
Tibetan (1956–1959)
Sino-Indian (1962)
Vietnamese (1965–1975)
Second Kashmir (1965)
Six Day (1967)
Israeli-Egyptian (1969–1970)
Football (1969)
Bangladesh (1971)
Philippine-MNLF (1972–)
Yom Kippur (1973)
Turco-Cypriot (1974)
Ethiopian-Eritrean (1974–)

(continued)

Appendix 2. *Continued*

Vietnamese-Cambodian (1975–)	Ugandan-Tanzanian (1978–1979)
Timor (1975–)	Sino-Vietnamese (1979)
Saharan (1975–)	Russo-Afghan (1979–)
Ogaden (1976–)	Iran-Iraqi (1980–)

Note: This table is taken from Melvin Small and J. David Singer (1982, pp. 79–80). This is a partial list of international wars fought between 1816 and 1980. In Appendices A and B, Small and Singer identify a total of 575 wars during this period, but approximately 159 of them appear to be largely domestic, or civil wars.

This list excludes covert interventions, some of which have been directed by liberal regimes against other liberal regimes—for example, the United States' effort to destabilize the Chilean election and Allende's government. Nonetheless, it is significant that such interventions are not pursued publicly as acknowledged policy. The covert destabilization campaign against Chile is recounted by the Senate Select Committee to Study Governmental Operations with Respect to Intelligence Activities (1975, *Covert Action in Chile, 1963–73*).

Following the argument of this article, this list also excludes civil wars. Civil wars differ from international wars, not in the ferocity of combat, but in the issues that engender them. Two nations that could abide one another as independent neighbors separated by a border might well be the fiercest of enemies if forced to live together in one state, jointly deciding how to raise and spend taxes, choose leaders, and legislate fundamental questions of value. Notwithstanding these differences, no civil wars that I recall upset the argument of liberal pacification.

REFERENCES

Banks, Arthur, and William Overstreet, eds. 1983. *A Political Handbook of the World; 1982–1983*. New York: McGraw Hill.

Barnet, Richard. 1968. *Intervention and Revolution*. Cleveland: World Publishing Co.

Chan, Steve. 1984. Mirror, Mirror on the Wall . . . : Are Freer Countries More Pacific? *Journal of Conflict Resolution*, 28:617–48.

Doyle, Michael W. 1983a. Kant, Liberal Legacies, and Foreign Affairs: Part 1. *Philosophy and Public Affairs*, 12:205–35.

Doyle, Michael W. 1983b. Kant, Liberal Legacies, and Foreign Affairs: Part 2. *Philosophy and Public Affairs*, 12:323–53.

Doyle, Michael W. 1986. *Empires*. Ithaca: Cornell University Press.

The Europa Yearbook for 1985. 1985. 2 vols. London: Europa Publications.

Gastil, Raymond. 1985. The Comparative Survey of Freedom 1985. *Freedom at Issue*, 82:3–16.

Haas, Michael. 1974. *International Conflict*. New York: Bobbs-Merrill.

Holmes, Stephen. 1979. Aristippus in and out of Athens. *American Political Science Review*, 73:113–28.

Huliung, Mark. 1983. *Citizen Machiavelli*. Princeton: Princeton University Press.

Hume, David. 1963. Of the Balance of Power. *Essays: Moral, Political, and Literary*. Oxford: Oxford University Press.

Kant, Immanuel. 1970. *Kant's Political Writings*. Hans Reiss, ed. H. B. Nisbet, trans. Cambridge: Cambridge University Press.

Kelly, George A. 1969. *Idealism, Politics, and History*. Cambridge: Cambridge University Press.

Langer, William L., ed. 1968. *The Encyclopedia of World History*. Boston: Houghton Mifflin.

Machiavelli, Niccolo. 1950. *The Prince and the Discourses*. Max Lerner, ed. Luigi Ricci and Christian Detmold, trans. New York: Modern Library.

Mansfield, Harvey C. 1970. Machiavelli's New Regime. *Italian Quarterly*, 13:63–95.

Montesquieu, Charles de. 1949. *Spirit of the Laws*. New York: Hafner. (Originally published in 1748.)

Murphy, Jeffrie. 1970. *Kant: The Philosophy of Right*. New York: St. Martins.

Pocock, J. G. A. 1975. *The Machiavellian Moment*. Princeton: Princeton University Press.

Powell, G. Bingham. 1982. *Contemporary Democracies*. Cambridge, MA: Harvard University Press.

Reagan, Ronald. June 9, 1982. Address to Parliament. *New York Times*.

Riley, Patrick. 1983. *Kant's Political Philosophy*. Totowa, NJ: Rowman and Littlefield.

Rummel, Rudolph J. 1983. Libertarianism and International Violence. *Journal of Conflict Resolution*, 27:27–71.

Russett, Bruce. 1985. The Mysterious Case of Vanishing Hegemony. *International Organization*, 39:207–31.

Schumpeter, Joseph. 1955. The Sociology of Imperialism. In *Imperialism and Social Classes*. Cleveland: World Publishing Co. (Essay originally published in 1919.)

Schwarz, Wolfgang. 1962. Kant's Philosophy of Law and International Peace. *Philosophy and Phenomenonological Research*, 23:71–80.

Skinner, Quentin. 1981. *Machiavelli*. New York: Hill and Wang.

Small, Melvin, and J. David Singer. 1976. The War-Proneness of Democratic Regimes. *The Jerusalem Journal of International Relations*, 1(4):50–69.

Small, Melvin, and J. David Singer. 1982. *Resort to Arms*. Beverly Hills: Sage Publications.

Thucydides. 1954. *The Peloponnesian War*. Rex Warner, ed. and trans. Baltimore: Penguin.

U.K. Foreign and Commonwealth Office. 1980. *A Yearbook of the Commonwealth 1980*. London: HMSO.

U.S. Congress. Senate. Select Committee to Study Governmental Operations with Respect to Intelligence Activities. 1975. *Covert Action in Chile, 1963–74*. 94th Cong., 1st sess., Washington, D.C.: U.S. Government Printing Office.

U.S. Department of State. 1981. *Country Reports on Human Rights Practices*. Washington, D.C.: U.S. Government Printing Office.

Weede, Erich. 1984. Democracy and War Involvement. *Journal of Conflict Resolution*, 28:649–64.

Wilkenfeld, Jonathan. 1968. Domestic and Foreign Conflict Behavior of Nations. *Journal of Peace Research*, 5:56–69.

Wright, Quincy. 1942. *A Study of History*. Chicago: Chicago University Press.

ALEXANDER WENDT

ANARCHY IS WHAT STATES MAKE OF IT: THE SOCIAL CONSTRUCTION OF POWER POLITICS

The debate between realists and liberals has reemerged as an axis of contention in international relations theory.[1] Revolving in the past around competing theories of human nature, the debate is more concerned today with the extent to which state action is influenced by "structure" (anarchy and the distribution of power) versus "process" (interaction and learning) and institutions.

From *International Organization* 46, no. 2 (spring 1992): 391–425. Some of the author's notes have been omitted.

Does the absence of centralized political authority force states to play competitive power politics? Can international regimes overcome this logic, and under what conditions? What in anarchy is given and immutable, and what is amenable to change?

*   *   *

* * * I argue that self-help and power politics do not follow either logically or causally from anarchy and that if today we find ourselves in a self-help world, this is due to process, not structure.

There is no "logic" of anarchy apart from the practices that create and instantiate one structure of identities and interests rather than another; structure has no existence or causal powers apart from process. Self-help and power politics are institutions, not essential features of anarchy. *Anarchy is what states make of it.*

*   *   *

Anarchy and Power Politics

Classical realists such as Thomas Hobbes, Reinhold Niebuhr, and Hans Morgenthau attributed egoism and power politics primarily to human nature, whereas structural realists or neorealists emphasize anarchy. The difference stems in part from different interpretations of anarchy's causal powers. Kenneth Waltz's work is important for both. In *Man, the State, and War,* he defines anarchy as a condition of possibility for or "permissive" cause of war, arguing that "wars occur because there is nothing to prevent them."[2] It is the human nature or domestic politics of predator states, however, that provide the initial impetus or "efficient" cause of conflict which forces other states to respond in kind.[3] Waltz is not entirely consistent about this, since he slips without justification from the permissive causal claim that in anarchy war is always possible to the active causal claim that "war may at any moment occur."[4] But despite Waltz's concluding call for third-image theory, the efficient causes that initialize anarchic systems are from the first and second images. This is reversed in Waltz's *Theory of International Politics*, in which first- and second-image theories are spurned as "reductionist," and the logic of anarchy seems by itself to constitute self-help and power politics as necessary features of world politics.[5]

This is unfortunate, since whatever one may think of first- and second-image theories, they have the virtue of implying that practices determine the character of anarchy. In the permissive view, only if human or domestic factors cause A to attack B will B have to defend itself. Anarchies may contain dynamics that lead to competitive power politics, but they also may not, and we can argue about when particular structures of identity and interest will emerge. In neorealism, however, the role of practice in shaping the character of anarchy is substantially reduced, and so there is less about which to argue: self-help and competitive power politics are simply given exogenously by the structure of the state system.

I will not here contest the neorealist description of the contemporary state system as a competitive, self-help world;[6] I will only dispute its explanation. I develop my argument in three stages. First, I disentangle the concepts of self-help and anarchy by showing that self-interested conceptions of security are not a constitutive property of anarchy. Second, I show how self-help and competitive power politics may be produced causally by processes of interaction between states in which anarchy plays only a permissive role. In both of these stages of my argument, I self-consciously bracket the first- and second-image determinants of state identity, not because they are unimportant (they are indeed important), but because like Waltz's objective, mine is to clarify the "logic" of anarchy. Third, I reintroduce first- and second-image determinants to assess their effects on identity-formation in different kinds of anarchies.

Anarchy, Self-Help, and Intersubjective Knowledge

Waltz defines political structure on three dimensions: ordering principles (in this case, anarchy), principles of differentiation (which here drop out), and the distribution of capabilities.[7] By itself, this definition predicts little about state behavior. It does not predict whether two states will be friends or foes, will recognize each other's sovereignty, will have dynastic ties, will be revisionist or status quo powers, and so on. These factors, which are fundamentally intersubjective, affect states' security interests and thus the character of their interaction under anarchy. In an important revision of Waltz's theory, Stephen Walt implies as much when he argues that the "balance of threats," rather than the balance of power, determines state action, threats being socially constructed.[8] Put more generally, without assumptions about the structure of identities and interests in the system, Waltz's definition of structure cannot predict the content or dynamics of anarchy. Self-help is one such intersubjective structure and, as such, does the decisive explanatory work in the theory. The question is whether self-help is a logical or contingent feature of anarchy. In this section, I develop the concept of a "structure of identity and interest" and show that no particular one follows logically from anarchy.

A fundamental principle of constructivist social theory is that people act toward objects, including other actors, on the basis of the meanings that the objects have for them.[9] States act differently toward enemies than they do toward friends because enemies are threatening and friends are not. Anarchy and the distribution of power are insufficient to tell us which is which. U.S. military power has a different significance for Canada than for Cuba, despite their similar "structural" positions, just as British missiles have a different significance for the United States than do Soviet missiles. The distribution of power may always affect states' calculations, but how it does so depends on the intersubjective understandings and expectations, on the "distribution of knowledge," that constitute their conceptions of self and other.[10] If society "forgets" what a university is, the powers and practices of professor and student cease to exist; if the United States and Soviet Union decide that they are no longer enemies, "the cold war is over." It is collective meanings that constitute the structures which organize our actions.

Actors acquire identities—relatively stable, role-specific understandings and expectations about self—by participating in such collective meanings.[11] Identities are inherently relational: "Identity, with its appropriate attachments of psychological reality, is always identity within a specific, socially constructed world," Peter Berger argues.[12] Each person has many identities linked to institutional roles, such as brother, son, teacher,

and citizen. Similarly, a state may have multiple identities as "sovereign," "leader of the free world," "imperial power," and so on.[13] The commitment to and the salience of particular identities vary, but each identity is an inherently social definition of the actor grounded in the theories which actors collectively hold about themselves and one another and which constitute the structure of the social world.

Identities are the basis of interests. Actors do not have a "portfolio" of interests that they carry around independent of social context; instead, they define their interests in the process of defining situations.[14] As Nelson Foote puts it: "Motivation . . . refer[s] to the degree to which a human being, as a participant in the ongoing social process in which he necessarily finds himself, defines a problematic situation as calling for the performance of a particular act, with more or less anticipated consummations and consequences, and thereby his organism releases the energy appropriate to performing it."[15] Sometimes situations are unprecedented in our experience, and in these cases we have to construct their meaning, and thus our interests, by analogy or invent them de novo. More often they have routine qualities in which we assign meanings on the basis of institutionally defined roles. When we say that professors have an "interest" in teaching, research, or going on leave, we are saying that to function in the role identity of "professor," they have to define certain situations as calling for certain actions. This does not mean that they will necessarily do so (expectations and competence do not equal performance), but if they do not, they will not get tenure. The absence or failure of roles makes defining situations and interests more difficult, and identity confusion may result. This seems to be happening today in the United States and the former Soviet Union: without the cold war's mutual attributions of threat and hostility to define their identities, these states seem unsure of what their "interests" should be.

An institution is a relatively stable set or "structure" of identities and interests. Such structures are often codified in formal rules and norms, but these have motivational force only in virtue of actors' socialization to and participation in collective knowledge. Institutions are fundamentally cognitive entities that do not exist apart from actors' ideas about how the world works.[16] This does not mean that institutions are not real or objective, that they are "nothing but" beliefs. As collective knowledge, they are experienced as having an existence "over and above the individuals who happen to embody them at the moment."[17] In this way, institutions come to confront individuals as more or less coercive social facts, but they are still a function of what actors collectively "know." Identities and such collective cognitions do not exist apart from each other; they are "mutually constitutive."[18] On this view, institutionalization is a process of internalizing new identities and interests, not something occurring outside them and affecting only behavior; socialization is a cognitive process, not just a behavioral one. Conceived in this way, institutions may be cooperative or conflictual, a point sometimes lost in scholarship on international regimes, which tends to equate institutions with cooperation. There are important differences between conflictual and cooperative institutions to be sure, but all relatively stable self-other relations—even those of "enemies"—are defined intersubjectively.

Self-help is an institution, one of various structures of identity and interest that may exist under anarchy. Processes of identity-formation under anarchy are concerned first and foremost with preservation or "security" of the self. Concepts of security therefore differ in the extent to which and the manner in which the self is identified cognitively with the other,[19] and, I want to suggest, it is upon this cognitive variation that the meaning of anarchy and the distribution of power depends. Let me illustrate with a standard continuum of security systems.[20]

At one end is the "competitive" security system, in which states identify negatively with each other's security so that ego's gain is seen as alter's loss. Negative identification under anarchy constitutes system of "realist" power politics: risk-averse actors that infer intentions from capabilities and worry about relative gains and losses. At the limit—in the Hobbesian war of all against all—collective action is nearly impossible in such a system because each actor must constantly fear being stabbed in the back.

In the middle is the "individualistic" security system, in which states are indifferent to the relationship between their own and others' security. This constitutes "neoliberal" systems: states are still self-regarding about their security but are concerned primarily with absolute gains rather than relative gains. One's position in the distribution of power is less important, and collective action is more possible (though still subject to free riding because states continue to be "egoists").

Competitive and individualistic systems are both "self-help" forms of anarchy in the sense that states do not positively identify the security of self with that of others but instead treat security as the individual responsibility of each. Given the lack of a positive cognitive identification on the basis of which to build security regimes, power politics within such systems will necessarily consist of efforts to manipulate others to satisfy self-regarding interests.

This contrasts with the "cooperative" security system, in which states identify positively with one another so that the security of each is perceived as the responsibility of all. This is not self-help in any interesting sense, since the "self" in terms of which interests are defined is the community; national interests are international interests.[21] In practice, of course, the extent to which states' identification with the community varies, from the limited form found in "concerts" to the full-blown form seen in "collective security" arrangements.[22] Depending on how well developed the collective self is, it will produce security practices that are in varying degrees altruistic or prosocial. This makes collective action less dependent on the presence of active threats and less prone to free riding.[23] Moreover, it restructures efforts to advance one's objectives, or "power politics," in terms of shared norms rather than relative power.[24]

On this view, the tendency in international relations scholarship to view power and institutions as two opposing explanations of foreign policy is therefore misleading, since anarchy and the distribution of power only have meaning for state action in virtue of the understandings and expectations that constitute institutional identities and interests. Self-help is one such institution, constituting one kind of anarchy but not the only kind. Waltz's three-part definition of structure therefore seems underspecified. In order to go from structure to action, we need to add a fourth: the intersubjectively constituted structure of identities and interests in the system.

This has an important implication for the way in which we conceive of states in the state of nature before their first encounter with each other. Because states do not have conceptions of self and other, and thus security interests, apart from or prior to interaction, we assume too much about the state of nature if we concur with Waltz that, in virtue of anarchy, "international political systems, like economic markets, are formed by the coaction of self-regarding units."[25] We also assume too much if we argue that, in virtue of anarchy, states in the state of nature necessarily face a "stag hunt" or "security dilemma."[26] These claims presuppose a history of interaction in which actors have acquired "selfish" identities and interests; before interaction (and still in abstraction from first- and second-image factors) they would have no experience upon which to base such definitions of self and other. To assume otherwise is to attribute to states in the state of nature qualities that they can only possess in society.[27] Self-help is an institution, not a constitutive feature of anarchy.

What, then, *is* a constitutive feature of the state of nature before interaction? Two things are left if we strip away those properties of the self which presuppose interaction with others. The first is the material substrate of agency, including its intrinsic capabilities. For human beings, this is the body; for states, it is an organizational apparatus of governance. In effect, I am suggesting for rhetorical purposes that the raw material out of which members of the state system are constituted is created by domestic society before states enter the constitutive process of international society,[28] although this process implies neither stable territoriality nor sovereignty, which are internationally negotiated terms of individuality (as discussed further below). The second is a desire to preserve this material substrate, to survive. This does not entail "self-regardingness," however, since actors do not have a self prior to interaction with an other; how they view the meaning and requirements of this survival therefore depends on the processes by which conceptions of self evolve.

This may all seem very arcane, but there is an important issue at stake: are the foreign policy identities and interests of states exogenous or endogenous to the state system? The former is the answer of an individualistic or undersocialized systemic theory for which rationalism is appropriate; the latter is the answer of a fully socialized systemic theory. Waltz seems to offer the latter and proposes two mechanisms, competition and socialization, by which structure conditions state action.[29] The content of his argument about this conditioning, however, presupposes a self-help system that is not itself a constitutive feature of anarchy. As James Morrow points out, Waltz's two mechanisms condition behavior, not identity and interest.[30] This explains how Waltz can be accused of both "individualism" and "structuralism."[31] He is the former with respect to systemic constitutions of identity and interest, the latter with respect to systemic determinations of behavior.

Anarchy and the Social Construction of Power Politics

If self-help is not a constitutive feature of anarchy, it must emerge causally from processes in which anarchy plays only a permissive role.[32] This reflects a second principle of constructivism: that the meanings in terms of which action is organized arise out of interaction.[33] This being said, however, the situation facing states as they encounter one another for the first time may be such that only self-regarding conceptions of identity can survive; if so, even if these conceptions are socially constructed, neorealists may be right in holding identities and interests constant and thus in privileging one particular meaning of anarchic structure over process. In this case, rationalists would be right to argue for a weak, behavioral conception of the difference that institutions make, and realists would be right to argue that any international institutions which are created will be inherently unstable, since without the power to transform identities and interests they will be "continuing objects of choice" by exogenously constituted actors constrained only by the transaction costs of behavioral change.[34] Even in a permissive causal role, in other words, anarchy may decisively restrict interaction and therefore restrict viable forms of systemic theory. I address these causal issues first by showing how self-regarding ideas about security might develop and then by examining the conditions under which a key efficient cause—predation—may dispose states in this direction rather than others.

Conceptions of self and interest tend to "mirror" the practices of significant others over time. This principle of identity-formation is captured by the symbolic interactionist notion of the "looking-glass self," which asserts that the self is a reflection of an actor's socialization.

Consider two actors—ego and alter—encountering each other for the first time.[35] Each wants to survive and has certain material capabilities, but neither actor has biological or domestic imperatives for power, glory, or conquest (still bracketed), and there is no history of security or insecurity between the two. What should they do? Realists would probably argue that each should act on the basis of worst-case assumptions about the other's intentions, justifying such an attitude as prudent in view of the possibility of death from making a mistake. Such a possibility always exists, even in civil society; however, society would be impossible if people made decisions purely on the basis of worst-case possibilities. Instead, most decisions are and should be made on the basis of probabilities, and these are produced by interaction, by what actors *do*.

In the beginning is ego's gesture, which may consist, for example, of an advance, a retreat, a brandishing of arms, a laying down of arms, or an attack.[36] For ego, this gesture represents the basis on which it is prepared to respond to alter. This basis is unknown to alter, however, and so it must make an inference or "attribution" about ego's intentions and, in particular, given that this is anarchy, about whether ego is a threat.[37] The content of this inference will largely depend on two considerations. The first is the gesture's and ego's physical qualities, which are in part contrived by ego and which include the direction of movement, noise, numbers, and immediate consequences of the gesture.[38] The second consideration concerns what alter would intend by such qualities were it to make such a gesture itself. Alter may make an attributional "error" in its inference about ego's intent, but there is also no reason for it to assume a priori—before the gesture—that ego is threatening, since it is only through a process of signaling and interpreting that the costs and probabilities of being wrong can be determined.[39] Social threats are constructed, not natural.

Consider an example. Would we assume, a priori, that we were about to be attacked if we are ever contacted by members of an alien civilization? I think not. We would be highly alert, of course, but whether we placed our military forces on alert or launched an attack would depend on how we interpreted the import of their first gesture for our security—if only to avoid making an immediate enemy out of what may be a dangerous adversary. The possibility of error, in other words, does not force us to act on the assumption that the aliens are threatening: action depends on the probabilities we assign, and these are in key part a function of what the aliens do; prior to their gesture, we have no systemic basis for assigning probabilities. If their first gesture is to appear with a thousand spaceships and destroy New York, we will define the situation as threatening and respond accordingly. But if they appear with one spaceship, saying what seems to be "we come in peace," we will feel "reassured" and will probably respond with a gesture intended to reassure them, even if this gesture is not necessarily interpreted by them as such.[40]

INSTITUTIONS   **PROCESS**

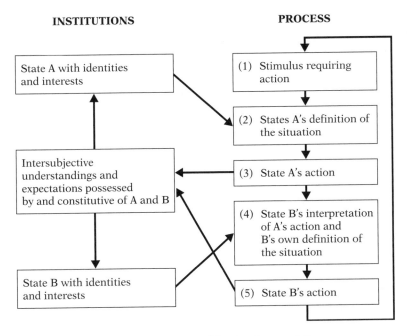

Figure 3.1. The Codetermination of Institutions and Process

This process of signaling, interpreting, and responding completes a "social act" and begins the process of creating intersubjective meanings. It advances the same way. The first social act creates expectations on both sides about each other's future behavior: potentially mistaken and certainly tentative, but expectations nonetheless. Based on this tentative knowledge, ego makes a new gesture, again signifying the basis on which it will respond to alter, and again alter responds, adding to the pool of knowledge each has about the other, and so on over time. The mechanism here is reinforcement; interaction rewards actors for holding certain ideas about each other and discourages them from holding others. If repeated long enough, these "reciprocal typifications" will create relatively stable concepts of self and other regarding the issue at stake in the interaction.[41]

It is through reciprocal interaction, in other words, that we create and instantiate the relatively enduring social structures in terms of which we define our identities and interests. Jeff Coulter

sums up the ontological dependence of structure on process this way: "The parameters of social organization themselves are reproduced only in and through the orientations and practices of members engaged in social interactions over time. . . . Social configurations are not 'objective' like mountains or forests, but neither are they 'subjective' like dreams or flights of speculative fancy. They are, as most social scientists concede at the theoretical level, intersubjective constructions."[42]

The simple overall model of identity- and interest-formation proposed in Figure 1 applies to competitive institutions no less than to cooperative ones. Self-help security systems evolve from cycles of interaction in which each party acts in ways that the other feels are threatening to the self, creating expectations that the other is not to be trusted. Competitive or egoistic identities are caused by such insecurity; if the other is threatening, the self is forced to "mirror" such behavior in its conception of the self's relationship to that other.[43] Being treated as an object for the gratification of others precludes the positive identification with others necessary for collective security; conversely, being treated by others in ways that are empathic with respect to the security of the self permits such identification.[44]

Competitive systems of interaction are prone to security "dilemmas," in which the efforts of actors to enhance their security unilaterally threatens the security of the others, perpetuating distrust and alienation. The forms of identity and interest that constitute such dilemmas, however, are themselves ongoing effects of, not exogenous to, the interaction; identities are produced in and through "situated activity."[45] We do not *begin* our relationship with the aliens in a security dilemma; security dilemmas are not given by anarchy or nature. Of course, once institutionalized such a dilemma may be hard to change (I return to this below), but the point remains: identities and interests are constituted by collective meanings that are always in process. As Sheldon Stryker emphasizes, "The social process is one of constructing and reconstructing self and social relationships."[46] If states find themselves in a self-help system, this is because their practices made it that way. Changing the practices will change the intersubjective knowledge that constitutes the system.

Predator States and Anarchy as Permissive Cause

The mirror theory of identity-formation is a crude account of how the process of creating identities and interests might work, but it does not tell us why a system of states—such as, arguably, our own—would have ended up with self-regarding and not collective identities. In this section, I examine an efficient cause, predation, which, in conjunction with anarchy as a permissive cause, may generate a self-help system. In so doing, however, I show the key role that the structure of identities and interests plays in mediating anarchy's explanatory role.

The predator argument is straightforward and compelling. For whatever reasons—biology, domestic politics, or systemic victimization—some states may become predisposed toward aggression. The aggressive behavior of these predators or "bad apples" forces other states to engage in competitive power politics, to meet fire with fire, since failure to do so may degrade or destroy them. One predator will best a hundred pacifists because anarchy provides no guarantees. This argument is powerful in part because it is so weak: rather than making the strong assumption that all states are inherently power-seeking (a purely reductionist theory of power politics), it assumes that just one is power-seeking and that the others have to follow suit because anarchy permits the one to exploit them.

In making this argument, it is important to reiterate that the possibility of predation does not in itself force states to anticipate it a priori with competitive power politics of their own. The possibility of predation does not mean that "war may at any moment occur"; it may in fact be extremely unlikely. Once a predator emerges, however, it may condition identity- and interest-formation in the following manner.

In an anarchy of two, if ego is predatory, alter must either define its security in self-help terms or pay the price. This follows directly from the above argument, in which conceptions of self mirror treatment by the other. In an anarchy of many, however, the effect of predation also depends on the level of collective identity already attained in the system. If predation occurs right after the first encounter in the state of nature, it will force others with whom it comes in contact to defend themselves, first individually and then collectively *if* they come to perceive a common threat. The emergence of such a defensive alliance will be seriously inhibited if the structure of identities and interests has already evolved into a Hobbesian world of maximum insecurity, since potential allies will strongly distrust each other and face intense collective action problems; such insecure allies are also more likely to fall out amongst themselves once the predator is removed. If collective security identity is high, however, the emergence of a predator may do much less damage. If the predator attacks any member of the collective, the latter will come to the victim's defense on the principle of "all for one, one for all," even if the predator is not presently a threat to other members of the collective. If the predator is not strong enough to withstand the collective, it will be defeated and collective security will obtain. But if it is strong enough, the logic of the two-actor case (now predator and collective) will activate, and balance-of-power politics will reestablish itself.

The timing of the emergence of predation relative to the history of identity-formation in the community is therefore crucial to anarchy's explanatory role as a permissive cause. Predation will always lead victims to defend themselves, but whether defense will be collective or not depends on the history of interaction within the potential collective as much as on the ambitions of the predator. Will the disappearance of the Soviet threat renew old insecurities among the members of the North Atlantic Treaty Organization? Perhaps, but not if they have reasons independent of that threat for identifying their security with one another. Identities and interests are relationship-specific, not intrinsic attributes of a "portfolio"; states may be competitive in some relationships and solidary in others. "Mature" anarchies are less likely than "immature" ones to be reduced by predation to a Hobbesian condition, and maturity, which is a proxy for structures of identity and interest, is a function of process.[47]

The source of predation also matters. If it stems from unit-level causes that are immune to systemic impacts (causes such as human nature or domestic politics taken in isolation), then it functions in a manner analogous to a "genetic trait" in the constructed world of the state system. Even if successful, this trait does not select for other predators in an evolutionary sense so much as it teaches other states to respond in kind, but since traits cannot be unlearned, the other states will continue competitive behavior until the predator is either destroyed or transformed from within. However, in the more likely event that predation stems at least in part from prior systemic interaction—perhaps as a result of

being victimized in the past (one thinks here of Nazi Germany or the Soviet Union)—then it is more a response to a learned identity and, as such, might be transformed by future social interaction in the form of appeasement, reassurances that security needs will be met, systemic effects on domestic politics, and so on. In this case, in other words, there is more hope that process can transform a bad apple into a good one.

The role of predation in generating a self-help system, then, is consistent with a systematic focus on process. Even if the source of predation is entirely exogenous to the system, it is what states *do* that determines the quality of their interactions under anarchy. In this respect, it is not surprising that it is classical realists rather than structural realists who emphasize this sort of argument. The former's emphasis on unit-level causes of power politics leads more easily to a permissive view of anarchy's explanatory role (and therefore to a processual view of international relations) than does the latter's emphasis on anarchy as a "structural cause";[48] neorealists do not need predation because the system is given as self-help.

This raises anew the question of exactly how much and what kind of role human nature and domestic politics play in world politics. The greater and more destructive this role, the more significant predation will be, and the less amenable anarchy will be to formation of collective identities. Classical realists, of course, assumed that human nature was possessed by an inherent lust for power or glory. My argument suggests that assumptions such as this were made for a reason: an unchanging Hobbesian man provides the powerful efficient cause necessary for a relentless pessimism about world politics that anarchic structure alone, or even structure plus intermittent predation, cannot supply. One can be skeptical of such an essentialist assumption, as I am, but it does produce determinate results at the expense of systemic theory. A concern with systemic process over structure suggests that perhaps it is time to revisit the debate over the relative importance of first-, second-, and third-image theories of state identity-formation.[49]

Assuming for now that systemic theories of identity-formation in world politics are worth pursuing, let me conclude by suggesting that the realist-rationalist alliance "reifies" self-help in the sense of treating it as something separate from the practices by which it is produced and sustained. Peter Berger and Thomas Luckmann define reification as follows: "[It] is the apprehension of the products of human activity *as if* they were something else than human products—such as facts of nature, results of cosmic laws, or manifestations of divine will. Reification implies that man is capable of forgetting his own authorship of the human world, and further, that the dialectic between man, the producer, and his products is lost to consciousness. The reified world is . . . experienced by man as a strange facticity, an *opus alienum* over which he has no control rather than as the *opus proprium* of his own productive activity."[50] By denying or bracketing states' collective authorship of their identities and interests, in other words, the realist-rationalist alliance denies or brackets the fact that competitive power politics help create the very "problem of order" they are supposed to solve—that realism is a self-fulfilling prophecy. Far from being exogenously given, the intersubjective knowledge that constitutes competitive identities and interests is constructed every day by processes of "social will formation."[51] It is what states have made of themselves.

Institutional Transformations of Power Politics

Let us assume that processes of identity- and interest-formation have created a world in which states do not recognize rights to territory or existence—a war of all against all. In this world, anarchy has a "realist" meaning for state action: be insecure and concerned with relative power. Anarchy has this meaning only in virtue of collective, insecurity-producing practices, but if those practices are relatively stable, they do constitute a system that may resist change. The fact that

worlds of power politics are socially constructed, in other words, does not guarantee they are malleable, for at least two reasons.

The first reason is that once constituted, any social system confronts each of its members as an objective social fact that reinforces certain behaviors and discourages others. Self-help systems, for example, tend to reward competition and punish altruism. The possibility of change depends on whether the exigencies of such competition leave room for actions that deviate from the prescribed script. If they do not, the system will be reproduced and deviant actors will not.[52]

The second reason is that systemic change may also be inhibited by actors' interests in maintaining relatively stable role identities. Such interests are rooted not only in the desire to minimize uncertainty and anxiety, manifested in efforts to confirm existing beliefs about the social world, but also in the desire to avoid the expected costs of breaking commitments made to others—notably domestic constituencies and foreign allies in the case of states—as part of past practices. The level of resistance that these commitments induce will depend on the "salience" of particular role identities to the actor.[53] The United States, for example, is more likely to resist threats to its identity as "leader of anticommunist crusades" than to its identity as "promoter of human rights." But for almost any role identity, practices and information that challenge it are likely to create cognitive dissonance and even perceptions of threat, and these may cause resistance to transformations of the self and thus to social change.[54]

For both systemic and "psychological" reasons, then, intersubjective understandings and expectations may have a self-perpetuating quality, constituting path-dependencies that new ideas about self and other must transcend. This does not change the fact that through practice agents are continuously producing and reproducing identities and interests, continuously "choosing now the preferences [they] will have later."[55] But it does mean that choices may not be experienced with meaningful degrees of freedom. This could be a constructivist justification for the realist position that only simple learning is possible in self-help systems. The realist might concede that such systems are socially constructed and still argue that after the corresponding identities and interests have become institutionalized, they are almost impossible to transform.

In the remainder of this article, I examine three institutional transformations of identity and security interest through which states might escape a Hobbesian world of their own making. In so doing, I seek to clarify what it means to say that "institutions transform identities and interests," emphasizing that the key to such transformations is relatively stable practice.

Sovereignty, Recognition, and Security

In a Hobbesian state of nature, states are individuated by the domestic processes that constitute them as states and by their material capacity to deter threats from other states. In this world, even if free momentarily from the predations of others, state security does not have any basis in social recognition—in intersubjective understandings or norms that a state has a right to its existence, territory, and subjects. Security is a matter of national power, nothing more.

The principle of sovereignty transforms this situation by providing a social basis for the individuality and security of states. Sovereignty is an institution, and so it exists only in virtue of certain intersubjective understandings and expectations; there is no sovereignty without an other. These understandings and expectations not only constitute a particular kind of state—the "sovereign" state—but also constitute a particular form of community, since identities are relational. The essence of this community is a mutual recognition of one another's right to exercise exclusive political authority within territorial limits. These reciprocal "permissions"[56] constitute a spatially rather than functionally differentiated world—a world in which fields of practice constitute and are organized around "domestic" and "international" spaces rather than around the performance of particular activities.[57] The location of

the boundaries between these spaces is of course sometimes contested, war being one practice through which states negotiate the terms of their individuality. But this does not change the fact that it is only in virtue of mutual recognition that states have "territorial property rights."[58] This recognition functions as a form of "social closure" that disempowers nonstate actors and empowers and helps stabilize interaction among states.[59]

Sovereignty norms are now so taken for granted, so natural, that it is easy to overlook the extent to which they are both presupposed by and an ongoing artifact of practice. When states tax "their" "citizens" and not others, when they "protect" their markets against foreign "imports," when they kill thousands of Iraqis in one kind of war and then refuse to "intervene" to kill even one person in another kind, a "civil" war, and when they fight a global war against a regime that sought to destroy the institution of sovereignty and then give Germany back to the Germans, they are acting against the background of, and thereby reproducing, shared norms about what it means to be a sovereign state.

If states stopped acting on those norms, their identity as "sovereigns" (if not necessarily as "states") would disappear. The sovereign state is an ongoing accomplishment of practice, not a once-and-for-all creation of norms that somehow exist apart from practice.[60] Thus, saying that "the institution of sovereignty transforms identities" is shorthand for saying that "regular practices produce mutually constituting sovereign identities (agents) and their associated institutional norms (structures)." Practice is the core of constructivist resolutions of the agent-structure problem. This ongoing process may not be politically problematic in particular historical contexts and, indeed, once a community of mutual recognition is constituted, its members—even the disadvantaged ones[61]—may have a vested interest in reproducing it. In fact, this is part of what having an identity means. But this identity and institution remain dependent on what actors do: removing those practices will remove their intersubjective conditions of existence.

This may tell us something about how institutions of sovereign states are reproduced through social interaction, but it does not tell us why such a structure of identity and interest would arise in the first place. Two conditions would seem necessary for this to happen: (1) the density and regularity of interactions must be sufficiently high and (2) actors must be dissatisfied with preexisting forms of identity and interaction. Given these conditions, a norm of mutual recognition is relatively undemanding in terms of social trust, having the form of an assurance game in which a player will acknowledge the sovereignty of the others as long as they will in turn acknowledge that player's own sovereignty. Articulating international legal principles such as those embodied in the Peace of Augsburg (1555) and the Peace of Westphalia (1648) may also help by establishing explicit criteria for determining violations of the nascent social consensus.[62] But whether such a consensus holds depends on what states do. If they treat each other as if they were sovereign, then over time they will institutionalize that mode of subjectivity; if they do not, then that mode will not become the norm.

Practices of sovereignty will transform understandings of security and power politics in at least three ways. First, states will come to define their (and our) security in terms of preserving their "property rights" over particular territories. We now see this as natural, but the preservation of territorial frontiers is not, in fact, equivalent to the survival of the state or its people. Indeed, some states would probably be more secure if they would relinquish certain territories—the "Soviet Union" of some minority republics, "Yugoslavia" of Croatia and Slovenia, Israel of the West Bank, and so on. The fact that sovereignty practices have historically been oriented toward producing distinct territorial spaces, in other words, affects states' conceptualization of what they must "secure" to function in that identity, a process that may help account for the "hardening" of territorial boundaries over the centuries.[63]

Second, to the extent that states successfully internalize sovereignty norms, they will be more respectful toward the territorial rights of others.[64] This restraint is *not* primarily because of the costs of violating sovereignty norms, although when violators do get punished (as in the Gulf War) it reminds everyone of what these costs can be, but because part of what it means to be a "sovereign" state is that one does not violate the territorial rights of others without "just cause." A clear example of such an institutional effect, convincingly argued by David Strang, is the markedly different treatment that weak states receive within and outside communities of mutual recognition.[65] What keeps the United States from conquering the Bahamas, or Nigeria from seizing Togo, or Australia from occupying Vanuatu? Clearly, power is not the issue, and in these cases even the cost of sanctions would probably be negligible. One might argue that great powers simply have no "interest" in these conquests, and this might be so, but this lack of interest can only be understood in terms of their recognition of weak states' sovereignty. I have no interest in exploiting my friends, not because of the relative costs and benefits of such action but because they are my friends. The absence of recognition, in turn, helps explain the Western states' practices of territorial conquest, enslavement, and genocide against Native American and African peoples. It is in *that* world that only power matters, not the world of today.

Finally, to the extent that their ongoing socialization teaches states that their sovereignty depends on recognition by other states, they can afford to rely more on the institutional fabric of international society and less on individual national means—especially military power—to protect their security. The intersubjective understandings embodied in the institution of sovereignty, in other words, may redefine the meaning of others' power for the security of the self. In policy terms, this means that states can be less worried about short-term survival and relative power and can thus shift their resources accordingly. Ironically, it is the great powers, the states with the greatest national means, that may have the hardest time learning this lesson; small powers do not have the luxury of relying on national means and may therefore learn faster that collective recognition is a cornerstone of security.

None of this is to say that power becomes irrelevant in a community of sovereign states. Sometimes states *are* threatened by others that do not recognize their existence or particular territorial claims, that resent the externalities from their economic policies, and so on. But most of the time, these threats are played out within the terms of the sovereignty game. The fates of Napoleon and Hitler show what happens when they are not.

Cooperation among Egoists and Transformations of Identity

We began this section with a Hobbesian state of nature. Cooperation for joint gain is extremely difficult in this context, since trust is lacking, time horizons are short, and relative power concerns are high. Life is "nasty, brutish, and short." Sovereignty transforms this system into a Lockean world of (mostly) mutually recognized property rights and (mostly) egoistic rather than competitive conceptions of security, reducing the fear that what states already have will be seized at any moment by potential collaborators, thereby enabling them to contemplate more direct forms of cooperation. A necessary condition for such cooperation is that outcomes be positively interdependent in the sense that potential gains exist which cannot be realized by unilateral action. States such as Brazil and Botswana may recognize each other's sovereignty, but they need further incentives to engage in joint action. One important source of incentives is the growing "dynamic density" of interaction among states in a world with new communications technology, nuclear weapons, externalities from industrial development, and so on.[66] Unfortunately, growing dynamic density does not ensure that states will in fact realize joint gains; interdependence also entails vulnerability and the risk of being "the sucker," which if exploited will become a source of conflict rather than cooperation.

This is the rationale for the familiar assumption that egoistic states will often find themselves facing prisoners' dilemma, a game in which the dominant strategy, if played only once, is to defect. As Michael Taylor and Robert Axelrod have shown, however, given iteration and a sufficient shadow of the future, egoists using a tit-for-tat strategy can escape this result and build cooperative institutions.[67] The story they tell about this process on the surface seems quite similar to George Herbert Mead's constructivist analysis of interaction, part of which is also told in terms of "games."[68] Cooperation is a gesture indicating ego's willingness to cooperate; if alter defects, ego does likewise, signaling its unwillingness to be exploited; over time and through reciprocal play, each learns to form relatively stable expectations about the other's behavior, and through these, habits of cooperation (or defection) form. Despite similar concerns with communication, learning, and habit-formation, however, there is an important difference between the game-theoretic and constructivist analysis of interaction that bears on how we conceptualize the causal powers of institutions.

In the traditional game-theoretic analysis of cooperation, even an iterated one, the structure of the game—of identities and interests—is exogenous to interaction and, as such, does not change.[69] A "black box" is put around identity- and interest-formation, and analysis focuses instead on the relationship between expectations and behavior. The norms that evolve from interaction are treated as rules and behavioral regularities which are external to the actors and which resist change because of the transaction costs of creating new ones. The game-theoretic analysis of cooperation among egoists is at base behavioral.

A constructivist analysis of cooperation, in contrast, would concentrate on how the expectations produced by behavior affect identities and interests. The process of creating institutions is one of internalizing new understandings of self and other, of acquiring new role identities, not just of creating external constraints on the behavior of exogenously constituted actors.[70] Even if not intended as such, in other words, the process by which egoists learn to cooperate is at the same time a process of reconstructing their interests in terms of shared commitments to social norms. Over time, this will tend to transform a positive interdependence of *outcomes* into a positive interdependence of *utilities* or collective interest organized around the norms in question. These norms will resist change because they are tied to actors' commitments to their identities and interests, not merely because of transaction costs. A constructivist analysis of "the cooperation problem," in other words, is at base cognitive rather than behavioral, since it treats the intersubjective knowledge that defines the structure of identities and interests, of the "game," as endogenous to and instantiated by interaction itself.

The debate over the future of collective security in Western Europe may illustrate the significance of this difference. A weak liberal or rationalist analysis would assume that the European states' "portfolio" of interests has not fundamentally changed and that the emergence of new factors, such as the collapse of the Soviet threat and the rise of Germany, would alter their cost-benefit ratios for pursuing current arrangements, thereby causing existing institutions to break down. The European states formed collaborative institutions for good, exogenously constituted egoistic reasons, and the same reasons may lead them to reject those institutions; the game of European power politics has not changed. A strong liberal or constructivist analysis of this problem would suggest that four decades of cooperation may have transformed a positive interdependence of outcomes into a collective "European identity" in terms of which states increasingly define their "self"-interests.[71] Even if egoistic reasons were its starting point, the process of cooperating tends to redefine those reasons by reconstituting identities and interests in terms of new intersubjective understandings and commitments. Changes in the distribution of power during the late twentieth century are undoubtedly a challenge to these new understandings, but it is not as if West European states have some inherent, exogenously given in-

terest in abandoning collective security if the price is right. Their identities and security interests are continuously in process, and if collective identities become "embedded," they will be as resistant to change as egoistic ones.[72] Through participation in new forms of social knowledge, in other words, the European states of 1990 might no longer be the states of 1950.

Critical Strategic Theory and Collective Security

The transformation of identity and interest through an "evolution of cooperation" faces two important constraints. The first is that the process is incremental and slow. Actors' objectives in such a process are typically to realize joint gains within what they take to be a relatively stable context, and they are therefore unlikely to engage in substantial reflection about how to change the parameters of that context (including the structure of identities and interests) and unlikely to pursue policies specifically designed to bring about such changes. Learning to cooperate may change those parameters, but this occurs as an unintended consequence of policies pursued for other reasons rather than as a result of intentional efforts to transcend existing institutions.

A second, more fundamental, constraint is that the evolution of cooperation story presupposes that actors do not identify negatively with one another. Actors must be concerned primarily with absolute gains; to the extent that antipathy and distrust lead them to define their security in relativistic terms, it will be hard to accept the vulnerabilities that attend cooperation.[73] This is important because it is precisely the "central balance" in the state system that seems to be so often afflicted with such competitive thinking, and realists can therefore argue that the possibility of cooperation within one "pole" (for example, the West) is parasitic on the dominance of competition between poles (the East–West conflict). Relations between the poles may be amenable to some positive reciprocity in areas such as arms control, but the atmosphere of distrust leaves little room for such cooperation and its transformative consequences.[74] The conditions of negative identification that make an "evolution of cooperation" most needed work precisely against such a logic.

This seemingly intractable situation may nevertheless be amenable to quite a different logic of transformation, one driven more by self-conscious efforts to change structures of identity and interest than by unintended consequences. Such voluntarism may seem to contradict the spirit of constructivism, since would-be revolutionaries are presumably themselves effects of socialization to structures of identity and interest. How can they think about changing that to which they owe their identity? The possibility lies in the distinction between the social determination of the self and the personal determination of choice, between what Mead called the "me" and the "I."[75] The "me" is that part of subjectivity which is defined in terms of others; the character and behavioral expectations of a person's role identity as "professor," or of the United States as "leader of the alliance," for example, are socially constituted. Roles are not played in mechanical fashion according to precise scripts, however, but are "taken" and adapted in idiosyncratic ways by each actor.[76] Even in the most constrained situations, role performance involves a choice by the actor. The "I" is the part of subjectivity in which this appropriation and reaction to roles and its corresponding existential freedom lie.

The fact that roles are "taken" means that, in principle, actors always have a capacity for "character planning"—for engaging in critical self-reflection and choices designed to bring about changes in their lives.[77] But when or under what conditions can this creative capacity be exercised? Clearly, much of the time it cannot: if actors were constantly reinventing their identities, social order would be impossible, and the relative stability of identities and interests in the real world is indicative of our propensity for habitual rather than creative action. The exceptional, conscious choosing to transform or transcend roles has at least two preconditions. First, there must

be a reason to think of oneself in novel terms. This would most likely stem from the presence of new social situations that cannot be managed in terms of preexisting self-conceptions. Second, the expected costs of intentional role change—the sanctions imposed by others with whom one interacted in previous roles—cannot be greater than its rewards.

When these conditions are present, actors can engage in self-reflection and practice specifically designed to transform their identities and interests and thus to "change the games" in which they are embedded. Such "critical" strategic theory and practice has not received the attention it merits from students of world politics (another legacy of exogenously given interests perhaps), particularly given that one of the most important phenomena in contemporary world politics, Mikhail Gorbachev's policy of "New Thinking," is arguably precisely that.[78] Let me therefore use this policy as an example of how states might transform a competitive security system into a cooperative one, dividing the transformative process into four stages.

The first stage in intentional transformation is the breakdown of consensus about identity commitments. In the Soviet case, identity commitments centered on the Leninist theory of imperialism, with its belief that relations between capitalist and socialist states are inherently conflictual, and on the alliance patterns that this belief engendered. In the 1980s, the consensus within the Soviet Union over the Leninist theory broke down for a variety of reasons, principal among which seem to have been the state's inability to meet the economic-technological-military challenge from the West, the government's decline of political legitimacy at home, and the reassurance from the West that it did not intend to invade the Soviet Union, a reassurance that reduced the external costs of role change.[79] These factors paved the way for a radical leadership transition and for a subsequent "unfreezing of conflict schemas" concerning relations with the West.[80]

The breakdown of consensus makes possible a second stage of critical examination of old ideas about self and other and, by extension, of the structures of interaction by which the ideas have been sustained. In periods of relatively stable role identities, ideas and structures may become reified and thus treated as things that exist independently of social action. If so, the second stage is one of denaturalization, of identifying the practices that reproduce seemingly inevitable ideas about self and other; to that extent, it is a form of "critical" rather than "problem-solving" theory.[81] The result of such a critique should be an identification of new "possible selves" and aspirations.[82] New Thinking embodies such critical theorizing. Gorbachev wants to free the Soviet Union from the coercive social logic of the cold war and engage the West in far-reaching cooperation. Toward this end, he has rejected the Leninist belief in the inherent conflict of interest between socialist and capitalist states and, perhaps more important, has recognized the crucial role that Soviet aggressive practices played in sustaining that conflict.

Such rethinking paves the way for a third stage of new practice. In most cases, it is not enough to rethink one's own ideas about self and other, since old identities have been sustained by systems of interaction with *other* actors, the practices of which remain a social fact for the transformative agent. In order to change the self, then, it is often necessary to change the identities and interests of the others that help sustain those systems of interaction. The vehicle for inducing such change is one's own practice and, in particular, the practice of "altercasting"—a technique of interactor control in which ego uses tactics of self-presentation and stage management in an attempt to frame alter's definitions of social situations in ways that create the role which ego desires alter to play.[83] In effect, in altercasting ego tries to induce alter to take on a new identity (and thereby enlist alter in ego's effort to change itself) by treating alter *as if* it already had that identity. The logic of this follows directly from the mirror theory of identity-formation, in which alter's identity is a reflection of ego's practices;

change those practices and ego begins to change alter's conception of itself.

What these practices should consist of depends on the logic by which the preexisting identities were sustained. Competitive security systems are sustained by practices that create insecurity and distrust. In this case, transformative practices should attempt to teach other states that one's own state can be trusted and should not be viewed as a threat to their security. The fastest way to do this is to make unilateral initiatives and self-binding commitments of sufficient significance that another state is faced with "an offer it cannot refuse."[84] Gorbachev has tried to do this by withdrawing from Afghanistan and Eastern Europe, implementing asymmetric cuts in nuclear and conventional forces, calling for "defensive defense," and so on. In addition, he has skillfully cast the West in the role of being morally required to give aid and comfort to the Soviet Union, has emphasized the bonds of common fate between the Soviet Union and the West, and has indicated that further progress in East–West relations is contingent upon the West assuming the identity being projected onto it. These actions are all dimensions of altercasting, the intention of which is to take away the Western "excuse" for distrusting the Soviet Union, which, in Gorbachev's view, has helped sustain competitive identities in the past.

Yet by themselves such practices cannot transform a competitive security system, since if they are not reciprocated by alter, they will expose ego to a "sucker" payoff and quickly wither on the vine. In order for critical strategic practice to transform competitive identities, it must be "rewarded" by alter, which will encourage more such practice by ego, and so on.[85] Over time, this will institutionalize a positive rather than a negative identification between the security of self and other and will thereby provide a firm intersubjective basis for what were initially tentative commitments to new identities and interests.[86]

Notwithstanding today's rhetoric about the end of the cold war, skeptics may still doubt whether

Gorbachev (or some future leader) will succeed in building an intersubjective basis for a new Soviet (or Russian) role identity. There are important domestic, bureaucratic, and cognitive-ideological sources of resistance in both East and West to such a change, not the least of which is the shakiness of the democratic forces' domestic position. But if my argument about the role of intersubjective knowledge in creating competitive structures of identity and interest is right, then at least New Thinking shows a greater appreciation—conscious or not—for the deep structure of power politics than we are accustomed to in international relations practice.

Conclusion

All theories of international relations are based on social theories of the relationship between agency, process, and social structure. Social theories do not determine the content of our international theorizing, but they do structure the questions we ask about world politics and our approaches to answering those questions. The substantive issue at stake in debates about social theory is what kind of foundation offers the most fruitful set of questions and research strategies for explaining the revolutionary changes that seem to be occurring in the late twentieth century international system. Put simply, what should systemic theories of international relations look like? How should they conceptualize the relationship between structure and process? Should they be based exclusively on "microeconomic" analogies in which identities and interests are exogenously given by structure and process is reduced to interactions within those parameters? Or should they also be based on "sociological" and "social psychological" analogies in which identities and interests and therefore the meaning of structure are endogenous to process? Should a behavioral-individualism or a cognitive-constructivism be the basis for systemic theories of world politics?

This article notwithstanding, this question is ultimately an empirical one in two respects.

First, its answer depends in part on how important interaction among states is for the constitution of their identities and interests. On the one hand, it may be that domestic or genetic factors, which I have systematically bracketed, are in fact much more important determinants of states' identities and interests than are systemic factors. To the extent that this is true, the individualism of a rationalist approach and the inherent privileging of structure over process in this approach become more substantively appropriate for systemic theory (if not for first- and second-image theory), since identities and interests are *in fact* largely exogenous to interaction among states. On the other hand, if the bracketed factors are relatively unimportant or if the importance of the international system varies historically (perhaps with the level of dynamic density and interdependence in the system), then such a framework would not be appropriate as an exclusive foundation for general systemic theory.

Second, the answer to the question about what systemic theories should look like also depends on how easily state identities and interests can change as a result of systemic interaction. Even if interaction is initially important in constructing identities and interests, once institutionalized its logic may make transformation extremely difficult. If the meaning of structure for state action changes so slowly that it becomes a de facto parameter within which process takes place, then it may again be substantively appropriate to adopt the rationalist assumption that identities and interests are given (although again, this may vary historically).

We cannot address these empirical issues, however, unless we have a framework for doing systemic research that makes state identity and interest an issue for both theoretical and empirical inquiry. Let me emphasize that this is *not* to say we should never treat identities and interests as given. The framing of problems and research strategies should be question-driven rather than method-driven, and if we are not interested in identity- and interest-formation, we may find the assumptions of a rationalist discourse perfectly reasonable. Nothing in this article, in other words, should be taken as an attack on rationalism per se. By the same token, however, we should not let this legitimate analytical stance become a de facto ontological stance with respect to the content of third-image theory, at least not until after we have determined that systemic interaction does not play an important role in processes of state identity- and interest-formation. We should not choose our philosophical anthropologies and social theories prematurely. By arguing that we cannot derive a self-help structure of identity and interest from the principle of anarchy alone—by arguing that anarchy is what states make of it—this article has challenged one important justification for ignoring processes of identity- and interest-formation in world politics. As such, it helps set the stage for inquiry into the empirical issues raised above and thus for a debate about whether communitarian or individualist assumptions are a better foundation for systemic theory.

I have tried to indicate by crude example what such a research agenda might look like. Its objective should be to assess the causal relationship between practice and interaction (as independent variable) and the cognitive structures at the level of individual states and of systems of states which constitute identities and interests (as dependent variable)—that is, the relationship between what actors *do* and what they *are*. We may have some a priori notion that state actors and systemic structures are "mutually constitutive," but this tells us little in the absence of an understanding of how the mechanics of dyadic, triadic, and *n*-actor interaction shape and are in turn shaped by "stocks of knowledge" that collectively constitute identities and interests and, more broadly, constitute the structures of international life. Particularly important in this respect is the role of practice in shaping attitudes toward the "givenness" of these structures. How and why do actors reify social structures, and under what conditions do they denaturalize such reifications?

The state-centrism of this agenda may strike some, particularly postmodernists, as "depress-

ingly familiar."[87] The significance of states relative to multinational corporations, new social movements, transnationals, and intergovernmental organizations is clearly declining, and "postmodern" forms of world politics merit more research attention than they have received. But I also believe, with realists, that in the medium run sovereign states will remain the dominant political actors in the international system. Any transition to new structures of global political authority and identity—to "postinternational" politics—will be mediated by and path-dependent on the particular institutional resolution of the tension between unity and diversity, or particularism and universality, that is the sovereign state.[88] In such a world there should continue to be a place for theories of anarchic interstate politics, alongside other forms of international theory; to that extent, I am a statist and a realist. I have argued in this article, however, that statism need not be bound by realist ideas about what "state" must mean. State identities and interests can be collectively transformed within an anarchic context by many factors—individual, domestic, systemic, or transnational—and as such are an important dependent variable. Such a reconstruction of state-centric international theory is necessary if we are to theorize adequately about the emerging forms of transnational political identity that sovereign states will help bring into being. To that extent, I hope that statism, like the state, can be historically progressive.

*   *   *

NOTES

1. See, for example, Joseph Grieco, "Anarchy and the Limits of Cooperation: A Realist Critique of the Newest Liberal Institutionalism," *International Organization* 42 (Summer 1988), pp. 485–507; Joseph Nye, "Neorealism and Neoliberalism," *World Politics* 40 (January 1988), pp. 235–51; Robert Keohane, "Neoliberal Institutionalism: A Perspective on World Politics," in his collection of essays en-

titled *International Institutions and State Power* (Boulder, Colo.: Westview Press, 1989), pp. 1–20; John Mearsheimer, "Back to the Future: Instability in Europe After the Cold War," *International Security* 13 (Summer 1990), pp. 5–56.

2. Kenneth Waltz, *Man, the State, and War* (New York: Columbia University Press, 1959), p. 232.

3. Ibid., pp. 169–70.

4. Ibid., p. 232. This point is made by Hidemi Suganami in "Bringing Order to the Causes of War Debates," *Millennium* 19 (Spring 1990), p. 34, fn. 11.

5. Kenneth Waltz, *Theory of International Politics* (Boston: Addison-Wesley, 1979).

6. The neorealist description is not unproblematic. For a powerful critique, see David Lumsdaine, [*Moral Vision in International Politics:*] *The Foreign Aid Regime, 1949–1989* (Princeton, N.J.: Princeton University Press, [1993]).

7. Waltz, *Theory of International Politics*, pp. 79–101.

8. Stephen Walt, *The Origins of Alliances* (Ithaca, N.Y.: Cornell University Press, 1987).

9. See, for example, Herbert Blumer, "The Methodological Position of Symbolic Interactionism," in his *Symbolic Interactionism: Perspective and Method* (Englewood Cliffs, N.J.: Prentice-Hall, 1969), p. 2. Throughout this article, I assume that a theoretically productive analogy can be made between individuals and states.

10. The phrase "distribution of knowledge" is Barry Barnes's, as discussed in his work *The Nature of Power* (Cambridge: Polity Press, 1988); see also Peter Berger and Thomas Luckmann, *The Social Construction of Reality* (New York: Anchor Books, 1966).

11. For an excellent short statement of how collective meanings constitute identities, see Peter Berger, "Identity as a Problem in the Sociology of Knowledge," *European Journal of Sociology*, vol. 7, no. 1, 1966, pp. 32–40.

12. Berger, "Identity as a Problem in the Sociology of Knowledge," p. 111.

13. While not normally cast in such terms, foreign policy scholarship on national role conceptions could be adapted to such identity language. See Kal Holsti, "National Role Conceptions in the Study of Foreign Policy," *International Studies Quarterly* 14 (September 1970), pp. 233–309; and Stephen Walker, ed., *Role Theory and Foreign Policy Analysis* (Durham, N.C.: Duke University Press, 1987). For an important effort to do so, see Stephen Walker, "Symbolic Interactionism and International Politics: Role Theory's Contribution to International Organization," in C. Shih and Martha Cottam, eds., *Contending Dramas: A Cognitive Approach to Post-War International Organizational Processes* (New York: Praeger, [1992]).

14. On the "portfolio" conception of interests, see Barry Hindess, *Political Choice and Social Structure* (Aldershot, U.K.: Edward Elgar, 1989), pp. 2–3. The "definition of the situation" is a central concept in interactionist theory.

15. Nelson Foote, "Identification as the Basis for a Theory of Motivation," *American Sociological Review* 16 (February 1951), p. 15. Such strongly sociological conceptions of interest have been criticized, with some justice, for being "oversocialized"; see Dennis Wrong, "The Oversocialized Conception of Man in Modern Sociology," *American Sociological Review* 26 (April 1961), pp. 183–93. For useful correctives, which focus on the activation of presocial but nondetermining human needs within social contexts, see Turner, *A Theory of Social Interaction*, pp. 23–69; and Viktor Gecas, "The Self-Concept as a Basis for a Theory of Motivation," in Judith Howard and Peter Callero, eds., *The Self-Society Dynamic* (Cambridge: Cambridge University Press, 1991), pp. 171–87.

16. In neo-Durkheimian parlance, institutions are "social representations." See Serge Moscovici, "The Phenomenon of Social Representations," in Rob Farr and Serge Moscovici, eds., *Social Representations* (Cambridge: Cambridge University Press, 1984), pp. 3–69.

17. Berger and Luckmann, *The Social Construction of Reality*, p. 58.

18. See Giddens, *Central Problems in Social Theory;* and Alexander Wendt and Raymond Duvall, "Institutions and International Order," in Ernst-Otto Czempiel and James Rosenau, eds., *Global Changes and Theoretical Challenges* (Lexington, Mass.: Lexington Books, 1989), pp. 51–74.

19. Proponents of choice theory might put this in terms of "interdependent utilities."

20. Security systems might also vary in the extent to which there is a functional differentiation or a hierarchical relationship between patron and client, with the patron playing a hegemonic role within its sphere of influence in defining the security interests of its clients. I do not examine this dimension here; for preliminary discussion, see Alexander Wendt, "The States System and Global Militarization," Ph.D. diss., University of Minnesota, Minneapolis, 1989; and Alexander Wendt and Michael Barnett, "The International System and Third World Militarization," unpublished manuscript, 1991.

21. This amounts to an "internationalization of the state." For a discussion of this subject, see Raymond Duvall and Alexander Wendt, "The International Capital Regime and the Internationalization of the State," unpublished manuscript, 1987. See also R. B. J. Walker, "Sovereignty, Identity, Community: Reflections on the Horizons of Contemporary Political Practice," in R. B. J. Walker and Saul Mendlovitz, eds., *Contending Sovereignties* (Boulder, Colo.: Lynne Rienner, 1990), pp. 159–85.

22. On the spectrum of cooperative security arrangements, see Charles Kupchan and Clifford Kupchan, "Concerts, Collective Security, and the Future of Europe," *International Security* 16 (Summer 1991), pp. 114–61; and Richard Smoke, "A Theory of Mutual Security," in Richard Smoke and Andrei Kortunov, eds., *Mutual Security* (New York: St. Martin's Press, 1991), pp. 59–111. These may be usefully set alongside Christopher Jencks' "Varieties of Altruism," in Jane Mansbridge, ed., *Beyond Self-Interest* (Chicago: University of Chicago Press, 1990), pp. 53–67.

23. On the role of collective identity in reducing collective action problems, see Bruce Fireman and William Gamson, "Utilitarian Logic in the Resource Mobilization Perspective," in Mayer Zald and John McCarthy, eds., *The Dynamics of Social Movements* (Cambridge, Mass.: Winthrop, 1979), pp. 8–44; Robyn Dawes et al., "Cooperation for the Benefit of Us—Not Me, or My Conscience," in Mansbridge, *Beyond Self-Interest*, pp. 97–110; and Craig Calhoun, "The Problem of Identity in Collective Action," in Joan Huber, ed., *Macro-Micro Linkages in Sociology* (Beverly Hills, Calif.: Sage, 1991), pp. 51–75.

24. See Thomas Risse-Kappen, "Are Democratic Alliances Special?" unpublished manuscript, Yale University, New Haven, Conn., 1991.

25. Waltz, *Theory of International Politics*, p. 91.

26. See Waltz, *Man, the State, and War;* and Robert Jervis, "Cooperation Under the Security Dilemma," *World Politics* 30 (January 1978), pp. 167–214.

27. My argument here parallels Rousseau's critique of Hobbes. For an excellent critique of realist appropriations of Rousseau, see Michael Williams, "Rousseau, Realism, and Realpolitik," *Millennium* 18 (Summer 1989), pp. 188–204. Williams argues that far from being a fundamental starting point in the state of nature, for Rousseau the stag hunt represented a stage in man's fall. On p. 190, Williams cites Rousseau's description of man prior to leaving the state of nature: "Man only knows himself; he does not see his own well-being to be identified with or contrary to that of anyone else; he neither hates anything nor loves anything; but limited to no more than physical instinct, he is no one, he is an animal." For another critique of Hobbes on the state of nature that parallels

my constructivist reading of anarchy, see Charles Landesman, "Reflections on Hobbes: Anarchy and Human Nature," in Peter Caws, ed., *The Causes of Quarrel* (Boston: Beacon, 1989), pp. 139–48.

28. Empirically, this suggestion is problematic, since the process of decolonization and the subsequent support of many Third World states by international society point to ways in which even the raw material of "empirical statehood" is constituted by the society of states. See Robert Jackson and Carl Rosberg, "Why Africa's Weak States Persist: The Empirical and the Juridical in Statehood," *World Politics* 35 (October 1982), pp. 1–24.

29. Waltz, *Theory of International Politics*, pp. 74–77.

30. See James Morrow, "Social Choice and System Structure in World Politics," *World Politics* 41 (October 1988), p. 89. Waltz's behavioral treatment of socialization may be usefully contrasted with the more cognitive approach taken by Ikenberry and the Kupchans in the following articles: G. John Ikenberry and Charles Kupchan, "Socialization and Hegemonic Power," *International Organization* 44 (Summer 1989), pp. 283–316; and Kupchan and Kupchan, "Concerts, Collective Security, and the Future of Europe." Their approach is close to my own, but they define socialization as an elite strategy to induce value change in others, rather than as a ubiquitous feature of interaction in terms of which all identities and interests get produced and reproduced.

31. Regarding individualism, see Richard Ashley, "The Poverty of Neorealism," *International Organization* 38 (Spring 1984), pp. 225–86; Wendt, "The Agent-Structure Problem in International Relations Theory"; and David Dessler, "What's at Stake in the Agent-Structure Debate?" *International Organization* 43 (Summer 1989), pp. 441–74. Regarding structuralism, see R. B. J. Walker, "Realism, Change, and International Political Theory,"

International Studies Quarterly 31 (March 1987), pp. 65–86; and Martin Hollis and Steven Smith, *Explaining and Understanding International Relations* (Oxford: Clarendon Press, 1989).

32. The importance of the distinction between constitutive and causal explanations is not sufficiently appreciated in constructivist discourse. See Wendt, "The Agent-Structure Problem in International Relations Theory," pp. 362–65; Wendt, "The States System and Global Militarization," pp. 110–13; and Wendt, "Bridging the Theory/Meta-Theory Gap in International Relations," *Review of International Studies* 17 (October 1991), p. 390.

33. See Blumer, "The Methodological Position of Symbolic Interactionism," pp. 2–4.

34. See Robert Grafstein, "Rational Choice: Theory and Institutions," in Kristen Monroe, ed., *The Economic Approach to Politics* (New York: Harper Collins, 1991), pp. 263–64. A good example of the promise and limits of transaction cost approaches to institutional analysis is offered by Robert Keohane in his *After Hegemony* (Princeton, N.J.: Princeton University Press, 1984).

35. This situation is not entirely metaphorical in world politics, since throughout history states have "discovered" each other, generating an instant anarchy as it were.

36. Mead's analysis of gestures remains definitive. See Mead's *Mind, Self, and Society*. See also the discussion of the role of signaling in the "mechanics of interaction" in Turner's *A Theory of Social Interaction*, pp. 74–79 and 92–115.

37. On the role of attribution processes in the interactionist account of identity-formation, see Sheldon Stryker and Avi Gottlieb, "Attribution Theory and Symbolic Interactionism," in John Harvey et al., eds., *New Directions in Attribution Research*, vol. 3 (Hillsdale, N.J.: Lawrence Erlbaum, 1981), pp. 425–58; and Kathleen Crittenden, "Sociological Aspects

of Attribution," *Annual Review of Sociology*, vol. 9, 1983, pp. 425–46. On attributional processes in international relations, see Shawn Rosenberg and Gary Wolfsfeld, "International Conflict and the Problem of Attribution," *Journal of Conflict Resolution* 21 (March 1977), pp. 75–103.

38. On the "stagecraft" involved in "presentations of self," see Erving Goffman, *The Presentation of Self in Everyday Life* (New York: Doubleday, 1959). On the role of appearance in definitions of the situation, see Gregory Stone, "Appearance and the Self," in Arnold Rose, ed., *Human Behavior and Social Processes* (Boston: Houghton Mifflin, 1962), pp. 86–118.

39. This discussion of the role of possibilities and probabilities in threat perception owes much to Stewart Johnson's comments on an earlier draft of my article.

40. On the role of "reassurance" in threat situations, see Richard Ned Lebow and Janice Gross Stein, "Beyond Deterrence," *Journal of Social Issues*, vol. 43, no. 4, 1987, pp. 5–72.

41. On "reciprocal typifications," see Berger and Luckmann, *The Social Construction of Reality*, pp. 54–58.

42. Jeff Coulter, "Remarks on the Conceptualization of Social Structure," *Philosophy of the Social Sciences* 12 (March 1982), pp. 42–43.

43. The following articles by Noel Kaplowitz have made an important contribution to such thinking in international relations: "Psychopolitical Dimensions of International Relations: The Reciprocal Effects of Conflict Strategies," *International Studies Quarterly* 28 (December 1984), pp. 373–406; and "National Self-Images, Perception of Enemies, and Conflict Strategies: Psychopolitical Dimensions of International Relations," *Political Psychology* 11 (March 1990), pp. 39–82.

44. These arguments are common in theories of narcissism and altruism. See Heinz Kohut, *Self-Psychology and the Humanities* (New

York: Norton, 1985); and Martin Hoffmann, "Empathy, Its Limitations, and Its Role in a Comprehensive Moral Theory," in William Kurtines and Jacob Gewirtz, eds., *Morality, Moral Behavior, and Moral Development* (New York: Wiley, 1984), pp. 283–302.

45. See C. Norman Alexander and Mary Glenn Wiley, "Situated Activity and Identity Formation," in Morris Rosenberg and Ralph Turner, eds., *Social Psychology: Sociological Perspectives* (New York: Basic Books, 1981), pp. 269–89.

46. Sheldon Stryker, "The Vitalization of Symbolic Interactionism," *Social Psychology Quarterly* 50 (March 1987), p. 93.

47. On the "maturity" of anarchies, see Barry Buzan, *People, States, and Fear* (Chapel Hill: University of North Carolina Press, 1983).

48. A similar intuition may lie behind Ashley's effort to reappropriate classical realist discourse for critical international relations theory. See Richard Ashley, "Political Realism and Human Interests," *International Studies Quarterly* 38 (June 1981), pp. 204–36.

49. Waltz has himself helped open up such a debate with his recognition that systemic factors condition but do not determine state actions. See Kenneth Waltz, "Reflections on *Theory of International Politics:* A Response to My Critics," in Robert Keohane, ed., *Neorealism and Its Critics* (New York: Columbia University Press, 1986), pp. 322–45. The growing literature on the observation that "democracies do not fight each other" is relevant to this question, as are two other studies that break important ground toward a "reductionist" theory of state identity: William Bloom's *Personal Identity, National Identity and International Relations* (Cambridge: Cambridge University Press, 1990) and Lumsdaine's *Ideals and Interests*.

50. See Berger and Luckmann, *The Social Construction of Reality*, p. 89. See also Douglas Maynard and Thomas Wilson, "On the Reification of Social Structure," in Scott McNall

and Gary Howe, eds., *Current Perspectives in Social Theory*, vol. 1 (Greenwich, Conn.: JAI Press, 1980), pp. 287–322.

51. See Richard Ashley, "Social Will and International Anarchy," in Hayward Alker and Richard Ashley, eds., *After Realism*, work in progress, Massachusetts Institute of Technology, Cambridge, and Arizona State University, Tempe, 1992.

52. See Ralph Turner, "Role-Taking: Process Versus Conformity," in Rose, *Human Behavior and Social Processes*, pp. 20–40; and Judith Howard, "From Changing Selves Toward Changing Society," in Howard and Callero, *The Self-Society Dynamic*, pp. 209–37.

53. On the relationship between commitment and identity, see Foote, "Identification as the Basis for a Theory of Motivation"; Howard Becker, "Notes on the Concept of Commitment," *American Journal of Sociology* 66 (July 1960), pp. 32–40; and Stryker, *Symbolic Interactionism*. On role salience, see Stryker, ibid.

54. On threats to identity and the types of resistance that they may create, see Glynis Breakwell, *Coping with Threatened Identities* (London: Methuen, 1986); and Terrell Northrup, "The Dynamic of Identity in Personal and Social Conflict," in Louis Kreisberg et al., eds., *Intractable Conflicts and Their Transformation* (Syracuse, N.Y.: Syracuse University Press, 1989), pp. 55–82. For a broad overview of resistance to change, see Timur Kuran, "The Tenacious Past: Theories of Personal and Collective Conservatism," *Journal of Economic Behavior and Organization* 10 (September 1988), pp. 143–71.

55. James March, "Bounded Rationality, Ambiguity, and the Engineering of Choice," *Bell Journal of Economics* 9 (Autumn 1978), p. 600.

56. Haskell Fain, *Normative Politics and the Community of Nations* (Philadelphia: Temple University Press, 1987).

57. This is the intersubjective basis for the principle of functional nondifferentiation among states, which "drops out" of Waltz's definition of structure because the latter has no explicit intersubjective basis. In international relations scholarship, the social production of territorial space has been emphasized primarily by poststructuralists. See, for example, Richard Ashley, "The Geopolitics of Geopolitical Space: Toward a Critical Social Theory of International Politics," *Alternatives* 12 (October 1987), pp. 403–34; and Simon Dalby, *Creating the Second Cold War* (London: Pinter, 1990). But the idea of space as both product and constituent of practice is also prominent in structurationist discourse. See Giddens, *Central Problems in Social Theory;* and Derek Gregory and John Urry, eds., *Social Relations and Spatial Structures* (London: Macmillan, 1985).

58. See John Ruggie, "Continuity and Transformation in the World Polity: Toward a Neorealist Synthesis," *World Politics* 35 (January 1983), pp. 261–85.

59. For a definition and discussion of "social closure," see Raymond Murphy, *Social Closure* (Oxford: Clarendon Press, 1988).

60. See Richard Ashley, "Untying the Sovereign State: A Double Reading of the Anarchy Problematique," *Millennium* 17 (Summer 1988), pp. 227–62.

61. See, for example, Mohammed Ayoob, "The Third World in the System of States: Acute Schizophrenia or Growing Pains?" *International Studies Quarterly* 33 (March 1989), pp. 67–80.

62. See William Coplin, "International Law and Assumptions About the State System," *World Politics* 17 (July 1965), pp. 615–34.

63. See Anthony Smith, "States and Homelands: The Social and Geopolitical Implications of National Territory," *Millennium* 10 (Autumn 1981), pp. 187–202.

64. This assumes that there are no other, competing, principles that organize political space and identity in the international system and coexist with traditional notions of sovereignty; in

fact, of course, there are. On "spheres of influence" and "informal empires," see Jan Triska,
ed., *Dominant Powers and Subordinate States*
(Durham, N.C.: Duke University Press, 1986);
and Ronald Robinson, "The Excentric Idea of
Imperialism, With or Without Empire," in
Wolfgang Mommsen and Jurgen Osterham-
mel, eds., *Imperialism and After: Continuities
and Discontinuities* (London: Allen & Unwin,
1986), pp. 267–89. On Arab conceptions of
sovereignty, see Michael Barnett, "Sovereignty, Institutions, and Identity: From Pan-
Arabism to the Arab State System,"
unpublished manuscript, University of Wisconsin, Madison, 1991.

65. David Strang, "Anomaly and Commonplace
in European Expansion: Realist and Institutional Accounts," *International Organization*
45 (Spring 1991), pp. 143–62.

66. On "dynamic density," see Ruggie, "Continuity and Transformation in the World Polity";
and Waltz, "Reflections on *Theory of International Politics*." The role of interdependence
in conditioning the speed and depth of social
learning is much greater than the attention
to which I have paid it. On the consequences
of interdependence under anarchy, see Helen
Milner, "The Assumption of Anarchy in International Relations Theory: A Critique," *Review of International Studies* 17 (January
1991), pp. 67–85.

67. See Michael Taylor, *Anarchy and Cooperation*
(New York: Wiley, 1976); and Robert Axelrod,
The Evolution of Cooperation (New York: Ba-
sic Books, 1984).

68. Mead, *Mind, Self, and Society*.

69. Strictly speaking, this is not true, since in iterated games the addition of future benefits to
current ones changes the payoff structure of
the game at T1, in this case from prisoners'
dilemma to an assurance game. This transformation of interest takes place entirely within
the actor, however, and as such is not a function of interaction with the other.

70. In fairness to Axelrod, he does point out that
internalization of norms is a real possibility

that may increase the resilience of institutions. My point is that this important idea
cannot be derived from an approach to theory that takes identities and interests as exogenously given.

71. On "European identity," see Barry Buzan et
al., eds., *The European Security Order Recast*
(London: Pinter, 1990), pp. 45–63.

72. On "embeddedness," see John Ruggie, "International Regimes, Transactions, and Change:
Embedded Liberalism in a Postwar Economic
Order," in Krasner, *International Regimes*,
pp. 195–232.

73. See Grieco, "Anarchy and the Limits of
Cooperation."

74. On the difficulties of creating cooperative security regimes given competitive interests,
see Robert Jervis, "Security Regimes," in
Krasner, *International Regimes*, pp. 173–94;
and Charles Lipson, "International Cooperation in Economic and Security Affairs,"
World Politics 37 (October 1984), pp. 1–23.

75. See Mead, *Mind, Self, and Society*.

76. Turner, "Role-Taking."

77. On "character planning," see Jon Elster, *Sour
Grapes: Studies in the Subversion of Rationality* (Cambridge: Cambridge University Press,
1983), p. 117.

78. For useful overviews of New Thinking, see
Mikhail Gorbachev, *Perestroika: New Think-
ing for Our Country and the World* (New York:
Harper & Row, 1987); and Allen Lynch, *Gor-
bachev's International Outlook: Intellectual
Origins and Political Consequences* (New
York: Institute for East–West Security Stud-
ies, 1989).

79. For useful overviews of these factors, see Jack
Snyder, "The Gorbachev Revolution: A Wan-
ing of Soviet Expansionism?" *World Politics*
12 (Winter 1987–88), pp. 93–121; and Stephen
Meyer, "The Sources and Prospects of Gorbachev's New Political Thinking on Security,"
International Security 13 (Fall 1988), pp.
124–63.

80. See Daniel Bar-Tal et al., "Conflict Termination: An Epistemological Analysis of Interna-

tional Cases," *Political Psychology* 10 (June 1989), pp. 233–55.

81. See Robert Cox, "Social Forces, States and World Orders: Beyond International Relations Theory," in Keohane, *Neorealism and Its Critics*, pp. 204–55. See also Brian Fay, *Critical Social Science* (Ithaca, N.Y.: Cornell University Press, 1987).

82. Hazel Markus and Paula Nurius, "Possible Selves," *American Psychologist* 41 (September 1986), pp. 954–69.

83. See Goffman, *The Presentation of Self in Everyday Life;* Eugene Weinstein and Paul Deutschberger, "Some Dimensions of Altercasting," *Sociometry* 26 (December 1963), pp. 454–66; and Walter Earle, "International Relations and the Psychology of Control: Alternative Control Strategies and Their Consequences," *Political Psychology* 7 (June 1986), pp. 369–75.

84. See Volker Boge and Peter Wilke, "Peace Movements and Unilateral Disarmament: Old Concepts in a New Light," *Anns Control* 7 (September 1986), pp. 156–70; Zeev Maoz and Daniel Felsenthal, "Self-Binding Commitments, the Inducement of Trust, Social Choice, and the Theory of International Cooperation," *International Studies Quarterly* 31 (June 1987), pp. 177–200; and V. Sakamoto, "Unilateral Initiative as an Alternative Strategy," *World Futures*, vol. 24, nos. 1–4, 1987, pp. 107–34.

85. On rewards, see Thomas Milburn and Daniel Christie, "Rewarding in International Politics," *Political Psychology* 10 (December 1989), pp. 625–45.

86. The importance of reciprocity in completing the process of structural transformation makes the logic in this stage similar to that in the "evolution of cooperation." The difference is one of prerequisites and objective: in the former, ego's tentative redefinition of self enables it to try and change alter by acting "as if" both were already playing a new game; in the latter, ego acts only on the basis of given interests and prior experience, with transformation emerging only as an unintended consequence.

87. Yale Ferguson and Richard Mansbach, "Between Celebration and Despair: Constructive Suggestions for Future International Theory," *International Studies Quarterly* 35 (December 1991), p. 375.

88. For excellent discussions of this tension, see Walker, "Sovereignty, Identity, Community"; and R. B. J. Walker, "Security, Sovereignty, and the Challenge of World Politics," *Alternatives* 15 (Winter 1990), pp. 3–27. On institutional path dependencies, see Stephen Krasner, "Sovereignty: An Institutional Perspective," *Comparative Political Studies* 21 (April 1988), pp. 66–94.

J. ANN TICKNER

MAN, THE STATE, AND WAR: GENDERED PERSPECTIVES ON NATIONAL SECURITY

It is not in giving life but in risking life that man is raised above the animal: that is why superiority has been accorded in humanity not to the sex that brings forth but to that which kills.

—*Simone de Beauvoir*

If we do not redefine manhood, war is inevitable.

—*Paul Fussell*

In the face of what is generally perceived as a dangerous international environment, states have ranked national security high in terms of their policy priorities. According to international relations scholar Kenneth Waltz, the state conducts its affairs in the "brooding shadow of violence," and therefore war could break out at any time.[1] In the name of national security, states have justified large defense budgets, which take priority over domestic spending, military conscription of their young adult male population, foreign invasions, and the curtailment of civil liberties. The security of the state is perceived as a core value that is generally supported unquestioningly by most citizens, particularly in time of war. While the role of the state in the twentieth century has expanded to include the provision of domestic social programs, national security often takes precedence over the social security of individuals.

When we think about the provision of national security we enter into what has been, and continues to be, an almost exclusively male domain. While most women support what they take to be legitimate calls for state action in the interests of international security, the task of defining, defending, and advancing the security interests of the

From J. Ann Tickner, *Gender in International Relations: Feminist Perspectives on Achieving Global Security* (New York: Columbia University Press, 1992); 27–66.

state is a man's affair, a task that, through its association with war, has been especially valorized and rewarded in many cultures throughout history. As Simone de Beauvoir's explanation for male superiority suggests, giving one's life for one's country has been considered the highest form of patriotism, but it is an act from which women have been virtually excluded. While men have been associated with defending the state and advancing its international interests as soldiers and diplomats, women have typically been engaged in the "ordering" and "comforting" roles both in the domestic sphere, as mothers and basic needs providers, and in the caring professions, as teachers, nurses, and social workers.[2] The role of women with respect to national security has been ambiguous: defined as those whom the state and its men are protecting, women have had little control over the conditions of their protection.

*   *   *

A Gendered Perspective on National Security

Morgenthau, Waltz, and other realists claim that it is possible to develop a rational, objective theory of international politics based on universal laws that operate across time and space. In her feminist critique of the natural sciences, Evelyn Fox Keller points out that most scientific communities share the "assumption that the universe they study is directly accessible, represented by concepts shaped not by language but only by the demands of logic and experiment." The laws of nature, according to this view of science, are beyond the relativity of language.[3] Like most contemporary feminists, Keller rejects this positivist view of science that, she asserts, imposes a coercive, hierarchical, and conformist pattern on scientific inquiry. Since most contemporary feminist scholars believe that knowledge is socially constructed, they are skeptical of finding an unmediated foundation for knowledge that realists claim is possible. Since they believe that it is language that transmits knowledge, many feminists suggest that the scholarly claims about the neutral uses of language and about objectivity must continually be questioned.[4]

I shall now investigate the individual, the state, and the international system—the three levels of analysis that realists use in their analysis of war and national security—and examine how they have been constructed in realist discourse. I shall argue that the language used to describe these concepts comes out of a Western-centered historical worldview that draws almost exclusively on the experiences of men. Underneath its claim to universality this worldview privileges a view of security that is constructed out of values associated with hegemonic masculinity.

"Political Man"

In his *Politics Among Nations*, a text rich in historical detail, Morgenthau has constructed a world almost entirely without women. Morgenthau claims that individuals are engaged in a struggle for power whenever they come into contact with one another, for the tendency to dominate exists at all levels of human life: the family, the polity, and the international system; it is modified only by the conditions under which the struggle takes place.[5] Since women rarely occupy positions of power in any of these arenas, we can assume that, when Morgenthau talks about domination, he is talking primarily about men, although not all men.[6] His "political man" is a social construct based on a partial representation of human nature abstracted from the behavior of men in positions of public power.[7] Morgenthau goes on to suggest that, while society condemns the violent behavior that can result from this struggle for power within the polity, it encourages it in the international system in the form of war.

While Morgenthau's "political man" has been criticized by other international relations scholars for its essentializing view of human nature, the social construction of hegemonic masculinity and its opposition to a devalued femininity have been central to the way in which the discourse of international politics has been constructed more generally. In Western political theory from the Greeks to Machiavelli, traditions upon which contemporary realism relies heavily for its analysis, this socially constructed type of masculinity has been projected onto the international behavior of states. The violence with which it is associated has been legitimated through the glorification of war.

*   *   *

The International System: The War of Everyman Against Everyman

According to Richard Ashley, realists have privileged a higher reality called "the sovereign state" against which they have posited anarchy understood in a negative way as difference, ambiguity, and contingency—as a space that is external and dangerous.[8] All these characteristics have also been attributed to women. Anarchy is an actual or potential site of war. The most common metaphor that realists employ to describe the anarchical international system is that of the seventeenth-century English philosopher Thomas Hobbes's depiction of the state of nature. Although Hobbes did not write much about international politics, realists have applied his description of individuals' behavior in a hypothetical precontractual state of nature, which Hobbes termed the war of everyman against everyman, to the behavior of states in the international system.[9]

Carole Pateman argues that, in all contemporary discussions of the state of nature, the differentiation between the sexes is generally ignored, even though it was an important consideration for contract theorists themselves.[10] Although Hobbes did suggest that women as well as men could be free and equal individuals in the state of nature, his description of human behavior in this environment refers to that of adult males whose behavior is taken as constitutive of human nature as a whole by contemporary realist analysis. According to Jane Flax, the individuals that Hobbes described in the state of nature appeared to come to full maturity without any engagement with one another; they were solitary creatures lacking any socialization in interactive behavior. Any interactions they did have led to power struggles that resulted in domination or submission. Suspicion of others' motives led to behavior characterized by aggression, self-interest, and the drive for autonomy.[11] In a similar vein, Christine Di Stephano uses feminist psychoanalytic theory to support her claim that the masculine dimension of atomistic egoism is powerfully underscored in Hobbes's state of nature, which, she asserts, is built on the foundation of denied maternity. "Hobbes' abstract man is a creature who is self-possessed and radically solitary in a crowded and inhospitable world, whose relations with others are unavoidably contractual and whose freedom consists in the absence of impediments to the attainment of privately generated and understood desires."[12]

As a model of human behavior, Hobbes's depiction of individuals in the state of nature is partial at best; certain feminists have argued that such behavior could be applicable only to adult males, for if life was to go on for more than one generation in the state of nature, women must have been involved in activities such as reproduction and child rearing rather than in warfare. Reproductive activities require an environment that can provide for the survival of infants and behavior that is interactive and nurturing.

*   *   *

* * * [W]ar is central to the way we learn about international relations. * * * War is a time when male and female characteristics become polarized; it is a gendering activity at a time when the discourse of militarism and masculinity permeates the whole fabric of society.[13]

As Jean Elshtain points out, war is an experience to which women are exterior; men have

inhabited the world of war in a way that women have not.[14] The history of international politics is therefore a history from which women are, for the most part, absent. Little material can be found on women's roles in wars; generally they are seen as victims, rarely as agents. While war can be a time of advancement for women as they step in to do men's jobs, the battlefront takes precedence, so the hierarchy remains and women are urged to step aside once peace is restored. When women themselves engage in violence, it is often portrayed as a mob or a food riot that is out of control.[15] Movements for peace, which are also part of our history, have not been central to the conventional way in which the evolution of the Western state system has been presented to us. International relations scholars of the early twentieth century, who wrote positively about the possibilities of international law and the collective security system of the League of Nations, were labeled "idealists" and not taken seriously by the more powerful realist tradition.

Metaphors, such as Hobbes's state of nature, are primarily concerned with representing conflictual relations between great powers. The images used to describe nineteenth-century imperialist projects and contemporary great power relations with former colonial states are somewhat different. Historically, colonial people were often described in terms that drew on characteristics associated with women in order to place them lower in a hierarchy that put their white male colonizers on top. As the European state system expanded outward to conquer much of the world in the nineteenth century, its "civilizing" mission was frequently described in stereotypically gendered terms. Colonized peoples were often described as being effeminate, masculinity was an attribute of the white man, and colonial order depended on Victorian standards of manliness. Cynthia Enloe suggests that the concept of "ladylike behavior" was one of the mainstays of imperialist civilization. Like sanitation and Christianity, feminine respectability was meant to convince colonizers and colonized alike that foreign conquest was right and necessary. Masculinity denoted protection of the respectable lady; she stood for the civilizing mission that justified the colonization of benighted peoples.[16] Whereas the feminine stood for danger and disorder for Machiavelli, the European female, in contrast to her colonial counterpart, came to represent a stable, civilized order in nineteenth-century representations of British imperialism.

An example of the way in which these gender identities were manipulated to justify Western policy with respect to the rest of the world can also be seen in attitudes toward Latin America prevalent in the United States in the nineteenth century. According to Michael Hunt, nineteenth-century American images of Latin society depicted a (usually black) male who was lazy, dishonest, and corrupt. A contrary image that was more positive—a Latin as redeemable—took the form of a fair-skinned senorita living in a marginalized society, yet escaping its degrading effects. Hunt suggests that Americans entered the twentieth century with three images of Latin America fostered through legends brought back by American merchants and diplomats. These legends, perpetuated through school texts, cartoons, and political rhetoric, were even incorporated into the views of policymakers. The three images pictured the Latin as a half-breed brute, feminized, or infantile. In each case, Americans stood superior; the first image permitted a predatory aggressiveness, the second allowed the United States to assume the role of ardent suitor, and the third justified America's need to provide tutelage and discipline. All these images are profoundly gendered: the United States as a civilizing warrior, a suitor, or a father, and Latin America as a lesser male, a female, or a child.[17]

Such images, although somewhat muted, remain today and are particularly prevalent in the thinking of Western states when they are dealing with the Third World. * * *

*   *   *

Feminist Perspectives on National Security

Women Define Security

It is difficult to find definitions by women of national security. While it is not necessarily the case that women have not had ideas on this subject, they are not readily accessible in the literature of international relations. When women speak or write about national security, they are often dismissed as being naive or unrealistic. An example of this is the women in the United States and Europe who spoke out in the early years of the century for a more secure world order. Addressing the International Congress of Women at the Hague during World War I, Jane Addams spoke of the need for a new internationalism to replace the self-destructive nationalism that contributed so centrally to the outbreak and mass destruction of that war. Resolutions adopted at the close of the congress questioned the assumption that women, and civilians more generally, could be protected during modern war. The conference concluded that assuring security through military means was no longer possible owing to the indiscriminate nature of modern warfare, and it called for disarmament as a more appropriate course for ensuring future security.[18]

At the Women's International Peace Conference in Halifax, Canada, in 1985, a meeting of women from all over the world, participants defined security in various ways depending on the most immediate threats to their survival; security meant safe working conditions and freedom from the threat of war or unemployment or the economic squeeze of foreign debt. Discussions of the meaning of security revealed divisions between Western middle-class women's concerns with nuclear war, concerns that were similar to those of Jane Addams and her colleagues, and Third World women who defined insecurity more broadly in terms of the structural violence associated with imperialism, militarism, racism, and sexism. Yet all agreed that security meant nothing if it was built on others' insecurity.[19]

The final document of the World Conference to Review and Appraise the Achievements of the United Nations Decade for Women, held in Nairobi in 1985, offered a similarly multidimensional definition of security. The introductory chapter of the document defined peace as "not only the absence of war, violence and hostilities at the national and international levels but also the enjoyment of economic and social justice."[20] All these definitions of security take issue with realists' assumptions that security is zero-sum and must therefore be built on the insecurity of others.

*   *   *

Citizenship Redefined

Building on the notion of hegemonic masculinity, the notion of the citizen-warrior depends on a devalued femininity for its construction. In international relations, this devalued femininity is bound up with myths about women as victims in need of protection; the protector/protected myth contributes to the legitimation of a militarized version of citizenship that results in unequal gender relations that can precipitate violence against women. Certain feminists have called for the construction of an enriched version of citizenship that would depend less on military values and more on an equal recognition of women's contributions to society. Such a notion of citizenship cannot come about, however, until myths that perpetuate views of women as victims rather than agents are eliminated.

One such myth is the association of women with peace, an association that has been invalidated through considerable evidence of women's support for men's wars in many societies.[21] In spite of a gender gap, a plurality of women generally support war and national security policies; Bernice Carroll suggests that the association of women and peace is one that has been imposed on women by their disarmed condition.[22] In the West, this association grew out of the Victorian ideology of women's moral superiority and the glorification of motherhood. This ideal was expressed by feminist Charlotte Perkins Gilman whose book *Herland* was first serialized in *The Forerunner* in 1915. Gilman glorified women as caring and nurturing mothers whose private sphere skills could benefit the world at large.[23] Most turn-of-the-century feminists shared Gilman's ideas. But if the implication of this view was that women were disqualified from participating in the corrupt world of political and economic power by virtue of their moral superiority, the result could only be the perpetuation of male dominance. Many contemporary feminists see dangers in the continuation of these essentializing myths that can only result in the perpetuation of women's subordination and reinforce dualisms that serve to make men more powerful. The association of femininity with peace lends support to an idealized masculinity that depends on constructing women as passive victims in need of protection. It also contributes to the claim that women are naive in matters relating to international politics. An enriched, less militarized notion of citizenship cannot be built on such a weak foundation.

While women have often been willing to support men's wars, many women are ambivalent about fighting in them, often preferring to leave that task to men. Feminists have also been divided on this issue; some argue, on the grounds of equality, that women must be given equal access to the military, while others suggest that women must resist the draft in order to promote a politics of peace. * * *

*   *   *

In spite of many women's support for men's wars, a consistent gender gap in voting on defense-related issues in many countries suggests that women are less supportive of policies that rest on the use of direct violence. Before the outbreak of the Persian Gulf war in 1990, women in the United States were overwhelmingly against the use of force and, for the first time, women alone turned the public opinion polls against opting for war.[24] During the 1980s, when the Reagan administration was increasing defense budgets, women were less likely to support defense at the expense of social programs, a pattern that, in the United States, holds true for women's behavior more generally.

Explanations for this gender gap, which in the United States appears to be increasing as time goes on, range from suggestions that women have not been socialized into the practice of violence to claims that women are increasingly voting their own interests. While holding down jobs, millions of women also care for children, the aged, and the sick—activities that usually take place outside the economy. When more resources go to the military, additional burdens are placed on such women as public sector resources for social services shrink. While certain women are able, through access to the military, to give service to their country, many more are serving in these traditional care-giving roles. A feminist challenge to the traditional definition of patriotism should therefore question the meaning of service to one's country.[25] In contrast to a citizenship that rests on the assumption that it is more glorious to die than to live for one's state, Wendy Brown suggests that a more constructive view of citizenship could center on the courage to sustain life.[26] In similar terms, Jean Elshtain asserts the need to move toward a politics that shifts the focus of political loyalty and identity from sacrifice to responsibility.[27] Only when women's contributions to society are seen as equal to men's can these reconstructed visions of citizenship come about.

Feminist Perspectives on States' Security-Seeking Behavior

Realists have offered us an instrumental version of states' security-seeking behavior, which, I have argued, depends on a partial representation of human behavior associated with a stereotypical hegemonic masculinity. Feminist redefinitions of citizenship allow us to envisage a less militarized version of states' identities, and feminist theories can also propose alternative models for states' in-

ternational security-seeking behavior, extrapolated from a more comprehensive view of human behavior.

Realists use state-of-nature stories as metaphors to describe the insecurity of states in an anarchical international system. I shall suggest an alternative story, which could equally be applied to the behavior of individuals in the state of nature. Although frequently unreported in standard historical accounts, it is a true story, not a myth, about a state of nature in early nineteenth-century America. Among those present in the first winter encampment of the 1804–1806 Lewis and Clark expedition into the Northwest territories was Sacajawea, a member of the Shoshone tribe. Sacajawea had joined the expedition as the wife of a French interpreter; her presence was proving invaluable to the security of the expedition's members, whose task it was to explore uncharted territory and establish contact with the native inhabitants to inform them of claims to these territories by the United States. Although unanticipated by its leaders, the presence of a woman served to assure the native inhabitants that the expedition was peaceful since the Native Americans assumed that war parties would not include women: the expedition was therefore safer because it was not armed.[28]

This story demonstrates that the introduction of women can change the way humans are assumed to behave in the state of nature. Just as Sacajawea's presence changed the Native American's expectations about the behavior of intruders into their territory, the introduction of women into our state-of-nature myths could change the way we think about the behavior of states in the international system. The use of the Hobbesian analogy in international relations theory is based on a partial view of human nature that is stereotypically masculine; a more inclusive perspective would see human nature as both conflictual and cooperative, containing elements of social reproduction and interdependence as well as domination and separation. Generalizing from this more comprehensive view of human nature, a feminist perspective would assume that the potential for international community also exists and that an atomistic, conflictual view of the international system is only a partial representation of reality. Liberal individualism, the instrumental rationality of the marketplace, and the defector's self-help approach in Rousseau's stag hunt [see p. 344] are all, in analogous ways, based on a partial masculine model of human behavior.[29]

*   *   *

Feminist perspectives on national security take us beyond realism's statist representations. They allow us to see that the realist view of national security is constructed out of a masculinized discourse that, while it is only a partial view of reality, is taken as universal. Women's definitions of security are multilevel and multidimensional. Women have defined security as the absence of violence whether it be military, economic, or sexual. Not until the hierarchical social relations, including gender relations, that have been hidden by realism's frequently depersonalized discourse are brought to light can we begin to construct a language of national security that speaks out of the multiple experiences of both women and men. * * *

NOTES

I owe the title of this chapter to Kenneth Waltz's book *Man, the State, and War.*

De Beauvoir epigraph from *The Second Sex* [New York: Knopf, 1972], p. 72. De Beauvoir's analysis suggests that she herself endorsed this explanation for male superiority; * * * Fussell epigraph quoted by Anna Quindlen in *The New York Times*, February 7, 1991, p. A25.

1. [Kenneth N.] Waltz, *Theory of International Politics* [Boston: Addison-Wesley, 1979], p. 102.
2. While heads of state, all men, discussed the "important" issues in world politics at the Group of Seven meeting in London in July 1991, Barbara Bush and Princess Diana were pictured on the "CBS Evening News" (July 17, 1991) meeting with British AIDS patients.
3. [Evelyn Fox] Keller, *Reflections on Gender and Science* [New Haven: Yale University Press 1985], p. 130.
4. For example, see [Donna] Haraway, *Primate Visions* [New York: Routledge, 1989], ch. 1. Considering scientific practice from the perspective of the way its factual findings are narrated, Haraway provocatively explores how scientific theories produce and are embedded in particular kinds of stories. This allows her to challenge the neutrality and objectivity of scientific facts. She suggests that texts about primates can be read as science fictions about race, gender, and nature.
5. [Hans J.] Morgenthau, *Politics Among Nations* [New York: Knopf, 1973], p. 34.
6. Morgenthau does talk about dominating mothers-in-law, but as feminist research has suggested, it is generally men, legally designated as heads of households in most societies, who hold the real power even in the family and certainly with respect to the family's interaction with the public sphere.
7. For an extended discussion of Morgenthau's "political man," see [J. Ann] Tickner, "Hans Morgenthau's Principles of Political Realism" [*Millennium* 17(3):429–440]. In neorealism's depersonalized structural analysis, Morgenthau's depiction of human nature slips out of sight.
8. [Richard K.] Ashley, "Untying the Sovereign State" [*Millennium* 17(2) (1988)], p. 230.
9. Hobbes, *Leviathan*, part 1, ch. 13, quoted in Vasquez, ed., *Classics of International Relations*, pp. 213–215.
10. [Carole] Pateman, *The Sexual Contract* [Stanford: Stanford University Press, 1988], p. 41.
11. [Jane] Flax, "Political Philosophy and the Patriarchal Unconscious: A Psychoanalytic Perspective on Epistemology and Metaphysics," in Harding and Hintikka, eds., *Discovering Reality* [Dordrecht, Holland: D. Reidel, 1983], pp. 245–281.

12. [Christine] Di Stephano, "Masculinity as Ideology in Political Theory" [Women's Studies International Forum 6(6) (1983):633–644]. Carole Pateman has disputed some of Di Stephano's assumptions about Hobbes's characterizations of women and the family in the state of nature. But this does not deny the fact that Di Stephano's characterization of men is the one used by realists in their depiction of the international system. See Pateman, "'God Hath Ordained to Man a Helper': Hobbes, Patriarchy, and Conjugal Right."

13. [Margaret Randolph] Higonnet et al., *Behind the Lines* [New Haven: Yale University Press, 1987], introduction.

14. [Jean Bethke] Elshtain, *Women and War* [New York: Basic Books, 1987], p. 194.

15. Ibid., p. 168.

16. [Cynthia] Enloe, *Bananas, Beaches, and Bases* [Berkeley: University of California Press, 1990], pp. 48–49.

17. [Michael H.] Hunt, *Ideology and U.S. Foreign Policy* [New Haven: Yale University Press, 1987], pp. 58–62.

18. [Jane] Addams et al., *Women at The Hague* [New York: Macmillan, 1916], pp. 150ff.

19. [Anne Sisson] Runyan, "Feminism, Peace, and International Politics" [Ph.D. diss., American University, 1988], ch. 6.

20. "Forward-looking Strategies for the Advancement of Women Towards the Year 2000." Quoted in [Hilkka] Pietilä and [Jeanne] Vickers, *Making Women Matter* [London: Zed Books, 1990], pp. 46–47.

21. See Elshtain, *Women and War*, ch. 3.

22. Carroll, "Feminism and Pacifism: Historical and Theoretical Connections," in [Ruth Roach] Pierson, ed., *Women and Peace* [London: Croom Helm, 1987], pp. 2–28.

23. Margaret Hobbs, "The Perils of 'Unbridled Masculinity': Pacifist Elements in the Feminist and Socialist Thought of Charlotte Perkins Gilman," in Pierson, ed., *Women and Peace*, pp. 149–169.

24. The *New York Times* of December 12, 1990 (p. A35) reported that while men were about evenly split on attacking Iraqi forces in Kuwait, women were 73 percent against and 22 percent in favor.

25. Suzanne Gordon, "Another Enemy," *Boston Globe*, March 8, 1991, p. 15.

26. [Wendy] Brown, *Manhood and Politics* [Totowa, N.J.: Rowman and Littlefield, 1988], p. 206.

27. Elshtain, "Sovereignty, Identity, Sacrifice," in [V. Spike] Peterson, ed., *Gendered States* [Boulder: Lynne Rienner, 1992].

28. I am grateful to Michael Capps, historian at the Lewis and Clark Museum in St. Louis, Missouri, for this information. The story of Sacajawea is told in one of the museum's exhibits.

29. In *Man, the State, and War* [New York: Columbia University Press, 1959], [Kenneth N.] Waltz argues that "in the stag-hunt example, the will of the rabbit-snatcher was rational and predictable from his own point of view" (p. 183), while "in the early state of nature, men were sufficiently dispersed to make any pattern of cooperation unnecessary" (p. 167). Neorealist revisionists, such as Snidal [see "Relative Gains and the Pattern of International Cooperation"] do not question the masculine bias of the stag hunt metaphor. Like Waltz and Rousseau, they also assume the autonomous, adult male (unparented and in an environment without women or children) in their discussion of the stag hunt; they do not question the rationality of the rabbit-snatching defector or the restrictive situational descriptions implied by their payoff matrices. Transformations in the social nature of an interaction are very hard to represent using such a model. Their reformulation of Waltz's position is instead focused on the exploration of different specifications of the game payoff in less conflictual ways (i.e., as an assurance game) and on inferences concerning the likely consequences of relative gain-seeking behavior in a gamelike interaction with more than two (equally autonomous and unsocialized) players.

4 THE INTERNATIONAL SYSTEM

Liberals, realists, and radicals offer different conceptions of the international system. One prominent strand of liberal thinking conceives the international system as an "international society." Hedley Bull's The Anarchical Society *(1977), a major statement of the so-called English School of international relations, argues that states in the international society, no matter how competitive, have nonetheless had common interests, developed common rules, and participated in common institutions. According to this variant of liberal thinking, these commonalities represent elements of order that regulate competition in the international system.*

Realists and radicals disagree about the amount of order found in the international system. Realist Hans Morgenthau writes in Politics among Nations *(1948) that the international system is characterized by the desire of state actors to maximize power. For international stability to be achieved, a balance-of-power system is necessary. In this selection, Morgenthau discusses what states can do to ensure the balance. For the radical world-system theorist and sociologist Immanuel Wallerstein, the international system is a capitalist world-system differentiated into three types of states: the core, the periphery, and the semiperiphery. Drawing on the historical trends developed in his widely read book,* The Modern World-System: Capitalist Agriculture and the Origins of the European World-Economy in the Sixteenth Century *(1974), Wallerstein traces the evolution of each group of states. He argues that with each group pursuing its own economic interest, the semiperiphery is the linchpin of the system, being exploited by the core and exploiting the periphery. In the radical vision, like the realist one, the international system is fundamentally conflictual.*

What are the characteristics of the contemporary international system? The last two selections offer answers. Drawing on centuries of historical and economic data, Indiana University's William Thompson asserts that unipolarity is a recurring but nonpermanent phenomenon. He finds that while the current international system has unipolar characteristics due to U.S. military superiority, American technological and hence economic superiority is being challenged. Unipolarity does not inevitably lead to empire. Anthony Pagden investigates the historic roots of the term, concluding that the U.S. is not an empire. The U.S. seeks to impose liberal democratic values along with a system of international free trade, but once those conditions are met the U.S. retreats, unlike empires of the past.

HEDLEY BULL

DOES ORDER EXIST IN WORLD POLITICS?

*   *   *

The Idea of International Society

Throughout the history of the modern states system there have been three competing traditions of thought: the Hobbesian or realist tradition, which views international politics as a state of war; the Kantian or universalist tradition, which sees at work in international politics a potential community of mankind; and the Grotian or internationalist tradition, which views international politics as taking place within an international society.[1] Here I shall state what is essential to the Grotian or internationalist idea of international society, and what divides it from the Hobbesian or realist tradition on the one hand, and from the Kantian or universalist tradition on the other. Each of these traditional patterns of thought embodies a description of the nature of international politics and a set of prescriptions about international conduct.

The Hobbesian tradition describes international relations as a state of war of all against all, an arena of struggle in which each state is pitted against every other. International relations, on the Hobbesian view, represent pure conflict between states and resemble a game that is wholly

distributive or zero-sum: the interests of each state exclude the interests of any other. The particular international activity that, on the Hobbesian view, is most typical of international activity as a whole, or best provides the clue to it, is war itself. Thus peace, on the Hobbesian view, is a period of recuperation from the last war and preparation for the next.

The Hobbesian prescription for international conduct is that the state is free to pursue its goals in relation to other states without moral or legal restrictions of any kind. Ideas of morality and law, on this view, are valid only in the context of a society, but international life is beyond the bounds of any society. If any moral or legal goals are to be pursued in international politics, these can only be the moral or legal goals of the state itself. Either it is held (as by Machiavelli) that the state conducts foreign policy in a kind of moral and legal vacuum, or it is held (as by Hegel and his successors) that moral behaviour for the state in foreign policy lies in its own self-assertion. The only rules or principles which, for those in the Hobbesian tradition, may be said to limit or circumscribe the behaviour of states in their relations with one another are rules of prudence or expediency. Thus agreements may be kept if it is expedient to keep them, but may be broken if it is not.

The Kantian or universalist tradition, at the other extreme, takes the essential nature of international politics to lie not in conflict among

From Hedley Bull, *The Anarchical Society: A Study of Order in World Politics*, 2d ed. (New York: Columbia University Press, 1977), Chap. 2.

states, as on the Hobbesian view, but in the trans-national social bonds that link the individual human beings who are the subjects or citizens of states. The dominant theme of international relations, on the Kantian view, is only apparently the relationship among states, and is really the relationship among all men in the community of mankind—which exists potentially, even if it does not exist actually, and which when it comes into being will sweep the system of states into limbo.[2]

Within the community of all mankind, on the universalist view, the interests of all men are one and the same; international politics, considered from this perspective, is not a purely distributive or zero-sum game, as the Hobbesians maintain, but a purely cooperative or non-zero-sum game. Conflicts of interest exist among the ruling cliques of states, but this is only at the superficial or transient level of the existing system of states; properly understood, the interests of all peoples are the same. The particular international activity which, on the Kantian view, most typifies international activity as a whole is the horizontal conflict of ideology that cuts across the boundaries of states and divides human society into two camps—the trustees of the immanent community of mankind and those who stand in its way, those who are of the true faith and the heretics, the liberators and the oppressed.

The Kantian or universalist view of international morality is that, in contrast to the Hobbesian conception, there are moral imperatives in the field of international relations limiting the action of states, but that these imperatives enjoin not coexistence and co-operation among states but rather the overthrow of the system of states and its replacement by a cosmopolitan society. The community of mankind, on the Kantian view, is not only the central reality in international politics, in the sense that the forces able to bring it into being are present; it is also the end or object of the highest moral endeavour. The rules that sustain coexistence and social intercourse among states should be ignored if the imperatives of this higher morality require it. Good faith with heretics has no meaning, except in terms of tacti-

cal convenience; between the elect and the damned, the liberators and the oppressed, the question of mutual acceptance of rights to sovereignty or independence does not arise.

What has been called the Grotian or internationalist tradition stands between the realist tradition and the universalist tradition. The Grotian tradition describes international politics in terms of a society of states or international society.[3] As against the Hobbesian tradition, the Grotians contend that states are not engaged in simple struggle, like gladiators in an arena, but are limited in their conflicts with one another by common rules and institutions. But as against the Kantian or universalist perspective the Grotians accept the Hobbesian premise that sovereigns or states are the principal reality in international politics; the immediate members of international society are states rather than individual human beings. International politics, in the Grotian understanding, expresses neither complete conflict of interest between states nor complete identity of interest; it resembles a game that is partly distributive but also partly productive. The particular international activity which, on the Grotian view, best typifies international activity as a whole is neither war between states, nor horizontal conflict cutting across the boundaries of states, but trade—or, more generally, economic and social intercourse between one country and another.

The Grotian prescription for international conduct is that all states, in their dealings with one another, are bound by the rules and institutions of the society they form. As against the view of the Hobbesians, states in the Grotian view are bound not only by rules of prudence or expediency but also by imperatives of morality and law. But, as against the view of the universalists, what these imperatives enjoin is not the overthrow of the system of states and its replacement by a universal community of mankind, but rather acceptance of the requirements of coexistence and co-operation in a society of states.

Each of these traditions embodies a great variety of doctrines about international politics, among which there exists only a loose connection. In different periods each pattern of thought appears in a different idiom and in relation to different issues and preoccupations. This is not the place to explore further the connections and distinctions within each tradition. Here we have only to take account of the fact that the Grotian idea of international society has always been present in thought about the states system, and to indicate in broad terms the metamorphoses which, in the last three to four centuries, it has undergone.

Christian International Society

In the fifteenth, sixteenth and seventeenth centuries, when the universal political organisation of Western Christendom was still in process of disintegration, and modern states in process of articulation, the three patterns of thought purporting to describe the new international politics, and to prescribe conduct within it, first took shape. On the one hand, thinkers like Machiavelli, Bacon and Hobbes saw the emerging states as confronting one another in the social and moral vacuum left by the receding *respublica Christiana*. On the other hand Papal and Imperialist writers fought a rearguard action on behalf of the ideas of the universal authority of Pope and Emperor. As against these alternatives there was asserted by a third group of thinkers, relying upon the tradition of natural law, the possibility that the princes now making themselves supreme over local rivals and independent of outside authorities were nevertheless bound by common interests and rules. * * *

*   *   *

European International Society

In the eighteenth and nineteenth centuries, when the vestiges of Western Christendom came almost to disappear from the theory and practice of international politics, when the state came to be fully articulated, first in its dynastic or absolutist phase, then in its national or popular

phase, and when a body of modern inter-state practice came to be accumulated and studied, the idea of international society assumed a different form. * * *

The international society conceived by theorists of this period was identified as European rather than Christian in its values or culture. References to Christendom or to divine law as cementing the society of states declined and disappeared, as did religious oaths in treaties. References to Europe took their place, for example in the titles of their books: in the 1740s the Abbe de Mably published his *Droit public de l'Europe*, in the 1770s J. J. Moser his *Versuch des neuesten Europaischen Volkerrechts*, in the 1790s Burke denounced the regicide Directory of France for having violated "the public law of Europe."[4]

As the sense grew of the specifically European character of the society of states, so also did the sense of its cultural differentiation from what lay outside: the sense that European powers in their dealings with one another were bound by a code of conduct that did not apply to them in their dealings with other and lesser societies. * * *

*   *   *

World International Society

*   *   *

In the twentieth century international society ceased to be regarded as specifically European and came to be considered as global or world wide. * * *

Today, when non-European states represent the great majority in international society and the United Nations is nearly universal in its membership, the doctrine that this society rests upon a specific culture or civilisation is generally rejected. * * *

In the twentieth century, * * * there has been a retreat from the confident assertions, made in the age of Vattel [France, eighteenth century], that the members of international society were states and nations, towards the ambiguity and imprecision on this point that characterised the era of Grotius [Holland, seventeenth century].

The state as a bearer of rights and duties, legal and moral, in international society today is widely thought to be joined by international organisations, by non-state groups of various kinds operating across frontiers, and—as implied by the Nuremberg and Tokyo War Crimes Tribunals, and by the Universal Declaration of Human Rights—by individuals. There is no agreement as to the relative importance of these different kinds of legal and moral agents, or on any general scheme of rules that would relate them one to another, but Vattel's conception of a society simply of states has been under attack from many different directions.

*   *   *

The twentieth-century emphasis upon ideas of a reformed or improved international society, as distinct from the elements of society in actual practice, has led to a treatment of the League of Nations, the United Nations and other general international organisations as the chief institutions of international society, to the neglect of those institutions whose role in the maintenance of international order is the central one. Thus there has developed the Wilsonian rejection of the balance of power, the denigration of diplomacy and the tendency to seek to replace it by international administration, and a return to the tendency that prevailed in the Grotian era to confuse international law with international morality or international improvement.

*   *   *

The Element of Society

My contention is that the element of a society has always been present, and remains present, in the modern international system, although only as one of the elements in it, whose survival is sometimes precarious. The modern international system in fact reflects all three of the elements singled out, respectively, by the Hobbesian, the Kantian and the Grotian traditions: the element of war and struggle for power among states, the element of transnational soli-

darity and conflict, cutting across the divisions among states, and the element of cooperation and regulated intercourse among states. In different historical phases of the states system, in different geographical theatres of its operation, and in the policies of different states and statesmen, one of these three elements may predominate over the others.

*   *   *

Because international society is no more than one of the basic elements at work in modern international politics, and is always in competition with the elements of a state of war and of transnational solidarity or conflict, it is always erroneous to interpret international events as if international society were the sole or the dominant element. This is the error committed by those who speak or write as if the Concert of Europe, the League of Nations or the United Nations were the principal factors in international politics in their respective times; as if international law were to be assessed only in relation to the function it has of binding states together, and not also in relation to its function as an instrument of state interest and as a vehicle of transnational purposes; as if attempts to maintain a balance of power were to be interpreted only as endeavours to preserve the system of states, and not also as manoeuvres on the part of particular powers to gain ascendancy; as if great powers were to be viewed only as "great responsibles" or "great indispensables," and not also as great predators; as if wars were to be construed only as attempts to violate the law or to uphold it, and not also simply as attempts to advance the interests of particular states or of transnational groups. The element of international society is real, but the elements of a state of war and of transnational loyalties and divisions are real also, and to reify the first element, or to speak as if it annulled the second and third, is an illusion.

Moreover, the fact that international society provides some element of order in international politics should not be taken as justifying an attitude of complacency about it, or as showing that the arguments of those who are dissatisfied with the order provided by international society are without foundation. The order provided within modern international society is precarious and imperfect. To show that modern international society has provided some degree of order is not to have shown that order in world politics could not be provided more effectively by structures of a quite different kind.

NOTES

1. This threefold division derives from Martin Wight. The best published account of it is his "Western Values in International Relations," in *Diplomatic Investigations*, ed. Herbert Butterfield and Martin Wight (London: Allen & Unwin, 1967). The division is further discussed in my "Martin Wight and The Theory of International Relations. The Second Martin Wight Memorial Lecture," *British Journal of International Studies*, vol. II, no. 2 (1976).

2. In Kant's own doctrine there is of course ambivalence as between the universalism of *The Idea of Universal History from a Cosmopolitical Point Of View* (1784) and the position taken up in *Perpetual Peace* (1795), in which Kant accepts the substitute goal of a league of "republican" states.

3. I have myself used the term "Grotian" in two senses: (i) as here, to describe the broad doctrine that there is a society of states; (ii) to describe the solidarist form of this doctrine, which united Grotius himself and the twentieth-century neo-Grotians, in opposition to the pluralist conception of international society entertained by Vattel and later positivist writers. See "The Grotian Conception of International Society," in *Diplomatic Investigations*.

4. See "Third Letter on the Proposals for Peace with the Regicide Directory of France," in *The Works of the Right Honourable Edmund Burke*, ed. John C. Nimmo (London: Bohn's British Classics, 1887).

HANS MORGENTHAU

THE BALANCE OF POWER[1]

The aspiration for power on the part of several nations, each trying either to maintain or overthrow the status quo, leads of necessity to a configuration that is called the balance of power and to policies that aim at preserving it. We say "of necessity" advisedly. For here again we are confronted with the basic misconception that has impeded the understanding of interna-

From Hans Morgenthau, *Politics among Nations: The Struggle for Power and Peace*, 4th ed. (New York: Knopf, 1967), Chaps. 11, 12, 14. Some of the author's notes have been omitted.

tional politics and has made us the prey of illusions. This misconception asserts that men have a choice between power politics and its necessary outgrowth, the balance of power, on the other hand, and a different, better kind of international relations on the other. It insists that a foreign policy based on the balance of power is one among several possible foreign policies and that only stupid and evil men will choose the former and reject the latter.

It will be shown * * * that the international balance of power is only a particular manifestation of a general social principle to which all societies composed of a number of autonomous units owe the autonomy of their component parts; that the balance of power and policies aiming at its preservation are not only inevitable but are an essential stabilizing factor in a society of sovereign nations; and that the instability of the international balance of power is due not to the faultiness of the principle but to the particular conditions under which the principle must operate in a society of sovereign nations.

Social Equilibrium

Balance of Power as Universal Concept

The concept of "equilibrium" as a synonym for "balance" is commonly employed in many sciences—physics, biology, economics, sociology, and political science. It signifies stability within a system composed of a number of autonomous forces. Whenever the equilibrium is disturbed either by an outside force or by a change in one or the other elements composing the system, the system shows a tendency to re-establish either the original or a new equilibrium. Thus equilibrium exists in the human body. While the human body changes in the process of growth, the equilibrium persists as long as the changes occurring in the different organs of the body do not disturb the body's stability. This is especially so if the quantitative and qualitative changes in the different organs are proportionate to each other. When, however, the body suffers a wound or loss of one of its organs through outside interference, or experiences a malignant growth or a pathological transformation of one of its organs, the equilibrium is disturbed, and the body tries to overcome the disturbance by reestablishing the equilibrium either on the same or a different level from the one that obtained before the disturbance occurred.[2]

The same concept of equilibrium is used in a social science, such as economics, with reference to the relations between the different elements of the economic system, e.g., between savings and investments, exports and imports, supply and demand, costs and prices. Contemporary capitalism itself has been described as a system of "countervailing power."[3] It also applies to society as a whole. Thus we search for a proper balance between different geographical regions, such as the East and the West, the North and the South; between different kinds of activities, such as agriculture and industry, heavy and light industries, big and small businesses, producers and consumers, management and labor, between different functional groups, such as city and country, the old, the middle-aged, and the young, the economic and the political sphere, the middle classes and the upper and lower classes.

Two assumptions are at the foundation of all such equilibriums: first, that the elements to be balanced are necessary for society or are entitled to exist and, second, that without a state of equilibrium among them one element will gain ascendancy over the others, encroach upon their interests and rights, and may ultimately destroy them. Consequently, it is the purpose of all such equilibriums to maintain the stability of the system without destroying the multiplicity of the elements composing it. If the goal were stability alone, it could be achieved by allowing one element to destroy or overwhelm the others and take their place. Since the goal is stability plus the preservation of all the elements of the system, the equilibrium must aim at preventing any element from gaining ascendancy over the others. The means employed to maintain the equilibrium consist in allowing the different elements to pursue their opposing tendencies up to the point where the tendency of one is not so strong as to overcome the tendency of the others, but strong enough to prevent the others from overcoming its own. * * *

*   *   *

DIFFERENT METHODS OF THE BALANCE OF POWER

The balancing process can be carried on either by diminishing the weight of the heavier scale or by increasing the weight of the lighter one.

B. The former alternative is exemplified by the policy of compensations and the armament race as well as by disarmament; the latter, by the policy of alliances.

Divide and Rule

The former method has found its classic manifestation, aside from the imposition of onerous conditions in peace treaties and the incitement to treason and revolution, in the maxim "divide and rule." It has been resorted to by nations who tried to make or keep their competitors weak by dividing them or keeping them divided. The most consistent and important policies of this kind in modern times are the policy of France with respect to Germany and the policy of the Soviet Union with respect to the rest of Europe. From the seventeenth century to the end of the Second World War, it has been an unvarying principle of French foreign policy either to favor the division of the German Empire into a number of small independent states or to prevent the coalescence of such states into one unified nation. * * * Similarly, the Soviet Union from the twenties to the present has consistently opposed all plans for the unification of Europe, on the assumption that the pooling of the divided strength of the European nations into a "Western bloc" would give the enemies of the Soviet Union such power as to threaten the latter's security.

The other method of balancing the power of several nations consists in adding to the strength of the weaker nation. This method can be carried out by two different means: Either B can increase its power sufficiently to offset, if not surpass, the power of A, and vice versa; or B can pool its power with the power of all the other nations that pursue identical policies with regard to A, in which case A will pool its power with all the nations pursuing identical policies with respect to

Compensations

Compensations of a territorial nature were a common device in the eighteenth and nineteenth centuries for maintaining a balance of power which had been, or was to be, disturbed by the territorial acquisitions of one nation. The Treaty of Utrecht of 1713, which terminated the War of the Spanish Succession, recognized for the first time expressly the principle of the balance of power by way of territorial compensations. It provided for the division of most of the Spanish possessions, European and colonial, between the Hapsburgs and the Bourbons *ad conservandum in Europa equilibrium,* as the treaty put it.

*   *   *

In the latter part of the nineteenth and the beginning of the twentieth century, the principle of compensations was again deliberately applied to the distribution of colonial territories and the delimitation of colonial or semicolonial spheres of influence. Africa, in particular, was during that period the object of numerous treaties delimiting spheres of influence for the major colonial powers. Thus the competition between France, Great Britain, and Italy for the domination of Ethiopia was provisionally resolved * * * by the treaty of 1906, which divided the country into three spheres of influence for the purpose of establishing in that region a balance of power among the nations concerned. * * *

Even where the principle of compensations is not deliberately applied, however, * * * it is nowhere absent from political arrangements, territorial or other, made within a balance-of-power system. For, given such a system, no nation will agree to concede political advantages to another nation without the expectation, which may or may not be well founded, of receiving proportionate advantages in return. The bargaining of diplomatic negotiations, issuing in political compromise, is but the principle of compensations in its most general form, and as such it is organically connected with the balance of power.

Armaments

The principal means, however, by which a nation endeavors with the power at its disposal to maintain or re-establish the balance of power are armaments. The armaments race in which Nation A tries to keep up with, and then to outdo, the armaments of Nation B, and vice versa, is the typical instrumentality of an unstable, dynamic balance of power. The necessary corollary of the armaments race is a constantly increasing burden of military preparations devouring an ever greater portion of the national budget and making for ever deepening fears, suspicions, and insecurity. The situation preceding the First World War, with the naval competition between Germany and Great Britain and the rivalry of the French and German armies, illustrates this point.

It is in recognition of situations such as these that, since the end of the Napoleonic Wars, repeated attempts have been made to create a stable balance of power, if not to establish permanent peace, by means of the proportionate disarmament of competing nations. The technique of stabilizing the balance of power by means of a proportionate reduction of armaments is somewhat similar to the technique of territorial compensations. For both techniques require a quantitative evaluation of the influence that the arrangement is likely to exert on the respective power of the individual nations. The difficulties in making such a quantitative evaluation—in correlating, for instance, the military strength of the French army of 1932 with the military power represented by the industrial potential of Germany—

have greatly contributed to the failure of most attempts at creating a stable balance of power by means of disarmament. The only outstanding success of this kind was the Washington Naval Treaty of 1922, in which Great Britain, the United States, Japan, France, and Italy agreed to a proportionate reduction and limitation of naval armaments. Yet it must be noted that this treaty was part of an over-all political and territorial settlement in the Pacific which sought to stabilize the power relations in that region on the foundation of Anglo-American predominance.

Alliances

The historically most important manifestation of the balance of power, however, is to be found not in the equilibrium of two isolated nations but in the relations between one nation or alliance of nations and another alliance.

*   *   *

Alliances are a necessary function of the balance of power operating within a multiple-state system. Nations A and B, competing with each other, have three choices in order to maintain and improve their relative power positions. They can increase their own power, they can add to their own power the power of other nations, or they can withhold the power of other nations from the adversary. When they make the first choice, they embark upon an armaments race. When they choose the second and third alternatives, they pursue a policy of alliances.

Whether or not a nation shall pursue a policy of alliances is, then, a matter not of principle but of expediency. A nation will shun alliances if it believes that it is strong enough to hold its own unaided or that the burden of the commitments resulting from the alliance is likely to outweigh the advantages to be expected. It is for one or the other or both of these reasons that, throughout the better part of their history, Great Britain and the United States have refrained from entering into peacetime alliances with other nations.

*   *   *

The "Holder" of the Balance

Whenever the balance of power is to be realized by means of an alliance—and this has been generally so throughout the history of the Western world—two possible variations of this pattern have to be distinguished. To use the metaphor of the balance, the system may consist of two scales, in each of which are to be found the nation or nations identified with the same policy of the status quo or of imperialism. The continental nations of Europe have generally operated the balance of power in this way.

The system may, however, consist of two scales plus a third element, the "holder" of the balance or the "balancer." The balancer is not permanently identified with the policies of either nation or group of nations. Its only objective within the system is the maintenance of the balance, regardless of the concrete policies the balance will serve. In consequence, the holder of the balance will throw its weight at one time in this scale, at another time in the other scale, guided only by one consideration—the relative position of the scales. Thus it will put its weight always in the scale that seems to be higher than the other because it is lighter. The balancer may become in a relatively short span of history consecutively the friend and foe of all major powers, provided they all consecutively threaten the balance by approaching predominance over the others and are in turn threatened by others about to gain such predominance. To paraphrase a statement of Palmerston: while the holder of the balance has no permanent friends, it has no permanent enemies either; it has only the permanent interest of maintaining the balance of power itself.

The balancer is in a position of "splendid isolation." It is isolated by its own choice; for, while the two scales of the balance must vie with each other to add its weight to theirs in order to gain the overweight necessary for success, it must refuse to enter into permanent ties with either side. The holder of the balance waits in the middle in watchful detachment to see which scale is likely to sink. Its isolation is "splendid"; for, since its support or lack of support is the decisive factor in the struggle for power, its foreign policy, if cleverly managed, is able to extract the highest price from those whom it supports. But since this support, regardless of the price paid for it, is always uncertain and shifts from one side to the other in accordance with the movements of the balance, its policies are resented and subject to condemnation on moral grounds. Thus it has been said of the outstanding balancer in modern times, Great Britain, that it lets others fight its wars, that it keeps Europe divided in order to dominate the continent, and that the fickleness of its policies is such as to make alliances with Great Britain impossible. "Perfidious Albion" has become a byword in the mouths of those who either were unable to gain Great Britain's support, however hard they tried, or else lost it after they had paid what seemed to them too high a price.

The holder of the balance occupies the key position in the balance-of-power system, since its position determines the outcome of the struggle for power. It has, therefore, been called the "arbiter" of the system, deciding who will win and who will lose. By making it impossible for any nation or combination of nations to gain predominance over the others, it preserves its own independence as well as the independence of all the other nations, and is thus a most powerful factor in international politics.

The holder of the balance can use this power in three different ways. It can make its joining one or the other nation or alliance dependent upon certain conditions favorable to the maintenance or restoration of the balance. It can make its support of the peace settlement dependent upon similar conditions. It can, finally, in either situation see to it that the objectives of its own national policy, apart from the maintenance of the balance of power, are realized in the process of balancing the power of others.

*   *   *

EVALUATION OF THE BALANCE OF POWER

*   *   *

The Unreality of the Balance of Power

[The] uncertainty of all power calculations not only makes the balance of power incapable of practical application but leads also to its very negation in practice. Since no nation can be sure that its calculation of the distribution of power at any particular moment in history is correct, it must at least make sure that, whatever errors it may commit, they will not put the nation at a disadvantage in the contest for power. In other words, the nation must try to have at least a margin of safety which will allow it to make erroneous calculations and still maintain the balance of power. To that effect, all nations actively engaged in the struggle for power must actually aim not at a balance—that is, equality—of power, but at superiority of power in their own behalf. And since no nation can foresee how large its miscalculations will turn out to be, all nations must ultimately seek the maximum of power obtainable under the circumstances. Only thus can they hope to attain the maximum margin of safety commensurate with the maximum of errors they might commit. The limitless aspiration for power, potentially always present * * * in the power drives of nations, finds in the balance of power a mighty incentive to transform itself into an actuality.

Since the desire to attain a maximum of power is universal, all nations must always be afraid that their own miscalculations and the power increases of other nations might add up to an inferiority for themselves which they must at all costs try to avoid. Hence all nations who have gained an apparent edge over their competitors tend to consolidate that advantage and use it for changing the distribution of power permanently in their favor. This can be done through diplomatic pressure by bringing the full weight of that advantage to bear upon the other nations, compelling them to make the concessions that will consolidate the temporary advantage into a permanent superiority. It can also be done by war. Since in a balance-of-power system all nations live in constant fear lest their rivals deprive them, at the first opportune moment, of their power position, all nations have a vital interest in anticipating such a development and doing unto the others what they do not want the others to do unto them. * * *

NOTES

1. The term "balance of power" is used in the text with four different meanings: (1) as a policy aimed at a certain state of affairs, (2) as an actual state of affairs, (3) as an approximately equal distribution of power, (4) as any distribution of power. Whenever the term is used without qualification, it refers to an actual state of affairs in which power is distributed among several nations with approximate equality. * * *

2. Cf., for instance, the impressive analogy between the equilibrium in the human body and in society in Walter B. Cannon, *The Wisdom of the Body* (New York: W. W. Norton and Company, 1932), pp. 293, 294: "At the outset it is noteworthy that the body politic itself exhibits some indications of crude automatic stabilizing processes. In the previous chapter I expressed the postulate that a certain degree of constancy in a complex system is itself evidence that agencies are acting or are ready to act to maintain that constancy. And moreover, that when a system remains steady it does so because any tendency towards change is met by increased effectiveness of the factor or factors which resist the change. Many familiar facts prove that these statements are to some degree true for soci-

ety even in its present unstabilized condition. A display of conservatism excites a radical revolt and that in turn is followed by a return to conservatism. Loose government and its consequences bring the reformers into power, but their tight reins soon provoke restiveness and the desire for release. The noble enthusiasms and sacrifices of war are succeeded by moral apathy and orgies of self-indulgence. Hardly any strong tendency in a nation continues to the stage of disaster; before that extreme is reached corrective forces arise which check the tendency and they commonly prevail to such an excessive degree as themselves to cause a reaction. A study of the nature of these social swings and their reversal might lead to valuable understanding and possibly to means of more narrowly limiting the disturbances. At this point, however, we merely note that the disturbances are roughly limited, and that this limitation suggests, perhaps, the early stages of social homeostasis." (Reprinted by permission of the publisher. Copyright 1932, 1939, by Walter B. Cannon.)

3. John K. Galbraith, *American Capitalism, the Concept of Countervailing Power* (Boston: Houghton Mifflin, 1952).

IMMANUEL WALLERSTEIN

THE RISE AND FUTURE DEMISE OF THE WORLD CAPITALIST SYSTEM: CONCEPTS FOR COMPARATIVE ANALYSIS

The growth within the capitalist world-economy of the industrial sector of production, the so-called industrial revolution, was accompanied by a very strong current of thought which defined this change as both a process of organic development and of progress. There were those who considered these economic developments and the concomitant changes in social organization to be some penultimate stage of world development whose final working out was but a matter of time. These included such diverse thinkers as Saint-Simon, Comte, Hegel, Weber, Durkheim. And then there were the critics, most notably Marx, who argued, if you will, that the nineteenth-century present was only an ante-

penultimate stage of development, that the capitalist world was to know a cataclysmic political revolution which would then lead in the fullness of time to a final societal form, in this case the classless society.

One of the great strengths of Marxism was that, being an oppositional and hence critical doctrine, it called attention not merely to the contradictions of the system but to those of its ideologists, by appealing to the empirical evidence of historical reality which unmasked the irrelevancy of the models proposed for the explanation of the social world. The Marxist critics saw in abstracted models concrete rationalization, and they argued their case fundamentally by pointing to the failure of their opponents to analyze the social whole. * * *

From *Comparative Studies in Society and History* 14, no. 4 (1974): 387–415. Some of the author's notes have been omitted.

*   *   *

We take the defining characteristic of a social system to be the existence within it of a division of labor, such that the various sectors or areas within are dependent upon economic exchange with others for the smooth and continuous provisioning of the needs of the area. Such economic exchange can clearly exist without a common political structure and even more obviously without sharing the same culture.

A minisystem is an entity that has within it a complete division of labor, and a single cultural framework. Such systems are found only in very simple agricultural or hunting and gathering societies. Such minisystems no longer exist in the world. Furthermore, there were fewer in the past than is often asserted, since any such system that became tied to an empire by the payment of tribute as "protection costs"[1] ceased by that fact to be a "system," no longer having a self-contained division of labor. For such an area, the payment of tribute marked a shift, in Polanyi's language, from being a reciprocal economy to participating in a larger redistributive economy.[2]

Leaving aside the now defunct minisystems, the only kind of social system is a world-system, which we define quite simply as a unit with a single division of labor and multiple cultural systems. It follows logically that there can, however, be two varieties of such world-systems, one with a common political system and one without. We shall designate these respectively as world-empires and world-economies.

It turns out empirically that world-economies have historically been unstable structures leading either towards disintegration or conquest by one group and hence transformation into a world-empire. Examples of such world-empires emerging from world-economies are all the so-called great civilizations of premodern times, such as China, Egypt, Rome (each at appropriate periods of its history). On the other hand, the so-called nineteenth-century empires, such as Great Britain or France, were not world-empires at all, but nation-states with colonial appendages operating within the framework of a world-economy.

World-empires were basically redistributive in economic form. No doubt they bred clusters of merchants who engaged in economic exchange (primarily long distance trade), but such clusters, however large, were a minor part of the total economy, and not fundamentally determinative of its fate. * * *

It was only with the emergence of the modern world-economy in sixteenth-century Europe that we saw the full development and economic predominance of market trade. This was the system called capitalism. Capitalism and a world-economy (that is, a single division of labor but multiple polities and cultures) are obverse sides of the same coin. One does not cause the other. We are merely defining the same indivisible phenomenon by different characteristics.

How and why it came about that this particular European world-economy of the sixteenth century did not become transformed into a redistributive world-empire but developed definitively as a capitalist world-economy I have explained elsewhere.[3] The genesis of this world-historical turning point is marginal to the issues under discussion in this paper, which is rather what conceptual apparatus one brings to bear on the analysis of developments within the framework of precisely such a capitalist world-economy.

Let us therefore turn to the capitalist world-economy. * * *

*   *   *

We must start with how one demonstrates the existence of a single division of labor. We can regard a division of labor as a grid which is substantially interdependent. Economic actors operate on some assumption (obviously seldom clear to any individual actor) that the totality of their essential needs—of sustenance, protection, and pleasure—will be met over a reasonable time span by a combination of their own productive activities and exchange in some form. The smallest grid that would substantially meet the expectations of the overwhelming majority of actors within those boundaries constitutes a single division of labor.

The reason why a small farming community whose only significant link to outsiders is the payment of annual tribute does not constitute such a single division of labor is that the assumptions of persons living in it concerning the provision of protection involve an "exchange" with other parts of the world-empire.

This concept of a grid of exchange relationships assumes, however, a distinction between *essential* exchanges and what might be called "luxury" exchanges. This is to be sure a distinction rooted in the social perceptions of the actors and hence in both their social organization and their culture. These perceptions can change. But this distinction is crucial if we are not to fall into the trap of identifying *every* exchange activity as evidence of the existence of a system. Members of a system (a minisystem or a world-system) can be linked in limited exchanges with elements located outside the system, in the "external arena" of the system.

The form of such an exchange is very limited. Elements of the two systems can engage in an exchange of preciosities. That is, each can export to the other what is in *its* system socially defined as worth little in return for the import of what in its system is defined as worth much. This is not a mere pedantic definitional exercise, as the exchange of preciosities *between* world-systems can be extremely important in the historical evolution of a given world-system. The reason why this is so important is that in an exchange of preciosities, the importer is "reaping a windfall" and not obtaining a profit. Both exchange partners can reap windfalls simultaneously but only one can obtain maximum profit, since the exchange of surplus value within a system is a zero-sum game.

We are, as you see, coming to the essential feature of a capitalist world-economy, which is production for sale in a market in which the object is to realize the maximum profit. In such a system production is constantly expanded as long as further production is profitable, and men constantly innovate new ways of producing things that will expand the profit margin. The classical economists tried to argue that such production for the market was somehow the "natural" state of man. But the combined writings of the anthropologists and the Marxists left few in doubt that such a mode of production (these days called "capitalism") was only one of several possible modes.

Since, however, the intellectual debate between the liberals and the Marxists took place in the era of the industrial revolution, there has tended to be a *de facto* confusion between industrialism and capitalism. This left the liberals after 1945 in the dilemma of explaining how a presumably noncapitalist society, the USSR, had industrialized. The most sophisticated response has been to conceive of "liberal capitalism" and "socialism" as two variants of an "industrial society," two variants destined to "converge." * * * But the same confusion left the Marxists, including Marx, with the problem of explaining what was the mode of production that predominated in Europe from the sixteenth to the eighteenth centuries, that is before the industrial revolution. Essentially, most Marxists have talked of a "transitional" stage, which is in fact a blurry nonconcept with no operational indicators. This dilemma is heightened if the unit of analysis used is the state, in which case one has to explain why the transition has occurred at different rates and times in different countries.

Marx himself handled this by drawing a distinction between "merchant capitalism" and "industrial capitalism." This I believe is unfortunate teminology, since it leads to such conclusions as that of Maurice Dobb who says of this "transitional" period:

> But why speak of this as a stage of capitalism at all? The workers were generally not proletarianized: that is, they were not separated from the instruments of production, nor even in many cases from occupation of a plot of land. Production was scattered and decentralized and not concentrated. *The capitalist was still predominantly a merchant* [italics mine] who did not control production directly and did not impose his own discipline upon the work of artisan-craftsmen, who both laboured as individual (or family) units and retained a considerable measure of independence (if a dwindling one).[4]

One might well say: why indeed? Especially if one remembers how much emphasis Dobb places a few pages earlier on capitalism as a mode of *production*—how then can the capitalist be primarily a merchant?—on the concentration of such ownership in the hands of a few, and on the fact that capitalism is not synonymous with private ownership, capitalism being different from a system in which the owners are "small peasant producers or artisan-producers." Dobb argues that a defining feature of private ownership under capitalism is that some are "obliged to [work for those that own] since [they own] nothing and [have] no access to means of production [and hence] have no other means of livelihood."[5] Given this contradiction, the answer Dobb gives to his own question is in my view very weak: "While it is true that at this date the situation was transitional, and capital-to-wage-labour relations were still immaturely developed, the latter were already beginning to assume their characteristic features."[6]

If capitalism is a mode of production, production for profit in a market, then we ought, I should have thought, to look to whether or not such production was or was not occurring. It turns out in fact that it was, and in a very substantial form. Most of this production, however, was not industrial production. What was happening in Europe from the sixteenth to the eighteenth centuries is that over a large geographical area going from Poland in the northeast westwards and southwards throughout Europe and including large parts of the Western Hemisphere as well, there grew up a world-economy with a single division of labor within which there was a world market, for which men produced largely agricultural products for sale and profit. I would think the simplest thing to do would be to call this agricultural capitalism.

This then resolves the problems incurred by using the pervasiveness of *wage* labor as a defining characteristic of capitalism. An individual is no less a capitalist exploiting labor because the state assists him to pay his laborers low wages (including wages in kind) and denies these laborers the right to change employment. Slavery and

so-called second serfdom are not to be regarded as anomalies in a capitalist system. Rather the so-called serf in Poland or the Indian on a Spanish *encomienda* in New Spain in this sixteenth-century world-economy were working for landlords who "paid" them (however euphemistic this term) for cash crop production. This is a relationship in which labor power is a commodity (how could it ever be more so than under slavery?), quite different from the relationship of a feudal serf to his lord in eleventh-century Burgundy, where the economy was not oriented to a world market, and where labor power was (therefore?) in no sense bought or sold.

Capitalism thus means labor as a commodity to be sure. But in the era of agricultural capitalism, wage labor is only one of the modes in which labor is recruited and recompensed in the labor market. Slavery, coerced cash-crop production (my name for the so-called second feudalism), sharecropping, and tenancy are all alternative modes. It would be too long to develop here the conditions under which differing regions of the world-economy tend to specialize in different agricultural products. * * *

What we must notice now is that this specialization occurs in specific and differing geographic regions of the world-economy. This regional specialization comes about by the attempts of actors in the market to avoid the normal operation of the market whenever it does not maximize their profit. The attempts of these actors to use non-market devices to ensure short-run profits makes them turn to the political entities which have in fact power to affect the market—the nation-states. * * *

In any case, the local capitalist classes—cash-crop landowners (often, even usually, nobility) and merchants—turned to the state, not only to liberate them from non-market constraints (as traditionally emphasized by liberal historiography) but to create new constraints on the new market, the market of the European world-economy.

By a series of accidents—historical, ecological, geographic—northwest Europe was better situated in the sixteenth century to diversify its agricultural specialization and add to it certain industries (such as textiles, shipbuilding, and metal wares) than were other parts of Europe. Northwest Europe emerged as the core area of this world-economy, specializing in agricultural production of higher skill levels, which favored (again for reasons too complex to develop) tenancy and wage labor as the modes of labor control. Eastern Europe and the Western Hemisphere became peripheral areas specializing in export of grains, bullion, wood, cotton, sugar—all of which favored the use of slavery and coerced cash-crop labor as the modes of labor control. Mediterranean Europe emerged as the semiperipheral area of this world-economy specializing in high-cost industrial products (for example, silks) and credit and specie transactions, which had as a consequence in the agricultural arena sharecropping as the mode of labor control and little export to other areas.

The three structural positions in a world-economy—core, periphery, and semiperiphery—had become stabilized by about 1640. How certain areas became one and not the other is a long story.[7] The key fact is that given slightly different starting points, the interests of various local groups converged in northwest Europe, leading to the development of strong state mechanisms, and diverged sharply in the peripheral areas, leading to very weak ones. Once we get a difference in the strength of the state machineries, we get the operation of "unequal exchange"[8] which is enforced by strong states on weak ones, by core states on peripheral areas. Thus capitalism involves not only appropriation of the surplus value by an owner from a laborer, but an appropriation of surplus of the whole world-economy by core areas. * * *

In the early Middle Ages, there was to be sure trade. But it was largely either "local," in a region that we might call the "extended" manor, or "long-distance," primarily of luxury goods. There was no exchange of "bulk" goods, of "staples" across intermediate-size areas, and hence no production for such markets. Later on in the Middle Ages, world-economies may be said to have come

into existence, one centering on Venice, a second on the cities of Flanders and the Hanse. For various reasons, these structures were hurt by the retractions (economic, demographic, and ecological) of the period 1300–1450. It is only with the creating of a *European* division of labor after 1450 that capitalism found firm roots.

Capitalism was from the beginning an affair of the world-economy and not of nation-states. It is a misreading of the situation to claim that it is only in the twentieth century that capitalism has become "world-wide," although this claim is frequently made in various writings, particularly by Marxists. Typical of this line of argument is Charles Bettelheim's response to Arghiri Emmanuel's discussion of unequal exchange:

> The tendency of the capitalist mode of production to become worldwide is manifested not only through the constitution of a group of national economies forming a complex and hierarchical structure, including an imperialist pole and a dominated one, and not only through the antagonistic relations that develop between the different "national economies" and the different states, but also through the constant "transcending" of "national limits" by big capital (the formation of "international big capital," "world firms," etc. . . .).[9]

The whole tone of these remarks ignores the fact that capital has never allowed its aspirations to be determined by national boundaries in a capitalist world-economy, and that the creation of "national" barriers—generically, mercantilism—has historically been a defensive mechanism of capitalists located in states which are one level below the high point of strength in the system. Such was the case of England *vis-à-vis* the Netherlands in 1660–1715, France *vis-à-vis* England in 1715–1815, Germany *vis-à-vis* Britain in the nineteenth century, the Soviet Union *vis-à-vis* the US in the twentieth. In the process a large number of countries create national economic barriers whose consequences often last beyond their initial objectives. At this later point in the process the very same capitalists who pressed their national governments to impose the restrictions now find these restrictions constraining.

This is not an "internationalization" of "national" capital. This is simply a new political demand by certain sectors of the capitalist classes who have at all points in time sought to maximize their profits within the real economic market, that of the world-economy.

If this is so, then what meaning does it have to talk of structural positions within this economy and identify states as being in one of these positions? And why talk of three positions, inserting that of "semiperiphery" in between the widely used concepts of core and periphery? The state machineries of the core states were strengthened to meet the needs of capitalist landowners and their merchant allies. But that does not mean that these state machineries were manipulable puppets. Obviously any organization, once created, has a certain autonomy from those who pressed it into existence for two reasons. It creates a stratum of officials whose own careers and interests are furthered by the continued strengthening of the organization itself, however the interests of its capitalist backers may vary. Kings and bureaucrats wanted to stay in power and increase their personal gain constantly. Secondly, in the process of creating the strong state in the first place, certain "constitutional" compromises had to be made with other forces within the state boundaries and these institutionalized compromises limit, as they are designed to do, the freedom of maneuver of the managers of the state machinery. The formula of the state as "executive committee of the ruling class" is only valid, therefore, if one bears in mind that executive committees are never mere reflections of the wills of their constituents, as anyone who has ever participated in any organization knows well.

The strengthening of the state machineries in core areas has as its direct counterpart the decline of the state machineries in peripheral areas. The decline of the Polish monarchy in the sixteenth and seventeenth centuries is a striking example of this phenomenon.[10] There are two reasons for this. In peripheral countries, the interests of the capitalist landowners lie in an opposite direction from those of the local commercial bourgeoisie. Their interests lie in maintaining an open economy to maximize their profit from world-market trade (no restrictions in exports and access to lower-cost industrial products from core countries) and in elimination of the commercial bourgeoisie in favor of outside merchants (who pose no local political threat). Thus, in terms of the state, the coalition which strengthened it in core countries was precisely absent.

The second reason, which has become ever more operative over the history of the modern world-system, is that the strength of the state machinery in core states is a function of the weakness of other state machineries. Hence intervention of outsiders via war, subversion, and diplomacy is the lot of peripheral states.

All this seems very obvious. I repeat it only in order to make clear two points. One cannot reasonably explain the strength of various state machineries at specific moments of the history of the modern world-system primarily in terms of a genetic-cultural line of argumentation, but rather in terms of the structural role a country plays in the world-economy at that moment in time. To be sure, the initial eligibility for a particular role is often decided by an accidental edge a particular country has, and the "accident" of which one is talking is no doubt located in part in past history, in part in current geography. But once this relatively minor accident is given, it is the operations of the world-market forces which accentuate the differences, institutionalize them, and make them impossible to surmount over the short run.

The second point we wish to make about the structural differences of core and periphery is that they are not comprehensible unless we realize that there is a third structural position: that of the semi-periphery. This is not the result merely of establishing arbitrary cutting-points on a continuum of characteristics. Our logic is not merely inductive, sensing the presence of a third category from a comparison of indicator curves. It is also deductive. The semiperiphery is needed to make a capitalist world-economy run smoothly. Both kinds of world-system, the world-empire with a redistributive economy and the world-economy with a capitalist market economy, involve markedly unequal distribution of rewards. Thus, logically, there is immediately posed the question of how it is possible politically for such a system to persist. Why do not the majority who are exploited simply overwhelm the minority who draw disproportionate benefits? The most rapid glance at the historic record shows that these world-systems have been faced rather rarely by fundamental system-wide insurrection. While internal discontent has been eternal, it has usually taken quite long before the accumulation of the erosion of power has led to the decline of a world-system, and as often as not, an external force has been a major factor in this decline.

There have been three major mechanisms that have enabled world-systems to retain relative political stability * * *. One obviously is the concentration of military strength in the hands of the dominant forces. * * *

A second mechanism is the pervasiveness of an ideological commitment to the system as a whole. I do not mean what has often been termed the "legitimation" of a system, because that term has been used to imply that the lower strata of a system feel some affinity with or loyalty towards the rulers, and I doubt that this has ever been a significant factor in the survival of world-systems. I mean rather the degree to which the staff or cadres of the system (and I leave this term deliberately vague) feel that their own well-being is wrapped up in the survival of the system as such and the competence of its leaders. It is this staff which not only propagates the myths; it is they who believe them.

But neither force nor the ideological commitment of the staff would suffice were it not for the division of the majority into a larger lower stratum and a smaller middle stratum. Both the revolutionary call for polarization as a strategy of change and the liberal encomium to consensus as the basis of the liberal polity reflect this proposition. The import is far wider than its use in the

analysis of contemporary political problems suggests. It is the normal condition of either kind of world-system to have a three-layered structure. When and if this ceases to be the case, the world-system disintegrates.

In a world-empire, the middle stratum is in fact accorded the role of maintaining the marginally desirable long-distance luxury trade, while the upper stratum concentrates its resources on controlling the military machinery which can collect the tribute, the crucial mode of redistributing surplus. By providing, however, for an access to a limited portion of the surplus to urbanized elements who alone, in premodern societies, could contribute political cohesiveness to isolated clusters of primary producers, the upper stratum effectively buys off the potential leadership of coordinated revolt. And by denying access to political rights for this commercial-urban middle stratum, it makes them constantly vulnerable to confiscatory measures whenever their economic profits become sufficiently swollen so that they might begin to create for themselves military strength.

In a world-economy, such "cultural" stratification is not so simple, because the absence of a single political system means the concentration of economic roles vertically rather than horizontally throughout the system. The solution then is to have three *kinds* of states, with pressures for cultural homogenization within each of them— thus, besides the upper stratum of core states and the lower stratum of peripheral states, there is a middle stratum of semiperipheral ones.

This semiperiphery is then assigned as it were a specific economic role, but the reason is less economic than political. That is to say, one might make a good case that the world-economy as an economy would function every bit as well without a semiperiphery. But it would be far less *politically* stable, for it would mean a polarized world-system. The existence of the third category means precisely that the upper stratum is not faced with the *unified* opposition of all the others because the *middle* stratum is both exploited and exploiter. It follows that the specific economic role is not all that important, and has thus changed through the various historical stages of the modern world-system. * * *

Where then does class analysis fit in all of this? And what in such a formulation are nations, nationalities, peoples, ethnic groups? First of all, without arguing the point now,[11] I would contend that all these latter terms denote variants of a single phenomenon which I will term "ethno-nations."

Both classes and ethnic groups, or status groups, or ethno-nations are phenomena of world-economies and much of the enormous confusion that has surrounded the concrete analysis of their functioning can be attributed quite simply to the fact that they have been analyzed as though they existed within the nation-states of this world-economy, instead of within the world-economy as a whole. This has been a Procrustean bed indeed.

The range of economic activities being far wider in the core than in the periphery, the range of syndical interest groups is far wider there. Thus, it has been widely observed that there does not exist in many parts of the world today a proletariat of the kind which exists in, say, Europe or North America. But this is a confusing way to state the observation. Industrial activity being disproportionately concentrated in certain parts of the world-economy, industrial wage workers are to be found principally in certain geographic regions. Their interests as a syndical group are determined by their collective relationship to the world-economy. Their ability to influence the political functioning of this world-economy is shaped by the fact that they command larger percentages of the population in one sovereign entity than another. The form their organizations take have, in large part, been governed too by these political boundaries. The same might be said about industrial capitalists. Class analysis is perfectly capable of accounting for the political position of, let us say, French skilled workers if we look at their structural position and interests in the world-economy. Similarly with ethno-nations. The meaning of ethnic consciousness in a core area is considerably different from that of

ethnic consciousness in a peripheral area precisely because of the different class position such ethnic groups have in the world-economy.[12]

Political struggles of ethno-nations or segments of classes within national boundaries of course are the daily bread and butter of local politics. But their significance or consequences can only be fruitfully analyzed if one spells out the implications of their organizational activity or political demands for the functioning of the world-economy. This also incidentally makes possible more rational assessments of these politics in terms of some set of evaluative criteria such as "left" and "right."

The functioning then of a capitalist world-economy requires that groups pursue their economic interests within a single world market while seeking to distort this market for their benefit by organizing to exert influence on states, some of which are far more powerful than others but none of which controls the world market in its entirety. Of course, we shall find on closer inspection that there are periods where one state is relatively quite powerful and other periods where power is more diffuse and contested, permitting weaker states broader ranges of action. We can talk then of the relative tightness or looseness of the world-system as an important variable and seek to analyze why this dimension tends to be cyclical in nature, as it seems to have been for several hundred years.

*   *   *

* * * We have adumbrated as our basic unit of observation a concept of world-systems that have structural parts and evolving stages. It is within such a framework, I am arguing, that we can fruitfully make comparative analyses—of the wholes and of parts of the whole. Conceptions precede and govern measurements. I am all for minute and sophisticated quantitative indicators. I am all for minute and diligent archival work that will trace a concrete historical series of events in terms of all its immediate complexities. But the point of either is to enable us to see better what has happened and what is happening. For that we need glasses with which to discern

the dimensions of difference, we need models with which to weigh significance, we need summarizing concepts with which to create the knowledge which we then seek to communicate to each other. And all this because we are men with hybris and original sin and therefore seek the good, the true, and the beautiful.

NOTES

1. See Frederic Lane's discussion of "protection costs" which is reprinted in part 3 of *Venice and History* (Baltimore: Johns Hopkins Press, 1966). For the specific discussion of tribute, see pp. 389–90, 416–20.

2. See Karl Polanyi, "The Economy as Instituted Process," in Karl Polanyi, Conrad M. Arsenberg and Harry W. Pearson (eds.), *Trade and Market in the Early Empire* (Glencoe: Free Press, 1957), pp. 243–70.

3. See my *The Modern World-System: Capitalist Agriculture and the Origins of the European World-Economy in the Sixteenth Century* (New York: Academic Press, 1974).

4. Maurice Dobb, *Capitalism Yesterday and Today* (London: Lawrence and Wishart, 1958), p. 21.

5. *Ibid.*, pp. 6–7.

6. *Ibid.*, p. 21.

7. I give a brief account of this in "Three Paths of National Development in the Sixteenth Century," *Studies in Comparative International Development*, 7: 2 (Summer 1972) 95–101, and below, ch. 2.

8. See Arghiri Emmanuel, *Unequal Exchange* (New York: Monthly Review Press, 1972).

9. Charles Bettelheim, "Theoretical Comments," in Emmanuel, *Unequal Exchange*, p. 295.

10. See J. Siemenski, "Constitutional Conditions in the Fifteenth and Sixteenth Centuries," in *Cambridge History of Poland*, vol. 1, W. F. Reddaway *et al.* (eds.), *From the Origins to Sobieski (to 1696)* (Cambridge: University Press, 1950), pp. 416–40; Janusz Tazbir, "The Commonwealth of the Gentry," in Aleksander Gieysztor *et al.*, *History of Poland* (Warszawa: PWN—Polish Scientific Publications, 1968), pp. 169–271.

11. See my fuller analysis in "Social Conflict in Post-Independence Black Africa: The Concepts of Race and Status-Group Reconsidered," in Ernest Q. Campbell (ed.), *Racial Tensions and National Identity* (Nashville: Vanderbilt University Press, 1972), pp. 207–26.

12. See my "The Two Modes of Ethnic Consciousness: Soviet Central Asia in Transition?" in Edward Allworth (ed.), *The Nationality Question in Soviet Central Asia* (New York: Praeger, 1973), pp. 168–75.

WILLIAM R. THOMPSON

SYSTEMIC LEADERSHIP, EVOLUTIONARY PROCESSES, AND INTERNATIONAL RELATIONS THEORY: THE UNIPOLARITY QUESTION

The Chinese curse—"may you live in interesting times"—applies fully to international relations theory, but in reverse. For people intrigued by such theory, interesting times are not a curse because noninteresting times encourage little in the way of theoretical novelty and progress. International change and turmoil—perhaps subject to some ceiling threshold—dramatize analytical puzzles that invite speculation and theory construction.

A case in point is systemic analysis. Periods of recognized macro-structural change tend to be good for systemic analyses. In particular, periods in which the leading power is in decline and other states seem to be catching up are especially good times for systemic analysis. Distributions of power seem to be in flux. The potential for great mischief, revised status quos, and intensive violence seem to be in the offing. Uncertain futures make people uneasy and especially attentive to structural arguments. The late 1970s through the early 1990s was such a period. But then some things happened. The Soviet Union fell apart. The Japanese economic challenge fizzled. The United States not only persisted as the world's sole superpower survivor, it was hard pressed to find any semblance of peer competitors. The world system seemingly had become unipolar literally overnight. For many analysts, this was the first instance of unipolarity in a planetary-wide international system that had so far swung only from multipolarity to bipolarity.

This structural change has generated continuing debate about what it means and how we should interpret it. The arguments, unfortunately, have not led to a widespread revival of systemic theorizing. But the renewed interest in such questions is most heartening in a world dominated by too many politicians who view international affairs through starkly monadic lenses and too many international relations analysts who are captivated (and captured) by exclusively dyadic frameworks. In the course of the debate, some very interesting new ideas have emerged as well as some that are less than fully persuasive.

Within this context, I propose to join the debate by tackling the "unipolar question" from a leadership long cycle perspective. At issue is where we are systemically and, as a consequence, what we might anticipate. First, I will sketch the leadership long cycle perspective to establish the ideational foundation on which this essay builds, and, then, examine fifteen assertions found in the unipolarity literature that I think are dubious or debatable. The point is not simply to throw critical rocks at a host of disconnected generalizations, although some of that is inevitable, but to highlight theoretical problems, positively and negatively, to see if we cannot improve on our ability to tell "system time"—that is, where we are in the evolution of the world's political-military structure and what it portends for world politics.

Unipolarity and the Leadership Long Cycle Perspective

Unipolarity is a relatively alien concept in most international relations theory. It is not something

From *International Studies Review* 8 no. 1 (March 2006), 1–22. The author's notes have been omitted.

that is supposed to happen, courtesy of balance-of-power reactions, according to most realists. Power concentration of this sort is rarely germane to liberals who prefer to focus on domestic attributes and processes anyway. Constructivists, for the most part, seem also unlikely to devote much time to categories of systemic power distributions. Historical-structural approaches, in contrast, are fairly comfortable with the notion of power concentration by a single leading actor because these approaches often assume intermittent unipolarity as a fundamental factor in their explanations.

One historical-structural approach, leadership long cycle theory, examines the systemic evolution of power, leadership, and structural order. A variety of circumstances in the first half of the second millennium CE gave Western Europe an opportunity to establish itself as the central region in the world system. Not all European states seized this opportunity and many of the most successful were marginal players by regional standards. Specializing in long-distance commerce, some states chose to focus on activities outside of their home region. Venice, Portugal, the Netherlands, and Britain proved to be the most successful of these maritime-commercial powers. Other states continued to pursue more traditional strategies of expanding their home bases within the local region. Still others tried to pursue both types of strategies, usually waffling back and forth between the two types of endeavors. Spain and France were the most prominent wafflers.

The distinctions between these two fundamental strategies lent themselves to a two-game differentiation between regional and global politics. The former game was mainly about territorial expansion carried out by large and increasingly well-armed armies in relatively adjacent space. The other revolved around the management of interregional trade, its associated problems, and the consequent need for maritime capabilities. From time to time, attempts to unify the European region spilled over into global politics because regional hegemony constituted direct and indirect threats to the status quo of the global political economy. Global wars, listed in Table 1, were fought in part to suppress the regional threats and in part to determine who would make policy at the global level. In this latter respect, global wars have served as periodic political selection instruments, not unlike elections in state political systems—only more deadly and primitive.

Yet, there is more to global warfare than the simple intermittent fusing of global and regional affairs. Long-term economic growth, according to the leadership long cycle perspective, is based

Table 1. Global Wars

Global War	Timing	Issues
Italian/Indian Ocean Wars	1490s–1510s	Franco-Spanish contest over Italian states; Portuguese breaking of Venetian/Mameluke eastern trade monopoly
Dutch Independence War	1580s–1600s	Opposition to Phillip II's expansion; Dutch breaking of Spanish/Portuguese eastern trade monopoly
Louis XIV Wars	1680s–1710s	Opposition to Louis XIV expansion; French attempt to break Dutch trading monopoly in Europe and elsewhere
French Revolutionary/ Napoleonic Wars	1790s–1810s	Opposition to French expansion; French attempt to resist British industrial lead and systemic leadership
World Wars I and II	1910s–1940s	Opposition to German expansion; German attempt to succeed Britain as system leader

on radical shifts in commercial and technological innovations that tend to be concentrated initially in one state at a time. A spurt of growth in one state revolutionizes best economic practices and also destabilizes the international system's pecking order. The ensuing global war, assuming a decisive outcome, restabilizes the global system by producing a clear winner—the state with the system's lead economy or principal source of innovation and, later, credit and finance. The benefits of war-induced growth and a world economy tilted in its direction then leads to a second, postwar spurt of innovation and growth. In this fashion, each lead economy experiences at least one "twin peak" set of growth built around a long global war period.

On the basis of the schedule of leading sector indicators in Table 2 (the activities or industries in which the radical innovations have taken place), Figure 4.1 plots the rough timing of the successive economic life cycles of the leading global powers (Portugal, the Netherlands, Britain, and the United States). The first two system leaders experienced one set of twin peaks. Britain enjoyed a double set or four successive peaks. The United States has led the world economy through one set of twin peaks and may be set to preside over a second set.

Another way of keeping track of systemic leadership is to look at the distribution of naval capabilities—the power medium that, historically, has been most appropriate for expanding and defending long distance trade, which was primarily maritime trade after 1500. Contrary to popular impressions, the leadership long cycle argument is not about cycles of sea power concentration. Rather, sea power has been the global reach capability of choice for much of the past five hundred years. Other types of capabilities are not dismissed as irrelevant. But they either tend to be of less significance for global reach or already hinted at by the distribution of sea power capabilities. As a consequence, fluctuations in naval power concentration are geared to the timing of global war and lead economy predominance. Global wars and the wealth gained from pioneering radical economic innovations facilitate systemic reconcentration in global reach capabilities, just as they select political–economic and military leadership in the global political system. The principal winner of the global war and the system's lead economy is also the global

Table 2. Leading Sector Timing and Indicators, Fifteenth to Twenty-First Centuries

Lead Economy	Leading Sector Indicators	Start-Up Phase	High Growth Phase
Portugal	Guinea gold	1430–1460	1460–1494
	Indian pepper	1494–1516	1516–1540
The Netherlands	Baltic and Atlantic trade	1540–1560	1560–1580
	Eastern trade	1580–1609	1609–1640
Britain I	Amerasian trade (especially sugar)	1640–1660	1660–1688
	Amerasian trade	1688–1713	1713–1740
Britain II	Cotton, iron	1740–1763	1763–1792
	Railroads, steam	1792–1815	1815–1850
United States I	Steel, chemicals, electronics	1850–1873	1873–1914
	Motor vehicles, aviation, electronics	1914–1945	1945–1973
United States II?	Information industries	1973–2000	2000–2030
	?	2030–2050	2050–2080

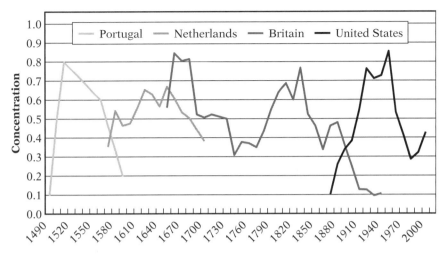

Figure 4.1. System Leader Leading-Sector Concentration

system's leading sea power. Thus, the primary foundations for systemic leadership are the periodic concentrations in economic innovation and growth and in global reach capabilities.

Figure 4.2 provides an updated look at the ups and downs of global reach—or naval capability concentration—by charting the proportion controlled by the four successive system leaders between 1494 and 2000. The causal relationships among leading sector growth, leading sector share concentration, and naval capability concentration have been established by Rasler and Thompson (1994) and Reuveny and Thompson (2004).

From this perspective, unipolarity in global politics—a high concentration of power favoring one state—is a recurring, if nonpermanent, phenomenon. Political–economic and military concentrations ultimately give way to systemic deconcentration—something easily discernible in Figures 4.1 and 4.2. There are fluctuations in year-to-year deconcentration. It is not simply an inexorable, negative slide from some early peak into great-power oblivion. The relative decline of systemic leadership can be quite gradual and protracted. There are also various ways in which

a trend toward deconcentration can be interrupted. One is the twin-peaks phenomenon in which another round of technological innovation revitalizes the basis of a system leader's capabilities. Other, although ultimately less significant, paths involve the defeat of major players or changes in the nature of global reach capabilities that cause short-term gains in the relative share of leading sector production and global reach capabilities.

From a leadership long cycle perspective, unipolarity is not so abnormal or extraordinary. Although not the norm, it is at least a familiar phenomenon at the global level. Moreover, it is not a static concept. Over time, the capabilities of unipolar powers have evolved and expanded as has the structural nature of world politics. Portuguese global unipolarity in the sixteenth century was by no means identical to U.S. global unipolarity in the twentieth and twenty-first centuries. In the sixteenth century, a global political system was very much an emergent phenomenon and Portugal was very weak in terms of its overall capability portfolio. Yet, it was sufficiently capable of playing the role of the first lead global power away from the European home region for

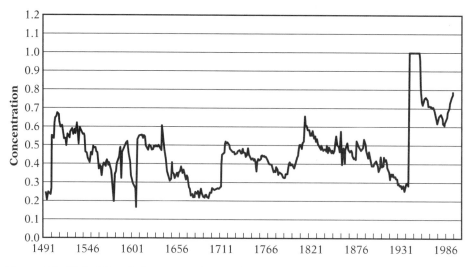

Figure 4.2. Global Reach Concentration, 1494–2000

a generation or two. Successive centuries of change and further evolution have seen the capabilities of the lead global power grow enormously, just as the world system has become far more complex than it was in the sixteenth century.

So, from this perspective, what are we to make of the contemporary concern about unipolarity in a post-Cold War world? However one views the various interpretations that have been put forward, perhaps the most welcome aspect of the debates about unipolarity is that they have enriched our theoretical inventory with new arguments. What follows then is a critique, based on a leadership long cycle perspective, of multiple points of view on the nature of contemporary unipolarity. The critique is structured around fifteen assertions that have been culled from the unipolarity literature, which are listed in Table 3. Even though a variety of disagreements with prevailing interpretations will be registered in what follows, an auxiliary goal is to highlight some new ideas that have emerged and that are well worth paying more empirical attention to as well as possibly co-opting.

Fifteen Assertions about Contemporary Unipolarity

(1) The well-known anarchy assumption is a good place to begin an analysis of the distribution of power and world order (or anything else).

Anarchy is not simply what you make of it. It is a major obstacle to theorizing about governance in the international system. With thanks in part to Thomas Hobbes' premature birth—possibly because his mother had become alarmed about an imminent invasion by the 1588 Spanish Armada—compounded by abandonment by his father shortly thereafter, we have inherited a major assumption in international relations that tends to be shared by realists and liberals alike (see, for example, McClelland 1996:192). The international relations concept of anarchy, of course, does not mean what our students frequently assume—that is, that anarchy is a synonym for chaos. Rather, anarchy, predicated on very mistaken ideas about security and insecurity in the state of nature, means the absence of

Table 3. Fifteen Assertions about Contemporary Unipolarity

(1) The anarchy assumption is a good place to begin an analysis of the distribution of power and world order.
(2) Polarity is the right "question."
(3) All major powers are identical in terms of their primary strategic orientation to world politics.
(4) Absolute gains have supplanted relative gains for all or most major powers, thereby rendering the search for primacy as outmoded.
(5) Technological change occurs randomly in space and time.
(6) A modern European state-system evolved into a global system.
(7) The relative restraint of the incumbent system leader can be attributed to American exceptionalism.
(8) The U.S. preeminent position shortly after 1945 was unusual and cannot be compared to its present position.
(9) The current U.S. unipolarity is unprecedented and indicates that the talk of decline in the 1980s was in error.
(10) The chief threat to prolonged unipolarity is not doing enough.
(11) The quick route to multipolarity is blocked by the absence of formidable challengers on the near horizon.
(12) The chief threats to prolonged unipolarity are the costs of leadership and the consequent loss of domestic support for system leadership activities.
(13) Balancing against a strong system leader is highly probable eventually.
(14) Unbalanced power encourages the emergence of new powers.
(15) Challengers must catch up to the system leader to cause significant levels of trouble.

central government. But the employment of the term "anarchy" implies rather strongly that the absence of central government is equated with a high potential for chaotic insecurity in which everyone needs to take care of themselves as best they can (namely, self-help). Call it the Mad Max approach to international politics.

If we put aside the understandable Hobbesian preference for a central government in the mid-seventeenth century, at a time when his own country was embroiled in a series of civil wars, the anarchy assumption can be reduced to a distinction between national and international politics. The former is often characterized by a central government and the latter rarely is. Expressed in this fashion, the anarchy assumption becomes another way of saying that domestic and international politics do not always proceed in precisely the same types of institutional environments—even though we can think of a number of exceptions in which states have no functioning central

governments. But keep in mind that even in the case of failed states, there is usually some minimal level of central governance being attempted, just as there are likely to be rival groups attempting to capture and regulate limited spatial domains within the state.

Without wishing to mince words, then, there is also a distinction to be made between *a* central government and central government or governance. Yes, by definition, there is no single central government that rules or reigns in contemporary international politics, but there are all sorts of phenomena and practices that generate variable amounts of governance. From a realist perspective, even the venerable balance-of-power practice is a primitive process for regulating conflict tendencies and power inequalities. From a liberal perspective, a number of international institutions increasingly attempt to supply governance in restricted domains. From an evolutionary perspective, systemic leadership, primarily focused on managing policy conflicts pertaining to intercontinental commerce, began to emerge some five hundred years ago. Anarchy, however defined, is, thus, not a constant. It is a variable, as is the amount of governance supplied from various sources in international politics. We would do well to reconsider our dependence on this concept and perhaps purge ourselves altogether of what Barry Buzan and Richard Little (2000) amusingly, but accurately, call "anarchophobia."

(2) Polarity is the right "question."

The appropriate answer to this question is the Janus-faced "yes" and "no." Discussions of polarity run the risk of falling into the conceptual and theoretical traps of older arguments about polarity, which are twofold. One is the reductionist tendency to think that polarity per se can explain a great deal. The reason why this argument is unlikely to be the case leads directly to the second problem with polarity—namely, polarity distinctions demand qualification. All multipolar situations are not the same. Charles Kegley and Gregory Raymond (1994), for instance, compare six multipolar periods over the last five hundred years and find that behavior is not uniform. The same problem applies equally to bipolar and unipolar settings. For that matter, we do not really have any consensus about the categorical thresholds separating unipolarity from bipolarity and multipolarity, making it difficult to systematically pursue different behavior within the nominal polarity categories. George Modelski (1974) offered a set of definitional criteria that might have helped create an empirical consensus, but, unfortunately, his proposed thresholds have not been widely adopted. As a consequence, polarity arguments often quickly bring in modifiers such as tight/loose or symmetrical/asymmetrical. In doing so, we have abruptly escalated what was initially three categories of polarity into twelve possible combinations without getting into hybrid possibilities, such as a system that is, say, unipolar in terms of military resources but multipolar in terms of the distribution of economic resources. Usually, though, polarity arguments have proceeded along the lines of generic distinctions between multipolarity and bipolarity, with little reference to unipolarity or the many possible qualifiers of various structural settings.

To the extent that contemporary discussions of unipolarity fall back into the sterility of the older polarity arguments (assuming that all unipolar settings are equal), we are unlikely to get very far. Fortunately, however, a number of the new unipolar arguments are theoretically rich and have raised interesting cognate questions that deserve further consideration. * * * Thus, structural change at the systemic level is at least good for one thing. It encourages analysts to think creatively about what is going on. Earlier instances of this phenomenon include the late nineteenth-century geopolitics of A. T. Mahan (1890) and Halford MacKinder (1904, 1919), arguably the beginning of modern international relations discourse, and the late twentieth-century arguments about "hegemonic decline."

(3) All major powers are identical in terms of their primary strategic orientation to world politics.

International relations theory tends to assume that all states participate in world politics on similar bases. All states seek security; all states seek to expand their power; or all states are in the process of becoming more concerned with low politics than with more traditional, high political questions. Such assumptions may be convenient for constructing some kinds of theory, but they do great damage to Robert Gilpin's (1981) essential duality in international relations. As we observed above, some states have a marked propensity for worrying primarily about territorial expansion, often in their home region. Others specialize in commercial and industrial expansion, concerned more about access to, and control of, distant markets than about territorial expansion closer to home. These are not "genetically based" instincts or orientations. In some cases, states wobble back and forth between the two fundamental orientations. In other cases, states adopt the commercial orientation after satiating their local territorial ambitions—or after being thwarted in satiating them. Consider the fact that English decision makers had to be convinced, through several centuries of coercive contestation over their claims to France, that they did, indeed, inhabit an island. However states come by their strategic orientations, two very different approaches to participating in world politics suggest rather strongly that we should seek to avoid assuming that one size fits all when it comes to motivations.

(4) Absolute gains have supplanted relative gains for all or most major powers. Therefore, primacy is an outmoded concept.

(5) Technological change is random in space and time.

There is ample room for disagreement about whether absolute gains in general have become the primary concern for certain sets of actors in world politics. We can also argue about whether such generalizations apply to all or some issues. One very important issue, however, tends to be overlooked in these debates. The history of the past several hundred years (if not longer) suggests that states with pronounced technological edges over their competitors tend to be the norm and not the exception. It is possible to take this observation one step further and argue that, in many years, one state tends to possess an economy that is more technologically advanced than any other in the system.

The reason for this tendency is not hard to discern. The most technologically advanced state in the system gained that status by generating more technological innovations than the other states. Technological innovation is, therefore, concentrated spatially. The economy that pioneers many innovations enjoys superiority in economic production for a finite time. It also accrues all sorts of rents and profits from its pioneering lead,

which, among other things, pays off in terms of higher standards of living for the population of the system's lead economy.

One area in which relative gains matter very much, therefore, is who has the system's lead economy and relative monopoly on technological innovation. To be sure, this status is not permanent. Pioneering innovations eventually are adopted and often improved on elsewhere. As technological innovation diffuses, some (but certainly not all) economies can catch up to the leader. Still, the preferred position is to have the lead economy, and this is one domain of relative gains that should persist even in a "postmodern" world. It may not matter as much as it once did who has the largest army or the most tanks. Who possesses the most innovative economy still matters very much.

(6) A modern European state-system evolved into a global system.

(7) The relative restraint of the current system leader is attributable to U.S. exceptionalism.

One widespread interpretation of the modern history of international relations is that the European region invented states and interstate politics in 1494 or 1648 and proceeded to extend the scope of what was initially a regional system to gradually encompass the rest of the world. According to this interpretation, Europeans stayed in charge until the late nineteenth-century advent of non-European great powers and the exhaustion of the West European powers by two world wars in the first half of the twentieth century. Along the way the modern European state-system morphed into a planetary-wide, global system presided over—for a time—by two superpowers: the United States and the Soviet Union. By the end of the twentieth century, the Soviet Union had disintegrated, leaving only one superpower survivor.

This story starts from a highly Eurocentric perspective. Europe may take credit for the first nation-states, but the existence of states and re-gional interstate systems outside the western edge of Eurasia long predated the modern era. Nor was European superiority over other regions manifested all that quickly. The penetration of the Caribbean and South America proved to be easier than it probably should have been. The African interior took centuries to penetrate. India and China were also able to resist European inroads until after local empires had either fallen apart or were in decline (see Thompson 1999).

*   *   *

A combination of factors contributed to the elevation of the European region. Some of these factors were exogenous to Europe in the sense that they depended on developments over which the Europeans had no control. Two examples are the successes of the Mongol conquests and the later exploitation of American silver that proved indispensable in breaking into Asian markets. Other factors were endogenous to Europe. Perhaps most important was the hyper-competitiveness of the European states, which led, in turn, to the development of increasingly lethal firepower with more than a little help from the late eighteenth-century industrial revolution.

Another critical factor was related closely to this hyper-competitiveness. Given the failure of any hegemonic aspirant to conquer the European region, weak, marginal states on the fringe of western Eurasia (Genoa, Venice, Portugal, the United Provinces of the Netherlands, and Britain) were permitted to survive and thrive as commercial-maritime powers. This type of actor had existed before (Minoans, Phoenicians, and Carthaginians). But they tended to run afoul of adjacent land empires that either swallowed or destroyed them. Between the eleventh and early twentieth centuries, a string of trading states worked hard to gain and maintain control over east-west trade initially within Eurasia but ultimately on a worldwide basis. Much of the time, they were able to evade conquest by nearby land empires.

But it was not just the absence of a coercively unified Europe that permitted the survival of these relative anomalies. Increasingly, they became crucial to the construction and financing of coalitions that thwarted aspiring regional hegemons. Philip II and Louis XIV might have managed to change the regional trajectory of a nonunified Europe, and world history in the bargain, were it not for the coalition wars of the 1580s–1600s and 1680s–1710s. The interdependence of the commercial-maritime states and multiple sovereignties within Europe was thus highly reciprocal.

Nonetheless, something else was going on besides the intermittent efforts to maintain a nonunified European region. The commercial-maritime powers were too weak and largely disinterested in competing with the regional powers for territorial expansion within their home region. Instead, their energies were focused principally on extending their influence and maritime networks at some distance from their home region. Territorial expansion tended to come later (somewhere other than Europe) and only after the powers initially attempted to avoid the expenses involved in maintaining extensive on-shore holdings.

The two very different strategic orientations—territorial expansion in the home region (certainly not distinctive to Europe) and market expansion abroad—created the sort of two-level game mentioned previously. Commercial-maritime powers concerned themselves first with managing global contests over interregional trade. Only when affairs in the home region threatened their survival did they turn to the task of managing contests at home over regional hegemony. At these times, the local and increasingly Central European region became fused with the global system of managing long distance trade. At other times, the affairs of the central region and the global system functioned somewhat separately.

*   *   *

Still, it is the two orientations that help explain leadership restraint. Regional territorial expansion is less likely to be characterized by restraint. Initial successes seem to encourage further expansion so that there have been concerted efforts to take over the whole European region. Global commercial expansion is more subtle (and distant) and, at least initially, attempts proceed by avoiding territorial conquest. The world is also a much bigger place than the European region. What might be contemplated in terms of dominance at the regional level is simply unthinkable at the global level. There is no need to fall back on U.S. exceptionalism (see Ikenberry 2002) to account for the reluctance of post-1945 U.S. policies to control fully the rest of the world. Constrained systemic leadership predated U.S. exceptionalism. In fact, restrained systemic leadership conforms to the global historical pattern and, therefore, is unexceptional.

(8) The preeminent U.S. position shortly after 1945 was unusual and cannot be compared to its present position.

This generalization is best deconstructed into two separate statements. The first one—that the 1945 position was unusual—is the more dubious of the two. From a leadership long cycle perspective, the U.S. position in 1945 was comparable to the British positions after 1713 and 1815, the Dutch position after 1608, and the Portuguese position after 1516. What these episodes had in common was that one state emerged from a period of global warfare as the preeminent global power. It controlled the lead economy in the system. Its control of global reach capabilities exceeded a threshold set at the sum of the capabilities held by all other global powers (50%). Its most acute enemies had just been defeated decisively in a generation of intensive war.

Do any of these assertions mean that the lead global power was "hegemonic"? No, not if "hegemony" implies absolute dominance over other actors. All of these global leaders have been limited in their ability to project their influence inland. None sought control of European affairs, and only the incumbent leading global power was in a position to strongly influence what took place within the west European region. Even that position proved to be temporary.

Do these assertions mean that each of the global leaders was equally powerful immediately after their global war triumph? Again, the answer is of course not. The magnitude of the lead enjoyed by the United States in 1945 did not spring forth at full force in the way the Portuguese lead of the early sixteenth century did. Nor could it have done so. The magnitude of the lead, and the types of capabilities upon which global systemic leadership rests, have evolved over time. Portugal possessed a very small population and a limited resource base. It was capable of stumbling its way around Africa and beyond, as well as seizing control of Indian Ocean trade for a period of time. The Dutch were twice as numerous and more formidable in war than the Portuguese but just as vulnerable to a hostile takeover on the western Eurasian continent. Ultimately, the Dutch were forced to hijack the English throne to augment their capabilities against the French. The British population base was about three times that of the Dutch. Moreover, their maritime-commercial network was augmented by a less vulnerable geopolitical location, two colonial empires, and an industrial revolution. The United States could claim even more people, a substantial resource endowment, the least vulnerable location possible, and a succession of more advanced industrial revolutions.

*   *   *

Where does that leave the second assertion—that the current U.S. position is incomparable to its earlier 1945 position? If incomparable means that the 1945 and 2005 positions are different, one would certainly have to agree. They are not the same. The earlier one was immediately post-global war, and the current position is a half-century away from the last global war. Although the global war enemies were defeated decisively by 1945, a Cold War with a wartime ally was about to commence. In 2005, the principal enemies are nonstate groups espousing variants on militant Islam and a handful of weak minor powers that have, or are threatening to acquire, nuclear weapons.

If incomparable means that the 1945 and 2005 positions cannot be compared, that is obviously not the case, as is demonstrated in the preceding paragraph. They are also not identical positions as Figure 4.3 demonstrates U.S. sea power had regained much of the relative positional losses incurred during the Cold War after 1960, but it is unlikely to improve much more than it already has. The leading sector picture is even clearer in some respects given that the relative decline in production was more precipitous after the 1950s peak. The economic relative position began to turn upward after the 1980s trough, but there is still some way to go to return to the 1950s relative position.

Unlike the global reach index, there is some possibility, however, that the U.S. leading sector position could return to a 1950s-like peak. Just as Britain led the way through two sets of twin-peaked technological innovation spurts, we may be in the beginning of a second set for the United States that is geared to information technology. It is fair to say that the U.S. economy has led the way in such technology in its start-up phase. It remains in a respectable leading position at the

beginning of the high-growth phase. The question is whether it can maintain the lead in the next few decades. That is a future outcome that is most difficult to predict.

(9) The current U.S. unipolarity is unprecedented and indicates that the talk of decline in the 1980s was in error.

Again, this assertion is best broken into two statements. Of the two statements, the second one is the easiest one to handle. The discussion of decline in the 1980s was entirely appropriate. The U.S. position had, indeed, declined relative to its earlier position. Relative decline cannot be equated with absolute decline, however. Absolute decline was not in question. Multiple indicators of relative decline were difficult to challenge. Actually, though, the real debate was not—and should not have been—about relative decline per se. The real question should have been about how much relative decline had taken place by the 1980s. With the advantage of hindsight and knowing how the Cold War played out, it is possible to say that the level of relative decline that had been experienced by the 1980s was easy to exaggerate.

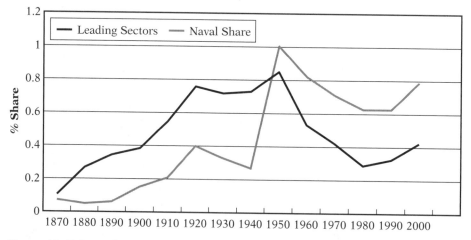

Figure 4.3. U.S. Leading Sectors and Naval Shares

In point of fact, there are "new things under the sun." The current U.S. position is unprecedented in some ways. Two important ones come immediately to mind. One is that the current system leader has no major power rivals. That condition may be temporary, but it is certainly unprecedented. It is also closely related to the unipolar outcome. The emergence of a genuine rival may end U.S. military unipolarity, although there are other ways that the unipolar status may end.

A second novelty is that the United States currently possesses the world system's lead army—not necessarily in size but in terms of lethality, technological competence, and ability to project force at long distance. Not all of these characteristics are entirely novel, but the total package is unusual. Normally, the leading whale is not also the leading elephant.

In other respects, though, the current U.S. position is not so unprecedented. Some sixty years after the last global war, its relative standing has diminished, not become stronger. The U.S. military reach can now penetrate the interior of Eurasia better than it could in 1945, but then so could Britain sixty years after 1815. The U.S. share of global reach has also not declined as much as its relative economic position. That was true of the United States' predecessor as well. Most important, the basic nature of the system has not seemed to have changed all that much. We are still dependent on a high concentration of technological innovation and global reach for the creation of world order. The odds of maintaining both attributes tend to diminish as one moves away from the last episode of structural clarification via global war. The United States may be able to claim a unipolar status, but it is in part due to default. That is not the same thing as being able to claim a unipolar status as the result of winning a global war. As a consequence, the United States has its hands full—not so much with near-term major power challenges, but with plenty of smaller challenges to the eroding world order that it established after the conclusion of World War II.

(10) The chief threat to prolonged unipolarity is not doing enough.

(11) The quick route to multipolarity is blocked by the absence of formidable challengers on the near horizon.

Presumably, the system leader's basic options are attempting much or little. Unlike Goldilocks, we do not know what level of activity is just right. Nonetheless, the main threat to a preeminent position from a leadership long cycle perspective is erosion in the economic foundation that supports systemic leadership. Put another way, there is more than one quick route to multipolarity. The loss of a commercial-technological edge due to diffusion will decrease the gap between the system leader just as fast as will the rise of a formidable challenger. Doing too much or too little need not influence the extent to which material power is concentrated in the system. Doing too much or too little, however, can affect how much world order is accomplished through the efforts of the system leader. So can performing the role of the system leader poorly and with no concern for the legitimacy of one's efforts.

(12) The chief threats to prolonged unipolarity are the costs of leadership and the consequent loss of domestic support for system leadership activities.

Although, empirically, it can be demonstrated that there are economic costs related to systemic leadership, it is also easy to exaggerate the role leadership costs play in facilitating the relative decline of the system leader. The principal cause of relative decline is the loss of advantage in technological innovation. Even though nothing is inevitable, the diffusion of technological innovation is highly probable. The only real antidote is being the first to catch the next long wave of economic growth and not hanging on too tightly to investments and ways of doing things from the last wave.

The potential loss of domestic support for systemic leadership activities is an area that is little explored. We know something about mass preferences for defense spending and interna-tionalism in the United States. The problem is that defense spending and international activities are rarely framed as systemic leadership func-tions. They are sold to public opinion as re-sponses to threats to U.S. interests. Germans, Japanese, Soviets, Chinese, unfriendly alleged possessors of weapons of mass destruction, and terrorists have so far been obliging in providing a series of apparent threats over the past sixty-five years. What might public opinion's reaction be to a major threat portrayed as something more ab-stract and generic—such as climate change, over-population, poverty, or disease—that call for equal or even greater sacrifices if we are to cope with their dangers? That remains to be seen.

Nonetheless, Charles Kupchan's (2002) con-tention that structural arguments tend to assume system leaders will choose to make use of their power advantage deserves more study. But it need not be the case. If the system leader chooses to withdraw from international activism, a struc-tural concentration of power will be less relevant. Other actors will become relatively more power-ful by default.

Kupchan (2002) argues that current U.S. unipolarity is likely to disappear as the U.S. com-mitment to internationalism wanes. Another way of looking at this possibility is that the distribu-tion of power described as unipolar might persist but that structural concentration would make less difference. The emphasis on whether strate-gic choices are pursued, as opposed to assuming they will be by a system leader, is most appropri-ate, but it raises a number of auxiliary questions also raised by Kupchan's discussion. Has U.S. in-ternationalism peaked? Is internationalism sus-tained by economic growth and reliance on casualty reducing tactics such as air power? How are new generations persuaded to accept com-mitments made in an earlier time? Or, should we integrate a generational decay factor into the problem of systemic leadership decline? The point here is not that none of these questions has ever been examined in the U.S. context. They have (see, for instance, Russett 1990 or Wittkopf

1990)—but not as questions directly tied to analyses of systemic leadership. Given the serial threats encountered by the United States over the last sixty-five years or so, separating elite and mass support for a response to threats as op-posed to a commitment to internationalism is not an easy task. Moreover, the empirical work that has been done on this particular theoretical approach to systemic leadership, call it the do-mestic political support for engaging in systemic leadership, for the most part has been conducted solely in the U.S. domain. More comparisons with earlier leadership life cycles are needed even though, or because, domestic politics presum-ably has evolved into a more significant compo-nent of systemic leadership over the past five centuries.

(13) Balancing against a strong system leader is highly probable eventually.

Historically, balancing against a system leader is not all that common. Note that Jack Levy and Thompson (2003) have found that the leading sea power is far less likely than the leading land power to provoke balancing coalitions. The main reason takes us back to the basic major power duality. System leaders have had maritime-commercial-industrial orientations. Whatever they may have done before becoming system leaders, their pri-mary expansionary interests have concerned ac-cess to markets not territory and, most especially, not territory in a home region populated by other major powers. As a consequence, their economic success may well be resented, but system leaders are not seen as representing overt threats to the sovereignty of other major powers.

Stephen Walt (2002) argues cogently that threats pertinent to balancing calculi are a func-tion of power, proximity, offensive capabilities, and aggressive intentions. However, these four factors need not be equally weighted. Of the four, aggressive intentions represent the most signifi-cant element. Yet, land powers that control a strong proportion of a region's resources tend to be viewed, rightly or wrongly, as possessing the intention of dominating the region coercively. Thus, leading regional powers, unlike global system leaders, do tend to be the target of balancing coalitions. Historically, and especially in the European cockpit of balancing, power and aggressive intentions have tended to become fused in the minds of decision makers contemplating the likelihood of maintaining their autonomy given the relative power of the Habsburg-Spanish, French, and Germans.

Balancing against the system leader, therefore, is not ruled out completely, but it is a low probability occurrence because system leaders do not seek hegemony and territorial control—at least not where it matters most to balancing considerations. But system leaders, as leaders, do need followers. More likely than balancing, then, is the probability that other states become disinclined to accept policy directions advocated by system leaders in relative decline or who are acting in ways thought to be lacking in legitimacy.

(14) Unbalanced power encourages the emergence of new powers.

Christopher Layne (1993) contends that unbalanced power creates situations that are conducive to the emergence of new major powers. Why this might be the case appears to be predicated on a combination of uneven growth rates and the anarchy-driven propensity to imitate rivals. This argument seems problematic in at least two respects. First, it is not clear why uneven growth should be viewed as a function of unbalanced power. No one would deny that uneven growth has characterized the major power subsystem. Yet, surely, uneven growth and power concentration can be separate processes. Power deconcentration may encourage growth elsewhere, as does the system leader's technological innovation, but it is not clear that concentration per se will stimulate growth.

A second problem is that Layne's evidence is based on two earlier cases that he finds similar in nature to the present situation: France in 1660 and Britain in 1860. From a leadership long cycle perspective (but not necessarily from Layne's perspective), the first case is inappropriate because it mixes regional apples with global oranges. (Layne appears to subscribe to the assumption that a European system evolved into a global system.) In the second half of the seventeenth century, France was the leading regional power in Europe, but it was not the global system leader. That is precisely why it sought to destroy the Netherlands and its European trade monopoly. But even if one accepted the case as analogous, it is also difficult to see how Britain and Austria should be seen as emerging in imitation of France's predominance. Both states had been considered major powers in Europe long before 1660. They had also been occasional foes of France for many years before 1660. That they coalesced against French ambitions in the 1688–1713 conflict was neither surprising nor emergent behavior.

The second case—Britain in 1860—is more interesting. It focuses on a system leader and, therefore, is more relevant than the earlier French case. A glance at Figure 4.4 is most suggestive. In 1860, Britain had declined considerably in relative economic position (in leading sector terms) from a peak attained around 1830. Its status then improved for a few years before beginning a steady plunge toward the bottom of the chart. Thanks to the defeat of Russia in the Crimean War and subsequent experimentation in battleship construction, Britain's naval position remained high and even re-exceeded the 50% threshold in the last two decades of the nineteenth century. That high position could no longer be sustained in the twentieth century.

Whether a strong case can be made for British unipolarity in 1860 or not, the comparison may be even more appropriate than what Layne thought. To the extent that it illustrates the transitoriness of leading powers on downward trajectories—and the problems of interpreting them without the benefit of hindsight—Britain in 1860 may prove to be analogous to the United States in the early twenty-first century. Just how analogous depends on whether the United States has resumed an upward trajectory as it moves into a second twin-peak set of technological innovations. If the United States is on this latter trajectory, the analogy will break down because Britain by 1860 had already enjoyed two sets of twin spurts of economic growth leadership and was not destined to lead in a third set.

Even so, it is difficult to accept the emergence of Germany, Japan, and the United States as responding, strictly speaking, to British predominance in the nineteenth century. That their ascendance resisted the implications of British predominance is clear. Both Germany and the United States erected high tariff barriers in the nineteenth century to hold off British productive superiority and to escape their role as suppliers of raw materials to the British industrial machine. They also imitated Britain's initial leading sectors (textiles, iron, steam, and rail). But that is the way modern economic growth and diffusion work. The center innovates and others either copy or fall behind. However, Germany, Japan, and the United States did not imitate Britain in all other respects. Both Germany and Japan stayed attached to, and mired in, dominating their home regions. The United States did so as well initially, but moved on to more global preoccupations af-

ter conquering a respectable proportion of North America without too much opposition. Both Japan and the United States chose to coalesce with Britain against the German threat in World War I. There seems to be much less "sameness" operating here than Layne sees.

On the contrary, exactly the opposite pattern to the imbalancing one that Layne advances has characterized the last five hundred years. Regional powers are encouraged to emerge and grow stronger in the context of systemic leadership decline. * * * Global powers are also encouraged to rebuild the foundation of their capability in response to regional hegemonic threats.

(15) Challengers must catch up to the system leader to cause significant levels of trouble.

The historical pattern of ascent and decline is more complex than this assertion allows. Some challengers win without a fight. The U.S. British transition is a case in point. Although the Dutch and English fought several less intense wars in the 1650s–1670s, the actual transition in global leadership from the Netherlands to Britain in the

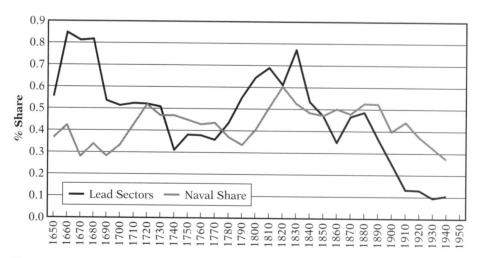

Figure 4.4. British Leading Sector and Naval Shares

early eighteenth century was resented but not resisted by the exhausted Dutch. There was never any once-and-for-all showdown between the Dutch and the Portuguese either—in large part because Spain absorbed Portugal before such a confrontation could take place.

Other challengers have taken on the system leader before they have fully caught up in economic or military terms. The point has been made that incomplete catch-ups are inherently conflict-prone. If one state has or is about to surpass the system leader in all the categories that count, there is much less reason to fight. It is probably too late for the incumbent to hope to reverse its relative decline on the battlefield. The challenger, to the contrary, has less to prove than if there is uncertainty as to who is actually ahead and in what way.

William Wohlforth (1999:20) has advanced the theory that uneven capability portfolios generate structural ambiguity that, in turn, is more dangerous than more unambiguous situations. Preponderance across the board should discourage all but the greatest risk takers. When the most powerful states are powerful in some respects but considered vulnerable in others, challenges become more conceivable. Challengers are empowered by superiority in some areas. At the same time, leaders still have reason to feel they can defend the status quo that they have largely created in an earlier era.

Even though this argument has yet to be fully tested, it has plausibility. It may also be useful in two contexts. The argument may help explain periods of reduced conflict sometimes associated with new system leaders. Newly incumbent system leaders may be most likely to be "preponderant across the board" at the outset of their political–military life cycle. To the extent that system leaders are likely to decline unevenly in different sectors (challengers are also likely to improve their relative positions unevenly), Wohlforth's interpretation may help explain what seem to be, with the advantage of hindsight, premature challenges.

Conclusion

So, where are we in the evolution of systemic structure? The current system has some unipolar features. Most evident is the persistent monopoly in global reach capabilities. One state continues to have a superior ability to project military power throughout the globe. But that is something less than a novelty of the post–Cold War era. It has been in place since at least 1945 in the U.S. iteration, even if the technology has certainly improved.

The same state continues to lead in pioneering technological innovation—something it has been doing since the late nineteenth century. What is less clear is whether the United States is on the technological ascent or descent. Is it introducing new sunrise industries or riding sunset industries into relative decline? The answer is probably some of both. The United States leads in information technology, but it remains heavily wedded to the old Fordist/assembly line/motor vehicle/petroleum paradigm that prevailed throughout most of the twentieth century.

The United States may be first among a small set of economic peers, but it is hardly unipolar economically. Its capability portfolio, in Wohlforth's terms, is not uniformly predominant. We will need to see how things shake out in the first quarter of the twenty-first century to assess whether the capability portfolio is becoming more uniform and more predominant or not. In the interim, one would have to acknowledge the slow relative decline of the U.S. economic position over the past sixty years.

Thus, the early decades of the twenty-first century, other things being equal, should be more like the last quarter or so of the eighteenth and nineteenth centuries. Assuming foremost that technological innovation continues to be concentrated spatially and temporally, one state will move to the front of the pack. This passage could resemble the late eighteenth century in which Britain re-emerged as the clear economic leader. Or, it could resemble the late nineteenth century in which the incumbent lead economy was supplanted gradually by challengers.

In either case, stressing the unipolar facets of the current period too much could prove to be a major error of interpretation. Whether it proves to be long lasting (a technologically ascendant United States) or temporary (a United States in relative technological decline), the current structure remains a weak and weakened form of military unipolarity created by Soviet default. Thus, I would agree with Randall Schweller (1999:37) and others that the current system is "both more unipolar and less concentrated" than before. But if forced to choose between a stand-alone military unipolarity or a more uniform concentration of political–military and economic resources as predictors of structural impact, leadership long cycle theory would opt for the latter over the former. Genuine or strong military unipolarity, at the very least, needs to be buttressed by strong technological and economic unipolarity. Some legitimacy for system leadership activities would not hurt either.

REFERENCES

Bacevich, Andrew J. (2002) *American Empire: The Realities and Consequences of U.S. Diplomacy*. Cambridge, M.A.: Harvard University Press.

Buzan, Barry. (2004) *The United States and the Great Powers: World Politics in the Twenty-First Century*. Cambridge: Polity.

Buzan, Barry, and Richard Little. (2000) *International Systems in World History: Remaking the Study of International Relations*. Oxford: Oxford University Press.

Carr, Edward H. (1946) *The Twenty Year's Crisis, 1919–1939*. 2nd edition. New York: Harper.

Doran, Charles F. (2003) Economics, Philosophy of History, and the "Single Dynamic" of Power Cycle Theory: Expectations, Competition, and Statecraft. *International Political Science Review* 24:13–49.

Ferguson, Niall. (2004) *Colossus: The Rise and Fall of the American Empire*. New York: Penguin.

Frieden, Jeffrey. (1988) Sectoral Conflict and U.S. Foreign Economic Policy. *International Organization* 42:59–90.

Gilpin, Robert. (1981) *War and Change in World Politics*. Cambridge: Cambridge University Press.

Hardt, Michael, and Antonio Negri. (2000) *Empire*. Cambridge, M.A.: Harvard University Press.

Huntington, Samuel P. (1993) Why International Primacy Matters. *International Security* 17(4):68–83.

Ikenberry, G. John. (2002) Democracy, Institutions, and American Restraint. In *America Unrivaled: The Future of the Balance of Power*, edited by John G. Ikenberry. Ithaca: Cornell University Press.

Jervis, Robert. (1993) International Primacy: Is the Game Worth the Candle? *International Security* 17(4):52–67.

Joffe, Josef. (2002) Defying History and Theory: The United States as the "Last Remaining Superpower." In *America Unrivaled: The Future of the Balance of Power*, edited by G. John Ikenberry. Ithaca: Cornell University Press.

Kegley, Charles W. Jr., and Gregory Raymond. (1994) *A Multipolar Peace? Great Power Politics in the Twenty-First Century*. New York: St. Martin's Press.

Knutsen, Torbjorn L. (1999) *The Rise and Fall of World Orders*. Manchester: Manchester University Press.

Kugler, Jacek, and Douglas Lemke, eds. (1996) *Parity and War: Evaluations and Extensions of the War Ledger*. Ann Arbor: University of Michigan Press.

Kupchan, Charles A. (2002) Hollow Hegemony or Stable Multipolarity? In *America Unrivaled: The Future of the Balance of Power*, edited by G. John Ikenberry. Ithaca: Cornell University Press.

Layne, Christopher. (1993) The Unipolar Illusion: Why New Great Powers Will Rise. *International Security* 17(4):5–51.

Levy, Jack S., and William R. Thompson. (2003) Balancing at Sea: Do States Coalesce Against the Leading Sea Power? Paper presented at the annual meeting of the American Political Science Association, Philadelphia, P.A., August.

MacKinder, Halford J. (1904) The Geographical Pivot of History. *Geographical Journal* 23:421–444.

MacKinder, Halford J. (1919) *Democratic Ideas and Reality: A Study in the Politics of Recon-struction*. New York: Henry Holt.

Mahan, A. T. (1890) *The Influence of Sea Power Upon History, 1600–1783*. Boston: Little, Brown.

Mann, Michael. (2004) The First Failed Empire of the Twenty-First Century. In *American Power in the 21st Century*, edited by David Held and Mathias Koenig-Archibugi. Cambridge: Polity.

Mastanduno, Michael. (1997) Preserving the Unipolar Moment: Realist Theories and U.S. Grand Strategy after the Cold War. *International Security* 21(4):49–88.

Mastanduno, Michael. (2002) Incomplete Hegemony and Security Order in the Asia-Pacific. In *America Unrivaled: The Future of the Balance of Power*, edited by G. John Ikenberry. Ithaca: Cornell University Press.

McClelland, U. S. (1996) *A History of Western Political Thought*. New York: Routledge.

Modelski, George. (1974) *World Power Concentrations: Typology, Data, Explanatory Framework*. Morristown: General Learning Press.

Modelski, George. (1987) *Long Cycles in World Politics*. London: Macmillan.

Modelski, George. (1996) An Evolutionary Paradigm for Global Politics. *International Studies Quarterly* 40:321–353.

Modelski, George. (2000) World System Evolution. In *World System History: The Social Science of Longterm Change*, edited by Robert A. Denemark, Jonathan Friedman, Barry K. Gills, and George Modelski. London: Routledge.

Modelski, George, and Sylvia Modelski, eds. (1988) *Documenting Global Leadership*. London: Macmillan.

Modelski, George, and William R. Thompson. (1988) *Sea Power in Global Politics, 1494–1993*. London: Macmillan.

Modelski, George, and William R. Thompson. (1989) Long Cycles and Global Wars. In *Handbook of War Studies*, edited by Manus Midlarsky. Boston: Allen and Unwin.

Modelski, George, and William R. Thompson. (1996) *Leading Sectors and World Powers: The Co-evolution of Global Politics and Economics*. Columbia: University of South Carolina Press.

Nau, Henry R. (1990) *The Myth of America's Decline: Leading the World Economy into the 1990s*. Oxford: Oxford University Press.

Nye, Joseph S. (1990) *Bound to Lead: The Changing Nature of U.S. Power*. New York: Basic Books.

O'Brien, Patrick K. (2002) Pax Britannica and American Hegemony: Precedent, Antecedent, or Just Another History? In *Two Hegemonies: Britain, 1846–1914 and the United States, 1941–2001*, edited by Patrick K. O'Brien and Armand Clesse. Aldershot: Ashgate.

Odom, William E., and Robert Dujarric. (2004) *America's Inadvertent Empire*. New Haven: Yale University Press.

Owen, John M. (2002) Transnational Liberalism and American Primacy or Benignity Is in the Eye of the Beholder. In *America Unrivaled: The Future of the Balance of Power*, edited by G. John Ikenberry. Ithaca: Cornell University Press.

Posen, Barry R. (2003) Command of the Commons: The Military Foundation of U.S. Hegemony. *International Security* 28(1): 5–46.

Rasler, Karen, and William R. Thompson. (1989) *War and State Making: The Shaping of the Global Powers*. Boston: Unwin Hyman.

Rasler, Karen, and William R. Thompson. (1994) *The Great Powers and Global Struggle, 1490–1990*. Lexington: University Press of Kentucky.

Rasler, Karen, and William R. Thompson. (2000) Global Wars and the Political Economy of

Structural Change. In *Handbook of War Studies II*, edited by Manus Midlarsky. Ann Arbor: University of Michigan Press.

Rasler, Karen, and William R. Thompson. (2005) *Puzzles of the Democratic Peace: Theory, Geopolitics, and the Transformation of World Politics*. New York: Palgrave-Macmillan.

Reuveny, Rafael, and William R. Thompson. (2004) *Growth, Trade, and Systemic Leadership*. Ann Arbor: University of Michigan Press.

Risse, Thomas. (2002) U.S. Power in a Liberal Security Community. In *America Unrivaled: The Future of the Balance of Power*, edited by G. John Ikenberry. Ithaca: Cornell University Press.

Rodman, Peter W. (2000) The World's Resentment: Anti-Americanism as a Global Phenomenon. *The National Interest* 60:33–41.

Rosecrance, Richard. (1999) *The Rise of the Virtual State: Wealth and Power in the Coming Century*. New York: Basic Books.

Russett, Bruce M. (1985) The Mysterious Case of Vanishing Hegemony, or, Is Mark Twain Really Dead? *International Organization* 10:207–231.

Russett, Bruce M. (1990) *Controlling the Sword: The Democratic Governance of National Security*. Cambridge, MA: Harvard University Press.

Schweller, Randall L. (1999) Realism and the Present Great Power System: Growth and Positional Conflict over Scarce Resources. In *Unipolar Politics: Realism and State Strategies After the Cold War*, edited by Ethan B. Kapstein and Michael Mastanduno. New York: Columbia University Press.

Strange, Susan. (1987) The Persistent Myth of Lost Hegemony. *International Organization* 41: 551–574.

Thompson, William R. (1988) *On Global War: Historical-Structural Approaches to World Politics*. Columbia: University of South Carolina Press.

Thompson, William R. (1999) The Military Superiority Thesis and the Ascendancy of Western Eurasia in the World System. *Journal of World History* 10:143–178.

Thompson, William R. (2000) *The Emergence of the Global Political Economy*. London: University College London Press.

Vasquez, John A. (1998) *The Power of Power Politics: From Classical Realism to Neotraditionalism*. Cambridge: Cambridge University Press.

Volgy, Thomas J., and Alison Bailin. (2003) *International Politics and State Strength*. Boulder: Lynne Rienner Publishers.

Walt, Stephen M. (2002) Keeping the World "Off Balance": Self Restraint and U.S. Foreign Policy. In *America Unrivaled: The Future of the Balance of Power*, edited by G. John Ikenberry. Ithaca: Cornell University Press.

Wilkinson, David. (1996) Configurations of the Indic States System. *Comparative Civilizations Review* 34:63–119.

Wilkinson, David. (1999) Power Polarity in the Far Eastern World System, 1025 B.C.–A.D. 1850: Narrative and 25-Year Interval Data. *Journal of World-Systems Research* 3.

Wilkinson, David. (2001) Problems in Power Configuration Sequences: The Southwest Asian Macrosystem to 1500 B.C. *Comparative Civilization* 17:1–13.

Wilkinson, David. (2004a) Power Configuration Sequences in the Northeast African World System to 1500 B.C. *Comparative Civilizations Review* 50:82–104.

Wilkinson, David. (2004b) The Power Configuration Sequence of the Central World System, 1500–700 B.C. *Journal of World-System Research* 10:655–720.

Wittkopf, Eugene. (1990) *Faces of Internationalism: Public Opinion and American Foreign Policy*. Durham: Duke University Press.

Wohlforth, William C. (1999) The Stability of a Unipolar World. *International Security* 24:5–41.

ANTHONY PAGDEN

IMPERIALISM, LIBERALISM AND THE QUEST FOR PERPETUAL PEACE

For at least two generations, "empire" and "imperialism" have been dirty words. Already by 1959, when neither the French nor the British Empire had yet quite ceased to exist, Raymond Aaron dismissed imperialism as a "name given by rivals, or spectators, to the diplomacy of a great power"—something, that is, that only others did or had. By the 1970s, a consensus had emerged in liberal circles in the West that all empires—or at least those of European or North American origin—had only ever been systems of power that constituted a denial by one people of the rights (above all, the right to self-determination) of countless others. They had never benefited anyone but their rulers; all of those who had lived under imperial rule would much rather not have and finally they had all risen up and driven out their conquerors.

Very recently this picture has begun to change. Now that empires are no more (the last serious imperial outpost, Hong Kong, vanished in 1997), a more nuanced account of their long histories is beginning to be written. It has become harder to avoid the conclusion that some empires were much weaker than was commonly claimed; that at least some of the colonized collaborated willingly, for at least some of the time, with their colonizers; that minorities often fared better under empires than under nation-states; and that empires were often more successful than nation-states at managing the murderous consequences of religious differences.

Ever since 9/11 and the war in Afghanistan, a few intrepid voices have even been heard to declare that some empires might in fact have been

From *Daedalus* (Spring 2005), 46–57. Some of the author's notes have been omitted.

forces for good. Books both for and against—with such titles as *The Sorrows of Empire, America's Inadvertent Empire, Resurrecting Empire,* and *The Obligation of Empire*—now appear almost daily. As these titles suggest, the current revival of interest in empire is not unrelated to the behavior of the current U.S. administration in international affairs, and to the widespread assumption that the United States has become a new imperial power. Even so, most Americans continue to feel uncomfortable with the designation, which (forgetting Hawaii, the Philippines, and Puerto Rico) they have long regarded as a European evil. Yet ever since the mid-1990s, the rhetoric of U.S. international relations has become increasingly imperial. "If we have to use force, it is because we are America," declared Madeleine Albright in 1998, taking care not to pronounce the word 'empire.' "We are the indispensable nation, We stand tall, We see further into the future."[1] No British proconsul could have put it better.

But for all the talk about a new American empire, is the United States today really, in Niall Ferguson's words, "the empire that does not dare to speak its name—an empire in denial"?[2]

This would appear to suggest that the United States behaves like and pursues the recognized objectives of an empire while being unprepared to commit itself ideologically to imperialism, or to take the necessary measures to ensure that those objectives constitute a long-term success. Is that really so?

Before these questions can be answered, we need to answer a rather more fundamental one—namely, what is an empire? The word has been used to describe societies as diverse as

Meso-american tribute-distribution systems (the so-called Aztec and Inca Empires), tribal conquest states (the Mongol and Ottoman Empires), European composite monarchies (the Hapsburg and Austro-Hungarian Empires), and even networks of economic and political clientage (the current relation of the First to the Third World)—not to mention the British Empire, which combined features of all of these. Faced with such diversity, simple definitions will clearly be of little use. It is, of course, possible to define the word so narrowly as to exclude all but the most obvious European (and a few Asian) megastates. On the other hand, defining it so widely as to include any kind of extensive international power runs the risk of rending the concept indeterminate.

So let me begin by saying that an empire is an extensive state in which one ethnic or tribal group, by one means or another, rules over several others—roughly what the first-century Roman historian Tacitus meant when he spoke of the Roman world as an "immense body of empire" (*immensum imperii corpus*).[3] As such, empires have always been more frequent, more extensive political and social forms than tribal territories or nations have ever been. Ever since antiquity, large areas of Asia were ruled by imperial states of one kind or another, and so too were substantial areas of Africa. Vishanagar, Assyria, Elam, Urartu, Benin, Maori New Zealand—all were, in this sense, empires.

All empires inevitably involve the exercise of imperium, or sovereign authority, usually acquired by force. Few empires have survived for long without suppressing opposition, and probably all were initially created to supply the metropolis with goods it could not otherwise acquire. In 1918, the great Austrian economist Joseph Schumpeter described territorial expansion as "the purely instinctual inclination towards war and conquest" and relegated it to an earlier atavistic period of human history that he believed was now past.[4] He would have to wait another half century for the final dismemberment of the world's last significant colonial outposts. But he could see that in the new global economies that he projected for the world in the wake of the Great War, conquest would no longer be possible and that without conquest there could be no empire.

But Schumpeter's view is only part of the picture. War and conquest would have achieved very little if that is all there had been. To survive for long, all empires have had to win over their conquered populations. The Romans learned this very early in their history. "An empire," declared the historian Livy at the end of the first century B.C., "remains powerful so long as its subjects rejoice in it."

Rome had a lot to offer its conquered populations—architecture, baths, the ability to bring fresh water from distant hills or to heat marble-lined rooms in villas in the wilds of Northumberland. (The historian Tacitus acidly commented that in adopting baths, porticos, and banquets, all the unwitting Britons had done was to describe as "humanity" what was in reality "an aspect of their slavery.") Ultimately, however, Rome's greatest attraction was citizenship—a concept that, in its recognizably modern form, the Romans invented and that, ever since the early days of the Republic, had been the main ideological prop of the Roman world. Of course, not all Rome's subject peoples wished for such things; but if a substantial number had not, its empire could not have survived as long as it did.

All the later European empires did the best they could to follow at least part of the example Rome had set them. The Spanish and the French both attempted to create something resembling a single society governed by a single body of law. Similarly, the British in India could never have succeeded in seizing control of the former Mughal Empire without the active and sometimes enthusiastic assistance of the emperors' former subjects. Without Indian bureaucrats, Indian judges, and, above all, Indian soldiers, the British Raj would have remained a private trading company. At the Battle of Plassey in 1757, which marked the beginning of the East India Company's political ascendancy over the Mughal Empire, twice as many Indians as Europeans fought on the British side.[5]

It was this process of absorption—and with it the ambition to create a single community that would embrace, as the Roman Empire had, both the mother country and the indigenous inhabitants of its colonies—that allowed Edmund Burke to speak of the victims of the brutal regime of Warren Hastings, governor of Bengal, as "our distressed fellow-citizens in India."[6] Empire was a sacred trust, "given," as Burke insisted, "by an incomprehensible dispensation of Divine providence into our hands." To abuse it, as Hastings had, was not just morally offensive; more significantly for Burke, it threatened the very existence not only of the "British constitution," but of "the civilization of Europe."[7]

Yet the idea of empire based upon universal citizenship created a paradox. If all the inhabitants of the empire were indeed fellow citizens, then a new kind of society, universal and cosmopolitan, would have had to come into being to accommodate them. With hindsight it was possible to argue, as Edward Gibbon did, that in the second century, when "the Roman Empire comprehended the fairest part of the earth and the most civilized portion of mankind," a new kind of society had indeed arisen.[8] But in the eighteenth century, things did not look quite so harmonious. Instead of one world community, the European overseas powers had created what the French philosopher and economist the Marquis de Mirabeau described in 1758 as "a new and monstrous system" that vainly attempted to combine three distinct types of political association (or, as he called them, *esprits*): domination, commerce, and settlement. The inevitable conflict that had arisen between these had thrown all the European powers into crisis. In Mirabeau's view, the only way forward was to abandon both settlement and conquest—especially conquest—in favor of commerce.

He was not alone. For those like Mirabeau and his near-contemporary Adam Smith, what in the eighteenth century was called "the commercial society" seemed to provide a means to create a new, more ecumenical form of empire that now would benefit all its members. For, in theory at least, commerce created a relationship between peoples that did not involve dependency of any kind and that, most importantly, avoided any use of force. In these new commercialized societies, the various peoples of the world would swap new technologies and basic scientific and cultural skills as readily as they would swap foodstuffs. These would not be empires of conquest, but "empires of liberty."[9]

But this vision never materialized because, as Smith fully recognized, the European empires were not, nor had ever been, merely means to economic ends; they were also matters of international prestige.[10] Smith knew that without colonies Britain would be nothing more than a small European state. The disparity in size between the mother country and the rest of the empire remained a constant worry. Furthermore, as David Hume pointed out, the "sweet commerce" in which Montesquieu and others had placed such trust was, at best, an uncertain panacea for the ills of mankind: in reality, even the most highly commercialized states tended to "look upon their neighbours with a suspicious eye, to consider all trading states as their rivals, and to suppose that it is impossible for any of them to flourish, but at their expence."[11]

Hume's skepticism proved all too accurate. It was in the long run more profitable, as both the British and the Dutch discovered in Asia, to exercise direct control over the sources of supply through conquest than it was to trade with them. But the Enlightenment vision of the future transvaluation of empire was finally swept aside not so much by the actual practice of the "empires of liberty" as by Napoleon's attempt to build quite a different kind of empire within Europe itself.

Initially the very brevity and bloodiness of the Napoleonic ambition to transform Europe into a series of satellite kingdoms seemed to the liberals who had suffered from it—Alexis de Tocqueville and Benjamin Constant in particular—to have rendered all such projects unrepeatable. In 1813, with Napoleon apparently out of the way, Constant felt able to declare that, at last, "pleasure and utility" had "opposed irony to every real or feigned enthusiasm" of the kind that had always been the driving force behind all modes of imperialism. Napoleon, and, above all, Napoleon's fall, had shown that postrevolutionary politics were to be conducted not in the name of "conquest and usurpation," but in accordance with public opinion. And public opinion, Constant confidently predicted, would have nothing to do with empire. "The force that a people needs to keep all others in subjection," he wrote,

> is today, more than ever, a privilege that cannot last. The nation that aimed at such an empire would place itself in a more dangerous position than the weakest of tribes. It would become the object of universal horror. Every opinion, every desire, every hatred, would threaten it, and sooner or later those hatreds, those opinions, and those desires would explode and engulf it.[12]

Like Smith, Constant also believed that commerce, or "civilized calculation," as he called it, would come to control all future relationships between peoples. Nearly a century later, Schumpeter expressed, in characteristically unquestioning terms, the same conviction. "It may be stated as beyond controversy," he declared, "that where free trade prevails no class has an interest in forcible expansion as such."[13]

Ironically, in view of the similarity of these claims, what separated Schumpeter from Constant in time was a phase of imperial expansion that was more atavistic, more "enthusiastic" even than the one Constant hoped he had seen the last of. For what in fact followed Napoleon's final defeat was not a return to the Enlightenment status quo ante, but the emergence of modern nationalism. After the Congress of Vienna, the newly self-conscious European states and, subsequently, the new nations of Europe—Belgium (founded in 1831), Italy (1861), and Germany (1876)—all began to compete with one another for the status and economic gains that empire was thought to bestow. Public opinion, far from turning an ironical eye on the imperialistic pretensions of the new European nations, embraced them with enthusiasm. National prestige was, for instance, the

main grounds on which Tocqueville supported the French invasion of Algeria in 1830.

The new imperialism turned out to be very different from the kind of empire of liberty for which Burke and Smith and Mirabeau had argued. No "sacred trust" was involved here—only, in Joseph Conrad's famous phrase, "the taking away [of the earth] from those who have a different complexion or slightly flatter noses than ourselves." In the new nationalist calculus, the more of this earth you could take away, the greater you became. By 1899, imperialism had indeed become, as Curzon remarked, "the faith of a nation."[14]

There was something else that was new about the new imperialism. With the exception of the Spanish, the earlier European powers had been only marginally concerned with changing the lives, beliefs, and customs of the peoples whose lands they had occupied. Missionaries—Catholic, Anglican, Lutheran, Calvinist—were present in British and French America, and even in British, French, and Dutch Asia, but their activities were always of secondary political importance and generally looked upon by the civilian authorities as something of a nuisance.

In the nineteenth century, however, Africa and even India became the testing grounds for a new missionary zeal. Driven partly by Christian ideals, partly by a belief in the overwhelming superiority of European culture, the new imperialists sought to make of the world one world—Christian, liberal, and, ultimately (since none of the virtues peddled by the missionaries could be sustained in any other kind of society), commercial and industrial.

In this vision of empire, the "natives," Rudyard Kipling's "new-caught sullen peoples, half devil and half child," had not merely to be ruled, they had to be ruled for their own good—however much they might resent it at first—and had to be made to recognize that one way of life was the inevitable goal of all mankind. This was empire as tutelage. Ironically, and fatally for the imperial powers as it turned out, it also implied that one day all the subjects of all the European empires would become self-governing.

"By good government," Lord Macaulay had declared as early as 1833, "we may educate our subjects into a capacity for better government; that having become instructed in European knowledge they may, in some future age, demand European institutions." He did not know when this would come about, but he was certain that when it did, "it will be the proudest day in English history."[15] In practice, self-determination would be postponed into the remote future. But Macaulay was forced to acknowledge that, theoretically at least, it could not be postponed indefinitely.

Nationalist imperialism, however, brought to the fore a question that had remained unanswered for a long time: in the modern world what, precisely, was the nature of empire? Ever since 1648, the modern nation-state has been one in which imperium has been regarded as indivisible. The monarchs of Europe had spent centuries wresting authority from nobles, bishops, towns, guilds, military orders, and any number of quasi-independent, quasi-sovereign bodies. Indivisibility had been one of the shibboleths of prerevolutionary Europe, and one which the French Revolution had gone on to place at the center of the conception of the modern state. The modern person is a rights-bearing individual, but—as the 1791 *Déclaration des droits de l'homme et du citoyen* had made clear—he or she is so only by virtue of being a citizen of a single indivisible state.[16]

Such a strong notion of sovereignty could apply, however, only within Europe. In the world beyond, things were very different. It had been impossible for any empire to thrive without sharing power with either local settler elites or with local inhabitants. As Henry Maine, a renowned jurist, historian, and legal member of the viceroy's council in India, had declared in 1887, "Sovereignty has always been regarded as divisible in international law."[17] Failure to cede this point had, after all, been the prime cause of the American Revolution, and, after 1810, of the revolt of the Spanish colonies in South America—and had almost driven the French settlers of Saint-Domingue, Guadeloupe, and Martinique into the waiting arms of the British.

Nowhere was the question of divided sovereignty so acute as in the British Empire, which by the early nineteenth century had become larger and more widespread, and consequently more varied, than any of its rivals or predecessors. "I know of no example of it either in ancient or modern history," wrote Disraeli in 1878. "No Caesar or Charlemagne ever presided over a dominion so peculiar." If such a conglomerate was to survive at all, it could insist on no single constitutional identity. It was this feature of the empire that led the historian Sir Robert Seeley in 1883 to make his famous remark that it seemed as if England had "conquered and peopled half the world in a fit of absence of mind."[18]

Nothing, it seems, could be further removed from the present position of the United States. Is then the United States really an empire?

I think if we look at the history of the European empires, the answer must be no. It is often assumed that because America possesses the military capability to become an empire, any overseas interest it does have must necessarily be imperial.[19] But if military muscle had been all that was required to make an empire, neither Rome nor Britain—to name only two—would have been one. Contrary to the popular image, most empires were, in fact, for most of their histories, fragile structures, always dependent on their subject peoples for survival. Universal citizenship was not created out of generosity. It was created out of need. "What else proved fatal to Sparta and Athens in spite of their power in arms," the emperor Claudius asked the Roman Senate when it attempted to deny citizenship to the Gauls in Italy, "but their policy of holding the conquered aloof as alien-born?"[20]

This is not to say that the United States has not resorted to some of the strategies of past empires. Today, for instance, Iraq and Afghanistan look remarkably like British protectorates. Whatever the administration may claim publicly about the autonomy of the current Iraqi and Afghan leadership, the United States in fact shares sovereignty with the civilian governments of both places, since it retains control over the countries' armed forces. What, however, the United States is not committed to is the view that empire—the exercise of imperium—is the best, or even a possible, way to achieve this.

In a number of crucial respects, the United States is, indeed, very unimperial. Despite allusions to the *Pax Americana*, twenty-first-century America bears not the slightest resemblance to ancient Rome. Unlike all previous European empires, it has no significant overseas settler populations in any of its formal dependencies and no obvious desire to acquire any. It does not conceive its hegemony beyond its borders as constituting a form of citizenship. It exercises no direct rule anywhere outside these areas; and it has always attempted to extricate itself as swiftly as possible from anything that looks as if it were about to develop into even indirect rule.

Cecil Rhodes once said that he would colonize the stars if he could. It is hard to image any prominent American policymaker, even Paul Wolfowitz, even secretly, harboring such desires. As Viscount James Bryce, one of the most astute observers of the Americas both North and South, said of the (North) Americans, "they have none of the earth-hunger which burns in the great nations of Europe."[21]

The one feature the United States does share with many past empires is the desire to impose its political values on the rest of the world. Like the "liberal" empires of nineteenth-century Britain and France, the United States is broadly committed to the liberal-democratic view that democracy is the highest possible form of government and should therefore be exported. This is the American mission to which Madeleine Albright alluded, and it has existed in one form or another ever since the creation of the republic.

In addressing the need to "contain" Communist China, Harry Truman—comparing America to Achaemenid Persia, Macedonian Greece, Antonine Rome, and Victorian Britain—claimed that the only way to save the world from totalitarianism was for the "whole world [to] adopt the American system." By this he meant, roughly, what George W. Bush means by freedom—democratic institutions and free trade. Truman, knowingly or unknowingly, took the phrase "American system" from Alexander Hamilton, who firmly believed that the new republic should one day be able to "concur in erecting one great American system superior to the control of all transatlantic force or influence and able to dictate the terms of the connections between the old world and the new."[22] "For the American system," Truman continued, could only survive "by becoming a world system."[23] What for Hamilton was to be a feature of international relations, for Truman was to be nothing less than a world culture.

But even making the rest of the world adopt the American system did not mean, as it had for all the other empires Truman cited, ruling the rest of the world. For Truman assumed, as has every American administration since, that the world's "others" no longer needed to be led and cajoled until one day they finally demanded their own democratic institutions. American values, as Bush put it in 2002, are not only "right and true for every person in every society"—they are self-evidently so.[24] All humanity is capable of recognizing that democracy, or "freedom," will always be in its own best interest. All that has ever prevented some peoples from grasping this simple truth is fanaticism, the misguided claims of (certain) religions, and the actions of malevolent, self-interested leaders. Rather than empire, the United States' objective, then, is to eliminate these internal obstacles, to establish the conditions necessary for democracy, and then to retreat.

There can be little doubt that this assumption has been the cause, in Iraq as much as in El Salvador, of the failure to establish regimes that are democratic in more than name. Humanity is not, as Iraq and Afghanistan have demonstrated, destined to find democracy more enticing than any other alternative. You may not need to be an

American to embrace "American values"—but you certainly need to be much closer to American beliefs and cultural expectations than most of the populations of the Middle East currently are. Tocqueville made a similar point about Algeria. It would have been impossible to make Algeria into a modern nation without "civilizing" the Arabs, he argued, a task that would be impossible to achieve unless Algeria was made into not a "colony," but "an extension of France itself on the far side of the Mediterranean."[25] The French government chose to ignore him and made it into a colony nonetheless.

But such an arrangement has never been an option for the United States. If only because the United States is the one modern nation in which no division of sovereignty is, at least conceptually, possible. The federal government shares sovereignty with the individual states of which the union is composed, but it could not contemplate, as former empires all had to, sharing sovereignty with the members of *other* nations. Only very briefly has the mainland United States ever been considered an empire rather than a nation. As each new U.S. territory was settled or conquered it became, within a very short space of time, a new state within the Union. This implied that any territories the United States might acquire overseas had, like Hawaii, to be incorporated fully into the nation—or returned to its native inhabitants. No American administration has been willing to tolerate any kind of colonialism for very long. Even so resolute an imperialist as Teddy Roosevelt could not imagine turning Cuba or the Philippines into colonies.[26] The United States does possess a number of dependent territories—Guam, the Virgin Islands, Samoa, etc.—but these are too few and too small to constitute an overseas colonial empire. The major exception to this rule is Puerto Rico. The existence of a vigorous debate over the status of this "commonwealth"—a term which itself suggests that Puerto Rico is an independent republic—and the fact that the status quo strikes everyone, even those who support its continuation, as an anomaly, largely proves the rule.[27]

Those advocating a more forceful U.S. imperial policy overlook that if America is in denial, it is in it for a very good reason. To become a true empire, as even the British were at the end of the nineteenth century, the United States would have to change radically the nature of its political culture. It is a liberal democracy (as most of the Western world now conceives it)—and liberal democracy and liberal empire (as Mill conceived it) are incompatible.[28] The form of empire championed by Mill existed to enforce the virtues and advantages that accompanied free or liberal government in places that otherwise would be, in Mill's language, "barbarous." The time might indeed come when the inhabitants of such places would demand European institutions—but as Mill and even Macaulay knew, when that happened, the empire would be at an end.

By contrast the United States makes no claim to be holding Iraq and Afghanistan in trust until such time as their peoples are able to govern themselves in a suitable—i.e., Western—manner. It seeks, however imperfectly, to confer free democratic institutions directly on those places, and then to depart, leaving the hapless natives to fabricate as best they can the social and political infrastructure without which no democratic process can survive for long.

In the end, perhaps, what Smith, Constant, and Schumpeter prophesied has come to pass: commerce has finally replaced conquest. True, it is commerce stripped of all its eighteenth-century attributes of benevolence, but it is commerce nonetheless. The long-term political objectives of the United States, which have varied little from administration to administration, have been to sustain and, where necessary, to create a world of democracies bound inexorably together by international trade. And the political forms best suited to international commerce are federations (such as the European Union) and trading partnerships (the OECD or NAFTA), not empires.

In *Paradise and Power: America and Europe in the New World Order*, Robert Kagan boasts that whereas the "old" Europeans had moved beyond "power into a self-contained world of laws and rules and transnational negotiation and cooperation . . . a post-historical paradise of peace and relative prosperity, the realization of Immanuel Kant's 'perpetual peace,'" the United States

> remains mired in history, exercising power in an anarchic Hobbesian world where international rules are unreliable, and where true security and the defense and promotion of a liberal order still depend on the possession and use of military might.[29]

It is difficult to know just what Kagan takes the words "Kant" and "Hobbes" to stand for. But on any reasoned understanding of the writings of Thomas Hobbes and Immanuel Kant, he would seem to have inverted the objectives of the Europeans and the Americans. For it is the Europeans (or at least the majority of them) who—by attempting to isolate the European Union as far as possible from all forms of external conflict that are considered to pose no immediate domestic threat—are the true Hobbesians. And in most respects the objectives of Kant's conception of a "universal *cosmopolitan existence*"—which would constitute the "matrix within which all the original capacities of the human race may develop"[30]— is, mutatis mutandis, what the current U.S. government claims to be attempting to achieve.

Kant argued that the peoples of the world would never be at peace so long as the existing world powers—what he called "universal monarchies"—were locked into internecine competition with one another. They had, he said, to be persuaded to join a league for their own mutual protection. To make this possible, however, it was not enough to rely on international trade agreements or peace treaties, because in the long run the parties to such agreements would honor them only if they perceived them to be in their interests. A true world federation could only come about once all the states of the world shared a common political order, what Kant called "representative republicanism." Only then would they all have the same interests, and only then would those interests be to promote mutual prosperity and to avoid warfare. The reason he believed this

to be so was that such societies were the only ones in which human beings were treated as ends not means; the only ones, therefore, in which human beings could be fully autonomous; and the only ones, consequently, in which no people would ever go to war to satisfy the greed or ambition of their rulers.

With due allowance for the huge differences between the late eighteenth century and the early twenty-first, and between what Kant understood by representative republics and what is meant today by liberal democracies, the United States' vision for the world is roughly similar: a union of democracies, certainly not equal in size or power, but all committed to the common goal of greater prosperity and peace through free trade. The members of this union have the right to defend themselves against aggressors and, in the pursuit of defense, they are also entitled to do their best to cajole so-called rogue states into mending their ways sufficiently to be admitted into the union. This is what Kant called the "cosmopolitan right."[31] We may assume that Truman had such an arrangement in mind when he said that the American system could only survive by becoming a world system.

For like the "American system," Kant's "cosmopolitan right" was intended to provide precisely the kind of harmonious environment in which it was possible to pursue what Kant valued most highly, namely, the interdependence of all human societies. This indisputably "liberal order" still depended "on the possession and use of military might," but there would be no permanent, clearly identifiable, perpetual enemy—only dissidents, "rogue" states, and the perverse malice of the excluded. Kant was also not, as Kagan seems to imply, some kind of high-minded idealist, in contrast to Hobbes, the indefatigably realist. He was in fact very suspicious of high-mindedness of any kind. "This rational idea of a *peaceful*, even if not friendly, thoroughgoing community of all the nations on the earth," he wrote, "is not a philanthropic (ethical), principle, but a principle *having to do with rights*."[32] It was based quite as firmly upon a calculation of reasonable self-interest as was Hobbes's suggestion for exiting from the "war of all against all."[33]

Kant, however, was also aware that bringing human beings to understand just what is in their own self-interest would always be a long and arduous task. In order to recognize that autonomy is the highest human good, humans have to disentangle themselves from the "leading strings" by which the "guardians"—priests, lawyers, and rulers—have made them "domesticated animals." Only he who could "throw off the ball and chain of his perpetual immaturity" would be properly "enlightened," and only the enlightened could create the kind of state in which true autonomy would be possible.[34] Because of this, the cosmopolitan right still lay for most at some considerable distance in the future.

It still does—few states today fulfill Kant's criteria. And of course Kant never addressed the problem of how the transition from one or another kind of despotism to "representative republicanism" was to be achieved (although he seems to have thought that the French Revolution, at least in its early phases, offered one kind of model).

Kant's project for perpetual peace has often been taken to be some kind of moral blueprint for the United Nations. But in my view, it is far closer to the final objective of the modern global state system in which the United States is undoubtedly, for the moment at least, the key player. It is also, precisely because it is a project for some future time, a far better guide to the overall ideological objectives of the United States than anything that now goes under the name of "empire."

NOTES

1. Quoted in Emmanuel Todd, *Après l'empire: essai sur la décomposition du système américain* (Paris: Gallimard, 2002), 22. Ironically—or perhaps not—she was justifying a missile attack on Iraq.

2. Niall Ferguson, *Empire: The Rise and Demise of the British World Order and the Lessons for Global Power* (New York: Basic Books, 2003),

317; Ferguson, *Colossus: The Price of America's Empire* (New York: Penguin Press, 2004), 3–7.

3. See P. A. Blunt, "Laus imperii," in Peter Garnsey and C. R. Whittaker, eds., *Imperialism in the Ancient World* (Cambridge: Cambridge University Press, 1978), 159–191.

4. Joseph Schumpeter, *Imperialism and Social Classes*, trans. Heinz Norden (New York: A. M. Kelley, 1951), 7.

5. Linda Colley, *Captives: Britain, Empire and the World, 1600–1850* (London: Jonathan Cape, 2002), 259.

6. "Speech on the Nabob of Arcot's Debts," quoted in Uday Singh Mehta, *Liberalism and Empire: A Study in Nineteenth-Century British Liberal Thought* (Chicago: University of Chicago Press, 1999), 157.

7. Edmund Burke, *On Empire, Liberty, and Reform: Speeches and Letters*, ed. David Bromwich (New Haven, Conn.: Yale University Press, 2000), 15–16.

8. Edward Gibbon, *Decline and Fall of the Roman Empire*, chap. 3.

9. See Anthony Pagden, *Lords of All the World: Ideologies of Empire in Spain, Britain and France c.1500–c.1800* (New Haven, Conn.: Yale University Press, 1995), 178–187.

10. Adam Smith, "Thoughts on the State of the Contest with America," in Ernest Campbell Mossner and Ian Simpson Ross, eds., *Correspondence of Adam Smith*, vol. 6 (Oxford: Clarendon Press, 1977), 383.

11. David Hume, "On the Jealousy of Trade," in Eugene F. Miller, ed., *Essays, Moral, Political, and Literary* (Indianapolis: Liberty Classics, 1985), 328.

12. Benjamin Constant, *The Spirit of Conquest and Usurpation and their Relation to European Civilization in Political Writings*, ed. and trans. Biancamaria Fontana (Cambridge: Cambridge University Press, 1988), 79.

13. Schumpeter, *Imperialism and Social Classes*, 99.

14. Quoted in Harold Nicolson, *Curzon: The Last Phase, 1919–1925: A Study in Post-War*

Diplomacy (New York: Houghton Mifflin Company, 1934), 13.

15. Quoted in Thomas R. Metcalf, *Ideologies of the Raj* (Cambridge: Cambridge University Press, 1994), 34.

16. See Anthony Pagden, "Human Rights, Natural Rights and Europe's Imperial Legacy," *Political Theory* 31 (2003): 171–199.

17. Quoted in Edward Keene, *Beyond the Anarchical Society: Grotius, Colonialism and Order in World Politics* (Cambridge: Cambridge University Press, 2002), 63.

18. Sir John Robert Seeley, *The Expansion of England* (London: Macmillan, 1883), 12.

19. This, for instance, is the argument behind Robert D. Kaplan's *Warrior Politics: Why Leadership Demands a Pagan Ethos* (New York: Random House, 2002), and in a very different and more measured tone, Chalmers A. Johnson's *The Sorrows of Empire: Militarism, Secrecy, and the End of the Republic* (New York: Metropolitan Books, 2004)—although Kaplan approves and Johnson disapproves.

20. Tacitus, *Annals* II, 23–24.

21. Quoted by Arthur Schelsinger, Jr. in "The Making of a Mess," *The New York Review of Books* 51 (14) (September 2004): 41.

22. Federalist 11 in *The Federalist Papers*, ed. Isaac Kramnick (Harmondsworth: Penguin, 1987), 133–134.

23. Quoted in Ferguson, *Colossus*, 80.

24. Quoted in Rashid Khalidi, *Resurrecting Empire: Western Footprints and America's Perilous Path in the Middle East* (Boston: Beacon Press, 2004), 3.

25. "Rapport fait par M. Tocqueville sur le projet de la loi relative aux credits extraordinaires demandés pour l'Algérie," in Seloua Luste Boulbina, ed., *Tocqueville sur l'Algérie, 1847* (Paris: Flammarion, 2003), 228.

26. Frank Ninkovich, *The United States and Imperialism* (Malden, Mass.: Blackwell Publishers, 2001), 75.

27. See Christina Duffy Burnett and Burke Marshall, eds., *Foreign in a Domestic Sense: Puerto Rico, American Expansion, and the Constitution* (Durham, N.C.: Duke University Press, 2001).

28. On this term, see Michael Mann, *Incoherent Empire* (London: Verso, 2003), 11.

29. Robert Kagan, *Paradise and Power: America and Europe in the New World Order* (London: Atlantic Books, 2003), 3.

30. Immanuel Kant, "Idea for a Universal History with a Cosmopolitan Purpose," in Hans Reiss, ed., *Political Writings* (Cambridge: Cambridge University Press, 1991), 51.

31. Immanuel Kant, *The Metaphysics of Morals*, trans. Mary Gregor (Cambridge: Cambridge University Press, 1991), 156.

32. Kant, *The Metaphysics of Morals*, 158; Anthony Pagden, "Stoicism, Cosmopolitanism and the Legacy of European Imperialism," *Constellations* 7 (2000): 3–22.

33. Immanuel Kant, "Perpetual Peace: A Philosophical Sketch," in Reiss, ed., *Political Writings*, 112.

34. Immanuel Kant, "An Answer to the Question: 'What Is Enlightenment?'" in Reiss, ed., *Political Writings*, 54–55.

5 THE STATE

The state remains the key actor in international relations, although challenges to the state are increasing, as explained in Chapter 5 of Essentials of International Relations. *The selections in this chapter examine issues concerning the state, its strength, and challenges to it. Stanford University professor Stephen Krasner discusses the principles of sovereignty but finds that they do not work for many parts of the world. Alternatives to state failure must entail new options, including shared sovereignty and de facto trusteeships. Other transnational processes may also "nibble" at state sovereignty. Anne-Marie Slaughter of Princeton University proposes that state sovereignty will increasingly be challenged by the growth of transgovernmental networks.*

The state is challenged in other ways as well. Globalization undermines state power and authority. Transnational religious and ideological movements and ethnonational movements are threats to states and state sovereignty. Samuel P. Huntington, a prominent Harvard University political scientist, predicts that the future international system will be characterized by a clash between Western and Islamic civilizations. The article included here and the book that elaborates the thesis, The Clash of Civilizations and the Remaking of World Order (*1996*), *have been widely discussed and criticized. Among the potent critiques is the argument that Islam is a more diverse "opponent" than Huntington suggests. Yahya Sadowski of American University of Beirut carefully describes the diversity of Muslims (Sunni and Shia; rural and urban; nationalist variations), and the diversity within political Islam (traditional, fundamentalist, Islamist). Sadowski's article traces the characteristics of political Islam as a social movement and its relationship with democracy.*

STEPHEN D. KRASNER

SHARING SOVEREIGNTY: NEW INSTITUTIONS FOR COLLAPSED AND FAILING STATES

Conventional sovereignty assumes a world of autonomous, internationally recognized, and well-governed states. Although frequently violated in practice, the fundamental rules of conventional sovereignty—recognition of juridically independent territorial entities and nonintervention in the internal affairs of other states—have rarely been challenged in principle. But these rules no longer work, and their inadequacies have had deleterious consequences for the strong as well as the weak. The policy tools that powerful and well-governed states have available to "fix" badly governed or collapsed states—principally governance assistance and transitional administration (whether formally authorized by the United Nations or engaged in by a coalition of the willing led by the United States)—are inadequate. In the future, better domestic governance in badly governed, failed, and occupied polities will require the transcendence of accepted rules, including the creation of shared sovereignty in specific areas. In some cases, decent governance may require some new form of trusteeship, almost certainly de facto rather than de jure.[1]

Many countries suffer under failed, weak, incompetent, or abusive national authority structures. The best that people living in such countries can hope for is marginal improvement in their material well-being; limited access to social services, including health care and education; and a moderate degree of individual physical security. At worst they will confront endemic violence, exploitative political leaders, falling life expectancy, declining per capita income, and even state-sponsored genocide. In the Democratic Republic of Congo (formerly Zaire), for example, civil wars that have persisted for more than two decades have resulted in millions of deaths. In Zimbabwe the policies of President Robert Mugabe, who was determined to stay in office regardless of the consequences for his country's citizens, led to an economic debacle that began in 2000 with falling per capita income, inflation above 500 percent, and the threat of mass starvation. In Colombia much of the territory is controlled by the Revolutionary Armed Forces of Colombia (FARC), a Marxist rebel group that derives most of its income from drug trafficking. In Rwanda more than 700,000 people were slaughtered in a matter of weeks in 1994 as a result of a government-organized genocide.

The consequences of failed and inadequate governance have not been limited to the societies directly affected. Poorly governed societies can generate conflicts that spill across international borders. Transnational criminal and terrorist networks can operate in territories not controlled by the internationally recognized government. Humanitarian disasters not only prick the conscience of political leaders in advanced democratic societies but also leave them with no policy options that are appealing to voters.

Challenges related to creating better governance also arise where national authority structures have collapsed because of external invasion and occupation rather than internal conflict. The availability of weapons of mass destruction and the presence of transnational terrorism have created a historically unprecedented situation in which polities with very limited material capability can threaten the security of much more powerful states. These polities can be conquered and

From *International Security* 29, no. 2 (Fall 2004): 85–120. Some of the author's notes have been omitted.

occupied with relative ease, leaving the occupying power with the more challenging task of establishing an acceptable domestic governing structure. Contemporary Afghanistan and Iraq are the obvious cases in point.

Left to their own devices, collapsed and badly governed states will not fix themselves because they have limited administrative capacity, not least with regard to maintaining internal security.[2] Occupying powers cannot escape choices about what new governance structures will be created and sustained. To reduce international threats and improve the prospects for individuals in such polities, alternative institutional arrangements supported by external actors, such as de facto trusteeships and shared sovereignty, should be added to the list of policy options.

The current menu of policy instruments for dealing with collapsed and failing states is paltry, consisting primarily of transitional administration and foreign assistance to improve governance, both of which assume that in more or less short order, targeted states can function effectively on their own. Nation-building or state-building efforts are almost always described in terms of empowering local authorities to assume the responsibilities of conventional sovereignty. The role of external actors is understood to be limited with regard to time, if not scope, in the case of transitional administration exercising full executive authority. Even as the rules of conventional sovereignty are de facto violated if not de jure challenged, and it is evident that in many cases effective autonomous national government is far in the future, the language of diplomacy, the media, and the street portrays nothing other than a world of fully sovereign states.

The next section of this article describes the basic elements that constitute the conventional understanding of sovereignty and provides a taxonomy of alternative institutional forms. It is followed by a discussion of the ways in which conventional sovereignty has failed in some states, threatening the well-being of their own citizens and others. The inadequacy of the current repertoire of policy options for dealing with collapsed, occupied, and badly governed states—governance assistance and transitional administration—is then assessed. The possibilities for new institutional forms—notably shared sovereignty and some de facto form of trusteeship—are examined. Included is a discussion of why such arrangements might be accepted by political leaders in target as well as intervening states.

Conventional Sovereignty and Some Alternatives

Conventional sovereignty has three elements: international legal sovereignty, Westphalian/Vatellian sovereignty, and domestic sovereignty.[3] The basic rule of international legal sovereignty is to recognize juridically independent territorial entities. These entities then have the right to freely decide which agreements or treaties they will enter into. In practice, this rule has been widely but not universally honored. Some entities that are not juridically independent have been recognized (e.g., Byelorussia and the Ukraine during the Cold War), and some entities that are juridically independent have not been recognized (e.g., the People's Republic of China from 1949 to the 1970s).

The fundamental rule of Westphalian/Vatellian sovereignty is to refrain from intervening in the internal affairs of other states. Each state has the right to determine its own domestic authority structures. In practice, Westphalian/Vatellian sovereignty has frequently been violated.

Domestic sovereignty does not involve a norm or a rule, but is rather a description of the nature of domestic authority structures and the extent to which they are able to control activities within a state's boundaries. Ideally, authority structures would ensure a society that is peaceful, protects human rights, has a consultative mechanism, and honors a rule of law based on a shared understanding of justice.

In the ideal sovereign state system, international legal sovereignty, Westphalian/Vatellian sovereignty, and domestic sovereignty are mutually supportive. Recognized authorities within territorial entities regulate behavior, enjoy independence from outside interference, and enter into mutually beneficial contractual relations (treaties) with other recognized entities. This is the conventional world of international politics in which state-to-state relations are what count. One of the most striking aspects of the contemporary world is the extent to which domestic sovereignty has faltered so badly in states that still enjoy international legal, and sometimes even Westphalian/Vatellian, sovereignty. Somalia, for instance, is still an internationally recognized entity, even though it has barely any national institutions; and external actors have not, in recent years, tried to do much about Somalia's domestic sovereignty, or the lack thereof.

Conventional sovereignty was not always the hegemonic structure for ordering political life. Obviously, the basic rules of medieval Europe or the pre-nineteenth-century Sinocentric world were very different. But even in the nineteenth century, by which time conventional sovereignty had become a well-recognized structure, there were also legitimated and accepted alternatives. Protectorates were one alternative to conventional sovereignty; the rulers of a protectorate relinquished control over foreign policy to a more powerful state but retained authority over domestic affairs. For instance, in 1899 the ruler of Kuwait signed an agreement that gave Britain control of most elements of his country's foreign policy because he needed external support against threats from both Iraq and members of his own family.[4] In nineteenth-century China the major powers established treaty ports where British, French, German, and Japanese authorities regulated commerce and exercised extraterritorial authority over their own citizens and sometimes Chinese as well.[5] Within the British Empire, Australia, Canada, and South Africa became dominions that enjoyed almost complete control over their domestic affairs, recognized the British ruler as the head of state, but to some

extent deferred to Britain in matters of foreign policy. Finally, colonization was a legitimated practice in the nineteenth century that allowed powerful states to assume international legal sovereignty and regulate the domestic authority structures of far-flung territories.

Conventional sovereignty is currently the only fully legitimated institutional form, but unfortunately, it does not always work. Honoring Westphalian/Vatellian sovereignty (and sometimes international legal sovereignty as well) makes it impossible to secure decent and effective domestic sovereignty, because the autochthonous political incentives facing political leaders in many failed, failing, or occupied states are perverse. These leaders are better able to enhance their own power and wealth by making exclusionist ethnic appeals or undermining even the limited legal routinized administrative capacity that might otherwise be available.

To secure decent domestic governance in failed, failing, and occupied states, new institutional forms are needed that compromise Westphalian/Vatellian sovereignty for an indefinite period. Shared sovereignty, arrangements under which individuals chosen by international organizations, powerful states, or ad hoc entities would share authority with nationals over some aspects of domestic sovereignty, would be a useful addition to the policy repertoire. Ideally, shared sovereignty would be legitimated by a contract between national authorities and an external agent. In other cases, external interveners may conclude that the most attractive option would be the establishment of a de facto trusteeship or protectorate. Under such an arrangement, the Westphalian/Vatellian sovereignty of the target polity would be violated, executive authority would be vested primarily with external actors, and international legal sovereignty would be suspended. There will not, however, be any effort to formalize through an international convention or treaty a general set of principles for such an option.[6] (For a summary of these different institutional possibilities, see Table 1.)

Table 1. Alternative Institutional Arrangements

	International Legal Sovereignty		Westphalian/Vatellian Sovereignty			Duration of Rule Violation		
	No	Yes	None	Some	Full	Short	Medium	Long
Conventional sovereignty		X			X	n/a	n/a	n/a
Colony	X		X					X
Transitional administration with full foreign executive authority	X		X			X		
Trusteeship	X		X or	X			X	X
Shared sovereignty		X		X				X
Nineteenth-century protectorate	X			X				X

Failures of Conventional Sovereignty

Failed, inadequate, incompetent, or abusive national authority structures have sabotaged the economic well-being, violated the basic human rights, and undermined the physical security of their countries' populations. In some cases, state authority has collapsed altogether for an extended period, although such instances are rare. Afghanistan in the early 1990s before the Taliban consolidated power, Liberia for much of the 1990s, and the Democratic Republic of Congo and Sierra Leone in the late 1990s are just a few of the examples. Governance challenges have also arisen in Afghanistan and Iraq, where authority structures collapsed as a result of external invasion rather than internal conflict. The occupying powers, most obviously the United States, were then confronted with the challenge of fashioning decent governance structures in both countries.

In some parts of the world, disorder (including civil war) has become endemic. For the period 1955 to 1998, the State Failure Task Force identified 136 occurrences of state failure in countries with populations larger than 500,000. The task force operationalized state failure as one of four kinds of internal political crisis: revolutionary war, ethnic war, "adverse regime change," or genocide. In 1955 fewer than 6 percent of the countries were in failure. In the early 1990s the figure had risen to almost 30 percent, falling to about 20 percent in 1998, the last year of the study. Adverse regime change was the most common form of state failure, followed by ethnic war, revolutionary war, and genocide. The task force identified partial democracy, trade closure, and low levels of economic well-being as indicated by high infant mortality rates as the primary causes of state failure. James Fearon and David Laitin show that internal strife is more likely in countries suffering from poverty, recent decolonization, high population, and mountainous terrain.

These conditions allow even relatively small guerrilla bands to operate successfully because recognized governments do not have the administrative competence to engage in effective rural policing and counterinsurgency operations.[7]

States that experience failure or poor governance more generally are beset by many problems. In such states, infrastructure deteriorates; corruption is widespread; borders are unregulated; gross domestic product is declining or stagnant; crime is rampant; and the national currency is not widely accepted. Armed groups operate within the state's boundaries but outside the control of the government. The writ of the central government, the entity that exercises the prerogatives of international legal sovereignty (e.g., signing treaties and sending delegates to international meetings), may not extend to the whole country; in some cases, it may not extend beyond the capital. Authority may be exercised by local entities in other parts of the country, or by no one at all.

Political leaders operating in an environment in which material and institutional resources are limited have often chosen policies that make a bad situation even worse. For some leaders, disorder and uncertainty are more attractive than order and stability because they are better able to extract resources from a disorderly society. Decisions affecting the distribution of wealth are based on personal connections rather than bureaucratic regulations or the rule of law. Leaders create multiple armed units that they can play off against each other. They find it more advantageous to take a bigger piece of a shrinking pie than a smaller piece of a growing pie.

The largest number of poorly governed states is found on the continent of Africa. Since the mid-1950s about a third of African states have been in failure.[8] In constant 1995 U.S. dollars, gross domestic product per capita for all of sub-Saharan Africa fell from $660 in 1980 to $587 in 1990 to $563 in 2000. Out of the sub-Saharan states for which data are available from the World Bank, eighteen had increases in their per capita gross domestic product from 1990 to 2000, seven had decreases of less than 5 percent,

and seventeen experienced decreases of more than 5 percent. With the exception of the former Soviet Union, no other area of the world fared so badly with regard to economic performance.[9]

*   *   *

Thus, for many countries domestic sovereignty is not working, and the situation is not improving in any substantive way. Although the number and percentage of countries suffering from civil war declined during the 1990s, the per capita gross national income in current U.S. dollars of the least developed countries continued to drop, falling by 9 percent from 1990 to 2000, a period of robust growth for the world as a whole.

Why Sovereignty Failures Matter

In the contemporary world, powerful states have not been able to ignore governance failures. Polities where domestic authority has collapsed or been inadequate have threatened the economic and security interests of these states. Humanitarian crises have engaged electorates in advanced democracies and created no-win situations for political leaders who are damned if they intervene and damned if they do not. And, most obviously, when a state has been invaded, the occupiers have been confronted with the problem of establishing effective domestic sovereignty.

The availability of weapons of mass destruction, the ease of movement across borders, and the emergence of terrorist networks have attenuated the relationship between the underlying capabilities of actors and the ability to kill large numbers of people. In the past, state and nonstate actors with limited resources could not threaten the security of states with substantial resources. The killing power of a nation's military depended on the underlying wealth of the country. Nonstate actors such as anarchist groups in the nineteenth century could throw bombs that might kill fifty or even several hundred people, but not more. This is no longer true. States with limited means can procure chemical and biological weapons. Nuclear weapons demand more re-sources, but they are not out of reach of even a dismally poor country such as North Korea. Weapons of mass destruction can be delivered in myriad ways, not only by missiles but also by commercial ships, trucks, planes, and even envelopes. Failed or weak states may provide terrorists with territory in which they can operate freely.

Moreover, political leaders who have effective control within their borders but limited resources to defend or deter an invasion present a tempting target if they adopt policies that threaten the core security interests of powerful states. For instance, throughout his rule Saddam Hussein sought and sometimes used weapons of mass destruction, and even when faced with invasion, failed to fully cooperate with UN inspectors. In Afghanistan the Taliban supported al-Qa'ida, which had already demonstrated that it could strike core targets in the United States. Neither Iraq nor Afghanistan could defend itself against, or deter, a U.S. attack. When the threat is high and invasion is easy, powerful states are likely to use military force to bring down a menacing regime. When, however, the old regime has collapsed, the occupiers confront the challenge of creating effective and decent domestic sovereignty.

Sovereignty failures may also present problems in the area of transnational criminality. Drug trafficking is difficult to control under any circumstances, but such activities are more likely to flourish where domestic sovereignty is inadequate. About 95 percent of illicit drug production takes place in areas of civil strife. Colombia, where the FARC controls a large part of the territory, has been one of the major sources of such drugs for the United States. In the late 1990s Afghanistan cultivated 75 percent of the world's opium poppies, and despite a ban by the Taliban at the end of its rule, production revived after the regime was overthrown because the new government in Kabul had only limited control over much of the country. Transnational trafficking in persons is more likely, although not limited to, countries where domestic authority and control are weak or ineffective. A 2004 State Department report lists ten countries—Bangladesh, Burma, Cuba, Ecuador, Equatorial Guinea, Guyana, North Korea, Sierra Leone, Sudan, and Venezuela—that have not met minimum efforts to control trafficking in persons. Most of the ten are failed or badly governed states.[10] In addition, it is more difficult to trace and punish the perpetrators of transnational financial fraud in countries where the police and judiciary do not function well.

Finally, gross violations of human rights present unpleasant political choices for democratic leaders in powerful states. There have been a number of humanitarian catastrophes in recent years, with the killings in Rwanda in the mid-1990s being one of the most appalling and most widely reported. Millions of people have died in other countries as well at the hands of their own government or rival political groups. These and other humanitarian disasters have engaged attentive elites. The Canadian ministry of foreign affairs, for instance, organized the International Commission on Intervention and State Sovereignty in 2000 in response to UN Secretary-General Kofi Annan's appeal for a new consensus on the right of humanitarian intervention. The commission, composed of twelve eminent persons, produced a widely circulated report entitled *The Responsibility to Protect*. The report defends the principle of humanitarian intervention when governments abuse or fail to protect their own citizens. Samantha Power's book, *A Problem from Hell: America and the Age of Genocide*, which describes the failure of the United States to act either to prevent or to mitigate a number of genocides throughout the twentieth century, won a Pulitzer Prize in 2003.[11]

*   *   *

Humanitarian crises, then, present decisionmakers in democratic countries with a no-win situation. If they fail to intervene and a humanitarian disaster occurs, they may lose the votes of citizens who are attentive to and care about the fate of particular countries, regions, ethnic groups, or principled issues in general. On the other hand, if a political leader does intervene, the costs in terms of soldiers killed will be readily apparent, but the number of lives saved can never be demonstrated with certainty.

The Existing Institutional Repertoire: Governance Assistance and Transitional Administration

Political leaders in powerful and weak states have been reluctant to challenge the conventional norms of sovereignty. The policy options currently available to repair occupied or badly governed states—governance assistance and transitional administration—are consistent with these norms. They have made some limited contribution to improving governance in badly run and collapsed states, but policymakers would be better served if they had a wider repertoire of policy choices.

Governance Assistance

For the last decade international organizations, the United States, and other donor countries have devoted substantial resources to promoting better governance. U.S. foreign aid has been given to train judges, rewrite criminal codes, increase fiscal transparency, professionalize the police, encourage an open media, strengthen political parties, and monitor elections. In 2004 President George W. Bush's administration launched a new foreign aid initiative, the Millennium Challenge Account (MCA), which, if fully funded, will increase U.S. foreign assistance by 50 percent and provide these resources to a relatively small number of poor countries that have demonstrated good governance in the areas of promoting economic freedom, governing justly, and investing in people.[12]

Since the 1950s, international financial institutions have been involved in questions of policy and sometimes institutional reform in borrowing countries. The conditions attached to lending by the World Bank and the International Monetary Fund (IMF) have covered a wide range of issues such as aggregate credit expansion, subsidies, number of government employees, indexation of salaries, tariffs, tax rates, and institution building. International financial institutions have placed their own personnel in key bureaus.[13] In the mid-1990s the managing director of the IMF and the president of the World Bank committed themselves to a more aggressive attack on corruption in developing states.[14] In 1997 the World Bank subtitled its world development report *The State in a Changing World*. The report declares that the "clamor for greater government effectiveness has reached crisis proportions in many developing countries where the state has failed to deliver even such fundamental public goods as property rights, roads, and basic health and education."[15] Further, it lists basic tasks for the state, including establishing a foundation of law, protecting the environment, and shielding the vulnerable; chastises governments for spending too much on rich and middle-class students in universities while neglecting primary education; and urges these governments to manage ethnic and social differences. Finally, and most ambitiously, the 1991 Agreement Establishing the European Bank for Reconstruction and Development explicitly includes a commitment to democracy as a condition of membership.

Foreign assistance to improve governance in weak states does not usually contradict the rules of conventional sovereignty. Governments contract with external agencies (e.g., countries, multilateral organizations, and nongovernmental organizations [NGOs]) to provide training in various areas. Such contracting is a manifestation of international legal sovereignty and is consistent with Westphalian/Vatellian sovereignty, so long as the influence of external actors on domestic authority structures is limited to specific policies or improvements in the capabilities of government employees. When bargaining power is highly asymmetric, as may be the case in some conditionality agreements between international financial institutions and borrowing countries,

Westphalian/Vatellian sovereignty can be compromised. External actors can influence not just policies but also institutional arrangements in target states. The borrowing country is better off with the agreement, conditions or no, than it would have been without it; otherwise it would not have signed. Nevertheless, political leaders may accept undesired and intrusive engagement from external actors because the alternative is loss of access to international capital markets.

The effectiveness of governance assistance will always be limited. Some leaders will find the exploitation of their own populations more advantageous than the introduction of reforms. The leverage of external actors will usually be constrained. International financial institutions are in the business of lending money; they cannot put too stringent restrictions on their loans lest their customers disappear. Many IMF agreements are renegotiated, sometimes several times. Small social democratic countries in Europe have been committed, because of the views of their electorates, to assisting the poor; they will be loath to allow their funding levels to drop below the generally recognized target of 0.7 percent of national income. The wealthier countries also routinely provide humanitarian assistance, regardless of the quality of governance in a particular country.

Moreover, those providing governance assistance are likely to adopt formulas that reflect their own domestic experience and that may be ill suited to the environments of particular target countries. The United States, for instance, has emphasized elections and independent legislatures. Interest groups have been regarded as independent of the state, whereas in European social democratic countries, they are legitimated by and sometimes created by the state.

Transitional Administration

Transitional administration is the one recognized alternative to conventional sovereignty that exists in the present international environment, but it is explicitly not meant as a challenge to the basic norms of sovereignty. The scope of transitional administration or peacekeeping and peacebuilding operations has ranged from the full assertion of executive authority by the UN for some period of time, East Timor being an example, to more modest efforts involving monitoring the implementation of peace agreements, as was the case in Guatemala in the 1990s. Transitional administration, usually authorized by the UN Security Council, has always been seen as a temporary, transitional measure designed to create the conditions under which conventional sovereignty can be restored. The U.S. occupation of Iraq has followed the same script, albeit without any UN endorsement of the occupation itself, although the Security Council did validate the restoration of international legal sovereignty in June 2004. Westphalian/Vatellian sovereignty and sometimes international legal sovereignty are violated in the short term so that they can be restored in the longer term; at least that is the standard explanation.

The record of peacebuilding efforts since World War II has been mixed. One recent study identified 124 cases of peacebuilding by the international community. Of these, 43 percent were judged to be successful based on the absence of hostilities. If progress toward democracy is added as a measure of success, only 35 percent were successful.[16]

More extensive peacekeeping operations, those that might accurately be called "transitional administration" because they involve the assertion of wide-ranging or full executive authority by the UN (or the United States), are difficult: the demands are high; advance planning, which must prejudge outcomes, is complicated, especially for the UN; and resources—economic, institutional, and military—are often limited. UN missions have run monetary systems, enforced laws, appointed officials, created central banks, decided property claims, regulated businesses, and operated public utilities. The resources to undertake these tasks have rarely been adequate. Each operation has been ad hoc; no cadres of bureaucrats, police, soldiers, or judges permanently committed to transitional administration exist;

and there is a tension between devolving authority to local actors and having international actors assume responsibility for all governmental functions because, at least at the outset, this latter course is seen as being more efficient.[17]

Transitional administration is particularly problematic in situations where local actors disagree about basic objectives among themselves and with external actors. Under these circumstances, as opposed to situations in which local actors agree on goals but need external monitoring to provide reassurances about the behavior of their compatriots, the inherently temporary character of transitional administration increases the difficulty of creating stable institutions. If indigenous groups disagree about the distribution of power and the constitutional structure of the new state, then the optimal strategy for their political leaders is to strengthen their own position in anticipation of the departure of external actors. They do so by maximizing support among their followers rather than backing effective national institutions. Alternatively, local leaders who become dependent on external actors during a transitional administration, but who lack support within their own country, do not have an incentive to invest in the development of new institutional arrangements that would allow their external benefactors to leave at an earlier date.[18]

Multiple external actors with varying interests and little reason to coordinate their activities have exacerbated the problems associated with transitional administration. The bureaucratic and financial interests of international organizations are not necessarily complementary. NGOs need to raise money and make a mark. The command structures for security and civilian activities have been separated. The permanent members of the Security Council, to whom UN peacekeeping authorities are ultimately responsible, have not always had the same interests.[19]

*   *   *

Transitional administration has been most effective when the level of violence in a country has been low, where there has been involvement by major powers, and where the contending parties within the country have reached a mutually acceptable agreement. The key role for the transitional administration is then to monitor the implementation of the agreement. For instance, in Namibia the contact group, comprising Canada, France, Germany, Great Britain, and the United States, was involved in UN discussions about the constitutional structure for an independent Namibia beginning in 1978. All of the major contending parties consented to the UN Transition Assistance Group (UNTAG) that was sent in 1989, allowing the lightly armed mission to play a neutral role between South Africa and Namibia. The strength of the major potential spoilers, hard-line whites, was undermined by the collapse of apartheid in South Africa. The major responsibility of UNTAG was to supervise the elections for the government that assumed power when Namibia secured international legal sovereignty.[20]

There were also successful missions in Central America in the 1990s. In both Guatemala and Nicaragua, government and rebel groups had reached a mutually acceptable settlement. Peacekeeping missions contributed to stability by supervising elections, helping to demobilize combatants, and training police.[21]

In sum, transitional administration has worked best for the easiest cases, those where the key actors have already reached a mutually acceptable agreement. In these situations, the transitional administration plays a monitoring role. It can be truly neutral among the contending parties. The mission does not have to be heavily armed. Transitional administration, however, is much more difficult in cases such as Bosnia, Kosovo, Afghanistan, and Iraq—that is, where local leaders have not reached agreement on what the ultimate outcome for their polity should be and where they must think about positioning themselves to win support from parochial constituencies when transitional administration, along with its large foreign military force, comes to an end.

New Institutional Options: De Facto Trusteeships and Shared Sovereignty

Given the limitations of governance assistance and transitional administration, other options for dealing with countries where international legal sovereignty and Westphalian/Vatellian sovereignty are inconsistent with effective and responsible domestic sovereignty need to be explored. At least two such arrangements would add to the available tool kit of policy options. The first would be to revive the idea of trusteeship or protectorate, probably de facto rather than de jure. The second would be to explore possibilities for shared sovereignty in which national rulers would use their international legal sovereignty to legitimate institutions within their states in which authority was shared between internal and external actors.

De Facto Trusteeships

In a prescient article published in 1993, Gerald Helman and Steven Ratner argued that in extreme cases of state failure, the establishment of trusteeships under the auspices of the UN Security Council would be necessary. By the end of the 1990s, such suggestions had become more common. Analysts have noted that de facto trusteeships have become a fact of international life. In a monograph published in 2002, Richard Caplan argues, "An idea that once enjoyed limited academic currency at best—international trusteeship for failed states and contested territories—has become a reality in all but name." Martin Indyk, an assistant secretary of state during President Bill Clinton's administration, has argued that the most attractive path to permanent peace in the Middle East would be to establish a protectorate in Palestine, legitimated by the United Nations and with the United States playing a key role in security and other areas. Even if final status talks were completed, the trusteeship would remain in place

until a responsible Palestinian government was established.[22]

Despite these recent observations, developing an alternative to conventional sovereignty, one that explicitly recognizes that international legal sovereignty will be withdrawn and that external actors will control many aspects of domestic sovereignty for an indefinite period of time, will not be easy. To date there has been no effort, for instance, to produce a treaty or convention that would define and embody in international law a new form of trusteeship. Just the opposite. The rhetorical commitment of all significant actors, including the United States, has been to restore authority to local actors at the soonest possible moment, a stance exemplified by the decision to give what U.S. officials insisted was full sovereignty to Iraq in June 2004.[23]

Codifying a general set of principles and rules for some new kind of trusteeship or protectorate would involve deciding who would appoint the authority and oversee its activities: the UN Security Council? A regional organization such as the European Union? A coalition of the willing? A single state? A treaty or convention would have to define the possible scope of authority of the governing entity: all activities of the state including security and international affairs? Only matters related to the provision of public goods such as roads, but not those related to the private sphere such as marriage? Given that there would be no fixed date for ending a trusteeship or protectorate, how would the appropriate moment for transferring authority to local actors be determined? What intermediate steps would be taken? Could a trusteeship, for instance, be granted international legal recognition and sovereignty, while some aspects of domestic governance remained under the control of the trustee or conservator?

The most substantial barrier to a general international treaty codifying a new form of trusteeship or protectorate is that it will not receive support from either the powerful, who would have to implement it, or the weak, who might be subject to it. There is widespread sentiment for the proposition that Westphalian/Vatellian sovereignty is not absolute and can be breached in cases of massive human rights violations. UN Secretary-General Annan expressed this view in 1999 to widespread international acclaim.[24] But arguing that Westphalian/Vatellian sovereignty is not absolute is quite different from codifying an explicit alternative that would deprive states of their international legal sovereignty as well as control over their domestic affairs.

An explicit and legitimated alternative to sovereignty would require, at minimum, agreement among the major powers. An arrangement supported by leading states that are not members of the OECD such as Brazil, China, India, Indonesia, Nigeria, and South Africa would be even better. Best of all would be an agreement endorsed by the Security Council and the General Assembly. There is no indication, however, that such widespread support would be given. None of the actors has a clear interest in doing so. The major powers, those with the capacity to create a trusteeship, want to be able to pick and choose not only where they intervene but also the policies they would follow. The endorsement of a new institutional arrangement would provide a new choice on the menu, but this option might make it difficult to engage in ad hoc arrangements better suited to specific circumstances. For states in the third world, any successor to the mandate system of the League of Nations, or the trusteeship system of the UN, would smell if not look too much like colonialism.[25]

Shared Sovereignty

Shared sovereignty would involve the engagement of external actors in some of the domestic authority structures of the target state for an indefinite period of time. Such arrangements would be legitimated by agreements signed by recognized national authorities. National actors would use their international legal sovereignty to enter into agreements that would compromise their Westphalian/Vatellian sovereignty with the goal of improving domestic sovereignty. One core element of sovereignty—voluntary agreements—would be preserved, while another core element—the principle of autonomy—would be violated.

National leaders could establish shared sovereignty through either treaties or unilateral commitments. To be effective, such arrangements would have to create self-enforcing equilibria involving either domestic players alone or some combination of domestic and international actors. Political elites in the target state would have to believe that they would be worse off if the shared sovereignty arrangement were violated.

For policy purposes, it would be best to refer to shared sovereignty as "partnerships." This would more easily let policymakers engage in organized hypocrisy, that is, saying one thing and doing another. Shared sovereignty or partnerships would allow political leaders to embrace sovereignty, because these arrangements would be legitimated by the target state's international legal sovereignty, even though they violate the core principle of Westphalian/Vatellian sovereignty: autonomy. Organized hypocrisy is not surprising in an environment such as the international system where there are competing norms (e.g., human rights vs. Westphalian/Vatellian sovereignty), power differentials that allow strong actors to pursue policies that are inconsistent with recognized rules, and exceptional complexity that makes it impossible to write any set of rules that could provide optimal outcomes under all conditions. Shared sovereignty or partnerships would make no claim to being an explicit alternative to conventional sovereignty. It would allow actors to obfuscate the fact that their behavior would be inconsistent with their principles.

HISTORICAL EXAMPLES OF SHARED SOVEREIGNTY

Shared sovereignty agreements have been used in the past. There are several late nineteenth-century shared sovereignty arrangements in which external actors assumed control over part of the revenue-generating stream of a state that had defaulted on its debt. The state wanted renewed access to international capital markets.

The lenders wanted assurance that they would be repaid. Direct control over the collection of specific taxes provided greater confidence than other available measures.

For example, a shared sovereignty arrangement between external lenders and the Porte (the government of the Ottoman Empire) was constructed for some parts of the revenue system of the empire during the latter part of the nineteenth century. The empire entered international capital markets in the 1850s to fund military expenditures associated with the Crimean War. By 1875, after receiving more than a dozen new loans, the empire was unable to service its foreign debt. To again secure access to international capital markets, the Ottomans agreed in 1881 to create, through government decree, the Council of the Public Debt. The members of the council— two from France; one each from Austria, Germany, Italy, and the Ottoman Empire itself; and one from Britain and the Netherlands together— were selected by foreign creditors. Until the debt was liquidated, the Porte gave control of several major sources of revenue to the council and authorized it to take initiatives that would increase economic activity. The council promoted, for instance, the export of salt (the tax on which it controlled) to India and introduced new technologies for the silk and wine industries. It increased the confidence of foreign investors in the empire's railways by collecting revenues that the government had promised to foreign companies. In the decade before World War I, the council controlled about one-quarter of the empire's revenue. It was disbanded after the war.[26]

Unlike classic gunboat diplomacy, where the governments of foreign creditors took over control of customs houses to secure repayment of loans, in the case of the Ottoman Council of the Public Debt, the norm of international legal sovereignty was honored, at least in form. The council was established by an edict issued by the Ottoman Empire at the behest of foreign creditors. International legal sovereignty was honored; Westphalian/Vatellian sovereignty was ignored. This arrangement was durable because

if the empire had revoked its decree, it would have lost access to international capital markets.

The relationship of the Soviet Union to the satellite states of Eastern Europe during the Cold War is another example of shared sovereignty. For more than forty years, Soviet penetration of domestic regimes, close oversight of officials, and policy direction from Moscow kept communist regimes in power. During the 1950s the Polish secret police, for instance, reported directly to Moscow. The militaries of the satellites were integrated into the Soviet command structure and unable to operate independently. The communist regimes that Moscow had put in place and sustained by violating Westphalian/Vatellian sovereignty dutifully signed off on the security arrangements that their overlord preferred. Except in a few instances, such as the invasion of Czechoslovakia in 1968, Soviet behavior was consistent with international legal sovereignty. The implicit and sometimes explicit use of force, however, was necessary to support these regimes because many of the citizens of the satellite states were alienated from their rulers.

The shared sovereignty arrangements established by the United States after World War II were more successful. Germany is the prime example. The Western allies wanted to internationally legitimate the Federal Republic of Germany (FRG or West Germany) but at the same time constrain its freedom of action. The Bonn agreements, signed in 1952 by the FRG, France, the United Kingdom, and the United States and revised in Paris in 1954, gave West Germany full authority over its internal and external affairs but with key exceptions in the security area. Not only did the FRG renounce its right to produce chemical, biological, and nuclear weapons; it also signed a status of forces agreement that gave the allies expansive powers. These included exclusive jurisdiction over the members of their armed forces and the right to patrol public areas including roads, railways, and restaurants. Allied forces could take any measures necessary to ensure order and discipline.[27] West Germany's military was fully integrated into NATO. Article 5(2) of the Convention on Relations gave the Western powers the right to declare a state of emergency until FRG officials obtained adequate powers enabling them to take effective action to protect the security of the foreign forces.[28] Without a clear definition of these adequate powers, the Western allies formally retained the right to resume their occupation of the Federal Republic until 1990, when the 1990 Treaty on the Final Settlement with Respect to Germany terminated the Bonn agreements.

The United States succeeded in the West German case because most Germans supported democracy, a market economy, and constraints on the FRG's security policies. Obviously the strength of this support reflected many factors, including the long-term economic success of the West relative to the Soviet bloc. Shared sovereignty arrangements for security in the FRG contributed to effective domestic governance by taking a potentially explosive issue off the table both within and, more important, without West Germany. Security dilemmas that might have strengthened undemocratic forces in the FRG never occurred because the Bonn government did not have exclusive control of the country's defense.

*   *   *

INCENTIVES FOR SHARED SOVEREIGNTY

Shared sovereignty arrangements can work only if they create a self-enforcing equilibrium, which might include external as well as domestic players. There are at least four circumstances that might make shared sovereignty arrangements attractive for political decision-makers, those who hold international legal sovereignty, in target states: avarice, postconflict occupation, desperation, and elections.

Natural Resources and Avarice. Rulers salivate at the wealth and power that natural resources, most notably oil, can bring them. Their bargaining position, however, depends on the acceptance of the precepts of conventional sovereignty: the state owns the oil and has the right to sign contracts and set rules governing its exploitation. Neither companies, nor consuming states, nor

international organizations have challenged the property rights of the state. No one, at least no one in a position of authority, has suggested, for instance, that oil in badly governed states ought to be declared part of the common heritage of mankind and placed under the control of perhaps the World Bank.

For poorly governed countries, however, natural resources, especially oil, have been a curse that has feathered the nests of rulers and undermined democracy and economic growth. Oil concentrates resources in the hands of the state. The road to wealth and power for any ambitious individual leads through the offices of the central government, not through individual enterprise or productive economic activity. With oil wealth, the state can buy off dissenters and build military machines that can be used to repress those who cannot be bought off.[29]

Shared sovereignty arrangements for extractive industries would offer an alternative to conventional practices that would provide better governance in oil-abundant states, more benefits for their people, and fewer incentives for corruption and conflict. Such arrangements would depend on the willingness of wealthier democratic states to constrain the options available to political leaders in poorly governed resource-rich states. Conventional sovereignty would not be challenged in principle but would be compromised in practice. Political leaders in host countries would then be confronted with a choice between nothing and something, although much less than they might have at their private disposal under conventional practices.

A shared sovereignty arrangement for natural resources could work in the following way. An agreement between the host country and, say, the World Bank would create a trust. The trust would be domiciled in an advanced industrialized country with effective rule of law. All funds generated by the natural resources project would be placed in an international escrow account controlled by the trust. All disbursements from the account would have to be approved by a majority of the directors of the trust. Half of the board of directors of the trust would be appointed by the host government, the other half by the World Bank; the bank could name directors from any country but would not designate its own employees. Directors would have to believe that their success depended on the success of the trust.

The trust agreement would stipulate that a large part of these funds would be used for social welfare programs, although specific allocations for, say, health care or education would be left to the host government. The trust would refuse to dispense funds that did not conform with these commitments. The trust might even be charged with implementing programs using the resources of the escrow account if the government failed to act expeditiously.

The laws of the advanced democracy in which the trust was incorporated would hold accountable the directors of the trust. Legislation enacted by the country in which the trust was domiciled would back the firms' responsibility to pay revenues into the escrow account, and only the escrow account.

No doubt the leaders of oil-rich or other natural resource–rich countries would cringe at such arrangements. They would have much more difficulty putting billions of dollars in foreign bank accounts, as did Sani Abacha, the late Nigerian military dictator. It would be hard to spend half a billion dollars on a European vacation as did some members of the Saudi royal family in 2002. But if the major democracies passed legislation requiring that any imported oil be governed by a trust arrangement, avarice might induce political leaders in resource-rich countries to accept shared sovereignty, because without shared sovereignty they would get nothing.[30]

Postconflict Occupation. Postconflict occupation might also be conducive to creating shared sovereignty arrangements. When there is military intervention and occupation, local leaders have limited choice. In Afghanistan, Bosnia, East Timor, Iraq, and Kosovo, the local leaders have been dependent to some extent on external actors. They have had to accept the presence of nonnationals. Foreigners have been running many of the ministries in Bosnia. In Kosovo joint implementation for administrative structures has been the norm: there are twenty administrative departments and four independent agencies, all of which are codirected by a Kosovar and a senior UNMIK staff person.[31] In Afghanistan and Iraq, security has been provided in part by foreign forces.

Shared sovereignty contracts would make such arrangements permanent, not transitional. The presence of external actors would not be the result of a unilateral decision by an external administrator but rather of a contract between external and domestic actors who would be granted international legal sovereignty. Because the contract would have no termination date, local actors could no longer assume that they could simply wait for the foreigners to leave. Some local leaders might still decide that acting as a spoiler might maximize their interests, but others would see cooperation as more likely to enhance their long-term prospects.

Such arrangements could be successful in the long run only if they were supported by a winning coalition in the host country. Unlike oil trusts, external enforcement mechanisms would be difficult to create. External actors might bolster domestic agents committed to shared sovereignty or threaten to impose sanctions or cut foreign assistance if the agreement were violated, but there could not be an ironclad guarantee of success.

Still, shared sovereignty arrangements would be more promising than constitution writing, which has been the center of attention in recent occupations. The problem with relying on a constitution or any other legal commitments made under pressure at a particular moment in time is that once the occupying power leaves, the incentives for domestic actors to honor their earlier commitments can radically change. Shared sovereignty, in contrast, could generate a self-enforcing equilibrium if it provided benefits to a large enough group of domestic actors.

Monetary policy is one area where shared sovereignty might work in a postconflict or even a more benign environment. Controlling inflation can be a daunting problem. A few countries,

East Timor being one example, have simply resorted to using the U.S. dollar. Others have tried to engineer credible commitments through domestic institutions, such as independent central banks. Appointment of the governors of the central bank by both government and external actors could enhance the credibility of such arrangements. In this regard, the IMF might be the right partner. Nonnational governors could be of any nationality. They would not be IMF employees. The fund would sign a contract with the host country setting up shared sovereignty on a permanent basis or until both parties agreed to end the arrangement. If the national government unilaterally abrogated the arrangement, it would be a clear signal to external actors that the government was abandoning the path of monetary responsibility. If the central bank were successful in constraining inflation, the arrangement would generate support from domestic actors. Like oil trusts, one major attraction of such an agreement is that it would not be costly for the IMF or any other external actor.

Commercial courts might be another area where shared sovereignty could be productive. Again, the opportunities in this area would not be limited to postconflict situations. In a state where the rule of law has been sketchy, the international legal sovereign would conclude a contract with an external entity—for instance, a regional organization such as the EU or the Organization of American States—to establish a separate commercial court system. The judges in these courts would be appointed by both the national government and its external partner. The expectation would be that local business interests would find this court system attractive. It would provide a venue in which they could resolve disagreements more effectively than would be the case within existing national institutions. The presence of such a court system might even attract higher levels of foreign investment. Like oil trusts and central banks, such an arrangement would not involve substantial costs for the external actor. The national government, or even to some extent the litigants, could fund commercial courts.

Desperation. Aside from the avarice associated with natural resources and the pressures arising from occupation, desperation for external resources might also motivate national authorities to enter into shared sovereignty arrangements. For countries that have spiraled into the abyss because of civil war or misgovernance, and that do not have easily exploited natural resources, foreign assistance might be a major potential source of revenue. The bargaining leverage of political leaders under such circumstances would be limited. The ability of external actors to negotiate shared sovereignty arrangements would be high.

As in the case of occupation, the most promising spheres for shared sovereignty, such as monetary policy and commercial courts, would not require substantial resources from external actors but would generate adequate domestic support. In collapsed or near-collapsed states, however, external actors would have to provide resources at least for some period of time. This would open additional possibilities for shared sovereignty for activities funded by external donors. A committee composed of national officials and individuals appointed by the education ministries of major donor countries might make, for instance, decisions about educational curriculum. A system of health care facilities administered by external aid workers or NGOs could be created separate from the national ministry of health. Because donors are not likely to be willing to provide aid on a quasi-permanent basis, however, such arrangements could be sustained only if a large enough domestic coalition were willing to support them even after foreign funding had been withdrawn.

Elections. Finally, in badly governed illiberal democracies, elections might provide an incentive for shared sovereignty contracts. Political candidates might make such policies part of their electoral platform. Illiberal democracies are polities that hold competitive elections but are deficient with regard to rule of law, an active civil society, and a free press. In illiberal democracies, government does not work very well. Public officials are disconnected from the citizenry. Individuals or parties might change, but policies remain more or less the same. Voters become cynical, and even potentially progressive political candidates have no way to make their campaign pledges credible. Shared sovereignty contracts could be an appealing political strategy for a dissident candidate. Such a political platform could win votes by signaling to the electorate that a politician would make a decisive break with the past by engaging external actors in domestic decisionmaking processes.

The long-term credibility of a shared sovereignty arrangement concluded by a successful dissident candidate in an illiberal democracy would depend both on the extent to which such practices have been internationally legitimated and on their effectiveness. The more common shared sovereignty agreements are, the easier it would be for any one leader to defend his actions against opponents who might claim that he had compromised the state's sovereignty. The greater the improvement in governance associated with shared sovereignty arrangements, the greater the likelihood that they would be honored over the long term.

Thus some form of de facto protectorate and, more promising, shared sovereignty are policy tools that could be added to the meager selection of options currently available to deal with bad governance or to create effective institutions following military occupations. Legitimacy for shared sovereignty would be provided by the agreement of those exercising the target state's international legal sovereignty.

Conclusion

During the twentieth century, the norms of international legal sovereignty and Westphalian/Vatellian sovereignty became universally accepted. It has often been tacitly assumed that these norms would be accompanied by effective domestic sovereignty, that is, by governance structures that exercised competent and ideally constructive control over their countries' populations and territory. This assumption has proven false. Poor, even malevolent, governance is a widespread problem. Badly governed states have become a threat to the interests of much more powerful actors: weapons of mass destruction have broken the connection between resources and the ability to do grievous harm; genocides leave political leaders in democratic polities with uncomfortable choices; and transnational disease and crime are persistent challenges.

The policy tools available to external actors—governance assistance and transitional administration—are inadequate, even when foreign powers have militarily occupied a country. Governance assistance can have positive results in occupied or badly governed states, but the available evidence suggests that the impact is weak. Transitional administration, which aims to restore conventional sovereignty in a relatively short time frame, can be effective only if indigenous political leaders believe that they will be better off allying with external actors not only while these actors are present but also after they leave.

The menu of options to deal with failing and collapsed states could be expanded in at least two ways. First, major states or regional or international organizations could assume some form of de facto trusteeship or protectorate responsibility for specific countries, even if there is no general international convention defining such arrangements. In a trusteeship, international actors would assume control over local functions for an indefinite period of time. They might also eliminate the international legal sovereignty of the entity or control treaty-making powers in whole or in part (e.g., in specific areas such as security or trade). There would be no assumption of a withdrawal in the short or medium term.

Second, domestic sovereignty in collapsed or poorly governed states could be improved through shared sovereignty contracts. These contracts would create joint authority structures in specific areas. They would not involve a direct assault on sovereignty norms because they would be formally consistent with international legal sovereignty, even though they would violate Westphalian/Vatellian sovereignty. Natural resources trusts, whose directors were appointed by national and nonnational entities, would be one possibility; central banks whose boards of governors comprised citizens and noncitizens would be another.

Political leaders in target states might accept such arrangements to secure external resources, either payments for raw materials' exploitation or foreign assistance, to encourage the departure of occupying forces or to attract voters. To be durable, shared sovereignty institutions either would require external enforcement, something that would be possible for natural resources trusts, or would have to create adequate domestic support, which would depend on the results delivered.

For external signatories—international organizations, regional organizations, and states—the most attractive shared sovereignty arrangements would be ones that did not require any significant commitment of resources over the long term. Natural resources trusts and central bank administration would meet this condition. In cases of states recovering from collapse, or something near to it, where foreign aid is the incentive for national leaders to accept shared sovereignty, resources commitments by external actors would be unavoidable for the short and medium terms. Over the longer term, though, shared sovereignty institutions could survive only if the services they provided were funded from internal sources of revenue.

De facto trusteeships or protectorates and shared sovereignty hardly exhaust the possibilities for improving domestic sovereignty in poorly governed states. Leaders in some polities have already used private firms to carry out some activities that have traditionally been in the hands of state officials. Indonesia, for instance, used a Swiss firm to collect its customs for more than eleven years. Other governments have hired private military companies (PMCs). Perhaps with stronger accountability mechanisms enforced by advanced industrial states, such as the ability to prosecute PMCs and their employees for abuses, the results might be more consistently salutary.

There is no panacea for domestic sovereignty failures. Even with the best of intentions and substantial resources, external actors cannot quickly eliminate the causes of these failures: poverty, weak indigenous institutions, insecurity, and the raw materials curse. But the instruments currently available to policy-makers to deal with places such as Congo, Liberia, and Iraq are woefully inadequate. De facto trusteeships, and especially shared sovereignty, would offer political leaders a better chance of bringing peace and prosperity to the populations of badly governed states and reduce the threat that such polities present to the wider international community.

NOTES

1. For a discussion of the requirements for successful international engagement that complements many of the points made in this article, see James D. Fearon and David D. Laitin, "Neotrusteeship and the Problem of Weak States," *International Security*, Vol. 28, No. 4 (Spring 2004), pp. 5–43.

2. See ibid., especially pp. 36–37.

3. Although the principle of nonintervention is traditionally associated with the Peace of Westphalia of 1648, the doctrine was not explicitly articulated until a century later by the Swiss jurist Emmerich de Vattel in his *The Law of Nations or Principles of the Law of Nature Applied to the Conduct and Affairs of Nations and Sovereigns*, originally published in French in 1758.

4. Mary Ann Tetreault, "Autonomy, Necessity, and the Small State: Ruling Kuwait in the Twentieth Century," *International Organization*, Vol. 45, No. 4 (Autumn 1991), pp. 565–591.

5. In Shanghai, for instance, the British established a municipal council that regulated the activities of Chinese living within Shanghai as well as non-Chinese. See Jean Chesneaux,

Marianne Bastid, and Marie-Claire Bergere, *China from the Opium Wars to the 1911 Revolution* (Hassocks, Sussex, U.K.: Harvester, 1977), pp. 61–68.

6. For two very similar analyses, see Robert O. Keohane, "Political Authority after Intervention: Gradations in Sovereignty," in J.L. Holzgrefe and Keohane, eds., *Humanitarian Intervention: Ethical, Legal, and Political Dilemmas* (Cambridge: Cambridge University Press, 2003), pp. 276–277; and Gerald B. Helman and Steven R. Ratner, "Saving Failed States," *Foreign Policy*, No. 89 (Winter 1993), pp. 3–21. Keohane argues that there should be gradations of sovereignty. Helman and Ratner suggest that there are three forms of what they call "guardianship": governance assistance, the delegation of government authority, and trusteeship. They also suggest the term "conservatorship" as an alternative to trusteeship.

7. James D. Fearon and David D. Laitin, "Ethnicity, Insurgency, and Civil War," *American Political Science Review*, Vol. 97, No. 1 (March 2003), pp. 1–17; and Fearon and Laitin, "Neotrusteeship and the Problem of Weak States," pp. 36–37.

8. Goldstone et al., *State Failure Task Force Report*, p. 21.

9. These figures are derived from data found at World Bank, *WDI Online*, http://devdata .worldbank.org/dataonline/.

10. U.S. Department of State, *Trafficking in Persons Report* (Washington, D.C.: U.S. Department of State, June 2004), http://www.state .gov/documents/organization/33614.pdf.

11. International Commission on Intervention and State Sovereignty, *The Responsibility to Protect* (Ottawa: International Development Research Centre, 2001), http://www.dfait -maeci.gc.ca/icissciise/pdf/Commission-Report.pdf. See also Gareth Evans and Mohamed Sahnoun, "The Responsibility to Protect," *Foreign Affairs*, Vol. 81, No. 6 (November/December 2002), pp. 99–110.

12. For the White House description of the MCA, see http://www.whitehouse.gov/infocus/ developingnations/millenium.html. For a list of the first set of countries to receive funding from the MCA, see MCA, press release, "The Millennium Challenge Corporation Names MCA Eligible Countries," May 6, 2004, http:// www.usaid.gov/mca/Documents/PR_Eligible .pdf. For a discussion of the World Bank's governance assistance programs, see http:// www.worldbank.org/wbi/governance/about .html. See also Arthur A. Goldsmith, "Foreign Aid and Statehood in Africa," *International Organization*, Vol. 55, No. 1 (Winter 2000), pp. 135–136.

13. International Monetary Fund, Fiscal Affairs Department, *Fund-Supported Programs, Fiscal Policy, and Income Distribution*, Occasional Paper No. 46 (Washington, D.C.: International Monetary Fund, 1986), p. 40; and Robin Broad, *Unequal Alliance: The World Bank, the International Monetary Fund, and the Philippines* (Berkeley: University of California Press, 1988), pp. 51–53, Table 12.

14. Paul Lewis, "Global Lenders Use Leverage to Combat Corruption," *New York Times*, late ed., August 11, 1997, p. 4; and James C. McKinley Jr., "Kenyan Who Charged 4 Officials with Graft Is Suspended," *New York Times*, late ed., July 31, 1998, p. 4.

15. World Bank, *World Development Report, 1997: The State in a Changing World* (Washington, D.C.: World Bank, 1997), p. 2.

16. Michael W. Doyle and Nicholas Sambanis, "International Peacebuilding: A Theoretical and Quantitative Analysis," *American Political Science Review*, Vol. 94, No. 4 (December 2000), pp. 779–802. For a second study with a different database but comparable findings, see George Downs and Stephen John Stedman, "Evaluating Issues in Peace Implementation," in Stedman, Donald Rothchild, and Elizabeth M. Cousens, eds., *Ending Civil Wars: The Implementation of Peace Agreements* (Boulder, Colo.: Lynne Rienner, 2002), pp. 50–52.

17. Richard Caplan, *A New Trusteeship? The International Administration of War-torn Territories* (London: International Institute for

Strategic Studies, 2002), pp. 8–9, 50–51; United Nations, *Report of the Panel on United Nations Peace Operations* (Brahimi report) (New York: United Nations, 2000), pp. 7, 14. In June 2003 Secretary of Defense Donald Rumsfeld discussed the possibility of a standing international peacekeeping force under the leadership of the United States. Ester Schrader, "U.S. Looks at Organizing Global Peacekeeping Force," *Los Angeles Times*, June 27, 2003, p. A1.

18. Fearon and Laitin, "Neotrusteeship and the Problem of Weak States," p. 37. See also David M. Edelstein, "Occupational Hazards: Why Military Occupations Succeed or Fail," *International Security*, Vol. 29, No. 1 (Summer 2004), pp. 49–81.

19. Michael Ignatieff points to the possibly negative consequences of competition among NGOs. Ignatieff, "State Failure and Nation-Building," p. 27.

20. For Namibia, see Downs and Stedman, "Evaluating Issues in Peace Implementation," pp. 59–61; and Roland Paris, *At War's End? Building Peace after Civil Conflict* (Cambridge: Cambridge University Press, 2004), chap. 8.

21. Downs and Stedman, "Evaluating Issues in Peace Implementation," pp. 62–63; and Paris, *At War's End*, chap. 7.

22. Helman and Ratner, "Saving Failed States," pp. 3–21; Caplan, *A New Trusteeship?* p. 7; Ignatieff, "State Failure and Nation-Building," p. 308; and Martin Indyk, "A Trusteeship for Palestine?" *Foreign Affairs*, Vol. 82, No. 3 (May/June 2003), pp. 51–66.

23. At least one way to interpret the strategy of U.S. decisionmakers is to understand the June transfer as one that gives Iraq international legal sovereignty. With this international legal sovereignty, the new Iraqi government will be able to legitimate agreements with external agents. Given the dependence of the new government on the United States for security and revenue, such agreements will allow the United States to continue to pursue its core interests.

24. Kofi Annan, "The Legitimacy to Intervene: International Action to Uphold Human Rights Requires a New Understanding of State and Individual Sovereignty," *Financial Times*, December 31, 1999.

25. Fearon and Laitin have suggested that "neotrusteeship" is the most appropriate term for arrangements that could cope with the postconflict security problems afflicting states suffering from weak administrative capacity, poverty, and rough terrain. Because such states are unlikely to be able to conduct effective policing and counterinsurgency operations on their own, maintaining security will require the engagement of external actors for an extended period of time. The authors do not, however, argue that neotrusteeship would involve a loss of international legal sovereignty. See Fearon and Laitin, "Neotrusteeship and the Problem of Weak States," especially pp. 24–41.

26. Donald C. Blaisdell, *European Financial Control in the Ottoman Empire: A Study of the Establishment, Activities, and Significance of the Administration of the Ottoman Public Debt* (New York: Columbia University Press, 1929), pp. 90–120, 124–130; Herbert Feis, *Europe, the World's Banker, 1870–1914: An Account of European Foreign Investment and the Connection of World Finance with Diplomacy before World War I* (New York: W. W. Norton, 1965), pp. 332–341; Bernard Lewis, *The Middle East: A Brief History of the Last 2,000 Years* (New York: Scribner, 1995), pp. 298–299; and Roger Owen, *The Middle East in the World Economy, 1800–1914* (Cambridge: Cambridge University Press, 1981), p. 101.

27. "Revised NATO SOFA Supplementary Agreement," articles 19, 22, 28. The full text of the agreement is available at http://www.oxc.army.mil/others/Gca/files%5Cgermany.doc.

28. "Convention on Relations between the Three Powers and the Federal Republic of Germany," *American Journal of International Law*, Vol. 49, No. 3 (July 1955), pp. 57–69. For a detailed examination of the retained rights of the

Western powers, see Joseph W. Bishop Jr., "The 'Contractual Agreements' with the Federal Republic of Germany," *American Journal of International Law*, Vol. 49, No. 2 (April 1955), pp. 125–147. For a general analysis of Germany's situation after World War II, see Peter J. Katzenstein, *Policy and Politics in West Germany: The Growth of a Semisovereign State* (Philadelphia: Temple University Press, 1987).

29. Michael Lewin Ross, "Does Oil Hinder Democracy?" *World Politics*, Vol. 53, No. 3 (April 2001), pp. 325–361.

30. This proposal assumes that oil could be exploited only by companies domiciled in advanced democratic polities interested in supporting good governance and that these countries cooperate with each other. Absent these conditions, the host country could play one oil company off against another and avoid the constraints that would come with a shared sovereignty trust.

31. Caplan, *A New Trusteeship?* p. 39.

ANNE-MARIE SLAUGHTER

THE REAL NEW WORLD ORDER

The State Strikes Back

Many thought that the new world order proclaimed by George Bush was the promise of 1945 fulfilled, a world in which international institutions, led by the United Nations, guaranteed international peace and security with the active support of the world's major powers. That world order is a chimera. Even as a liberal internationalist ideal, it is infeasible at best and dangerous at worst. It requires a centralized rule-making authority, a hierarchy of institutions, and universal membership. Equally to the point, efforts to create such an order have failed. The United Nations cannot function effectively independent of the major powers that compose it, nor will those nations cede their power and sovereignty to an international institution. Efforts to expand supranational authority, whether by the U.N. secretary-general's office, the European Commission, or the World Trade Organization (WTO),

From *Foreign Affairs* 75, no. 5 (September/October 1997): 183–97.

have consistently produced a backlash among member states.

The leading alternative to liberal internationalism is "the new medievalism," a back-to-the-future model of the 21st century. Where liberal internationalists see a need for international rules and institutions to solve states' problems, the new medievalists proclaim the end of the nation-state. Less hyperbolically, in her article, "Power Shift," in the January/February 1997 *Foreign Affairs*, Jessica T. Mathews describes a shift away from the state—up, down, and sideways—to supra-state, sub-state, and, above all, nonstate actors. These new players have multiple allegiances and global reach.

Mathews attributes this power shift to a change in the structure of organizations: from hierarchies to networks, from centralized compulsion to voluntary association. The engine of this transformation is the information technology revolution, a radically expanded communications capacity that empowers individuals and groups while diminishing traditional authority. The result is not world government, but global governance. If government denotes the formal exercise of power by established institutions, governance denotes cooperative problem-solving by a changing and often uncertain cast. The result is a world order in which global governance networks link Microsoft, the Roman Catholic Church, and Amnesty International to the European Union, the United Nations, and Catalonia.

The new medievalists miss two central points. First, private power is still no substitute for state power. Consumer boycotts of transnational corporations destroying rain forests or exploiting child labor may have an impact on the margin, but most environmentalists or labor activists would prefer national legislation mandating control of foreign subsidiaries. Second, the power shift is not a zero-sum game. A gain in power by nonstate actors does not necessarily translate into a loss of power for the state. On the contrary, many of these nongovernmental organizations (NGOs) network with their foreign counterparts to apply additional pressure on the traditional levers of domestic politics.

A new world order is emerging, with less fanfare but more substance than either the liberal internationalist or new medievalist visions. The state is not disappearing, it is disaggregating into its separate, functionally distinct parts. These parts—courts, regulatory agencies, executives, and even legislatures—are networking with their counterparts abroad, creating a dense web of relations that constitutes a new, transgovernmental order. Today's international problems—terrorism, organized crime, environmental degradation, money laundering, bank failure, and securities fraud—created and sustain these relations. Government institutions have formed networks of their own, ranging from the Basle Committee of Central Bankers to informal ties between law enforcement agencies to legal networks that make foreign judicial decisions more and more familiar. While political scientists Robert Keohane and Joseph Nye first observed its emergence in the 1970s, today trans-governmentalism is rapidly becoming the most widespread and effective mode of international governance.

Compared to the lofty ideals of liberal internationalism and the exuberant possibilities of the new medievalism, transgovernmentalism seems mundane. Meetings between securities regulators, antitrust or environmental officials, judges, or legislators lack the drama of high politics. But for the internationalists of the 1990s—bankers, lawyers, businesspeople, public-interest activists, and criminals—transnational government networks are a reality. Wall Street looks to the Basle Committee rather than the World Bank. Human rights lawyers are more likely to develop transnational litigation strategies for domestic courts than to petition the U.N. Committee on Human Rights.

Moreover, transgovernmentalism has many virtues. It is a key element of a bipartisan foreign policy, simultaneously assuaging conservative fears of a loss of sovereignty to international institutions and liberal fears of a loss of regulatory power in a globalized economy. While presidential candidate Pat Buchanan and Senator Jesse Helms (R-N.C.) demonize the U.N. and the WTO as supranational bureaucracies that seek to dictate to national governments, Senators Ted Kennedy (D-Mass.) and Paul Wellstone (D-Mich.) inveigh against international capital mobility as the catalyst of a global "race to the bottom" in regulatory standards. Networks of bureaucrats responding to international crises and planning to prevent future problems are more flexible than international institutions and expand the regulatory reach of all participating nations. This combination of flexibility and effectiveness offers something for both sides of the aisle.

Transgovernmentalism also offers promising new mechanisms for the Clinton administration's "enlargement" policy, aiming to expand the community of liberal democracies. Contrary to Samuel Huntington's gloomy predictions in *The Clash of Civilizations and the New World Order* (1996), existing government networks span civilizations, drawing in courts from Argentina to Zimbabwe and financial regulators from Japan to Saudi Arabia. The dominant institutions in these networks remain concentrated in North

America and Western Europe, but their impact can be felt in every corner of the globe. Moreover, disaggregating the state makes it possible to assess the quality of specific judicial, administrative, and legislative institutions, whether or not the governments are liberal democracies. Regular interaction with foreign colleagues offers new channels for spreading democratic accountability, governmental integrity, and the rule of law.

An offspring of an increasingly borderless world, transgovernmentalism is a world order ideal in its own right, one that is more effective and potentially more accountable than either of the current alternatives. Liberal internationalism poses the prospect of a supranational bureaucracy answerable to no one. The new medievalist vision appeals equally to states' rights enthusiasts and supranationalists, but could easily reflect the worst of both worlds. Transgovernmentalism, by contrast, leaves the control of government institutions in the hands of national citizens, who must hold their governments as accountable for their transnational activities as for their domestic duties.

Judicial Foreign Policy

Judges are building a global community of law. They share values and interests based on their belief in the law as distinct but not divorced from politics and their view of themselves as professionals who must be insulated from direct political influence. At its best, this global community reminds each participant that his or her professional performance is being monitored and supported by a larger audience.

National and international judges are networking, becoming increasingly aware of one another and of their stake in a common enterprise. The most informal level of transnational judicial contact is knowledge of foreign and international judicial decisions and a corresponding willingness to cite them. The Israeli Supreme Court and the German and Canadian constitutional courts have long researched U.S. Supreme Court precedents

in reaching their own conclusions on questions like freedom of speech, privacy rights, and due process. Fledgling constitutional courts in Central and Eastern Europe and in Russia are eagerly following suit. In 1995, the South African Supreme Court, finding the death penalty unconstitutional under the national constitution, referred to decisions from national and supranational courts around the world, including ones in Hungary, India, Tanzania, Canada, and Germany and the European Court of Human Rights. The U.S. Supreme Court has typically been more of a giver than a receiver in this exchange, but Justice Sandra Day O'Connor recently chided American lawyers and judges for their insularity in ignoring foreign law and predicted that she and her fellow justices would find themselves "looking more frequently to the decisions of other constitutional courts."

Why should a court in Israel or South Africa cite a decision by the U.S. Supreme Court in reaching its own conclusion? Decisions rendered by outside courts can have no authoritative value. They carry weight only because of their intrinsic logical power or because the court invoking them seeks to gain legitimacy by linking itself to a larger community of courts considering similar issues. National courts have become increasingly aware that they and their foreign counterparts are often engaged in a common effort to delimit the boundaries of individual rights in the face of an apparently overriding public interest. Thus, the British House of Lords recently rebuked the U.S. Supreme Court for its decision to uphold the kidnapping of a Mexican doctor by U.S. officials determined to bring him to trial in the United States.

Judges also cooperate in resolving transnational or international disputes. In cases involving citizens of two different states, courts have long been willing to acknowledge each other's potential interest and to defer to one another when such deference is not too costly. U.S. courts now recognize that they may become involved in a sustained dialogue with a foreign court. For instance, Judge Guido Calabresi of the Second

Circuit recently allowed a French litigant to invoke U.S. discovery provisions without exhausting discovery options in France, reasoning that it was up to the French courts to identify and protest any infringements of French sovereignty. U.S. courts would then respond to such protests.

Judicial communication is not always harmonious, as in a recent squabble between a U.S. judge and a Hong Kong judge over an insider trading case. The U.S. judge refused to decline jurisdiction in favor of the Hong Kong court on grounds that "in Hong Kong they practically give you a medal for doing this sort of thing [insider trading]." In response, the Hong Kong judge stiffly defended the adequacy of Hong Kong law and asserted his willingness to apply it. He also chided his American counterpart, pointing out that any conflict "should be approached in the spirit of judicial comity rather than judicial competitiveness." Such conflict is to be expected among diplomats, but what is striking here is the two courts' view of themselves as quasi-autonomous foreign policy actors doing battle against international securities fraud.

The most advanced form of judicial cooperation is a partnership between national courts and a supranational tribunal. In the European Union (EU), the European Court of Justice works with national courts when questions of European law overlap national law. National courts refer cases up to the European Court, which issues an opinion and sends the case back to national courts; the supranational recommendation guides the national court's decision. This cooperation marshals the power of domestic courts behind the judgment of a supranational tribunal. While the Treaty of Rome provides for this reference procedure, it is the courts that have transformed it into a judicial partnership.

Finally, judges are talking face to face. The judges of the supreme courts of Western Europe began meeting every three years in 1978. Since then they have become more aware of one another's decisions, particularly with regard to each other's willingness to accept the decisions handed down by the European Court of Justice.

Meetings between U.S. Supreme Court justices and their counterparts on the European Court have been sponsored by private groups, as have meetings of U.S. judges with judges from the supreme courts of Central and Eastern Europe and Russia.

The most formal initiative aimed at bringing judges together is the recently inaugurated Organization of the Supreme Courts of the Americas. Twenty-five supreme court justices or their designees met in Washington in October 1995 and drafted the OCSA charter, dedicating the organization to "promot[ing] and strengthen[ing] judicial independence and the rule of law among the members, as well as the proper constitutional treatment of the judiciary as a fundamental branch of the state." The charter calls for triennial meetings and envisages a permanent secretariat. It required ratification by 15 supreme courts, achieved in spring 1996. An initiative by judges, for judges, it is not a stretch to say that OCSA is the product of judicial foreign policy.

Champions of a global rule of law have most frequently envisioned one rule for all, a unified legal system topped by a world court. The global community of law emerging from judicial networks will more likely encompass many rules of law, each established in a specific state or region. No high court would hand down definitive global rules. National courts would interact with one another and with supranational tribunals in ways that would accommodate differences but acknowledge and reinforce common values.

The Regulatory Web

The densest area of transgovernmental activity is among national regulators. Bureaucrats charged with the administration of antitrust policy, securities regulation, environmental policy, criminal law enforcement, banking and insurance supervision—in short, all the agents of the modern regulatory state—regularly collaborate with their foreign counterparts.

National regulators track their quarry through cooperation. While frequently ad hoc, such cooperation is increasingly cemented by bilateral and multilateral agreements. The most formal of these are mutual legal assistance treaties, whereby two states lay out a protocol governing cooperation between their law enforcement agencies and courts. However, the preferred instrument of cooperation is the memorandum of understanding, in which two or more regulatory agencies set forth and initial terms for an ongoing relationship. Such memorandums are not treaties; they do not engage the executive or the legislature in negotiations, deliberation, or signature. Rather, they are good-faith agreements, affirming ties between regulatory agencies based on their like-minded commitment to getting results.

"Positive comity," a concept developed by the U.S. Department of Justice, epitomizes the changing nature of transgovernmental relations. Comity of nations, an archaic and notoriously vague term beloved by diplomats and international lawyers, has traditionally signified the deference one nation grants another in recognition of their mutual sovereignty. For instance, a state will recognize another state's laws or judicial judgments based on comity. Positive comity requires more active cooperation. As worked out by the Antitrust Division of the U.S. Department of Justice and the EU's European Commission, the regulatory authorities of both states alert one another to violations within their jurisdiction, with the understanding that the responsible authority will take action. Positive comity is a principle of enduring cooperation between government agencies.

In 1988 the central bankers of the world's major financial powers adopted capital adequacy requirements for all banks under their supervision—a significant reform of the international banking system. It was not the World Bank, the International Monetary Fund, or even the Group of Seven that took this step. Rather, the forum was the Basle Committee on Banking Supervision, an organization composed of 12 central bank governors. The Basle Committee was created by a simple agreement among the governors themselves. Its members meet four times a year and follow their own rules. Decisions are made by consensus and are not formally binding; however, members do implement these decisions within their own systems. The Basle Committee's authority is often cited as an argument for taking domestic action.

National securities commissioners and insurance regulators have followed the Basle Committee's example. Incorporated by a private bill of the Quebec National Assembly, the International Organization of Securities Commissioners has no formal charter or founding treaty. Its primary purpose is to solve problems affecting international securities markets by creating a consensus for enactment of national legislation. Its members have also entered into information-sharing agreements on their own initiative. The International Association of Insurance Supervisors follows a similar model, as does the newly created Tripartite Group, an international coalition of banking, insurance, and securities regulators the Basle Committee created to improve the supervision of financial conglomerates.

Pat Buchanan would have had a field day with the Tripartite Group, denouncing it as a prime example of bureaucrats taking power out of the hands of American voters. In fact, unlike the international bogeymen of demagogic fantasy, transnational regulatory organizations do not aspire to exercise power in the international system independent of their members. Indeed, their main purpose is to help regulators apprehend those who would harm the interests of American voters. Transgovernmental networks often promulgate their own rules, but the purpose of those rules is to enhance the enforcement of national law.

Traditional international law requires states to implement the international obligations they incur through their own law. Thus, if states agree to a 12-mile territorial sea, they must change their domestic legislation concerning the interdiction of vessels in territorial waters accordingly. But this legislation is unlikely to overlap with domestic law, as national legislatures do not usually seek to regulate global commons issues and interstate relations.

Transgovernmental regulation, by contrast, produces rules concerning issues that each nation already regulates within its borders: crime, securities fraud, pollution, tax evasion. The advances in technology and transportation that have fueled globalization have made it more difficult to enforce national law. Regulators benefit from coordinating their enforcement efforts with those of their foreign counterparts and from ensuring that other nations adopt similar approaches.

The result is the nationalization of international law. Regulatory agreements between states are pledges of good faith that are self-enforcing, in the sense that each nation will be better able to enforce its national law by implementing the agreement if other nations do likewise. Laws are binding or coercive only at the national level. Uniformity of result and diversity of means go hand in hand, and the makers and enforcers of rules are national leaders who are accountable to the people.

Bipartisan Globalization

Secretary of State Madeleine Albright seeks to revive the bipartisan foreign policy consensus of the late 1940s. Deputy Secretary of State Strobe Talbott argues that promoting democracy worldwide satisfies the American need for idealpolitik as well as realpolitik. President Clinton, in his second inaugural address, called for a "new government for a new century," abroad as well as at home. But bipartisanship is threatened by divergent responses to globalization, democratization is a tricky business, and Vice President Al Gore's efforts to "reinvent government" have focused on domestic rather than international institutions. Transgovernmentalism can address all these problems.

Globalization implies the erosion of national boundaries. Consequently, regulators' power to implement national regulations within those boundaries declines both because people can eas-

ily flee their jurisdiction and because the flows of capital, pollution, pathogens, and weapons are too great and sudden for any one regulator to control. The liberal internationalist response to these assaults on state regulatory power is to build a larger international apparatus. Globalization thus leads to internationalization, or the transfer of regulatory authority from the national level to an international institution. The best example is not the WTO itself, but rather the stream of proposals to expand the WTO's jurisdiction to global competition policy, intellectual property regulation, and other trade-related issues. Liberals are likely to support expanding the power of international institutions to guard against the global dismantling of the regulatory state.

Here's the rub. Conservatives are more likely to favor the expansion of globalized markets without the internationalization that goes with it, since internationalization, from their perspective, equals a loss of sovereignty. According to Buchanan, the U.S. foreign policy establishment "want[s] to move America into a New World Order where the World Court decides quarrels between nations; the WTO writes the rules for trade and settles all disputes; the IMF and World Bank order wealth transfers from continent to continent and country to country; the Law of the Sea Treaty tells us what we may and may not do on the high seas and ocean floor, and the United Nations decides where U.S. military forces may and may not intervene." The rhetoric is deliberately inflammatory, but echoes resound across the Republican spectrum.

Transgovernmental initiatives are a compromise that could command bipartisan support. Regulatory loopholes caused by global forces require a coordinated response beyond the reach of any one country. But this coordination need not come from building more international institutions. It can be achieved through transgovernmental cooperation, involving the same officials who make and implement policy at the national level. The transgovernmental alternative is fast, flexible, and effective.

A leading example of transgovernmentalism in action that demonstrates its bipartisan appeal is a State Department initiative christened the New Transatlantic Agenda. Launched in 1991 under the Bush administration and reinvigorated by Secretary of State Warren Christopher in 1995, the initiative structures the relationship between the United States and the EU, fostering cooperation in areas ranging from opening markets to fighting terrorism, drug trafficking, and infectious disease. It is an umbrella for ongoing projects between U.S. officials and their European counterparts. It reaches ordinary citizens, embracing efforts like the Transatlantic Business Dialogue and engaging individuals through people-to-people exchanges and expanded communication through the Internet.

Democratization, Step by Step

Transgovernmental networks are concentrated among liberal democracies but are not limited to them. Some nondemocratic states have institutions capable of cooperating with their foreign counterparts, such as committed and effective regulatory agencies or relatively independent judiciaries. Transgovernmental ties can strengthen institutions in ways that will help them resist political domination, corruption, and incompetence and build democratic institutions in their countries, step by step. The Organization of Supreme Courts of the Americas, for instance, actively seeks to strengthen norms of judicial independence among its members, many of whom must fend off powerful political forces.

Individuals and groups in nondemocratic countries may also "borrow" government institutions of democratic states to achieve a measure of justice they cannot obtain in their own countries. The court or regulatory agency of one state may be able to perform judicial or regulatory functions for the people of another. Victims of human rights violations, for example, in countries such as Argentina, Ethiopia, Haiti, and the Philippines have sued for redress in the courts of

the United States. U.S. courts accepted these cases, often over the objections of the executive branch, using a broad interpretation of a moribund statute dating back to 1789. Under this interpretation, aliens may sue in U.S. courts to seek damages from foreign government officials accused of torture, even if the torture allegedly took place in the foreign country. More generally, a nongovernmental organization seeking to prevent human rights violations can often circumvent their own government's corrupt legislature and politicized court by publicizing the plight of victims abroad and mobilizing a foreign court, legislature, or executive to take action.

Responding to calls for a coherent U.S. foreign policy and seeking to strengthen the community of democratic nations, President Clinton substituted the concept of "enlargement" for the Cold War principle of "containment." Expanding transgovernmental outreach to include institutions from nondemocratic states would help expand the circle of democracies one institution at a time.

A New World Order Ideal

Transgovernmentalism offers its own world order ideal, less dramatic but more compelling than either liberal internationalism or the new medievalism. It harnesses the state's power to find and implement solutions to global problems. International institutions have a lackluster record on such problem-solving; indeed, NGOs exist largely to compensate for their inadequacies. Doing away with the state, however, is hardly the answer. The new medievalist mantra of global governance is "governance without government." But governance without government is governance without power, and government without power rarely works. Many pressing international and domestic problems result from states' insufficient power to establish order, build infrastructure, and provide minimum social services. Private actors may take up some slack, but there is no substitute for the state.

Transgovernmental networks allow governments to benefit from the flexibility and decentralization of nonstate actors. Jessica T. Mathews argues that "businesses, citizens' organizations, ethnic groups, and crime cartels have all readily adopted the network model," while governments "are quintessential hierarchies, wedded to an organizational form incompatible with all that the new technologies make possible." Not so. Disaggregating the state into its functional components makes it possible to create networks of institutions engaged in a common enterprise even as they represent distinct national interests. Moreover, they can work with their subnational and supranational counterparts, creating a genuinely new world order in which networked institutions perform the functions of a world government—legislation, administration, and adjudication—without the form.

These globe-spanning networks will strengthen the state as the primary player in the international system. The state's defining attribute has traditionally been sovereignty, conceived as absolute power in domestic affairs and autonomy in relations with other states. But as Abram and Antonia Chayes observe in *The New Sovereignty* (1995), sovereignty is actually "status—the vindication of the state's existence in the international system." More importantly, they demonstrate that in contemporary international relations, sovereignty has been redefined to mean "membership . . . in the regimes that make up the substance of international life." Disaggregating the state permits the disaggregation of sovereignty as well, ensuring that specific state institutions derive strength and status from participation in a transgovernmental order.

Transgovernmental networks will increasingly provide an important anchor for international organizations and nonstate actors alike. U.N. officials have already learned a lesson about the limits of supranational authority; mandated cuts in the international bureaucracy will further tip the balance of power toward national regulators. The next generation of international institutions is also likely to look more like the Basle Committee, or, more formally, the Organization of Economic Co-

operation and Development, dedicated to providing a forum for transnational problem-solving and the harmonization of national law. The disaggregation of the state creates opportunities for domestic institutions, particularly courts, to make common cause with their supranational counterparts against their fellow branches of government. Nonstate actors will lobby and litigate wherever they think they will have the most effect. Many already realize that corporate self-regulation and states' promises to comply with vague international agreements are no substitute for national law.

The spread of transgovernmental networks will depend more on political and professional convergence than on civilizational boundaries. Trust and awareness of a common enterprise are more vulnerable to differing political ideologies and corruption than to cultural differences. Government networks transcend the traditional divide between high and low politics. National militaries, for instance, network as extensively as central bankers with their counterparts in friendly states. Judicial and regulatory networks can help achieve gradual political convergence, but are unlikely to be of much help in the face of a serious economic or military threat. If the coming conflict with China is indeed coming, transgovernmentalism will not stop it.

The strength of transgovernmental networks and of transgovernmentalism as a world order ideal will ultimately depend on their accountability to the world's peoples. To many, the prospect of transnational government by judges and bureaucrats looks more like technocracy than democracy. Critics contend that government institutions engaged in policy coordination with their foreign counterparts will be barely visible, much less accountable, to voters still largely tied to national territory.

Citizens of liberal democracies will not accept any form of international regulation they cannot control. But checking unelected officials is a familiar problem in domestic politics. As national legislators become increasingly aware of transgovernmental networks, they will expand their oversight capacities and develop networks of their own. Transnational NGO networks will develop a similar monitoring capacity. It will be harder to monitor themselves.

Transgovernmentalism offers answers to the most important challenges facing advanced industrial countries: loss of regulatory power with economic globalization, perceptions of a "democratic deficit" as international institutions step in to fill the regulatory gap, and the difficulties of engaging nondemocratic states. Moreover, it pro-vides a powerful alternative to a liberal internationalism that has reached its limits and to a new medievalism that, like the old Marxism, sees the state slowly fading away. The new medievalists are right to emphasize the dawn of a new era, in which information technology will transform the globe. But government networks are government for the information age. They offer the world a blueprint for the international architecture of the 21st century.

SAMUEL P. HUNTINGTON

THE CLASH OF CIVILIZATIONS?

The Next Pattern of Conflict

World politics is entering a new phase, and intellectuals have not hesitated to proliferate visions of what it will be—the end of history, the return of traditional rivalries between nation states, and the decline of the nation state from the conflicting pulls of tribalism and globalism, among others. Each of these visions catches aspects of the emerging reality. Yet they all miss a crucial, indeed a central, aspect of what global politics is likely to be in the coming years.

It is my hypothesis that the fundamental source of conflict in this new world will not be primarily ideological or primarily economic. The great divisions among humankind and the dominating source of conflict will be cultural. Nation states will remain the most powerful actors in world affairs, but the principal conflicts of global politics will occur between nations and groups of different civilizations. The clash of civilizations will dominate global politics. The fault lines between civilizations will be the battle lines of the future.

From *Foreign Affairs* 72, no. 3 (summer 1993): 22–49.

Conflict between civilizations will be the latest phase in the evolution of conflict in the modern world. For a century and a half after the emergence of the modern international system with the Peace of Westphalia, the conflicts of the Western world were largely among princes—emperors, absolute monarchs and constitutional monarchs attempting to expand their bureaucracies, their armies, their mercantilist economic strength and, most important, the territory they ruled. In the process they created nation states, and beginning with the French Revolution the principal lines of conflict were between nations rather than princes. * * * [A]s a result of the Russian Revolution and the reaction against it, the conflict of nations yielded to the conflict of ideologies, first among communism, fascism-Nazism and liberal democracy, and then between communism and liberal democracy. During the Cold War, this latter conflict became embodied in the struggle between the two superpowers, neither of which was a nation state in the classical European sense and each of which defined its identity in terms of its ideology.

* * * With the end of the Cold War, international politics moves out of its Western phase,

and its centerpiece becomes the interaction between the West and non-Western civilizations and among non-Western civilizations. In the politics of civilizations, the peoples and governments of non-Western civilizations no longer remain the objects of history as targets of Western colonialism but join the West as movers and shapers of history.

The Nature of Civilizations

During the Cold War the world was divided into the First, Second and Third Worlds. Those divisions are no longer relevant. It is far more meaningful now to group countries not in terms of their political or economic systems or in terms of their level of economic development but rather in terms of their culture and civilization.

What do we mean when we talk of a civilization? A civilization is a cultural entity. Villages, regions, ethnic groups, nationalities, religious groups, all have distinct cultures at different levels of cultural heterogeneity. The culture of a village in southern Italy may be different from that of a village in northern Italy, but both will share in a common Italian culture that distinguishes them from German villages. European communities, in turn, will share cultural features that distinguish them from Arab or Chinese communities. Arabs, Chinese and Westerners, however, are not part of any broader cultural entity. They constitute civilizations. A civilization is thus the highest cultural grouping of people and the broadest level of cultural identity people have short of that which distinguishes humans from other species. It is defined both by common objective elements, such as language, history, religion, customs, institutions, and by the subjective self-identification of people. * * *

* * * Civilizations are nonetheless meaningful entities, and while the lines between them are seldom sharp, they are real. Civilizations are dynamic; they rise and fall; they divide and merge. And, as any student of history knows, civilizations disappear and are buried in the sands of time.

Westerners tend to think of nation states as the principal actors in global affairs. They have been that, however, for only a few centuries. The broader reaches of human history have been the history of civilizations. In *A Study of History*, Arnold Toynbee identified 21 major civilizations; only six of them exist in the contemporary world.

Why Civilizations Will Clash

Civilization identity will be increasingly important in the future, and the world will be shaped in large measure by the interactions among seven or eight major civilizations. These include Western, Confucian, Japanese, Islamic, Hindu, Slavic-Orthodox, Latin American and possibly African civilization. The most important conflicts of the future will occur along the cultural fault lines separating these civilizations from one another.

Why will this be the case?

First, differences among civilizations are not only real; they are basic. Civilizations are differentiated from each other by history, language, culture, tradition and, most important, religion. The people of different civilizations have different views on the relations between God and man, the individual and the group, the citizen and the state, parents and children, husband and wife, as well as differing views of the relative importance of rights and responsibilities, liberty and authority, equality and hierarchy. These differences are the product of centuries. They will not soon disappear. * * *

Second, the world is becoming a smaller place. The interactions between peoples of different civilizations are increasing; these increasing interactions intensify civilization consciousness and awareness of differences between civilizations and commonalities within civilizations. * * *

Third, the processes of economic modernization and social change throughout the world are separating people from longstanding local identities. They also weaken the nation state as a source of identity. In much of the world religion has moved in to fill this gap, often in the form of movements that are labeled "fundamentalist."

Such movements are found in Western Christianity, Judaism, Buddhism and Hinduism, as well as in Islam. * * * The "unsecularization of the world," George Weigel has remarked, "is one of the dominant social facts of life in the late twentieth century." * * *

Fourth, the growth of civilization-consciousness is enhanced by the dual role of the West. On the one hand, the West is at a peak of power. At the same time, however, and perhaps as a result, a return to the roots phenomenon is occurring among non-Western civilizations. Increasingly one hears references to trends toward a turning inward and "Asianization" in Japan, the end of the Nehru legacy and the "Hinduization" of India, the failure of Western ideas of socialism and nationalism and hence "re-Islamization" of the Middle East, and now a debate over Westernization versus Russianization in Boris Yeltsin's country. A West at the peak of its power confronts non-Wests that increasingly have the desire, the will and the resources to shape the world in non-Western ways.

*   *   *

Fifth, cultural characteristics and differences are less mutable and hence less easily compromised and resolved than political and economic ones. In the former Soviet Union, communists can become democrats, the rich can become poor and the poor rich, but Russians cannot become Estonians and Azeris cannot become Armenians. * * * Even more than ethnicity, religion discriminates sharply and exclusively among people. A person can be half-French and half-Arab and simultaneously even a citizen of two countries. It is more difficult to be half-Catholic and half-Muslim.

Finally, economic regionalism is increasing. * * * On the one hand, successful economic regionalism will reinforce civilization-consciousness. On the other hand, economic regionalism may succeed only when it is rooted in a common civilization. The European Community rests on the shared foundation of European culture and Western Christianity. The success of the North American Free Trade Area depends on the convergence now underway of Mexican, Canadian and American cultures. Japan, in contrast, faces difficulties in creating a comparable economic entity in East Asia because Japan is a society and civilization unique to itself. * * *

*   *   *

As people define their identity in ethnic and religious terms, they are likely to see an "us" versus "them" relation existing between themselves and people of different ethnicity or religion. The end of ideologically defined states in Eastern Europe and the former Soviet Union permits traditional ethnic identities and animosities to come to the fore. Differences in culture and religion create differences over policy issues, ranging from human rights to immigration to trade and commerce to the environment. * * * Most important, the efforts of the West to promote its values of democracy and liberalism as universal values, to maintain its military predominance and to advance its economic interests engender countering responses from other civilizations. * * *

The clash of civilizations thus occurs at two levels. At the micro-level, adjacent groups along the fault lines between civilizations struggle, often violently, over the control of territory and each other. At the macro-level, states from different civilizations compete for relative military and economic power, struggle over the control of international institutions and third parties, and competitively promote their particular political and religious values.

The Fault Lines between Civilizations

The fault lines between civilizations are replacing the political and ideological boundaries of the Cold War as the flash points for crisis and bloodshed. The Cold War began when the Iron Curtain divided Europe politically and ideologically. The Cold War ended with the end of the Iron Curtain. As the ideological division of Europe has disappeared, the cultural division of

Europe between Western Christianity, on the one hand, and Orthodox Christianity and Islam, on the other, has reemerged. The most significant dividing line in Europe, as William Wallace has suggested, may well be the eastern boundary of Western Christianity in the year 1500. This line runs along what are now the boundaries between Finland and Russia and between the Baltic states and Russia, cuts through Belarus and Ukraine separating the more Catholic western Ukraine from Orthodox eastern Ukraine, swings westward separating Transylvania from the rest of Romania, and then goes through Yugoslavia almost exactly along the line now separating Croatia and Slovenia from the rest of Yugoslavia. In the Balkans this line, of course, coincides with the historic boundary between the Hapsburg and Ottoman empires. The peoples to the north and west of this line are Protestant or Catholic; they shared the common experiences of European history—feudalism, the Renaissance, the Reformation, the Enlightenment, the French Revolution, the Industrial Revolution; they are generally economically better off than the peoples to the east; and they may now look forward to increasing involvement in a common European economy and to the consolidation of democratic political systems. The peoples to the east and south of this line are Orthodox or Muslim; they historically belonged to the Ottoman or Tsarist empires and were only lightly touched by the shaping events in the rest of Europe; they are generally less advanced economically; they seem much less likely to develop stable democratic political systems. The Velvet Curtain of culture has replaced the Iron Curtain of ideology as the most significant dividing line in Europe. As the events in Yugoslavia show, it is not only a line of difference; it is also at times a line of bloody conflict.

Conflict along the fault line between Western and Islamic civilizations has been going on for 1,300 years. * * *

*   *   *

This centuries-old military interaction between the West and Islam is unlikely to decline. It could become more virulent. The Gulf War left some Arabs feeling proud that Saddam Hussein had attacked Israel and stood up to the West. It also left many feeling humiliated and resentful of the West's military presence in the Persian Gulf, the West's overwhelming military dominance, and their apparent inability to shape their own destiny. Many Arab countries, in addition to the oil exporters, are reaching levels of economic and social development where autocratic forms of government become inappropriate and efforts to introduce democracy become stronger. Some openings in Arab political systems have already occurred. The principal beneficiaries of these openings have been Islamist movements. * * *

Those relations are also complicated by demography. The spectacular population growth in Arab countries, particularly in North Africa, has led to increased migration to Western Europe. The movement within Western Europe toward minimizing internal boundaries has sharpened political sensitivities with respect to this development. * * *

*   *   *

Historically, the other great antagonistic interaction of Arab Islamic civilization has been with the pagan, animist, and now increasingly Christian black peoples to the south. In the past, this antagonism was epitomized in the image of Arab slave dealers and black slaves. It has been reflected in the on-going civil war in the Sudan between Arabs and blacks, the fighting in Chad between Libyan-supported insurgents and the government, the tensions between Orthodox Christians and Muslims in the Horn of Africa, and the political conflicts, recurring riots and communal violence between Muslims and Christians in Nigeria. The modernization of Africa and the spread of Christianity are likely to enhance the probability of violence along this fault line. Symptomatic of the intensification of this conflict was the Pope John Paul II's speech in Khartoum in February 1993 attacking the actions of the Sudan's Islamist government against the Christian minority there.

On the northern border of Islam, conflict has increasingly erupted between Orthodox and Muslim peoples, including the carnage of Bosnia and Sarajevo, the simmering violence between Serb and Albanian, the tenuous relations between Bulgarians and their Turkish minority, the violence between Ossetians and Ingush, the unremitting slaughter of each other by Armenians and Azeris, the tense relations between Russians and Muslims in Central Asia. * * *

The conflict of civilizations is deeply rooted elsewhere in Asia. The historic clash between Muslim and Hindu in the subcontinent manifests itself now not only in the rivalry between Pakistan and India but also in intensifying religious strife within India between increasingly militant Hindu groups and India's substantial Muslim minority. The destruction of the Ayodhya mosque in December 1992 brought to the fore the issue of whether India wll remain a secular democratic state or become a Hindu one. * * *

*   *   *

Groups or states belonging to one civilization that become involved in war with people from a different civilization naturally try to rally support from other members of their own civilization. * * *

*   *   *

Civilization rallying to date has been limited, but it has been growing, and it clearly has the potential to spread much further. As the conflicts in the Persian Gulf, the Caucasus and Bosnia continued, the positions of nations and the cleavages between them increasingly were along civilizational lines. Populist politicians, religious leaders and the media have found it a potent means of arousing mass support and of pressuring hesitant governments. In the coming years, the local conflicts most likely to escalate into major wars will be those, as in Bosnia and the Caucasus, along the fault lines between civilizations. The next world war, if there is one, will be a war between civilizations.

The West versus the Rest

The West is now at an extraordinary peak of power in relation to other civilizations. Its superpower opponent has disappeared from the map. Military conflict among Western states is unthinkable, and Western military power is unrivaled. Apart from Japan, the West faces no economic challenge. It dominates international political and security institutions and with Japan international economic institutions. Global political and security issues are effectively settled by a directorate of the United States, Britain and France, world economic issues by a directorate of the United States, Germany and Japan, all of which maintain extraordinarily close relations with each other to the exclusion of lesser and largely non-Western countries. Decisions made at the U.N. Security Council or in the International Monetary Fund that reflect the interests of the West are presented to the world as reflecting the desires of the world community. The very phrase "the world community" has become the euphemistic collective noun (replacing "the Free World") to give global legitimacy to actions reflecting the interests of the United States and other Western powers.[1] * * *

*   *   *

* * * V. S. Naipaul has argued that Western civilization is the "universal civilization" that "fits all men." At a superficial level much of Western culture has indeed permeated the rest of the world. At a more basic level, however, Western concepts differ fundamentally from those prevalent in other civilizations. Western ideas of individualism, liberalism, constitutionalism, human rights, equality, liberty, the rule of law, democracy, free markets, the separation of church and state often have little resonance in Islamic, Confucian, Japanese, Hindu, Buddhist or Orthodox cultures. Western efforts to propagate such ideas produce instead a reaction against "human rights imperialism" and a reaffirmation of indigenous values, as can be seen in the support for religious fundamentalism by the younger generation in non-Western cultures. The very notion that there

could be a "universal civilization" is a Western idea, directly at odds with the particularism of most Asian societies and their emphasis on what distinguishes one people from another. Indeed, the author of a review of 100 comparative studies of values in different societies concluded that "the values that are most important in the West are least important worldwide."[2] In the political realm, of course, these differences are most manifest in the efforts of the United States and other Western powers to induce other peoples to adopt Western ideas concerning democracy and human rights. Modern democratic government originated in the West. When it has developed in non-Western societies it has usually been the product of Western colonialism or imposition.

The central axis of world politics in the future is likely to be, in Kishore Mahbubani's phrase, the conflict between "the West and the Rest" and the responses of non-Western civilizations to Western power and values.[3] Those responses generally take one or a combination of three forms. At one extreme, non-Western states can, like Burma and North Korea, attempt to pursue a course of isolation, to insulate their societies from penetration or "corruption" by the West, and, in effect, to opt out of participation in the Western-dominated global community. The costs of this course, however, are high, and few states have pursued it exclusively. A second alternative, the equivalent of "band-wagoning" in international relations theory, is to attempt to join the West and accept its values and institutions. The third alternative is to attempt to "balance" the West by developing economic and military power and cooperating with other non-Western societies against the West, while preserving indigenous values and institutions; in short, to modernize but not to Westernize.

*   *   *

Implications for the West

This article does not argue that civilization identities will replace all other identities, that nation states will disappear, that each civilization will become a single coherent political entity, that groups within a civilization will not conflict with and even fight each other. This paper does set forth the hypotheses that differences between civilizations are real and important; civilization-consciousness is increasing; conflict between civilizations will supplant ideological and other forms of conflict as the dominant global form of conflict; international relations, historically a game played out within Western civilization, will increasingly be de-Westernized and become a game in which non-Western civilizations are actors and not simply objects; successful political, security and economic international institutions are more likely to develop within civilizations than across civilizations; conflicts between groups in different civilizations will be more frequent, more sustained and more violent than conflicts between groups in the same civilization; violent conflicts between groups in different civilizations are the most likely and most dangerous source of escalation that could lead to global wars; the paramount axis of world politics will be the relations between "the West and the Rest"; the elites in some torn non-Western countries will try to make their countries part of the West, but in most cases face major obstacles to accomplishing this; a central focus of conflict for the immediate future will be between the West and several Islamic-Confucian states.

This is not to advocate the desirability of conflicts between civilizations. It is to set forth descriptive hypotheses as to what the future may be like. If these are plausible hypotheses, however, it is necessary to consider their implications for Western policy. These implications should be divided between short-term advantage and long-term accommodation. In the short term it is clearly in the interest of the West to promote greater cooperation and unity within its own civilization, particularly between its European and North American components; to incorporate into the West societies in Eastern Europe, and Latin America whose cultures are close to those of the West; to promote and maintain cooperative relations with Russia and

Japan; to prevent escalation of local inter-civilization conflicts into major inter-civilization wars; to limit the expansion of the military strength of Confucian and Islamic states; to moderate the reduction of Western military capabilities and maintain military superiority in East and Southwest Asia; to exploit differences and conflicts among Confucian and Islamic states; to support in other civilizations groups sympathetic to Western values and interests; to strengthen international institutions that reflect and legitimate Western interests and values and to promote the involvement of non-Western states in those institutions.

In the longer term other measures would be called for. Western civilization is both Western and modern. Non-Western civilizations have attempted to become modern without becoming Western. To date only Japan has fully succeeded in this quest. Non-Western civilizations will continue to attempt to acquire the wealth, technology, skills, machines and weapons that are part of being modern. They will also attempt to reconcile this modernity with their traditional culture and values. Their economic and military strength relative to the West will increase. Hence the West will increasingly have to accommodate these non-Western modern civilizations whose power approaches that of the West but whose values and interests differ significantly from those of the West. This will require the West to maintain the economic and military power necessary to protect its interests in relation to these civilizations. It will also, however, require the West to develop a more profound understanding of the basic religious and philosophical assumptions underlying other civilizations and the ways in which people in those civilizations see their interests. It will require an effort to identify elements of commonality between Western and other civilizations. For the relevant future, there will be no universal civilization, but instead a world of different civilizations, each of which will have to learn to coexist with the others.

NOTES

1. Almost invariably Western leaders claim they are acting on behalf of "the world community." One minor lapse occurred during the run-up to the Gulf War. In an interview on "Good Morning America," Dec. 21, 1990, British Prime Minister John Major referred to the actions "the West" was taking against Saddam Hussein. He quickly corrected himself and subsequently referred to "the world community." He was, however, right when he erred.

2. Harry C. Triandis, *The New York Times*, Dec. 25, 1990, p. 41, and "Cross-Cultural Studies of Individualism and Collectivism," Nebraska Symposium on Motivation, vol. 37, 1989, pp. 41–133.

3. Kishore Mahbubani, "The West and the Rest," *The National Interest*, Summer 1992, pp. 3–13.

YAHYA SADOWSKI

POLITICAL ISLAM: ASKING THE WRONG QUESTIONS?

Introduction

The men who destroyed the World Trade Center on 9/11 were not political clones who subscribed to a single ideology. Muhammad Atta, whose Hamburg Cell actually executed the attacks, grew up in a white-collar Egyptian household; held ardently to a Sufi-influenced version of Islam; and lived much of his life in Europe. Yet he hated the West, believing that it supported genocide against Muslims in Bosnia and Chechnya. Osama bin Ladin, who organized the attacks, came from a wealthy family in insular Saudi Arabia; was a pious follower of a sectarian, anti-Sufi brand of Islam (Salafism); and never really worked outside the Muslim world. His primary objective seems to have been to drive U.S. troops out of the Middle East, particularly away from the Islamic holy places in Saudi Arabia. Khalid Shaykh Muhammad, who dreamed up the skyjacking attack, came from a working-class Baluchi (Pakistani) family in Kuwait; was never a pious Muslim of any variety; and had lived everywhere from North Carolina to the Philippines. His great obsession was the Palestine question, and he hoped to punish America for supporting Israel (Blanchard 2005, Marlin 2004).

It is doubtful that these men could have agreed on an answer to the question that has obsessed the West since 2001: "Why do they hate us?" Their objectives overlapped but they were never identical. Al Qaeda, the organization that brought them together, was not a disciplined political party that maintained internal ideological homogeneity. Rather, it was a network that pooled the funds and talents of diverse *jihadi* Muslims, shopping around for opportunities to

From *Annual Review of Political Science* 9 (2006): 215–40.

work together against common enemies (Burke 2004). If it is not easy to generalize about the motives and characteristics of the two dozen men who organized one single atrocity, imagine how difficult it must be to make broad inferences about the millions of Muslims who participate in other forms of political Islam.

Yet studies of political Islam usually try to do precisely this: to make homogenous claims about how religion affects the lives of more than a billion individuals who live everywhere from the jungles of Surinam to the steppes of Mongolia and whose political activity is channeled through regimes as different as the Emirate of Sharja and the French Republic. Despite this diversity, scholars have felt free to make sweeping claims about political Islam. They assert that Islam encourages war—or peace. It is deeply authoritarian—or compatible with democracy. It promotes fatalism and quiescence—or it requires activism and revolution. It is irrational and obstructs modernization—or it resembles "the Protestant ethic" and lays the foundations for modernity.

The contradictory nature of these claims suggests that there is something fundamentally wrong with the way scholars try to generalize about Islam.

The Diversity Debate

Studies of political Islam commonly begin from two faulty assumptions, guaranteeing that whatever questions are asked will generate misleading answers. The first assumption is that Muslims around the world share a common, relatively homogenous body of doctrine on a wide array of religious, social, and political matters. The second is that this doctrine is actually the primary determinant of Muslim behavior. These assumptions inform recent works, such as Huntington's (1995) famous "clash of civilizations" doctrine. But Huntington and his peers are building on the older work of Orientalist scholars who explicitly claimed that the evolution of the Muslim world was primarily determined by its common culture and that this culture derives from a single source: the text of the Holy Qur'an (Lockman 2004).

Orientalism was already challenged in the 1960s by a number of scholars, particularly anthropologists (Abdel-Malek 1963, Geertz 1971, Gilsenan 1983), who noted that although orthodox, literate, urban Muslims might share similar doctrines, "folk Islam" in the villages tended to be heterodox and heterogeneous. Their critique was popularized by Said (1978) in his famous study *Orientalism* and other works. Said argued:

[A]fter Muhammad's preaching and career, the faith spread into hundreds of different regions and cultures, from China and India in the east to Morocco in the West, to Europe in the north, and to Africa in the south. Each region and people who came under its sway developed its own kind of Islam. Thus, Islam is a world of many histories, many peoples, many languages, traditions, schools of interpretation, proliferating developments, disputations, cultures, and countries. A vast world of 1.2 billion people stretched out over every continent, north and south, including now the Americas, it can't adequately be apprehended or understood simply as "Islam." (Said 2002, pp. 69–70)

He concluded that serious scholarship should not begin from a presumed unity of Islamic civilization, but should "talk about different kinds of Islam, at different moments, for different people, in different fields." Serious studies should begin by focusing on specific groups of Muslims in defined periods and be very cautious about making universal claims about Muslims. There may be certain traits that are shared by Muslims and not by other populations, but they are not obvious, and they need to be discovered rather than simply posited (for a pioneering effort in this direction, see Eickelman & Piscatori 1996).

*   *   *

Empirical studies have shown time and again that most of the traits that Muslims have in common are the ones they share with the rest of humanity. A recent study by Inglehart & Norris (2003) compared surveys of attitudes in 11 Muslim-majority countries during 1995 and 2000 with identical surveys in 69 non-Muslim countries. These surveys showed that with respect to questions of political culture and values, Muslims did not differ significantly from Christians and other populations. Indeed, Muslims tended to show slightly more enthusiasm for democracy than Christians. The one significant difference was with respect to gender questions, where the majority of Muslims shared the same illiberal attitudes found among a minority of Christians. Even in this area, Muslim attitudes appeared to derive more from social circumstances than from Islamic dogma: Gender attitudes in more literate and industrialized Muslim countries such as Turkey tended to be distinctly more liberal than those in less developed ones such as Bangladesh.

*   *   *

If, at the global level, Muslims do not appear strikingly different from the heirs of other religious traditions, at the local level they differ from each other in manifold ways that the Orientalist approach has tended to neglect or occlude. Most obviously, there is the difference between Sunni and Shia Muslims (although even this is more pronounced in cities than in villages). Sunni thinkers, being part of the political and numerical majority, are more comfortable with writing their ethical edicts into public law and participating in quotidian politics. For the Shia, in contrast, individual clerics rather than formal legal canons are the primary arbiters of private and political morality (Cole & Keddie 1986).

The urban-rural divide among Muslims may actually be more important than doctrinal differences. Urban Muslims tend to be more literate and connected by long-distance trade networks than their country cousins, so they rely more on the classical texts of the faith and have preserved greater homogeneity from one place to the next. Rural Muslims, in contrast, tend to be not only more heterodox but more heterogeneous, relying more on local holy men for interpretations of the faith and developing idiosyncratic practices in different places (Keddie 1972, Zaman 2002).

Since the nineteenth century, a third differentiation among Muslims has become increasingly potent: the development of discrete national versions of the faith. There have long been regional differences between such places as Morocco, where exclusivist traditions prevailed, and Indonesia, where many Muslims were enthusiastically syncretic (Eickelman 1975, Geertz 1976). But this tendency was exaggerated when the overthrow of the Ottoman and Mughal empires delivered political power to new nationalist elites. Turkish Islam, battered by a Kemalist elite that was actively hostile to traditional religion, wound up evolving in a very different direction from Islam in Egypt, where Arab nationalists sought to co-opt religion as part of the Arab cultural heritage. * * * The collapse of the old empires severed many of the transnational networks through which the Ulema (clerics) had communicated, and the new nationalist states imposed central control over the education of the Ulema and the management of mosques.

Perhaps the most profound, yet least understood, difference among Muslims emerged over the past two centuries with the rise of mass Islamic movements. These come in two distinct and rival varieties. Some of the largest and most widespread are "pietistic" movements, which feel that Islam must advance by inculcating faith in individuals rather than through the creation of an Islamic state. * * *

Pietist movements are largely ignored in the West, precisely because they are apolitical. They do not make revolutions or coups or breed terrorists. When scholars claim that "Islam is a religion of *jihad*," they are not thinking of (or perhaps even aware of) the pietists. They are focusing on the opposing wing of the Islamic mass movements: political Islam.

A Typology of Islamic Movements

Political Islam consists of a broad array of mass movements in the Muslim world, which share a conviction that political power is an essential instrument for constructing a God-fearing society. They believe that Muslims can fulfill their religious obligations only when public law sanctions and encourages pious behavior. To this end, the majority of these movements work to take control of state power, whether by propaganda, plebiscite, or putsch.

But political Islam, like other varieties, takes very different forms at distinct places and times. Other than the Qur'an itself, which provides inspiration but no unambiguous program for action, its proponents have never adhered to a single text or theory. Unlike the socialists of the nineteenth century, its advocates have never affiliated with a single "international," and, unlike the communists of the twentieth century, its branches have never been supervised by a single Comintern. If its members share any common trait, it is that they all seem to fear alternative, competing interpretations of political Islam—which, for them, smack of heresy—even more than they fear non-Islamic political groups. It should not be surprising, then, that when Islamic movements engage in violence, it is usually fratricidal and targets other Muslims (Sadowski 1998).

To grasp the diversity of political Islam, it is useful to begin with a typology. The best available was constructed by the French scholar Olivier Roy, who wandered around the mountains of Afghanistan in the 1980s, examining the difficulties that different groups of *Mujahidin* had in cooperating against the invading Russians. Roy (1990) discovered that these groups varied not only in terms of sect and ethnic background, but also in the organizational forms they preferred and the social constituencies from which they recruited. The main subforms of political Islam that he identified were traditionalist, fundamentalist, and Islamist.

Traditionalist Groups

Traditionalist groups tend to conflate Islam with local cultural practice, and to accept the political authority of local notables, saints, and holy families. Precisely because their focus is so parochial, they do not easily amalgamate into national groupings, much less attain international recognition. Perhaps the most famous traditionalist group today is the cult of the monarchy in Morocco, in which various groups of Sufis and clerics unite in support of the religious and secular authority of the king in Rabat (Hammoudi 1997). Traditionalists affiliate through a host of different organizational forms—tribes, patronage networks, and Sufi brotherhoods—but their preferred institutions are highly personalistic (Eickelman 1985, Gellner & Waterbury 1977). As other versions of political Islam have become increasingly common in the cities, traditionalist movements have been increasingly confined to rural areas, recruiting their supporters among peasants, mountaineers, and tribesmen.

Fundamentalist Groups

Fundamentalist groups share a mission that can be both revolutionary and reactionary: They seek to purge Islam of local or non-Muslim practices that may have crept in over the centuries and to return it to the pure practice of the faith that prevailed during the life of the Prophet. They thus make heavy use of the *hadith*, the sayings of the Prophet and his companions, which describe life in the first Islamic state (although, since dozens of compilations of the *hadith* exist, various fundamentalist movements offer quite different pictures of that state). Fundamentalists believe that only carefully trained clerics, the Ulema, can properly interpret the Qur'an and *hadith,* and they tend to accord this caste privileged authority both in their leadership and in their plans for an Islamic state. Fundamentalists can organize around a variety of vehicles (Sufi orders, again, often being important), but given their clerical bent, perhaps their most natural instrument is the Islamic college, known as a *madrassa* among Sunnis or a *hawza* among Shia (Del Castillo 2001, Nakash 2003). It was the graduates of such colleges who led the Islamic revolution in Iran and who legitimated the monarchy in Saudi Arabia (Akhavi 1980, Yassini 1985).

The traditional recruiting ground of the fundamentalists has been among urban elites and the traditional middle classes (*bazaaris*) (see Fischer 1980). Indeed, during much of the twentieth century, fundamentalism served to reinforce the authority of these literate elites against displaced peasants and other groups that had begun to crowd into the cities. But in the 1980s, the spread of *madrassas* gave rise to a new generation of clerics recruited from the urban poor, espousing a rival—rough and vulgar—variant of fundamentalism. Roy has dubbed this tendency, which gave rise to the Taliban in Afghanistan, "neo-fundamentalism" (Rashid 2000, Roy 1994).

The fundamentalists made one great contribution to the arsenal of political Islam. At some point in the eighteenth century, adherents of the Naqshibandi Sufi order discovered an organizational technique that has been called the Muhammadan paradigm (*at-tariqa al-muhammadiyya*). So that followers could fully appreciate Islam as it was experienced during the life of the Prophet, they formed small groups that sought to replicate the general stages of his career: exposure to the corrupt practices of non-Islamic society (*jahiliyya*), retreat into a pure community where each member reinforces the piety of others (*hijra*), and finally a return to the wider world with the discipline and power necessary to propagate Islam (*fath*). Although this technique for promoting religiosity by retreating into small, self-policing groups was invented by fundamentalists, it proved so fruitful that it is now widely practiced by all of the Islamic movements (Buehler 1998, Ruthven 1986).

Islamist Groups

*   *   *

The Islamists, with their cosmopolitan backgrounds, introduced various tools they had borrowed from the West into their organizational arsenal. Ideologically, they drew on antimodernist philosophies that embodied Western dissatisfaction with the consequences of industrialization and positivism: Spengler, Althusser, and Feyerabend supplied some of their favorite texts (Ahmed 1992, Majid 2000). They rearticulated Islam as a modern ideology in which control of a totalistic Islamic state would permit the transformation of society in a manner that promoted not only piety but progress. Recruiting from the same intellectual groups through which Marxism penetrated the Muslim world—and often doing jail time in the same prisons as persecuted communists—they quickly learned the advantages of organizing into parties of disciplined cadres, organized into discrete cells, that could work to lay the foundations for revolution among wider groups. This idea that Islamists should focus on building "vanguard" parties (*tali'a*) was propounded by two figures at opposite ends of the Muslim world, who created two of its most effective movements: Sayyid Qutb, who led the Muslim Brotherhood in Egypt, and Abul-A'la Mawdudi, who established the Jama'at-i Islami in India and Pakistan (Moussalli 1993, Nasr 1994). Although never quite as prominent as it was in the Sunni world, Islamism also penetrated the Shia community through the Liberation Party of Iran and its offshoots, including the Mojahedin-i Khalq (Abrahamian 1989, Chehabi 1990, Rahnema 2000).

This typology does not exhaust the variety of modern Islamic politics; it simply describes the major forms that have sustained stand-alone mass movements. There are also, for example, large numbers of Islamic modernists who believe that the state must represent all citizens, not just Muslims, and that application of religious law (Sharia) should be largely a private matter. This viewpoint is particularly common in countries where orthodox Muslims do not form a majority, such as India and Indonesia. (Modernism is not the same thing as pietism, which is agnostic with respect to the form of the state.) But modernists have not, except in Iran and Indonesia, formed their own mass movements. Instead, modernists have tended to associate with other political groups, sometimes affiliating with fundamentalist or Islamist movements but most often attaching themselves to nationalist groups (Kurzman 1998).

The Islamic Reformation

In fact, for a full century before 1975, the majority of politically active Muslims tended to join nationalist rather than Islamic movements. Then, over the course of a single decade, the appeal of nationalism seemed to collapse and the allure of Islamic movements exploded. By 1985 many nationalist parties and the regimes they had established were on the defensive, battered by electoral challenges or even armed insurrections by political Islam.

Why did this happen? Certainly one major factor was the 1979 Islamic revolution in Iran, which established a fundamentalist regime [although the insurrection against the Shah had originally involved a coalition of nationalists, Marxists, and Islamists (Abrahamian 1993)]. The Iranian example of an Islamic regime that could take and hold power, despite an array of challenges that included a full-scale foreign invasion, inspired Muslims around the globe. But although the Iranian paradigm encouraged the Islamic resurgence, it did not trigger it. By 1979 Islamic movements already formed the largest political parties in Egypt and Indonesia, and were mounting insurrections in Syria and Afghanistan. The Islamic resurgence of the 1980s built upon a broad array of trends, including political, economic, and cultural developments.

Political Factors

By 1975 it was already clear that nationalist regimes in the Muslim world had failed to create an inclusive sense of national unity. They had not been able to fulfill interstate national unity projects (such as pan-Arab aspirations or retaining the Bengalis within Pakistan). Large groups— Kurds in Turkey and Iraq, Chinese in Malaysia and Indonesia, Dinka in the Sudan, Berbers in Algeria, etc.—felt excluded from the political community. Worse, nationalist regimes had not even made adequate provision for national security, leaving Lebanon, Syria, Egypt, Jordan, Afghanistan, Pakistan, and Somalia open to defeat or invasion by foreign powers. The fatal error of many nationalist regimes lay in their failure to deliver elementary services to their citizens: education, health, infrastructure, and civil order. Even poor states may provide some sense of justice to their citizens, but the nationalist regimes had become increasingly corrupt and aloof, ruled by inbred elites.

Economic Factors

Of course, the most important service that nationalist regimes had promised their supporters was economic development. But the populist policies (price controls, nationalization, state investment in heavy industry) initially pursued by most nationalists benefited only a minority while alienating large sections of the population, including the merchants and shopkeepers who formed the backbone of many Islamic movements. During the 1970s, the global rise of oil prices pumped more money into the economies of countries from Algeria to Indonesia, and (through workers' remittances) from Morocco to Pakistan. Yet petrodollars also fueled a rise of inflation, an appreciation of the currency, and lavish opportunities for graft and corruption. In the 1980s, when oil prices collapsed, states had to cut their subsidies and public employment programs, and the gross domestic product in many Muslim countries fell by half. Azerbaijanis, for example, had to endure not only the drop of oil prices but also the economic crisis that attended the collapse of the Soviet Union (which also affected Muslim states across Central Asia) and even came under pressure during the 1997 Asian economic crisis (which devastated Indonesia and caused massive dislocations as far away as Turkey).

Cultural Factors

Although nationalist regimes may not have delivered economic development, they did preside over an epochal growth of urbanization and the bloating of Cairo, Istanbul, Karachi, and Djakarta into megalopoli with populations of over ten million. Urbanization, in turn, triggered a host of cultural changes. Heterodox Muslims coming from the countryside began to interact with established urban elites, usually in a way that expanded the constituency of literate, orthodox versions of Islam. Both pietist and fundamentalist groups played a prominent role in this transformation. Cities were also where Muslims came into increasing contact with the non-Muslim world through cinemas, television, tourism, and shopping malls (Adelkhah 2000, Verkaaik 2004). The share of their societies that could afford to connect to the world via satellite television, the internet, and international travel steadily grew (Henry & Springborg 2001, Roy 2004, Sageman 2004). This altered consumption patterns and, more importantly, raised disturbing questions about traditional sexual expectations.

History of Modern Islamic Movements

*　　*　　*

The Islamic movements only began to make a comeback in the 1930s—under the "new management" of the Islamists. The first Islamist movement was the Muslim Brotherhood, founded in Egypt in 1928 by Hassan al-Banna; but in 1937, Abul-A'la Mawdudi organized a similar group in India that evolved into the Jama'at-i Is-lami (Mitchell 1993, Nasr 1996). Islamist groups mobilized lay communities that were less suscep-tible to state pressure than clerics, they espoused a transnational Islamic ideology that many found more satisfying than nationalism, and their doc-trine and tactics were as modern as anything that fundamentalists, nationalists, or colonial powers could deploy against them. They quickly estab-lished disciplined branches in multiple countries.

But nationalist movements continued to dom-inate the Muslim world until the 1970s, when their shortcomings catalyzed the Islamic resur-gence. This unfolded in two distinct phases. Dur-ing the 1970s and early 1980s, Islamist movements were most prominent: the Muslim Brotherhood staged revolts or launched coups in Syria, Egypt, Palestine (Hamas), and the Sudan; the Jama'at-i Islami and the Hizb-i Islami led the revolt against the Soviets in Afghanistan; and the Mojahedin-i Khalq provided the shock troops for the revolu-tion in Iran. But as these movements were sup-pressed, fundamentalist movements pushed to the fore: Khomeini and his disciples in Iran, Hizbul-lah in Lebanon, the Groupe Islamique Arme in Al-geria, the Naqshibandis and the Qadiris in Chechnya and the Philippines. Finally, in the 1990s, a series of neo-fundamentalist movements edged aside their more established rivals: the Tal-iban in Afghanistan, the Salafis in Saudi Arabia and Yemen, the Ahl-i Hadith and its offshoots in Pakistan and Kashmir, and the Lashkar Jihad in Indonesia (Rana 2004, Roy & Abu-Zahab 2004).

The Islamic resurgence led to a dizzying ar-ray of political conflicts, affecting virtually every Muslim society. Yet Islamic parties actually took power in only five countries: in Iran and Afghan-istan by revolution, in Sudan and Pakistan through military coups, and in Turkey by means of the ballot box. Everywhere else, insurgencies were suppressed or contained. The nationalist movements still retained broad (if less enthusias-tic) social support in many Muslim countries and controlled the state, thus enjoying an enormous advantage during internal conflicts even when opposed by well-organized Muslim movements.

Social Power in Weak States

*   *   *

The great majority of Muslims who are associated with the Islamic movements experience them pri-marily as social rather than political organiza-tions. Indeed, many Islamic activists believe that transforming society is a necessary first step in the quest for political power. The influential Sudanese Islamist Hassan al-Turabi has argued that if Mus-lims reorganize society properly, they can let the state wither away into a vestigial role (Hamdi 1998). The Islamic movements have invested enormous energy in the construction of social net-works, which include employment agencies, food banks and charities, schools and nurseries, sav-ings clubs and financial institutions, student and professional associations, and even sports clubs and cultural gatherings. They have also gained a foothold in more traditional social solidarities: tribes, family associations, castes, guilds, village councils, and, of course, mosques (Fandy 2001, Simone 1994, Wickham 2002, Wiktorowicz 2004).

Through these agencies, the Islamic move-ments have attracted support from large groups of people who may not be particularly pious, much less attracted by complex political doc-trines, but who simply need the services that the movements supply. The Islamic movements ap-peal particularly to those who need the services that religious groups deliver with particular effec-tiveness. Like faith-based organizations in the United States and elsewhere, the Islamic move-ments offer unique solutions for communities coping with crime and corruption, as well as for individuals grappling with alcoholism or drugs, trying to claw their way up from poverty by start-ing a small business, or striving to hold a family together after the death of a breadwinner (Wuth-now 2004). The Muhammadan paradigm of small groups whose members pool their resources and provide intimate moral support functions as well as any twelve-step program ever devised.

*   *   *

The Problems of the Islamic Movements

This pattern of organization is responsible for what Muslims themselves consider some of the most serious problems of the Islamic movements. For example, in all varieties of political Islam, existing state borders, usually delineated by colonial powers, are deemed illegitimate. Many Islamic activists insist that the entire Muslim world forms one political community that should be united into a single state. One of their central complaints against secular nationalism has been that it failed to efface the borders that divided the Arab world, much less those that divided Arabs from Turks or Tajiks.

Yet the Islamic movements have been no more successful in this regard. Only a handful of Islamic movements (Tablighi Jamaat, the Muslim Brotherhood) have even created transnational networks, and these have involved only tiny numbers of people. No Islamic regime has merged with any other state. Instead, the parochial organization of the Islamic movements seems to have accentuated divisions between one group of Muslims and another: between Sunni and Shia, between Sharia literalists and Sufi inclusivists, and between adherents of different interpretations of political Islam.

Indeed, relations between Muslim communities have grown dramatically worse since the 1990s. Neo-fundamentalist groups such as the Salafis [Wahhabis who reject the authority of the traditional Saudi clerics; see Wiktorowicz (2001)] in Algeria and Syria, the Taliban in Afghanistan, the Jama'at-i Ulema-i Islam in Pakistan, and the Jaysh-i Muhammad in Kashmir are strikingly less tolerant than older Islamic movements. These organizations share three frightening characteristics. First, they uphold the doctrine of *takfir*, according to which any Muslim who fails in his or her religious duties may be denounced as an unbeliever. Second, they subscribe to some version of an anti-Semitic conspiracy theory according to which Jewish-controlled economic institutions,

the United States government, local Muslim regimes, and impious Muslims are all working together to subvert Islam. Finally, they are violently anti-Shia, refusing to acknowledge that the Shia are even Muslims and calling for their violent suppression.

The growth of this neo-fundamentalist "inquisition" was partly a spontaneous response of certain Sunni groups to the rising prominence of the Shia after the successes of the revolution in Iran and of Hizbullah in Lebanon. These movements were also deliberately armed and cultivated by the governments of Saudi Arabia and Pakistan, who viewed them as tools in a regional struggle for influence against Tehran. But the governments have lost control. The same neo-fundamentalists that targeted the Shia minority in Pakistan and the Hazara in Afghanistan are the ones who now attack the Shia-dominated security forces in Iraq and seek to topple the Saudi government.

Shia Islamic movements have countermobilized against the neo-fundamentalists, but, beyond raising their own militias, they are not well equipped to address this problem. Because they are not organized as parties, the Islamic movements have little practical experience at negotiating with nonmembers, forming coalitions, sharing power, or even amalgamating demands. Despite their claim that *al-islam huwa al-hall* ("Islam is the solution"), the Islamic movements lack the skill to address many of the problems states routinely face. This raises a second question for members of the Islamic movements: They have learned to thrive in opposition, but how would they handle the new responsibilities that would face them if they ever came to power?

Some analysts have noted that the Islamic movements have failed to develop a coherent program for dealing with the large-scale problems that confront Muslim societies (Roy 1994). Their economic policies, for example, differ little from the variety of populism that prevailed in the region (even among secular regimes) in the 1960s: a version of state capitalism in which price controls and consumer subsidies are supposed to combine with state control of finance and heavy industry to produce both equity and growth. This approach has not produced satisfactory results, even when applied by pious regimes with popular support, such as the Islamic republic of Iran (Nomani & Rahnema 1994).

*   *   *

Democratization in the Muslim World

As the Islamic movements come closer to taking and exercising state power, one concern is whether they will promote or reverse democratic trends in regional politics. Some scholars have argued that Islam is "essentially" incompatible with democracy (Kedourie 1994, Berman 2003). They claim that Islam requires a totalitarian submission to God and obedience to legitimate political authorities. And in fact, some Islamic movements (particularly the Salafis) are ardently authoritarian, seeking to return to the earliest form of Islamic government: the autocratic Caliphate.

But on this issue, as on so many others, there is enormous diversity in Islam. All Muslims agree that the Sharia was originally designed to place limits on the power of rulers, guaranteeing citizens many rights and liberties (Peletz 2002, Hooker 2003). Some passages of the Qur'an require that politicians consult regularly with their followers, and the majority of Islamic movements are actually led by representative councils rather than by autocrats. An elaborate body of doctrine insisting that Islam requires some form of democracy has already developed (Hefner 2004, Esposito & Voll 2001).

In the past few decades, these democratic tendencies have been reinforced by the practical experience of the Islamic movements. As their popular support has grown, Islamic activists have come to see that the ballot box might offer a shortcut to power. There is an element of opportunism in this; one U.S. government official complained that political Islam views democracy as a matter of "one man, one vote, one time." But the logic of democracy has tended to temper and restrain this opportunism. Even where the leaders of the Islamic movements are not deeply committed to democracy, they are learning that aspirations for freedom are very widespread in the Muslim world and that if they want to retain public support they need to play by democratic rules. Thus, not only the AK party in Turkey but Hizbullah in Lebanon, the Islamic Constitutional Movement in Kuwait (a branch of the Muslim Brotherhood), and the Jama'at-i Islami in Pakistan have consistent records of democratic practice. Indeed, in Indonesia the major Islamic movements (the Muhammadiyya and the Nahdat ul-Ulema) have become key pillars of the democratic regime (Hefner 2000, Bowen 2003).

Iran offers an excellent example of the prospects and perils that confront democratization in the Muslim world. Although Ayatullah Khomeini could easily have ruled as a "benign" dictator, he and his followers actually constructed an electoral form of government that allowed the diverse subtrends of the Islamic movements to compete for a voice. Iran had fair and regular elections (untainted by the military interventions that plague Turkey) for 20 years after the revolution. In 2000, the 15 Khordad reform movement swept to power on a liberal platform; the reformers had learned during their years in opposition that democracy requires not just balloting but a wide array of civil liberties. Conservative clerics, their authority threatened by these reforms, then began using their control of the judiciary to proscribe reformist candidates from future elections, but this was not enough to terminate Iran's democratic experiment. The struggle to expand, consolidate, and define Iranian democracy goes on today, with all the participants in the debate claiming the support of Islam for their position (Jahanbaksh 2001, Moslem 2002).

*   *   *

The one really original idea to emerge from studies of the Muslim world in recent years is the theory of the "rentier state," which explains why countries with large petrodollar revenues tend to remain authoritarian (Crystal 1990, Karl 1997, Luciani 1990, Ross 2001). States that enjoy large and regular revenues (rents) from oil, gas, and other resources do not need to rely on taxes from their citizens. And where citizens are untaxed (and are dependent on subsidies and jobs supplied by the central government), they are in a very weak position to demand representative government. This tendency appears to be strong not only among Muslims or Arabs but in Russia and Angola, or in any country where democracy is not already well institutionalized before the petrodollars begin to flow (Bayulgen 2005).

Fortunately for the Arabs (although not for the world economy), the value of their oil production is likely to decline markedly over the next 20 years as their reservoirs are exhausted and the world begins to shift to alternative sources of energy (Roberts 2004, Simmons 2005). This sea change may improve the economic foundations for democracy, since oil—through the "Dutch disease" or "resource curse" (see Auty 1993, Kim 2003)—tends to inhibit economic development. If the Islamic movements are still serious contenders for power at that time, we will get to see a fairer test of how they respond to opportunities for democratization.

Political Islam and Terrorism

The sudden growth of interest in the democratization of the Muslim world since 9/11 derives from the hope that in a democratic society Muslims would be less inclined to resort to terrorism. Many Westerners, reeling from the attacks in New York, London, and Madrid, believe that Islam makes its followers more warlike than the adherents of other religions. No less an authority than Samuel Huntington has claimed precisely this, arguing that "in the early 1990s Muslims were engaged in more intergroup violence than non-Muslims, and that two-thirds to three-quarters of intercivilizational wars were between Muslims and non-Muslims. Islam's borders are bloody, and so are its innards" (Huntington 1995).

Yet Huntington reached this conclusion using only data for the years 1992 and 1993, which were far from typical. This was the period immediately following the "Leninist extinction" of 1989, when several non-Muslim conflicts (El Salvador, Nicaragua, Angola) came to an end and the break-up of Yugoslavia and the Soviet Union fueled a host of new ones—many of them involving Muslims (Bosnia, Kosovo, Azerbaijan, Tajikistan). If Huntington had used data for a period 10 years earlier or later, his picture would have been more balanced. If he had used data for a period 30 years earlier, when Europe was struggling to hold onto its overseas colonies, the West would have appeared more violent than Islam. Indeed, the war and conflict databases maintained by international relations experts suggest that during the two centuries prior to World War II and the nuclear stalemate that emerged around 1950, the vast majority of wars involved Western powers. Does this mean—as some scholars have suggested (Moore 1991, Nirenberg 1998)—that Christian civilization is more prone to violence than others?

Indeed, the statistics of the U.S. National Counterterrorism Center suggest that Muslims are involved in ~19% of terrorist attacks annually—just what you would expect relative to their share of the global population (Sevastopulo 2005). Detailed studies of Muslim terrorists suggest that the links between religion and their tactics are extremely weak. Many are not especially pious; most of the 9/11 terrorists spent the weeks before the attack drinking and whoring (McDermott 2005). We have particularly good studies of Palestinian suicide bombers, and these suggest that their character is essentially the same as that of non-Muslim terrorists (Victor 2003, Davis 2003). First, they are not crazy or irrational; they are men (or women) who believe in a cause and think that their tactics are a necessary means for advancing that cause. They are "good soldiers" whose mindset is not significantly different from that of the crews that piloted nuclear bombers during the Cold War. [Strategic bombing was, in fact, considered a form of terrorism until World

War II (Lindqvist 2003).] Second, terrorists fit no single social profile. Some, particularly the foot soldiers who actually conduct the attacks, come from lower-class backgrounds and are relatively uneducated. But others, especially the managers who plan the attacks, are highly educated and raised in conditions of privilege (Burke 2004, Hudson 2002).

The doctrines of terrorists do tend to share certain common features. They make absolute claims to the truth, they demand blind obedience, they idealize one particular period of history, they claim that their ends justify any means, and they deploy a formal concept of holy war (Kimball 2002, Stern 2003). But these doctrines do not cause people to be terrorists; rather, potential terrorists seem to select or construct these types of doctrines, even when they are aware of alternative, contradictory positions. Muslim suicide bombers are aware that the overwhelming majority of Muslim clerics have condemned their tactics.

Most Islamic movements, in fact, do not advocate or practice terrorism, and terrorists form a miniscule element within the politically active Muslim population. This does not mean that Muslim terrorism is a minor problem; a very small number of men or women can cause a massive amount of terror. However, terrorism among Muslims appears to be concentrated in three distinct domains, each of which has its particular rationale and traits.

Protracted suicide-bombing campaigns have been supported by some large Islamic movements: Hizbullah in Lebanon, Hamas in Palestine, and the Salafis in Iraq. They have also won popular approval among large numbers of Muslims, even those not directly involved in the conflict (Pew 2005). Most Muslims would—rightly or wrongly—reject the idea that these are terrorist actions. The bombings are directed against foreigners, Israelis or Americans, whom many Muslims feel have lost their status as noncombatants because they are occupying another country. There is nothing particularly Islamic about this attitude: Vietnamese, Tamils in Sri Lanka, and

secular Algerian nationalists have made precisely the same claims and employed similar tactics (Pape 2005).

A different type of terrorism has emerged in conflicts between Muslim groups. Smaller, extremist Muslim organizations have used bombs and machine guns to kill large numbers of Muslims whom they consider to be unbelievers or apostates. The Groupe Islamique Arme massacred supporters of the secular government in Algeria; the Sipah-i Sahaba Pakistan have systematically attacked their country's Shia minority, as did the Taliban in their campaigns against the Hazara, and the various Salafi groups in Iraq have increasingly redirected their attacks from American troops to Shia gatherings. Neofundamentalist movements seem particularly inclined toward this type of terror. The objective and strategy behind these pogroms is quite different from assaults on foreign occupiers; they are more akin to the type of ethnic cleansing that plagued Bosnia and Rwanda (Kalyvas 2005).

The least common form of terrorism among Muslims is precisely the one that concerns Westerners most: the global jihad in which small groups of Muslims, not affiliated with any large Islamic movement, volunteer to conduct attacks in Washington, Nairobi, or other locations far outside the Muslim world. Ironically, the very marginality of these movements makes them more difficult to combat. Although officials often give them names (al Qaeda in the Middle East or Jama'a Islamiyya in Southeast Asia) that suggest the existence of formal organizations, these terrorists really work through informal networks. They raise funds and acquire weapons from diverse sources, acting independently and without central leadership. They lack sustained support from the larger Muslim population, at least partly because their objectives remain unclear.

Because these different forms of terrorism have distinct social foundations, strategies for curbing (or promoting) them need to take different forms. Suicide bombings against foreign occupiers enjoy wide public support and can best be terminated by a political process that addresses the underlying grievances. Global jihad, on the other hand, is a marginal, underground movement that requires no public support. Even regime change is not going to seriously curb it. It must be fought through police actions, systematically hunting down its adherents and collapsing their cells.

Why Do They Hate Us?

Much of the literature on Islam since 9/11 has actually obscured the differences between these strains of terror by implying that all but a few Muslims are fundamentally hostile to Western civilization as a whole. No question produced so much hand-wringing after 9/11 as "Why do they hate us?" But this question reflects two false premises: first, the assumption (again) that all or most Muslims behave the same way; second, the assumption that Western values, institutions, and practices evoke a deep-seated revulsion among Muslims. Nothing could be further from the truth. Most Muslims admire Western technology, industry, education, egalitarianism, and liberty. They send their children to study in the West, and, given the chance, are quite happy to emigrate there (Zogby 2002a,b). There are features of Western society that they do not admire, but these are typically the same ones that Westerners (particularly conservatives) denounce: the decline of the family and leisure, high rates of illegitimate births and crime, greed and crass materialism.

Most Muslims do not view the West as something that must be accepted or rejected in toto; rather they see it as a kind of smorgasbord from which they can select attractive bits while leaving others. Muslims everywhere display an eagerness to learn, borrow, and emulate features of modern society. Many Westerners tend to ignore or dismiss this activity, seeing it as incompatible with the antipathy that Muslims display for other aspects of the West. But there is no contradiction. Europeans borrow Indian cuisine, Chinese prints, Japanese gizmos, and Buddhist philoso-phy without embracing other parts of Asian cultures. Cultural exchange is not like a roller coaster ride, where once you have started you have to stay for the entire course (*Economist* 2005).

Even the unattractive features of the West do not lead Muslims to "hate" it. The decline of the family in the West is something most Muslims would want to avoid repeating, but it usually generates pity rather than rage. The only features of the West that engender real anger among Muslims are its foreign policies—and even here the fury is directed at particular states rather than at Western civilization per se (Defense Science Board 2004). Chechens and Afghans hate the Russians. Moroccans and Algerians despise the French. The Indonesians loathe tourists. More Muslims rage against the United States than any other country—because Washington has a longer global reach and intervenes in the Muslim world more often. Yet even those Muslims who denounce the United States do not all do so for the same reasons. Hamas in Palestine, Hizbullah in Lebanon, and the Muslim Brotherhood in Egypt hate America for its support of Israel; Saudi and Kuwaiti militants hate Washington for its support of their ruling dynasties (while their loyalist cousins may respect it for the same reason); Malaysian and Indonesian Muslims denounce the United States for its role in the 1997 Asian currency crisis. Islamic militants are the first to recognize the difficulties this diversity presents for trying to unite with their brethren in other countries. Many do not feel hatred toward Western countries, and those that do cannot agree on a common focus.

Some Lessons

Meaningful generalizations about a subject can only be made after completing a broad survey of its particulars. Thus, in the 1960s and 1970s, political scientists were able to propose some interesting—if not really conclusive—theories about how revolutions occurred because they

could build on excellent studies of particular revolts in the American colonies, in France, and in
Russia. But the study of political Islam is not yet
ripe for this kind of induction; the ratio of noise
to signal in the existing literature is still too high.
We actually have better studies of the broad social trends behind the 1979 revolution in Iran
(Arjomand 1989, Foran 1994, Kazemi 1980) than
we do of the Islamic movements that participated in it.

Useful studies of political Islam can be written, despite the forbidding obstacles that curb research on the subject, only if scholars avoid the
pitfalls and prejudices that have been sketched in
this essay. The following facts, in particular, need
to be kept in mind:

- Muslim societies tend to be at least as diverse
  as they are similar;
- There is a large gap between Islamic doctrine
  and Muslim practice;
- The aspirations of Muslims do not differ
  markedly from those of other cultures, although the means they deploy to pursue
  them may [this is an instance of the famous
  "fundamental attribution error" (Reed
  1993)];
- Despite the criticisms made during the Enlightenment, religion neither prevents people
  from behaving rationally nor prevents them
  from innovating;
- The great struggles in which Muslims are
  caught up are structured by history but not
  determined by it. Their outcomes may still be
  uncertain.

These are not facts that apply to Islam and
Muslims uniquely. If you substitute Hindu, Jew,
or Christian for Muslim in these statements, they
remain true. It is precisely the growing respect
for these facts by students of political religion in
the West, and particularly of the religious right in
the United States, that has led to an explosion of
new and more valuable studies (Ammerman
1987, Wilcox 2000).

*   *   *

REFERENCES

Abdel-Malek A. 1963. Orientalism in crisis. *Dio-
genes* 44:107–8

Abrahamian E. 1989. *The Iranian Mojahedin.*
New Haven, CT: Yale Univ. Press

Abrahamian E. 1993. *Khomeinism: Essays on the
Islamic Republic.* Berkeley: Univ. Calif. Press

Abun-Nasr J. 1965. *The Tijaniyya: A Sufi Order in
the Modern World.* London: Oxford Univ. Press

Adelkhah F. 2000. *Being Modern in Iran.* New
York: Columbia Univ. Press

Ahmed A. 1992. *Postmodernism and Islam:
Predicament and Promise.* London: Routledge

Akhavi S. 1980. *Religion and Politics in Contemporary Iran: Clergy-State Relations in the
Pahlavi Period.* Albany: State Univ. NY Press

Almond G, Appleby R, Sivan E. 2003. *Strong Religions: The Rise of Fundamentalisms around
the World.* Chicago: Chicago Univ. Press

Ammerman N. 1987. *Bible Believers: Fundamentalists in the Modern World.* New Brunswick,
NJ: Rutgers Univ. Press

Arjomand SA. 1989. *The Turban for the Crown:
The Islamic Revolution in Iran.* Oxford, UK:
Oxford Univ. Press

Auty R. 1993. *Sustaining Development in Mineral
Economies: The Resource Curse Thesis.* London: Routledge

Ayubi N. 1993. *Political Islam: Religion and Politics in the Arab World.* London: Routledge

Bayat M. 1982. *Mysticism and Dissent: So-
cioreligious Thought in Qajar Iran.* Syracuse,
NY: Syracuse Univ. Press

Bayulgen O. 2005. Foreign investment, oil curse,
and democratization: a comparison of Azerbaijan and Russia. *Business Polit.* 7: article 3.
http://www.bepress.com/bap/vol7/iss1/art3/

Berman P. 2003. *Terror and Liberalism.* New York:
W.W. Norton

Blanchard C. 2005. *Al Qaeda: statements and
evolving ideology.* CRS Rep. for Congr. Washington, DC: Congr. Res. Serv.

Bowen J. 2003. *Islam, Law, and Equality in Indonesia: An Anthropology of Public Reasoning.*
Cambridge, UK: Cambridge Univ. Press

Buehler A. 1998. *Sufi Heirs of the Prophet: The Indian Naqshbandiyya and the Rise of the Mediating Sufi Shaykh*. Columbia: Univ. South Carolina Press

Burke J. 2004. *Al-Qaeda: The True Story of Radical Islam*. London: I.B. Tauris

Carapico S. 1998. *Civil Society in the Yemen: The Political Economy of Activism in Modern Arabia*. Cambridge, UK: Cambridge Univ. Press

Carpenter J. 1997. *Revive Us Again: The Reawakening of American Fundamentalism*. Oxford, UK: Oxford Univ. Press

Chehabi H. 1990. *Iranian Politics and Religious Modernism: The Liberation Movement of Iran under the Shah and Khomeini*. London: I.B. Tauris

Cleveland W. 1985. *Islam against the West: Shakib Arslan and the Campaign for Islamic Nationalism*. Austin: Univ. Texas Press

Cole J, Keddie R, eds. 1986. *Shi'ism and Social Protest*. New Haven, CT: Yale Univ. Press

Crenshaw M, ed. 1994. *Terrorism in Context*. Philadelphia: Penn. State Univ. Press

Crystal J. 1990. *Oil and Politics in the Gulf: Rulers and Merchants in Kuwait and Qatar*. New York: Cambridge Univ. Press

Davis J. 2003. *Martyrs: Innocence, Vengeance and Despair in the Middle East*. New York: Palgrave

Defense Science Board. 2004. *Task Force on Strategic Communication*. Washington, DC: Off. Undersecretary for Defense

Del Castillo D. 2001. Pakistan's Islamic colleges provide the Taliban's spiritual fire. *Chron. Higher Educ.* Sept. 28:A19

DeLong J. 2001. *Dealing with the Islamic reformation: parallels between today and the sixteenth century*. http://econ161.berkeley.edu/TotW/Islamic_reformation.html

Delong-bas N. 2004. *Wahhabi Islam: From Revival and Reform to Global Jihad*. Oxford, UK: Oxford Univ. Press

Duverger M. 1954. *Political Parties: Their Organization and Activity in the Modern State*. London: Methuen

Economist. 2005. How others see Americans: still not loved. Now not envied. *Economist* 25 June. http://economist.com/world/na/displayStory.cfm?story_id/4105223

Eickelman D. 1975. *Moroccan Islam: Tradition and Society in a Pilgrimage Center*. Austin: Univ. Texas Press

Eickelman D. 1985. *Knowledge and Power in Morocco: The Education of a Twentieth-Century Notable*. Princeton, NJ: Princeton Univ. Press

Eickelman D, Piscatori J. 1996. *Muslim Politics*. Princeton, NJ: Princeton Univ. Press

Ellens H, ed. 2003. *The Destructive Power of Religion: Violence in Judaism, Christianity, and Islam*. Vols. 1–4. New York: Praeger

Esmer Y. 2003. Is there an Islamic civilization? In *Human Values and Social Change: Findings from the Values Survey*, ed. R Inglehart, pp. 35–68. Leiden: Brill

Esposito J, Voll J. 2001. *Makers of Contemporary Islam*. Oxford: Oxford Univ. Press

Fandy M. 2001. *Saudi Arabia and the Politics of Dissent*. New York: Palgrave Macmillan

Fischer M. 1980. *Iran: From Religious Dispute to Revolution*. Cambridge, MA: Harvard Univ. Press

Foran J. 1994. *A Century of Revolutions: Social Movements in Iran*. Minneapolis: Univ. Minnesota Press

Geertz C. 1971. *Islam Observed: Religious Development in Morocco and Indonesia*. Chicago: Univ. Chicago Press

Geertz C. 1976. *The Religion of Java*. Chicago: Chicago Univ. Press

Gellner E. 1994. *Conditions of Liberty: Civil Society and Its Rivals*. New York: Penguin

Gellner E, Waterbury J. 1977. *Patrons and Clients in Mediterranean Societies*. London: Cent. Mediterr. Stud.

Gilsenan M. 1983. *Recognizing Islam: An Anthropologist's Introduction*. London: Croom Helm

Hamdi M. 1998. *The Making of an Islamic Leader: Conversations with Hasan al-Turabi*. Boulder, CO: Westview

Hammoudi A. 1997. *Master and Disciple: The*

Cultural Foundations of Moroccan Authoritarianism. Chicago: Univ. Chicago Press

Hamzeh A. 2004. *In the Path of Hizbullah*. Syracuse, NY: Syracuse Univ. Press

Harik J. 2004. *Hezbollah: The Changing Face of Terrorism*. London: I.B. Tauris

Hefner R. 2000. *Civil Islam: Muslims and Democratization in Indonesia*. Princeton, NJ: Princeton Univ. Press

Hefner R, ed. 2004. *Remaking Muslim Politics: Pluralism, Contestation, Democratization*. Princeton, NJ: Princeton Univ. Press

Henry C, Springborg R. 2001. *Globalization and the Politics of Development in the Middle East*. Cambridge, UK: Cambridge Univ. Press

Hermansen M. 1995. *The Conclusive Argument from God: Shah Wali Allah of Delhi's Hujjat Allah al-Baligha*. Leiden: E.J. Brill

Hooker M. 2003. *Indonesian Islam: Social Change through Contemporary Fatawa*. Honolulu: Univ. Hawaii

Hudson R. 2002. *Who Becomes a Terrorist and Why: The 1999 Government Report on Profiling Terrorists*. Guilford, UK: Lyons Press

Huntington S. 1995. *The Clash of Civilizations and the Remaking of World Order*. New York: Simon & Schuster

Inglehart R, Norris P. 2003. The true clash of civilizations. *For. Policy*, Mar.–Apr.: 67–74

Jahanbaksh F. 2001. *Islam, Democracy and Modernism in Iran, 1953–2000: From Bazargan to Soroush*. Leiden: E.J. Brill

Kalyvas S. 2005. *The Logic of Violence in Civil War*. Cambridge, UK: Cambridge Univ. Press

Karl T. 1997. *The Paradox of Plenty: Oil Booms and Petro-states*. Berkeley: Univ. Calif. Press

Kazemi F. 1980. *Poverty and Revolution in Iran: The Migrant Poor, Marginality, and Politics*. New York: NY Univ. Press

Keddie N, ed. 1972. *Scholars, Saints and Sufis: Muslim Religious Institutions in the Middle East since 1500*. Berkeley: Univ. Calif. Press

Kedourie E. 1994. *Democracy and Arab Political Culture*. London: Frank Cass

Kepel G. 2003. *Jihad: The Trail of Political Islam*. London: Belknap

Khalid A. 1999. *The Politics of Muslim Cultural Reform: Jadidism in Asia*. Berkeley: Univ. Calif. Press

Kim Y. 2003. *The Resource Curse in a Post-Communist Regime: Russia in Comparative Perspective*. New York: Ashgate

Kimball C. 2002. *When Religion Becomes Evil*. San Francisco: Harper

Kuczynski P, Williamson J, eds. 2003. *After the Washington Consensus: Restarting Growth and Reform in Latin America*. Washington, DC: Inst. Int. Econ.

Kurzman C, ed. 1998. *Liberal Islam: A Sourcebook*. Oxford, UK: Oxford Univ. Press

Lewis B. 1990. The roots of Muslim rage. *Atl. Mon.* 266:47–60

Lewis B. 2002. *What Went Wrong?: The Clash between Islam and Modernity in the Middle East*. New York: Perennial

Lindqvist S. 2003. *A History of Bombing*. New York: W.W. Norton

Lipset S. 1959. Some social requisites of democracy: economic development and political legitimacy. *Am. Polit. Sci. Rev.* 53:69–105

Lockman Z. 2004. *Contending Visions of the Middle East: The History and Politics of Orientalism*. Cambridge, UK: Cambridge Univ. Press

Luciani G, ed. 1990. *The Arab State*. Berkeley: Univ. Calif. Press

Majid A. 2000. *Unveiling Islam: Postcolonial Islam in a Polycentric World*. Raleigh, NC: Duke Univ. Press

Mandaville P. 2001. *Transnational Muslim Politics: Reimagining the Umma*. London: Routledge

Marlin R. 2004. *What Does al-Qaeda Want?: Unedited Communiques*. Berkeley, CA: North Atlantic Books

Martin W. 1996. *With God on Our Side: The Rise of the Religious Right in America*. New York: Broadway Books

Marty M, Appleby R. 1991. *Fundamentalisms Observed*. Chicago: Univ. Chicago

McDermott T. 2005. *Perfect Soldiers: The Hijackers: Who They Were, Why They Did It*. New York: HarperCollins

McKenna T. 1998. *Muslim Rulers and Rebels: Everyday Politics and Armed Separatism in the Southern Philippines*. Berkeley: Univ. Calif. Press

Masud M. 2000. *Travellers in Faith: Studies of the Tablighi Jama'at as a Transnational Islamic Movement for Faith Renewal*. Leiden: E.J. Brill

Mitchell R. 1993. *The Society of the Muslim Brothers*. Oxford, UK: Oxford Univ. Press

Moaddel M. 2002. *Jordanian Exceptionalism: A Comparative Analysis of State-Religion Relationships in Egypt, Iran, Jordan and Syria* New York: Palgrave Macmillan

Moslem M. 2002. *Factional Politics in Post-Khomeini Iran*. Syracuse, NY: Syracuse Univ. Press

Moore RI. 1991. *The Formation of a Persecuting Society: Power and Deviance in Western Europe, 950–1250*. Oxford, UK: Blackwell

Moussalli A. 1993. *Radical Islamic Fundamentalism: The Ideological and Political Discourse of Islamic Fundamentalism*. Syracuse, UK: Syracuse Univ. Press

Nakash Y. 2003. *The Shi'is of Iraq*. Princeton, NJ: Princeton Univ. Press

Nasr S. 1994. *The Vanguard of the Islamic Revolution: the Jama'at-i Islami of Pakistan* Berkeley: Univ. Calif. Press

Nasr S. 1996. *Mawdudi & the Making of Islamic Revivalism*. New York: Oxford Univ. Press

Navaro-Yashin Y. 2002. *Faces of the State: Secularism and Public Life in Turkey*. Princeton, NJ: Princeton Univ. Press

Nirenberg D. 1998. *Communities of Violence*. Princeton, NJ: Princeton Univ. Press

Nomani F, Rahnema A. 1994. *Islamic Economic Systems*. London: Zed Books

Paden J. 1973. *Religion and Political Culture in Kano*. Berkeley: Univ. Calif. Press

Pape R. 2005. *Dying to Win: The Strategic Logic of Suicide Terrorism*. New York: Random House

Peletz M. 2002. *Islamic Modern: Religious Courts and Cultural Politics in Malaysia*. Princeton, NJ: Princeton Univ. Press

Pew Global Attitudes Survey. 2005. *Islamic Extremism: Common Concern for Muslim and Western Publics*. Washington, DC: Pew Global Attitudes

Rahnema A. 2000. *An Islamic Utopian: A Political Biography of Ali Shariati*. London: I.B. Tauris

Rana M. 2004. *A to Z of Jehadi Organizations in Pakistan*. Lahore, Pakistan: Mashal

Rashid A. 2000. *Taliban: Militant Islam, Oil and Fundamentalism in Central Asia*. New Haven, CT: Yale Univ. Press

Reed S. 1993. *Making Common Sense of Japan*. Pittsburgh, PA: Univ. Pittsburgh Press

Riesebrodt M. 1993. *Pious Passion: The Emergence of Modern Fundamentalism in the United States and Iran*. Berkeley: Univ. Calif.

Rizvi S. 1980. *Shah Wali-Allah and His Times: A Study of Eighteenth Century Islam, Politics and Society in India*. Islamabad, Pakistan: Ma'rifat

Roberts P. 2004. *The End of Oil: On the Edge of a Perilous New World*. Boston: Houghton Mifflin

Ross M. 2001. Does oil hinder democracy? *World Polit.* 53: 325–61

Roy O. 1990. *Islam and Resistance in Afghanistan*. Cambridge, UK: Cambridge Univ. Press. 2nd ed.

Roy O. 1994. *The Failure of Political Islam*. Cambridge, MA: Harvard Univ. Press

Roy O. 2004. *Globalized Islam: The Search for a New Ummah*. New York: Columbia Univ.

Roy O, Abou Zahab M. 2004. *Islamist Networks: The Afghan-Pakistan Connection*. London: Hurst & Co.

Ruthven M. 1986. *Islam in the World*. Oxford, UK: Oxford Univ. Press

Sadowski Y. 1998. *The Myth of Global Chaos*. Washington, DC: Brookings Inst.

Sageman M. 2004. *Understanding Terror Networks*. Philadelphia: Univ. Penn.

Said E. 1978. *Orientalism*. New York: Pantheon

Said E. 2002. Impossible histories: why the many Islams cannot be simplified. *Harper's Mag.* July:69–74

Schatz E. 2004. *Modern Clan Politics: The Power of "Blood" in Kazakhstan and Beyond*. Seattle: Univ. Wash. Press

Schwedler J, ed. 1995. *Toward Civil Society in the Middle East?: A Primer*. Boulder, CO: Lynne Rienner

Sevastopulo D. 2005. U.S. raises figures for terror attacks to 3,200. *Financ. Times* (6 July)

Simmons M. 2005. *Twilight in the Desert: The Coming Saudi Oil Shock and the World Economy*. New York: Wiley

Simone TA. 1994. *In Whose Image?: Political Islam and Urban Practices in the Sudan*. Chicago: Univ. Chicago

Stepan A. 2003. An 'Arab' more than a 'Muslim' democracy gap. *J. Democr.* July:30–44

Stern J. 2003. *Terror in the Name of God: Why Religious Militants Kill*. New York: Harper-Collins

Tammam H, Haenni P. 2003. Egypt's air-conditioned Islam. *Monde dipl.* Sept. http://mondediplo.com/2003/09/03egyptislam

Varshney A. 2003. *Ethnic Conflict and Civic Life: Hindus and Muslims in India*. New Haven, CT: Yale Univ. Press

Verkaaik O. 2004. *Migrants and Militants: Fun and Urban Violence in Pakistan*. Princeton, NJ: Princeton Univ. Press

Victor B. 2003. *Army of Roses: Inside the World of Palestinian Women Suicide Bombers*. New York: Rodale

Voll J. 1994. *Islam: Continuity and Change in the Modern World*. Syracuse, NY: Syracuse Univ. Press

Wickham C. 2002. *Mobilizing Islam: Religion, Activism, and Political Change in Egypt*. New York: Columbia Univ. Press

Wiktorowicz Q. 2001. *The Management of Islamic Activism: Salafis, the Muslim Brotherhood, and State Power in Jordan*. Albany: State Univ. NY Press

Wiktorowicz Q, ed. 2004. *Islamic Activism: A Social Movement Theory Approach*. Bloomington: Indiana Univ. Press

Wilcox C. 2000. *Onward Christian Soldiers?: The Religious Right in American Politics*. Boulder, CO: Westview. 2nd ed.

Wuthnow R. 2004. *Saving America? Faith-Based Initiatives and the Future of Civil Society*. Princeton, NJ: Princeton Univ. Press

al-Yassini A. 1985. *Religion and State in the Kingdom of Saudi Arabia*. Boulder, CO: Westview

Yavuz MH. 2001. *Islamic Political Identity in Turkey*. Oxford, UK: Oxford Univ. Press

Yavuz MH, Esposito J, eds. 2003. *Turkish Islam and the Secular State: The Gulen Movement*. Syracuse, NY: Syracuse Univ. Press

Zaman M. 2002. *The Ulama in Contemporary Islam: Custodians of Change*. Princeton, NJ: Princeton Univ. Press

Zogby J. 2002a. *Impressions of America*. Washington, DC: Zogby Int.

Zogby J. 2002b. *What Arabs Think*. Washington, DC: Zogby Int.

6 THE INDIVIDUAL

Individual psychology is also important in shaping international relations. Individuals include not only foreign policy elites—the leaders who move the world—but also the diplomats, warriors, activists, and voters whose attitudes and perceptions animate the politics of international issues. In a now-classic piece originally published in 1968, Robert Jervis articulates hypotheses on the origins of misperceptions. Drawing heavily on psychology, he suggests strategies for decision makers to mitigate the effects of misperception.

John Mueller's book Retreat from Doomsday: The Obsolescence of Major War *argues that the turning away from warfare among the major developed powers in the twentieth century did not depend on nuclear deterrence or on the spread of democracy, but on the horrible costs of even non-nuclear war. Mueller argues that Adolf Hitler was perhaps the last man in Europe to embrace major war and that World War II would never have happened except for the decisive influence of this individual on history.*

ROBERT JERVIS

HYPOTHESES ON MISPERCEPTION

In determining how he will behave, an actor must try to predict how others will act and how their actions will affect his values. The actor must therefore develop an image of others and of their intentions. This image may, however, turn out to be an inaccurate one; the actor may, for a number of reasons, misperceive both others' actions and their intentions. * * * I wish to discuss the types of misperceptions of other states' intentions which states tend to make. * * *

From *World Politics* 20, no. 3 (April 1968): 454–79. Some of the author's notes have been omitted.

*   *   *

Theories—Necessary and Dangerous

* * * The evidence from both psychology and history overwhelmingly supports the view (which may be labeled Hypothesis 1) that decision-makers tend to fit incoming information into their existing theories and images. Indeed, their theories and images play a large part in determining what they notice. In other words, actors tend to perceive what they expect. Furthermore (Hypothesis 1a), a theory will have greater impact on an actor's interpretation of data (a) the greater the ambiguity of the data and (b) the higher the degree of confidence with which the actor holds the theory.[1]

*   *   *

* * * Hypothesis 2: scholars and decision-makers are apt to err by being too wedded to the established view and too closed to new information, as opposed to being too willing to alter their theories. Another way of making this point is to argue that actors tend to establish their theories and expectations prematurely. In politics, of course, this is often necessary because of the need for action. But experimental evidence indicates that the same tendency also occurs on the unconscious level. * * *

However, when we apply these and other findings to politics and discuss kinds of misperception, we should not quickly apply the label of cognitive distortion. We should proceed cautiously for two related reasons. The first is that the evidence available to decision-makers almost always permits several interpretations. It should be noted that there are cases of visual perception in which different stimuli can produce exactly the same pattern on an observer's retina. Thus, for an observer using one eye the same pattern would be produced by a sphere the size of a golf ball which was quite close to the observer, by a baseball-sized sphere that was further away, or by a basketball-sized sphere still further away. Without other clues, the observer cannot possibly determine which of these stimuli he is presented with, and we would not want to call his incorrect perceptions examples of distortion. Such cases, relatively rare in visual perception, are frequent in international relations. The evidence available to decision-makers is almost always very ambiguous since accurate clues to others' intentions are surrounded by noise[2] and deception. In most cases, no matter how long, deeply, and "objectively" the evidence is analyzed, people can differ in their interpretations, and there are no general rules to indicate who is correct.

The second reason to avoid the label of cognitive distortion is that the distinction between perception and judgment, obscure enough in individual psychology, is almost absent in the making of inferences in international politics. Decision-makers who reject information that contradicts their views—or who develop complex interpretations of it—often do so consciously and explicitly. Since the evidence available contains contradictory information, to make any inferences requires that much information be ignored or given interpretations that will seem tortuous to those who hold a different position.

Indeed, if we consider only the evidence available to a decision-maker at the time of decision, the view later proved incorrect may be supported by as much evidence as the correct one—or even by more. Scholars have often been too unsympathetic with the people who were proved wrong. On closer examination, it is frequently difficult to point to differences between those who were right and those who were wrong with respect to their openness to new information and willingness to modify their views. Winston Churchill, for example, did not open-mindedly view each Nazi action to see if the explanations provided by the appeasers accounted for the data better than his own beliefs. Instead, like Chamberlain, he fitted each bit of ambiguous information into his own hypotheses. That he was correct should not lead us to overlook the fact that his methods of analysis and use of theory to produce cognitive consistency did not basically differ from those of the appeasers.

A consideration of the importance of expectations in influencing perception also indicates that the widespread belief in the prevalence of "wishful thinking" may be incorrect, or at least may be based on inadequate data. The psychological literature on the interaction between affect and perception is immense and cannot be treated here, but it should be noted that phenomena that at first were considered strong evidence for the impact of affect on perception often can be better treated as demonstrating the influence of expectations.[3] Thus, in international relations, cases like the United States' misestimation of the political climate in Cuba in April 1961, which may seem at first glance to have been instances of wishful thinking, may instead be more adequately explained by the theories held by the decision-makers (e.g., Communist governments are unpopular). Of course, desires may have an impact on perception by influencing expectations, but since so many other factors affect expectations, the net influence of desires may not be great.

There is evidence from both psychology[4] and international relations that when expectations and desires clash, expectations seem to be more important. The United States would like to believe that North Vietnam is about to negotiate or that the USSR is ready to give up what the United States believes is its goal of world domination, but ambiguous evidence is seen to confirm the opposite conclusion, which conforms to the United States' expectations. Actors are apt to be especially sensitive to evidence of grave danger if they think they can take action to protect themselves against the menace once it has been detected.

Safeguards

Can anything then he said to scholars and decision-makers other than "Avoid being either too open or too closed, but be especially aware of the latter danger"? Although decision-makers will always be faced with ambiguous and confusing evidence and will be forced to make inferences about others which will often be inaccurate,

a number of safeguards may be suggested which could enable them to minimize their errors. First, and most obvious, decision-makers should be aware that they do not make "unbiased" interpretations of each new bit of incoming information, but rather are inevitably heavily influenced by the theories they expect to be verified. They should know that what may appear to them as a self-evident and unambiguous inference often seems so only because of their preexisting beliefs. To someone with a different theory the same data may appear to be unimportant or to support another explanation. Thus many events provide less independent support for the decision-makers' images than they may at first realize. Knowledge of this should lead decision-makers to examine more closely evidence that others believe contradicts their views.

Second, decision-makers should see if their attitudes contain consistent or supporting beliefs that are not logically linked. These may be examples of true psycho-logic. While it is not logically surprising nor is it evidence of psychological pressures to find that people who believe that Russia is aggressive are very suspicious of any Soviet move, other kinds of consistency are more suspect. For example, most people who feel that it is important for the United States to win the war in Vietnam also feel that a meaningful victory is possible. And most people who feel defeat would neither endanger U.S. national security nor be costly in terms of other values also feel that we cannot win. Although there are important logical linkages between the two parts of each of these views (especially through theories of guerrilla warfare), they do not seem strong enough to explain the degree to which the opinions are correlated. Similarly, in Finland in the winter of 1939, those who felt that grave consequences would follow Finnish agreement to give Russia a military base also believed that the Soviets would withdraw their demand if Finland stood firm. And those who felt that concessions would not lead to loss of major values also believed that Russia would fight if need be.[5] In this country, those who favored a nuclear test ban tended to argue that fallout was very harmful, that only limited improvements in technology would flow from further testing, and that a test ban would increase the chances for peace and security. Those who opposed the test ban were apt to disagree on all three points. This does not mean, of course, that the people holding such sets of supporting views were necessarily wrong in any one element. The Finns who wanted to make concessions to the USSR were probably correct in both parts of their argument. But decision-makers should be suspicious if they hold a position in which elements that are not logically connected support the same conclusion. This condition is psychologically comfortable and makes decisions easier to reach (since competing values do not have to be balanced off against each other). The chances are thus considerable that at least part of the reason why a person holds some of these views is related to psychology and not to the substance of the evidence.

Decision-makers should also be aware that actors who suddenly find themselves having an important shared interest with other actors have a tendency to overestimate the degree of common interest involved. This tendency is especially strong for those actors (e.g., the United States, at least before 1950) whose beliefs about international relations and morality imply that they can cooperate only with "good" states and that with those states there will be no major conflicts. On the other hand, states that have either a tradition of limited cooperation with others (e.g., Britain) or a strongly held theory that differentiates occasional from permanent allies[6] (e.g., the Soviet Union) find it easier to resist this tendency and need not devote special efforts to combating its danger.

A third safeguard for decision-makers would be to make their assumptions, beliefs, and the predictions that follow from them as explicit as possible. An actor should try to determine, before events occur, what evidence would count for and against his theories. By knowing what to expect he would know what to be surprised by, and surprise could indicate to that actor that his beliefs needed reevaluation.[7]

A fourth safeguard is more complex. The decision-maker should try to prevent individuals and organizations from letting their main task, political future, and identity become tied to specific theories and images of other actors.[8] If this occurs, subgoals originally sought for their contribution to higher ends will take on value of their own, and information indicating possible alternative routes to the original goals will not be carefully considered. For example, the U.S. Forest Service was unable to carry out its original purpose as effectively when it began to see its distinctive competence not in promoting the best use of lands and forests but rather in preventing all types of forest fires.[9]

Organizations that claim to be unbiased may not realize the extent to which their definition of their role has become involved with certain beliefs about the world. Allen Dulles is a victim of this lack of understanding when he says, "I grant that we are all creatures of prejudice, including CIA officials, but by entrusting intelligence coordination to our central intelligence service, which is excluded from policy-making and is married to no particular military hardware, we can avoid, to the greatest possible extent, the bending of facts obtained through intelligence to suit a particular occupational viewpoint."[10] This statement overlooks the fact that the CIA has developed a certain view of international relations and of the cold war which maximizes the importance of its information-gathering, espionage, and subversive activities. Since the CIA would lose its unique place in the government if it were decided that the "back alleys" of world politics were no longer vital to U.S. security, it is not surprising that the organization interprets information in a way that stresses the continued need for its techniques.

Fifth, decision-makers should realize the validity and implications of Roberta Wohlstetter's argument that "a willingness to play with material from different angles and in the context of unpopular as well as popular hypotheses is an essential ingredient of a good detective, whether the end is the solution of a crime or an intelligence estimate."[11] However, it is often difficult, psychologically and politically, for any one person to do this. Since a decision-maker usually cannot get "unbiased" treatments of data, he should instead seek to structure conflicting biases into the decision-making process. The decision-maker, in other words, should have devil's advocates around. Just as, as Neustadt points out,[12] the decision-maker will want to create conflicts among his subordinates in order to make appropriate choices, so he will also want to ensure that incoming information is examined from many different perspectives with many different hypotheses in mind. To some extent this kind of examination will be done automatically through the divergence of goals, training, experience, and information that exists in any large organization. But in many cases this divergence will not be sufficient. The views of those analyzing the data will still be too homogeneous, and the decision-maker will have to go out of his way not only to cultivate but to create differing viewpoints.

While all that would be needed would be to have some people examining the data trying to validate unpopular hypotheses, it would probably be more effective if they actually believed and had a stake in the views they were trying to support. If in 1941 someone had had the task of proving the view that Japan would attack Pearl Harbor, the government might have been less surprised by the attack. And only a person who was out to show that Russia would take objectively great risks would have been apt to note that several ships with especially large hatches going to Cuba were riding high in the water, indicating the presence of a bulky but light cargo that was not likely to be anything other than strategic missiles. And many people who doubt the wisdom of the administration's Vietnam policy would be somewhat reassured if there were people in the government who searched the statements and actions of both sides in an effort to prove that North Vietnam was willing to negotiate and that the official interpretation of such moves as the Communist activities during the Têt truce of 1967 was incorrect.

Of course all these safeguards involve costs. They would divert resources from other tasks and would increase internal dissension. Determining whether these costs would be worth the gains would depend on a detailed analysis of how the suggested safeguards might be implemented. Even if they were adopted by a government, of course, they would not eliminate the chance of misperception. However, the safeguards would make it more likely that national decision-makers would make conscious choices about the way data were interpreted rather than merely assuming that they can be seen in only one way and can mean only one thing. Statesmen would thus be reminded of alternative images of others just as they are constantly reminded of alternative policies.

These safeguards are partly based on Hypothesis 3: actors can more easily assimilate into their established image of another actor information contradicting that image if the information is transmitted and considered bit by bit than if it comes all at once. In the former case, each piece of discrepant data can be coped with as it arrives and each of the conflicts with the prevailing view will be small enough to go unnoticed, to be dismissed as unimportant, or to necessitate at most a slight modification of the image (e.g., addition of exceptions to the rule). When the information arrives in a block, the contradiction between it and the prevailing view is apt to be much clearer and the probability of major cognitive reorganization will be higher.

Sources of Concepts

An actor's perceptual thresholds—and thus the images that ambiguous information is apt to produce—are influenced by what he has experienced and learned about.[13] If one actor is to perceive that another fits in a given category he must first have, or develop, a concept for that category. We can usefully distinguish three levels at which a concept can be present or absent. First, the concept can be completely missing. The actor's cognitive structure may not include anything corresponding to the phenomenon he is encountering. This situation can occur not only in science fiction, but also in a world of rapid change or in the meeting of two dissimilar systems. Thus China's image of the Western world was extremely inaccurate in the mid-nineteenth century, her learning was very slow, and her responses were woefully inadequate. The West was spared a similar struggle only because it had the power to reshape the system it encountered. Once the actor clearly sees one instance of the new phenomenon, he is apt to recognize it much more quickly in the future.[14] Second, the actor can know about a concept but not believe that it reflects an actual phenomenon. Thus Communist and Western decision-makers are each aware of the other's explanation of how his system functions, but do not think that the concept corresponds to reality. Communist elites, furthermore, deny that anything *could* correspond to the democracies' description of themselves. Third, the actor may hold a concept, but not believe that another actor fills it at the present moment. Thus the British and French statesmen of the 1930's held a concept of states with unlimited ambitions. They realized that Napoleons were possible, but they did not think Hitler belonged in that category. Hypothesis 4 distinguishes these three cases: misperception is most difficult to correct in the case of a missing concept and least difficult to correct in the case of a recognized but presumably unfilled concept. All other things being equal (e.g., the degree to which the concept is central to the actor's cognitive structure), the first case requires more cognitive reorganization than does the second, and the second requires more reorganization than the third.

However, this hypothesis does not mean that learning will necessarily be slowest in the first case, for if the phenomena are totally new the actor may make such grossly inappropriate responses that he will quickly acquire information clearly indicating that he is faced with something he does not understand. And the sooner the actor realizes that things are not—or may not be—what they seem, the sooner he is apt to correct his image.[15]

Three main sources contribute to decision-makers' concepts of international relations and of other states and influence the level of their perceptual thresholds for various phenomena. First, an actor's beliefs about his own domestic political system are apt to be important. In some cases, like that of the USSR, the decision-makers' concepts are tied to an ideology that explicitly provides a frame of reference for viewing foreign affairs. Even where this is not the case, experience with his own system will partly determine what the actor is familiar with and what he is apt to perceive in others. Louis Hartz claims, "It is the absence of the experience of social revolution which is at the heart of the whole American dilemma. . . . In a whole series of specific ways it enters into our difficulty of communication with the rest of the world. We find it difficult to understand Europe's 'social question'. . . . We are not familiar with the deeper social struggles of Asia and hence tend to interpret even reactionary regimes as 'democratic.'"[16] Similarly, George Kennan argues that in World War I the Allied, powers, and especially America, could not understand the bitterness and violence of others' internal conflicts: ". . . The inability of the Allied statesmen to picture to themselves the passions of the Russian civil war [was partly caused by the fact that] we represent . . . a society in which the manifestations of evil have been carefully buried and sublimated in the social behavior of people, as in their very consciousness. For this reason, probably, despite our widely traveled and outwardly cosmopolitan lives, the mainsprings of political behavior in such a country as Russia tend to remain concealed from our vision."[17]

Second, concepts will be supplied by the actor's previous experiences. An experiment from another field illustrates this. Dearborn and Simon presented business executives from various divisions (e.g., sales, accounting, production) with the same hypothetical data and asked them for an analysis and recommendations from the standpoint of what would be best for the company as a whole. The executives' views heavily reflected their departmental perspectives.[18] William W. Kaufmann shows how the perceptions of Ambassador Joseph Kennedy were affected by his past: "As befitted a former chairman of the Securities Exchange and Maritime Commissions, his primary interest lay in economic matters. . . . The revolutionary character of the Nazi regime was not a phenomenon that he could easily grasp. . . . It was far simpler, and more in accord with his own premises, to explain German aggressiveness in economic terms. The Third Reich was dissatisfied, authoritarian, and expansive largely because her economy was unsound."[19] Similarly it has been argued that Chamberlain was slow to recognize Hitler's intentions partly because of the limiting nature of his personal background and business experiences. The impact of training and experience seems to be demonstrated when the background of the appeasers is compared to that of their opponents. One difference stands out: "A substantially higher percentage of the anti-appeasers (irrespective of class origins) had the kind of knowledge which comes from close acquaintance, mainly professional, with foreign affairs."[20] Since members of the diplomatic corps are responsible for meeting threats to the nation's security before these grow to major proportions and since they have learned about cases in which aggressive states were not recognized as such until very late, they may be prone to interpret ambiguous data as showing that others are aggressive. It should be stressed that we cannot say that the professionals of the 1930's were more apt to make accurate judgments of other states. Rather, they may have been more sensitive to the chance that others were aggressive. They would then rarely take an aggressor for a status-quo power, but would more often make the opposite error. Thus in the years before World War I the permanent officials in the British Foreign Office overestimated German aggressiveness.[21]

A parallel demonstration in psychology of the impact of training on perception is presented by an experiment in which ambiguous pictures were shown to both advanced and beginning police-administration students. The advanced group perceived more violence in the pictures than did the beginners. The probable explanation is that "the law enforcer may come to accept crime as a familiar personal experience, one which he himself is not surprised to encounter. The acceptance of crime as a familiar experience in turn increases the ability or readiness to perceive violence where clues to it are potentially available."[22] This experiment lends weight to the view that the British diplomats' sensitivity to aggressive states was not totally a product of personnel selection procedures.

A third source of concepts, which frequently will be the most directly relevant to a decision-maker's perception of international relations, is international history. As Henry Kissinger points out, one reason why statesmen were so slow to recognize the threat posed by Napoleon was that previous events had accustomed them only to actors who wanted to modify the existing system, not overthrow it.[23] The other side of the coin is even more striking: historical traumas can heavily influence future perceptions. They can either establish a state's image of the other state involved or can be used as analogies. An example of the former case is provided by the fact that for at least ten years after the Franco-Prussian War most of Europe's statesmen felt that Bismarck had aggressive plans when in fact his main goal was to protect the status quo. Of course the evidence was ambiguous. The post-1871 Bismarckian maneuvers, which were designed to keep peace, looked not unlike the pre-1871 maneuvers designed to set the stage for war. But that the post-1871 maneuvers were seen as indicating aggressive plans is largely attributable to the impact of Bismarck's earlier actions on the statesmen's image of him.

A state's previous unfortunate experience with a type of danger can sensitize it to other examples of that danger. While this sensitivity may lead the state to avoid the mistake it committed in the past, it may also lead it mistakenly to believe that the present situation is like the past one. Santayana's maxim could be turned around: "Those who remember the past are condemned to make the opposite mistakes." As Paul Kecskemeti shows, both defenders and critics of the unconditional surrender plan of the Second World War thought in terms of the conditions of World War I.[24] Annette Baker Fox found that the Scandinavian countries' neutrality policies in World War II were strongly influenced by their experiences in the previous war, even though vital aspects of the two situations were different. Thus "Norway's success [during the First World War] in remaining non-belligerent though pro-Allied gave the Norwegians confidence that their country could again stay out of war."[25] And the lesson drawn from the unfortunate results of this policy was an important factor in Norway's decision to join NATO.

The application of the Munich analogy to various contemporary events has been much commented on, and I do not wish to argue the substantive points at stake. But it seems clear that the probabilities that any state is facing an aggressor who has to be met by force are not altered by the career of Hitler and the history of the 1930's. Similarly the probability of an aggressor's announcing his plans is not increased (if anything, it is decreased) by the fact that Hitler wrote *Mein Kampf*. Yet decision-makers are more sensitive to these possibilities, and thus more apt to perceive ambiguous evidence as indicating they apply to a given case, than they would have been had there been no Nazi Germany.

Historical analogies often precede, rather than follow, a careful analysis of a situation (e.g., Truman's initial reaction to the news of the invasion of South Korea was to think of the Japanese invasion of Manchuria). Noting this precedence, however, does not show us which of many analogies will come to a decision-maker's mind. Truman could have thought of nineteenth-century European wars that were of no interest to the United States. Several factors having nothing to do with the event under consideration influence what analogies a decision-maker is apt to make. One factor is the number of cases similar to the analogy with which the decision-maker is familiar. Another is the importance of the past event to the political system of which the decision-maker is a part. The more times such an event occurred and the greater its consequences were, the more a decision-maker will be sensitive to the particular danger involved and the more he will be apt to see ambiguous stimuli as indicating another instance of this kind of event. A third factor is the degree of the decision-maker's personal involvement in the past case—in time, energy, ego, and position. The last-mentioned variable will affect not only the event's impact on the decision-maker's cognitive structure, but also the way he perceives the event and the lesson he draws. Someone who was involved in getting troops into South Korea after the attack will remember the Korean War differently from someone who was involved in considering the possible use of nuclear weapons or in deciding what messages should be sent to the Chinese. Greater personal involvement will usually give the event greater impact, especially if the decision-maker's own views were validated by the event. One need not accept a total application of learning theory to nations to believe that "nothing fails like success."[26] It also seems likely that if many critics argued at the time that the decision-maker was wrong, he will be even more apt to see other situations in terms of the original event. For example, because Anthony Eden left the government on account of his views and was later shown to have been correct, he probably was more apt to see as Hitlers other leaders with whom he had conflicts (e.g., Nasser). A fourth factor is the degree to which the analogy is compatible with the rest of his belief system. A fifth is the absence of alternative concepts and analogies. Individuals and states vary in the amount of direct or indirect political experience they have had which can provide different ways of interpreting data. Decision-makers who are aware of multiple possibilities of states' intentions may be less likely to seize on an analogy prematurely. The perception of citizens of nations like the United States which have relatively little history of international politics may be more apt to be heavily influenced by the few major international events that have been important to their country.

The first three factors indicate that an event is more apt to shape present perceptions if it occurred in the recent rather than the remote past. If it occurred recently, the statesman will then know about it at first hand even if he was not involved in the making of policy at the time. Thus if generals are prepared to fight the last war, diplomats may be prepared to avoid the last war. Part of the Anglo-French reaction to Hitler can be explained by the prevailing beliefs that the First World War was to a large extent caused by misunderstandings and could have been avoided by farsighted and nonbelligerent diplomacy. And part of the Western perception of Russia and China can be explained by the view that appeasement was an inappropriate response to Hitler.[27]

The Evoked Set

The way people perceive data is influenced not only by their cognitive structure and theories about other actors but also by what they are concerned with at the time they receive the information. Information is evaluated in light of the small part of the person's memory that is presently active—the "evoked set." My perceptions of the dark streets I pass walking home from the movies will be different if the film I saw had dealt with spies than if it had been a comedy. If I am working on aiding a country's education system and I hear someone talk about the need for economic development in that state, I am apt to think he is concerned with education, whereas if I had been working on, say, trying to achieve political stability in that country, I would have placed his remarks in that framework.[28]

Thus Hypothesis 5 states that when messages are sent from a different background of concerns and information than is possessed by the receiver,

misunderstanding is likely. Person A and person B will read the same message quite differently if A has seen several related messages that B does not know about. This difference will be compounded if, as is frequently the case, A and B each assume that the other has the same background he does. This means that misperception can occur even when deception is neither intended nor expected. Thus Roberta Wohlstetter found not only that different parts of the United States government had different perceptions of data about Japan's intentions and messages partly because they saw the incoming information in very different contexts, but also that officers in the field misunderstood warnings from Washington: "Washington advised General Short [in Pearl Harbor] on November 27 to expect 'hostile action' at any moment, by which it meant 'attack on American possessions from without,' but General Short understood this phrase to mean 'sabotage.'"[29] Washington did not realize the extent to which Pearl Harbor considered the danger of sabotage to be primary, and furthermore it incorrectly believed that General Short had received the intercepts of the secret Japanese diplomatic messages available in Washington which indicated that surprise attack was a distinct possibility. Another implication of this hypothesis is that if important information is known to only part of the government of state A and part of the government of state B, international messages may be misunderstood by those parts of the receiver's government that do not match, in the information they have, the part of the sender's government that dispatched the message.[30]

Two additional hypotheses can be drawn from the problems of those sending messages. Hypothesis 6 states that when people spend a great deal of time drawing up a plan or making a decision, they tend to think that the message about it they wish to convey will be clear to the receiver.[31] Since they are aware of what is to them the important pattern in their actions, they often feel that the pattern will be equally obvious to others, and they overlook the degree to which the message is apparent to them only because they know what to look for. Those who have not participated in the endless meetings may not understand what information the sender is trying to convey. George Quester has shown how the German and, to a lesser extent, the British desire to maintain target limits on bombing in the first eighteen months of World War II was undermined partly by the fact that each side knew the limits it was seeking and its own reasons for any apparent "exceptions" (e.g., the German attack on Rotterdam) and incorrectly felt that these limits and reasons were equally clear to the other side.[32]

Hypothesis 7 holds that actors often do not realize that actions intended to project a given image may not have the desired effect because the actions themselves do not turn out as planned. Thus even without appreciable impact of different cognitive structures and backgrounds, an action may convey an unwanted message. For example, a country's representatives may not follow instructions and so may give others impressions contrary to those the home government wished to convey. The efforts of Washington and Berlin to settle their dispute over Samoa in the late 1880's were complicated by the provocative behavior of their agents on the spot. These agents not only increased the intensity of the local conflict, but led the decision-makers to become more suspicious of the other state because they tended to assume that their agents were obeying instructions and that the actions of the other side represented official policy. In such cases both sides will believe that the other is reading hostility into a policy of theirs which is friendly. Similarly, Quester's study shows that the attempt to limit bombing referred to above failed partly because neither side was able to bomb as accurately as it thought it could and thus did not realize the physical effects of its actions.[33]

Further Hypotheses from the Perspective of the Perceiver

From the perspective of the perceiver several other hypotheses seem to hold. Hypothesis 8 is that there is an overall tendency for decision-makers to see other states as more hostile than they are.[34] There seem to be more cases of statesmen incorrectly believing others are planning major acts against their interest than of statesmen being lulled by a potential aggressor. There are many reasons for this which are too complex to be treated here (e.g., some parts of the bureaucracy feel it is their responsibility to be suspicious of all other states; decision-makers often feel they are "playing it safe" to believe and act as though the other state were hostile in questionable cases; and often, when people do not feel they are a threat to others, they find it difficult to believe that others may see them as a threat). It should be noted, however, that decision-makers whose perceptions are described by this hypothesis would not necessarily further their own values by trying to correct for this tendency. The values of possible outcomes as well as their probabilities must be considered, and it may be that the probability of an unnecessary arms-tension cycle arising out of misperceptions, multiplied by the costs of such a cycle, may seem less to decision-makers than the probability of incorrectly believing another state is friendly, multiplied by the costs of this eventuality.

Hypothesis 9 states that actors tend to see the behavior of others as more centralized, disciplined, and coordinated than it is. This hypothesis holds true in related ways. Frequently, too many complex events are squeezed into a perceived pattern. Actors are hesitant to admit or even see that particular incidents cannot be explained by their theories.[35] Those events not caused by factors that are important parts of the perceiver's image are often seen as though they were. Further, actors see others as more internally united than they in fact are and generally overestimate the degree to which others are following a coherent policy. The degree to which the other side's policies are the product of internal bargaining,[36] internal misunderstandings, or subordinates' not following instructions is underestimated. This is the case partly because actors tend to be unfamiliar with the details of another state's policy-making processes. Seeing only the finished product, they find it simpler to try to construct a rational explanation for the policies, even though they know that such an analysis could not explain their own policies.[37]

Familiarity also accounts for Hypothesis 10: because a state gets most of its information about the other state's policies from the other's foreign office, it tends to take the foreign office's position for the stand of the other government as a whole. In many cases this perception will be an accurate one, but when the other government is divided or when the other foreign office is acting without specific authorization, misperception may result. For example, part of the reason why in 1918 Allied governments incorrectly thought "that the Japanese were preparing to take action [in Siberia], if need be, with agreement with the British and French alone, disregarding the absence of American consent,"[38] was that Allied ambassadors had talked mostly with Foreign Minister Motono, who was among the minority of the Japanese favoring this policy. Similarly, America's NATO allies may have gained an inaccurate picture of the degree to which the American government was committed to the MLF because they had greatest contact with parts of the government that strongly favored the MLF. And states that tried to get information about Nazi foreign policy from German diplomats were often misled because these officials were generally ignorant of or out of sympathy with Hitler's plans. The Germans and the Japanese sometimes purposely misinformed their own ambassadors in order to deceive their enemies more effectively.

Hypothesis 11 states that actors tend to overestimate the degree to which others are acting in response to what they themselves do when the others behave in accordance with the actor's desires; but when the behavior of the other is undesired, it is usually seen as derived from internal forces. If the *effect* of another's action is to injure or threaten the first side, the first side is apt to believe that such was the other's *purpose*. An example of the first part of the hypothesis is provided by Kennan's account of the activities of official and unofficial American representatives who

protested to the new Bolshevik government against several of its actions. When the Soviets changed their position, these representatives felt it was largely because of their influence.[39] This sort of interpretation can be explained not only by the fact that it is gratifying to the individual making it, but also, taking the other side of the coin mentioned in Hypothesis 9, by the fact that the actor is most familiar with his own input into the other's decision and has less knowledge of other influences. The second part of Hypothesis 11 is illustrated by the tendency of actors to believe that the hostile behavior of others is to be explained by the other side's motives and not by its reaction to the first side. Thus Chamberlain did not see that Hitler's behavior was related in part to his belief that the British were weak. More common is the failure to see that the other side is reacting out of fear of the first side, which can lead to self-fulfilling prophecies and spirals of misperception and hostility.

This difficulty is often compounded by an implication of Hypothesis 12: when actors have intentions that they do not try to conceal from others, they tend to assume that others accurately perceive these intentions. Only rarely do they believe that others may be reacting to a much less favorable image of themselves than they think they are projecting.[40]

For state A to understand how state B perceives A's policy is often difficult because such understanding may involve a conflict with A's image of itself. Raymond Sontag argues that Anglo-German relations before World War I deteriorated partly because "the British did not like to think of themselves as selfish, or unwilling to tolerate 'legitimate' German expansion. The Germans did not like to think of themselves as aggressive, or unwilling to recognize 'legitimate' British vested interest."[41]

Hypothesis 13 suggests that if it is hard for an actor to believe that the other can see him as a menace, it is often even harder for him to see that issues important to him are not important to others. While he may know that another actor is on an opposing team, it may be more difficult for him to realize that the other is playing an entirely different game. This is especially true when the game he is playing seems vital to him.[42]

The final hypothesis, Hypothesis 14, is as follows: actors tend to overlook the fact that evidence consistent with their theories may also be consistent with other views. When choosing between two theories we have to pay attention only to data that cannot be accounted for by one of the theories. But it is common to find people claiming as proof of their theories data that could also support alternative views. This phenomenon is related to the point made earlier that any single bit of information can be interpreted only within a framework of hypotheses and theories. And while it is true that "we may without a vicious circularity accept some datum as a fact because it conforms to the very law for which it counts as another confirming instance, and reject an allegation of fact because it is already excluded by law,"[43] we should be careful lest we forget that a piece of information seems in many cases to confirm a certain hypothesis only because we already believe that hypothesis to be correct and that the information can with as much validity support a different hypothesis. For example, one of the reasons why the German attack on Norway took both that country and England by surprise, even though they had detected German ships moving toward Norway, was that they expected not an attack but an attempt by the Germans to break through the British blockade and reach the Atlantic. The initial course of the ships was consistent with either plan, but the British and Norwegians took this course to mean that their predictions were being borne out.[44] This is not to imply that the interpretation made was foolish, but only that the decision-makers should have been aware that the evidence was also consistent with an invasion and should have had a bit less confidence in their views.

The longer the ships would have to travel the same route whether they were going to one or another of two destinations, the more information would be needed to determine their plans. Taken as a metaphor, this incident applies generally to the treatment of evidence. Thus as long as Hitler made demands for control only of ethnically German areas, his actions could be explained either by the hypothesis that he had unlimited ambitions or by the hypothesis that he wanted to unite all the Germans. But actions against non-Germans (e.g., the takeover of Czechoslovakia in March 1938) could not be accounted for by the latter hypothesis. And it was this action that convinced the appeasers that Hitler had to be stopped. It is interesting to speculate on what the British reaction would have been had Hitler left Czechoslovakia alone for a while and instead made demands on Poland similar to those he eventually made in the summer of 1939. The two paths would then still not have diverged, and further misperception could have occurred.

NOTES

1. Floyd Allport, *Theories of Perception and the Concept of Structure* (New York 1955), 382; Ole Holsti, "Cognitive Dynamics and Images of the Enemy," in David Finlay, Ole Holsti, and Richard Fagen, *Enemies in Politics* (Chicago 1967), 70.

2. For a use of this concept in political communication, see Roberta Wohlstetter, *Pearl Harbor* (Stanford 1962).

3. See, for example, Donald Campbell, "Systematic Error on the Part of Human Links in Communications Systems," *Information and Control*, I (1958), 346–50; and Leo Postman, "The Experimental Analysis of Motivational Factors in Perception," in Judson S. Brown, ed., *Current Theory and Research in Motivation* (Lincoln, Neb., 1953), 59–108.

4. Dale Wyatt and Donald Campbell, "A Study of Interviewer Bias as Related to Interviewer's Expectations and Own Opinions," *International Journal of Opinion and Attitude Research*, IV (Spring 1950), 77–83.

5. Max Jacobson, *The Diplomacy of the Winter War* (Cambridge, Mass., 1961), 136–39.

6. Raymond Aron, *Peace and War* (Garden City 1966), 29.

7. Cf. Kuhn, *The Structure of Scientific Revolution*, 65. A fairly high degree of knowledge is needed before one can state precise expectations. One indication of the lack of international relations theory is that most of us are not sure what "naturally" flows from our theories and what constitutes either "puzzles" to be further explored with the paradigm or "anomalies" that cast doubt on the basic theories.

8. See Philip Selznick, *Leadership in Administration* (Evanston 1957).

9. Ashley Schiff, *Fire and Water: Scientific Heresy in the Forest Service* (Cambridge, Mass., 1962). Despite its title, this book is a fascinating and valuable study.

10. *The Craft of Intelligence* (New York 1963), 53.

11. P. 302. See Beveridge, 93, for a discussion of the idea that the scientist should keep in mind as many hypotheses as possible when conducting and analyzing experiments.

12. *Presidential Power* (New York 1960).

13. Most psychologists argue that this influence also holds for perception of shapes. For data showing that people in different societies differ in respect to their predisposition to experience certain optical illusions and for a convincing argument that this difference can be explained by the societies' different physical environments, which have led their people to develop different patterns of drawing inferences from ambiguous visual cues, see Marshall Segall, Donald Campbell, and Melville Herskovits, *The Influence of Culture on Visual Perceptions* (Indianapolis 1966).

14. Thus when Bruner and Postman's subjects first were presented with incongruous playing cards (i.e., cards in which symbols and colors of the suits were not matching, producing red spades or black diamonds), long exposure times were necessary for correct identification. But once a subject correctly perceived the card and added this type of card to his repertoire of categories, he was able to identify other incongruous cards much more quickly. For an analogous example—in this case, changes in the analysis of aerial reconnaissance photographs of an enemy's secret weapons-testing facilities produced by the belief that a previously unknown object may be present—see David Irving, *The Mare's Nest* (Boston 1964), 66–67, 274–75.

15. Bruner and Postman, 220.

16. *The Liberal Tradition in America* (New York 1955), 306.

17. *Russia and the West Under Lenin and Stalin* (New York 1962), 142–43.

18. DeWitt Dearborn and Herbert Simon, "Selective Perception: A Note on the Departmental Identification of Executives," *Sociometry*, XXI (June 1958), 140–44.

19. "Two American Ambassadors: Bullitt and Kennedy," in Craig and Gilbert, 358–59.

20. Donald Lammer, *Explaining Munich* (Stanford 1966), 15.

21. George Monger, *The End of Isolation* (London 1963). I am also indebted to Frederick Collignon for his unpublished manuscript and several conversations on this point.

22. Hans Toch and Richard Schulte, "Readiness to Perceive Violence as a Result of Police Training," *British Journal of Psychology*, LII (November 1961), 392 (original italics omitted). It should be stressed that one cannot say whether or not the advanced police students perceived the pictures "accurately." The point is that their training predisposed them to see violence in ambiguous situations. Whether on balance they would make fewer perceptual errors and better decisions is very hard to determine. For an experiment showing that training can lead people to "recognize" an expected stimulus even when that stimulus is in fact not shown, see Israel Goldiamond and William F. Hawkins, "Vexierversuch: The Log Relationship Between

Word-Frequency and Recognition Obtained in the Absence of Stimulus Words," *Journal of Experimental Psychology*, LVI (December 1958), 457–63.

23. *A World Restored* (New York 1964), 2–3.

24. *Strategic Surrender* (New York 1964), 215–41.

25. *The Power of Small States* (Chicago 1959), 81.

26. William Inge, *Outspoken Essays*, First Series (London 1923), 88.

27. Of course, analogies themselves are not "unmoved movers." The interpretation of past events is not automatic and is informed by general views of international relations and complex judgments. And just as beliefs about the past influence the present, views about the present influence interpretations of history. It is difficult to determine the degree to which the United States' interpretation of the reasons it went to war in 1917 influenced American foreign policy in the 1920's and 1930's and how much the isolationism of that period influenced the histories of the war.

28. For some psychological experiments on this subject, see Jerome Bruner and A. Leigh Minturn, "Perceptual Identification and Perceptual Organization" *Journal of General Psychology*, LIII (July 1955), 22–28; Seymour Feshbach and Robert Singer, "The Effects of Fear Arousal and Suppression of Fear Upon Social Perception," *Journal of Abnormal and Social Psychology*, LV (November 1957), 283–88; and Elsa Sippoal, "A Group Study of Some Effects of Preparatory Sets," *Psychology Monographs*, XLVI, No. 210 (1935), 27–28. For a general discussion of the importance of the perceiver's evoked set, see Postman, 87.

29. Pp. 73–74.

30. For example, Roger Hilsman points out, "Those who knew of the peripheral reconnaissance flights that probed Soviet air defenses during the Eisenhower administration and the U-2 flights over the Soviet Union itself . . . were better able to understand some of the things the Soviets were saying and doing than people who did not know of these activities" (*To Move a Nation* [Garden City 1967], 66). But it is also possible that those who knew about the U-2 flights at times misinterpreted Soviet messages by incorrectly believing that the sender was influenced by, or at least knew of, these flights.

31. I am grateful to Thomas Schelling for discussion on this point.

32. *Deterrence Before Hiroshima* (New York 1966), 105–22.

33. *Ibid.*

34. For a slightly different formulation of this view, see Holsti, 27.

35. The Soviets consciously hold an extreme version of this view and seem to believe that nothing is accidental. See the discussion in Nathan Leites, *A Study of Bolshevism* (Glencoe 1953), 67–73.

36. A. W. Marshall criticizes Western explanations of Soviet military posture for failing to take this into account. See his "Problems of Estimating Military Power," a paper presented at the 1966 Annual Meeting of the American Political Science Association, 16.

37. It has also been noted that in labor-management disputes both sides may be apt to believe incorrectly that the other is controlled from above, either from the international union office or from the company's central headquarters (Robert Blake, Herbert Shepard, and Jane Mouton, *Managing Intergroup Conflict in Industry* [Houston 1964], 182). It has been further noted that both Democratic and Republican members of the House tend to see the other party as the one that is more disciplined and united (Charles Clapp, *The Congressman* [Washington 1963], 17–19).

38. George Kennan, *Russia Leaves the War* (New York 1967), 484.

39. *Ibid.*, 404, 408, 500.

40. Herbert Butterfield notes that these assumptions can contribute to the spiral of "Hobbesian fear. . . . You yourself may vividly feel the terrible fear that you have of the other party, but you cannot enter into the other man's

counter-fear, or even understand why he should be particularly nervous. For you know that you yourself mean him no harm, and that you want nothing from him save guarantees for your own safety; and it is never possible for you to realize or remember properly that since he cannot see the inside of your mind, he can never have the same assurance of your intentions that you have" (*History and Human Conflict* [London 1951], 20).

41. *European Diplomatic History 1871–1932* (New York 1933), 125. It takes great mental effort to realize that actions which seem only the natural consequence of defending your vital interests can look to others as though you are refusing them any chance of increasing their influence. In rebutting the famous Crowe "balance of power" memorandum of 1907, which justified a policy of "containing" Germany on the grounds that she was a threat to British national security, Sanderson, a former permanent undersecretary in the Foreign Office, wrote, "It has sometimes seemed to me that to a foreigner reading our press the British Empire must appear in the light of some huge giant sprawling all over the globe, with gouty fingers and toes stretching in every direction, which cannot be approached without eliciting a scream" (quoted in Monger, 315). But few other Englishmen could be convinced that others might see them this way.

42. George Kennan makes clear that in 1918 this kind of difficulty was partly responsible for the inability of either the Allies or the new Bolshevik government to understand the motivations of the other side: "There is . . . nothing in nature more egocentric than the embattled democracy. . . . It . . . tends to attach to its own cause an absolute value which distorts its own vision of everything else. . . . It will readily be seen that people who have got themselves into this frame of mind have little understanding for the issues of any contest other than the one in which they are involved. The idea of people wasting time and substance on any *other* issue seems to them preposterous" (*Russia and the West*, 11–12).

43. Kaplan, 89.

44. Johan Jorgen Holst, "Surprise, Signals, and Reaction: The Attack on Norway," *Cooperation and Conflict*, No. 1 (1966), 34. The Germans made a similar mistake in November 1942 when they interpreted the presence of an Allied convoy in the Mediterranean as confirming their belief that Malta would be resupplied. They thus were taken by surprise when landings took place in North Africa (William Langer, *Our Vichy Gamble* [New York 1966], 365).

JOHN MUELLER

FROM *RETREAT FROM DOOMSDAY: THE OBSOLESCENCE OF MAJOR WAR*

Introduction

*   *   *

The holocaust of World War I turned peace advocates into a pronounced majority in the developed world and virtually destroyed war romanticism. Were it not for the astoundingly successful machinations of Adolf Hitler, just about the last European who was willing to risk major war, and for the anachronistic forays of distant Japan, World War I might have been the last major war.

*   *   *

Hitler's War

It is not true that no one in Europe besides Adolf Hitler wanted war, or at any rate the gains of war. Obviously, he found enough residual war spirit to inflame, and others found his vision of an expanded Germany attractive. It does seem true, however, that after 1918 Hitler was the only person left in Europe who combined the requisite supreme political skills with a willingness to risk major conflagration to quest after his vision. Not only did he manufacture a reason for war, but against great internal and external opposition, he crafted a military strategy that promised to achieve these gains without repeating World War I; and for a decade he experienced an amazing record of success against his timorous opponents.

There was great discontent with the status quo in Germany after the defeat of 1918 and after the punishing, often gratuitously insulting terms

From *Retreat from Doomsday: The Obsolescence of Major War* (New York Basic Books, 1989).

that were imposed upon it, and there was enormous frustration with the enervating domestic combat between the political left and right, and with the waffling, ineffectual center. In places the war spirit lingered: in the 1920s Germany produced not only Erich Maria Remarque's famous antiwar novel, *All Quiet on the Western Front*, but also Ernst Jünger's popular and blood-curdling, if less well-remembered, *The Storm of Steel*. Moreover, there was economic chaos, political instability, class hostility, and ethnic turmoil throughout Central and Eastern Europe. Some limited military clashes might have developed out of the various festering national resentments and rivalries—perhaps some border conflicts or land seizures, bitter but brief. However, given the overwhelming horror of major war that prevailed throughout the continent, and the profound exhaustion with it, the idea that another world war would somehow have naturally evolved out of the conflict and chaos in Europe is singularly unconvincing. A spectacularly skilled, and unusually lucky, entrepreneur was necessary for war.

Hitler needed the chaos and discontent to work with—although he created much of it, too. And surely he needed assistance—colleagues who were worshipfully subservient; a superb army that could be manipulated and whipped into action; a population capable of being mesmerized and led to slaughter; foreign opponents who were confused, disorganized, gullible, myopic, and faint-hearted; neighbors who would rather be prey than fight—although he created much of this as well. Hitler took the conditions of the world as he found them and then shaped and manipulated them to his own ends. He created the machinery to allow him to carry out his war plans and then ran the machinery himself. To a considerable degree, World War II came about because one man wanted it to occur and, with astonishingly single-minded and ruthless guile and craft, made it happen.

Hitler's Centrality

Hitler was central to the Nazi system both creatively and operationally. As Norman Rich observes, "The point cannot be stressed too strongly; Hitler was master of the Third Reich." Hitler received "dictatorial powers" within his own party in 1921; and after seizing control of the country in 1933, he moved quickly and decisively to persuade, browbeat, dominate, outmaneuver, downgrade, and, in many instances, murder opponents or would-be opponents. He possessed enormous energy and stamina, exceptional persuasive powers, an excellent memory, strong powers of concentration, an overwhelming craving for power, a fanatical belief in his mission, a monumental self-confidence, a unique daring, a spectacular facility for lying, a mesmerizing oratory style, and an ability to be utterly ruthless to anyone who got in his way or attempted to divert him from his intended course of action.[1] Although he could be laughable with his struttings and fulminations and Chaplinesque moustache, he was, as historians like Rich, Allan Bullock, and Hugh Trevor-Roper have suggested, "a political genius." Because he was a moral criminal, a monster, it is easy to conclude that he must also have been an irrational fanatic with little grasp of reality. Trevor-Roper calls this the error of "extrapolating low intelligence from moral degradation."[2] To conclude that he could not recognize reality and manipulate it to his benefit would be to continue the underestimation of his talents that helped drag his contemporaries into history's most terrible war.

Hitler, in short, was neither symptom nor figurehead. He invented Nazism, he made it work, and he caused World War II.

Hitler's Theory of Conquest

Although he was quite capable of seizing political opportunities when they arose, Hitler was at core a man with a plan that derived from a cosmic, if appalling, theory. The German people, he had convinced himself, were destined to dominate the world—with himself, of course, at the helm. As he figured it, this destiny derived from their racial superiority. As the master race, they naturally needed something to master; and the races to the east, which Hitler had concluded were inferior, seemed to him ideal for this role. The essence of Hitler's thought, according to Rich, was that "the German population was too small and its territorial base too limited to guarantee the survival of the racially superior Germans in the world arena of racial competition; if the German race was to survive, both its population and territorial base would have to be extended—at once and on a vast scale." It was therefore necessary for the German people to gain land, particularly in the east, for agricultural settlement and industrial development. The inferior people on the newly conquered territories would in no sense be assimilated; instead, they would be used for labor, expelled, or exterminated.[3] There was substantial enthusiasm in Germany for Hitler's demand that Germans in Central Europe all be incorporated into a single state, and the major countries in Europe proved to be sympathetic to that demand. What brought war was Germany's quest to occupy and control non-German lands, and that idea appears to have appealed to few but Hitler.

Hitler's Military Strategy

Conquest, therefore, was central to Hitler's theory. Although war was obviously ultimately necessary as a means to this end, it is not clear that Hitler was enamored of war for its own sake: unlike Mussolini, he does not seem to have been all that romantic about it. As Gerhard Weinberg has suggested, if the peoples Hitler wanted to conquer offered him "subservience" rather than "defiance," he was quite willing to accept it.[4] To be sure, Hitler had been a war enthusiast in his youth. In his autobiographical and ideological testament, *Mein Kampf*, he recalls a childhood fascination with books on military subjects and says he "raved more and more about everything connected with war or with militarism." He also relates that when war broke out in 1914, he was "overwhelmed by passionate enthusiasm" and fell on his knees to thank "Heaven" from his "overflowing heart" for granting him "the good fortune of being allowed to live" during those times. But these attitudes, as suggested in the previous chapter, were far from unusual at the time.[5] And Hitler also relates that as the Great War continued "the romance of battle had turned into horror. The enthusiasm gradually cooled down and the exuberant joy was suffocated by the fear of death."[6] Hitler certainly sought war, he apparently enjoyed being commander-in-chief during World War II (at least when things were going well for him), and he sometimes voiced Social Darwinist ideas at the time, arguing, for example, that a war every fifteen or twenty years was "good for the German people." But these unofficial pronouncements were often in the context of providing justification for the sacrifices he was demanding of his country. He saw expansion as racially invigorating and necessary, and wars that accompanied such expansion were therefore desirable. However, since war tends to call out "the best racial elements," too much of it could lead to the "slow bleeding away of the best, most valuable elements of a nation." Therefore, war should never become the "aim of the life of the people, but only a means for the preservation of this life."[7]

Given the realities of the situation, war was clearly necessary because the peoples he wanted to conquer were hardly likely to join his foreign, racist regime by their own will. In seeking to gain an effective consensus within Germany in support of his policy, however, Hitler inevitably came up against the argument put forward by not only his military chiefs but just about everybody else: However desirable his goals might be, any effort to achieve them by force would ultimately devolve into a long, eviscerating war of attrition like World War I or worse.

Hitler's response was to argue that the wrong lessons were almost universally being adduced

from the experience of the Great War. He agreed that Germany could never win a war of attrition from its present position. His policy was for rapid rearmament and for a series of separate isolated wars, avoiding the multifront war that overextended and ultimately doomed Germany in World War I. The mobility of airpower and tanks would be stressed in these wars, and upon the success of each, more geography would be added to the empire. Should total war eventually evolve out of this process (which Hitler may have expected and certainly was planning to be ready for), Germany would be in a good position to win, given its vast new territorial base.[8]

Hitler's Successes

Hitler invented, then, not only a theory of expansion and conquest but also a military methodology for carrying it out. Then, riding over internal and external opposition, he proceeded to put it into action. Under his leadership and through the direct application of his will Germany regained the Saarland in the west; rearmed; reintroduced conscription; reoccupied the Rhineland between Germany and France; took over Austria and then the Sudetenland section of Czechoslovakia; invaded the rest of Czechoslovakia; and invaded, in succession, Poland, Denmark, Norway, Holland, Belgium, Luxembourg, and France.

All these ventures were successful, and all were accomplished at remarkably little cost. It was a truly virtuosic performance. Given the experience of 1914–18, it might not be unreasonable to consider Hitler's deft destruction of Dutch, Belgian, British, and French forces in 1940 to be the most spectacular military success in history. At each step there were doubters and opponents within the regime; but, impressed by Hitler's steadily lengthening record of unalloyed success, they became fewer and fewer, and the objections gradually focused less on strategic judgment and more on minor matters of tactics.[9]

The German people seem to have reacted similarly. Hitler had achieved great popularity by the mid-1930s because he had reestablished domestic order and because he seemed to have gotten the lurching economy to function productively. But, in great contrast with 1914, there was no widespread enthusiasm for war. Conscription was not popular, and the public reacted to one of Hitler's greatest triumphs, acquiring by bloodless intimidation the Sudetenland section of Czechoslovakia, by cheering the English peacemaker, Neville Chamberlain. And they watched silently and sullenly as Hitler publicly oversaw the sending of motorized units to Czechoslovakia, causing Hitler to reportedly mutter, "With these people I cannot make war." Hitler's military advances into Poland in 1939 or into the Low Countries and France in 1940 did not inspire enthusiasm, although the Germans did apparently permit themselves an optimistic victory celebration when their old enemy, France, fell with such amazing quickness.[10]

The war, then, was Adolf Hitler's personal project. As Weinberg has put it, "Whether any other German leader would indeed have taken the plunge is surely doubtful, and the very warnings Hitler received from some of his generals can only have reinforced his belief in his personal role as the one man able, willing, and even eager to lead Germany and drag the world into war."[11] Hitler himself told his generals in 1939 that "essentially all depends on me, on my existence, because of my political talents." "In all modesty," he boasted, he was "irreplaceable. Neither a military man nor a civilian could replace me."[12]

Opposing Hitler

Given Hitler's plans and ideological need for geographic expansion and conquest, it seems likely that he could have been stopped only if his opponents had banded together either by militarily restraining him early in his path of adventure (when he was assuring all listeners that his appetite was moderate, conventionally nationalistic, and entirely satiable) or by putting together a truly effective alliance with the Soviets and oth-

ers that could have credibly threatened Germany with an immediate multifront war, thereby undercutting the very premise upon which Hitler's strategy rested. And, of course, major war in Europe could in all probability have been prevented if at any time Adolf Hitler had gotten in the way of a lethal germ, a well-placed bullet, or a speeding truck.[13]

But Hitler's opponents in Europe were horrified by the experience of the Great War and appalled by the prospect of going through anything like that again. They had concluded that only a monster or a lunatic could want, or even want to risk, another Great War, and they paid Hitler the undue compliment of assuming that he did not fall into those categories. As Williamson Murray puts it, the British were "firmly convinced that wars were something that twentieth-century statesmen did not consider." There was thus broad consensus—shared even by the curmudgeonly Winston Churchill, then out of office— that great efforts should be expended to reach a general peaceful settlement of any remaining grievances in Europe.[14]

Hitler exploited this desire like the master orchestrator and consummate liar he was. It is true that in *Mein Kampf*, written in the mid-1920s, he had envisioned a vast German empire through expansion toward the east; but now as the responsible and undisputed leader of Germany, he claimed that he only sought a settlement in which Germany would embrace all the various Germanic factions scattered around Central Europe in the Saarland, the Rhineland, Austria, and the mostly German Sudetenland section of Czechoslovakia. This last acquisition was, he assured his appeasers, the "last territorial claim I have to make in Europe." Moreover, he repeatedly proclaimed his peaceful intentions. He said he regarded "the forcible amalgamation of one people with another alien people not only as a worthless political aim, but in the long run as a danger to the internal unity and hence the strength of a nation. . . . Our racial theory therefore regards every war for subjection and domination of an alien people as a proceeding which sooner or later changes and weakens the victor internally. . . . Germany wants peace because of its fundamental convictions. . . . Germany has nothing to gain by a European war of any kind" (1935); "There is not a single German who desires war. The last war cost us two million dead and seven and a half million wounded. Even if we had been victorious, no victory would have been worth the payment of such a price" (1936); "We have no interest in breaking the peace" (1938); For years past I have expressed my abhorrence of war and, it is true, also my abhorrence of warmongers. . . . I love peace" (1939).

The British and French reluctantly approved his demands in hopes that Hitler really had moderated the visions expressed in *Mein Kampf*. As archappeaser, Chamberlain observed wishfully at the time, "In spite of the hardness and ruthlessness I thought I saw on his face, I got the impression that here was a man who could be relied upon when he has given his word." Meanwhile, the Allies belatedly began to build up their military forces and anticipated that in a war they could rely on the dominance of the defensive (a lesson, they thought, of the Great War) and on a sea blockade. After the Sudetenland agreement at Munich in 1938, Hitler showed his truer colors in 1939 by taking over the rest of Czechoslovakia. The British and French then guaranteed the safety of Poland and, when that country was invaded by Germany in September, declared war after thinking it over for a few days. Even at that, however, war was purely declaratory: Britain and France hunkered down behind their defensive fortifications and did no actual fighting until Germany invaded France eight months later—an idea that was Hitler's alone. It seems entirely possible that had Hitler remained content with his conquests to that point, no general war would have taken place, and Hitler and his racist Reich might still be there now, festering in Central Europe.[15]

Most of the smaller countries of Europe were even less effective in dealing with Hitler. Instead of seeking to ally themselves with larger and stronger countries, many of them responded to the German menace by trying to become as un-threatening as possible in hopes, apparently, that they might become invisible to him. Thus, Holland decided to remain quiet and neutral, Belgium broke off its alliance with France, and Denmark disarmed, while Poland and Yugoslavia strained to remain on good terms with the Germans. Hitler, of course, encouraged these developments, solemnly pledging that he would respect the small countries' neutrality.[16]

When the menace became fully manifest, many countries were so horrified by the prospect of presumably fruitless battle that they simply capitulated. Thus, Austria opened its gates to the Germans in 1938; Czechoslovakia, which was well armed, gave up without a fight in 1938 and 1939; and Denmark, which wasn't, surrendered precipitously in 1940. Those who fought—the Poles, the Norwegians, the Dutch, and the Belgians—collapsed quickly, as did the divided and demoralized French. Although the British, armed with Winston Churchill's inspiring rhetoric, managed to hold out behind their English Channel moat, their armies in France mostly reacted to Hitler's advances with retreat, and in Malaya a year and a half later their army of 100,000 meekly surrendered to an invading Japanese army of 30,000. To a notable degree, Europeans had lost all will for waging a substantial war. The only ones besides Germany that seem to have been fully willing to fight were Poland (which held out rather well for a while against impossible odds), Finland (which battled the lumbering Soviet Union in 1939–40), and Switzerland.

After the fall of France in 1940, Hitler continued to pursue his visions. With the war stalemated in the west at the Channel, he turned his attention to the east, where he had always wanted to carry out his dreams of expansion. Impressed by the Soviets' incredible ineptitude in their war with tiny Finland, and noting that Soviet dictator Josef Stalin had recently killed off most of his best officers in a typical fit of paranoia, Hitler abrogated his 1939 nonaggression pact with the Soviet Union and invaded in June 1941, a decision the German people greeted with dismay.[17] As anticipated, initial victory was swift and sure, but as the brutal winter hit, the Soviets had not collapsed. It is probably not going too far to suggest that by Nazi standards the invasion of the Soviet Union was the first visible and consequential mistake Hitler had made in at least ten years.

But now he was bogged down in a war with enemies, including eventually the United States, on all sides. He had his empire, and he also had a total multifront war. Gradually the tide turned against him, but the Germans fought tenaciously for him, and the war raged on until May 1945, when Adolf Hitler finally removed himself from the scene by pointing a pistol into his mouth and pulling the trigger.

It seems a reasonable, if depressing, prediction that hundreds of years from now when the twentieth century for most people will have been reduced to a few catch words, the name that will represent it in the popular imagination will not be Winston Churchill, Pablo Picasso, George Balanchine, Franklin Roosevelt, Albert Einstein, or even Fred Astaire. Our best-remembered figure will be Adolf Hitler.

*   *   *

NOTES

1. Norman Rich, *Hitler's War Aims: Ideology, the Nazi State, and the Course of Expansion* (New York: Norton, 1973) pp. 11, xxxvi–xxxix; Albert Speer, *Inside the Third Reich* (New York: Macmillan, 1970), pp. 15–18.

2. "political genius": Rich 1973, p. xxxii; Alan Bullock, *Hitler: A Study in Tyranny* (London: Odhams, 1952), p. 735; H. R. Trevor-Roper, "The Mind of Adolf Hitler" in *Hitler's Secret Conversations 1941–1944* (New York: Farrar, Strauss, and Young, 1953), pp. viii, xiv, xxx. "extrapolating": Eberhard Jäckel, "The Evolution of Hitler's Foreign Policy Aims" in Henry A. Turner, Jr. (ed.), *Nazism and the Third Reich* (New York: Quadrangle, 1972), p. 202. See also P. M. H. Bell, *The Origins of the Second World War in Europe* (London: Longman, 1986), p. 75.

3. Rich 1973, p.xiii; Jäckel 1972; Gerhard L. Weinberg, *The Foreign Policy of Hitler's Germany: Starting World War II, 1937–1939* (Chicago: University of Chicago Press, 1980), pp. 18, 657; *Norman Rich, Hitler's War Aims: The Establishment of the New Order* (New York: Norton, 1974), p. 420; Trevor-Roper 1953, p. xxiii. See also Adolf Hitler, *Mein Kampf* (New York: Reynal and Hitchcock, 1939), pp. 944–53; Alan Bullock, "Hitler and the Origins of the Second World War" in Henry A. Turner, Jr. (ed.), *Nazism and the Third Reich* (New York: Quadrangle, 1972); Alan S. Milward, *War, Economy, and Society* (Berkelely, CA: University of California Press, 1977), pp. 6–8; William T. Bluhm, *Ideologies and Attitudes: Modern Political Culture* (Englewood, NJ: Prentice-Hall, 1974), ch. 7. So overwhelming was Hitler's theory that (after blaming international Jewry for starting the war and his generals for losing it) he concluded his last written statement by restating his central objective: "The aim must still be to win territory in the east for the German people" (Bullock 1952, p. 729).

4. Weinberg 1980, p. 670. See also Adolf Hitler, *Hitler's Secret Book* (New York: Grove Press, 1961), pp. 22–23.

5. Compare the 1914 comment of a British radical reformer: "I feel nothing but gratitude to the gods for sending [this war] in my time" (Joll 1984, p. 183).

6. Hitler 1939, pp. 8, 210, 214–15.

7. Hitler 1961, pp. 9–10. "Good for the German People": Adolf Hitler, *Hitler's Secret Conversations 1941–1944* (New York: Farrar, Strauss, and Young, 1953), pp. 23–24, 43. For war-glorifying statements by other Nazis, see Vernon Van Dyke, *International Politics* (New York: Appleton-Century-Crofts, 1966), p. 33.

8. Weinberg 1980, pp. 657–59; Bullock 1972, pp. 226; Richard Rosecrance, *The Rise of the Trading State: Commerce and Conquest in the*

Modern World (New York: Basic Books, 1986), pp. 105–6. R. J. Overy argues that an eventual total war was part of Hitler's grand scheme—a scheme he carefully kept from military and industrial leaders who he knew would find it "unthinkable"; the Hitler blitzkrieg, therefore, emerged not so much by plan as "by default" (R. J. Overy, "Hitler's War and the German Economy: A Reinterpretation," *Economic History Review,* vol. 35, no. 2, p. 279 and passim; Richard Overy, *Goering: The "Iron Man"* [London: Routledge and Kegan Paul, 1984], chs. 3–8; see also Williamson Murray, *The Change in the European Balance of Power, 1938–1939* [Princeton, NJ: Princeton University Press, 1984]). Hitler apparently recognized that his attack on France in 1940 could lead to a (one-front) struggle of attrition: see MacGregor Knox, *Mussolini Unleashed 1939–1941: Politics and Strategy in Fascist Italy's Last War* (New York: Cambridge University Press, 1982), p. 87. On Hitler's procedures for persuading his generals to attack France and the Low countries in 1940, see John J. Mearsheimer, *Conventional Deterrence* (Ithaca, NY: Cornell University Press, 1983), ch. 4. For Hitler's correct rejection of the popular notion that air power could deliver a quick "knock-out blow," see Uri Bialer, *Shadow of the Bombers: The Fear of Air Attack and British Politics, 1932–1939* (London: Royal Historical Society, 1980), pp. 133–34. On the lack of enthusiasm for a war of conquest by established political and military leaders in Germany, see Bell 1986, p. 44.

9. MacGregor Knox, "Conquest, Foreign and Domestic, in Fascist Italy and Nazi Germany," *Journal of Modern History,* vol. 56 (March, 1984), pp. 42–43, 49–57; Marlis Steinert, *Hitler's War and the Germans: Public Mood and Attitude during the Second World War* (Athens, OH: Ohio University Press, 1977), pp. 25–102; Rich 1973, p. 211. The 1940 victory: see also Mearsheimer 1983, p. 99.

10. Telford Taylor, *Munich: The Price of Peace* (New York: Doubleday, 1979), p. 877; George H. Quester, *Offense and Defense in the International System* (New York: Wiley, 1977), p. 137; Weinberg 1980, pp. 451–52, 458, 677; Knox 1984, pp. 42, 51, 55; Bell 1986, p. 12.; Speer 1970, pp. 166–67; Friedrich Percyval Reck-Malleczewen, *Diary of a Man in Despair* (New York: Macmillan, 1970), pp. 103–9. One analyst of German public opinion characterizes it as "dead set" against major war: Steinert 1977, p. 50.

11. As Hitler biographer Allan Bullock puts it forcefully, "It is no good saying that it was 'the machine' that did this, not Hitler. Hitler was never the prisoner of 'the machine.' If 'the machine' had been left to decide things, it would never have taken the risk of attacking the West. . . . If it had been left to 'the machine,' German rearmament would never have been carried out at the pace on which Hitler insisted, or on the blitzkrieg pattern which proved to be as applicable to war with the Western powers as to the limited Polish campaign." It was "Hitler, not the German military leaders or the German people" who "decided that enough was not enough, that war must go on," and "the one thing no one thought of except Hitler was to attack Russia." "Of course he could not have done this without the military machine and skill in using it which the German armed forces put at his disposal, but the evidence leaves no doubt that the decision where and when to use that machine was in every case Hitler's, not his staff's, still less that all Hitler was doing was to react to the initiative of his opponents"(1972, pp. 241–43).

12. Weinberg 1980, p. 664. "Essentially": Alan Alexandroff and Richard Rosecrance, "Deterrence in 1939," *World Politics,* vol. 29, no. 3 (April 1977), pp. 416–17. "Irreplaceable": *Documents on German Foreign Policy, 1918–1945,* Series D, Vol. 8 (Washington: U.S. Government Printing Office, 1954).

13. For a discussion of Hitler's concern about assassination and of the elaborate security

measures taken to protect him, see Peter Hoffman, *Hitler's Personal Security* (Cambridge, MA: MIT Press, 1979).

14. Murray 1984, p. 369. Weinberg 1980, pp. 668–70.

15. On this point and Hitler's idea about attacking France, see Mearsheimer 1983, pp. 95–96, 102, 131–33. Allied plans: Weinberg 1980, pp. 6–7. On the delays in the West on declaring war even after the Germans had invaded Poland, see Leonard Moseley, *On Borrowed Time: How World War II Began* (New York: Random House, 1969), chs. 20–21. "in spite of": Taylor 1979, p. 743. "last territorial claim," peaceful proclamations: Adolf Hitler, *The Speeches of Adolf Hitler* (London: Oxford University Press, 1942), pp. 1517, 1218, 1220, 1235, 1260, 1514, 1639–40, 1661.

16. Weinberg 1980, p. 631.

17. Steinert 1977, p. 118.

IGOS, NGOS, AND INTERNATIONAL LAW

International organizations such as the United Nations are undisputed actors in international relations. Debate over the United Nations Security Council's role in legitimizing use of force has continued since the beginning of the 1990s. Eric Voeten examines why and how the "elite pact" (the Security Council) has become the legitimizer of force. The UN influences the behavior of states because officials have made it important through their actions and statements. Just as the United Nations has been criticized for accruing power, so too has the European Union. The national referendums of 2005 rejecting the proposed European constitution were a signal. Princeton University's Andrew Moravcsik argues that leaders must return to more incremental reforms, although the European Union project, in his assessment, remains stable and legitimate.

In addition to intergovernmental organizations (IGOs), research on nongovernmental organizations (NGOs), social movements, and transnational advocacy networks has expanded since the 1990s. Using a constructivist approach, Margaret Keck and Kathryn Sikkink, in an excerpt from their award-winning book, Activists beyond Borders: Advocacy Networks in International Politics (1998), show how such networks develop and operate, by "building new links among actors in civil societies, states, and international organizations. . . ."

One particularly controversial issue in international relations is humanitarian intervention. Humanitarian intervention involves the application of international law for intergovernmental and nongovernmental organizations and state actors. In a selection from the Atlantic Monthly, Samantha Power examines why the United States did not do more to stop the 1994 genocide in Rwanda. According to Power, not only are American decision makers to blame, but so is the United Nations and its bureaucracy.

In the international legal community and among policy makers, the issue of universal jurisdiction has gained considerable attention, particularly since the establishment of the International Criminal Court. Henry Kissinger, academician and former Secretary of State and National Security Advisor (rumored

to be under indictment by national courts himself), argues against the prac-
tice. Tyranny of judges replaces that of governments, he contends, and political
disagreements should not be resolved by legal means. Kenneth Roth of Human
Rights Watch disagrees.

John Mearsheimer, the quintessential realist, is openly skeptical about the
impact of international institutions. In this excerpt, he carefully delineates the
flaws of liberal institutionalist theory and concludes that policies based on
these theories are bound to fail.

ERIK VOETEN

THE POLITICAL ORIGINS OF THE UN SECURITY COUNCIL'S ABILITY TO LEGITIMIZE THE USE OF FORCE

In a 1966 article, Claude observed that the function of collective legitimization in global politics is increasingly conferred on international organizations (IOs), and that the United Nations (UN) has become the primary custodian of this legitimacy. Claude argued that "the world organization has come to be regarded, and used, as a dispenser of politically significant approval and disapproval of the claims, policies, and actions of states."[1] This assertion is even more relevant now than it was in 1966. States, including the United States, have shown the willingness to incur significant cost in terms of time, policy compromise, and side-payments simply to obtain the stamp of approval from the UN Security Council (SC) for military actions. To be sure, if the attempt to achieve a SC compromise proved unsuccessful, the United States has not shied away from using other means to pursue its ends. Nevertheless, the failure to acquire SC approval is generally perceived as costly, giving SC decisions considerable clout in international politics.

From *International Organization* 59 no. 3 (summer 2005): 527–57. Some of the author's notes have been omitted.

Given its lack of enforcement capabilities, the SC's leverage resides almost entirely in the perceived legitimacy its decisions grant to forceful actions. Governments across the globe appear more willing to cooperate voluntarily once the SC has conferred its blessing on a use of force. Why has the SC become the most impressive source of international legitimacy for the use of military force? That it would be so is far from obvious. Claude, for instance, thought of the UN General Assembly (GA) as the ultimate conferrer of legitimacy.[2] Franck argued in his influential 1990 treatise on legitimacy that if one were interested in identifying rules in the international system with a strong compliance pull, the provisions in the UN Charter that grant the SC military enforcement powers (Chapter VII) should be set aside.[3] Since then, these provisions have been invoked with great regularity to legitimize uses of force.

The development is also puzzling from a theoretical perspective. Most theorists seek the origins of modern institutional legitimacy in legal or moral principles. However, the SC has been inconsistent at best in applying legal principles; its decision-making procedures are not inclusive, transparent, or based on egalitarian principles; its decisions are frequently clouded by the threat of outside action; and the morality of its (non-) actions is widely debated. Hence, it is unlikely that the institution has the ability to appear depoliticized, an argument that motivates most constructivist accounts of institutional legitimacy in the international arena.[4]

On the other hand, scholars who study the strategic aspects of international politics have largely dismissed the UN from their analyses.[5] This article provides a firmer base for the role of the SC in strategic interactions. I argue that when governments and citizens look for an authority to legitimize the use of force, they generally do not seek an independent judgment on the appropriateness of an intervention; rather, they want political reassurance about the consequences of proposed military adventures. The rationale is based on an analysis of the strategic dilemmas that impede cooperation in a unipolar world. In the absence of credible limits to power, fears of exploitation stifle cooperation. Because no single state can credibly check the superpower, enforcing limits on the superpower's behavior involves overcoming a complex coordination dilemma. A cooperative equilibrium that implies self-enforcing limits to the exercise of power exists but is unlikely to emerge spontaneously given that governments have conflicting perceptions about what constitute legitimate actions and fundamental transgressions by the superpower. The SC provides a focal solution that has the characteristics of an elite pact: an agreement among a select set of actors that seeks to neutralize threats to stability by institutionalizing nonmajoritarian mechanisms for conflict resolution. The elite pact's authority depends on the operation of a social norm in which SC approval provides a green light for states to cooperate, whereas its absence triggers a coordinated response that imposes costs on violators. The observance of this norm allows for more cooperation and restraint than can be achieved in the absence of coordination on the SC as the proper institutional device. Hence the extent to which the SC confers legitimacy on uses of force

depends not on the perceived normative qualities of the institution, but on the extent to which actors in international politics believe that norm compliance produces favorable outcomes.

The attractiveness of the elite pact account resides partly in its ability to explain the emergence of a limited degree of governance in the international system without assuming the existence of a collective global identity that generates an ideological consensus over appropriate forms of global governance. There is little evidence that such a consensus exists. Thus accounts that require only a limited set of a priori common values appear more plausible. Furthermore, the elite pact model better fits the SC's institutional design than alternative accounts and provides a plausible explanation for the sudden surge in authority following the Gulf War. Finally, the model stresses that elite pacts need to be self-enforcing. This opens a more promising avenue for analyzing norm stability than the constructivist assumption that norms are internalized.

The article proceeds with a broad overview of temporal fluctuations in the extent to which states have historically put weight on SC decisions. The next section explains why SC authority stems from its ability to legitimize uses of force and provides an operational definition. While there is a large literature that asserts that SC decisions confer legitimacy on uses of force, explanations for this phenomenon are rarely made explicit. One of the contributions of this article is to more precisely identify the various plausible roles of the SC in the international system. After discussing the four most common (though often implicit) explanations, the elite pact argument is introduced more elaborately. The conclusion discusses the implications for theories of international legitimacy and the future of SC legitimacy.

The Security Council and Its Authority over Uses of Force

When states sign the UN Charter, they pledge not to use or threaten force "against the territorial integrity or political independence of any state, or in any manner inconsistent with the Purposes of the United Nations."[6] The Charter delegates significant authority to the SC to decide whether particular uses of force meet these purposes. This delegation is necessitated by the incompleteness of any contract that seeks to regulate the use of force but falls short of forbidding it outright. The Charter provides some guidance by explicitly specifying two general circumstances in which force may be exercised.

First, Article 51 of the Charter affirms the inherent right of states to use force in individual or collective self-defense against armed attacks. In principle, states are not obliged to obtain the approval of the SC for invoking this right. However, states routinely resort to expanded conceptions of self-defense in attempts to justify unilateral uses of force. SC resolutions conceivably provide judgments on the merit of self-defense claims. An example is Resolution 1373, which reaffirms the right of the United States to act forcefully in its self-defense against terrorist activities and de facto legitimized the U.S. military action in Afghanistan.[7] This resolution, however, was quite exceptional. In nearly all other controversial claims to self-defense the SC has been unable or unwilling to rule on the legitimacy of self-defense claims; instead allowing the GA to adopt highly politicized and mostly ignored resolutions about the legitimacy of uses of force.[8]

Second, Chapter VII of the Charter defines a more active role for the SC in the management of international security. This chapter lays out a set of procedures through which the SC can authorize uses of force in response to the "existence of any threat to the peace, breach of the peace, or act of aggression."[9] Before 1990, the SC adopted only twenty-two resolutions under Chapter VII, most of which authorized sanctions rather than uses of force.[10] The two most important exceptions were the Congo peacekeeping force and the Korean War (1950). In the latter case, authorization was possible only because of the temporary absence of the Union of Soviet Socialist Republics (USSR) to protest the exclusion of the People's Republic of China from the Council. In anticipation of deadlock when the USSR would retake its seat, the SC adopted the 1950 "Uniting for Peace Resolution," which allowed the GA to take responsibility in security affairs if the SC were unable to act. It has been invoked ten times, most notably in 1956 to order the French and British to stop their military intervention in the Suez Canal and to create the UN Emergency Force to provide a buffer between Egyptian and Israeli forces.

Although the UN's effectiveness and decisiveness were often limited, the UN was actively involved in the management of many international conflicts in the first twenty-five years of its existence. Decisions by the UN's political organs carried some weight, even to realists such as Hans Morgenthau, who argued that the United States should be willing to compromise to "to keep the United Nations in existence and make it an effective instrument of international government."[11] Between the late-1960s and 1989, however, neither the GA nor the SC exercised much influence over when or whether states resorted to force, a development characterized by Haas as evidence for "regime decay."[12] States, including the great powers, repeatedly intervened militarily without considering UN authorization and routinely ignored resolutions condemning their actions. Most obviously, this holds for major Cold War interventions, such as the Soviet invasion of Afghanistan and the U.S. military action in Vietnam. But it also pertains to smaller conflicts. U.S. President Ronald Reagan famously claimed that the 1983 GA resolution condemning the United States for its intervention in Grenada "didn't upset his breakfast at all."[13] This disregard for the authority of the UN over uses of force continued at least until December 1989, when the United States invaded Panama without considering asking approval from any IO. A GA resolution deploring the intervention had no discernable impact on domestic public or elite support for the intervention, and neither did a SC resolution that the United States vetoed.[14]

The successful cooperation between states in the first Persian Gulf War abruptly turned the SC into the natural first stop for coalition building.[15] It is important to appreciate the magnitude of the sudden the shift in SC activity immediately after operation Desert Storm. Between 1977 and the start of the Gulf War, the SC had adopted only two resolutions under Chapter VII.[16] Between 1990 and 1998, the Council approved 145 Chapter VII resolutions.[17] The number of UN commanded missions that used force beyond traditional peacekeeping principles went from one (Congo) before 1990 to five thereafter.[18] The number of missions where the authority to exercise force was delegated to interested parties went from one (Korea) to twelve.[19] Since 1990, the SC has authorized uses of force by coalitions of able and willing states in Europe (for example, the former Yugoslavia), Africa (for example, Sierra Leone, Somalia, the Great Lakes Region), Latin America (for example, Haiti), Oceania (for example, East-Timor), and Asia (For example, Afghanistan).

This spurt in activity does not simply reflect a newfound harmony in the preferences of the five veto powers. China and Russia frequently abstained from SC votes and often accompanied their abstentions with statements of discontent.[20] Reaching agreement often involved difficult compromises that had a noticeable impact on the implementation of operations, as exemplified most prolifically by the Bosnia case.[21] On several occasions, the United States made significant side-payments to obtain SC blessing for operations it could easily, and de facto did, execute alone or with a few allies. For instance, in exchange for consent for the U.S. intervention in Haiti, China and Russia obtained sizeable concessions, including a favorable World Bank loan and U.S. support for peacekeeping in Georgia.[22] Thus, attaining SC approval for a use of force is no easy task.

Governments outside the United States have also placed considerable weight on SC decisions. SC authorization was crucial to Australia's willingness to intervene in East-Timor.[23] India has since 1992 committed to a "pro-active" approach toward UN peacekeeping missions, providing generous troop contributions across the globe to

UN-approved missions while refusing to supply to troops for non-UN approved missions.[24] New interpretations of Basic Law provisions that restrict German military activity abroad have made exceptions for German participation in UN peacekeeping and peacemaking missions, as well as North Atlantic Treaty Organization (NATO) and West European Union (WEU) operations directed at implementing SC resolutions. Japan has adopted a law that makes military contributions of most kinds conditional on SC authorization.[25] Thus even for these powerful states that lack permanent membership, SC approval has become almost imperative for participation in cooperative military endeavors.

The increased significance of SC authorization is also apparent in public opinion, both in the United States and elsewhere. There is a wealth of evidence that Americans consistently prefer UN actions to other types of multilateral interventions and even more so to unilateral initiatives. For example, in a January 2003 poll, the Program on International Policy Attitudes (PIPA) asked respondents whether they "think the UN Security Council has the right to authorize the use of military force to prevent a country that does not have nuclear weapons from acquiring them." Of all respondents, 76 percent answered affirmatively to this question, whereas only 48 percent believes the United States without UN approval has this right.[26] What is impressive about these findings is their consistency across interventions, question formats, and time.[27] Public opinion outside the United States tends to insist even more strongly on UN authorization.[28] This suggests that SC authorization may facilitate foreign leaders to participate in military actions.

The observation that, since the Persian Gulf War, it has become costly to circumvent the authority of the SC is not completely undermined by the two main cases where this authority has been ignored: the Kosovo intervention and the 2003 Iraq intervention. The absence of SC authorization for the Kosovo intervention was generally (and explicitly) perceived as unfortunate by the U.S. administration and even more so by its allies in the North Atlantic Treaty Organization (NATO).[29] NATO motivated its actions by referring to previous SC resolutions and obtained SC authorization for the peacekeeping mission and transitional authority that were set up in the immediate aftermath of the military campaign. Similarly, the United States went to considerable length to persuade the SC to authorize the Iraq intervention, argued repeatedly that it was implementing past SC resolutions, and returned to the SC in the immediate aftermath of the intervention. Moreover, the absence of SC authorization is often used domestically in the argument that the lack of allies makes the war unnecessarily expensive. That NATO and the United States eventually went ahead without SC authorization does demonstrate, however, that the SC may raise the costs of unilateral action but cannot prevent it altogether. As former U.S. Secretary of Defense William Cohen said about SC authorization for the Kosovo intervention: "It's desirable, not imperative."[30]

Legitimacy

The previous section illustrates that since the Persian Gulf War, the main states in world politics have behaved "as if" it is costly to circumvent the authority of the SC when deciding on uses of force. How can one explain this observation given that the SC lacks independent capabilities to enforce its decisions? Several commonplace explanations for IO authority apply poorly to the SC. There are few, if any, institutional mechanisms that allow states to create credible long-term commitments to the institution, making it an unlikely candidate for locking in policies, along the lines suggested by Ikenberry.[31] The tasks that the SC performs are not routine and do not require high levels of specific expertise or knowledge. Thus, delegation of decision-making authority to the SC does not result in similar gains from specialization that plausibly explain why states are willing to delegate authority to IOs

such as the World Bank[32] and the International Monetary Fund (IMF).[33]

In the absence of obvious alternative sources, the origins of the SC authority are usually assumed to lie in the legitimacy it confers on forceful actions.[34] Actions that are perceived as legitimate are obeyed voluntarily rather than challenged. Hence, obtaining legitimacy for proposed interventions is valuable. This clearly implies that legitimacy resides entirely in the subjective beliefs of actors.[35] This contrasts with the conception that legitimacy properly signifies an evaluation on normative grounds, usually derived from democratic theory. In this view, if an institution fails to meet a set of specified standards it is illegitimate, regardless of how individual actors perceive the institution. While it is important to evaluate how democratic principles ought to be extended to a global arena, such a normative approach is unlikely to generate much insight into the question why SC decisions confer the legitimacy they do.

I define legitimacy perceptions as the beliefs of actors that the convention or social norm that the SC authorizes and forbids discretionary uses of force by states against states should be upheld. Discretionary uses of force are those that do not involve direct and undisputed self-defense against an attack. Thus the authority of the SC resides in the beliefs of actors that violating this social norm is costly, undesirable, or inappropriate. This focus on perceptions and on the social aspect of legitimacy is consistent with constructivist approaches. It also fits rationalist accounts of self-enforcing conventions and social norms.

The primary actors are governments, who decide on uses of force and are the members of the UN. However, because governments, especially democratically elected ones, rely on the support of citizens, the perceptions of individuals also matter in an indirect way. In addition, it may well be that actors in the state with the intent to use force, most often the United States in our examples, and actors in other states may have different motivations for insisting on SC authorization.

Explanations

Why do state actors believe that a failure to achieve SC authorization is undesirable? What sustains these beliefs? To find convincing answers to these questions one needs to appreciate not only why states demand some form of multilateralism, but also the reasons that would lead actors to rely on the SC rather than alternatives, such as the GA, regional institutions (for example, NATO), or multilateral coalitions that are not embedded in formal IOs. Thus, pointing to a general inclination toward multilateralism does not form a satisfactory explanation of the empirical pattern. Besides institutional form, a persuasive account must provide useful insights about the sources for temporal variation in the authority of the SC, including its sudden surge following the Gulf War. Moreover, it should give a plausible explanation for how these beliefs can be sustained given the behavior of the SC.

Most theoretical accounts argue that the legitimacy of international institutions resides in their ability to appear depoliticized by faithfully applying a set of rules, procedures, and norms that are deemed desirable by the international community.[36] I discuss three variants of this general argument that each stresses a different role for institutions: consistently applying legal rules, facilitating deliberation, and increasing accountability and fairness. Alternatively, the origins of the SC's legitimacy may lie in beliefs that granting the SC the authority to legitimize force generally lead to more desirable outcomes. The public goods explanation discussed below fits this mold, as does the elite pact account.

Legal Consistency

Much legal scholarship assumes that the SC derives its ability to legitimize and delegitimize the use of force from its capacity to form judgments about the extent to which proposed actions fit a legal framework that defines a system of collective security. Although the SC is explicitly a political institution rather than a court, there is a body of customary and written international law that provides a basis for determinations about the legality of self-defense actions and other uses of force. The indiscriminatory nature of legal norms potentially makes legal uses of force more acceptable to governments and citizens than actions that do not meet legal standards. To maintain its standing as a legitimate conferrer of legal judgments, an institution must thus strive for consistency in its rulings and motivate deviations from past practice with (developing) legal principles. This standard has usefully been applied to other bodies, such as dispute resolution mechanisms in trade organizations[37] and the European Court of Justice (ECJ).[38] That legal consistency is the institutional behavior that reinforces legitimacy beliefs also motivates concerns by legal scholars that the SC squanders its legitimacy when it behaves in ways that are inconsistent with general principles of international law.[39]

There is, however, no empirical evidence that legal consistency has been a driving force behind SC decisions. During the Cold War, the judgments by UN bodies on the legality of self-defense actions were widely perceived as politically motivated and not persuasive on the issue of lawfulness.[40] The SC has not developed a consistent doctrine on this matter since the end of the Cold War. The most noteworthy decision is the previously noted Resolution 1373, which affirms the right of the United States to act forcefully in its self-defense against terrorist activities. The extensive scope of the resolution has led some to question its legal foundations. As Farer puts it: "At this point, there is simply no cosmopolitan body of respectable legal opinion that could be invoked to support so broad a conception of self-defense."[41]

With regard to Chapter VII authorizations, the most basic determination is whether a situation presents a threat to international peace and security. Such "Article 39 determinations" have been stretched on multiple occasions to accommodate immediate political objectives. For example, Iraqi actions in Kurdish areas in 1991, the humanitarian tragedy in Somalia in 1992, the civil war in Angola in 1993, the failure to implement election results in Haiti in 1994, and Libya's unwillingness to surrender its citizens accused of terrorism have all been deemed threats to international peace.[42] Most importantly, there has been no serious effort at motivating the Article 39 determination on these resolutions. As Kirgis points out: "[I]f we are concerned about the responsible use of power by a marginally representative international organ that at present is not subject to recall or judicial review, we should expect the Security Council to be conscious of how and why it is expanding the definition. It should also contemplate the limits to be applied to the broader definition. It should, in other words, make principled Article 39 determinations, publicly explicated, that do not set unlimited or unintended precedents."[43]

Legal scholars have noted a variety of other difficulties considering SC decisions, including the common practice to delegate the use of force to individual states or groupings of states, the failure to define a greater role for judicial review through the International Court of Justice, and the extent to which the Charter obliges states to seek peaceful resolutions before authorizing force.[44] Glennon has concluded that coherent international law concerning intervention by states no longer exists.[45] Others counter that the Charter does not impose meaningful restrictions on the set of cases in which the SC can legally authorize forceful means.[46] Clearly, either view precludes that legal consistency is the driving force behind the SC's legitimizing ability. This does not mean that legal norms do not affect the use of force. The norm to ask for approval from the SC for the use of force can itself be understood as a legal norm. The observation that this norm is mostly obeyed even though the SC itself has shown little regard for legal principles warrants an explanation.

Forum for Deliberation

A second set of scholars claim that while legal arguments are not decisive in the SC, law plays a broader role in the process of justificatory discourse. This view relies on the notion that governments generally feel compelled to justify their actions on something other than self-interest. This may be so because governments seek to acquire the support of other governments, domestic political actors, or public opinion. Or, it may be that governments have internalized standards for appropriate behavior that are embedded in international legal norms. The importance of law in persuasion resides in its ability to put limits on the set of arguments that can acceptably be invoked.[47] Moreover, professional experts (international lawyers) help distinguish good arguments from poor ones in the evaluation of truth claims. Of course, the extent to which legal specialists can perform this function depends on the presence of a relatively coherent body of international law that regulates uses of force.

Alternatively, discourse in the SC may be guided by rules that the international community collectively understands to guide the process of acquiring approval for uses of force, even if not codified by law.[48] This thesis relies on the presence of easily recognizable common values that facilitate the evaluation of arguments.

The above view provides a promising account for why states frequently appeal to legal arguments, precedents, and collective security rules, even if final decisions often violate those rules. However, this view does not provide a plausible explanation for the role of the SC in this discursive process. It is widely recognized that the SC falls far short of Habermasian conditions for effective communicative action.[49] There is only a shallow set of common values, participants are unequal, and the SC relies extensively on unrecorded and informal consultations between subsets of the permanent members.[50] U.S. Secretary of State Colin Powell's public exposition of evidence for the case against Iraq was highly unusual and of questionable efficacy as a persuasive effort.[51] More frequently, the most visible efforts at persuasion occur outside of the institutional context of the SC. SC debates are usually recitations by representatives of statements prepared by their state departments. Strategic incentives further impede deliberation. There are clear and obvious incentives for states to misrepresent their positions, as the stakes are clear and the relevant actors few. In short, it is hard to see how the institutional setting of the SC contributes to the process of justificatory discourse and why, if deliberation were so important, institutional reforms have not been undertaken or alternative venues such as the GA have not grown more relevant.

Appropriate Procedures

An institution's decisions may be seen as legitimate because the institution's decision-making process corresponds to practice deemed desirable by members of the community. Beliefs about the appropriateness of a decision-making process constitute an important source of authority for domestic political institutions, particularly in democracies. Citizens may attach inherent value to procedures that conform to principles widely shared in a society. As a consequence, decisions of an institution may be perceived as legitimate even if these produce outcomes deemed undesirable.[52] In a similar vein, accountability, procedural fairness, and broad participation are often seen as inherent elements of the legitimacy of IOs. This assumption underlies the common argument that the main threat to SC legitimacy is that the institution is dominated by a few countries and that its procedures are opaque and unfair. The assertion is that the SC's decisions would carry greater legitimacy if its procedures more closely matched liberal norms, which allegedly have become increasingly important in international society.

The many attempts to reform the SC indicate that the legitimacy of the SC may be enhanced from the perspective of some if its decision-making procedures more closely corresponded to liberal principles. But one cannot plausibly explain the legitimacy the SC does confer on uses of force from the assumption that governments and citizens demand appropriate process. As outlined earlier, SC practice sets a low standard if measured against any reasonable set of liberal principles. One may object that a use of force authorized by the SC more closely approximates standards of appropriate procedure than unilateral actions. But if demands for appropriate procedure were strong, one would surely expect a greater use of more inclusive IOs, such as a return to the "uniting for peace" procedure popular in the 1950s and 1960s, perhaps under a weighted voting system. Instead, the GA has grown increasingly irrelevant for legitimizing uses of force. Alternatively, one might have expected reforms that increase transparency and accountability, which have been moderately successful in international financial institutions. Some argue that accountability has worsened in the 1990s, as the GA can no longer hold the SC accountable through the budget by qualified majority rule,[53] and because of the increasingly common practice of delegating the authority to use force to states and regional organizations.[54]

It is equally implausible that the general public appreciates the SC for its procedures. The public knows little about how the SC makes its decisions. Even in the midst of the Iraq controversy, 32 percent of the U.S. public claimed that the United States does not have the right to veto SC decisions,[55] and only 16 percent could name the five members with veto power.[56] Knowledge is not much better elsewhere, with correct identification of permanent members varying in a nine-country study from 5 percent in Portugal to 24 percent in Germany.[57]

Finally and most fundamentally, there is no set of common values that generate consensus about what constitutes appropriate global governance. Disagreements have become especially apparent in debates about voting rules and membership questions, but they have also surfaced in virtually any other area where meaningful reforms have been proposed.[58] Even liberal democracies generally disagree on if and how liberal principles ought to be extended to global governance.[59] Explanations that emphasize strong common values are less likely to be successful for a diverse global organization than for an institution with more homogenous membership.

Global Public Goods

An alternative view is that the SC helps solve collective action problems that arise in the production of global public goods. Successful peacekeeping operations reduce suffering and save lives. Globalization and the end of the Cold War may have increased demands for international actions that produce such effects.[60] In addition, UN-authorized interventions may provide a measure of stability and security that benefits virtually all nations. For example, the first Gulf War reinforced the norm that state borders not be changed forcibly and secured the stability of the global oil supply.[61] These benefits accrue to all status quo powers and are not easily excludable.

Models of public good provision predict that poor nations will be able to free ride off the contributions of wealthier nations and that the public good will be under-provided because contributors do not take into account the spillover benefits that their support confers to others. The SC may help alleviate underprovision and free riding in three ways. First, the fixed burden-sharing mechanism for peacekeeping operations provides an institutional solution that helps reduce risks of bargaining failures and lessens transaction costs. Second, the delegation of decision-making authority to a small number of states may facilitate compromise on the amount of public good that ought to be produced.[62] Third, the SC helps states pool resources.[63] The existence of selective incentives induces some states to incur more than their required share of the peacekeeping burden. For example, Kuwait paid two-thirds of the bill for the UN Iraq-Kuwait Observation Mission through voluntary contributions. Australia proved willing to shoulder a disproportionate share of the peacekeeping burden in East-Timor. States are more likely to make such contributions when these add to the efforts of others in a predictable manner.

The absence of enforcement mechanisms implies that the survival of this cooperative solution depends on a social norm. This norm first and foremost requires states to pay their share of the burden. The more states believe that this norm is followed, the fewer incentives they have to free ride in any particular case. In individual instances, states must be willing to shoulder a larger share of the burden than they would with a voluntary mechanism, because they believe that the benefits from upholding the social norm (greater public good production in the long run) exceed the short-term benefits of shirking. Hence, interventions authorized by the SC could be perceived as more legitimate in the sense that they signal a longer-term commitment to global public good production.

Although this argument is plausible theoretically, it fails to account for some noticeable empirical patterns. First, the belief among rational actors that the SC plays this role should and probably has weakened considerably since the early 1990s. The much-publicized failures in Somalia, Rwanda, and Bosnia should have reduced beliefs that the SC is the appropriate mechanism for coordination that helps solve problems of public good production. Moreover, several wealthy states, most notably the United States, have failed repeatedly to meet their peacekeeping assessments. As of 31 January 2003, the United States had $789 million in peacekeeping arrears.[64] Other states owe the UN $1.4 billion in payments for peacekeeping. These arrears constitute a sizeable portion of the total peacekeeping budget.[65] Under the collective action model, the failure of states to meet their assessments gives other states clear incentives to shirk.

Second, the public goods rationale does not explain why states value SC authorization even when they do not use its fixed burden-sharing mechanism. Between 1996 and 2000, estimated expenditures on non–UN-financed peacekeeping missions have exceeded spending on UN-financed operations by $11.5 billion. Interestingly, many of these non–UN-financed operations have taken place with the explicit authorization of the SC. For example, the mandates of the various peacekeeping and peacemaking forces in Bosnia, Kosovo, and Afghanistan were all authorized at some point by SC resolutions, but none of them are financed primarily through the UN system or executed by the UN.

Third, the decision-making procedures grant veto power to states that contribute little to UN operations and exclude some of the most significant contributors. Japan and Germany are the second and third largest contributors but have no permanent seat at the table. China contributes less than small European states such as Belgium, Sweden, and the Netherlands, but has the right to veto any resolution.[66] If public good provision were the prime concern, reform of these decision-making mechanisms would be in every state's best interest. It would prevent large contributors from abandoning the institution or refusing to pay their dues. International financial institutions, such as the World Bank and the IMF, have adopted weighted voting rules that better fit these objectives.

The value states attach to SC authorization rests not entirely in the extent to which it forms an institutional solution to free-rider problems that lead to underproduction of public goods. However, the public good argument is not completely without merit. Several SC-authorized peacekeeping missions have helped resolve conflicts and have contributed to the implementation of peace agreements.[67] Moreover, a global alternative is not readily available. The elite pact rationale suggests that the main function of the SC in this may be that it addresses a distributional issue that frequently impedes successful collective action.

The Security Council as an Elite Pact

An alternative perspective is that the SC is an institutional manifestation of a central coalition of great powers.[68] This view does not proclaim that the SC enforces a broad system of collective security, but rather that it may serve as a useful mechanism that facilitates cooperative efforts in an anarchic world characterized by the security dilemma.[69] Concerts were historically designed to deal with situations of multipolarity that followed the defeat of hegemony. However, similar incentives for cooperation exist in a unipolar world characterized by interdependence. There are substantial potential gains from cooperation between the superpower and other states on economic issues such as trade and financial stability. Moreover, many governments face common security threats such as terrorism and states with the capacity and intention to challenge status quo boundaries or produce nuclear weapons. The main impediment to cooperation under the security dilemma is fear of exploitation.[70] Such fears are also relevant in a unipolar world where the superpower can use its preponderant capabilities to extract concessions, set the terms for cooperation, and act against the interests of individual states without being checked by a single credible power.

In such asymmetrical situations, credible limits to the use of force potentially benefit both the superpower and the rest of the world.[71] In the absence of credible guarantees, one observes suboptimal levels of cooperation as states pay a risk premium, captured for instance by increased military expenditure or other actions targeted at limiting the superpower's relative primacy. Institutions, such as NATO, help increase the credibility of security guarantees by raising the cost of reneging from a commitment. However, the absence of an outside threat and strong collective identity make such arrangements much more difficult to achieve at the global level.

Game-theoretic analyses that treat institutions as self-enforcing equilibria suggest an alternative route by which institutions help achieve better outcomes: they aid in solving the coordination dilemma among those actors that fear exploitation. Potential individual challenges are unlikely to deter a superpower from engaging in transgressions. However, the prospect of a coordinated challenge may well persuade the superpower to follow restraint. For this to succeed, states would have to agree on a mechanism that credibly triggers a coordinated response. For example, Greif, Milgrom, and Weingast argue that merchant guilds during the late medieval period provided a credible threat of costly boycotts if trade centers violated merchants' property rights.[72] Without these guilds, trade centers were unable to credibly commit to not exploit individual merchants and consequentially, merchants traded less than desired by the trade centers. As such, cooperation with the guilds became self-enforcing: it was in the self-interest of all actors to abide by the cooperative norm and defend against violations of the norm. Therefore, breaches of the norm came to be seen as illegitimate actions.

There is, however, a complicating factor in applying this analogy to the international arena. One can reasonably assume that merchants agreed on a common definition of what constituted a fundamental transgression by a trade center. Such consensus surely does not exist in the global arena. As the recent conflict over Iraq illustrates, what some states perceive as a proper use of force, others see as an encroachment. This introduces a political component to the problem. The strategic dilemma in the international system therefore more closely resembles that of achieving limited governance and rule of law in the context of ethnically, linguistically, and religiously heterogeneous societies, as analyzed by Weingast.

In heterogeneous societies, actors usually have conflicting interests about many aspects of governance. Weingast's model assumes that each actor can classify each move by the superpower[73] as either a transgression or a legitimate action. However, actors do not necessarily agree on these classifications. A superpower can exploit this by rewarding a subset of actors and infringing on the interests of the others. Although there are many such uncooperative equilibria, in a dynamic setting the Pareto-optimal cooperative outcome is also an equilibrium. In this equilibrium, no transgressions occur and states can cooperate beneficially. However, this equilibrium entails that states agree on a mechanism that triggers a coordinated response against an identifiable action by the superpower. It also requires that states use trigger strategies to punish one another for failing to cooperate in a coordinated challenge. The heterogeneous actors that occupy the international system are unlikely to resolve their coordination dilemma in a wholly decentralized manner.

In accordance with the literature on comparative politics, Weingast suggests that the most effective manner to induce limited governance in divided societies is through elite pacts. An elite pact is an agreement among a select set of actors that seeks to neutralize threats to stability by institutionalizing nonmajoritarian mechanisms for conflict resolution. The SC can usefully be understood as such a pact that functions as a focal point that helps state actors coordinate what limits to the exercise of power should be defended. If the SC authorizes a use of force, the superpower and the states that cooperate should not be challenged. If, however, the United States exercises force in the absence of SC authorization, other states should challenge it and its allies, for instance, by reducing cooperation elsewhere. This equilibrium behavior can be understood as a social norm or convention. For a convention to be successful, it needs to be self-enforcing. This means that actors should find it in their interest to punish unilateral defections from the pact, for example, because they believe that deviations have the potential to steer international society down a conflict-ridden path. SC authorizations thus legitimize uses of force in that they form widely accepted political judgments that signal whether a use of force transgresses a limit that should be defended. This fits with the conventional interpretation that legitimate power is limited power.

To domestic publics this convention performs a signaling function. Citizens are generally unprepared to make accurate inferences about the likely consequences of forceful actions. If the convention operates as specified above, SC agreement provides the public with a shortcut on the likely consequences of foreign adventures. SC authorization indicates that no costly challenges will result from the action. The absence of SC authorization on the other hand, signals the possibility of costly challenges and reduced cooperation. A U.S. public that generally wants the United States to be involved internationally but is fearful of overextension[74] may value such a signaling function. To foreign publics, SC approval signals that a particular use of force does not constitute an abuse of power that should lead to a coordinated, costly response. Clearly this conception of the SC poses fewer informational demands on general publics than alternatives. Moreover, it does not rely on the assumption that citizens share common values about the normative qualities of global governance. All citizens need to understand is that SC authorization implies some measure of consent and cooperation, whereas the absence of authorization signals potential challenges. The symbolic (focal point) aspect of SC approval allows for analogies to past experiences in a way that cooperative efforts through ad hoc coalitions do not.

More generally, the elite pact account does not depend on the existence of a broad set of common values that generates a consensus about what global governance should look like. For a cooperative equilibrium to survive, it is not necessary that each actor believe that the norm that sustains the equilibrium is morally appropriate, as long as most nonbelievers assume that other actors would react to violations. This is consistent with Weber's view on why a social order is binding on an individual level.[75] It helps explain the observation that governments insist on SC authorizations of uses of force even if they challenge the normative qualities of the institution. As observed earlier, powerful states such as Germany, Japan, and India, as well as many developing countries, regularly criticize the SC for its composition and decision-making procedures. Yet, they also insist on SC authorization of uses of force and in some cases even adjust their domestic laws to make cooperation conditional on SC.

The elite pact account has several other interesting implications that put it at odds with the alternative accounts. The remainder of this section discusses three of these: the mode of transformation, institutional design, and the self-enforcing character of the pact.

Mode of Transformation

The alternative explanations either do not give a clear prediction of how a shift in the authority of the SC takes place or (implicitly) assume that change occurs in response to gradual normative shifts toward greater reliance on liberal values or globalization.[76] The elite pact model predicts that if a shift toward a more cooperative equilibrium occurs, it will be in response to a discrete event. Elite pacts cannot be formed at just any time. In the most natural uncoordinated equilibrium, groups of actors exploit others and have no direct incentive to stop this practice. Elite pacts are therefore imposed following galvanizing events that disturb the beliefs on which a preceding equilibrium rested.[77] The conclusion of major wars is particularly likely to upset previously held beliefs and payoff structures.

This is compatible with the empirical record. Concerts were imposed following the defeat of a hegemon in a major war; a characterization that also fits the formation of the SC in the immediate aftermath of World War II. Nevertheless, the pact was not self-enforcing and had little bearing on whatever stability there was during most of the Cold War. The end of the Cold War created uncertainty in the perceptions of states about new equilibrium behavior. In such a situation it is highly likely that the manner by which a cooperative resolution to the first major international conflict was reached greatly influenced beliefs among policymakers, politicians and citizens about the future resolution of conflicts, and hence that adherence to the norm that the SC authorizes force helps enforce a stable (but limited) form of governance.

It is important to emphasize that the strategic dilemma that states faced in the Gulf War matches the game that motivates the elite pact account. First, there were clear incentives for cooperation. The Iraqi conquest of Kuwait constituted a violation of an international norm that nearly all states would prefer to uphold. Moreover, many states had strategic interests in the region that could be harmed by a unilateral response. Second, there were fears of exploitation. These were especially apparent in the USSR and motivated its initial preference for prolonged economic sanctions over multilateral intervention. Such fears were also evident in China,[78] Arab states,[79] and even Europe, especially in France, where President Francois Mitterrand had to force the resignation of his defense minister over the issue. Mitterrand explained to U.S. Secretary of State James Baker that SC approval was necessary even if lawyers believed that the intervention was legally justifiable without explicit authorization:[80] "Fifty-five million French people are not international lawyers. We need that resolution to ensure the consequences it will entail."[81] Thus, Mitterrand believed that his domestic audience desired reassurance and that SC approval would provide it. Finally, the U.S. motivation for seeking SC approval hinged strongly on the acquisition of political approval that would remove suspicions of exploitative behavior. Baker explained his logic of going through the SC in the following way:

> But to my way of thinking our disagreement about legalities was academic. As a practical matter, the United States had no real choice initially but to try a coalition approach in dealing with the crisis. . . . The credibility of our cause would be suspect, not just in the Arab world, but even to some in the West, including the United States.[82]

The Persian Gulf War was successful in that the first major conflict after the Cold War was resolved in a cooperative manner without the United States overextending. As I established earlier, there was a surge in SC activity immediately following the Persian Gulf War. Whereas the United States never considered asking for SC authorization for its intervention in Panama in December 1989, such requests became commonplace after the successful cooperative effort to remove Iraq from Kuwait. The suggestion here is that this development was directly related to the experience of the Gulf War in the uncertain environment of the end of the Cold War rather than an ideational change that stipulated greater sympathy for legal or liberal values.

There is much anecdotal evidence that policymakers and politicians across the globe were indeed at least moderately optimistic about the prospects for cooperation through the SC in the aftermath of the Gulf War.[83] That the experience would make a big impression on policymakers is also supported by studies of foreign policy decision making. For example, Khong has shown that war experiences that have consensual interpretations are likely to be uncritically, and perhaps inappropriately, used as analogies for future decisions.[84] Even those who believed that the legitimacy of the SC was based on false perceptions of reality usually did not argue that it was irrelevant, but rather that it was dangerous.[85] The success of cooperation also shaped perceptions among the general public. In a December 1992 *Newsweek* poll, 87 percent agreed with the statement: "The US should commit its troops only as part of a United Nations operation."[86] Before 1990, questions that suggested a primacy for the UN or the need for UN authorization for interventions were not even asked to the American public. This too suggests a change in expectations about what the SC could and should do.

Institutional Design

The argument advanced here does not presume that it was inevitable that the SC would play the role it did in the Persian Gulf War or that it would have risen to the same prominence had the Yugoslavian crisis occurred before the Gulf War. Rather, I maintain that given that the SC functioned as it did at a time of great uncertainty about equilibrium behavior, it is plausible that it impressed beliefs on state actors that a cooperative equilibrium could be played with the SC as a focal solution. Nevertheless, the institutional design of the SC did make it a more viable candidate for such a role than alternative institutions.

First, elite pacts eschew majoritarian decision making and commonly grant influential actors the power to veto decisions.[87] This is understandable because the goal of elite pacts is stability, not proper procedure. Stability is threatened if those with the power to disturb it are overruled in the decision process. Thus the GA would be a poor coordination device and indeed has been largely irrelevant in security affairs throughout the 1990s.

Second, the process by which compromises in elite cartels are achieved is generally secretive rather than transparent. Public deliberation manifests heterogeneity and commits actors to take stands from which it is costly to recede. For the most part, the public record of SC meetings is uninformative about true motivations actors have as most compromises are achieved in unrecorded negotiations. Extensive public debate is uncommon and counterproductive, as commented on in the section on deliberation.

Third, elite cartels usually embrace principles of subsidiarity or segmental authority.[88] Delegating discretion to influential actors within their own domain helps preserve satisfaction with the status quo. It has become the modal option for the SC to de facto delegate the authority to use force to regional organizations (for example, NATO, Economic Community of West African States) or regional powers (for example, United States, Australia). This creates serious problems of accountability and has questionable legal foundations in the Charter.[89] It fits, however, within the purpose of an elite pact.

Although the elite pact's primary focus is to define instances of appropriate uses of power by the United States and hence to identify the circumstances under which other states may legitimately cooperate with the United States, it may also confer judgments on the use of force by regional powers. For instance, SC approval of Australia's intervention in East-Timor signals that this use of force is legitimate in that it should not trigger a coordinated response by other states. In the absence of such an assurance, a military intervention that enhances peace and security in the region may be more difficult to undertake for Australia in that the risks may be less clear to the

government and the public. In this sense, the SC may enhance the production of public goods, although through a different mechanism than discussed in the previous section. It provides a political judgment on whether a particular use of force is sufficiently in the "public interest" such that it can be supported rather than challenged.

Although the SC's institutional characteristics reflect the general properties of an elite pact well, one can surely think of alternative and perhaps more efficient designs to tackle the coordination problem. For example, it may not be obvious why states would rely on a formal institution rather than a club-based organization with less explicit decision-making procedures, such as the Group of 7 (G-7) or the Concert of Europe. First, formal institutions help solve time-inconsistency problems that sometimes impede mutually beneficial resolutions of distributional conflicts.[90] A formal SC authorization for military action raises the cost for China or Russia to withdraw from endorsing it because everyone knows they had the opportunity to veto the action. These costs may be lower in a club-based organization. Second, fixed decision-making procedures help clarify expectations and thus reduce uncertainties that may impede compromises to distributive conflicts. Third, the institutional context of the UN facilitates the symbolic function that the SC performs for domestic publics. Finally, negotiating an entirely new elite pact is difficult. The fact that the SC is substantively charged with authorizing force and had some experience with doing so may help explain the pull toward the institution.

Norm Stability

Constructivists have criticized rationalist approaches for being ontologically inclined to revisionism and therefore unable to adequately explain the persistence of norms, since self-interested actors do not value the norms themselves, just the benefits directly accruing from them. Instead, constructivists typically assume that actors internalize social norms. The concept of internalization is borrowed from the developmental and social psychology literature, where it is used to characterize the process by which humans absorb norms and values present in their social environment to develop standards for appropriate behavior. Once these standards are internalized, actors do not reevaluate adherence to them when choosing between alternative courses of action. There are both good theoretical and empirical reasons to suspect that internalization is not a prominent source of norm stability in the case under investigation. Theoretically, it is not at all obvious how the internalization concept extends to state actors, especially when these are making decisions regarding behavior than can hardly be described as habitual: the use of military force. Empirically, there are examples aplenty where state actors consciously and explicitly evaluated the trade-off between the legitimacy benefits of the SC and the costs of compromise necessary to obtain those benefits.[91] This suggests a different thought process than internalization would.

That internalization is unlikely does imply that norm stability is a concern. In the elite pact model, a stable norm reflects a self-enforcing equilibrium. This indeed requires that governments must find that their expected utility of abiding by the norm exceeds their utility from acting otherwise. Whether the norm is self-enforcing depends at least partly on the behavior of the institution itself. If the SC conforms to the expectations of actors regarding its function, the legitimacy beliefs on which its authority is based are reinforced. If, however, the SC defies those expectations, these beliefs are undermined. If the behavior of the SC reinforces the social norm, more actors in more situations perceive it to be in their interest to adhere to it. If the behavior of the SC undermines the social norm, fewer actors in fewer situations support it. This self-undermining process can reach a critical level at which the equilibrium is no longer self-enforcing and institutional change should follow. This point is consistent with the common assumption that regimes weaken when actual practice is inconsistent with the rules and norms that constitute the regime.[92]

Behavior associated with the SC reinforces the social norm if it contributes to keeping U.S. power in check while avoiding costly challenges and maintaining beneficial forms of global cooperation. It undermines the social norm if it either fails to provide an adequate check on U.S. power or leads to costly challenges. In observing a SC authorization for the use of force, one should not observe meaningful challenges to the United States by other states. If important states would retaliate even after the United States obtains SC authorization, the United States may be less inclined to follow the social norm in future instances. In addition, the decision to authorize force cannot merely be a rubber stamp. If those states that are delegated the responsibilities to constrain U.S. power give too much leeway, SC decisions lose their utility to other states. This implies that to maintain the equilibrium it will sometimes be necessary for permanent members to defend the interests of important states not represented in the Council. If they would fail to do so, the social norm would be of little use to these states and they might challenge it.

Besides the Persian Gulf War, other reinforcing examples include the Haitian and Somalian invasions, and the various resolutions on Bosnia. These cases may not have been resolved in a manner that is satisfactory from a moral, legal, or efficiency standpoint, but they did not result in an overextension of U.S. power or in costly challenges against its power, despite disagreements between states over the proper courses of action.

If the United States uses force in the absence of SC agreement, one should see countermeasures that are costly to the United States. If states fail to react, more people within the United States will believe that a lack of SC authorization carries no serious consequences and thus fewer believe that the social norm should be adhered to. To other states, the utility of the SC as an institution to limit power is diminished if the United States can engage in unpunished transgressions. Moreover, states should seek to punish other states that cooperate with the United States in the absence of SC authorization.

The Kosovo intervention presents the first important deviation from the norm. The decision by the United States and its NATO allies to intervene forcefully without SC authorization did elicit protest from various sources, but it did not trigger an extensive coordinated response. There were two circumstances that modify the weakening implications for the SC somewhat, though not entirely. First, the action was executed by NATO, which implied some checks to U.S. power. Of course, if going through NATO would establish itself as an easier and risk-free alternative strategy the social norm that grants the SC authority is undermined. Second, although there was no explicit SC authorization to use force, there were two previous resolutions that at least implied a forceful response.[93] More importantly, the SC adopted new resolutions that defined an extensive role for the UN once the fighting ended.[94] The United States and its allies were willing to delegate authority to the UN in implementing their victory, thus alleviating fears of overextension somewhat. Nevertheless, the Kosovo episode should at least have had the consequence that fewer people in fewer situations believe that the absence of SC authorization for an intervention carries great costs.

The decision by the Bush administration in 2003 to invade Iraq in the absence of SC authorization presents a more serious challenge. A large number of countries clearly perceived the U.S.-led intervention as a transgression of acceptable limits to U.S. power. Failure to generate a coordinated response should seriously weaken the legitimacy of the SC. It leads U.S. decision makers to perceive that the benefit of SC authorization for future interventions is minor. Moreover, it should reduce the belief among states that the SC can provide a credible check on U.S. power, perhaps inducing these states to resort to other means.

The early evidence is that challenging behavior is moderate. Pape has referred to it as "soft balancing," meaning that it relies on recalcitrance in international institutions, the use of economic leverage, and diplomatic efforts to frustrate American intentions.[95] The leaders of several European countries strongly opposed to the military action announced their intentions to increase military spending, strengthen military cooperation within Europe, and strengthen military ties with China.[96] Several states, most notably India and Japan, have made troop contributions conditional on SC resolutions. There is also some evidence that states who perceived the U.S. action as a transgression sought to "punish" states that cooperated in the absence of SC authorization. For instance, French President Jacques Chirac said the East European leaders who signed letters of support for the U.S. position on Iraq had "missed an opportunity to shut up," adding that he "felt they acted frivolously because entry into the European Union implies a minimum of understanding for the others."[97] These actions should reinforce beliefs that there are some costs associated with acting and cooperating without SC authorization. While it is too early to draw more definitive conclusions, the actions should also reinforce beliefs that, at least in the short run, the costs from disobeying the norm are not prohibitively large.

Conclusions

The ability of the SC to successfully restrain the United States is at the heart of its aptitude to play a legitimizing role in international politics. In this conception, a legitimate exercise of power abides by certain accepted limits. SC authorization signals the observance of these limits, which are defined not by legal, moral, or efficiency standards, but by an undemocratic political process that seeks to achieve compromise among elite actors. It is important to understand that although the role of the SC depends entirely on the configuration of state interests, this fact does not make the institution epiphenomenal. There are many potential equilibria and convergence on a particular (semicooperative) equilibrium has important implications. This is true even if the restraint on the exercise of power is limited to raising the cost of unilateralism.

Theoretically, this conception of legitimacy corresponds best to those classical realists who did not consider power and legitimacy to be antithetical, but complementary.[98] Legitimacy, these theorists argued, helps convert power into authority. Authority is a much cheaper regulatory device than the constant exercise of coercion. Therefore, attempts to legitimize power are a persistent feature of political life, even in the anarchical global arena. However, these realists had little faith in legalities or moral values as the source for legitimacy. Instead, the process of legitimation primarily involves the acquisition of political judgments about the proper way in which the exercise of power ought to be limited. As Claude wrote in 1966: "[T]he process of legitimization is ultimately a political phenomenon, a crystallization of judgment that may be influenced but is unlikely to be wholly determined by legal norms and moral principles."[99] This statement contrasts sharply with the view that IOs derive their legitimacy precisely from their ability to appear depoliticized. One way of reconciling these views is that the latter focuses mostly on the role of IOs as bureaucracies or courts, whereas the first stresses their political arena role. The UN encompasses both roles, but the ability of the SC to legitimize the use of force stems from its function as a political meeting place. This political arena function of IOs has hitherto received too little attention in the theoretical literature.

The implications of this argument differ in important ways from alternative accounts. The common claim among scholars of international law that the SC threatens to lose its legitimacy if it adopts resolutions that do not fit a broader legal framework depends strongly on the (usually implicit) assumption that its legitimacy depends primarily on its ability to fulfill the role of legal adjudicator. This is the premise of Glennon's argument that the SC was a "grand attempt to subject the use of force to the rule of law," which has "fallen victim to geopolitical forces too strong for a legalist institution to withstand."[100] If the SC's legitimacy does not critically depend on its functioning as a guardian of a legal system, as I argue

here, the legal consistency of SC resolutions should not per se be of great consequence to the legitimacy of the institution.[101]

Others claim that the gravest threat to the legitimacy of the SC is that a few countries dominate it and that its procedures are opaque and unfair.[102] If demand for proper procedures were the motivating factor behind the SC's authority, secretive backroom deals among the great powers would be considered illegitimate. Such deals are part of the elite pact account of legitimacy. This does not imply that actors view the procedural aspects of elite politics as desirable per se, but that these are useful to the higher purpose of stability. This situation suggests that successful reforms to make the SC more transparent may actually have adverse effects in that powerful states may flee the forum. In the public goods rationale, the legitimacy of the SC depends critically on preventing free riding and effectiveness in producing global public goods. This is not necessarily the primary concern in the elite-pact rationale, although the proper functioning of the elite pact increases public good production in comparison to uncooperative equilibria. Nevertheless, the failures of the SC in Rwanda and other places and the failure of the United States to meet its peacekeeping burden may have diminished esteem for the institution, but these failures appear to have had little effect on the belief that the SC is the proper authority to legitimize force.

The conclusion from this study should not be that states are not concerned with legal and moral principles or global public goods, but that the existing and persistent belief that the SC is the most desirable institution to approve the use of force cannot be explained persuasively from the assumption that states do. Legitimacy that relies on the effectiveness of an institution to resolve a particular dilemma is often thought to be inherently unstable. For example, it depends on outcomes that could be caused by a multitude of factors, not just the decisions of the institution. I agree that if the SC's legitimacy were based on a convergence of opinions on its normative properties, its legitimacy would be more stable than it is today. However, such agreement does not exist and is unlikely to emerge in the near future. The collective legitimation function of the UN helps shape state behavior because state officials have made it important by their actions and statements.[103] Those actions and statements could also undermine the Council's legitimacy.

REFERENCES

Abbot, Kenneth, and Duncan Snidal. 1998. Why States Act Through Formal International Organizations. *Journal of Conflict Resolution* 42 (1):3–32.

Alvarez, Jose E. 1995. The Once and Future Security Council. *The Washington Quarterly* (spring): 3–20.

Andeweg, Rudy B. 2000. Consociational Democracy. *Annual Review of Political Science* 3: 509–36.

Bailey, Sidney D., and Sam Daws. 1998. *The Procedure of the UN Security Council.* 3d ed. Oxford: Clarendon Press.

Baker, James A. III 1995. *The Politics of Diplomacy: Revolution, War and Peace 1989–1992.* New York: Putnam's Sons.

Barnett, Michael N. 1997. Bringing in the New World Order: Liberalism, Legitimacy, and the United Nations. *World Politics* 49 (4):526–51.

Barnett, Michael N., and Martha Finnemore. 1999. The Politics, Power, and Pathologies of International Organizations. *International Organization* 53 (4):699–732.

Bennett, Andrew, and Joseph Lepgold. 1993. Reinventing Collective Security after the Cold War and the Gulf Conflict. *Political Science Quarterly* 108 (2):213–237.

Bennett, Andrew, Joseph Lepgold, and Danny Unger. 1994. Burden-Sharing in the Persian Gulf War. *International Organization* 48 (1):39–75.

Blokker, Niels. 2000. Is the Authorization Authorized? Powers and Practice of the UN Security Council to Authorize the Use of Force by 'Coalitions of the Able and Willing.' *European Journal of International Law* 11 (3): 541–68.

Bobrow, Davis B., and Mark A. Boyer. 1997. Maintaining System Stability: Contributions to Peacekeeping Operations. *Journal of Conflict Resolution* 41 (6):723–48.

Buchanan, Allen, and Robert O. Keohane. 2004. The Preventive Use of Force: A Cosmopolitan Institutional Proposal. *Ethics and International Affairs* 18 (1):1–23.

Burley, Anne-Marie, and Walter Mattli. 1993. Europe Before the Court: A Political Theory of Legal Integration. *International Organization* 47 (1):41–76.

Caron, David C. 1993. The Legitimacy of the Collective Authority of the Security Council. *American Journal of International Law* 87 (4):552–88.

Christopher, Warren. 1998. *In the Stream of History: Shaping Foreign Policy for a New Era.* Stanford, Calif.: Stanford University Press.

Claude, Inis L. 1964. *Swords into Plowshares: The Problems and Progress of International Organization.* 3d ed. New York: Random House.

———. 1966. Collective Legitimation as a Political Function of the United Nations. *International Organization* 20 (3):367–79.

Coleman, Katharina P. 2004. States, International Organizations, and Legitimacy: The Role of International Organizations in Contemporary Peace Enforcement Operations. Ph.D. diss., Princeton University, Princeton, N.J.

Daalder, Ivo H., and Michael E. O'Hanlon. 2000. *Winning Ugly: NATO's War to Save Kosovo.* Washington, D.C.: Brookings Institution.

Downs, George, and Keisuke Iida, eds. 1994. *Collective Security Beyond the Cold War.* Ann Arbor: University of Michigan Press.

Doyle, Michael W., and Nicholas Sambanis. 2000. International Peacebuilding: A Theoretical and Quantitative Analysis, *American Political Science Review* 94 (4):779–801.

Drezner, Daniel. 2003. Clubs, Neighborhoods, and Universes: The Governance of Global Finance. Unpublished manuscript, University of Chicago, Chicago.

Faksh, Mahmud A., and Ramzi F. Faris. 1993. The Saudi Conundrum: Squaring the Security-Stability Circle. *Third World Quarterly* 14 (2):277–94.

Farer, Tom. 2002. Beyond the Charter Frame: Unilateralism or Condominium Frame? *American Journal of International Law* 96 (2):359–64.

Franck, Thomas M. 1990. *The Power of Legitimacy Among Nations*. Oxford: Oxford University Press.

———. 1999. Sidelined in Kosovo? The United Nation's Demise Has Been Exaggerated. *Foreign Affairs* 78 (4):116–18.

———. 2001. Terrorism and the Right of Self-Defense. *American Journal of International Law* 95 (4):839–43.

Fravel, Taylor M. 1996. China's Attitude Toward U.N. Peacekeeping Operations Since 1989. *Asian Survey* 36 (11):1102–21.

Frederking, Brian. 2003. Constructing Post–Cold War Collective Security *American Political Science Review* 97 (3):363–78.

Freedman, Lawrence, and Efraim Karsh. 1993. *The Gulf Conflict, 1990–91: Diplomacy and War in the New World Order*. Princeton, N.J.: Princeton University Press.

Garrett, Geoffrey, and Barry Weingast. 1993. Ideas, Interests and Institutions: Constructing the European Community's Internal Market. In *Ideas and Foreign Policy: Beliefs, Institutions, and Political Change*, edited by Judith Goldstein and Robert O. Keohane, 173–206. Ithaca, N.Y.: Cornell University Press.

German Marshall Fund and Compagnia di San Paolo. 2003. *Transatlantic Trends 2003*. Washington, D.C.: German Marshall Fund of the United States.

Gibson, James L. 1989. Understandings of Justice: Institutional Legitimacy, Procedural Justice and Political Tolerance. *Law and Society Review* 23 (3):469–96.

Glennon, Michael J. 1999. The New Interventionism. *Foreign Affairs* 78 (3):2–7.

———. 2001. *Limits of Law, Prerogatives of Power: Intervention After Kosovo*. New York: Palgrave.

———. 2003. Why the Security Council Failed. *Foreign Affairs* 82 (3):16–35.

Gordon, Ruth. 1994. United Nations Intervention in Internal Conflicts: Iraq, Somalia, and Beyond. *Michigan Journal of International Law* 15(2):519–89.

Greif, Avner, and David Laitin. 2004. A Theory of Endogenous Institutional Change. *American Political Science Review* 98 (4):633–52.

Greif, Avner, Paul Milgrom, and Barry R. Weingast. 1994. Coordination, Commitment, and Enforcement: The Case of the Merchant Guild. *Journal of Political Economy* 102 (4):745–76.

Haas, Ernst B. 1983. Regime Decay: Conflict Management and International Organizations, 1945–1981. *International Organization* 37 (2):189–256.

Held, David. 1995. *Democracy and the Global Order: From the Modern State to Cosmopolitan Governance*. Cambridge: Polity Press.

Hoffmann, Stanley. 1998. *World Disorders: Troubled Peace in the Post–Cold War Era*. Lanham, Md.: Rowman & Littlefield.

Holsti, Ole. 2004. *Public Opinion and American Foreign Policy*. Ann Arbor: University of Michigan Press.

Hurd, Ian. 1997. Security Council Reform: Informal Membership and Practice. In *The Once and Future Security Council*, edited by Bruce Russett and Ian Hurd, 135–52, New York: St. Martin's Press.

———. 1999. Legitimacy and Authority in International Politics. *International Organization* 53 (2):379–408.

———. 2002. Legitimacy, Power, and the Symbolic Life of the UN Security Council. *Global Governance* 8 (1):35–51.

———. 2003. Stayin' Alive: The Rumours of the UN's Death Have Been Exaggerated: Too Legit to Quit. *Foreign Affairs* 82 (4):204–5.

Ikenberry, John. 2001. *After Victory*. Princeton, N.J.: Princeton University Press.

Jakobsen, Peter Viggo. 2002. The Transformation of United Nations Peace Operations in the 1990s. *Cooperation and Conflict* 37 (3):267–82.

Jervis, Robert. 1985. From Balance to Concert: A Study of International Security Cooperation. *World Politics* 38 (1):58–79.

Johnstone, Ian. 2003. Security Council Deliberations: The Power of the Better Argument. *European Journal of International Law* 14 (3): 437–80.

Kelemen, R. Daniel. 2001. The Limits of Judicial Power: Trade-Environment Disputes in the GATT/ WTO and the EU *Comparative Political Studies* 34 (6):622–50.

Keohane, Robert O., and Joseph S. Nye Jr. 2001. Democracy, Accountability, and Global Governance. Politics Research Group Working Paper 01–04. Cambridge, Mass.: Harvard University.

Khanna, Jyoti, Todd Sandler, and Hirofumi Shimizu. 1998. Sharing the Financial Burden for U.N. and NATO Peacekeeping, 1976–1996. *The Journal of Conflict Resolution* 42 (2): 176–95.

Khong, Yuen Foong. 1992. *Analogies at War*. Princeton, N.J.: Princeton University Press.

Kirgis, Frederic L. 1995. The Security Council's First Fifty Years. *The American Journal of International Law* 89 (3):506–39.

Krasner, Stephen D. 1982. Structural Causes and Regime Consequences: Regimes as Intervening Variables. *International Organization* 36 (2): 185–205.

Krauthammer, Charles. 1990/1991. The Unipolar Moment. *Foreign Affairs* 70 (1):5–12.

Krishnasamy, Kabilan. 2003. The Paradox of India's Peacekeeping. *Contemporary South Asia* 12 (2):263–64.

Kull. Steven. 2002. Public Attitudes Towards Multilateralism. In *Multilateralism and U.S. Foreign Policy*, edited by Stewart Patrick and Shepard Forman, 99–120. London: Lynne Rienner.

Lefever, Ernest W. 1993. Reining in the U.N.: Mistaking the Instrument for the Actor. *Foreign Affairs* 72 (3):17–20.

Lesch, Ann M. 1991. Contrasting Reactions to the Persian Gulf Crisis: Egypt, Syria, Jordan, and the Palestinians. *Middle East Journal* 45 (1): 30–50.

Lewis, David. 1969. *Convention, A Philosophical Study*. Cambridge, Mass.: Harvard University Press.

Lijphart, Arend. 1969. Consociational Democracy. *World Politics* 21 (2):207–25.

Luck, Edward C. 2002. The United States, International Organizations, and the Quest for Legitimacy. In: *Multilateralism and U.S. Foreign Policy*, edited by Stewart Patrick and Shepard Forman, 47–74, London: Lynne Rienner.

———. 2003. Reforming the United Nations: Lessons from a History in Progress. International Relations Studies and the United Nations Occasional Paper 2003:1. Waterloo, Canada: Academic Council on the United Nations System.

Malone, David M. 1998. *Decision-Making in the UN Security Council: The Case of Haiti, 1990–1997*. New York: Oxford University Press.

Martin, Lisa L. 1992. Interests, Power, and Multilateralism. *International Organization* 46 (4): 765–92.

———. 2003. Distribution, Information, and Delegation to International Organizations: The Case of IMF Conditionality. Unpublished manuscript, Harvard University, Cambridge, Mass.

Morgenthau, Hans. 1954. The United Nations and the Revision of the Charter. *Review of Politics* 16 (1):3–21.

Morrow, James D. 1994. Modeling the Forms of International Cooperation: Distribution Versus Information. *International Organization* 48 (3):387–423.

Murphy, John F. 1997. Force and Arms. In *The United Nations and International Law*, edited by Christopher C. Joyner, 97–130. Cambridge: Cambridge University Press.

Nielson, Daniel, and Michael Tierney. 2003. Delegation to International Organizations: Agency Theory and World Bank Environmental Reform. *International Organization* 57 (2): 241–76.

Program on International Policy Attitudes (PIPA). 2003a. PIPA Knowledge Networks Poll: Americans on Iraq and the UN Inspections I, 21–26 January 2003.

PIPA. 2003b. PIPA Knowledge Networks Poll: Americans on Iraq and the UN Inspections II, 21 February 2003.

Risse, Thomas. 2000. "Let's Argue!": Communicative Action in World Politics. *International Organization* 54 (1):1–40.

Rosecrance, Richard. 1992. A New Concert of Powers. *Foreign Affairs* 71 (2):64–82.

Ruggie, John Gerard. 1993. Multilateralism: The Anatomy of an Institution. In *Multilateralism Matters*, edited by John G. Ruggie, 3–48. New York: Columbia University Press.

Russett, Bruce, and James Sutterlin. 1991. The UN in a New World Order. *Foreign Affairs* 70 (2): 69–83.

Rustow, Dankwart. 1970. Transitions to Democracy: Toward a Dynamic Model. *Comparative Politics* 2 (3):337–63.

Sandholtz, Wayne, and Alec Stone Sweet. 2004. Law, Politics and International Governance In *The Politics of International Law*, edited by Christian Reus-Smit, 238–71. Cambridge: Cambridge University Press.

Schachter, Oscar. 1989. Self-Defense and the Rule of Law. *American Journal of International Law* 83(2):259–77.

Schmitz, Hans Peter, and Kathryn Sikkink. 2002. International Human Rights. In *Handbook of International Relations*, edited by Walter Carlsnaes, Thomas Risse-Kappen, and Beth A. Simmons, 517–37, London: Sage Publications.

Shimizu, Hirofumi, and Todd Sandler. 2002. Peacekeeping and Burden-Sharing, 1994–2000. *Journal of Peace Research* 39 (6):651–68.

Slaughter, Anne-Marie. 1995. International Law in a World of Liberal States. *The European Journal of International Law* 6 (4):503–38.

———. 2003. Misreading the Record. *Foreign Affairs* 82 (4):202–4.

Thompson, Alexander. 2004. Understanding IO Legitimation. Unpublished paper, Ohio State University, Columbus.

Tsebelis. George. 1990. *Nested Games: Rational Choice in Comparative Politics*. Berkeley: University of California Press.

Urquhart, Brian. 1991. Learning from the Gulf. *New York Review of Books* 38 (5):34–37.

Voeten, Erik. 2001. Outside Options and the Logic of Security Council Action. *American Political Science Review* 95 (4):845–58.

Weber, Max. 1978. The Types of Legitimate Domination. In *Economy and Society: An Outline of Interpretive Sociology*, edited by Guenther Roth and Claus Wittich, 212–301. Berkeley: University of California Press.

Weingast, Barry. 1997. The Political Foundations of Democracy and the Rule of Law. *American Political Science Review* 91 (2):245–63.

Weingast, Barry, and William J. Marshall. 1988. The Industrial Organization of Congress; or, Why Legislatures, like Firms, Are Not Organized as Markets. *Journal of Political Economy* 96 (1):132–63.

Wendt, Alexander. 1999. *Social Theory of International Politics*. Cambridge: Cambridge University Press.

Wood, Michael. 1996. Security Council Working Methods and Procedure: Recent Developments. *International and Comparative Law Quarterly* 45 (1):150–61.

Woods, Ngaire. 1999. Good Governance in International Organizations. *Global Governance* 5 (1):39–61.

Young, H. Peyton. 1993. The Evolution of Conventions. *Econometrica* 61 (1):57–84.

NOTES

1. Claude 1966, 367.
2. Claude 1966, 373.
3. Franck 1990, 42.
4. See especially Barnett and Finnemore 1999.
5. Hoffmann 1998, 179.
6. UN Charter, Article 2(4).
7. SC Resolution 1373, 28 September 2001.
8. Schachter 1989.
9. UN Charter, Article 39.
10. Bailey and Daws 1998, 271.
11. Morgenthau 1954, 11.
12. Haas 1983.

13. Cited in Luck 2002, 63.
14. Luck 2002, 64.
15. Baker 1995, 278.
16. See SC Resolution 502, 3 April 1982; SC Resolution 598, 20 July 1987; and Bailey and Daws 1998, 272.
17. Bailey and Daws 1998, 271.
18. Jakobsen 2002.
19. Ibid.
20. Voeten 2001.
21. See Christopher 1998.
22. Malone 1998.
23. Coleman 2004.
24. Krishnasamy 2003.
25. Law Concerning Cooperation for United Nations Peacekeeping Operations and Other Operations (the International Peace Cooperation Law) originally passed in June 1992. For other examples, see Hurd 1999.
26. PIPA 2003a. Poll conducted among 1,063 American adults, margin of error +/–3 percent. The order of the questions was randomized.
27. Kull 2002.
28. See German Marshall Fund and Compagnia di San Paolo 2003; and Thompson 2004.
29. Daalder and O'Hanlon 2000, 218–19.
30. See *New York Times*, 12 June 1998, A1.
31. Ikenberry 2001. Accordingly, Ikenberry focuses on NATO and GATT/WTO.
32. Nielson and Tierney 2003.
33. Martin 2003.
34. See Caron 1993; and Hurd 1999.
35. Weber 1978.
36. Barnett and Finnemore 1999, 708.
37. Kelemen 2001.
38. Burley and Mattli 1993.
39. See Alvarez 1995; Farer 2002; Glennon 2001; and Kirgis 1995.
40. Schachter 1989.
41. Farer 2002, 359.
42. See SC Resolution 688, 5 April 1991; SC Resolution 794, 3 December 1992; and SC Resolution 940, 31 July 1994.
43. Kirgis 1995, 517. See also Gordon 1994.

44. See Alvarez 1995; Glennon 2001; and Kirgis 1995.
45. Glennon 1999 and 2001.
46. Franck 1999.
47. Johnstone 2003.
48. Frederking 2003.
49. See Johnstone 2003; and Risse 2000.
50. See Bailey and Daws 1998; Woods 1999; and Wood 1996.
51. Colin Powell, "Remarks to the United Nations Security Council," New York City, 5 February 2003.
52. Gibson 1989.
53. Woods 1999.
54. Blokker 2000.
55. According to PIPA 2003b, 55 percent thought that the United States does have that right.
56. German Marshall Fund and Compagnia di San Paolo 2003.
57. Ibid.
58. Luck 2003.
59. See Schmitz and Sikkink 2002, 521; and Slaughter 1995.
60. Jakobsen 2002.
61. Bennett, Lepgold, and Unger 1994.
62. Martin 1992, 773.
63. Abbott and Snidal 1998.
64. See <http://www.globalpolicy.org/finance/tables/core/un-us-03.htm>. Accessed 10 March 2005.
65. In the 2000–2002 period, yearly peacekeeping budgets were around $2.6 billion.
66. Based on data in Shimizu and Sandler 2002.
67. Doyle and Sambanis 2000.
68. Rosecrance 1992.
69. Jervis 1985. Other realists believe that concerts were mostly epiphenomenal. See Downs and Iida 1994.
70. Jervis 1985, 69.
71. Ikenberry 2001.
72. Greif, Milgrom, and Weingast 1994.
73. Sovereign in Weingast's case.
74. Holsti 2004.
75. Weber 1978.
76. See Barnett 1997; and Jakobsen 2002.

77. Weingast 1997. See also Rustow 1970.
78. Fravel 1996.
79. See Faksh and Faris 1993; and Lesch 1991.
80. Namely through the previously mentioned Article 51 procedure.
81. Baker 1995, 315. Also cited in Thompson 2004.
82. Baker 1995, 279.
83. See, for example, the discussions in Bennett and Lepgold 1993; Russett and Sutterlin 1991; and Urquhart 1991.
84. Khong 1992.
85. See Krauthammer 1990/1991; and Lefever 1993.
86. 10 percent disagreed and 3 percent answered "don't know." Poll executed by Gallup on 3–4 December 1992.
87. Andeweg 2000.
88. Ibid.
89. Blokker 2000.
90. Weingast and Marshall 1988.
91. For example, Voeten 2001.

92. Krasner 1982.
93. See SC Resolution 1199, 23 September 1998; and SC Resolution 1203, 24 October 1998.
94. In particular, see SC Resolution 1239, 14 May 1999; and SC Resolution 1244, 10 June 1999.
95. *Boston Globe*, 23 April 2003, H1.
96. Joint Declaration Meeting of the Heads of State and Government of Germany, France, Luxembourg and Belgium on European Defense, Brussels, 29 April 2003.
97. *International Herald Tribune*, 19 February 2003, 3.
98. On the UN see: Claude 1964, 1966; and Morgenthau 1954, 10–11. Unfortunately, contemporary Realists have mostly ignored legitimacy. See Barnett 1997, 529.
99. Claude 1966, 369.
100. Glennon 2003, 16.
101. Slaughter 2003; and Hurd 2003 make similar arguments in response to Glennon.
102. Caron 1993.
103. See also Claude 1966, 543.

ANDREW MORAVCSIK

A TOO PERFECT UNION?: WHY EUROPE SAID "NO"

The people of France and the Netherlands have spoken. As a result of their referendums this spring, the European Union constitution is dead, as is Turkish membership in the EU, and progress in areas from services deregulation to Balkan enlargement will now be much more difficult. Yet for the chattering classes the outcome was an opportunity to repolish long-held positions. In the face of implacable opposition to Turkish membership, *The Economist* blithely in-terpreted the rejection of a proposed EU constitution as evidence that Europe has gone too far, too fast—except, of course, on enlargement. Oxford's Timothy Garton Ash, a perennial optimist about the reconciliation of Britain's transatlantic and European vocations, espied another promising moment for Blairite diplomacy. The court philosopher of continental social democracy, Jürgen Habermas, called on European leaders (read: his former student, German Foreign Minister Joschka Fischer) to recapture the "idealism of 1968" by leading a leftist movement against neoliberal US hegemony. With quintessentially French

From *Current History* 104, no. 685 (November 2005): 355–59.

misanthropy, Serge July of *Libération* accused French politicians of opportunism and French voters of racism. Across the Atlantic, *Weekly Standard* editor Bill Kristol, undeterred by the massive protest vote against European economic reform, called for rejection of the welfare state, open borders to immigration, and an embrace of America.

It is time to view Europe as it really is. Far from demonstrating that the European Union is in decline or disarray, the constitutional crisis demonstrates its essential stability and legitimacy. The central error of the European constitutional framers was one of style and symbolism rather than substance. The constitution contained a set of modest reforms, very much in line with European popular preferences. Yet European leaders upset the emerging pragmatic settlement by dressing up the reforms as a grand scheme for constitutional revision and popular democratization of the EU.

Looking back in 50 years, historians will not see this year's referendums as the end of the EU— or as the beginning of the end. The union remains the most successful experiment in political institution building since World War II. Historians will see instead the last gasp of idealistic European federalism born in the mid-1940s, symbolized by the phrase "ever closer union" and aimed at establishing a United States of Europe. It is time to recognize that the EU can neither aspire to replace nation states nor seek democratic legitimacy in the same way nations do. The current EU constitutional settlement, which has defined a stable balance between Brussels and national capitals and democratic legitimacy through indirect accountability and extensive checks and balances, is here to stay. To see why this is so, we must understand the nature of the current constitutional compromise, the reasons European leaders called it into question, and the deeper lessons this teaches us about the limits of European integration.

Just Say No

Voting patterns in the referendums were a reflection of three related motivations that have domi-

nated every EU election in history. First is ideological extremism. The center supported Europe while the extreme right and left, which now account for almost one-third of the French and Dutch electorates, voted "no." Second is protest voting against unpopular governments. Third, and most important, is a reaction against the insecurity felt by poorer Europeans. Whereas business, the educated elite, and wealthier Europeans favored the constitution, those fearful of unemployment, labor market reform, globalization, privatization, and the consolidation of the welfare state opposed it. Today these concerns dovetail with the perceived economic and cultural threat posed by Muslim immigration.

This type of disaffection is the primary political problem for European governments today, since it is directed both against poor economic performance and against reform measures designed to improve it. As *Newsweek*'s Fareed Zakaria has observed, the tragedy is that "Europe needs more of what's producing populist paranoia: economic reform to survive in an era of economic competition, young immigrants to sustain its social market, and a more strategic relationship with the Muslim world, which would be dramatically enhanced by Turkish membership in the EU."

Forgotten in the electoral chaos this spring was the document itself. The constitution is, after all, a conservative text containing incremental improvements that consolidate EU developments of the past 20 years. The "no" campaigns conceded the desirability of the modest reforms from the start—including appointment of a foreign minister, formulation of a stronger anti-crime policy, and streamlining of voting procedures. Such changes are popular, not least in France, which proposed most of them. One is forced to conclude that the constitution became controversial not because its content was objectionable, but because the content was so innocuous that citizens saw a chance to cast an inexpensive protest vote.

What were they protesting against? Here, too, the referendums cannot be viewed as plebiscites directed at the EU's policies. Although the EU is associated, through its advisory "Lisbon process," with labor market and welfare reform, these matters remain firmly within the competence of the member states. The EU's activities as a whole, while they include oversight of state subsidies and trade policy, may just as reasonably be seen as part of a European effort to manage globalization rather than promote it. Opponents made occasional mention of EU policies not contained in the constitution, such as the recent enlargement to 25 members, the introduction of the euro, the deregulation of electricity, and Turkish accession. Yet only the last of these seems to have swayed many voters, and they seem to have been unaware that free migration has been ruled out even before negotiations begin.

So what lesson should the EU take away? The relative lack of direct criticism of the constitution, the lack of fundamental objections to EU policies, and, above all, the stunning lack of positive proposals for reform are striking evidence of the underlying stability of the EU system. The 16 years since the fall of the Berlin Wall have been, after all, the most successful period in EU history. The single market, the euro, and a nascent European foreign and defense policy came into being. EU enlargement was carried out with surprisingly little disruption in existing member states, and proved the most cost-effective Western instrument for advancing global democracy and security. In sum, notwithstanding the rejection of the proposed charter, the EU appears to have quietly reached a stable constitutional settlement.

Fixing the Unbroken

What is this settlement? The EU is now preeminent in trade, agriculture, fishing, eurozone monetary policy, and some business regulation, and helps to coordinate cooperation in foreign policy. Contrary to statistics one often reads, this amounts to only about 20 percent of European regulation and legislation. Most areas of greatest public concern—taxes, health, pensions, education, crime, infrastructure, defense,

and immigration—remain firmly national. With a tax base one-fiftieth the size of the member states', an administration smaller than that of a small city, no police force or army, and a narrow legal mandate, the EU will never encompass these fiscally and administratively demanding tasks.

There is no new *grand projet*, akin to the single market of the 1980s or the single currency of the 1990s, to justify change. In 18 months of deliberation, the constitutional convention devoted only two days to the expansion of EU competencies. European health, pension, fiscal, and education policies have little support, while a US-style military buildup exceeds Europe's means and insults its "civilian power" ideals. There was always less to the constitution than both its proponents and its detractors proclaimed.

Many believe that a European defense independent of the United States poses an imminent threat to US interests. Of course, it is true that if the United States were again to attempt an operation on the scale of Iraq with so little substantive justification or multilateral legitimation, European nations would be uniformly opposed. (Even the British government has already declared that it does not see any useful military options for regime change in Iran.) But another Iraq is an unlikely possibility, given the evident costs of that imbroglio; the United States is militarily incapable of repeating this adventure at the current time. More important is the fact that the United States and the EU have agreed on every other major use of force since the 1989 Gulf War. More than 100,000 European troops are currently stationed out of their home countries, most involved in operations that involve the United States.

The ambition to form a European Union military or diplomatic superpower with a principal mission of opposing American "hyperpower" is little more than—and always was little more than—idle talk. Only the combination of ignorance and bias regarding the EU that is so uniquely concentrated among self-reinforcing groups of US neoconservatives and British Euroskeptics could construe the EU as a military or geopolitical threat. As recently as a year ago, many conservatives pleaded with the Bush administration to oppose the EU constitution, encourage British withdrawal, and insist on the unconditional predominance of NATO. With the recent European trips by Secretary of State Condoleezza Rice and President George W. Bush, these demands for an aggressive policy toward Europe have been definitively rebuffed.

Consider also European social policy, of which we heard so much in the referendum campaigns. What concrete EU policies should this imply? Blocking sensible efforts to reform the welfare state for long-term sustainability is shortsighted. While many studies show that a division of labor between the new and old members of the EU will generate growth, there is little evidence of a regulatory or fiscal "race to the bottom" driven by the EU, and plenty of room remains for social policy at the national level. The neoliberal "Anglo-Saxon" threat is a myth. Britain is building up its welfare state faster than any of its partners, based partly on a Scandinavian model. Indeed, with continental liberalization and British social democratization, Europe's social systems are converging—through the pressure of national politics, not as the result of some EU social policy pipe dream.

A similar constitutional compromise has emerged with regard to institutions. Although Anglo-American Euroskeptics have sought to resurrect the bogeyman of a Brussels superstate headed by the European Commission, treaty changes since 1970 have consistently moved Europe in the opposite direction. They have increased the power of the council of ministers (favored by France and Britain, particularly for matters outside the economic core) and the directly elected European parliament (favored by Germany) at the expense of the technocratic commission.

The proposed constitution sought to marginally improve the EU's efficiency and transparency while retaining its basic structure. All of this is the sensible stuff policy wonks love and publics generally support. The constitution called for expanding the role of the directly elected European parliament in EU legislation (termed "codecision" in Brussels-speak), giving national parliaments an advisory and gate keeping role, abolishing the rotating presidency, adjusting voting weights to represent large countries more fairly, and centralizing foreign policy coordination in a foreign minister. The proposal was a multinational constitutional compromise that attended to the interests of large and small countries, left and right parties, and Europhile and Euroskeptic tendencies.

The reforms enjoyed broad support among member states, and none met a serious challenge in the referendum debates. The biggest change—creation of a European foreign minister empowered to recommend, though not impose, a more coordinated foreign policy—enjoys 70 percent approval across Europe. And recognizing the EU as it is, the constitution struck the classic idealist phrase "ever closer union" from the Treaty of Rome, and substituted the more balanced "unity in diversity."

Undone by Idealism

So it was not the substance of the emerging constitutional settlement that triggered opposition. The objectionable aspect was its form: an idealistic constitution. Since the 1970s, lawyers have regarded the 1957 Treaty of Rome as a de facto constitution. The new document was an unnecessary public relations exercise based on the seemingly intuitive, but in fact peculiar, notion that democratization and the European ideal could legitimate the EU. In the wake of the Nice and Amsterdam treaties, which consolidated the union, Euro-enthusiast scholars, politicians, and commentators have argued that the EU is unpopular primarily because it is secretive, complex, unaccountable, and distant from the public—in sum, because it suffers from a "democratic deficit." Fischer, the German foreign minister, gave the idea of constitutional legitimation a big push with his celebrated lecture on the ultimate goal of integration at Humboldt University in 2000. But like the other European leaders who jumped on his band-wagon, Fischer, while ostensibly transcending a narrow, national discourse, was in fact framing the argument in a familiar domestic manner: in his case 1968-style German anti-nationalism.

The idea was to legitimate the EU not through trade, economic growth, and useful regulation, as had been the case for 50 years, but by politicizing and democratizing it. This was to be done through a constitutional convention. Enthused by the prospect of a reenactment of Philadelphia 1787, millions of web-savvy Europeans were supposed to deliberate the meaning of Europe. More pragmatic voices hoped to combat cynicism by simplifying the treaty and delineating EU prerogatives. To justify the need for change, reformers also seized on the perception that the EU would require a radical overhaul to avoid gridlock with 25 rather than 15 members—a fear that now seems unjustified, both because the new states are proving constructive and because the EU is not moving as far or fast as it once did.

Of course, the constitutional deliberation did not mobilize Europeans. Few citizens were even aware of the 200 *conventionnels'* deliberations. When testimony from civil society was requested, professors turned up. When a youth conference was called, would-be Eurocrats attended. When those who did attend came to consider democracy, they found that the arrangement Europe currently has is appropriate to a diverse polity in which member states insist on checks and balances at every level. There was little popular or elite support for democratic reform beyond the modest increases in scrutiny by national and European parliaments the constitution contains.

This is as it should be, for there is no "democratic deficit" in the EU—or not much of one. Once we set aside ideal notions of democracy and look to real-world standards, we see that the EU is as transparent, responsive, accountable, and honest as its member states. The relative lack of centralized financial or administrative discretion all but eliminates corruption. The EU's areas of autonomous authority—trade policy, constitutional adjudication, and central banking—are the same

as those in most democracies, where these functions are politically insulated for sound reasons.

The notion of imposing democratic control through multiple checks and balances, rather than through elections to a single sovereign parliament, is more American than European—but it is no less legitimate for that. Everyone gets a say in a system in which a European directive needs approval from a technocratic commission, a supermajority of democratic national governments, and a directly elected parliament, and must then be implemented by national regulators. Studies show that EU legislation is both consensual and relatively responsive to shifts in partisan and popular opinion.

Enthusiasts for democracy fail to grasp its limits. Engaging European citizens will not necessarily create rational (let alone supportive) debate, because those with intense preferences about the EU tend to be its opponents. Average citizens and political parties keep but a few issues—usually those involving heavy taxing and spending—in mind at any one time, and thus respond only to highly salient ideals and issues. The pull of Europe remains weak, while the bread and butter policies citizens care about most, including the welfare and identity issues that dominated the referendum debates, remain almost exclusively in national hands. The failure of European elections to generate high turnouts or focus on EU issues over the years suggests that citizens fail to participate in EU politics not because they are blocked from doing so, but because they have insufficient incentive.

Some democratic enthusiasts propose jump-starting EU democracy by incorporating hot-button issues like social policy and immigration, despite the lack of popular support for doing so. This is, in essence, Habermas's vision. Yet anyone except a philosopher like Habermas can see that this is the sort of extreme cure that will kill the patient. There is little that could lead the European public to decisively reject an institution as deeply embedded as the EU, but transferring controversial issues like social policy to it without justification might just do it.

More sober voices propose to empower national parliaments, which the constitution sought to do in a modest way. Yet this reveals a final fallacy of the democratizers. There is little reason to believe that turning policy over to a legislature makes it more legitimate. In Western democracies, popularity is inversely correlated with direct electoral accountability. The most popular institutions are the courts, the police, and the military. Parliaments are generally disliked. Whatever the source of Europe's declining popularity—a general decline in political trust, unfamiliarity with institutions, xenophobia, discontent with economic performance—it has little to do with Europe's democratic mandate.

Forcing an unstructured debate about an institution that handles matters like telecommunications standardization, the composition of the Bosnia stabilization force, and the privatization of electricity production inexorably drove debate to the lowest common denominator. When pro-European political elites found themselves defending a constitution with modest content, they felt they had no alternative but to oversell it using inflated notions of what the EU does and rhetoric drawn from 1950s European idealism. Small wonder they were outgunned by grumpy populists with stronger symbols rooted in class, nation, and race (and even more inflated views of what the EU does). Publics became confused and alarmed by the scare tactics of both sides. The referendums came to inhabit a strange twilight zone of symbolic politics, in which claims about the EU bore little relationship to reality, and support and opposition for a status quo constitution became a potent symbol for the myriad hopes and fears of modern electorates.

A Union That Works

In the wake of this debacle, European politicians must find a constructive path forward. They should start with a collective mea culpa. The document itself must be renounced. Then, over the next few years, the EU should return to its successful tradition of quiet and pragmatic reform.

Europeans consistently support incremental advances in the union's foreign, internal security, and economic policies along the lines set forth in the constitution.

Turkish membership is off the agenda, as it probably would have been even without the referendums, which revealed a considerable degree of popular concern and some virulent opposition to Turkish membership. To quell it, France committed itself to another referendum, should the question arise—a procedure also required by some other EU national constitutions. It is clear that a high-profile move toward Turkey at this point would bolster popular fear of and opposition to the EU—which are otherwise likely to wither away. Negotiations with Turkey should and will be pursued, so as to maintain the momentum of reform in that country. It should be obvious, however, that no further movement on accession is likely for some time. The best outcome would be for talks to continue quietly for a decade or two while Europeans attend to more pressing and practical plans for Balkan enlargement. Politicians need to concede this, and concede it loud and clear, not least in order to preserve continued EU enlargement in the Balkans.

A halfway arrangement acceptable to both EU and Turkish publics remains a realistic goal over the next 20 years, and may be better for Turkey than the limited type of EU membership that is currently on offer. This arrangement might provide for even freer trade, substantial regulatory convergence, and close cooperation on foreign and internal security policies, perhaps culminating in a privileged associate status. No other European policy could contribute as much to global peace and security.

Above all, European politicians need to acknowledge explicitly the existence of a stable European constitutional settlement. The unique genius of the EU is that it locks in policy coordination while respecting the powerful rhetoric and symbols that still attach to national identity. Publics will be reassured if it is portrayed as stable and successful. There is no shameful compromise with grand principles here. On the contrary, it is a highly appealing constitutional order that preserves national democratic politics for the issues most salient to citizens while delegating to more indirect democratic forms those issues that are of less concern—or on which there is an administrative, technical, or legal consensus.

The EU's distinctive system of multilevel governance is the only new form of state organization to emerge and prosper since the rise of the welfare state at the turn of the twentieth century. Now it is a mature constitutional order, one that no longer needs to move forward to legitimate its past and present successes. Left behind must be the European centralizers and democratizers for whom "ever closer union" remains an end in itself. They will insist that the answer to failed democracy is more democracy and the answer to a failed constitution is another constitution. But Europe has moved beyond them. Disowning this well-meaning, even admirable, band of idealists may seem harsh, but it is both necessary and just. On this basis, Europeans can develop a new discourse of national interest, pragmatic cooperation, and constitutional stability—a discourse that sees Europe as it is. The constitution is dead, long live the constitution!

MARGARET E. KECK AND KATHRYN SIKKINK

TRANSNATIONAL ADVOCACY NETWORKS IN INTERNATIONAL POLITICS

World politics at the end of the twentieth century involves, alongside states, many nonstate actors that interact with each other, with states, and with international organizations. These interactions are structured in terms of networks, and transnational networks are increasingly visible in international politics. [Networks are forms of organization characterized by voluntary, reciprocal, and horizontal patterns of communication and exchange.] Some involve economic actors and firms. Some are networks of scientists and experts whose professional ties and shared causal ideas underpin their efforts to influence policy.[1] Others are networks of activists, distinguishable largely by the centrality of principled ideas or values in motivating their formation.[2] We will call these *transnational advocacy networks*. [A transnational advocacy network includes those relevant actors working internationally on an issue who are bound together by shared values, a common discourse, and dense exchanges of information and services.]

Advocacy networks are significant transnationally and domestically. By building new links among actors in civil societies, states, and international organizations, they multiply the channels of access to the international system. In such issue areas as the environment and human rights, they also make international resources available to new actors in domestic political and social struggles. By thus blurring the boundaries between a state's relations with its own nationals and the recourse both citizens and states have to the international system, advocacy networks are helping to transform the practice of national sovereignty.

From Margaret E. Keck and Kathryn Sikkink, *Activists beyond Borders: Advocacy Networks in International Politics* (Ithaca, N.Y.: Cornell University Press, 1998), Chaps. 1, 3.

*   *   *

Transnational advocacy networks are proliferating, and their goal is to change the behavior of states and of international organizations. Simultaneously principled and strategic actors, they "frame" issues to make them comprehensible to target audiences, to attract attention and encourage action, and to "fit" with favorable institutional venues.[3] Network actors bring new ideas, norms, and discourses into policy debates, and serve as sources of information and testimony. * * *

They also promote norm implementation, by pressuring target actors to adopt new policies, and by monitoring compliance with international standards. Insofar as is possible, they seek to maximize their influence or leverage over the target of their actions. In doing so they contribute to changing perceptions that both state and societal actors may have of their identities, interests, and preferences, to transforming their discursive positions, and ultimately to changing procedures, policies, and behavior.[4]

Networks are communicative structures. To influence discourse, procedures, and policy, activists may engage and become part of larger policy communities that group actors working on an issue from a variety of institutional and value perspectives. Transnational advocacy networks must also be understood as political spaces, in which differently situated actors negotiate—formally or informally—the social, cultural, and political meanings of their joint enterprise.

*   *   *

Major actors in advocacy networks may include the following: (1) international and domestic nongovernmental research and advocacy organizations; (2) local social movements; (3) foundations; (4) the media; (5) churches, trade unions, consumer organizations, and intellectuals; (6) parts of regional and international intergovernmental organizations; and (7) parts of the executive and/or parliamentary branches of governments. Not all these will be present in each advocacy network. Initial research suggests, however, that in-

ternational and domestic NGOs play a central role in all advocacy networks, usually initiating actions and pressuring more powerful actors to take positions. NGOs introduce new ideas, provide information, and lobby for policy changes.

Groups in a network share values and frequently exchange information and services. The flow of information among actors in the network reveals a dense web of connections among these groups, both formal and informal. The movement of funds and services is especially notable between foundations and NGOs, and some NGOs provide services such as training for other NGOs in the same and sometimes other advocacy networks. Personnel also circulate within and among networks, as relevant players move from one to another in a version of the "revolving door."

*   *   *

We cannot accurately count transnational advocacy networks to measure their growth over time, but one proxy is the increase in the number of international NGOs committed to social change. Because international NGOs are key components of any advocacy network, this increase suggests broader trends in the number, size, and density of advocacy networks generally. Table 1 suggests that the number of international nongovernmental social change groups has increased across all issues, though to varying degrees in different issue areas. There are five times as many organizations working primarily on human rights as there were in 1950, but proportionally human rights groups have remained roughly a quarter of all such groups. Similarly, groups working on women's rights accounted for 9 percent of all groups in 1953 and in 1993. Transnational environmental organizations have grown most dramatically in absolute and relative terms, increasing from two groups in 1953 to ninety in 1993, and from 1.8 percent of total groups in 1953 to 14.3 percent in 1993. The percentage share of groups in such issue areas as international law, peace, ethnic unity, and Esperanto, has declined.[5]

*   *   *

Table 1. International Nongovernmental Social Change Organizations
(categorized by the major issue focus of their work)

Issue area (N)	1953 (N=110)	1963 (N=141)	1973 (N=183)	1983 (N=348)	1993 (N=631)
Human rights	33 30.0%	38 27.0%	41 22.4%	79 22.7%	168 26.6%
World order	8 7.3	4 2.8	12 6.6	31 8.9	48 7.6
International law	14 12.7	19 13.4	25 13.7	26 7.4	26 4.1
Peace	11 10.0	20 14.2	14 7.7	22 6.3	59 9.4
Women's rights	10 9.1	14 9.9	16 8.7	25 7.2	61 9.7
Environment	2 1.8	5 3.5	10 5.5	26 7.5	90 14.3
Development	3 2.7	3 2.1	7 3.8	13 3.7	34 5.4
Ethnic unity/Group rts.	10 9.1	12 8.5	18 9.8	37 10.6	29 4.6
Esperanto	11 10.0	18 12.8	28 15.3	41 11.8	54 8.6

SOURCE: Union of International Associations, *Yearbook of International Organizations* (1953, 1963, 1973, 1983, 1993). We are indebted to Jackie Smith, University of Notre Dame, for the use of her data from 1983 and 1993, and the use of her coding form and codebook for our data collection for the period 1953–73.

How Do Transnational Advocacy Networks Work?

Transnational advocacy networks seek influence in many of the same ways that other political groups or social movements do. Since they are not powerful in a traditional sense of the word, they must use the power of their information, ideas, and strategies to alter the information and value contexts within which states make policies. The bulk of what networks do might be termed persuasion or socialization, but neither process is devoid of conflict. Persuasion and socialization often involve not just reasoning with opponents, but also bringing pressure, arm-twisting, encouraging sanctions, and shaming. * * *

Our typology of tactics that networks use in their efforts at persuasion, socialization, and pressure includes (1) *information politics*, or the ability to quickly and credibly generate politically usable information and move it to where it will have the most impact; (2) *symbolic politics*, or the ability to call upon symbols, actions, or stories that make sense of a situation for an audience that is frequently far away;[6] (3) *leverage politics*, or the ability to call upon powerful actors to affect a situation where weaker members of a network are unlikely to have influence; and (4) *accountability politics*, or the effort to hold powerful actors to their previously stated policies or principles.

A single campaign may contain many of these elements simultaneously. For example, the human rights network disseminated information about human rights abuses in Argentina in the period 1976–83. The Mothers of the Plaza de Mayo marched in circles in the central square in Buenos Aires wearing white handkerchiefs to draw symbolic attention to the plight of their missing children. The network also tried to use both material and moral leverage against the Argentine regime, by pressuring the United States and other governments to cut off military and economic aid, and by efforts to get the UN and the Inter-American Commission on Human Rights to condemn Argentina's human rights practices. Monitoring is a variation on information politics, in which activists use information strategically to ensure accountability with public statements, existing legislation and international standards.

*   *   *

Network members actively seek ways to bring issues to the public agenda by framing them in innovative ways and by seeking hospitable venues. Sometimes they create issues by framing old problems in new ways; occasionally they help transform other actors' understanding of their identities and their interests. Land use rights in the Amazon, for example, took on an entirely different character and gained quite different allies viewed in a deforestation frame than they did in either social justice or regional development frames. In the 1970s and 1980s many states decided for the first time that promotion of human rights in other countries was a legitimate foreign policy goal and an authentic expression of national interest. This decision came in part from interaction with an emerging global human rights network. We argue that this represents not the victory of morality over self-interest, but a transformed understanding of national interest, possible in part because of structured interactions between state components and networks. * * *

*   *   *

Under What Conditions Do Advocacy Networks Have Influence?

To assess the influence of advocacy networks we must look at goal achievement at several different levels. We identify the following types or stages of network influence: (1) issue creation and agenda setting; (2) influence on discursive positions of states and international organizations; (3) influence on institutional procedures; (4) influence on policy change in "target actors" which may be states, international organizations like the World Bank, or private actors like the Nestlé Corporation; and (5) influence on state behavior.

Networks generate attention to new issues and help set agendas when they provoke media attention, debates, hearings, and meetings on issues that previously had not been a matter of public debate. Because values are the essence of advocacy networks, this stage of influence may require a modification of the "value context" in which policy debates takes place. The UN's theme years and decades, such as International Women's Decade and the Year of Indigenous Peoples, were international events promoted by networks that heightened awareness of issues.

Networks influence discursive positions when they help persuade states and international organizations to support international declarations or to change stated domestic policy positions. The role environmental networks played in shaping state positions and conference declarations at the 1992 "Earth Summit" in Rio de Janeiro is an example of this kind of impact. They may also pressure states to make more binding commitments by signing conventions and codes of conduct.

The targets of network campaigns frequently respond to demands for policy change with changes in procedures (which may affect policies in the future). The multilateral bank campaign is largely responsible for a number of changes in internal bank directives mandating greater NGO and local participation in discussions of projects. It also opened access to formerly restricted information, and led to the establishment of an independent inspection panel for World Bank projects. Procedural changes can greatly increase the opportunity for advocacy organizations to develop regular contact with other key players on an issue, and they sometimes offer the opportunity to move from outside to inside pressure strategies.

A network's activities may produce changes in policies, not only of the target states, but also of other states and/or international institutions. Explicit policy shifts seem to denote success, but even here both their causes and meanings may be elusive. We can point with some confidence to network impact where human rights network pressures have achieved cutoffs of military aid to repressive regimes, or a curtailment of repressive practices. Sometimes human rights activity even affects regime stability. But we must take care to distinguish between policy change and change in behavior; official policies regarding timber extraction in Sarawak, Malaysia, for example, may say little about how timber companies behave on the ground in the absence of enforcement.

We speak of stages of impact, and not merely types of impact, because we believe that increased attention, followed by changes in discursive positions, make governments more vulnerable to the claims that networks raise. (Discursive changes can also have a powerfully divisive effect on networks themselves, splitting insiders from outsiders, reformers from radicals.[7]) A government that claims to be protecting indigenous areas or ecological reserves is potentially more vulnerable to charges that such areas are endangered than one that makes no such claim. At that point the effort is not to make governments change their position but to hold them to their word. Meaningful policy change is thus more likely when the first three types or stages of impact have occurred.

Both issue characteristics and actor characteristics are important parts of our explanation of how networks affect political outcomes and the conditions under which networks can be effective. Issue characteristics such as salience and resonance within existing national or institutional agendas can tell us something about where networks are likely to be able to insert new ideas and discourses into policy debates. Success in influencing policy also depends on the strength and density of the network and its ability to achieve leverage. * * *

* * *

Toward a Global Civil Society?

Many other scholars now recognize that "the state does not monopolize the public sphere,"[8] and are seeking, as we are, ways to describe the sphere of international interactions under a variety of names: transnational relations, international civil society, and global civil society.[9] In these views, states no longer look unitary from the outside. Increasingly dense interactions among individuals, groups, actors from states, and international institutions appear to involve much more than representing interests on a world stage.

We contend that the advocacy network concept cannot be subsumed under notions of transnational social movements or global civil society. In particular, theorists who suggest that a global civil society will inevitably emerge from economic globalization or from revolutions in communication and transportation technologies ignore the issues of agency and political opportunity that we find central for understanding the evolution of new international institutions and relationships.

* * *

We lack convincing studies of the sustained and specific processes through which individuals and organizations create (or resist the creation of) something resembling a global civil society. Our research leads us to believe that these interactions involve much more agency than a pure diffusionist perspective suggests. Even though the implications of our findings are much broader than most political scientists would admit, the findings themselves do not yet support the strong claims about an emerging global civil society.[10] We are much more comfortable with a conception of transnational civil society as an arena of struggle, a fragmented and contested area where "the politics of transnational civil society is centrally about the way in which certain groups emerge and are legitimized (by governments, institutions, and other groups)."[11]

*   *   *

HUMAN RIGHTS ADVOCACY NETWORKS IN LATIN AMERICA

Argentina

Even before the military coup of March 1976, international human rights pressures had influenced the Argentine military's decision to cause political opponents to "disappear," rather than imprisoning them or executing them publicly.[12] (The technique led to the widespread use of the verb "to disappear" in a transitive sense.) The Argentine military believed they had "learned" from the international reaction to the human rights abuses after the Chilean coup. When the Chilean military executed and imprisoned large numbers of people, the ensuing uproar led to the international isolation of the regime of Augusto Pinochet. Hoping to maintain a moderate international image, the Argentine military decided to secretly kidnap, detain, and execute its victims, while denying any knowledge of their whereabouts.[13]

Although this method did initially mute the international response to the coup, Amnesty International and groups staffed by Argentine political exiles eventually were able to document and condemn the new forms of repressive practices. To counteract the rising tide of criticism, the Argentina junta invited AI for an on-site visit in 1976. In March 1977, on the first anniversary of the military coup, AI published the report on its visit, a well-documented denunciation of the abuses of the regime with emphasis on the problem of the disappeared. Amnesty estimated that the regime had taken six thousand political prisoners, most without specifying charges, and had abducted between two and ten thousand people. The report helped demonstrate that the disappearances were part of a deliberate government policy by which the military and the police kidnapped perceived opponents, took them to secret detention centers where they tortured, interrogated, and killed them, then secretly disposed of their bodies.[14] Amnesty International's denunciations of the Argentine regime were legitimized when it won the Nobel Peace Prize later that year.

Such information led the Carter administration and the French, Italian, and Swedish governments to denounce rights violations by the junta. France, Italy, and Sweden each had citizens who had been victims of Argentine repression, but their concerns extended beyond their own citizens. Although the Argentine government claimed that such attacks constituted unacceptable intervention in their internal affairs and violated Argentine sovereignty, U.S. and European officials persisted. In 1977 the U.S. government reduced the planned level of military aid for Argentina because of human rights abuses. Congress later passed a bill eliminating all military assistance to Argentina, which went into effect on 30 September 1978.[15] A number of high-level U.S. delegations met with junta members during this period to discuss human rights.

Early U.S. action on Argentina was based primarily on the human rights documentation provided by AI and other NGOs, not on information received through official channels at the embassy or the State Department.[16] For example, during a 1977 visit, Secretary of State Cyrus Vance carried a list of disappeared people prepared by human rights NGOs to present to members of the junta.[17] When Patricia Derian met with junta member Admiral Emilio Massera during a visit in 1977, she brought up the navy's use of torture. In response to Massera's denial, Derian said she had seen a rudimentary map of a secret detention center in the Navy Mechanical School, where their meeting was being held, and asked whether perhaps under their feet someone was being tortured. Among Derian's key sources of information were NGOs and especially the families of the disappeared, with whom she met frequently during her visits to Buenos Aires.[18]

Within a year of the coup, Argentine domestic human rights organizations began to develop significant external contacts. Their members traveled frequently to the United States and Europe, where they met with human rights organizations, talked to the press, and met with parliamentarians and government officials. These groups sought foreign contacts to publicize the human rights situation, to fund their activities, and to help protect themselves from further repression by their government, and they provided evidence to U.S. and European policymakers. Much of their funding came from European and U.S.-based foundations.[19]

Two key events that served to keep the case of Argentine human rights in the minds of U.S. and European policymakers reflect the impact of transnational linkages on policy. In 1979 the Argentine authorities released Jacobo Timerman, whose memoir describing his disappearance and torture by the Argentine military helped human rights organizations, members of the U.S. Jewish community, and U.S. journalists to make his case a cause célèbre in U.S. policy circles.[20] Then in 1980 the Nobel Peace Prize was awarded to an Argentine human rights activist, Adolfo Pérez Es-

quivel. Peace and human rights groups in the United States and Europe helped sponsor Pérez Esquivel's speaking tour to the United States exactly at the time that the OAS was considering the IACHR report on Argentina and Congress was debating the end of the arms embargo to Argentina.

The Argentine military government wanted to avoid international human rights censure. Scholars have long recognized that even authoritarian regimes depend on a combination of coercion and consent to stay in power. Without the legitimacy conferred by elections, they rely heavily on claims about their political efficacy and on nationalism.[21] Although the Argentine military mobilized nationalist rhetoric against foreign criticism, a sticking point was that Argentines, especially the groups that most supported the military regime, thought of themselves as the most European of Latin American countries. The military junta claimed to be carrying out the repression in the name of "our Western and Christian civilization."[22] But the military's intent to integrate Argentina more fully into the liberal global economic order was being jeopardized by deteriorating relations with countries most identified with that economic order, and with "Western and Christian civilization."

The junta adopted a sequence of responses to international pressures. From 1976 to 1978 the military pursued an initial strategy of denying the legitimacy of international concern over human rights in Argentina. At the same time it took actions that appear to have contradicted this strategy, such as permitting the visit of the Amnesty International mission to Argentina in 1976. The "failure" of the Amnesty visit, from the military point of view, appeared to reaffirm the junta's resistance to human rights pressures. This strategy was most obvious at the UN, where the Argentine government worked to silence international condemnation in the UN Commission on Human Rights. Ironically, the rabidly anticommunist Argentine regime found a diplomatic ally in the Soviet Union, an importer of Argentine wheat, and the two countries collaborated to block UN consideration of the Argentine human rights situation.[23] Concerned states circumvented this blockage by creating the UN Working Group on Disappearances in 1980. Human rights NGOs provided information, lobbied government delegations, and pursued joint strategies with sympathetic UN delegations.

By 1978 the Argentine government recognized that something had to be done to improve its international image in the United States and Europe, and to restore the flow of military and economic aid.[24] To these ends the junta invited the Inter-American Commission on Human Rights for an on-site visit, in exchange for a U.S. commitment to release Export-Import Bank funds and otherwise improve U.S.-Argentine relations.[25] During 1978 the human rights situation in Argentina improved significantly. [T]he practice of disappearance as a tool of state policy was curtailed only after 1978, when the government began to take the "international variable" seriously.[26]

The value of the network perspective in the Argentine case is in highlighting the fact that international pressures did not work independently, but rather in coordination with national actors. Rapid change occurred because strong domestic human rights organizations documented abuses and protested against repression, and international pressures helped protect domestic monitors and open spaces for their protest. International groups amplified both information and symbolic politics of domestic groups and projected them onto an international stage, from which they echoed back into Argentina. This classic boomerang process was executed nowhere more skillfully than in Argentina, in large part due to the courage and ability of domestic human rights organizations.

Some argue that repression stopped because the military had finally killed all the people that they thought they needed to kill. This argument disregards disagreements within the regime about the size and nature of the "enemy." International pressures affected particular factions within the military regime that had differing ideas about how much repression was "necessary." Although by the military's admission 90 percent of the *armed* opposition had been eliminated by April

1977, this did not lead to an immediate change in human rights practices.[27] By 1978 there were splits within the military about what it should do in the future. One faction was led by Admiral Massera, a right-wing populist, another by Generals Carlos Suarez Mason and Luciano Menéndez, who supported indefinite military dictatorship and unrelenting war against the left, and a third by Generals Jorge Videla and Roberto Viola, who hoped for eventual political liberalization under a military president. Over time, the Videla-Viola faction won out, and by late 1978 Videla had gained increased control over the Ministry of Foreign Affairs, previously under the influence of the navy.[28] Videla's ascendancy in the fall of 1978, combined with U.S. pressure, helps explain his ability to deliver on his promise to allow the Inter-American Commission on Human Rights visit in December.

The Argentine military government thus moved from initial refusal to accept international human rights interventions, to cosmetic cooperation with the human rights network, and eventually to concrete improvements in response to increased international pressures. Once it had invited IACHR and discovered that the commission could not be co-opted or confused, the government ended the practice of disappearance, released political prisoners, and restored some semblance of political participation. Full restoration of human rights in Argentina did not come until after the Malvinas War and the transition to democracy in 1983, but after 1980 the worst abuses had been curtailed.

In 1985, after democratization, Argentina tried the top military leaders of the juntas for human rights abuses, and a number of key network members testified: Theo Van Boven and Patricia Derian spoke about international awareness of the Argentine human rights situation, and a member of the IACHR delegation to Argentina discussed the OAS report. Clyde Snow and Eric Stover provided information about the exhumation of cadavers from mass graves. Snow's testimony, corroborated by witnesses, was a key part of the prosecutor's success in establishing that top military officers were guilty of murder.[29] A public opinion poll taken during the trials showed that 92 percent of Argentines were in favor of the trials of the military juntas.[30] The tribunal convicted five of the nine defendants, though only two—ex-president Videla, and Admiral Massera—were given life sentences. The trials were the first of their kind in Latin America, and among the very few in the world ever to try former leaders for human rights abuses during their rule. In 1990 President Carlos Menem pardoned the former officers. By the mid-1990s, however, democratic rule in Argentina was firmly entrenched, civilian authority over the military was well established, and the military had been weakened by internal disputes and severe cuts in funding.[31]

The Argentine case set important precedents for other international and regional human rights action, and shows the intricate interactions of groups and individuals within the network and the repercussions of these interactions. The story of the Grandmothers of the Plaza de Mayo is an exemplar of network interaction and unanticipated effects. The persistence of the Grandmothers helped create a new profession—what one might call "human rights forensic science." (The scientific skills existed before, but they had never been put to the service of human rights.) Once the Argentine case had demonstrated that forensic science could illuminate mass murder and lead to convictions, these skills were diffused and legitimized. Eric Stover, Clyde Snow, and the Argentine forensic anthropology team they helped create were the prime agents of international diffusion. The team later carried out exhumations and training in Chile, Bolivia, Brazil, Venezuela, and Guatemala.[32] Forensic science is being used to prosecute mass murderers in El Salvador, Honduras, Rwanda, and Bosnia. By 1996 the UN International Criminal Tribunal for the former Yugoslavia had contracted with two veterans of the Argentine forensic experiment, Stover and Dr. Robert Kirschner, to do forensic investigations for its war crimes tribunal. "'A war crime creates a crime scene,' said Dr. Kirschner, 'That's how we treat it. We recover forensic evidence for prosecu-

tion and create a record which cannot be successfully challenged in court.'"[33]

*　　*　　*

[Conclusions]

A realist approach to international relations would have trouble attributing significance either to the network's activities or to the adoption and implementation of state human rights policies. Realism offers no convincing explanation for why relatively weak nonstate actors could affect state policy, or why states would concern themselves with the internal human rights practices of other states even when doing so interferes with the pursuit of other goals. For example, the U.S. government's pressure on Argentina on human rights led Argentina to defect from the grain embargo of the Soviet Union. Raising human rights issues with Mexico could have undermined the successful completion of the free trade agreement and cooperation with Mexico on antidrug operations. Human rights pressures have costs, even in strategically less important countries of Latin America.

In liberal versions of international relations theory, states and nonstate actors cooperate to realize joint gains or avoid mutually undesirable outcomes when they face problems they cannot resolve alone. These situations have been characterized as cooperation or coordination games with particular payoff structures.[34] But human rights issues are not easily modeled as such. Usually states can ignore the internal human rights practices of other states without incurring undesirable economic or security costs.

In the issue of human rights it is primarily principled ideas that drive change and cooperation. We cannot understand why countries, organizations, and individuals are concerned about human rights or why countries respond to human rights pressures without taking into account the role of norms and ideas in international life. Jack Donnelly has argued that such moral interests are as real as material interests, and that a sense of moral interdependence has led to the emergence of human rights regimes.[35] For human rights * * * the primary movers behind this form of principled international action are international networks.

NOTES

1. Peter Haas has called these "knowledge-based" or "epistemic communities." See Peter Haas, "Introduction: Epistemic Communities and International Policy Coordination," *Knowledge, Power and International Policy Coordination*, special issue, *International Organization* 46 (Winter 1992), pp. 1–36.

2. Ideas that specify criteria for determining whether actions are right and wrong and whether outcomes are just or unjust are shared principled beliefs or values. Beliefs about cause-effect relationships are shared casual beliefs. Judith Goldstein and Robert Keohane, eds., *Ideas and Foreign Policy: Beliefs, Institutions, and Political Change* (Ithaca: Cornell University Press, 1993), pp. 8–10.

3. David Snow and his colleagues have adapted Erving Goffman's concept of framing. We use it to mean "conscious strategic efforts by groups of people to fashion shared understandings of the world and of themselves that legitimate and motivate collective action." Definition from Doug McAdam, John D. McCarthy, and Mayer N. Zald, "Introduction," *Comparative Perspectives on Social Movements: Political Opportunities, Mobilizing Structures, and Cultural Framings*, ed. McAdam, McCarthy, and Zald (New York: Cambridge University Press, 1996), p. 6. See also Frank Baumgartner and Bryan Jones, "Agenda Dynamics and Policy Subsystems," *Journal of Politics* 53:4 (1991): 1044–74.

4. With the "constructivists" in international relations theory, we take actors and interests to be constituted in interaction. See Martha Finnemore, *National Interests in International Society* (Ithaca: Cornell University Press, 1996), who argues that "states are embedded in dense networks of transnational and international social relations that shape their perceptions of the world and their role in that world. States are *socialized* to want certain things by the international society in which they and the people in them live" (p. 2).

5. Data from a collaborative research project with Jackie G. Smith. We thank her for the use of her data from the period 1983–93, whose results are presented in Jackie G. Smith, "Characteristics of the Modern Transnational Social Movement Sector," in Jackie G. Smith, et al., eds. *Transnational Social Movements and World Politics: Solidarity beyond the State* (Syracuse: Syracuse University Press, forthcoming 1997), and for permission to use her coding form and codebook for our data collection for the period 1953–73. All data were coded from Union of International Associations, *The Yearbook of International Organizations*, 1948–95 (published annually).

6. Alison Brysk uses the categories "information politics" and "symbolic politics" to discuss strategies of transnational actors, especially networks around Indian rights. See "Acting Globally: Indian Rights and International Politics in Latin America," in *Indigenous Peoples and Democracy in Latin America*, ed. Donna Lee Van Cott (New York: St. Martin's Press/Inter-American Dialogue, 1994), pp. 29–51; and "Hearts and Minds: Bringing Symbolic Politics Back In," *Polity* 27 (Summer 1995): 559–85.

7. We thank Jonathan Fox for reminding us of this point.

8. M. J. Peterson, "Transnational Activity, International Society, and World Politics," *Millennium* 21:3 (1992): 375–76.

9. See, for example, Ronnie Lipschutz, "Reconstructing World Politics: The Emergence of Global Civil Society," *Millennium* 21:3 (1992): 389–420; Paul Wapner, "Politics beyond the State: Environmental Activism and World Civic Politics," *World Politics* 47 (April

1995): 311–40; and the special issue of *Millennium* on social movements and world politics, 23:3 (Winter 1994).

10. Sidney Tarrow, *Power in Movement: Social Movements and Contentious Politics*, rev. ed. (Cambridge: Cambridge University Press, forthcoming 1998), Chapter 11. An earlier version appeared as "Fishnets, Internets and Catnets: Globalization and Transnational Collective Action," Instituto Juan March de Estudios e Investigaciones, Madrid: Working Papers 1996/78, March 1996; and Peterson, "Transnational Activity."

11. Andrew Hurrell and Ngaire Woods, "Globalisation and Inequality," *Millennium* 24:3 (1995), p. 468.

12. This section draws upon some material from an earlier co-authored work: Lisa L. Martin and Kathryn Sikkink, "U.S. Policy and Human Rights in Argentina and Guatemala, 1973–1980," in *Double-Edged Diplomacy: International Bargaining and Domestic Politics*, ed., Peter B. Evans, Harold K. Jacobson, and Robert D. Putnam (Berkeley: University of California Press, 1993), pp. 330–62.

13. See Emilio Mignone, *Derechos humanos y sociedad: el caso argentino* (Buenos Aires: Ediciones del Pensamiento Nacional and Centro de Estudios Legales y Sociales, 1991), p. 66; Claudio Uriarte, *Almirante Cero: Biografía No Autorizada de Emilio Eduardo Massera* (Buenos Aires: Planeta, 1992), p. 97; and Carlos H. Acuña and Catalina Smulovitz, "Adjusting the Armed Forces to Democracy: Successes, Failures, and Ambiguities in the Southern Cone," in *Constructing Democracy: Human Rights, Citizenship, and Society in Latin America*, ed. Elizabeth Jelin and Eric Hershberg (Boulder, Colo.: Westview, 1993), p. 15.

14. Amnesty International, *Report of an Amnesty International Mission to Argentina* (London: Amnesty International, 1977).

15. Congressional Research Service, Foreign Affairs and National Defense Division, *Human Rights and U.S. Foreign Assistance: Experiences and Issues in Policy Implementation (1977–1978)*, report prepared for U.S. Senate Committee on Foreign Relations, November 1979, p. 106.

16. After the 1976 coup, Argentine political exiles set up branches of the Argentine Human Rights Commission (CADHU) in Paris, Mexico, Rome, Geneva, and Washington, D.C. In October two of its members testified on human rights abuses before the U.S. House Subcommittee on Human Rights and International Organization. Iain Guest, *Behind the Disappearances: Argentina's Dirty War against Human Rights and the United Nations* (Philadelphia: University of Pennsylvania Press, 1990), pp. 66–67.

17. Interview with Robert Pastor, Wianno, Massachusetts, 28 June 1990.

18. Testimony given by Patricia Derian to the National Criminal Appeals Court in Buenos Aires during the trials of junta members. "Massera sonrió y me dijo: Sabe qué pasó con Poncio Pilatos . . . ?" *Diario del Juicio*, 18 June 1985, p. 3; Guest, *Behind the Disappearances*, pp. 161–63. Later it was confirmed that the Navy Mechanical School was one of the most notorious secret torture and detention centers. *Nunca Más: The Report of the Argentine National Commission for the Disappeared* (New York: Farrar Straus & Giroux, 1986), pp. 79–84.

19. The Mothers of the Plaza de Mayo received grants from Dutch churches and the Norwegian Parliament, and the Ford Foundation provided funds for the Center for Legal and Social Studies (CELS) and the Grandmothers of the Plaza de Mayo.

20. Jacobo Timerman, *Prisoner without a Name, Cell without a Number* (New York: Random House, 1981).

21. See Guillermo O'Donnell, "Tensions in the Bureaucratic Authoritarian State and the Question of Democracy," in *The New Authoritarianism in Latin America*, ed. David Collier

(Princeton: Princeton University Press, 1979), pp. 288, 292–94.

22. Daniel Frontalini and Maria Cristina Caiati, *El Mito de la Guerra Sucia* (Buenos Aires: Centro de Estudios Legales y Sociales, 1984), p. 24.

23. Guest, *Behind the Disappearances*, pp. 118–19, 182–83.

24. *Carta Política*, a news magazine considered to reflect the junta's views concluded in 1978 that "the principal problem facing the Argentine State has now become the international siege (cerco internacional)." "Cuadro de Situación," *Carta Política* 57 (August 1978):8.

25. Interviews with Walter Mondale, Minneapolis, Minnesota, 20 June 1989, and Ricardo Yofre, Buenos Aires, 1 August 1990.

26. See Asamblea Permanente por los Derechos Humanos, *Las Cifras de la Guerra Sucia* (Buenos Aires, 1988), pp. 26–32.

27. According to a memorandum signed by General Jorge Videla, the objectives of the military government "go well beyond the simple defeat of subversion." The memorandum called for a continuation and intensification of the "general offensive against subversion," including "intense military action." "Directivo 504," 20 April 1977, in "La orden secreta de Videla," *Diario del Juicio* 28 (3 December 1985): 5–8.

28. David Rock, *Argentina, 1516–1987: From Spanish Colonization to Alfonsín* (Berkeley: University of California Press, 1985), pp. 370–71; Timerman, *Prisoner without a Name*, p. 163.

29. *Diario del Juicio* 1 (27 May 1985), and 9 (23 July 1985).

30. *Diario del Juicio* 25 (12 November 1985).

31. Acuña and Smulovitz, "Adjusting the Armed Forces to Democracy," pp. 20–21.

32. Cohen Salama, *Tumbas anónimas [informe sobre la identificación de restos de víctimas de la represión* (Buenos Aires: Catálogos Editora, 1992)], p. 275.

33. Mike O'Connor, "Harvesting Evidence in Bosnia's Killing Fields," *New York Times,* 7 April 1996, p. E3.

34. See, e.g., Arthur A. Stein, "Coordination and Collaboration: Regimes in an Anarchic World," *International Organization* 36:2 (Spring 1982): 299–324.

35. Donnelly, *Universal Human Rights [in Theory and Practice* (Ithaca: Cornell University Press, 1989)], pp. 211–12.

SAMANTHA POWER

BYSTANDERS TO GENOCIDE: WHY THE UNITED STATES LET THE RWANDAN TRAGEDY HAPPEN

I. People Sitting in Offices

In the course of a hundred days in 1994 the Hutu government of Rwanda and its extremist allies very nearly succeeded in exterminating the country's Tutsi minority. Using firearms, machetes,

From *The Atlantic Monthly* (Sept. 2001), 84–108.

and a variety of garden implements, Hutu militiamen, soldiers, and ordinary citizens murdered some 800,000 Tutsi and politically moderate Hutu. It was the fastest, most efficient killing spree of the twentieth century.

A few years later, in a series in *The New Yorker,* Philip Gourevitch recounted in horrific detail the story of the genocide and the world's failure to stop it. President Bill Clinton, a famously avid reader, expressed shock. He sent copies of Gourevitch's articles to his second-term national-security adviser, Sandy Berger. The articles bore confused, angry, searching queries in the margins. "Is what he's saying true?" Clinton wrote with a thick black felt-tip pen beside heavily underlined paragraphs. "How did this happen?" he asked, adding, "I want to get to the bottom of this." The President's urgency and outrage were oddly timed. As the terror in Rwanda had unfolded, Clinton had shown virtually no interest in stopping the genocide, and his Administration had stood by as the death toll rose into the hundreds of thousands.

Why did the United States not do more for the Rwandans at the time of the killings? Did the President really not know about the genocide, as his marginalia suggested? Who were the people in his Administration who made the life-and-death decisions that dictated U.S. policy? Why did they decide (or decide not to decide) as they did? Were any voices inside or outside the U.S. government demanding that the United States do more? If so, why weren't they heeded? And most crucial, what could the United States have done to save lives?

So far people have explained the U.S. failure to respond to the Rwandan genocide by claiming that the United States didn't know what was happening, that it knew but didn't care, or that regardless of what it knew there was nothing useful to be done. The account that follows is based on a three-year investigation involving sixty interviews with senior, mid-level, and junior State Department, Defense Department, and National Security Council officials who helped to shape or inform U.S. policy. It also reflects dozens of interviews with Rwandan, European, and United Nations officials and with peacekeepers, journalists, and nongovernmental workers in Rwanda. Thanks to the National Security Archive (www.nsarchive .org), a nonprofit organization that uses the Freedom of Information Act to secure the release of classified U.S. documents, this account also draws on hundreds of pages of newly available government records. This material provides a clearer picture than was previously possible of the interplay among people, motives, and events. It reveals that the U.S. government knew enough about the genocide early on to save lives, but passed up countless opportunities to intervene.

In March of 1998, on a visit to Rwanda, President Clinton issued what would later be known as the "Clinton apology," which was actually a carefully hedged acknowledgment. He spoke to the crowd assembled on the tarmac at Kigali Airport: "We come here today partly in recognition of the fact that we in the United States and the world community did not do as much as we could have and should have done to try to limit what occurred" in Rwanda.

This implied that the United States had done a good deal but not quite enough. In reality the United States did much more than fail to send troops. It led a successful effort to remove most of the UN peacekeepers who were already in Rwanda. It aggressively worked to block the subsequent authorization of UN reinforcements. It refused to use its technology to jam radio broadcasts that were a crucial instrument in the coordination and perpetuation of the genocide. And even as, on average, 8,000 Rwandans were being butchered each day, U.S. officials shunned the term "genocide," for fear of being obliged to act. The United States in fact did virtually nothing "to try to limit what occurred." Indeed, staying out of Rwanda was an explicit U.S. policy objective.

With the grace of one grown practiced at public remorse, the President gripped the lectern with both hands and looked across the dais at the Rwandan officials and survivors who surrounded him. Making eye contact and shaking his head, he explained, "It may seem strange to you here, especially the many of you who lost members of your family, but all over the world there were people like me sitting in offices, day after day after day, who *did not fully appreciate* [pause] the depth [pause] and the speed [pause] with which you were being engulfed by this *unimaginable* terror."

Clinton chose his words with characteristic care. It was true that although top U.S. officials could not help knowing the basic facts—thousands of Rwandans were dying every day—that were being reported in the morning papers, many did not "fully appreciate" the meaning. In the first three weeks of the genocide the most influential American policymakers portrayed (and, they insist, perceived) the deaths not as astrocities or the components and symptoms of genocide but as wartime "casualties"—the deaths of combatants or those caught between them in a civil war.

Yet this formulation avoids the critical issue of whether Clinton and his close advisers might reasonably have been expected to "fully appreciate" the true dimensions and nature of the massacres. During the first three days of the killings U.S. diplomats in Rwanda reported back to Washington that well-armed extremists were intent on eliminating the Tutsi. And the American press spoke of the door-to-door hunting of unarmed civilians. By the end of the second week informed nongovernmental groups had already begun to call on the Administration to use the term "genocide," causing diplomats and lawyers at the State Department to begin debating the word's applicability soon thereafter. In order not to appreciate that genocide or something close to it was under way, U.S. officials had to ignore public reports and internal intelligence and debate.

The story of U.S. policy during the genocide in Rwanda is not a story of willful complicity with evil. U.S. officials did not sit around and conspire to allow genocide to happen. But whatever their convictions about "never again," many of them did sit around, and they most certainly did allow genocide to happen. In examining how and why the United States failed Rwanda, we see that without strong leadership the system will incline toward risk-averse policy choices. We also see that with the possibility of deploying U.S. troops to Rwanda taken off the table early on—and with crises elsewhere in the world unfolding—the slaughter never received the top-level attention it deserved. Domestic political forces that might have pressed for action were absent. And most U.S. officials opposed to American involvement in Rwanda were firmly convinced that they were doing all they could—and, most important, all they *should*—in light of competing American interests and a highly circumscribed understanding of what was "possible" for the United States to do.

One of the most thoughtful analyses of how the American system can remain predicated on the noblest of values while allowing the vilest of crimes was offered in 1971 by a brilliant and earnest young foreign-service officer who had just resigned from the National Security Council to protest the 1970 U.S. invasion of Cambodia. In an article in *Foreign Policy*, "The Human Reality of Realpolitik," he and a colleague analyzed the process whereby American policymakers with moral sensibilities could have waged a war of such immoral consequence as the one in Vietnam. They wrote,

> The answer to that question begins with a basic intellectual approach which views foreign policy as a lifeless, bloodless set of abstractions. "Nations," "interests," "influence," "prestige"—all are disembodied and dehumanized terms which encourage easy inattention to the real people whose lives our decisions affect or even end.

Policy analysis excluded discussion of human consequences. "It simply is not *done*," the authors wrote. "Policy—good, steady policy—is made by the 'tough-minded.' To talk of suffering is to lose 'effectiveness,' almost to lose one's grip. It is seen as a sign that one's 'rational' arguments are weak."

In 1994, fifty years after the Holocaust and twenty years after America's retreat from Vietnam, it was possible to believe that the system had changed and that talk of human consequences had become admissible. Indeed, when the machetes were raised in Central Africa, the White House official primarily responsible for the shaping of U.S. foreign policy was one of the authors of that 1971 critique: Anthony Lake, President Clinton's first-term national-security adviser. The genocide in Rwanda presented Lake and the rest of the Clinton team with an opportunity to prove that "good, steady policy" could be made in the interest of saving lives.

II. The Peacekeepers

Rwanda was a test for another man as well: Romeo Dallaire, then a major general in the Canadian army who at the time of the genocide was the commander of the UN Assistance Mission in Rwanda. If ever there was a peacekeeper who believed wholeheartedly in the promise of humanitarian action, it was Dallaire. A broad-shouldered French-Canadian with deep-set sky-blue eyes, Dallaire has the thick, calloused hands of one brought up in a culture that prizes soldiering, service, and sacrifice. He saw the United Nations as the embodiment of all three.

Before his posting to Rwanda Dallaire had served as the commandant of an army brigade that sent peacekeeping battalions to Cambodia and Bosnia, but he had never seen actual combat himself. "I was like a fireman who has never been to a fire, but has dreamed for years about how he would fare when the fire came," the fifty-five-year-old Dallaire recalls. When, in the summer of 1993, he received the phone call from UN headquarters offering him the Rwanda posting, he was ecstatic. "It was answering the aim of my life," he says. "It's *all* you've been waiting for."

Dallaire was sent to command a UN force that would help to keep the peace in Rwanda, a nation the size of Vermont, which was known as "the land of a thousand hills" for its rolling terrain. Before Rwanda achieved independence from Belgium, in 1962, the Tutsi, who made up 15 percent of the populace, had enjoyed a privileged status. But independence ushered in three decades of Hutu rule, under which Tutsi were systematically discriminated against and periodically subjected to waves of killing and ethnic cleansing. In 1990 a group of armed exiles, mainly Tutsi, who had been clustered on the Ugandan border, invaded Rwanda. Over the next several years the rebels, known as the Rwandan Patriotic Front, gained ground against Hutu gov-

ernment forces. In 1993 Tanzania brokered peace talks, which resulted in a power-sharing agreement known as the Arusha Accords. Under its terms the Rwandan government agreed to share power with Hutu opposition parties and the Tutsi minority. UN peacekeepers would be deployed to patrol a cease-fire and assist in de-militarization and demobilization as well as to help provide a secure environment, so that exiled Tutsi could return. The hope among moderate Rwandans and Western observers was that Hutu and Tutsi would at last be able to coexist in harmony.

Hutu extremists rejected these terms and set out to terrorize Tutsi and also those Hutu politicians supportive of the peace process. In 1993 several thousand Rwandans were killed, and some 9,000 were detained. Guns, grenades, and machetes began arriving by the planeload. A pair of international commissions—one sent by the United Nations, the other by an independent collection of human-rights organizations—warned explicitly of a possible genocide.

But Dallaire knew nothing of the precariousness of the Arusha Accords. When he made a preliminary reconnaissance trip to Rwanda, in August of 1993, he was told that the country was committed to peace and that a UN presence was essential. A visit with extremists, who preferred to eradicate Tutsi rather than cede power, was not on Dallaire's itinerary. Remarkably, no UN officials in New York thought to give Dallaire copies of the alarming reports from the international investigators.

The sum total of Dallaire's intelligence data before that first trip to Rwanda consisted of one encyclopedia's summary of Rwandan history, which Major Brent Beardsley, Dallaire's executive assistant, had snatched at the last minute from his local public library. Beardsley says, "We flew to Rwanda with a Michelin road map, a copy of the Arusha agreement, and that was it. We were under the impression that the situation was quite straightforward: there was one cohesive government side and one cohesive rebel side, and they had come together to sign the peace agreement and had then requested that we come in to help them implement it."

Though Dallaire gravely underestimated the tensions brewing in Rwanda, he still felt that he would need a force of 5,000 to help the parties implement the terms of the Arusha Accords. But when his superiors warned him that the United States would never agree to pay for such a large deployment, Dallaire reluctantly trimmed his written request to 2,500. He remembers, "I was told, 'Don't ask for a brigade, because it ain't there.'"

Once he was actually posted to Rwanda, in October of 1993, Dallaire lacked not merely intelligence data and manpower but also institutional support. The small Department of Peacekeeping Operations in New York, run by the Ghanaian diplomat Kofi Annan, now the UN secretary general, was overwhelmed. Madeleine Albright, then the U.S. ambassador to the UN, recalls, "The global nine-one-one was always either busy or nobody was there." At the time of the Rwanda deployment, with a staff of a few hundred, the UN was posting 70,000 peacekeepers on seventeen missions around the world. Amid these widespread crises and logistical headaches the Rwanda mission had a very low status.

Life was not made easier for Dallaire or the UN peacekeeping office by the fact that American patience for peacekeeping was thinning. Congress owed half a billion dollars in UN dues and peacekeeping costs. It had tired of its obligation to foot a third of the bill for what had come to feel like an insatiable global appetite for mischief and an equally insatiable UN appetite for missions. The Clinton Administration had taken office better disposed toward peacekeeping than any other Administration in U.S. history. But it felt that the Department of Peacekeeping Operations needed fixing and demanded that the UN "learn to say no" to chancy or costly missions.

Every aspect of the UN Assistance Mission in Rwanda was run on a shoestring. UNAMIR (the acronym by which it was known) was equipped

with hand-me-down vehicles from the UN's Cambodia mission, and only eighty of the 300 that turned up were usable. When the medical supplies ran out, in March of 1994, New York said there was no cash for resupply. Very little could be procured locally, given that Rwanda was one of Africa's poorest nations. Replacement spare parts, batteries, and even ammunition could rarely be found. Dallaire spent some 70 percent of his time battling UN logistics.

Dallaire had major problems with his personnel, as well. He commanded troops, military observers, and civilian personnel from twenty-six countries. Though multinationality is meant to be a virtue of UN missions, the diversity yielded grave discrepancies in resources. Whereas Belgian troops turned up well armed and ready to perform the tasks assigned to them, the poorer contingents showed up "bare-assed," in Dallaire's words, and demanded that the United Nations suit them up. "Since nobody else was offering to send troops, we had to take what we could get," he says. When Dallaire expressed concern, he was instructed by a senior UN official to lower his expectations. He recalls, "I was told, 'Listen, General, you are NATO-trained. This is not NATO.'" Although some 2,500 UNAMIR personnel had arrived by early April of 1994, few of the soldiers had the kit they needed to perform even basic tasks.

The signs of militarization in Rwanda were so widespread that even without much of an intelligence-gathering capacity, Dallaire was able to learn of the extremists' sinister intentions. In January of 1994 an anonymous Hutu informant, said to be high up in the inner circles of the Rwandan government, had come forward to describe the rapid arming and training of local militias. In what is now referred to as the "Dallaire fax," Dallaire relayed to New York the informant's claim that Hutu extremists "had been ordered to register all the Tutsi in Kigali." "He suspects it is for their extermination," Dallaire wrote. "Example he gave was that in 20 minutes his personnel could kill up to 1000 Tutsis." "Jean-Pierre," as the informant became known, had said that the militia planned first to provoke and murder a number of Belgian peacekeepers, to "thus guarantee Belgian withdrawal from Rwanda." When Dallaire notified Kofi Annan's office that UNAMIR was poised to raid Hutu arms caches, Annan's deputy forbade him to do so. Instead Dallaire was instructed to notify the Rwandan President, Juvénal Habyarimana, and the Western ambassadors of the informant's claims. Though Dallaire battled by phone with New York, and confirmed the reliability of the informant, his political masters told him plainly and consistently that the United States in particular would not support aggressive peacekeeping. (A request by the Belgians for reinforcements was also turned down.) In Washington, Dallaire's alarm was discounted. Lieutenant Colonel Tony Marley, the U.S. military liaison to the Arusha process, respected Dallaire but knew he was operating in Africa for the first time. "I thought that the neophyte meant well, but I questioned whether he knew what he was talking about," Marley recalls.

III. The Early Killings

On the evening of April 6, 1994, Romeo Dallaire was sitting on the couch in his bungalow residence in Kigali, watching CNN with Brent Beardsley. Beardsley was preparing plans for a national Sports Day that would match Tutsi rebel soldiers against Hutu government soldiers in a soccer game. Dallaire said, "You know, Brent, if the shit ever hit the fan here, none of this stuff would really matter, would it?" The next instant the phone rang. Rwandan President Habyarimana's Mystère Falcon jet, a gift from French President François Mitterrand, had just been shot down, with Habyarimana and Burundian President Cyprien Ntaryamira aboard. Dallaire and Beardsley raced in their UN jeep to Rwandan army headquarters, where a crisis meeting was under way.

Back in Washington, Kevin Aiston, the Rwanda desk officer, knocked on the door of Deputy Assistant Secretary of State Prudence

Bushnell and told her that the Presidents of Rwanda and Burundi had gone down in a plane crash. "Oh, shit," she said. "Are you sure?" In fact nobody was sure at first, but Dallaire's forces supplied confirmation within the hour. The Rwandan authorities quickly announced a curfew, and Hutu militias and government soldiers erected roadblocks around the capital.

Bushnell drafted an urgent memo to Secretary of State Warren Christopher. She was concerned about a probable outbreak of killing in both Rwanda and its neighbor Burundi. The memo read,

> If, as it appears, both Presidents have been killed, there is a strong likelihood that widespread violence could break out in either or both countries, particularly if it is confirmed that the plane was shot down. Our strategy is to appeal for calm in both countries, both through public statements and in other ways.

A few public statements proved to be virtually the only strategy that Washington would muster in the weeks ahead.

Lieutenant General Wesley Clark, who later commanded the NATO air war in Kosovo, was the director of strategic plans and policy for the Joint Chiefs of Staff at the Pentagon. On learning of the crash, Clark remembers, staff officers asked, "Is it Hutu and Tutsi or Tutu and Hutsi?" He frantically called for insight into the ethnic dimension of events in Rwanda. Unfortunately, Rwanda had never been of more than marginal concern to Washington's most influential planners.

America's best-informed Rwanda observer was not a government official but a private citizen, Alison Des Forges, a historian and a board member of Human Rights Watch, who lived in Buffalo, New York. Des Forges had been visiting Rwanda since 1963. She had received a Ph.D. from Yale in African history, specializing in Rwanda, and she could speak the Rwandan language, Kinyarwanda. Half an hour after the plane crash Des Forges got a phone call from a close friend in Kigali, the human-rights activist Monique Mujawamariya. Des Forges had been worried about Mujawamariya for weeks, because the Hutu extremist radio station, Radio Mille Collines, had branded her "a bad patriot who deserves to die." Mujawamariya had sent Human Rights Watch a chilling warning a week earlier: "For the last two weeks, all of Kigali has lived under the threat of an instantaneous, carefully prepared operation to eliminate all those who give trouble to President Habyarimana."

Now Habyarimana was dead, and Mujawamariya knew instantly that the hard-line Hutu would use the crash as a pretext to begin mass killing. "This is it," she told Des Forges on the phone. For the next twenty-four hours Des Forges called her friend's home every half hour. With each conversation Des Forges could hear the gunfire grow louder as the militia drew closer. Finally the gunmen entered Mujawamariya's home. "I don't want you to hear this," Mujawamariya said softly. "Take care of my children." She hung up the phone.

Mujawamariya's instincts were correct. Within hours of the plane crash Hutu militiamen took command of the streets of Kigali. Dallaire quickly grasped that supporters of the Arusha peace process were being targeted. His phone at UNAMIR headquarters rang constantly as Rwandans around the capital pleaded for help. Dallaire was especially concerned about Prime Minister Agathe Uwilingiyimana, a reformer who with the President's death had become the titular head of state. Just after dawn on April 7 five Ghanaian and ten Belgian peacekeepers arrived at the Prime Minister's home in order to deliver her to Radio Rwanda, so that she could broadcast an emergency appeal for calm.

Joyce Leader, the second-in-command at the U.S. embassy, lived next door to Uwilingiyimana. She spent the early hours of the morning behind the steel-barred gates of her embassy-owned house as Hutu killers hunted and dispatched their first victims. Leader's phone rang. Uwilingiyimana was on the other end. "Please hide me," she begged.

Minutes after the phone call a UN peacekeeper attempted to hike the Prime Minister over the wall separating their compounds. When Leader heard shots fired, she urged the peacekeeper to abandon the effort. "They can see you!" she shouted. Uwilingiyimana managed to slip with her husband and children into another compound, which was occupied by the UN Development Program. But the militiamen hunted them down in the yard, where the couple surrendered. There were more shots. Leader recalls, "We heard her screaming and then, suddenly, after the gunfire the screaming stopped, and we heard people cheering." Hutu gunmen in the Presidential Guard that day systematically tracked down and eliminated Rwanda's moderate leadership.

The raid on Uwilingiyimana's compound not only cost Rwanda a prominent supporter of the Arusha Accords; it also triggered the collapse of Dallaire's mission. In keeping with the plan to target the Belgians which the informant Jean-Pierre had relayed to UNAMIR in January, Hutu soldiers rounded up the peacekeepers at Uwilingiyimana's home, took them to a military camp, led the Ghanaians to safety, and then killed and savagely mutilated the ten Belgians. In Belgium the cry for either expanding UNAMIR's mandate or immediately withdrawing was prompt and loud.

In response to the initial killings by the Hutu government, Tutsi rebels of the Rwandan Patriotic Front—stationed in Kigali under the terms of the Arusha Accords—surged out of their barracks and resumed their civil war against the Hutu regime. But under the cover of that war were early and strong indications that systematic genocide was taking place. From April 7 onward the Hutu-controlled army, the gendarmerie, and the militias worked together to wipe out Rwanda's Tutsi. Many of the early Tutsi victims found themselves specifically, not spontaneously, pursued: lists of targets had been prepared in advance, and Radio Mille Collines broadcast names, addresses, and even license-plate numbers. Killers often carried a machete in one hand and a transistor radio in the other. Tens of thousands of Tutsi fled their homes in panic and were snared and butchered at checkpoints. Little care was given to their disposal. Some were shoveled into landfills. Human flesh rotted in the sunshine. In churches bodies mingled with scattered hosts. If the killers had taken the time to tend to sanitation, it would have slowed their "sanitization" campaign.

IV. The "Last War"

The two tracks of events in Rwanda—simultaneous war and genocide—confused policymakers who had scant prior understanding of the country. Atrocities are often carried out in places that are not commonly visited, where outside expertise is limited. When country-specific knowledge is lacking, foreign governments become all the more likely to employ faulty analogies and to "fight the last war." The analogy employed by many of those who confronted the outbreak of killing in Rwanda was a peacekeeping intervention that had gone horribly wrong in Somalia.

On October 3, 1993, ten months after President Bush had sent U.S. troops to Somalia as part of what had seemed a low-risk humanitarian mission, U.S. Army Rangers and Delta special forces in Somalia attempted to seize several top advisers to the warlord Mohammed Farah Aideed. Aideed's faction had ambushed and killed two dozen Pakistani peacekeepers, and the United States was striking back. But in the firefight that ensued the Somali militia killed eighteen Americans, wounded seventy-three, and captured one Black Hawk helicopter pilot. Somali television broadcast both a video interview with the trembling, disoriented pilot and a gory procession in which the corpse of a U.S. Ranger was dragged through a Mogadishu street.

On receiving word of these events, President Clinton cut short a trip to California and convened an urgent crisis-management meeting at the White House. When an aide began recapping the situation, an angry President interrupted him. "Cut the bullshit," Clinton snapped. "Let's work this out." "Work it out" meant walk out. Republican Congressional pressure was intense. Clinton appeared on American television the next day, called off the manhunt for Aideed, temporarily reinforced the troop presence, and announced that all U.S. forces would be home within six months. The Pentagon leadership concluded that peacekeeping in Africa meant trouble and that neither the White House nor Congress would stand by it when the chips were down.

Even before the deadly blowup in Somalia the United States had resisted deploying a UN mission to Rwanda. "Anytime you mentioned peacekeeping in Africa," one U.S. official remembers, "the crucifixes and garlic would come up on every door." Having lost much of its early enthusiasm for peacekeeping and for the United Nations itself, Washington was nervous that the Rwanda mission would sour like so many others. But President Habyarimana had traveled to Washington in 1993 to offer assurances that his government was committed to carrying out the terms of the Arusha Accords. In the end, after strenuous lobbying by France (Rwanda's chief diplomatic and military patron), U.S. officials accepted the proposition that UNAMIR could be the rare "UN winner." On October 5, 1993, two days after the Somalia firefight, the United States reluctantly voted in the Security Council to authorize Dallaire's mission. Even so, U.S. officials made it clear that Washington would give no consideration to sending U.S. troops to Rwanda. Somalia and another recent embarrassment in Haiti indicated that multilateral initiatives for humanitarian purposes would likely bring the United States all loss and no gain.

Against this backdrop, and under the leadership of Anthony Lake, the national-security adviser, the Clinton Administration accelerated the development of a formal U.S. peacekeeping doctrine. The job was given to Richard Clarke, of the National Security Council, a special assistant to the President who was known as one of the most effective bureaucrats in Washington. In an interagency process that lasted more than a year, Clarke managed the production of a presidential decision directive, PDD-25, which listed sixteen factors that policymakers needed to consider when deciding whether to support peacekeeping activities: seven factors if the United States was to vote in the UN Security Council on peace operations carried out by non-American soldiers, six additional and more stringent factors if U.S. forces were to participate in UN peacekeeping missions, and three final factors if U.S. troops were likely to engage in actual combat. In the words of Representative David Obey, of Wisconsin, the restrictive checklist tried to satisfy the American desire for "zero degree of involvement, and zero degree of risk, and zero degree of pain and confusion." The architects of the doctrine remain its strongest defenders. "Many say PDD-25 was some evil thing designed to kill peacekeeping, when in fact it was there to save peacekeeping," Clarke says. "Peacekeeping was almost dead. There was no support for it in the U.S. government, and the peacekeepers were not effective in the field." Although the directive was not publicly released until May 3, 1994, a month into the genocide, the considerations encapsulated in the doctrine and the Administration's frustration with peacekeeping greatly influenced the thinking of U.S. officials involved in shaping Rwanda policy.

V. The Peace Processors

Each of the American actors dealing with Rwanda brought particular institutional interests and biases to his or her handling of the crisis. Secretary of State Warren Christopher knew little about Africa. At one meeting with his top advisers, several weeks after the plane crash, he pulled an atlas off his shelf to help him locate the country. Belgian Foreign Minister Willie Claes recalls trying to discuss Rwanda with his American counterpart and being told, "I have other responsibilities." Officials in the State Department's Africa Bureau were, of course, better informed. Prudence Bushnell, the deputy assistant secretary, was one of them. The daughter of a diplomat, Bushnell had joined the foreign service in 1981, at the age of thirty-five. With her agile mind and sharp tongue, she had earned the attention

of George Moose when she served under him at the U.S. embassy in Senegal. When Moose was named the assistant secretary of state for African affairs, in 1993, he made Bushnell his deputy. Just two weeks before the plane crash the State Department had dispatched Bushnell and a colleague to Rwanda in an effort to contain the escalating violence and to spur the stalled peace process.

Unfortunately, for all the concern of the Americans familiar with Rwanda, their diplomacy suffered from three weaknesses. First, ahead of the plane crash diplomats had repeatedly threatened to pull out UN peacekeepers in retaliation for the parties' failure to implement Arusha. These threats were of course counterproductive, because the very Hutu who opposed power-sharing wanted nothing more than a UN withdrawal. One senior U.S. official remembers, "The first response to trouble is 'Let's yank the peacekeepers.' But that is like believing that when children are misbehaving, the proper response is 'Let's send the baby-sitter home.'"

Second, before and during the massacres U.S. diplomacy revealed its natural bias toward states and toward negotiations. Because most official contact occurs between representatives of states, U.S. officials were predisposed to trust the assurances of Rwandan officials, several of whom were plotting genocide behind the scenes. Those in the U.S. government who knew Rwanda best viewed the escalating violence with a diplomatic prejudice that left them both institutionally oriented toward the Rwandan government and reluctant to do anything to disrupt the peace process. An examination of the cable traffic from the U.S. embassy in Kigali to Washington between the signing of the Arusha agreement and the downing of the presidential plane reveals that setbacks were perceived as "dangers to the peace process" more than as "dangers to Rwandans." American criticisms were deliberately and steadfastly leveled at "both sides," though Hutu government and militia forces were usually responsible.

The U.S. ambassador in Kigali, David Rawson, proved especially vulnerable to such bias.

Rawson had grown up in Burundi, where his father, an American missionary, had set up a Quaker hospital. He entered the foreign service in 1971. When, in 1993, at age fifty-two, he was given the embassy in Rwanda, his first, he could not have been more intimate with the region, the culture, or the peril. He spoke the local language—almost unprecedented for an ambassador in Central Africa. But Rawson found it difficult to imagine the Rwandans who surrounded the President as conspirators in genocide. He issued pro forma demarches over Habyarimana's obstruction of power-sharing, but the cable traffic shows that he accepted the President's assurances that he was doing all he could. The U.S. investment in the peace process gave rise to a wishful tendency to see peace "around the corner." Rawson remembers, "We were naive policy optimists, I suppose. The fact that negotiations can't work is almost not one of the options open to people who care about peace. We were looking for the hopeful signs, not the dark signs. In fact, we were looking away from the dark signs . . . One of the things I learned and should have already known is that once you launch a process, it takes on its own momentum. I had said, 'Let's try this, and then if it doesn't work, we can back away.' But bureaucracies don't allow that. Once the Washington side buys into a process, it gets pursued, almost blindly." Even after the Hutu government began exterminating Tutsi, U.S. diplomats focused most of their efforts on "re-establishing a cease-fire" and "getting Arusha back on track."

The third problematic feature of U.S. diplomacy before and during the genocide was a tendency toward blindness bred by familiarity: the few people in Washington who were paying attention to Rwanda before Habyarimana's plane was shot down were those who had been tracking Rwanda for some time and had thus come to expect a certain level of ethnic violence from the region. And because the U.S. government had done little when some 40,000 people had been killed in Hutu-Tutsi violence in Burundi in October of 1993, these officials also knew that Washington was prepared to tolerate substantial bloodshed. When the massacres began in April, some U.S. regional specialists initially suspected that Rwanda was undergoing "another flare-up" that would involve another "acceptable" (if tragic) round of ethnic murder.

Rawson had read up on genocide before his posting to Rwanda, surveying what had become a relatively extensive scholarly literature on its causes. But although he expected internecine killing, he did not anticipate the scale at which it occurred. "Nothing in Rwandan culture or history could have led a person to that forecast," he says. "Most of us thought that if a war broke out, it would be quick, that these poor people didn't have the resources, the means, to fight a sophisticated war. I couldn't have known that they would do each other in with the most economic means." George Moose agrees: "We were psychologically and imaginatively too limited."

*   *   *

VII. Genocide? What Genocide?

Just when did Washington know of the sinister Hutu designs on Rwanda's Tutsi? Writing in *Foreign Affairs* last year [2000], Alan Kuperman argued that President Clinton "could not have known that a nationwide genocide was under way" until about two weeks into the killing. It is true that the precise nature and extent of the slaughter was obscured by the civil war, the withdrawal of U.S. diplomatic sources, some confused press reporting, and the lies of the Rwandan government. Nonetheless, both the testimony of U.S. officials who worked the issue day to day and the declassified documents indicate that plenty was known about the killers' intentions.

A determination of genocide turns not on the numbers killed, which is always difficult to ascertain at a time of crisis, but on the perpetrators' intent: Were Hutu forces attempting to destroy Rwanda's Tutsi? The answer to this question was available early on. "By eight A.M. the morning after the plane crash we knew what was happening, that there was systematic killing of Tutsi,"

Joyce Leader recalls. "People were calling me and telling me who was getting killed. I knew they were going door to door." Back at the State Department she explained to her colleagues that three kinds of killing were going on: war, politically motivated murder, and genocide. Dallaire's early cables to New York likewise described the armed conflict that had resumed between rebels and government forces, and also stated plainly that savage "ethnic cleansing" of Tutsi was occurring. U.S. analysts warned that mass killings would increase. In an April 11 memo prepared for Frank Wisner, the undersecretary of defense for policy, in advance of a dinner with Henry Kissinger, a key talking point was "Unless both sides can be convinced to return to the peace process, a massive (hundreds of thousands of deaths) bloodbath will ensue."

Whatever the inevitable imperfections of U.S. intelligence early on, the reports from Rwanda were severe enough to distinguish Hutu killers from ordinary combatants in civil war. And they certainly warranted directing additional U.S. intelligence assets toward the region—to snap satellite photos of large gatherings of Rwandan civilians or of mass graves, to intercept military communications, or to infiltrate the country in person. Though there is no evidence that senior policy-makers deployed such assets, routine intelligence continued to pour in. On April 26 an unattributed intelligence memo titled "Responsibility for Massacres in Rwanda" reported that the ringleaders of the genocide, Colonel Théoneste Bagosora and his crisis committee, were determined to liquidate their opposition and exterminate the Tutsi populace. A May 9 Defense Intelligence Agency report stated plainly that the Rwandan violence was not spontaneous but was directed by the government, with lists of victims prepared well in advance. The DIA observed that an "organized parallel effort of *genocide* [was] being implemented by the army to destroy the leadership of the Tutsi community."

From April 8 onward media coverage featured eyewitness accounts describing the widespread targeting of Tutsi and the corpses piling up on Kigali's streets. American reporters relayed stories of missionaries and embassy officials who had been unable to save their Rwandan friends and neighbors from death. On April 9 a front-page *Washington Post* story quoted reports that the Rwandan employees of the major international relief agencies had been executed "in front of horrified expatriate staffers." On April 10 a *New York Times* front-page article quoted the Red Cross claim that "tens of thousands" were dead, 8,000 in Kigali alone, and that corpses were "in the houses, in the streets, everywhere." The *Post* the same day led its front-page story with a description of "a pile of corpses six feet high" outside the main hospital. On April 14 *The New York Times* reported the shooting and hacking to death of nearly 1,200 men, women, and children in the church where they had sought refuge. On April 19 Human Rights Watch, which had excellent sources on the ground in Rwanda, estimated the number of dead at 100,000 and called for use of the term "genocide." The 100,000 figure (which proved to be a gross underestimate) was picked up immediately by the Western media, endorsed by the Red Cross, and featured on the front page of *The Washington Post*. On April 24 the *Post* reported how "the heads and limbs of victims were sorted and piled neatly, a bone-chilling order in the midst of chaos that harked back to the Holocaust." President Clinton certainly could have known that a genocide was under way, if he had wanted to know.

Even after the reality of genocide in Rwanda had become irrefutable, when bodies were shown choking the Kagera River on the nightly news, the brute fact of the slaughter failed to influence U.S. policy except in a negative way. American officials, for a variety of reasons, shunned the use of what became known as "the g-word." They felt that using it would have obliged the United States to act, under the terms of the 1948 Genocide Convention. They also believed, understandably, that it would harm U.S. credibility to name the crime and then do nothing to stop it. A discussion paper on Rwanda, prepared by an official in the Office of the Secretary of Defense and dated May 1, testifies to the nature of official thinking. Regarding issues that might be brought up at the next interagency working group, it stated,

> 1. Genocide Investigation: Language that calls for an international investigation of human rights abuses and possible violations of the genocide convention. *Be Careful. Legal at State was worried about this yesterday—Genocide finding could commit [the U.S. government] to actually "do something."* [Emphasis added.]

At an interagency teleconference in late April, Susan Rice, a rising star on the NSC who worked under Richard Clarke, stunned a few of the officials present when she asked, "If we use the word 'genocide' and are seen as doing nothing, what will be the effect on the November [congressional] election?" Lieutenant Colonel Tony Marley remembers the incredulity of his colleagues at the State Department. "We could believe that people would wonder that," he says, "but not that they would actually voice it." Rice does not recall the incident but concedes, "If I said it, it was completely inappropriate, as well as irrelevant."

The genocide debate in U.S. government circles began the last week of April, but it was not until May 21, six weeks after the killing began, that Secretary Christopher gave his diplomats permission to use the term "genocide"—sort of. The UN Human Rights Commission was about to meet in special session, and the U.S. representative, Geraldine Ferraro, needed guidance on whether to join a resolution stating that genocide had occurred. The stubborn U.S. stand had become untenable internationally.

The case for a label of genocide was straightforward, according to a May 18 confidential analysis prepared by the State Department's assistant secretary for intelligence and research, Toby Gati: lists of Tutsi victims' names and addresses had reportedly been prepared; Rwandan government troops and Hutu militia and youth squads were the main perpetrators; massacres were reported all over the country; humanitarian agencies were now "claiming from 200,000 to 500,000 lives" lost. Gati offered the intelligence bureau's view: "We believe 500,000 may be an exaggerated estimate, but no accurate figures are available. Systematic killings began within hours of Habyarimana's death. Most of those killed have been Tutsi civilians, including women and children." The terms of the Genocide Convention had been met. "We weren't quibbling about these numbers," Gati says. "We can never know precise figures, but our analysts had been reporting huge numbers of deaths for weeks. We were basically saying, 'A rose by any other name . . .'"

Despite this straightforward assessment, Christopher remained reluctant to speak the obvious truth. When he issued his guidance, on May 21, fully a month after Human Rights Watch had put a name to the tragedy, Christopher's instructions were hopelessly muddied.

> The delegation is authorized to agree to a resolution that states that "acts of genocide" have occurred in Rwanda or that "genocide has occurred in Rwanda." Other formulations that suggest that some, but not all of the killings in Rwanda are genocide . . . e.g. "genocide is taking place in Rwanda"—are authorized. Delegation is not authorized to agree to the characterization of any specific incident as genocide or to agree to any formulation that indicates that all killings in Rwanda are genocide.

Notably, Christopher confined permission to acknowledge full-fledged genocide to the upcoming session of the Human Rights Commission. Outside that venue State Department officials were authorized to state publicly only that *acts* of genocide had occurred.

Christine Shelly, a State Department spokesperson, had long been charged with publicly articulating the U.S. position on whether events in Rwanda counted as genocide. For two months she had avoided the term, and as her June 10 exchange with the Reuters correspondent Alan Elsner reveals, her semantic dance continued.

> *Elsner*: How would you describe the events taking place in Rwanda?
>
> *Shelly*: Based on the evidence we have seen from observations on the ground, we have every

reason to believe that acts of genocide have occurred in Rwanda.

Elsner: What's the difference between "acts of genocide" and "genocide"?

Shelly: Well, I think the—as you know, there's a legal definition of this . . . clearly not all of the
killings that have taken place in Rwanda are
killings to which you might apply that label . . .
But as to the distinctions between the words,
we're trying to call what we have seen so far as
best as we can; and based, again, on the evidence, we have every reason to believe that acts
of genocide have occurred.

Elsner: How many acts of genocide does it take to
make genocide?

Shelly: Alan, that's just not a question that I'm in a
position to answer.

The same day, in Istanbul, Warren Christopher, by then under severe internal and external
pressure, relented: "If there is any particular
magic in calling it genocide, I have no hesitancy
in saying that."

VIII. "Not Even a Sideshow"

Once the Americans had been evacuated, Rwanda
largely dropped off the radar of most senior Clinton Administration officials. In the situation
room on the seventh floor of the State Department a map of Rwanda had been hurriedly
pinned to the wall in the aftermath of the plane
crash, and eight banks of phones had rung off the
hook. Now, with U.S. citizens safely home, the
State Department chaired a daily interagency
meeting, often by teleconference, designed to coordinate mid-level diplomatic and humanitarian
responses. Cabinet-level officials focused on
crises elsewhere. Anthony Lake recalls, "I was obsessed with Haiti and Bosnia during that period,
so Rwanda was, in William Shawcross's words, a
'sideshow,' but not even a sideshow—a no-show."
At the NSC the person who managed Rwanda
policy was not Lake, the national-security adviser,
who happened to know Africa, but Richard

Clarke, who oversaw peacekeeping policy, and for
whom the news from Rwanda only confirmed a
deep skepticism about the viability of UN deploy-
ments. Clarke believed that another UN failure
could doom relations between Congress and the
United Nations. He also sought to shield the President from congressional and public criticism.
Donald Steinberg managed the Africa portfolio at
the NSC and tried to look out for the dying Rwandans, but he was not an experienced infighter
and, colleagues say, he "never won a single argument" with Clarke.

*   *   *

During the entire three months of the genocide
Clinton never assembled his top policy advisers to
discuss the killings. Anthony Lake likewise never
gathered the "principals"—the Cabinet-level
members of the foreign-policy team. Rwanda was
never thought to warrant its own top-level meeting. When the subject came up, it did so along
with, and subordinate to, discussions of Somalia,
Haiti, and Bosnia. Whereas these crises involved
U.S. personnel and stirred some public interest,
Rwanda generated no sense of urgency and could
safely be avoided by Clinton at no political cost.
The editorial boards of the major American newspapers discouraged U.S. intervention during the
genocide. They, like the Administration, lamented
the killings but believed, in the words of an April
17 *Washington Post* editorial, "The United States
has no recognizable national interest in taking a
role, certainly not a leading role." Capitol Hill was
quiet. Some in Congress were glad to be free of
the expense of another flawed UN mission. Others, including a few members of the Africa sub-
committees and the Congressional Black Caucus,
eventually appealed tamely for the United States
to play a role in ending the violence—but again,
they did not dare urge U.S. involvement on the
ground, and they did not kick up a public fuss.
Members of Congress weren't hearing from their
constituents. Pat Schroeder, of Colorado, said on
April 30, "There are some groups terribly concerned about the gorillas . . . But—it sounds
terrible—people just don't know what can be

done about the people." Randall Robinson, of the nongovernmental organization TransAfrica, was preoccupied, staging a hunger strike to protest the U.S. repatriation of Haitian refugees. Human Rights Watch supplied exemplary intelligence and established important one-on-one contacts in the Administration, but the organization lacks a grassroots base from which to mobilize a broader segment of American society.

IX. The UN Withdrawal

When the killing began, Romeo Dallaire expected and appealed for reinforcements. Within hours of the plane crash he had cabled UN headquarters in New York: "Give me the means and I can do more." He was sending peacekeepers on rescue missions around the city, and he felt it was essential to increase the size and improve the quality of the UN's presence. But the United States opposed the idea of sending reinforcements, no matter where they were from. The fear, articulated mainly at the Pentagon but felt throughout the bureaucracy, was that what would start as a small engagement by foreign troops would end as a large and costly one by Americans. This was the lesson of Somalia, where U.S. troops had gotten into trouble in an effort to bail out the beleaguered Pakistanis. The logical outgrowth of this fear was an effort to steer clear of Rwanda entirely and be sure others did the same. Only by yanking Dallaire's entire peacekeeping force could the United States protect itself from involvement down the road.

One senior U.S. official remembers, "When the reports of the deaths of the ten Belgians came in, it was clear that it was Somalia redux, and the sense was that there would be an expectation everywhere that the U.S. would get involved. We thought leaving the peacekeepers in Rwanda and having them confront the violence would take us where we'd been before. It was a foregone conclusion that the United States wouldn't intervene and that the concept of UN peacekeeping could not be sacrificed again."

A foregone conclusion. What is most remarkable about the American response to the Rwandan genocide is not so much the absence of U.S. military action as that during the entire genocide the possibility of U.S. military intervention was never even debated. Indeed, the United States resisted intervention of any kind.

The bodies of the slain Belgian soldiers were returned to Brussels on April 14. One of the pivotal conversations in the course of the genocide took place around that time, when Willie Claes, the Belgian Foreign Minister, called the State Department to request "cover." "We are pulling out, but we don't want to be seen to be doing it alone," Claes said, asking the Americans to support a full UN withdrawal. Dallaire had not anticipated that Belgium would extract its soldiers, removing the backbone of his mission and stranding Rwandans in their hour of greatest need. "I expected the excolonial white countries would stick it out even if they took casualties," he remembers. "I thought their pride would have led them to stay to try to sort the place out. The Belgian decision caught me totally off guard. I was truly stunned."

Belgium did not want to leave ignominiously, by itself. Warren Christopher agreed to back Belgian requests for a full UN exit. Policy over the next month or so can be described simply: no U.S. military intervention, robust demands for a withdrawal of all of Dallaire's forces, and no support for a new UN mission that would challenge the killers. Belgium had the cover it needed.

On April 15 Christopher sent one of the most forceful documents to be produced in the entire three months of the genocide to Madeleine Albright at the UN—a cable instructing her to demand a full UN withdrawal. The cable, which was heavily influenced by Richard Clarke at the NSC, and which bypassed Donald Steinberg and was never seen by Anthony Lake, was unequivocal about the next steps. Saying that he had "fully" taken into account the "humanitarian reasons put forth for retention of UNAMIR elements in Rwanda," Christopher wrote that there was "insufficient justification" to retain a UN presence.

The international community must give highest priority to full, orderly withdrawal of all UNAMIR personnel as soon as possible . . . We will oppose any effort at this time to preserve a UNAMIR presence in Rwanda . . . Our opposition to retaining a UNAMIR presence in Rwanda is firm. It is based on our conviction that the Security Council has an obligation to ensure that peacekeeping operations are viable, that they are capable of fulfilling their mandates, and that UN peacekeeping personnel are not placed or retained, knowingly, in an untenable situation.

"Once we knew the Belgians were leaving, we were left with a rump mission incapable of doing anything to help people," Clarke remembers. "They were doing nothing to stop the killings."

But Clarke underestimated the deterrent effect that Dallaire's very few peacekeepers were having. Although some soldiers hunkered down, terrified, others scoured Kigali, rescuing Tutsi, and later established defensive positions in the city, opening their doors to the fortunate Tutsi who made it through roadblocks to reach them. One Senegalese captain saved a hundred or so lives single-handedly. Some 25,000 Rwandans eventually assembled at positions manned by UNAMIR personnel. The Hutu were generally reluctant to massacre large groups of Tutsi if foreigners (armed or unarmed) were present. It did not take many UN soldiers to dissuade the Hutu from attacking. At the Hotel des Mille Collines ten peacekeepers and four UN military observers helped to protect the several hundred civilians sheltered there for the duration of the crisis. About 10,000 Rwandans gathered at the Amohoro Stadium under light UN cover. Brent Beardsley, Dallaire's executive assistant, remembers, "If there was any determined resistance at close quarters, the government guys tended to back off." Kevin Aiston, the Rwanda desk officer at the State Department, was keeping track of Rwandan civilians under UN protection. When Prudence Bushnell told him of the U.S. decision to demand a UNAMIR withdrawal, he turned pale. "We can't," he said. Bushnell replied, "The train has already left the station."

On April 19 the Belgian Colonel Luc Marchal delivered his final salute and departed with the last of his soldiers. The Belgian withdrawal reduced Dallaire's troop strength to 2,100. More crucially, he lost his best troops. Command and control among Dallaire's remaining forces became tenuous. Dallaire soon lost every line of communication to the countryside. He had only a single satellite phone link to the outside world.

The UN Security Council now made a decision that sealed the Tutsi's fate and signaled the militia that it would have free rein. The U.S. demand for a full UN withdrawal had been opposed by some African nations, and even by Madeleine Albright; so the United States lobbied instead for a dramatic drawdown in troop strength. On April 21, amid press reports of some 100,000 dead in Rwanda, the Security Council voted to slash UNAMIR's forces to 270 men. Albright went along, publicly declaring that a "small, skeletal" operation would be left in Kigali to "show the will of the international community."

After the UN vote Clarke sent a memorandum to Lake reporting that language about "the safety and security of Rwandans under UN protection had been inserted by US/UN at the end of the day to prevent an otherwise unanimous UNSC from walking away from the at-risk Rwandans under UN protection as the peacekeepers drew down to 270." In other words, the memorandum suggested that the United States was *leading* efforts to ensure that the Rwandans under UN protection were not abandoned. The opposite was true.

Most of Dallaire's troops were evacuated by April 25. Though he was supposed to reduce the size of his force to 270, he ended up keeping 503 peacekeepers. By this time Dallaire was trying to deal with a bloody frenzy. "My force was standing knee-deep in mutilated bodies, surrounded by the guttural moans of dying people, looking into the eyes of children bleeding to death with their wounds burning in the sun and being invaded by maggots and flies," he later wrote. "I found myself walking through villages where the only sign of life was a goat, or a chicken, or a songbird, as all the people were dead, their bodies being eaten by voracious packs of wild dogs."

Dallaire had to work within narrow limits. He attempted simply to keep the positions he held and to protect the 25,000 Rwandans under UN supervision while hoping that the member states on the Security Council would change their minds and send him some help while it still mattered.

By coincidence Rwanda held one of the rotating seats on the Security Council at the time of the genocide. Neither the United States nor any other UN member state ever suggested that the representative of the genocidal government be expelled from the council. Nor did any Security Council country offer to provide safe haven to Rwandan refugees who escaped the carnage. In one instance Dallaire's forces succeeded in evacuating a group of Rwandans by plane to Kenya. The Nairobi authorities allowed the plane to land, sequestered it in a hangar, and, echoing the American decision to turn back the *S.S. St. Louis* during the Holocaust, then forced the plane to return to Rwanda. The fate of the passengers is unknown.

Throughout this period the Clinton Administration was largely silent. The closest it came to a public denunciation of the Rwandan government occurred after personal lobbying by Human Rights Watch, when Anthony Lake issued a statement calling on Rwandan military leaders by name to "do everything in their power to end the violence immediately." When I spoke with Lake six years later, and informed him that human-rights groups and U.S. officials point to this statement as the sum total of official public attempts to shame the Rwandan government in this period, he seemed stunned. "You're kidding," he said. "That's truly pathetic."

At the State Department the diplomacy was conducted privately, by telephone. Prudence Bushnell regularly set her alarm for 2:00 A.M. and phoned Rwandan government officials. She spoke several times with Augustin Bizimungu, the Rwandan military chief of staff. "These were the most bizarre phone calls," she says. "He spoke in perfectly charming French. 'Oh, it's so nice to hear from you,' he said. I told him, 'I am calling to tell you President Clinton is going to hold you accountable for the killings.' He said, 'Oh, how nice it is that your President is thinking of me.'"

X. The Pentagon "Chop"

The daily meeting of the Rwanda interagency working group was attended, either in person or by teleconference, by representatives from the various State Department bureaus, the Pentagon, the National Security Council, and the intelligence community. Any proposal that originated in the working group had to survive the Pentagon "chop." "Hard intervention," meaning U.S. military action, was obviously out of the question. But Pentagon officials routinely stymied initiatives for "soft intervention" as well.

The Pentagon discussion paper on Rwanda, referred to earlier, ran down a list of the working group's six short-term policy objectives and carped at most of them. The fear of a slippery slope was persuasive. Next to the seemingly innocuous suggestion that the United States "support the UN and others in attempts to achieve a cease-fire" the Pentagon official responded, "Need to change 'attempts' to 'political efforts'—without 'political' there is a danger of signing up to troop contributions."

The one policy move the Defense Department supported was a U.S. effort to achieve an arms embargo. But the same discussion paper acknowledged the ineffectiveness of this step: "We do not envision it will have a significant impact on the killings because machetes, knives and other hand implements have been the most common weapons."

Dallaire never spoke to Bushnell or to Tony Marley, the U.S. military liaison to the Arusha process, during the genocide, but they all reached the same conclusions. Seeing that no troops were forthcoming, they turned their attention to measures short of full-scale deployment which might alleviate the suffering. Dallaire pleaded with New York, and Bushnell and her team recommended in Washington, that something be done to "neutralize" Radio Mille Collines.

The country best equipped to prevent the genocide planners from broadcasting murderous instructions directly to the population was the United States. Marley offered three possibilities. The United States could destroy the antenna. It could transmit "counter-broadcasts" urging perpetrators to stop the genocide. Or it could jam the hate radio station's broadcasts. This could have been done from an airborne platform such as the Air Force's Commando Solo airplane. Anthony Lake raised the matter with Secretary of Defense William Perry at the end of April. Pentagon officials considered all the proposals non-starters. On May 5 Frank Wisner, the undersecretary of defense for policy, prepared a memo for Sandy Berger, then the deputy national-security adviser. Wisner's memo testifies to the unwillingness of the U.S. government to make even financial sacrifices to diminish the killing.

> We have looked at options to stop the broadcasts within the Pentagon, discussed them interagency and concluded jamming is an ineffective and expensive mechanism that will not accomplish the objective the NSC Advisor seeks.

> International legal conventions complicate airborne or ground based jamming and the mountainous terrain reduces the effectiveness of either option. Commando Solo, an Air National Guard asset, is the only suitable DOD jamming platform. It costs approximately $8500 per flight hour and requires a semi-secure area of operations due to its vulnerability and limited self-protection.

> I believe it would be wiser to use air to assist in Rwanda in the [food] relief effort . . .

The plane would have needed to remain in Rwandan airspace while it waited for radio transmissions to begin. "First we would have had to figure out whether it made sense to use Commando Solo," Wisner recalls. "Then we had to get it from where it was already and be sure it could be moved. Then we would have needed flight clearance from all the countries nearby. And then we would need the political go-ahead. By the time we got all this, weeks would have passed. And it was not going to solve the fundamental problem, which was one that needed to be addressed militarily." Pentagon planners understood that stopping the genocide required a military solution. Neither they nor the White House wanted any part in a military solution. Yet instead of undertaking other forms of intervention that might have at least saved some lives, they justified inaction by arguing that a military solution was required.

Whatever the limitations of radio jamming, which clearly would have been no panacea, most of the delays Wisner cites could have been avoided if senior Administration officials had followed through. But Rwanda was not their problem. Instead justifications for standing by abounded. In early May the State Department Legal Advisor's Office issued a finding against radio jamming, citing international broadcasting agreements and the American commitment to free speech. When Bushnell raised radio jamming yet again at a meeting, one Pentagon official chided her for naiveté: "Pru, radios don't kill people. *People* kill people!"

*   *   *

However significant and obstructionist the role of the Pentagon in April and May, Defense Department officials were stepping into a vacuum. As one U.S. official put it, "Look, nobody senior was paying any attention to this mess. And in the absence of any political leadership from the top, when you have one group that feels pretty strongly about what *shouldn't* be done, it is extremely likely they are going to end up shaping U.S. policy." Lieutenant General Wesley Clark looked to the White House for leadership. "The Pentagon is always going to be the last to want to intervene," he says. "It is up to the civilians to tell us they want to do something and we'll figure out how to do it."

*   *   *

XI. PDD-25 in Action

No sooner had most of Dallaire's forces been withdrawn, in late April, than a handful of non-permanent members of the Security Council, aghast at the scale of the slaughter, pressed the major powers to send a new, beefed-up force (UNAMIR II) to Rwanda.

When Dallaire's troops had first arrived, in the fall of 1993, they had done so under a fairly traditional peacekeeping mandate known as a Chapter VI deployment—a mission that assumes a cease-fire and a desire on both sides to comply with a peace accord. The Security Council now had to decide whether it was prepared to move from peacekeeping to peace *enforcement*—that is, to a Chapter VII mission in a hostile environment. This would demand more peacekeepers with far greater resources, more-aggressive rules of engagement, and an explicit recognition that the UN soldiers were there to protect civilians.

Two proposals emerged. Dallaire submitted a plan that called for joining his remaining peacekeepers with about 5,000 well-armed soldiers he hoped could be gathered quickly by the Security Council. He wanted to secure Kigali and then fan outward to create safe havens for Rwandans who had gathered in large numbers at churches and schools and on hillsides around the country. The United States was one of the few countries that could supply the rapid airlift and logistic support needed to move reinforcements to the region. In a meeting with UN Secretary General Boutros Boutros-Ghali on May 10, Vice President Al Gore pledged U.S. help with transport.

Richard Clarke, at the NSC, and representatives of the Joint Chiefs challenged Dallaire's plan. "How do you plan to take control of the airport in Kigali so that the reinforcements will be able to land?" Clarke asked. He argued instead for an "outside-in" strategy, as opposed to Dallaire's "inside-out" approach. The U.S. proposal would have created protected zones for refugees at Rwanda's borders. It would have kept any U.S. pilots involved in airlifting the peacekeepers safely out of Rwanda. "Our proposal was the most feasible, doable thing that could have been done in the short term," Clarke insists. Dallaire's proposal, in contrast, "could not be done in the short term and could not attract peacekeepers." The U.S. plan—which was modeled on Operation Provide Comfort, for the Kurds of northern Iraq—seemed to assume that the people in need were refugees fleeing to the border, but most endangered Tutsi could not make it to the border. The most vulnerable Rwandans were those clustered together, awaiting salvation, deep inside Rwanda. Dallaire's plan would have had UN soldiers move to the Tutsi in hiding. The U.S. plan would have required civilians to move to the safe zones, negotiating murderous roadblocks on the way. "The two plans had very different objectives," Dallaire says. "My mission was to save Rwandans. Their mission was to put on a show at no risk."

America's new peacekeeping doctrine, of which Clarke was the primary architect, was unveiled on May 3, and U.S. officials applied its criteria zealously. PDD-25 did not merely circumscribe U.S. participation in UN missions; it also limited U.S. support for other states that hoped to carry out UN missions. Before such missions could garner U.S. approval, policymakers had to answer certain questions: Were U.S. interests at stake? Was there a threat to world peace? A clear mission goal? Acceptable costs? Congressional, public, and allied support? A working cease-fire? A clear command-and-control arrangement? And, finally, what was the exit strategy?

The United States haggled at the Security Council and with the UN Department of Peacekeeping Operations for the first two weeks of May. U.S. officials pointed to the flaws in Dallaire's proposal without offering the resources that would have helped him to overcome them. On May 13 Deputy Secretary of State Strobe Talbott sent Madeleine Albright instructions on how the United States should respond to Dallaire's plan. Noting the logistic hazards of airlifting troops into the capital, Talbott wrote, "The U.S. is not prepared at this point to lift heavy equipment and troops into Kigali." The "more manageable" operation would

be to create the protected zones at the border, secure humanitarian-aid deliveries, and "promot[e]
restoration of a ceasefire and return to the Arusha
Peace Process." Talbott acknowledged that even
the minimalist American proposal contained
"many unanswered questions":

> Where will the needed forces come from; how will
> they be transported . . . where precisely should
> these safe zones be created; . . . would UN forces be
> authorized to move out of the zones to assist af-
> fected populations not in the zones . . . will the
> fighting parties in Rwanda agree to this arrange-
> ment . . . what conditions would need to obtain for
> the operation to end successfully?

Nonetheless, Talbott concluded, "We would urge
the UN to explore and refine this alternative and
present the Council with a menu of at least two
options in a formal report from the [Secretary
General] along with cost estimates before the Security Council votes on changing UNAMIR's
mandate." U.S. policymakers were asking valid
questions. Dallaire's plan certainly would have
required the intervening troops to take risks in an
effort to reach the targeted Rwandans or to confront the Hutu militia and government forces.
But the business-as-usual tone of the American
inquiry did not seem appropriate to the unprecedented and utterly unconventional crisis that was
under way.

On May 17, by which time most of the Tutsi
victims of the genocide were already dead, the
United States finally acceded to a version of
Dallaire's plan. However, few African countries
stepped forward to offer troops. Even if troops
had been immediately available, the lethargy of
the major powers would have hindered their use.
Though the Administration had committed the
United States to provide armored support if the
African nations provided soldiers, Pentagon
stalling resumed. On May 19 the UN formally requested fifty American armored personnel carri-
ers. On May 31 the United States agreed to send
the APCs from Germany to Entebbe, Uganda.
But squabbles between the Pentagon and UN
planners arose. Who would pay for the vehicles?

Should the vehicles be tracked or wheeled?
Would the UN buy them or simply lease them?
And who would pay the shipping costs? Com-
pounding the disputes was the fact that Department of Defense regulations prevented the U.S.
Army from preparing the vehicles for transport
until contracts had been signed. The Defense Department demanded that it be reimbursed $15
million for shipping spare parts and equipment
to and from Rwanda. In mid-June the White
House finally intervened. On June 19, a month
after the UN request, the United States began
transporting the APCs, but they were missing the
radios and heavy machine guns that would be
needed if UN troops came under fire. By the time
the APCs arrived, the genocide was over—halted
by Rwandan Patriotic Front forces under the
command of the Tutsi leader, Paul Kagame.

XII. The Stories We Tell

It is not hard to conceive of how the United
States might have done things differently. Ahead
of the plane crash, as violence escalated, it could
have agreed to Belgian pleas for UN reinforcements. Once the killing of thousands of Rwandans a day had begun, the President could have
deployed U.S. troops to Rwanda. The United
States could have joined Dallaire's beleaguered
UNAMIR forces or, if it feared associating with
shoddy UN peacekeeping, it could have intervened unilaterally with the Security Council's
backing, as France eventually did in late June.
The United States could also have acted without
the UN's blessing, as it did five years later in
Kosovo. Securing congressional support for U.S.
intervention would have been extremely difficult,
but by the second week of the killing Clinton
could have made the case that something ap-
proximating genocide was under way, that a
supreme American value was imperiled by its occurrence, and that U.S. contingents at relatively
low risk could stop the extermination of a people.

Alan Kuperman wrote in *Foreign Affairs* that
President Clinton was in the dark for two weeks;

by the time a large U.S. force could deploy, it would not have saved "even half of the ultimate victims." The evidence indicates that the killers' intentions were known by mid-level officials and knowable by their bosses within a week of the plane crash. Any failure to fully appreciate the genocide stemmed from political, moral, and imaginative weaknesses, not informational ones. As for what force could have accomplished, Kuperman's claims are purely speculative. We cannot know how the announcement of a robust or even a limited U.S. deployment would have affected the perpetrators' behavior. It is worth noting that even Kuperman concedes that belated intervention would have saved 75,000 to 125,000—no small achievement. A more serious challenge comes from the U.S. officials who argue that no amount of leadership from the White House would have overcome congressional opposition to sending U.S. troops to Africa. But even if that highly debatable point was true, the United States still had a variety of options. Instead of leaving it to mid-level officials to communicate with the Rwandan leadership behind the scenes, senior officials in the Administration could have taken control of the process. They could have publicly and frequently denounced the slaughter. They could have branded the crimes "genocide" at a far earlier stage. They could have called for the expulsion of the Rwandan delegation from the Security Council. On the telephone, at the UN, and on the Voice of America they could have threatened to prosecute those complicit in the genocide, naming names when possible. They could have deployed Pentagon assets to jam—even temporarily—the crucial, deadly radio broadcasts.

Instead of demanding a UN withdrawal, quibbling over costs, and coming forward (belatedly) with a plan better suited to caring for refugees than to stopping massacres, U.S. officials could have worked to make UNAMIR a force to contend with. They could have urged their Belgian allies to stay and protect Rwandan civilians. If the Belgians insisted on withdrawing, the White House could have done everything within its power to make sure that Dallaire was immediately reinforced. Se-nior officials could have spent U.S. political capital rallying troops from other nations and could have supplied strategic airlift and logistic support to a coalition that it had helped to create. In short, the United States could have led the world.

Why did none of these things happen? One reason is that all possible sources of pressure—U.S. allies, Congress, editorial boards, and the American people—were mute when it mattered for Rwanda. American leaders have a circular and deliberate relationship to public opinion. It is circular because public opinion is rarely if ever aroused by foreign crises, even genocidal ones, in the absence of political leadership, and yet at the same time, American leaders continually cite the absence of public support as grounds for inaction. The relationship is deliberate because American leadership is not absent in such circumstances: it was present regarding Rwanda, but devoted mainly to suppressing public outrage and thwarting UN initiatives so as to avoid acting.

Strikingly, most officials involved in shaping U.S. policy were able to define the decision not to stop genocide as ethical and moral. The Administration employed several devices to keep down enthusiasm for action and to preserve the public's sense—and, more important, its own—that U.S. policy choices were not merely politically astute but also morally acceptable. First, Administration officials exaggerated the extremity of the possible responses. Time and again U.S. leaders posed the choice as between staying out of Rwanda and "getting involved everywhere." In addition, they often presented the choice as one between doing nothing and sending in the Marines. On May 25, at the Naval Academy graduation ceremony, Clinton described America's relationship to ethnic trouble spots: "We cannot turn away from them, but our interests are not sufficiently at stake in so many of them to justify a commitment of our folks."

Second, Administration policymakers appealed to notions of the greater good. They did not simply frame U.S. policy as one contrived in order to advance the national interest or avoid U.S. casualties. Rather, they often argued against intervention from the standpoint of people committed to protecting human life. Owing to recent failures in UN peacekeeping, many humanitarian interventionists in the U.S. government were concerned about the future of America's relationship with the United Nations generally and peacekeeping specifically. They believed that the UN and humanitarianism could not afford another Somalia. Many internalized the belief that the UN had more to lose by sending reinforcements and failing than by allowing the killings to proceed. Their chief priority, after the evacuation of the Americans, was looking after UN peacekeepers, and they justified the withdrawal of the peacekeepers on the grounds that it would ensure a future for humanitarian intervention. In other words, Dallaire's peacekeeping mission in Rwanda had to be destroyed so that peacekeeping might be saved for use elsewhere.

A third feature of the response that helped to console U.S. officials at the time was the sheer flurry of Rwanda-related activity. U.S. officials with a special concern for Rwanda took their solace from mini-victories—working on behalf of specific individuals or groups (Monique Mujawamariya; the Rwandans gathered at the hotel). Government officials involved in policy met constantly and remained "seized of the matter"; they neither appeared nor felt indifferent. Although

little in the way of effective intervention emerged from midlevel meetings in Washington or New York, an abundance of memoranda and other documents did.

Finally, the almost willful delusion that what was happening in Rwanda did not amount to genocide created a nurturing ethical framework for inaction. "War" was "tragic" but created no moral imperative.

What is most frightening about this story is that it testifies to a system that in effect worked. President Clinton and his advisers had several aims. First, they wanted to avoid engagement in a conflict that posed little threat to American interests, narrowly defined. Second, they sought to appease a restless Congress by showing that they were cautious in their approach to peacekeeping. And third, they hoped to contain the political costs and avoid the moral stigma associated with allowing genocide. By and large, they achieved all three objectives. The normal operations of the foreign-policy bureaucracy and the international community permitted an illusion of continual deliberation, complex activity, and intense concern, even as Rwandans were left to die.

*   *   *

HENRY A. KISSINGER

THE PITFALLS OF UNIVERSAL JURISDICTION

Risking Judicial Tyranny

In less than a decade, an unprecedented movement has emerged to submit international poli-

From Henry Kissinger, *Does America Need a Foreign Policy?: Toward a Diplomacy for the 21st Century* (New York: Simon & Schuster, 2002): 274–82.

tics to judicial procedures. It has spread with extraordinary speed and has not been subjected to systematic debate, partly because of the intimidating passion of its advocates. To be sure, human rights violations, war crimes, genocide, and torture have so disgraced the modern age and in such a variety of places that the effort to interpose legal norms to prevent or punish such outrages does credit to its advocates. The danger lies in pushing the effort to extremes that risk substituting the tyranny of judges for that of governments; historically, the dictatorship of the virtuous has often led to inquisitions and even witch-hunts.

The doctrine of universal jurisdiction asserts that some crimes are so heinous that their perpetrators should not escape justice by invoking doctrines of sovereign immunity or the sacrosanct nature of national frontiers. Two specific approaches to achieve this goal have emerged recently. The first seeks to apply the procedures of domestic criminal justice to violations of universal standards, some of which are embodied in United Nations conventions, by authorizing national prosecutors to bring offenders into their jurisdictions through extradition from third countries. The second approach is the International Criminal Court (ICC), the founding treaty for which was created by a conference in Rome in July 1998 and signed by 95 states, including most European countries. It has already been ratified by 30 nations and will go into effect when the total reaches 60. On December 31, 2000, President Bill Clinton signed the ICC treaty with only hours to spare before the cutoff date. But he indicated that he would neither submit it for Senate approval nor recommend that his successor do so while the treaty remains in its present form.

The very concept of universal jurisdiction is of recent vintage. The sixth edition of *Black's Law Dictionary*, published in 1990, does not contain even an entry for the term. The closest analogous concept listed is *hostes humani generis* ("enemies of the human race"). Until recently, the latter term has been applied to pirates, hijackers, and similar outlaws whose crimes were typically committed outside the territory of any state. The notion that heads of state and senior public officials should have the same standing as outlaws before the bar of justice is quite new.

In the aftermath of the Holocaust and the many atrocities committed since, major efforts have been made to find a judicial standard to deal with such catastrophes: the Nuremberg tri-als of 1945–46, the Universal Declaration of Human Rights of 1948, the genocide convention of 1948, and the antitorture convention of 1988. The Final Act of the Conference on Security and Cooperation in Europe, signed in Helsinki in 1975 by President Gerald Ford on behalf of the United States, obligated the 35 signatory nations to observe certain stated human rights, subjecting violators to the pressures by which foreign policy commitments are generally sustained. In the hands of courageous groups in Eastern Europe, the Final Act became one of several weapons by which communist rule was delegitimized and eventually undermined. In the 1990s, international tribunals to punish crimes committed in the former Yugoslavia and Rwanda, established ad hoc by the U.N. Security Council, have sought to provide a system of accountability for specific regions ravaged by arbitrary violence.

But none of these steps was conceived at the time as instituting a "universal jurisdiction." It is unlikely that any of the signatories of either the U.N. conventions or the Helsinki Final Act thought it possible that national judges would use them as a basis for extradition requests regarding alleged crimes committed outside their jurisdictions. The drafters almost certainly believed that they were stating general principles, not laws that would be enforced by national courts. For example, Eleanor Roosevelt, one of the drafters of the Universal Declaration of Human Rights, referred to it as a "common standard." As one of the negotiators of the Final Act of the Helsinki conference, I can affirm that the administration I represented considered it primarily a diplomatic weapon to use to thwart the communists' attempts to pressure the Soviet and captive peoples. Even with respect to binding undertakings such as the genocide convention, it was never thought that they would subject past and future leaders of one nation to prosecution by the national magistrates of another state where the violations had not occurred. Nor, until recently, was it argued that the various U.N. declarations subjected past and future leaders to the possibility of prosecution by national magistrates of third countries without either due process safeguards or institutional restraints.

Yet this is in essence the precedent that was set by the 1998 British detention of former Chilean President Augusto Pinochet as the result of an extradition request by a Spanish judge seeking to try Pinochet for crimes committed against Spaniards on Chilean soil. For advocates of universal jurisdiction, that detention—lasting more than 16 months—was a landmark establishing a just principle. But any universal system should contain procedures not only to punish the wicked but also to constrain the righteous. It must not allow legal principles to be used as weapons to settle political scores. Questions such as these must therefore be answered: What legal norms are being applied? What are the rules of evidence? What safeguards exist for the defendant? And how will prosecutions affect other fundamental foreign policy objectives and interests?

A Dangerous Precedent

It is decidedly unfashionable to express any degree of skepticism about the way the Pinochet case was handled. For almost all the parties of the European left, Augusto Pinochet is the incarnation of a right-wing assault on democracy because he led a coup d'état against an elected leader. At the time, others, including the leaders of Chile's democratic parties, viewed Salvador Allende as a radical Marxist ideologue bent on imposing a Castro-style dictatorship with the aid of Cuban-trained militias and Cuban weapons. This was why the leaders of Chile's democratic parties publicly welcomed—yes, welcomed—Allende's overthrow. (They changed their attitude only after the junta brutally maintained its autocratic rule far longer than was warranted by the invocation of an emergency.)

Disapproval of the Allende regime does not exonerate those who perpetrated systematic human rights abuses after it was overthrown. But neither should the applicability of universal jurisdiction as a policy be determined by one's view of the political history of Chile. The appropriate

solution was arrived at in August 2000 when the Chilean Supreme Court withdrew Pinochet's senatorial immunity, making it possible to deal with the charges against him in the courts of the country most competent to judge this history and to relate its decisions to the stability and vitality of its democratic institutions.

On November 25, 1998, the judiciary committee of the British House of Lords (the United Kingdom's supreme court) concluded that "international law has made it plain that certain types of conduct . . . are not acceptable conduct on the part of anyone." But that principle did not oblige the lords to endow a Spanish magistrate—and presumably other magistrates elsewhere in the world—with the authority to enforce it in a country where the accused had committed no crime, and then to cause the restraint of the accused for 16 months in yet another country in which he was equally a stranger. It could have held that Chile, or an international tribunal specifically established for crimes committed in Chile on the model of the courts set up for heinous crimes in the former Yugoslavia and Rwanda, was the appropriate forum.

The unprecedented and sweeping interpretation of international law in *Ex parte Pinochet* would arm any magistrate anywhere in the world with the power to demand extradition, substituting the magistrate's own judgment for the reconciliation procedures of even incontestably democratic societies where alleged violations of human rights may have occurred. It would also subject the accused to the criminal procedures of the magistrate's country, with a legal system that may be unfamiliar to the defendant and that would force the defendant to bring evidence and witnesses from long distances. Such a system goes far beyond the explicit and limited mandates established by the U.N. Security Council for the tribunals covering war crimes in the former Yugoslavia and Rwanda as well as the one being negotiated for Cambodia.

Perhaps the most important issue is the relationship of universal jurisdiction to national reconciliation procedures set up by new democratic governments to deal with their countries' questionable pasts. One would have thought that a Spanish magistrate would have been sensitive to the incongruity of a request by Spain, itself haunted by transgressions committed during the Spanish Civil War and the regime of General Francisco Franco, to try in Spanish courts alleged crimes against humanity committed elsewhere.

The decision of post-Franco Spain to avoid wholesale criminal trials for the human rights violations of the recent past was designed explicitly to foster a process of national reconciliation that undoubtedly contributed much to the present vigor of Spanish democracy. Why should Chile's attempt at national reconciliation not have been given the same opportunity? Should any outside group dissatisfied with the reconciliation procedures of, say, South Africa be free to challenge them in their own national courts or those of third countries?

It is an important principle that those who commit war crimes or systematically violate human rights should be held accountable. But the consolidation of law, domestic peace, and representative government in a nation struggling to come to terms with a brutal past has a claim as well. The instinct to punish must be related, as in every constitutional democratic political structure, to a system of checks and balances that includes other elements critical to the survival and expansion of democracy.

Another grave issue is the use in such cases of extradition procedures designed for ordinary criminals. If the Pinochet case becomes a precedent, magistrates anywhere will be in a position to put forward an extradition request without warning to the accused and regardless of the policies the accused's country might already have in place for dealing with the charges. The country from which extradition is requested then faces a seemingly technical legal decision that, in fact, amounts to the exercise of political discretion—whether to entertain the claim or not.

Once extradition procedures are in train, they develop a momentum of their own. The accused is not allowed to challenge the substantive merit of the case and instead is confined to procedural issues: that there was, say, some technical flaw in the extradition request, that the judicial system of the requesting country is incapable of providing a fair hearing, or that the crime for which the extradition is sought is not treated as a crime in the country from which extradition has been requested—thereby conceding much of the merit of the charge. Meanwhile, while these claims are being considered by the judicial system of the country from which extradition is sought, the accused remains in some form of detention, possibly for years. Such procedures provide an opportunity for political harassment long before the accused is in a position to present any defense. It would be ironic if a doctrine designed to transcend the political process turns into a means to pursue political enemies rather than universal justice.

The Pinochet precedent, if literally applied, would permit the two sides in the Arab-Israeli conflict, or those in any other passionate international controversy, to project their battles into the various national courts by pursuing adversaries with extradition requests. When discretion on what crimes are subject to universal jurisdiction and whom to prosecute is left to national prosecutors, the scope for arbitrariness is wide indeed. So far, universal jurisdiction has involved the prosecution of one fashionably reviled man of the right while scores of East European communist leaders—not to speak of Caribbean, Middle Eastern, or African leaders who inflicted their own full measures of torture and suffering—have not had to face similar prosecutions.

Some will argue that a double standard does not excuse violations of international law and that it is better to bring one malefactor to justice than to grant immunity to all. This is not an argument permitted in the domestic jurisdictions of many democracies—in Canada, for example, a charge can be thrown out of court merely by showing that a prosecution has been selective enough to amount to an abuse of process. In any case, a universal standard of justice should not be based on the proposition that a just end warrants unjust means, or that political fashion trumps fair judicial procedures.

An Indiscriminate Court

The ideological supporters of universal jurisdiction also provide much of the intellectual compass for the emerging International Criminal Court. Their goal is to criminalize certain types of military and political actions and thereby bring about a more humane conduct of international relations. To the extent that the ICC replaces the claim of national judges to universal jurisdiction, it greatly improves the state of international law. And, in time, it may be possible to negotiate modifications of the present statute to make the ICC more compatible with U.S. constitutional practice. But in its present form of assigning the ultimate dilemmas of international politics to unelected jurists—and to an international judiciary at that—it represents such a fundamental change in U.S. constitutional practice that a full national debate and the full participation of Congress are imperative. Such a momentous revolution should not come about by tacit acquiescence in the decision of the House of Lords or by dealing with the ICC issue through a strategy of improving specific clauses rather than as a fundamental issue of principle.

The doctrine of universal jurisdiction is based on the proposition that the individuals or cases subject to it have been clearly identified. In some instances, especially those based on Nuremberg precedents, the definition of who can be prosecuted in an international court and in what circumstances is self-evident. But many issues are much more vague and depend on an understanding of the historical and political context. It is this fuzziness that risks arbitrariness on the part of prosecutors and judges years after the event and that became apparent with respect to existing tribunals.

For example, can any leader of the United States or of another country be hauled before international tribunals established for other purposes? This is precisely what Amnesty International implied when, in the summer of 1999, it supported a "complaint" by a group of European and Canadian law professors to Louise Arbour, then the prosecutor of the International Criminal Tribunal for the Former Yugoslavia (ICTY). The complaint alleged that crimes against humanity had been committed during the NATO air campaign in Kosovo. Arbour ordered an internal staff review, thereby implying that she did have jurisdiction if such violations could, in fact, be demonstrated. Her successor, Carla Del Ponte, in the end declined to indict any NATO official because of a general inability "to pinpoint individual responsibilities," thereby implying anew that the court had jurisdiction over NATO and American leaders in the Balkans and would have issued an indictment had it been able to identify the particular leaders allegedly involved.

Most Americans would be amazed to learn that the ICTY, created at U.S. behest in 1993 to deal with Balkan war criminals, had asserted a right to investigate U.S. political and military leaders for allegedly criminal conduct—and for the indefinite future, since no statute of limitations applies. Though the ICTY prosecutor chose not to pursue the charge—on the ambiguous ground of an inability to collect evidence—some national prosecutor may wish later to take up the matter as a valid subject for universal jurisdiction.

The pressures to achieve the widest scope for the doctrine of universal jurisdiction were demonstrated as well by a suit before the European Court of Human Rights in June 2000 by families of Argentine sailors who died in the sinking of the Argentine cruiser *General Belgano* during the Falklands War. The concept of universal jurisdiction has moved from judging alleged political crimes against humanity to second-guessing, 18 years after the event, military operations in which neither civilians nor civilian targets were involved.

Distrusting national governments, many of the advocates of universal jurisdiction seek to place politicians under the supervision of magistrates and the judicial system. But prosecutorial discretion without accountability is precisely one of the flaws of the International Criminal Court. Definitions of the relevant crimes are vague and highly susceptible to politicized application. Defendants will not enjoy due process as understood in the United States. Any signatory state has the right to trigger an investigation. As the U.S. experience with the special prosecutors investigating the executive branch shows, such a procedure is likely to develop its own momentum without time limits and can turn into an instrument of political warfare. And the extraordinary attempt of the ICC to assert jurisdiction over Americans even in the absence of U.S. accession to the treaty has already triggered legislation in Congress to resist it.

The independent prosecutor of the ICC has the power to issue indictments, subject to review only by a panel of three judges. According to the Rome statute, the Security Council has the right to quash any indictment. But since revoking an indictment is subject to the veto of any permanent Security Council member, and since the prosecutor is unlikely to issue an indictment without the backing of at least one permanent member of the Security Council, he or she has virtually unlimited discretion in practice. Another provision permits the country whose citizen is accused to take over the investigation and trial. But the ICC retains the ultimate authority on whether that function has been adequately exercised and, if it finds it has not, the ICC can reassert jurisdiction. While these procedures are taking place, which may take years, the accused will be under some restraint and certainly under grave public shadow.

The advocates of universal jurisdiction argue that the state is the basic cause of war and cannot be trusted to deliver justice. If law replaced politics, peace and justice would prevail. But even a cursory examination of history shows that there is no evidence to support such a theory. The role of the statesman is to choose the best option when seeking to advance peace and justice, realizing that there is frequently a tension between the two and that any reconciliation is likely to be partial. The choice, however, is not simply between universal and national jurisdictions.

Modest Proposals

The precedents set by international tribunals established to deal with situations where the enormity of the crime is evident and the local judicial system is clearly incapable of administering justice, as in the former Yugoslavia and Rwanda, have shown that it is possible to punish without removing from the process all political judgment and experience. In time, it may be possible to renegotiate the ICC statute to avoid its shortcomings and dangers. Until then, the United States should go no further toward a more formal system than one containing the following three provisions. First, the U.N. Security Council would create a Human Rights Commission or a special subcommittee to report whenever systematic human rights violations seem to warrant judicial action. Second, when the government under which the alleged crime occurred is not authentically representative, or where the domestic judicial system is incapable of sitting in judgment on the crime, the Security Council would set up an ad hoc international tribunal on the model of those of the former Yugoslavia or Rwanda. And third, the procedures for these international tribunals as well as the scope of the prosecution should be precisely defined by the Security Council, and the accused should be entitled to the due process safeguards accorded in common jurisdictions.

In this manner, internationally agreed procedures to deal with war crimes, genocide, or other crimes against humanity could become institutionalized. Furthermore, the one-sidedness of the current pursuit of universal jurisdiction would be avoided. This pursuit could threaten the very purpose for which the concept has been developed. In the end, an excessive reliance on universal jurisdiction may undermine the political will to sustain the humane norms of international behavior so necessary to temper the violent times in which we live.

KENNETH ROTH

THE CASE FOR UNIVERSAL JURISDICTION

Behind much of the savagery of modern history lies impunity. Tyrants commit atrocities, including genocide, when they calculate they can get away with them. Too often, dictators use violence and intimidation to shut down any prospect of domestic prosecution. Over the past decade, however, a slowly emerging system of international justice has begun to break this pattern of impunity in national courts.

The United Nations Security Council established international war crimes tribunals for the former Yugoslavia in 1993 and Rwanda in 1994 and is now negotiating the creation of mixed national-international tribunals for Cambodia and Sierra Leone. In 1998, the world's governments gathered in Rome to adopt a treaty for an International Criminal Court (ICC) with potentially global jurisdiction over genocide, war crimes, and crimes against humanity.

With growing frequency, national courts operating under the doctrine of universal jurisdiction are prosecuting despots in their custody for atrocities committed abroad. Impunity may still be the norm in many domestic courts, but international justice is an increasingly viable option, promising a measure of solace to victims and their families and raising the possibility that would-be tyrants will begin to think twice before embarking on a barbarous path.

In "The Pitfalls of Universal Jurisdiction" (July/August 2001), former Secretary of State Henry Kissinger catalogues a list of grievances against the juridical concept that people who commit the most severe human rights crimes can be tried wherever they are found. But his objections are misplaced, and the alternative he proposes is little better than a return to impunity.

From *Foreign Affairs* 80, no. 5 (September/October 2001): 150–154.

Kissinger begins by suggesting that universal jurisdiction is a new idea, at least as applied to heads of state and senior public officials. However, the exercise by U.S. courts of jurisdiction over certain heinous crimes committed overseas is an accepted part of American jurisprudence, reflected in treaties on terrorism and aircraft hijacking dating from 1970. Universal jurisdiction was also the concept that allowed Israel to try Adolf Eichmann in Jerusalem in 1961.

Kissinger says that the drafters of the Helsinki Accords—the basic human rights principles adopted by the Conference on Security and Cooperation in Europe in 1975—and the U.N.'s 1948 Universal Declaration of Human Rights never intended to authorize universal jurisdiction. But this argument is irrelevant, because these hortatory declarations are not legally binding treaties of the sort that could grant such powers.

As for the many formal treaties on human rights, Kissinger believes it "unlikely" that their signatories "thought it possible that national judges would use them as a basis for extradition requests regarding alleged crimes committed outside their jurisdictions." To the contrary, the Torture Convention of 1984, ratified by 124 governments including the United States, requires states either to prosecute any suspected torturer found on their territory, regardless of where the torture took place, or to extradite the suspect to a country that will do so. Similarly, the Geneva Conventions of 1949 on the conduct of war, ratified by 189 countries including the United States, require each participating state to "search for" persons who have committed grave breaches of the conventions and to "bring such persons, regardless of nationality, before its own courts." What is new is not the concept of extraterritorial jurisdiction but the willingness of some governments to fulfill this duty against those in high places.

Order and the Court

Kissinger's critique of universal jurisdiction has two principal targets: the soon-to-be-formed International Criminal Court and the exercise of universal jurisdiction by national courts. (Strictly speaking, the ICC will use not universal jurisdiction but, rather, a delegation of states' traditional power to try crimes committed on their own territory.) Kissinger claims that the crimes detailed in the ICC treaty are "vague and highly susceptible to politicized application." But the treaty's definition of war crimes closely resembles that found in the Pentagon's own military manuals and is derived from the widely ratified Geneva Conventions and their Additional Protocols adopted in 1977. Similarly, the ICC treaty's definition of genocide is borrowed directly from the Genocide Convention of 1948, which the United States and 131 other governments have ratified and pledged to uphold, including by prose-cuting offenders. The definition of crimes against humanity is derived from the Nuremberg Charter, which, as Kissinger acknowledges, proscribes conduct that is "self-evident[ly]" wrong.

Kissinger further asserts that the ICC prosecutor will have "discretion without accountability," going so far as to raise the specter of Independent Counsel Kenneth Starr and to decry "the tyranny of judges." In fact, the prosecutor can be removed for misconduct by a simple majority of the governments that ratify the ICC treaty, and a two-thirds vote can remove a judge. Because joining the court means giving it jurisdiction over crimes committed on the signatory's territory, the vast majority of member states will be democracies, not the abusive governments that self-protectively flock to U.N. human rights bodies, where membership bears no cost.

Kissinger criticizes the "extraordinary attempt of the ICC to assert jurisdiction over Americans even in the absence of U.S. accession to the treaty." But the United States itself asserts such jurisdiction over others' citizens when it prosecutes terrorists or drug traffickers, such as Panamanian dictator Manuel Noriega, without the consent of the suspect's government. Moreover, the ICC will assert such power only if an American commits a specified atrocity on the territory of a government that has joined the ICC and has thus delegated its prosecutorial authority to the court.

Kissinger claims that ICC defendants "will not enjoy due process as understood in the United States"—an apparent allusion to the lack of a jury trial in a court that will blend civil and common law traditions. But U.S. courts martial also do not provide trials by jury. Moreover, U.S. civilian courts routinely approve the constitutionality of extradition to countries that lack jury trials, so long as their courts otherwise observe basic due process. The ICC clearly will provide such due process, since its treaty requires adherence to the full complement of international fair-trial standards.

Of course, any court's regard for due process is only as good as the quality and temperament of its judges. The ICC's judges will be chosen by the governments that join the court, most of which, as noted, will be democracies. Even without ratifying the ICC treaty, the U.S. government could help shape a culture of respect for due process by quietly working with the court, as it has done successfully with the international war crimes tribunals for Rwanda and the former Yugoslavia. Regrettably, ICC opponents in Washington are pushing legislation—the misnamed American Servicemembers Protection Act—that would preclude such cooperation.

The experience of the Yugoslav and Rwandan tribunals, of which Kissinger speaks favorably, suggests that international jurists, when forced to decide the fate of a particular criminal suspect, do so with scrupulous regard for fair trial standards. Kissinger's only stated objection to these tribunals concerns the decision of the prosecutor of the tribunal for the former Yugoslavia to pursue a brief inquiry into how NATO conducted its air war against the new Yugoslavia—an inquiry that led her to exonerate NATO.

It should be noted, in addition, that the jurisdiction of the Yugoslav tribunal was set not by the prosecutor but by the U.N. Security Council, with

U.S. consent. The council chose to grant jurisdiction without prospective time limit, over serious human rights crimes within the territory of the former Yugoslavia committed by anyone—not just Serbs, Croats, and Bosnian Muslims. In light of that mandate, the prosecutor would have been derelict in her duties not to consider NATO's conduct; according to an extensive field investigation by Human Rights Watch, roughly half of the approximately 500 civilian deaths caused by NATO's bombs could be attributed to NATO's failure, albeit not criminal, to abide by international humanitarian law.

Kissinger claims that the ICC would violate the U.S. Constitution if it asserted jurisdiction over an American. But the court is unlikely to prosecute an American because the Rome treaty deprives the ICC of jurisdiction if, after the court gives required notice of its intention to examine a suspect, the suspect's government conducts its own good-faith investigation and, if appropriate, prosecution. It is the stated policy of the U.S. government to investigate and prosecute its own war criminals.

Moreover, the ICC's assertion of jurisdiction over an American for a crime committed abroad poses no greater constitutional problem than the routine practice under status-of-forces agreements of allowing foreign prosecution of American military personnel for crimes committed overseas, such as Japan's arrest in July of a U.S. Air Force sergeant for an alleged rape on Okinawa. An unconstitutional delegation of U.S. judicial power would arguably take place only if the United States ratified the ICC treaty; then an American committed genocide, war crimes, or crimes against humanity on U.S. soil; and then U.S. authorities did not prosecute the offender. Yet that remote possibility would signal a constitutional crisis far graver than one spawned by an ICC prosecution.

No Place To Hide

National courts come under Kissinger's fire for selectively applying universal jurisdiction. He characterizes the extradition request by a Spanish judge seeking to try former Chilean President Augusto Pinochet for crimes against Spanish citizens on Chilean soil as singling out a "fashionably reviled man of the right." But Pinochet was sought not, as Kissinger writes, "because he led a coup d'état against an elected leader" who was a favorite of the left. Rather, Pinochet was targeted because security forces under his command murdered and forcibly "disappeared" some 3,000 people and tortured thousands more.

Furthermore, in recent years national courts have exercised universal jurisdiction against a wide range of suspects: Bosnian war criminals, Rwandan *génocidaires*, Argentine torturers, and Chad's former dictator. It has come to the point where the main limit on national courts empowered to exercise universal jurisdiction is the availability of the defendant, not questions of ideology.

Kissinger also cites the Pinochet case to argue that international justice interferes with the choice by democratic governments to forgive rather than prosecute past offenders. In fact, Pinochet's imposition of a self-amnesty at the height of his dictatorship limited Chile's democratic options. Only after 16 months of detention in the United Kingdom diminished his power was Chilean democracy able to begin prosecution. Such imposed impunity is far more common than democratically chosen impunity.

Kissinger would have had a better case had prosecutors sought, for example, to overturn the compromise negotiated by South Africa's Nelson Mandela, widely recognized at the time as the legitimate representative of the victims of apartheid. Mandela agreed to grant abusers immunity from prosecution if they gave detailed testimony about their crimes. In an appropriate exercise of prosecutorial discretion, no prosecutor has challenged this arrangement, and no government would likely countenance such a challenge.

Kissinger legitimately worries that the nations exercising universal jurisdiction could include governments with less-entrenched traditions of due process than the United Kingdom's. But his fear of governments robotically extraditing suspects for sham or counterproductive trials is overblown.

Governments regularly deny extradition to courts that are unable to ensure high standards of due process. And foreign ministries, including the U.S. State Department, routinely deny extradition requests for reasons of public policy.

If an American faced prosecution by an untrustworthy foreign court, the United States undoubtedly would apply pressure for his or her release. If that failed, however, it might prove useful to offer the prosecuting government the face-saving alternative of transferring the suspect to the ICC, with its extensive procedural protections, including deference to good-faith investigations and prosecutions by a suspect's own government. Unfortunately, the legislation being pushed by ICC opponents in Washington would preclude that option.

Until the ICC treaty is renegotiated to avoid what Kissinger sees as its "short-comings and dangers," he recommends that the U.N. Security Council determine which cases warrant an international tribunal. That option was rejected during the Rome negotiations on the ICC because it would allow the council's five permanent members, including Russia and China as well as the United States, to exempt their nationals and those of their allies by exercising their vetoes.

As a nation committed to human rights and the rule of law, the United States should be embracing an international system of justice, even if it means that Americans, like everyone else, might sometimes be scrutinized.

JOHN J. MEARSHEIMER

THE FALSE PROMISE OF INTERNATIONAL INSTITUTIONS

*　*　*

What Are Institutions?

There is no widely-agreed upon definition of institutions in the international relations literature.[1] The concept is sometimes defined so broadly as to encompass all of international relations, which gives it little analytical bite.[2] For example, defining institutions as "recognized patterns of behavior or practice around which expectations converge" allows the concept to cover almost every regularized pattern of activity between states, from war to tariff bindings negotiated under the General Agreement on Tariffs and Trade (GATT), thus rendering

From *International Security* 19, no. 3 (Winter 1994/95): 5–49.

it largely meaningless.[3] Still, it is possible to devise a useful definition that is consistent with how most institutionalist scholars employ the concept.

I define institutions as a set of rules that stipulate the ways in which states should cooperate and compete with each other.[4] They prescribe acceptable forms of state behavior, and proscribe unacceptable kinds of behavior. These rules are negotiated by states, and according to many prominent theorists, they entail the mutual acceptance of higher norms, which are "standards of behavior defined in terms of rights and obligations."[5] These rules are typically formalized in international agreements, and are usually embodied in organizations with their own personnel and budgets.[6] Although rules are usually incorporated into a formal international organization, it is not the organization *per se* that compels states to obey the rules. Institutions are not a form of world government. States themselves must choose to obey the rules they created. Institutions, in short, call for the "decentralized cooperation of individual sovereign states, without any effective mechanism of command."[7]

*   *   *

Institutions in a Realist World

Realists * * * recognize that states sometimes operate through institutions. However, they believe that those rules reflect state calculations of self-interest based primarily on the international distribution of power. The most powerful states in the system create and shape institutions so that they can maintain their share of world power, or even increase it. In this view, institutions are essentially "arenas for acting out power relationships."[8] For realists, the causes of war and peace are mainly a function of the balance of power, and institutions largely mirror the distribution of power in the system. In short, the balance of power is the independent variable that explains war; institutions are merely an intervening variable in the process.

NATO provides a good example of realist thinking about institutions. NATO is an institution, and it certainly played a role in preventing World War III and helping the West win the Cold War. Nevertheless, NATO was basically a manifestation of the bipolar distribution of power in Europe during the Cold War, and it was that balance of power, not NATO *per se*, that provided the key to maintaining stability on the continent. NATO was essentially an American tool for managing power in the face of the Soviet threat. Now, with the collapse of the Soviet Union, realists argue that NATO must either disappear or reconstitute itself on the basis of the new distribution of power in Europe.[9] NATO cannot remain as it was during the Cold War.

*   *   *

Liberal Institutionalism

Liberal institutionalism does not directly address the question of whether institutions cause peace, but instead focuses on the less ambitious goal of explaining cooperation in cases where state interests are not fundamentally opposed.[10] Specifically, the theory looks at cases where states are having difficulty cooperating because they have "mixed" interests; in other words, each side has incentives both to cooperate and not to cooperate.[11] Each side can benefit from cooperation, however, which liberal institutionalists define as "goal-directed behavior that entails mutual policy adjustments so that all sides end up better off than they would otherwise be."[12] The theory is of little relevance in situations where states' interests are fundamentally conflictual and neither side thinks it has much to gain from cooperation. In these circumstances, states aim to gain advantage over each other. They think in terms of winning and losing, and this invariably leads to intense security competition, and sometimes war. But liberal institutionalism does not deal directly with these situations, and thus says little about how to resolve or even ameliorate them.

Therefore, the theory largely ignores security issues and concentrates instead on economic and, to a lesser extent, environmental issues.[13] In fact, the theory is built on the assumption that international politics can be divided into two realms—security and political economy—and that liberal institutionalism mainly applies to the latter, but not the former. * * *

*   *   *

According to liberal institutionalists, the principal obstacle to cooperation among states with mutual interests is the threat of cheating.[14] The famous "prisoners' dilemma," which is the analytical centerpiece of most of the liberal institutionalist literature, captures the essence of the problem that states must solve to achieve cooperation.[15] Each of two states can either cheat or cooperate with the other. Each side wants to maximize its own gain, but does not care about the size of the other side's gain; each side cares about the other side only so far as the other side's chosen strategy affects its own prospects for maximizing gain. The most attractive strategy for each state is to cheat and hope the other state pursues a cooperative strategy. In other words, a state's ideal outcome is to "sucker" the other side into thinking it is going to cooperate, and then cheat. But both sides understand this logic, and therefore both sides will try to cheat the other. Consequently, both sides will end up worse off than if they had cooperated, since mutual cheating leads to the worst possible outcome. Even though mutual cooperation is not as attractive as suckering the other side, it is certainly better than the outcome when both sides cheat.

The key to solving this dilemma is for each side to convince the other that they have a collective interest in making what appear to be short-term sacrifices (the gain that might result from successful cheating) for the sake of long-term benefits (the substantial payoff from mutual long-term cooperation). This means convincing states to accept the second-best outcome, which is mutual collaboration. The principal obstacle to reaching this cooperative outcome will be fear of getting suckered, should the other side cheat. This, in a nutshell, is the problem that institutions must solve.

To deal with this problem of "political market failure," institutions must deter cheaters and protect victims.[16] Three messages must be sent to potential cheaters: you will be caught, you will be punished immediately, and you will jeopardize future cooperative efforts. Potential victims, on the other hand, need early warning of cheating to avoid serious injury, and need the means to punish cheaters.

Liberal institutionalists do not aim to deal with cheaters and victims by changing fundamental norms of state behavior. Nor do they suggest transforming the anarchical nature of the international system. They accept the assumption that states operate in an anarchic environment and behave in a self-interested manner.[17] * * * Liberal institutionalists instead concentrate on showing how rules can work to counter the cheating problem, even while states seek to maximize their own welfare. They argue that institutions can change a state's calculations about how to maximize gains. Specifically, rules can get

states to make the short-term sacrifices needed to resolve the prisoners' dilemma and thus to realize long-term gains. Institutions, in short, can produce cooperation.

Rules can ideally be employed to make four major changes in "the contractual environment."[18] First, rules can increase the number of transactions between particular states over time.[19] This *institutionalized iteration* discourages cheating in three ways. It raises the costs of cheating by creating the prospect of future gains through cooperation, thereby invoking "the shadow of the future" to deter cheating today. A state caught cheating would jeopardize its prospects of benefiting from future cooperation, since the victim would probably retaliate. In addition, iteration gives the victim the opportunity to pay back the cheater: it allows for reciprocation, the tit-for-tat strategy, which works to punish cheaters and not allow them to get away with their transgression. Finally, it rewards states that develop a reputation for faithful adherence to agreements, and punishes states that acquire a reputation for cheating.[20]

Second, rules can tie together interactions between states in different issue areas. *Issue-linkage* aims to create greater interdependence between states, who will then be reluctant to cheat in one issue area for fear that the victim—and perhaps other states as well—will retaliate in another issue area. It discourages cheating in much the same way as iteration: it raises the costs of cheating and provides a way for the victim to retaliate against the cheater.

Third, a structure of rules can increase the amount of *information* available to participants in cooperative agreements so that close monitoring is possible. Raising the level of information discourages cheating in two ways: it increases the likelihood that cheaters will be caught, and more importantly, it provides victims with early warning of cheating, thereby enabling them to take protective measures before they are badly hurt.

Fourth, rules can reduce the *transaction costs* of individual agreements.[21] When institutions perform the tasks described above, states can devote less effort to negotiating and monitoring cooperative agreements, and to hedging against possible defections. By increasing the efficiency of international cooperation, institutions make it more profitable and thus more attractive for self-interested states.

Liberal institutionalism is generally thought to be of limited utility in the security realm, because fear of cheating is considered a much greater obstacle to cooperation when military issues are at stake.[22] There is the constant threat that betrayal will result in a devastating military defeat. This threat of "swift, decisive defection" is simply not present when dealing with international economics. Given that "the costs of betrayal" are potentially much graver in the military than the economic sphere, states will be very reluctant to accept the "one step backward, two steps forward" logic which underpins the tit-for-tat strategy of conditional cooperation. One step backward in the security realm might mean destruction, in which case there will be no next step—backward or forward.[23]

* * * There is an important theoretical failing in the liberal institutionalist logic, even as it applies to economic issues. The theory is correct as far as it goes: cheating can be a serious barrier to cooperation. It ignores, however, the other major obstacle to cooperation: relative-gains concerns. As Joseph Grieco has shown, liberal institutionalists assume that states are not concerned about relative gains, but focus exclusively on absolute gains.[24] * * *

This oversight is revealed by the assumed order of preference in the prisoners' dilemma game: each state cares about how its opponent's strategy will affect its own (absolute) gains, but not about how much one side gains relative to the other. In other words, each side simply wants to get the best deal for itself, and does not pay attention to how well the other side fares in the process.[25] Nevertheless, liberal institutionalists cannot ignore relative-gains considerations, because they assume that states are self-interested actors in an anarchic system, and they recognize that military power matters to states. A theory that explicitly accepts realism's core assumptions—and liberal institutionalism does that—must confront the issue of relative gains if it hopes to develop a sound explanation for why states cooperate.

One might expect liberal institutionalist to offer the counterargument that relative-gains logic applies only to the security realm, while absolute-gains logic applies to the economic realm. Given that they are mainly concerned with explaining economic and environmental cooperation, leaving relative-gains concerns out of the theory does not matter.

There are two problems with this argument. First, if cheating were the only significant obstacle to cooperation, liberal institutionalists could argue that their theory applies to the economic, but not the military realm. In fact, they do make that argument. However, once relative-gains considerations are factored into the equation, it becomes impossible to maintain the neat dividing line between economic and military issues, mainly because military might is significantly dependent on economic might. The relative size of a state's economy has profound consequences for its standing in the international balance of military power. Therefore, relative-gains concerns must be taken into account for security reasons when looking at the economic as well as military domain. The neat dividing line that liberal institutionalists employ to specify when their theory applies has little utility when one accepts that states worry about relative gains.[26]

Second, there are non-realist (i.e., nonsecurity) logics that might explain why states worry about relative gains. Strategic trade theory, for example, provides a straightforward economic logic for why states should care about relative gains.[27] It argues that states should help their own firms gain comparative advantage over the firms of rival states, because that is the best way to insure national economic prosperity. There is also a psychological logic, which portrays individuals as caring about how well they do (or their state does) in a cooperative agreement, not for material reasons, but because it is human nature to compare one's progress with that of others.[28]

Another possible liberal institutionalist counterargument is that solving the cheating problem renders the relative-gains problem irrelevant. If states cannot cheat each other, they need not fear each other, and therefore, states would not have to worry about relative power. The problem with this argument, however, is that even if the cheating problem were solved, states would still have to worry about relative gains because gaps in gains can be translated into military advantage that can be used for coercion or aggression. And in the international system, states sometimes have conflicting interests that lead to aggression.

There is also empirical evidence that relative-gains considerations mattered during the Cold War even in economic relations among the advanced industrialized democracies in the Organization for Economic Cooperation and Development (OECD). One would not expect realist logic about relative gains to be influential in this case: the United States was a superpower with little to fear militarily from the other OECD states, and those states were unlikely to use a relative-gains advantage to threaten the United States.[29] Furthermore, the OECD states were important American allies during the Cold War, and thus the United States benefited strategically when they gained substantially in size and strength.

Nonetheless, relative gains appear to have mattered in economic relations among the advanced industrial states. Consider three prominent studies. Stephen Krasner considered efforts at cooperation in different sectors of the international communications industry. He found that states were remarkably unconcerned about cheating but deeply worried about relative gains, which led him to conclude that liberal institutionalism "is not relevant for global communications." Grieco examined American and EC efforts to implement, under the auspices of GATT, a number of agreements relating to non-tariff barriers to trade. He found that the level of success was not a function of concerns about cheating but was influenced primarily by concern about the distribution of gains. Similarly, Michael Mastanduno found that concern about relative gains, not about cheating, was an impor-

tant factor in shaping American policy towards Japan in three cases: the FSX fighter aircraft, satellites, and high-definition television.[30]

I am not suggesting that relative-gains considerations make cooperation impossible; my point is simply that they can pose a serious impediment to cooperation and must therefore be taken into account when developing a theory of cooperation among states. This point is apparently now recognized by liberal institutionalists. Keohane, for example, acknowledges that he "did make a major mistake by underemphasizing distributive issues and the complexities they create for international cooperation."[31]

CAN LIBERAL INSTITUTIONALISM BE REPAIRED?

Liberal institutionalists must address two questions if they are to repair their theory. First, can institutions facilitate cooperation when states seriously care about relative gains, or do institutions only matter when states can ignore relative-gains considerations and focus instead on absolute gains? I find no evidence that liberal institutionalists believe that institutions facilitate cooperation when states care deeply about relative gains. They apparently concede that their theory only applies when relative-gains considerations matter little or hardly at all.[32] Thus the second question: when do states not worry about relative gains? The answer to this question would ultimately define the realm in which liberal institutionalism applies.

Liberal institutionalists have not addressed this important question in a systematic fashion, so any assessment of their efforts to repair the theory must be preliminary. * * *

*   *   *

PROBLEMS WITH THE EMPIRICAL RECORD

Although there is much evidence of cooperation among states, this alone does not constitute support for liberal institutionalism. What is needed is evidence of cooperation that would not have occurred in the absence of institutions because of fear of cheating, or its actual presence. But

scholars have provided little evidence of cooperation of that sort, nor of cooperation failing because of cheating. Moreover, as discussed above,
there is considerable evidence that states worry
much about relative gains not only in security
matters, but in the economic realm as well.

This dearth of empirical support for liberal
institutionalism is acknowledged by proponents
of that theory.[33] The empirical record is not completely blank, however, but the few historical cases
that liberal institutionalists have studied provide
scant support for the theory. Consider two prominent examples.

Keohane looked at the performance of the International Energy Agency (IEA) in 1974–81, a period that included the 1979 oil crisis.[34] This case
does not appear to lend the theory much support.
First, Keohane concedes that the IEA failed outright when put to the test in 1979: "regimeoriented
efforts at cooperation do not always succeed, as
the fiasco of IEA actions in 1979 illustrates."[35] He
claims, however, that in 1980 the IEA had a minor
success "under relatively favorable conditions" in
responding to the outbreak of the Iran-Iraq War.
Although he admits it is difficult to specify how
much the IEA mattered in the 1980 case, he notes
that "it seems clear that 'it [the IEA] leaned in the
right direction',", a claim that hardly constitutes
strong support for the theory.[36] Second, it does not
appear from Keohane's analysis that either fear of
cheating or actual cheating hindered cooperation
in the 1979 case, as the theory would predict.
Third, Keohane chose the IEA case precisely because it involved relations among advanced Western democracies with market economies, where
the prospects for cooperation were excellent.[37]
The modest impact of institutions in this case is
thus all the more damning to the theory.

Lisa Martin examined the role that the European Community (EC) played during the Falklands War in helping Britain coax its reluctant
allies to continue economic sanctions against Argentina after military action started.[38] She concludes that the EC helped Britain win its allies'
cooperation by lowering transaction costs and facilitating issue linkage. Specifically, Britain made

concessions on the EC budget and the Common
Agricultural Policy (CAP); Britain's allies agreed
in return to keep sanctions on Argentina.

This case, too, is less than a ringing endorsement for liberal institutionalism. First, British efforts to maintain EC sanctions against Argentina
were not impeded by fears of possible cheating,
which the theory identifies as the central impediment to cooperation. So this case does not present an important test of liberal institutionalism,
and thus the cooperative outcome does not tell us
much about the theory's explanatory power. Second, it was relatively easy for Britain and her allies to strike a deal in this case. Neither side's
core interests were threatened, and neither side
had to make significant sacrifices to reach an
agreement. Forging an accord to continue sanctions was not a difficult undertaking. A stronger
test for liberal institutionalism would require
states to cooperate when doing so entailed significant costs and risks. Third, the EC was not essential to an agreement. Issues could have been
linked without the EC, and although the EC may
have lowered transaction costs somewhat, there
is no reason to think these costs were a serious
impediment to striking a deal.[39] It is noteworthy
that Britain and America were able to cooperate
during the Falklands War, even though the
United States did not belong to the EC.

There is also evidence that directly challenges
liberal institutionalism in issue areas where one
would expect the theory to operate successfully.
The studies discussed above by Grieco, Krasner,
and Mastanduno test the institutionalist argument in a number of different political economy
cases, and each finds the theory has little explanatory power. More empirical work is needed before
a final judgment is rendered on the explanatory
power of liberal institutionalism. Nevertheless, the
evidence gathered so far is unpromising at best.

In summary, liberal institutionalism does not
provide a sound basis for understanding international relations and promoting stability in the
post–Cold War world. It makes modest claims
about the impact of institutions, and steers clear
of war and peace issues, focusing instead on the

less ambitious task of explaining economic cooperation. Furthermore, the theory's causal logic is flawed, as proponents of the theory now admit. Having overlooked the relative-gains problem, they are now attempting to repair the theory, but their initial efforts are not promising. Finally, the available empirical evidence provides little support for the theory.

*   *   *

Conclusion

*   *   *

The attraction of institutionalist theories for both policymakers and scholars is explained, I believe, not by their intrinsic value, but by their relationship to realism, and especially to core elements of American political ideology. Realism has long been and continues to be an influential theory in the United States.[40] Leading realist thinkers such as George Kennan and Henry Kissinger, for example, occupied key policymaking positions during the Cold War. The impact of realism in the academic world is amply demonstrated in the institutionalist literature, where discussions of realism are pervasive.[41] Yet despite its influence, Americans who think seriously about foreign policy issues tend to dislike realism intensely, mainly because it clashes with their basic values. The theory stands opposed to how most Americans prefer to think about themselves and the wider world.[42]

There are four principal reasons why American elites, as well as the American public, tend to regard realism with hostility. First, realism is a pessimistic theory. It depicts a world of stark and harsh competition, and it holds out little promise of making that world more benign. Realists, as Hans Morgenthau wrote, are resigned to the fact that "there is no escape from the evil of power, regardless of what one does."[43] Such pessimism, of course, runs up against the deep-seated American belief that with time and effort, reasonable individuals can solve important social problems. Americans regard progress as both desirable and possible in politics, and they are therefore un

comfortable with realism's claim that security competition and war will persist despite our best efforts to eliminate them.[44]

Second, realism treats war as an inevitable, and indeed sometimes necessary, form of state activity. For realists, war is an extension of politics by other means. Realists are very cautious in their prescriptions about the use of force: wars should not be fought for idealistic purposes, but instead for balance-of-power reasons. Most Americans, however, tend to think of war as a hideous enterprise that should ultimately be abolished. For the time being, however, it can only justifiably be used for lofty moral goals, like "making the world safe for democracy"; it is morally incorrect to fight wars to change or preserve the balance of power. This makes the realist conception of warfare anathema to many Americans.

Third, as an analytical matter, realism does not distinguish between "good" states and "bad" states, but essentially treats them like billiard balls of varying size. In realist theory, all states are forced to seek the same goal: maximum relative power.[45] A purely realist interpretation of the Cold War, for example, allows for no meaningful difference in the motives behind American and Soviet behavior during that conflict. According to the theory, both sides must have been driven by concerns about the balance of power, and must have done what was necessary to try to achieve a favorable balance. Most Americans would recoil at such a description of the Cold War, because they believe the United States was motivated by good intentions while the Soviet Union was not.[46]

Fourth, America has a rich history of thumbing its nose at realism. For its first 140 years of existence, geography and the British navy allowed the United States to avoid serious involvement in the power politics of Europe. America had an isolationist foreign policy for most of this period, and its rhetoric explicitly emphasized the evils of entangling alliances and balancing behavior. Even as the United States finally entered its first European war in 1917, Woodrow Wilson railed against realist thinking. America has a long tradition of antirealist rhetoric, which continues to influence us today.

Given that realism is largely alien to American culture, there is a powerful demand in the United States for alternative ways of looking at the world, and especially for theories that square with basic American values. Institutionalist theories nicely meet these requirements, and that is the main source of their appeal to policymakers and scholars. Whatever else one might say about these theories, they have one undeniable advantage in the eyes of their supporters: they are not realism. Not only do institutionalist theories offer an alternative to realism, but they explicitly seek to undermine it. Moreover, institutionalists offer arguments that reflect basic American values. For example, they are optimistic about the possibility of greatly reducing, if not eliminating, security competition among states and creating a more peaceful world. They certainly do not accept the realist stricture that war is politics by other means. Institutionalists, in short, purvey a message that Americans long to hear.

There is, however, a downside for policymakers who rely on institutionalist theories: these theories do not accurately describe the world, hence policies based on them are bound to fail. The international system strongly shapes the behavior of states, limiting the amount of damage that false faith in institutional theories can cause. The constraints of the system notwithstanding, however, states still have considerable freedom of action, and their policy choices can succeed or fail in protecting American national interests and the interests of vulnerable people around the globe. The failure of the League of Nations to address German and Japanese aggression in the 1930s is a case in point. The failure of institutions to prevent or stop the war in Bosnia offers a more recent example. These cases illustrate that institutions have mattered rather little in the past; they also suggest that the false belief that institutions matter has mattered more, and has had pernicious effects. Unfortunately, misplaced reliance on institutional solutions is likely to lead to more failures in the future.

NOTES

1. Regimes and institutions are treated as synonymous concepts in this article. They are also used interchangeably in the institutionalist literature. See Robert O. Keohane, "International Institutions: Two Approaches," *International Studies Quarterly*, Vol. 32, No. 4 (December 1988), p. 384; Robert O. Keohane, *International Institutions and State Power: Essays in International Relations Theory* (Boulder, Colo.: Westview Press, 1989), pp. 3–4; and Oran R. Young, *International Cooperation: Building Regimes for Natural Resources and the Environment* (Ithaca, N.Y.: Cornell University Press, 1989), chaps. 1 and 8. The term "multilateralism" is also virtually synonymous with institutions. To quote John Ruggie, "the term 'multilateral' is an adjective that modifies the noun 'institution.' Thus, multilateralism depicts a *generic institutional form* in international relations. . . . [Specifically,] multilateralism is an institutional form which coordinates relations among three or more states on the basis of 'generalized' principles of conduct." Ruggie, "Multilateralism [The Anatomy of an Institution]," [*International Organization*, Vol. 46, No. 3 (Summer 1992),] pp. 570–571.

2. For discussion of this point, see Arthur A. Stein, *Why Nations Cooperate: Circumstance and Choice in International Relations* (Ithaca, N.Y.: Cornell University Press, 1990), pp. 25–27. Also see Susan Strange, "*Cave! Hic Dragones:* A Critique of Regime Analysis," in Stephen D. Krasner, ed., *International Regimes*, special issue of *International Organization*, Vol. 36, No. 2 (Spring 1982), pp. 479–496.

3. Oran R. Young, "Regime Dynamics: The Rise and Fall of International Regimes," in Krasner, *International Regimes*, p. 277.

4. See Douglass C. North and Robert P. Thomas, "An Economic Theory of the Growth of the Western World," *The Economic History Re-*

view, 2nd series, Vol. 23, No. 1 (April 1970), p. 5.

5. Krasner, *International Regimes*, p. 186. Nonrealist institutions are often based on higher norms, while few, if any, realist institutions are based on norms. The dividing line between norms and rules is not sharply defined in the institutionalist literature. See Robert O. Keohane, *After Hegemony: Cooperation and Discord in the World Political Economy* (Princeton, N.J.: Princeton University Press, 1984), pp. 57–58. For example, one might argue that rules, not just norms, are concerned with rights and obligations. The key point, however, is that for many institutionalists, norms, which are core beliefs about standards of appropriate state behavior, are the foundation on which more specific rules are constructed. This distinction between norms and rules applies in a rather straightforward way in the subsequent discussion. Both collective security and critical theory challenge the realist belief that states behave in a self-interested way, and argue instead for developing norms that require states to act more altruistically. Liberal institutionalism, on the other hand, accepts the realist view that states act on the basis of self-interest, and concentrates on devising rules that facilitate cooperation among states.

6. International organizations are public agencies established through the cooperative efforts of two or more states. These administrative structures have their own budget, personnel, and buildings. John Ruggie defines them as "palpable entities with headquarters and letterheads, voting procedures, and generous pension plans." Ruggie, "Multilateralism," p. 573. Once rules are incorporated into an international organization, "they may seem almost coterminous," even though they are "distinguishable analytically." Keohane, *International Institutions and State Power*, p. 5.

7. Charles Lipson, "Is the Future of Collective Security Like the Past?" in George W. Downs, ed., *Collective Security beyond the Cold War*

(Ann Arbor: University of Michigan Press), p. 114.

8. Tony Evans and Peter Wilson, "Regime Theory and the English School of International Relations: A Comparison," *Millennium: Journal of International Studies*, Vol. 21, No. 3 (Winter 1992), p. 330.

9. See Gunther Hellmann and Reinhard Wolf, "Neorealism Neoliberal Institutionalism, and the Future of NATO," *Security Studies*, Vol. 3, No. 1 (Autumn 1993), pp. 3–43.

10. Among the key liberal institutionalist works are: Robert Axelrod and Robert O. Keohane, "Achieving Cooperation under Anarchy: Strategies and Institutions," *World Politics*, Vol. 38, No. 1 (October 1985), pp. 226–254; Keohane, *After Hegemony*; Keohane, "International Institutions: Two Approaches," pp. 379–396; Keohane, *International Institutions and State Power*, chap. 1; Charles Lipson, "International Cooperation in Economic and Security Affairs," *World Politics*, Vol. 37, No. 1 (October 1984), pp. 1–23; Lisa L. Martin, "Institutions and Cooperation: Sanctions During the Falkland Islands Conflict," *International Security*, Vol. 16, No. 4 (Spring 1992), pp. 143–178; Lisa L. Martin, *Coercive Cooperation: Explaining Multilateral Economic Sanctions* (Princeton, N.J.: Princeton University Press, 1992); Kenneth A. Oye, "Explaining Cooperation Under Anarchy: Hypotheses and Strategies," *World Politics*, Vol. 38, No. 1 (October 1985), pp. 1–24; and Stein, *Why Nations Cooperate*.

11. Stein, *Why Nations Cooperate*, chap. 2. Also see Keohane, *After Hegemony*, pp. 6–7, 12–13, 67–69.

12. Milner, "International Theories of Cooperation [among Nations: Strengths and Weaknesses]," [*World Politics*, Vol. 44, No. 3 (April 1992),] p. 468.

13. For examples of the theory at work in the environmental realm, see Peter M. Haas, Robert O. Keohane, and Marc A. Levy, eds., *Institutions for the Earth: Sources of Effective International Environmental Protection*

(Cambridge, Mass.: MIT Press, 1993), especially chaps. 1 and 9. Some of the most important work on institutions and the environment has been done by Oran Young. See, for example, Young, *International Cooperation*. The rest of my discussion concentrates on economic, not environmental issues, for conciseness, and also because the key theoretical works in the liberal institutionalist literature focus on economic rather than environmental matters.

14. Cheating is basically a "breach of promise." Oye, "Explaining Cooperation Under Anarchy," p. 1. It usually implies unobserved noncompliance, although there can be observed cheating as well. Defection is a synonym for cheating in the institutionalist literature.

15. The centrality of the prisoners' dilemma and cheating to the liberal institutionalist literature is clearly reflected in virtually all the works cited in footnote 10. As Helen Milner notes in her review essay on this literature: "The focus is primarily on the role of regimes [institutions] in solving the defection [cheating] problem." Milner, "International Theories of Cooperation," p. 475.

16. The phrase is from Keohane, *After Hegemony*, p. 85.

17. Kenneth Oye, for example, writes in the introduction to an issue of *World Politics* containing a number of liberal institutionalist essays: "Our focus is on non-altruistic cooperation among states dwelling in international anarchy." Oye, "Explaining Cooperation Under Anarchy," p. 2. Also see Keohane, "International Institutions: Two Approaches," pp. 380–381; and Keohane, *International Institutions and State Power*, p. 3.

18. Haas, Keohane, and Levy, *Institutions for the Earth*, p. 11. For general discussions of how rules work, which inform my subsequent discussion of the matter, see Keohane, *After Hegemony*, chaps. 5–6; Martin, "Institutions and Cooperation," pp. 143–178; and Milner,

"International Theories of Cooperation," pp. 474–478.

19. See Axelrod and Keohane, "Achieving Cooperation Under Anarchy," pp. 248–250; Lipson, "International Cooperation," pp. 4–18.

20. Lipson, "International Cooperation," p. 5.

21. See Keohane, *After Hegemony*, pp. 89–92.

22. This point is clearly articulated in Lipson, "International Cooperation," especially pp. 12–18. The subsequent quotations in this paragraph are from ibid. Also see Axelrod and Keohane, "Achieving Cooperation Under Anarchy," pp. 232–233.

23. See Roger B. Parks, "What if 'Fools Die'? A Comment on Axelrod," Letter to *American Political Science Review*, Vol. 79, No. 4 (December 1985), pp. 1173–1174.

24. See Grieco, "Anarchy and the Limits of Cooperation [A Realist Critique of the Newest Liberal Institutionalism,]" [*International Organization*, Vol. 42, No. 3 (Summer 1988)]. Other works by Grieco bearing on the subject include: Joseph M. Grieco, "Realist Theory and the Problem of International Cooperation: Analysis with an Amended Prisoner's Dilemma Model," *The Journal of Politics*, Vol. 50, No. 3 (August 1988), pp. 600–624; Grieco, *Cooperation among Nations: Europe, America, and Non-Tariff Barriers to Trade* (Ithaca, N.Y.: Cornell University Press, 1990); and Grieco, "Understanding the Problem of International Cooperation: The Limits of Neoliberal Institutionalism and the Future of Realist Theory," in Baldwin, [ed.,] *Neorealism and Neoliberalism* [*The Contempory Debate* (New York: Columbia University Press, 1993)], pp. 301–338. The telling effect of Grieco's criticism is reflected in ibid., which is essentially organized around the relative gains vs. absolute gains debate, an issue given little attention before Grieco raised it in his widely cited 1988 article. The matter was briefly discussed by two other scholars before Grieco. See Joanne Gowa, "Anarchy, Egoism, and Third Images: *The Evolution of*

Cooperation and International Relations," *International Organization*, Vol. 40, No. 1 (Winter 1986), pp. 172–179; and Oran R. Young, "International Regimes: Toward a New Theory of Institutions," *World Politics*, Vol. 39, No. 1 (October 1986), pp. 118–119.

25. Lipson writes: "The Prisoner's Dilemma, in its simplest form, involves two players. Each is assumed to be a self-interested, self-reliant maximizer of his own utility, an assumption that clearly parallels the Realist conception of sovereign states in international politics." Lipson, "International Cooperation," p. 2. Realists, however, do not accept this conception of international politics and, not surprisingly, have questioned the relevance of the prisoners' dilemma (at least in its common form) for explaining much of international relations. See Gowa, "Anarchy, Egoism, and Third Images"; Grieco, "Realist Theory and the Problem of International Cooperation"; and Stephen D. Krasner, "Global Communications and National Power: Life on the Pareto Frontier," *World Politics*, Vol. 43, No. 3 (April 1991), pp. 336–366.

26. My thinking on this matter has been markedly influenced by Sean Lynn-Jones, in his June 19, 1994, correspondence with me.

27. For a short discussion of strategic trade theory, see Robert Gilpin, *The Political Economy of International Relations* (Princeton, N.J.: Princeton University Press, 1987), pp. 215–221. The most commonly cited reference on the subject is Paul R. Krugman, ed., *Strategic Trade Policy and the New International Economics* (Cambridge, Mass.: MIT Press, 1986).

28. See Robert Axelrod, *The Evolution of Cooperation* (New York: Basic Books, 1984), pp. 110–113.

29. Grieco maintains in *Cooperation among Nations* that realist logic should apply here. Robert Powell, however, points out that "in the context of negotiations between the European Community and the United States . . .

it is difficult to attribute any concern for relative gains to the effects that a relative loss may have on the probability of survival." Robert Powell, "Absolute and Relative Gains in International Relations Theory," *American Political Science Review*, Vol. 85, No. 4 (December 1991), p. 1319, footnote 26. I agree with Powell. It is clear from Grieco's response to Powell that Grieco includes non-military logics like strategic trade theory in the realist tent, whereas Powell and I do not. See Grieco's contribution to "The Relative-Gains Problem for International Relations," *American Political Science Review*, Vol. 87, No. 3 (September 1993), pp. 733–735.

30. Krasner, "Global Communications and National Power," pp. 336–366; Grieco, *Cooperation among Nations*; and Michael Mastanduno, "Do Relative Gains Matter? America's Response to Japanese Industrial Policy," *International Security*, Vol. 16, No. 1 (Summer 1991), pp. 73–113. Also see Jonathan B. Tucker, "Partners and Rivals: A Model of International Collaboration in Advanced Technology," *International Organization*, Vol. 45, No. 1 (Winter 1991), pp. 83–120.

31. Keohane, "Institutional Theory and the Realist Challenge," [in Baldwin, *Neorealism and Neoliberalism*,] p. 292.

32. For example, Keohane wrote after becoming aware of Grieco's argument about relative gains: "Under specified conditions—where mutual interests are low and relative gains are therefore particularly important to states—neoliberal theory expects neorealism to explain elements of state behavior." Keohane, *International Institutions and State Power*, pp. 15–16.

33. For example, Lisa Martin writes that "scholars working in the realist tradition maintain a well-founded skepticism about the empirical impact of institutional factors on state behavior. This skepticism is grounded in a lack of studies that show precisely how and when institutions have constrained state

decision-making." According to Oran Young, "One of the more surprising features of the emerging literature on regimes [institutions] is the relative absence of sustained discussions of the significance of . . . institutions, as determinants of collective outcomes at the international level." Martin, "Institutions and Cooperation," p. 144; Young, *International Cooperation*, p. 206.

34. Keohane, *After Hegemony*, chap. 10.

35. Ibid., p. 16.

36. Ibid., p. 236. A U.S. Department of Energy review of the IEA's performance in the 1980 crisis concluded that it had "failed to fulfill its promise." Ethan B. Kapstein, *The Insecure Alliance: Energy Crises and Western Politics Since 1944* (New York: Oxford University Press, 1990), p. 198.

37. Keohane, *After Hegemony*, p. 7.

38. Martin, "Institutions and Cooperation." Martin looks closely at three other cases in *Coercive Cooperation* to determine the effect of institutions on cooperation. I have concentrated on the Falklands War case, however, because it is, by her own admission, her strongest case. See ibid., p. 96.

39. Martin does not claim that agreement would not have been possible without the EC. Indeed, she appears to concede that even without the EC, Britain still could have fashioned "separate bilateral agreements with each EEC member in order to gain its cooperation, [although] this would have involved much higher transaction costs." Martin, "Institutions and Cooperation," pp. 174–175. However, transaction costs among the advanced industrial democracies are not very high in an era of rapid communications and permanent diplomatic establishments.

40. See Michael J. Smith, *Realist Thought from Weber to Kissinger* (Baton Rouge: Lousiana State University Press, 1986), chap. 1.

41. Summing up the autobiographical essays of 34 international relations scholars, Joseph Kruzel notes that "Hans Morgenthau is more frequently cited than any other name in these memoirs." Joseph Kruzel, "Reflections on the Journeys," in Joseph Kruzel and James N. Rosenau, eds., *Journeys through World Politics: Autobiographical Reflections of Thirty-four Academic Travelers* (Lexington, Mass.: Lexington Books, 1989), p. 505. Although "Morgenthau is often cited, many of the references in these pages are negative in tone. He seems to have inspired his critics even more than his supporters." Ibid.

42. See Keith L. Shimko, "Realism, Neorealism, and American Liberalism," *Review of Politics*, Vol. 54, No. 2 (Spring 1992), pp. 281–301.

43. Hans J. Morgenthau, *Scientific Man vs. Power Politics* (Chicago: University of Chicago Press, 1974), p. 201. Nevertheless, Keith Shimko convincingly argues that the shift within realism, away from Morgenthau's belief that states are motivated by an unalterable will to power, and toward Waltz's view that states are motivated by the desire for security, provides "a residual, though subdued optimism, or at least a possible basis for optimism [about international politics]. The extent to which this optimism is stressed or suppressed varies, but it is there if one wants it to be." Shimko, "Realism, Neorealism, and American Liberalism," p. 297. Realists like Stephen Van Evera, for example, point out that although states operate in a dangerous world, they can take steps to dampen security competition and minimize the danger of war. See Van Evera, *Causes of War* [Vol. II: *National Misperception and the Origins of War*, forthcoming].

44. See Reinhold Niebuhr, *The Children of Light and The Children of Darkness: A Vindication of Democracy and a Critique of Its Traditional Defense* (New York: Charles Scribner's, 1944), especially pp. 153–190. See also Samuel P. Huntington, *The Soldier and the State: The Theory and Politics of Civil-Military Relations* (New York: Vintage Books, 1964).

45. It should be emphasized that many realists have strong moral preferences and are driven by deep moral convictions. Realism is not a normative theory, however, and it provides no criteria for moral judgment. Instead, realism merely seeks to explain how the world works. Virtually all realists would prefer a world without security competition and war, but they believe that goal is unrealistic given the structure of the international system. See, for example, Robert G. Gilpin, "The Richness of the Tradition of Political Realism," in Keohane, [ed.,] *Neorealism and Its Critics*, [New York: Columbia University Press, 1986] p. 321.

46. Realism's treatment of states as billiard balls of different sizes tends to raise the hackles of comparative politics scholars, who believe that domestic political and economic factors matter greatly for explaining foreign policy behavior.

8 WAR AND STRIFE

Warfare and military intervention continue to be central problems of international relations. Two of the readings in this section address a core issue: the relationship between the use of force and politics. Excerpts from classic books by Karl von Clausewitz, On War (originally published in the 1830s), and Thomas Schelling, Arms and Influence (1966), remind us that warfare is not simply a matter of brute force; war needs to be understood as a continuation of political bargaining. In the most influential treatise on warfare ever written, the Prussian general Clausewitz reminded the generation that followed the devastating Napoleonic Wars that armed conflict should not be considered a blind, all-out struggle governed by the logic of military operations. Rather, he said, the conduct of war had to be subordinated to its political objectives. These ideas resonated strongly with American strategic thinkers of Schelling's era, who worried that military plans for total nuclear war would outstrip the ability of political leaders to control them. Schelling, a Harvard professor who also spent time at the RAND Corporation advising the U.S. Air Force on its nuclear weapons strategy, explained that political bargaining and risk taking, not military victory, lay at the heart of the use and threat of force in the nuclear era.

Like Schelling, Robert Jervis drew on mathematical game theory and theories of bargaining in his influential 1978 article on the "security dilemma," which explains how war can arise even among states that seek only to defend themselves. Like the realists, these analysts are interested in studying how states' strategies for survival can lead to tragic results. However, they go beyond the realists in examining how differences in bargaining tactics and perceptions can intensify or mitigate the struggle for security.

The advent of nuclear weapons has led to a lively debate over the relationship between nuclear proliferation and international-system stability. Kenneth Waltz and Scott Sagan took up the discussion in their book The Spread of Nuclear Weapons: A Debate, republished in 2003. In his Foreign Affairs article reprinted here, Scott Sagan reexamines his contention that nuclear deterrence is destabilizing and risks eventually breaking down, applying the *argument to Iran. Unable to maintain centralized control over nuclear weapons or materials, Iran's emergent nuclear capability is destabilizing. Policy options are explored to convince Tehran to give up its nuclear ambitions.*

In the armed violence of the twentieth century, deaths of noncombatants have often vastly outnumbered the number of fighters who are killed. Benjamin Valentino argues against the common view that the mass slaughter of civilians is due to irrational barbarism or popular hatreds. Instead, he contends that powerful leaders backed by relatively small groups of perpetrators use violence to advance what they consider their strategic interests—for example, draining the civilian "sea" in which rebels "swim," to use Mao Tse-tung's metaphor for counterinsurgency warfare.

The 1990s and early years of the twenty-first century have been marked by both ethnic conflict and terrorism. Barry Posen shows how realist theories of conflict in anarchy, long used by scholars to understand the dynamics of international wars, can also illuminate the strategic incentives that intensify ethnic rivalries when states or empires collapse. Posen draws heavily on the seminal ideas in Jervis's "security dilemma" article. This shows how fundamental theoretical concepts, grounded in a powerful logical framework, can serve as general-purpose tools to be adapted to new practical problems as the current agenda of international issues changes.

While terrorism has long been used as a substitute for war, the attention of the international community has been drawn to this phenomenon following the September 11, 2001, attacks. Max Abrahms refutes the conventional wisdom that terrorism is an effective coercive strategy. Based on an empirical assessment of twenty-eight foreign terrorist organizations operating since 2001, he finds that the groups' objectives were achieved only 7 percent of the time. Targeting of civilians even worsens the probability of achieving policy objectives. Robert Pape of the University of Chicago also conducts empirical research for the American Political Science Review *piece excerpted below. His data is on the least-understood aspect of terrorism: suicide terrorism. Contrary to conventional expectations, he finds that suicide bombers cannot be directly tied to Islamic fundamentalism, but rather they share a common goal, which is to rid their homelands of domination by foreign democratic regimes. Responding to suicide terrorists by trying to reassert this dominance is apt to only increase the number of terrorists, says Pape.*

While international wars have declined in number, civil wars have increased. Political scientist Michael Ross shows in an empirical study of fifteen recent civil wars how natural resources play a role. The duration of a civil war is affected by the characteristics of the disputed natural resource, namely its lootability, obstructability, and legality.

Not all see war as a viable policy option. Political scientist Carol Cohn and philosopher/activist Sara Ruddick draw on a long feminist tradition that opposes war making. Using a methodology that focuses on individual experience, the authors trace the broader social costs of weaponization and the particularly devastating effects on women.

CARL VON CLAUSEWITZ

WAR AS AN INSTRUMENT OF POLICY

*   *   *

* * * War is only a part of political intercourse, therefore by no means an independent thing in itself.

We know, certainly, that War is only called forth through the political intercourse of Governments and Nations; but in general it is supposed that such intercourse is broken off by War, and that a totally different state of things ensues, subject to no laws but its own.

We maintain, on the contrary, that War is nothing but a continuation of political intercourse, with a mixture of other means. We say mixed with other means in order thereby to maintain at the same time that this political intercourse does not cease by the War itself, is not changed into something quite different, but that, in its essence, it continues to exist, whatever may be the form of the means which it uses, and that the chief lines on which the events of the War progress, and to which they are attached, are only the general features of policy which run all through the War until peace takes place. And how can we conceive it to be otherwise? Does the cessation of diplomatic notes stop the political relations between different Nations and Governments? Is not War merely another kind of writing and language for political thoughts? It has certainly a grammar of its own, but its logic is not peculiar to itself.

Accordingly, War can never be separated from political intercourse, and if, in the consideration of the matter, this is done in any way, all the threads of the different relations are, to a certain extent, broken, and we have before us a senseless thing without an object.

From Carl von Clausewitz, *On War* (Harmondsworth: Penguin Books, 1968), Bk. 5, Chap. 6. The author's notes have been omitted.

This kind of idea would be indispensable even if War was perfect War, the perfectly unbridled element of hostility, for all the circumstances on which it rests, and which determine its leading features, viz. our own power, the enemy's power, Allies on both sides, the characteristics of the people and their Governments respectively, etc.—are they not of a political nature, and are they not so intimately connected with the whole political intercourse that it is impossible to separate them? But this view is doubly indispensable if we reflect that real War is no such consistent effort tending to an extreme, as it should be according to the abstract idea, but a half-and-half thing, a contradiction in itself; that, as such, it cannot follow its own laws, but must be looked upon as a part of another whole—and this whole is policy.

Policy in making use of War avoids all those rigorous conclusions which proceed from its nature; it troubles itself little about final possibilities, confining its attention to immediate probabilities. If such uncertainty in the whole action ensues therefrom, if it thereby becomes a sort of game, the policy of each Cabinet places its confidence in the belief that in this game it will surpass its neighbour in skill and sharp-sightedness.

Thus policy makes out of the all-overpowering element of War a mere instrument, changes the tremendous battle-sword, which should be lifted with both hands and the whole power of the body to strike once for all, into a light handy weapon, which is even sometimes nothing more than a rapier to exchange thrusts and feints and parries.

Thus the contradictions in which man, naturally timid, becomes involved by War may be solved, if we choose to accept this as a solution.

If War belongs to policy, it will naturally take its character from thence. If policy is grand and powerful, so also will be the War, and this may be carried to the point at which War attains to *its absolute form.*

In this way of viewing the subject, therefore, we need not shut out of sight the absolute form of War, we rather keep it continually in view in the background.

Only through this kind of view War recovers unity; only by it can we see all Wars as things of *one* kind; and it is only through it that the judgement can obtain the true and perfect basis and point of view from which great plans may be traced out and determined upon.

It is true the political element does not sink deep into the details of War. Vedettes are not planted, patrols do not make their rounds from political considerations; but small as is its influence in this respect, it is great in the formation of a plan for a whole War, or a campaign, and often even for a battle.

For this reason we were in no hurry to establish this view at the commencement. While engaged with particulars, it would have given us little help, and, on the other hand, would have distracted our attention to a certain extent; in the plan of a War or campaign it is indispensable.

There is, upon the whole, nothing more important in life than to find out the right point of view from which things should be looked at and judged of, and then to keep to that point; for we can only apprehend the mass of events in their unity from *one* standpoint; and it is only the keeping to one point of view that guards us from inconsistency.

If, therefore, in drawing up a plan of a War, it is not allowable to have a two-fold or three-fold point of view, from which things may be looked at, now with the eye of a soldier, then with that of an administrator, and then again with that of a politician, etc., then the next question is, whether *policy* is necessarily paramount and everything else subordinate to it.

That policy unites in itself, and reconciles all the interests of internal administrations, even those of humanity, and whatever else are rational subjects of consideration is presupposed, for it is nothing in itself, except a mere representative and exponent of all these interests towards other States. That policy may take a false direction, and may promote unfairly the ambitious ends, the private interests, the vanity of rulers, does not concern us here; for, under no circumstances can the Art of War be regarded as its preceptor, and we can only look at policy here as the representative of the interests generally of the whole community.

The only question, therefore, is whether in framing plans for a War the political point of view should give way to the purely military (if such a point is conceivable), that is to say, should disappear altogether, or subordinate itself to it, or whether the political is to remain the ruling point of view and the military to be considered subordinate to it.

That the political point of view should end completely when War begins is only conceivable in contests which are Wars of life and death, from pure hatred: as Wars are in reality, they are, as we before said, only the expressions or manifestations of policy itself. The subordination of the political point of view to the military would be contrary to common sense, for policy has declared the War; it is the intelligent faculty, War only the instrument, and not the reverse. The subordination of the military point of view to the political is, therefore, the only thing which is possible.

If we reflect on the nature of real War, and call to mind what has been said, *that every War should be viewed above all things according to the probability of its character, and its leading features as they are to be deduced from the political forces and proportions*, and that often—indeed we may safely affirm, in our days, *almost* always—War is to be regarded as an organic whole, from which the single branches are not to be separated, in which therefore every individual activity flows into the whole, and also has its origin in the idea of this whole, then it becomes certain and palpable to us that the superior standpoint for the conduct of the War, from which its leading lines must proceed, can be no other than that of policy.

From this point of view the plans come, as it were, out of a cast; the apprehension of them and the judgement upon them become easier and more natural, our convictions respecting them gain in force, motives are more satisfying and history more intelligible.

At all events from this point of view there is no longer in the nature of things a necessary conflict between the political and military interests, and where it appears it is therefore to be regarded as imperfect knowledge only. That policy makes demands on the War which it cannot respond to, would be contrary to the supposition that it knows the instrument which it is going to use, therefore, contrary to a natural and indispensable supposition. But if policy judges correctly of the march of military events, it is entirely its affair to determine what are the events and what the direction of events most favourable to the ultimate and great end of the War.

In one word, the Art of War in its highest point of view is policy, but, no doubt, a policy which fights battles instead of writing notes.

According to this view, to leave a great military enterprise or the plan for one, to *a purely military judgement and decision* is a distinction which cannot be allowed, and is even prejudicial; indeed, it is an irrational proceeding to consult professional soldiers on the plan of a War, that they may give a *purely military opinion* upon what the Cabinet ought to do; but still more absurd is the demand of Theorists that a statement of the available means of War should be laid before the General, that he may draw out a purely military plan for the War or for a campaign in accordance with those means. Experience in general also teaches us that notwithstanding the multifarious branches and scientific character of military art in the present day, still the leading outlines of a War are always determined by the Cabinet, that is, if we would use technical language, by a political not a military organ.

This is perfectly natural. None of the principal plans which are required for a War can be made without an insight into the political relations; and, in reality, when people speak, as they often do, of the prejudicial influence of policy on the conduct of a War, they say in reality something

very different to what they intend. It is not this influence but the policy itself which should be found fault with. If policy is right, that is, if it succeeds in hitting the object, then it can only act with advantage on the War. If this influence of policy causes a divergence from the object, the cause is only to be looked for in a mistaken policy.

It is only when policy promises itself a wrong effect from certain military means and measures, an effect opposed to their nature, that it can exercise a prejudicial effect on War by the course it prescribes. Just as a person in a language with which he is not conversant sometimes says what he does not intend, so policy, when intending right, may often order things which do not tally with its own views.

This has happened times without end, and it shows that a certain knowledge of the nature of War is essential to the management of political intercourse.

But before going further, we must guard ourselves against a false interpretation of which this is very susceptible. We are far from holding the opinion that a War Minister smothered in official papers, a scientific engineer, or even a soldier who has been well tried in the field, would, any of them, necessarily make the best Minister of State where the Sovereign does not act for himself; or, in other words, we do not mean to say that this acquaintance with the nature of War is the principal qualification for a War Minister; elevation, superiority of mind, strength of character, these are the principal qualifications which he must possess; a knowledge of War may be supplied in one way or the other. * * *

*　　*　　*

We shall now conclude with some reflections derived from history.

In the last decade of the past century, when that remarkable change in the Art of War in Europe took place by which the best Armies found that a part of their method of War had become utterly unserviceable, and events were brought about of a magnitude far beyond what any one had any previous conception of, it certainly appeared that a false calculation of everything was to be laid to the charge of the Art of War. * * *

*   *   *

But is it true that the real surprise by which men's minds were seized was confined to the conduct of War, and did not rather relate to policy itself? That is: Did the ill success proceed from the influence of policy on the War, or from a wrong policy itself?

The prodigious effects of the French Revolution abroad were evidently brought about much less through new methods and views introduced by the French in the conduct of War than through the changes which it wrought in state-craft and civil administration, in the character of Governments, in the condition of the people, etc. That other Governments took a mistaken view of all these things; that they endeavoured, with their ordinary means, to hold their own against forces of a novel kind and overwhelming in strength— all that was a blunder in policy.

Would it have been possible to perceive and mend this error by a scheme for the War from a purely military point of view? Impossible. For if there had been a philosophical strategist, who merely from the nature of the hostile elements had foreseen all the consequences, and prophesied remote possibilities, still it would have been practically impossible to have turned such wisdom to account.

If policy had risen to a just appreciation of the forces which had sprung up in France, and of the new relations in the political state of Europe, it might have foreseen the consequences which must follow in respect to the great features of War, and it was only in this way that it could arrive at a correct view of the extent of the means required as well as of the best use to make of those means.

We may therefore say, that the twenty years' victories of the Revolution are chiefly to be ascribed to the erroneous policy of the Governments by which it was opposed.

It is true these errors first displayed themselves in the War, and the events of the War completely disappointed the expectations which policy entertained. But this did not take place because policy neglected to consult its military advisers. That Art of War in which the politician of the day could believe, namely, that derived from the reality of War at that time, that which belonged to the policy of the day, that familiar instrument which policy had hitherto used—*that* Art of War, I say, was naturally involved in the error of policy, and therefore could not teach it anything better. It is true that War itself underwent important alterations both in its nature and forms, which brought it nearer to its absolute form; but these changes were not brought about because the French Government had, to a certain extent, delivered itself from the leading-strings of policy; they arose from an altered policy, produced by the French Revolution, not only in France, but over the rest of Europe as well. This policy had called forth other means and other powers, by which it became possible to conduct War with a degree of energy which could not have been thought of otherwise.

Therefore, the actual changes in the Art of War are a consequence of alterations in policy; and, so far from being an argument for the possible separation of the two, they are, on the contrary, very strong evidence of the intimacy of their connexion.

Therefore, once more: War is an instrument of policy; it must necessarily bear its character, it must measure with its scale: the conduct of War, in its great features, is therefore policy itself, which takes up the sword in place of the pen, but does not on that account cease to think according to its own laws.

THOMAS C. SCHELLING

THE DIPLOMACY OF VIOLENCE

The usual distinction between diplomacy and force is not merely in the instruments, words or bullets, but in the relation between adversaries—in the interplay of motives and the role of communication, understandings, compromise, and restraint. Diplomacy is bargaining: it seeks outcomes that, though not ideal for either party, are better for both than some of the alternatives. In diplomacy each party somewhat controls what the other wants, and can get more by compromise, exchange, or collaboration than by taking things in his own hands and ignoring the other's wishes. The bargaining can be polite or rude, entail threats as well as offers, assume a status quo or ignore all rights and privileges, and assume mistrust rather than trust. But whether polite or impolite, constructive or aggressive, respectful or vicious, whether it occurs among friends or antagonists and whether or not there is a basis for trust and goodwill, there must be some common interest, if only in the avoidance of mutual damage, and an awareness of the need to make the other party prefer an outcome acceptable to oneself.

With enough military force a country may not need to bargain. Some things a country wants it can take, and some things it has it can keep, by sheer strength, skill and ingenuity. It can do this *forcibly*, accommodating only to opposing strength, skill, and ingenuity and without trying to appeal to an enemy's wishes. Forcibly a country can repel and expel, penetrate and occupy, seize, exterminate, disarm and disable, confine, deny access, and directly frustrate intrusion or attack. It can, that is, if it has enough strength.

From Thomas C. Schelling, *Arms and Influence* (New Haven: Yale University Press, 1966), Chap. 1. Some of the author's notes have been omitted.

"Enough" depends on how much an opponent has.

There is something else, though, that force can do. It is less military, less heroic, less impersonal, and less unilateral; it is uglier, and has received less attention in Western military strategy. In addition to seizing and holding, disarming and confining, penetrating and obstructing, and all that, military force can be used *to hurt*. In addition to taking and protecting things of value it can *destroy* value. In addition to weakening an enemy militarily it can cause an enemy plain suffering.

Pain and shock, loss and grief, privation and horror are always in some degree, sometimes in terrible degree, among the results of warfare; but in traditional military science they are incidental, they are not the object. If violence can be done incidentally, though, it can also be done purposely. The power to hurt can be counted among the most impressive attributes of military force.

Hurting, unlike forcible seizure or self-defense, is not unconcerned with the interest of others. It is measured in the suffering it can cause and the victims' motivation to avoid it. Forcible action will work against weeds or floods as well as against armies, but suffering requires a victim that can feel pain or has something to lose. To inflict suffering gains nothing and saves nothing directly; it can only make people behave to avoid it. The only purpose, unless sport or revenge, must be to influence somebody's behavior, to coerce his decision or choice. To be coercive, violence has to be anticipated. And it has to be avoidable by accommodation. The power to hurt is bargaining power. To exploit it is diplomacy—vicious diplomacy, but diplomacy.

The Contrast of Brute Force with Coercion

There is a difference between taking what you want and making someone give it to you, between fending off assault and making someone afraid to assault you, between holding what people are trying to take and making them afraid to take it, between losing what someone can forcibly take and giving it up to avoid risk or damage. It is the difference between defense and deterrence, between brute force and intimidation, between conquest and blackmail, between action and threats. It is the difference between the unilateral, "undiplomatic" recourse to strength, and coercive diplomacy based on the power to hurt.

The contrasts are several. The purely "military" or "undiplomatic" recourse to forcible action is concerned with enemy strength, not enemy interests; the coercive use of the power to hurt, though, is the very exploitation of enemy wants and fears. And brute strength is usually measured relative to enemy strength, the one directly opposing the other, while the power to hurt is typically not reduced by the enemy's power to hurt in return. Opposing strengths may cancel each other, pain and grief do not. The willingness to hurt, the credibility of a threat, and the ability to exploit the power to hurt will indeed depend on how much the adversary can hurt in return; but there is little or nothing about an adversary's pain or grief that directly reduces one's own. Two sides cannot both overcome each other with superior strength; they may both be able to hurt each other. With strength they can dispute objects of value; with sheer violence they can destroy them.

And brute force succeeds when it is used, whereas the power to hurt is most successful when held in reserve. It is the *threat* of damage, or of more damage to come, that can make someone yield or comply. It is *latent* violence that can influence someone's choice—violence that can still be withheld or inflicted, or that a victim believes can be withheld or inflicted. The threat of pain tries to structure someone's motives, while brute force tries to overcome his strength. Unhappily, the power to hurt is often communicated by some performance of it. Whether it is sheer terroristic violence to induce an irrational response, or cool premeditated violence to persuade somebody that you mean it and may do it again, it is not the pain and damage itself but its influence on somebody's behavior that matters. It is the expectation of *more* violence that gets the wanted behavior, if the power to hurt can get it at all.

To exploit a capacity for hurting and inflicting damage one needs to know what an adversary treasures and what scares him and one needs the adversary to understand what behavior of his will cause the violence to be inflicted and what will cause it to be withheld. The victim has to know what is wanted, and he may have to be assured of what is not wanted. The pain and suffering have to appear *contingent* on his behavior; it is not alone the threat that is effective—the threat of pain or loss if he fails to comply—but the corresponding assurance, possibly an implicit one, that he can avoid the pain or loss if he does comply. The prospect of certain death may stun him, but it gives him no choice.

Coercion by threat of damage also requires that our interests and our opponent's not be absolutely opposed. If his pain were our greatest delight and our satisfaction his greatest woe, we would just proceed to hurt and to frustrate each other. It is when his pain gives us little or no satisfaction compared with what he can do for us, and the action or inaction that satisfies us costs him less than the pain we can cause, that there is room for coercion. Coercion requires finding a bargain, arranging for him to be better off doing what we want—worse off not doing what we want—when he takes the threatened penalty into account.

It is this capacity for pure damage, pure violence, that is usually associated with the most vicious labour disputes, with racial disorders, with civil uprisings and their suppression, with racketeering. It is also the power to hurt rather than brute force that we use in dealing with criminals; we hurt them afterward, or threaten to, for their misdeeds rather than protect ourselves with cordons of electric wires, masonry walls, and armed guards. Jail, of course, can be either forcible restraint or threatened privation; if the object is to keep criminals out of mischief by confinement, success is measured by how many of them are gotten behind bars, but if the object is to *threaten* privation, success will be measured by how few have to be put behind bars and success then depends on the subject's understanding of the consequences. Pure damage is what a car threatens when it tries to hog the road or to keep its rightful share, or to go first through an intersection. A tank or a bulldozer can force its way regardless of others' wishes; the rest of us have to threaten damage, usually mutual damage, hoping the other driver values his car or his limbs enough to give way, hoping he sees us, and hoping he is in control of his own car. The threat of pure damage will not work against an unmanned vehicle.

This difference between coercion and brute force is as often in the intent as in the instrument. To hunt down Comanches and to exterminate them was brute force; to raid their villages to make them behave was coercive diplomacy, based on the power to hurt. The pain and loss to the Indians might have looked much the same one way as the other; the difference was one of purpose and effect. If Indians were killed because they were in the way, or somebody wanted their land, or the authorities despaired of making them behave and could not confine them and decided to exterminate them, that was pure unilateral force. If *some* Indians were killed to make *other* Indians behave, that was coercive violence—or intended to be, whether or not it was effective. The Germans at Verdun perceived themselves to be chewing up hundreds of thousands of French soldiers in a gruesome "meat-grinder." If the purpose was to eliminate a military obstacle—the French infantryman, viewed as a military "asset" rather than as a warm human being—the offensive at Verdun was a unilateral exercise of military force. If instead the object was to make the loss of young men—not of impersonal "effectives," but of

sons, husbands, fathers, and the pride of French manhood—so anguishing as to be unendurable, to make surrender a welcome relief and to spoil the foretaste of an Allied victory, then it was an exercise in coercion, in applied violence, intended to offer relief upon accommodation. And of course, since any use of force tends to be brutal, thoughtless, vengeful, or plain obstinate, the motives themselves can be mixed and confused. The fact that heroism and brutality can be either coercive diplomacy or a contest in pure strength does not promise that the distinction will be made, and the strategies enlightened by the distinction, every time some vicious enterprise gets launched.

The contrast between brute force and coercion is illustrated by two alternative strategies attributed to Genghis Khan. Early in his career he pursued the war creed of the Mongols: the vanquished can never be the friends of the victors, their death is necessary for the victor's safety. This was the unilateral extermination of a menace or a liability. The turning point of his career, according to Lynn Montross, came later when he discovered how to use his power to hurt for diplomatic ends. "The great Khan, who was not inhibited by the usual mercies, conceived the plan of forcing captives—women, children, aged fathers, favorite sons—to march ahead of his army as the first potential victims of resistance."[1] Live captives have often proved more valuable than enemy dead; and the technique discovered by the Khan in his maturity remains contemporary. North Koreans and Chinese were reported to have quartered prisoners of war near strategic targets to inhibit bombing attacks by United Nations aircraft. Hostages represent the power to hurt in its purest form.

Coercive Violence in Warfare

This distinction between the power to hurt and the power to seize or hold forcibly is important in modern war, both big war and little war, hypothetical war and real war. For many years the Greeks and the Turks on Cyprus could hurt each other indefinitely but neither could quite take or hold forcibly what they wanted or protect themselves from violence by physical means. The Jews in Palestine could not expel the British in the late 1940s but they could cause pain and fear and frustration through terrorism, and eventually influence somebody's decision. The brutal war in Algeria was more a contest in pure violence than in military strength; the question was who would first find the pain and degradation unendurable. The French troops preferred—indeed they continually tried—to make it a contest of strength, to pit military force against the nationalists' capacity for terror, to exterminate or disable the nationalists and to screen off the nationalists from the victims of their violence. But because in civil war terrorists commonly have access to victims by sheer physical propinquity, the victims and their properties could not be forcibly defended and in the end the French troops themselves resorted, unsuccessfully, to a war of pain.

Nobody believes that the Russians can take Hawaii from us, or New York, or Chicago, but nobody doubts that they might destroy people and buildings in Hawaii, Chicago, or New York. Whether the Russians can conquer West Germany in any meaningful sense is questionable; whether they can hurt it terribly is not doubted. That the United States can destroy a large part of Russia is universally taken for granted; that the United States can keep from being badly hurt, even devastated, in return, or can keep Western Europe from being devastated while itself destroying Russia, is at best arguable; and it is virtually out of the question that we could conquer Russia territorially and use its economic assets unless it were by threatening disaster and inducing compliance. It is the power to hurt, not military strength in the traditional sense, that inheres in our most impressive military capabilities at the present time [1966]. We have a Department of *Defense* but emphasize *retaliation*—"to return evil for evil" (synonyms: requital, reprisal, revenge, vengeance, retribution). And it is pain and violence, not force in the traditional sense, that inheres also in some of the least impressive

military capabilities of the present time—the plastic bomb, the terrorist's bullet, the burnt crops, and the tortured farmer.

War appears to be, or threatens to be, not so much a contest of strength as one of endurance, nerve, obstinacy, and pain. It appears to be, and threatens to be, not so much a contest of military strength as a bargaining process—dirty, extortionate, and often quite reluctant bargaining on one side or both—nevertheless a bargaining process.

The difference cannot quite be expressed as one between the *use* of force and the *threat* of force. The actions involved in forcible accomplishment, on the one hand, and in fulfilling a threat, on the other, can be quite different. Sometimes the most effective direct action inflicts enough cost or pain on the enemy to serve as a threat, sometimes not. The United States threatens the Soviet Union with virtual destruction of its society in the event of a surprise attack on the United States; a hundred million deaths are awesome as pure damage, but they are useless in stopping the Soviet attack—especially if the threat is to do it all afterward anyway. So it is worth while to keep the concepts distinct—to distinguish forcible action from the threat of pain— recognizing that some actions serve as both a means of forcible accomplishment and a means of inflicting pure damage, some do not. Hostages tend to entail almost pure pain and damage, as do all forms of reprisal after the fact. Some modes of self-defense may exact so little in blood or treasure as to entail negligible violence; and some forcible actions entail so much violence that their threat can be effective by itself.

The power to hurt, though it can usually accomplish nothing directly, is potentially more versatile than a straightforward capacity for forcible accomplishment. By force alone we cannot even lead a horse to water—we have to drag him—much less make him drink. Any affirmative action, any collaboration, almost anything but physical exclusion, expulsion, or extermination, requires that an opponent or a victim *do* something, even if only to stop or get out. The threat of pain and damage may make him want to do it, and anything he can do is potentially susceptible to inducement. Brute force can only accomplish what requires no collaboration. The principle is illustrated by a technique of unarmed combat: one can disable a man by various stunning, fracturing, or killing blows, but to take him to jail one has to exploit the man's own efforts. "Come-along" holds are those that threaten pain or disablement, giving relief as long as the victim complies, giving him the option of using his own legs to get to jail.

We have to keep in mind, though, that what is pure pain, or the threat of it, at one level of decision can be equivalent to brute force at another level. Churchill was worried, during the early bombing raids on London in 1940, that Londoners might panic. Against people the bombs were pure violence, to induce their undisciplined evasion; to Churchill and the government, the bombs were a cause of inefficiency, whether they spoiled transport and made people late to work or scared people and made them afraid to work. Churchill's decisions were not going to be coerced by the fear of a few casualties. Similarly on the battlefield: tactics that frighten soldiers so that they run, duck their heads, or lay down their arms and surrender represent coercion based on the power to hurt; to the top command, which is frustrated but not coerced, such tactics are part of the contest in military discipline and strength.

The fact that violence—pure pain and damage—can be used or threatened to coerce and to deter, to intimidate and to blackmail, to demoralize and to paralyze, in a conscious process of dirty bargaining, does not by any means imply that violence is not often wanton and meaningless or, even when purposive, in danger of getting out of hand. Ancient wars were often quite "total" for the loser, the men being put to death, the women sold as slaves, the boys castrated, the cattle slaughtered, and the buildings leveled, for the sake of revenge, justice, personal gain, or merely custom. If an enemy bombs a city, by design or by carelessness, we usually bomb his if we can. In the excitement and fatigue of warfare, revenge is one of the few satisfactions that can be savored; and

justice can often be construed to demand the enemy's punishment, even if it is delivered with more enthusiasm than justice requires. When Jerusalem fell to the Crusaders in 1099 the ensuing slaughter was one of the bloodiest in military chronicles. "The men of the West literally waded in gore, their march to the church of the Holy Sepulcher being gruesomely likened to 'treading out the wine press'. . . . ," reports Montross (p. 138), who observes that these excesses usually came at the climax of the capture of a fortified post or city. "For long the assailants have endured more punishment than they were able to inflict; then once the walls are breached, pent up emotions find an outlet in murder, rape and plunder, which discipline is powerless to prevent." The same occurred when Tyre fell to Alexander after a painful siege, and the phenomenon was not unknown on Pacific islands in the Second World War. Pure violence, like fire, can be harnessed to a purpose; that does not mean that behind every holocaust is a shrewd intention successfully fulfilled.

But if the occurrence of violence does not always bespeak a shrewd purpose, the absence of pain and destruction is no sign that violence was idle. Violence is most purposive and most successful when it is threatened and not used. Successful threats are those that do not have to be carried out. By European standards, Denmark was virtually unharmed in the Second World War; it was violence that made the Danes submit. Withheld violence—successfully threatened violence—can look clean, even merciful. The fact that a kidnap victim is returned unharmed, against receipt of ample ransom, does not make kidnapping a nonviolent enterprise. * * *

*   *   *

The Strategic Role of Pain and Damage

Pure violence, nonmilitary violence, appears most conspicuously in relations between unequal countries, where there is no substantial military challenge and the outcome of military engagement is not in question. Hitler could make his threats contemptuously and brutally against Austria; he could make them, if he wished, in a more refined way against Denmark. It is noteworthy that it was Hitler, not his generals, who used this kind of language; proud military establishments do not like to think of themselves as extortionists. Their favorite job is to deliver victory, to dispose of opposing military force and to leave most of the civilian violence to politics and diplomacy. But if there is no room for doubt how a contest in strength will come out, it may be possible to bypass the military stage altogether and to proceed at once to the coercive bargaining.

A typical confrontation of unequal forces occurs at the *end* of a war, between victor and vanquished. Where Austria was vulnerable before a shot was fired, France was vulnerable after its military shield had collapsed in 1940. Surrender negotiations are the place where the threat of civil violence can come to the fore. Surrender negotiations are often so one-sided, or the potential violence so unmistakable, that bargaining succeeds and the violence remains in reserve. But the fact that most of the actual damage was done during the military stage of the war, prior to victory and defeat, does not mean that violence was idle in the aftermath, only that it was latent and the threat of it successful.

Indeed, victory is often but a prerequisite to the exploitation of the power to hurt. When Xenophon was fighting in Asia Minor under Persian leadership, it took military strength to disperse enemy soldiers and occupy their lands; but land was not what the victor wanted, nor was victory for its own sake.

> Next day the Persian leader burned the villages to the ground, not leaving a single house standing, so as to strike terror into the other tribes to show them what would happen if they did not give in. . . . He sent some of the prisoners into the hills and told them to say that if the inhabitants did not come down and settle in their houses to submit to him, he would burn up their villages too and destroy their crops, and they would die of hunger.[2]

Military victory was but the *price of admission.* The payoff depended upon the successful threat of violence.

*   *   *

The Nuclear Contribution to Terror and Violence

Man has, it is said, for the first time in history enough military power to eliminate his species from the earth, weapons against which there is no conceivable defense. War has become, it is said, so destructive and terrible that it ceases to be an instrument of national power. "For the first time in human history," says Max Lerner in a book whose title, *The Age of Overkill*, conveys the point, "men have bottled up a power . . . which they have thus far not dared to use."[3] And Soviet military authorities, whose party dislikes having to accommodate an entire theory of history to a single technological event, have had to reexamine a set of principles that had been given the embarrassing name of "permanently operating factors" in warfare. Indeed, our era is epitomized by words like "the first time in human history," and by the abdication of what was "permanent."

For dramatic impact these statements are splendid. Some of them display a tendency, not at all necessary, to belittle the catastrophe of earlier wars. They may exaggerate the historical novelty of deterrence and the balance of terror. More important, they do not help to identify just what is new about war when so much destructive energy can be packed in warheads at a price that permits advanced countries to have them in large numbers. Nuclear warheads are incomparably more devastating than anything packaged before. What does that imply about war?

It is not true that for the first time in history man has the capability to destroy a large fraction, even the major part, of the human race. Japan was defenseless by August 1945. With a combination of bombing and blockade, eventually invasion, and if necessary the deliberate spread of disease, the United States could probably have exterminated the population of the Japanese islands without nuclear weapons. It would have been a gruesome, expensive, and mortifying campaign; it would have taken time and demanded persistence. But we had the economic and technical capacity to do it; and, together with the Russians or without them, we could have done the same in many populous parts of the world. Against defenseless people there is not much that nuclear weapons can do that cannot be done with an ice pick. And it would not have strained our Gross National Product to do it with ice picks.

It is a grisly thing to talk about. We did not do it and it is not imaginable that we would have done it. We had no reason; if we had had a reason, we would not have the persistence of purpose, once the fury of war had been dissipated in victory and we had taken on the task of executioner. If we and our enemies might do such a thing to each other now, and to others as well, it is not because nuclear weapons have for the first time made it feasible.

*   *   *

* * * In the past it has usually been the victors who could do what they pleased to the enemy. War has often been "total war" for the loser. With deadly monotony the Persians, Greeks, or Romans "put to death all men of military age, and sold the women and children into slavery," leaving the defeated territory nothing but its name until new settlers arrived sometime later. But the defeated could not do the same to their victors. The boys could be castrated and sold only after the war had been won, and only on the side that lost it. The power to hurt could be brought to bear only after military strength had achieved victory. The same sequence characterized the great wars of this century; for reasons of technology and geography, military force has usually had to penetrate, to exhaust, or to collapse opposing military force—to achieve military victory—before it could be brought to bear on the enemy nation itself. The Allies in World War I could not inflict coercive pain and suffering directly on the Germans

in a decisive way until they could defeat the German army; and the Germans could not coerce the French people with bayonets unless they first beat the Allied troops that stood in their way. With two-dimensional warfare, there is a tendency for troops to confront each other, shielding their own lands while attempting to press into each other's. Small penetrations could not do major damage to the people; large penetrations were so destructive of military organization that they usually ended the military phase of the war.

Nuclear weapons make it possible to do monstrous violence to the enemy without first achieving victory. With nuclear weapons and today's means of delivery, one expects to penetrate an enemy homeland without first collapsing his military force. What nuclear weapons have done, or appear to do, is to promote this kind of warfare to first place. Nuclear weapons threaten to make war less military, and are responsible for the lowered status of "military victory" at the present time. *Victory is no longer a prerequisite for hurting the enemy.* And it is no assurance against being terribly hurt. One need not wait until he has won the war before inflicting "unendurable" damages on his enemy. One need not wait until he has lost the war. There was a time when the assurance of victory—false or genuine assurance—could make national leaders not just willing but sometimes enthusiastic about war. Not now.

Not only *can* nuclear weapons hurt the enemy before the war has been won, and perhaps hurt decisively enough to make the military engagement academic, but it is widely assumed that in a major war that is *all* they can do. Major war is often discussed as though it would be only a contest in national destruction. If this is indeed the case—if the destruction of cities and their populations has become, with nuclear weapons, the primary object in an all-out war—the sequence of war has been reversed. Instead of destroying enemy forces as a prelude to imposing one's will on the enemy nation, one would have to destroy the nation as a means or a prelude to destroying the enemy forces. If one cannot disable enemy forces without virtually destroying the country, the victor does not even have the option of sparing the conquered nation. He has already destroyed it. Even with blockade and strategic bombing it could be supposed that a country would be defeated before it was destroyed, or would elect surrender before annihilation had gone far. In the Civil War it could be hoped that the South would become too weak to fight before it became too weak to survive. For "all-out" war, nuclear weapons threaten to reverse this sequence.

So nuclear weapons do make a difference, marking an epoch in warfare. The difference is not just in the amount of destruction that can be accomplished but in the role of destruction and in the decision process. Nuclear weapons can change the speed of events, the control of events, the sequence of events, the relation of victor to vanquished, and the relation of homeland to fighting front. Deterrence rests today on the threat of pain and extinction, not just on the threat of military defeat. We may argue about the wisdom of announcing "unconditional surrender" as an aim in the last major war, but seem to expect "unconditional destruction" as a matter of course in another one.

Something like the same destruction always *could* be done. With nuclear weapons there is an expectation that it *would* be done. It is not "overkill" that is new; the American army surely had enough 30 caliber bullets to kill everybody in the world in 1945, or if it did not it could have bought them without any strain. What is new is plain "kill"—the idea that major war might be just a contest in the killing of countries, or not even a contest but just two parallel exercises in devastation.

That is the difference nuclear weapons make. At least they *may* make that difference. They also may not. If the weapons themselves are vulnerable to attack, or the machines that carry them, a successful surprise might eliminate the opponent's means of retribution. That an enormous explosion can be packaged in a single bomb does not by itself guarantee that the victor will receive deadly punishment. Two gunfighters facing each other in a Western town had an unquestioned capacity to kill one another; that did not guarantee that both would die in a gunfight—only the slower of the two. Less deadly weapons, permitting an injured one to shoot back before he died, might have been more conducive to a restraining balance of terror, or of caution. The very efficiency of nuclear weapons could make them ideal for starting war, if they can suddenly eliminate the enemy's capability to shoot back.

And there is a contrary possibility: that nuclear weapons are not vulnerable to attack and prove not to be terribly effective against each other, posing no need to shoot them quickly for fear they will be destroyed before they are launched, and with no task available but the systematic destruction of the enemy country and no necessary reason to do it fast rather than slowly. Imagine that nuclear destruction *had* to go slowly—that the bombs could be dropped only one per day. The prospect would look very different, something like the most terroristic guerilla warfare on a massive scale. It happens that nuclear war does not have to go slowly; but it may also not have to go speedily. The mere existence of nuclear weapons does not itself determine that everything must go off in a blinding flash, any more than that it must go slowly. Nuclear weapons do not simplify things quite that much.

*   *   *

War no longer looks like just a contest of strength. War and the brink of war are more a contest of nerve and risk-taking, of pain and endurance. Small wars embody the threat of a larger war; they are not just military engagements but "crisis diplomacy." The threat of war has always been somewhere underneath international diplomacy, but for Americans it is now much nearer the surface. Like the threat of a strike in industrial relations, the threat of divorce in a family dispute, or the threat of bolting the party at a political convention, the threat of violence continuously circumscribes international politics. Neither strength nor goodwill procures immunity.

Military strategy can no longer be thought of, as it could for some countries in some eras, as the science of military victory. It is now equally, if not more, the art of coercion, of intimidation and deterrence. The instruments of war are more punitive than acquisitive. Military strategy, whether we like it or not, has become the diplomacy of violence.

NOTES

1. Lynn Montross, *War Through the Ages* (3d ed. New York, Harper and Brothers, 1960), p. 146.

2. Xenophon, *The Persian Expedition*, Rex Warner, transl. (Baltimore, Penguin Books, 1949), p. 272. "The 'rational' goal of the threat of violence," says H. L. Nieburg, "is an accommodation of interests, not the provocation of actual violence. Similarly the 'rational' goal of actual violence is demonstration of the will and capability of action, establishing a measure of the credibility of future threats, not the exhaustion of that capability in unlimited conflict." "Uses of Violence," *Journal of Conflict Resolution*, 7 (1963), 44.

3. New York, Simon and Schuster, 1962, p. 47.

ROBERT JERVIS

COOPERATION UNDER THE SECURITY DILEMMA

I. Anarchy and the Security Dilemma

The lack of an international sovereign not only permits wars to occur, but also makes it difficult for states that are satisfied with the status quo to arrive at goals that they recognize as being in their common interest. Because there are no institutions or authorities that can make and enforce international laws, the policies of cooperation that will bring mutual rewards if others cooperate may bring disaster if they do not. Because states are aware of this, anarchy encourages behavior that leaves all concerned worse off than they could be, even in the extreme case in which all states would like to freeze the status quo. This is true of the men in Rousseau's "Stag Hunt." If they cooperate to trap the stag, they will all eat well. But if one person defects to chase a

From *World Politics* 30, no. 2 (January 1978): 167–214. Some of the author's notes have been omitted.

rabbit—which he likes less than stag—none of the others will get anything. Thus, all actors have the same preference order, and there is a solution that gives each his first choice: (1) cooperate and trap the stag (the international analogue being cooperation and disarmament); (2) chase a rabbit while others remain at their posts (maintain a high level of arms while others are disarmed); (3) all chase rabbits (arms competition and high risk of war); and (4) stay at the original position while another chases a rabbit (being disarmed while others are armed). Unless each person thinks that the others will cooperate, he himself will not. And why might he fear that any other person would do something that would sacrifice his own first choice? The other might not understand the situation, or might not be able to control his impulses if he saw a rabbit, or might fear that some other member of the group is unreliable. If the person voices any of these suspicions, others are more likely to fear that he will defect, thus making them more likely to defect, thus making it more rational for him to defect. Of course in this simple case—and in many that are more realistic—there are a number of arrangements that could permit cooperation. But the main point remains: although actors may know that they seek a common goal, they may not be able to reach it.

Even when there is a solution that is everyone's first choice, the international case is characterized by three difficulties not present in the Stag Hunt. First, to the incentives to defect given above must be added the potent fear that even if the other state now supports the status quo, it may become dissatisfied later. No matter how much decision makers are committed to the status quo, they cannot bind themselves and their successors to the same path. Minds can be changed, new leaders can come to power, values can shift, new opportunities and dangers can arise.

The second problem arises from a possible solution. In order to protect their possessions, states often seek to control resources or land outside their own territory. Countries that are not self-sufficient must try to assure that the necessary supplies will continue to flow in wartime. This was part of the explanation for Japan's drive into China and Southeast Asia before World War II. If there were an international authority that could guarantee access, this motive for control would disappear. But since there is not, even a state that would prefer the status quo to increasing its area of control may pursue the latter policy.

When there are believed to be tight linkages between domestic and foreign policy or between the domestic politics of two states, the quest for security may drive states to interfere preemptively in the domestic politics of others in order to provide an ideological buffer zone. * * *

More frequently, the concern is with direct attack. In order to protect themselves, states seek to control, or at least to neutralize, areas on their borders. But attempts to establish buffer zones can alarm others who have stakes there, who fear that undesirable precedents will be set, or who believe that their own vulnerability will be increased. When buffers are sought in areas empty of great powers, expansion tends to feed on itself in order to protect what is acquired * * *.

Though this process is most clearly visible when it involves territorial expansion, it often operates with the increase of less tangible power and influence. The expansion of power usually brings with it an expansion of responsibilities and commitments; to meet them, still greater power is required. The state will take many positions that are subject to challenge. It will be involved with a wide range of controversial issues unrelated to its core values. And retreats that would be seen as normal if made by a small power would be taken as an index of weakness inviting predation if made by a large one.

The third problem present in international politics but not in the Stag Hunt is the security dilemma: many of the means by which a state tries to increase its security decrease the security of others. In domestic society, there are several ways to increase the safety of one's person and property without endangering others. One can move to a safer neighborhood, put bars on the windows, avoid dark streets, and keep a distance from suspicious-looking characters. Of course these measures are not convenient, cheap, or certain of success. But no one save criminals need be alarmed if a person takes them. In international politics, however, one state's gain in security often inadvertently threatens others. In explaining British policy on naval disarmament in the interwar period to the Japanese, Ramsey MacDonald said that "Nobody wanted Japan to be insecure."[1] But the problem was not with British desires, but with the consequences of her policy. In earlier periods, too, Britain had needed a navy large enough to keep the shipping lanes open. But such a navy could not avoid being a menace to any other state with a coast that could be raided, trade that could be interdicted, or colonies that could be isolated. When Germany started building a powerful navy before World War I, Britain objected that it could only be an offensive weapon aimed at her. As Sir Edward Grey, the Foreign Secretary, put it to King

Edward VII: "If the German Fleet ever becomes superior to ours, the German Army can conquer this country. There is no corresponding risk of this kind to Germany; for however superior our Fleet was, no naval victory could bring us any nearer to Berlin." The English position was half correct: Germany's navy was an anti-British instrument. But the British often overlooked what the Germans knew full well: "in every quarrel with England, German colonies and trade were . . . hostages for England to take." Thus, whether she intended it or not, the British Navy constituted an important instrument of coercion.[2]

II. What Makes Cooperation More Likely?

Given this gloomy picture, the obvious question is, why are we not all dead? Or, to put it less starkly, what kinds of variables ameliorate the impact of anarchy and the security dilemma? The working of several can be seen in terms of the Stag Hunt or repeated plays of the Prisoner's Dilemma.[3] The Prisoner's Dilemma differs from the Stag Hunt in that there is no solution that is in the best interests of all the participants; there are offensive as well as defensive incentives to defect from the coalition with the others; and, if the game is to be played only once, the only rational response is to defect. But if the game is repeated indefinitely, the latter characteristic no longer holds and we can analyze the game in terms similar to those applied to the Stag Hunt. It would be in the interest of each actor to have others deprived of the power to defect; each would be willing to sacrifice this ability if others were similarly restrained. But if the others are not, then it is in the actor's interest to retain the power to defect.[4] The game theory matrices for these two situations are given below, with the numbers in the boxes being the order of the actor's preferences.

We can see the logical possibilities by rephrasing our question: "Given either of the above situations, what makes it more or less

STAG HUNT		PRISONER'S DILEMMA	
A		A	
COOPERATE DEFECT		COOPERATE DEFECT	

STAG HUNT — A (COOPERATE / DEFECT), B (COOPERATE / DEFECT): CC = 1,1; A DEFECT / B COOPERATE = 2,4; A COOPERATE / B DEFECT = 4,2; DD = 3,3.

PRISONER'S DILEMMA — A (COOPERATE / DEFECT), B (COOPERATE / DEFECT): CC = 2,2; A DEFECT / B COOPERATE = 1,4; A COOPERATE / B DEFECT = 4,1; DD = 3,3.

likely that the players will cooperate and arrive at CC?" The chances of achieving this outcome will be increased by: (1) anything that increases incentives to cooperate by increasing the gains of mutual cooperation (CC) and/or decreasing the costs the actor will pay if he cooperates and the other does not (CD); (2) anything that decreases the incentives for defecting by decreasing the gains of taking advantage of the other (DC) and/or increasing the costs of mutual noncooperation (DD); (3) anything that increases each side's expectation that the other will cooperate.[5]

The Costs of Being Exploited (CD)

The fear of being exploited (that is, the cost of CD) most strongly drives the security dilemma; one of the main reasons why international life is not more nasty, brutish, and short is that states are not as vulnerable as men are in a state of nature. People are easy to kill, but as Adam Smith replied to a friend who feared that the Napoleonic Wars would ruin England, "Sir, there is a great deal of ruin in a nation."[6] The easier it is to destroy a state, the greater the reason for it either to join a larger and more secure unit, or else to be especially suspicious of others, to require a large army, and, if conditions are favorable, to attack at the slightest provocation rather than wait to be attacked. If the failure to eat that day—be it venison or rabbit—means that he will starve, a person is likely to defect in the Stag Hunt even if he really likes venison and has a high level of trust in his colleagues. (Defection is especially likely if the others are also starving or if they know that he is.) By contrast, if the costs of CD are lower, if people are well-fed or states are resilient, they can afford to take a more relaxed view of threats.

A relatively low cost of CD has the effect of transforming the game from one in which both players make their choices simultaneously to one in which an actor can make his choice after the other has moved. He will not have to defect out of fear that the other will, but can wait to see what the other will do. States that can afford to be cheated in a bargain or that cannot be destroyed by a surprise attack can more easily trust others and need not act at the first, and ambiguous, sign of menace. Because they have a margin of time and error, they need not match, or more than match, any others' arms in peacetime. They can mobilize in the prewar period or even at the start of the war itself, and still survive. For example, those who opposed a crash program to develop the H-bomb felt that the U.S. margin of safety was large enough so that even if Russia managed to gain a lead in the race, America would not be endangered. The program's advocates disagreed: "If we let the Russians get the super first, catastrophe becomes all but certain."[7]

When the costs of CD are tolerable, not only is security easier to attain but, what is even more important here, the relatively low level of arms and relatively passive foreign policy that a status-quo power will be able to adopt are less likely to threaten others. Thus it is easier for status-quo states to act on their common interests if they are hard to conquer. All other things being equal, a world of small states will feel the effects of anarchy much more than a world of large ones. Defensible borders, large size, and protection against sudden attack not only aid the state, but facilitate cooperation that can benefit all states.

Of course, if one state gains invulnerability by being more powerful than most others, the problem will remain because its security provides a base from which it can exploit others. When the price a state will pay for DD is low, it leaves others with few hostages for its good behavior. Others who are more vulnerable will grow apprehensive, which will lead them to acquire more arms and

will reduce the chances of cooperation. The best situation is one in which a state will not suffer greatly if others exploit it, for example, by cheating on an arms control agreement (that is, the costs of CD are low); but it will pay a high long-run price if cooperation with the others breaks down—for example, if agreements cease functioning or if there is a long war (that is, the costs of DD are high). The state's invulnerability is then mostly passive; it provides some protection, but it cannot be used to menace others. As we will discuss below, this situation is approximated when it is easier for states to defend themselves than to attack others, or when mutual deterrence obtains because neither side can protect itself.

The differences between highly vulnerable and less vulnerable states are illustrated by the contrasting policies of Britain and Austria after the Napoleonic Wars. Britain's geographic isolation and political stability allowed her to take a fairly relaxed view of disturbances on the Continent. Minor wars and small changes in territory or in the distribution of power did not affect her vital interests. An adversary who was out to overthrow the system could be stopped after he had made his intentions clear. And revolutions within other states were no menace, since they would not set off unrest within England. Austria, surrounded by strong powers, was not so fortunate; her policy had to be more closely attuned to all conflicts. By the time an aggressor-state had clearly shown its colors, Austria would be gravely threatened. And foreign revolutions, be they democratic or nationalistic, would encourage groups in Austria to upset the existing order. So it is not surprising that Metternich propounded the doctrine summarized earlier, which defended Austria's right to interfere in the internal affairs of others, and that British leaders rejected this view. Similarly, Austria wanted the Congress system to be a relatively tight one, regulating most disputes. The British favored a less centralized system. In other words, in order to protect herself, Austria had either to threaten or to harm others, whereas Britain did not. For Austria and her neighbors the security dilemma was acute; for Britain it was not.

The ultimate cost of CD is of course loss of sovereignty. This cost can vary from situation to situation. The lower it is (for instance, because the two states have compatible ideologies, are similar ethnically, have a common culture, or because the citizens of the losing state expect economic benefits), the less the impact of the security dilemma; the greater the costs, the greater the impact of the dilemma. Here is another reason why extreme differences in values and ideologies exacerbate international conflict.

*   *   *

SUBJECTIVE SECURITY DEMANDS

Decision makers act in terms of the vulnerability they feel, which can differ from the actual situation; we must therefore examine the decision makers' subjective security requirements. Two dimensions are involved. First, even if they agree about the objective situation, people can differ about how much security they desire—or, to put it more precisely, about the price they are willing to pay to gain increments of security. The more states value their security above all else (that is, see a prohibitively high cost in CD), the more they are likely to be sensitive to even minimal threats, and to demand high levels of arms. And if arms are positively valued because of pressures from a military-industrial complex, it will be especially hard for status-quo powers to cooperate. By contrast, the security dilemma will not operate as strongly when pressing domestic concerns increase the opportunity costs of armaments. In this case, the net advantage of exploiting the other (DC) will be less, and the costs of arms races (that is, one aspect of DD) will be greater; therefore the state will behave as though it were relatively invulnerable.

The second aspect of subjective security is the perception of threat (that is, the estimate of whether the other will cooperate). A state that is predisposed to see either a specific other state as an adversary, or others in general as a menace, will react more strongly and more quickly than a state that sees its environment as benign. Indeed, when a state believes that another not only is not likely to be an adversary, but has sufficient interests in common with it to be an ally, then it will actually welcome an increase in the other's power.

*   *   *

Geography, Commitments, Beliefs, and Security through Expansion

* * * Situations vary in the ease or difficulty with which all states can simultaneously achieve a high degree of security. The influence of military technology on this variable is the subject of the next section. Here we want to treat the impact of beliefs, geography, and commitments (many of which can be considered to be modifications of geography, since they bind states to defend areas outside their homelands). In the crowded continent of Europe, security requirements were hard to mesh. Being surrounded by powerful states, Germany's problem—or the problem created by Germany—was always great and was even worse when her relations with both France and Russia were bad, such as before World War I. In that case, even a status-quo Germany, if she could not change the political situation, would almost have been forced to adopt something like the Schlieffen Plan. Because she could not hold off both of her enemies, she had to be prepared to defeat one quickly and then deal with the other in a more leisurely fashion. If France or Russia stayed out of a war between the other state and Germany, they would allow Germany to dominate the Continent (even if that was not Germany's aim). They therefore had to deny Germany this ability, thus making Germany less secure. Although Germany's arrogant and erratic behavior, coupled with the desire for an unreasonably high level of security (which amounted to the desire to escape from her geographic plight), compounded the problem, even wise German statesmen would have been hard put to gain a high degree of security without alarming their neighbors.

*   *   *

III. Offense, Defense, and the Security Dilemma

Another approach starts with the central point of the security dilemma—that an increase in one state's security decreases the security of others—and examines the conditions under which this proposition holds. Two crucial variables are involved: whether defensive weapons and policies can be distinguished from offensive ones, and whether the defense or the offense has the advantage. The definitions are not always clear, and many cases are difficult to judge, but these two variables shed a great deal of light on the question of whether status-quo powers will adopt compatible security policies. All the variables discussed so far leave the heart of the problem untouched. But when defensive weapons differ from offensive ones, it is possible for a state to make itself more secure without making others less secure. And when the defense has the advantage over the offense, a large increase in one state's security only slightly decreases the security of the others, and status-quo powers can all enjoy a high level of security and largely escape from the state of nature.

Offense-Defense Balance

When we say that the offense has the advantage, we simply mean that it is easier to destroy the other's army and take its territory than it is to defend one's own. When the defense has the advantage, it is easier to protect and to hold than it is to move forward, destroy, and take. If effective defenses can be erected quickly, an attacker may be able to keep territory he has taken in an initial victory. Thus, the dominance of the defense made it very hard for Britain and France to push Germany out of France in World War I. But when superior defenses are difficult for an aggressor to improvise on the battlefield and must be constructed during peacetime, they provide no direct assistance to him.

The security dilemma is at its most vicious when commitments, strategy, or technology dic-tate that the only route to security lies through expansion. Status-quo powers must then act like aggressors; the fact that they would gladly agree to forego the opportunity for expansion in return for guarantees for their security has no implica-tions for their behavior. Even if expansion is not sought as a goal in itself, there will be quick and drastic changes in the distribution of territory and influence. Conversely, when the defense has the advantage, status-quo states can make them-selves more secure without gravely endangering others.[8] Indeed, if the defense has enough of an advantage and if the states are of roughly equal size, not only will the security dilemma cease to inhibit status-quo states from cooperating, but aggression will be next to impossible, thus ren-dering international anarchy relatively unimpor-tant. If states cannot conquer each other, then the lack of sovereignty, although it presents prob-lems of collective goods in a number of areas, no longer forces states to devote their primary atten-tion to self-preservation. Although, if force were not usable, there would be fewer restraints on the use of nonmilitary instruments, these are rarely powerful enough to threaten the vital interests of a major state.

Two questions of the offense-defense balance can be separated. First, does the state have to spend more or less than one dollar on defensive forces to offset each dollar spent by the other side on forces that could be used to attack? If the state has one dollar to spend on increasing its security, should it put it into offensive or defensive forces? Second, with a given inventory of forces, is it bet-ter to attack or to defend? Is there an incentive to strike first or to absorb the other's blow? These two aspects are often linked: if each dollar spent on offense can overcome each dollar spent on de-fense, and if both sides have the same defense budgets, then both are likely to build offensive forces and find it attractive to attack rather than to wait for the adversary to strike.

These aspects affect the security dilemma in different ways. The first has its greatest impact on arms races. If the defense has the advantage, and if the status-quo powers have reasonable subjective security requirements, they can probably avoid an arms race. Although an increase in one side's arms and security will still decrease the other's security, the former's increase will be larger than the latter's decrease. So if one side increases its arms, the other can bring its security back up to its previous level by adding a smaller amount to its forces. And if the first side reacts to this change, its increase will also be smaller than the stimulus that produced it. Thus a stable equilibrium will be reached. Shifting from dynamics to statics, each side can be quite secure with forces roughly equal to those of the other. Indeed, if the defense is much more potent than the offense, each side can be willing to have forces much smaller than the other's, and can be indifferent to a wide range of the other's defense policies.

The second aspect—whether it is better to attack or to defend—influences short-run stability. When the offense has the advantage, a state's reaction to international tension will increase the chances of war. The incentives for pre-emption and the "reciprocal fear of surprise attack" in this situation have been made clear by analyses of the dangers that exist when two countries have first-strike capabilities.[9] There is no way for the state to increase its security without menacing, or even attacking, the other. Even Bismarck, who once called preventive war "committing suicide from fear of death," said that "no government, if it regards war as inevitable even if it does not want it, would be so foolish as to leave to the enemy the choice of time and occasion and to wait for the moment which is most convenient for the enemy."[10] In another arena, the same dilemma applies to the policeman in a dark alley confronting a suspected criminal who appears to be holding a weapon. Though racism may indeed be present, the security dilemma can account for many of the tragic shootings of innocent people in the ghettos.

Beliefs about the course of a war in which the offense has the advantage further deepen the security dilemma. When there are incentives to strike first, a successful attack will usually so weaken the other side that victory will be relatively quick, bloodless, and decisive. It is in these periods when conquest is possible and attractive that states consolidate power internally—for instance, by destroying the feudal barons—and expand externally. There are several consequences that decrease the chance of cooperation among status-quo states. First, war will be profitable for the winner. The costs will be low and the benefits high. Of course, losers will suffer; the fear of losing could induce states to try to form stable cooperative arrangements, but the temptation of victory will make this particularly difficult. Second, because wars are expected to be both frequent and short, there will be incentives for high levels of arms, and quick and strong reaction to the other's increases in arms. The state cannot afford to wait until there is unambiguous evidence that the other is building new weapons. Even large states that have faith in their economic strength cannot wait, because the war will be over before their products can reach the army. Third, when wars are quick, states will have to recruit allies in advance.[11] Without the opportunity for bargaining and re-alignments during the opening stages of hostilities, peacetime diplomacy loses a degree of the fluidity that facilitates balance-of-power policies. Because alliances must be secured during peacetime, the international system is more likely to become bipolar. It is hard to say whether war therefore becomes more or less likely, but this bipolarity increases tension between the two camps and makes it harder for status-quo states to gain the benefits of cooperation. Fourth, if wars are frequent, statesmen's perceptual thresholds will be adjusted accordingly and they will be quick to perceive ambiguous evidence as indicating that others are aggressive. Thus, there will be more cases of status-quo powers arming against each other in the incorrect belief that the other is hostile.

When the defense has the advantage, all the foregoing is reversed. The state that fears attack does not pre-empt—since that would be a wasteful use of its military resources—but rather prepares to receive an attack. Doing so does not decrease the security of others, and several states can do it simultaneously; the situation will therefore be stable, and status-quo powers will be able to cooperate. * * *

More is involved than short-run dynamics. When the defense is dominant, wars are likely to become stalemates and can be won only at enormous cost. Relatively small and weak states can hold off larger and stronger ones, or can deter attack by raising the costs of conquest to an unacceptable level. States then approach equality in what they can do to each other. Like the .45-caliber pistol in the American West, fortifications were the "great equalizer" in some periods. Changes in the status quo are less frequent and cooperation is more common wherever the security dilemma is thereby reduced.

Many of these arguments can be illustrated by the major powers' policies in the periods preceding the two world wars. Bismarck's wars surprised statesmen by showing that the offense had the advantage, and by being quick, relatively cheap, and quite decisive. Falling into a common error, observers projected this pattern into the future. The resulting expectations had several effects. First, states sought semi-permanent allies. In the early stages of the Franco-Prussian War, Napoleon III had thought that there would be plenty of time to recruit Austria to his side. Now, others were not going to repeat this mistake. Second, defense budgets were high and reacted quite sharply to increases on the other side. * * * Third, most decision makers thought that the next European war would not cost much blood and treasure.[12] That is one reason why war was generally seen as inevitable and why mass opinion was so bellicose. Fourth, once war seemed likely, there were strong pressures to pre-empt. Both sides believed that whoever moved first could penetrate the other deep enough to disrupt mobilization and thus gain an insurmountable advantage. (There was no such belief about the use of naval forces. Although Churchill made an ill-advised speech saying that if German ships "do not come out and fight in time of war they will be dug out like rats in a hole,"[13] everyone knew that submarines, mines, and coastal fortifications made

this impossible. So at the start of the war each navy prepared to defend itself rather than attack, and the short-run destabilizing forces that launched the armies toward each other did not operate.)[14] Furthermore, each side knew that the other saw the situation the same way, thus increasing the perceived danger that the other would attack, and giving each added reasons to precipitate a war if conditions seemed favorable. In the long and the short run, there were thus both offensive and defensive incentives to strike. This situation casts light on the common question about German motives in 1914: "Did Germany unleash the war deliberately to become a world power or did she support Austria merely to defend a weakening ally," thereby protecting her own position?[15] To some extent, this question is misleading. Because of the perceived advantage of the offense, war was seen as the best route both to gaining expansion and to avoiding drastic loss of influence. There seemed to be no way for Germany merely to retain and safeguard her existing position.

Of course the war showed these beliefs to have been wrong on all points. Trenches and machine guns gave the defense an overwhelming advantage. The fighting became deadlocked and produced horrendous casualties. It made no sense for the combatants to bleed themselves to death. If they had known the power of the defense beforehand, they would have rushed for their own trenches rather than for the enemy's territory. Each side could have done this without increasing the other's incentives to strike. War might have broken out anyway, * * * but at least the pressures of time and the fear of allowing the other to get the first blow would not have contributed to this end. And, had both sides known the costs of the war, they would have negotiated much more seriously. The obvious question is why the states did not seek a negotiated settlement as soon as the shape of the war became clear. Schlieffen had said that if his plan failed, peace should be sought.[16] The answer is complex, uncertain, and largely outside of the scope of our concerns. But part of the reason was the hope and sometimes the expectation that break-throughs could be made and the dominance of the offensive restored. Without that hope, the po-litical and psychological pressures to fight to a decisive victory might have been overcome.

The politics of the interwar period were shaped by the memories of the previous conflict and the belief that any future war would resem-ble it. Political and military lessons reinforced each other in ameliorating the security dilemma. Because it was believed that the First World War had been a mistake that could have been avoided by skillful conciliation, both Britain and, to a lesser extent, France were highly sensitive to the possibility that interwar Germany was not a real threat to peace, and alert to the danger that re-acting quickly and strongly to her arms could create unnecessary conflict. And because Britain and France expected the defense to continue to dominate, they concluded that it was safe to adopt a more relaxed and non-threatening mili-tary posture.[17] Britain also felt less need to main-tain tight alliance bonds. The Allies' military posture then constituted only a slight danger to Germany; had the latter been content with the status quo, it would have been easy for both sides to have felt secure behind their lines of fortifica-tions. Of course the Germans were not content, so it is not surprising that they devoted their money and attention to finding ways out of a defense-dominated stalemate. *Blitzkrieg* tactics were necessary if they were to use force to change the status quo.

The initial stages of the war on the Western Front also contrasted with the First World War. Only with the new air arm were there any incen-tives to strike first, and these forces were too weak to carry out the grandiose plans that had been both dreamed and feared. The armies, still the main instrument, rushed to defensive posi-tions. Perhaps the allies could have successfully attacked while the Germans were occupied in Poland.[18] But belief in the defense was so great that this was never seriously contemplated. Three months after the start of the war, the French Prime Minister summed up the view held by almost everyone but Hitler: on the Western Front there is "deadlock. Two Forces of equal strength and the one that attacks seeing such enormous casualties that it cannot move without endangering the continuation of the war or of the aftermath."[19] The Allies were caught in a dilemma they never fully recognized, let alone solved. On the one hand, they had very high war aims; although unconditional surrender had not yet been adopted, the British had decided from the start that the removal of Hitler was a neces-sary condition for peace.[20] On the other hand, there were no realistic plans or instruments for allowing the Allies to impose their will on the other side. The British Chief of the Imperial Gen-eral Staff noted, "The French have no intention of carrying out an offensive for years, if at all"; the British were only slightly bolder.[21] So the Al-lies looked to a long war that would wear the Germans down, cause civilian suffering through shortages, and eventually undermine Hitler. There was little analysis to support this view—and indeed it probably was not supportable—but as long as the defense was dominant and the numbers on each side relatively equal, what else could the Allies do?

To summarize, the security dilemma was much less powerful after World War I than it had been before. In the later period, the expected power of the defense allowed status-quo states to pursue compatible security policies and avoid arms races. Furthermore, high tension and fear of war did not set off short-run dynamics by which each state, trying to increase its security, inadvertently acted to make war more likely. The expected high costs of war, however, led the Allies to believe that no sane German leader would run the risks entailed in an attempt to dominate the Continent, and discouraged them from risking war themselves.

TECHNOLOGY AND GEOGRAPHY

Technology and geography are the two main fac-tors that determine whether the offense or the de-fense has the advantage. As Brodie notes, "On the tactical level, as a rule, few physical factors favor the attacker but many favor the defender. The defender usually has the advantage of cover. He characteristically fires from behind some form of shelter while his opponent crosses open ground."[22] Anything that increases the amount of ground the attacker has to cross, or impedes his progress across it, or makes him more vulnerable while crossing, increases the advantage accruing to the defense. When states are separated by barriers that produce these effects, the security dilemma is eased, since both can have forces adequate for defense without being able to attack.* * *

Oceans, large rivers, and mountain ranges serve the same function as buffer zones. Being hard to cross, they allow defense against superior numbers. The defender has merely to stay on his side of the barrier and so can utilize all the men he can bring up to it. The attacker's men, however, can cross only a few at a time, and they are very vulnerable when doing so. If all states were self-sufficient islands, anarchy would be much less of a problem. A small investment in shore defenses and a small army would be sufficient to repel invasion. Only very weak states would be vulnerable, and only very large ones could menace others. As noted above, the United States, and to a lesser extent Great Britain, have partly been able to escape from the state of nature because their geographical positions approximated this ideal.

Although geography cannot be changed to conform to borders, borders can and do change to conform to geography. Borders across which an attack is easy tend to be unstable. States living within them are likely to expand or be absorbed. Frequent wars are almost inevitable since attacking will often seem the best way to protect what one has. This process will stop, or at least slow down, when the state's borders reach—by expansion or contraction—a line of natural obstacles. Security without attack will then be possible. Furthermore, these lines constitute salient solutions to bargaining problems and, to the extent that they are barriers to migration, are likely to divide ethnic groups, thereby raising the costs and lowering the incentives for conquest.

Attachment to one's state and its land reinforce one quasi-geographical aid to the defense. Conquest usually becomes more difficult the deeper the attacker pushes into the other's territory. Nationalism spurs the defenders to fight harder; advancing not only lengthens the attacker's supply lines, but takes him through unfamiliar and often devastated lands that require troops for garrison duty. These stabilizing dynamics will not operate, however, if the defender's war materiel is situated near its borders, or if the people do not care about their state, but only about being on the winning side. * * *

*   *   *

The other major determinant of the offense-defense balance is technology. When weapons are highly vulnerable, they must be employed before they are attacked. Others can remain quite invulnerable in their bases. The former characteristics are embodied in unprotected missiles and many kinds of bombers. (It should be noted that it is not vulnerability *per se* that is crucial, but the location of the vulnerability. Bombers and missiles that are easy to destroy only after having been launched toward their targets do not create destabilizing dynamics.) Incentives to strike first are usually absent for naval forces that are threatened by a naval attack. Like missiles in hardened silos, they are usually well protected when in their bases. Both sides can then simultaneously be prepared to defend themselves successfully.

In ground warfare under some conditions, forts, trenches, and small groups of men in prepared positions can hold off large numbers of attackers. * * *

*   *   *

Concerning nuclear weapons, it is generally agreed that defense is impossible—a triumph not of the offense, but of deterrence. Attack makes no sense, not because it can be beaten off, but because the attacker will be destroyed in turn. In terms of the questions under consideration here, the result is the equivalent of the primacy of the defense. First, security is relatively cheap. Less than one percent of the G.N.P. is devoted to deterring a direct attack on the United States; most of it is spent on acquiring redundant systems to provide a lot of insurance against the worst conceivable contingencies. Second, both sides can simultaneously gain security in the form of second-strike capability. Third, and related to the foregoing, second-strike capability can be maintained in the face of wide variations in the other side's military posture. There is no purely military reason why each side has to react quickly and strongly to the other's increases in arms. Any spending that the other devotes to trying to achieve first-strike capability can be neutralized by the state's spending much smaller sums on protecting its second-strike capability. Fourth, there are no incentives to strike first in a crisis.

*   *   *

Offense-Defense Differentiation

The other major variable that affects how strongly the security dilemma operates is whether weapons and policies that protect the state also provide the capability for attack. If they do not, the basic postulate of the security dilemma no longer applies. A state can increase its own security without decreasing that of others. The advantage of the defense can only ameliorate the security dilemma. A differentiation between offensive and defensive stances comes close to abolishing it. Such differentiation does not mean, however, that all security problems will be abolished. If the offense has the advantage, conquest and aggression will still be possible. And if the offense's advantage is great enough, status-quo powers may find it too expensive to protect themselves by defensive forces and decide to procure offensive weapons even though this will menace others. Furthermore, states will still have to worry that even if the other's military posture shows that it is peaceful now, it may develop aggressive intentions in the future.

Assuming that the defense is at least as potent as the offense, the differentiation between them allows status-quo states to behave in ways that are clearly different from those of aggressors. Three beneficial consequences follow. First, status-quo powers can identify each other, thus laying the foundations for cooperation. Conflicts growing out of the mistaken belief that the other side is expansionist will be less frequent. Second, status-quo states will obtain advance warning when others plan aggression. Before a state can attack, it has to develop and deploy offensive weapons. If procurement of these weapons cannot be disguised and takes a fair amount of time, as it almost always does, a status-quo state will have the time to take countermeasures. It need not maintain a high level of defensive arms as long as its potential adversaries are adopting a peaceful posture.* * *

*   *   *

* * * [I]f all states support the status quo, an obvious arms control agreement is a ban on weapons that are useful for attacking. As President Roosevelt put it in his message to the Geneva Disarmament Conference in 1933: "If all nations will agree wholly to eliminate from possession and use the weapons which make possible a successful attack, defenses automatically will become impregnable, and the frontiers and independence of every nation will become secure."[23] The fact that such treaties have been rare * * * shows either that states are not always willing to guarantee the security of others, or that it is hard to distinguish offensive from defensive weapons.

*   *   *

IV. Four Worlds

The two variables we have been discussing—whether the offense or the defense has the advantage, and whether offensive postures can be distinguished from defensive ones—can be combined to yield four possible worlds.

The first world is the worst for status-quo states. There is no way to get security without menacing others, and security through defense is terribly difficult to obtain. Because offensive and defensive postures are the same, status-quo states acquire the same kind of arms that are sought by aggressors. And because the offense has the advantage over the defense, attacking is the best route to protecting what you have; status-quo states will therefore behave like aggressors. The situation will be unstable. Arms races are likely. Incentives to strike first will turn crises into wars. Decisive victories and conquests will be common. States will grow and shrink rapidly, and it will be hard for any state to maintain its size and influence without trying to increase them. Cooperation among status-quo powers will be extremely hard to achieve.

	Offense Has the Advantage	Defense Has the Advantage
Offensive Posture Not distinguishable from Defensive One	1 Doubly dangerous	2 Security dilemma, but security requirements may be compatible.
Offensive Posture Distinguishable from Defensive One	3 No security dilemma, but aggression possible. Status-quo states can follow different policy than aggressors. Warning given.	4 Doubly stable

There are no cases that totally fit this picture, but it bears more than a passing resemblance to Europe before World War I. Britain and Germany, although in many respects natural allies, ended up as enemies. Of course much of the explanation lies in Germany's ill-chosen policy. And from the perspective of our theory, the powers' ability to avoid war in a series of earlier crises cannot be easily explained. Nevertheless, much of the behavior in this period was the product of technology and beliefs that magnified the security dilemma. Decision makers thought that the offense had a big advantage and saw little difference between offensive and defensive military postures. The era was characterized by arms races. And once war seemed likely, mobilization races created powerful incentives to strike first.

In the nuclear era, the first world would be one in which each side relied on vulnerable weapons that were aimed at similar forces and each side understood the situation. In this case, the incentives to strike first would be very high—so high that status-quo powers as well as aggressors would be sorely tempted to pre-empt. And since the forces could be used to change the status quo as well as to preserve it, there would be no way for both sides to increase their security simultaneously. Now the familiar logic of deterrence leads both sides to see the dangers in this world. Indeed, the new understanding of this situation was one reason why vulnerable bombers and missiles were replaced. Ironically, the 1950's would have been more hazardous if the decision makers had been aware of the dangers of their posture and had therefore felt greater pressure to strike first. This situation could be recreated if both sides were to rely on MIRVed ICBMs.

In the second world, the security dilemma operates because offensive and defensive postures cannot be distinguished; but it does not operate as strongly as in the first world because the defense has the advantage, and so an increment in one side's strength increases its security more than it decreases the other's. So, if both sides have reasonable subjective security requirements, are of roughly equal power, and the variables discussed earlier are favorable, it is quite likely that status-quo states can adopt compatible security policies. * * *

This world is the one that comes closest to matching most periods in history. Attacking is usually harder than defending because of the strength of fortifications and obstacles. But purely defensive postures are rarely possible because fortifications are usually supplemented by armies and mobile guns which can support an attack. In the nuclear era, this world would be one in which both sides relied on relatively invulnerable ICBM's and believed that limited nuclear war was impossible. * * *

In the third world there may be no security dilemma, but there are security problems. Because states can procure defensive systems that do not threaten others, the dilemma need not operate. But because the offense has the advantage, aggression is possible, and perhaps easy. If the offense has enough of an advantage, even a status-quo state may take the initiative rather than risk being attacked and defeated. If the offense has less of an advantage, stability and cooperation are likely because the status-quo states will procure defensive forces. They need not react to others who are similarly armed, but can wait for the warning they would receive if others started to deploy offensive weapons. But each state will have to watch the others carefully, and there is room for false suspicions. The costliness of the defense and the allure of the offense can lead to unnecessary mistrust, hostility, and war, unless some of the variables discussed earlier are operating to restrain defection.

* * *

The fourth world is doubly safe. The differentiation between offensive and defensive systems permits a way out of the security dilemma; the advantage of the defense disposes of the problems discussed in the previous paragraphs. There is no reason for a status-quo power to be tempted to procure offensive forces, and aggressors give notice of their intentions by the posture they adopt. Indeed, if the advantage of the defense is great enough, there are no security problems. The loss of the ultimate form of the power to alter the status quo would allow greater scope for the exercise of nonmilitary means and probably would tend to freeze the distribution of values.

* * *

NOTES

1. Quoted in Gerald Wheeler, *Prelude to Pearl Harbor* (Columbia: University of Missouri Press 1963), 167.
2. Quoted in Leonard Wainstein, "The Dreadnought Gap," in Robert Art and Kenneth Waltz, eds., *The Use of Force* (Boston: Little, Brown 1971), 155 * * *.
3. In another article, Jervis says: "International politics sometimes resembles what is called a Prisoner's Dilemma (PD). In this scenario, two men have been caught redhanded committing a minor crime. The district attorney knows that they are also guilty of a much more serious offense. He tells each of them separately that if he confesses and squeals on his buddy, he will go free and the former colleague will go to jail for thirty years. If both of them refuse to give any information, they will be prosecuted for the minor crime and be jailed for thirty days; if they both squeal, plea-bargaining will get them ten years. In other words, as long as each criminal cares only about himself, he will confess to the more serious crime no matter what he thinks his colleague will do. If he confesses and his buddy does not, he will get the best possible outcome (freedom); if he confesses and his buddy also does so, the outcome will not be good (ten years in jail), but it will be better than keeping silent and going to jail for thirty years. Since both can see this, both will confess. Paradoxically, if they had both been irrational and kept quiet, they would have gone to jail for only a month." (Robert Jervis, "A Political Science Perspective on the Balance of Power and the Concert," *American Historical Review* 97, no. 3 (June 1992): 720.)
4. Experimental evidence for this proposition is summarized in James Tedeschi, Barry Schlenker, and Thomas Bonoma, *Conflict, Power, and Games* (Chicago: Aldine 1973), 135–41.
5. The results of Prisoner's Dilemma games played in the labouratory support this argument. See Anatol Rapoport and Albert Chammah, *Prisoner's Dilemma* (Ann Arbor: University of Michigan Press 1965), 33–50. Also see Robert Axelrod, *Conflict of Interest* (Chicago: Markham 1970), 60–70.

6. Quoted in Bernard Brodie, *Strategy in the Missile Age* (Princeton: Princeton University Press 1959), 6.

7. Herbert York, *The Advisors: Oppenheimer, Teller, and the Superbomb* (San Francisco: Freemar, 1976), 56–60.

8. Thus, when Wolfers, [*Discord and Collaboration* (Baltimore: Johns Hopkins Press 1962),] 126, argues that a status-quo state that settles for rough equality of power with its adversary, rather than seeking preponderance, may be able to convince the other to reciprocate by showing that it wants only to protect itself, not menace the other, he assumes that the defense has an advantage.

9. Schelling, [*The Strategy of Conflict* (New York: Oxford University Press 1963),] chap. 9.

10. Quoted in Fritz Fischer, *War of Illusions* (New York: Norton 1975), 377, 461.

11. George Quester, *Offense and Defense in the International System* (New York: John Wiley 1977), 105–06; Sontag [*European Diplomatic History, 1871–1932* (New York: Appleton-Century-Crofts 1933)], 4–5.

12. Some were not so optimistic. Gray's remark is well-known: "The lamps are going out all over Europe; we shall not see them lit again in our life-time." The German Prime Minister, Bethmann Hollweg, also feared the consequences of the war. But the controlling view was that it would certainly pay for the winner.

13. Quoted in Martin Gilbert, *Winston S. Churchill*, III, *The Challenge of War, 1914–1916* (Boston: Houghton Mifflin 1971), 84.

14. Quester (fn. 33), 98–99. Robert Art, *The Influence of Foreign Policy on Seapower*, II (Beverly Hills: Sage Professional Papers in International Studies Series, 1973), 14–18, 26–28.

15. Konrad Jarausch, "The Illusion of Limited War: Chancellor Bethmann Hollweg's Calculated Risk, July 1914," *Central European History*, II (March 1969), 50.

16. Brodie (fn. 6), 58.

17. President Roosevelt and the American delegates to the League of Nations Disarmament Conference maintained that the tank and mobile heavy artillery had re-established the dominance of the offensive, thus making disarmament more urgent (Boggs, [*Attempts to Define and. Limit "Aggressive" Armament in Diplomacy and Strategy* (Columbia: University of Missouri Studies, XVI, No. 1, 1941)], pp. 31, 108), but this was a minority position and may not even have been believed by the Americans. The reduced prestige and influence of the military, and the high pressures to cut government spending throughout this period also contributed to the lowering of defense budgets.

18. Jon Kimche, *The Unfought Battle* (New York: Stein 1968); Nicholas William Bethell, *The War Hitler Won: The Fall of Poland, September 1939* (New York: Holt 1972); Alan Alexandroff and Richard Rosecrance, "Deterrence in 1939," *World Politics*, XXIX (April 1977), 404–24.

19. Roderick Macleod and Denis Kelly, eds., *Time Unguarded: The Ironside Diaries, 1937–1940* (New York: McKay 1962), 173.

20. For a short time, as France was falling, the British Cabinet did discuss reaching a negotiated peace with Hitler. The official history ignores this, but it is covered in P.M.H. Bell, *A Certain Eventuality* (Farnborough, England: Saxon House 1974), 40–48.

21. Macleod and Kelly (fn. 19), 174. In flat contradiction to common sense and almost everything they believed about modern warfare, the Allies planned an expedition to Scandinavia to cut the supply of iron ore to Germany and to aid Finland against the Russians. But the dominant mood was the one described above.

22. Brodie (fn. 6), 179.

23. Quoted in Merze Tate, *The United States and Armaments* (Cambridge: Harvard University Press 1948), 108.

SCOTT D. SAGAN

HOW TO KEEP THE BOMB FROM IRAN

Preventing the Unthinkable

The ongoing crisis with Tehran is not the first time Washington has had to face a hostile government attempting to develop nuclear weapons. Nor is it likely to be the last. Yet the reasoning of U.S. officials now struggling to deal with Iran's nuclear ambitions is clouded by a kind of historical amnesia, which leads to both creeping fatalism about the United States' ability to keep Iran from getting the bomb and excessive optimism about the United States' ability to contain Iran if it does become a nuclear power. Proliferation fatalism and deterrence optimism reinforce each other in a disturbing way. As nuclear proliferation comes to be seen as inevitable, wishful thinking can make its consequences seem less severe, and if faith in deterrence grows, incentives to combat proliferation diminish.

A U.S. official in the executive branch anonymously told *The New York Times* in March 2006, "The reality is that most of us think the Iranians are probably going to get a weapon, or the technology to make one, sooner or later." Such proliferation fatalists argue that over the long term, it maybe impossible to stop Iran—or other states for that matter—from getting the bomb. Given the spread of nuclear technology and know-how, and the right of parties to the Nuclear Nonproliferation Treaty (NPT) to enrich uranium and separate plutonium, the argument goes, any foreign government determined to acquire nuclear weapons will eventually do so. Moreover, the 1981 Israeli attack on the Osirak nuclear reactor in Iraq may have delayed Iraq's progress, but similar air strikes are unlikely to disable Iran's capacities, since its uranium-enrichment facilities can be hidden underground or widely dis-

persed. Imposing economic sanctions through the UN Security Council is clearly a preferable option. But as Washington learned with India and Pakistan in the 1980s and 1990s, sanctions only increase the costs of going nuclear; they do not reduce the ability of a determined government to get the bomb.

Faced with only unattractive options to stem proliferation, some Bush administration officials are reluctantly preparing to live with a nuclear Iran. Military planners and intelligence officers have reportedly been tasked with developing strategies to deter Tehran if negotiations fail. Washington officials cry that the sky is falling whenever they face the prospect of a hostile state's getting the bomb, yet they seem to find solace in the recollection that deterrence and containment did work to maintain the peace during the Cold War. So why worry that the latest crop of rogue regimes might prove less deterrable than the Soviet Union and China? The Bush administration already appears to have adopted this logic with respect to North Korea. According to *The New York Times*, administration officials privately predict that deterrence will work against Pyongyang: "The North Koreans know . . . that a missile attack on the United States would result in the vaporization of Pyongyang," the paper quoted an official as saying. And if deterrence can work with Kim Jong Il, why not with Ayatollah Ali Khamenei? "Iran is just one instance of the [proliferation] problem, and in Iran's case, containment might work," argues Brent Scowcroft, who was national security adviser to President George H. W. Bush.

But both deterrence optimism and proliferation fatalism are wrongheaded. Deterrence optimism is based on mistaken nostalgia and a faulty analogy. Although deterrence did work with the Soviet Union and China, there were many close calls; maintaining nuclear peace during the Cold

From *Foreign Affairs* 85, no. 5 (Sept./Oct. 2006): 45–59.

War was far more difficult and uncertain than U.S. officials and the American public seem to remember today. Furthermore, a nuclear Iran would look a lot less like the totalitarian Soviet Union and the People's Republic of China and a lot more like Pakistan, Iran's unstable neighbor—a far more frightening prospect. Fatalism about nuclear proliferation is equally unwarranted. Although the United States did fail to prevent its major Cold War rivals from developing nuclear arsenals, many other countries curbed their own nuclear ambitions. After flirting with nuclear programs in the 1960s, West Germany and Japan decided that following the NPT and relying on the protection of the U.S. nuclear umbrella would bring them greater security in the future; South Korea and Taiwan gave up covert nuclear programs when the United States threatened to sever security relations with them; North Korea froze its plutonium production in the 1990s; and Libya dismantled its nascent nuclear program in 2003.

Given these facts, Washington should work harder to prevent the unthinkable rather than accept what falsely appears to be inevitable. The lesson to be drawn from the history of nonproliferation is not that all states eyeing the bomb eventually get it but that nonproliferation efforts succeed when the United States and other global actors help satisfy whatever concerns drove a state to want nuclear weapons in the first place. Governments typically pursue nuclear power for one of three reasons: to protect themselves against an external security threat, to satisfy the parochial interests of domestic actors, or to acquire an important status symbol. Iran is, mostly, a classic case of a state that wants nuclear weapons to dissuade an attack. It sits in a perennially unstable region, has long faced a belligerent Iraq, and now wants to stand up to Washington's calls for regime change in Tehran. Any viable solution to Tehran's appetite for nuclear weapons will therefore require that Washington learn to coexist peacefully with Iran's deeply problematic government. U.S. officials should not assume that Iran will go nuclear no matter what and draw up plans for containing it

when it does. Nor should Washington rely exclusively on UN sanctions, which might not work. Instead, the U.S. government must dig into its diplomatic toolbox and offer—in conjunction with China, Russia, and the EU-3 (France, Germany, and the United Kingdom)—contingent security guarantees to Tehran.

Delusions of Deterrence

The nuclear monopoly the United States enjoyed at the end of World War II did not last long. Nonproliferation discussions in the United Nations soon after the war came to naught because the Soviet Union understandably distrusted any plan that gave the United States a monopoly on the scientific knowledge and engineering experience needed to build a nuclear weapon. As Cold War hostilities grew, first President Harry Truman and then President Dwight Eisenhower considered launching attacks against the Soviet Union to prevent it from developing a nuclear arsenal. Moscow had tested its first atomic bomb in 1949, but it was the prospect of the Soviets' amassing a large H-bomb arsenal that particularly alarmed Eisenhower. In 1953, he asked Secretary of State John Foster Dulles if "our duty to future generations did not require us to initiate war at the most propitious time that we could designate." Eisenhower eventually rejected the idea, however, because he feared the Red Army would respond by invading U.S. allies in Europe. Even if the United States did emerge victorious from such a conflict, Eisenhower told his advisers in 1954, "the colossal job of occupying the territories of a defeated enemy would be far beyond the resources of the United States at the conclusion of this war."

As the Soviet nuclear arsenal expanded, it triggered a chain reaction. The United Kingdom and France raced to develop their own nuclear weapons (which they first detonated in 1952 and 1960, respectively), partly as an independent deterrent to Soviet aggression in Europe but also as a symbol of their continuing great-power status. That U.S. allies developed such capacities did not much concern Washington, but the U.S. government became deeply worried that China under Mao Zedong might acquire its own bomb. Still, the Kennedy administration rejected plans to launch a preventive air strike on Chinese nuclear facilities in 1963 for fear that it would spark a major war and because the Soviets had rejected Washington's secret request for their assistance.

It is common today to look back nostalgically on those years as "the long peace." But this oversimplifies the challenges of the Cold War. Nuclear weapons did seem to have a sobering influence on the great powers, but that effect was neither automatic nor foolproof. Both the Soviet and the Chinese governments originally hoped that having the bomb would allow them to engage in more aggressive policies with impunity. Moscow repeatedly threatened West Berlin in the late 1950s and early 1960s, for example, confident that its growing arsenal would dissuade the United States from coming to West Germany's defense. Soviet Premier Nikita Khrushchev also believed that if the Soviet Union could place nuclear weapons in Cuba, the United States, once faced with the fait accompli, would be deterred by the Soviet arsenal from attacking Fidel Castro's regime.

What could be called dangerous learning by "trial and terror" also characterized relations with China. Mao appears to have genuinely believed that nuclear weapons were "paper tigers" and that China could survive any large-scale nuclear war. Beijing's foreign policy certainly did not turn moderate after its 1964 nuclear tests. Mao ordered military ambushes of Soviet armed forces on the disputed Chinese-Soviet border in March 1969, instructing Chinese generals not to worry about Moscow's response because "we, too, have atomic bombs." Soviet leaders retaliated against Chinese units along the border and threatened a preventive nuclear strike against China's nuclear facilities. Mao eventually accepted a negotiated settlement of the territorial dispute, but only after evacuating the Chinese leadership to the countryside and putting China's nuclear arsenal on alert.

A Regime Is Born

The frightening crises of the 1960s led U.S. and Soviet leaders to understand that nuclear weapons guaranteed only a precarious peace. Increasingly, the two superpowers pursued bilateral arms control measures—such as the Strategic Arms Limitation Talks and the Anti-Ballistic Missile Treaty—to try to manage their nuclear relationship. They also recognized that a new multilateral approach was needed to stop the spread of nuclear weapons.

In March 1963, President John F. Kennedy told the press that he was "haunted" by the fear that by the 1970s the United States would "face a world in which 15 or 20 or 25 nations" possessed nuclear weapons. Five years of negotiations later, the United States, the Soviet Union, the United Kingdom, and 59 non-nuclear-weapons states signed the NPT. Under the terms of the treaty, states possessing nuclear weapons agreed not to transfer weapons or knowledge about how to build them to their friends and allies. (This commitment effectively ended Washington's hope of supplying West Germany and other NATO powers with "a multilateral force" of nuclear weapons, a prospect that had deeply troubled Moscow.) They also undertook "to work in good faith" toward the eventual elimination of nuclear weapons. The non-nuclear-weapons states, for their part, agreed not to seek nuclear weapons and to cooperate with inspectors from the International Atomic Energy Agency (IAEA) to allow monitoring of their peaceful nuclear research and energy facilities. The idea behind this "I won't if you won't" provision was to reduce the security threats, potential or real, that non-nuclear-weapons states posed to one another. The treaty also guaranteed that non-nuclear-weapons states in good standing would gain the full benefits of peaceful nuclear energy production, creating a "sovereign right," Iran has since argued, for any such state to develop a full nuclear-fuel production cycle of its own. The broad ambition behind the NPT was to slow down proliferation by reducing the demand for nuclear weapons. By both providing some assurance that states subscribing to the treaty would not develop nuclear bombs and creating, through the IAEA, a system to detect their efforts if they did, the NPT assuaged the security concerns of many states. It also reduced the bomb's appeal as a status symbol by creating an international norm according to which "responsible" states followed NPT commitments and only "rogue" states did not. And by offering hope that the nuclear states would take significant steps toward eventual disarmament, the treaty made it easier for nonnuclear governments to justify their own self-restraint to their domestic constituencies.

The NPT system proved reasonably successful for quite a long while. Although they are less discussed than the failures, the nonproliferation successes—the nuclear dogs that did not bark—are more numerous. Many non-nuclear-weapons states did continue to develop nuclear energy facilities after the NPT was signed, and some—such as Japan, with its massive plutonium stockpile—kept nuclear materials and continued their nuclear research in case the NPT regime fell apart. (Uncertainty about the treaty was so strong at first that Japan and other nonnuclear states insisted that they be allowed to review and renew their membership every five years.) But the NPT and U.S. security guarantees eventually reduced those countries' interest in proliferation. Other U.S. allies were caught cheating—most notably South Korea in the 1970s and Taiwan in the 1980s—but they ended suspected military-related activities when Washington confronted them and threatened to withdraw its security assistance. Egypt sought nuclear weapons in the early 1960s, but it signed the NPT in 1968 and ratified it in 1979 after striking a peace deal with Israel that reduced its national security concerns. Belarus, Kazakhstan, and Ukraine were nuclear powers from the moment of their independence, having inherited arsenals when the Soviet Union collapsed in 1991. But they soon handed over the weapons to Russia in exchange for economic assistance, highly limited security assurances from the United States, and a chance to join the NPT in good standing. The

NPT has been enough of a success that at the 1995 NPT Review Conference, all 178 states that have ratified it agreed to extend it permanently.

Perils of Proliferation

A few outliers have bucked the system, however, and it is their actions that have bred the fatalism about proliferation that now dominates in Washington. Israel has never officially admitted to possessing nuclear weapons, but it is widely known to have constructed (with France's help) a small arsenal in the 1970s. South Africa secretly built seven nuclear devices under the apartheid regime in the 1980s (but unilaterally destroyed them well before a black-majority-rule government took over in 1994). India and Pakistan developed nuclear capabilities in the late 1980s and came out of the closet with them in May 1998. Iraq had been inching along, too, and after the 1981 Israeli air strike on its Osirak reactor, it started an underground gaseous diffusion facility to produce bomb-grade uranium, which was belatedly discovered and destroyed by UN inspectors after the 1991 Gulf War.

A number of political and military developments since the 1990s have further weakened the nonproliferation regime. The Pakistani scientist A. Q. Khan, among others, began secretly selling uranium-enrichment capabilities and even bomb designs to potential proliferators. The emergence of new nuclear states has threatened those states' neighbors, and the United States itself is increasingly seen as a security threat by some potential proliferators. Some states—Iran in particular—insist that they have a "right" to develop nuclear-fuel-production capabilities, which would get them uncomfortably close to developing nuclear bombs if they were subsequently to quit the treaty. In 1999, the U.S. Senate also dealt the regime a blow by voting against ratification of the Comprehensive Test Ban Treaty despite the Clinton administration's promise to ratify it during the 1995 NPT conference as proof of the U.S. commitment to eventual disarmament.

Most important, some new nuclear states have proved to be particularly risky actors. Consider the unsettling case of Pakistan. Islamabad has been dangerously lax since its 1998 nuclear tests, exercising weak control over its military personnel, intelligence officials, and scientists who have access to nuclear weapons, materials, and technology. Soon after the 1998 tests, Pakistani military planners developed more belligerent strategies against India. Dusting off an old plan, in the winter of 1999, Pakistani infantry units disguised as mujahideen snuck into Indian-held Kashmir. The incursion sparked the 1999 Kargil War, in which over 1,000 soldiers were killed on both sides before Pakistani forces reluctantly withdrew. According to U.S. and Indian intelligence, before the fighting ended, the Pakistani military had started to ready its nuclear-capable missiles for potential use. But when President Bill Clinton raised the possibility that this had happened with Pakistani Prime Minister Nawaz Sharif, he displayed a disturbing lack of knowledge about what his own military was doing. Similarly, Pakistani leaders gave important nuclear command-and-control responsibilities to the notorious Inter-Services Intelligence (ISI), which has intimate ties to both the Taliban and jihadist groups fighting in Kashmir. Doing so was a recipe for trouble, raising the risks that a rogue faction could steal a weapon or give it to terrorists. According to credible reports, during the Kargil War, Pakistani military planners and the ISI considered hiding Pakistan's nuclear weapons in western Afghanistan to protect them from a potential preemptive attack by India; they even contacted Taliban officials to explore the option. Islamabad has also exercised incredibly loose control over Pakistani nuclear scientists. After the 9/11 attacks, it was discovered that a number of individual scientists—including Sultan Bashiruddin Mahmood, a senior official of the Pakistan Atomic Energy Commission (PAEC)—had met with Osama bin Laden in Afghanistan and discussed techniques for developing nuclear weapons and other weapons of mass destruction. In April 2002, Pakistani President Pervez Mushar-

raf admitted that PAEC scientists had been in contact with al Qaeda but claimed that "the scientists involved had only very superficial knowledge." Most proliferation experts also believe that senior Pakistani military officers were involved in many, if not all, of the deals in which A. Q. Khan and his associates sold nuclear centrifuge components to Iran and Libya, offered to help Saddam Hussein build a bomb just before the 1991 Gulf War, and provided North Korea with uranium-enrichment technology.

The Most Dangerous Game

Dealing with a nuclear Iran in the near future would be more like dealing with Pakistan than with nuclearized democracies such as Israel and India or even nuclear totalitarian states such as the Soviet Union and China. Not only does Iranian President Mahmoud Ahmadinejad spew belligerent anti-Israel and Holocaust-denying statements, but the Iranian government as a whole continues to nurture revolutionary ambitions toward Iran's conservative Sunni neighbors and to support Hezbollah and other terrorist organizations. Tehran, like Islamabad, would be unlikely to maintain centralized control over its nuclear weapons or materials. In order to deter Tehran from giving nuclear weapons to terrorists, in January 2006 the French government announced that it would respond to nuclear terrorism with a nuclear strike of its own against any state that had served as the terrorists' accomplice. But this "attribution deterrence" posture glosses over the difficult question of what do if the source of nuclear materials for a terrorist bomb is uncertain. It also ignores the possibility that Tehran, once in possession of nuclear weapons, would feel emboldened to engage in aggressive naval actions against tankers in the Persian Gulf or to assist terrorist attacks as it did with the Hezbollah bombing of the U.S. barracks at the Khobar Towers in Saudi Arabia in 1996.

There is no reason to assume that, even if they wanted to, central political authorities in Tehran could completely control the details of nuclear operations by the Islamic Revolutionary Guard Corps. The IRGC recruits young "true believers" to join its ranks, subjects them to ideological indoctrination (but not psychological-stability testing), and—as the IAEA discovered when it inspected Iran's centrifuge facilities in 2003—gives IRGC units responsibility for securing production sites for nuclear materials. The IRGC is known to have ties to terrorist organizations, which means that Iran's nuclear facilities, like its chemical weapons programs, are under the ostensible control of the organization that manages Tehran's contacts with foreign terrorists. It is misguided simply to hope that eventual regime change in Tehran would end the nuclear danger because, in the words of one Bush administration official, who spoke to *The New York Times* anonymously, Washington would then "have a different relationship with a different Iranian government." This wish assumes that another Iranian revolution would end gently, with an orderly transfer of power, rather than in chaos and with the control of nuclear weapons left unclear.

The Reasons Why

If Iran must not be allowed to go nuclear, what then can be done to stop it? A U.S. military strike on Iran today should be avoided for the same prudent reasons that led Eisenhower and Kennedy to choose diplomacy and arms control over preventive war in their dealings with the Soviet Union and China. Even if U.S. intelligence services were confident that they had identified all major nuclear-related sites in Iran (they are not) and the Pentagon could hit all the targets, the United States would expose itself (especially its bases in the Middle East and U.S troops in Afghanistan and Iraq), and its allies, to the possibility of severe retaliation. When asked about possible U.S. air strikes in August 2004, Iranian Defense Minister Ali Shamkhani said, "You may be surprised to know that the U.S. military presence near us is not power for the United States because this power may under certain circumstances become a

hostage in our hands. . . . The United States is not the only power present in the region. We are also present from Khost to Kandahar in Afghanistan and we are present in the Gulf and can be present in Iraq." Iran might also support attacks by terrorist groups in Europe or the United States. Bush administration officials have sought to give some teeth to the threat of a military attack by hinting that Israel might strike on Washington's behalf. The Pentagon notified Congress in April 2005 of its intention to sell conventional GBU-28 "bunker-buster" bombs to Israel, and President George W. Bush reasserted Washington's commitment to "support Israel if her security is threatened." But an Israeli air strike on Iran's nuclear facilities would do no more good than a U.S. one: it could not destroy all the facilities and thus would leave Tehran to resume its uranium-enrichment program at surviving sites and would give Iran strong incentives to retaliate against U.S. forces in the Middle East. Muslim sentiment throughout the world would be all the more inflamed, encouraging terrorist responses against the West.

With no viable military option at hand, the only way for Washington to move forward is to give Tehran good reason to relinquish its pursuit of nuclear weapons. That, in turn, requires understanding why Tehran wants them in the first place. Iran's nuclear energy program began in the 1960s under the shah, but even he wanted to create a breakout option to get the bomb quickly if necessary. One of his senior energy advisers once recalled, "The shah told me that he does not want the bomb yet, but if anyone in the neighborhood has it, we must be ready to have it." At first, Ayatollah Ruhollah Khomeini objected to nuclear weapons and other weapons of mass destruction on religious grounds, but the mullahs abandoned such restraint after Saddam ordered chemical attacks on Iranian forces during the Iran-Iraq War. As former Iranian President Hashemi Rafsanjani, then the speaker of Iran's Parliament, noted in 1988, the conflict with Saddam showed that "the moral teachings of the world are not very effective when war reaches a serious stage," and so Iranians must "fully equip ourselves in the defensive and offensive use of chemical, bacteriological, and radiological weapons." Tehran began purchasing centrifuge components from A. Q. Khan's network in 1987 and received, according to the IAEA, documents on how to cast enriched uranium into the form needed for nuclear weapons. Iran's nuclear-development efforts were further accelerated when, after the 1991 Gulf War, UN inspectors discovered and disclosed that Iraq had been just one or two years away from developing nuclear weapons of its own.

The end of Saddam's rule in 2003 significantly reduced the security threat to Tehran. But by then the United States had already taken Iraq's place, Washington having made it clear that it wanted regime change in Iran, too. In his January 2002 State of the Union address, President Bush had denounced the governments of Iran, Iraq, and North Korea as members of an "axis of evil" with ties to international terrorism. Increasingly, Bush administration spokespeople were advocating "preemption" to counter proliferation. After the fall of Baghdad, an unidentified senior U.S. official told a *Los Angeles Times* reporter that Tehran should "take a number," hinting that it was next in line for regime change. It did not help that the 2002 Nuclear Posture Review, which was leaked to the press, listed Iran as one of the states to be considered as a potential target by U.S. nuclear war planners. When asked, in April 2006, whether the Pentagon was considering a potential preventive nuclear strike against Iranian nuclear facilities, President Bush pointedly replied, "All options are on the table."

In the meantime, Iran's program has advanced. The last official U.S. intelligence estimate given to Congress, in February 2006, vaguely stated that if Iran "continues on its current path . . . [it] will likely have the capacity to produce a nuclear weapon within the next decade"—an estimate that has since been widely interpreted to mean five to ten years. Last April, Tehran began operating a cascade of 164 uranium-enrichment centrifuges at Natanz. According to the State Department, it will take over 13 years for an experimental cascade of this size to produce enough

highly enriched uranium for even a single nuclear weapon. But without an arms control agreement, Iran is free to construct more centrifuge cascades at Natanz, and without intrusive IAEA inspections in place, Iran could build a covert enrichment facility elsewhere. What was once a proliferation problem is now a proliferation crisis.

Agreed Framework in Farsi

The depth of Tehran's security concerns is precisely the reason that, despite the Bush administration's hopes, Libya cannot be a model for how to deal with Iran now. Libyan President Muammar al-Qaddafi finally relinquished the pursuit of nuclear weapons in 2003 in exchange for both an end to trade sanctions and positive economic incentives. But Tripoli was always a very different foe from Tehran. For one thing, the Libyans turned out to be the gang that could not proliferate straight. For years, Qaddafi reportedly tried but failed to purchase complete nuclear weapons directly from China, India, and Pakistan. When he did purchase 20 centrifuges and components for another 200 from A. Q. Khan in 1997, he could not get enough of the machines assembled in the right way. In the late 1990s, moreover, as Qaddafi's regime was becoming more concerned with domestic threats—economic stagnation and the rise of jihadist insurgents—than it was with external ones, its nuclear program began to turn into a liability. Tehran today is in a very different position: it is much closer to being able to develop weapons, and it continues to have serious external security reasons for wanting them.

A better source of inspiration for handling Iran would be the 1994 Agreed Framework that the United States struck with North Korea. The Bush administration has severely criticized the deal, but it contained several elements that could prove useful for solving the Iranian nuclear crisis.

After the North Koreans were caught violating their NPT commitments in early 1993 (they were covertly removing nuclear materials from the Yongbyon reactor), they threatened to withdraw from the treaty. Declaring that "North Korea cannot be allowed to develop a nuclear bomb," President Clinton threatened an air strike on the Yongbyon reactor site if the North Koreans took further steps to reprocess plutonium. In June 1994, as the Pentagon was reinforcing military units on the Korean Peninsula and briefing Clinton on war preparations, Pyongyang froze its plutonium production, agreed to let IAEA inspectors monitor the reactor site, and entered into bilateral negotiations with a view to eventually eliminating its nuclear capability. It is unclear whether North Korea blinked out of fear of military intervention, because of concerns about economic sanctions, or because Washington's proposal held out the promise of security guarantees and normalized relations. But the talks produced the October 1994 Agreed Framework, under which North Korea agreed to eventually dismantle its reactors, remain in the NPT, and implement full IAEA safeguards. In exchange, the United States promised to provide it with limited oil supplies, construct two peaceful light-water reactors for energy production, "move toward full normalization of political and economic relations," and extend "formal assurances to [North Korea] against the threat or use of nuclear weapons by the U.S."

By 2002, however, the Agreed Framework had broken down, not only because Pyongyang was suspected of cheating but also because it believed that the United States, by delaying construction of the light-water reactors and failing to start normalizing relations, had not honored its side of the bargain. When confronted with evidence of its secret uranium program, in November 2002, Pyongyang took advantage of the fact that the U.S. military was tied down in preparations for the invasion of Iraq and withdrew from the NPT, kicked out the inspectors, and started reprocessing plutonium. Pyongyang is now thought to have six to eight nuclear weapons, to be producing more plutonium in the Yongbyon reactor, and to be constructing a larger one.

President Bush famously promised, in his 2002 State of the Union address, that the United States "will not permit the world's most danger-

ous regimes to threaten us with the world's most destructive weapons." Yet when North Korea kicked out the IAEA inspectors, Secretary of State Colin Powell proclaimed that the situation was "not a crisis," and Bush repeatedly declared that the United States had "no intention of invading North Korea." Deputy Secretary of State Richard Armitage quickly underscored the position: "The president has no hostile intentions and no plans to invade. That's an indication that North Korea can have the regime that [it] want[s] to have." The point was not lost on Tehran.

The 1994 Agreed Framework thus serves as a reminder of what to do, and its failure as a warning about what to avoid. If Washington is to offer security assurances to Tehran, it would be wise to do so soon (making the assurances contingent on Tehran's not developing nuclear weapons), rather than offering them too late, as it did with North Korea (and thus making them contingent on Tehran's getting rid of any existing nuclear weapons). As with North Korea, any deal with Iran must be structured in a series of steps, each offering a package of economic benefits (light-water reactors, aircraft parts, or status at the World Trade Organization) in exchange for constraints placed on Iran's future nuclear development.

Both Washington and Tehran will need to make major compromises. The Bush administration has said that a condition of any deal must be that "not a single centrifuge can spin" in Iran. But it might have to soften its stance. Allowing Tehran to maintain its experimental 164-centrifuge cascade, which poses no immediate danger and yet is an important status symbol for the Iranian regime, could help Tehran save face and sell a deal with Washington to its domestic constituencies by allowing it to claim that the arrangement protects Iran's "sovereign right" to have a full nuclear fuel cycle. One way to do this would be to draw a line between research on uranium enrichment (which would be allowed) and significant production of enriched uranium (which would be prohibited). In exchange, Tehran would have to accept verifiable safeguards on all its enrichment operations, permit throughout the country the more intrusive type of inspections required by the Additional Protocol of the IAEA, supply the IAEA with full documentation about suspected past violations, and freeze the construction of more centrifuges and heavy-water reactors that could produce plutonium.

History, particularly that of U.S.–North Korean relations, suggests that such agreements are just the start of serious negotiations. Even if a deal is struck, delays and backsliding should be expected. To limit their impact and keep them from leading to the agreement's dissolution, it would be necessary for Washington to both keep its promises and maintain credible threats that it would impose sanctions or even use limited force against Iran if Tehran violated its commitments.

Most important, however, would be a reduction in the security threat that the United States poses to Iran. Given the need for Washington to have a credible deterrent against, say, terrorist attacks sponsored by Iran, it would be ill advised to offer Tehran a blanket security guarantee. But more limited guarantees, such as a commitment not to use nuclear weapons and other commitments of the type offered North Korea under the Agreed Framework, could be effective today. They would reassure Tehran and pave the way toward the eventual normalization of U.S.-Iranian relations while signaling to other states that nuclear weapons are not the be all and end all of security. None of this will happen, however, if U.S. officials keep threatening to topple the Iranian government. In any final settlement, Tehran will need to agree to freeze its nuclear program and end its support for terrorism, and Washington—along with China, Russia, and the EU-3—must issue a joint security guarantee that respects Iran's political sovereignty, thus committing the United States to promote democracy only by peaceful means. Peaceful coexistence does not require friendly relations, but it does mean exercising mutual restraint. Relinquishing the threat of regime change by force is a necessary and acceptable price for the United States to pay to stop Tehran from getting the bomb.

BENJAMIN A. VALENTINO

FROM *FINAL SOLUTIONS: MASS KILLING AND GENOCIDE IN THE TWENTIETH CENTURY*

Introduction: Mass Killing in Historical and Theoretical Perspective

* * * Episodes of mass killing in the former Yugoslavia and Rwanda are but the latest entries on a long list of atrocities extending back to earliest

From *Final Solutions: Mass Killing and Genocide in the Twentieth Century* (Ithaca, NY: Cornell University Press, 2004). Some of the author's note have been omitted.

recorded history, even into the archeological record.[1] Mass killings have been perpetrated by and against a wide range of nations, cultures, forms of government, and ethnic and religious groups. Between 60 million and 150 million people probably have perished in episodes of mass killings during the twentieth century alone.[2] By comparison, international and civil wars have accounted for approximately 34 million battle deaths during the same period.[3] * * *

Many of the most widely accepted explanations of genocide and mass killing see the causes of these events in the social structures, forms of government, or collective psychology of the societies in which they take place. In particular, many scholars have focused on the dangers of dehumanizing attitudes and deep cleavages between social groups, on the psychological and political consequences of major societal crises such as wars or revolutions, and on the concentration of unchecked power in undemocratic political systems.

Although these theories have generated many important insights, each of them also has significant problems or limitations. Structural factors such as severe ethnic, racial, national, or religious divisions between social groups fail to provide a reliable indicator of mass killing. Indeed, some of the bloodiest mass killings in history have occurred in relatively homogeneous societies, between groups of the same or closely related ethnicity, nationality, religion, or class. Conversely, many deeply divided societies have endured for extended periods without experiencing mass killing.

Nor can mass killing adequately be explained by the presence of highly undemocratic governments or the occurrence of major social crises. While there is substantial evidence that these factors increase the risk that mass killing will occur, the great majority of undemocratic governments and social crises are not associated with massive violence against civilians, suggesting that other important causes are at work.

I believe that an understanding of mass killing must begin with the specific goals and strategies of high political and military leaders, not with broad social or political factors. Previous theoretical studies of genocide have tended to diminish the role of leadership on the grounds that the interests and ideas of a few elites cannot account for the participation of the rest of society in the violence. My research, however, suggests that society at large plays a smaller role in mass killing than is commonly assumed. Mass killing is rarely a popular enterprise in which neighbor turns against neighbor. On the contrary, the impetus for mass killing usually originates from a relatively small group of powerful political or military leaders. Sometimes even individual leaders can play a decisive role in instigating and determining the course of the slaughter. Scholars have long struggled, for example, to imagine the Great Terror without Stalin, the Holocaust without Hitler, or the Cultural Revolution without Mao.

It is true that these tyrants could not have accomplished their crimes without help from others in their societies. Nevertheless, a broad examination of the phenomenon of mass killing in the twentieth century reveals that the minimum level of social support necessary to carry out mass killing has been uncomfortably easy to achieve. Leaders have powerful methods to recruit the individuals needed to carry out mass killing and to secure the compliance or at least the passivity of the rest of society. The broader public sometimes approves of mass killing, but often it does not. Whatever the sympathies of the public, the active support of a large portion of society is usually not required to carry out mass killing. The violence itself is typically performed by a relatively small group of people, usually members of military or paramilitary organizations. They carry out their bloody work often with little more than the passive acceptance of the rest of society, including members of the perpetrators' own social groups.

In light of these unsettling findings, I argue that the causes of mass killing will be best understood when the phenomenon is studied from what I call a strategic perspective. The strategic perspective suggests that mass killing is most accurately viewed as an instrumental policy—a brutal strategy designed to accomplish leaders' most important ideological or political objectives and counter what they see as their most dangerous threats.

Like war, mass killing can be a powerful political and military tool. Unfortunately, leaders throughout history have proved all too ready to use this tool when it seemed to serve their purposes. Many scholars have sought to draw a clear line between warfare and mass killing, but I believe that the two phenomena are closely related.

This is not merely because mass killing so often occurs during times of war. Rather, it is because both phenomena involve the use of organized violence to compel others to do what they would not otherwise do. Contrary to common perceptions, perpetrators seldom view mass killing as an end in itself. Violence against victim groups is rarely intended to physically exterminate entire populations as such. More often, its purpose is to force victims to submit to radically new ways of life, to give up their homes and possessions, or to cease their support for political or military opposition groups. Some perpetrators, most notably the Nazis, have attempted to totally exterminate victim populations. Policies of extermination, however, usually emerge only after leaders have concluded that other options for achieving their ends, including less violent forms of repression or even limited concessions to victim groups, are ineffective or impractical.

The most meaningful distinction between war and mass killing, therefore, is not the purpose of its violence but the nature of its victims. War merges with mass killing when its intended targets become unarmed civilians rather than soldiers.

Thus, perpetrators see mass killing as a "final solution" in two respects. Mass killing is a final solution because it is permanent. It obviates the need for future efforts to resolve the perceived problems posed by its victims. Mass killing is also final, however, because it is usually the last in a series of efforts to "solve" these problems using other means. It usually emerges out of leaders' frustration with conventional military and political strategies for dealing with their victims. Perhaps perpetrators hesitate to resort immediately to this level of violence because some shred of humanity or compassion compels them to consider alternatives. More likely, perpetrators first seek less violent solutions because strategies of mass killing can carry substantial risks— inciting violent resistance from victim groups, alienating domestic populations and foreign powers, or provoking intervention by third parties. When perpetrators perceive the stakes to be high enough, and when less violent alternatives

appear to be blocked or unworkable, however, the incentives to consider mass killing multiply.

As with war, even the most despotic leaders do not see mass killing as the most appropriate solution to every problem. Many scholars have noted that perpetrators may view genocide or mass killing as a "rational" response to a perceived threat, but few have attempted to explain why perpetrators see this kind of violence as an appropriate response to some threats but not others. I contend that leaders are likely to perceive mass killing as an attractive means to achieve their ends only in very specific circumstances. My research identifies several real-world scenarios that seem to generate powerful incentives for leaders to consider mass killing. Three of these scenarios, which account for the greatest number of episodes of mass killing in the twentieth century as well as the greatest number of victims, serve as the major focus of this book.

First, mass killing can be an attractive strategy for regimes seeking to achieve the radical communization of their societies. Indeed, communist regimes probably have been responsible for the most violent mass killings in human history. Radical communist regimes have been so closely associated with mass killing because the changes they have sought to bring about in their societies have resulted in the nearly complete material dispossession of vast populations. Communist policies such as agricultural collectivization have stripped tens of millions of people of their homes and property and have obliterated traditional ways of life. In practice, few people have been willing to submit to such severe changes in the absence of violence and coercion. * * *

Second, regimes seeking to implement policies of large-scale ethnic cleansing also face significant incentives to consider mass killing. The mass killing of ethnic, national, or religious groups has often been portrayed as the result of deep-seated hatred of victims by perpetrators, or sometimes simply as killing for killing's sake. I argue, however, that ethnic mass killing occurs when leaders believe that their victims pose a threat that can be countered only by removing them from society or by permanently destroying their ability to organize politically or militarily. This perception may be based on perpetrators' racist or nationalistic ideological beliefs, or it may be a reaction to real, although almost always exaggerated, threatening actions of victim groups. Ethnic cleansing and mass killing are not one and the same, but they have often gone hand in hand. Forcing people to abandon their homes, belongings, and history for an unknown life in distant lands often requires considerable coercion. Even after victims have been coerced into flight, the process and aftermath of large population movements can be deadly. The bloodiest episodes of ethnic mass killing, however, occur when perpetrators conclude that physically expelling victims from society is impossible or impractical. Perpetrators may reach this conclusion when there simply are no territories available to receive large numbers of victims, or because they fear that victims will continue to pose a threat from across the border. Whatever the reasons, once perpetrators reject the possibility of expulsion as an effective of dealing with victim groups, the impulse for ethnic cleansing can escalate to systematic extermination.

Third, regimes seeking to defeat major guerrilla insurgencies may be drawn to strategies of mass killing. My research suggests that the intentional slaughter of civilians in the effort to defeat guerrilla insurgencies was the most common impetus for mass killing in the twentieth century. Guerrilla warfare has so often led to mass killing because the use of guerrilla tactics by insurgent groups generates powerful incentives for counterinsurgency forces to target civilians. Much more than conventional armies, guerrilla forces must rely directly on the civilian population for food, shelter, and information. Although the support of the civilian population is one of the primary strengths of guerrilla warfare, it can also be a weakness. Unlike guerrilla forces themselves, the civilian populations upon which insurgents rely are largely defenseless, immobile, and impossible to conceal. Military organizations seeking to defeat guerrillas therefore often find it easier to target their base of support in the people than to engage the guerrillas themselves. This effort to isolate the guerrillas from their civilian support has often resulted in mass killing.

*   *   *

1. Mass Killing and Genocide

No generally accepted terminology exists to describe the intentional killing of large numbers of noncombatants. The most likely contender, of course, is the term "genocide." This term, however, fails to capture the broad range of events I wish to examine. The most important limitation of "genocide" is its relatively narrow meaning, both in its etymology and in the formal United Nations definition of groups that qualify as its victims.

Raphael Lemkin, a Polish jurist of Jewish descent, first coined the word "genocide" in 1944. To create the term, Lemkin combined the Greek word *genos*, meaning "race or tribe," with the Latin derivative *cide*, which means "to kill." Lemkin defined genocide as "a coordinated plan of different actions aiming at the destruction of essential foundations of the life of national groups, with the aim of annihilating the groups themselves."[4] The United Nations Genocide Convention of 1948, which Lemkin played a major role in drafting, limits the victims of genocide to "national, ethnical, racial or religious" groups.[5] Similarly, the *Oxford English Dictionary* defines genocide as "the deliberate and systematic extermination of an ethnic or national group."[6]

Many of the most infamous and important "genocidal" events of this century, however, including the deliberate killing of between 10 million and 23 million people in the Soviet Union, between 10 million and 46 million in China, and between 1 million and 2 million in Cambodia, have not primarily involved clashes between different ethnic or national groups. In many other episodes of large-scale, systematic killing, ethnic, national or religious groups have been targeted, but not because of their group identity per se.

Because "genocide" is a term of general interest to society, however, and because it carries with it the weight of powerful moral sanction, many authors have been reluctant to give it up. Indeed, so politically powerful is the term that activists have applied it to policies such as abortion, interracial adoption, and lack of government funding for AIDS treatment and research.[7] As a result, the precise definition of the term has become the subject of intense debate among genocide scholars, policy makers, and human rights advocates.[8] Ever since the Genocide Convention was drafted, many authors have dissented from the UN definition, taking issue with, among other things, its apparent exclusion of political and other non-ethnic groups from the definition of genocide.

I strongly believe that understanding the causes of the systematic murder of noncombatants is important, regardless of the group identity of the victims. In academic works, however, it is useful if central terms coincide with their common English usage and etymology so that they can be readily understood, even by readers from outside the field. From a political perspective, it may be more effective to include non-ethnic groups in the definition of genocide and in the international agreements designed to prevent this kind of violence. From a scholarly perspective, however, clarity is paramount.

What Is Mass Killing?

In order to avoid this and other difficulties with the term "genocide," I utilize the term "mass killing"—defined here simply as *the intentional killing of a massive number of noncombatants*.[9] Victims of mass killing may be members of any kind of group (ethnic, political, religious, etc.) as long as they are noncombatants and as long as their deaths were caused intentionally. Three aspects of the definition of mass killing warrant further elaboration.

First, the mass killing must be intentional, which distinguishes it from deaths caused by natural disasters, outbreaks of disease, or the un-

intentional killing of civilians during war.[10] This definition is not limited to "direct" methods of killing such as execution, gassing, and bombing. It includes deaths caused by starvation, exposure, or disease resulting from the intentional confiscation, destruction, or blockade of the necessities of life. It also includes deaths caused by starvation, exhaustion, exposure, or disease during forced relocation or forced labor.

Determining the intentionality of deaths due to these causes can be extremely difficult, since it requires knowledge of the specific aims of the perpetrators. For the purposes of this definition, deaths need not be the result of policies designed specifically to kill in order to be considered mass killing. I also consider deaths to be intentional if they result from policies designed to compel or coerce civilian populations to change their behavior—and if the perpetrators could have reasonably expected that these policies would result in widespread death. Thus, civilians killed by aerial bombardment would be considered victims of mass killing only if their attackers intentionally aimed to kill or terrorize civilians as part of an effort to coerce survivors to surrender. If the civilians were killed as the attackers attempted to destroy nearby military forces or infrastructure, however, these deaths would be considered unintentional even though the attacker might have expected a certain level of civilian casualties. Deaths resulting from forced marches, forced labor, or forced deportation are considered intentional if perpetrators could have reasonably expected that implementing these policies would lead to large numbers of civilian deaths—even if perpetrators did not set out to kill these victims, per se. Unlike the civilian deaths caused by the bombing of factories or nearby military installations, civilian populations are the direct objects of forced marches, forced labour and deportation, not the coincidental victims of policies targeted against soldiers or physical structures.

*   *   *

The second aspect of the definition of mass killing that requires further specification is the meaning of "a massive number." Unlike most scholarly definitions of genocide, mass killing does not specify that perpetrators must possess the intent to destroy an entire group or even a specific percentage of it.[11] Rather, for the purposes of this definition, a massive number is defined simply as at least fifty thousand intentional deaths over the course of five or fewer years.[12] * * *

* * *

The third aspect of the definition of mass killing that warrants clarification is the term "noncombatant." This definition focuses on the killing of noncombatants because it is violence directed against noncombatants that distinguishes mass killing from other forms of warfare and that most offends our moral sensibilities. A noncombatant is defined as any unarmed person who is not a member of an organized military group and who does not actively participate in hostilities by intending to cause physical harm to enemy personnel or property.[13] It should be noted that simply associating with combatants, providing food or other nonlethal military supplies to them, or participating in nonviolent political activities in support of armed forces does not convert a noncombatant to a combatant. Because these activities pose no immediate threat of physical harm to combatants, individuals who engage in them deserve protection from killing—although they may be subject to judicial punishments. * * *

* * *

3. The Strategic Logic of Mass Killing

To identify societies at high risk for mass killing, I have suggested, we must first understand the specific goals, ideas, and beliefs of powerful groups and leaders, not necessarily the broad social structures or systems of government of the societies over which these leaders preside. * * *

* * * I contend that mass killing occurs when powerful groups come to believe it is the best available means to accomplish certain radical goals, counter specific types of threats, or solve difficult military problems. From this perspective, mass killing should be viewed as an instrumental policy calculated to achieve important political and military objectives with respect to other groups—a "final solution" to its perpetrators' most urgent problems.

Because mass killing is a means to an end, it is rarely a policy of first resort. Perpetrators commonly experiment with other, less violent or even conciliatory means in the attempt to achieve their ends. When these means fail or are deemed too costly or demanding, however, leaders are forced to choose between compromising their most important goals and interests or resorting to more violent methods to achieve them. Regardless of perpetrators' original intentions or attitudes toward their victims, the failure or frustration of other means can make mass killing a more attractive option.

It is important to emphasize that a strategic understanding of mass killing does not imply that perpetrators always evaluate objectively the problems they face in their environment, nor that they accurately assess the ability of mass killing to resolve these problems. Human beings act on the basis of their subjective perceptions and beliefs, not objective reality. Indeed, the powerful role that small groups and individuals play in the conception and implementation of policies of mass killing can amplify the influence of misperceptions in promoting such violence. The often misguided and sometimes outrightly bizarre ideas and beliefs of perpetrator groups can persist at least in part because they usually are shielded from the critical scrutiny of a wider audience. A profound obsession with secrecy, frequently engendered by years spent in political or military opposition, is common in perpetrator organizations and tends to exacerbate misperceptions.

A strategic approach to mass killing, therefore, suggests only that perpetrators are likely to employ mass killing when they perceive it to be both necessary and effective, not when it is actually so. In many cases, the threat posed by the victims of mass killing is more imagined than real. The Jews of Europe, after all, posed no conceivable threat to Germany in the 1930s. This reality mattered little, however, since Germany's leaders were steadfastly convinced of the contrary, and they possessed the power to act on their convictions. Perpetrators also frequently have overestimated the capacity of mass killing to achieve their goals, especially in the long term. While mass killing can be a powerful political or military strategy, it also can be decidedly counterproductive, even from the point of view of those who instigate it. In practice, the use of massive violence has often backfired, diverting scarce resources away from real threats, provoking increased resistance from victim groups, mobilizing third parties on behalf of the victims, or discrediting the ideologies in the service of which it has been employed.

Mass killing failed to achieve its perpetrators' objectives, at least in the long run, in all of the cases examined in this book. In the Soviet Union, China, and Cambodia communist leaders resorted to mass killing in an effort to force peasants to accept new, supposedly more productive means of agriculture. While the violence succeeded in coercing the peasantry, it also resulted in massive starvation, the near collapse of the economy, and eventually contributed to the decision to abandon radical communist agricultural methods. In Turkey, Nazi Germany, and Rwanda perpetrators used mass killing to eliminate perceived threats from ethnic minorities. In each case, the task of murdering defenseless civilians drew resources away from ongoing wars, contributing to major military defeats. During the civil war in Guatemala and the Soviet occupation of Afghanistan, mass killing was intended to destroy civilian support for insurgent movements. In Afghanistan, the violence simply drove millions to support the rebels and provoked increased international opposition to the Soviet occupation. In Guatemala, the tactic was more successful in the short run, but popular resentment of the military government remained high and the regime ultimately was forced to negotiate with the rebels and implement democratic reforms.

A Typology of Mass Killing

*   *   *

* * * I have identified six specific motives—corresponding to six "types" of mass killing—that, under certain specific conditions, appear to generate strong incentives for leaders to initiate mass killing.

These six motives can be grouped into two general categories. First, when leaders' plans result in the near-complete material disenfranchisement of large groups of people, leaders are likely to conclude that mass killing is necessary to overcome resistance by these groups or, more radically, that mass killing is the only practical way to physically remove these groups or their influence from society. I refer to this general class as "dispossessive" mass killings. Second, mass killing can become an attractive solution in military conflicts in which leaders perceive conventional military tactics to be hopeless or unacceptably costly. When leaders' efforts to defeat their enemies' military forces directly are frustrated, they face powerful incentives to target the civilian populations they suspect of supporting those forces. I refer to this class of mass killing as "coercive" mass killings.

The specific real-world scenarios in which each type of mass killing occurs, as well as several selected historical examples of each scenario, are presented in table 1. I will briefly describe each of the types of mass killing in this table in subsequent sections of this chapter.

Of the six types mass killing, three have accounted for the majority of episodes of mass killing as well as the greatest number of victims in the twentieth century: communist mass killings, ethnic mass killings, and counterguerrilla mass killings. * * *

*   *   *

Table 1. A Typology of Mass Killing

Motive/Type	Scenario	Examples*
DISPOSSESSIVE MASS KILLING		
Communist	Agricultural collectivization and political terror	Soviet Union (1917–53) China (1950–76) Cambodia (1975–79)
Ethnic	Ethnic cleansing	Turkish Armenia (1915–18) The Holocaust (1939–45) Rwanda (1994)
Territorial	Colonial enlargement	European colonies in North and South America Genocide of the Herero in German South-West Africa (1904–7)
	Expansionist wars	German annexation of western Poland (1939–45)
COERCIVE MASS KILLING		
Counterguerrilla	Guerrilla wars	Algerian war of independence from France (1954–62) Soviet invasion of Afghanistan (1979–88) Ethiopian civil war (1970s and 1980s) Guatemalan civil war (1980s)
Terrorist	Terror bombing	Allied bombings of Germany and Japan (1940–45)
	Starvation blockades/siege warfare	Allied naval blockade of Germany (1914–19) Nigerian land blockade of Biafra (1967–70)
	Sub-state/insurgent terrorism	FLN terrorism in Algerian war of independence against France (1954–62) Viet Cong terrorism in South Vietnam (1957–75) RENAMO terrorism in Mozambique (1976–92)
Imperialist	Imperial conquests and rebellions	German occupation of Western Europe (1940–45) Japan's empire in East Asia (1910–45)

Note: This typology does not exhaust the entire universe of motives for mass killing in the twentieth century, but it does appear to account for the great majority of these episodes. At least two notable cases—the mass killing of between 250,000 and 1,000,000 people in Indonesia in 1965 and the mass killing of between 100,000 and 500,000 people in Uganda under Idi Amin from 1971 to 1979—do not appear entirely consistent with any of the motives described in this book.

*Selected examples only, not a complete list of all instances of mass killings within each category. Some examples combine aspects of more than one motive.

Dispossessive Mass Killings

Dispossessive mass killings are the result of policies that, by design or by consequence, suddenly strip large groups of people of their possessions, their homes, or their way of life. These kinds of policies do not aim at mass killing as such, but in practice their implementation often leads to it.

*   *   *

Communist Mass Killing

The most deadly mass killings in history have resulted from the effort to transform society according to communist doctrine. Radical communist regimes have proven so exceptionally violent because the changes they have sought to bring about have resulted in the nearly complete material dispossession of vast numbers of people. Radical communist policies have extended well beyond the restriction of personal and political freedoms characteristic of authoritarian or dictatorial regimes. The most radical communist regimes have attempted to bring about the wholesale transformation of their societies, often including the abrupt destruction of traditional ways of life and means of production, and the subordination of personal choices and daily activities to the dictates of the state. Not surprisingly, many people have chosen to resist these drastic changes. Faced with the choice between moderating their revolutionary goals to allow for voluntary change and forcing change on society using whatever means necessary, communist leaders like Stalin, Mao, and Pol Pot opted for mass killing over compromise.

Mass killings associated with the collectivization of agriculture and other radical communist agricultural policies provide the most striking examples of this process. Communist agricultural policies like collectivization have tended to go hand in hand with mass killing because, more than any other communist program, these policies have stripped vast numbers of people of their most valued possessions—their homes and their way of life. The imposition of radical communist agricultural policies on the peasantry of the Soviet Union, China, and Cambodia resulted in millions of deaths. Many victims were executed outright in the effort to crush real or suspected resistance to the socialization of the countryside, but most died in the massive famines sparked by collectivization. Communist leaders did not deliberately engineer these famines, as some have suggested, but they did use hunger as a weapon by directing the worst effects of the famines against individuals and social groups perceived to oppose collectivization.

*   *   *

Ethnic Mass Killing

Ethnic, national, or religious groups may become preferential targets in any of the types of mass killing described in this book. In these pages, however, "ethnic mass killings" are distinguished from the other types of mass killing by the explicitly racist or nationalist motives of the perpetrators. Ethnic mass killing, I argue, is not simply the result of perpetrators' bitter hatred of other ethnic groups, or of a racist ideology that calls for the extermination of these groups as such. Ethnic mass killing has deeper roots in perpetrators' fears than in their hatreds. I find that mass killing is most likely to occur when perpetrators believe that their ethnic opponents pose a threat that can be countered only by physically removing them from society, in other words, by implementing a policy of ethnic cleansing. This perception may be shaped by perpetrators' ideological beliefs about other ethnic groups, as it was in Nazi Germany, but it may also be a reaction to real, if almost always misperceived or exaggerated, threatening actions of some victim group members, as it was in Rwanda in 1994. In many cases, a combination of ideological beliefs and real-world conflicts seem to shape perpetrators' perceptions of victim groups.

The decision to engage in ethnic cleansing, however, is not always a decision to perpetrate mass killing. Ethnic cleansing and mass killing

Table 2. Communist Mass Killings in the Twentieth Century

Location-Dates	Description	Additional Motives	Deaths
Soviet Union (1917–23)	Russian Civil War and Red Terror	Counterguerrilla	250,000–2,500,000
Soviet Union and Eastern Europe (1927–45)	Collectivization, Great Terror, occupation/communization of Baltic states and western Poland	Counterguerrilla	10,000,000–20,000,000
China (including Tibet) (1949–72)	Land reform, Great Leap Forward, Cultural Revolution, and other political purges	Counterguerrilla	10,000,000–46,000,000
Cambodia (1975–79)	Collectivization and political repression	Ethnic	1,000,000–2,000,000
		POSSIBLE CASES*	
Bulgaria (1944–?)	Agricultural collectivization and political repression		50,000–100,000
East Germany (1945–?)	Political repression by Soviet Union		80,000–100,000
Romania (1945–?)	Agricultural collectivization and political repression		60,000–300,000
North Korea (1945–?)	Agricultural collectivization and political repression	Counterguerrilla	400,000–1,500,000
North and South Vietnam (1953–?)	Agricultural collectivization and political repression		80,000–200,000

Note: All figures in this and subsequent tables are author's estimates based on numerous sources.

*Episodes are listed under the heading "possible cases" in this and subsequent tables when the available evidence suggests a mass killing *may* have occurred, but documentation is insufficient to make a definitive judgment regarding the number of people killed, the intentionality of the killing, or the motives of the perpetrators.

are often conflated in popular parlance, but they are not synonymous. Ethnic cleansing refers to the removal of certain groups from a given territory, a process that may or may not involve mass killing. Nevertheless, like communist policies such as collectivization, large-scale ethnic cleansing frequently has been associated with mass killing because it often results in the near-complete material dispossession of large groups of people. Violence is often required to force people to relinquish their homes and their possessions. Even after victims have been coerced into flight, the process and aftermath of large population movements itself can be deadly.

The bloodiest episodes of ethnic mass killing, however, occur when leaders conclude that they have no practical options for the physical relocation of victim groups. In such cases, perpetrators may see violent repression on a massive scale as the only way to meet the perceived threat posed by their victims. The killing may be designed to deprive the victim group of its ability to organize

Table 3. Ethnic Mass Killings in the Twentieth Century

Location-Dates	Description	Additional Motives	Deaths
Turkey (1915–18)	Genocide of Armenians	Counterguerrilla	500,000–1,500,000
Soviet Union (1941–53)	Deportation of nationalities	Counterguerrilla	300,000–600,000
Germany (1939–45)	Genocide of Jews and other Nazi race enemies		5,400,000–6,800,000
Yugoslavia (1941–45)	Ustasha violence against Serbs	Counterguerrilla	350,000–530,000
Eastern Europe (1945–47)	Post–WW II expulsion of ethnic Germans from Poland, Czechoslovakia, Yugoslavia, and elsewhere		2,000,000–2,300,000
India (1947–48)	Partition of India		500,000–1,000,000
Bangladesh (1971)	Partition of East Pakistan		500,000–3,000,000
Burundi (1972)	Genocide of Hutu	Counterguerrilla	100,000–200,000
Bosnia-Herzegovina (1990–95)	Ethnic cleansing of Muslims from Bosnia	Counterguerrilla	25,000–155,000
Rwanda (1994)	Genocide of Tutsi	Counterguerrilla	500,000–800,000

politically or militarily by eliminating its elites, intellectuals, or males of military age. At the most extreme, perpetrators may conclude that systematic extermination is the only available means to counter the threat. Ethnic mass killing, therefore, is best seen as an instrumental strategy that seeks the physical removal or permanent military or political subjugation of ethnic groups, not the annihilation of these groups as an end in itself.

*　　*　　*

Territorial Mass Killing

The third general motive for dispossessive mass killing arises when powerful groups attempt to resettle territories already inhabited by large, preexisting populations. Unlike the ethnic mass killings described above, perpetrators of territorial mass killing do not seek to cleanse a given territory of its inhabitants because they believe these people themselves pose a threat, but rather because perpetrators want to populate (and usually cultivate) the land with their own people. As with ethnic mass killings, however, territorial mass killing occurs because the process and aftermath of rapidly removing large numbers of people from their homes often involves considerable violence.

Territorial mass killings have emerged in two closely related scenarios. First, mass killing can result when settler colonies attempt to expand their territory into regions already populated by indigenous people.[14] This scenario has occurred primarily in colonial settings. * * *

*　　*　　*

Table 4. Territorial (Colonial and Expansionist) Mass Killings in the Twentieth Century

Location-Dates	Description	Additional Motives	Deaths
Namibia (1904–7)	Genocide of Herero and Nama	Counterguerrilla	60,000–65,000
Eastern Europe (1939–45)	Nazi territorial expansion	Counterguerrilla, imperialist	10,000,000– 15,000,000

Coercive Mass Killings

Sometimes mass killing is simply war by other means. Coercive mass killings occur in major armed conflicts when combatants lack the capabilities to defeat their opponents' military forces with conventional military techniques. When such conflicts threaten highly important goals, leaders must search for alternative means to defeat their adversaries. Under such circumstances, military and political leaders may conclude that the most effective way to achieve victory is to target the civilians that they suspect of providing material and political support to their adversaries' military forces. Perpetrators of this kind of mass killing usually do not seek to exterminate entire populations; rather, they use massive violence and the threat of even greater violence to coerce large numbers of civilians or their leaders into submission. When more "selective" mass killing fails to dissuade civilian supporters or induce surrender, however, coercive mass killing can escalate to the genocidal targeting of suspect ethnic groups or the enemy populations of entire geographical regions.[15]

I divide coercive mass killings into three major types: counterguerrilla, terrorist, and imperialist.

Counterguerrilla Warfare

Mass killing can become an attractive strategy for governments engaged in counterguerrilla warfare. Although many observers have characterized mass killing in counterguerrilla warfare as the result of the actions of undisciplined, frustrated, or racist troops, the strategic approach suggests that counterguerrilla mass killing is a calculated military response to the unique challenges posed by guerrilla warfare.

Unlike conventional armies, guerrilla forces often depend on the local civilian population for food, shelter, and supplies. Guerrillas also depend on the local population to reveal information about enemy outposts and troop movements and as a form of "human camouflage" into which guerrillas can blend to avoid detection. Thus, according to Mao Zedong's famous analogy, "the guerrillas are as the fish and the people the sea in which they swim."[16]

Civilian support can be a major source of strength for guerrilla armies, but it can also be a weakness. Regimes facing guerrilla opponents either at home or abroad have sometimes been able to turn the guerrillas' dependency on the local population to their own advantage. Unlike the guerrillas themselves, the civilian support network upon which guerrillas rely is virtually defenseless and impossible to conceal. Some regimes have found it easier, therefore, to wage war against a guerrilla army by depriving it of its base of support in the people than by attempting to target the guerrillas directly. In the terms of Mao's analogy, this strategy seeks to catch the fish by draining the sea. Not surprisingly, this strategy of counterinsurgency has frequently resulted in mass killing.

Theorists of counterguerrilla warfare have often advocated "selective" violence targeted only against those who provide active support for the guerrillas. In practice, however, such distinctions have been difficult to maintain. * * * Counterguerrilla warfare has often been characterized by

Table 5. Counterguerrilla Mass Killings in the Twentieth Century

Location-Dates	Description	Additional Motives	Deaths
Philippines (1899–1902)	U.S. occupation of the Philippines		100,000–200,000
China (1927–49)	Nationalist repression in Chinese civil war		6,000,000–10,000,000
Spain (1936–43?)	Nationalist violence in Spanish civil war	Terrorist	185,000–410,000
Algeria (1954–63)	Algerian war of independence from France		70,000–570,000
Sudan (1956–71)	Suppression of southern Sudanese	Ethnic	250,000–500,000
Tibet (1959–60)	Suppression of Tibetan rebellion	Communist	65,000–90,000
Iraq (1963–91)	Suppression of Kurdish rebellions		85,000–265,000
Guatemala (1966–85)	Guatemalan civil war		100,000–200,000
Ethiopia (1974–91)	Ethiopian civil war	Communist	500,000–1,000,000
Angola (1975–2002)	Angolan civil war		60,000–375,000
Indonesia (East Timor) (1975–99)	Suppression of East Timorese secession		100,000–200,000
Afghanistan (1978–89)	Soviet invasion and occupation	Communist	950,000–1,280,000
El Salvador (1979–92)	Salvadoran civil war		40,000–70,000
Sudan (1983–2002)	Suppression of southern Sudanese	Ethnic	1,000,000–1,500,000
Somalia (1988–91)	Suppression of Isaaq clan/SNM	Ethnic	50,000–60,000
Burundi (1993–98)	Suppression of Hutu	Ethnic	100,000–200,000
Russia (Chechnya) (1994–2000)	Suppression of Chechen secession movement		55,000–60,000
		POSSIBLE CASES	
Tanzania (German Southwest Africa) (1905–7)	Suppression of Maji-Maji uprising		200,000–300,000
Vietnam (1945–54)	French suppression of Vietminh guerrillas		60,000–250,000
Colombia (1948–58)	"Conservative" violence against "Liberals" in Colombian civil war	Terrorist	50,000–150,000
Vietnam (South) (1965–75)	U.S. and South Vietnamese suppression of NLF		110,000–310,000
Cambodia (1969–73)	U.S. invasion-bombardment of Cambodia	Terrorist	30,000–150,000
Uganda (1979–87)	Suppression of suspected NRA supporters		100,000–300,000

reliance on indiscriminate tactics such as "free-fire zones," the intentional destruction of crops, livestock and dwellings, massive programs of population resettlement, and the use of torture and large-scale massacres designed to intimidate guerrilla supporters.

Guerrilla warfare, of course, has been one of the most common forms of combat in the twentieth century. Although it has seldom spared civilian populations, in most cases it has not provoked mass killing by counterinsurgent forces. * * * When leaders believe that the guerrillas are not receiving significant support from the local population or do not pose a threat to the regime's critical goals or interests, they have little reason to order the killing of large numbers of civilians.

* * *

Mass Killing as Mass Terror

A second scenario of coercive mass killing occurs when combatants engaged in protracted wars of attrition search for means to swiftly end the war. As in counterguerrilla killings, leaders may choose to target enemy civilians in the hopes of coercing surrender without having to defeat the enemy's military forces directly. * * *

* * *

The advent of strategic air and missile power in the second half of this century has rendered the strategy of terror during war an especially attractive and extremely destructive weapon. During the Second World War, Britain and the United States intentionally bombed German cities in an effort to weaken German public support for the war and force an early surrender. In the early stages of the war, British civilian and military leaders considered the possibility of using air power to attack Germany's military forces and industrial assets without targeting civilians, but they soon discovered that these techniques were not technically practical.[17] British strategic bombing planners ultimately decided that in or-

der to crush the German will to fight, the Allies "must achieve two things: first, we must make [German towns] physically uninhabitable and, secondly, we must make the people conscious of constant personal danger. The immediate aim is therefore two-fold, namely to produce: (i) destruction; and (ii) the fear of death."[18] By 1942 the British government had directed the Royal Air Force to abandon its efforts to conduct precision bombing of military and industrial targets and stated that "a primary object" of RAF bombing raids should be "the morale of the enemy civil population."[19]

In public, of course, the allies were careful to justify their attacks by claiming that the raids were intended to destroy German war industries or military targets. The high proportion of incendiary bombs used by the allies, however, casts doubt on whether military targets were the first priority of these operations.[20] As for industrial targets, while the destruction of German industry was undoubtedly the primary objective of some attacks, many cities without significant industrial resources were also destroyed.[21] Arthur Harris, the head of the RAF Bomber Command, admitted in his memoirs that the destruction of several factories in the devastating 1943 raid on Hamburg—an attack that killed more than forty thousand people—had been "a bonus."[22] By the end of the war, British and American bombing probably killed between 300,000 and 600,000 civilians in Europe.[23]

Long-range bombers and missiles may have perfected the instruments of terror warfare, but the strategy of targeting enemy civilians in the effort to force a military surrender is probably as old as war itself. Military forces throughout history have relied on the practice of siege warfare and the use of starvation blockades to achieve the same effect. Famine is often an unintended consequence of war, but it too can be used as a military tool, like the bombing of cities, to induce capitulation without a conventional military victory.[24] During the First World War, for example, more than 250,000 people died of starvation and malnutrition when the British blockaded Germany and Austria-Hungary in an effort to starve them into surrender.[25] More recently, at least half a million people died in the late 1960s when Nigeria blockaded food supplies to the eastern part of the country, which was attempting to secede.[26]

In addition to strategic bombing and siege warfare, powerful sub-state insurgent groups have sometimes used coercive mass killing to terrorize their enemies, typically colonial governments and their loyalists among the native population. By killing large numbers of civilians from specifically targeted groups, these insurgents hope to achieve their political goals without directly engaging the superior military forces of their enemies. Algerian resistance groups relied heavily on this strategy during their war for independence from France, killing almost seventy thousand people—nearly all of them native Algerians.[27] Communist guerrillas in Vietnam also utilized mass terror in their fight for liberation against France and the United States.[28]

The incentives to resort to mass terror probably exist in most major conflicts, particularly for the weaker side. Yet terrorist mass killing has remained relatively rare compared to the number of conflicts waged in the last century. Three main factors seem to account for this pattern. First, many groups simply lack the physical capabilities needed to implement a military strategy of mass terror. While I have argued that mass killing does not require large or highly capable forces in the absence of organized resistance, terrorist mass killings take place during war and are often directed against civilian groups protected by substantial military organizations of their own. Large, expensive, and technologically sophisticated forces are often required to overcome or bypass enemy military defenses and kill civilians in large numbers. Few states throughout history, for example, have possessed the military forces necessary to carry out large-scale strategic bombing campaigns or to implement effective starvation blockades even if they wished to do so.

Sub-state groups, in particular, have seldom been able to muster the capabilities and organization necessary to carry out violence on the pace and scale of mass killing as defined in this book. Sub-state terrorism may be a "weapon of the weak," but mass killing through terrorism has eluded even the most determined international terrorist organizations. The increasing ease with which weapons of mass destruction, especially biological weapons, can be produced and delivered to their targets, however, seems likely to increase the capabilities of sub-state groups to carry out mass killing in the future.

Second, because mass killing can be a risky and costly strategy, even groups that possess the means to carry out mass terror have employed it only rarely. Mass killing can be counterproductive if it draws in concerned third parties. * * *

*   *   *

Imperialist Mass Killing

The third scenario of coercive mass killing is closely linked to empire. Imperial powers have garnered a well-deserved reputation for the brutal treatment of civilian populations. The Roman empire, the Aztec empire in Central America, Nazi Germany's empire in Europe, and Japan's empire in China and Korea each perpetrated mass killing against at least some of their conquests. Like territorial mass killing, however, imperialist mass killing has declined in frequency in the twentieth century as the great European empires have steadily dissolved.

Much of the violence associated with imperialism seems to be motivated by the effort to diminish the costs of building and administering large empires.[29] The purpose of an empire is to extract wealth from conquests, but empires would be prohibitively expensive to maintain if each subject city, state, or province had to be defeated by force and then policed to a man. Imperial leaders, therefore, have strong incentives to adopt a strategy of mass killing as a means of deterring rebellions and resistance within their empire and as a method of intimidating future conquests into submission. The large-scale killing of rebellious subjects is intended to demonstrate

Table 6. Terrorist Mass Killings in the Twentieth Century

Location-Dates	Description	Additional Motives	Deaths
Germany (1914–18)	Allied blockade of Germany in WWI		250,000–425,000
China (1927–49)	Communist terror in Chinese civil war	Communist	1,800,000–3,500,000
Spain (1936–39)	Republican terrorism in Spanish civil war	Communist	20,000–55,000
United Kingdom (1940–45)	German bombardment of UK in WW II		60,000–62,000
Germany (1940–45)	Allied bombardment of Germany in WW II		300,000–600,000
Japan (1942–45)	American bombardment of Japan in WWII		268,000–900,000
Algeria (1954–63)	FLN terrorism		70,000–235,000
Vietnam (1954–75)	NLF (Viet-Cong) terrorism in Vietnam war	Communist	45,000–80,000
Nigeria (1967–70)	Suppression of secession of Biafra	Counterguerrilla?	450,000–2,000,000
Angola (1975–2002)	UNITA terrorism		125,000–560,000
Mozambique (1975–1992)	RENAMO terrorism in Mozambican civil war		100,000–700,000
Algeria (1992–2002)	Civil war/antigovernment terrorism		75,000–150,000
POSSIBLE CASES			
North Korea (1950–54)	U.S./R.O.K. bombing and other killing in Korean War	Counterguerrilla	500,000–1,500,000
Colombia (1948–58)	Liberal violence against conservatives in Colombian civil war		50,000–150,000
Iraq (1990–97)	Economic embargo of Iraq by UN/U.S. (prior to "oil for food" program)		80,000–170,000

to all others considering resistance the terrible fate awaiting those who refuse to accept imperial rule.

The Mongol empire ruled by Genghis Khan and his progeny was one of the earliest and most efficient practitioners of this strategy of mass killing. According to Paul Ratchnevsky, "Genghis Khan used terror as a strategic weapon in his military plans. . . . Terrible destruction was threatened in the event of resistance; bloody examples were designed to spread fear and reduce the populace's will to resist."[30] Because imperial powers intend mass killing to deter future resistance throughout the empire, they frequently employ it even after rebellious states or regions have capitulated. To ensure the greatest effect, the violence often is carried out in an exceptionally grisly and highly public manner. One of the bloodiest examples of this strategy in recent history occurred during the Japanese campaign to expand its empire into the Chinese mainland. In December 1937, Japanese troops descended on the city of Nanking in an orgy of rape, murder, and mutilation that ultimately left between 200,000 and 350,000 people dead.[31] Many explanations of the brutality of the Japanese empire in China have emphasized the racism, indiscipline, and vengefulness of Japanese troops.[32] However, the violence also represented a calculated strategy designed to terrify China's vast population into submission without a fight.[33] Indeed, it is likely that Nanking was singled out for especially harsh treatment because of the fierce resistance Japanese forces had encountered as they advanced on the city, and because of Nanking's symbolic value as the capital city of Nationalist China.

Of course, not all empires engage in mass killing, and even empires that have perfected this brutal strategy seldom unleash it against all of their conquests. The incentives for imperialist mass killing seem to be greatest when empires are relatively weak or overstretched, or when they make extreme demands on their subjects. Under these conditions, resistance to imperial rule is likely to be especially determined, and the empire's ability to police far-flung territories with conventional means will be heavily strained.

*   *   *

*   *   *

Conclusion: Anticipating and Preventing Mass Killing

The evidence presented in this book points to three central conclusions about the causes of mass killing. First, small groups often play an important role in instigating and carrying out this kind of violence. Mass killing is usually conceived of and organized by a relatively small number of powerful political or military leaders acting in the service of their own interests, ideas, hatreds, fears, and misperceptions—not reacting to the attitudes or desires of the societies over which they preside. Indeed, in the Soviet Union, Nazi Germany, China, and Cambodia—the four bloodiest mass killings I investigated—there are strong reasons to believe that, but for the influence of a single dictatorial leader, the violence might have been averted or at least substantially diminished. Perpetrators do not need widespread social support to carry out mass killing. Compliance with authority or simply passivity and indifference to the suffering of victims, what I have called negative support, is more important than active support or participation in the killing itself. In each of the eight cases I examined, relatively small military or paramilitary groups, acting under direct orders from political and military authorities, carried out the majority of the

Table 7. Imperialist Mass Killings in the Twentieth Century

Location-Dates	Description	Additional Motives	Deaths
East Asia 1937–45	Japanese occupation of East Asia (especially China)	Counterguerrilla	3,000,000– 10,600,000
Western Europe 1940–45	German occupation of Western Europe	Counterguerrilla	425,000– 625,000

actual killing. Civilians did play a significant role in the violence in Rwanda and the Chinese Cultural Revolution, but even in these cases the killers represented only a small fraction of society, and military or paramilitary forces killed many or most of the victims.

Second, because small groups can play such a central role in causing mass killing, I find that characteristics of society at large, such as preexisting cleavages, hatred and discrimination between groups, and nondemocratic forms of government, are of limited utility in distinguishing societies at high risk for mass killing. There is substantial evidence of preexisting hatreds or discrimination directed against at least some victim groups in each of the cases examined in this book—especially the genocides in Turkey, Nazi Germany, and Rwanda. There is little indication, however, that these attitudes were more severe than they were in many other countries that never experienced mass killing. In Guatemala and Afghanistan, perpetrators made efforts, albeit halfhearted ones, to minimize the extent of social differences and ameliorate discrimination against victims in an effort to draw support away from insurgent movements. In the Soviet Union, Nazi Germany, China, Cambodia, and Rwanda, on the other hand, leaders deliberately promoted hatred and discrimination through propaganda and indoctrination in the effort to increase public support for attacks on victim groups. Preexisting animosity between groups is a particularly weak explanation for the communist mass killings * * * since many victims of these regimes were never objects of intense hatred by society at large. In fact, in all three countries, the perpetrators directed much of the killing against the communist party itself.

Third, mass killing usually is driven by instrumental, strategic calculations. Perpetrators see mass killing as a means to an end, not an end in itself. None of the cases of mass killing considered here can be accurately described as killing for killing's sake. Indeed, mass killing was never the only strategy that leaders considered to achieve their ends. Mass killing has not always been a policy of last resort, but rarely has it been a policy of first resort either. With the possible exception of Cambodia, leaders in all eight cases examined in this book appear to have seriously considered or actively experimented with options short of mass killing to achieve their ends. Leaders adopted mass killing in frustration, only after they came to believe, although often mistakenly, that other strategies for achieving their goals were impossible or impractical.

The history of all eight cases suggests that leaders conceived of mass killing as a instrumental strategy designed to achieve their most important political or ideological goals, counter their most dangerous threats, or solve their most difficult military problems. Leaders saw mass killing as a bloody but effective solution to such problems. I have also tried to demonstrate, however, that leaders are likely to perceive mass killing as an attractive strategy only in a few, relatively uncommon situations. Three specific historical scenarios—the implementation of radical communist policies, large-scale ethnic cleansing, and counterguerrilla wars—have generated the incentives for the majority of episodes of mass killings in this century. Even in these situations, however, mass killing is not inevitable. A variety of factors and conditions, including the size of the targeted civilian population, the pace with which dispossessive changes are implemented, and the ability of victim groups to flee to safer areas can impact the incentives and ability of perpetrators to carry out mass killing.

*   *   *

NOTES

1. Shepard Krech, "Genocide in Tribal Society," *Nature*, September 1994, pp. 14–15.
2. Estimate based on numerous sources. See tables 2–7 in chapter 3. The term "mass killing" is defined below. Using a more expansive definition, Rudolph Rummel estimates that between 76 million and 360 million people

were killed in "democides" from 1900 to 1987—with a "prudent or conservative midrange estimate" of 169,198,000 deaths. Rummel's estimates tend to be considerably higher than those of most other scholars. See Rudolph Rummel, *Statistics of Democide: Genocide and Mass Murder Since 1900* (Charlottesville, Va.: Center for National Security Law, 1997), p. 355; and Rudolph Rummel, *Death by Government* (New Brunswick, N.J.: Transaction, 1994), pp. xviii–xx. Zbigniew Brzezinski estimates more than 80 million politically motivated deaths from 1900 to 1993, not including civilian or military deaths during war. See Zbigniew Brzezinski, *Out of Control: Global Turmoil on the Eve of the Twenty-First Century* (New York: Charles Scribner's Sons, 1993), p. 17. Matthew White estimates 83 million deaths from "genocide and tyranny" and an additional 44 million in "man-made famines" during the twentieth century. See Matthew White, "Historical Atlas of the Twentieth Century" http://users.erols.com/mwhite28/warstat8.htm [June 2003]. Using a more restricted definition, Barbara Harff estimates that between 8.9 and 19.8 million people were killed in forty-eight episodes of genocide and "politicide" between 1945 and 1994. See Barbara Harff and Ted Robert Gurr, "Victims of the State: Genocides, Politicides and Group Repression from 1945 to 1995," in Albert Jongman, ed., *Contemporary Genocide: Causes, Cases, Consequences* (Leiden: Den Haag, 1996), pp. 49–51.

3. Rummel, *Death by Government*, p. 15. Rummel's estimate is for the period between 1900 and 1987. William Eckhardt estimates 85,527,000 war-related deaths between 1900 and 1988, of which approximately 50 percent were civilians. Estimates of civilian war-related deaths by Eckhardt appear to include many episodes of intentional killing and therefore overlap considerably with genocide and mass killing. See William Eckhardt, "Civilian Deaths in Wartime," *Bulletin of Peace Proposals* 20, no. 1 (1989): 90.

4. Raphael Lemkin, *Axis Rule in Occupied Europe: Laws of Occupation, Analysis of Government, Proposals for Redress* (Washington, D.C.: Carnegie Endowment for International Peace, 1944), p. 79.

5. For the complete text of the genocide convention, see Lawrence J. LeBlanc, *The United States and the Genocide Convention* (Durham, N.C.: Duke University Press, 1991), pp. 245–249. For a description of Lemkin's efforts to draft and ratify the convention, see Samantha Power, *"A Problem from Hell": America and the Age of Genocide* (New York: Basic Books, 2002), pp. 17–85.

6. *Oxford English Dictionary*, 2d ed., 6:445.

7. For one example, see Robert Johnson and Paul S. Leighton, "American Genocide: The Destruction of the Black Underclass," in Craig Summers and Eric Markusen, eds., *Collective Violence: Harmful Behavior in Groups and Governments* (Lanham, Md.: Rowman and Littlefield, 1999), pp. 95–140. The use of the term "holocaust" has generated a similar political debate. See Samuel G. Freedman, "Laying Claim to Sorrow beyond Words," *New York Times*, December 13, 1997, p. A19.

8. For reviews of the debate on the definition of genocide, see Scott Straus, "Contested Meanings and Conflicting Imperatives: A Conceptual Analysis of Genocide," *Journal of Genocide Research* 3, no. 3 (November 2001): 349–375; Helen Fein, *Genocide: A Sociological Perspective* (London: Sage, 1993), pp. xi–xix, 1–31; Eric Markusen and David Kopf, *The Holocaust and Strategic Bombing: Genocide and Total War in the Twentieth Century* (Boulder: Westview, 1995), pp. 39–64; and Frank Chalk and Kurt Jonassohn, *The History and Sociology of Genocide* (New Haven: Yale University Press, 1990), pp. 12–23.

9. This definition is similar in some respects to Rummel's concept of "democide." Rummel's definition, however, includes the killing of any number of civilians, no matter how small. In addition, Rummel specifies that democide must be carried out by government

groups, while the perpetrators of mass killing can belong to any kind of group. See Rudolph Rummel, *Death by Government* (New Brunswick, N.J.: Transaction, 1994), pp. 31–43.

10. Disease can also be spread intentionally as part of an effort to exterminate large numbers of people. European colonists, for example, appear to have made deliberate efforts to spread fatal diseases among native American populations, although it remains unclear whether these early experiments with biological warfare proved "successful." See William H. McNeill, *Plagues and Peoples* (Garden City: Doubleday, 1976), p. 222; and Russell Thornton, *American Indian Holocaust and Survival: A Population History since 1492* (Norman: University of Oklahoma Press, 1987), pp. 78–79.

11. Steven Katz, for example, argues that "the concept of genocide applies *only* when there is an actualized intent, however successfully carried out, to physically destroy an *entire* group." Steven Katz, *The Holocaust in Historical Context: The Holocaust and Mass Death before the Modern Age* (New York: Oxford University Press, 1994), p. 128; italics in original.

12. If an episode of mass killing continues for more than five years, all deaths resulting from it are included as long as at least 50,000 civilians were killed in any five-year period during the episode. For example, approximately 80,000 civilians were intentionally killed during the civil war in El Salvador from 1979 to 1992. Although this figure represents an average of less than 50,000 deaths every five years, more than 50,000 of these occurred in the five-year period from 1980 to 1985. All intentional civilian deaths resulting from the civil war are therefore included as mass killing.

13. This definition is generally consistent with the definition of "civilian" adopted by the two 1977 additional protocols of the Geneva Convention. See Michael Bothe, Karl Josef Partsch, and Waldemar A. Solf, *New Rules for Victims of Armed Conflicts: Commentary on the Two 1977 Protocols Additional to the Geneva Conventions of 1949* (The Hague: Martinus Nijhoff Publishers, 1982), pp. 274–318. For more on the history and evolution of the international legal protection of civilian populations during war, see Yvonne van Dongen, *The Protection of Civilian Populations in Time of Armed Conflict* (Amsterdam: Thesis Publishers, 1991).

14. Settler colonies should be distinguished from imperial possessions. Settler colonies are territories intended to be permanently inhabited by large numbers of people from the colonizing state. Imperial possessions are not densely settled. Rather, subjects of empire are required to provide goods and services for the empire. Empires have also been frequent perpetrators of mass killing, although for very different reasons that will be described below.

15. On the distinction between coercion and the "brute force" use of violence, see Thomas Schelling, *Arms and Influence* (New Haven: Yale University Press, 1966), pp. 2–18.

16. Mao Tse-Tung, *On Guerrilla Warfare*, trans. Samuel B. Griffith (New York: Praeger, 1961), pp. 44, 92–93.

17. See Robert A. Pape, *Bombing to Win: Air Power and Coercion in War* (Ithaca, N.Y.: Cornell University Press, 1996), p. 269.

18. Quoted in ibid., p. 261.

19. Quoted in Ronald Schaffer, *Wings of Judgment: American Bombing in World War II* (Oxford: Oxford University Press, 1985), p. 36.

20. Ibid., p. 270.

21. See David Irving, *The Destruction of Dresden* (New York: Ballantine, 1965), p. 76, Anthony Verrier, *The Bomber Offensive* (London: B. T. Batsford, 1968), p. 301; and Michael Sherry, *The Rise of American Air Power* (New Haven: Yale University Press, 1987), p. 154.

22. Quoted in Sherry, *Rise of American Air Power*, p. 154.

23. Ibid., p. 260.

24. For more on the political and military use of famine, see Kurt Jonassohn, "Famine, Genocide and Refugees," *Society* 30, no. 6 (September/October 1993) pp. 73–74; John Mueller and Karl Mueller, "The Methodology of Mass Destruction: Assessing Threats in the New World Order," *Journal of Strategic Studies* 23, no. 1 (March 2000): 163–187; David Keen, *The Benefits of Famine: A Political Economy of Famine and Relief in Southwestern Sudan, 1983–1989* (Princeton: Princeton University Press, 1994); Jean Mayer, "Time to Ban the Use of Starvation as a Weapon of War," *Christian Science Monitor*, December 24, 1984, p. 12; and Karl Zinsmeister, "All the Hungry People," *Reason* 20, no. 2 (June 1988): 22–30.

25. Martin Gilbert, *The First World War* (New York: Henry Holt, 1994), p. 391. William Eckhardt estimates that eight hundred thousand civilians died as a result of blockade from 1914 to 1918. See "Civilian Deaths in Wartime," *Bulletin of Peace Proposals* 20 no. 1 (1989): 95.

26. John de St. Jorre, *The Brothers' War: Biafra and Nigeria* (Boston: Houghton Mifflin, 1972), p. 412; and Dan Jacobs, The Brutality of Nations (New York: Paragon House, 1988).

27. Alistair Horne, *A Savage War of Peace: Algeria 1954–1962* (New York: Viking, 1977), p. 538. On the strategic use of terror by Islamist guerrillas in Algeria in the 1990s, see Stathis N. Kalyvas, "Wanton and Senseless? The Logic of Massacres in Algeria," *Rationality and Society* II, no. 3 (1999): 243–285.

28. See Guenter Lewy, *America in Vietnam* (New York: Oxford University Press, 1978), pp. 272–279; and Douglas Pike, *The Viet-Cong Strategy of Terror* (Saigon: United States Mission to Viet-Nam, 1970).

29. For a similar argument, see Kurt Jonassohn and Frank Chalk, "A Typology of Genocide and Some Implications for the Human Rights Agenda," in Isidor Wallimann and Michael Dobkowski, eds., *Genocide and the Modern Age* (New York: Greenwood, 1987), pp. 13–14.

30. Paul Ratchnevsky, *Genghis Khan: His Life and Legacy* (Oxford: Basil Blackwell, 1991), pp. 160, 173.

31. Iris Chang, *The Rape of Nanking: The Forgotten Holocaust of World War II* (New York: Basic Books, 1997).

32. John Dower, *War without Mercy: Race and Power in the Pacific War* (New York: Pantheon Books, 1986).

33. Callum MacDonald, "'Kill All, Burn All, Loot All': The Nanking Massacres of December 1937 and Japanese Policy in China," in Mark Levene and Penny Roberts eds., *The Massacre in History* (New York: Berghahn Books, 1999), pp. 223–245.

BARRY R. POSEN

THE SECURITY DILEMMA AND ETHNIC CONFLICT

The end of the Cold War has been accompanied by the emergence of nationalist, ethnic and religious conflict in Eurasia. However,

From *Survival* 35, no. 1 (spring 1993): 27–47. Some of the author's notes have been omitted.

the risks and intensity of these conflicts have varied from region to region: Ukrainians and Russians are still getting along relatively well; Serbs and Slovenians had a short, sharp clash; Serbs, Croats and Bosnian Muslims have waged open warfare; and Armenians and Azeris seem destined to fight a slow-motion attrition war. The claim that newly released, age-old antipathies account for this violence fails to explain the considerable variance in observable intergroup relations.

The purpose of this article is to apply a basic concept from the realist tradition of international relations theory, "the security dilemma," to the special conditions that arise when proximate groups of people suddenly find themselves newly responsible for their own security. A group suddenly compelled to provide its own protection must ask the following questions about any neighbouring group: is it a threat? How much of a threat? Will the threat grow or diminish over time? Is there anything that must be done immediately? The answers to these questions strongly influence the chances for war.

This article assesses the factors that could produce an intense security dilemma when imperial order breaks down, thus producing an early resort to violence. The security dilemma is then employed to analyse * * * the break-up of Yugoslavia * * * to illustrate its utility. Finally, some actions are suggested to ameliorate the tendency towards violence.

The Security Dilemma

The collapse of imperial regimes can be profitably viewed as a problem of "emerging anarchy." The longest standing and most useful school of international relations theory—realism—explicitly addresses the consequences of anarchy—the absence of a sovereign—for political relations among states.[1] In areas such as the former Soviet Union and Yugoslavia, "sovereigns" have disappeared. They leave in their wake a host of groups—ethnic, religious, cultural—of greater or lesser cohesion. These groups must pay attention to the first thing that states have historically addressed—the problem of security—even though many of these groups still lack many of the attributes of statehood.

Realist theory contends that the condition of anarchy makes security the first concern of states. It can be otherwise only if these political organizations do not care about their survival as independent entities. As long as some do care, there will be competition for the key to security—power. The competition will often continue to a point at which the competing entities have amassed more power than needed for security and, thus, consequently begin to threaten others. Those threatened will respond in turn.

Relative power is difficult to measure and is often subjectively appraised; what seems sufficient to one state's defence will seem, and will often be, offensive to its neighbours. Because neighbours wish to remain autonomous and secure, they will react by trying to strengthen their own positions. States can trigger these reactions even if they have no expansionist inclinations. This is the security dilemma: what one does to enhance one's own security causes reactions that, in the end, can make one less secure. Cooperation among states to mute these competitions can be difficult because someone else's "cheating" may leave one in a militarily weakened position. All fear betrayal.

Often statesmen do not recognize that this problem exists: they do not empathize with their neighbours; they are unaware that their own actions can seem threatening. Often it does not matter if they know of this problem. The nature of their situation compels them to take the steps they do.

The security dilemma is particularly intense when two conditions hold. First, when offensive and defensive military forces are more or less identical, states cannot signal their defensive intent—that is, their limited objectives—by the kinds of military forces they choose to deploy. Any forces on hand are suitable for offensive campaigns. For example, many believe that armoured forces are the best means of defence against an attack by armoured forces. However, because armour has a great deal of offensive potential, states so outfitted cannot distinguish one another's intentions. They must assume the worst because the worst is possible.

A second condition arises from the effectiveness of the offence versus the defence. If offensive operations are more effective than defensive operations, states will choose the offensive if they wish to survive. This may encourage pre-emptive war in the event of a political crisis because the perceived superiority of the offensive creates incentives to strike first whenever war appears likely. In addition, in the situation in which offensive capability is strong, a modest superiority in numbers will appear to provide greatly increased prospects for military success. Thus, the offensive advantage can cause preventive war if a state achieves a military advantage, however fleeting.

The barriers to cooperation inherent in international politics provide clues to the problems that arise as central authority collapses in multi-ethnic empires. The security dilemma affects relations among these groups, just as it affects relations among states. Indeed, because these groups have the added problem of building new state structures from the wreckage of old empires, they are doubly vulnerable.

Here it is argued that the process of imperial collapse produces conditions that make offensive and defensive capabilities indistinguishable and make the offence superior to the defence. In addition, uneven progress in the formation of state structures will create windows of opportunity and vulnerability. These factors have a powerful influence on the prospects for conflict, regardless of the internal politics of the groups emerging from old empires. Analysts inclined to the view that most of the trouble lies elsewhere, either in the specific nature of group identities or in the short-term incentives for new leaders to "play the nationalist card" to secure their power, need to understand the security dilemma and its consequences. Across the board, these strategic problems show that very little nationalist rabble-rousing or nationalistic combativeness is required to generate very dangerous situations.

The Indistinguishability of Offence and Defence

Newly independent groups must first determine whether neighbouring groups are a threat. They will examine one another's military capabilities to do so. Because the weaponry available to these groups will often be quite rudimentary, their offensive military capabilities will be as much a function of the quantity and commitment of the soldiers they can mobilize as the particular characteristics of the weapons they control. Thus, each group will have to assess the other's offensive military potential in terms of its cohesion and its past military record.

The nature of military technology and organization is usually taken to be the main factor affecting the distinguishability of offence and defence. Yet, clear distinctions between offensive and defensive capabilities are historically rare, and they are particularly difficult to make in the realm of land warfare. For example, the force structures of armed neutrals such as Finland, Sweden and Switzerland are often categorized as defensive. These countries rely more heavily on infantry, which is thought to have weak offensive potential, than on tanks and other mechanized weaponry, which are thought to have strong offensive potential. However, their weak offensive capabilities have also been a function of the massive military power of what used to be their most plausible adversary, the former Soviet Union. Against states of similar size, similarly armed, all three countries would have considerable offensive capabilities—particularly if their infantries were extraordinarily motivated—as German and French infantry were at the outset of World War I, as Chinese and North Vietnamese infantry were against the Americans and as Iran's infantry was against the Iraqis.

Ever since the French Revolution put the first politically motivated mass armies into the field, strong national identity has been understood by both scholars and practitioners to be a key ingredient of the combat power of armies.[2] A group identity helps the individual members cooperate to achieve their purposes. When humans can readily cooperate, the whole exceeds the sum of the parts, creating a unit stronger relative to those groups with a weaker identity. Thus, the "groupness" of the ethnic, religious, cultural and linguistic collectivities that emerge from collapsed empires gives each of them an inherent offensive military power.

The military capabilities available to newly independent groups will often be less sophisticated; infantry-based armies will be easy to organize, augmented by whatever heavier equipment is inherited or seized from the old regime. Their offensive potential will be stronger the more cohesive their sponsoring group appears to be. Particularly in the close quarters in which these groups often find themselves, the combination of infantry-based, or quasi-mechanized, ground forces with strong group solidarity is likely to encourage groups to fear each other. Their capabilities will appear offensive.

The solidarity of the opposing group will strongly influence how each group assesses the magnitude of the military threat of the others. In general, however, it is quite difficult to perform such assessments. One expects these groups to be "exclusive" and, hence, defensive. Frenchmen generally do not want to turn Germans into Frenchmen, or the reverse. Nevertheless, the drive for security in one group can be so great that it produces near-genocidal behaviour towards neighbouring groups. Because so much conflict has been identified with "group" identity throughout history, those who emerge as the leaders of any group and who confront the task of self-defence for the first time will be sceptical that the strong group identity of others is benign.

What methods are available to a newly independent group to assess the offensive implications of another's sense of identity?[3] The main mechanism that they will use is history: how did other groups behave the last time they were unconstrained? Is there a record of offensive military activity by the other? Unfortunately, the conditions under which this assessment occurs suggest that these groups are more likely to assume that their neighbours are dangerous than not.

The reason is that the historical reviews that new groups undertake rarely meet the scholarly standards that modern history and social science hold as norms (or at least as ideals) in the West.

First, the recently departed multi-ethnic empires probably suppressed or manipulated the facts of previous rivalries to reinforce their own rule; the previous regimes in the Soviet Union and Yugoslavia lacked any systemic commitment to truth in historical scholarship. Second, the members of these various groups no doubt did not forget the record of their old rivalries; it was preserved in oral history. This history was undoubtedly magnified in the telling and was seldom subjected to critical appraisal. Third, because their history is mostly oral, each group has a difficult time divining another's view of the past. Fourth, as central authority begins to collapse and local politicians begin to struggle for power, they will begin to write down their versions of history in political speeches. Yet, because the purpose of speeches is domestic political mobilization, these stories are likely to be emotionally charged.

The result is a worst-case analysis. Unless proven otherwise, one group is likely to assume that another group's sense of identity, and the cohesion that it produces, is a danger. Proving it to be otherwise is likely to be very difficult. Because the cohesion of one's own group is an essential means of defence against the possible depredations of neighbours, efforts to reinforce cohesion are likely to be undertaken. Propagandists are put to work writing a politicized history of the group, and the mass media are directed to disseminate that history. The media may either willingly, or under compulsion, report unfolding events in terms that magnify the threat to the group. As neighbouring groups observe this, they do the same.

In sum, the military capability of groups will often be dependent on their cohesion, rather than their meagre military assets. This cohesion is a threat in its own right because it can provide the emotional power for infantry armies to take the offensive. An historical record of large-scale armed clashes, much less wholesale mistreatment of unarmed civilians, however subjective, will further the tendency for groups to see other groups as threats. They will all simultaneously "arm"—militarily and ideologically—against each other.

The Superiority of Offensive over Defensive Action

Two factors have generally been seen as affecting the superiority of offensive over defensive action—technology and geography. Technology is usually treated as a universal variable, which affects the military capabilities of all the states in a given competition. Geography is a situational variable, which makes offence particularly appealing to specific states for specific reasons. This is what matters most when empires collapse.

In the rare historical cases in which technology has clearly determined the offence-defence balance, such as World War I, soldiers and statesmen have often failed to appreciate its impact. Thus, technology need not be examined further, with one exception: nuclear weapons. If a group inherits a nuclear deterrent, and its neighbours do as well, "groupness" is not likely to affect the security dilemma with as much intensity as would be the case in non-nuclear cases. Because group solidarity would not contribute to the ability of either side to mount a counterforce nuclear attack, nationalism is less important from a military standpoint in a nuclear relationship.

Political geography will frequently create an "offence-dominant world" when empires collapse. Some groups will have greater offensive capabilities because they will effectively surround some or all of the other groups. These other groups may be forced to adopt offensive strategies to break the ring of encirclement. Islands of one group's population are often stranded in a sea of another. Where one territorially concentrated group has "islands" of settlement of its members distributed across the nominal territory of another group (irredenta), the protection of these islands in the event of hostile action can seem extremely difficult. These islands may not be able to help one another; they may be subject to blockade and siege, and by virtue of their numbers relative to the surrounding population and because of topography, they may be militarily indefensible. Thus, the brethren of the stranded group may come to believe that only rapid offensive military action can save their irredenta from a horrible fate.[4]

The geographic factor is a variable, not a constant. Islands of population can be quite large, economically autonomous and militarily defensible. Alternatively, they can have large numbers of nearby brethren who form a powerful state, which could rescue them in the event of trouble. Potentially, hostile groups could have islands of another group's people within their states; these islands could serve as hostages. Alternatively, the brethren of the "island" group could deploy nuclear weapons and thus punish the surrounding group if they misbehave. In short, it might be possible to defend irredenta without attacking or to deter would-be aggressors by threatening to retaliate in one way or another.

Isolated ethnic groups—ethnic islands—can produce incentives for preventive war. Theorists argue that perceived offensive advantages make preventive war more attractive: if one side has an advantage that will not be present later and if security can best be achieved by offensive military action in any case, then leaders will be inclined to attack during this "window of opportunity."[5] For example, if a surrounding population will ultimately be able to fend off relief attacks from the home territory of an island group's brethren, but is currently weak, then the brethren will be inclined to attack sooner rather than later.

In disputes among groups interspersed in the same territory, another kind of offensive advantage exists—a tactical offensive advantage. Often the goal of the disputants is to create ever-growing areas of homogeneous population for their brethren. Therefore, the other group's population must be induced to leave. The Serbs have introduced the term "ethnic cleansing" to describe this objective, a term redolent with the horrors of 50 years earlier. The offence has tremendous tactical military advantages in operations such as these. Small military forces directed against unarmed or poorly armed civilians can generate tremendous terror. This has always been true, of course, but even simple modern weapons, such as machine guns and mortars, increase the havoc that small bands of fanatics can wreak against the defenceless: Consequently, small bands of each group have an incentive to attack the towns of the other in the hopes of driving the people away.[6] This is often quite successful, as the vast populations of war refugees in the world today attest.

The vulnerability of civilians makes it possible for small bands of fanatics to initiate conflict. Because they are small and fanatical, these bands are hard to control. (This allows the political leadership of the group to deny responsibility for the actions those bands take.) These activities produce disproportionate political results among the opposing group—magnifying initial fears by confirming them. The presence or absence of small gangs of fanatics is thus itself a key determinant of the ability of groups to avoid war as central political authority erodes. Although almost every society produces small numbers of people willing to engage in violence at any given moment, the rapid emergence of organized bands of particularly violent individuals is a sure sign of trouble.

The characteristic behaviour of international organizations, especially the United Nations (UN), reinforces the incentives for offensive action. Thus far, the UN has proven itself unable to anticipate conflict and provide the credible security guarantees that would mitigate the security dilemma. Once there is politically salient trouble in an area, the UN may try to intervene to "keep the peace." However, the conditions under which peacekeeping is attempted are favourable to the party that has had the most military success. As a general rule, the UN does not make peace: it negotiates cease-fires. Two parties in dispute generally agree to a cease-fire only because one is successful and happy with its gains, while the other has lost, but fears even worse to come. Alternatively, the two sides have fought to a bloody stalemate and would like to rest. The UN thus protects, and to some extent legitimates, the military gains of the winning side, or gives both a respite to recover. This approach by the international community to intervention in ethnic conflict, helps create an incentive for offensive military operations.

Windows of Vulnerability and Opportunity

Where central authority has recently collapsed, the groups emerging from an old empire must calculate their power relative to each other at the time of collapse and make a guess about their relative power in the future. Such calculations must account for a variety of factors. Objectively, only one side can be better off. However, the complexity of these situations makes it possible for many competing groups to believe that their prospects in a war would be better earlier, rather than later. In addition, if the geographic situation creates incentives of the kind discussed earlier, the temptation to capitalize on these windows of opportunity may be great. These windows may also prove tempting to those who wish to expand for other reasons.

The relative rate of state formation strongly influences the incentives for preventive war. When central authority has collapsed or is collapsing, the groups emerging from the political rubble will try to form their own states. These groups must choose leaders, set up bureaucracies to collect taxes and provide services, organize police forces for internal security and organize military forces for external security. The material remnants of the old state (especially weaponry, foreign currency reserves, raw material stocks and industrial capabilities) will be unevenly distributed across the territories of the old empire. Some groups may have had a privileged position in the old system. Others will be less well placed.

The states formed by these groups will thus vary greatly in their strength. This will provide immediate military advantages to those who are farther along in the process of state formation. If those with greater advantages expect to remain in that position by virtue of their superior numbers, then they may see no window of opportunity. However, if they expect their advantage to wane or disappear, then they will have an incentive to solve outstanding issues while they are much stronger than the opposition.

This power differential may create incentives for preventive expropriation, which can generate a spiral of action and reaction. With military resources unevenly distributed and perhaps artificially scarce for some due to arms embargoes, cash shortages or constrained access to the outside world, small caches of armaments assume large importance. Any military depot will be a tempting target, especially for the poorly armed. Better armed groups also have a strong incentive to seize these weapons because this would increase their margin of superiority.

In addition, it matters whether or not the old regime imposed military conscription on all groups in society. Conscription makes arms theft quite easy because hijackers know what to look for and how to move it. Gains are highly cumulative because each side can quickly integrate whatever it steals into its existing forces. High cumulativity of conquered resources has often motivated states in the past to initiate preventive military actions.

Expectations about outside intervention will also affect preventive war calculations. Historically, this usually meant expectations about the intervention of allies on one side or the other, and the value of such allies. Allies may be explicit or tacit. A group may expect itself or another to find friends abroad. It may calculate that the other group's natural allies are temporarily preoccupied, or a group may calculate that it or its adversary has many other adversaries who will attack in the event of conflict. The greater the number of potential allies for all groups, the more complex this calculation will be and the greater the chance for error. Thus, two opposing groups could both think that the expected behaviour of others makes them stronger in the short term.

A broader window-of-opportunity problem has been created by the large number of crises and conflicts that have been precipitated by the end of the Cold War. The electronic media provide free global strategic intelligence about these problems to anyone for the price of a shortwave radio, much less a satellite dish. Middle and great

powers, and international organizations, are able to deal with only a small number of crises simultaneously. States that wish to initiate offensive military actions, but fear outside opposition, may move quickly if they learn that international organizations and great powers are preoccupied momentarily with other problems.

Croats and Serbs

Viewed through the lens of the security dilemma, the early stages of Yugoslavia's disintegration were strongly influenced by the following factors. First, the parties identified the re-emerging identities of the others as offensive threats. The last time these groups were free of constraint, during World War II, they slaughtered one another with abandon. In addition, the Yugoslav military system trained most men for war and distributed infantry armament widely across the country. Second, the offensive appeared to have the advantage, particularly against Serbs "marooned" in Croatian and Muslim territory. Third, the new republics were not equally powerful. Their power assets varied in terms of people and economic resources; access to the wealth and military assets of the previous regime; access to external allies; and possible outside enemies. Preventive war incentives were consequently high. Fourth, small bands of fanatics soon appeared on the scene. Indeed, the political and military history of the region stressed the role of small, violent, committed groups; the resistance to the Turks; the Ustashe in the 1930s; and the Ustashe state and Serbian Chetniks during World War II.

Serbs and Croats both have a terrifying oral history of each other's behaviour. This history goes back hundreds of years, although the intense Croat-Serb conflict is only about 125 years old. The history of the region is quite warlike: the area was the frontier of the Hapsburg and Turkish empires, and Croatia had been an integral part of the military apparatus of the Hapsburg empire. The imposition of harsh Hungarian rule in Croatia in 1868; the Hungarian divide-and-conquer strategy that pitted Croats and Serbs in Croatia against each other; the rise of the independent Serbian nation-state out of the Ottoman empire, formally recognized in Europe in 1878; and Serbian pretensions to speak for all south Slavs were the main origins of the Croat-Serb conflict. When Yugoslavia was formed after World War I, the Croats had a very different vision of the new state than the Serbs. They hoped for a confederal system, while the Serbs planned to develop a centralized nation-state.[7] The Croats did not perceive themselves to be treated fairly under this arrangement, and this helped stimulate the development of a violent resistance movement, the Ustashe, which collaborated with the Fascist powers during the 1930s.

The Serbs had some reasons for assuming the worst about the existence of an independent Croatian state, given Croatian behaviour during World War II. Ustashe leadership was established in Croatia by Nazi Germany. The Serbs, both communist and non-communist, fought the Axis forces, including the Croats, and each other. (Some Croats also fought in Josef Tito's communist partisan movement against the Nazis.) Roughly a million people died in the fighting—some 5.9% of Yugoslavia's pre-war population.[8] The Croats behaved with extraordinary brutality towards the Serbs, who suffered nearly 500,000 dead, more than twice as many dead as the Croats.[9] (Obviously, the Germans were responsible for many Serbian deaths as well.) Most of these were not killed in battle; they were civilians murdered in large-scale terrorist raids.

The Croats themselves suffered some 200,000 dead in World War II, which suggests that depredations were inflicted on many sides. (The non-communist, "nationalist" Chetniks were among the most aggressive killers of Croats, which helps explain why the new Croatian republic is worried by the nationalist rhetoric of the new Serbian republic.) Having lived in a pre- and post-war Yugoslavia largely dominated by Serbs, the Croats had reason to suspect that the demise of the Yugoslavian Communist Party would be followed by a Serbian bid for hegemony. In 1971,

the Croatian Communist Party had been purged of leaders who had favoured greater autonomy. In addition, the historical record of the Serbs during the past 200 years is one of regular efforts to establish an ever larger centralized Serbian national state on the Balkan Peninsula. Thus, Croats had sufficient reason to fear the Serbs.

Serbs in Croatia were scattered in a number of vulnerable islands; they could only be "rescued" by offensive action from Serbia. Such a rescue, of course, would have been enormously complicated by an independent Bosnia, which in part explains the Serbian war there. In addition, Serbia could not count on maintaining absolute military superiority over the Croats forever: almost twice as many Serbs as Croats inhabit the territory of what was once Yugoslavia, but Croatia is slightly wealthier than Serbia.[10] Croatia also has some natural allies within former Yugoslavia, especially Bosnian Muslims, and seemed somewhat more adept at winning allies abroad. As Croatia adopted the trappings of statehood and achieved international recognition, its military power was expected to grow. From the Serbian point of view, Serbs in Croatia were insecure and expected to become more so as time went by.

From a military point of view, the Croats probably would have been better off postponing their secession until after they had made additional military preparations. However, their experience in 1971, more recent political developments and the military preparations of the Yugoslav army probably convinced them that the Serbs were about to strike and that the Croatian leadership would be rounded up and imprisoned or killed if they did not act quickly.

Each side not only had to assess the other's capabilities, but also its intentions, and there were plenty of signals of malign intent. Between 1987 and 1990, Slobodan Milosevic ended the administrative autonomy within Serbia that had been granted to Kosovo and Vojvodina in the 1974 constitution.[11] In August 1990, Serbs in the Dalmatia region of Croatia held a cultural autonomy referendum, which they defended with armed roadblocks against expected Croatian interference.[12]

By October, the Yugoslav army began to impound all of the heavy weapons stored in Croatia for the use of the territorial defence forces, thus securing a vast military advantage over the nascent armed forces of the republic.[13] The Serbian window of opportunity, already large, grew larger. The Croats accelerated their own military preparations.

It is difficult to tell just how much interference the Croats planned, if any, in the referendum in Dalmatia. However, Croatia had stoked the fires of Serbian secessionism with a series of ominous rulings. In the spring of 1990, Serbs in Croatia were redefined as a minority, rather than a constituent nation, and were asked to take a loyalty oath. Serbian police were to be replaced with Croats, as were some local Serbian officials. No offer of cultural autonomy was made at the time. These Croatian policies undoubtedly intensified Serbian fears about the future and further tempted them to exploit their military superiority.

It appears that the Croats overestimated the reliability and influence of the Federal Republic of Germany as an ally due to some combination of World War II history, the widespread misperception created by the European media and by Western political leaders of Germany's near-superpower status, the presumed influence of the large Croatian émigré community in Germany and Germany's own diplomacy, which was quite favourable to Croatia even before its June 1991 declaration of independence.[14] These considerations may have encouraged Croatia to secede. Conversely, Serbian propaganda was quick to stress the German-Croatian connection and to speculate on future German ambitions in the Balkans.[15] Fair or not, this prospect would have had an impact on Serbia's preventive war calculus.

*   *   *

Conclusion

Three main conclusions follow from the preceding analysis. First, the security dilemma and realist international relations theory more generally have considerable ability to explain and predict the probability and intensity of military conflict among groups emerging from the wreckage of empires.

Second, the security dilemma suggests that the risks associated with these conflicts are quite high. Several of the causes of conflict and war highlighted by the security dilemma operate with considerable intensity among the groups emerging from empires. The kind of military power that these groups can initially develop and their competing versions of history will often produce mutual fear and competition. Settlement patterns, in conjunction with unequal and shifting power, will often produce incentives for preventive war. The cumulative effect of conquered resources will encourage preventive grabs of military equipment and other assets.

Finally, if outsiders wish to understand and perhaps reduce the odds of conflict, they must assess the local groups' strategic view of their situation. Which groups fear for their physical security and why? What military options are open to them? By making these groups feel less threatened and by reducing the salience of windows of opportunity, the odds of conflict may be reduced.

Because the international political system as a whole remains a self-help system, it will be difficult to act on such calculations. Outsiders rarely have major material or security interests at stake in regional disputes. It is difficult for international institutions to threaten credibly in advance to intervene, on humanitarian grounds, to protect groups that fear for the future. Vague humanitarian commitments will not make vulnerable groups feel safe and will probably not deter those who wish to repress them. In some cases, however, such commitments may be credible because the conflict has real security implications for powerful outside actors.

Groups drifting into conflict should be encouraged to discuss their individual histories of mutual relations. Competing versions of history should be reconciled if possible. Domestic policies that raise bitter memories of perceived past injustices or depredations should be examined. This exercise need not be managed by an international political institution; non-governmental organizations could play a role. Discussions about regional history would be an intelligent use of the resources of many foundations. A few conferences will not, of course, easily undo generations of hateful, politicized history, bolstered by reams of more recent propaganda. The exercise would cost little and, therefore, should be tried.

In some cases, outside powers could threaten not to act; this would discourage some kinds of aggressive behaviour. For example, outside powers could make clear that if a new state abuses a minority and then gets itself into a war with that minority and its allies, the abuser will find little sympathy abroad if it begins to lose. To accomplish this, however, outside powers must have a way of detecting mistreatment of minorities.

In other cases, it may be reasonable for outside powers to provide material resources, including armaments, to help groups protect themselves. However, this kind of hard-bitten policy is politically difficult for liberal democratic governments now dominating world politics to pursue, even on humanitarian grounds. In addition, it is an admittedly complicated game in its own right because it is difficult to determine the amount and type of military assistance needed to produce effective defensive forces, but not offensive capabilities. Nevertheless, considerable diplomatic leverage may be attained by the threat to supply armaments to one side or the other.

*   *   *

It will frequently prove impossible, however, to arrange military assets, external political commitments and political expectations so that all neighbouring groups are relatively secure and perceive themselves as such. War is then likely. These wars will confirm and intensify all the fears that led to their initiation. Their brutality will tempt outsiders to intervene, but peace efforts originating from the outside will be unsuccessful if they do not realistically address the fears that triggered the conflicts initially. In most cases, this will require a willingness to commit large numbers of troops and substantial amounts of military equipment to troubled areas for a very long time.

NOTES

1. The following realist literature is essential for those interested in the analysis of ethnic conflict: Kenneth Waltz, *Theory of International Politics* (Reading, MA: Addison Wesley, 1979), Chapters 6 and 8; Robert Jervis, "Cooperation under the security dilemma," *World Politics*, no. 2, January 1978, pp. 167–213; Robert Jervis, *Perception and Misperception in International Politics* (Princeton, NJ: Princeton University Press, 1976), Chapter 3; Thomas C. Schelling, *Arms and Influence* (New Haven, CT: Yale University Press, 1966, 1976), Chapters 1 and 6.

2. See Carl Von Clausewitz, *On War* (Princeton, NJ: Princeton University Press, 1984), pp. 591–92; Robert Gilpin, "The Richness of the Tradition of Political Realism," in Robert E. Keohane, *Neorealism and its Critics* (New York: Columbia University Press, 1986), pp. 300–21, especially pp. 304–308.

3. This problem shades into an assessment of "intentions," another very difficult problem for states in international politics. This issue is treated as a capabilities problem because the emergence of anarchy forces leaders to focus on military potential, rather than on intentions. Under these conditions, every group will ask whether neighbouring groups have the cohesion, morale and martial spirit to take the offensive if their leaders call on them to do so.

4. It is plausible that the surrounding population will view irredenta in their midst as an offensive threat by the outside group. They may be perceived as a "fifth column," that must be controlled, repressed or even expelled.

5. See Stephen Van Evera, "The cult of the offensive and the origins of the First World War," *International Security*, vol. 9, no. 1, Summer 1984, pp. 58–107.

6. Why do they not go to the defence of their own, rather than attack the other? Here, it is hypothesized that such groups are scarce relative to the number of target towns and villages, so they cannot "defend" their own with any great confidence.

7. James Gow, "Deconstructing Yugoslavia," *Survival*, vol. 33, no. 4, July/August 1991, p. 292; J.B. Hoptner, *Yugoslavia in Crisis 1934–1941* (New York: Columbia University Press, 1962), pp. 1–9.

8. Ivo Banac, "Political change and national diversity," *Daedalus*, vol. 119, no. 1, Winter 1990, pp. 145–150, estimates that 487,000 Serbs, 207,000 Croats, 86,000 Bosnian Muslims and 60,000 Jews died in Yugoslavia during the war.

9. Aleksa Djilas, *The Contested Country* (Cambridge, MA: Harvard University Press, 1991), pp. 103–28. See especially, Chapter 4, "The National State and Genocide: The Ustasha Movement, 1929–1945," especially pp.

120–27, which vividly describes large-scale Croatian murders of Serbs, as well as Jews and Gypsies; however, Djilas does not explain how 200,000 Croats also died.

10. See Sabrina Ramet, *Nationalism and Federalism in Yugoslavia 1962–1991* (Bloomington, IN: Indiana University Press, 2nd ed., 1992), Appendix 2, p. 286.

11. Gow, *op. cit.* in note 7, p. 294. Vojvodina contains the only petroleum and gas in Yugoslavia proximate to Serbia, so this act probably had a strategic motive; see Central Intelligence Agency, *Atlas of Eastern Europe* (Washington, DC: US Government Printing Office, August 1990), p. 10.

12. International Institute for Strategic Studies, *Strategic Survey 1990–1991* (London: Brassey's for the IISS, 1991), p. 167.

13. Gow, *op. cit.* in note 7, p. 299.

14. See John Newhouse, "The diplomatic round," *The New Yorker*, 24 August 1992, especially p. 63. See also John Zametica, *The Yugoslav Conflict*, Adelphi Paper 270 (London: Brassey's for the IISS, 1992), pp. 63–65.

15. Ramet, *op. cit.* in note 10, p. 265.

ROBERT A. PAPE

THE STRATEGIC LOGIC OF SUICIDE TERRORISM

Terrorist organizations are increasingly relying on suicide attacks to achieve major political objectives. For example, spectacular suicide terrorist attacks have recently been employed by Palestinian groups in attempts to force Israel to abandon the West Bank and Gaza, by the Liberation Tigers of Tamil Eelam to compel

From *American Political Science Review* 97.3 (August 2003): 343–361. Some of the author's notes have been omitted.

the Sri Lankan government to accept an independent Tamil homeland, and by Al Qaeda to pressure the United States to withdraw from the Saudi Arabian Peninsula. Moreover, such attacks are increasing both in tempo and location. Before the early 1980s, suicide terrorism was rare but not unknown (Lewis 1968; O'Neill 1981; Rapoport 1984). However, since the attack on the U.S. embassy in Beirut in April 1983, there have been at least 188 separate suicide terrorist attacks worldwide, in Lebanon, Israel, Sri Lanka,

India, Pakistan, Afghanistan, Yemen, Turkey, Russia and the United States. The rate has increased from 31 in the 1980s, to 104 in the 1990s, to 53 in 2000–2001 alone (Pape 2002). The rise of suicide terrorism is especially remarkable, given that the total number of terrorist incidents worldwide fell during the period, from a peak of 666 in 1987 to a low of 274 in 1998, with 348 in 2001 (Department of State 2001).

What accounts for the rise in suicide terrorism, especially, the sharp escalation from the 1990s onward? Although terrorism has long been part of international politics, we do not have good explanations for the growing phenomenon of suicide terrorism. Traditional studies of terrorism tend to treat suicide attack as one of many tactics that terrorists use and so do not shed much light on the recent rise of this type of attack (e.g., Hoffman 1998; Jenkins 1985; Laqueur 1987). The small number of studies addressed explicitly to suicide terrorism tend to focus on the irrationality of the act of suicide from the perspective of the individual attacker. As a result, they focus on individual motives—either religious indoctrination (especially Islamic Fundamentalism) or psychological predispositions that might drive individual suicide bombers (Kramer 1990; Merari 1990; Post 1990).

The first-wave explanations of suicide terrorism were developed during the 1980s and were consistent with the data from that period. However, as suicide attacks mounted from the 1990s onward, it has become increasingly evident that these initial explanations are insufficient to account for which individuals become suicide terrorists and, more importantly, why terrorist organizations are increasingly relying on this form of attack (Institute for Counter-Terrorism 2001). First, although religious motives may matter, modern suicide terrorism is not limited to Islamic Fundamentalism. Islamic groups receive the most attention in Western media, but the world's leader in suicide terrorism is actually the Liberation Tigers of Tamil Eelam (LTTE), a group who recruits from the predominantly Hindu Tamil population in northern and eastern

Sri Lanka and whose ideology has Marxist/Leninist elements. The LTTE alone accounts for 75 of the 186 suicide terrorist attacks from 1980 to 2001. Even among Islamic suicide attacks, groups with secular orientations account for about a third of these attacks (Merari 1990; Sprinzak 2000).

Second, although study of the personal characteristics of suicide attackers may someday help identify individuals terrorist organizations are likely to recruit for this purpose, the vast spread of suicide terrorism over the last two decades suggests that there may not be a single profile. Until recently, the leading experts in psychological profiles of suicide terrorists characterized them as uneducated, unemployed, socially isolated, single men in their late teens and early 20s (Merari 1990; Post 1990). Now we know that suicide terrorists can be college educated or uneducated, married or single, men or women, socially isolated or integrated, from age 13 to age 47 (Sprinzak 2000). In other words, although only a tiny number of people become suicide terrorists, they come from a broad cross section of lifestyles, and it maybe impossible to pick them out in advance.

In contrast to the first-wave explanations, this article shows that suicide terrorism follows a strategic logic. Even if many suicide attackers are irrational or fanatical, the leadership groups that recruit and direct them are not. Viewed from the perspective of the terrorist organization, suicide attacks are designed to achieve specific political purposes: to coerce a target government to change policy, to mobilize additional recruits and financial support, or both. Crenshaw (1981) has shown that terrorism is best understood in terms of its strategic function; the same is true for suicide terrorism. In essence, suicide terrorism is an extreme form of what Thomas Schelling (1966) calls "the rationality of irrationality," in which an act that is irrational for individual attackers is meant to demonstrate credibility to a democratic audience that still more and greater attacks are sure to come. As such, modern suicide terrorism is analogous to instances of international coercion. For states, air power and economic sanctions are often the preferred coercive tools (George et al. 1972; Pape 1996, 1997). For terrorist groups, suicide attacks are becoming the coercive instrument of choice.

To examine the strategic logic of suicide terrorism, this article collects the universe suicide terrorist attacks worldwide from 1980 to 2001, explains how terrorist organizations have assessed the effectiveness of these attacks, and evaluates the limits on their coercive utility.

Five principal findings follow. First, suicide terrorism is strategic. The vast majority of suicide terrorist attacks are not isolated or random acts by individual fanatics but, rather, occur in clusters as part of a larger campaign by an organized group to achieve a specific political goal. Groups using suicide terrorism consistently announce specific political goals and stop suicide attacks when those goals have been fully or partially achieved.

Second, the strategic logic of suicide terrorism is specifically designed to coerce modern democracies to make significant concessions to national self-determination. In general, suicide terrorist campaigns seek to achieve specific territorial goals, most often the withdrawal of the target state's military forces from what the terrorists see as national homeland. From Lebanon to Israel to Sri Lanka to Kashmir to Chechnya, every suicide terrorist campaign from 1980 to 2001 has been waged by terrorist groups whose main goal has been to establish or maintain self-determination for their community's homeland by compelling an enemy to withdraw. Further, every suicide terrorist campaign since 1980 has been targeted against a state that had a democratic form of government.

Third, during the past 20 years, suicide terrorism has been steadily rising because terrorists have learned that it pays. Suicide terrorists sought to compel American and French military forces to abandon Lebanon in 1983, Israeli forces to leave Lebanon in 1985, Israeli forces to quit the Gaza Strip and the West Bank in 1994 and 1995, the Sri Lankan government to create an independent Tamil state from 1990 on, and the Turkish government to grant autonomy to the Kurds in the late 1990s. Terrorist groups did not achieve their full objectives in all these cases. However, in all but the case of Turkey, the terrorist political cause made more gains after the resort to suicide operations than it had before. Leaders of terrorist groups have consistently credited suicide operations with contributing to these gains. These assessments are hardly unreasonable given the timing and circumstances of many of the concessions and given that other observers within the terrorists' national community, neutral analysts, and target government leaders themselves often agreed that suicide operations accelerated or caused the concession. This pattern of making concessions to suicide terrorist organizations over the past two decades has probably encouraged terrorist groups to pursue even more ambitious suicide campaigns.

Fourth, although moderate suicide terrorism led to moderate concessions, these more ambitious suicide terrorist campaigns are not likely to achieve still greater gains and may well fail completely. In general, suicide terrorism relies on the threat to inflict low to medium levels of punishment on civilians. In other circumstances, this level of punishment has rarely caused modern nation states to surrender significant political goals, partly because modern nation states are often willing to countenance high costs for high interests and partly because modern nation states are often able to mitigate civilian costs by making economic and other adjustments. Suicide terrorism does not change a nation's willingness to trade high interests for high costs, but suicide attacks can overcome a country's efforts to mitigate civilian costs. Accordingly, suicide terrorism may marginally increase the punishment that is inflicted and so make target nations somewhat more likely to surrender modest goals, but it is unlikely to compel states to abandon important interests related to the physical security or national wealth of the state. National governments have in fact responded aggressively to ambitious suicide terrorist campaigns in recent years, events which confirm these expectations.

Finally, the most promising way to contain suicide terrorism is to reduce terrorists' confidence in their ability to carry out such attacks on the target society. States that face persistent suicide terrorism should recognize that neither offensive military action nor concessions alone are likely to do much good and should invest significant resources in border defenses and other means of homeland security.

The Logic of Suicide Terrorism

Most suicide terrorism is undertaken as a strategic effort directed toward achieving particular political goals; it is not simply the product of irrational individuals or an expression of fanatical hatreds. The main purpose of suicide terrorism is to use the threat of punishment to coerce a target government to change policy, especially to cause democratic states to withdraw forces from territory terrorists view as their homeland. The record of suicide terrorism from 1980 to 2001 exhibits tendencies in the timing, goals, and targets of attack that are consistent with this strategic logic but not with irrational or fanatical behavior.

Defining Suicide Terrorism

Terrorism involves the use of violence by an organization other than a national government to cause intimidation or fear among a target audience (Department of State 1983–2001; Reich 1990; Schmid and Jongman 1988). Although one could broaden the definition of terrorism so as to include the actions of a national government to cause terror among an opposing population, adopting such a broad definition would distract attention from what policy makers would most like to know: how to combat the threat posed by subnational groups to state security. Further, it could also create analytic confusion. Terrorist organizations and state governments have different levels of resources, face different kinds of incen-

tives, and are susceptible to different types of pressures. Accordingly, the determinants of their behavior are not likely to be the same and, thus, require separate theoretical investigations.

In general, terrorism has two purposes—to gain supporters and to coerce opponents. Most terrorism seeks both goals to some extent, often aiming to affect enemy calculations while simultaneously mobilizing support for the terrorists' cause and, in some cases, even gaining an edge over rival groups in the same social movement (Bloom 2002). However, there are trade-offs between these objectives and terrorists can strike various balances between them. These choices represent different forms of terrorism, the most important of which are demonstrative, destructive, and suicide terrorism.

Demonstrative terrorism is directed mainly at gaining publicity, for any or all of three reasons: to recruit more activists, to gain attention to grievances from softliners on the other side, and to gain attention from third parties who might exert pressure on the other side. Groups that emphasize ordinary, demonstrative terrorism include the Orange Volunteers (Northern Ireland), National Liberation Army (Columbia), and Red Brigades (Italy) (Clutterbuck 1975; Edler Baumann 1973; St. John 1991). Hostage taking, airline hijacking, and explosions announced in advance are generally intended to use the possibility of harm to bring issues to the attention of the target audience. In these cases, terrorists often avoid doing serious harm so as not to undermine sympathy for the political cause. Brian Jenkins (1975, 4) captures the essence of demonstrative terrorism with his well-known remark, "Terrorists want a lot of people watching, not a lot of people dead."

Destructive terrorism is more aggressive, seeking to coerce opponents as well as mobilize support for the cause. Destructive terrorists seek to inflict real harm on members of the target audience at the risk of losing sympathy for their cause. Exactly how groups strike the balance between harm and sympathy depends on the nature of the political goal. For instance, the

Baader-Meinhoft group selectively assassinated rich German industrialists, which alienated certain segments of German society but not others. Palestinian terrorists in the 1970s often sought to kill as many Israelis as possible, fully alienating Jewish society but still evoking sympathy from Muslim communities. Other groups that emphasize destructive terrorism include the Irish Republican Army, the Revolutionary Armed Forces of Colombia (FARC), and the nineteenth-century Anarchists (Elliott 1998; Rapoport 1971; Tuchman 1966).

Suicide terrorism is the most aggressive form of terrorism, pursuing coercion even at the expense of losing support among the terrorists' own community. What distinguishes a suicide terrorist is that the attacker does not expect to survive a mission and often employs a method of attack that requires the attacker's death in order to succeed (such as planting a car bomb, wearing a suicide vest, or ramming an airplane into a building). In essence, a suicide terrorist kills others at the same time that he kills himself.[1] In principle, suicide terrorists could be used for demonstrative purposes or could be limited to targeted assassinations.[2] In practice, however, suicide terrorists often seek simply to kill the largest number of people. Although this maximizes the coercive leverage that can be gained from terrorism, it does so at the greatest cost to the basis of support for the terrorist cause. Maximizing the number of enemy killed alienates those in the target audience who might be sympathetic to the terrorists cause, while the act of suicide creates a debate and often loss of support among moderate segments of the terrorists' community, even if also attracting support among radical elements. Thus, while coercion is an element in all terrorism, coercion is the paramount objective of suicide terrorism.

The Coercive Logic of Suicide Terrorism

At its core, suicide terrorism is a strategy of coercion, a means to compel a target government to change policy. The central logic of this strategy is simple: Suicide terrorism attempts to inflict enough pain on the opposing society to overwhelm their interest in resisting the terrorists' demands and, so, to cause either the government to concede or the population to revolt against the government. The common feature of all suicide terrorist campaigns is that they inflict punishment on the opposing society, either directly by killing civilians or indirectly by killing military personnel in circumstances that cannot lead to meaningful battlefield victory. As we shall see, suicide terrorism is rarely a one time event but often occurs in a series of suicide attacks. As such, suicide terrorism generates coercive leverage both from the immediate panic associated with each attack and from the risk of civilian punishment in the future.

Suicide terrorism does not occur in the same circumstances as military coercion used by states, and these structural differences help to explain the logic of the strategy. In virtually all instances of international military coercion, the coercer is the stronger state and the target is the weaker state; otherwise, the coercer would likely be deterred or simply unable to execute the threatened military operations (Pape 1996). In these circumstances, coercers have a choice between two main coercive strategies, punishment and denial. Punishment seeks to coerce by raising the costs or risks to the target society to a level that overwhelms the value of the interests in dispute. Denial seeks to coerce by demonstrating to the target state that it simply cannot win the dispute regardless of its level of effort, and therefore fighting to a finish is pointless—for example, because the coercer has the ability to conquer the disputed territory. Hence, although coercers may initially rely on punishment, they often have the resources to create a formidable threat to deny the opponent victory in battle and, if necessary, to achieve a brute force military victory if the target government refuses to change its behavior. The Allied bombing of Germany in World War II, American bombing of North Vietnam in 1972, and Coalition attacks against Iraq in 1991 all fit this pattern.

Suicide terrorism (and terrorism in general) occurs under the reverse structural conditions. In suicide terrorism, the coercer is the weaker actor and the target is the stronger. Although some elements of the situation remain the same, flipping the stronger and weaker sides in a coercive dispute has a dramatic change on the relative feasibility of punishment and denial. In these circumstances, denial is impossible, because military conquest is ruled out by relative weakness. Even though some groups using suicide terrorism have received important support from states and some have been strong enough to wage guerrilla military campaigns as well as terrorism, none have been strong enough to have serious prospects of achieving their political goals by conquest. The suicide terrorist group with the most significant military capacity has been the LTTE, but it has not had a real prospect of controlling the whole of the homeland that it claims, including Eastern and Northern Provinces of Sri Lanka.

As a result, the only coercive strategy available to suicide terrorists is punishment. Although the element of "suicide" is novel and the pain inflicted on civilians is often spectacular and gruesome, the heart of the strategy of suicide terrorism is the same as the coercive logic used by states when they employ air power or economic sanctions to punish an adversary: to cause mounting civilian costs to overwhelm the target state's interest in the issue in dispute and so to cause it to concede the terrorists' political demands. What creates the coercive leverage is not so much actual damage as the expectation of future damage. Targets may be economic or political, military or civilian, but in all cases the main task is less to destroy the specific targets than to convince the opposing society that they are vulnerable to more attacks in the future. These features also make suicide terrorism convenient for retaliation, a tit-for-tat interaction that generally occurs between terrorists and the defending government (Crenshaw 1981).

The rhetoric of major suicide terrorist groups reflects the logic of coercive punishment. Abdel Karim, a leader of Al Aksa Martyrs Brigades, a militant group linked to Yasir Arafat's Fatah movement, said the goal of his group was "to increase losses in Israel to a point at which the Israeli public would demand a withdrawal from the West Bank and Gaza Strip" (Greenberg 2002). The infamous fatwa signed by Osama Bin Laden and others against the United States reads, "The ruling to kill the Americans and their allies—civilians and military—is an individual duty for every Muslim who can do it in any country in which it is possible to do it, in order to liberate the al-Aqsa Mosque and the holy mosque [Mecca] from their grip, and in order for their armies to move out of all the lands of Islam, defeated and unable to threaten any Muslim" (World Islamic Front 1998).

Suicide terrorists' willingness to die magnifies the coercive effects of punishment in three ways. First, suicide attacks are generally more destructive than other terrorist attacks. An attacker who is willing to die is much more likely to accomplish the mission and to cause maximum damage to the target. Suicide attackers can conceal weapons on their own bodies and make last-minute adjustments more easily than ordinary terrorists. They are also better able to infiltrate heavily guarded targets because they do not need escape plans or rescue teams. Suicide attackers are also able to use certain especially destructive tactics such as wearing "suicide vests" and ramming vehicles into targets. The 188 suicide terrorist attacks from 1980 to 2001 killed an average of 13 people each, not counting the unusually large number of fatalities on September 11 and also not counting the attackers themselves. During the same period, there were about 4,155 total terrorist incidents worldwide, which killed 3,207 people (also excluding September 11), or less than one person per incident. Overall, from 1980 to 2001, suicide attacks amount to 3% of all terrorist attacks but account for 48% of total deaths due to terrorism, again excluding September 11 (Department of State 1983–2001).

Second, suicide attacks are an especially convincing way to signal the likelihood of more pain to come, because suicide itself is a costly signal, one that suggests that the attackers could not have been deterred by a threat of costly retaliation. Organizations that sponsor suicide attacks can also deliberately orchestrate the circumstances around the death of a suicide attacker to increase further expectations of future attacks. This can be called the "art of martyrdom" (Schalk 1997). The more suicide terrorists justify their actions on the basis of religious or ideological motives that match the beliefs of a broader national community, the more the status of terrorist martyrs is elevated, and the more plausible it becomes that others will follow in their footsteps. Suicide terrorist organizations commonly cultivate "sacrificial myths" that include elaborate sets of symbols and rituals to mark an individual attacker's death as a contribution to the nation. Suicide attackers' families also often receive material rewards both from the terrorist organizations and from other supporters. As a result, the art of martyrdom elicits popular support from the terrorists' community, reducing the moral backlash that suicide attacks might otherwise produce, and so establishes the foundation for credible signals of more attacks to come.

Third, suicide terrorist organizations are better positioned than other terrorists to increase expectations about escalating future costs by deliberately violating norms in the use of violence. They can do this by crossing thresholds of damage, by breaching taboos concerning legitimate targets, and by broadening recruitment to confound expectations about limits on the number of possible terrorists. The element of suicide itself helps increase the credibility of future attacks, because it suggests that attackers cannot be deterred. Although the capture and conviction of Timothy McVeigh gave reason for some confidence that others with similar political views might be deterred, the deaths of the September 11 hijackers did not, because Americans would have to expect that future Al Qaeda attackers would be equally willing to die.

The Record of Suicide Terrorism, 1980 to 2001

To characterize the nature of suicide terrorism, this study identified every suicide terrorist attack from 1980 to 2001 that could be found in Lexis Nexis's on-line database of world news media (Pape 2002).[3] Examination of the universe shows that suicide terrorism has three properties that are consistent with the above strategic logic but not with irrational or fanatical behavior: (1) *timing*—nearly all suicide attacks occur in organized, coherent campaigns, not as isolated or randomly timed incidents; (2) *nationalist goals*—suicide terrorist campaigns are directed at gaining control of what the terrorists see as their national homeland territory, specifically at ejecting foreign forces from that territory; and (3) *target selection*—all suicide terrorist campaigns in the last two decades have been aimed at democracies, which make more suitable targets from the terrorists' point of view. Nationalist movements that face nondemocratic opponents have not resorted to suicide attack as a means of coercion.

TIMING

As Table 1 indicates, there have been 188 separate suicide terrorist attacks between 1980 and 2001. Of these, 179, or 95%, were parts of organized, coherent campaigns, while only nine were isolated or random events. Seven separate disputes have led to suicide terrorist campaigns: the presence of American and French forces in Lebanon, Israeli occupation of West Bank and Gaza, the independence of the Tamil regions of Sri Lanka, the independence of the Kurdish region of Turkey, Russian occupation of Chechnya, Indian occupation of Kashmir, and the presence of American forces on the Saudi Arabian Peninsula. Overall, however, there have been 16 distinct campaigns, because in certain disputes the terrorists elected to suspend operations one or more times either in response to concessions or for other reasons. Eleven of the campaigns have ended and five were ongoing as of the end of 2001. The attacks

Table 1. Suicide Terrorist Campaigns, 1980–2001

Date	Terrorist Group	Terrorists' Goal	No. of Attacks	No. Killed	Target Behavior
		Completed Campaigns			
1. Apr–Dec 1983	Hezbollah	U.S./France out of Lebanon	6	384	Complete withdrawal
2. Nov 1983– Apr 1985	Hezbollah	Israel out of Lebanon	6	96	Partial withdrawal
3. June 1985– June 1986	Hezbollah	Israel out of Lebanon security zone	16	179	No change
4. July 1990– Nov 1994	LTTE	Sri Lanka accept Tamil state	14	164	Negotiations
5. Apr 1995– Oct 2000	LTTE	Sri Lanka accept Tamil state	54	629	No change
6. Apr 1994	Hamas	Israel out of Palestine	2	15	Partial withdrawal from Gaza
7. Oct 1994– Aug 1995	Hamas	Israel out of Palestine	7	65	Partial withdrawal from West Bank
8. Feb–Mar 1996	Hamas	Retaliation for Israeli assassination	4	58	No change
9. Mar–Sept 1997	Hamas	Israel out of Palestine	3	24	Hamas leader released
10. June–Oct 1996	PKK	Turkey accept Kurd autonomy	3	17	No change
11. Mar–Aug 1999	PKK	Turkey release jailed leader	6	0	No change
		Ongoing Campaigns, as of December 2001			
12. 1996–	Al Qaeda	U.S. out of Saudi Peninsula	6	3,329	TBD[a]
13. 2000–	Chechen Rebels	Russia out of Chechnya	4	53	TBD
14. 2000–	Kashmir Rebels	India out of Kashmir	3	45	TBD
15. 2001–	LTTE	Sri Lanka accept Tamil state	6	51	TBD
16. 2000–	Several	Israel out of Palestine	39	177	TBD
Total incidents	188				
No. in campaigns	179				
No. isolated	9				

Source: Pape (2002).

[a]To be determined.

comprising each campaign were organized by the same terrorist group (or, sometimes, a set of cooperating groups as in the ongoing "second *intifada*" in Israel/Palestine), clustered in time, publically justified in terms of a specified political goal, and directed against targets related to that goal.

The most important indicator of the strategic orientation of suicide terrorists is the timing of the suspension of campaigns, which most often occurs based on a strategic decision by leaders of the terrorist organizations that further attacks would be counterproductive to their coercive purposes—for instance, in response to full or partial concessions by the target state to the terrorists' political goals. Such suspensions are often accompanied by public explanations that justify the decision to opt for a "cease-fire." Further, the terrorist organizations' discipline is usually fairly good; although there are exceptions, such announced ceasefires usually do stick for a period of months at least, normally until the terrorist leaders take a new strategic decision to resume in pursuit of goals not achieved in the earlier campaign. This pattern indicates that both terrorist leaders and their recruits are sensitive to the coercive value of the attacks.

As an example of a suicide campaign, consider Hamas's suicide attacks in 1995 to compel Israel to withdraw from towns in the West Bank. Hamas leaders deliberately withheld attacking during the spring and early summer in order to give PLO negotiations with Israel an opportunity to finalize a withdrawal. However, when in early July, Hamas leaders came to believe that Israel was backsliding and delaying withdrawal, Hamas launched a series of suicide attacks. Israel accelerated the pace of its withdrawal, after which Hamas ended the campaign. Mahmud al-Zahar, a Hamas leader in Gaza, announced, following the cessation of suicide attacks in October 1995:

> We must calculate the benefit and cost of continued armed operations. If we can fulfill our goals without violence, we will do so. Violence is a means, not a goal. Hamas's decision to adopt self-restraint does not contradict our aims, which include the establishment of an Islamic state instead of Israel. . . . We will never recognize Israel, but it is possible that a truce could prevail between us for days, months, or years. (Mishal and Sela 2000, 71)

If suicide terrorism were mainly irrational or even disorganized, we would expect a much different pattern in which either political goals were not articulated (e.g., references in news reports to "rogue" attacks) or the stated goals varied considerably even within the same conflict. We would also expect the timing to be either random or, perhaps, event-driven, in response to particularly provocative or infuriating actions by the other side, but little if at all related to the progress of negotiations over issues in dispute that the terrorists want to influence.

NATIONALIST GOALS

Suicide terrorism is a high-cost strategy, one that would only make strategic sense for a group when high interests are at stake and, even then, as a last resort. The reason is that suicide terrorism maximizes coercive leverage at the expense of support among the terrorists' own community and so can be sustained over time only when there already exists a high degree of commitment among the potential pool of recruits. The most important goal that a community can have is the independence of its homeland (population, property, and way of life) from foreign influence or control. As a result, a strategy of suicide terrorism is most likely to be used to achieve nationalist goals, such as gaining control of what the terrorists see as their national homeland territory and expelling foreign military forces from that territory.

In fact, every suicide campaign from 1980 to 2001 has had as a major objective—or as its central objective—coercing a foreign government that has military forces in what they see as their homeland to take those forces out. Table 2 summarizes the disputes that have engendered suicide terrorist campaigns. Since 1980, there has not been a suicide terrorist campaign directed mainly against domestic opponents or against foreign opponents who did not have military forces in the terrorists homeland. Although attacks against civilians are often the most salient to Western observers, actually every suicide terrorist campaign in the past two decades has included attacks directly against the foreign military forces in the country, and most have been waged by guerrilla organizations that also use more conventional methods of attack against those forces.

Even Al Qaeda fits this pattern. Although Saudi Arabia is not under American military occupation per se and the terrorists have political objectives against the Saudi regime and others, one major objective of Al Qaeda is the expulsion of U.S. troops from the Saudi Peninsula and there have been attacks by terrorists loyal to Osama Bin Laden against American troops in Saudi Arabia. To be sure, there is a major debate among Islamists over the morality of suicide attacks, but within Saudi Arabia there is little debate over Al Qaeda's objection to American forces in the region and over 95% of Saudi society reportedly agrees with Bin Laden on this matter (Sciolino 2002).

Still, even if suicide terrorism follows a strategic logic, could some suicide terrorist campaigns be irrational in the sense that they are being waged for unrealistic goals? The answer is that some suicide terrorist groups have not been realistic in expecting the full concessions demanded of the target, but this is normal for disputes involving overlapping nationalist claims and even for coercive attempts in general. Rather, the ambitions of terrorist leaders are realistic in two other senses. First, suicide terrorists' political aims, if not their methods, are often more mainstream than observers realize; they generally reflect quite common, straightforward nationalist self-determination claims of their community. Second, these groups often have significant support for their policy goals versus the target state, goals that are typically much the same as those of other nationalists within their community. Differences between the terrorists and more "moderate" leaders usually concern the usefulness of a certain level of violence and—sometimes—the legitimacy of attacking additional targets besides foreign troops in the country, such as attacks in other countries or

Table 2. Motivation and Targets of Suicide Terrorist Campaigns, 1980–2001

Region Dispute	Homeland Status	Terrorist Goal	Target a Democracy?
Lebanon, 1983–86	U.S./F/IDF military presence	U.S./F/IDF withdrawal	Yes
West Bank/Gaza, 1994–	IDF military presence	IDF withdrawal	Yes
Tamils in Sri Lanka, 1990–	SL military presence	SL withdrawal	Yes (1950)[a]
Kurds in Turkey, 1990s	Turkey military presence	Turkey withdrawal	Yes (1983)[a]
Chechnya, 2000–	Russia military presence	Russian withdrawal	Yes (1993)[a]
Kashmir, 2000–	Indian military presence	Indian withdrawal	Yes
Saudi Peninsula, 1996–	U.S. military presence	U.S. withdrawal	Yes

SOURCE: Pape (2002). Przeworski et al. 2000 identifies four simple rules for determining regime type: (1) The chief executive must be elected, (2) the legislature must be elected, (3) there must be more than one party, and (4) there must be at least one peaceful transfer of power. By these criteria all the targets of suicide terrorism were and are democracies. Przeworski et al. codes only from 1950 to 1990 and is updated to 1999 by Boix and Rosato 2001. Freedom House also rates countries as "free," "partly free," and "not free," using criteria for degree of political rights and civil liberties. According to Freedom House's measures, Sri Lanka, Turkey, and Russia were all partly free when they were the targets of suicide terrorism, which puts them approximately in the middle of all countries, a score that is actually biased against this study since terrorism itself lowers a country's civil liberties rating (freedomhouse.org).

[a]Date established as a democracy (if not always a democracy).

against third parties and civilians. Thus, it is not that the terrorists pursue radical goals and then seek others' support. Rather, the terrorists are simply the members of their societies who are the most optimistic about the usefulness of violence for achieving goals that many, and often most, support.

The behavior of Hamas illustrates the point. Hamas terrorism has provoked Israeli retaliation that has been costly for Palestinians, while pursuing the—apparently unrealistic—goal of abolishing the state of Israel. Although prospects of establishing an Arab state in all of "historic Palestine" may be poor, most Palestinians agree that it would be desirable if possible. Hamas's terrorist violence was in fact carefully calculated and controlled. In April 1994, as its first suicide campaign was beginning, Hamas leaders explained that "martyrdom operations" would be used to achieve intermediate objectives, such as Israeli withdrawal from the West Bank and Gaza, while the final objective of creating an Islamic state from the Jordan River to the Mediterranean may require other forms of armed resistance (Shiqaqi 2002; Hroub 2000; Nusse 1998).

DEMOCRACIES AS THE TARGETS

Suicide terrorism is more likely to be employed against states with democratic political systems than authoritarian governments for several reasons. First, democracies are often thought to be especially vulnerable to coercive punishment. Domestic critics and international rivals, as well as terrorists, often view democracies as "soft," usually on the grounds that their publics have low thresholds of cost tolerance and high ability to affect state policy. Even if there is little evidence that democracies are easier to coerce than other regime types (Horowitz and Reiter 2001), this image of democracy matters. Since terrorists can inflict only moderate damage in comparison to even small interstate wars, terrorism can be expected to coerce only if the target state is viewed as especially vulnerable to punishment. Second, suicide terrorism is a tool of the weak,

which means that, regardless of how much punishment the terrorists inflict, the target state almost always has the capacity to retaliate with far more extreme punishment or even by exterminating the terrorists' community. Accordingly, suicide terrorists must not only have high interests at stake, they must also be confident that their opponent will be at least somewhat restrained. While there are infamous exceptions, democracies have generally been more restrained in their use of force against civilians, at least since World War II. Finally, suicide attacks may also be harder to organize or publicize in authoritarian police states, although these possibilities are weakened by the fact that weak authoritarian states are also not targets.

In fact, the target state of every modern suicide campaign has been a democracy. The United States, France, Israel, India, Sri Lanka, Turkey, and Russia were all democracies when they were attacked by suicide terrorist campaigns, even though the last three became democracies more recently than the others. To be sure, these states vary in the degree to which they share "liberal" norms that respect minority rights; Freedom House rates Sri Lanka, Turkey, and Russia as "partly free" (3.5–4.5 on a seven-point scale) rather than "free" during the relevant years, partly for this reason and partly because terrorism and civil violence themselves lowers the freedom rating of these states. Still, all these states elect their chief executives and legislatures in multiparty elections and have seen at least one peaceful transfer of power, making them solidly democratic by standard criteria (Boix and Rosato 2001; Huntington 1991; Przeworski et al. 2000).

The Kurds, which straddle Turkey and Iraq, illustrate the point that suicide terrorist campaigns are more likely to be targeted against democracies than authoritarian regimes. Although Iraq has been far more brutal toward its Kurdish population than has Turkey, violent Kurdish groups have used suicide attacks exclusively against democratic Turkey and not against the authoritarian regime in Iraq. There are plenty of national groups living under authoritarian regimes with grievances that could possibly inspire suicide terrorism, but none have. Thus, the fact that rebels have resorted to this strategy only when they face the more suitable type of target counts against arguments that suicide terrorism is a nonstrategic response, motivated mainly by fanaticism or irrational hatreds.

Terrorists' Assessments of Suicide Terrorism

The main reason that suicide terrorism is growing is that terrorists have learned that it works. Even more troubling, the encouraging lessons that terrorists have learned from the experience of the 1980s and 1990s are not, for the most part, products of wild-eyed interpretations or wishful thinking. They are, rather, quite reasonable assessments of the outcomes of suicide terrorist campaigns during this period.

To understand how terrorists groups have assessed the effectiveness of suicide terrorism * * *, it is important to assess whether the lessons that the terrorists drew were reasonable conclusions from the record. The crucial cases are the Hamas and Islamic Jihad campaigns against Israel during the 1990s, because they are most frequently cited as aimed at unrealistic goals and therefore as basically irrational.

*   *   *

The Apparent Success of Suicide Terrorism

Perhaps the most striking aspect of recent suicide terrorist campaigns is that they are associated with gains for the terrorists' political cause about half the time. As Table 1 shows, of the 11 suicide terrorist campaigns that were completed during 1980–2001, six closely correlate with significant policy changes by the target state toward the terrorists' major political goals. In one case, the terrorists' territorial goals were fully achieved (Hezbollah v. US/F, 1983); in three cases, the ter-rorists territorial aims were partly achieved (Hezbollah v. Israel, 1983–85; Hamas v. Israel, 1994; and Hamas v. Israel, 1994–95); in one case, the target government to entered into sovereignty negotiations with the terrorists (LTTE v. Sri Lanka, 1993–94); and in one case, the terrorist organization's top leader was released from prison (Hamas v. Israel, 1997). Five campaigns did not lead to noticeable concessions (Hezbollah's second effort against Israel in Lebanon, 1985–86; a Hamas campaign in 1996 retaliating for an Israeli assassination; the LTTE v. Sri Lanka, 1995–2002; and both PKK campaigns). Coercive success is so rare that even a 50% success rate is significant, because international military and economic coercion, using the same standards as above, generally works less than a third of the time (Art and Cronin 2003).

There were limits to what suicide terrorism appeared to gain in the 1980s and 1990s. Most of the gains for the terrorists' cause were modest, not involving interests central to the target countries' security or wealth, and most were potentially revocable. For the United States and France, Lebanon was a relatively minor foreign policy interest. Israel's apparent concessions to the Palestinians from 1994 to 1997 were more modest than they might appear. Although Israel withdrew its forces from parts of Gaza and the West Bank and released Sheikh Yassin, during the same period Israeli settlement in the occupied territories almost doubled, and recent events have shown that Israel is not deterred from sending force back in when necessary. In two disputes, the terrorists achieved initial success but failed to reach greater goals. Although Israel withdrew from much of Lebanon in June 1985, it retained a six-mile security buffer zone along the southern edge of the country for another 15 years from which a second Hezbollah suicide terrorist campaign failed to dislodge it. The Sri Lankan government did conduct apparently serious negotiations with the LTTE from November 1994 to April 1995, but did not concede the Tamil's main demand, for independence, and since 1995, the government has preferred to prosecute the war rather than consider permitting Tamil secession.

Still, these six concessions, or at least apparent concessions, help to explain why suicide terrorism is on the rise. * * *

*   *   *

The Crucial Case of Hamas

The Hamas and Islamic Jihad suicide campaigns against Israel in 1994 and 1995 are crucial tests of the reasonableness of terrorists' assessments. In each case, Israel made significant concessions in the direction of the terrorists' cause and terrorist leaders report that these Israeli concessions increased their confidence in the coercive effectiveness of suicide attack. However, there is an important alternative explanation for Israel's concessions in these cases—the Israeli government's obligations under the Oslo Accords. Accordingly, evaluating the reasonableness of the terrorists' assessments of these cases is crucial because many observers characterize Hamas and Islamic Jihad as fanatical, irrational groups, extreme both within Palestinian society and among terrorists groups in general (Kramer 1996). Further, these campaigns are also of special interest because they helped to encourage the most intense ongoing campaign, the second *intifada* against Israel, and may also have helped to encourage Al Qaeda's campaign against the United States.

Examination of these crucial cases demonstrates that the terrorist groups came to the conclusion that suicide attacks accelerated Israeli's withdrawal in both cases. Although the Oslo Accords formally committed to withdrawing the IDF from Gaza and the West Bank, Israel routinely missed key deadlines, often by many months, and the terrorists came to believe that Israel would not have withdrawn when it did, and perhaps not at all, had it not been for the coercive leverage of suicide attack. Moreover, this interpretation of events was hardly unique. Numerous other observers and key Israeli government leaders themselves came to the same conclusion. To be clear, Hamas may well have had motives other than coercion for launching particular attacks, such as retaliation (De Figueredo and Weingast 1998), gaining local support (Bloom 2002), or disrupting negotiated outcomes it considered insufficient (Kydd and Walter 2002). However, the experience of observing how the target reacted to the suicide campaigns appears to have convinced terrorist leaders of the coercive effectiveness of this strategy.

To evaluate these cases, we need to know (1) the facts of each case, (2) how others interpreted the events, and (3) how the terrorists interpreted these events. Each campaign is discussed in turn.

ISRAEL'S WITHDRAWAL FROM GAZA, MAY 1994

The Facts. Israel and the Palestinian Liberation Organization signed the Oslo Accords on September 13, 1993. These obligated Israel to withdraw its military forces from the Gaza Strip and West Bank town of Jericho beginning on December 13 and ending on April 13, 1994. In fact, Israel missed both deadlines. The major sticking points during the implementation negotiations in Fall and Winter of 1993–94 were the size of the Palestinian police force (Israel proposed a limit of 1,800, while the Palestinians demanded 9,000) and jurisdiction for certain criminal prosecutions, especially whether Israel could retain a right of hot pursuit to prosecute Palestinian attackers who might flee into Palestinian ruled zones. As of April 5, 1994, these issues were unresolved. Hamas then launched two suicide attacks, one on April 6 and another on April 13, killing 15 Israeli civilians. On April 18, the Israeli Knesset voted to withdraw, effectively accepting the Palestinian positions on both disputed issues. The suicide attacks then stopped and the withdrawal was actually conducted in a few weeks starting on May 4, 1994.[4]

These two suicide attacks may not originally have been intended as coercive, since Hamas leaders had announced them in March 1994 as part of a planned series of five attacks in retaliation for the February 24th Hebron massacre in which an Israeli settler killed 29 Palestinians and had strong reservations about negotiating a compromise settlement with Israel (Kydd and Walter 2002). However, when Israel agreed to withdraw more promptly than expected, Hamas decided to forgo the remaining three planned attacks. There is thus a circumstantial case that these attacks had the effect of coercing the Israelis into being more forthcoming in the withdrawal negotiations and both Israeli government leaders and Hamas leaders publically drew this conclusion.

Israeli and Other Assessments. There are two main reasons to doubt that terrorist pressure accelerated Israel's decision to withdraw. First, one might think that Israel would have withdrawn in any case, as it had promised to do in the Oslo Accords of September 1993. Second, one might argue that Hamas was opposed to a negotiated settlement with Israel. Taking both points together, therefore, Hamas' attacks could not have contributed to Israel's withdrawal.

The first of these arguments, however, ignores the facts that Israel had already missed the originally agreed deadline and, as of early April 1994, did not appear ready to withdraw at all if that meant surrendering on the size of the Palestinian police force and legal jurisdiction over terrorists. The second argument is simply illogical. Although Hamas objected to surrendering claims to all of historic Palestine, it did value the West Bank and Gaza as an intermediate goal, and certainly had no objection to obtaining this goal sooner rather than later.

Most important, other observers took explanations based on terrorist pressure far more seriously, including the person whose testimony must count most, Israeli Prime Minister Yitzhak Rabin. On April 13, 1994, Rabin said,

> I can't recall in the past any suicidal terror acts by the PLO. We have seen by now at least six acts of this type by Hamas and Islamic Jihad. . . . The only response to them and to the enemies of peace on the part of Israel is to accelerate the negotiations. (Makovsky and Pinkas 1994).

On April 18, 1994, Rabin went further, giving a major speech in the Knesset explaining why the withdrawal was necessary:

> Members of the Knessett: I want to tell the truth. For 27 years we have been dominating another people against its will. For 27 years Palestinians in the territories . . . get up in the morning harboring a fierce hatred for us, as Israelis and Jews. Each morning they get up to a hard life, for which we are also, but not solely responsible. We cannot deny that our continuing control over a foreign people who do not want us exacts a painful price. . . . For two or three years we have been facing a phenomenon of extremist Islamic terrorism, which recalls Hezbollah, which surfaced in Lebanon and perpetrated attacks, including suicide missions. . . . There is no end to the targets Hamas and other terrorist organizations have among us. Each Israeli, in the territories and inside sovereign Israel, including united Jerusalem, each bus, each home, is a target for their murderous plans. Since there is no separation between the two populations, the current situation creates endless possibilities for Hamas and the other organizations.

Independent Israeli observers also credited suicide terrorism with considerable coercive effectiveness. The most detailed assessment is by Efraim Inbar (1999, 141–42):

> A significant change occurred in Rabin's assessment of the importance of terrorist activities. . . . Reacting to the April 1994 suicide attack in Afula, Rabin recognized that terrorists activities by Hamas and other Islamic radicals were "a form of terrorism different from what we once knew from the PLO terrorist organizations. . . ." Rabin admitted that there was no "hermitic" solution available to protect Israeli citizens against such terrorist attacks. . . . He also understood that such incidents intensified the domestic pressure to freeze the Palestinian track of the peace process. Islamic terrorism thus initially contributed to the pressure for accelerating the negotiations on his part.

Arab writers also attributed Israeli accommodation to the suicide attacks. Mazin Hammad wrote in an editorial in a Jordanian newspaper:

> It is unprecedented for an Israeli official like Y. Rabin to clearly state that there is no future for the

settlements in the occupied territories.... He would not have said this [yesterday] if it was not for the collapse of the security Israel.... The martyrdom operation in Hadera shook the faith of the settlers in the possibility of staying in the West Bank and Gaza and increased their motivation to pack their belongings and dismantle their settlements. ("Hamas Operations" 1994)

Terrorists' Assessments. Even though the favorable result was apparently unexpected by Hamas leaders, given the circumstances and the assessments voiced by Rabin and others, it certainly would have been reasonable for them to conclude that suicide terrorism had helped accelerate Israeli withdrawal, and they did.

Hamas leader Ahmed Bakr (1995) said that "what forced the Israelis to withdraw from Gaza was the intifada and not the Oslo agreement," while Imad al-Faluji judged that

> all that has been achieved so far is the consequence of our military actions. Without the so-called peace process, we would have gotten even more.... We would have got Gaza and the West Bank without this agreement.... Israel can beat all Arab Armies. However, it can do nothing against a youth with a knife or an explosive charge on his body. Since it was unable to guarantee security within its borders, Israel entered into negotiations with the PLO.... If the Israelis want security, they will have to abandon their settlements ... in Gaza, the West Bank, and Jerusalem. ("Hamas Leader" 1995)

Further, these events appear to have persuaded terrorists that future suicide attacks could eventually produce still greater concessions. Fathi al-Shaqaqi (1995), leader of Islamic Jihad, said,

> Our jihad action has exposed the enemy weakness, confusion, and hysteria. It has become clear that the enemy can be defeated, for if a small faithful group was able to instill all this horror and panic in the enemy through confronting it in Palestine and southern Lebanon, what will happen when the nation confronts it with all its potential.... Martyrdom actions will escalate in the face of all pressures ... [they] are a realistic option in confronting the unequal balance of power. If we are un-

able to effect a balance of power now, we can achieve a balance of horror.

ISRAEL'S WITHDRAWAL FROM WEST BANK TOWNS, DECEMBER 1995

The second Hamas case, in 1995, tells essentially the same story as the first. Again, a series of suicide attacks was associated with Israeli territorial concessions to the Palestinians, and again, a significant fraction of outside observers attributed the concessions to the coercive pressure of suicide terrorism, as did the terrorist leaders themselves.

The Facts. The original Oslo Accords scheduled Israel to withdraw from the Palestinian populated areas of the West Bank by July 13, 1994, but after the delays over Gaza and Jericho all sides recognized that this could not be met. From October 1994 to April 1995, Hamas, along with Islamic Jihad, carried out a series of seven suicide terrorist attacks that were intended to compel Israel to make further withdrawals and suspended attacks temporarily at the request of the Palestinian Authority after Israel agreed on March 29, 1995, to begin withdrawals by July 1. Later, however, the Israelis announced that withdrawals could not begin before April 1996 because bypass roads needed for the security of Israeli settlements were not ready. Hamas and Islamic Jihad then mounted new suicide attacks on July 24 and August 21, 1995, killing 11 Israeli civilians. In September, Israel agreed to withdraw from the West Bank towns in December (Oslo II) even though the roads were not finished. The suicide attacks then stopped and the withdrawal was actually carried out in a few weeks starting on December 12, 1995.[5]

Israeli and Other Assessments. Although Israeli government spokesmen frequently claimed that suicide terrorism was delaying withdrawal, this claim was contradicted by, among others, Prime Minister Rabin. Rabin (1995) explained that the decision for the second withdrawal was, like the first in 1994, motivated in part by the goal of reducing suicide terrorism:

Interviewer: Mr. Rabin, what is the logic of withdrawing from towns and villages when you know that terror might continue to strike at us from there? *Rabin:* What is the alternative, to have double the amount of terror? As for the issue of terror, take the suicide bombings. Some 119 Israelis . . . have been killed or murdered since 1st January 1994, 77 of them in suicide bombings perpetrated by Islamic radical fanatics. . . . All the bombers were Palestinians who came from areas under our control.

*   *   *

Terrorists' Assessments. As in 1994, Hamas and Islamic Jihad came to the conclusion that suicide terrorism was working. Hamas's spokesman in Jordan explained that new attacks were necessary to change Israel's behavior:

> Hamas, leader Muhammad Nazzal said, needed military muscle in order to negotiate with Israel from a position of strength. Arafat started from a position of weakness, he said, which is how the Israelis managed to push on him the solution and get recognition of their state and settlements without getting anything in return. (Theodoulou 1995)

After the agreement was signed, Hamas leaders also argued that suicide operations contributed to the Israeli withdrawal. Mahmud al-Zahhar (1996), a spokesman for Hamas, said,

> The Authority told us that military action embarrasses the PA because it obstructs the redeployment of the Israeli's forces and implementation of the agreement. . . . We offered many martyrs to attain freedom. . . . Any fair person knows that the military action was useful for the Authority during negotiations.

*   *   *

The bottom line is that the ferocious escalation of the pace of suicide terrorism that we have witnessed in the past several years cannot be considered irrational or even surprising. Rather, it is simply the result of the lesson that terrorists have quite reasonably learned from their experience of the previous two decades: Suicide terrorism pays.

The Limits of Suicide Terrorism

Despite suicide terrorists' reasons for confidence in the coercive effectiveness of this strategy, there are sharp limits to what suicide terrorism is likely to accomplish in the future. During the 1980s and 1990s, terrorist leaders learned that moderate punishment often leads to moderate concessions and so concluded that more ambitious suicide campaigns would lead to greater political gains. However, today's more ambitious suicide terrorist campaigns are likely to fail. Although suicide terrorism is somewhat more effective than ordinary coercive punishment using air power or economic sanctions, it is not drastically so.

Suicide Terrorism Is Unlikely to Achieve Ambitious Goals

In international military coercion, threats to inflict military defeat often generate more coercive leverage than punishment. Punishment, using anything short of nuclear weapons, is a relatively weak coercive strategy because modern nation states generally will accept high costs rather than abandon important national goals, while modern administrative techniques and economic adjustments over time often allow states to minimize civilian costs. The most punishing air attacks with conventional munitions in history were the American B-29 raids against Japan's 62 largest cities from March to August 1945. Although these raids killed nearly 800,000 Japanese civilians—almost 10% died on the first day, the March 9, 1945, firebombing of Tokyo, which killed over 85,000—the conventional bombing did not compel the Japanese to surrender.

Suicide terrorism makes adjustment to reduce damage more difficult than for states faced with military coercion or economic sanctions. However, it does not affect the target state's interests in the issues at stake. As a result, suicide terrorism can coerce states to abandon limited or modest goals, such as withdrawal from territory of low strategic importance or, as in Israel's case in 1994 and 1995, a temporary and partial withdrawal from a more important area. However, suicide terrorism is unlikely to cause targets to abandon goals central to their wealth or security, such as a loss of territory that would weaken the economic prospects of the state or strengthen the rivals of the state.

*   *   *

The data on suicide terrorism from 1980 to 2001 support this conclusion. While suicide terrorism has achieved modest or very limited goals, it has so far failed to compel target democracies to abandon goals central to national wealth or security. When the United States withdrew from Lebanon in 1984, it had no important security, economic, or even ideological interests at stake. Lebanon was largely a humanitarian mission and not viewed as central to the national welfare of the United States. Israel withdrew from most of Lebanon in June 1985 but remained in a security buffer on the edge of southern Lebanon for more than a decade afterward, despite the fact that 17 of 22 suicide attacks occurred in 1985 and 1986. Israel's withdrawals from Gaza and the West Bank in 1994 and 1995 occurred at the same time that settlements increased and did little to hinder the IDF's return, and so these concessions were more modest than they may appear. Sri Lanka has suffered more casualties from suicide attack than Israel but has not acceded to demands that it surrender part of its national territory. Thus, the logic of punishment and the record of suicide terrorism suggests that, unless suicide terrorists acquire far more destructive technologies, suicide attacks for more ambitious goals are likely to fail and will continue to provoke more aggressive military responses.

Policy Implications for Containing Suicide Terrorism

While the rise in suicide terrorism and the reasons behind it seem daunting, there are important policy lessons to learn. The current policy debate is misguided. Offensive military action or concessions alone rarely work for long. For over 20 years, the governments of Israel and other states targeted by suicide terrorism have engaged in extensive military efforts to kill, isolate, and jail suicide terrorist leaders and operatives, sometimes with the help of quite good surveillance of the terrorists' communities. Thus far, they have met with meager success. Although decapitation of suicide terrorist organizations can disrupt their operations temporarily, it rarely yields long-term gains. Of the 11 major suicide terrorist campaigns that had ended as of 2001, only one—the PKK versus Turkey—did so as a result of leadership decapitation, when the leader, in Turkish custody, asked his followers to stop. So far, leadership decapitation has also not ended Al Qaeda's campaign. Although the United States successfully toppled the Taliban in Afghanistan in December 2001, Al Qaeda launched seven successful suicide terrorist attacks from April to December 2002, killing some 250 Western civilians, more than in the three years before September 11, 2001, combined.

Concessions are also not a simple answer. Concessions to nationalist grievances that are widely held in the terrorists' community can reduce popular support for further terrorism, making it more difficult to recruit new suicide attackers and improving the standing of more moderate nationalist elites who are in competition with the terrorists. Such benefits can be realized, however, only if the concessions really do substantially satisfy the nationalist or self-determination aspirations of a large fraction of the community.

Partial, incremental, or deliberately staggered concessions that are dragged out over a substantial period of time are likely to become the worst of both worlds. Incremental compromise may appear—or easily be portrayed—to the terrorists' community as simply delaying tactics and, thus, may fail to reduce, or actually increase, their distrust that their main concerns will ever be met. Further, incrementalism provides time and opportunity for the terrorists to intentionally provoke the target state in hopes of derailing the smooth progress of negotiated compromise in the short term, so that they can reradicalize their own community and actually escalate their efforts toward even greater gains in the long term. Thus, states that are willing to make concessions should do so in a single step if at all possible.

Advocates of concessions should also recognize that, even if they are successful in undermining the terrorist leaders' base of support, almost any concession at all will tend to encourage the terrorist leaders further about their own coercive effectiveness. Thus, even in the aftermath of a real settlement with the opposing community, some terrorists will remain motivated to continue attacks and, for the medium term, may be able to do so, which in turn would put a premium on combining concessions with other solutions.

Given the limits of offense and of concessions, homeland security and defensive efforts generally must be a core part of any solution. Undermining the feasibility of suicide terrorism is a difficult task. After all, a major advantage of suicide attack is that it is more difficult to prevent than other types of attack. However, the difficulty of achieving perfect security should not keep us from taking serious measures to prevent would-be terrorists from easily entering their target society. As Chaim Kaufmann (1996) has shown, even intense ethnic civil wars can often be stopped by demographic separation because it greatly reduces both means and incentives for the sides to attack each other. This logic may apply with even more force to the related problem of suicide terrorism, since, for suicide attackers, gaining physical access to the general area of the target is the only genuinely demanding part of an operation, and as we have seen, resentment of foreign occupation of their national homeland is a key part of the motive for suicide terrorism.

The requirements for demographic separation depend on geographic and other circumstances that may not be attainable in all cases. For example, much of Israel's difficulty in con-

taining suicide terrorism derives from the deeply intermixed settlement patterns of the West Bank and Gaza, which make the effective length of the border between Palestinian and Jewish settled areas practically infinite and have rendered even very intensive Israeli border control efforts ineffective (Kaufmann 1998). As a result, territorial concessions could well encourage terrorists leaders to strive for still greater gains while greater repression may only exacerbate the conditions of occupation that cultivate more recruits for terrorist organizations. Instead, the best course to improve Israel's security may well be a combined strategy: abandoning territory on the West Bank along with an actual wall that physically separates the populations.

Similarly, if Al Qaeda proves able to continue suicide attacks against the American homeland, the United States should emphasize improving its domestic security. In the short term, the United States should adopt stronger border controls to make it more difficult for suicide attackers to enter the United States. In the long term, the United States should work toward energy independence and, thus, reduce the need for American troops in the Persian Gulf countries where their presence has helped recruit suicide terrorists to attack America. These measures will not provide a perfect solution, but they may make it far more difficult for Al Qaeda to continue attacks in the United States, especially spectacular attacks that require elaborate coordination.

Perhaps most important, the close association between foreign military occupations and the growth of suicide terrorist movements in the occupied regions should give pause to those who favor solutions that involve conquering countries in order to transform their political systems. Conquering countries may disrupt terrorist operations in the short term, but it is important to recognize that occupation of more countries may well increase the number of terrorists coming at us.

*　　*　　*

NOTES

1. A suicide attack can be defined in two ways, a narrow definition limited to situations in which an attacker kills himself and a broad definition that includes any instance when an attacker fully expects to be killed by others during an attack. My research relies on the narrow definition, partly because this is the common practice in the literature and partly because there are so few instances in which it is clear that an attacker expected to be killed by others that adding this category of events would not change my findings.

2. Hunger strikes and self-immolation are not ordinarily considered acts of terrorism, because their main purpose is to evoke understanding and sympathy from the target audience, and not to cause terror (Niebuhr 1960).

3. This survey sought to include every instance of a suicide attack in which the attacker killed himself except those explicitly authorized by a state and carried out by the state government apparatus.

4. There were no suicide attacks from April to October 1994.

5. There were no suicide attacks from August 1995 to February 1996. There were four suicide attacks in response to an Israeli assassination from February 25 to March 4, 1996, and then none until March 1997.

REFERENCES

al-Shaqaqi, Fathi. 1995. "Interview with Secretary General of Islamic Jihad." *Al-Quds*, 11 April. FBIS-NES-95-70, 12 April 1995.

al-Zahhar, Mahmud. 1996. "Interview." *Al-Dustur* (Amman), 19 February. FBIS-NES-96-034, 20 February 1996.

Art, Robert J., and Patrick M. Cronin. 2003. *The United States and Coercive Diplomacy*. Washington, DC: United States Institute of Peace.

Bakr, Ahmed. 1995. "Interview." *The Independent* (London), 14 March. FBIS-NES-95-086, 4 May 1995.

Bearden, Milton. 2002. Personal correspondence. University of Chicago, March 26.

Bloom, Mia. 2002. "Rational Interpretations of Palestinian Suicide Bombing." Paper presented at the Program on International Security Policy, University of Chicago.

Boix, Carlos, and Sebastian Rosato. 2001. "A Complete Dataset of Regimes, 1850–1999." University of Chicago. Typescript.

"Bus Attack Said to Spur Rabin to Speed Talks." 1995. *Yediot Aharonot*, July 25. FBIS-NES-94-142, 25 July 1995.

Clutterbuck, Richard. 1975. *Living with Terrorism*. London: Faber & Faber.

Crenshaw, Martha. 1981. "The Causes of Terrorism." *Comparative Politics* 13 (July): 397–99.

De Figueiredo, Rui, and Barry R. Weingast. 1998. "Vicious Cycles: Endogenous Political Extremism and Political Violence." Paper presented at the annual meeting of the American Political Science Association.

Department of State. 1983–2001. *Patterns of Global Terrorism*. Washington, DC: DOS.

Edler Baumann, Carol. 1973. *Diplomatic Kidnapings: A Revolutionary Tactic of Urban Terrorism*. The Hague: Nijhoff.

Elliott, Paul. 1998. *Brotherhoods of Fear*. London: Blandford.

George, Alexander, et al. 1972. *Limits of Coercive Diplomacy*. Boston: Little, Brown.

Greenberg, Joel. 2002. "Suicide Planner Expresses Joy Over His Missions," *New York Times*, 9 May.

Hamas Communique No. 125. 1995. *Filastin al-Muslimah* (London), August. FBIS-NES-95-152, 8 August 1995.

"Hamas Leader Discusses Goals." 1995. *Frankfurter Runschau*, 3 May. FBIS-NES-95-086, 4 May 1995.

"Hamas Operations Against Israel Said to Continue," 1994. *Al-Dustur* (Amman, Jordan), 14 April. FBIS-NES-94-072, 14 April 1994.

Hamas Statement. 2000. *BBC Summary of World Broadcasts*, 23 July.

Hoffman, Bruce. 1998. *Inside Terrorism*. New York: Columbia University Press.

Horowitz, Michael, and Dan Reiter, 2001. "When Does Aerial Bombing Work? Quantitative Empirical Tests, 1917–1999." *Journal of Conflict Resolution* 45 (April): 147–73.

Hroub, Khaled. 2000. *Hamas: Political Thought and Practice*. Washington, DC: Institute for Palestine Studies.

Huntington, Samuel P. 1991. *The Third Wave: Democratization in the Twentieth Century*. Norman: University of Oklahoma Press.

Inbar, Efraim. 1999. *Rabin and Israel's National Security*. Baltimore: Johns Hopkins University Press.

Institute for Counter-Terrorism (ICT). 2001. *Countering Suicide Terrorism*. Herzliya, Israel: International Policy Institute for Counter-Terrorism.

Jenkins, Brian N. 1975. "Will Terrorists Go Nuclear?" Rand Report P-5541. Santa Monica, CA: Rand Corp.

Jenkins, Brian N. 1985. *International Terrorism*. Washington, DC: Rand Corp.

Jervis, Robert. 1976. *Perception and Misperception in International Politics*. Princeton, NJ: Princeton University Press.

Kaufmann, Chaim D. 1996. "Possible and Impossible Solutions to Ethnic Civil Wars." *International Security* 20 (Spring): 136–75.

Kaufmann, Chaim D. 1998. "When All Else Fails: Ethnic Population Transfers and Partitions in the Twentieth Century." *International Security* 23 (Fall): 120–56.

Kramer, Martin. 1990. "The Moral Logic of Hitzballah." In *Origins of Terrorism*, ed. Walter Reich. New York: Cambridge University Press.

Kramer, Martin. 1996. "Fundamentalist Islam at Large: Drive for Power." *Middle East Quarterly* 3 (June): 37–49.

Kydd, Andrew, and Barbara F. Walter. 2002. "Sabotaging the Peace: The Politics of Extremist Violence." *International Organization* 56 (2): 263–96.

Laqueur, Walter. 1987. *The Age of Terrorism*. Boston: Little, Brown.

Lebow, Richard Ned. 1981. *Between Peace and War: The Nature of International Crisis*. Baltimore, MD: Johns Hopkins University Press.

Lewis, Bernard. 1968. *The Assassins*. New York: Basic Books.

Makovsky, David, and Alon Pinkas. 1994. "Rabin: Killing Civilians Won't Kill the Negotiations." *Jerusalem Post*, 13 April.

Merari, Ariel. 1990. "The Readiness to Kill and Die: Suicidal Terrorism in the Middle East." In *Origins of Terrorism*, ed. Walter Reich. New York: Cambridge University Press.

Mish'al, Khalid. 2000. "Interview." *BBC Summary of World Broadcasts*, 17 November.

Mishal, Shaul, and Avraham Sela. 2000. *The Palestinian Hamas*. New York: Columbia University Press.

Niebuhr, Reinhold. 1960. *Moral Man and Immoral Society*. New York: Scribner.

Nusse, Andrea. 1998. *Muslim Palestine: The Ideology of Hamas*. Amsterdam: Harwood Academic.

O'Neill, Richard. 1981. *Suicide Squads*. New York: Ballantine Books.

Pape, Robert A. 1996. *Bombing to Win: Air Power and Coercion in War*. Ithaca, NY: Cornell University Press.

Pape, Robert A. 1997. "Why Economic Sanctions Do Not Work." *International Security* 22 (Fall): 90–136.

Pape, Robert A. 2002. "The Universe of Suicide Terrorist Attacks Worldwide, 1980–2001." University of Chicago. Typescript.

Post, Jerrold M. 1990. "Terrorist Psycho-Logic: Terrorist Behavior as a Product of Psychological Forces." In *Origins of Terrorism*, ed. Walter Reich. New York: Cambridge University Press.

Przeworski, Adam, Michael E. Alvarez, Jose Antonio Cheibub, and Fernando Limongi. 2000. *Democracy and Development: Political Institutions and Well-Being in the World, 1950–1990*. Cambridge, UK: Cambridge University Press.

Rabin, Yitzhaq. 1994. "Speech to Knessett." *BBC Summary of World Broadcasts*, 20 April.

Rabin, Yitzhaq. 1995. "Interview." *BBC Summary of World Broadcasts.* 8 September.

Rapoport, David C. 1971. *Assassination and Terrorism*, Toronto: CBC Merchandising.

Rapoport, David C. 1984. "Fear and Trembling: Terrorism in Three Religious Traditions." *American Political Science Review* 78 (September): 655–77.

Reagan, Ronald. 1990. *An American Life.* New York: Simon and Schuster.

Reich, Walter, ed. 1990. *Origins of Terrorism.* New York: Cambridge University Press.

Sauvagnargues, Philippe. 1994. "Opposition Candidate." *Agence France Presse*, 14 August.

Schalk, Peter. 1997. "Resistance and Martyrdom in the Process of State Formation of Tamililam." In *Martyrdom and Political Resistance*, ed. Joyed Pettigerw. Amsterdam: VU University Press, 61–83.

Schelling, Thomas. 1996. *Arms and Influence.* New Haven, CT: Yale University Press.

Schmid, Alex P., and Albert J. Jongman. 1988. *Political Terrorism.* New Brunswick, NJ: Transaction Books.

Sciolino, Elaine. 2002. "Saudi Warns Bush." *New York Times*, 27 January.

Shallah, Ramadan. 2001. "Interview." *BBC Summary of World Broadcasts*, 3 November.

Shiqaqi, Khalil, et al. 2002. *The Israeli-Palestinian Peace Process.* Portland, OR: Sussex Academic Press.

Sprinzak, Ehud. 2000. "Rational Fanatics." *Foreign Policy*, No. 120 (September/October): 66–73.

"Sri Lanka Opposition Leader Promises Talk with Rebels." 1994. *Japan Economic Newswire*, 11 August.

St. John, Peter. 1991. *Air Piracy, Airport Security, and International Terrorism.* New York: Quorum Books.

Theodoulou, Michael. 1995. "New Attacks Feared." *The Times* (London), 21 August. FBIS-NES-95-165, 25 August 1995.

Tuchman, Barbara W. 1966. *The Proud Tower.* New York: Macmillan.

World Islamic Front. 1998. "Jihad Against Jews and Crusaders." Statement, 23 February.

MAX ABRAHMS

WHY TERRORISM DOES NOT WORK

Terrorist groups attack civilians to coerce their governments into making policy concessions, but does this strategy work? If target countries systematically resist rewarding terrorism, the international community is armed with a powerful message to deter groups from terrorizing civilians. The prevailing view within the field of political science, however, is that terrorism is an effective coercive strategy. The implications of this perspective are grim; as target

countries are routinely coerced into making important strategic and ideological concessions to terrorists, their victories will reinforce the strategic logic for groups to attack civilians, spawning even more terrorist attacks.

This pessimistic outlook is unwarranted; there has been scant empirical research on whether terrorism is a winning coercive strategy, that is, whether groups tend to exact policy concessions from governments by attacking their civilian populations. In the 1980s, Martha Crenshaw observed that "the outcomes of campaigns of terrorism have been largely ignored," as "most analy-

From *International Security* 31, no. 2 (fall 2006): 42–78. Some of the author's notes have been omitted.

ses have emphasized the causes and forms rather than the consequences of terrorism."[1] Ted Robert Gurr added that terrorism's policy effectiveness is "a subject on which little national-level research has been done, systematically or otherwise."[2] This lacuna within terrorism studies is both a symptom and a cause of the lack of data sets with coded information on the outcomes of terrorist campaigns.[3] Within the past several years, numerous scholars have purported to show that terrorism is an effective coercive strategy, but their research invariably rests on game-theoretic models, single case studies, or a handful of well-known terrorist victories.[4] To date, political scientists have neither analyzed the outcomes of a large number of terrorist campaigns nor attempted to specify the antecedent conditions for terrorism to work. In light of its policy relevance, terrorism's record in coercing policy change requires further empirical analysis.

This study analyzes the political plights of twenty-eight terrorist groups—the complete list of foreign terrorist organizations (FTOs) as designated by the U.S. Department of State since 2001.[5] The data yield two unexpected findings. First, the groups accomplished their forty-two policy objectives only 7 percent of the time. Second, although the groups achieved certain types of policy objectives more than others, the key variable for terrorist success was a tactical one: target selection. Groups whose attacks on civilian targets outnumbered attacks on military targets systematically failed to achieve their policy objectives, regardless of their nature. These findings suggest that (1) terrorist groups rarely achieve their policy objectives, and (2) the poor success rate is inherent to the tactic of terrorism itself. Together, the data challenge the dominant scholarly opinion that terrorism is strategically rational behavior.[6] The bulk of the article develops a theory to explain why terrorist groups are unable to achieve their policy objectives by targeting civilians.

This article has five main sections. The first section summarizes the conventional wisdom that terrorism is an effective coercive strategy and highlights the deficit of empirical research sustaining this position. The second section explicates the methods used to assess the outcomes of the forty-two terrorist objectives included in this study and finds that terrorist success rates are actually extremely low. The third section examines the antecedent conditions for terrorism to work. It demonstrates that although terrorist groups are more likely to succeed in coercing target countries into making territorial concessions than ideological concessions, groups that primarily attack civilian targets do not achieve their policy objectives, regardless of their nature. The fourth section develops a theory derived from the social psychology literature for why terrorist groups that target civilians are unable to compel policy change. Its external validity is then tested against two case studies: the September 11, 2001, attacks on the United States, and Palestinian terrorism in the first intifada. The article concludes with four policy implications for the war on terrorism and suggestions for future research.

The Notion That Terrorism Works

Writers are increasingly contending that terrorism is an effective coercive strategy. In his 2002 best-seller, *Why Terrorism Works*, Alan Dershowitz argues that Palestinian gains since the early 1970s reveal that terrorism "works" and is thus "an entirely rational choice to achieve a political objective."[7] David Lake recently adapted James Fearon's rationalist bargaining model to argue that terrorism is a "rational and strategic" tactic because it enables terrorists to achieve a superior bargain by increasing their capabilities relative to those of target countries.[8] Based on their game-theoretic model and case study on Hamas, Andrew Kydd and Barbara Walter likewise conclude that terrorist groups are "surprisingly successful in their aims."[9] According to Scott Atran, terrorist groups "generally" achieve their policy objectives. As evidence, he notes that the Lebanese-based Shiite terrorist group, Hezbollah, successfully compelled the United

States and France to withdraw their remaining forces from Lebanon in 1984 and that in 1990 the Tamil Tigers of Sri Lanka wrested control of Tamil areas from the Sinhalese-dominated government.[10] For Ehud Sprinzak, the plights of Hezbollah and the Tamil Tigers testify to terrorism's "gruesome effectiveness," which explains its growing popularity since the mid-1980s.[11]

Robert Pape has developed this thesis in a prominent article that was recently expanded into a major book.[12] Pape contends that "over the past two decades, suicide terrorism has been rising largely because terrorists have learned that it pays."[13] He reports that from 1980 to 2003, six of the eleven terrorist campaigns in his sample were associated with "significant policy changes by the target state" and that "a 50 percent success rate is remarkable."[14] The perception that terrorism is an effective method of coercion, he affirms, is thus grounded in "reasonable assessments of the relationship between terrorists' coercive efforts and the political gains that the terrorists have achieved."[15] Pape's research, although confined to suicide terrorist groups, is frequently cited as evidence that terrorism in general is "effective in achieving a terrorist group's political aims."[16]

This emerging consensus lacks a firm empirical basis. The notion that terrorism is an effective coercive instrument is sustained by either single case studies or a few well-known terrorist victories, namely, by Hezbollah, the Tamil Tigers, and Palestinian terrorist groups. Pape's research appears to offer the strongest evidence that terrorist groups regularly accomplish their policy objectives, but on closer analysis his thesis is also empirically weak. Not only is his sample of terrorist campaigns modest, but they targeted only a handful of countries: ten of the eleven campaigns analyzed were directed against the same three countries (Israel, Sri Lanka, and Turkey), with six of the campaigns directed against the same country (Israel).[17] More important, Pape does not examine whether the terrorist campaigns achieved their core policy objectives. In his assessment of Palestinian terrorist campaigns, for example, he counts the limited withdrawals of

the Israel Defense Forces from parts of the Gaza Strip and the West Bank in 1994 as two separate terrorist victories, ignoring the 167 percent increase in the number of Israeli settlers during this period—the most visible sign of Israeli occupation.[18] Similarly, he counts as a victory the Israeli decision to release Hamas leader Sheik Ahmed Yassin from prison in October 1997, ignoring the hundreds of imprisonments and targeted assassinations of Palestinian terrorists throughout the Oslo "peace process."[19] Pape's data therefore reveal only that select terrorist campaigns have occasionally scored tactical victories, not that terrorism is an effective strategy for groups to achieve their policy objectives. The two sections that follow are intended to help bridge the gap between the growing interest in terrorism's efficacy and the current weakness of empirical research on this topic.

Measuring Terrorism's Effectiveness

Terrorist campaigns come in two varieties: strategic terrorism aims to coerce a government into changing its policies; redemptive terrorism is intended solely to attain specific human or material resources such as prisoners or money.[20] Because my focus is on terrorism's ability to compel policy change, terrorism in this study refers only to strategic terrorism campaigns. Terrorism's effectiveness can be measured along two dimensions: combat effectiveness describes the level of damage inflicted by the coercing power; strategic effectiveness refers to the extent to which the coercing power achieves its policy objectives.[21] This study is confined to analyzing the notion that terrorism is strategically effective, not whether it succeeds on an operational or tactical level.[22] Finally, because this study is concerned with terrorism's effect on the target country, intermediate objectives—namely, the ability of terrorist groups to gain international attention and support—are outside the scope of analysis.[23]

This study analyzes the strategic effectiveness of the twenty-eight terrorist groups designated by the U.S. Department of State as foreign terrorist organizations since 2001. The only selection bias would come from the State Department. Using this list provides a check against selecting cases on the dependent variable, which would artificially inflate the success rate because the most well known policy outcomes involve terrorist victories (e.g., the U.S. withdrawal from southern Lebanon in 1984). Furthermore, because all of the terrorist groups have remained active since 2001, ample time has been allowed for each group to make progress on achieving its policy goals, thereby reducing the possibility of artificially deflating the success rate through too small a time frame. In fact, the terrorist groups have had significantly more time than five years to accomplish their policy objectives: the groups, on average, have been active since 1978; the majority has practiced terrorism since the 1960s and 1970s; and only four were established after 1990.

For terrorist groups, policy outcomes are easier to assess than policy objectives. Instead of arbitrarily defining the objectives of the terrorist groups in this study, I define them as the terrorists do. In general, the stated objectives of terrorist groups are a stable and reliable indicator of their actual intentions. This assumption undergirds the widely accepted view within terrorism studies that groups use terrorism as a communication strategy to convey to target countries the costs of noncompliance.[24] Because these groups seek political change and because their stated objectives represent their intentions, terrorism's effectiveness is measured by comparing their stated objectives to policy outcomes. A potential objection to this approach is that terrorists possess extreme policy goals relative to those of their supporters, and thus terrorist campaigns may be judged unsuccessful even when they compel policy changes of significance to their broader community. What distinguish terrorists from "moderates," however, are typically not their policy goals, but the belief that terrorism is the optimal means to achieve them.[25] As Pape has

observed, "It is not that terrorists pursue radical goals" relative to those of their supporters. Rather, it is that "terrorists are simply the members of their societies who are the most optimistic about the usefulness of violence for achieving goals that many, and often most, support."[26] There are no broadly based data sets with coded information on the objectives of terrorist campaigns, but those ascribed to the terrorist groups in this study are all found in standard descriptions of them, such as in RAND's MIPT Terrorism Knowledge Base and the Federation of American Scientists' Directory of Terrorist Organizations (see Table 1).[27]

To capture the range of policy outcomes, this study employs a four-tiered rating scale. A "total success" denotes the full attainment of a terrorist group's policy objective. Conversely, "no success" describes a scenario in which a terrorist group does not make any perceptible progress on realizing its stated objective. Middling achievements are designated as either a "partial success" or a "limited success" in descending degrees of effectiveness. Several groups are counted more than once to reflect their multiple policy objectives. Hezbollah, for example, is credited with two policy successes: repelling the multinational peacekeepers and Israelis from southern Lebanon in 1984 and again in 2000. By contrast, Revolutionary Nuclei is tagged with two policy failures: its inability either to spark a communist revolution in Greece or to sever U.S.-Greek relations.

To construct a hard test for the argument that terrorism is an ineffective means of coercion, I afforded generous conditions to limit the number of policy failures. First, for analytic purposes both a "total success" and a "partial success" are counted as policy successes, while only completely unsuccessful outcomes ("no successes") are counted as failures. A "limited success" is counted as neither a success nor a failure, even though the terrorist group invariably faces criticism from its natural constituency that the means employed have been ineffective, or even counterproductive. Thus, a policy objective is deemed a success even if the terrorist group was

Table 1. Terrorist Groups: Objectives, Targets, and Outcomes

Group	Objective	Type	Main Target	Outcome
Abu Nidal Organization	Destroy Israel	Maximalist	Civilian	No success
Abu Sayyaf Group	Establish Islamic state in Philippines	Maximalist	Civilian	No success
Al-Qaida	Expel the United States from Persian Gulf	Limited	Civilian	Limited success
Al-Qaida	Sever U.S.-Israel relations	Idiosyncratic	Civilian	No success
Al-Qaida	Sever U.S.-apostate relations	Idiosyncratic	Civilian	No success
Al-Qaida	Spare Muslims from "Crusader wars"	Idiosyncratic	Civilian	No success
Armed Islamic Group	Establish Islamic state in Algeria	Maximalist	Civilian	No success
United Forces of Colombia	Eliminate left-wing insurgents	Idiosyncratic	Civilian	No success
Aum Shinrikyo	Establish utopian society in Japan	Maximalist	Civilian	No success
People's Liberation Front	Establish Marxism in Turkey	Maximalist	Civilian	No success
People's Liberation Front	Sever U.S.-Turkish relations	Idiosyncratic	Civilian	No success
Egyptian Islamic Jihad	Establish Islamic state in Egypt	Maximalist	Civilian	No success
National Liberation Army	Establish Marxism in Colombia	Maximalist	Civilian	No success
Revolutionary Armed Forces of Colombia	Establish peasant rule in Colombia	Maximalist	Military	Limited success
Fatherland and Liberty	Establish Basque state	Limited	Civilian	No success
Hamas	Establish state in historic Palestine	Maximalist	Civilian	Limited success
Hamas	Destroy Israel	Maximalist	Civilian	No success
Harakat ul-Mujahidin	Rule Kashmir	Limited	Military	No success
Harakat ul-Mujahidin	Eliminate Indian insurgents	Idiosyncratic	Military	No success
Hezbollah (Lebanese)	Expel peacekeepers	Limited	Military	Total success
Hezbollah (Lebanese)	Expel Israel	Limited	Military	Total success
Hezbollah (Lebanese)	Destroy Israel	Maximalist	Military	No success
Islamic Movement of Uzbekistan	Establish Islamic state in Uzbekistan	Maximalist	Military	No success
Islamic Group	Establish Islamic state in Egypt	Maximalist	Civilian	No success
Islamic Jihad	Establish state in historic Palestine	Maximalist	Civilian	Limited success
Islamic Jihad	Destroy Israel	Maximalist	Civilian	No success
Kach	Transfer Palestinians from Israel	Idiosyncratic	Civilian	No success
Mujahideen-e-Khalq	End clerical rule in Iran	Maximalist	Military	No success
Popular Front for the Liberation of Palestine (PFLP)	Destroy Israel	Maximalist	Civilian	No success
PFLP	Establish Marxist Palestine	Maximalist	Civilian	No success
PFLP-General Command	Destroy Israel	Maximalist	Military	No success
PFLP-General Command	Establish Marxist Palestine	Maximalist	Military	No success

Kurdistan Workers' Party	Establish Kurdish state in Middle East	Limited	Civilian	No success
Kurdistan Workers' Party	Establish communism in Turkey	Maximalist	Civilian	No success
Palestine Liberation Front	Destroy Israel	Maximalist	Civilian	No success
Real Irish Republican Army	Establish Irish unification	Limited	Military	No success
Revolutionary Nuclei	Establish Marxism in Greece	Maximalist	Military	No success
Revolutionary Nuclei	Sever U.S.-Greek relations	Idiosyncratic	Military	No success
Seventeen November	Establish Marxism in Greece	Maximalist	Civilian	No success
Seventeen November	Sever U.S.-Greek relations	Idiosyncratic	Civilian	No success
Shining Path	Establish communism in Peru	Maximalist	Civilian	No success
Tamil Tigers	Establish Tamil state	Limited	Military	Partial success

SOURCES: RAND, MIPT Terrorism Knowledge Base, http://www.tkb.org/Home.jsp; and Federation of American Scientists, "Liberation Movements, Terrorist Organizations, Substance Cartels, and Other Para-state Entities," http://www.fas.org/irp/world/para.

only partially successful in accomplishing it, whereas an objective receives a failing grade only if the group has not made any noticeable progress toward achieving it. Second, an objective is judged successful even if the group accomplished it before 2001, the year the State Department assembled its official list of foreign terrorist organizations. Third, all policy successes are attributed to terrorism as the causal factor, regardless of whether important intervening variables, such as a peace process, may have contributed to the outcome. Fourth, terrorist groups are not charged with additional penalties for provoking responses from the target country that could be considered counterproductive to their policy goals.[28] Fifth, the objectives of al-Qaida affiliates are limited to their nationalist struggles. Groups such as the Kashmiri Harakat ul-Mujahidin and the Egyptian Islamic Jihad are not evaluated on their ability to sever U.S.-Israeli relations, for example, even though many of their supporters claim to support this goal.

Based on their policy platforms, the twenty-eight terrorist groups examined in this study have a combined forty-two policy objectives, a healthy sample of cases for analysis. Several well-known terrorist campaigns have accomplished their objectives. As frequently noted, Hezbollah successfully coerced the multinational peacekeepers and Israelis from southern Lebanon in 1984 and 2000, and the Tamil Tigers won control over the northern and eastern coastal areas of Sri Lanka from 1990 on. In the aggregate, however, the terrorist groups achieved their main policy objectives only three out of forty-two times—a 7 percent success rate.[29] Within the coercion literature, this rate of success is considered extremely low. It is substantially lower, for example, than even the success rate of economic sanctions, which are widely regarded as only minimally effective.[30] The most authoritative study on economic sanctions has found a success rate of 34 percent—nearly five times greater than the success rate of the terrorist groups examined in my study—while other studies have determined that economic sanctions accomplish their policy ob-

jectives at an even higher rate.[31] Compared to even minimally effective methods of coercion, terrorism is thus a decidedly unprofitable coercive instrument.[32]

When Terrorism Works: The Paramountcy of Target Selection

The terrorist groups in this study were far more likely to achieve certain types of policy objectives than others. Yet predicting the outcomes of terrorist campaigns based on their policy goals is problematic. The objectives of terrorist groups are sometimes difficult to code. More important, the terrorist groups did not tend to achieve their policy aims regardless of their nature. The key variable for terrorist success was a tactical one: target selection. Groups whose attacks on civilian targets outnumbered attacks on military targets systematically failed to achieve their policy objectives. Below I examine the effects of objective type and target selection on the outcomes of the forty-two terrorist campaigns included in this study.

Importance of Objective Type

Since the mid-1960s, international mediation theorists have asserted that limited objectives are more conducive to locating a mutually acceptable resolution than disputes over maximalist objectives, which foreclose a bargaining range.[33] In the international mediation literature, limited objectives typically refer to demands over territory (and other natural resources); maximalist objectives, on the other hand, refer to demands over beliefs, values, and ideology, which are more difficult to divide and relinquish.[34] Empirical research on interstate bargaining has demonstrated that limited issues are more likely to be resolved than demands over maximalist issues; in one study, Jacob Bercovitch, Theodore Anagnoson, and Donnette Willie showed that in the latter half of the twentieth century only one out of ten Cold War disputes resulted in political compromise, compared to thirteen of thirty-one nonideological disputes in which the coercing party succeeded in winning concessions.[35] More recently, scholars have applied the distinction between limited and maximalist objectives to civil wars. Unlike traditional interstate conflicts, which often end in territorial compromise, civil wars were found to defy political resolution because they are frequently fought over competing ideologies where the costs of retreating are comparatively high.[36]

Disaggregating the terrorist campaigns by objective type offers preliminary evidence that it influences their success rate (see Figure 8.1). As in other political contexts, a terrorist group is said to have limited objectives when its demands are over territory. Specifically, the group is fighting to either (1) evict a foreign military from occupying another country, or (2) win control over a piece of territory for the purpose of national self-determination. By contrast, a terrorist group has maximalist objectives when its demands are over ideology. In this scenario, the group is attacking a country to either (1) transform its political system (usually to either Marxist or Islamist), or (2) annihilate it because of its values.[37] The data suggest that, for terrorist groups, limited objectives are far more likely to be conciliated than maximalist objectives. Coercion suc-

ceeded in three out of eight cases when territory was the goal, but it failed in all twenty-two cases when groups aimed to destroy a target state's society or values. This result is not only consistent with previous studies on interstate and civil conflict mediation; it is intuitively understandable that target countries would resist making concessions to groups believed to hold maximalist intentions.

There are, however, major limitations to predicting the outcomes of terrorist campaigns based on the nature of their policy objectives. First, even when their objectives are territorial, terrorist groups do not usually achieve them. The Kurdistan Workers' Party (PKK), Harakat ul-Mujahidin (HUM), Basque terrorists (ETA), and the Real Irish Republican Army (RIRA) have all failed to end what they regard as foreign occupations: the PKK's aspirations of an independent Kurdish state remain elusive; HUM has had little success establishing a Kashmiri state; the ETA has made some progress gaining civil and political rights, but not on its core demand of sovereignty; and Irish unification is not imminent. Second, in some cases terrorist objectives can be difficult to code. As an explanatory variable, objective type lacks robustness; terrorist objectives frequently do not conform to the territory-ideology organizing scheme. In this sample, 20 percent of the policy objectives are termed "idiosyncratic"; campaigns aiming to eliminate other militant groups (e.g., HUM) or

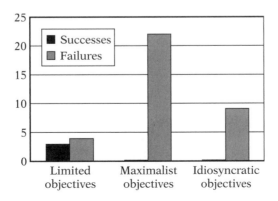

Figure 8.1. Terrorist Objectives Matter

sever relations between states (e.g., Revolutionary Nuclei) do not readily fit into the territory-ideology dichotomy (see Table 1). Furthermore, terrorist groups sometimes have ambiguous policy objectives. The al-Aqsa Martyrs Brigades, for example, routinely makes contradictory claims about whether its goal is to destroy Israel or merely establish a Palestinian state in the West Bank and Gaza Strip.[38]

The Key: Target Selection

Target selection is a superior explanatory variable for predicting the outcomes of terrorist campaigns. The Department of State defines "foreign terrorist organizations" as groups that engage in "premeditated, politically motivated violence perpetrated against noncombatant targets."[39] Like other lists of terrorist groups, the Department of State's does not distinguish between (1) groups that focus their attacks primarily on civilian targets and (2) those that mostly attack military targets, but occasionally attack civilians. By convention, any group whose strategy includes the intentional targeting of noncombatants is deemed a terrorist organization. This classification scheme may be defensible on normative grounds, but it obscures significant differences in the coercion rates of guerrilla groups and what I call "civilian-centric terrorist groups" (CCTGs). Guerrilla groups, by definition, mostly attack

military and diplomatic targets, such as military assets, diplomatic personnel, and police forces.[40] CCTGs, on the other hand, primarily attack innocent bystanders and businesses. Conflating the two types of groups contributes to the view that attacking civilians is an effective tactic for groups to attain their policy goals.[41] In fact, for terrorist groups the targeting of civilians is strongly associated with policy failure.

RAND's MIPT Terrorism Incident database provides statistics on the target selections of every terrorist group.[42] When groups are classified by target selection, a trend emerges: guerrilla groups—that is, groups whose attacks on "military" and "diplomatic" targets outnumber attacks on "civilian" targets—accounted for all of the successful cases of political coercion. Conversely, CCTGs never accomplished their policy goals, even when they were limited, ambiguous, or idiosyncratic (see Figure 8.2). The remainder of the article develops a theory to explain why terrorist groups that target civilians systematically fail to achieve their policy objectives, even when they are not maximalist.

Why Attacking Civilians Is Strategically Ineffective

Terrorism is a coercive instrument intended to communicate to target countries the costs of

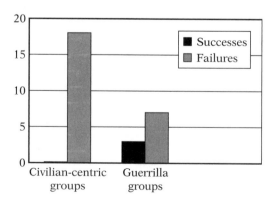

Figure 8.2. Paramountcy of Target Selection

noncompliance with their policy demands. This notion has important implications for explaining the poor track record of terrorist groups. The following analysis develops a theory for why terrorist groups—especially ones that primarily target civilians—do not achieve their policy objectives. The basic contention is that civilian-centric terrorist groups fail to coerce because they miscommunicate their policy objectives. Even when a terrorist group has limited, ambiguous, or idiosyncratic objectives, target countries infer from attacks on their civilians that the group wants to destroy these countries' values, society, or both. Because countries are reluctant to appease groups that are believed to harbor maximalist objectives, CCTGs are unable to win political concessions (see Figure 8.3).[43]

This model is grounded in two ways. First, it is consistent with attributional research in the social psychology literature; correspondent inference theory offers a framework to show that target countries infer that CCTGs—regardless of their policy demands—have maximalist objectives. Second, correspondent inference theory is applied to three case studies: the responses of Russia to the

September 1999 apartment bombings, the United States to the September 11 attacks, and Israel to Palestinian terrorism in the first intifada. The three cases offer empirical evidence that (1) target countries infer that groups have maximalist objectives when they target civilians, and (2) the resultant belief that terrorist groups have maximalist objectives dissuades target countries from making political concessions. The two methodological approaches combine to offer an externally valid theory for why terrorist groups, when their attacks are directed against civilians, do not achieve their policy goals regardless of their nature.

Objectives Encoded in Outcomes

Correspondent inference theory provides a framework for understanding why target countries infer that CCTGs have maximalist objectives, even when their policy demands suggest otherwise. Correspondent inference theory was developed in the 1960s and 1970s by the social psychologist Edward Jones to explain the cognitive process by which an observer infers the motives of an actor. The theory is derived from the foundational work

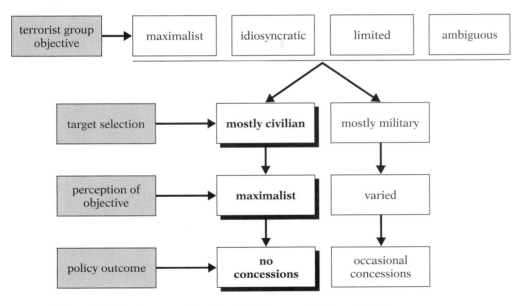

Figure 8.3. Contingency Model of Civilian-centric Terrorist Groups

of Fritz Heider, the father of attributional theory. Heider saw individuals as "naïve psychologists" motivated by a practical concern: a need to simplify, comprehend, and predict the motives of others. Heider postulated that individuals process information by applying inferential rules that shape their response to behavior. In laboratory experiments, he found that people attribute the behavior of others to inherent characteristics of their personality—or dispositions—rather than to external or situational factors.[44]

Correspondent inference theory attempted to resolve a crucial question that Heider left unanswered: How does an observer infer the motives of an actor based on its behavior?[45] Jones showed that observers tend to interpret an actor's objective in terms of the consequence of the action.[46] He offered the following simple example to illustrate the observer's assumption of similarity between the effect and objective of an actor: a boy notices his mother close the door, and the room becomes less noisy; the correspondent inference is that she wanted quiet.[47] The essential point is what Jones called the "attribute-effect linkage," whereby the objectives of the actor are presumed to be encoded in the outcome of the behavior.[48] Levels of correspondence describe the extent to which the objectives of the actor are believed to be reflected in the effects of the action.[49] When an action has high correspondence, the observer infers the objectives of the actor directly from the consequences of the action. With low correspondence, the observer either does not perceive the behavior as intentional or attributes it to external factors, rather than to the actor's disposition.[50]

High Correspondence of Terrorism

The theory posited here is that terrorist groups that target civilians are unable to coerce policy change because terrorism has extremely high correspondence. Countries believe that their civilian populations are attacked not because the terrorist group is protesting unfavorable external conditions such as territorial occupation or poverty. Rather, target countries infer from the short-term consequences of terrorism—the deaths of innocent citizens, mass fear, loss of confidence in the government to offer protection, economic contraction, and the inevitable erosion of civil liberties—the objectives of the terrorist group. In short, target countries view the negative consequences of terrorist attacks on their societies and political systems as evidence that the terrorists want them destroyed. Target countries are understandably skeptical that making concessions will placate terrorist groups believed to be motivated by these maximalist objectives. As a consequence, CCTGs are unable to coerce target countries into entering a political compromise, even when their stated goals are not maximalist.

The two case studies that follow provide preliminary evidence that terrorism is a flawed method of coercion because (1) terrorism has high correspondence, and (2) inferences derived from its effects militate against political compromise. To highlight the effect of the independent variable—terrorist attacks—on the proclivity of target states to bargain, a supporting case must conform to five empirical criteria: (1) the coercing party is not motivated by a maximalist objective, that is, the desire to destroy the target state's values or society; (2) the coercing party either uses terrorism or is suspected of doing so to further its policy objectives; (3) the target country fixates on the short-term effects of the terrorist acts, rather than the coercing party's policy demands; (4) the target country infers from the effects of the terrorist acts that the coercing party has maximalist objectives; and (5) the target country's inference that the coercing party wants to destroy its society, values, or both impedes it from making political concessions.

*   *   *

U.S. Response to the September 11 Terrorist Attacks

The response of the United States to the September 11 attacks * * * illustrates why terrorist groups that target civilians are unable to coerce policy change. The U.S. response provides supporting evidence that (1) terrorism has high correspondence, and (2) inferences derived from the effects of the attacks have not been conducive to offering concessions. The following case study shows that Americans—especially in the immediate aftermath of the terrorist attacks—have tended to ignore al-Qaida's rationale for violence. Instead of focusing on al-Qaida's policy demands, they have fixated on the effects of the terrorist attacks and inferred from them that the terrorists are targeting the United States to destroy its society and values. These inferences have hampered al-Qaida from translating its violence into policy successes in the Muslim world.

Al-Qaida's Stated Objectives

Al-Qaida describes its use of terrorism as a communication strategy to demonstrate to the United States the costs of maintaining its unpopular foreign policies in the Muslim world. Osama bin Laden has implored Americans to rid themselves of their "spiritless materialistic life," but a comprehensive perusal of al-Qaida's public statements reveals scant references to American popular culture. Bin Laden has threatened that "freedom and human rights in America are doomed," but American political values are also not a recurrent theme in al-Qaida communiqués. The relative silence on these issues suggests that American values are not a principal grievance. In fact, bin Laden has explicitly rejected the claim that al-Qaida's goal is to change these values. On multiple occasions, he has warned American audiences that those who repeat this "lie" either suffer from "confusion" or are intentionally "misleading you."[51]

Since bin Laden declared war on the United States in February 1998, his policy demands have remained notably consistent. First, his most well-known ultimatum is for the United States to withdraw its troops from Saudi Arabia, "Land of the Two Holy Places." His statements indicate that he objects not only to the U.S. stationing of troops in "the holiest of places," but also to U.S. bases serving as a "spearhead through which to fight the neighboring Muslim peoples." In al-Qaida communiqués, criticisms of U.S. military interference in Saudi Arabia have invariably been coupled with complaints about the treatment of its "neighbors," especially Iraq. For the al-Qaida leadership, deploying U.S. troops to Saudi Arabia during the lead-up to the 1991 Persian Gulf War was not only an egregious provocation in itself; the bases represented and facilitated the occupation of "its most powerful neighboring Arab state." Bin Laden and his lieutenants have thus threatened that the United States will remain a target until its military forces withdraw from the entire Persian Gulf.

Second, al-Qaida spokesmen say that its terrorist acts are intended to dissuade the United States from supporting military interventions that kill Muslims around the world. In the 1990s these interventions included "Crusader wars" in Chechnya, Bosnia, and East Timor. Bloodshed in Israel and Iraq during this period generated the most intense opposition. Since the September 11 attacks, al-Qaida's condemnation of the United States has focused on events in these two countries.[52]

Third, al-Qaida communiqués emphasize the goal of ending U.S. support for pro-Western Muslim rulers who suppress the will of their people. Al-Qaida leaders routinely denounce the House of Saud and President Pervez Musharraf's Pakistan in particular as the most "oppressive, corrupt, and tyrannical regimes" whose very existence depends on the "supervision of America."[53] A prominent al-Qaida website has equated U.S. financial and political support of Saudi Arabia and Pakistan to colonization.[54]

Fourth, al-Qaida leaders describe Israel in similar terms, as a colonial outpost. Based on the organization's communiqués, al-Qaida's final objective is thus to destroy the "Zionist-Crusader alliance," which enables Israel to maintain its "occupation of Jerusalem" and "murder Muslims there."[55]

Effects Trump Rationale

Americans have focused on the effects of al-Qaida violence, not on al-Qaida's stated purpose. Ronald Steel noted in the *New Republic* after the June 1996 attack on the Khobar Towers in Saudi Arabia, which killed 19 Americans, that American journalists fixated on "who or what bin Laden attacked" and "the method of attack." By contrast, "what bin Laden had been saying about why he and his al-Qaida forces were attacking was given short shrift."[56] The British journalist Robert Fisk similarly observed that after the August 1998 attacks on the U.S. embassies in Kenya and Tanzania, U.S. leaders emphasized the carnage and devastation, but "not in a single press statement, press conference, or interview did a U.S. leader or diplomat explain why the enemies of America hate America."[57] Since September 11, 2001, major Western journalists have devoted generous coverage to the fallout of terrorist attacks, but only since 2004, with the publication of Michael Schueur's *Imperial Hubris*, have they consistently published excerpts of al-Qaida's communiqués.[58]

High Correspondence of September 11

President George W. Bush's public pronouncements indicate that he deduces al-Qaida's motives directly from the short-term consequences of the terrorist attacks of September 11. According to Bush, "We have seen the true nature of these terrorists in the nature of their attacks," rather than in their professed political agenda.[59] For Bush, September 11 demonstrated that the enemy "hates not our policies, but our existence."[60] In the resulting panic weeks after the attacks, he concluded, "These acts of mass murder were intended to frighten our nation into chaos." With Americans hesitant to fly after the four planes were hijacked, he asserted, "They [the terrorists] want us to stop flying."[61] The toppling of the World Trade Center and the economic contraction that followed revealed that "the terrorists wanted our economy to stop." With American

civil liberties inevitably restricted in the wake of the attacks, he proclaimed that al-Qaida's goals, inter alia, were to curtail "our freedom of religion, our freedom of speech, our freedom to vote and assemble and disagree with each other."[62] Given that al-Qaida and its affiliates are mute on these topics, it is difficult to imagine Bush ascribing them to the terrorists had Americans not been greatly frightened for their safety, hesitant to fly, and worried about their political and economic future in the wake of the terrorist attacks.

For President Bush, any group that deliberately attacks American civilians is evidently motivated by the desire to destroy American society and its democratic values. When asked by a reporter in October 2001 if there was any direct connection between the September 11 attacks and the spate of anthrax attacks that followed, he replied: "I have no direct evidence but there are some links . . . both series of actions are motivated to disrupt Americans' way of life."[63] This interpretation of the motives of the unknown terrorist perpetrator(s) is revealing: the identity of the person(s) who sent the anthrax is irrelevant because all terrorists who disrupt the American way of life must be motivated by this maximalist objective.

The American public has tended to share President Bush's interpretation of the terrorists' motives. Polls conducted after September 11 show that most Americans believed that al-Qaida was not responding to unpopular U.S. foreign policies. After the attacks, only one in five respondents agreed with the statement that "there is any way that the United States has been unfair in its dealings with other countries that might have motivated the terrorist attacks."[64] In a separate poll, only 15 percent of Americans agreed that "American foreign policies are partly the reason" for al-Qaida terrorism.[65] Instead of attributing al-Qaida terrorism to U.S. foreign policies, large segments of American society shared Bush's belief that the goal of the terrorists was to destroy American society and values. Since September 11, more Americans have polled that the terrorists are targeting the United States because of its "democracy," "freedom," "values," and "way of life" than because of its interference in the Muslim world.[66]

Al-Qaida's Miscommunication Strategy

Bin Laden and his lieutenants frequently complain that the United States has failed to "understand" the "true reason" for the September 11 attacks. Instead of attacking because "we hate freedom," the attacks are a response to the fact that "you spoil our security" and "attack us."[67] Attributional research provides a framework to explain why al-Qaida's communication strategy has failed. As correspondent inference theory predicts, supporting evidence suggests that President Bush and large segments of American society focused on the disastrous effects of al-Qaida's behavior and inferred from them that the terrorists must want to destroy American society and its values—despite al-Qaida's relative silence on these issues.[68]

To be sure, even if terrorism had not delegitimized al-Qaida's policy demands, it is inconceivable the United States would have ever fully complied with them. Paul Wilkinson has observed that in deciding whether to negotiate with terrorists, the target government must first decide whether their demands are "corrigible" or "incorrigible." When demands are perceived as corrigible, the target government engages in a "roots debate"—an assessment of the pros and cons of appeasing the terrorists. When terrorists are perceived as incorrigible, concessions are rejected outright because the demands are deemed so extreme that they fall outside of the realm of consideration. In Wilkinson's model, incorrigible terrorists are not categorically implacable, but placating them would exact a prohibitive cost.[69] In the discourse of international relations theory, realists would support the view that the United States has not entered a post–September 11 roots debate because it is strategically wedded to the Middle East.

Realists are on strong ground in their prediction that the world's most powerful country would not willingly concede a geographically vital region of the world to terrorists. But it is doubtful that had Americans viewed al-Qaida's stated grievances as credible, they would have embraced a counterterrorism strategy after September 11 that systematically aggravated them. In response to the September 11 attacks, the United States took four steps: (1) increased troop levels in the Persian Gulf fifteenfold; (2) strengthened military relations with pro-U.S. Muslim rulers, especially in Pakistan and Saudi Arabia; (3) supported counterterrorism operations—either directly or indirectly—that have killed tens of thousands of Muslims around the world; and (4) became an even less partial mediator in the Israeli-Palestinian conflict.[70] Although the September 11 attacks achieved al-Qaida's intermediate objectives of gaining supporters and attention, its post–September 11 policy failures are a testament, at least in part, to its flawed communication strategy.

Israel's Response to the First Intifada

The first intifada may seem like an unlikely case study to illustrate the limitations of terrorism as a coercive strategy. The mass uprising in the Gaza Strip and the West Bank was an exceptionally moderate period in the history of Palestinian terrorism. The revolt from December 1987 to January 1991 killed only twenty Israeli civilians. Compared with the "Revolutionary Violence" campaign of the 1970s and the outbreak of the second intifada in September 2000, the first intifada was a peaceful interlude.[71] Furthermore, the spontaneous insurrection was a bottom-up initiative. It circumvented Palestinian terrorist groups, which were ideologically opposed to a two-state solution. These groups were momentarily sidelined for three reasons. First, the Marxist groups (e.g., the Popular Front for the Liberation of Palestine and the PFLP–General Command) were reeling from the recent loss of their Soviet patron with the end of the Cold War.

Second, the Islamist groups (e.g., Hamas and Islamic Jihad) did not yet pose a significant challenge to the Palestine Liberation Organization (PLO). Third, the PLO was based in Tunis during this period, largely detached from Palestinian life in the territories.[72] Facing relatively little competition from other Palestinian groups, the PLO co-opted the mass uprising in the late 1980s by recognizing the Israeli state within its pre-1967 borders and formally renouncing terrorism. Despite the unusually moderate tactics and objectives of the intifada, the Israeli response to it underscores that (1) the limited use of Palestinian terrorism had high correspondence, and (2) Israeli inferences of Palestinian objectives undermined support for making concessions.

Edy Kaufman has noted that "the primary purpose of the first intifada was to communicate to Israelis the need to end the occupation of the territories."[73] Terrorist acts, even in small numbers, interfered with the message. Throughout the intifada, only 15 percent of Palestinian demonstrations were violent.[74] Yet an absolute majority of Israelis (80 percent) believed that the means employed by the Palestinians to protest Israeli rule were "mainly violent." Of the violent Palestinian acts, the vast majority consisted of rock throwing against the Israel Defense Forces in the territories, with few incidences of terrorism inside the Green Line. An even broader consensus of Israelis (93 percent) felt that the intifada was directed "both towards civilians and towards the army."[75] Notwithstanding the intifada's restrained use of violence, Israelis appear to have fixated on the intermittent attacks against Israeli civilians.

The Louis Guttman Israel Institute of Applied Social Research conducted a series of polls in December 1990 to assess the Israeli public's views of Palestinian objectives in the first intifada. As correspondent inference theory predicts, a strong majority of the respondents surveyed (85 percent) believed its purpose was to "cause damage and injury"—as it surely did—while only a fraction (15 percent) believed the goal was to "express protest." Similarly, the majority (66 percent)

believed that the intifada was directed against "the existence of the state of Israel," while a minority (34 percent) believed the purpose was to liberate the West Bank and Gaza Strip.[76] The disconnect between the PLO's policy demands and Israeli perceptions of Palestinian objectives has been explained by (1) inconsistent rhetoric on the part of Palestinian leaders about the aims of the intifada, and (2) Jewish apprehension that contemporary violence against Israel is akin to previous traumatic experiences in which Jewish survival in the Diaspora was threatened.

Compelling evidence suggests, however, that terrorism informed the Israeli view of Palestinian objectives. In a fascinating study based on the polling data contained in the Guttman report, Kaufman observed that the respondents who perceived Palestinian tactics as "mainly violent" were more likely to believe that the Palestinian goal was to "destroy Israel." Conversely, the more Israelis perceived Palestinian tactics as nonviolent, the more they believed the goal was to liberate the territories. The positive correlation between perceived Palestinian terrorism and maximalist objectives existed independent of the respondents' political affiliation, suggesting that the association was not a function of their preexisting political attitudes.[77] Not surprisingly, Israelis were twice as likely to believe "less in the idea of peace" than before the intifada.[78] Because the majority of Israelis regarded the intifada as a protracted terrorist campaign, and Israelis inferred from Palestinian terrorism their intentions of wanting to destroy Israel, the intifada undermined Israeli confidence in the Palestinians as a credible partner for peace.

In the early 1990s, Israeli Prime Ministers Yitzhak Shamir and Yitzhak Rabin came under increased pressure to trade "land for peace" with the Palestinians. The sources of pressure were twofold. First, President George H.W. Bush, determined to improve U.S.-Arab relations after Israel had lost its strategic utility as a Cold War satellite, "forced the Israelis to the negotiating table" by linking U.S. financial assistance to Shamir's participation in the Madrid peace conference in October 1991. Second, Israeli military strategists recognized that the Jewish state faced a long-term demographic problem in occupying a growing and restive Palestinian population.[79] In September 1993 Israel consented to the land-for-peace formula outlined in the Declaration of Principles known as the Oslo accords, but the pattern persisted: although Palestinian terrorism demonstrated to Israel the costs of the occupation, it undercut Israeli confidence in the Palestinians as a credible partner for peace, reducing support for making territorial concessions. Throughout the 1990s, the Jaffee Center for Strategic Studies periodically polled Israeli respondents on their perceptions of Palestinian aspirations. The "dominant" response was that the Palestinians wanted to "conquer Israel" and "destroy a large portion of the Jewish population," a position that peaked during heightened levels of terrorist activity.[80] The perception that the Palestinians hold maximalist aspirations has been the principal impediment to Israel's willingness to make significant territorial concessions. Since 1994 the Tami Steinmetz Center for Peace Research has polled a representative sample of Israelis on two questions: Do you believe the Palestinians are viable partners for peace? And do you support the peace process? Instances of Palestinian terrorism systematically incline Israelis to answer "no" to both questions.[81]

In sum, since the first intifada, Palestinian violence has created pressure on Israel to change the status quo. Paradoxically, terrorism has simultaneously convinced Israelis that the Palestinians are not committed to a two-state solution, which has eroded support for making the territorial concessions necessary to achieving it.

Conclusion

Thomas Schelling asserted more than a decade ago that terrorists frequently accomplish "intermediate means toward political objectives . . . but with a few exceptions it is hard to see that the attention and publicity have been of much value

except as ends in themselves."[82] This study corroborates that view; the twenty-eight groups of greatest significance to U.S. counterterrorism policy have achieved their forty-two policy objectives less than 10 percent of the time. As the political mediation literature would predict, target countries did not make concessions when terrorist groups had maximalist objectives. Yet even when groups expressed limited, ambiguous, or idiosyncratic policy objectives, they failed to win concessions by primarily attacking civilian targets. This suggests not only that terrorism is an ineffective instrument of coercion, but that its poor success rate is inherent to the tactic of terrorism itself.

Why are terrorist groups unable to coerce governments when they primarily attack civilian targets? Terrorism miscommunicates groups' objectives because of its extremely high correspondence. * * * The [responses of the] United States to the attacks of September 11, and Israel to Palestinian terrorism in the first intifada provide evidence that target countries infer the objectives of terrorist groups not from their stated goals, but from the short-term consequences of terrorist acts. Target countries view the deaths of their citizens and the resulting turmoil as proof that the perpetrators want to destroy their societies, their publics, or both. Countries are therefore reluctant to make concessions when their civilians are targeted irrespective of the perpetrators' policy demands.

Four policy implications follow for the war on terrorism. First, terrorists will find it extremely difficult to transform or annihilate a country's political system. Second, the jihadists stand to gain from restricting their violence to military targets. Already, mounting U.S. casualties in Iraq and the absence of a post–September 11 attack on the homeland have eroded U.S. support for maintaining a military presence in Iraq.[83] Terrorist strikes on the U.S. homeland will only undermine the terrorists' message that their purpose is to alter unpopular U.S. policies in the Muslim world. Even sporadic attacks on American civilians—if seen as the dominant component of al-Qaida's overall strategy—will undermine support for an exit strategy. Third, the self-defeating policy consequences of terrorism will ultimately dissuade potential jihadists from supporting it. Although guerrilla attacks against U.S. forces in Iraq show no signs of abating, polling data from Muslim countries suggest that the terrorism backlash is already under way. The Pew Research Center reported in its July 2005 Global Attitudes Project that compared with its polls conducted in 2002, "In most majority-Muslim countries surveyed support for suicide bombings and other acts of violence in defense of Islam has declined significantly," as has "confidence in Osama bin Laden to do the right thing in world affairs."[84] Similarly, major Islamist groups and leaders are increasingly denouncing terrorist attacks as counterproductive, even as they encourage guerrilla warfare against the Iraqi occupation.[85] Fourth, it is commonly said that terrorists cannot be deterred because they are willing to die for their cause and that they lack a "return address" to threaten with a retaliatory strike.[86] But perhaps the greatest reason deterrence breaks down is because of the widespread, albeit erroneous, belief that attacking civilians is an effective strategy for terrorist groups to advance their policy goals. Disabusing terrorists of this notion would go a long way toward defusing the cycles of violent reprisal.

Further research is needed in three areas. First, why do terrorist groups target civilians if doing so is strategically ineffective? Testing of the following four hypotheses could yield useful results: (1) groups have an exaggerated sense of terrorism's ability to coerce policy change;[87] (2) terrorist groups attach equal importance to achieving their intermediate objectives; (3) even though terrorism almost never pays, it is a superior strategy to the alternatives, such as conducting a peaceful protest; and (4) only comparatively weak groups target civilians, because attacking military targets requires a higher level of combat sophistication. Of these hypotheses, only the fourth one appears empirically dubious. Nascent terrorist groups generally focus their attacks on military targets and then graduate to attacking civilian targets. This progression from military to civilian targets was evident between the two Chechen wars, between al-Qaida's declaration of war on the United States in 1998 and the September 11 attacks, and from the beginning of the first intifada to its more violent conclusion. In each campaign, the terrorists initially confined their attacks to military targets and then, upon becoming stronger organizationally and technologically, took aim at civilians.

Second, future research may demonstrate that in international relations the attribute-effect linkage diminishes over time. In this study, the target countries inferred from attacks on their civilians that the perpetrators held maximalist objectives that could not be satisfied. As time elapsed from the terrorist attacks, however, the publics of Russia and the United States began expressing greater receptivity to curtailing their country's influence in Chechnya and the Muslim world, respectively.[88]

Third, correspondent inference theory may have prescriptive utility for conducting a more strategic and humane war on terrorism. If countries impute terrorists' motives from the consequences of their actions, then the communities in which terrorists thrive may impute states' motives from the consequences of their counterterrorism policies, reinforcing the strategic logic of minimizing collateral damage. Correspondent inference theory can explain not only why terrorist campaigns rarely work, but also perhaps why counterterrorism campaigns tend to breed even more terrorism.

NOTES

1. Martha Crenshaw, ed., *Terrorism, Legitimacy, and Power: The Consequences of Political Violence* (Middletown, Conn.: Wesleyan University Press, 1983), p. 5.
2. Ted Robert Gurr, "Empirical Research on Political Terrorism," in Robert O. Slater and Michael Stohl, eds., *Current Perspectives on International Terrorism* (New York: St. Martin's, 1988), p. 125.

3. See ibid., p. 120.

4. See, for example, Max Abrahms, "Are Terrorists Really Rational? The Palestinian Example," *Orbis*, Vol. 48, No. 3 (Summer 2004), pp. 533–549; Max Abrahms, "Al-Qaida's Scorecard: A Progress Report on al-Qaida's Objectives," *Studies in Conflict and Terrorism;* Sprinzak, "Rational Fanatics," p. 68; Lake, "Rational Extremism," p. 15; Kydd and Walter, "The Strategies of Terrorism," p. 49; Pape, *Dying to Win*, p. 40; and Pape, "The Strategic Logic of Suicide Terrorism," p. 13. The sample Pape used to determine the motivations of suicide terrorist groups is impressive, incorporating data from every suicide attack from 1980 to 2003. His secondary argument on terrorism's effectiveness relies on a less convincing sample of cases. For a critique of the methods Pape used to analyze the effectiveness of suicide terrorist groups, see Max Abrahms, "Dying to Win," *Middle East Policy*, Vol. 12, No. 4 (Winter 2005), pp. 176–178.

5. U.S. Department of State, "Foreign Terrorist Organizations (FTOs)," October 11, 2005, http://www.state.gov/s/ct/rls/fs/37191.htm.

6. Herbert Simon noted that there are two types of rationality. "Substantive rationality" is based on the actual "achievement of given goals." By contrast, "procedural rationality" depends only on "the [thought] process that generated it." In other words, substantive rationality is concerned with the consequences of the decision, whereas procedural rationality makes no claim that the actor correctly anticipates the consequences of his decision. Simon, "From Substantive to Procedural Rationality," in Spiro Latsis, ed., *Method and Appraisal in Economics* (Cambridge: Cambridge University Press, 1976), pp. 130–131; and Simon, *Models of Bounded Rationality*, Vol. 3: *Empirically Grounded Economic Research* (Cambridge, Mass.: MIT Press, 1997), pp. 8–9. My article addresses the question of whether terrorism is substantively rational behavior, not whether it is procedurally rational.

7. Dershowitz, *Why Terrorism Works*, p. 86. In the past several years, a flurry of editorials has likewise warned that the tendency for states to reward terrorism is encouraging other groups to use it. See John Derbyshire, "Terrorism Works," *National Review Online*, October 12, 2000; Evelyn Gordon, "Terrorism Works," *Jerusalem Post*, July 14, 2005; and R.W. Johnson, "Why Bush Might Yet Give In to the Terrorists," *Daily Telegraph* (London), September 29, 2001. See also Kruglanski and Fishman, "The Psychology of Terrorism," p. 207; and Chomsky, "The New War against Terror."

8. Lake, "Rational Extremism," pp. 20, 15.

9. Kydd and Walter, "Sabotaging the Peace," p. 264.

10. Atran, "Trends in Suicide Terrorism."

11. Sprinzak, "Rational Fanatics," p. 68.

12. Pape, "The Strategic Logic of Suicide Terrorism"; and Pape, *Dying to Win*.

13. Pape, "The Strategic Logic of Suicide Terrorism," p. 343.

14. Ibid., p. 9; and Pape, *Dying to Win*, pp. 64–65.

15. Pape, *Dying to Win*, pp. 61, 64–65.

16. See, for example, Kydd and Walter, "The Strategies of Terrorism," p. 49.

17. Pape, "The Strategic Logic of Suicide Terrorism," p. 9.

18. Abrahms, "Dying to Win," p. 177.

19. See Abrahms, "Dying to Win."

20. Gary C. Gambill, "The Balance of Terror: War by Other Means in the Contemporary Middle East," *Journal of Palestine Studies*, Vol. 28, No. 1 (Autumn 1998), p. 61.

21. Robert A. Pape, *Bombing to Win: Air Power and Coercion in War* (Ithaca, N.Y.: Cornell University Press, 1996), pp. 56–57.

22. See James T. Tedeschi, "A Reinterpretation of Research on Aggression," *Psychological Bulletin*, Vol. 81, No. 9 (September 1974), p. 562.

23. There is little debate that terrorism often facilitates the achievement of intermediate objectives. This position gained acceptance after the 1967 Arab-Israeli war, when a spate

of terrorist attacks galvanized Palestinian nationalist sentiment and propelled the Palestinian cause onto the international agenda. In September 1969, just three months after the Popular Front for the Liberation of Palestine hijacked a U.S. jet departing from Athens, the United Nations General Assembly recognized the "inalienable rights of the Palestinian people." Eighteen months after Palestinian terrorists killed eleven Israeli Olympians at the 1972 Munich Games, Yassir Arafat was officially invited to speak before this body. Bruce Hoffman has observed, "It is doubtful whether the terrorists could ever have received this success had they not resorted to international terrorism." Hoffman, *Inside Terrorism* (New York: Columbia University Press, 1998), p. 75. See also Abrahms, "Are Terrorists Really Rational?" p. 341; and Thomas C. Schelling, "What Purposes Can 'International Terrorism' Serve?" in R.G. Frey and Christopher W. Morris, eds., *Violence, Terrorism, and Justice* (New York: Cambridge University Press, 1991), p. 20.

24. See Crenshaw, "The Causes of Terrorism," p. 379; Ronald D. Crelinsten, "Terrorism as Political Communication: The Relationship between the Controller and the Controlled," in Paul Wilkinson and Alasdair M. Stewart, eds., *Contemporary Research on Terrorism* (Aberdeen, Scotland: Aberdeen University Press, 1987), pp. 3–31; Bruce Hoffman and Gordon H. McCormick, "Terrorism, Signaling, and Suicide Attack," *Studies in Conflict and Terrorism*, Vol. 27, No. 4 (July/August 2004), pp. 243–281; Max Abrahms, "Al-Qaeda's Miscommunication War: The Terrorism Paradox," *Terrorism and Political Violence*, Vol. 17, No. 4 (Autumn 2005), pp. 529–549; and Kydd and Walter, "The Strategies of Terrorism," p. 59.

25. U.S. Department of Defense, "The National Military Strategic Plan for the War on Terrorism," February 1, 2006, p. 3.

26. Pape, "The Strategic Logic of Suicide Terrorism," p. 7.

27. Gurr, "Empirical Research on Political Terrorism," p. 120; RAND, MIPT Terrorism Knowledge Base: A Comprehensive Databank of Global Terrorist Incidents and Organizations, "Groups Subcategories," http://www.tkb.org/Category.jsp?catID?1; and Federation of American Scientists, "Liberation Movements, Terrorist Organizations, Substance Cartels, and Other Para-state Entities," http://www.fas.org/irp/world/para/. See also Kydd and Walter, "The Strategies of Terrorism," pp. 54–55.

28. That the Israel Defense Forces reoccupied large sections of the West Bank in April 2002 in response to terrorist activity, for example, is relevant only insofar as it may have prevented Palestinian terrorist organizations from accomplishing their stated objectives.

29. Even when "limited successes" are counted as policy successes, the success rate is only 17 percent.

30. Robert A. Pape, "Why Economic Sanctions Do Not Work," *International Security*, Vol. 22, No. 2 (Fall 1997), p. 99.

31. Robert A. Hart, "Democracy and the Successful Use of Economic Sanctions," *Political Research Quarterly*, Vol. 53, No. 2 (June 2000), p. 279.

32. To say that the coercive skills of terrorist groups are poor relative to those of states because these groups are considerably weaker is to concede the point that compelling policy change is a low-probability affair for terrorist groups.

33. Robert A. Dahl, *Who Governs? Democracy and Power in an American City* (New Haven, Conn.: Yale University Press, 1961); Theodore J. Lowi, "American Business, Public Policy, Case Studies, and Political Theory," *World Politics*, Vol. 16, No. 3 (July 1964), pp. 677–715; and Marvin Ott, "Mediation as a Method of Conflict Resolution, Two Cases," *International Organization*, Vol. 26, No. 4 (Autumn 1972), p. 613. The distinction between limited and maximalist issues is also expressed in terms of tangible versus intangible

issues, respectively. See John A. Vasquez, "The Tangibility of Issues and Global Conflict: A Test of Rosenau's Issue Area Typology," *Journal of Peace Research*, Vol. 20, No. 2 (Summer 1983), p. 179; and I. William Zartman, *Elusive Peace: Negotiating an End to Civil Conflicts* (Washington, D.C.: Brookings, 1995).

34. Kalevi J. Holsti, "Resolving International Conflicts: A Taxonomy of Behavior and Some Figures on Procedure," *Journal of Conflict Resolution*, Vol. 10, No. 3 (September 1966), p. 272; Robert Jervis, *Perception and Misperception in International Politics* (Princeton, N.J.: Princeton University Press, 1976), p. 101; and Daniel Druckman and Benjamin J. Broome, "Value Differences and Conflict Resolution: Facilitation or Delinking?" *Journal of Conflict Resolution*, Vol. 32, No. 3 (September 1988), p. 491.

35. Jacob J. Bercovitch, Theodore J. Anagnoson, and Donnette L. Willie, "Some Conceptual Issues and Empirical Trends in the Study of Successful Mediation in International Relations," *Journal of Peace Research*, Vol. 28, No. 1 (June 1991), pp. 7–17; Druckman and Broome, "Value Differences and Conflict Resolution," pp. 489–510; and Jacob J. Bercovitch and Jeffrey Langley, "The Nature of the Dispute and the Effectiveness of International Mediation," *Journal of Conflict Resolution*, Vol. 37, No. 4 (Autumn 1993), pp. 670–691.

36. Jacob J. Bercovitch and Karl DeRouen, "Managing Ethnic Civil Wars: Assessing the Determinants of Successful Mediation," *Civil Wars*, Vol. 7, No. 1 (Spring 2005), p. 100.

37. There is no suggestion that groups with limited objectives lack ideological convictions, only that the object of change is territorial possession, not the target country's ideology.

38. The al-Aqsa Martyrs Brigades is not in the sample because the State Department began listing it as an FTO after 2001.

39. U.S. Department of State, "Foreign Terrorist Organizations (FTOs)."

40. The terms "guerrilla warfare" and "insurgency" are often used interchangeably to denote an asymmetric campaign by subnational actors against a conventional army. I have opted against using the term "insurgency" because it also denotes a separatist struggle. The term "guerrilla group," by contrast, refers only to a subnational group's target selection. See "Guerrilla," *Encyclopedia of Terrorism* (London: Sage, 2003), p. 54; and Cathal J. Nolan, *The Greenwood Encyclopedia of International Relations* (Westport, Conn.: Greenwood, 2002), p. 669.

41. In Pape's research, for example, six of the thirteen terrorist campaigns are actually waged by guerrilla groups, which account for all of the terrorist victories in his sample. See Pape, *Dying to Win*, p. 40.

42. RAND, MIPT Terrorism Knowledge Base, http://www.tkb.org/Home.jsp.

43. Thomas C. Schelling makes a related point that coercion stands to work only when the coerced party understands the coercing party's demands. See Schelling, *Arms and Influence* (New Haven, Conn.: Yale University Press, 1966), p. 3. Several studies analyze how groups use terrorism to signal their capabilities and resolve. These studies tend to ignore the question of whether terrorism effectively conveys to the target government the terrorist group's policy objectives. See Harvey E. Lapan and Todd Sandler, "Terrorism and Signaling," *European Journal of Political Economy*, Vol. 9, No. 3 (August 1993), pp. 383–397; Per Baltzer Overgaard, "The Scale of Terrorist Attacks as a Signal of Resources," *Journal of Conflict Resolution*, Vol. 38, No. 3 (September 1994), pp. 452–478; and Hoffman and McCormick, "Terrorism, Signaling, and Suicide Attack," pp. 243–281.

44. Fritz Heider, *The Psychology of Interpersonal Relations* (New York: Wiley, 1958), p. 79.

45. Kathleen S. Crittenden, "Sociological Aspects of Attribution," *Annual Review of Sociology*, Vol. 9 (1983), p. 426.

46. Edward E. Jones and Daniel McGillis, "Correspondence Inferences and the Attribution Cube: A Comparative Reappraisal," in John H. Harvey, William J. Ickes, and Robert F. Kidd, ed., *New Directions in Attribution Research*, Vol. 1 (Hillsdale, N.J.: Erlbaum, 1976), pp. 389–420; and Edward E. Jones and Richard E. Nisbett, "The Actor and the Observer," in Jones, David E. Kanouse, Harold H. Kelley, Richard E. Nisbett, Stuart Valins, and Bernard Weiner, eds., *Attribution: Perceiving the Causes of Behavior* (Morristown, N.J.: General Learning Press, 1972), p. 87.

47. See "A Conversation with Edward E. Jones and Harold H. Kelley," in Harvey, Ickes, and Kidd, *New Directions in Attribution Research*, p. 378; and Edward E. Jones and Keith E. Davis, "From Acts to Dispositions: The Attribution Process in Person Perception," in Leonard Berkowitz, ed., *Advances in Experimental Social Psychology*, Vol. 2 (New York: Academic Press, 1965), p. 225.

48. Jones and Davis, "From Acts to Dispositions," p. 227.

49. Crittenden, "Sociological Aspects of Attribution," p. 427; and Jones and Davis, "From Acts to Dispositions," p. 263.

50. Jones and Davis, "From Acts to Dispositions," p. 264. Social psychologists stress two important points: first, that an observer believes an action has high correspondence does not mean the effect of the action actually reflects the actor's objectives (correspondent inferences can lead ob servers to assign mistaken objectives to the actor); and second, perceptions believed to be real have real consequences. Regardless of their accuracy, inferences of the actor's objectives influence the observer's attitude toward the actor. See Jones and McGillis, "Correspondence Inferences and the Attribution Cube," p. 417; and Harold H. Kelley and John L.Michela, "Attribution Theory and Research," *Annual Review of Psychology*, Vol. 31 (New York: Academic Press, 1980), p. 494.

51. "Bin Laden: 'Your Security Is in Your Own Hands,'" October 30, 2004 http://edition.cnn.com/2004/WORLD/meast/10/29/bin.laden.transcript.

52. See, for example, "Bin Laden Rails against Crusaders and UN," November 3, 2002, *BBC.com*, http://news.bbc.co.uk/1/hi/world/monitoring/media_reports/1636782.stm. Statement first broadcast on *Aljazeera.com*, November 3, 2002. See also "Bin Laden's Warning: Full Text," October 7, 2001, *BBC.com*, http://news.bbc.co.uk/1/hi/world/south_asia/1585636.stm. Statement first broadcast on *Aljazeera.com*, July 7, 2001.

53. *ABC News*, "Interview: Osama Bin Laden," May 1998, http://www.pbs.org/wgbh/pages/frontline/shows/binladen/who/interview.html; and Ayman Zawahiri, quoted in Bergen, *Holy War, Inc.*, p. 208. See also *Observer*, "Full Text: Bin Laden's 'Letter to America,'" November 24, 2002, http://observer.guardian.co.uk/worldview/story/0,11581,845725,00.html. The letter first appeared on the internet and was then circulated by supporters in Britain.

54. This statement is based on conclusions reported by the Center for Islamic Studies and Research in The Operation of 11 Rabi al-Awwal: *The East Riyadh Operation and Our War with the United States and Its Agents*, published in 2003. The book was translated by the Foreign Broadcast Information Service. For excerpts, see http://www.why-war.com/files/2004/01/qaeda_east_riyadh.html.

55. Middle East Media Research Institute, "Osama bin Laden Speech Offers Peace Treaty with Europe"; and World Islamic Front, "Jihad against the Jews and the Crusaders," February 23, 1998, http://www.fas.org/irp/world/para/ladin.htm.

56. Ronald Steel, "Blowback: Terrorism and the U.S. Role in the Middle East," *New Republic*, July 28, 1996, pp. 7–11.

57. Robert Fisk, "As My Grocer Said: Thank You Mr. Clinton for the Fine Words . . . ," *Independent* (London), August 22, 1998, p. 3.

58. See Anonymous, *Imperial Hubris*, p. 128.

59. George W. Bush, speech by the president to the Warsaw Conference, Warsaw, Poland, November 6, 2001.

60. George W. Bush, remarks by the president to the United Nations General Assembly, New York, November 10, 2001, http://www .usunnewyork.usmission.gov/01_162.htm.

61. Richard A. Clarke, *Against All Enemies: Inside America's War on Terror* (New York: Free Press, 2004), p. 17; and George W. Bush, presidential speech to the California Business Association, Sacramento, November 17, 2001.

62. Quoted in Clarke, *Against All Enemies*, p. 17; and George W. Bush, address by the president to a joint session of Congress, Washington, D.C., September 23, 2001.

63. George W. Bush, remarks by the president to the Dixie Printing Company, Glen Burnie, Maryland, October 24, 2001, http://www .globalsecurity.org/military/library/news/2001 /10/ mil-011024-usa03c.htm.

64. Pew Research Center, Roper Center, September 21, 2001. Seventy percent of Americans rejected the idea that "unfair" U.S. foreign policies contributed to the terrorist attacks.

65. IPSOS-REID, Roper Center, September 21, 2001.

66. Roper Center, Harris poll, September 19–24, 2001, http://www.pollingreport.com/terror9 .htm, October 20, 2005.

67. Quoted in Anonymous, *Imperial Hubris*, p. 153; and *Aljazeera.com*, "Bin Laden: 'Your Security Is in Your Own Hands.'"

68. Ronald Spiers, "Try Clearer Thinking About Terrorists," *International Herald Tribune*, January 14, 2003; Bergen, *Holy War, Inc.*, p. 223; and Gunaratna, *Inside Al Qaeda*, p. 45. See also Anonymous, *Imperial Hubris*, p. x.

69. Paul Wilkinson, "Security Challenges in the New Reality," lecture, Tufts University, Medford, Massachusetts, October 16, 2002.

70. For a detailed analysis of al-Qaida's effect on U.S. policies in the Muslim world, see Abrahms, "Al-Qaeda's Scorecard." In this study, al-Qaida is tagged with failures in three of the core policy objectives outlined in its 1998 declaration of war: ending U.S. support for Muslim "apostate" regimes, Israel, and what it derides as "Crusader wars," such as Operation Iraqi Freedom. Al-Qaida's policy effectiveness in the Persian Gulf is designated as a "limited success." Overall, the September 11 attacks did not reduce U.S. involvement in the Gulf. On the contrary, the attacks served as the critical impetus for the American public's decision to support the operation, which has led to the long-term occupation of Iraq and unprecedented U.S. military cooperation with the Gulf monarchy countries. The one modest success was the U.S. decision to draw down its troop presence in the Saudi Arabian Peninsula after September 11, 2001. Al-Qaida does not regard this policy outcome as noteworthy, for two reasons. First, the decision to withdraw hundreds of American troops from the Saudi desert after September 11 palls in comparison to the roughly 150,000 additional U.S. troops that were deployed to the same theater during this period. Second, U.S. interference in the political affairs of the Saudi kingdom increased markedly after the September 11 attacks, owing to the joint U.S.-Saudi interest in fighting the jihadists. I thank Michael Knights of *Jane's Intelligence Review* for offering his expertise in this area. For supporting analysis, see Chaim Kaufmann, "Threat Inflation and the Failure of the Marketplace of Ideas: The Selling of the Iraq War," *International Security*, Vol. 29, No. 1 (Summer 2004), p. 31; and Pape, *Dying to Win*, pp. 46, 84.

71. B'Tselem, "Fatalities in the First Intifada," http://www.btselem.org/english/statistics/ first_Intifada_Tables.asp.

72. See Bloom, *Dying to Kill*, p. 24; and Council on Foreign Relations, "Terrorism: Questions and Answers," October 31, 2005, http:// cfrterrorism.org/groups/pflp.html.

73. Edy Kaufman, "Israeli Perceptions of the Palestinians' 'Limited Violence' in the

Intifada," *Terrorism and Political Violence*, Vol. 3, No. 4 (Winter 1991), p. 4.

74. Gene Sharp, "The Intifada and Nonviolent Struggle," *Journal of Palestine Studies*, Vol. 19, No. 1 (Autumn 1989), p. 7.

75. Kaufman, "Israeli Perceptions of the Palestinians 'Limited Violence' in the Intifada," p. 4.

76. Louis Guttman Israel Institute of Applied Social Research, Jerusalem, "Public Assessment of the Activities and Violence of the Intifada," No. (s)IK1124/E&H (December 1990).

77. Kaufman, "Israeli Perceptions of the Palestinians 'Limited Violence' in the Intifada," p. 13.

78. *Jerusalem Post International Edition*, No. 1 (weekend ed., August 27, 1988), p. 451.

79. Avi Shlaim, "When Bush Comes to Shove: America and the Arab-Israeli Peace Process," *Oxford International Review*, Vol. 3, No. 2 (Spring 1992), p. 4.

80. Asher Arian, *Israeli Public Opinion on National Security, 2000* (Tel Aviv: Jaffee Center for Strategic Studies, 2000), p. 14.

81. Tami Steinmetz Center for Peace Research, Tel Aviv University, "Peace Index," http://www.tau.ac.il/peace. See also David Fielding and Madeline Penny, "What Causes Changes in Opinion about the Israeli-Palestinian Peace Process?" Economics Discussion Paper, No. 0601 (Dunedin, New Zealand: School of Business, University of Otago, March 2006), p. 8.

82. Schelling, "What Purposes Can 'International Terrorism' Serve?" p. 20.

83. See "Bush Urges Patience as Support for War Shrinks," *CNN.com*, October 30, 2005.

84. Since 2002, public support for terrorism has dropped by 64 percent in Pakistan, 80 percent in Indonesia, 87 percent in Lebanon, and 200 percent in Morocco. Pew Global Attitudes Project, "Support for Terror Wanes among Muslim Publics," July 14, 2005, pp. 2, 6, http://www.pewglobal.org.reports/pdf/248.pdf.

85. Fareed Zakaria, "How We Can Prevail," *Newsweek*, July 18, 2005, p. 38.

86. See, for example, George W. Bush, "National Security Strategy of the United States of America" (Washington, D.C.: White House, September 17, 2002), http://www.whitehouse.gov/nsc/nss.html.

87. Bin Laden, for example, has frequently said that terrorism works, especially against the United States, such as when it withdrew from Lebanon following the 1983 U.S. Marine barracks bombing and from Somalia in 1993 after the deaths of the eighteen U.S. Army Rangers. See Bruce Hoffman, "Rethinking Terrorism and Counterterrorism since 9/11," *Studies in Conflict and Terrorism*, Vol. 25, No. 5 (September 2002), p. 310.

88. See A. Petrova, "Approval for Russian Military Actions in Chechnya Is Steadily Declining," Public Opinion Foundation Database, September 5, 2002, http://bd.english.fom.ru/report/cat/societas/Chechnya/truck_war/eof023305; and Susan Page, "Poll: American Attitudes on Iraq Similar to Vietnam Era," *USA Today*, December 15, 2005.

MICHAEL L. ROSS

OIL, DRUGS, AND DIAMONDS: THE VARYING ROLES OF NATURAL RESOURCES IN CIVIL WAR

According to several recent studies, when states rely more heavily on the export of natural resources, they are more likely to suffer from civil war. But are all types of commercially valuable natural resources—including oil, hard-rock minerals, gemstones, timber, agricultural commodities, and illegal drugs—equally likely to lead to civil war? Do different types of resources have different effects on conflict?

This chapter is a modest effort to describe how different types of resources have influenced recent conflicts, as well as to develop hypotheses that can be tested in future studies. It begins by showing that of all major types of natural resources, diamonds and drugs are most strongly associated with the civil wars that occurred between 1990 and 2000. The second section offers seven hypotheses about how three characteristics of natural resources—their lootability, their obstructability, and their legality—are likely to influence civil wars. The hypotheses are illustrated by evidence from fifteen recent conflicts in which natural resources played some role (documented in Table 1). The chapter concludes with a discussion of the implications of these hypotheses for different types of natural resources.

This chapter advances four main arguments. First, resources have sharply different effects in separatist conflicts compared to nonseparatist conflicts. Second, the impact of a particular resource largely depends on whether or not it is "lootable"—that is, whether it can be easily appropriated by individuals or small groups of unskilled workers. Third, lootable resources—such

From Karen Ballentine and Jake Sherman, eds. *The Political Economy of Armed Conflict: Beyond Greed and Grievance* (Boulder, CO: Lynne Rienner, 2003), 47–70. Some of the author's notes have been omitted.

as diamonds and drugs—are more likely to ignite nonseparatist conflicts, which once begun are harder to resolve; but they pose little danger of igniting separatist conflicts. Finally, unlootable resources—like oil, natural gas, and deep-shaft minerals—tend to produce separatist conflicts, but seldom influence nonseparatist conflicts. In sum, lootable resources negatively affect nonseparatist conflicts, and unlootable resources negatively affect separatist conflicts.

This chapter illustrates but does not test these arguments, and the hypotheses that undergird them. The hypotheses were derived from the fifteen case studies. To determine whether they are valid beyond these scenarios—and hence have predictive and not just descriptive value—they should be tested with a different data set.

Civil Wars among Resource-Rich States

There is good evidence that resources and civil wars are causally linked.[1] Several studies have found a strong statistical correlation between a state's reliance on the export of natural resources, and either the likelihood it will suffer from civil war,[2] or alternatively, the duration of a civil war once commenced.[3]

There is also good evidence at the case-study level that natural resources have contributed to the onset, duration, and intensity of many civil wars. An earlier study by Michael Ross, drawing on case studies of thirteen conflicts between 1994 and 2000, confirms this conclusion, and also finds that natural resources tend to influence separatist conflicts differently than they influence nonseparatist conflicts, further distinguished by the lootability of a resource.[4] But are all natural resources equally at fault? Are some types of resources more likely than others to generate, or lengthen, civil conflict?

One way to address these questions is to observe a sample of civil wars in which resources played some role, and take note of what types of resources were involved. Table 1 summarizes information about twelve civil wars, plus three low-level conflicts, that occurred between 1994 and 2001 and have been causally linked to the exploitation of natural resources in case studies.[5] The resources most frequently linked to civil conflict are diamonds and other gemstones (seven conflicts, all of them civil wars); oil and natural gas (seven conflicts, six of them civil wars); illicit drugs (five conflicts, all of them civil wars); copper or gold (four conflicts, two of them civil wars); and timber (three conflicts, all of them civil

wars). Legal agricultural crops played a role in two conflicts (both civil wars), although in each case other natural resources played larger roles.

While this type of analysis has some value, it is unsatisfying in at least two ways. First, some types of natural resources are more common than others; this alone might explain why there are more civil wars in states that produce oil (which is a relatively common resource) than in states that produce copper (which is a less common resource). What we would like to know is whether civil wars occur at anomalously high rates among the producers of a given commodity. For example, do civil wars occur more frequently among oil producers than among nonproducers, more frequently among copper producers than among nonproducers? Second, there may be subtle causal links between civil wars and natural resources that are difficult to observe in case

Table 1. Civil Conflicts Linked to Resource Wealth, 1994–2001

	Duration	Type	Resources
Afghanistan	1978–2001	Lootable	Gems, opium
Angola (UNITA)	1975–	Both	Oil, diamonds
Angola (Cabinda)[a]	1975–	Unlootable	Oil
Burma	1949–	Lootable	Timber, gems, opium
Cambodia	1978–1997	Lootable	Timber, gems
Colombia	1984–	Both	Oil, opium, coca
Congo Republic	1997	Unlootable	Oil
Democratic Republic of Congo	1996–1998	Both	Copper, coltan, diamonds, gold, cobalt, coffee
Indonesia (Aceh)	1975–	Unlootable	Natural gas
Indonesia (West Papua)[a]	1969–	Unlootable	Copper, gold
Liberia	1989–1996	Lootable[b]	Timber, diamonds, iron, palm oil, cocoa, coffee, marijuana, rubber, gold
Papua New Guinea[a]	1988–	Unlootable	Copper, gold
Peru	1980–1995	Lootable	Coca
Sierra Leone	1991–2000	Lootable	Diamonds
Sudan	1983–	Unlootable	Oil

Source: Figures on conflict duration taken from Paul Collier and Anke Hoeffler, "Greed and Grievance in Civil War," Policy Research Working Paper no. 2355 (Washington, D.C.: World Bank, 2001).

Notes: Italic denotes separatist conflict.

[a]Conflict did not generate 1,000 battle deaths in any twelve-month period.

[b]Since the resources in Liberia's conflict were overwhelmingly lootable, I classify it as "lootable" rather than "both."

studies; for this reason some conflicts may have been wrongly excluded from Table 1.

One simple way to address these problems is to observe whether civil wars occur at different rates among states that are highly dependent, moderately dependent, or minimally dependent on the export or production of a given resource. If civil wars occur at above-average rates among states that are highly dependent on a given resource, it would imply that the resource is tied to the occurrence of conflict.[6]

Table 2 shows a simple tabulation of civil war rates between 1990 and 2000, by level of resource dependence. Resources are divided into four categories, as used by the World Bank: oil, gas, and other fuel-based minerals; nonfuel minerals, excluding gemstones; food-based agricultural exports; and nonfood agricultural exports, including timber but excluding illegal drugs.[7] The cross-tabulations show the civil war rates among countries that ranked in the top, middle, or bottom third of all states in the ratio of re-

source exports to gross domestic product (GDP) in the midpoint year of 1995.[8] Between 1990 and 2000, 32 out of 161 countries surveyed had civil wars; this means that for any random country, there is an approximately 20 percent chance that it suffered a civil war at some point in the 1990s.[9] As Table 2 shows, civil wars occurred at slightly lower rates among states that were highly dependent on resource exports in all four categories.[10]

One reason why there is no obvious correlation in this table between resource dependence and civil war rates is that other factors—most important, income per capita—are not controlled for. A second reason is that these standard four categories exclude (or in the case of timber, fail to isolate) several types of resources that have been most visibly linked to conflict in the media: diamonds, timber, and illicit drugs. To address the first shortcoming, Table 3 adjusts the figures in Table 2 by dividing the ratio of resource exports to GDP by each country's income per

Table 2. Civil War Rates 1990–2000, by 1995 Ratios of Resource Exports to GDP

	Oil and Gas	Minerals[a]	Food Crops	Nonfood Crops
Top Third	.146	.122	.133	.100
Middle Third	.208	.146	.166	.100
Bottom Third	.188	.195	.133	.233

Sources: For civil war occurrences, Paul Collier and Anke Hoeffler, "Greed and Grievance in Civil War," Policy Research Working Paper no. 2355 (Washington, D.C.: World Bank, 2001). All other data taken from World Bank, *World Development Indicators 2001* (Washington, D.C.: World Bank, 2001), CD-ROM.

Note:[a] Nonfuel minerals, not including gemstones.

Table 3. Civil War Rates 1990–2000, Adjusted for GDP per Capita

	Oil and Gas	Minerals[a]	Food Crops	Nonfood Crops
Top Third	.207	.172	.241	.207
Middle Third	.166	.133	.166	.166
Bottom Third	.100	.138	.033	.067

Sources: For civil war occurrences, Paul Collier and Anke Hoeffler, "Greed and Grievance in Civil War," Policy Research Working Paper no. 2355 (Washington, D.C.: World Bank, 2001). All other data taken from World Bank, *World Development Indicators 2001* (Washington, D.C.: World Bank, 2001), CD-ROM.

Note:[a]Nonfuel minerals, not including gemstones.

capita, producing a figure that simultaneously re- flects both resource dependence and per capita wealth. In this table, resource-dependent coun- tries are at a notably higher risk of civil war. There is no obvious difference among types of re- source dependence, as all seem to make conflicts more likely once per capita income has been ac- counted for.[11]

Tables 4, 5, and 6 address the second short- coming. Table 4 shows the civil war rates among timber-producing states, measured in four differ- ent ways—each representing an effort to deter- mine whether timber production or export is in some way correlated with the incidence of con- flict. The first column of numbers divides states by the quantity of commercial timber (i.e., industrial roundwood) they produced from both natural forests and plantations in 1995. Thus these data may suggest whether conflict became more likely when more commercial timber was harvested. Of

course, other things influence the amount of tim- ber produced, such as the size of the country: the United States and Russia cut more timber than Gabon or Honduras, but this reflects in part their greater size. Hence the second column, timber per capita, divides states by the volume of timber they produced per capita. Once again, states that are more timber-intensive do not seem to face a higher risk of civil war; in fact, they appear to face a lower risk.

Perhaps, however, civil war becomes more likely as states grow more dependent on the ex- port of unprocessed timber. The third column in Table 4 divides states by the value of their unpro- cessed timber exports as a ratio of their GDP— making these data comparable to the figures in Table 2.[12] As in Table 2, there is no obvious corre- lation between a country's reliance on the com- modity and the likelihood that it suffered a civil war in the 1990s. Finally, the fourth column

Table 4. Civil War Rates 1990–2000, by 1995 Timber Production and Exports

	Timber Production	Timber per capita	Timber Exports per GDP	Adjusted for GDP per capita
Top Third	.116	.047	.111	.194
Middle Third	.250	.273	.243	.189
Bottom Third	.250	.318	.270	.243

Sources: For civil war occurrences, Paul Collier and Anke Hoeffler, "Greed and Grievance in Civil War," Policy Re- search Working Paper no. 2355 (Washington, D.C.: World Bank, 2001). For timber production and export figures, Food and Agriculture Administration Statistics Database (FAOSTAT), http://apps.fao.org/. For GDP figures (mea- sured in purchasing power parity), World Bank, World Development Indicators 2001 (Washington, D.C.: World Bank, 2001), CD-ROM.

Table 5. Civil War Rates 1990–2000, by 1995 Diamond and Drug Production

	Diamonds	Alluvial Diamonds	Opium and Coca
Producers	.278 (5/18)	.500 (4/8)	.444 (4/9)
Nonproducers	.188 (27/143)	.183 (28/153)	.184 (28/152)

Sources: For civil war occurrences, Paul Collier and Anke Hoeffler, "Greed and Grievance in Civil War," Policy Re- search Working Paper no. 2355 (Washington, D.C.: World Bank, 2001). For diamond production, Ronald F. Balazik, "Industrial Diamonds" (Washington D.C.: U.S. Geological Survey, 1998). For opium and coca production, UN Office for Drug Control and Crime Prevention, "World Drug Report, 2000" (New York: Oxford University Press, 2000).

Table 6. Civil War Rates 1990–2000, by Cannabis Production

Primary Source Countries	.300 (3/10)
Secondary Source Countries	.132 (9/68)
All Other Countries	.241 (20/83)

Sources: For civil war occurrences, Paul Collier and Anke Hoeffler, "Greed and Grievance in Civil War," Policy Research Working Paper no. 2355 (Washington, DC: World Bank, 2001). For cannabis production, UN Office for Drug Control and Crime Prevention, "World Drug Report, 2000" (New York: Oxford University Press, 2000).

adjusts the figures in the third column by dividing them by GDP per capita, to account for the influence of income on civil war. Even here, however, there is no evidence to suggest that greater timber dependence is associated with higher rates of conflict. This appears to contradict accounts like those of Michael Klare, who suggests that timber production or export is linked to civil conflict.[13]

Table 5 shows civil war rates by production of three other commodities that are commonly faulted for "fueling" civil wars: diamonds, coca, and opium. The first column lists the civil war rates among diamond producers and nonproducers, with the second column distinguishing the production of alluvial diamonds—that is, diamonds that can be extracted from riverbeds and alluvial plains, typically at a minimal cost. Although the numbers are small, the civil war rate among diamond producers (five wars in eighteen states) is anomalously high—and among the producers of alluvial diamonds (four wars in eight states), it is exceptionally high.

The third column of Table 5 compares the civil war rates among coca and opium producers with rates among nonproducers.[14] I combine opium and coca producers for several reasons: they are an overlapping group of countries; the production of these drugs is highly similar in land use, transportability, and value per weight; and it is easier to make inferences about larger categories of states than about smaller categories. The civil war rate is much higher among the drug-producing states than among nonproducers.

Finally, Table 6 records the civil war rates among states that, according to Interpol, were primary producers, secondary producers, or nonproducers of cannabis—a drug that is more widely grown, is less penalized against, and has a much lower value-to-weight ratio than coca or opium products.[15] Although the civil war rate is higher among primary producers than among secondary producers, this finding appears somewhat fragile statistically, because nonproducers have a higher civil war rate than secondary producers, and because dropping just a single civil war from the category of primary producers would no longer create an anomalously high rate.

The analysis in this section is exceedingly simple in statistical terms, and has several important limitations: it only considers civil wars that occurred in the 1990s, not before; it is purely cross-sectional, and does not include a time-series dimension; it does not properly control for other factors that influence civil war rates; it compares civil war rates among the top, middle, and bottom thirds of countries rather than examining the continuous effect of resource dependence on civil war risks; and it compares decade-long civil war rates to levels of resource dependence in 1995, the year for which the greatest quantity of data are available.

Despite these limitations, the data suggest three things. First, there is no obvious difference in the civil war rates among states dependent on the four general categories of natural resources. Second, higher rates of timber production and export do not appear to be linked to higher rates of civil wars. Finally, there is a strong association between civil war and both the production of diamonds—especially alluvial diamonds—and the production of drugs, especially coca and opium. What accounts for this pattern?

Few prior studies have addressed this question. An important exception is Philippe Le Billon, who makes two key distinctions: between those that are proximate to a national capital (and hence easier for governments to capture) and those that are distant (and hence easier for rebels to hold); and between "point-source" resources, which are concentrated in a small area (and therefore more easily controlled by a single group), and diffuse resources, which are scattered over a larger area (and hence harder for any single group to capture).[16] These two categories, Le Billon suggests, yield a fourfold typology of conflict: point-source resources near the capital create violent incentives to control the state, and hence produce coups d'état; point-source resources far from the capital produce secession movements; diffuse resources near the capital lead to rebellions and rioting; and diffuse resources far from the capital lead to "warlordism," areas of de facto sovereignty with economies built around the resource itself. The Le Billon study provides an important precedent for the analysis below.

Seven Hypotheses on Resources and Conflict

This section develops seven hypotheses about the ways that natural resources tend to influence civil wars. It suggests that the role played by any natural resource depends largely on its lootability, and to a lesser extent on its obstructability and its legality.

A resource's lootability is the ease with which it can be extracted and transported by individuals or small teams of unskilled workers.[17] Drugs, alluvial gemstones, agricultural products, and timber are relatively lootable; deep-shaft minerals and gemstones, oil, and natural gas are relatively unlootable.

A resource is obstructable if its transportation can be easily blocked by a small number of individuals with few weapons; it is relatively unobstructable if it can only be blocked with many soldiers and heavy equipment. A resource's obstructability is in part a function of its physical characteristics. Resources that have a high value-to-weight ratio, such as gemstones, coca, and opium, are usually transported by air and are difficult to obstruct, since they can be flown out of remote areas. Resources with a lower value-to-weight ratio that must be transported by truck or train—like minerals and timber—are moderately obstructable, if they must cross long distances. Resources that are transported in liquid form and travel long distances through above-ground pipelines (e.g., oil and natural gas) are highly obstructable, since pipelines are continuously vulnerable to disruption along their entire length. A resource's location also helps determine its obstructability: if an oil field is in a remote, land-locked location, it is highly obstructable; if it is located near a port or offshore, it is relatively unobstructable.

Finally, most resources can be legally traded on international markets; drugs—coca, opium, cannabis, and their derivatives—are the main types of illegal natural resources.[18] Figure 8.4

	Lootable	Unlootable
Highly Obstructable	—	Onshore, remote oil and gas
Moderately Obstructable	Agricultural products Timber	Deep-shaft minerals
Unobstructable	**Coca** **Opium** Alluvial gems	Deep-shaft gems Offshore oil and gas

Note: **Bold** denotes illegal resources.

Figure 8.4. Natural Resources, by Lootability, Obstructability, and Legality

categorizes most types of resources according to these criteria, which yield seven hypotheses about the social and political consequences of resource extraction, summarized in Table 7.

Hypothesis 1: The more lootable a resource is, the more likely it is to benefit local peoples and the poor.

This first hypothesis does not directly address the issues of conflict, but it provides the basis for the other hypotheses that do. The extraction of highly lootable resources relies more heavily on the use of unskilled labour; the extraction of unlootable resources relies more heavily on skilled labor and capital. Hence lootable resources are more likely to generate income for local communities, and for unskilled workers—for example, the poor. Unlootable resources are more likely to produce revenues for skilled workers, for those who provide the requisite capital, and for the government. In developing countries, where skilled labor and capital tend to be scarce, these factors are more likely to come from outside the region—possibly from other countries.

If true, this hypothesis implies that the extraction of lootable resources such as alluvial gems, drugs, timber, and agricultural products is more likely to have a popular local constituency than is the extraction of unlootable resources such as oil, gas, and deep-shaft minerals. This also means that efforts to stop the flow of lootable

resources are more likely to face opposition from local communities, and to harm low- and moderate-income sectors of the economy.

Hypothesis 2: The more unlootable a resource is, the more likely it will lead to separatist conflicts.

This hypothesis follows directly from the previous one. If a resource is highly lootable, it is more likely to generate direct benefits for the poor, and to benefit local peoples; if it is relatively unlootable, it is more likely to generate revenues for skilled workers (who are less likely to originate from the region), the extraction firm, and the government—and hence to produce grievances about the distribution of resource wealth. This has important consequences for separatist conflicts, which in resource-rich areas are commonly incited by grievances over the distribution of resource revenue.

Figure 8.5 divides the six separatist conflicts from Table 1 into those involving lootable resources and those involving unlootable resources. The nine nonseparatist conflicts from Table 1 are similarly divided for comparison. Of the six separatist conflicts, five feature unlootable resources: the Cabinda conflict in Angola (over oil); the Aceh conflict (over natural gas) and the West Papua (Irian Jaya) conflict in Indonesia (over copper and gold); the Bougainville conflict in Papua New Guinea (over copper); and the conflict in Sudan

Table 7. Hypotheses on Resources and Civil War

1. The more lootable a resource is, the more likely it is to benefit local peoples and the poor.
2. The more unlootable a resource is, the more likely it will lead to separatist conflicts.
3. The more lootable a resource is, the more likely it is to benefit a rebel group; the more unlootable it is, the more likely it is to benefit the government.
4. The more lootable the resource, the more likely it is to create discipline problems inside the army that controls it.
5. The more lootable the resource, the more likely it is to prolong nonseparatist conflicts.
6. If a resource is obstructable, it is more likely to increase the duration and intensity of conflicts.
7. If the resource is illegal, it is more likely to benefit the rebels—unless the government is willing to endure international sanctions.

(over oil). In each of these five cases, grievances over the distribution of resource wealth have helped spark or exacerbate the conflict. Just one separatist conflict features lootable resources: Burma, where rebel groups have used opium and gemstones to fund themselves, but the production of those goods has not in itself caused separatist grievances.

Hypothesis 3: The more lootable a resource is, the more likely it is to benefit a rebel group; the more unlootable it is, the more likely it is to benefit the government.

If a resource is highly lootable, whichever party controls the surrounding territory can use it for funding. But if it is unlootable, it is more likely to benefit the government, since the government is more able to credibly provide the security guarantees necessary to attract and maintain the requisite skilled labor and capital. Both sides in a conflict can benefit from controlling an area that produces alluvial diamonds or drugs, but only the government is likely to benefit from controlling an area that produces oil or copper.

Skeptics may point out that a rebel army still profits from gaining control of an unlootable resource, since this action will deny resource revenues to the government. This is true, but an unlootable resource will still be of less value to the rebels than a lootable resource. Imagine that a rebel army captures from the government an unlootable resource. The net change in the government's revenue from this event is the amount of annual revenue lost in exploiting this resource, plus the amount of annual revenue gained by the rebels, which is zero since they cannot extract the resource. Now imagine that the rebel army captures a lootable resource from the government, which produces the same revenue as the unlootable resource above. In this case, the loss to the government's revenue is doubled, since the rebels can now exploit the resource. Hence lootable resources should be more valuable than unlootable resources to the rebels; unlootable resources should be more valuable than lootable resources to the government.

Figure 8.6 shows that the cases in Table 1 are consistent with this pattern.[19] In all ten conflicts over lootable resources, resource revenues flowed to either the rebels exclusively, or to both sides.

	Separatist	Nonseparatist
Lootable	Burma	Afghanistan Angola (UNITA)[a] Cambodia Colombia[a] DRC[a] Liberia Peru Sierra Leone
Unlootable	Angola (Cabinda) Indonesia (Aceh) Idonesia (West Papua) Papua New Guinea Sudan	Angola (UNITA)[a] Colombia[a] Congo Republic DRC[a]

[a]Conflict entails both lootable and unlootable resources.

Figure 8.5. Lootability and Separatism

	Rebels	Government	Both Sides
Lootable	Afghanistan (gems) Cambodia Liberia Peru DRC[a]	—	Afghanistan (opium) Angola (gems) Burma Colombia (drugs) Sierra Leone DRC
Unlootable	—	Angola (oil) Angola-Cabinda Indonesia-Aceh Indonesia-W. Papua	Colombia (oil) Congo Republic Sudan DRC[b]

[a]Including coltan, gold, coffee, and timber.
[b]Including cobalt and kimberlite diamonds.

Figure 8.6. Which Side Earns Revenues from Resource Wealth?

In the eight cases with unlootable resources, revenues went exclusively to the government in four cases, to both sides in four cases, and to the rebels exclusively in none. Of the four conflicts in which unlootable resources produced revenues for both sides, in two cases (Colombia and Sudan) it was because long oil pipelines made the resource obstructable, and hence susceptible to holdups (see Hypothesis 6).

It is also notable that in the three conflicts with both lootable and unlootable resources—Angola (UNITA), Colombia, and the Democratic Republic of Congo—in two cases (Angola and the Democratic Republic of Congo), the government has continuously controlled the unlootable resources, while the rebels have periodically controlled the lootable resources. In the third case (Colombia), the leftist guerrillas as well as the right-wing paramilitaries have raised money from both resources.

Hypothesis 4: The more lootable the resource, the more likely it is to create discipline problems inside the army that controls it.

If a resource is unlootable—such as oil or natural gas—then it will most likely help fund the military of the side that controls it through a centralized process. Unlootable resources must be managed by large firms or state-owned enterprises, which will generate revenues for the government; these in turn will be appropriated to military forces through some type of budgetary mechanism. This centralized process should help give commanding officers fiscal tools to help them maintain control over lower-ranking officers and soldiers.

If a resource is lootable, however, it is less likely to generate funds for the government. It also creates opportunities for soldiers of all ranks to earn money by extracting or transporting the resources themselves, or extorting money from others who do.[20] The result is likely to be a reduced level of discipline and central control in the armed forces of the party that controls the resource.

There is only sporadic data on discipline problems within government and rebel forces. It is noteworthy, however, that of the fifteen cases in this sample, there were five cases in which a breakdown of military cohesion was so severe that some units defected to the other side, or did battle with each other. Four cases involved lootable resources: Cambodia (among the rebels), the Democratic Republic of Congo (among the rebels), Liberia (among the rebels), and Sierra Leone (on the government side). The fifth case, Sudan (among the rebels), involved oil, an obstructable resource.

Hypothesis 5: The more lootable the resource, the more likely it is to prolong nonseparatist conflicts.

There are three rationales behind this hypothesis. The first is based on Hypothesis 3. When resource revenue flows to the rebels, it is likely to prolong a conflict, since the rebels are typically the weaker party, and without this funding they are more likely to be forced to the negotiating table or extinguished. Conversely, if resource revenue accrues to the government, it is likely to shorten a conflict by bringing about a quicker victory or settlement—provided that the government is the stronger party.[21] If both parties carry out resource looting, the net effect should be to lengthen the conflict, since combat is likely to continue as long as the weaker party does not run out of money. Hence unlootable resources are more likely to shorten a war, by strengthening the stronger side; lootable resources are more likely to lengthen a war, by strengthening the weaker side, or both sides. The second rationale is based on Hypothesis 4. Discipline problems— which should be more strongly associated with lootable resources—are also likely to lengthen

conflicts by making it harder for commanding officers to impose the terms of a settlement on their own forces.[22] There is also a third possibility: that wartime resource exploitation will become so profitable for rebels that they prefer war to peace. Again, this is more likely if resources are lootable—and hence can generate profits for rebels—than if they are unlootable.

This hypothesis only applies to nonseparatist conflicts. As James Fearon points out, separatist and nonseparatist conflicts appear to have substantially different characteristics: separatist conflicts tend to last longer, and often continue even when the separatist movement is at an overwhelming financial, disadvantage.[23] This may be because separatist movements can often sustain themselves indefinitely in a territory dominated by members of their own ethnic group, where government forces are considered alien.

This is a difficult hypothesis to investigate empirically, in part because so many of the conflicts in this sample are ongoing—meaning that we do not know much about their ultimate duration. One way to examine the hypothesis is to put this problem aside and compare the duration of nonseparatist conflicts over lootable resources to those over unlootable resources. Table 8 shows this comparison. The only nonseparatist conflict with unlootable resources—the 1997 war in the Congo Republic, which lasted just four months— is also the briefest conflict.

Table 8. Duration of Nonseparatist Conflicts

	Type	Period	Duration (years)
Afghanistan	Lootable	1978–2001	23
Cambodia	Lootable	1978–1997	19
Peru	Lootable	1980–1995	15
Sierra Leone	Lootable	1991–2000	9
Liberia	Lootable	1989–1996	7
Angola (UNITA)	Both	1975–	26+
Colombia	Both	1984–	17+
Democratic Republic of Congo	Both	1996–	5+
Congo Republic	Unlootable	1997	<1

This hypothesis can also be examined indirectly by determining whether any of these three causal processes—resource exploitation by the weaker side, discipline problems that impede a settlement, and resource profiteering that impedes a settlement—have occurred in the fifteen cases. While this will not tell us if these conflicts have actually been lengthened by resources, it can tell us if any of the three processes, which I argue are likely to lengthen the conflicts, have occurred.

Table 9 codes the fifteen conflicts according to whether or not the three processes have occurred. Since three conflicts include both lootable and unlootable resources, these conflicts are each listed twice, and the effects of each type of resource are coded independently. I included both the separatist and nonseparatist conflicts in this table to provide additional data on the incidence of these three processes, even though the hypothesis only applies to nonseparatist conflicts.

Table 9 shows that resource revenues went to the weak side in nine out of nine conflicts over lootable resources, but in only five of nine conflicts over unlootable resources. In two of these five cases (Angola and the Democratic Republic of Congo), the unlootable resource still benefited the government (Hypothesis 3), but at junctures when the government was the weaker party. In

Table 9. Resources and Duration of Conflict

	Weak Fund	Discipline	Incentive
Lootable Resources			
Afghanistan (opium, gems)	Yes	No	No
Angola-UNITA (gems)	Yes	No	No
Burma (gems, opium)	Yes	No	Yes[a]
Cambodia (gems, timber)	Yes	Yes[a]	No
Colombia (coca)	Yes	Yes	No
Democratic Republic of Congo (gems, coltan, gold)	Yes	Yes	Yes
Liberia (gems, etc.)	Yes	Yes	Yes
Peru (coca)	Yes	No	No
Sierra Leone (gems)	Yes	Yes	No
Unlootable Resources			
Angola-UNITA (oil)	Yes	No	No
Angola-Cabinda (oil)	No	No	No
Colombia (oil)	Yes	No	No
Congo Republic (oil)	Yes	No	Yes[a]
Democratic Republic of Congo (cobalt, copper)	Yes	No	Yes
Indonesia-Aceh (gas)	No	No	No
Indonesia-W. Papua (copper)	No	No	No
Papua New Guinea (copper)	No	No	No
Sudan (oil)	Yes	No	No

Notes: *Italic* denotes separatist conflicts. The conflicts are coded "yes" for weak fund if the weaker side received revenues from the extraction, transport, or sale of resources, and "no" otherwise; "yes" for discipline if the presence of resources created substantial discipline problems within the military force that controlled it, and "no" otherwise; and "yes" for incentive if the resource created an economic incentive for one side or the other that undermined a proposed peace agreement. Note that in two cases, Burma and the Congo Republic, the resource appeared to create an economic incentive in favor of a peace settlement; and in the case of Cambodia, the discipline problems created by the resources led to a quicker end to the conflict.

[a] Made the conflict shorter.

two other cases (Colombia and Sudan), the weak side profited from an unlootable resource (oil) due to its obstructability.

Major discipline problems were observed in five of the nine conflicts over lootable resources, but in none of the conflicts over unlootable resources.[24] The evidence is somewhat harder to interpret regarding the third process. Resources appeared to create an economic incentive that undermined peace treaties in Liberia and the Democratic Republic of Congo.[25] In the former case, the resources were lootable; in the latter, they were both lootable and unlootable. In two other cases, Burma and the Congo Republic, resource wealth appeared to create incentives that hastened a settlement.[26] It is difficult to draw any general conclusions about this final dynamic.

In short, there is indirect evidence that both lootable and unlootable resources may trigger at least two processes that prolong conflicts, and that—as Hypothesis 5 suggests—lootable resources tend to trigger these processes more frequently than unlootable resources.

Hypothesis 6: If a resource is obstructable, it is more likely to increase the duration and intensity of conflicts.

There are two reasons why this may be so. First, obstructable resources are subject to holdups, a tactic that benefits a weaker party in its campaign against a stronger opponent, and hence will tend to lengthen a conflict. The most easily obstructed resource, oil, has been a factor in five of the fifteen conflicts in the sample. In three cases the oil has been offshore and hence impervious to holdups (Angola-Cabinda, Angola-UNITA, and the Congo Republic); but in the other two cases (Colombia and Sudan), rebels have bombed pipelines to extort money from the government or oil firms, and to disrupt the government's revenues.[27]

In Colombia, for example, the country's oil must be transported to the coast from the unstable interior through two exceptionally long pipelines.[28] In 2000 the pipelines were bombed

ninety-eight times. Colombia's rebel groups have used these attacks to extort an estimated U.S. $140 million annually; this windfall has enabled one group, the National Liberation Army (ELN), to grow from fewer than 40 members to at least 3,000.[29]

Obstructable resources can also have a second effect: a government may anticipate that its resources will be subject to holdups by aggrieved local peoples, and decide to act preemptively by using terror and repression against them. Here we might not witness a full-blown civil war—if the repression is "successful" in the government's eyes—but nonetheless have a large number of resource-related casualties. Such preemptive campaigns have occurred in the Indonesian province of Aceh, where a natural gas facility was threatened by a proseparatist movement; and even more lethally in Sudan.

Sudan has witnessed both holdups by the rebel group and preemptive repression by the government. Sudan's oil reserves are located in the country's south, a region with long-standing separatist aspirations. The north's efforts to gain access to the south's oil have been a major source of grievance, which has been evident in both the rhetoric and the actions of the Sudan People's Liberation Army (SPLA): it has issued complaints that the north is stealing the south's resources, and between 1983 and 1999 it repeatedly demanded that work cease on a pipeline that would take oil from wells in the south to a refinery in the north. It also periodically attacked the workers and equipment associated with pipeline construction. These attacks helped the SPLA to fund itself by extorting money from Western oil firms that wished to protect their equipment.[30]

To counter the rebels, the government has tried to forcibly create a cordon sanitaire around the pipeline, and to clear whole populations from the oil fields. Clearances in the upper Nile region began in 1980, halted in the mid-1980s when oil development temporarily ceased, then commenced anew in the late 1990s when oil development resumed. Since early 1999 the government has used summary executions, rape, ground attacks, helicopter gunships, and high-altitude bombing to force tens of thousands of people from their homes in the oil regions. It has also razed houses, destroyed crops, and looted livestock to prevent people from returning. Although foreign observers have often been prevented from entering the affected areas, the pattern of displacements has been documented by both a special rapporteur for the UN Commission on Human Rights and several nongovernmental organizations.

Hypothesis 7: If the resource is illegal, it is more likely to benefit the rebels—unless the government is willing to endure international sanctions.

There are strong international sanctions against the production of illegal natural resources—for example, coca, opium, and cannabis; these sanctions are more effective against states than against nonstate entities, like rebel movements. If illegal substances are cultivated in a country suffering a civil war, it will be hard for the government's forces to profit from their presence, since they are likely to be subjected to international sanctions; a rebel group should be less responsive to international sanctions and hence should be more likely to seek funding from drug sales. This should not hold true, however, for governments that are willing to endure international sanctions, and pursue autarkic economic policies.

There are just four drug-producing states in the sample, which makes it difficult to know if this is a valid generalization. Table 10 lists these states, along with the side that benefited from the drug trade. In one case (Peru), only the rebels systematically raised money from the drug trade. In the other cases, both sides earned money from drugs—in two cases (Afghanistan and Burma) because the government was willing to endure international sanctions, and in the third case (Colombia) because drug revenues were collected by paramilitary forces, which were allied with the government but sufficiently independent from it (at least nominally) to allow the government to avoid international sanctions.

Table 10. Which Side Profits from Illegal Drugs?

	Substance	Beneficiary
Afghanistan	Opium	Both
Burma	Opium	Both
Colombia	Coca, opium	Both
Peru	Coca	Rebels

Implications and Conclusions

The aim of this chapter is to help determine whether some types of natural resources are more closely tied to civil wars than others, and if so, why. The first section, using simple cross-tabulations, showed that alluvial diamonds and illegal drugs appear to be more strongly linked to civil war than other resources; that timber is not associated with civil war; and that other categories of natural resources are about equally tied to civil wars. The second section used evidence from fifteen recent civil wars to develop hypotheses about why this pattern may hold. I argued that three qualities of any natural resource—most important, its susceptibility to low-cost extraction, or "looting"—tend to influence the incidence and duration of civil wars. The data also suggested that different types of resources have different consequences for separatist wars than for nonseparatist wars. Below I describe the implications of these seven hypotheses for both unlootable and lootable resources.

Unlootable Resources

Unlootable resources include oil, natural gas, and all types of deep-shaft minerals. The seven hypotheses have both positive and negative implications for states with unlootable resources; in general, the good news concerns nonseparatist conflicts and the bad news concerns separatist conflicts.

The good news is that unlootable resources should make nonseparatist conflicts briefer, because they tend to be of greater benefit to the government. If the government is the stronger party—which is true in most of the fifteen cases presented here—this should hasten the end of the conflict by bringing about a quicker government victory. On the other hand, if the government is the weaker party, but still receives revenues from unlootable resources—as in the case of Angola in 1993–1994, and in the Democratic Republic of Congo in 1997–1998—it may prolong the conflict by averting the government's defeat.

The bad news about unlootable resources is that they are more likely than lootable resources to cause separatist conflicts; moreover, separatist conflicts tend to last longer than nonseparatist conflicts. Five separatist conflicts in this sample were in part caused by grievances over the distribution of resource wealth; such grievances appear more likely to arise over unlootable resources than over lootable resources. In cases where the resource is obstructable—in particular, when it must travel through a long, above-ground pipeline—it creates a further class of problems, by presenting rebel groups with an unceasing flow of extortion opportunities.

These two dangers—that unlootable resources will be a source of grievance (in separatist conflicts), or a source of finance (if they are obstructable)—are depicted in Figure 8.7. The upper-right quadrant contains nonseparatist con-

flicts with an obstructable resource; in this cell, natural resources should be a source of rebel finance (because they are obstructable) but not a source of rebel grievance (because they are not separatist conflicts). The Colombia case fits this description closely.

The lower-left quadrant contains cases where the resource cannot be used for finance (since it is relatively unobstructable) but where it is a source of grievance (since it is found in a province with separatist aspirations). Each of the four cases in this cell are persistent, long-running conflicts in which violence has been minimal—generally producing fewer than 100 deaths per year. This pattern is consistent with a conflict over a long-standing grievance (the perceived maldistribution of resource revenues), in which the separatist group does not have a major source of finance, and hence is unable to fight a war that produces a large number of casualties.

The conflict in the Indonesian province of West Papua (formerly Irian Jaya) provides an illustration. Indonesia invaded the former Dutch colony in 1962, and later annexed it; a small proindependence army, the Organisasi Papua Merdeka (OPM), has been active since around 1965. In the early 1970s a U.S. firm, Freeport-McMoran, began to operate a major copper mine on the southern part of the island; since then, the mine has been a further source of

	Separatist (⟶ grievance)	Nonsepartist (⟶ no grievance)
Obstructable (⟶ finance)	Sudan	Colombia[a]
Unobstructable (⟶ no finance)	Indonesia (Aceh) Indonesia (W. Papua) Papua New Guinea Angola (Cabinda)	Angola (UNITA)[a] Congo Republic DRC[a]

[a]Has both lootable and unlootable resources.

Figure 8.7. Conflicts Involving Unlootable Resources

grievance for the island's indigenous population. The mine has intermittently been the target of OPM attacks. Proseparatist propaganda, including that generated by the OPM, argues that West Papua's resource wealth is wrongfully appropriated by the central government, and that Papuans would be wealthier if the province were independent. The government's military operations around the mine site, in turn, have led to human rights violations and have further heightened anti-Indonesia sentiment. There is no indication, however, that the OPM has used resource looting or extortion around the mine site to fund itself. Moreover, resource wealth has helped the stronger side in the conflict—the Indonesian military—not the OPM, which remains small and ill equipped. The OPM has perhaps several hundred "hard-core" members, and several dozen firearms—mostly old and rusted weapons from World War II. The conflict generates fewer than 100 casualties a year.

The upper-left quadrant of Figure 8.7 contains the most troubled category of conflicts: separatist conflicts over obstructable resources, in which an unlootable resource becomes both a source of grievance and a source of finance. There is, fortunately, just one state from the sample that fits into this cell: Sudan.

The lower-right quadrant includes states with unlootable, unobstructable resources engaged in nonseparatist conflicts. These three cases—Angola (UNITA), the Congo Republic, and the Democratic Republic of Congo—feature conflicts in which the resource is neither a source of grievance nor a source of finance via extortion. Two of these conflicts (Angola and the Democratic Republic of Congo) have both lootable and unlootable resources, and it has largely been their lootable resources that have made these conflicts long and bloody. The only case that has unlootable, unobstructable resources exclusively—the Congo Republic—was an unusual conflict, in that the opposition group received funding from a foreign oil firm and expected an imminent takeover of the government. After a four-month war, financed in part by this payment, the opposition group was proven right.

Lootable Resources

Alluvial gemstones and agricultural crops, including drugs, are all lootable resources. Diamonds and drugs were strongly associated with civil conflict in the 1990s, and are commonly viewed as the most troublesome resources. But this chapter suggests that there is another side to these commodities: they also tend to produce more widespread benefits for local peoples, and the poor, than do unlootable resources. The seven hypotheses have positive and negative implications for countries with lootable resources. In this case, the positive implications are for separatist conflicts, the negative for nonseparatist conflicts.

The good news is that lootable resources do not seem to generate separatist conflicts. Since lootable resources produce more revenues for unskilled workers, and for local peoples, they also seem to generate fewer grievances. There are six separatist conflicts in the sample. Five entail grievances over unlootable resources (see Figure 8.5).

The bad news about lootable resources is that they appear to prolong nonseparatist conflicts, due to two factors: their tendency to benefit rebel groups, and their tendency to cause discipline problems in the army that exploits them. These two effects have helped produce long, chaotic civil wars in eight of the fifteen cases in the sample: Afghanistan, Angola, Cambodia, Colombia, the Democratic Republic of Congo, Liberia, Peru, and Sierra Leone. If the resource is also illegal, this makes it even more likely to favor the rebel side.

For these reasons, lootable resources appear to create more complicated civil wars, with greater fragmentation and shifting alliances among the armies that control the resource. They may also be harder to resolve, due to this fragmentation, and because the widespread benefits they produce may make sanctions harder to implement and more costly for poor and local peoples.

In short, this study suggests that some resources are more dangerous to exploit than others; and that different resources are associated with different types of conflicts: unlootable resources are more likely to produce separatist conflicts, and lootable resources are more likely to produce nonseparatist conflicts. These patterns appear to hold true for the fifteen conflicts in the sample; to know whether they are true for a larger set of conflicts, they would have to be subjected to further testing, especially with a different data set. Still, they may hint at the complicated and contradictory effects that a country's natural resource endowment may have organized violence occuring inside its own borders.

*   *   *

Appendix 1. Diamond and Drug Producers, 1995

Diamond producers: **Angola,** Australia, Botswana, Brazil, Central African Republic, China, **Democratic Republic of Congo,** Côte d'Ivoire, Ghana, Guinea, **Liberia,** Namibia, **Russia, Sierra Leone,** South Africa, Venezuela, Zimbabwe.

Alluvial diamond producers: **Angola,** Brazil, Central African Republic, **Democratic Republic of Congo,** Côte d'Ivoire, Ghana, **Liberia, Sierra Leone.**

Opium producers: **Afghanistan, Burma, Colombia,** Laos, Mexico, Pakistan, Vietnam.

Coca producers: Bolivia, **Colombia, Peru.**

Cannabis producers: **Afghanistan, Cambodia, Colombia,** Jamaica, Morocco, Mexico, Nigeria, Pakistan, South Africa, Thailand.

Sources: Ronald F. Balazik, "Industrial Diamonds" (Washington, D.C.: U.S. Geological Survey, 1998); UN Office for Drug Control and Crime Prevention (UN-OCCP), "World Drug Report, 2000" (New York: Oxford University Press, 2000).

Note: **Bold** denotes countries that experienced civil wars in the 1990s.

NOTES

1. Like most scholars, I define civil wars as conflicts that occur within the recognized boundaries of a single state; involve combat between the state and at least one organized rebel force; and result in at least 1,000 deaths during a single calendar year. I use the database assembled by Paul Collier and Anke Hoeffler to determine when civil wars have occurred. See Paul Collier and Anke Hoeffler, "Greed and Grievance in Civil War," Policy Research Working Paper no. 2355 (Washington, D.C.: World Bank, 2001).

2. Paul Collier and Anke Hoeffler, "On the Economic Causes of Civil War," *Oxford Economic Papers* 50, no. 4 (October 1998): 563–573; Collier and Hoeffler, "Greed and Grievance"; Indra de Soysa, "Natural Resources and Civil War: Shrinking Pie or Honey Pot?" paper presented at the International Studies Association, Los Angeles, March 2000; and Ibrahim Elbadawi and Nicholas Sambanis, "How Much War Will We See? Estimating the Prevalence of Civil War in 161 Countries, 1960–1999," *Journal of Conflict Resolution* 46, no. 2 (June 2002): 307–334.

3. James D. Fearon, "Why Do Some Civil Wars Last So Much Longer Than Others?" paper presented at the World Bank–UC Irvine conference on "Civil Wars and Post-Conflict Transition," Irvine, Calif., May 18, 2001.

4. Michael L. Ross, "How Does Natural Resource Wealth Influence Civil War? Evidence from 13 Case Studies," paper presented at the World Bank–UC Irvine conference on "Civil Wars and Post-Conflict Transition," Irvine, Calif., May 18, 2001.

5. Ibid.

6. Collier and Hoeffler suggest that the relationship between resource dependence and civil wars is curvilinear, so that the danger of civil war peaks when resource dependence reaches a relatively high level, but declines at the very highest levels. Other scholars estimate the

relationship between resource dependence and civil war to be linear. Both estimates would predict a higher civil war rate among the top one-third of resource-dependent states than among the middle and bottom thirds. Collier and Hoeffler, "Greed and Grievance."

7. World Bank, *World Development Indicators 2001* (Washington, D.C.: World Bank, 2001), CD-ROM.

8. I chose 1995 because it is the year for which the greatest quantity of data are available, by far. By comparing 1995 levels of resource dependence to decade-long civil war rates, I am increasing the danger of endogeneity—that is, that causation may be running in both directions. On the problem of endogeneity in assessing the relationship between natural resources and civil conflict, see Ross, "How Does Natural Resource Wealth Influence Civil War?"

9. Collier and Hoeffler, "Greed and Grievance." Of these 161 states, 15 failed to produce any data on their export of natural resources, leaving a sample of 146 states with 29 civil wars for Table 3.2. The rate of civil wars in this smaller sample, however, is identical to the rate in the larger sample: 19.9 percent.

10. I use the period 1990–2000 because it is easier to use in analyzing more recent conflicts. The end of the Cold War may have produced an unusually large number of resource-related wars during this decade, since it may have forced combatants in some developing countries (such as Cambodia, Afghanistan, and Angola) to replace funding from superpowers with funding from natural resource exploitation. See David Keen, *The Economic Functions of Violence in Civil Wars* (Oxford: Oxford University Press for the International Institute for Strategic Studies, 1998).

11. Collier and Hoeffler find that oil is somewhat more closely tied to conflict than mining and agricultural products—although their database does not appear to include diamonds or drugs. Collier and Hoeffler, "Greed and Grievance."

12. Note that the first and second columns measure the quantity of timber harvested, while the third and fourth measure the value of timber exports, as a fraction of GDP.

13. Michael Klare, *Resource Wars: The New Landscape of Global Conflict* (New York: Metropolitan Books, 2001).

14. I define "nonproducers" as states that produced five or fewer tons of opium and coca.

15. "Primary producers" are the main sources of internationally traded cannabis, while "secondary producers" export lesser amounts.

16. Philippe Le Billon, "The Political Ecology of War: Natural Resources and Armed Conflicts," *Political Geography* 20, no. 5 (June 2001): 561–584.

17. I am borrowing the concept of lootability from Collier and Hoeffler, "Greed and Grievance," and Le Billon, "Political Ecology of War," although the definition is my own.

18. There is also an illegal international trade in endangered species and their products; I have found only one instance of their sale by military forces. See Ros Reeve and Stephen Ellis, "An Insider's Account of the South African Security Forces' Role in the Ivory Trade," *Journal of Contemporary African Studies* 13, no. 2 (July 1995): 227–244.

19. Note that for conflicts in which both lootable and unlootable resources mattered (Angola, Colombia, and the Democratic Republic of Congo), I have listed separately which party generated money from which resource.

20. Le Billon makes a similar point. Le Billon, "Political Ecology of War."

21. An important assumption is that conflicts will tend to last longer when the two sides have more equal resources. This assumption is supported by evidence from interstate conflicts. D. Scott Bennett, and Alan C. Stam III, "The Duration of Interstate Wars, 1816–1985," *American Political Science Review* 90, no. 2 (June 1996): 239–257.

22. Fearon, "Why Do Some Civil Wars Last So Much Longer Than Others?"; and Ross, "How

Does Natural Resource Wealth Influence Civil War?"

23. Fearon, "Why Do Some Civil Wars Last So Much Longer Than Others?"

24. Note, however, that in the case of Cambodia, these discipline problems led to an earlier end to the conflict when a rebel faction defected to the government side in order to retain its access to timber and gems.

25. Stephen Ellis, *The Mask of Anarchy: The Destruction of Liberia and the Religious Dimension of an African Civil War* (New York: New York University Press, 1999); UN Panel of Experts, "Report of the Panel of Experts on the Illegal Exploitation of Natural Resources and Other Forms of Wealth of the Democratic Republic of Congo," S/2001/357, UN Security Council, April 12, 2001.

26. Bertil Lintner, *Burma in Revolt* (Bangkok: Silkworm Press, 1999).

27. Obstructable resources are similar to lootable resources, since small bands of unskilled troops can use them to generate revenues.

28. One pipeline, operated by BP Amoco, is 444 miles long; the other, operated by Occidental Petroleum, is 485 miles long.

29. Thad Dunning and Leslie Wirpsa, "Andean Gulf? The Political Economy of Oil and Violence in Colombia," paper presented at the University of California, Davis, conference on "The Wars in Colombia," May 17–19, 2001, mimeo.

30. Edgar O'Ballance, *Sudan, Civil War, and Terrorism, 1956–1999* (New York: St. Martin's Press, 2000); and G. Norman, *Sudan in Crisis* (Gainesville: University Press of Florida, 1999).

CAROL COHN AND SARA RUDDICK

A FEMINIST ETHICAL PERSPECTIVE ON WEAPONS OF MASS DESTRUCTION

The world will note that the first atomic bomb was dropped on Hiroshima, a military base. That was because we wished in this first attack to avoid, insofar as possible, the killing of civilians.

—*President Harry Truman, August 9, 1945*[1]

I heard her voice calling "Mother, Mother." I went towards the sound. She was completely burned. The skin had come off her head altogether, leaving a twisted knot at the top. My daughter said, "Mother,

From Sohail H. Hashimi and Steven P. Lee, eds. *Ethics and Weapons of Mass Destruction: Religious and Secular Perspectives* (Cambridge, UK: Cambridge UP, 2004), 405–35. Some of the author's notes have been comitted.

you're late, please take me back quickly." She said it was hurting a lot. But there were no doctors. There was nothing I could do. So I covered up her naked body and held her in my arms for nine hours. At about eleven o'clock that night she cried out again "Mother," and put her hand around my neck. It was already ice-cold. I said, "Please say Mother again." But that was the last time.

—*A Hiroshima survivor*[2]

We are reporting on a feminist tradition that we label antiwar feminism. We consider ourselves inheritors of this tradition and draw on it to formulate a position on weapons of mass destruction. To put our position briefly: Antiwar feminism rejects both the military and political use of weapons of mass destruction in warfare or for deterrence. It is also deeply critical of the discourses that have framed public discussion of weapons of mass destruction. It calls for ways of thinking that reveal the complicated effects on possessor societies of developing and deploying these weapons, that portray the terror and potential suffering of target societies, and that grapple with the moral implications of the willingness to risk such massive destruction.

Antiwar Feminism

There is no single feminist position on war, armament, and weapons of mass destruction. Some feminists fight for women's right to fight and command fighters; some participate in armed nationalist struggles; some are pacifists; some believe that peace and war are not "women's issues." Most feminists do not divorce feminism from national, ethnic, religious, class, or other identities and politics that together create their attitudes toward war.

We report on one particular feminist tradition that opposes war making as a practice and seeks to replace it with practices of nonviolent contest and reconciliation. We call this tradition "antiwar feminism" and see ourselves as its inheritors and continuers; despite disagreements with some of its aspects, we refer to it as "ours." Our tradition is represented by groups as much as by individuals. Among the most venerable is the Women's International League for Peace and Freedom (WILPF), which was founded in 1915 to protest World War I and which today is actively involved in disarmament and nonproliferation issues, as well as in advocacy for gender analysis in security affairs at the United Nations. During the cold war, many women's movements protested nuclear weapons. Many other women's protest movements represent some but not all aspects of antiwar feminism. The courageous protest of the Madres of Argentina against a military dictatorship only gradually became antimilitarist and

seems never to have been conventionally feminist. Women in Black began in Israel/Palestine and has moved to many conflict-ridden sites around the world; though it nearly everywhere engages in struggles for peace, its members differ about the extent and generality of its antimilitarism. In armed conflict zones around the world, there are many other women's peace initiatives and groups; although many would identify themselves as antiwar, fewer would adopt the label "feminist." An excellent place to start researching these groups is the website www.peacewomen.org, which was started to provide a clearinghouse of information and website links for women's peace groups.

Antiwar feminists' opposition to the practice of war is simultaneously pragmatic and moral. We have an abiding suspicion of the use of violence, even in the best of causes. The ability of violence to achieve its stated aims is routinely overestimated, while the complexity of its costs is overlooked. Our opposition also stems from the perception that the practice of war entails far more than the killing and destroying of armed combat itself. It requires the creation of a "war system," which entails arming, training, and organizing for possible wars; allocating the resources these preparations require; creating a culture in which wars are seen as morally legitimate, even alluring; and shaping and fostering the masculinities and femininities that undergird men's and women's acquiescence to war. Even when it appears to achieve its aims, war is a source of enormous individual suffering and loss. Modern warfare is also predictably destructive to societies, civil liberties and democratic processes, and the nonhuman world. State security may sometimes be served by war, but too often human security is not.

Though they oppose war as a practice—and some individual antiwar feminists are committed to nonviolence—the tradition as a whole is not typically "pacifist" as that term is usually understood. It neither rejects all wars as wrong in principle nor condemns people just because they resort to violence. Some antiwar feminists support particular military campaigns. As a Northern Irish woman explained to Cynthia Cockburn, "We've always given each other a lot of leeway on [violence]." We continue to call these temporary militarists antiwar because they continue to oppose war making as a practice, mourn the suffering of *all* of wars' victims, and, in the midst of war, imagine the details of a future culture of peace. Although they do not reject violence in principle, they are committed to "translating" or "transfiguring violence into creative militant nonviolence." This requires letting go of "dangerous day dreams whether of promised homes of our own or of an apocalyptic demolition of all walls ... [and replacing these dreams] with the idea of something we could perhaps really have: a careful and a caring struggle in a well lit space."

Nor is the feminist antiwar tradition a version of just war theory. In contrast to antiwar feminists who oppose war as a practice even if they support a particular military campaign, just war theorists implicitly accept war as a practice even when condemning particular wars. Just war theory accepts war only as a defense against serious attacks on one's state or one's people or as intervention on behalf of other states or people who suffer such aggression (*jus ad bellum*). Antiwar feminists may agree that the cause is just, but for us it does not automatically follow that war is therefore justified—for at least two reasons. First, while just war theorists claim that war must be a "last resort" after all nonviolent alternatives have failed, in our view they barely explore nonviolent alternatives once just cause is determined nor seek to return to nonviolent struggle once war has begun. Antiwar feminists continue to explore nonviolent alternatives even after war starts and seek every opportunity to return to nonviolent means of fighting. Second, just war theorists tend to abstract particular wars from the war system on which they rely and which they strengthen, whereas antiwar feminists are acutely critical of the political, economic, social, and moral costs of that system.

However just the cause, just war theorists set moral limits to permissible strategies of war (*jus in bello*). Ideally, only armed combatants or, at most, people contributing directly to combat should be targeted. Weapons must be able to target discriminately and then should cause only the suffering required to render combatants harmless. Antiwar feminists are skeptical of these "rules of war." Some argue that they depend on unworkable abstractions, including, in much contemporary warfare, the central distinction between combatants and noncombatants. Others document the routine, often willful, violation of these rules, beginning with the use of weapons that cannot discriminate. Generally, antiwar feminists, like many pacifists, do not so much argue as point insistently to the facts of suffering and destruction that cannot be limited, in place or time, to battlefield and soldier.

To suggest the distinctive character of our tradition as contrasted with just war and pacifism, we identify four of its constitutive positions.

War Is a Gendered Practice

It is a common perception that war making is an activity primarily engaged in by men and governed by norms of masculinity. Antiwar feminism both asserts and challenges the association of war and masculinity in at least three ways.

First, antiwar feminists insistently underline the gendered character of war, stressing its domination by men and masculinity, thus making visible what has been taken for granted. But they also stress that women's labour has always been central to war making—although it has also consistently been either unacknowledged or represented as tangential in order to protect war's "masculinity."

Second, they challenge the view that war is inherently gendered—in particular, the view that biology renders men "naturally" war-like and war therefore a "natural" male activity. They stress that multiple masculinities (and femininities) are required by the mobilization for war and argue that the simple link of some "innate" male aggression to the conduct of war is belied both by what men actually *do* in war and by many men's reluctance to fight. Whatever the role of biology in gender and gender in war, antiwar feminists identify the association of manliness with militarized violence as the product of specific social processes that they try to analyze and change.[3]

Finally, antiwar feminists not only explore the multiple gendered *identities* needed for and shaped by the practice of war making; they also analyze the ways that warmaking is shaped by a gendered *system of meanings*. We understand gender not just as a characteristic of individuals but as a symbolic system—a central organizing discourse in our culture, a set of ways of thinking, images, categories, and beliefs that not only shape how we experience, understand, and represent ourselves as men and women but that also provide a familiar set of metaphors, dichotomies, and values that structure ways of thinking about other aspects of the world, including war and security. In other words, we see the ways in which human characteristics and endeavors are culturally divided into those seen as "masculine" and those seen as "feminine" (e.g., mind is opposed to body, culture to nature, thought to feeling, logic to intuition, objectivity to subjectivity, aggression to passivity, confrontation to accommodation, war to peace, abstraction to particularity, public to private, political to personal, and realism to moral reflection.), and the terms coded "male" are valued more highly than those coded "female."

Once the gender coding takes place—once certain ways of thinking are marked as masculine and feminine, entwining metaphors of masculinity with judgments of legitimacy and power—then any system of thought or action comes to have gendered positions within it. For example, we see the devaluation and exclusion of "the feminine" as shaping and distorting basic national security paradigms and policies. And once the devaluation-by-association-with-the-feminine takes place, it becomes extremely difficult for anyone, female or male, to take the devalued position, to express concerns or ideas marked as "feminine." What then gets left out is the emotional, the concrete,

the particular, human bodies and their vulnerability, human lives and their subjectivity.[4]

The characteristics that are excluded as "feminine" are characteristics of women and men. They are also characteristics that women often ascribe to themselves "as women" and that feminists also sometimes ascribe to women. There is considerable disagreement among feminists, in print and casual conversation, about the degree to which women and men differ from each other, how these differences arise, and whether they are subject to change. Our own understanding of gender has changed over time and is affected by the circumstances in which we reflect and speak. In the circumstances of this discussion, we allude to women's actual differences from men only when describing the distinctive effects of war on women and the particular experiences and insights women themselves say that they would bring to peace negotiations.

Start from Women's Lives

Our second position applies a central tenet of feminist methodology to the particular case of weapons of mass destruction. We attempt to look at war and weapons from the perspective of women's lives, making women's experiences a central rather than marginal concern. In the context of war, "women's lives" has two primary referents: the work women do and the distinctive bodily assaults war inflicts on women.

Women's work traditionally includes life-shaping responsibilities of caring labour: giving birth to and caring for children, protecting and sustaining ill, frail, or other dependents, maintaining households, and fostering and protecting kin, village, and neighborhood relations. Seen from the standpoint of caring labour, war is at least disruptive and usually destructive. In war women often can't get or keep the goods on which they depend, whether medicine, cattle, or food. War threatens the well-being and even existence of the people, relations, and homes that women maintain.

Caring labour may be intertwined with or depend on other labour. In many economies, women "work" to secure the cash to get the goods that "women's work" requires. Whether or not they are responsible for care, women work for wages in jobs that are lower paid and often in the service of others. In war, women's work typically expands to include "comfort" and prostitution, low-skilled workers/servants, secretaries, and many others who keep militaries functioning. Notoriously, war gives some women special job opportunities, training, and experience unavailable elsewhere. Some survive postwar downsizing and the return of men to "their" jobs. But other women are in effect conscripted for dangerous or demeaning work whose effects may also survive the official end of war.

The practice of war implies a willingness to inflict pain and damage on bodies, to "out-injure" in pursuit of war's aim.[5] Women are no more or less embodied than men, but their bodies are differently at risk. There has been a quantitative shift in the ratio of women to men sufferers as civilian casualties come to outnumber those of the military. Women also suffer sexually more than men and distinctly. Rape is the conqueror's reward and taunt. It is a weapon against "woman" and also against the men and community to whom she "belongs." The woman who becomes pregnant by rape may be seen by the rapist or may see herself as forced to join the enemy, to create him. She may fear and her rapist may hope that she is contributing to the destruction of her own people.

Given the effects of war on women's work and the multiple ways that war commits violence against women, it is suspect, at the least, to look for "security" from militaries. Conceptions of security based in the military defense of state borders and interests often mean greater insecurity for women.

War Is Not Spatially or Temporally Bounded

Antiwar feminism rejects the conception of war as a discrete event, with clear locations, and a beginning and an end. It is not that we fail to dis-

tinguish between war and peace or to make distinctions between kinds of violence, but in our vision, and in contrast to much just war theory, it is crucial not to separate war either from the preparations made for it (preparations taken in the widest possible sense, including the social costs of maintaining large standing armies and the machinery of deterrence) or from its long-term physical, psychological, socio-economic, environmental, and gendered effects. This conception of war is sometimes explicit in feminist writings, typically implied by the rhetoric and symbols of feminist movements and fundamental to our response to the questions being asked in this volume.

Women's war and postwar stories underline the unboundedness of war in at least two different dimensions: cultural and practical. Culturally, war is understood as a creation and creator of the culture in which it thrives. War's violence is *not* understood as separate and apart from other social practices. There is a continuum of violence running from bedroom to boardroom, factory, stadium, classroom, and battlefield, "traversing our bodies and our sense of self."[6] Weapons of violence and representations of those weapons travel through interlocking institutions—economic, political, familial, technological, and ideological. These institutions prepare some people but not others to believe in the effectiveness of violence, to imagine and acquire weapons, to use and justify using force to work their will. They prepare some but not others to renounce, denounce, or passively submit to force, to resist or accept the war plans put before them.

Practically, feminists see war as neither beginning with the first gunfire nor ending when the treaties are signed. Before the first gunfire is the research, development, and deployment of weapons; the maintaining of standing armies; the cultural glorification of the power of armed force; and the social construction of masculinities and femininities that support a militarized state. When the organized violence of war is over, what remains is a ripped social fabric: the devastation of the physical, economic, and social infrastructure through which people provision themselves and their families; the havoc wrought in the lives and psyches of combatants, noncombatants, and children who have grown up in war; the surfeit of arms on the streets and of ex-soldiers trained to kill; citizens who have been schooled and practiced in the methods of violence but not in nonviolent methods of dealing with conflict; "nature" poisoned, burned, made ugly and useless. Typically, "peace" includes official ongoing "punishment"—retribution, reparations, domination, and deprivation. At best, even the most laudable treaty is only the beginning of making peace.

Alternative Epistemology: The Inadequacy of Dominant Ways of Thinking about War

Most Western philosophers have thought that knowledge is more trust worthy when generated by people who have transcended institutional constraints, social identities, gender identifications, and emotion. Many feminists propose an "alternative epistemology" that stresses that all thinkers are "situated" within "epistemic communities" that ask some but not other questions and legitimate some but not other ways of knowing. We are each of us also situated by social identities and personal histories. To take an example at hand: Some of us address this volume's questions as heirs of the "victims" of nuclear weapons or associate ourselves with them.[7] Others are heirs of the attackers. Some address the issue of "proliferation" of nuclear weapons from the situation of a possessor state, others from a situation in which they would find the term "proliferation" inappropriate. None of us speaks from nowhere; there is no phenomenon—including nuclear attack or proliferation—that can be seen independently of the situation of the seers.

Three tenets of this "alternative epistemology" seem especially relevant to our work. Knowing is never wholly separated from feelings. Indeed, in many kinds of inquiry the capacity to feel and to account for one's feelings are both a source and a test of knowledge. Second, as useful as hypothetical thought experiments and imagined scenarios may be, we begin with and return to concrete open-ended questions about actual people in actual situations. Finally, we measure arguments, and ideals of objectivity, partly in terms of the goods that they yield, the pleasures they make possible, and the suffering they prevent.

Grounded in this alternative epistemology, antiwar feminists criticize the dominant political/strategic paradigm for thinking about weapons of mass destruction, which we call "technostrategic discourse."[8] In contrast to just war theory, this discourse is explicitly centered not on the ethics of warfare but on its material and political practicalities. As a tool for thinking about weapons of mass destruction, it essentially restricts the thinker to three issues: the actual use, that is, the detonation, of these weapons in state warfare or by terrorists; the physical and geo-political effects of this use; and the deployment of these weapons to deter attacks involving either conventional weapons or weapons of mass destruction. In other words, the concerns of the dominant strategic discourse are limited to the destructive effects of the weapons when *and only when* they are detonated and to the possible deterrent effects of possessing these weapons. There is scant attention to the potential suffering of targeted societies and no attempt to evaluate complicated effects on possessor societies of deploying and developing these weapons, nor to grapple with the moral significance of willingly risking such massive, total destruction.

When antiwar feminists think about wars, they take into consideration the political, social, economic, psychological, and moral consequences of accepting the practice of war. When assessing weapons, they do not single out or isolate weapons' physical, military, and strategic effects from their embeddedness in and impact on social and political life as a whole nor from the effects of the discourses that constitute "knowledge" about these weapons. Hence, when asked to think about weapons of mass destruction, we strive to consider the totality of the web of social, economic, political, and environmental relationships within which weapons of mass destruction are developed, deployed, used, and disposed of—all the while starting from the perspective of women's lives. It is not possible to do so from within the bounds of "just war" and/or "technostrategic" frameworks—yet those are the very discourses that have shaped the questions we are asked to answer in this volume. Thus, as we respond to the editors' questions, we find we need to both think inside their frame and about the frame itself.

Sources and Principles

The first question asks whether our tradition includes general norms governing the use of weapons in war. It does not. If, as it appears, the question assumes the inevitability, perhaps even the acceptability, of war making, we do not. And granted the existence of wars, we are ambivalent about making ethical distinctions between weapons. We recognize that some weapons, and uses of weapons, are worse than others. Some weapons can be sparingly used and carefully aimed to cause minimal damage; others cannot. Some weapons may be deliberately cruel (e.g., dum dum bullets), outlast the occasion that apparently justified them (e.g., land mines), harm indiscriminately (e.g., cluster bombs, land mines again, or poison gas in a crowded subway), or injure massively and painfully (e.g., incendiary bombs). While respecting these distinctions, we nonetheless fear that stressing the horror of some weapons diminishes the horrors that more "acceptable" weapons wreak. For us the crucial question is not "How do we choose among weapons?" but rather, "How can we identify and attend to the specific horrors of any weapon?"

Moreover, it is striking that the criteria by which some weapons are declared less horrible than others do not fare well by feminist antiwar criteria. We consider two kinds: small arms and light weapons, and high-tech weapons aimed precisely from a distance.

"Small arms and light weapons" are weapons light enough to be packed over a mountain on a mule. Among them are stinger missiles, AK47s, machine guns, grenades, assault rifles, small explosives, and hand guns. Far more than weapons of mass destruction (WMD), these weapons can allow for distinguishing attackers and combatants from bystanders. Some, such as hand guns, can be accurately aimed to incapacitate without killing a dangerous attacker. Of course, the weapons may be misused. But if they are carefully aimed by properly trained gunners, they can satisfy conventional moral criteria of doing the least harm commensurate with protection from violence.

If, however, we start looking at weapons from the perspectives of women's lives, small arms and light weapons become visible as the cause of enormous, sustained, and pervasive suffering of very specific kinds. Light weapons are a staple of the arms market, and the principal instrument of violence in armed conflicts throughout the world. They are inexpensive, require little or no training to use, and are easily available, often unregulated by state, military, civic, or even parental authority. They have a long shelf life, travel easily, and therefore can, in the course of time, be traded, turned against various enemies, and brought home.

These weapons are so easy to get that they threaten to turn any conflict violent—whether between peoples, neighbors, or family members. Women can carry them, but they more often remain the property of men and late adolescent boys, increasing the imbalance of power between men and women.

These weapons can wreak havoc among the relationships women have tended and destroy women's capacity to obtain food, water, and other necessary staples or to farm and to keep their animals safe. Thus, it is not surprising that current international feminist attention to war is often focused on ethno-nationalist armed conflicts that are fought with light weapons. These wars, brutal in their effects, often in gender-related ways, are undeterred by—indeed, unaffected by—the existence of weapons of mass destruction.

Ironically, by contrast with small arms and light weapons, nuclear weapons can in some ways seem attractive. They are expensive and difficult to produce, complicated to deploy, require training if they are to be used, and rarely make their way onto main street or into homes, except as waste material. In the lives of women around the world, it is small arms and light weapons, more than weapons of mass destruction, that constitute a clear and daily present danger.

Consider the "virtues" of a quite different class of weapons, precision-guided munitions (PGM). Modern, high-tech PGM can reputedly be precisely aimed at carefully selected targets, a virtue often on verbal and graphic display during the Gulf War – although the degree of precision of both weapons and target selection are sometimes more illusory than real. PGM are typically launched from great distances, the human "targets" invisible to the attacker and the weapons' effects transmuted into unreality by video game-like imagery. Neither the attackers nor civilians at home need to be aware of the destruction they cause. Moreover, PGM on "electronic battlefields" appear to make warfare safer for the warriors who use them.

From our perspective, these virtues, too, become suspect. Critics charge that we—citizens, military, political leaders—are too easily reassured by images of PGM's precision. In fact, PGM are notoriously subject to "mistakes" of judgment, information, and technological control. While we agree with these critics, we emphasize two other moral doubts.

With PGM, not only is the discourse of war abstract, but war fighting itself becomes increasingly abstract and unreal to those who kill, mutilate, and destroy. Antimilitarists have often seen war as a fiction, an Old Lie, that obscures brutality through patriotic rhetoric, euphemistic language, abstract theories, and discourse. To these are now added the abstracted illusion of precision strikes displayed on video screens. By contrast, we consider it a virtue if the brutality of war is evident to the combatants, to those who order them to war, and to the society they represent.

Second, we cannot unambivalently applaud the relative safety that PGM accord those who use them. This safety is purchased by an ignorance of injuries, ultimately an indifference toward "the targets." We understand the military obligation and human desire to save one's own fighters. But we cannot praise a weapon for its ability to save "us" while endangering the lives and destroying the resources of "the enemy" we don't see, whose humanity we never confront. Indeed, people who reject war, including feminists, refuse to construe an enemy as killable.

By calling into question the criteria by which weapons are judged, we do not in any way minimize the horror of weapons of mass destruction. Women and feminists of our tradition have been protesting the development, testing, deployment, and possible use of nuclear weapons, in particular, since Hiroshima. But antiwar feminism urges that we appreciate the specificity of horror and learn to mourn the damage that each kind of weapon inflicts on both its possessor and the injured. This would be both an expression and a development of our tradition.

WMD Utilization

The second question asks us whether it is ever morally permissible to use weapons of mass destruction. We are tempted to answer with only three words: "of course not."

Rather than pondering the question of when, if ever, it is morally justified to use WMD, we move in two directions. First, we note that antiwar feminists' energies have not been focused on when to use these weapons, but rather on attempting to explain why, over many years, there has been widespread acceptance of the deployment of nuclear weapons and of the stated willingness to use them. Second, we move to question the question itself.

Antiwar feminist attention to WMD has largely focused on nuclear weapons—their horrors, the urgency of abolishing them, and the question of how anyone could think it sane to develop and deploy them. In this chapter, we, too, write primarily about nuclear weapons—as a reflection of the tradition on which we report, but also because they are the weapons whose magnitude of destructive power seems distinctive and to best warrant the description "weapons of mass destruction." However, as we learned in the course of our research, many elements of the antiwar feminist critique of nuclear weapons hold for chemical and biological weapons as well.

Rather than seeing acceptance of nuclear weapons as a "realistic" acknowledgment of the "technologically inevitable," antiwar feminists have seen the political and intellectual acceptance of nuclear weapons' deployment as something to be explained. Some feminists have noted the allure of nuclear weapons, particularly the excitement and awe evoked by actual or imagined nuclear explosions. Some have seen the appeal of exploding or launching nuclear weapons as reflecting and reinforcing masculine desires and identities.

Several antiwar feminists have focused less on the weapons themselves and more on the discourse through which the weapons (and their use) are theorized and legitimated. They have written about both the sexual and domestic metaphors that turn the mind's eye toward the pleasant and familiar, rather than toward images of indescribable devastation. They have identified in nuclear discourse techniques of denial and conceptual fragmentation. They have emphasized the ways that the abstraction and euphemism of nuclear discourse protect nuclear planners and politicians from the grisly realities behind their words. Speaking generally, antiwar feminists invite women and men to attend to the identities, emotions, and discourses that allow us to accept the possible use of nuclear weapons.[9]

Perhaps the most general feminist concern is the willingness of intellectuals to talk as usual about nuclear weapons (or about any atrocity). And this brings us back to the issue of the framing of the second question. The question as it is posed seems in some ways similar to the abstract, distancing thinking that we have criticized—but in which we also participate. There is no mention of the horror, let alone a pause to rest with it. We move or are moved quickly to an abstract moral tone: "any circumstances" "might be morally permissible . . ." and then to comparisons.

Abstract language and a penchant for distinctions are typical of philosophy, intrinsically unobjectionable, and often a pleasure. It is continuous abstraction while speaking of actual or imagined horror that disturbs us. Abstract discussion of warfare is both the tool and the privilege of those who imagine themselves as the (potential) users of weapons. The victims, if they can speak at all, speak quite differently.

An account of a nuclear blast's effects by a U.S. defense intellectual:

> [You have to have ways to maintain communications in a] nuclear environment, a situation bound to include EMP blackout, brute force damage to systems, a heavy jamming environment, and so on.[10]

An account by a Hiroshima survivor:

> Everything was black, had vanished into the black dust, was destroyed. Only the flames that were beginning to lick their way up had any color. From the dust that was like a fog, figures began to loom up, black, hairless, faceless. They screamed with voices that were no longer human. Their screams drowned out the groans rising everywhere from the rubble, groans that seemed to rise from the very earth itself.[11]

It should become apparent then, that our concern about abstract language is not only relevant to the *framing* of the second question, about utilization, but to its *content*—the justifiability of nuclear weapons' use—as well. It is easier to contemplate and "justify" the use of nuclear weapons in the abstract language of defense intellectuals than in the descriptive, emotionally resonant language of the victim; from the perspective of the user rather than the victim. Antiwar feminists note that detailed, focal attention to the human impact of weapons' use is not only considered out of bounds in security professionals' discourse; it is also *delegitimated* by its association with the "feminine," with insufficient masculinity, as is evident in this excerpt of an interview with a physicist:

> Several colleagues and I were working on modeling counterforce nuclear attacks, trying to get realistic estimates of the number of immediate fatalities that would result from different deployments. At one point, we re-modeled a particular attack, using slightly different assumptions, and found that instead of there being 36 million immediate fatalities, there would only be 30 million. And everybody was sitting around nodding, saying, "Oh yeh, that's great, only 30 million," when all of a sudden, I heard what we were saying. And I blurted out, "Wait, I've just heard how we're talking—Only 30 million! Only 30 million human beings killed instantly?" Silence fell upon the room. Nobody said a word. They didn't even look at me. It was awful. I felt like a woman.

After telling this story to one of the authors, the physicist added that he was careful to never blurt out anything indicating that he was thinking about the victims again.[12] Fear of feeling like a woman (or being seen as unmanly) silently works to maintain the boundaries of a distanced, abstract discourse and to sustain the tone of the second question—a tone that invites us to think abstractly, "objectively" about WMD use, without pausing to consider human particularities, passions, and suffering.

WMD Deterrence

The third question asks whether it is ethical to develop and deploy WMD as deterrents only. That is, it asks the classic question of whether it is ethical to have weapons and threaten to use then, even if it is not ethical to use those weapons militarily. As the question is framed, then, "development" and "deployment" appear not as phenomena subject to ethical scrutiny unto themselves but merely as way-stations, as adjuncts subsumed under what is taken to be the core ethical issue, which is seen as deterrence.

This formulation does not work for us. We need to pause and recognize that there are really several questions enfolded in that one. We must ask not only about the ethical status of deterrence, but also whether its entailments—development and deployment—are themselves ethical.

One of the constitutive positions of antiwar feminism is that in thinking about weapons and wars, we must accord full weight to their daily effects on the lives of women. We then find that the development and deployment of nuclear weapons, even when they are not used in warfare, exacts immense economic costs that particularly affect women. In the recent words of an Indian feminist:

> The social costs of nuclear weaponisation in a country where the basic needs of shelter, food and water, electricity, health and education have not been met are obvious. . . . [S]ince patriarchal family norms place the task of looking after the daily needs of the family mainly upon women, scarcity of resources always hits women the hardest. Less food for the family inevitably means an even smaller share for women and female children just as water shortages mean an increase in women's labour who have to spend more time and energy in fetching water from distant places at odd hours of the day.

While the United States is not as poor a nation as India, Pakistan, or Russia, it has remained, throughout the nuclear age, a country in which poverty and hunger are rife, health care is still unaffordable to many, low-cost housing is unavailable, and public schools and infrastructure crumbling, are all while the American nuclear weapons program has come at the cost of $4.5 trillion.

In addition to being economically costly, nuclear weapons development has medical and political costs. In the U.S. program, many people have been exposed to high levels of radiation, including uranium miners, workers at reactors and processing facilities, the quarter of a million military personnel who took part in "atomic battlefield" exercises, "downwinders" from test sites, and Marshall Islanders.[13] Politically, nuclear regimes require a level of secrecy and security measures that excludes the majority of citizens and, in most countries, all women from defense policy and decision making.[14]

From the perspective of women's lives, we see not only the costs of the *development* of nuclear weapons, but also the spiritual, social, and psychological costs of *deployment*. One cost, according to some feminists, is that "Nuclearisation produces social consent for increasing levels of violence.[15] Another cost for many is that nuclear weapons create high levels of tension, insecurity, and fear. As Arundhati Roy puts it, nuclear weapons "[i]nform our dreams. They bury themselves like meat hooks deep in the base of our brains."[16]

Further, feminists are concerned about the effect of nuclear policy on moral thought, on ideas about gender, and how the two intersect. Nuclear development may legitimize male aggression and breed the idea that nuclear explosions give "virility" to the nation, which men as individuals can somehow also share.

> [T]he strange character of nuclear policy-making not only sidelines moral and ethical questions, but genders them. This elite gets to be represented as rational, scientific, modern, and of course masculine, while ethical questions, questions about the social and environmental costs are made to seem emotional, effeminate, regressive and not modern. This rather dangerous way of thinking, which suggests that questions about human life and welfare are somehow neither modern nor properly masculine questions, or that men have no capacity and concern for peace and morality, can have disastrous consequences for both men and women.[17]

All in all, we find the daily costs of WMD development and deployment staggeringly high—in and of themselves sufficient to prevent deterrence from being an ethical moral option.

A so-called realist response to this judgment might well pay lip-service to the "moral niceties"

it embodies, but then argue that deterrence is worth those costs. Or perhaps to be more accurate, it might argue that the results of a nuclear attack would be so catastrophic that the rest of these considerations are really an irrelevant distraction; deterring a WMD attack on our homeland is the precondition on which political freedom and social life depend, and so it must be thought about in a class by itself.

We make two rejoinders to this claim. First, we note that in the culture of nuclear defense intellectuals, even raising the issue of costs is delegitimized, in large part through its association with "the feminine." It is the kind of thing that "hysterical housewives" do; something done by people not tough and hard enough to look harsh "reality" in the eye, unsentimentally; not strong enough to separate their feelings from theorizing mass death; people who don't have "the stones for war." Feminist analysis rejects the cultural division of meaning that devalues anything associated with women or femininity. It sees in that same cultural valuing of the so-called masculine over the so-called feminine an explanation of why it appears so self-evident to many that what is called "military necessity" should appropriately be prioritized over all other human necessities. And it questions the assumptions that bestow the mantle of "realism" on such a constrained focus on weapons and state power. Rather than simply being an "objective" reflection of political reality, we understand this thought system as (1) a partial and distorted picture of reality and (2) a major contributor to creating the very circumstances it purports to describe and protect against.

Second, just as feminists tend to be skeptical about the efficacy of violence, they might be equally skeptical about the efficacy of deterrence. Or to put it another way, if war is a "lie," so is deterrence. This is not, of course, to say that deterrence *as a phenomenon* never, occurs; no doubt, one opponent is sometimes deterred from attacking another by the fear of retaliation. But rather, deterrence *as a theory, a discourse,* and a set of practices underwritten by that discourse is a fiction.

Deterrence theory is an elaborate, abstract conceptual edifice, which posits a hypothetical relation between two different sets of weapons systems—or rather, between abstractions of two different sets of weapons systems, for in fact, as both common sense and military expertise tell us, human error and technological imperfection mean that one could not actually expect real weapons to function in the ways simply assumed in deterrence theory. Because deterrence theory sets in play the hypothetical representations of various weapons systems, rather than assessments of how they would actually perform or fail to perform in warfare, it can be nearly infinitely elaborated, in a never-ending regression of intercontinental ballistic missile gaps and theater warfare gaps and tactical "mini-nuke" gaps, ad infinitum, thus legitimating both massive vertical proliferation and arms racing.

Deterrence theory is also a fiction in that it depends on "rational actors," for whom what counts as "rational" is the same, independent of culture, history, or individual difference. It depends on those "rational actors" perfectly understanding the meaning of "signals" communicated by military actions, despite dependence on technologies that sometimes malfunction, despite cultural difference and the lack of communication that is part of being political enemies, despite the difficulties of ensuring mutual understanding even when best friends make direct face-to-face statements to each other. It depends on those same "rational actors" engaging in a very specific kind of calculus that includes one set of variables (e.g., weapons size, deliverability, survivability, as well as the "credibility" of their and their opponent's threats) and excludes other variables (such as domestic political pressures, economics, or individual subjectivity). What is striking from a feminist perspective is that even while "realists" may worry that some opponents are so "insufficiently rational" as to be undeterrable, this does not lead them to search for a more reliable form of ensuring security or to an approach that is not so weapons-dependent.

Cynthia Cockburn, in her study of women's peace projects in conflict zones, describes one of the women's activities as helping each other give up "dangerous day dreams."[18] From a feminist antiwar perspective, having WMD as deterrents is a dangerous dream. The dream of perfect rationality and control that underwrites deterrence theory is a dangerous dream, since it legitimates constructing a system that could be (relatively) safe only if that perfect rationality and control were actually possible. Deterrence theory itself is a dangerous dream because it justifies producing and deploying WMD, thereby making their accidental or purposive use possible (and far more likely) than if they were not produced at all nor deployed in such numbers. "Realists" are quick to point out the dangers of *not having* WMD for deterrence when other states have them. Feminist perspectives suggest that that danger appears so self-evidently greater than the danger of *having* WMD only if you discount as "soft" serious attention to the costs of development and deployment.

WMD Proliferation

The fourth question asks: "If some nations possess weapons of mass destruction (either licitly or illicitly) for defensive and deterrent purposes, is it proper to deny such possession to others for the same purposes?"

We believe that the rampant proliferation of weapons of *all kinds*, from handguns to nuclear weapons, is a massive tragedy, the direct and indirect source of great human suffering. Given this starting point, we of course oppose the proliferation of weapons of mass destruction. But our opposition does not allow us to give a simple "yes" answer to the fourth question as it is posed. Before turning to proliferation as a *phenomenon*, we must first consider current proliferation *discourse*.

Proliferation as a Discourse

"Proliferation" is not a mere description or mirror of a phenomenon that is "out there," but rather a very specific way of identifying and constructing a problem. "Proliferation," as used in Western political discourse, does not simply refer to the "multiplication" of weapons of mass destruction on the planet. Rather, it constructs some WMD as a problem and others as unproblematic. It does so by assuming preexisting, legitimate possessors of the weapons, implicitly not only entitled to those weapons but to "modernize" and develop new "generations" of them as well. The "problematic" WMD are only those that "spread" into the arsenals of other, formerly nonpossessor states. This is presumably the basis for the "licit/illicit" distinction in the question; it does not refer to the nature of the weapons themselves nor even to the purposes for which they are intended—only, in the case of nuclear weapons, to who the possessor is, where "licitness" is based on the treaty-enshrined "we got there first."

Thus, use of the term "proliferation" tends to locate the person who uses it within a possessor state and aligns him or her with the political stance favoring the hierarchy of state power enshrined in the current distribution of WMD. The framing of the fourth question, ". . . is it proper to deny [WMD] possession to others for the same purposes?" seems similarly based in a possessor state perspective, as it is presumably the possessor states who must decide whether it is proper to deny possession to others.

As we have already stated, we find WMD themselves intrinsically morally indefensible, no matter who possesses them, and we are concerned about the wide array of costs *to any state* of development and deployment. We therefore reject the discourse's implicit division of "good" and "bad," "safe" and "unsafe" WMD (defined as good or bad depending on who possesses them). Our concern is to understand how some WMD are rendered invisible ("ours") and some visible ("theirs"); some rendered malignant and others benign.

Here, we join others in noting that the language in which the case against "proliferation" is made is ethno-racist and contemptuous. Gener-

ally, in Western proliferation discourse as a whole, a distinction is drawn between "the 'Self' (seen as responsible) vs. the non-Western Unruly Other.[19] The United States represents itself as a rational actor, while representing the Unruly Other as emotional, unpredictable, irrational, immature, misbehaving. Not only does this draw on and reconstruct an Orientalist portrayal of third world actors;[20] it does so through the medium of gendered terminology. By drawing the relations between possessors and nonpossessors in gendered terms—the prudential, rational, advanced, mature, restrained, technologically and bureaucratically competent (and thus "masculine") Self versus the emotional, irrational, unpredictable, uncontrolled, immature, primitive, undisciplined, technologically incompetent (and thus "feminine") Unruly Other—the discourse naturalizes and legitimates the Self/possessor states having weapons that the Other does not. By drawing on and evoking gendered imagery and resonances, the discourse naturalizes the idea that "We"/the United States/the responsible father must protect, control, and limit "her," the emotional, out-of-control state, for her own good, as well as for ours.

This Western proliferation discourse has had a function in the wider context of U.S. national security politics. With the end of the "Evil Empire" in the late 1980s, until the attacks of September 11, 2001, the United States appeared to be without an enemy of grand enough proportions to justify maintaining its sprawling military-industrial establishment. This difficulty was forestalled by the construction of the category of "rogue states"—states seen as uncontrollable, irresponsible, irrational, malevolent, and antagonistic to the West.[21] Their unruliness and antagonism were represented as intrinsic to their irrational nature; if it were not in their "nature," the United States would have needed to ask more seriously if actions on the part of the West had had any role in producing that hostility and disorder.

The discourse of WMD proliferation has been one of the principal means of producing these states as major threats. To say this is neither to back away from our position of opposing weapons of mass destruction nor to assess the degree to which WMD in the hands of "Other" states actually do threaten the United States, the "Other" states' regional opponents, or their own population. But it is an assessment of the role of WMD proliferation discourse in naturalizing and legitimating programs and expenditures such as National Missile Defense that are otherwise difficult to make appear rational.[22]

Proliferation as a Phenomenon

Within the logic of deterrence theory and proliferation discourse, the phenomenon of WMD proliferation is understandable in two main ways. States acquire WMD either for purposes of aggression—that is, to use WMD or to threaten their use in acts of aggression, intimidation, and/or coercion against other states or populations within their own state—or to enhance their own security by deterring an opponent's attack. Within a strategic calculus, either is understood as a "rational" motivation for WMD possession, even if not everyone would view these reasons as equally morally defensible.

Some in the security community have argued that this "realist consensus" about states' motivations for development of WMD "is dangerously inadequate." They argue that "nuclear weapons, like other weapons, are more than tools of national security; they are political objects of considerable importance in domestic debates and internal bureaucratic struggles and can also serve as international normative symbols of modernity and identity."[23] We agree, but would add that understanding any of those motivations will be incomplete without gender analysis.

We argue that gendered terms and images are an integral part of the ways national security issues are thought about and represented—and that it matters. During the 1991 Gulf War, for example, the mass media speculated about whether George Bush had finally "beat the wimp factor." When in the spring of 1998, India exploded five

nuclear devices, Hindu nationalist leader Balasaheb Thackeray explained, "We had to prove that we are not eunuchs." An Indian newspaper cartoon "depicted Prime Minister Atal Behari Vajpayee propping up his coalition government with a nuclear bomb. 'Made with Viagra,' the caption read."[24]

Feminists argue that these images are not trivial, but instead deserve analysis. Metaphors that equate political and military power with sexual potency and masculinity serve to both shape and limit the ways in which national security is conceptualized.[25] Political actors incorporate sexual metaphors in their representations of nuclear weapons as a way to mobilize gendered associations and symbols in creating assent, excitement, support for, and identification with the weapons and their own political regime. Moreover, gendered metaphor is not only an integral part of accomplishing domestic power aims. The use of these metaphors also appropriates the test of a nuclear weapon into the occasion for reinforcing patriarchal gender relations.

That a nation wishing to stake a claim to being a world power (or a regional one) should choose nuclear weapons as its medium for doing so is often seen as "natural": The more advanced military destructive capacity you have, the more powerful you are. The "fact" that nuclear weapons would be the coin of the realm in establishing a hierarchy of state power is fundamentally unremarked, unanalyzed, taken for granted by most (non-feminist) analysts. Some antiwar feminists, by contrast, have looked with a historical and postcolonial eye and seen nuclear weapons' enshrinement as the emblem of power not as a natural fact but as a social one, produced by the actions of states. They argue that when the United States, with the most powerful economy and conventional military in the world, acts as though its power and security are guaranteed only by a large nuclear arsenal, it creates a context in which nuclear weapons become the ultimate necessity for and symbol of state security.[26] And when the United States or any other nuclear power works hard to ensure that other states do not obtain nuclear weapons, it is creating a context in which nuclear weapons become the ultimate arbiter of political power.[27]

An Ethical Nonproliferation Politics?

Finally, after our critique of both the framing and political uses of Western proliferation discourse and our questioning of the adequacy of the models through which proliferation as a phenomenon is understood, there remains the question: "If some nations possess weapons of mass destruction (either licitly or illicitly) for defensive and deterrent purposes, is it proper to deny such possession to others for the same purposes?"

We have spoken of the multiple costs of developing and deploying nuclear weapons *to their possessors* (third question) and the immense suffering that weapons of mass destruction would bring. Given what we have said, we should not be indifferent to other states' developing nuclear weapons unless we were indifferent to them. Additionally, as we argue in response to the fifth question, we believe that more WMD in more places would make their "accidental" or purposive use by states, as well as their availability to terrorists, more likely. So we are opposed to the development and deployment of any WMD, by any state or nonstate actor.

Despite this clear opposition to the spread of WMD, we are uneasy simply answering "yes" to the question *as it is posed*. The question assumes that some states already have WMD and asks only whether it is proper to deny WMD to others. Denying WMD to others implies maintaining the current international balance of power, in which the West is privileged, politically and economically. As feminists, we oppose the extreme inequality inherent in the current world order and are troubled by actions that will further enshrine it. But at the same time, we cannot endorse WMD proliferation as a mode of equalization, nor do we see it as an effective form of redress.

Second, we come to the question not only as feminists but as citizens of the most highly armed possessor state. As such, we must ask: Are citizens of possessor states entitled to judge, threaten, allow, or encourage the decisions of nonpossessor states to develop WMD? On what grounds? In what discursive territory? As we have outlined above, we find the existing proliferation discourse too ethno-racist, too focused on horizontal rather than vertical proliferation, and too sanguine about the justifiability of "our" having what "they" are not fit to have.

Our task, then, as antiwar feminists, is to learn how to participate in a constructive conversation,[28] eschewing the vocabulary of "proliferation," learning to listen, perhaps publicizing the warnings that women—and men—are issuing about the multiple costs and risks of WMD in their particular states. As citizens of the most highly armed possessor state, our credibility as participants in this conversation will be contingent on our committed efforts to bring about nuclear disarmament in our own state and our efforts to redress the worldwide inequalities that are underwritten by our military superiority.

WMD Disarmament

Our tradition has advocated and will continue to advocate unilateral reduction in nuclear arms. Our commitment to nuclear disarmament originates in a general understanding of the use and dangers of weapons. We begin by noting that conflict is endemic to human relationships. "Peace" means, among other things, engaging in conflicts, that is, "fighting," without actually injuring or damaging others, without trying to do so, at best without being willing to do so.

There will always be something at hand to use as a weapon and threaten the "peace"; it is impossible to create a weaponless scene of conflict. A child's block, a kitchen knife, a passenger airliner can injure or kill. There is no substitute, then, for learning to fight without resorting to weapons.

But having "real" weapons at hand makes conflict far more dangerous. It makes injuring more likely, whether accidental, deliberate, unwitting, or willing. It also tends to expand the scale of injury; for example, while two airliners hitting the World Trade Center resulted in more than 3,000 deaths, a "small" nuclear warhead dropped on the twin towers would have instantly killed at least 100,000, with another 100,000 deaths in the days that followed. Deliberately relying on weapons—purchasing them, learning to use them, keeping them nearby—makes less likely the development of other strategies of self-protection. Once on the scene, weapons may be used in anger or ignorance, just because they are nearby. Weapons injure; as far as possible they should be cleared out.

Nonetheless, individuals and states continue to keep weapons at hand. States and citizens draw lessons from history that show the dangers of disarmament. We believe that the recourse to weapons underestimates their complex costs and dangers. People equate being armed with being safe, unarmed with being vulnerable. They overlook the risk of guns at hand and exaggerate the protection guns may give. But we understand that the issue of weapons arises from personal experience and collective identities, that it is deeply felt and in no way simple. We would insist only that weapons are never a substitute for negotiation and nonviolent fighting and that they may well hinder the success of nonviolent methods.

When we turn to weapons of mass destruction, we have only three additional comments. First, given the political will, nuclear weapons are among the most easily reduced. The scale of the effort required to produce them, the scientific and technological expertise and financial investment involved, have all militated toward state ownership and control of nuclear weapons. Thus, in contrast to weapons such as small arms—which are unregulated, can travel anywhere, and often become the property of near-children—nuclear weapons are relatively controllable and so can be selectively destroyed.

Second, unilateral disarmament is not an all-or-nothing matter, in which weapons disappear almost overnight. Would that this were possible. In reality, destroying nuclear weapons would be a massively complicated feat, slow and gradual at best. It is often said, rightly, that the United States can never disarm itself completely, can never lose the capacity to develop nuclear weapons. We are saying that the United States would lose *nothing* by beginning to destroy its remaining weapons. It would always have weapons, remain a nuclear "power," even if it wished otherwise. The example of unilateral disarmament might, on the other hand, lend credibility to the stated desire for a more stable world less endangered by nuclear weapons.

Finally, George W. Bush's nuclear missile defense, Reagan's impenetrable shield *redux*, symbolizes the sense of safety and power that nuclear weapons of all kinds appear to bestow. We know that even if such a shield were technologically feasible, it would be porous, "penetrable," not only by nuclear warheads on missiles but by nuclear weapons in suitcases, on boats, and in Piper Cubs; by biological weapons sent through the mail; by chemical weapons sprayed by crop-dusters; by passenger airliners employed as tools of mass destruction. But "giving up" weapons and giving up the promise (no matter how far-fetched) of a means to defend against them makes one feel vulnerable—and, thus, by extension, "feminine." There is nothing shameful—and nothing masculine or feminine—about the desire to be safe and to provide safety for others. But the hope of finding safety in weapons is another "dangerous dream" that nuclear weapons inspire.

Concrete Options

The final question asks us to evaluate current or proposed treaty agreements concerning nuclear, biological, and chemical weapons. We are offered a place at the negotiating table, a position few women, probably fewer feminists, have occupied.

For feminists there are two questions: How should we respond to the invitation? And what should we say about particular treaties if we accept? The second question is not one to which antiwar feminists have a distinctive answer arising from our tradition. It is the first question, whether to come to the table and how to act effectively once there, that traditionally and today preoccupies feminists.

Peace making, like war, has been dominated by men. Few women have been asked to participate in negotiations; when asked, it has usually been late, after the agenda was already set. But women are now claiming their place in negotiations.[29] They have participated in the struggles and have a right to be present; many feel that only they will represent women's distinctive interests.

Getting and accepting an invitation is only the first step in being able to participate effectively. Often women have to overcome outright hostility and ridicule from male participants. When they are treated with courtesy, they may still feel unable to express their concerns and ignored or dismissed when they try. Even when present in large numbers, women may be unable fully to engage. In South Africa women were welcomed to the peace table and occupied half its seats, but no one had contended with the divisions of work and responsibility in their lives. When negotiations lasted well into the night, no one was taking care of their husbands and children; women who stayed became tense and preoccupied.[30]

Women's difficulties participating in peace negotiations may be especially marked when the topic is weapons, a subject that, as we have said, is particularly liable to lend itself to abstraction. A report by a woman participant at biological weapons treaty negotiations sounds familiar themes. What counts as "reason" prevailed, what gets coded as "emotions" were excluded. Disturbing concerns, for example, with the effects of a vaccine on troops or the populace, were labeled "emotional." Speakers engaged in "cool, detached reasoning about the possible uses of weapons against an adversary. . . . 'Useful' in this context means ability to cause serious loss of life." Talking about a vaccine's negative effects was tantamount to "complaining," "whining," "carrying on."[31]

In discussions of biological weapons, as in issues of proliferation, the dichotomous division between reason and emotion is entwined with a similar division between [Western] Self and [unruly] Other, a particular instance of self and other, Us and Enemy typical of peace and arms negotiation. "One test of belonging and being heard in this group was whether one accepted the nature of the source of the BW problem. Did one accept the identity of the adversary?" That identity was often described in racist terms—for example, "[they] don't value human life the way we do"—and these remarks elicited no comment.[32]

"To belong and speak and be heard" would mean ignoring the rules and interrupting the cool detached voice of reason. Again the gender discourse system is at work, frustrating these efforts. An objection that acknowledges emotion, that talks about the fate of bodies or lives, becomes an "outburst." Reason ignores them in order to continue the discussion of weapons and their effects. Outbursts are "feminine"; in the silence that follows an outburst, anyone, male or female, can "feel like a woman." The effect of gender discourse depends on a person's complex personal and social identities. But for a feminist, who aims to speak as herself-who-is-a-woman, the *accusation* of "being a woman" or a wimp has to be poignantly inhibiting.

For feminists struggling to participate effectively, the final insult may be the realization that the negotiations, especially if they are presented as inclusive and democratic, are more ritualistic displays than political action. "In reality, major decisions are made in secret in the capitals, based on calculations that seek military (and increasingly commercial) advantages."[33] In the words of a male political scientist: "Arms control is war by other means." Real power is always already somewhere else by the time a woman takes her place at the table.[34]

Should women then give up the effort to join in negotiations? It seems that many do. They "get intimidated, and don't put up with it, so they step aside."[35] But other women in increasing numbers are resisting ridicule and discrimination in order to make their views known. There are many reasons, personal and social, why some women persevere where others do not. Cultural attitudes toward women vary; women are more easily heard when many women are present, especially if they are linked in alliances that include all parties in conflict.

One reason that some women persevere is their belief that they have a distinctive perspective to bring to negotiation. Women participants in peace negotiations have said that they bring to the table an ability to attest to "the severe human consequences of conflict" and a commitment to expose the "underbelly of war." They stress the importance of speaking openly about pain and fear and loss, of building trust among adversaries, of opening up difficult, divisive issues rather than cloaking them in rhetoric or postponing them. They are apt to "see more clearly the continuum of conflict that stretches from the beating at home to the rape on the street to the killing on the battlefield." "They witness vivid links between violence, poverty and inequality in daily lives." They define peace in terms of "basic universal human needs" and advocate practical solutions to the building of peace, focusing on ordinary safety, housing, education, and child care.[36]

In sum, these women introduce a perspective that satisfies the criteria of the "feminine" as it functions metaphorically in gender discourse. The women only sometimes compare themselves with men, occasionally with some anger, more often speaking quietly of what women are more likely to believe and do. But it would be hard to *accuse* them of acting like women; and if women are present in sufficient numbers, they may be less vulnerable to the silencing power of gendered national security discourse.

Making treaties is only a small part of making peace. There are virtues in treaty making even when individual treaties are seriously flawed. Negotiating requires structured places in which opponents can talk; signed treaties require further conversation and negotiation. Prolonged negoti-

ations create relations that at the least survive post-treaty crises and at best may help to resolve them. But treaties are no substitute for peace-building processes. They are made in formal contexts where participants are apt to cling to their ethno-national political identities and to keep their eye on political boundaries, rewards, and positions.[37] Among treaties, arms control negotiations, which extrapolate weapons from their context of injury and pain, may be the least amenable to the perspectives attributed to and claimed by women.

But if there are to be treaties, if weapons of mass destruction are to be subject to negotiation, then our tradition would encourage the participation of women. This is not because we believe that women offer a perspective "different" from men's—though that may be the case in many cultures at this historical moment. What gets left out of dominant ways of thinking about weapons— the emotional, the concrete, the particular, the human bodies and their vulnerability, human lives and their subjectivity—is neither masculine nor feminine but human. Rather, we would hope that the power of gender discourse to exclude what is now coded as "feminine" would be weakened by the presence of numbers of women for whom "acting and feeling like a woman" were a matter of course, even sometimes a source of strength, and not an occasion for self-doubt and silence.

NOTES

1. From a speech by Harry S. Truman. The full text was published in the *New York Times*, August 10, 1945, p 12.

2. Cited in Bel Mooney, "Beyond the Wasteland," in *Over Our Dead Bodies: Women against the Bomb*, ed. Dorothy Thompson (London: Virago Press, 1983), 7.

3. See Enloe, especially *Maneuvers* and *Bananas, Beaches, and Bases*; Jacklyn Cock, *Women and War in South Africa* (Cleveland, Ohio: Pilgrim Press, 1993).

4. Carol Cohn, "War, Wimps and Women," in *Gendering War Talk*, 227–46. See also idem, "Sex and Death in the Rational World of Defense Intellectuals," *Signs* 12:4 (1987): 687–728.

5. Elaine Scarry, *The Body in Pain* (Oxford: Oxford University Press, 1985).

6. Cockburn, *Space between Us*, 8.

7. See David Chappell, Chapter 11 in this volume.

8. Cohn, "Sex and Death," 15–28.

9. See Cohn, "Wars, Wimps and Women" and "Sex and Death." For a very different presentation of these points, see Susan Griffin, *A Chorus of Stones* (New York: Doubleday, 1992); Christa Wolf, *Cassandra* (New York: Farrar, Straus & Giroux, 1984), and *Accident: A Day's News* (New York: Farrar, Straus & Giroux, 1989).

10. General Robert Rosenberg, formerly on the National Security Council staff during the Carter administration, speaking at the Harvard Seminar on C3I. "The Influence of Policy Making on C3I," in "Incidental Paper: Seminar on Command, Control, Communications and Intelligence," Spring 1980, Center for Information Policy Research, Harvard University, p. 59.

11. Hisako Matsubara, *Cranes at Dusk* (Garden City, N.Y.: Dial Press, 1985). The author was a child in Kyoto at the time the atomic bomb was dropped. Her description is based on the memories of survivors.

12. Cohn, "Wars, Wimps and Women."

13. Schwartz, "Four Trillion Dollars."

14. This point is made by Sangari et al., "Why Women Must Reject," 47.

15. Ibid., 48.

16. Roy, "End of Imagination," 101. She writes: "It is such supreme folly to believe that nuclear weapons are deadly only if they're used. The fact that they exist at all, their very presence in our lives, will wreak more havoc than we can begin to fathom."

17. Sangari et al., "Why Women Must Reject," 48.

18. Cockburn, *Space between Us*, 11.

19. Susan Wright, "Feminist Tales from the Arms Control Front," lecture at University of Michigan, March 24, 2001. Transcript by courtesy of the author.

20. Edward Said, *Orientalism* (New York: Pantheon, 1978); Hugh Gusterson, "Orientalism and the Arms Race: An Analysis of the Neocolonial Discourse on Nuclear Nonproliferation," working paper no. 47, Center for Transcultural Studies, 1991; Shampa Biswas, "'Nuclear Apartheid' as Political Position: Race as a Postcolonial Resource?" *Alternatives* 26:4 (October-December 2001): 485–522.

21. For "rogue states," see Michael Klare, *Rogue States and Nuclear Outlaws: America's Search for a New Foreign Policy* (New York: Hill and Wang, 1995). See also Wright, "Feminist Tales."

22. Nicholas Berry, "Too Much Hysteria Exists over the Increasing Proliferation of Weapons of Mass Destructions and Ballistic Missile Technology: A More Modest Hysteria Would Be Wiser," *Asia Forum*, January 21, 2000.

23. Scott Sagan, for example, has argued that "nuclear weapons programs also serve other, more parochial and less obvious objectives." Sagan, "Why Do States Build Nuclear Weapons? Three Models in Search of a Bomb," *International Security* 21:3 (Winter 1996/97): 54–86. In our view all three of the models Sagan outlines—the "security model," the "domestic politics model," and the "norms model"—are seriously weakened by their failure to incorporate gender analysis.

24. Basu and Basu, "India: Of Men, Women, and Bombs," 39.

25. Cohn, "Wars, Wimps, and Women."

26. Arundhati Roy put it this way: "But let us pause to give credit where it's due. Whom must we thank for all this? The Men who made it happen. The Masters of the Universe. Ladies and gentlemen, the United States of America! Come on up here, folks, stand up

and take a bow. Thank you for doing this to the world. Thank you for making a difference. Thank you for showing us the way. Thank you for altering the very meaning of life." Roy, "End of Imagination," 100–101.

27. Some Indian feminists have combined this attention to weapons-as-symbols-in-world-power-relations with an analysis of the gendered meanings of power. Basu and Basu argue that the BJP's decision to explode five nuclear bombs was in part an attempt "to shatter stereotypes about the 'effeminate' Indian that date back to the period of British colonialism." The British particularly disparaged "feminized" Hindu masculinity, while seeing Muslims as "robust and brave." Basu and Basu, "India: Of Men, Women, and Bombs," 39.

28. The term "constructive conversation" was introduced to us through a conversation Carol had with Laura Chasin, the director of the Public Conversations Project. Their website, http://www.publicconversations.org, would be a valuable resource for anyone who is trying to think about political conflict.

29. "Women Building Peace: From the Village Council to the Negotiating Table" is a network of grassroots activists and national and international organizations focused on getting women included in peace processes. See their website, www.international-alert.org/women, as well as the website of "Women Waging Peace," www.womenwagingpeace.net,

for more information on women's participation in peace-building efforts, including peace negotiations. In October 2000, the UN Security Council passed Resolution 1325 on Women, International Peace and Security, which affirmed the importance of women's role in peace building and stressed the importance of women's equal participation in all efforts for the promotion of peace and security.

30. Sanam Naraghi Anderlini, *Women at the Peace Table: Making a Difference* (New York: UNIFEM, 2000), 30.

31. Wright, "Feminist Tales." For further discussion of the place of what counts as "emotion" in international political discourse, see Neta C. Crawford, "The Passion of World Politics: Propositions on Emotion and Emotional Relationships," *International Security* 24:4 (Spring 2000): 116–56.

32. Wright, "Feminist Tales."

33. Ibid.

34. Ibid. Wright cites Barry Posen, "Military Lessons of the Gulf War—Implications for Middle East Arms Control," in *Arms Control and the New Middle East Security Environment*, ed. Shai Feldman and Ariel Levite (Jerusalem: Jaffee Center for Strategic Studies, 1994), 64.

35. Hanan Ashrawi, cited in Anderlini, *Women at the Peace Table*, 29.

36. Quotes and paraphrases from ibid., 29–36 and passim.

37. Ibid.

9 INTERNATIONAL POLITICAL ECONOMY

A plethora of economic issues are critical to understanding international relations in the twenty-first century. In the first selection here, a classic from U.S. Power and the Multinational Corporation *(1975), Princeton University's Robert Gilpin clearly and concisely discusses the relationship between economics and politics. He examines the three basic conceptions of political economy (liberalism, radicalism, and mercantilism), comparing them along a number of dimensions, including their perspectives on the nature of economic relations, actors, goals of economic relations; their theories of change; and how they characterize the relationship between economics and politics.*

International economic institutions play a key role in the liberal economy. Helen Milner of Princeton University examines the impact of these institutions—the IMF, World Bank, and World Trade Organization—on developing countries. She finds mixed economic outcomes, leading her to explore possible explanations. Martin Wolf, in his 2004 book Why Globalization Works, *responds to critics of neoliberal economic globalization. In this book chapter, he asks whether human welfare is rising. He finds that never before have so many individuals enjoyed such high standards of living. The poorest countries have not been hurt by the effects of economic liberalization, they have just failed to participate in it.*

Economic globalization has led to unanticipated consequences. Among the most vexing is the rise of the illicit political economy. Foreign Policy *editor Moisés Naím discusses how open borders and new technologies have led to illegal markets in people, drugs, weapons, and financial flows. Governments and state structures are challenged in new ways. Another unintended consequence of globalization has been identified by* New York Times *columnist Thomas Friedman as the First Law of Petropolitics: as oil-exporting states benefit from increasing oil prices, the less likely they are to initiate political reforms. Wealthy oil-rich regimes are able to provide political patronage, spend for coercive forces, and use revenues to relieve societal pressures, without introducing liberal political measures.*

Economic globalization has its radical critics. Sociologist Valentine M. Moghadam investigates how women have been affected by growing employment in the formal and informal sector, unionization, and greater social and gender inequities.

ROBERT GILPIN

THE NATURE OF POLITICAL ECONOMY

The international corporations have evidently declared ideological war on the "antiquated" nation state. . . . The charge that materialism, modernization and internationalism is the new liberal creed of corporate capitalism is a valid one. The implication is clear: the nation state as a political unit of democratic decision-making must, in the interest of "progress," yield control to the new mercantile mini-powers.[1]

While the structure of the multinational corporation is a modern concept, designed to meet the requirements of a modern age, the nation state is a very old-fashioned idea and badly adapted to serve the needs of our present complex world.[2]

These two statements—the first by Kari Levitt, a Canadian nationalist, the second by George Ball, a former United States undersecretary of state—express a dominant theme of contemporary writings on international relations. International society, we are told, is increasingly rent between its economic and its political organization. On the one hand, powerful economic and technological forces are creating a highly interdependent world economy, thus diminishing the traditional significance of national boundaries. On the other hand, the nation-state continues to command men's loyalties and to be the basic unit of political decision making. As one writer has put the issue, "The conflict of our era is be-

From Robert Gilpin, *U.S. Power and the Multinational Corporation* (New York: Basic Books, 1975), Chap. 1.

tween ethnocentric nationalism and geocentric technology."[3]

Ball and Levitt represent two contending positions with respect to this conflict. Whereas Ball advocates the diminution of the power of the nation-state in order to give full rein to the productive potentialities of the multinational corporation, Levitt argues for a powerful nationalism which could counterbalance American corporate domination. What appears to one as the logical and desirable consequence of economic rationality seems to the other to be an effort on the part of American imperialism to eliminate all contending centers of power.

Although the advent of the multinational corporation has put the question of the relationship between economics and politics in a new guise, it is an old issue. In the nineteenth century, for example, it was this issue that divided classical liberals like John Stuart Mill from economic nationalists, represented by Georg Friedrich List. Whereas the former gave primacy in the organization of society to economics and the production of wealth, the latter emphasized the political determination of economic relations. As this issue is central both to the contemporary debate on the multinational corporation and to the argument of this study, this chapter analyzes the three major treatments of the relationship between economics and politics—that is, the three major ideologies of political economy.

The Meaning of Political Economy

The argument of this study is that the relationship between economics and politics, at least in the modern world, is a reciprocal one. On the one hand, politics largely determines the framework of economic activity and channels it in directions intended to serve the interests of dominant groups; the exercise of power in all its forms is a major determinant of the nature of an economic system. On the other hand, the economic process itself tends to redistribute power and wealth; it transforms the power relationships among groups. This in turn leads to a transformation of the political system, thereby giving rise to a new structure of economic relationships. Thus, the dynamics of international relations in the modern world is largely a function of the reciprocal interaction between economics and politics.

First of all, what do I mean by "politics" or "economics"? Charles Kindleberger speaks of economics and politics as two different methods of allocating scarce resources: the first through a market mechanism, the latter through a budget.[4] Robert Keohane and Joseph Nye, in an excellent analysis of international political economy, define economics and politics in terms of two levels of analysis: those of structure and of process.[5] Politics is the domain "having to do with the establishment of an order of relations, a structure. . . ."[6] Economics deals with "short-term allocative behavior (i.e., holding institutions, fundamental assumptions, and expectations constant). . . ."[7] Like Kindleberger's definition, however, this definition tends to isolate economic and political phenomena except under certain conditions, which Keohane and Nye define as the "politicization" of the economic system. Neither formulation comes to terms adequately with the dynamic and intimate nature of the relationship between the two.

In this study, the issue of the relationship between economics and politics translates into that between wealth and power. According to this statement of the problem, economics takes as its province the creation and distribution of wealth;

politics is the realm of power. I shall examine their relationship from several ideological perspectives, including my own. But what is wealth? What is power?

In response to the question, What is wealth?, an economist-colleague responded, "What do you want, my thirty-second or thirty-volume answer?" Basic concepts are elusive in economics, as in any field of inquiry. No unchallengeable definitions are possible. Ask a physicist for his definition of the nature of space, time, and matter, and you will not get a very satisfying response. What you will get is an *operational* definition, one which is usable: it permits the physicist to build an intellectual edifice whose foundations would crumble under the scrutiny of the philosopher.

Similarly, the concept of wealth, upon which the science of economics ultimately rests, cannot be clarified in a definitive way. Paul Samuelson, in his textbook, doesn't even try, though he provides a clue in his definition of economics as "the study of how men and society *choose* . . . to employ *scarce* productive resources . . . to produce various commodities . . . and distribute them for consumption."[8] Following this lead, we can say that wealth is anything (capital, land, or labor) that can generate future income; it is composed of physical assets and human capital (including embodied knowledge).

The basic concept of political science is power. Most political scientists would not stop here; they would include in the definition of political science the purpose for which power is used, whether this be the advancement of the public welfare or the domination of one group over another. In any case, few would dissent from the following statement of Harold Lasswell and Abraham Kaplan:

> The concept of power is perhaps the most fundamental in the whole of political science: the political process is the shaping, distribution, and exercise of power (in a wider sense, of all the deference values, or of influence in general.)[9]

Power as such is not the sole or even the principal goal of state behavior. Other goals or values constitute the objectives pursued by nation-states: welfare, security, prestige. But power in its several forms (military, economic, psychological) is ultimately the necessary means to achieve these goals. For this reason, nation-states are intensely jealous of and sensitive to their relative power position. The distribution of power is important because it profoundly affects the ability of states to achieve what they perceive to be their interests.

The nature of power, however, is even more elusive than that of wealth. The number and variety of definitions should be an embarrassment to political scientists. Unfortunately, this study cannot bring the intradisciplinary squabble to an end. Rather, it adopts the definition used by Hans Morgenthau in his influential *Politics Among Nations*: "man's control over the minds and actions of other men."[10] Thus, power, like wealth, is the capacity to produce certain results.

Unlike wealth, however, power can not be quantified; indeed, it cannot be overemphasized that power has an important psychological dimension. Perceptions of power relations are of critical importance; as a consequence, a fundamental task of statesmen is to manipulate the perceptions of other statesmen regarding the distribution of power. Moreover, power is relative to a specific situation or set of circumstances; there is no single hierarchy of power in international relations. Power may take many forms—military, economic, or psychological—though, in the final analysis, force is the ultimate form of power. Finally, the inability to predict the behavior of others or the outcome of events is of great significance. Uncertainty regarding the distribution of power and the ability of the statesmen to control events plays an important role in international relations. Ultimately, the determination of the distribution of power can be made only in retrospect as a consequence of war. It is precisely for this reason that war has had, unfortunately, such a central place in the history of international relations. In short, power is an elusive concept indeed upon which to erect a science of politics.

*   *   *

The distinction * * * between economics as the science of wealth and politics as the science of power is essentially an analytical one. In the real world, wealth and power are ultimately joined. This, in fact, is the basic rationale for a political economy of international relations. But in order to develop the argument of this study, wealth and power will be treated, at least for the moment, as analytically distinct.

To provide a perspective on the nature of political economy, the next section of the chapter will discuss the three prevailing conceptions of political economy: liberalism, Marxism, and mercantilism. Liberalism regards politics and economics as relatively separable and autonomous spheres of activities; I associate most professional economists as well as many other academics, businessmen, and American officials with this outlook. Marxism refers to the radical critique of capitalism identified with Karl Marx and his contemporary disciples; according to this conception, economics determines politics and political structure. Mercantilism is a more questionable term because of its historical association with the desire of nation-states for a trade surplus and for treasure (money). One must distinguish, however, between the specific form mercantilism took in the seventeenth and eighteenth centuries and the general outlook of mercantilistic thought. The essence of the mercantilistic perspective, whether it is labeled economic nationalism, protectionism, or the doctrine of the German Historical School, is the subservience of the economy to the state and its interests—interests that range from matters of domestic welfare to those of international security. It is this more general meaning of mercantilism that is implied by the use of the term in this study.

*   *   *

Three Conceptions of Political Economy

The three prevailing conceptions of political economy differ on many points. Several critical differences will be examined in this brief comparison. (See Table)

The Nature of Economic Relations

The basic assumption of liberalism is that the nature of international economic relations is essentially harmonious. Herein lay the great intellectual innovation of Adam Smith. Disputing his mercantilist predecessors, Smith argued that international economic relations could be made a positive-sum game; that is to say, everyone could gain, and no one need lose, from a proper ordering of economic relations, albeit the distribution of these gains may not be equal. Following Smith, liberalism assumes that there is a basic harmony between true national interest and cosmopolitan economic interest. Thus, a prominent member of this school of thought has written, in response to a radical critique, that the economic efficiency of the sterling standard in the nineteenth century and that of the dollar standard in the twentieth century serve "the cosmopolitan interest in a national form."[11] Although Great Britain and the United States gained the most from the international role of their respective currencies, everyone else gained as well.

Liberals argue that, given this underlying identity of national and cosmopolitan interests in a free market, the state should not interfere with economic transactions across national boundaries. Through free exchange of commodities, removal of restrictions on the flow of investment, and an international division of labor, everyone will benefit in the long run as a result of a more efficient utilization of the world's scarce resources. The national interest is therefore best served, liberals maintain, by a generous and cooperative attitude regarding economic relations with other countries. In essence, the pursuit of self-interest in a free, competitive economy achieves the greatest good for the greatest number in international no less than in the national society.

Both mercantilists and Marxists, on the other hand, begin with the premise that the essence of economic relations is conflictual. There is no underlying harmony; indeed, one group's gain is another's loss. Thus, in the language of game theory, whereas liberals regard economic relations as a nonzero-sum game, Marxists and mercantilists view economic relations as essentially a zero-sum game.

The Goal of Economic Activity

For the liberal, the goal of economic activity is the optimum or efficient use of the world's scarce resources and the maximization of world welfare. While most liberals refuse to make value judgments regarding income distribution, Marxists and mercantilists stress the distributive effects of economic relations. For the Marxist the

Comparison of the Three Conceptions of Political Economy

	Liberalism	Marxism	Mercantilism
Nature of economic relations	Harmonious	Conflictual	Conflictual
Nature of the actors	Households and firms	Economic classes	Nation-states
Goal of economic activity	Maximization of global welfare	Maximization of class interests	Maximization of national interest
Relationship between economics and politics	Economics *should* determine politics	Economics *does* determine politics	Politics determines economics
Theory of change	Dynamic equilibrium	Tendency toward disequilibrium	Shifts in the distribution of power

distribution of wealth among social classess is central; for the mercantilist it is the distribution of employment, industry, and military power among nation-states that is most significant Thus, the goal of economic (and political) activity for both Marxists and mercantilists is the redistribution of wealth and power.

The State and Public Policy

These three perspectives differ decisively in their views regarding the nature of the economic actors. In Marxist analysis, the basic actors in both domestic and international relations are economic classes; the interests of the dominant class determine the foreign policy of the state. For mercantilists, the real actors in international economic relations are nation-states; national interest determines foreign policy. National interest may at times be influenced by the peculiar economic interests of classes, elites, or other subgroups of the society; but factors of geography, external configurations of power, and the exigencies of national survival are primary in determining foreign policy. Thus, whereas liberals speak of world welfare and Marxists of class interests, mercantilists recognize only the interests of particular nation-states.

Although liberal economists such as David Ricardo and Joseph Schumpeter recognized the importance of class conflict and neoclassical liberals analyze economic growth and policy in terms of national economies, the liberal emphasis is on the individual consumer, firm, or entrepreneur. The liberal ideal is summarized in the view of Harry Johnson that the nation-state has no meaning as an economic entity.[12]

Underlying these contrasting views are differing conceptions of the nature of the state and public policy. For liberals, the state represents an aggregation of private interests: public policy is but the outcome of a pluralistic struggle among interest groups. Marxists, on the other hand, regard the state as simply the "executive committee of the ruling class," and public policy reflects its interests. Mercantilists, however, regard the state

as an organic unit in its own right: the whole is greater than the sum of its parts. Public policy, therefore, embodies the national interest or Rousseau's "general will" as conceived by the political élite.

The Relationship between Economics and Politics; Theories of Change

Liberalism, Marxism, and mercantilism also have differing views on the relationship between economics and politics. And their differences on this issue are directly relevant to their contrasting theories of international political change.

Although the liberal ideal is the separation of economics from politics in the interest of maximizing world welfare, the fulfillment of this ideal would have important political implications. The classical statement of these implications was that of Adam Smith in *The Wealth of Nations*.[13] Economic growth, Smith argued, is primarily a function of the extent of the division of labor, which in turn is dependent upon the scale of the market Thus he attacked the barriers erected by feudal principalities and mercantilistic states against the exchange of goods and the enlargement of markets. If men were to multiply their wealth, Smith argued, the contradiction between political organization and economic rationality had to be resolved in favor of the latter. That is, the pursuit of wealth should determine the nature of the political order.

Subsequently, from nineteenth-century economic liberals to twentieth-century writers on economic integration, there has existed "the dream . . . of a great republic of world commerce, in which national boundaries would cease to have any great economic importance and the web of trade would bind all the people of the world in the prosperity of peace."[14] For liberals the long-term trend is toward world integration, wherein functions, authority, and loyalties will be transferred from "smaller units to larger ones; from states to federalism; from federalism to supranational unions and from these to superstates."[15] The logic of economic and technological development, it is argued, has set mankind on an inexorable course toward global political unification and world peace.

In Marxism, the concept of the contradiction between economic and political relations was enacted into historical law. Whereas classical liberals—although Smith less than others—held that the requirements of economic rationality *ought* to determine political relations, the Marxist position was that the mode of production does in fact determine the superstructure of political relations. Therefore, it is argued, history can be understood as the product of the dialectical process—the contradiction between the evolving techniques of production and the resistant sociopolitical system.

Although Marx and Engels wrote remarkably little on international economics, Engels, in his famous polemic, *Anti-Duhring*, explicitly considers whether economics or politics is primary in determining the structure of international relations.[16] E. K. Duhring, a minor figure in the German Historical School, had argued, in contradiction to Marxism, that property and market relations resulted less from the economic logic of capitalism than from extraeconomic political factors: "The basis of the exploitation of man by man was an historical act of force which created an exploitative economic system for the benefit of the stronger man or class."[17] Since Engels, in his attack on Duhring, used the example of the unification of Germany through the Zollverein or customs union of 1833, his analysis is directly relevant to this discussion of the relationship between economics and political organization.

Engels argued that when contradictions arise between economic and political structures, political power adapts itself to the changes in the balance of economic forces; politics yields to the dictates of economic development. Thus, in the case of nineteenth-century Germany, the requirements of industrial production had become incompatible with its feudal, politically fragmented structure. "Though political reaction was victorious in 1815 and again in 1848," he argued, "it

was unable to prevent the growth of large-scale industry in Germany and the growing participation of German commerce in the world market."[18] In summary, Engels wrote, "German unity had become an economic necessity."[19]

In the view of both Smith and Engels, the nation-state represented a progressive stage in human development, because it enlarged the political realm of economic activity. In each successive economic epoch, advances in technology and an increasing scale of production necessitate an enlargement of political organization. Because the city-state and feudalism restricted the scale of production and the division of labor made possible by the Industrial Revolution, they prevented the efficient utilization of resources and were, therefore, superseded by larger political units. Smith considered this to be a desirable objective; for Engels it was an historical necessity. Thus, in the opinion of liberals, the establishment of the Zollverein was a movement toward maximizing world economic welfare;[20] for Marxists it was the unavoidable triumph of the German industrialists over the feudal aristocracy.

Mercantilist writers from Alexander Hamilton to Frederich List to Charles de Gaulle, on the other hand, have emphasized the primacy of politics; politics, in this view, determines economic organization. Whereas Marxists and liberals have pointed to the production of wealth as the basic determinant of social and political organization, the mercantilists of the German Historical School, for example, stressed the primacy of national security, industrial development, and national sentiment in international political and economic dynamics.

In response to Engels's interpretation of the unification of Germany, mercantilists would no doubt agree with Jacob Viner that "Prussia engineered the customs union primarily for political reasons, in order to gain hegemony or at least influence over the lesser German states. It was largely in order to make certain that the hegemony should be Prussian and not Austrian that Prussia continually opposed Austrian entry into the Union, either openly or by pressing for a customs union tariff lower than highly protectionist Austria could stomach."[21] In pursuit of this strategic interest, it was "Prussian might, rather than a common zeal for political unification arising out of economic partnership, (that) . . . played the major role."[22]

In contrast to Marxism, neither liberalism nor mercantilism has a developed theory of dynamics. The basic assumption of orthodox economic analysis (liberalism) is the tendency toward equilibrium; liberalism takes for granted the existing social order and given institutions. Change is assumed to be gradual and adaptive—a continuous process of dynamic equilibrium. There is no necessary connection between such political phenomena as war and revolution and the evolution of the economic system, although they would not deny that misguided statesmen can blunder into war over economic issues or that revolutions are conflicts over the distribution of wealth; but neither is inevitably linked to the evolution of the productive system. As for mercantilism, it sees change as taking place owing to shifts in the balance of power; yet, mercantilist writers such as members of the German Historical School and contemporary political realists have not developed a systematic theory of how this shift occurs.

On the other hand, dynamics is central to Marxism; indeed Marxism is essentially a theory of social *change*. It emphasizes the tendency toward *dis*equilibrium owing to changes in the means of production, and the consequent effects on the everpresent class conflict. When these tendencies can no longer be contained, the sociopolitical system breaks down through violent upheaval. Thus war and revolution are seen as an integral part of the economic process. Politics and economics are intimately joined.

Why an International Economy?

From these differences among the three ideologies, one can get a sense of their respective explanations for the existence and functioning of the international economy.

An interdependent world economy constitutes the normal state of affairs for most liberal economists. Responding to technological advances in transportation and communications, the scope of the market mechanism, according to this analysis, continuously expands. Thus, despite temporary setbacks, the long-term trend is toward global economic integration. The functioning of the international economy is determined primarily by considerations of efficiency. The role of the dollar as the basis of the international monetary system, for example, is explained by the preference for it among traders and nations as the vehicle of international commerce.[23] The system is maintained by the mutuality of the benefits provided by trade, monetary arrangements, and investment.

A second view—one shared by Marxists and mercantilists alike—is that every interdependent international economy is essentially an imperial or hierarchical system. The imperial or hegemonic power organizes trade, monetary, and investment relations in order to advance its own economic and political interests. In the absence of the economic and especially the political influence of the hegemonic power, the system would fragment into autarkic economies or regional blocs. Whereas for liberalism maintenance of harmonious international market relations is the norm, for Marxism and mercantilism conflicts of class or national interests are the norm.

*   *   *

NOTES

1. Kari Levitt, "The Hinterland Economy," *Canadian Forum* 50 (July–August 1970): 163.
2. George W. Ball, "The Promise of the Multinational Corporation," *Fortune*, June 1, 1967, p. 80.
3. Sidney Rolfe, "Updating Adam Smith," *Interplay* (November 1968): 15.
4. Charles Kindleberger, *Power and Money: The Economics of International Politics and the Politics of International Economics* (New York: Basic Books, 1970), p. 5.

5. Robert Keohane and Joseph Nye, "World Politics and the International Economic System," in *The Future of the International Economic Order: An Agenda for Research*, ed. C. Fred Bergsten (Lexington, Mass.: D. C. Heath, 1973), p. 116.

6. Ibid.

7. Ibid., p. 117.

8. Paul Samuelson, *Economics: An Introductory Analysis* (New York: McGraw-Hill, 1967), p. 5.

9. Harold Lasswell and Abraham Kaplan, *Power and Society: A Framework for Political Inquiry* (New Haven: Yale University Press, 1950), p. 75.

10. Hans Morgenthau, *Politics Among Nations* (New York: Alfred A. Knopf), p. 26. For a more complex but essentially identical view, see Robert Dahl, *Modern Political Analysis* (Englewood Cliffs, N.J.: Prentice-Hall, 1963).

11. Kindleberger, *Power and Money*, p. 227.

12. For Johnson's critique of economic nationalism, see Harry Johnson, ed., *Economic Nationalism in Old and New States* (Chicago: University of Chicago Press, 1967).

13. Adam Smith, *The Wealth of Nations* (New York: Modem Library, 1937).

14. J. B. Condliffe, *The Commerce of Nations* (New York: W. W. Norton, 1950), p. 136.

15. Amitai Etzioni, "The Dialectics of Supranational Unification" in *International Political Communities* (New York: Doubleday, 1966), p. 147.

16. The relevant sections appear in Ernst Wangerman, ed., *The Role of Force in History: A Study of Bismarck's Policy of Blood and Iron*, trans. Jack Cohen (New York: International Publishers, 1968).

17. Ibid., p. 12.

18. Ibid., p. 13.

19. Ibid., p. 14.

20. Gustav Stopler, *The German Economy* (New York: Harcourt, Brace and World, 1967), p. 11.

21. Jacob Viner, *The Customs Union Issue*, Studies in the Administration of International Law and Organization, no. 10 (New York: Carnegie Endowment for International Peace, 1950), pp. 98–99.

22. Ibid., p. 101.

23. Richard Cooper, "Eurodollars, Reserve Dollars, and Asymmetrics in the International Monetary System," *Journal of International Economics* 2 (September 1972): 325–44.

HELEN V. MILNER

GLOBALIZATION, DEVELOPMENT, AND INTERNATIONAL INSTITUTIONS: NORMATIVE AND POSITIVE PERSPECTIVES

Introduction

At the conclusion of World War II, several international institutions were created to manage the world economy and prevent

From *Perspectives on Politics* 3, no. 4 (December 2005): 833–54. Some of the author's notes have been omitted.

another Great Depression. These institutions include the International Monetary Fund (IMF), the International Bank for Reconstruction and Development (now called the World Bank), and the General Agreement on Tariffs and Trade (GATT), which was expanded and institutionalized into the World Trade Organization (WTO) in 1995. These institutions have not only persisted for over five decades, but they have also expanded their mandates, changed their missions, and increased their membership. They have, however, become highly contested. As Stiglitz notes, "International bureaucrats—the faceless symbols of the world economic order—are under attack everywhere.... Virtually every major meeting of the International Monetary Fund, the World Bank and the World Trade Organization is now the scene of conflict and turmoil."[1]

Their critics come from both the left and right wings of the political spectrum. Antiglobalization forces from the left see them as instruments for the domination of the developing countries by both the rich countries or the forces of international capitalism. Critics from the right view these institutions as usurping the role of the market and easing pressures on developing states to adopt efficient, market-promoting policies. These debates often occur in a highly ideological and polemical fashion; they would benefit from being more informed by social science. By reviewing some of the recent social science literature, this essay addresses three questions: what has been the impact of these institutions on the developing countries, why have they had this impact, and what should be their role in the development process.

Conventional wisdom in international and comparative political economy has held that international institutions, like the IMF, World Bank, and WTO (and its predecessor, the GATT), have been largely beneficial for the countries in them. These institutions, it is claimed, constrain the behavior of the most powerful countries and provide information and monitoring capacities that enable states to cooperate.[2] All states involved are better off with these institutions than otherwise. Recently, however, evidence has mounted that these institutions may not be so beneficial for the developing countries.

Discerning the impact of these institutions requires that one address difficult counterfactual questions.[3] Would the developing countries have been better off if these institutions had not existed? Would resources for aid and crisis man-

agement have been as plentiful or more so if they had not existed? Would globalization have occurred as fast and extensively, or even faster and deeper, if these international institutions had not been present? Counterfactuals cannot be answered directly because they presume a situation which did not occur and rely on speculation about what this hypothetical world would have been like.[4] Researchers can only make indirect counterfactual speculations. First, longitudinal comparison asks whether a developing country performed as well before it joined the institution (or participated in its programs) as after it did so. This enables the researcher to hold constant many characteristics of the country that do not change over time. Second, cross-sectional comparison asks if countries belonging to the institution (or participating in its programs) fare better or worse than those countries who do not. These comparisons are usually not enough. Part of the problem of knowing what the "right" counterfactual is depends on why countries join. Selection bias arises if the countries are joining or participating for nonrandom reasons which are not held constant. If countries choose to participate only under certain conditions, then the counterfactual experiment must correct for this or its results are likely to be biased. Because selection bias can arise from both observed and unobserved factors, correcting for selection effects is not straightforward. Little of the research on these international institutions addresses all of these methodological issues.

Assessing the impact of these institutions involves addressing this counterfactual. But recent normative scholarship claims that answering this counterfactual is not enough for assessing their role. It proposes different standards for evaluation and raises the contentious question of what standard one should use to assess the responsibility of these institutions for the developing countries. This debate involves the extent of moral obligations that the rich countries and the institutions they created have regarding the poor countries, ranging from a limited "duty of assistance" to a cosmopolitan striving for equality.

Combining normative and empirical scholarship may be unusual, but it may be fruitful. As Beitz claims, "reflection about reform of global governance is well advanced in other venues, both academic and political, almost never with the benefit of the moral clarity that might be contributed by an articulate philosophical conception of global political justice."[5]

*   *   *

The Role of the International Economic Institutions

The roles of the three main institutions have changed over time; in addition, their membership has become nearly universal. All of these institutions were created by the victors in World War II and were intended to help them avoid another global depression. Part of the problem for these institutions lies in their legacy. They were designed to help the developed countries create a cooperative and stable world economy in a non-globalized world.

The IMF was established to support the fixed exchange rate system created at the Bretton Woods Conference in 1944; its role was to aid countries that were experiencing difficulties in maintaining their fixed exchange rate by providing them with short term loans. It was a lender of last resort and a provider of funds in crisis, enabling countries to avoid competitive devaluations. Ensuring a stable international monetary system to promote trade and growth was its central mission. From an initial membership of 29 countries, it has become almost universal with 184 members.

With the collapse of the Bretton Woods fixed exchange rate system in the early 1970s, this role changed. The IMF dealt less with the developed countries and more with the developing ones. It provided long and short term loans at below-market interest rates for countries in all sorts of economic difficulty, making it less distinct from the World Bank. It began attaching increasing

numbers of conditions to those loans ("conditionality"), negotiating with countries to make major changes in their domestic policies and institutions. Promoting economic growth as well as resolving specific crises became its mission, which meant that ever more countries became involved in these so-called structural adjustment programs. Indeed, as Vreeland notes, in 2000 alone the IMF had programs with sixty countries, or more than one-third of the developing world. These changes made the IMF more similar to the World Bank.

Formed after World War II, the Bank concentrated mostly on reconstruction and later on development; in 1960, with the formation of the International Development Association (IDA), the Bank moved further toward economic development programs.[6] Many countries over the years have received both IMF and World Bank loans, often simultaneously.[7] The World Bank also gives interest-free loans and grants (similar to foreign aid) to the poorest developing countries. This aid has been heavily used in Africa; indeed, in 2003, 51 percent of it went to sub-Saharan Africa. This overlap of missions, proliferation of adjustment loans, and expansion of conditionality are central issues today.

The WTO's central mission has been to promote trade liberalization by fostering negotiations among countries to reciprocally lower their trade barriers and providing information about countries' trade policies. Membership in the GATT/WTO has grown importantly over the years, from a mere 23 in 1947 to 146 countries in 2003.[8] Like the IMF and World Bank, the GATT was originally a negotiating forum for the developed countries; its impact on the developing countries has grown slowly over time. The liberalization of trade policy has become an accepted doctrine for most developing countries; barriers in the developing world have fallen significantly since 1980.[9] In addition, the WTO's mission has increasingly involved the connections between domestic policies and trade barriers. With significant lowering of tariffs and quotas, many domestic policies such as intellectual property laws, environmental policy, domestic subsidies, and tax laws, are now seen to affect trade flows and hence to reside within the WTO's jurisdiction. As with conditionality in the monetary domain, the attack on trade barriers has increasingly brought this international institution into contact with domestic politics.

The GATT/WTO system has sponsored numerous trade negotiation rounds over the past fifty years. The most recently concluded negotiations, called the Uruguay Round, ended in late 1994 with the debut of the WTO and accords lowering trade barriers and extending agreements into other areas such as intellectual property and foreign investment. This system relies on reciprocity, attempting to balance countries' gains and losses. The WTO is now conducting the new Doha Round of trade negotiations, which is intended to address the problems of the developing countries more directly.

The Experience of the Developing Countries

Debate over these institutions has arisen from the seeming lack of progress in the developing world. Except for the World Bank, the original and primary mission of these institutions was not promoting growth in the developing world. Nevertheless, since the change in their roles from the 1970s onward, they have increasingly been judged by their impact on the poor. Fairly or not, the question has been whether these institutions have fostered development.[10]

Each of these institutions has promoted the adoption of market-friendly policies, and part of the reaction against them has been connected to these policies. "The widespread recourse of indebted developing countries to structural adjustment loans from the Bretton Woods institutions in the aftermath of the debt crisis of the early 1980s played a pivotal role in the redefinition of trade and industrialization strategies. Prominent among the conditions attached to these loans was the liberalization of policies towards trade

and FDI (foreign direct investment). This was in line with the rising influence of pro-market economic doctrines during this period. Under these structural adjustment programs, there was a significant increase in the number of cases of trade and investment liberalization in many developing countries."[11]

But concerns abound over whether trade and capital market liberalization, privatization, deregulation, austerity, and the other elements of the so-called "Washington Consensus" that these institutions advocated promote development in poor countries. If one looks solely at the economic side, progress has been mixed in many developing countries. As Easterly concludes, "there was much lending, little adjustment, and little growth in the 1980s and 1990s" in the developing world.[12] Annual per capita growth for the developing countries averaged 0 percent for the years from 1980 to 1998, whereas from 1960–1979 their growth had averaged about 2.5 percent annually.[13] Poverty remains very high, with roughly 20 percent of the world's population living on less than a dollar a day and more than 45 percent on less than two dollars a day.[14] Because of these conditions, some 18 million people a year die of easily preventable causes, many of them children.[15] A sizable number of these countries were worse off economically in 2000 than they were in the 1980. World Bank data indicate, for instance, that per capita income was lower in 1999 in at least nine countries (for which we have data) than in 1960: Haiti, Nicaragua, Central African Republic, Chad, Ghana, Madagascar, Niger, Rwanda, and Zambia.[16] From 1980 to 2002, twenty countries experienced a decrease in their human development indexes, which include more than just economic growth.[17]

Since 1980 the world's poorest countries have done worse economically than the richest.[18] In the 1980s the high income countries of the Organisation for Economic Co-operation and Development (OECD) grew at 2.5 percent annually and in the 1990s at 1.8 percent; the developing countries grew at 0.7 percent and 1.7 percent, respectively.[19] Moreover, if one excludes East Asia where the growth was extraordinary (5.6 percent in the 1980s and 6.4 percent in the 1990s), the developing countries grew much more slowly than the developed ones. Thus, they have been falling further behind the rich countries, increasing the gap between the two. As Lant Pritchett has shown, over the period 1820 to 1992 the divergence in incomes between the world's rich and poor has grown enormously.[20] In 1820 the richest country had three times the income that the poorest did; in the early 1990s this number was thirty.[21] Much of this divergence is due to the rich countries' rapid growth.[22]

Economic crises among the developing countries have also proliferated after the 1970s. In addition, the debt problems of many developing countries have increased. "Total debt of developing countries increased until 1999 and then stabilized at about $3 trillion as of last year [that is, 2003]. Furthermore, while debt has declined as a proportion of GDP, it remains high at some 40 percent, and the ratio of debt to exports at 113 percent. More importantly, the net resource transfer—the resources available for use after paying interest—has been negative in recent years for all regions. These magnitudes suggest that it is difficult to consider current levels of debt sustainable and helping growth."[23]

The performance of the developing countries has not been uniformly poor, however. From 1960 to 2000, life expectancy increased from 46 to 63 years in the developing world. Child mortality rates were halved in the same period, as were illiteracy rates.[24] Poverty as a percentage of the developing countries' populations has declined recently.[25] Including China, where the declines have been enormous, the percentage of people in the developing countries living on the poverty threshold of $1 a day has fallen from over 28 percent in 1990 to below 22 percent in 2000.[26] The percentage living on $2 a day in the developing world also fell from 61 percent to 54 percent in this period.[27] Unfortunately, the absolute numbers of the desperately poor have not fallen much, if at all, because of high growth population rates.[28]

The developing countries have also upgraded their role in the world economy. They now are producers and exporters of manufactures and not primarily of primary products. In 2000, about 64 percent of low and middle income countries' exports were manufactures, while only 10 percent were agriculture, and their share of world trade in manufactures rose over this period from 9 percent to 26 percent.[29] Especially in East and South Asia, the developing economies have become tightly integrated into the world production and trading system led by multinational corporations. This increase in the value-added and the diversification of developing countries' production and trade has been a boon for many.

This mixed record of economic outcomes has raised questions about the impact of these international economic institutions. But one must pose the counterfactual to assess their impact: would the performance of these countries have been better, the same, or even worse had these institutions not existed?

Theories about the Functions and Benefits of International Institutions

Many international relations scholars have argued that countries should benefit from these institutions. States rationally decide to join them; therefore, they join only if the net benefits are greater than those offered by staying out of the organization. Membership is voluntary. The net utility derived from joining could be negative, but less negative than that incurred by remaining outside the institution. As Gruber has argued, if the most powerful states define the alternatives open to the developing countries and set up multilateral institutions, the developing countries can be better off by joining them than staying outside, but worse off than if the institutions never existed.[30] The rush lately by all countries to join these institutions suggests that developing countries have found them to be more beneficial than the alternative of staying out, but it does not moot the question of whether they would be better of without any of these multilateral institutions in the first place. Four reasons are often theorized for the existence of these institutions: (1) constraining the great powers, (2) providing information and reducing transaction costs, (3) facilitating reciprocity, and (4) promoting reform in domestic politics.

Constraining the Great Powers

International institutions may exert a constraint on the underlying anarchy of the international system. They make the use of force and power by states to achieve their goals less likely; the rules, norms, and procedures established by these institutions replace to some extent the pursuit of national interest by power. Most importantly, as Ikenberry claims, they help to harness the behavior of the most powerful states.[31] By creating and complying with these institutions, the Great Powers, or hegemon, can reassure other states that they will not take advantage of them. The strongest bind themselves to a set of norms and rules that the other states voluntarily agree to accept.

Evidence for this effect is mixed. As the WTO points out, "trade is likely to expand and be more profitable under conditions of certainty and security as to the terms of market access and the rules of trade—precommitment around a set of rules also diminishes the role of power and size in determining outcomes."[32] This motivation is important in trade where countries with large markets, and hence market power, can use this to obtain more favorable trading arrangements in bilateral negotiations with smaller countries.

Nevertheless, critics maintain that developing countries have not gained much from the GATT trade rounds; most of the gains have gone to developed countries. Some scholars even allege that the trade rounds have allowed the developed countries to exploit the developing ones by engaging them in unfair agreements. As Stiglitz

says, "previous rounds of trade negotiations [in the GATT/WTO] had protected the interests of the advanced industrial countries—or more accurately, special interests within those countries—without concomitant benefits for the lesser developed countries."[33] The unbalanced outcome of the recent Uruguay trade round is an important issue. "Several computable general equilibrium models have shown that the Uruguay Round results disproportionately benefit developed country gross domestic products (GDPs) compared to developing countries, and that some developing countries would actually suffer a net GDP loss from the Uruguay Round—at least in the short run."[34]

Developing countries have raised concerns about the equity of the outcome of this and other rounds. "With hindsight, many developing country governments perceived the outcome of the Uruguay Round to have been unbalanced. For most developing countries (some did gain), the crux of the unfavourable deal was the limited market access concessions they obtained from developed countries in exchange for the high costs they now realize they incurred in binding themselves to the new multilateral trade rules."[35] Others note that asymmetric outcomes are an intrinsic part of the GATT/WTO bargaining process. "[Trade] rounds have been concluded through power-based bargaining that has yielded asymmetrical contracts favoring the interests of powerful states. The agenda-setting process (the formulation of proposals that are difficult to amend), which takes place between launch and conclusion, has been dominated by powerful states; the extent of that domination has depended upon the extent to which powerful countries have planned to use their power to conclude the round."[36]

The counterfactual one must pose is the following: without the GATT or WTO would the developing countries be better off if they had to negotiate bilaterally with the large, rich countries? Multilateralism seems well suited to giving the developing countries a better outcome than would such bilateral negotiations.[37] "Multilateralism ensures transparency, and provides protection—however inadequate—against the asymmetries of power and influence in the international community."[38] It may not only place some constraints on the behavior of the large, developed countries, but it may also encourage developing countries to realize their common interests and counterbalance the rich countries. By giving them more political voice than otherwise, institutions like the WTO may enhance their capacity to influence outcomes.

Evidence of the constraining power of the IMF or World Bank is less apparent. Decisions in the IMF and World Bank are taken by weighted voting, with the rich countries—and especially the United States—having the lion's share of votes. Since the end of the fixed exchange rate system in the early 1970s, these institutions have basically collected funds from the developed countries and private capital markets to give to the developing ones under increasing conditions. Conditionality has been designed by these institutions with the tacit support of the developed countries, and it has been negotiated with the poor ones. Since the late 1970s few, if any, developed countries have not been subject to IMF programs; only the developing world has. Article IV of the IMF charter requires surveillance of all members and discussion of the problems in their fiscal and monetary policies, but since the late 1970s, de facto this has not applied to the developed countries.[39] The IMF has remarked on its own inefficacy: "Nowhere is the difficulty of conducting surveillance more apparent than in the relations between the IMF and the major industrial countries. Effective oversight over the policies of the largest countries is obviously essential if surveillance is to be uniform and symmetric across the membership, but progress in achieving that goal has been slow and hesitant."[40] It is difficult to argue that the IMF and World Bank constrain the exercise of power by the developed countries. Indeed, these multilateral institutions may enhance the capacity of the rich countries to collectively enforce their will on the poor countries, as Rodrik argues.[41]

Does their existence change the behavior of the rich? Without the two institutions, would the developed countries lend or donate as much as they do now? Does multilateral lending and aid substitute for or complement bilateral giving? Would the least well-off and the most politically insignificant countries be left to fend for themselves if they ran into economic crises, should the World Bank and IMF not exist? And would the terms of any aid or loans given bilaterally be worse for these countries than they are now? Evidence exists that bilateral aid tends to be more oriented toward the political and economic interests of donors than is multilateral aid.[42] Some critics of the IMF and World Bank claim that countries would experience fewer crises since they would be more attentive to their financial situation in the absence of the moral hazard presented by the existence of these multilateral organizations.[43] Others scholars have demonstrated that the distribution of aid and loans even with these institutions is weighted toward the economically better off and the politically more important developing countries.[44] For instance, Stone shows that in lending to the transition countries the IMF gave more and imposed lighter conditions on those states with stronger political ties to the United States.[45] Further, he shows how this political process undermines the credibility of the IMF's position and induces the recipient countries to ignore its conditionality. His research, however, does not really address the question of whether the IMF's presence affected the overall amount of lending or the allocation of those loans, relative to a situation where the Fund did not exist. These counterfactuals are essential for addressing questions about these multilateral institutions, but they are difficult to assess.

Providing Information and Reducing Transaction Costs

Following New Institutionalism theories, some argue that a major reason for these institutions is the lowering of transaction costs and the provision of information to facilitate multilateral cooperation in an anarchic world. As Keohane writes, international institutions "facilitate agreements by raising the anticipated costs of violating others' property rights, by altering transaction costs through clustering of issues, and by providing reliable information to members. [They] are relatively efficient institutions, compared to the alternative of having a myriad of unrelated agreements, since their principles, rules, and institutions create linkages among issues that give actors incentives to reach mutually beneficial agreements."[46] For him, international institutions also reduce uncertainty by monitoring the member states' behavior and allowing decentralized enforcement through reciprocity strategies.[47]

Scholars such as Anne Krueger have suggested just such an informational role for the IMF and World Bank.[48] Surveying and reporting on the policy behavior of member countries, providing information about the likelihood of crises, and being a repository of expert information are key roles for these institutions. The Meltzer Commission also emphasizes this role, and the most severe critics on the right imply that the IMF and World Bank should give up all roles except monitoring and providing expert information to member states. Others have noted the expertise role of the IFIs. "The World Bank is widely recognized to have exercised power over development policies far greater than its budget, as a percentage of North/South aid flows, would suggest because of the expertise it houses. . . . This expertise, coupled with its claim to "neutrality" and its "apolitical" technocratic decision-making style, have given the World Bank an authoritative voice with which it has successfully dictated the content, direction, and scope of global development over the past fifty years."[49]

The WTO has also been seen as an information-provision institution. It monitors and reports on the compliance of states with the commitments they have made to each other. This task reassures other member countries and domestic publics about the behavior of their political leaders, making cooperation more likely and sustainable.[50]

Informational arguments suggest that all states gain from participation in such institutions.[51] This mutual gain explains the voluntary participation of states in these multilateral forums. The expectation would be that developing countries join largely for these informational benefits, but there remains the issue of who provides what information for whose benefit. Are the developing countries providing more information than otherwise? Are the principal beneficiaries private investors in the developing countries or in the developed world, other domestic groups, or the institutions themselves? Do the IMF and World Bank provide developing countries with useful information about other members or with expertise that would otherwise be unavailable? These empirical questions have not been examined much.

One central complaint against the IMF and World Bank is that the policy advice they give (especially the "Washington Consensus" advice) has been unhelpful, if not detrimental, since it failed to take into account the circumstances of the developing countries.[52] The claim is that the policy expertise given (or imposed via conditionality) has not been beneficial. For instance, Stiglitz, Bhagwati, and others have all criticized the IMF for pushing the developing countries into opening their capital markets.[53] They have argued that little, if any, economic evidence or theory supports this, the consequences have been negative for most countries, and the main beneficiaries have been private investors in the developed world. As Stiglitz writes, "the [main] problem is that the IMF (and sometimes the other international economic organizations) presents as received doctrines propositions and policy recommendations for which there is not widespread agreement; indeed, in the case of capital market liberalization, there was scant evidence in support and a massive amount of evidence against."[54] Even the advice to open their economies to trade has not been unquestioned. Economic analysis shows that the impact of trade openness on economic growth can be positive but also insignificant.[55]

Easterly's book is also an indictment of the economic policy prescriptions of the Bank and Fund. Each chapter shows how the prevailing wisdom guiding economic policy prescriptions in the IFIs has either been proven wrong or never been attempted to be proven right or wrong. As he concludes, "in part II, we saw that the search for a magic formula to turn poverty into prosperity failed . . . Growth failed to respond to any of these formulas . . ."[56]

Vreeland's book supports these claims about the failed policy advice of the IMF. His research shows that IMF programs lower economic growth and redistribute income away from the most needy; the impact of conditionality is to retard development. As he concludes, this result means that either the IMF's policy prescriptions are incorrect or economic growth and poverty reduction are not the goals of the IMF. Stone's findings counter these; he shows that IMF programs do reduce inflation and return greater macroeconomic stability but only when they are not interfered with by political factors. Thus, even the informational value of the international institutions has been questioned.

Facilitating Reciprocity

International institutions facilitate reciprocity strategies among countries in an anarchic environment. Cooperation in anarchy relies on reciprocity, but more cooperation can be sustained if it need not require simultaneous and perfectly balanced exchanges. "International regimes can be thought of in part as arrangements that facilitate nonsimultaneous exchange."[57] Bagwell and Staiger have developed the most rigorous claims about the importance of reciprocity for the international trading system.[58] If countries are sizable economic actors in world markets, then they can use trade policy to manipulate their terms of trade and gain advantages over their trading partners. If these big countries set trade policy unilaterally, they will arrive at an inefficient outcome, sacrificing the gains to be had from mutual trade liberalization. Reciprocity enhanced

by the WTO's rules and monitoring can provide a context in which these big countries can achieve more efficient, cooperative outcomes. The main function of international institutions is to make reciprocity credible and feasible.

In the case of the large, rich countries in world trade this motivation seems apparent. The United States, European Union and Japan have used the GATT/WTO to enforce reciprocity strategies and lower their trade barriers. However, there is little evidence that this reciprocity has extended to the developing world. Many developing countries did not join the WTO until recently; most of the developing country members did not reciprocally liberalize their trade in the trade rounds.

"In the period until the launch of the Uruguay Round and the formation of the WTO, only the industrial countries were meaningful participants in multilateral trade negotiations. They bargained amongst themselves to reduce trade barriers, while developing countries were largely out of this process and had few obligations to liberalize. The latter availed themselves of the benefits of industrial country liberalization, courtesy of the Most Favored Nation (MFN) principle, but that defined pretty much the limits of their contribution to or benefits from the General Agreement on Tariffs and Trade (GATT). Industrial countries were content with this arrangement, in part because it alleviated the pressure on them to liberalize sensitive sectors such as agriculture and clothing, but perhaps more importantly because the markets of developing countries were not at that stage sufficiently attractive."[59]

This situation is not unexpected. Theories about the value of reciprocity in trade depend on the assumption that the country is a large trader (that is, it can affect prices); for most developing countries, this is not a realistic assumption.[60] "Countries with small markets are just not attractive enough for larger trading partners to engage in meaningful reciprocity negotiations."[61] The 100 largest developing countries (excluding the transition economies) accounted for 29 percent of total world exports in 2003; the United States alone accounted for 10 percent, the EU (excluding intra-EU trade) for 15 percent and Japan for 6.5 percent.[62]

In addition, many of the developing countries received preferential access to developed countries' markets, as noted above. Ironically, this access has reduced their interest in reciprocal multilateral liberalization since it simply reduces their preference margins.[63] "The problem with granting preferential access in goods trade as the payoff to small and poor countries is that it is counterproductive and even perverse. Although preferential access does provide rents in the short run, the empirical evidence suggests that preferences do not provide a basis for sustaining long-run growth.[64] In addition, preferences create an incentive for recipients to have more protectionist regimes.[65] For most of the developing world then, ensuring reciprocity has not been a main function of the trade regime.[66]

Facilitating Reform in Domestic Politics

Some scholars have speculated that joining an international institution and publicly agreeing to abide by its rules, norms, and practices has important domestic political consequences. It can help domestic leaders to alter policies at home that they otherwise would not be able to do. It can help them lock in "good" policies (that is, ones that enhance general welfare) and resist pressures by special interests to adopt "bad" policies (that is, ones that benefit special interests only). Or it can help domestic leaders to activate interest groups to counterbalance other groups' pressures and thus introduce different policies than otherwise.

Several logics exist to support these claims. For some, once leaders join an institution it becomes hard for them to violate its practices since leaders who do so tarnish their international reputations and are less capable of making new agreements; their publics lose from this and are more likely to evict the leader, making noncompliance more costly than otherwise.[67] Others argue that domestic publics receive signals from the monitoring of international institutions and that when the institution sounds a violation alarm, some domestic groups hear this and know their leaders are probably giving in to special interests and become more likely to vote them out of office.[68] For others the key is that achieving cooperative agreements with other countries brings advantages for some domestic groups that otherwise would not be involved in a change of policy; once their interests are engaged through the multilateral process, they can become strong proponents for policy change at home.[69]

Evidence for this binding effect is not extensive in the trade area. Mattoo and Subramanian, for instance, show that the poorest countries (roughly a third of all countries) have not used the WTO to make commitments. "For a vast majority of the poor and small countries, both the proportion of [tariff] bindings in the industrial sector is small and the wedge between actual and committed tariffs is large, indicating that countries have given themselves a large margin of flexibility to reverse their trade policies without facing adverse consequences in the WTO."[70]

Moreover, as others have noted, many of the developing countries chose to liberalize their trade regimes unilaterally.[71] That is, they decided to open their markets before joining the WTO; membership in the WTO was not necessary for them to liberalize. Once they liberalized, however, membership then became more important; it helped to prevent the raising of trade barriers.

The domestic political consequences of IMF and World Bank membership may be important but little research addresses this directly. Vreeland notes that countries underwent IMF programs out of choice as much as necessity. Governments were using the IMF to produce changes in policies that they desired, but unfortunately, these changes did not produce economic growth or poverty reduction. His analysis demonstrates that the programs were used instead to promote the welfare of capital owners, who tend to be the richest groups in developing countries and thus may have further hurt developing countries. Stone's analysis also shows that compliance with the IMF has been variable, and that, especially for important borrowers, domestic binding or compliance has been low. In sum, we do not know what the overall domestic effect of IMF and World Bank membership on countries has been.

Four Sources of the Problems with International Institutions

If the WTO, IMF, and World Bank do not provide the benefits for developing countries that scholars predict they might, what could explain this? Four claims have been advanced. Some argue that these institutions have minimal impact. Others argue that they are captured by either the powerful rich countries or by private producers and investors and so do not focus on the interests of the poor countries. Finally, the problems may lie with the internal organization and dynamics of the institutions themselves and the failure of the member countries to monitor their behavior.

1. No Impact. It may be that these institutions had little or no impact on the developing countries. Their fate could be far more sensitive to other forces, such as globalization and domestic politics.

Because of technological innovation, reduced communications and transportation costs, and policy changes, the developing countries have been increasingly exposed to the world economy.[72] But the capacity of the IMF and World Bank has not grown proportionately, and thus, they are less able to help, especially at times of crisis. "The IFIs seek to fulfill their role of technical and financial support, but the relative size of their financing remains low. They constitute only about 19 per cent of total debt outstanding by developing countries, and only 13 per cent among middle-income countries."[73] The developing countries have thus experienced increasing globalization while the IFIs capacity has not kept up with the rising demand for funds.

The debate over the impact of globalization on the developing countries is too vast to join here, but suffice it to say that many scholars have argued that globalization is having a large effect on such countries (whether it is positive or negative is much debated).[74] Globalization, however, is not disconnected from the WTO, World Bank, and IMF. These institutions were intended to help manage the process of integrating the developing economies into the world one. Nevertheless, the larger point is that globalization may have done more to affect these countries than these international institutions.

Others have attributed the outcomes of the developing countries to their own domestic problems. Political instability, corruption, civil war, lack of the rule of law, and authoritarianism are viewed as the bigger sources of their problems. Recent research touting the importance of domestic political institutions supports this line of argument. Without institutions that protect private property rights for broad segments of the population, growth is unlikely.[75] In this view, reforming domestic institutions is a first priority to promote sustained growth.[76] To the extent that the international institutions have advanced such institutional reform, they have helped the developing world. To the degree they have permitted developing nations to avoid or postpone such domestic change, they have hurt their prospects for development. From this perspective, it is essential not to attribute too much impact to the three international economic institutions. Much as realists in international relations maintain, these institutions may be more epiphenomenal; whatever impact they have, if any, is derived from their role in some larger political or economic structure.

2. Capture by the Powerful Developed Countries. For many scholars, Realists and others, these institutions were created by and for the interests of the large, rich countries. They were established at American initiative during its hegemony following World War II. American and European dominance in these organizations has been sealed by their sizable market power and their de facto control over the institutions' operations. Serving the interests of the advanced industrial nations has meant either that the interests of the poor countries were at best neglected and at worst damaged. "There are thus serious problems with the current structure and processes of global governance. Foremost among these is the vast inequality in the power and capacity of different nation states. At the root of this is the inequality in the economic power of different nations. The industrialized countries have far higher per capita incomes, which translates into economic clout in negotiations to shape global governance. They are the source of much-needed markets, foreign investments, financial capital, and technology. The ownership and control of these vital assets gives them immense economic power. This creates a built-in tendency for the process of global governance to be in the interests of powerful players, especially in rich nations."[77] In this view, the international institutions have not helped much since they are oriented to promote the interests of the developed countries.

This bias operates in a number of ways in each organization. World Bank aid has been questioned. It has been heavily used in sub-Saharan Africa, but this region has done least well. Scholars have argued that this aid has been used to prop up authoritarian governments and to continue with failed policies longer than they otherwise could have.[78] The link between the amount of aid a country received and its growth rate remains disputed; many find that aid alone has no significant impact on economic growth.[79] But aid flows have not been allocated to the neediest countries. Studies show that donor interests, both economic and foreign policy ones, often dictate which countries receive what aid, and when.[80] Countries with poor governments and policies may for other reasons receive large allocations of aid; the priorities of rich donors may undermine the developmental impact of aid.

According to other scholars, policy recommendations the developing countries were given reflected the experiences and interests of the rich countries. Trade liberalization promoted by the WTO and IMF occurred too quickly and without

(enough) concern for finding alternative means for the poor countries to fund their budgets and develop social safety nets. For others, the problem is more how the agenda is set and how negotiating power is distributed. In the WTO, Steinberg shows the enormous power of the rich countries. "The secretariat's bias in favor of great powers has been largely a result of who staffs it and the shadow of power under which it works. From its founding until 1999, every GATT and WTO Director-General was from Canada, Europe, or the United States, and most of the senior staff of the GATT/WTO secretariat have been nationals of powerful countries. Secretariat officials'...actions have usually been heavily influenced or even suggested by representatives of the most powerful states. For example...the package of proposals that became the basis for the final stages of negotiation in the Uruguay Round...was largely a collection of proposals prepared by and developed and negotiated between the EC and the United States."[81]

IMF and World Bank conditionality programs mandating capital market liberalization, privatization and governmental austerity programs often ran aground because the developing countries did not have the financial or legal institutions to support such policies. These policies might work in the context of the developed world where these institutions existed. An example of this is Russia, which Stiglitz and Stone discuss in detail. They show that American government officials pushed the IMF to loan and continue loaning large sums to Russia, that the IMF promoted policy changes that the Russian political economy could not handle, and finally that American pressure undercut the ability of the IMF to induce Russia to reform. "The officials who applied Washington Consensus policies failed to appreciate the social context of the transition economies";[82] privatization in the absence of a legal framework of corporate governance only helped cause economic and political problems. Stone, who presents a more optimistic picture of the IMF largely because his central focus is on reducing inflation and not increasing growth or equality, shows that American influence on the IMF is pervasive and pernicious. In the Russian case, for instance, he claims that the IMF made some mistakes (for example, in advising capital market liberalization in 1996, which was pushed by the Americans) but that most of the problems came not from IMF advice but from Russia's failure to listen to the IMF. American pressure on the IMF and support for Russia were largely to blame for this outcome; Russian politicians knew that the IMF would never carry out their threats since the United States would never let them. Stone's identification of the credibility problems that big country interference with the IMF engenders is a novel and subtle mechanism for rich country influence on the developing world.

Pressure from the rich countries has been seen as causing the international institutions at times to provide unhelpful advice as well as to shift the agenda and negotiating outcomes away from those favorable to the developing world. Bhagwati notes that "the rush to abandon controls on capital flows . . . was hardly a consequence of finance ministers and other policy makers in the developing countries suddenly acknowledging the folly of their ways. It reflected instead external pressures . . . from both the IMF and the U.S. Treasury."[83] Thacker shows that the United States exerts a great deal of influence over which countries get IMF loans.[84] Countries voting similarly to the United States in the United Nations do better at the IMF. The literature on foreign aid also suggests that a country's relationship to powerful sponsors makes a difference. Countries tend to get more aid from all sources the more ties they have to powerful, rich countries, especially the once-colonial powers. Loans, aid, and advice may respond to the pressures of the most powerful developed countries, while trade agreements may promote the agendas and interests of these rich countries, but are these effects more or less likely when multilateral institutions exist than when these relations must be negotiated bilaterally?

3. *Capture by Private Producers and Investors.* Some have argued that the mission of the WTO,

IMF, and World Bank have been increasingly dominated by the interests of private producers and investors.[85] Sometimes their influence over these institutions operates through the power of the United States and European governments, and other times it operates independently or even at cross purposes from the developed countries' interests. The impression given is that these commercial and financial interests have hijacked the agenda of these institutions and have turned them into enforcers of open access to the markets of the poor countries. Furthermore, globalization has increased the influence of these private actors. "The governance structure of the global financial system has also been transformed. As private financial flows have come to dwarf official flows, the role and influence of private actors such as banks, hedge funds, equity funds and rating agencies has increased substantially. As a result, these private financial agencies now exert tremendous power over the economic policies of developing countries, especially the emerging market economies."[86]

Stiglitz claims that "financial interests have dominated the thinking at the IMF, [and] commercial interests have had an equally dominant role at the WTO."[87] Even Bhagwati, who holds one of the most positive views about globalization, indicts the "Wall Street–U.S. Treasury complex" for many of the undesirable policies promoted by the international institutions and resultant problems they created for the developing countries.[88] Is there strong evidence for this? One area that many scholars have pointed to is the WTO's promotion of trade-related aspects of intellectual property rights (TRIPs), especially in drugs and pharmaceuticals. As Bhagwati claims, "the multinationals have, through their interest-driven lobbying, helped set the rules in the world trading, intellectual property, aid and other regimes that are occasionally harmful to the interest of the poor countries."[89] He notes that a key example of this harmful effect has been in intellectual property protection where "the pharmaceutical and software companies muscled their way into the WTO and turned it into a royalty-collection agency because the WTO can apply trade sanctions."[90] He goes on to describe how the industries lobbied to get their views onto the American trade policy agenda and then used the United States government to force this onto the WTO and the developing countries.[91]

The impact of private actors seems most well-documented in the case of the IMF. Gould's research, for example, shows that the number and nature of conditionality in the IMF have responded increasingly to private investors. Their influence has grown because such investors play such a prominent role in international financing. As she claims,

> many of the controversial changes in the terms of Fund conditionality agreements reflect the interests and preferences of supplementary financiers. The Fund often provides only a fraction of the amount of financing that a borrowing country needs in order to balance its payments that year and implement the Fund's recommended program. Both the Fund and the borrower rely (often explicitly) on outside financing to supplement the Fund's financing. This reliance gives the supplementary financiers some leverage over the design of Fund programs. The supplementary financiers, in turn, want to influence the design of Fund programs because these programs help them ensure that borrowers are using their financing in the ways they prefer.[92]

Perhaps international economic institutions like the IMF, World Bank, and WTO are a means for private actors to affect policies in the developing countries, particularly when globalization is high. Scholars "have pointed out that liberal international regimes improve the bargaining power of private investors vis-à-vis governments and other groups in society."[93] Again, the counterfactual deserves consideration: would the developing countries have been more or less subject to the pressure of private capital if these institutions had not existed?

4. Internal Dysfunctions and Failure of Accountability. Some scholars have been sensitive to the internal dynamics of the institutions themselves.

They claim these organizations have developed their own internal logics, which may not serve the interests of the poor (or rich) countries. Effective control over them by either the advanced industrial countries or the developing ones may be difficult; long chains of delegation allow them much slack and make adequate monitoring of their behavior costly.[94] Principal-agent models suggest such outcomes are especially likely when multiple principals (that is, countries) try to control a single agent (that is, the institution); in these situations, the ability of the bureaucracy to play off different countries' interests and to avoid monitoring is maximized. Unlike the previous explanations that treated international institutions as mere servants of either powerful states or private producers and investors, this claim gives the organizations broad independence and wide latitude for autonomous action.

Vaubel has been one of the foremost proponents of this view.[95] He produces evidence showing that bureaucratic incentives within the IMF and other international institutions lead to policies and practices inappropriate for their stated purposes. Concerns over career advancement and budget size induce actors within these agencies to focus on making loans and giving aid, but not on monitoring the results. Giving more loans and aid is always preferred to giving fewer, and recipients know this and use it to extract more. "If both institutions [that is, the IMF and World Bank] are left to themselves, they will likely revert to internal bureaucratic politics determining loans. The act of making loans will be rewarded rather than the act of helping the poor in each country."[96]

As noted by Barnett and Finnemore, the IR literature has tended to take a benign view of international organizations, viewing them as instruments for facilitating cooperation and making efficient agreements.[97] But "IOs often produce undesirable and even self-defeating outcomes repeatedly, without punishment much less dismantlement . . . In this view, decisions are not made after a rational decision process but rather through a competitive bargaining process over turf, budgets, and staff that may benefit parts of the organization at the expense of overall goals."[98] For instance, they point to the case of the World Bank: "Many scholars and journalists, and even the current head of the World Bank, have noticed that the bank has accumulated a rather distinctive record of 'failures' but continues to operate with the same criteria and has shown a marked lack of interest in evaluating the effectiveness of its own projects."[99] A series of internal problems could be responsible thus for the performance of these institutions vis-à-vis the developing countries.

These four problems are not exclusive or exhaustive. Enumerating them is important. Figuring out which problems affect which institutions seems important and understudied. Moreover, the type of reform desired depends on the problem. For example, Stone recommends further insulation of the IMF from the pressures of the donors, especially the United States. He wants the IMF to be more like an independent central bank. Insulation is desirable if the main problem is that they are too easily pressured by the rich countries or by private investors. Stiglitz, among others, however, has the opposite view. He thinks they should be more transparent and open to developing-country influence. Studies of bureaucracy in general see insulation as necessary, if undesirable, outside influences are strong and leaders are tempted to yield to them; but they see insulation as the problem itself if the bureaucracy's unaccountability and standard operating procedures are the failings. If the IMF's problem results mainly from its own internal organization and logic, then further insulation is only going to worsen the problem. Without further systematic evidence about the sources of these institutions' main problems in delivering benefits, to the developing countries, reform proposals may do more harm than good.

In sum, today's international economic institutions seem to be falling short of the goals that theories expect of them, and the reasons seem numerous. The current state of our knowledge does not warrant advocating the abolition of these international institutions, however. They appear to provide some benefits to the poor countries over the most likely counterfactual scenarios. But they probably could be reformed to provide even greater benefits.

*   *   *

Conclusions: What is to Be Done?

What do we know about the impact of the major international economic institutions, the IMF, World Bank, and the WTO, on the developing countries? Have these institutions improved the lives of the poor in these countries? Have they made the developing countries better off than they would have been in the absence of these global institutions? Is this counterfactual the appropriate standard to evaluate them by? What is the moral obligation of the rich countries and their international institutions to the poor ones? Should the institutions be reformed to better fulfill their "duty of assistance" to the poor? Or is a better standard for their evaluation one that asks whether the institutions could be reformed at low cost to the rich countries so that they would provide more benefits to the poor ones? How do normative and positive analyses together shed light on these institutions?

In terms of the four major functions that theories of international institutions identify, these three global institutions seem to have failed to live up to the expectations of these theories in their impact on the developing countries. They have had a difficult time constraining the large, developed countries; most of the time these countries have bargained hard to maximize their advantage vis-à-vis the developing nations. Perhaps they have left the developing countries better off than if they had to negotiate bilaterally for access to trade, aid, and loans, but it seems as if these institutions could have bargained less hard with the developing countries at little cost to themselves or the developed countries and thus provided more benefits for the poor.

The IMF, World Bank, and WTO have certainly helped provide monitoring and information. But the monitoring and information provision have been asymmetric; it is the developing countries that are monitored and provide more information than otherwise. This action, however, may make the developed countries and private investors more likely to trade with, invest in, and provide loans to the poor countries, but the terms of these agreements have often imposed multiple and powerful conditions on the developing countries that may have impeded their growth.

Facilitating reciprocity has been a central function attributed to international institutions. For these three organizations, reciprocity vis-à-vis the developing world has not been a central mission; trade agreements have often been very asymmetric and the aid and lending programs are one way. Finally, the ability to alter domestic politics by creating support or locking it in for reform has been less studied, but seems to clearly have had an impact. The impact of the international institutions on the developing countries and their domestic situation has been powerful but not always benign.

The difficulties faced by the international institutions in providing benefits for the developing countries have arisen from at least four sources. It may be the case that globalization has simply overwhelmed these institutions and that their impact is minor compared to other factors, especially with a large and open world economy, and it is likely that domestic weaknesses account for part of their poor performance. But their problems may also lie in the pressures exerted by the large, developed countries and private producers and investors. Both of these groups have shaped the functioning of the WTO, IMF, and World Bank. The powerful, rich countries have bargained hard within these institutions to advance their own interests. Private producers and investors have directly and indirectly affected the performance of the institutions through their central role in the world economy. All of these institutions were established to support and facilitate private trade and capital flows, not to supplant them. Finally, one cannot overlook the claim that part of the problems arises from the internal organization and procedures of the institutions themselves. Making loans and imposing conditions may be more important for career advancement than measuring the impact of these activities on the developing nations.

Positive, empirical research asks the question of whether the developing world would have been better or worse off with the presence of these international institutions than without them. The evidence suggests that even though problems abound with the institutions, one cannot rule out the counterfactual: without these institutions many developing countries could be worse off as they faced bilateral negotiations with the most powerful countries. Thus, advocating their abolition is premature.

Nevertheless, one has to ask if this question is the right one. Arguments from one stream of moral philosophers imply that it is not. Cosmopolitan versions of global distributive justice see this question as insufficient. They propose one ask whether these institutions could be reformed at low cost to the wealthy countries to provide more benefits to the poor. Are these institutions the best feasible ones that could help the developing countries without imposing large costs on the developed ones?

By many accounts, the answer is negative. A number of feasible and low cost reforms could be enacted that would render these institutions much more helpful to the poor at limited cost to the rich. Pogge makes such a case for the WTO.[100] By the standards posed in global distributive justice arguments, reforming the international institutions is imperative. Interestingly, normative and positive analyses sometimes agree; some international economists such as Bhagwati and Stiglitz propose similar reforms.

In addition to policy implications, several ramifications for future research arise from the arguments surveyed here. Pogge's point about the "nationalist" research agenda in the field is salient. His prescription that we include more international factors in research on the sources of poverty and economic and political development is not unfamiliar and seems a worthy one. Including global factors and their interactions with domestic ones in comparative studies is an important step that cannot be emphasized enough.

The field would benefit from more research on the actual effects of international institutions, rather than debates about whether they are autonomous agents. More empirical research on the ways in which these institutions function and on the forces that prevent them from functioning as our theories predict is essential. This is particularly the case vis-à-vis the developing countries, many of whom do not have the capacity to evaluate the impact of these institutions on their fortunes. "Identifying who gains and who loses from existing policies is important both to determine the need for policy change and to build support for such change. For example, documenting how specific OECD policies hurt the poor both at home and in developing countries can have a powerful effect on mobilizing support for welfare improving reforms. . . . Building coalitions with NGOs and other groups that care about development is vital in generating the political momentum that is needed to improve access in sensitive sectors and improve the rules of the game in the WTO."[101] Generating greater academic knowledge thus may contribute vastly to producing better policy and outcomes, which may be a moral imperative given the grave problems of the developing countries.

NOTES

1. Stiglitz 2002, 3.
2. For example, Keohane 1984; Ikenberry 2001.
3. Counterfactuals are defined as "subjunctive conditionals in which the antecedent is known . . . to be false" (Tetlock and Belkin 1996, 4). A critical issue is how can one know what would have happened if the antecedent was false, that is, if factor X, which was present, had not been present. This problem of cotenability, identified by Elster (1978) early on, remains crucial: counterfactuals require connecting principles that sustain but do not require the conditional claim, and these connecting principles must specify all else that would have to be true for the false conditional claim to have been true.
4. Tetlock and Belkin 1996.
5. Beitz 2005, 26.
6. In fiscal 2003, IBRD provided loans totaling $11.2 billion in support of 99 projects in 37 countries. In 2003, the grant arm of the Bank, the International Development Association (IDA), provided $7.3 billion in financing for 141 projects in 55 low-income countries (World Bank *Annual Report* 2004).
7. In the fourteen years between 1980 and 1994, Ghana received nineteen adjustment loans from the IMF and World Bank; Argentina, fifteen; Peru, eight; and Zambia, twelve (Easterly 2001a, 104–5).
8. WTO, World Trade Report 2003.
9. Studies show that WTO membership by developing countries has had little, if any, impact on the level of either their trade flows or their trade barriers (Rose 2002; Rose 2004; Milner with Kubota 2005; Subramanian and Wei 2003; Özden and Reinhardt 2002; Özden and Reinhardt 2004). Many developing countries were members of the GATT but retained very high trade barriers.
10. Defining development itself is an issue. Sen (2000) provides an excellent discussion and a rationale for a broad conception.
11. International Labor Organization 2004, 33.
12. Easterly 2001a, 102–3.
13. Easterly 2001b; Easterly 2001a, 101.
14. Chen and Ravaillon 2005, table 2.
15. Pogge 2002, 2.
16. This data from World Bank WDI 2003 is measured in 1995 $ using the chain method. Using constant dollar purchasing parity data from the World Bank, the number of countries whose GNP per capita was lower in 2000 than in 1975 rises to 37, most in Africa,

then Latin America and the Middle East. Even this calculation is likely to understate the problem; the worst off countries are most likely not to have any data, for example, Afghanistan, North Korea, Yemen, and Somalia.

17. UNDP 2004, 132.
18. Easterly 2001a, 60.
19. World Bank 2004, 43.
20. Pritchett 1997.
21. Easterly 2001a, 62.
22. The debate over whether inequality is falling or rising is too extensive to reproduce here. The answer depends on how it is measured (for example, Sala-i-Martin 2002a and Sala-i-Martin 2002b).
23. Loser 2004, 2.
24. UNDP 2004, 129.
25. Pogge and Reddy (2005) dispute these poverty figures, claiming they understate absolute poverty greatly.
26. World Bank 2004, 46. Even excluding China, this ratio fell from 27 percent to 23 percent. China joined the IMF and World Bank in 1980 and used their facilities often for the first fifteen years or so. It acceded to the WTO in 2003.
27. World Bank 2004, 46.
28. See Aisbett (2005) for a discussion of different interpretations of the data on globalization and poverty.
29. World Bank 2004, 40.
30. Gruber 2000.
31. Ikenberry 2001.
32. WTO 2003, xviii.
33. Stiglitz 2002, 61.
34. Steinberg 2002, 366.
35. ILO 2004, 33.
36. Steinberg 2002, 341.
37. If the large countries compete for access to the small countries' markets in a bilateral system, the small may find advantages. The recent Mercosur negotiations with the EU for a PTA have had an impact on the US position in its negotiations with the Mercosur countries for the Free Trade Area of the Americas.

38. ILO 2004, 6.
39. It is not clear that the IMF would tolerate some of the recurrent practices of the developed countries; many have run persistent government budget and current account deficits of a magnitude that the IMF condemns in the developing countries.
40. Boughton 2001, 135–36.
41. Rodrik 1996.
42. For example, Maizels and Nissanke 1984; Lumsdaine 1993; Milner 2004.
43. For example, Meltzer 2000. Moral hazard is a situation in which doing something for someone changes their incentives to help themselves. The common example is home insurance; when owners have insurance that fully replaces their house, they may be less attentive to making sure it does not burn down.
44. For example, Alesina and Dollar 2000.
45. Stone 2002.
46. Keohane 1984, 97.
47. These arguments tend to overlook the distributional effects of institutions, and to focus on the mutual gains from cooperation within the institution. See Martin and Simmons 1998.
48. Krueger 1998.
49. Barnett and Finnemore 1999, 709–10.
50. For example, Mansfield, Milner and Rosendorff 2002; Milner, Rosendorff and Mansfield, 2004.
51. Keohane is ambivalent, arguing throughout much of the book that membership is voluntary and rational, meaning members should be better off than otherwise if they join and remain. But in his final chapter, he notes that these institutions reflect the interests of the rich countries, and that while the poor countries gain from them, they might gain more if they were reformed (1984, 256).
52. "Many critics of the IMF's handling of the Asian financial crises have argued that the IMF inappropriately applied a standardized formula of budget cuts plus high interest rates to combat rapid currency depreciation

without appreciating the unique and local causes of this depreciation. These governments were not profligate spenders, and austerity policies did little to reassure investors, yet the IMF prescribed roughly the same remedy that it had in Latin America. The result, by the IMF's later admission, was to make matters worse" (Barnett and Finnemore 1999, 721).

53. Stiglitz 2002, chap. 3; Bhagwati 2004, 204.

54. Stiglitz 2002, 220.

55. For example, Sachs and Warner 1995; Frankel and Romer 1999; Rodriguez and Rodrik 2001; UNCTAD 2004.

56. Stiglitz 2002, 143.

57. Keohane 1984, 129.

58. Bagwell and Staiger 2002.

59. Mattoo and Subramanian 2004, 6.

60. Mattoo and Subramanian (2004) survey 62 small and poor countries, which account for about one-third of the world's total countries but they individually account for less than 0.05 percent of world trade, and collectively for only 1.1 percent of global trade. China is the only developing country that has a significant share of the world market; its share of world exports has risen from less than 1 percent in 1980 to 6 percent in 2003.

61. Mattoo and Subramanian 2004, 11.

62. WTO, International Trade Statistics, 2004.

63. Mattoo and Subramanian 2004, 19.

64. Romalis 2003.

65. Özden and Reinhardt 2004.

66. The IMF and World Bank do not seem to play much of a role in enforcing reciprocity. As noted before, they obtain their funds and mandates from the developed countries and do their lending and aid giving in the developing world. The symmetric treatment of rich and poor countries is not evident.

67. E.g., McGillivray and Smith 2000.

68. For example, Mansfield, Milner and Rosendorff 2002.

69. For example, Gilligan 1997; Bailey, Goldstein and Weingast 1997.

70. Mattoo and Subramanian 2004, 11.

71. For example, Milner with Kubota 2005.

72. Their trade dependence has grown significantly from approximately 50 percent in 1960 to over 80 percent in 2000, or nearly a 60 percent increase, for the about 80 developing countries accounting for more than 70 percent of world population.

73. UNCTAD, Ext Debt #24, 2004, 2.

74. For example, Rodrik 1997; Kaufman and Segura-Ubiergo 2001; Adsera and Boix 2002; Mosley 2003.

75. For example, Acemoglu, Johnson, and Robinson 2001; Acemoglu, Johnson, and Robinson 2002; Rodrik, Subramanian, and Trebbi 2002; Easterly and Levine 2002.

76. For example, Acemoglu, Johnson, and Robinson 2001; Acemoglu, Johnson, and Robinson 2002; Rodrik, Subramanian, and Trebbi 2002; Easterly and Levine 2002. The causes of differential growth may lie in international politics. The way in which the great powers colonized the developing countries centuries ago is strongly related to their growth prospect now. It is not easy to disentangle domestic and international factors.

77. ILO, 2004, 76.

78. For example, Bueno de Mesquita and Root 2002; Van de Walle 2001.

79. For example, Burnside and Dollar 2000; Easterly 2003.

80. For example, Schraeder et al. 1998; McKinlay and Little 1977; McKinlay and Little 1978; Alesina and Dollar 2000.

81. Steinberg 2002, 356.

82. Stiglitz 2002, 160.

83. Bhagwati 2004, 204.

84. Thacker 1999.

85. The articles of agreement of the IBRD and the IMF give as one of their main purposes the promotion of private foreign investment in the developing countries. So it is not a surprise that the two institutions are susceptible to pressures from private investors.

86. ILO 2004, 35.

87. Stiglitz 2002, 216.

88. Bhagwati 2004, 205.

89. Bhagwati 2004, 182.

90. Bhagwati 2004, 182.

91. Chaudhuri, Goldberg, and Jia (2003) show in a sophisticated counterfactual analysis that in a key segment of the pharmaceuticals market in India, the losses to Indian consumers are far greater than the increased profits of foreign producers from the introduction of TRIPs.

92. Gould 2004, ch8, p. 1. For Gould, supplementary financiers are both public and private actors.

93. Keohane 1984, 253.

94. For example, Vreeland 2003, 157.

95. Vaubel 1986; Vaubel 1996.

96. Easterly 2001a, 290.

97. Barnett and Finnemore 1999, 701.

98. Barnett and Finnemore 1999, 701, 717.

99. Barnett and Finnemore 1999, 723.

100. Pogge 2002, 162.

101. Hoekman 2002, 26.

REFERENCES

Acemoglu, Daron, Simon Johnson, and James Robinson. 2001. The colonial origins of comparative development: An empirical investigation. *American Economic Review* 91 (5): 1369–1401.

Acemoglu, Daron, Simon Johnson, and James Robinson. 2002. Reversal of fortune: Geography and institutions in the making of the modern world income distribution. *Quarterly Journal of Economics* 117 (4): 1231–94.

Adsera, Alicia, and Carles Boix. 2002. Trade, democracy and the size of the public sector: The political underpinnings of openness. *International Organization* 56 (2): 229–62.

Alesina, Alberto, and David Dollar. 2000. Who gives foreign aid to whom and why? *Journal of Economic Growth* 5(1): 33–63.

Aisbett, Emma. 2005. Why are the critics so convinced that globalization is bad for the poor? *National Bureau of Economic Research Working Paper* 11066.

Bagwell, Kyle, and Robert W. Staiger. 2002. *The economics of the world trading system*. Cambridge: MIT Press.

Bailey, Michael A., Judith Goldstein, Barry R. Weingast. 1997. The institutional roots of American trade policy: Politics, coalitions, and international trade. *World Politics* 49(3): 309–338.

Barnett, Michael N., and Martha Finnemore. 1999. The politics, power, and pathologies of international organizations. *International Organization* 53 (4): 699–732.

Barry, Brian M. 1995. *Justice as impartiality*. Oxford: Oxford University Press.

Beitz, Charles R. 1979. *Political theory and international relations*. Princeton; Princeton University Press.

———. 1999. International liberalism and distributive justice: A survey of recent thought. *World Politics* 51(2): 269–96.

———. 2000. Rawls's law of peoples. *Ethics* 110(4): 669–696.

———. 2005. Cosmopolitanism and global justice. *The Journal of Ethics* 9 (1–2): 11–27.

Bhagwati, Jagdish. 2004. *In defense of globalization*. New York: Oxford University Press.

Bird, Graham, and Dane Rowlands. 2001. IMF Lending: How is it affected by economic, political and institutional factors? *Policy Reform* 4 (3): 243–70.

Blake, Michael. 2001. Distributive justice, state coercion and autonomy. *Philosophy and Public Affairs* 30 (3): 257–95.

Boughton, James M. 2001. *Silent revolution: The International Monetary Fund 1979–1989*. Washington, DC: IMF.

Buchanan, Allen. 2000. Rawls's law of peoples: Rules for a vanished Westphalian world. *Ethics* 110 (4): 697–721.

Bueno de Mesquita, Bruce, and Hilton Root, eds. 2002. *Governing for prosperity*. New Haven: Yale University Press.

Burnside, Craig, and David Dollar. 2000. Aid, policies and growth. *American Economic Review* 90(4): 847–68.

Caney, Simon. 2001. International distributive justice. *Political Studies* 49 (4): 974–97.

Chaudhuri, Shubham, Pinelopi Goldberg, and Panle Jia. 2003. Estimating the effects of global patent protection for pharmaceuticals: A case study of fluoroquinolones in India. Unpublished manuscript.

Chen, Shaohua, and Martin Ravaillon. 2005. How have the world's poorest fared since the early 1980s? World Bank Staff Paper 3341.

Cullity, Garrett. 1994. International aid and the scope of kindness. *Ethics* 105 (1): 99–127.

Elster, Jon. 1978. *Logic and society: Contradictions and possible worlds.* New York: John Wiley.

Easterly, William, and Ross Levine. 2002. Tropics, germs and crops: How endowments influence economic development. National Bureau of Economic Research Working Paper 9106.

Easterly, William. 2001a. *The elusive quest for growth: Economists' adventures and misadventures in the tropics.* Cambridge: MIT Press.

———. 2001b. The lost decades: Developing countries' stagnation in spite of policy reform, 1980–1998. Journal of Economic Growth 6 (2): 135–57.

———. 2003. Can foreign aid buy growth? *Journal of Economic Perspectives* 17 (3): 23–48.

Frankel, Jeffrey A., and David Romer. 1999. Does trade cause growth? *American Economic Review* 89 (3): 379–99.

Gilligan, Michael J. 1997. *Empowering exporters.* Ann Arbor, MI: University of Michigan Press.

Gould, Erica R. 2004. Money talks: The International Monetary Fund, conditionality and supplementary financiers. Unpublished manuscript.

Grant, Ruth W., and Robert O. Keohane. 2005. Accountability and abuses of power in world politics. *American Political Science Review* 99 (1): 29–43.

Gruber, Lloyd. 2000. *Ruling the world: Power politics and the rise of supranational institutions.* Princeton: Princeton University Press.

Hoekman, Bernard. 2002. Economic development and the WTO after Doha. World Bank Policy Research Working Paper 2851.

Ikenberry, G. John. 2001. *After victory: Institutions, strategic restraint, and the rebuilding of order after major wars.* Princeton: Princeton University Press.

International Labor Organization. 2004. *A fair globalization: Creating opportunities for all.* Geneva: International Labor Office.

Kaufman, Robert R., and Alex Segura-Ubiergo. 2001. Globalization, domestic politics, and social spending in Latin America: A time-series cross-section analysis, 1973–97. *World Politics* 53 (4): 553–87.

Keohane, Robert O. 1984. *After hegemony: Cooperation and discord in the world political economy.* Princeton: Princeton University Press.

Krueger, Anne O. 1998. Whither the World Bank and the IMF? *Journal of Economic Literature* 36 (4): 1983–2020.

Kuper, Andrews. 2004. *Democracy beyond borders: Justice and representation in global institutions.* New York: Oxford University Press.

Loser, Claudio M. 2004. External debt sustainability: Guidelines for low- and middle-income countries. G-24 Discussion Paper Series 26. Geneva.

Lumsdaine, David Halloran. 1993. *Moral vision in international politics: The foreign aid regime, 1949–1989.* Princeton: Princeton University Press.

Maizels, Alfred, and Machiko K. Nissanke. 1984. Motivations for aid to developing countries. *World Development* 12 (9): 879–900.

Macedo, Stephen. 2004. What self-governing peoples owe to one another: Universalism, diversity and the law of peoples. *Fordham Law Review* 72 (5): 1721–38.

Mansfield, Edward D., Helen V. Milner, and B. Peter Rosendorff. 2002. Why democracies cooperate more: Electoral control and international trade agreements. *International Organization* 56 (3): 477–514.

Martin, Lisa, and Beth Simmons. 1998. Theories and empirical studies of international institutions. *International Organization* 52 (4): 729–57.

Mattoo, Aaditya, and Arvind Subramanian. 2004. The WTO and the poorest countries: The stark reality. IMF Working Paper 04/81.

McGillivray, Fiona, and Alastair Smith. 2000. Trust and cooperation through agent specific punishments. *International Organization* 54 (4): 809–24.

McKinlay, Robert D, and Richard Little. 1977. A foreign policy model of US bilateral aid allocation. *World Politics* 30 (1): 58–86.

———. 1978. A foreign policy model of the distribution of British bilateral aid, 1960–70. *British Journal of Political Science* 8 (3): 313–31.

Meltzer, Alan. 2000. Report of the international financial institutions advisory commission. Meltzer Commission. Washington, DC.

Milner, Helen V. 1998. Rationalizing politics: The emerging synthesis of international, American, and comparative politics. *International Organization* 52 (4): 759–86.

———. 2004. Why multilateralism? Foreign aid and domestic principal-agent problems. Unpublished manuscript.

Milner, Helen V., with Keiko Kubota. 2005. Why the move to free trade? Democracy and trade policy in the developing countries, 1970–1999. *International Organization* 59 (1): 107–43.

Milner, Helen V., B. Peter Rosendorff, and Edward Mansfield. 2004. International trade and domestic politics: The domestic sources of international trade agreements and organizations. *The impact of international law on international cooperation.* Eyal Benvenisti and Moshe Hirsch, eds. Cambridge UK, Cambridge University Press.

Mosley, Layna. 2003. *Global capital and national governments.* New York: Cambridge University Press.

Nagel, Thomas. 2005. The problem of global justice. *Philosophy and Public Affairs.* 33 (2): 113–47.

Özden, Çaglar, and Eric Reinhardt. 2002. The perversity of preferences: GSP and developing countries trade policies, 1976–2000. World Bank Working Papers 2955.

Özden, Çaglar, and Eric Reinhardt. 2004. First do no harm: The effect of trade preferences on developing country exports. World Bank Research Paper.

Pogge, Thomas W. 2002. *World poverty and human rights.* Cambridge, UK: Polity.

Pogge, Thomans, and Sanjay Reddy. 2005. How *not* to count the poor. Forthcoming in *Measuring global poverty,* Sudhir Anand and Joseph Stiglitz, eds. Oxford: Oxford University Press.

Pritchett, Lant. 1997. Divergence, big time. *Journal of Economic Perspectives* 11 (3): 3–17.

Rawls, John. 1999. *The law of peoples; with, the idea of public reason revisited.* Cambridge: Harvard University Press.

Risse, Mathias. 2004a. Does the global order harm the poor? Unpublished manuscript, Harvard University, John F. Kennedy School of Government.

———. 2004b. What we owe to the global poor. *Journal of Ethics* 9 (1/2): 81–117.

Rodriguez, Francisco, and Dani Rodrik. 2001. Trade policy and economic growth: A skeptic's guide to the cross-national evidence. *NBER macroeconomics annual 2000.* Ben S. Bernancke and Kenneth Rogoff. Cambridge MA: MIT Press for NBER: 261–325.

Rodrik, Dani. 1996. Why is there multilateral lending? In *Annual World Bank conference on development economics, 1995,* ed. Michael Bruno and Boris Pleeskovic, 167–93. Washington, DC: International Monetary Fund.

———. 1997. *Has globalization gone too far?* Washington, DC: Institute for International Economics.

———. 2000. Development strategies for the next century. Paper prepared for the conference on "Developing Economies in the Twenty-First Century", Ciba, Japan, January 26–27. http://ksghome.harvard.edu/~.drodrik.academic.ksg/.

Rodrik, Dani, Arvind Subramanian, and Francesco Trebbi. 2002. Institutions rule: The primacy of institutions over geography and integration in economic development. National Bureau of Economic Research Working Paper 9305.

Romalis, John. 2003. Would rich country trade preferences help poor countries grow? Evidence from the generalized system of preferences. Manuscript. http://gsbwww.uchicago.edu/fac/john.romalis/research/

Rose, Andrew K. 2002. Do WTO members have a more liberal trade policy? National Bureau of Economic Research Working Paper 9347.

———. 2004. Do we really know that the WTO increases trade? *American Economic Review* 94(1): 98–114.

Sachs, Jeffrey, and Andrew Warner. 1995. Economic reform and the process of global integration. *Brookings Papers on Economic Activity* (1): 1–118.

Sala-i-Martin, Xavier. 2002a. The world distribution of income (estimated from individual country distributions). NBER working paper #8933.

———. 2002b. The disturbing "rise" of global income inequality. NBER Working Paper 8904.

Schraeder, Peter J., Stephen W. Hook, and Bruce Taylor. 1998. Clarifying the foreign aid puzzle: A comparison of American, Japanese, French and Swedish aid flows. *World Politics* 50 (2): 294–323.

Sen, Amartya. 2000. *Development as freedom.* New York: Alfred A. Knopf.

Singer, Peter. 1972. Famine, affluence, and morality. *Philosophy & Public Affairs* 1 (3): 229–243.

———. 2002. *One world: The ethics of globalization.* New Haven: Yale University Press.

Steinberg, Richard. 2002. In the shadow of law or power? Consensus-based bargaining and outcomes in the in the GATT/WTO. *International Organization* 56 (2): 339–74.

Stiglitz, Joseph E. 2002. *Globalization and its discontents.* New York, NY: W. W. Norton.

Stone, Randall W. 2002. *Lending credibility: The International Monetary Fund and the postcommunist transition.* Princeton: Princeton University Press.

Subramanian, Arvind, and Shang-Jin Wei. 2003. The WTO promotes trade, strongly but unevenly. National Bureau of Economic Research Working Paper 10024.

Tetlock, Philip E., and Aaron Belkin, eds. 1996. *Counterfactual thought experiments in world politics: Logical, methodological, and psychological perspectives.* Princeton: Princeton University Press.

Thacker, Strom Cronan. 1999. The high politics of IMF lending. *World Politics* 52 (1): 38–75.

United Nations Conference on Trade and Development (UNCTAD). 2004. *Trade and poverty.* Geneva: UNCTAD.

UNDP. 2004. *Human development report 2004.* New York: UNDP.

Van de Walle, Nicolas. 2001. *African economies and the politics of permanent crisis, 1979–1999.* New York: Cambridge University Press.

Vaubel, Roland. 1986. A public choice approach to international organization. *Public Choice* 51 (1): 39–57.

———. 1996. Bureaucracy at the IMF and the World Bank: A comparison of the evidence. *World Economy* 19 (2): 195–210.

Vreeland, James Raymond. 2003. *The IMF and economic development.* New York: Cambridge University.

World Bank. 2002. *World development indicators.* Washington, DC: World Bank.

———. 2003. *Annual report 2003.* Washington, DC: World Bank.

———. 2004. *Annual report 2004.* Washington, DC: World Bank.

———. 2004. *Global economic prospects.* Washington, DC: World Bank.

World Trade Organization. 2003. *World trade report 2003.* Geneva: World Trade Organization.

———. 2004. *International trade statistics.* Geneva: World Trade Organization.

MARTIN WOLF

FROM *WHY GLOBALIZATION WORKS*

*   *   *

Chapter 9

Incensed about Inequality

Globalization has dramatically increased inequality between and within nations, even as it connects people as never before. A world in which the assets of the 200 richest people are greater than the combined income of the more than 2bn people at the other end of the economic ladder should give everyone pause.

—*Jay Mazur, president of the Union of Needletrades, Industrial and Textile Employees.*[1]

—Jay Mazur is not alone. Ignacio Ramonet has written on similar lines, in *Le Monde Diplomatique*, that:

the dramatic advance of globalization and neoliberalism . . . has been accompanied by an *explosive growth in inequality* and a return of mass poverty and unemployment. The very opposite of everything which the modern state and modern citizenship is supposed to stand for.

The net result is a *massive growth in inequality*. The United States, which is the richest country in the world, has more than 60 million poor. The world's foremost trading power, the European Union, has over 50 million. In the United States, 1 percent of the population owns 39 percent of the country's wealth. Taking the planet as a whole, the combined wealth of the 358 richest people (all of them dollar billionaires) is greater than the total annual income of 45 percent of the world's poorest inhabitants, that is, 2.6bn people.[2]

From *Why Globalization Works* (New Haven and London: Yale UP 2004), 138–72. Some of the author's notes have been omitted.

Let us, for a moment, ignore the assumption that the number of poor (how defined?) in two of the richest regions in the world tells one anything about global inequality, or about poverty for that matter, or even about inequality within the U.S. and the European Union. Let us also ignore the comparison between the *assets* of one group of people, the richest, and the *incomes* of another, the poor, which is a comparison of apples and oranges. (In order to obtain the permanent incomes of the rich, one would need to divide the value of their assets by at least twenty.) These absurdities merely make Ramonet's diatribe representative of the empty rhetoric of many critics of globalization. But the questions that underlie his remarks need to be tackled. Here are seven propositions that can be advanced about what has happened in the age of so-called neo-liberal globalization over the past two decades.

First, the ratio of average incomes in the richest countries to those in the poorest has continued to rise.

Second, the absolute gap in living standards between today's high-income countries and most developing countries has also continued to rise.

Third, global inequality among individuals has risen.

Fourth, the number of people in extreme poverty has risen.

Fifth, the proportion of people in extreme poverty in the world's population has also risen.

Sixth, the poor of the world are worse off not just in terms of incomes, but in terms of a wide range of other indicators of human welfare.

Seventh, income inequality has risen in every country and particularly in countries most exposed to international economic integration.

In the rest of this chapter I will consider what we know about these propositions and how the answers relate to international economic integration. Before examining them, however, we need to ask what matters to us. Most of the debate has been either about whether inequality has risen between the world's rich and poor or about whether the number of people in income poverty has risen. But critics of globalization have themselves often rightly argued that there is more to life than income. What is most important must be the living standards of the poor, not just in terms of their incomes, narrowly defined, but in terms of their health, life expectancy, nourishment and education.

Equally, we need to understand that rises in inequality might occur in very different ways. Three possibilities come to mind at once: a rise in incomes of the better off, at the expense of the poor; a rise in the incomes of the better off, with no effects on the welfare of the poor; or rises in incomes of the better off that, in various ways, benefit the poor, but not by proportionately as much as they benefit the better off. It seems clear that the first of these is malign, the second desirable, unless the welfare of the better off counts for nothing, and the third unambiguously desirable, though one might wish more of the gains to accrue to the poor. True egalitarians would differ on these judgements, of course. Indeed, an extreme egalitarian might take the view that a world in which everybody was an impoverished subsistence farmer would be better than the world we now have, because it would be less unequal. Most people—including, I imagine, many protesters against globalization—would regard this as crazy. Few are that egalitarian. Most people are not even as egalitarian as the late philosopher John Rawls, who argued that inequality was permissible only to the extent that it benefited the poor.

We need to be equally careful in considering the role of globalization in relation to inequality and poverty. International economic integration may affect global inequality in several different ways. Here are a few possibilities: it may increase inequality by lowering the incomes of the poor; it may raise the incomes of the better off, without having any impact on the incomes of the poor; it

may raise the incomes of the poor by proportionately less than it raises the incomes of the better off; or it may raise the incomes of the poor by proportionately more than it raises those of the better off. Only the first is unambiguously bad, but all of the first three would be associated with increasing inequality. Yet both of the last two mean higher living standards for the poor.

Again, it may not be globalization, as such, that delivers these outcomes, but a combination of globalization with non-globalization. Globalization may raise incomes of globalizers, while non-globalization lowers the incomes of non-globalizers. Then an era of globalization may be associated with rising inequality that is caused not by globalization, but by its opposite, the refusal (or inability) of some countries to participate.

The most important questions to bear in mind in the discussions below are, therefore, these. Is human welfare, broadly defined, rising? Is the proportion of humanity living in desperate misery declining? If inequality is rising, are the rich profiting at the expense of the poor? Is globalization damaging the poor or is it rather non-globalization that is doing so? To answer all these questions, one must start at the beginning, with economic growth.

Economic Growth and Globalization

In the mid-1970s I was the World Bank's senior divisional economist on India during the country's worst post-independence decade. After a spurt of growth in the early phase of its inward-looking development, growth in incomes per head had ground virtually to a halt. Hundreds of millions of people seemed, as a result, to be mired in hopeless and unending poverty. In a book published in 1968, a well-known environmentalist doomsayer, Paul Ehrlich, had written the country off altogether.[3] For a young man from the UK, work in India as an economist was both fascinating and appalling: so much poverty; so much frustration; so much complacency. Yet I was convinced then, as I am now, that, with perfectly feasible policy changes, this vast country could generate rapid rates of economic growth and reductions in poverty. No iron law imposed levels of real output (and so real incomes) per head at only 10 percent of those in high-income countries.

Since those unhappy days, India has enjoyed the fruit of two revolutions: the green revolution, which transformed agricultural productivity; and a liberalizing revolution, which began, haltingly, under Rajiv Gandhi's leadership, in the 1980s and then took a "great leap forward" in 1991, in response to a severe foreign exchange crisis, under the direction of one of the country's most remarkable public servants, Manmohan Singh, the then finance minister. Slowly, India abandoned the absurdities of its pseudo-Stalinist "control raj" in favor of individual enterprise and the market. As a result, between 1980 and 2000, India's real GDP per head more than doubled. Stagnation has become a thing of the past.

India was not alone. On the contrary, it was far behind a still more dynamic and even bigger liberalizing country—China, which achieved a rise in real incomes per head of well over 400 percent between 1980 and 2000. China and India, it should be remembered, contain almost two-fifths of the world's population. China alone contains more people than Latin America and sub-Saharan Africa together. Many other countries in east and south Asia have also experienced rapid growth. According to the 2003 *Human Development Report* from the United Nations Development Programme, between 1975 and 2001, GDP per head rose at 5.9 percent a year in east Asian developing countries (with 31 percent of the world's population in 2000). The corresponding figure for growth of GDP per head for south Asia (with another 22 percent of the world's population) was 2.4 percent a year. Between 1990 and 2001, GDP per head rose at 5.5 percent a year in east Asia, while growth rose to 3.2 percent a year in south Asia.

Never before have so many people—or so large a proportion of the world's population—

enjoyed such large rises in their standards of living. Meanwhile, GDP per head in high-income countries (with 15 percent of the world's population) rose by 2.1 percent a year between 1975 and 2001 and by only 1.7 percent a year between 1990 and 2001. This then was a period of partial convergence: the incomes of poor developing countries, with more than half the world's population, grew substantially faster than those of the world's richest countries.

This, in a nutshell, is why Mazur and the many people who think like him are wrong. Globalization has not increased inequality. It has reduced it, just as it has reduced the incidence of poverty. How can this be, critics will demand? Are absolute and proportional gaps in living standards between the world's richest and poorest countries not rising all the time? Yes is the answer. And is inequality not rising in most of the world's big countries? Yes, is again the answer. So how can global inequality be falling? To adapt Bill Clinton's campaign slogan, it is the growth, stupid. Rapid economic growth in poor countries with half the world's population has powerful effects on the only sort of inequality which matters, that among individuals. It has similarly dramatic effects on world poverty. The rise of Asia is transforming the world, very much for the better. It is the "Asian drama" of our times, to plagiarize the title of a celebrated work by a Nobel-laureate economist, the late Gunnar Myrdal.

What, the reader may ask, has this progress to do with international economic integration? In its analysis of globalization, published in 2002, the World Bank divided seventy-three developing countries, with aggregate population, in 1997, of 4 billion (80 percent of all people in developing countries), into two groups: the third that had increased ratios of trade to GDP, since 1980, by the largest amount and the rest.[4] The former group, with an aggregate population of 2.9 billion, managed a remarkable combined increase of 104 percent in the ratio of trade to GDP. Over the same period, the increase in the trade ratio of the high-income countries was 71 percent, while the "less globalized" two-thirds of countries in the sample of developing countries experienced a decline in their trade ratios.

The average incomes per head of these twenty-four globalizing countries rose by 67 percent (a compound rate of 3.1 percent a year) between 1980 and 1997. In contrast, the other forty-nine countries managed a rise of only 10 percent (a compound rate of 0.5 percent a year) in incomes per head over this period. As Table 1 shows, these more globalized countries did not have particularly high levels of education in 1980. At that time, they were also a little poorer, as a group, than the rest. Subsequently, the new globalizers, as the World Bank calls them, cut their import tariffs by 34 percentage points, on average, against 11 percentage points for the other group. They also achieved a better reading on the rule of law than the others. The World Bank's conclusion is that, "as they reformed and integrated with the world market, the 'more globalized' developing countries started to grow rapidly, accelerating steadily from 2.9 percent in the 1970s to 5 percent in the 1990s."[5]

While what the Bank says is both true and important, it should be observed that its notion of a group of twenty-four countries is something of a fiction. China and India contain, between them, 75 percent of the group's combined population. With Brazil, Bangladesh, Mexico, the Philippines and Thailand, one has 92 percent of the group's population. Moreover, Asian countries dominate: they make up 85 percent of the population of this group of globalizing countries.

What then do we learn from the success of the countries picked out as globalizers by the World Bank? We can say, with confidence, that the notion that international economic integration necessarily makes the rich richer and the poor poorer is nonsense. Here is a wide range of countries that increased their integration with the world economy and prospered, in some cases dramatically so. A subtler question, to which we shall return in subsequent chapters, is precisely what policies relatively successful developing countries have followed. Critics are right to argue that success has not required adoption of the full range of so-called neo-liberal policies—privatization, free trade, and capital-account liberalization. But, in insisting upon this point, critics are wilfully mistaking individual policy trees for the market-oriented forest. What the successful

Table 1. Characteristics of More Globalized and Less Globalized Developing Economies (Population-Weighted Average)

Socioeconomic characteristics	More globalized (24)	Less globalized (49)
Population, 1997 (billions)	2.9	1.1
Per-capita GDP, 1980	$1,488	$1,947
Per-capita GDP, 1997	$2,485	$2,133
Compound annual growth rate of GDP per head, 1980–1997	3.1%	0.5%
Rule of law index, 1997 (world average=0)	−0.04	−0.48
Average years primary schooling, 1980	2.4	2.5
Average years primary schooling, 1997	3.8	3.1
Average years secondary schooling, 1980	0.8	0.7
Average years secondary schooling, 1997	1.3	1.3
Average years tertiary schooling, 1980	0.08	0.09
Average years tertiary schooling, 1997	0.18	0.22

Source: World Bank, *Globalization, Growth & Poverty: Building an Inclusive World Economy* (Washington DC: World Bank, 2002), Table 1.1.

countries all share is a move towards the market economy, one in which private property rights, free enterprise and competition increasingly took the place of state ownership, planning and protection. They chose, however haltingly, the path of economic liberalization and international integration. This is the heart of the matter. All else is commentary.

If one compares the China of today with the China of Mao Zedong or the India of today with the India of Indira Gandhi, the contrasts are overwhelming. Market forces have been allowed to operate in ways that would have been not just unthinkable but criminal a quarter of a century ago. Under Mao, economic freedom had been virtually eliminated. Under the Indian control system, no significant company was allowed to produce, invest, or import without government permission. From this starting-point, much of the most important liberalization was, necessarily and rightly, internal. Given where it was in the 1970s, liberalizing agriculture alone started China on the path towards rapid development. Similarly, eliminating the more absurd controls on industry permitted an acceleration in Indian economic growth. In both cases then these initial reforms and the abundance of cheap and hard-working labor guaranteed accelerated growth.

Yet in neither case can the contribution of economic integration be ignored. This is spectacularly true of China. The volume of China's exports grew at 13 percent a year between 1980 and 1990 and then at 11 percent between 1990 and 1999. Between 1990 and 2000 the ratio of trade in goods to Chinese GDP, at market prices, jumped from 33 to 44 percent, an extraordinarily high ratio for such a large economy. The ratio of merchandise trade to output of goods in the economy rose from 47 percent to 66 percent over the same period.[6] In 2001, China's gross merchandize exports of $266 billion amounted to 4.3 percent of the world total, up from a mere 0.7 percent in 1977.[7] By that year, China was the world's sixth largest merchandise exporter (including intra-European Union trade in the total), just behind the UK, but already ahead of Canada

and Italy. Meanwhile, private capital flows into China jumped from 3 percent of GDP in 1990 to 13 percent in 2000. By 2001, the stock of inward foreign direct investment in China was $395 billion, 6 percent of the world's total, up from $25 billion in 1990. In 2000, inward direct investment financed 11 percent of the giant's gross fixed capital formation, while foreign affiliates generated 31 percent of China's manufacturing sales and, more astonishingly, 50 percent of its exports.[8] It is possible to argue that China's dramatic economic growth somehow had nothing to do with its headlong rush into the global market economy. But it would be absurd to do so.

India's integration was much less spectacular. So, not coincidentally, was its growth. Yet here, too, the change was palpable. India's volume of merchandise exports fell in the 1980s, which contributed mightily to the foreign exchange crisis that brought to an end its overwhelmingly inward-looking liberalization of the 1980s. But export volume rose at 5.3 percent a year between 1990 and 1999, after external liberalization had begun. India's share in world merchandise exports had fallen from 2.1 percent in 1951 to a low of 0.4 percent in 1980. But by 2001 this share was modestly back up, to 0.7 percent, putting it in thirtieth place globally. Between 1990 and 2000, the share of trade in goods also rose from 13 to 20 percent of GDP. India did achieve a significant success in exports of commercial services (particularly software). By 2001, its exports of such services were $20 billion, almost half as much as its $44 billion in merchandise exports. Its share in world exports of commercial services was 1.4 percent, double its share in exports of goods, while its rank in the world was nineteenth, though even here it was behind China's exports of $33 billion (2.3 percent of the world total). India also lagged in openness to inward direct investment, which only reached $3.4 billion in 2001. But even this was close to revolutionary in a country that had, for decades, discouraged all inward FDI. In 1990, the total stock of inward FDI was a mere $1.7 billion. By 2001, it had reached $22 billion. The 1990s were, in all, India's most economically successful post-independence decade. They were also the decade in which the country liberalized both internal and external transactions and increased its integration into the global economy. An accident? Hardly.

Now consider an even more fascinating example in the Bank's list of globalizing economies —Bangladesh, certainly the poorest sizeable country in the world in the 1970s and, as I remember well, almost universally deemed a hopeless case. Even this country has benefited from international economic integration. The GDP per head of Bangladesh rose at 2.3 percent a year between 1975 and 2001, generating a 60 percent rise in real income per head over more than a quarter of a century. Between 1990 and 2001, GDP per head grew considerably faster, at 3.1 percent a year, as the economy opened. In 1975, Bangladesh's real GDP per head (measured at purchasing power parity) was roughly half that of sub-Saharan Africa. By 2000, its real GDP per head was close to the average level of sub-Saharan Africa. In the 1980s, Bangladesh's volume of merchandise exports barely rose. In the 1990s, it rose at a remarkable 15 percent a year. Between 1990 and 2000, the ratio of exports to GDP jumped from 18 to 32 percent. The volume of trade also grew 6 percentage points a year faster than GDP in the decade. Bangladesh did not suddenly become a magnet for foreign direct investment. That is hardly surprising, since it has been ranked bottom of seventy-five countries in the cost of corruption.[9] But the stock of inward direct investment did reach $1.1 billion by 2001, up from $150 million in 1990. Even for Bangladesh, international economic integration has paid off. It is only a start. But it is, at least, that.

If a successful move to the market, including increasing integration in the world economy, explains the success stories of the past two decades, what explains the failures, that is, those which have failed to take advantage of the opportunities for global economic integration? Failure to develop has involved a complex interplay of institutions, endowments and policies.

Emphasis on institutions and their evolution has, quite properly, become a dominant focus of analysts of development. It is discovered, not surprisingly, that poor performers have corrupt, predatory or brutal governments or, sometimes even worse, no government at all, but rather civil war among competing warlords.[10] The failure of the state to provide almost any of the services desperately needed for development is at the root of the African disaster. This reflects both the artificiality of the states and the weak—if not nonexistent—sense of moral responsibility of Africa's "big men." Mobutu's Zaire was perhaps the most catastrophic example. But he was also one of many. Today, Robert Mugabe's destruction of once-prosperous Zimbabwe is almost equally horrifying.[11] An even more depressing case is that of sub-Sahara's giant, Nigeria. Today, Nigeria's GDP per head, at PPP, is the same as it was in 1970, despite three decades of abundant oil revenues, all of which has been wasted in foolish public spending and capital flight. The proportion of Nigeria's population in extreme poverty (real incomes of less than a dollar a day, at PPP) has doubled over this period. The élite has been predatory in the extreme: in 2000, the top 2 percent had the same income as the bottom 55 percent.[12] Much of Nigeria's wealth has been squirrelled away abroad. Alas, Nigeria is merely an extreme case. It is estimated that about 40 percent of Africa's private wealth was held overseas by 1990. But bad governments have also failed to provide the infrastructure on which development depends. As a result, African countries trade even less with one another and the rest of the world than would be predicted from their adverse locations.[13]

The second obstacle to development is a country's natural endowments. There is much evidence that location in the tropics is a handicap, though whether this is only via the impact on the evolution of countries' institutions, or independently, remains controversial. The probability is that it is a bit of both. Debilitating diseases have long been rife in the tropics. But it is also true that colonial regimes tended to create predatory institutions in their tropical possessions. Distance from the sea is also a handicap and particularly being landlocked. The disadvantages faced by the landlocked—a natural form of protection against foreign trade—also underline the costs of non-globalization.[14]

Endowments enter into development in another way, as resources. Natural resources, especially mineral wealth, seem to be an obstacle, not a spur, to economic development. This "resource curse" has many dimensions: resources tend to corrupt politics, turning it into a race to seize the incomes produced by resources, often generating debilitating civil wars; they generate unstable terms of trade, because prices of natural resources or agricultural commodities fluctuate widely; and they produce a high real exchange rate that, among other things, hinders development of internationally competitive manufacturing.

Data on real GDP per head show that developing countries with few natural resources grew two to three times faster between 1960 and 1990 than countries with abundant natural resources. The World Bank demonstrates that no fewer than forty-five countries experienced "unsustained growth" over the past four decades: they matched their 1999 level of real income per head in a previous decade, many as far back as the 1960s. All but six of these countries possess "point-source natural resources"—oil or minerals. Nigeria is one example of a country ruined by an abundance of oil. Angola is another: its GDP per head is lower today than it was in 1960.[15] So much, by the way, for the view that what countries need for successful development is more aid. If foreign resources were all that was needed to make a country rich, Angola and Nigeria would not be in the state they are in.

Even where natural resources do not generate corrupt, rent-seeking societies, they can be an obstacle to sustained development. In the postwar era, the most successful route to development seems to have been via the export of labor-intensive manufactures, the route on which China has followed Hong Kong, Singapore, Taiwan, and South Korea. The success of developing countries with exports of manufactures has been astonishing: in 1980 only 25 percent of the merchandise exports of developing countries were manufactures. By 1998, this had risen to 80 percent. The old view in which developing countries exported commodities in return for manufactures is entirely outmoded. Today, they are just as likely to export manufactures (and services, too, since their share in total exports of developing countries has risen to 17 percent, from 9 percent in the early 1980s) in return for commodities.[16]

The path of manufactures offers a number of significant advantages. World markets for manufactures, while not free, have been relatively open and dynamic. Markets for agricultural commodities have either been slow-growing and price-insensitive (as for the classic tropical commodities—cocoa, tea, and coffee), highly protected in the world's most important markets (as for temperate agricultural commodities), or both (as for sugar). Manufactures also offer a natural ladder up the chain of comparative advantage. A country that has specialized in natural-resource exports will find it hard to shift into competitive manufactures as it must break into world markets after having already achieved quite high real wages and, correspondingly, must do so at relatively high levels of productivity. Since there is learning-by-doing (and other spillovers) in manufacturing, achieving this transition to exports of manufactures can be tricky at relatively high-wages. The transition can be thwarted altogether by policies of blanket protection used, as they were in Argentina and other resource-rich countries, to spread resource rents to a politically influential working class. The task is not hopeless: the U.S. itself is an example of such a transition, successfully completed a century or so ago. More recently, Chile has had great success with a path based on commodity exports.

A final aspect of resources is human resources, both latent and overt. Under latent resources are the underlying cultural and behavioural assumptions of a society—its software, so to speak. Under overt human resources is the level of education achieved by the population. It cannot be altogether an accident that the most successful region of the world, after Europe and the British offshoots in the New World, is east Asia, long home to sophisticated agrarian states, with established bureaucratic cultures and developed mercantile traditions. From this point of view, sub-Saharan Africa has been doubly handicapped, long isolated from Eurasia, still enveloped in tribal traditions and lacking a sizeable number of highly educated people at the time of independence, when many mistakes were made.

Finally, there are policies. If all that mattered were endowments and institutions, one would never have seen sudden take-offs by some countries in response to policy changes. But the rapid growth of South Korea and Taiwan in the 1960s only followed a move to realistic exchange rates and export promotion. The mistakes repeatedly made by other countries have included overvalued real exchange rates, often used to suppress the inflationary consequences of fiscal imprudence (as in Zimbabwe today), creation of corrupt and incompetent public sector monopolies in vital areas, such as electric power generation and distribution or marketing of export commodities; and high and variable protection against imports, often via corruption-fuelling controls. How much these mistakes matter tends to depend on a country's comparative advantage. If a country possesses a supply of very cheap and highly motivated labor, as China does today, it seems easier to survive mistakes (and institutional failings) that would cripple an Argentina or a Mexico. Nevertheless, it was only after a series of reforms that China began to integrate into the world economy. Countries without China's human resources must try even harder to get policy right.

Growth and Inequality

Now what does the performance of those who have succeeded in growing through economic integration mean for inequality? Inequality is a measure of relative incomes. If the average real incomes of poor countries containing at least half of the world's population have been rising faster than those of the relatively rich, inequality among countries, weighted by population, will have fallen. This will be true even if the ratio of the incomes of the world's richest to the world's poorest countries and the absolute gaps in average incomes per head between rich countries and almost all developing countries have risen (as they have).

These two points may need a little explanation. First, compare, say, the U.S. with China. Between 1980 and 2000, according to the World Bank, Chinese average real incomes rose by about 440 percent. Over the same period, U.S. average real incomes per head rose by about 60 percent. The ratio of Chinese real incomes per head, at purchasing power parity, to those of the U.S. rose, accordingly, from just over 3 percent in 1980 to just under 12 percent in 2000. This is a big reduction in relative inequality. But the absolute gap in real incomes between China and the U.S. rose from $20,600 to $30,200 per head (at PPP). The reason is simple: since China's standard of living was, initially, about a thirtieth of that of the U.S. the absolute gap could have remained constant only if China's growth had been thirty times faster than that of the U.S. That would have been impossible. If China continues to grow faster than the U.S. however, absolute gaps will ultimately fall, as happened with Japan in the 1960s and 1970s.

Second, while the *ratio* of the average incomes per head in the richest country to those in the world's least successful countries is rising all the time, the *proportion* of the world's population living in the world's poorest countries has, happily, been falling. Thirty years ago, China and India were among the world's poorest countries. Today, the poorest seems to be Sierra Leone, a country with a population of only 5 million. China's average real income per head is now some ten times higher than Sierra Leone's. The largest very poor country today is Nigeria, with a population of 127 million in 2000 and a real income, at PPP, just a fortieth of that of the U.S.

(and a fifth of China's). Again, this means that rising ratios between the average incomes of the world's richest and poorest countries are consistent with declining inequality among countries, weighted by their populations. Moreover, it is also perfectly possible for inequality to have risen in every single country in the world (as Mazur alleges, wrongly) while global inequality has fallen. Unless the increase in inequality among individuals within countries offsets the reduction in population-weighted inequality among countries, not only inequality among (population-weighted) countries, but also inequality among individuals will have declined.

Andrea Boltho of Oxford University and Gianni Toniolo of Rome University have computed population-weighted inequality among forty-nine countries that contain 80 percent of the world's population, back to 1900. To compute their measure of inequality, the gini coefficient, the authors weight the average income, at purchasing power parity (in order to compare standards of living), of each country by its population.[17] They conclude that inequality among countries, weighted in this way, reached its maximum in 1980, at a value of 0.54, but has fallen by 9 percent since then, to 0.50, a level not seen since some six decades ago. This decline in inequality among countries, weighted by their population size, is exactly what one would expect.

The reason for weighting distribution among countries by population is that it is people who matter, not countries. Then the right thing to do must be to take account of changes in distribution of income within countries as well. A paper by François Bourguignon and Christian Morrison, for the World Bank, has attempted this heroic task for 1820 to 1992. As Figure 9.1 shows, they reach five significant conclusions.

First, global inequality among individuals rose progressively, from 1820 to a peak in 1980.

Second, all the increase in global inequality over those 160 years was the result of increases in inequality *among* countries, not *within* them. Within-country inequality was, they estimate (albeit roughly), lower in 1980 than 1820.

Third, back in 1820, only 13 percent of the inequality of individuals was determined by differences in the average prosperity among countries. By 1980, however, just over 60 percent of inequality among individuals was determined by differences in the average prosperity of countries. In the words of the authors, "differences in country economic growth rates practically explain all the increase in world inequality."[18] By 1980, the most important determinant of one's prosperity was not one's class or profession, but where one lived.

Fourth, inequality within countries reached a peak in 1910, subsequently fell to a trough in 1960 and then started to rise, modestly, once again.

Finally, because of a fall in inequality among countries, which offset a modest rise in inequality within them, global inequality among individuals fell, at last, between 1980 and 1992.

The most important conclusion then is that, since the beginning of the nineteenth century, changes in inequality among the world's individuals have been driven by changes in the relative wealth of nations. In particular, the steeply rising inequality among the people of the world in the nineteenth and first half of the twentieth century was driven by the divergent performance of Europe and the British offshoots, on the one hand, and Asia, on the other. What matters then is relative rates of economic growth over extended periods. Consequently, Asia's improved growth performance, and especially that of the Asian giants, has started to reverse this picture of rising inequality over the past two decades.

This World Bank study suffers from two defects: to take the analysis so far back, it had to rely on highly limited, indeed sketchy, data; and it ended in 1992, at the beginning of yet another decade of rapid growth in Asia, not least in China. More recent studies, on similar lines, remedy these defects. These are by another group of three authors at the World Bank, by Surjit Bhalla, formerly a World Bank economist, and by Xavier Sala-I-Martin of Columbia University

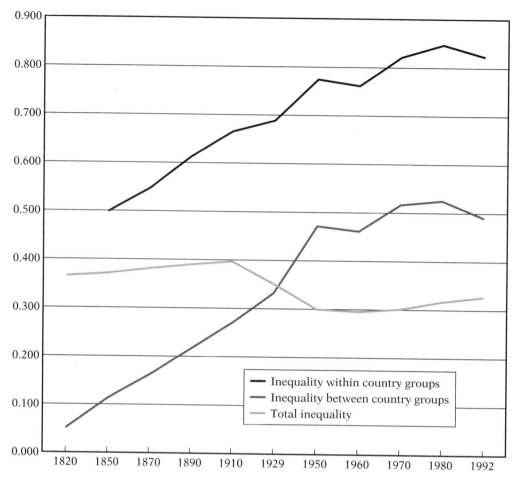

Figure 9.1. Decomposition of World Income Inequality (Mean Logarithmic Deviation)

Source: François Bourguignon and Christian Morrison, "Inequality among World Citizens" (*American Economic Review*, Vol. 92, No. 4 (September 2002), pp. 727–44).

(see Figure 9.2). All three reach a very similar conclusion: global inequality among households, or individuals, peaked in the 1970s, whereupon it started to fall. This decline happened not because of greater equality within countries, but because of greater population-weighted equality among them.

The three World Bank authors found, for example, that income inequality increased within high-income countries between 1980 and 1995, but fell quite sharply, world-wide, from its peak in 1965–9. This happened entirely because of reductions in (population-weighted) inequality among countries. Bhalla's results are similar, but even stronger. Global inequality in 2000 was lower, he argues, than at any time since 1910. It had fallen from its peak in 1980 by 5 percent (on the gini-coefficient measure). He agrees that inequality rose among people living in high-income countries after 1980, though it was well below levels in 1960. Inequality had fallen sharply among the people of the developing countries,

Figure 9.2. Inequality among People in the Age of Globalization (Mean Logarithmic Deviation)

Source: Xavier Sala-I-Martin, "The World Distribution of Income (Estimated from Individual Country Distributions)" (May 2002, mimeo), Table 8.

with China and India included, but not with these two giants excluded. Finally, Professor Sala-I-Martin concludes that global inequality peaked in the 1970s (in 1978, to be precise). Between then and 1998, he, too, found inequality had fallen by 5 percent (also on the gini-coefficient measure). It fell substantially more, however, on some of the other measures (see Figure 9.2).

Others contest this relatively sunny picture of global interpersonal inequality in the age of globalization. Perhaps the most important challenge has come from other World Bank researchers. Branko Milanovic, in particular, has written an influential paper, assessing what he calls "true world income distribution" for 1988 and 1993. The important difference between this study (as well as Bank analyses of changes in global poverty, to which I will turn below) and the studies cited above is that it ignores data from national accounts. It relies, instead, only on household surveys of income and expenditure. This has advantages: surveys include home consumption, which is important for poor people in poor countries, and exclude undistributed profits and increases in inventories, which do not affect the current welfare of a population. But it also has a significant disadvantage: the level and rate of rise of spending in such surveys frequently bear little relation to figures in national accounts. This is worrying. National accounts may be flawed, but they do have the virtue of being self-checking, since they are put together from independent evidence on output, income and expenditure. No comparable internal checks can be made on surveys of household incomes and spending.

Milanovic concluded from the evidence he uses that inequality rose substantially between 1988 and 1993. Measured by the gini coefficient, the rise was from 0.63 to 0.66 (a remarkably large 5 percent jump over such a short period). He also concludes that "The most important contributors were: rising urban–rural differences in China, and slow growth of rural purchasing-power adjusted incomes in South Asia, compared to several large developed market economies."[19] The results, though significantly different from those of the other researchers cited above, do at least support them in one respect. Milanovic concludes that "the difference between countries' mean incomes . . . is the most important factor behind world inequality. It explains between 75 and 88 percent of overall inequality" (depending on the measure used).[20] Milanovic also comes up with a number of additional statistics: the richest 1 percent of people in the world receive as much (in PPP terms) as the bottom 57 percent; and an

American with the average income of the bottom decile (the bottom 10 percent) is better off than two-thirds of the world's people.

Milanovic's conclusion that inequality increased sharply over five years was, subsequently, the basis of an influential article in *The Economist* newspaper by Robert Wade of the London School of Economics.[21] But are his results both credible and meaningful? A part of the answer is that this was an exceptional period, which makes the results more credible but less meaningful. Chinese economic growth slowed at the time of the Tiananmen Square massacre in 1989. Similarly, India suffered an economic crisis in 1991. Thus Milanovic's analysis was, accidentally, timed to coincide with the one period in the last two decades of the twentieth century when the two giant developing countries were growing quite modestly. Even Sala-I-Martin found that global inequality rose between 1986 and 1989, before falling, once again, after 1990 (see Figure 9.2). It would, for this reason, be dangerous to generalize from an analysis that covers this period. All the same, the size of the increase in inequality estimated by Milanovic is remarkable. According to Bhalla, the relative incomes of the high-income countries would need to rise by 27 percent to generate a 5 percent increase in global income inequality (measured by the gini coefficient). That simply did not happen. So the question of credibility remains.

Milanovic's data indicate, for example, that there was no increase in rural incomes in China between 1988 and 1993. National accounts give quite a different picture. So what is going on? A part of the answer, as suggested above, is that average household incomes and spending generally rise much more slowly in surveys of household income and expenditure than in national accounts. To take a significant example, the survey data relied upon by two authoritative World Bank researchers for their estimates of changes in absolute poverty between 1987 and 1999 show a rise in real consumption in developing countries of just 11 percent.[22] Over the same period, observes Bhalla, national accounts data (converted with

PPP exchange rates) show rises in average real incomes of 24 percent and in consumption of 21 percent. This is not some small discrepancy—it is a yawning chasm.

Bhalla also observes that, between 1987 and 1998, the ratio of average incomes in surveys of incomes to those in national accounts fell from 56 to 46 percent in east Asia, from 75 to 62 percent in south Asia and from 69 to 63 percent in sub-Saharan Africa. For consumption surveys, the ratio of averages fell from 82 to 81 percent in east Asia, 73 to 56 percent in south Asia and 125 to 115 percent in sub-Saharan Africa. On similar lines, Milanovic shows that, for Africa, average household income/expenditure in the surveys he used was 79 percent of levels in national accounts in 1988, but only 70 percent by 1993. For Asia, the ratio fell more modestly, from 61 to 59 percent. Nevertheless, in Milanovic's study, growth in average incomes, between 1988 and 1993, in the developing regions with the largest number of poor people was lower than in national accounts (at PPP): 49 percent, against 54 percent, for Asia, and 19 percent, against 33 percent for sub-Saharan Africa. This, in turn, must be a part of the explanation for the discrepancy between Milanovic's results and those of researchers who use national accounts.

How then is one to explain this discrepancy between the growth shown in surveys and the growth shown in national accounts? Logically, there are three alternatives.

The first is that the surveys are correct in their estimate of the level of consumption and incomes, in which case economic growth has been far slower in many important developing countries than we have believed. The national accounts are not reliable estimates, but propaganda. The second possibility is that both national accounts and the surveys are correct, for what they cover. This would be possible if virtually all the spending (and income) under-recorded in the surveys was by (and of) the rich *and* if the true share of the rich in both incomes and spending in the economy was also rising rapidly. This would mean that in many developing

countries income and spending were becoming more unequal, more quickly, than the standard estimates of inequality suggest. The third possibility is that household surveys have become ever less reliable as a way of estimating the rise in real incomes and spending over time (though they still remain all we have if we want to calculate changes in the distribution of income and spending over time).

The first possibility seems hugely implausible. If we did reject national accounts data for economic growth, we would be left with no idea of what has been going on in developing countries. Moreover, while there are questions about national accounts data, notably for China, they are probably the most carefully constructed national data in any country. This leaves the second and third possibilities. We cannot, on the evidence we now have, distinguish between them. In other words, either countries have been becoming more unequal more quickly than all the evidence suggests (because of rapid increases in unrecorded incomes and spending of the rich) or the household surveys themselves are unreliable.

This is not, however, the only difficulty. Converting incomes at average PPP exchange rates will itself create important distortions because the consumption of tradable goods and non-tradable services will vary across households. In general, the poor in developing countries will consume more of the former and the rich more of the latter. Every visitor from the west to a developing country must have been struck by the ability of the prosperous to employ hordes of servants, long vanished in the west, even though they cannot afford the latest high-technology machinery. If this were taken into account, the income distribution, properly measured at PPP, would be more unequal than the measured income distribution at domestic relative prices. The reverse side of this is that, in rapidly growing countries, the prices of services rise in relation to those of goods. If the poor consume goods more intensively than the rich, then they gain more from growth than the rich do. Thus, while the initial income distribution would be more unequal than calculations at domestic relative prices suggest, it would also be becoming more equal more quickly than they suggest. This reinforces the assumption that the poor are likely to have benefited substantially from growth in rapidly growing developing countries.

The bottom line is that it is plausible that inequality among individuals across the world has been falling over the past two decades, because of the relatively rapid growth of the Asian giants. This is consistent with rising inequality within many countries, rising relative gaps between the average incomes of the richest and very poorest countries, and increasing absolute gaps between the average incomes in the high-income countries, on the one hand, and virtually all developing countries, on the other. But the latter simply shows the tyranny of history. By 1980, inequality among countries was so large that it was impossible for absolute gaps to close, until there was much greater convergence of relative incomes.

Yet this ignores the fact that a great many countries have not enjoyed rapid growth, most notably in Africa, but also, to a lesser extent, in Latin America, the Middle East and, in the 1990s, the countries in transition from communism, especially the former Soviet Union. In the 1990s, for example, according to the Human Development Report, fifty-four countries, with 12 percent of the world's population, had negative growth rates in real incomes per head, while another seventy-one countries, with 26 percent of the world's population, had growth of between zero and 3 percent a year in real incomes per head.[23] Similarly, in the World Bank's study of globalization, countries containing 1.1 million people had virtually stagnant real incomes between 1980 and 1997 (see Table 1). While the poor performance of so many countries may not have prevented global income distribution from improving (though it will tend to do so once China's average incomes rise above the world average), it has certainly had a significant impact on the scale and regional distribution of world poverty. To that topic, just as vexed as income distribution, we now turn.

Growth and Poverty

On all measures, global inequality rose until about the early 1980s. Since then, it appears, inequality among individuals has declined as a result of the rapid growth of much of Asia and, above all, China. But it is also important to understand what drove the long-term trend towards global inequality over almost two centuries. It is the consequence of the dynamic growth that spread, unevenly, from the UK in the course of the nineteenth and twentieth centuries. In the process a growing number of people became vastly better off than any one had ever been before, but few can have become worse off. Such dynamic growth is bound to be uneven. Some regions of the world proved better able to take advantage of the new opportunities for growth, because of superior climates, resources and policies. In just the same way, some parts of countries, particularly huge countries such as China or India, are today better able to take advantage of new opportunities than others. To bemoan the resulting increase in inequality is to bemoan the growth itself. It is to argue that it would be better for everybody to be equally poor than for some to become significantly better off, even if, in the long run, this will almost certainly lead to advances for everybody.

For this reason, it makes more sense to focus on what has happened to poverty than to inequality. Again, the statistical debate is a vexed one. But some plausible conclusions can be reached.

The World Bank has, for some time, defined extreme poverty as an income of a dollar a day at 1985 international prices (PPP). Bourguignon and Morrison also used that figure in an analysis of extreme poverty since 1820, on the same lines as their analysis of inequality (see Figure 9.3).[24] It comes to three intriguing conclusions. First, the number of desperately poor people rose from about 900 million in 1820 to a peak of from 1.3 to 1.4 billion between 1960 and 1980, before falling, modestly, to just under 1.3 billion in 1992. Second, the proportion of the world's population living on less than a dollar a day fell dramatically, over time, from over 80 percent in 1820, a time when living on the margins of subsistence was the norm, to about two-thirds at the beginning of the twentieth century, to close to 50 percent by 1950, then 32 percent in 1980 and, finally, 24 percent by 1992. The contrast between rising numbers and falling proportions of the world's population in extreme poverty reflects the race between higher output and rising population, particularly in poor countries. In 1820, the world's population was a little over a billion. By 1910 it was 1.7 billion and by 1992 it had risen to 5.5 billion.

Again, the results from Bourguignon and Morrison are cause for qualified optimism. From

being universal, extreme poverty has become, if not rare, the affliction of less than a quarter of a vastly increased human population. But, again, it is necessary to look more closely at what has happened in the supposed period of globalization, the years since 1980. Here, the authoritative voice is that of the World Bank, the institution whose "dream is a world without poverty."[25] The numbers in Tables 2 and 3 come from two recent World Bank publications.[26] They reach the following conclusions.

First, the number of people in extreme poverty fell from 1.18 billion in 1987 to 1.17 billion in 1999, but not before jumping upwards to 1.29 billion in

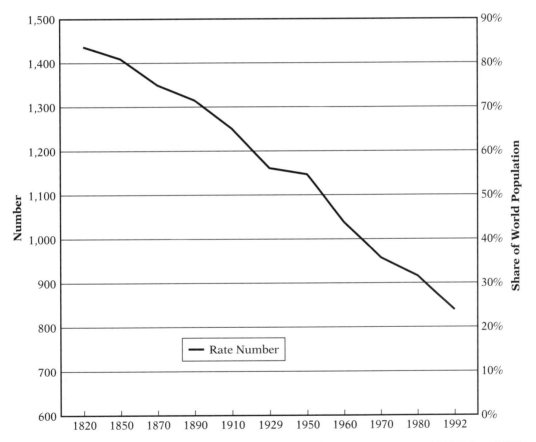

Figure 9.3. Extreme Poverty in the Long Run (Less than a Dollar a Day at PPP, in 1985 Prices, Millions and World Population Share)

Source: François Bourguignon and Christian Morrison, "Inequality among World Citizens" (*American Economic Review*, Vol. 92, No. 4 (September 2002), pp. 727–44).

Table 2. Income Poverty, by Region (Millions of People Living on Less than $1.08 a Day at 1993 PPP)

Regions	1987	1990	1999
East Asia and Pacific	418	486	279
(Excluding China)	114	110	57
China	304	376	222
Europe and Central Asia	1	6	24
Latin America and Caribbean	64	48	57
Middle East and North Africa	9	5	6
South Asia	474	506	488
Sub-Saharan Africa	217	241	315
Total	1,183	1,292	1,169
Total, excluding China	880	917	945

Sources: World Bank, *World Development Report 2000/2001: Attacking Poverty* (Washington DC: World Bank, 2000), Table 1.1, and World Bank, *Global Economic Prospects and the Developing Countries 2003: Investing to Unlock Global Opportunities* (Washington DC: World Bank, 2003), Table 1.9.

Table 3. Regional Incidence of Income Poverty (Share of People Living on Less than $1.08 a Day at 1993 PPP, in Regional Populations, Percent)

Regions	1987	1990	1999
East Asia and Pacific	26.6	30.5	15.6
(Excluding China)	23.9	24.2	10.6
China	27.8	33.0	17.7
Europe and Central Asia	0.2	1.4	5.1
Latin America and Caribbean	15.3	11.0	11.1
Middle East and North Africa	4.3	2.1	2.2
South Asia	44.9	45.0	36.6
Sub-Saharan Africa	46.6	47.4	49.0
Total	28.3	29.6	23.2
Total, excluding China	28.5	28.5	25.0
World total	23.7	24.6	19.5

Sources: World Bank, *World Development Report 2000/2001: Attacking Poverty*, Table 1.1, and World Bank, *Global Economic Prospects 2003*, Table 1.9.

1990, underlining the extent to which the 1988–93 period chosen by Milanovic was exceptional.

Second, enormous declines in the number of people in extreme poverty have occurred in dynamic east Asia, from 486 million in 1990 to 279 million in 1999, including China, and from 114 million to 57 million, excluding China. In China itself, the decline, between 1990 and 1999, was from 376 million to 222 million. Rapid growth reduces poverty dramatically. This remains today, as it has been for two centuries, an abiding truth.

Third, the number of people in extreme poverty fell very modestly in south Asia between 1990 and 1999, while it rose sharply in eastern Europe and central Asia (the former Soviet empire) and, above all, sub-Saharan Africa, from

217 million in 1987 to 241 million in 1990, and then 315 million in 1999.

Fourth, the regional incidence of poverty fell dramatically in east Asia, from 30.5 percent of the population in 1990 to just 15.6 percent in 1999. Excluding China, it fell from 24.2 to 10.6 percent. In China, it fell from 33 percent of the population to just under 18 percent over nine years. This was, without doubt, the most rapid reduction in the incidence of extreme poverty anywhere, ever.

Fifth, the incidence of poverty also fell sharply in south Asia (dominated by India) in the 1990s,

from 45.0 percent of the population in 1990 to 36.6 percent in 1999. But it rose sharply in eastern Europe and central Asia and also increased in sub-Saharan Africa, from 47.4 percent of the population to 49.0 percent.

As with the numbers of inequality, so with those on poverty, controversy abounds. In the optimistic corner are, once again, Bhalla and Sala-I-Martin. A comparison between their results and those of the World Bank for the number of people in absolute poverty over the 1990s (on slightly different definitions) appears in Figure 9.4. All

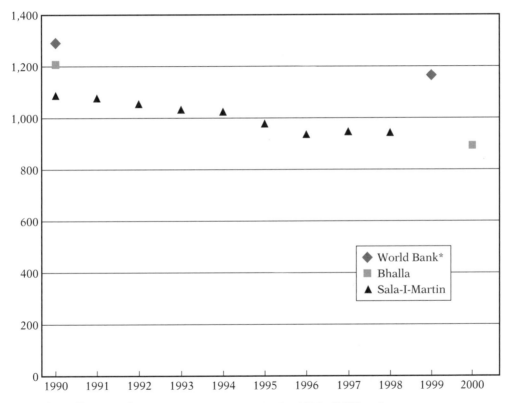

Figure 9.4. The Fall in Numbers in Extreme Poverty in the 1990s (Millions)

Source: World Bank, *Global Economic Prospects and the Developing Countries 2003: Investing to Unlock Global Opportunities* (Washington DC: World Bank, 2003), Table 1.9; Surjit S. Bhalla, *Imagine There's No Country: Poverty, Inequality and Growth in the Era of Globalization* (Washington DC: Institute for International Economics, 2002), Table 9.1; and Sala-I-Martin, "The World Distribution of Income (Estimated from Individual Country Distributions)" (May 2002, mimeo), Table 3A.

*To make these data roughly comparable, those chosen are as follows: for the World Bank, the $1.08 poverty line, at 1993 PPP, which appears to apply to consumption; for Bhalla, a $1.30 poverty line, at 1993 prices and, for Sala-I-Martin, his consumption poverty rates (applied to world population, to derive levels) for a dollar a day (probably at 1993 PPP).

three show substantial declines between 1990 and the end of the decade. But the World Bank's is a 9.5 percent decline over nine years; Sala-I-Martin has one of 13.1 percent over eight years; and Bhalla one of 25.6 percent over ten years.

What is one to make of these discrepancies? As Sala-I-Martin notes, the difference between his results and those of the World Bank, after some adjustments, are not large.[27] The big discrepancy is with the results of Bhalla. The most important source of those differences seems to be his use of national accounts data for the growth in average incomes and spending, along with household surveys for distribution of income and spending, against the Bank's use of surveys for both.

The implication of this difference is shown most clearly for what is, in many ways, the most surprising single case: India. For in India, as we know, real incomes per head rose by around a half in the 1990s yet the number of people in extreme poverty appears, on the World Bank data, to have fallen quite modestly. In south Asia, as a whole, dominated by India, it fell only from 506 million to 488 million between 1990 and 1999. This, Bhalla suggests, does not look very plausible. Since the latter figure is 42 percent of all the people in extreme poverty in the world, any significant error in calculating it is bound to create equally significant mistakes in the totals.

One thing we do know is that between 1987 and 1998 the proportion of the consumption shown in national accounts covered by the household surveys fell from 73 percent to only 56 percent in south Asia. It looks then as though the surveys missed a great deal of the rise in consumption in these countries. Moreover, as Bhalla points out, surveys of wages and unemployment in India indicate rises in rural wages that are far more consistent with consumption figures in the national accounts than in the household surveys of expenditure. In addition, India's official estimate of the poverty rate in 1999 (at a threshold rate of $1.25 a day, at PPP, in 1993 prices, which is higher than the Bank's $1.08 and should generate a significantly higher number of poor people)

was 26 percent, or 260 million. Yet the Bank apparently calculates this figure, on its own lower threshold, at around 360 million. It also calculates the level of poverty, on the Indian government's $1.25 line, at 470 million, which is 210 million more than the Indian government does itself. The government's estimates are themselves at the high end. Other estimates—from the respected National Council for Applied Economic Research, for example—give far lower numbers still for the population in extreme poverty in India, at 150 million in 1999.[28]

In short, there are good reasons to believe that the Bank has overestimated the number of people in extreme poverty – and underestimated its decline. If that is not so, then it must surely mean that the increase in inequality in India since the early 1990s has been very large indeed. That is logically possible, since so many of the poor live in the most backward states, such as Uttar Pradesh and Bihar. But it is not what India's own data show. One may not wish to go as far as Bhalla, who argues that the proportion of the developing world's population below $1.25 a day (at 1993 PPP) fell from 44 percent in 1980 to 13 percent in 2000. But the decline in poverty in India, and so the world, may well be substantially greater than the Bank suggests.

This, needless to say, is not universally accepted. Professors Thomas Pogge and Sanjay Reddy, also of Columbia University, like Professor Sala-I-Martin, argue that the Bank's numbers, if not necessarily too optimistic, are unsoundly based. They suggest, in particular, that this admittedly heroic attempt to compare poverty across the globe with the use of one measuring rod ($1.08 a day at PPP, in 1993 prices) is fundamentally flawed, in three ways. First, the international poverty line used by the Bank "fails to meet elementary requirements of consistency." As a result, "the Bank's poverty line leads to meaningless poverty estimates." Second, "the Bank's poverty line is not anchored in any assessment of the basic resource requirements of human beings." And third, "the poverty estimates currently available are subject to massive uncertainties because of their sensitivity to the values of crucial parameters that are estimated on the basis of limited data or none at all."[29]

Let us grant most of this. It is evident that converting national data with PPP exchange rates that are themselves both averages for economies and variable from year to year is a rough-and-ready procedure, to put it mildly. Equally, the dollar-a-day line is both inherently arbitrary and bound to mean different things in different countries. It is also true, as Pogge and Reddy argue, that PPP adjustments, which are largely for the relative price of non-tradable services, will create large, and growing, mismeasurement of the real incomes of the poor, since the latter consume commodities more intensively than the better off. That could well justify higher poverty lines. At the same time, it might mean that the rate of decline in poverty is higher than estimated by the Bank, since relative prices of commodities normally fall in fast-growing countries.

The big question, however, is whether it would be easy to do better. Pogge and Reddy suggest that the exercise should be conducted in terms not of arbitrary levels of income, but of capabilities—"calories and essential nutrients." They argue that "the income persons need to avoid poverty at some particular time and place can then be specified in terms of the least expensive locally available set of commodities containing the relevant characteristics needed to achieve the elementary human capabilities."[30] This sounds, straightforward. In fact, long experience suggests that reaching agreement on such poverty levels across countries is nigh on impossible.

Pogge and Reddy provide a warning. All poverty estimates are inherently arbitrary. Certainly, there is no good reason to believe in anybody's estimates of the levels of poverty at any moment. Trends are another matter. It is certain that the share of those in extreme (absolute, as opposed to relative) income poverty in the world's population has fallen enormously over the last two centuries, a decline that has, equally certainly, continued since 1980. It is almost equally certain that the numbers in extreme income poverty fell in east Asia over the past few decades and particularly over the past two. That is likely, though less certain, for India. Encouragingly, both China and India show enormous declines in estimates of numbers in extreme poverty on their different national measures (about 100 million for India, between 1980 and 2000, and 220 million for China, between 1978 and 1999, despite large increases in population in both countries over this period). Given these changes in east and south Asia, it is plausible, though not certain, that numbers in absolute income poverty declined world-wide. What is more than merely plausible is the proposition that, where numbers in extreme poverty have declined, the cause has been accelerated growth. This is as true of regions within countries (especially where mobility is hindered, as in China) as among them.

Poverty and Human Welfare

In the absence of any of the internationally comparable measures of capabilities that Pogge and Reddy call for, one has to look at other supporting evidence. It is here that we find unambiguous good news. For it is clear that human welfare has improved greatly in recent decades.[31] As an independent analyst, Indur Goklany, persuasively argues, it is possible, in addition, for people to enjoy better health and longer lives, at lower incomes, than before.[32] This is the result of technological and organizational improvements that have come from the world's rich countries. In 1913, life expectancy at birth in the U.S. was fifty-two years. U.S. GDP per head, at PPP, was then about 50 percent higher than China's would be in 2000, and 150 percent higher than India's.[33] Yet, in 2000, life expectancy in China was seventy and in India sixty-three. In 1900, Sweden seems to have had the world's highest life expectancy, at fifty-six. In 2000, only very poor countries, mostly in Africa, had life expectancy as low as (or lower than) this. As Goklany shows, the curve relating life expectancy to average GDP per head has shifted upwards over time. Similarly, the curve relating infant mortality to incomes has shifted downwards over time. Much the same desirable pattern can be observed for the relationship between other indicators of human welfare and income.

In the developing world as a whole, life expectancy rose by four months each year after 1970, from fifty-five years in 1970 to sixty-four years in 2000. It rose from forty-nine in 1970 to sixty-two in south Asia and from fifty-nine to sixty-nine in east Asia. Tragically, life expectancy fell in thirty-two countries in the 1990s, mostly because of the AIDS epidemic, or the gross incompetence (or worse) of governments, as in North Korea and Zimbabwe. It also fell because of western hysteria about DDT, which removed the only effective way of controlling that dreadful curse, malaria. Improvements in life expectancy have meant a decline in global inequality as well. In 1950, average life expectancy in developing countries was two-thirds of the levels in high-income countries (forty-four and sixty-six years of age, respectively). By 2000, it was 82 percent (sixty-four and seventy-eight).

Meanwhile, in the developing world as a whole, infant mortality rates have fallen from 107 per thousand in 1970 to eighty-seven in 1980 and fifty-eight in 2000. In east Asia, the region with the fastest-growing economy, they have fallen from fifty-six in 1980 to thirty-five in 2000. In south Asia, infant mortality fell from 119 in 1980 to seventy-three in 2000. In sub-Saharan Africa progress was, once again, slower. But infant mortality fell even there, from 116 in 1980 to ninety-one in 2000.

Losing a child must inflict the sharpest grief human beings can suffer. The decline in infant mortality is thus a tremendous blessing in itself. So, too, is the rise in life expectancy. But these improvements also mean that it makes sense to invest in education. The world increasingly produces smaller families with much better-educated children. On average, adult literacy in developing countries rose from 53 percent in 1970 to 74 percent in 1998. By 2000, adult male illiteracy was down to 8 percent in east Asia, though it was still 30 percent in sub-Saharan Africa and (a real scandal this) 34 percent in south Asia. Adult female illiteracy was more widespread than that for men, but was also improving. Between 1990 and 2000, female illiteracy fell from 29 percent to 21 percent in east Asia. In south Asia, it fell from 66 percent to 57 percent (an even worse scandal than the low rate for men), while in sub-Saharan Africa it fell from 60 to 47 percent. Illiteracy is much lower among the young. This guarantees that rates will continue to fall, as time passes.

The reduction in fertility rates has also been remarkable. In the developing world as a whole, births per woman (the fertility rate) have fallen from 4.1 in 1980 to 2.8 in 2000. In east Asia, the fertility rate, down from 3.0 to 2.1, is already at close to the replacement rate. In Latin America, the fertility rate has fallen from 4.1 to 2.6. Even in south Asia it has fallen from 5.3 in 1980 to 3.3 in 2000. Again, progress has been slowest in sub-Saharan Africa, where the birth rate has only fallen from 6.6 in 1980 to 5.2 in 2000. But, in all, these reductions tell us of improved control by women of their fertility, of fewer children with more parental investment in each and of far stronger confidence that children will survive to maturity. The demographic transition that is now under way in the developing world is immensely encouraging. It is also an indication—as well as a source—of rising welfare.

Now, let us look at hunger. Growth in food production has substantially outpaced that of population. Between 1961 and 1999, the average daily food supply per person increased 24 percent globally. In developing countries, it rose by 39 percent, to 2,684 calories. By 1999, China's average daily food supply had gone up 82 percent, to 3,044 calories, from a barely subsistence level of 1,636 in 1961. India's went up by 48 percent to 2,417 calories, from 1,635 calories in 1950–1. According to estimates by the United Nations Food and Agricultural Organization, the average active adult needs between 2,000 and 2,310 calories per person. Thus the developing-country food supply has gone, on average, from inadequate to adequate. Hunger persists. But the FAO estimates that the number of people suffering from chronic undernourishment fell from 920 million in 1969–71 to 790 million in 1997–9, or from 35 to 17 percent of the population of developing countries. Trends in sub-Saharan Africa, the continent that did not grow, were far worse. Between 1979–81 and 1997–9, the share of the population that was undernourished declined from 38 to 34 percent, but absolute numbers, in a rapidly growing population, rose from 168 million to 194 million.[34]

Now, turn to what has become one of the most controversial indicators: child labor. One would expect that more prosperous parents, with fewer children, who are also expected to live longer, would wish to see their children being educated rather than at work. So, happily, it has proved. The proportion of children aged ten to fourteen in the labor force has, according to the World Bank, fallen from 23 percent in all developing countries in 1980 to 12 percent in 2000. The fall in east Asia has, once again, been astonishing, from 26 to 8 percent. In south Asia, it has fallen from 23 to 15 percent. In sub-Saharan Africa, the decline has been less impressive, from 35 to 29 percent. China's transformation has been breathtaking, with a fall from 30 percent in 1980 to just 8 percent in 2000. In lagging India, the fall was from 21 to 12 percent. Thus, just as one would expect, countries whose economies have done well in the era of globalization have been ones in which parents have chosen to withdraw their children from the labor force. Parents have never put their children to work out of indifference or malevolence, but only out of necessity.

Finally, let us remember some of the other features of the last two decades: the world-wide shift to democracy, however imperfect; the disappearance of some of the worst despotisms in history; the increase in personal economic opportunity in vast swathes of the world, notably China and India; and the improving relative position of women almost, although not quite, everywhere.

All these are very encouraging trends. People in developing countries and, particularly, in the fast-growing ones are enjoying longer and healthier lives than before. They are better fed and better educated. They treat their fewer children better. All these good things have not happened only because of rising incomes. Learning from the high-income countries has helped. Developing countries are reaching higher levels of social progress at lower levels of income than the high-income countries of today. But, as one would expect, social progress has been greatest where incomes have risen fastest. It remains "the growth, stupid."

Inequality within Countries

If Mazur was wrong about global inequality, is he at least right about inequality within countries? For, as I have argued above, it is perfectly possible that globalization has worsened income distribution within every country, while improving it in the world as a whole. But has it done so? The answer is: up to a point. To be more precise, one needs to look at what has happened within developing and high-income countries separately.

Inequality within Developing Countries

Inequality has increased among what the World Bank calls the "new globalizers," its twenty-four countries with an aggregate population of close to 3 billion people, but only because of China.[35] The widening of inequality in China over the past two decades, almost entirely because of growing inter-regional inequality, was, however, inevitable, for four reasons: first, the distribution of incomes in Mao Zedong's gigantic prison was at least highly equal; second, the growth has been driven, since the initial surge in rural incomes, after abolition of the communes, by integration into the world economy, which has been dominated by the coastal regions of the country; third, in a country as enormous as China, as in the world as a whole, any imaginable growth process is certain to be regionally uneven (as is also becoming increasingly evident in India); and, last but not least, the Chinese authorities have done their best to limit migration from the rural hinterland to the booming coast. Thus, in many ways, to-day's China replicates, on a smaller scale, what has happened in the world as a whole over the past two decades. The reason for the growing internal inequality is, as it has been at the world level, the rising gap between the living standards of regions (countries) that are integrating successfully into the world economy and regions (countries) that are not. The poorest regions (countries) were not hurt by globalization. They just failed to be part of it. The challenge for China (as for the world) is to improve the ability of these lagging regions to participate, not to accept the clamour from some critics to separate itself from the world economy (hardly likely, as it happens).

If we look at other globalizing developing countries, we find they are as likely to have an improved distribution of income as a worsening one. David Dollar and Aart Kraay, in an already well-known paper, have argued that trade helps growth and that the poor tend to share in equal proportions with the rich in any rise in subsequent incomes. The paper, based on an analysis of 137 countries, finds that the poorest 20 percent of the population does, on average, share equally in growth.[36] This, interestingly, is a contradiction of a previously accepted idea, originally proposed by the Nobel-laureate Simon Kuznets, that inequality rises initially with growth, before declining once again. Bhalla, in his subsequent analysis, argues that in fact Kuznets was right and Dollar and Kraay are wrong. The evidence continues to suggest modest widening in inequality in growing economies.[37] But note that, even if the Kuznets hypothesis were true, growth would still be very much better for the poor than stagnation all round.

What seems clear is that the poor do share in growth. Viet Nam is an interesting example. Of the poorest 5 percent of households in 1992–3, some 98 percent had higher incomes six years later. Similar declines in income poverty were observed in Uganda in the 1990s.[38] Two qualifications, however, need to be made about this story. First, even if the poor do share equally in any proportionate increase in incomes, as Dollar and Kraay argue, the absolute increase in incomes they enjoy depends on their initial share. This is one sense in which growth can be more, or less, "pro-poor." Second, whether or not the poor share more or less equally in the benefits of the faster growth stimulated by greater trade depends on a country's comparative advantage. This is particularly important in understanding the contrasting experience with the moves towards outward-looking policies of the east Asian tigers and Latin American countries.

Standard theory (and experience) suggests that liberalization is good for the incomes of the relatively abundant factor of production. In east Asia, initial comparative advantage was based on cheap labor. One would expect international integration to be especially good for the relative incomes of the poor—and, on the whole, it was. Latin America is, however, a land-abundant continent with relatively high wages and a history of protection aimed at distributing income from the agricultural sector to the industrial working class. In these cases, one would expect liberalization to create greater inequality. The negative impact on the wages of the unskilled in Latin America has also probably been exacerbated by the entry of China and the rest of east Asia into the world economy.

Inequality within High-Income Countries

Let us turn, then, from the developing countries to the high-income countries. Here there seems to be less ambiguity: inequality has risen in most high-income countries. Where it has not risen, unemployment has tended to increase instead. In these countries, moreover, changes in inequality tend to be driven by changes in relative wages, while in developing countries wage-earners, especially in the modern sector, tend to be an élite. Widening of gaps in relative pay between the skilled and unskilled was substantial in the U.S. and UK in the 1980s and early 1990s. In the U.S. in particular, "the widening has been severe enough that lower-skilled groups had no gain and probably a slight loss, in real pay, over the whole quarter century 1973–1998, this despite a healthy growth of real earnings for the labor force as a whole."

This pattern of rising relative pay between skilled and unskilled workers does not seem to apply to other important high-income countries, however, such as Germany, France, Italy and Japan, at least for full-time workers. But when one takes work hours and unemployment into account, the same applies. Unskilled workers were more likely to be unemployed or to work part-time. As a result, from the mid-1980s to the mid-1990s, twenty out of twenty-one members of the Organization for Economic Co-operation and Development experienced a rise in inequality, largely because of rising inequality of labor earnings.[39]

If these are the facts, what are the causes? Logically, there could be several, some that work via the demand for labor and others that work on the supply. These include: trade, particularly rising imports of labor-intensive manufactures, partly as a result of growing outsourcing by multinational companies; a general growth in competition, eroding the monopoly position of industries (such as steel and automobile manufacture) that have, historically, granted large wage premia to trade-union-organized unskilled and semi-skilled labor; laws and other social and economic changes that have weakened the bargaining position of trades unions; technology, particularly skill-biased technological change or, less technically, innovations which raise the relative demand for skilled labor; a failure of the education system to improve the supply of skilled labor with sufficient speed; and immigration of unskilled labor.

Trade, reinforced by immigration, is then one of a number of possible explanations for the growth in inequality or, more precisely, the declining relative position of unskilled workers in high-income countries. Some would further argue that trade has caused the skill-bias in technical change—to save on what is, by world standards, relatively expensive unskilled labor, companies have developed technologies that save on its use. But, even if this were not true, a well-known economic theorem, the Stolper-Samuelson theorem, named after its two inventors, argues that prices of factors of production, including wages of labor, will be equalized in trade.[40] If so, since unskilled labor is enormously abundant in the world and a far higher proportion of that labor is engaged—actually and potentially—in the world economy than ever before, the wages of such labor in the high-income countries are bound to fall, relatively if not absolutely. To put this point more brutally, the working people of the high-income countries have historically benefited from the monopoly of their countries in manufacturing. Now, however, they are in competition with the unskilled of the world, with potentially devastating results.

I will return to some of these points in the next chapter, when considering the impact of trade, more narrowly. At this point, one must note that there are a number of powerful assumptions underlying the applicability of the Stolper-Samuelson theorem. Among others, productive efficiency must be the same in all countries, which it is not. Moreover, if this theorem applied, there would have been an improvement in the terms of trade (a reduction in the price of labor-intensive imports relative to exports), followed by a switch in methods of production towards those that use what had become redundant unskilled labor more intensively, everywhere. Yet, as Jagdish Bhagwati of Columbia University and others have argued, neither seems to have happened since the early 1980s. Particularly striking is the shift to greater use of skilled labor in almost every industry. This suggests to most observers that skill-biased technological change has been the dominant forces. Professors Lindert and Williamson summarize the broad consensus among economists on the rise in inequality in the U.S. (where the rise has been particularly large) that somewhere between 15 percent and a third is due to trade.[41]

The bottom line then is that the increased inequality in high-income countries over the past two decades may have been caused, in modest part, by increased exports from the developing world. Even so, two essential qualifications must be made.

First, if this has been the case, it is the result of an economic process that has benefited both the exporting countries *and* the importing countries as a whole. The right response is to help those adversely affected by low-wage imports, through retraining, improved education, generalized wage subsidies for low-wage labor and, if all else fails, simple transfers of income. It would be immoral for rich countries to deprive the poor of the world of so large an opportunity for betterment merely because they are unable to handle sensibly and justly the distribution of the internal costs of a change certain to be highly beneficial overall.

Second, remember above all that this upheaval in the high-income countries is part of a benign broadening of global prosperity. Bhalla has a particularly telling way of illustrating this. He defines the global middle class as those earning between $3,650 and $14,600 a year, at PPP, in 1993 prices. On his analysis, in 1960, some 64 percent of all the middle-class people in the world lived in the high-income countries. Today, this is down to 17 percent, with 51 percent living in Asia, the Middle East and North Africa, up from just 6 percent in 1960 and 16 percent in 1980. Only the most selfish westerners can complain about a transformation that has brought so much to so many so quickly.

Conclusion

Let us return then to the propositions with which this exploration of growth, poverty and inequality began. Here they are, together with what we now know.

First, the ratio of average incomes in the richest countries to those in the very poorest has continued to rise in the age of globalization. Response: correct.

Second, the absolute gap in living standards between today's high-income countries and the vast proportion of developing countries has continued to rise. Response: also correct and inevitably so, given the starting-point two decades ago.

Third, global inequality among individuals has risen. Response: false. Global inequality among individuals has, in all probability, fallen since the 1970s.

Fourth, the number of people in extreme income poverty has also risen. Response: probably false. The number of people in extreme poverty may well have fallen since 1980, for the first time in almost two centuries, because of the rapid growth of the Asian giants.

Fifth, the proportion of people in extreme poverty in the world's population has also risen. Response: false. The proportion of the world's population in extreme poverty has certainly fallen.

Sixth, the poor of the world are worse off not just in terms of incomes, but in terms of a wide range of indicators of human welfare and capability. Response: unambiguously false. The welfare of humanity, judged by life expectancies, infant mortality, literacy, hunger, fertility, and the incidence of child labor has improved enormously. It has improved least in sub-Saharan Africa, partly because of disease and partly because of the continent's failure to grow.

Seventh, income inequality has risen in every country and particularly in countries most exposed to international economic integration. Response: false. Income inequality has not risen in most of the developing countries that have integrated with the world economy, though it has risen in China. Inequality has apparently risen in the high-income countries, but the role of globalization in this change is unclear and, in all probability, not decisive.

We can also make some propositions of our own. Human welfare, broadly defined, has risen.

The proportion of humanity living in desperate misery is declining. The problem of the poorest is not that they are exploited, but that they are almost entirely unexploited: they live outside the world economy. The soaring growth of the rapidly integrating developing economies has transformed the world for the better. The challenge is to bring those who have failed so far into the new web of productive and profitable global economic relations.

NOTES

1. "Labor's New Internationalism," *Foreign Affairs*, Vol. 79, January–February 2000.
2. Ignacio Ramonet, *Le Monde Diplomatique*, May 1998. Cited in Xavier Sala-I-Martin, "The Myth of Exploding Income Inequality in Europe and the World," in Henryk Kierzkowski (ed.), *Europe and Globalization* (Basingstoke: Palgrave Macmillan, 2002), p. 11.
3. Paul Ehrlich, *The Population Bomb* (New York: Ballantine Books, 1968).
4. World Bank, *Globalization, Growth & Poverty: Building an Inclusive World Economy* (Washington DC: 2002), Table 1.1, p. 34.
5. *Ibid.*, p. 36.
6. These data are from World Bank, *World Development Indicators 2002* (Washington DC: World Bank, 2002).
7. World Trade Organization, *International Trade Statistics 2002* (Geneva: WTO, 2002), and T. N. Srinivasan, *Eight Lectures on India's Economic Reforms* (New York: Oxford University Press, 2000), p. 73, for the data on China in the 1970s and a comparison between China and India.
8. United Nations Conference on Trade and Development, *World Investment Report 2002: Transnational Corporations and Export Competitiveness* (New York: United Nations, 2002).
9. World Economic Forum, *The Global Competitiveness Report 2001–02* (New York: Oxford University Press, 2002).
10. See, on the role of government, particularly chapter 5, above.
11. See, on this, Johan Norberg's splendid tract, *In Defence of Global Capitalism* (Timbro, 2001), pp. 102 and, more generally, 98–113.
12. See, for example, Xavier Sala-I-Martin and Arvind Subramanian, "Addressing the Natural Resource Curse: An Illustration from Nigeria," May 2003, mimeo.
13. See World Bank, *Globalization, Growth & Poverty*, pp. 38–40.
14. A study that brought out the benefits of trade by focusing on natural barriers of distance is: Jeffrey Frankel and David Romer, "Does Trade Cause Growth?," *American Economic Review*, June 1999.
15. See, on the role of resources in development, World Bank, *World Development Report 2003: Sustainable Development in a Dynamic World: Transforming Institutions, Growth and Quality of Life* (New York: Oxford University Press, for the World Bank, 2003), pp. 148–56.
16. See World Bank, *Globalization, Growth & Poverty*, pp. 32–3.
17. Data come from Angus Maddison, *Monitoring the World Economy, 1820–1992* (Paris: Development Centre of the Organization for Economic Co-operation and Development, 1995 and 1998) and the International Monetary Fund's *World Economic Outlook*. See Andrea Boltho and Gianni Toniolo, "The Assessment: The Twentieth Century—Achievements, Failures, Lessons," *Oxford Review of Economic Policy*, Vol. 15, No. 4 (Winter 1999), pp. 1–17, Table 4.
18. Bourguignon and Morrison, "Inequality among World Citizens," p. 733.
19. Milanovic, "True World Income Distribution," Abstract.
20. *Ibid.*, p. 51.
21. Robert Wade, "Winners and Losers," *The Economist*, 26 April 2001. Professor Wade also cites another World Bank study, using the same data sets: Yuri Dikhanov and Michael Ward, "Measuring the Distribution of Global Income," World Bank, 2000, mimeo.

22. Shaohua Chen and Martin Ravallion, "How did the World's Poorest Fare in the 1990s?," World Bank, Washington DC, 2000, mimeo. This discrepancy between surveys and national accounts is discussed at length by Bhalla, *Imagine There's No Country*, pp. 78–87 and chapter 7.

23. See United Nations Development Programme, *Human Development Report 2003: Millennium Development Goals: A Compact among Nations to End Human Poverty* (New York: Oxford University Press, for the United Nations Development Programme, 2003), p. 40.

24. Bourguignon and Morrison, "Inequality among World Citizens," Table 1.

25. Cynics might suppose this is the Bank's nightmare. Fortunately for the Bank, though not for the world, poverty seems most unlikely to be eliminated in the near future, particularly since richer societies tend to define their poverty lines upwards, more or less *pari passu*.

26. Poverty lines are defined as $1.08 a day at 1993 PPP.

27. Professor Sala-I-Martin discusses those discrepancies in section 3D of his paper, "The World Distribution of Income."

28. See on this debate, Bhalla, *Imagine There's No Country*, chapter 7, World Bank, *Global Economic Prospects*, pp. 32–3, and Martin Ravallion, "The Debate on Globalization, Poverty and Inequality: Why Measurement Matters," World Bank, no date, www .worldbank.org.

29. See Thomas W. Pogge and Sanjay G. Reddy, "Unknown: The Extent, Distribution and Trend of Global Income Poverty," 16 July 2003, mimeo, pp. 1–2.

30. *Ibid.*, p. 12.

31. Where not otherwise indicated, data in this section come from World Bank, *World Devel-opment Indicators 2002* (Washington DC: World Bank, 2002).

32. Indur M. Goklany, "The Globalization of Human Well-Being," Policy Analysis No. 447, Cato Institute, Washington DC, 22 August 2002.

33. Maddison, *The World Economy*.

34. The data from the FAO are cited in *ibid.*, p. 7.

35. World Bank, *Globalization, Growth and Poverty*, p. 48.

36. David Dollar and Aart Kraay, "Growth is Good for the Poor," Policy Research Working Paper No. 2587 (Washington DC: World Bank, 2001).

37. Bhalla, *Imagine There's No Country*, pp. 36–46. Bhalla argues that the conclusion of Dollar and Kraay is biased by the inclusion of central and eastern Europe (including the former Soviet Union), where a huge widening in inequality coincided with a fall in incomes. This tends to make the elasticity of the incomes of the poor with respect to rising average incomes, in the sample as a whole, closer to unity (i.e. the falling shares in income of the eastern European poor as income falls is interpreted in the pooled cross-section regression as a rising share as income rises).

38. World Bank, *Globalization, Growth & Poverty*, pp. 49–50.

39. See Jean-Marc Burniaux, Thai-Thanh Dang, Douglas Fore, Michael Forster, Mario Mira d'Ercole and Howard Oxley, "Income Distribution and Poverty in Selected OECD Countries," OECD Economics Department Working Paper 189, Paris, OECD, March 1998, www.oecd.org.

40. Wolfgang Stolper and Paul A. Samuelson, "Protection and Real Wages," *Review of Economic Studies*, Vol. 9 (1941), pp. 58–73.

41. Lindert and Williamson, "Does Globalization Make the World More Unequal?," p. 33.

MOISÉS NAÍM

THE FIVE WARS OF GLOBALIZATION

The persistence of al Qaeda underscores how hard it is for governments to stamp out stateless, decentralized networks that move freely, quickly, and stealthily across national borders to engage in terror. The intense media coverage devoted to the war on terrorism, however, obscures five other similar global wars that pit governments against agile, well-financed networks of highly dedicated individuals. These are the fights against the illegal international trade in drugs, arms, intellectual property, people, and money. Religious zeal or political goals drive terrorists, but the promise of enormous financial gain motivates those who battle governments in these five wars. Tragically, profit is no less a motivator for murder, mayhem, and global insecurity than religious fanaticism.

In one form or another, governments have been fighting these five wars for centuries. And losing them. Indeed, thanks to the changes spurred by globalization over the last decade, their losing streak has become even more pronounced. To be sure, nation-states have benefited from the information revolution, stronger political and economic linkages, and the shrinking importance of geographic distance. Unfortunately, criminal networks have benefited even more. Never fettered by the niceties of sovereignty, they are now increasingly free of geographic constraints. Moreover, globalization has not only expanded illegal markets and boosted the size and the resources of criminal networks, it has also imposed more burdens on governments: Tighter public budgets, decentralization, privatization, deregulation, and a more open environment for international trade and investment all make the task of fighting global criminals more difficult. Governments are made up of cumbersome

bureaucracies that generally cooperate with difficulty, but drug traffickers, arms dealers, alien smugglers, counterfeiters, and money launderers have refined networking to a high science, entering into complex and improbable strategic alliances that span cultures and continents.

Defeating these foes may prove impossible. But the first steps to reversing their recent dramatic gains must be to recognize the fundamental similarities among the five wars and to treat these conflicts not as law enforcement problems but as a new global trend that shapes the world as much as confrontations between nation-states did in the past. Customs officials, police officers, lawyers, and judges alone will never win these wars. Governments must recruit and deploy more spies, soldiers, diplomats, and economists who understand how to use incentives and regulations to steer markets away from bad social outcomes. But changing the skill set of government combatants alone will not end these wars. Their doctrines and institutions also need a major overhaul.

The Five Wars

Pick up any newspaper anywhere in the world, any day, and you will find news about illegal migrants, drug busts, smuggled weapons, laundered money, or counterfeit goods. The global nature of these five wars was unimaginable just a decade ago. The resources—financial, human, institutional, technological—deployed by the combatants have reached unfathomable orders of magnitude. So have the numbers of victims. The tactics and tricks of both sides boggle the mind. Yet if you cut through the fog of daily headlines and orchestrated photo ops, one inescapable truth emerges: The world's governments are fighting a qualitatively new phenomenon with

From *Foreign Policy* no. 134 (Jan./Feb., 2003): 28–37.

obsolete tools, inadequate laws, inefficient bureaucratic arrangements, and ineffective strategies. Not surprisingly, the evidence shows that governments are losing.

Drugs

The best known of the five wars is, of course, the war on drugs. In 1999, the United Nations' "Human Development Report" calculated the annual trade in illicit drugs at $400 billion, roughly the size of the Spanish economy and about 8 percent of world trade. Many countries are reporting an increase in drug use. Feeding this habit is a global supply chain that uses everything from passenger jets that can carry shipments of cocaine worth $500 million in a single trip to custom-built submarines that ply the waters between Colombia and Puerto Rico. To foil eavesdroppers, drug smugglers use "cloned" cell phones and broadband radio receivers while also relying on complex financial structures that blend legitimate and illegitimate enterprises with elaborate fronts and structures of cross-ownership.

The United States spends between $35 billion and $40 billion each year on the war on drugs; most of this money is spent on interdiction and intelligence. But the creativity and boldness of drug cartels has routinely outstripped steady increases in government resources. Responding to tighter security at the U.S.-Mexican border, drug smugglers built a tunnel to move tons of drugs and billions of dollars in cash until authorities discovered it in March 2002. Over the last decade, the success of the Bolivian and Peruvian governments in eradicating coca plantations has shifted production to Colombia. Now, the U.S.-supported Plan Colombia is displacing coca production and processing labs back to other Andean countries. Despite the heroic efforts of these Andean countries and the massive financial and technical support of the United States, the total acreage of coca plantations in Peru, Colombia, and Bolivia has increased in the last decade from 206,200 hectares in 1991 to 210,939 in 2001. Between 1990 and 2000, according to economist Jeff DeSimone, the median price of a gram of cocaine in the United States fell from $152 to $112.

Even when top leaders of drug cartels are captured or killed, former rivals take their place. Authorities have acknowledged, for example, that the recent arrest of Benjamin Arellano Felix, accused of running Mexico's most ruthless drug cartel, has done little to stop the flow of drugs to the United States. As Arellano said in a recent interview from jail, "They talk about a war against the Arellano brothers. They haven't won. I'm here, and nothing has changed."

Arms Trafficking

Drugs and arms often go together. In 1999, the Peruvian military parachuted 10,000 AK-47s to the Revolutionary Armed Forces of Colombia, a guerrilla group closely allied to drug growers and traffickers. The group purchased the weapons in Jordan. Most of the roughly 80 million AK-47s in circulation today are in the wrong hands. According to the United Nations, only 18 million (or about 3 percent) of the 550 million small arms and light weapons in circulation today are used by government, military, or police forces. Illicit trade accounts for almost 20 percent of the total small arms trade and generates more than $1 billion a year. Small arms helped fuel 46 of the 49 largest conflicts of the last decade and in 2001 were estimated to be responsible for 1,000 deaths a day; more than 80 percent of those victims were women and children.

Small arms are just a small part of the problem. The illegal market for munitions encompasses top-of-the-line tanks, radar systems that detect Stealth aircraft, and the makings of the deadliest weapons of mass destruction. The International Atomic Energy Agency has confirmed more than a dozen cases of smuggled nuclear-weapons-usable material, and hundreds more cases have been reported and investigated over the last decade. The actual supply of stolen nuclear-, biological-, or chemical-weapons materials and technology may still be small. But the potential demand is strong and growing from both would-be nuclear powers and and cause prices to rise and create enormous incentives for illegal activities. More than one fifth of the 120,000 workers in Russia's former "nuclear cities"—where more than half of all employees earn less than $50 a month—say they would be willing to work in the military complex of another country.

Governments have been largely ineffective in curbing either supply or demand. In recent years, two countries, Pakistan and India, joined the declared nuclear power club. A U.N. arms embargo failed to prevent the reported sale to Iraq of jet fighter engine parts from Yugoslavia and the Kolchuga anti-Stealth radar system from Ukraine. Multilateral efforts to curb the manufacture and distribution of weapons are faltering, not least because some powers are unwilling to accept curbs on their own activities. In 2001, for example, the United States blocked a legally binding global treaty to control small arms in part because it worried about restrictions on its own citizens' rights to own guns. In the absence of effective international legislation and enforcement, the laws of economics dictate the sale of more weapons at cheaper prices: In 1986, an AK-47 in Kolowa, Kenya, cost 15 cows. Today, it costs just four.

Other Fronts

Drugs, arms, intellectual property, people, and money are not the only commodities traded illegally for huge profits by international networks. They also trade in human organs, endangered species, stolen art, and toxic waste. The illegal global trades in all these goods share several fundamental characteristics: Technological innovations and political changes open new markets, globalization is increasing both the geographical reach and the profit opportunities for criminal networks, and governments are on the losing end of the fight to stop them. Some examples:

Human organs: Corneas, kidneys, and livers are the most commonly traded human parts in a market that has boomed thanks to technology, which has improved preservation techniques and made transplants less risky. In the United States, 70,000 patients are on the waiting list for major organ transplants while only 20,000 of them succeed in getting the organ they need. Unscrupulous "organ brokers" partly meet this demand by providing, for a fee, organs and transplant services. Some of the donors, especially of kidneys, are desperately poor. In India, an estimated 2,000 people a year sell their organs. Many organs, however, come from nonconsenting donors forced to undergo operations or from cadavers in police morgues. For example, medical centers in Germany and Austria were recently found to have used human heart valves taken without consent from the cadavers of poor South Africans.

Endangered species: From sturgeon for caviar in gourmet delicatessens to tigers or elephants for private zoos, the trade in endangered animals and plants is worth billions of dollars and includes hundreds of millions of plant and animal types. This trade ranges from live animals and plants to all kinds of wildlife products derived from them, including food products, exotic leather goods, wooden musical instruments, timber, tourist curiosities, and medicines.

Stolen art: Paintings and sculptures taken from museums, galleries, and private homes, from Holocaust victims, or from "cultural artifacts" poached from archeological digs and other ancient ruins are also illegally traded internationally in a market worth an estimated $2 billion to $6 billion each year. The growing use of art-based transactions in money laundering has spurred demand over the last decade. The supply has boomed because the Soviet Union's collapse flooded the world's market with art that had been under state control. The Czech Republic, Poland, and Russia are three of the five countries most affected by art crime worldwide.

Toxic waste: Innovations in maritime transport, tighter environmental regulations in industrialized countries coupled with increased integration of poor countries to the global economy and better telecommunications have created a market where waste is traded internationally. Greenpeace estimates that during the 20 years prior to 1989, just 3.6 million tons of hazardous waste were exported; in the five years after 1989, the trade soared to about 6.7 billion tons. The environmental organization also reckons that 86 to 90 percent of all hazardous waste shipments destined for developing countries—purportedly for recycling, reuse, recovery, or humanitarian uses—are toxic waste.

Intellectual Property

In 2001, two days after recording the voice track of a movie in Hollywood, actor Dennis Hopper was in Shanghai where a street vendor sold him an excellent pirated copy of the movie with his voice already on it. "I don't know how they got my voice into the country before I got here," he wondered. Hopper's experience is one tiny slice of an illicit trade that cost the United States an estimated $9.4 billion in 2001. The piracy rate of business software in Japan and France is 40 percent, in Greece and South Korea it is about 60 percent, and in Germany and Britain it hovers around 30 percent. Forty percent of Procter & Gamble shampoos and 60 percent of Honda motorbikes sold in China in 2001 were pirated. Up to 50 percent of medical drugs in Nigeria and Thailand are bootleg copies. This problem is not limited to consumer products: Italian makers of industrial valves worry that their $2 billion a year export market is eroded by counterfeit Chinese valves sold in world markets at prices that are 40 percent cheaper.

The drivers of this bootlegging boom are complex. Technology is obviously boosting both the demand and the supply of illegally copied products. Users of Napster, the now defunct Internet company that allowed anyone, anywhere to download and reproduce copyrighted music for free, grew from zero to 20 million in just one year. Some 500,000 film files are traded daily through file-sharing services such as Kazaa and Morpheus; and in late 2002, some 900 million music files could be downloaded for free on the Internet—that is, almost two and a half times more files than those available when Napster reached its peak in February 2001.

Global marketing and branding are also playing a part, as more people are attracted to products bearing a well-known brand like Prada or Cartier. And thanks to the rapid growth and integration into the global economy of countries, such as China, with weak central governments and ineffective laws, producing and exporting near perfect knockoffs are both less expensive and less risky. In the words of the CEO of one of the best known Swiss watchmakers: "We now compete with a product manufactured by Chinese prisoners. The business is run by the Chinese military, their families and friends, using roughly the same machines we have, which they purchased at the same industrial fairs we go to. The way we have rationalized this problem is by assuming that their customers and ours are different. The person that buys a pirated copy of one of our $5,000 watches for less than $100 is not a client we are losing. Perhaps it is a future client that some day will want to own the real thing instead of a fake. We may be wrong and we do spend money to fight the piracy of our products. But given that our efforts do not seem to protect us much, we close our eyes and hope for the better." This posture stands in contrast to that of companies that sell cheaper products such as garments, music, or videos, whose revenues are directly affected by piracy.

Governments have attempted to protect intellectual property rights through various means, most notably the World Trade Organization's Agreement on Trade-Related Aspects of Intellectual Property Rights (TRIPS). Several other organizations such as the World Intellectual Property Organization, the World Customs Union, and Interpol are also involved. Yet the large and growing volume of this trade, or a simple stroll in the streets of Manhattan or Madrid, show that governments are far from winning this fight.

Alien Smuggling

The man or woman who sells a bogus Hermes scarf or a Rolex watch in the streets of Milan is likely to be an illegal alien. Just as likely, he or she was transported across several continents by a trafficking network allied with another network that specializes in the illegal copying, manufacturing, and distributing of high-end, brand-name products.

Alien smuggling is a $7 billion a year enterprise and according to the United Nations is the fastest growing business of organized crime.

Roughly 500,000 people enter the United States illegally each year—about the same number as illegally enter the European Union, and part of the approximately 150 million who live outside their countries of origin. Many of these back-door travelers are voluntary migrants who pay smugglers up to $35,000, the top-dollar fee for passage from China to New York. Others, instead, are trafficked—that is, bought and sold internationally—as commodities. The U.S. Congressional Research Service reckons that each year between 1 million and 2 million people are trafficked across borders, the majority of whom are women and children. A woman can be "bought" in Timisoara, Romania, for between $50 and $200 and "resold" in Western Europe for 10 times that price. The United Nations Children's Fund estimates that cross-border smugglers in Central and Western Africa enslave 200,000 children a year. Traffickers initially tempt victims with job offers or, in the case of children, with offers of adoption in wealthier countries, and then keep the victims in subservience through physical violence, debt bondage, passport confiscation, and threats of arrest, deportation, or violence against their families back home.

Governments everywhere are enacting tougher immigration laws and devoting more time, money, and technology to fight the flow of illegal aliens. But the plight of the United Kingdom's government illustrates how tough that fight is. The British government throws money at the problem, plans to use the Royal Navy and Royal Air Force to intercept illegal immigrants, and imposes large fines on truck drivers who (generally unwittingly) transport stowaways. Still, 42,000 of the 50,000 refugees who have passed through the Sangatte camp (a main entry point for illegal immigration to the United Kingdom) over the last three years have made it to Britain. At current rates, it will take 43 years for Britain to clear its asylum backlog. And that country is an island. Continental nations such as Spain, Italy, or the United States face an even greater challenge as immigration pressures overwhelm their ability to control the inflow of illegal aliens.

Money Laundering

The Cayman Islands has a population of 36,000. It also has more than 2,200 mutual funds, 500 insurance companies, 60,000 businesses, and 600 banks and trust companies with almost $800 billion in assets. Not surprisingly, it figures prominently in any discussion of money laundering. So does the United States, several of whose major banks have been caught up in investigations of money laundering, tax evasion, and fraud. Few, if any, countries can claim to be free of the practice of helping individuals and companies hide funds from governments, creditors, business partners, or even family members, including the proceeds of tax evasion, gambling, and other crimes. Estimates of the volume of global money laundering range between 2 and 5 percent of the world's annual gross national product, or between $800 billion and $2 trillion.

Smuggling money, gold coins, and other valuables is an ancient trade. Yet in the last two decades, new political and economic trends coincided with technological changes to make this ancient trade easier, cheaper, and less risky. Political changes led to the deregulation of financial markets that now facilitate cross-border money transfers, and technological changes made distance less of a factor and money less "physical." Suitcases full of banknotes are still a key tool for money launderers, but computers, the Internet, and complex financial schemes that combine legal and illegal practices and institutions are more common. The sophistication of technology, the complex web of financial institutions that crisscross the globe, and the ease with which "dirty" funds can be electronically morphed into legitimate assets make the regulation of international flows of money a daunting task. In Russia, for example, it is estimated that by the mid-1990s organized crime groups had set up 700 legal and financial institutions to launder their money.

Faced with this growing tide, governments have stepped up their efforts to clamp down on rogue international banking, tax havens, and money laundering. The imminent, large-scale introduction of e-money—cards with microchips that can store large amounts of money and thus can be easily transported outside regular channels or simply exchanged among individuals—will only magnify this challenge.

Why Governments Can't Win

The fundamental changes that have given the five wars new intensity over the last decade are likely to persist. Technology will continue to spread widely; criminal networks will be able to exploit these technologies more quickly than governments that must cope with tight budgets, bureaucracies, media scrutiny, and electorates. International trade will continue to grow, providing more cover for the expansion of illicit trade. International migration will likewise grow, with much the same effect, offering ethnically based gangs an ever growing supply of recruits and victims. The spread of democracy may also help criminal cartels, which can manipulate weak public institutions by corrupting police officers or tempting politicians with offers of cash for their increasingly expensive election campaigns. And ironically, even the spread of international law—with its growing web of embargoes, sanctions, and conventions—will offer criminals new opportunities for providing forbidden goods to those on the wrong side of the international community.

These changes may affect each of the five wars in different ways, but these conflicts will continue to share four common characteristics:

They are not bound by geography.

Some forms of crime have always had an international component: The Mafia was born in Sicily and exported to the United States, and smuggling has always been by definition international. But the five wars are truly global. Where is the theater or front line of the war on drugs? Is it Colombia or Miami? Myanmar (Burma) or Milan? Where are the battles against money launderers being fought? In Nauru or in London? Is

China the main theater in the war against the infringement of intellectual property, or are the trenches of that war on the Internet?

They defy traditional notions of sovereignty.

Al Qaeda's members have passports and nationalities—and often more than one—but they are truly stateless. Their allegiance is to their cause, not to any nation. The same is also true of the criminal networks engaged in the five wars. The same, however, is patently *not* true of government employees—police officers, customs agents, and judges—who fight them. This asymmetry is a crippling disadvantage for governments waging these wars. Highly paid, hypermotivated, and resource-rich combatants on one side of the wars (the criminal gangs) can seek refuge in and take advantage of national borders, but combatants of the other side (the governments) have fewer resources and are hampered by traditional notions of sovereignty. A former senior CIA official reported that international criminal gangs are able to move people, money, and weapons globally faster than he can move resources inside his own agency, let alone worldwide. Coordination and information sharing among government agencies in different countries has certainly improved, especially after September 11. Yet these tactics fall short of what is needed to combat agile organizations that can exploit every nook and cranny of an evolving but imperfect body of international law and multilateral treaties.

They pit governments against market forces.

In each of the five wars, one or more government bureaucracies fight to contain the disparate, uncoordinated actions of thousands of independent, stateless organizations. These groups are motivated by large profits obtained by exploiting international price differentials, an unsatisfied demand, or the cost advantages produced by theft. Hourly wages for a Chinese cook are far higher in

Manhattan than in Fujian. A gram of cocaine in Kansas City is 17,000 percent more expensive than in Bogotá. Fake Italian valves are 40 percent cheaper because counterfeiters don't have to cover the costs of developing the product. A well-funded guerrilla group will pay anything to get the weapons it needs. In each of these five wars, the incentives to successfully overcome government-imposed limits to trade are simply enormous.

They pit bureaucracies against networks.

The same network that smuggles East European women to Berlin may be involved in distributing opium there. The proceeds of the latter fund the purchase of counterfeit Bulgari watches made in China and often sold on the streets of Manhattan by illegal African immigrants. Colombian drug cartels make deals with Ukrainian arms traffickers, while Wall Street brokers controlled by the U.S.-based Mafia have been known to front for Russian money launderers. These highly decentralized groups and individuals are bound by strong ties of loyalty and common purpose and organized around semiautonomous clusters or "nodes" capable of operating swiftly and flexibly. John Arquilla and David Ronfeldt, two of the best known experts on these types of organizations, observe that networks often lack central leadership, command, or headquarters, thus "no precise heart or head that can be targeted. The network as a whole (but not necessarily each node) has little to no hierarchy; there may be multiple leaders. . . . Thus the [organization's] design may sometimes appear acephalous (headless), and at other times polycephalous (Hydra-headed)." Typically, governments respond to these challenges by forming interagency task forces or creating new bureaucracies. Consider the creation of the new Department of Homeland Security in the United States, which encompasses 22 former federal agencies and their 170,000 employees and is responsible for, among other things, fighting the war on drugs.

Rethinking the Problem

Governments may never be able to completely eradicate the kind of international trade involved in the five wars. But they can and should do better. There are at least four areas where efforts can yield better ideas on how to tackle the problems posed by these wars:

Develop more flexible notions of sovereignty.

Governments need to recognize that restricting the scope of multilateral action for the sake of protecting their sovereignty is often a moot point. Their sovereignty is compromised daily, not by nation-states but by stateless networks that break laws and cross borders in pursuit of trade. In May 1999, for example, the Venezuelan government denied U.S. planes authorization to fly over Venezuelan territory to monitor air routes commonly used by narcotraffickers. Venezuelan authorities placed more importance on the symbolic value of asserting sovereignty over air space than on the fact that drug traffickers' planes regularly violate Venezuelan territory. Without new forms of codifying and "managing" sovereignty, governments will continue to face a large disadvantage while fighting the five wars.

Strengthen existing multilateral institutions.

The global nature of these wars means no government, regardless of its economic, political, or military power, will make much progress acting alone. If this seems obvious, then why does Interpol, the multilateral agency in charge of fighting international crime, have a staff of 384, only 112 of whom are police officers, and an annual budget of $28 million, less than the price of some boats or planes used by drug traffickers? Similarly, Europol, Europe's Interpol equivalent, has a staff of 240 and a budget of $51 million.

One reason Interpol is poorly funded and staffed is because its 181 member governments don't trust each other. Many assume, and perhaps rightly so, that the criminal networks they are fighting have penetrated the police departments of other countries and that sharing information with such compromised officials would not be prudent. Others fear today's allies will become tomorrow's enemies. Still others face legal impediments to sharing intelligence with fellow nation-states or have intelligence services and law enforcement agencies with organizational cultures that make effective collabouration almost impossible. Progress will only be made if the world's governments unite behind stronger, more effective multilateral organizations.

Devise new mechanisms and institutions.

These five wars stretch and even render obsolete many of the existing institutions, legal frameworks, military doctrines, weapons systems, and law enforcement techniques on which governments have relied for years. Analysts need to rethink the concept of war "fronts" defined by geography and the definition of "combatants" according to the Geneva Convention. The functions of intelligence agents, soldiers, police officers, customs agents, or immigration officers need rethinking and adaptation to the new realities. Policymakers also need to reconsider the notion that ownership is essentially a physical reality and not a "virtual" one or that only sovereign nations can issue money when thinking about ways to fight the five wars.

Move from repression to regulation.

Beating market forces is next to impossible. In some cases, this reality may force governments to move from repressing the market to regulating it.

In others, creating market incentives may be better than using bureaucracies to curb the excesses of these markets. Technology can often accomplish more than government policies can. For example, powerful encryption techniques can better protect software or CDs from being copied in Ukraine than would making the country enforce patents and copyrights and trademarks.

In all of the five wars, government agencies fight against networks motivated by the enormous profit opportunities created by other government agencies. In all cases, these profits can be traced to some form of government intervention that creates a major imbalance between demand and supply and makes prices and profit margins skyrocket. In some cases, these government interventions are often justified and it would be imprudent to eliminate them—governments can't simply walk away from the fight against trafficking in heroin, human beings, or weapons of mass destruction. But society can better deal with other segments of these kinds of illegal trade through regulation, not prohibition. Policymakers must focus on opportunities where market regulation can ameliorate problems that have defied approaches based on prohibition and armed interdiction of international trade.

Ultimately, governments, politicians, and voters need to realize that the way in which the world is conducting these five wars is doomed to fail—not for lack of effort, resources, or political will but because the collective thinking that guides government strategies in the five wars is rooted in wrong ideas, false assumptions, and obsolete institutions. Recognizing that governments have no chance of winning unless they change the ways they wage these wars is an indispensable first step in the search for solutions.

THOMAS L. FRIEDMAN

THE FIRST LAW OF PETROPOLITICS

When I heard the president of Iran, Mahmoud Ahmadinejad, declare that the Holocaust was a "myth," I couldn't help asking myself: "I wonder if the president of Iran would be talking this way if the price of oil were $20 a barrel today rather than $60 a barrel." When I heard Venezuela's President Hugo Chávez telling British Prime Minister Tony Blair to "go right to hell" and telling his supporters that the U.S.-sponsored Free Trade Area of the Americas "can go to hell," too, I couldn't help saying to myself, "I wonder if the president of Venezuela would be saying all these things if the price of oil today were $20 a barrel rather than $60 a barrel, and his country had to make a living by empowering its own entrepreneurs, not just drilling wells."

As I followed events in the Persian Gulf during the past few years, I noticed that the first Arab Gulf state to hold a free and fair election, in which women could run and vote, and the first Arab Gulf state to undertake a total overhaul of its labor laws to make its own people more employable and less dependent on imported labor, was Bahrain. Bahrain happened to be the first Arab Gulf state expected to run out of oil. It was also the first in the region to sign a free trade agreement with the United States. I couldn't help asking myself: "Could that all just be a coincidence? Finally, when I looked across the Arab world, and watched the popular democracy activists in Lebanon pushing Syrian troops out of their country, I couldn't help saying to myself: "Is it an accident that the Arab world's first and only real democracy happens not to have a drop of oil?"

The more I pondered these questions, the more it seemed obvious to me that there must be a correlation—a literal correlation that could be measured and graphed—between the price of oil

and the pace, scope, and sustainability of political freedoms and economic reforms in certain countries. A few months ago I approached the editors of this magazine and asked them to see if we could do just that—try to quantify this intuition in graph form. Along one axis we would plot the average global price of crude oil, and along the other axis we would plot the pace of expanding or contracting freedoms, both economic and political, as best as research organizations such as Freedom House could measure them. We would look at free and fair elections held, newspapers opened or closed, arbitrary arrests, reformers elected to parliaments, economic reform projects started or stopped, companies privatized and companies nationalized, and so on.

I would be the first to acknowledge that this is not a scientific lab experiment, because the rise and fall of economic and political freedom in a society can never be perfectly quantifiable or interchangeable. But because I am not trying to get tenure anywhere, but rather to substantiate a hunch and stimulate a discussion, I think there is value in trying to demonstrate this very real correlation between the price of oil and the pace of freedom, even with its imperfections. Because the rising price of crude is certain to be a major factor shaping international relations for the near future, we must try to understand any connections it has with the character and direction of global politics. And the graphs assembled here certainly do suggest a strong correlation between the price of oil and the pace of freedom—so strong, in fact, that I would like to spark this discussion by offering the First Law of Petropolitics.

The First Law of Petropolitics posits the following: The price of oil and the pace of freedom always move in opposite directions in oil-rich petrolist states. According to the First Law of Petropolitics, the higher the average global crude oil

From *Foreign Policy* no. 154 (May/June, 2006): 28–36.

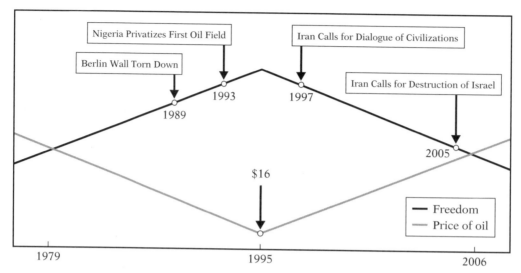

Figure 9.5. Freedom vs. Price of Oil

price rises, the more free speech, free press, free and fair elections, an independent judiciary, the rule of law, and independent political parties are eroded. And these negative trends are reinforced by the fact that the higher the price goes, the less petrolist leaders are sensitive to what the world thinks or says about them. Conversely, according to the First Law of Petropolitics, the lower the price of oil, the more petrolist countries are forced to move toward a political system and a society that is more transparent, more sensitive to opposition voices, and more focused on building the legal and educational structures that will maximize their people's ability, both men's and women's, to compete, start new companies, and attract investments from abroad. The lower the price of crude oil falls, the more petrolist leaders are sensitive to what outside forces think of them.

I would define petrolist states as states that are both dependent on oil production for the bulk of their exports or gross domestic product and have weak state institutions or outright authoritarian governments. High on my list of petrolist states would be Azerbaijan, Angola, Chad, Egypt, Equatorial Guinea, Iran, Kazakhstan, Nigeria, Russia, Saudi Arabia, Sudan, Uzbekistan, and Venezuela. (Countries that have a lot of crude oil but were well-established states, with solid democratic institutions and diversified economies before their oil was discovered—Britain, Norway, the United States, for example—would not be subject to the First Law of Petropolitics.)

To be sure, professional economists have, for a long time, pointed out in general the negative economic and political impacts that an abundance of natural resources can have on a country. This phenomenon has been variously diagnosed as "Dutch Disease" or the "resource curse." Dutch Disease refers to the process of deindustrialization that can result from a sudden natural resource windfall. The term was coined in the Netherlands in the 1960s, after it discovered huge deposits of natural gas. What happens in countries with Dutch Disease is that the value of their currency rises, thanks to the sudden influx of cash from oil, gold, gas, diamonds, or some other natural resource discovery. That then makes the country's manu-

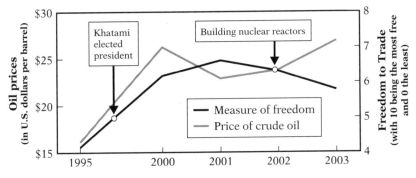

Figure 9.6. Iran: Freedom to Trade Internationally vs. Crude Oil Prices

Sources: BP Statistical Review of Word Energy 2005 and IEA; and Fraser Institute *Economic Freedom of the World Report*

factured exports uncompetitive and its imports very cheap. The citizens, flush with cash, start importing like crazy, the domestic industrial sector gets wiped out and, presto, you have deindustrialization. The "resource curse" can refer to the same economic phenomenon, as well as, more broadly speaking, the way a dependence on natural resources always skews a country's politics and investment and educational priorities, so that everything revolves around who controls the oil tap and who gets how much from it—not how to compete, innovate, and produce real products for real markets.

Beyond these general theories, some political scientists have explored how an abundance of oil wealth, in particular, can reverse or erode democratizing trends. One of the most trenchant analyses that I have come across is the work of UCLA political scientist Michael L. Ross. Using a statistical analysis from 113 states between 1971 and 1997, Ross concluded that a state's "reliance on either oil or mineral exports tends to make it less democratic; that this effect is not caused by other types of primary exports; that it is not limited to the Arabian Peninsula, to the Middle East, or sub-Saharan Africa; and that it is not limited to small states."

What I find particularly useful about Ross's analysis is his list of the precise mechanisms by which excessive oil wealth impedes democracy. First, he argues, there is the "taxation effect." Oil-

rich governments tend to use their revenues to "relieve social pressures that might otherwise lead to demands for greater accountability" from, or representation in, the governing authority. I like to put it this way: The motto of the American Revolution was "no taxation without representation." The motto of the petrolist authoritarian is "no representation without taxation." Oil-backed regimes that do not have to tax their people in order to survive, because they can simply drill an oil well, also do not have to listen to their people or represent their wishes.

The second mechanism through which oil dampens democratization, argues Ross, is the "spending effect." Oil wealth leads to greater patronage spending, which in turn dampens pressures for democratization. The third mechanism he cites is the "group formation effect." When oil revenues provide an authoritarian state with a cash windfall, the government can use its new-found wealth to prevent independent social groups—precisely those most inclined to demand political rights—from forming. In addition, he argues, an overabundance of oil revenues can create a "repression effect," because it allows governments to spend excessively on police, internal security, and intelligence forces that can be used to choke democratic movements. Finally, Ross sees a "modernization effect" at work. A massive influx of oil wealth can diminish social pressures for occupational specialization, urban-

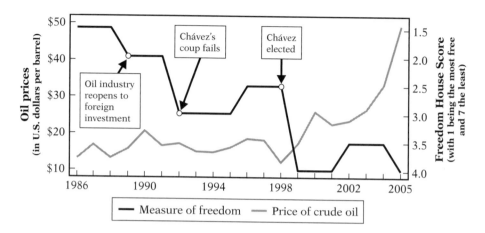

Figure 9.7. Venezuela: Freedom House *Freedom in the World* Rankings vs. Crude Oil Prices

Sources: BP Statistical Review of World Energy 2005 and IEA; and Freedom House *Freedom in the World 2005*

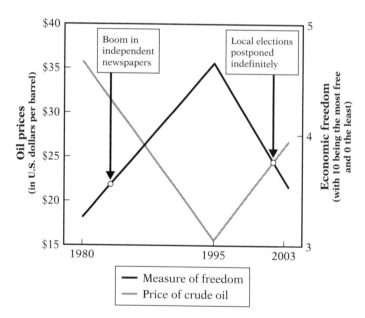

Figure 9.8. Nigeria: Legal System and Property Rights vs. Crude Oil Prices

Sources: BP Statistical Review of World Energy 2005 and IEA; and Fraser Institute *Economic Freedom of the World Report*

ization, and the securing of higher levels of education—trends that normally accompany broad economic development and that also produce a public that is more articulate, better able to organize, bargain, and communicate, and endowed with economic power centers of its own.

The First Law of Petropolitics tries to build on such arguments but to take the correlation between oil and politics one step further. What I am arguing in positing the First Law of Petropolitics is not only that an overdependence on crude oil can be a curse in general but also that one can actually correlate rises and falls in the price of oil with rises and falls in the pace of freedom in petrolist countries. The connection is very real. As these graphs demonstrate, the pace of freedom really starts to decline as the price of oil really starts to take off.

An Axis of Oil?

The reason this connection between the price of oil and the pace of freedom is worth focusing on today is that we appear to be at the onset of a structural rise in global crude oil prices. If that is the case, this higher price level is almost certain to have a long-term effect on the character of politics in many weak or authoritarian states. That, in turn, could have a negative global impact on the post-Cold War world as we have come to know it. In other words, the price of crude should now be a daily preoccupation of the U.S. secretary of state, not just the treasury secretary.

Since 9/11, oil prices have structurally shifted from the $20–$40 range to the $40–$60 range. Part of this move has to do with a general sense of insecurity in global oil markets due to violence in Iraq, Nigeria, Indonesia, and Sudan, but even more appears to be the result of what I call the "flattening" of the world and the rapid influx into the global marketplace of 3 billion new consumers, from China, Brazil, India, and the former Soviet Empire, all dreaming of a house, a car, a microwave, and a refrigerator. Their rising energy appetites are enormous. This already is, and will continue to

be, a steady source of pressure on the price of oil. Without a dramatic move toward conservation in the West, or the discovery of an alternative to fossil fuels, we are going to be in this $40-to-$60 range, or higher, for the foreseeable future.

Politically, that will mean that a whole group of petrolist states with weak institutions or outright authoritarian governments will likely experience an erosion of freedoms and an increase in corruption and autocratic, antidemocratic behaviors. Leaders in these countries can expect to have a significant increase in their disposable income to build up security forces, bribe opponents, buy votes or public support, and resist international norms and conventions. One need only pick up the newspaper on any day of the week to see evidence of this trend.

Consider a February 2005 article in the *Wall Street Journal* about how the mullahs in Tehran—who now are flush with cash thanks to high oil prices—are turning their backs on some foreign investors instead of rolling out the welcome mat. Turkcell, a Turkish mobile-phone operator, had signed a deal with Tehran to build the country's first privately owned cell-phone network. It was an attractive deal: Turkcell agreed to pay Iran $300 million for the license and invest $2.25 billion in the venture, which would have created 20,000 Iranian jobs. But the mullahs in the Iranian Parliament had the contract frozen, claiming it might help foreigners spy on Iran. Ali Ansari, an Iran expert at the University of St. Andrews in Scotland, told the *Journal* that Iranian analysts had been arguing in favor of economic reform for 10 years. "In actual fact, the scenario is worse now," said Ansari. "They have all this money with the high oil price, and they don't need to do anything about reforming the economy."

Or, how about a Feb. 11, 2006, story in *The Economist* about Iran, which stated: "Nationalism is easier on a full stomach and Mr. Ahmadinejad is the rare and fortunate president who expects to receive, over the coming Iranian year, some $36 billion in oil export revenues to help buy loyalty. In his first budget bill, now before parliament, the government has promised to build 300,000 housing units, two-thirds of them outside big towns, and to maintain energy subsidies that amount to a staggering 10% of [gross domestic product]."

Or, consider the drama now unfolding in Nigeria. Nigeria has a term limit for its presidents—two four-year terms. President Oluse-gun Obasanjo came to office in 1999, after a pe-riod of military rule, and was then reelected by a popular vote in 2003. When he took over from the generals in 1999, Obasanjo made headlines by in-vestigating human rights abuses by the Nigerian military, releasing political prisoners, and even making a real attempt to root out corruption. That was when oil was around $25 a barrel. To-day, with oil at $60 a barrel, Obasanjo is trying to persuade the Nigerian legislature to amend the constitution to allow him to serve a third term. A Nigerian opposition leader in the House of Repre-sentatives, Wunmi Bewaji, has alleged that bribes of $1 million were being offered to lawmakers who would vote to extend Obasanjo's tenure. "What they are touting now is $1 million per

vote," Bewaji was quoted as saying in a March 11, 2006, article by VOA News. "And it has been coor-dinated by a principal officer in the Senate and a principal officer in the House."

Clement Nwankwo, one of Nigeria's leading human rights campaigners, told me during a visit to Washington in March that since the price of oil has started to climb, "civil liberties [have been] on a huge decline—people have been arbitrarily arrested, political opponents have been killed, and institutions of democracy have been crippled." Oil accounts for 90 percent of Nigeria's exports, added Nwankwo, and that explains, in part, why there has been a sudden upsurge in the kidnapping of foreign oil workers in Nigeria's oil-rich Niger Delta. Many Nigerians think they must be stealing oil, because so little of the revenue is trickling down to the Nigerian people.

Very often in petrolist states, not only do all politics revolve around who controls the oil tap, but the public develops a distorted notion of

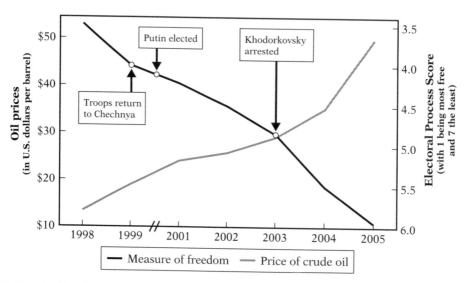

Figure 9.9. Russia: Freedom House *Nations in Transit* Rankings vs. Crude Oil Prices

Sources: BP Statistical Review of World Energy 2005 and IEA; and Freedom House *Nations in Transit*

what development is all about. If they are poor and the leaders are rich, it is not because their country has failed to promote education, innovation, rule of law, and entrepreneurship. It is because someone is getting the oil money and they are not. People start to think that, to get rich, all they have to do is stop those who are stealing the country's oil, not build a society that promotes education, innovation, and entrepreneurship. "If Nigeria had no oil, then the entire political equation would be different," said Nwankwo. "The income would not be coming from oil and therefore the diversification of the economy would become an issue and private enterprise would matter more, and people would have to expand their own creativity."

Indeed, the link between oil prices and the pace of freedom is so tight in some countries that even a farsighted leadership can be diverted from the path of economic and political reform by a sudden spike in crude prices. Consider Bahrain, which knows it is running out of oil, and has been a case study of how falling oil revenues can spur reform. Even it has not been able to resist the temporary seduction of higher oil prices. "We are having good times now because of high oil prices. This may lead officials to be complacent," Jasim Husain Ali, head of the University of Bahrain's economic research unit, recently told the *Gulf Daily News*. "This is a very dangerous trend, as oil income is not sustainable. [Bahrain's] [d]iversification may be enough by Gulf standards, but not by international standards." No wonder a young Iranian journalist once remarked to me while we were on a stroll in Tehran: "If only we didn't have oil, we could be just like Japan."

Geology Trumps Ideology

With all due respect to Ronald Reagan, I do not believe he brought down the Soviet Union. There were obviously many factors, but the collapse in global oil prices around the late 1980s and early 1990s surely played a key role. (When the Soviet Union officially dissolved on Christmas Day

1991, the price of a barrel of oil was hovering around $17.) And lower oil prices also surely helped tilt the postcommunist Boris Yeltsin government toward more rule of law, more openness to the outside world, and more sensitivity to the legal structures demanded by global investors. And then came Russian President Vladimir Putin. Think about the difference between Putin when oil was in the $20–$40 range and now, when it is $40–$60. When oil was $20–$40, we had what I would call "Putin I." President Bush said after their first meeting in 2001 that he had looked into Putin's "soul" and saw in there a man he could trust. If Bush looked into Putin's soul today—Putin II, the Putin of $60 a barrel—it would look very black down there, black as oil. He would see that Putin has used his oil windfall to swallow (nationalize) the huge Russian oil company, Gazprom, various newspapers and television stations, and all sorts of other Russian businesses and once independent institutions.

When oil prices were at a nadir in the early 1990s, even Arab oil states, such as Kuwait, Saudi Arabia, and Egypt, which has substantial gas deposits, were at least talking about economic reform, if not baby-step political reforms. But as prices started to climb, the whole reform process slowed, particularly on the political side.

As more and more oil wealth piles up in petrolist countries, it could really begin to distort the whole international system and the very character of the post-Cold War world. When the Berlin Wall fell, there was a widespread belief that an unstoppable tide of free markets and democratization had also been unleashed. The proliferation of free elections around the world for the next decade made that tide very real. But that tide is now running into an unanticipated counter-wave of petro-authoritarianism, made possible by $60-a-barrel oil. Suddenly, regimes such as those in Iran, Nigeria, Russia, and Venezuela are retreating from what once seemed like an unstoppable process of democratization, with elected autocrats in each country using their sudden oil windfalls to ensconce themselves in power, buy up opponents and supporters, and extend their state's chokehold into the private sector, after many thought it had permanently receded. The unstoppable tide of democratization that followed the fall of the Berlin Wall seems to have met its match in the black tide of petro-authoritarianism.

Although petro-authoritariansim does not represent the sort of broad strategic and ideological threat that communism posed to the West, its longterm impact could nevertheless corrode world stability. Not only will some of the worst regimes in the world have extra cash for longer than ever to do the worst things, but decent, democratic countries—India and Japan, for instance—will be forced to kowtow or turn a blind eye to the behavior of petro-authoritarians, such as Iran or Sudan, because of their heavy dependence on them for oil. That cannot be good for global stability.

Let me stress again that I know that the correlations suggested by these graphs are not perfect and, no doubt, there are exceptions that readers will surely point out. But I do believe they illustrate a general trend that one can see reflected in the news every day: The rising price of oil clearly has a negative impact on the pace of freedom in many countries, and when you get enough countries with enough negative impacts, you start to poison global politics.

Although we cannot affect the supply of oil in any country, we can affect the global price of oil by altering the amounts and types of energy we consume. When I say "we," I mean the United States in particular, which consumes about 25 percent of the world's energy, and the oil-importing countries in general. Thinking about how to alter our energy consumption patterns to bring down the price of oil is no longer simply a hobby for high-minded environmentalists or some personal virtue. It is now a national security imperative.

Therefore, any American democracy-promotion strategy that does not also include a credible and sustainable strategy for finding alternatives to oil and bringing down the price of crude is utterly meaningless and doomed to fail. Today, no matter where you are on the foreign-policy spectrum, you have to think like a Geo-Green. You cannot be either an effective foreign-policy realist or an effective democracy-promoting idealist without also being an effective energy environmentalist.

VALENTINE M. MOGHADAM

FEMALE LABOR, REGIONAL CRISES, AND FEMINIST RESPONSES

*　*　*

The Feminization of Labor and the Global Economy

Through institutions such as the nation-state and the transnational corporation, the world economy generates capital largely through the exploitation of labor, but it is not indifferent to the gender and ethnicity of that labor. Gender and racial ideologies have been deployed to favor white male workers and exclude others, but they also have been used to integrate and exploit the labor power of women and of members of disadvantaged racial and ethnic groups in the interest of profit making. In the current global environment of open economies, new trade regimes, and competitive export industries, global accumulation relies heavily on the work of women, both waged and unwaged, in formal sectors and in the home, in manufacturing, and in public and private services. Generally speaking, the situation is better or worse for women depending on the type of state and the strength of the economy. Women workers in the welfare states of northern Europe fare best, followed by women in other core economies. In Eastern Europe and the former Soviet Union, the economic status of working women changed dramatically for the worse following the collapse of communism. In much of the developing world, a class of women professionals and workers employed in the public sector and in the private sec-

From *Globalizing Women: Transnational Feminist Networks* (Baltimore: Johns Hopkins UP, 2005).

tor has certainly emerged due to rising educational attainment, changing aspirations, economic need, and the demand for relatively cheap labor. However, vast numbers of economically active women in the developing world lack formal training, work in the informal sector, have no access to social security, and live in poverty.

Proletarianization and Professionalization: Industry and Services

Let me begin with a definitional note. In my usage, *proletarianization* refers to the formation of a female working class. I distinguish this from the entry of middle-class women into the professions, which I refer to here as *professionalization*.[1] Proletarianization and professionalization coincide with the involvement of working women in trade unions and feminist organizations, including transnational feminist networks that promote women's human rights or that critique neoliberal economic policies for their adverse impact on low-income women.

As world markets expanded in the 1970s, a process of female proletarianization began to take place. In developing countries—and especially in Southeast and East Asia, parts of Latin America and the Caribbean, and Tunisia and Morocco—growing numbers of women were drawn into the labor-intensive and low-wage industries of textiles, garments, sportswear, electronics, and pharmaceuticals that produced for export as well as for the home market. The surge in women's waged employment in developing countries began in the 1970s, following an earlier period of capitalist development and economic growth that was characterized by the displacement of labor and craft work, commercialization of agriculture, and rural-urban migration.[2] Some called the marginalization of women "housewifeization";[3] others have described it as the initial part of the "U pattern" of female labor-force participation in early modernization.[4]

During the 1970s, it was observed that export-processing zones (EPZs) along the U.S.-Mexico border and in Southeast Asia, established by transnational corporations to take advantage of low labor costs in developing countries, were hiring mainly women. By the early 1980s, it was clear that the new industrialization in what was then called the Third World was drawing heavily on women workers. Many studies by WID specialists and socialist-feminists centered on the role played by the available pool of relatively cheap female labor.[5] Gender ideologies emphasizing the "nimble fingers" of young women workers and their capacity for hard work, especially in the Southeast Asian economies, justified the recruitment of women for unskilled and semi-skilled work in labor-intensive industries at wages lower than men would accept, and in conditions that unions would not permit. In Latin America, women entered the labor force at a time when average wages were falling dramatically. Around the world, women's share of total industrial labor rarely exceeds 30 to 40 percent, but as Ruth Pearson pointed out, the proportion of women workers in export processing factories producing textiles, electronics components, and garments was much higher, "with figures as high as 90% in some cases."[6] An INSTRAW (Institute for Research and Training on Women) study found that exports of manufactures from developing countries were largely comprised of the kinds of products typically produced by female labor, leading Susan Joekes to conclude that industrialization had been "as much *female* led as *export* led."[7]

The process of the feminization of labor continued throughout the recessionary 1980s and into the 1990s, encompassing countries like Bangladesh, which had one of the largest increases in the share of women participating in the labor force—from 5 percent in 1965 to 42 percent in 1995. In 1978 the country had four garment factories; by 1995 it had 2,400. These factories employed 1.2 million workers, 90 percent of whom were women under the age of twenty-five.[8] Female proletarianization continues apace in China's highly globalized and integrated economy, where huge plants producing for the world market employ thousands of women each.[9] In 2000 it was reported that 90 percent of the workers in the 850 EPZs around the world were women—and "in the majority of cases workers' rights and social protection are non-existent in EPZs. Although they work in factories, what EPZ workers have in common with informal sector workers is that they are unprotected, largely unorganized, female labor."[10]

Feminization occurred also in public services, where throughout the world women's share grew to 30–50 percent—at a time when public-sector wages, like industrial wages, were declining. In Iran, Egypt, and Turkey, women's share of public-service employment (including jobs as teachers and university professors in public schools and state universities, nurses and doctors in state hospitals, and workers and administrators across government agencies) increased during the 1990s. This occurred at a time when salaries had eroded tremendously and more men were gravitating toward the more lucrative and expanding private sector.[11]

As world trade in services has increased and global firms continue to engage in out-sourcing, the involvement of women in various occupations and professions of the service sector has grown. Women around the world have made impressive inroads into professional services such as law, banking, accounting, computing, and architecture; in tourism-related occupations; and in the information services, including offshore airline booking, mail order, credit cards, word-processing for publishers, telephone operators, and all manner of data entry and teleservices. In Barbados, according to one source, some three thousand people, or one in fifty of the country's labor force, were working in informatics in 1997, largely processing airline tickets and insurance forms. Low-cost typesetting is done in China, even by workers who do not understand what they are typing.[12] In India, Bangalore has become a technology hub, where thousands of young women work in offshore customer service centers for such firms as General Electric, British Airways, Amazon.com, and American Express.[13] Women in India represented 30 percent of employees in the computer industry in 2001, and 250,000 jobs were opened for women in the country's mobile phone industry. On the other hand, "many of these jobs are casual or part-time, and of much lower quality than men's."[14] The new technologies have enabled the reorganization of work based on the concept of flexibility.

The world trade in services favors women's labor migration, in contrast to the demand for male manufacturing workers during the earlier periods of industrialization in Europe and the United States.[15] Mexican, Central American, and Caribbean women have migrated to the United States to work as nurses, nannies, or domestics; Argentine women, to Italy to work as nurses; Filipinas and Sri Lankans, to the Middle East to work as waitresses, nurses, nannies, or domestics. Labor shortages in Europe and the growing demand for nurses has led to an out-migration of nurses from Ghana, South Africa, Jamaica, and Trinidad and Tobago.[16] In at least two countries—the Philippines and Sri Lanka—the majority of emigrants have been women.[17] There is also considerable intra-regional female labor migration, such as within Europe (e.g., East and Central Europeans to Western Europe) and Southeast and East Asia (e.g., women from the Philippines to Hong Kong).[18]

During the oil-boom years of the 1970s and afterwards, labor migration in the MENA region involved Palestinians, Egyptians, Jordanians, and Yemenis working in the oil-rich Gulf kingdoms. The remittances sent back by the predominantly male labor migrants allowed households in the capital-poor and labor-sending countries to maintain a relatively good standard of living. For both economic and political reasons, intra-Arab labor migration declined in the 1990s.[19] But this period also saw an increasing number of Moroccan, Tunisian, and Algerian women migrating alone to work in various occupations in France, Italy, and Spain, among other European countries.

The proletarianization and professionalization of women have cultural repercussions and sometimes entail backlashes and gender conflicts. In some advanced capitalist countries, working women often have encountered serious forms of sexual harassment. In the semiperipheral countries of the Middle East, the increasing participation of women in the labor force was accompanied in the 1980s by subtle or overt pressures on them to conform to religious dictates concerning dress. Hence in Egypt, many professional women came to don modest dress and to cover their heads. In the earlier stage of the Islamist movement, the influx of women in the work force raised fears of competition with men, leading to calls for the redomestication of women, as occurred in Iran immediately after the Islamic revolution. Later, although Islamists in Turkey, Iran, Egypt, Jordan, and Morocco did not call on women to withdraw from the labor force—indeed, among their female adherents are educated and employed women from the lower middle class—they did insist on veiling and on spatial and functional segregation. On the other hand, Islamists in Algeria and Palestine have continued to emphasize female domesticity, for reasons of both ideology/theology and male material interests.

The surge in women's employment is characteristic not only of semi-peripheral countries. In sixteen European countries, the increase in the number of women in the labor force over the period 1983–91 was quite dramatic, whereas it was relatively modest for men. In six countries the number of employed men actually fell over the period, most significantly by 3.4 percent in Belgium. During the 1990s, the Nordic countries, including Finland, had the highest rate of employment among women, with North America following close behind.[20] The feminization of labor, it should be noted, refers to the influx of women into relatively low-paying jobs, but also to the growth of part-time and temporary work among *men*. This trend was especially noticeable in New Zealand, the United Kingdom, and the Netherlands, mainly in retail trade, hotels and catering, banking, and insurance.[21] Indeed, in the Netherlands, men's part-time work in 1992 was as high as 13.4 percent of total male employment, up from 5.5 percent in 1979. These employment trends for European women and men continued through the end of the 1990s.[22] Unemployment rates vary across the European Union, where some countries show very high rates of unemployment among the young. At the start of the new millennium, Spain had the highest unemployment rate for both women and men (15.4 percent), followed by France (10.8 percent). Spain and France also had the highest female unemployment rates (22.7 percent and 12.8 percent respectively) and highest unemployment rates for young women (36.3 percent and 26.3 percent respectively). Other European countries with two-digit unemployment rates were Finland, Ireland, Slovakia, and Poland. Female unemployment rates exceeded men's in the following countries: Belgium, the United States, Iceland, the Netherlands, Finland, Switzerland, France, Denmark, Luxembourg, Germany, Italy, Spain, Greece, Portugal, Czech Republic, Slovakia, Poland, Mexico. Even in Turkey, with a much lower female participation rate, women's unemployment rate was 99 percent of men's. Clearly women have experienced a disadvantaged position in labor markets in the industrial countries.[23]

The Informal Sector, the Income Gap, and Unemployment

At the same time that women entered the formal labor force in record numbers in the core countries, much of the observed increase in female labor-force participation in semiperipheral countries occurred in the informal sectors of the economy. The extent of the urban informal sector and its links to the formal sector are matters of dispute, and women's involvement in it is rarely cap-

tured in the official statistics, but some studies have suggested significant increases in the size of the informal sector and in women's informal economic activities.[24] In Sub-Saharan Africa in the late 1990s, more than one-third of women in non-agricultural activities worked in the urban informal sector. Rates were as high as 65 to 80 percent in Senegal, Benin, Zambia, and Gambia.[25] Rates of urban informal activity among women have become high in parts of Peru, Indonesia, and Iran. Unregistered and small-scale urban enterprises, home-based work, and some self-employment fall into this category, and they include an array of commercial and productive activities. In the urban areas of developing countries, many formal jobs became informalized as employers sought to increase flexibility and lower labor and production costs through subcontracting, as Beneria and Roldan showed in their study of Mexico City and as Cinar revealed for Istanbul and Bursa.[26] Drawing on existing gender ideologies regarding women's roles, their attachment to family, and the perceived lower value of their work, subcontracting arrangements encourage the persistence of home-based work.[27] There is some debate concerning the reasons for women's concentration in such types of work, but some studies suggest that many women accept home-based employment—with its insecurity, low wages, and absence of benefits—as a convenient form of income generation that allows them to carry out domestic responsibilities and care for their children.[28]

The social relations of gender account for the pervasive income gap between men and women workers, a gap that is detrimental to women but lucrative to employers. On average women earn 75 percent of men's wages, with a narrower wage gap in the public sector than in the private sector.[29] Explanations for the gender gap are varied. Some point out that the gender difference in the income gap is based on lower education and intermittent employment among women workers. Others emphasize the role of gender bias. For example, in Ecuador, Jamaica, and the Philippines, women earn less than men despite higher qualifications, a problem that is especially acute in the private sector.[30] Labor-market segmentation along gender lines perpetuates the income gap. Pearson and Mitter found that in the computing and information processing sectors, the majority of high-skilled jobs went to male workers, while women were concentrated in the low-skilled ones.[31] In fact, all of the above factors are true and are consistent. For if "the uneven distribution of rewards has been the necessary pendant of capital accumulation," as Hopkins and Wallerstein argued,[32] then it is the deployment of female labor along the commodity chains of the global economy that guarantees a supply of relatively cheap labor, along with the desired higher profit margins.

Considering the social relations of gender and the function of gender ideologies, it should come as no surprise that despite women's key role in the global economy, the unemployment rates of women in the semiperiphery are very high, as we saw in the previous section in connection with the industrial countries. Global unemployment is partly a function of the nature of neoliberal economic policies, which have entailed massive retrenchment of labor in many semiperipheral countries, in the former socialist countries that underwent marketization, and in the core countries. In many developing countries unemployed women are new entrants to the labor force, who are seeking but not finding jobs. In certain countries where restructuring occurred in enterprises employing large numbers of women, or in export sectors that lost markets, the unemployment rates of women may also reflect job losses by previously employed women. This was the case in Malaysia in the mid-1980s, Viet Nam in the late 1980s, Poland, Bulgaria, and Russia in the early 1990s, and Morocco, Tunisia, and Turkey in the latter part of the 1990s. The Asian financial crisis of the late 1990s entailed further job and income losses for women workers, especially in South Korea, Thailand, and Indonesia. In South Korea, women lost jobs at twice the rate of men, despite the fact that before the crisis, they had been the preferred labor supply with an unemployment rate half that of men.[33]

In some cases, women have experienced job loss as a result of technological advances in the workplace. As has been noted above, many enterprises producing textiles and electronics for export have relied heavily on women workers. And yet as more sophisticated technology is used to produce these goods, women workers have tended to be replaced by men or recruited at a slower pace, as appears to have occurred in the Mexican *maquiladoras*,[34] and in the textiles industries of Spain and Italy. In all regions, high unemployment represents the downside of economic globalization, especially for women workers, who must contend with not only the class biases but also the gender biases of neoliberal economics. The feminization of unemployment, therefore, is as much a characteristic of the global economy as is the feminization of labor.

The analysis thus far may raise questions about the contingency versus permanence of the female labor force, and the possibility that female labor remains a reserve army of labor. Because the mass incorporation of women as proletarians and professionals is a relatively recent phenomenon, it is perhaps too soon to tell definitively.[35] However, I would argue that the incorporation of female labor is indeed a secular trend, due to the structural requirements of the capitalist world-system in the era of globalization, and also due to women's own aspirations. In turn, the contradictions of female labor incorporation have led women workers to join unions and women's organizations.

Women and Unionization

As part of the employment trends described above, more women have been joining trade unions, and have indeed been more likely than men to join unions, at a time when overall union membership has been in decline. In a number of advanced industrialized countries, such as the United States, Australia, and the Nordic countries, women have been the largest growing union constituency. Many unions, in response, are actively recruiting women workers, establishing women's departments, and appointing women trade unionists to decision-making positions. The growth of women's involvement in paid employment and in national-level unions has resulted in greater interest in women workers by the international trade unions.[36]

The International Confederation of Free Trade Unions (ICFTU) and the Public Services International (PSI) have active women's departments—and now, so does the AFL-CIO of the United States. In March 2002 the ICFTU—where women were 35 percent of members, compared with barely 7 percent when the union was formed about fifty years earlier—launched a three-year campaign called "Unions for Women, Women for Unions." The main theme for 2002 was "women's right to decent work." At the same time, the Executive Board and Women's Committee of the PSI identified pay equity as a priority issue, and launched a two-year campaign around it. For the major unions, the key issues identified by their women members are maternity protection, sexual harassment, balancing work and family life, job security, and decent wages. In addition, the International Labor Organization has determined that organizing women workers, especially in the informal sector, will strengthen unions as well as provide women workers with security and improved working conditions.[37]

Women trade unionists worked with other women's groups during the March 1995 Social Summit and the September 1995 Beijing conference. At the latter, and in recognition of women's growing importance in the global economy, as well as their growing union membership, Objective F of the 1995 Beijing Platform for Action affirmed the unions' important role in regulating and protecting women workers' rights, particularly where women constitute a very vulnerable group, as in export processing zones. Women trade unionists were also involved in the five-year reviews of the Social Summit and the Beijing conference, in 2000.

Both the PSI and the ICFTU attend the annual meetings of the UN's Commission on the Status of Women. Their statements usually describe the exploitative employment conditions that many women workers face, the dangers of "free trade," and the need for implementation of ILO labor standards and other conventions on worker rights, human rights, and women's rights. The PSI has a comprehensive website called WomeNet, which contains news and data about working women around the world. The theme of the ICFTU's Seventh Conference, held in May 1999 in Rio de Janeiro, was "Working Women in the 21st Century: Demanding Our Space, Taking Our Place." As mentioned above, the ICFTU took part in the Beijing+5 meetings and produced a number of policy briefs. According to one report published during the meetings:

> At Beijing+5, women trade unionists are concentrating on Strategic Objective F: Women and the Economy. Unions believe that government progress in this area has been poor for a number of reasons—the weakness of democratic political institutions and the absence of a vigorous civil society, defense spending and the devastation caused by armed conflicts. Globalization has had a negative impact with more exploitation in the export processing zones, where the majority of workers are women and the growth of low-paid 3D (dirty, dangerous and degrading) jobs. Cuts in public services have also hit women disproportionately. Job losses have forced women to emigrate to find work and so migrant women's needs are increasingly important.[38]

The report noted that although women workers have found traditional union structures unwelcoming, they now constituted "the future of the trade union movement" and were much more likely than men to account for the increases in union membership. As a result, "one of the important lessons of the Women's Summit is that unions must change to incorporate women's enthusiasm and ideas to fight globalization. Women need unions and unions need women."[39]

In many developing countries, women workers face difficulties in unionization, including employer harassment, state repression, and the masculine character of the existing trade unions. Still, increasing female labor force participation in

Latin American, Asian, and African countries has placed issues pertaining to women workers on the agendas of trade unions and of women's organizations in those regions. In Guatemala, women workers at an export shirt-making factory won a union contract, the first in a Guatemala *maquiladora*.[40] In Japan, the Asia-Japan Women's Resource Center studies and promotes the rights of women workers throughout East and Southeast Asia and publishes a newsletter called *Resource Materials on Women's Labor in Japan*.[41] In Taiwan the Grassroots Women Workers Centre, established in 1988, engages in various activities, including defense of the rights of immigrant women workers, and publishes a newsletter called *Female Workers in Taiwan*. According to its spring 1994 newsletter, "the Centre intends to provide opportunities for factory women and family subcontractors to reform the male-dominated workers' union, and to develop women workers' unions and workers' movements through the promotion of feminism." Similar activities and goals are shared by the Committee for Asian Women in Hong Kong. One important development came about in 2001, when the Hong Kong Domestic Workers Union was formed as an affiliate of the Hong Kong Confederation of Trade Unions. India's famous Self-Employed Women's Association (SEWA) operates as a trade union and a consciousness-raising feminist organization. A similar organization was formed in Durban, South Africa, in 1994 and is called the Self-employed Women's Union.

In the Middle East and North Africa, the involvement of women in paid employment has resulted in the politicization of women and of gender issues, but women have also responded by joining unions (though their proportions remain small), forming their own organizations, and engaging in collective action. In Tunisia, the National Commission on Working Women was created in July 1991 within the Tunisian General Federation of Workers. The commission has twenty-seven branches throughout Tunisia, and carries out surveys and studies pertaining to women and the workplace. Israeli Arab women workers ignored by the Histadrut formed the

Arab Women Workers Project, and Palestinian women activists in the West Bank and Gaza formed the Palestine Working Women Society. Morocco's Democratic League of Women's Rights organized a Roundtable on the Rights of Workers in 1995; subsequently a committee structure consisting of twelve participating organizations was formed. The group sought to revise the labor code to take into account women's conditions, to include domestic workers in the definition of wage workers and the delineation of their rights and benefits, to set the minimum work age at fifteen, and to provide workers on maternity leave with full salary and a job-back guarantee. In November 1995, some five hundred women textile workers employed by the Manufacture du Maroc factory outside Rabat went on strike for two weeks to protest "repeated violence" against several women employees. This included the arbitrary dismissal of the general secretary of the factory's union of women workers, her subsequent rape by a foreman, and the firing of seventeen women workers who protested the union leader's dismissal and rape. Morocco's Association of Democratic Women, a feminist organization, then set out to "mobilize human rights organizations and all the women's organizations" in defense of the women workers. The incident shows not only the vulnerability of women at the workplace, but the capacity of women workers to fight in defense of their rights, and the ability of the feminist organizations to mobilize support for women workers.

There are other examples of bold action by women trade unionists in the MENA region, some of which have been followed by state repression. In September 2000, thirty-five women affiliated to the Turkish union KESK who wanted to send letters of support to the UN concerning the Women's Global March 2000 were "detained and ill-treated." The following month, some women who wanted to begin a march to Ankara were confronted by police and arrested in Duzce.[42] And since 1998, Iranian working-class and professional women have formed unions of journalists, publishers, lawyers, teachers, and nurses, despite a political climate that is hostile to independent organizing.

Various transnational advocacy networks have emerged to support women workers. Women Working Worldwide, based in Manchester, England, has links with women worker groups in Central America and in South and Southeast Asia. IRENE (International Restructuring Education Network Europe), based in Tilburg, Holland, organizes educational seminars for unions from around the world, and disseminates a newsletter. Mujer a Mujer coordinates women workers' activities across the U.S.-Mexico border.[43] STITCH is a Chicago-based network of U.S. women that supports Central American women organizing in the maquila apparel-for-export industries. Some of its activists are associated with the International Textile, Garment, and Leather Workers Federation, which has a maquila project.[44]

As Gallin has pointed out, trade unions have championed women's rights since their beginnings and have included many charismatic women among their leaders, including Flora Tristan, Louise Michel, Clara Zetkin, Mary "Mother" Jones, Federica Montseny, Marie Nielsen, and Margarethe Faas.[45] However, the labor movement has been dominated by the culture of the male industrial workers, and the culture of unions has been rather masculine and often unfriendly to women workers. Thus in some cases women created their own unions. In Canada, the Federation of Women Teachers' Associations of Ontario is a women-only organization.[46] Denmark produced the Danish Women Workers' Union, KAD.[47] In more recent years, however, and particularly in northern Europe, Italy, Australia, and North America, union membership is taking on a female face.[48] In 2001, Germany's Trade Union Confederation had a female membership of 2.5 million women, or 31 percent of total members. According to the AFL-CIO, whereas U.S. women accounted for 19 percent of union members in 1962, by 1997 fully 39 percent of all union members were women, and they numbered 5.5 million. In 2002, two out of three new members were women,

which is no doubt why the AFL-CIO launched its own "Unions for Women, Women for Unions" campaign.[49] U.S. labor organizations such as UNITE (a textile and garment workers' union) and the Hotel and Restaurant Employees "now understand that feminist issues like sweatshops, comparable worth for women, sexual harassment and education provide the vital pathway toward the expansion and revitalization of their movement."[50]

Since the mid-1980s, women have made their way into positions of power in Australian trade unions at a time when overall union membership began to decline. The numbers of women on the foremost national council, the Australian Council of Trade Unions, rose from zero to one-third; in the mid-1990s in the State of South Australia the three major white-collar unions (teachers, nurses, public servants) were all led by women.[51] In Canada, where 31 percent of women workers (and 38 percent of men workers) were unionized in 1992,[52] women's committees succeeded not only in bringing benefits to women workers but also in bringing "increased energy" to unions such as the Ontario Public Service Employees Union.[53] According to Linda Briskin, "Canada has a strong movement of union women, and a vibrant autonomous women's movement," and these movements have "successfully pressured the unions to take up the issues of childcare, abortion, sexual harassment, pay equity, affirmative action and employment equity, etc.—as women's issues and as union issues."[54] According to Rosemary Warskett, Canadian "union feminism" effectively challenged the narrow vision of industrial unionism. "It is now well established in Canada that collective bargaining demands should address the needs of women and other discriminated groups."[55]

In global terms, the highest union density is found in northern Europe—Denmark, Finland, Norway, and Sweden—where women's participation as workers and as union officials is the greatest. In those countries, union density is very high in community, social, and personal services (68–87 percent), in trade, restaurants, and hotels (47–49 percent), and in manufacturing (80–100 percent), in both the public and private sectors.

Women are making up an increasing share of union membership, especially in services, with the most impressive figures found in Denmark. In the 1990s Danish women represented 42 and 62 percent of the two main union federations; they were 30 and 39 percent of the delegates to the union Congress and 13 and 41 percent of members of leading committees, as well as 10 and 30 percent of leaders of individual unions.[56] On at least one occasion that I know of, during the 1990s the Danish labor movement sent an all-woman delegation to the annual Congress of the International Labor Organization in Geneva. In Finland during the 1990s women comprised 45 percent of the membership of one of the two labor confederations (SAK); they also constituted about 37.5 percent of delegates to the SAK Congress, and 40 percent of the union council. The proportions of women in union leadership positions also increased in other European countries, as well as in some of the large international unions.

According to an ICFTU report released in June 2000, many unions have organized campaigns against violence and sexual harassment at work. These include Argentina's CGTA, the CDT in the Democratic Republic of Congo, and Malaysia's MTUC. Spanish unions concluded agreements with the government on job security and part-time work. Poland's NSZZ campaigned for better maternity protection within the ILO Convention. India's HMS drew up a detailed Charter of Demands for women workers, while Japan's RENGO campaigned for the strict implementation of the Equal Employment Opportunity Law. The ICFTU maintains that "unions have strengthened relations with NGOs and women's organizations and together they have been effective in putting forward women's views and demands to the government."[57] Gallin reports that "unions have increasingly entered partnerships with women's NGOs, organizing drives and forming alliances to represent informal workers' interests."[58]

Female labor incorporation and trends in women's unionization provide the social basis for women's mobilization on a world scale, but they also have occurred in a context of growing inequalities and economic crises. What follows is a cross-regional review of developments that have adversely affected women, and the ways that TFNs have responded.

Global Inequalities, Regional Crises, and Impacts on Women

As more women were drawn into the processes of economic globalization, they became aware not only of persistent social and gender inequalities but also of the creation of new forms of inequalities and the emergence of periodic economic crises that threaten the well-being of entire communities. Although many economists, particularly those wedded to neoliberalism or globalism, argue that free markets benefit all, others gather convincing empirical data to show that inequalities have been increasing within and across countries. Feminists use the same data to highlight the adverse impacts on women.

According to the UNDP's 1999 *Human Development Report*, while globalization offers great opportunities for human advancement, enriching people's lives, expanding choices, and creating a community based on shared values, markets have been allowed to dominate the process, at the expense of building these shared values and achieving common goals."[59] Market volatility has been behind a number of regional macroeconomic crises, which affect the poor in various ways. Declining labor earnings, unemployment, and inflation combine to reduce household income. Many poor households react to a crisis by postponing preventive or curative health measures, or by reducing the nutritional intake of children, or by withdrawing their children from school.

Sub-Saharan Africa has been in economic decline since the 1970s, and it has the largest proportion of people living on less than $1 a day. Stagnation set in after governments submitted to structural adjustment policies in hopes of attracting foreign investment and loans. Yet the region accounts for only 2 percent of all international trade, less than it did during the last days of colonialism fifty years ago. Although corrupt governments, excessive military spending, armed conflicts, and natural disasters such as drought can explain part of the problem, it is also true that deteriorating terms of trade in the form of steep declines in prices for African commodities are also salient. In countries where socialist-style economies were replaced by deregulated free-market models, farmers and industrialists lost business, workers lost jobs, and many women turned to prostitution—including export prostitution in Europe.

Latin America went through a severe economic recession in the 1980s, and crises erupted again in the 1990s, most notably in Mexico and Argentina in 1995, and Brazil in 1999. According to studies by the Inter-American Development Bank, at the turn of the new century, the wealthiest 10 percent received 40 percent of national incomes, while the poorest 30 percent received just 7.5 percent. One of the reasons is that the vast majority of the working population, and mostly women, work in poor-quality jobs. The crises in Mexico and Argentina imposed severe hardship on the poor, and contributed to the feminization of poverty. In Argentina poverty rose from 16.9 percent in 1993 to 24.8 percent in 1995. Argentina's economy deteriorated further in 2001 and 2002, leading to public riots, the downfall of several governments, and widespread disillusionment with the U.S.-backed free-market policies that were adopted in the 1990s. The IMF prescribed its usual austerity package.[60]

In the 1980s social funds were implemented to help offset the effects of structural adjustment policies (SAPs), but most neglected to improve the income-generating capacity of the poor. The IFIs focused on assisting stabilization and liberalization efforts and generally neglected to help governments protect pro-poor services from public spending cuts. Fiscal strategies to protect pro-poor spending began to take place only during Brazil's devaluation crisis of 1999. Latin America's basic services remain underfunded.[61] As a result, poverty may have increased in Mexico during the 1990s, despite economic growth and NAFTA. At least forty million (or 40 percent) of Mexico's population of 97 million live in poverty, and of that number, seventeen million live in misery.[62] Between 1994 and 1998, the share of the nation's income earned by the 20 percent of wealthiest Mexicans leaped from 49 to 54 percent while the earning of the poorest 40 percent of families fell from 14 to 12 percent.[63] Small wonder that illegal immigration from Mexico to the United States shows no sign of abatement.

During the decade of economic reform, unemployment rose at a rapid rate, according to a 1999 ILO report on Latin America and the Caribbean. The majority of new jobs were in the informal sector, where wages, productivity and social protection are much lower than in the formal sector. The ILO reports that youth unemployment rates usually have been double the national average (and triple for workers aged 15–19), and that women's unemployment rates are between 10–60 percent higher than the rates for men.[64]

The transition to a market economy in Eastern Europe and the former Soviet Union has been associated with increased inequality and social stratification. In the 1990s, living standards fell for a majority of people, unemployment and poverty grew, the distribution of assets and earnings changed radically, and social benefits fell. In particular, the FSU countries saw inequality climb to levels comparable to Latin America.[65] According to research by UNICEF, mortality rates rose considerably, particularly among men in Russia, leaving behind widows who had to cope with unemployment or low wages as household heads. In Central Asia, women were the targets of dramatic job cuts as state-owned companies were sold to the private sector. In many countries of the former socialist world, according to data from the ILO's *Key Indicators of the Labor Market 1999*, female unemployment rates are very high: 12.5 percent in Slovakia; 14.6 percent in Latvia; 20.1 percent in Croatia; 27.4 percent in Bulgaria; 44.5 percent in Macedonia.

Unemployment rates similarly have been very high in the Middle East and North Africa, especially for women: 24 percent in Algeria, Egypt, and Morocco; 14 percent in Syria; 20 percent in Turkey during most of the 1990s.[66] Morocco and Algeria have seen a high rate of impoverishment, a dangerous curtailment of social protection, and a heightened sense of exclusion among the marginalized and the excluded. In 1994, Algeria became unable to service its $26 billion foreign debt, which was consuming 93.4 percent of export earnings, and it had to resort to an IMF and World Bank SAP in exchange for debt relief. The SAP led to a 40 percent devaluation of the dinar, the lifting of subsidies on basic food, and the liberalization of foreign trade. Between 1994 and 1998, 815 public enterprises were dissolved, and Public Economic Enterprises laid off 60 percent of their workers.[67] Although the retrenchments affected mainly men, women's livelihood was adversely affected. More women sought jobs to augment deteriorating household budgets, but gender biases as well as structural economic problems foreclosed employment opportunities. Meanwhile, poverty increased, and government data showed that the percentage of the population living below the poverty line in 1995 was 8.9 percent in the urban areas and 19.3 percent in the rural areas. The poor and vulnerable population, however, was calculated to be 14.7 percent in urban areas and 30.4 percent in rural areas.[68]

Inequalities are wide and the poverty level high in Morocco, too. In 1999 it was estimated that around 20 percent of the population of 30 million lived in poverty, 10 percent in sheer misery, while 30 percent—mostly the young and the elderly—were classified as vulnerable. Around 56 percent of Moroccans were illiterate, and only 18 percent of women could read and write. Unemployment hovers at around 20 percent, though again much higher for women than for men, and the quality of the educational system has fallen markedly. According to Layachi, the socialist government of Abdelrahman Yousoufi was caught "between the pressing problems of his people, on the one hand, and the demands of international institutions which are likely to result in even more hardship, on the other."[69] Or as a Moroccan feminist rhetorically asked at an AWMR annual meet-

ing in July 2000, "How can the state improve the status of women, children, and the poor when international financial institutions are in control?"[70]

Tunisia has done much better in preventing the spread of poverty and has put into place an extensive social welfare system, which may be the only one of its kind in the MENA region. And yet, its trade with Europe may be endangered when the Free Trade Agreement that it signed with the EU comes into effect in 2007. It is estimated that between fifteen hundred and three thousand firms—many of them textiles and garment firms that employ women—will go out of business. The association agreement, which calls for abolishing tariff barriers in Tunisia, could increase imports and trade deficits, and is likely to diminish state revenue from tariffs.[71] This could have an adverse impact on the social welfare programs administered by the state, as well as retrench thousands of women workers.

The Asian financial crisis that swept across South and Southeast Asia exposed the dangers of the global trade economy. The crisis imposed significant costs in Thailand, Indonesia, the Republic of Korea, and to lesser extents, Malaysia and the Philippines. Economic crisis set in when skittish international investors began dumping their Asian holdings, resulting in financial panic, bankruptcy, massive unemployment, and increases in poverty. National governments were unable to stabilize the economic free-fall or cushion the shocks to workers and families. The countries had few policy tools (e.g., social insurance) available to combat poverty directly. (There were limited benefits provided by "provident funds," which are lump-sum benefits for pensioners or disabled workers.) The Republic of Korea did offer unemployment insurance, but its program covered only 22 percent of the labor force and provided only a few months of benefits at a fraction of workers' earnings.[72] Thus, when the Asian economies nosedived, their own safety nets were insufficient to meet the needs of the five million workers thrown out of their jobs or the countless families thrown into poverty. Meanwhile, the IMF response was the traditional austerity regime. As former World Bank chief economist Joseph Stiglitz put it, the IMF demanded reductions in government spending and elimination of subsidies for basic necessities like food and fuel "at the very time when contractionary policies made those subsidies more desperately needed than ever." Moreover, "not only was the IMF not restoring economic confidence in East Asia, it was undermining the region's social fabric."[73] This aggravated the crisis while preventing the affected governments from spending on antipoverty social services and income supports. The IMF later recognized this mistake and reversed its policy.

There is some evidence that women were the special victims of the Asian crisis. Women in these countries, as elsewhere, continue to confront social barriers that crowd them into some industries and occupations, foreclose entry into others, and generally push them onto the margins of economic life. Women are the last hired, the first fired, and the least likely to qualify for benefits provided by their employers or by their governments. Country papers circulated at the January 2000 consultation of the Bangkok-based Committee for Asian Women found that in Hong Kong, the female unemployment rate was as high as 25.8 percent and that women made up a high proportion of irregular workers; that during the crisis in South Korea many married women were made redundant or asked to resign from their jobs; that two thousand Malaysian women were laid off when a world market factory in Penang closed its operations in January 2000; and that even before the crisis, Indonesian women experienced higher rates of unemployment as well as various forms of employment discrimination.[74]

The Republic of Korea was the most industrialized of the affected countries. Prior to the crisis, labor markets were tight, with unemployment at a low 2 percent in 1995 and 1996. But between April 1997 and April 1998, overall employment shrank by 5.1 percent. Women workers suffered the worst of the crisis-induced job losses; employment fell 3.8 percent for men but fully 7.1 percent for women. As jobs became harder to find, both men

and women fell out of the labor force, but again, the effect was more pronounced for women. Between spring 1997 and 1998, the participation rate for men in the labor force fell by 0.5 percent, while for women the decline was 2.8 percent.[75]

Younger workers suffered the greatest share of job losses, and younger women suffered more than younger men. Employment rates in the 15-to-19-year-old age bracket fell 8.7 percent for men, but 20.2 percent for women. Unexpectedly, job losses for the 20-to-29-year-old age group were roughly equal: 13.3 percent for men and 13.7 percent for women. Older women also bore a disproportionate share of the job losses. Men between 50 and 59 saw employment rates fall 5.5 percent; for women the same age, employment shrank by 6.6 percent. Employment of men sixty years and older fell negligibly by 0.8 percent, but employment of older women declined 7.5 percent.[76]

In Thailand, 54,000 workers were laid off between January 1997 and February 1998. Slightly more than half were women. But these figures account for only the minority of the work force covered by employer-provided severance benefits and greatly understate the number of layoffs that actually occurred. According to one survey, 60 percent of the workers who lost jobs in Thailand were women over thirty years of age, one quarter of whom had been textile and garment workers.[77]

In Indonesia, during 1998, the garment and textile sector, a major employer of women, was responsible for retrenching 240,000 from paying jobs. Before the crisis, just over 49 percent of Indonesian women were working. By August 1998, this number had increased to more than 56 percent. But this increase was entirely the result of women working as unpaid labor in family-run enterprises. The fraction of women surveyed working at paid employment increased by a statistically insignificant 1 percent, from 36 percent to 37 percent. Meanwhile, job-creation programs by the government, which focused on infrastructure development, benefited men, because women make up only a small fraction of the construction and forestry work forces.[78]

The regional crises briefly described above became the target of criticism from various quarters. Well-known economists such as Joseph Stiglitz and Jeffrey Sachs pointed to misguided policies imposed by the World Bank, the IMF, and the U.S. Treasury, blaming them in particular for exacerbating the "Asian flu" that resulted in job loss and impoverishment. Women trade unionists and feminist economists did the same, while also stressing the class and gender inequalities and the North-South asymmetries that underpin these policy prescriptions.

*   *   *

Conclusions

In this chapter I have tried to show that women have been incorporated into the global economy as a source of relatively cheap labor, and that the social-gender effects of economic globalization have been mixed. The simultaneous emergence and expansion of formal and informal employment among women should be understood in terms of the cyclical processes and secular trends in capitalist development and expansion, and the necessary unevenness of those processes. At a meso level of analysis, we can understand trends in female employment and unemployment in terms of labor-market stratification, various management strategies to extract surplus-value or increase profitability, and (during the 1980s and 1990s) the depressed status of unions. At the macro level of analysis, the capitalist world-economy is maintained by *gendered* labor, with definitions of skill, allocation of resources, occupational distribution, and modes of remuneration shaped by asymmetrical gender relations. Moreover, gender ideologies define the roles and rights of men and women and the relative value of their labor. But the effects of this incorporation have not been uniformly negative, for there have been unintended consequences of women's economic participation.

In separate writings, Susan Tiano and Seung-Kyung Kim provide detailed accounts of how women workers in the Mexican maquilas and in a South Korean free export zone, respectively, accommodate and resist the dominating forces of global capitalism and patriarchy. Others, such as Helen Safa, have shown that the entry of women into the labor force in such large numbers has important implications for changes in gender relations and ideologies within the household and the larger society, and for women's gender consciousness and activism.[79] The emergence of working-class consciousness and the labor movement during the nineteenth and early twentieth centuries is paralleled by the emergence of gender consciousness and the women's movement in the late twentieth century and into the new century.

*   *   *

NOTES

1. In this book, I use the term *professionalization* in two ways: in this chapter to refer to the entry of middle-class women into the professions and in the next chapter to refer to a choice made by movement organizations.
2. See Boserup 1970.
3. Mies 1986.
4. See Pampel and Tanaka 1986 for a discussion of the "feminization U" and test of the hypothesis regarding the curvilinear relationship between economic development and female labor force participation.
5. Elson and Pearson 1981; Nash and Fernandez-Kelly 1983; Lim 1985.
6. Pearson 1992: 231.
7. Joekes/INSTRAW 1987: 81.
8. UN 1999.
9. Chandler 2001.
10. Gallin 2000: 19.
11. Moghadam 1998b
12. Nathan 2000.
13. Duff-Brown 2001.
14. ICFTU, "The New Economy Is Dominated by Women in Precarious Employment," 5/11/2001.

15. See Stalker 2000.
16. See Zachary 2001. On domestic workers, see G. Chang (2000) and K. Chang and L. H. M. Ling (2000).
17. Chang 2000; Stalker 2000: 72; Chang and Ling 2000.
18. Kofman 2000.
19. On patterns of labor migration see Serageldin, Socknat, and Birks 1983; on return migration and unemployment see Shaban, Assaad, and al-Qudsi 1995.
20. OECD 1994: 11–14.
21. UN 1991: 190.
22. UN 2000.
23. Data from EuroStat 2001. See also UNDP 2002b, table 18.
24. See, e.g., UNDP 1995; Charmes 1999.
25. UN 1999; Charmes 1999; CAWTAR 2001.
26. Beneria and Roldan 1987; Cinar 1994.
27. Boris and Prugl 1996.
28. For example, in a controversial study that disputes notions of gender discrimination and emphasizes women's own preferences, Hakim (1998) provides a detailed analysis of part-time work and homework in Britain, among other types of employment. She argues that women's lower wages and concentration in female-dominated occupations shows their "preference" for family and for part-time work.
29. UNDP 1995: 36.
30. World Bank 1995: 45.
31. Pearson and Mitter 1993: 50.
32. Hopkins and Wallerstein 1996: 4.
33. UN 1999; Moghadam 1995; CAWTAR 2001.
34. Sklair 2002.
35. On the other hand, the proletarianization of women was an integral part of early industrialization in England, France, and parts of the United States (e.g., the textile mills of Lowell, Massachusetts).
36. On women and unionization, see Hastings and Coleman 1992; Cobble 1993; Martens and Mitter 1994; Chhachhi and Pittin 1996; Needleman 1998; Dannecker 2000.

37. See, for example, "The ILO's on-line conference on organized labor in the 21st century," www.ilo.org/public/english/bureau/inst/papers/2000/dp125, accessed 30 May 2001.
38. ICFTU 2002.
39. Ibid.
40. The union contract had been won at the Camisas Modernas Phillips-Van Heusen plant in 1996. Early in 1999 Phillips-Van Heusen closed the factory.
41. See www.jca.ax.apc.org/ajwrc.
42. ICFTU 2000.
43. Gabriel and Macdonald (1994) described its role in new forms of cooperation among women from Mexico, the United States, and Canada who were critical of NAFTA.
44. Franklin 2001; "STITCH-ing across Borders," *Off Our Backs*, March 2001.
45. Gallin 2000: 17.
46. Briskin 1993.
47. The Danish Women Workers Union was formed in the early 1900s because the General Workers' Union refused to admit women workers. See Gallin 2000: 17.
48. Eaton 1992; Hastings and Coleman 1992.
49. AFL-CIO Fact Sheet: "Facts about Working Women," http://aflcio.org/women/wwfacts.htm, accessed 15 April 2002.
50. Spillane 2001: 6.
51. Franzway 1994.
52. Briskin 1998a.
53. Briskin 1998b: 24.
54. Briskin 1998a: 7.
55. Warskett 2001: 4.
56. See Hastings and Coleman 1992; Klausen 1997.
57. ICFTU, "After Beijing: Progress Sketchy," 15 June 2000, www.icftu.org, accessed 10 April 2002.
58. Gallin 2000: 19.
59. UNDP 1999.
60. Blustein 2002; Samuelson 2002; Faiola 2002.
61. Oxfam 2000; Lustig 1999.
62. Goering 2000.
63. Ibid.

64. ILO 1999b.
65. Mikhalev 1999; UNDP 2002b.
66. ILO 1999b; Moghadam 2001a.
67. Layachi 2001.
68. Ibid., 11.
69. Ibid., 18.
70. Al-Feddy 2000.
71. Layachi 2001: 25.
72. "Working without a Net: Women and the Asian Financial Crisis," *Gender Matters Quarterly*, January 2000, p. 6.
73. Stiglitz 2000: 58. See also Sachs 1998.
74. "The Situation of Women Workers in Asia," excerpts from *Asian Women Workers Newsletter* [The Committee for Asian Women, Bangkok]. The article reported on country papers circulated in CAW's regional consultation, held in Bangkok 23–26 January 2000.
75. "Working without a Net," p. 2.
76. Ibid.
77. Ibid.
78. Ibid., 4, 6.
79. Tiano 1994; Kim 1997; Safa 1996.

REFERENCES

Beneria, Lourdes, and Martha Roldan. 1987. *The Crossroads of Class and Gender: Industrial Homework, Subcontracting, and Household Dynamics in Mexico City*. Chicago: University of Chicago Press.

Blustein, Paul. 2002. "IMF, White House Fumble for a Strategy as Argentina Founders." *Washington Post*, 18 January.

Boris, Eileen, and Elisabeth Prugl, eds. 1996. *Homeworkers in Global Perspective*. Totawa, NJ.: Rowman and Littlefield.

Boserup, Ester. 1970. *Women and Economic Development*. New York: St. Martin's.

Briskin, Linda. 1993. "Union Women and Separate Organizing." In Linda Briskin and Patricia McDermott, eds., *Women Challenging Unions: Feminism, Democracy, and Militancy*. Toronto: University of Toronto Press, 1993.

———. 1998a. "Unions and Women's Organizing in Canada and Sweden." Paper presented at the World Congress of Sociology, Montreal (26 July-1 August). Forthcoming in Linda Briskin and Mona Eliasson, eds., *Women's Organizing, Public Policy and Social Change in Canada and Sweden*. Montreal: McGill-Queen's University Press, 1999.

———. 1998b. "Autonomy, Diversity and Integration: Union Women's Separate Organizing in North America and Western Europe in the Context of Restructuring and Globalization." Paper presented at the World Congress of Sociology, Montreal, 26 July–1 August.

CAWTAR. 2001. *Globalization and Gender: Economic Participation of Arab Women*. Tunis: CAWTAR Arab Women's Development Report.

Chandler, Clay. 2001. "A Factory to the World: China's Vast Labor Pool, Low Wages Lure Manufacturers." *Washington Post*, 25 November.

Chang, Grace. 2000. *Disposable Domestics: Immigrant Women Workers in the Global Economy*. Boston: South End Press.

Chang, Kimberly, and L. H. M. Ling. 2000. "Globalization and Its Intimate Other: Filipina Domestic Workers in Hong Kong." In Anne Sisson Runyan and Marianne Marchand, eds., *Gender and Global Restructuring: Sightings, Sites and Resistances*. London: Routledge.

Charmes, Jacques. 1999. "Gender and the Informal Sector." Background Paper for the World's Women 2000: Trends and Statistics. New York: United Nations.

Chhachhi, Amrita, and Renee Pittin, eds. 1996. *Confronting State, Capital, and Patriarchy: Women Organizing in the Process of Industrialization*. New York: St. Martin's.

Cinar, Mine. 1994. "Unskilled Urban Migrant Women and Disguised Employment: Homeworking Women in Istanbul, Turkey." *World Development* 22, no. 3: 369–80.

Cobble, Dorothy Sue. 1993. *Women and Unions: Forging a Partnership*. Ithaca, N.Y.: ILR Press.

Dannecker, Petra. 2000. "Collective Action, Organization Building, and Leadership: Women Workers in the Garment Sector in Bangladesh." *Gender & Development* 8, no. 3: 31–39.

Duff-Brown, Beth. 2001. "Services Boom in India, but Some See Sweatshops." *Chicago Tribune*, 9 July.

Eaton, Susan C. 1992. "Women Workers, Unions and Industrial Sectors in North America." Geneva: International Labor Office, IDP Women Working Paper 1 (October).

Elson, Diane, and Ruth Pearson. 1981. "Nimble Fingers Make Cheap Workers: An Analysis of Women's Employment in Third World Export Manufacturing." *Feminist Review* (Spring): 87–107.

Faiola, Anthony. 2002. "Argentina Signals Shift away from U.S." *Washington Post*, 16 January.

Franklin, Stephen. 2001. "Organizing Workers against Fear." *Chicago Tribune*, 27 March.

Franzway, Suzanne. 1994. "Women Working in Australian Unions." Paper prepared for the International Sociological Association, RC44, Bielefeld, Germany, 18–23 July.

Gabriel, Christina, and Laura Macdonald. 1994. "NAFTA, Women and Organising in Canada and Mexico: Forging a 'Feminist Internationality.'" *Millennium: Journal of International Studies* 23, no. 3: 535–62.

Gallin, Dan. 2000. "Trade Unions and NGOs: A Necessary Partnership for Social Development." Civil Society and Social Movements Programme, Paper No. 1 (June). Geneva: UNRISD.

Goering, Laurie. 2000. "Mexican Anomaly: Boom Sees More Poor." *Chicago Tribune*, 7 September.

Hakim, Catherine. 1998. *Social Change and Innovation in the Labor Market: Evidence from the Census SARs on Occupational Segregation and Labor Mobility, Part-time Work and Student Jobs, Homework and Self-Employment.* New York: Oxford University Press.

Hastings, Sue, and Martha Coleman. 1992. "Women Workers and Unions in Europe: An Analysis by Industrial Sector." IDP Working Paper 4. Geneva: International Labor Office.

Hopkins, Terence K., and Immanuel Wallerstein. 1996. "The World System: Is There a Crisis?" In Wallerstein et al., eds., *The Age of Transition: Trajectory of the World-System 1945–2025.* London: Zed.

ICFTU. 2000. "International Survey of Violation of Trade Union Rights, 2001 www.icftu.org, accessed 10 April 2002.

———. "3000 Trade Unionists March in Protest at Poverty and Violence against Women in Durban on April 5." www.icftu.org, accessed 15 April 2002.

ILO. 1999. *Key Indicators of the Labor Market* CD-ROM. Geneva: ILO.

Joekes, Susan, and INSTRAW. 1987. *Women in the Global Economy: An INSTRAW Study.* New York: Oxford University Press.

Kim, Seung-Kyung. 1997. *Class Struggle or Family Struggle? The Lives of Women Factory Workers in South Korea.* Cambridge, UK: Cambridge University Press.

Klausen, Jytte. 1997. "The Declining Significance of Male Workers: Trade Unions' Responses to Changing Labor Markets." In Peter Lange et al., eds., *Crisis and Conflict in Contemporary Capitalism.* Cambridge: Cambridge University Press.

Kofman, Eleonore. 2000. "Beyond a Reductionist Analysis of Female Migrants in Global European Cities: The Unskilled, Deskilled, and Professional." In Anne Sisson Runyan and Marianne Marchand, eds., *Gender and Global Restructuring: Sightings, Sites and Resistances.* London: Routledge.

Layachi, Azzedine. 2001. "Reform and the Politics of Inclusion in the Maghrib." *Journal of North African Studies* 53 (Autumn): 15–47.

Lim, Linda. 1985. *Women Workers in Multinational Enterprises in Developing Countries.* Geneva: ILO.

Lustig, Nora. 1999. "Containing the Human Impact of Economic Crisis." *WIDER Angle* 1, no. 99: 5–6.

Martens, Margaret Hosmer, and Swasti Mitter, eds. 1994. *Women in Trade Unions: Organizing the Unorganised*. Geneva: ILO.

Mies, Maria. 1986. *Patriarchy and Accumulation on a World Scale*. London: Zed Books.

Moghadam, Valentine M., ed. 1995. "Gender Aspects of Employment and Unemployment in a Global Perspective." In Mihaly Simai, ed., *Global Employment: An Investigation into the Future of Work*. London: Zed Books; Tokyo: United Nations University Press.

———. 1998. "The UN Decade for Women and Beyond." In Nellie Stromquist, ed., *Women in the Third World: An Encyclopedia of Contemporary Issues*. New York: Garland Publishing.

———. 2001. "Globalization and Women's Unemployment in the Arab Region." Background Paper prepared for the CAWTAR Report *Globalization and Gender: Economic Participation of Arab Women*.

Nash, June, and Maria Fernandez-Kelly, eds. 1983. *Women, Men, and the International Division of Labor*. Albany, N.Y.: SUNY Press.

Nathan, Debbie. 2000. "Sweating Out the Words." *The Nation*, 21 February: 27–30.

Needleman, Ruth. 1998. "Women Workers: Strategies for Inclusion and Rebuilding Unionism." In Gregory Mantsios, ed., *A New Labor Movement for the New Century*. New York: Garland.

OECD. 1994. *Employment Observatory 1994*. Paris: OECD.

Oxfam. 2000. "Poverty at Work Has a Human Face." *Links* (March): 2.

Pampel, Fred C., and Kazuko Tanaka. 1996. "Economic Development and Female Labor Force Participation: A Reconsideration." *Social Forces* 64, no. 3 (March): 599–620.

Pearson, Ruth. 1992. "Gender Issues in Industrialization." In Tom Hewitt, Hazel Johnson, and David Wield, eds., *Industrialization and Development*. Oxford: Oxford University Press.

Pearson, Ruth, and Swasti Mitter. 1993. "Employment and Working Conditions of Low-skilled Information-processing Workers in Less-developed Countries." *International Labor Review* 132, no. 1: 49–64.

Sachs, Jeffrey. 1998. "The IMF and the Asian Flu." *American Prospect* (March–April): 16–21.

Safa, Helen. 1996. "Gender Inequality and Women's Wage Labor: A Theoretical and Empirical Analysis." In V. M. Moghadam, ed., *Patriarchy and Development*. Oxford: Clarendon Press.

Samuelson, Robert J. 2002. "Do Cry for Argentina." *Washington Post*, 16 January.

Serageldin, Ismail, James A. Socknat, and John S. Birks. 1983. "Human Resources in the Arab World: The Impact of Migration." In I. Ibrahim, ed., *Arab Resources: The Transformation of a Society*. London: Croom Helm; Washington, D.C.: Center for Contemporary Arab Studies.

Shaban, Radwan A., Ragui Assaad, and Sulayman S. Al-Qudsi. 1995. "The Challenge of Unemployment in the Arab Region." *International Labor Review* 134, no. 1: 65–81.

Sklair, Leslie. 2002. *Globalization: Capitalism and Its Alternatives*. 3rd ed. Oxford: Oxford University Press.

Spillane, Margaret. 2001. "The V-Word is Heard." *The Nation*, 5 March: 6.

Stalker, Peter. 2000. *Workers without Frontiers: The Impact of Globalization on International Migration*. Boulder and Geneva: Lynne Rienner Publishers and the ILO.

Stiglitz, Joseph. 2000. "The Insider: What I Learned at the World Economic Crisis." *New Republic*, 17 and 24 April: 56–60.

Tiano, Susan. 1994. *Patriarchy on the Line: Labor, Gender, and Ideology in the Mexican Maquila Industry*. Philadelphia, Pa.: Temple University Press.

UN. 1991. *World Economic Survey 1991*. New York: UN/DIESA.

———. 1996. *The Beijing Declaration and Platform for Action*. New York: UN.

———. 1999. *World Survey on the Role of Women in Development: Globalization, Women, and Work*. New York: UN.

———. 2000. *The World's Women 2000: Trends and Statistics.* New York: UN.

UNDP. 1995. *The Human Development Report 1995.* New York: Oxford University Press.

———. 1999. *Human Development Report 1999* [on globalization]. New York: Oxford University Press.

———. 2002. *Human Development Report 2002* [on democracy]. New York: Oxford University Press.

Warskett, Rosemary. 2001. "Feminism's Challenge to Unions in the North: Possibilities and Contradictions." *Socialist Register 2001: Working Classes, Global Realities.* New York: Monthly Review Press.

World Bank. 1995. *World Development Report 1995: Workers in an Integrating World.* New York: Oxford University Press.

Zachary, G. Pascal. 2001. "Shortage of Nurses Hits Hardest Where They Are Needed the Most." *Wall Street Journal,* 24 January.

10 GLOBALIZATION AND GLOBALIZING ISSUES

Of the recent changes in international relations, none has been as complex as globalization, a multifaceted phenomenon involving economic, political, social, and cultural factors. Arising out of the interconnectedness of globalization, new issues have become part of the global agenda—issues of population, disease, the environment, human rights. Together these represent the new security issues for the twenty-first century.

Among the issues that have been affected by globalization is health. William Easterly, former World Bank economist and critic, examines two disturbing paradoxes in his chapter from The White Man's Burden. *Foreign aid has done much to improve health around the world, yet policy makers have been glacially slow to respond to AIDS. Cheaper alternatives aimed at preventing AIDS could actually save lives, yet policy makers have focused on expensive AIDS treatment. Council on Foreign Relations Senior Fellow Laurie Garrett is also concerned with the capacity of the global community to respond to global health threats, namely H5N1 avian flu, or "bird flu."*

In many of these globalizing issues, the rights of the individual are pitted against the rights of the global community. Does a couple have the right of unlimited procreation? Do the rights of the individual take precedence over the right of the community in the use of land and natural resources? In trying to resolve some of these dilemmas, some people have argued in favor of enforcement of a universal definition of human rights. These are human rights applicable across all peoples and all cultures. Other writers think that the notion of a universality of human rights is but an illusion. Cambridge University's Amartya Sen suggests that there is a great diversity of human rights experiences among both Western and non-Western cultures. The application of Western human rights standards across cultures may be problematic. Harvard University's Michael Ignatieff analyzes the same issue, suggesting that Western activist defenders of human rights may be compromising too much in their response to cultural relativists. Adopting notions of individual human rights does not mean adopting Western lifestyles. These questions of the entitlements of the individual versus the entitlements of the community address core issues of culture, legality, and morality.

WILLIAM EASTERLY

THE HEALERS: TRIUMPH AND TRAGEDY

Oh tear-filled figure who, like a sky held back grows heavy above the landscape of her sorrow. . . .
—*Rainer Maria Rilke, "O Lacrimosa," Translated by Stephen Mitchell, 1995*

In 1989, a team of field researchers in southern Uganda, near the Tanzanian border, stumbled on an older man living by himself in a thatched hut. The man himself was incoherent, but neighbors told his story: his wife and eight children had all died of AIDS. Asked about the man's future, villagers said, "He will not marry again."

Fourteen years later, I am sitting in a health clinic in Soweto, South Africa, talking to a sad young woman named Constance. Constance tells me she is HIV-positive and is too sick to work to support her three children. Even when she is feeling better, she cannot find a job. The father of her children is also unemployed, and she rarely sees him. Constance didn't tell her mother that she is HIV-positive, for fear that her mother and stepfather would eject her and her children from the household. She says her stepfather complains bitterly about her not working and not contributing to the maintenance of her children. Left unspoken between us is Constance's fate, and the fate of her three children when she succumbs to AIDS.

Southern Uganda was one of the places where AIDS first appeared in the early 1980s, but in the years since then, the epidemic has spread to most of southern and eastern Africa. South Africa is the most recent casualty of its spread. Thirty percent of pregnant women in their twen-

From *The White Man's Burden: Why the West's Efforts to Aid the Rest Have Done So Much Ill and So Little Good* (New York: Penguin Press, 2006), 238–63.

ties test HIV-positive in South African antenatal clinics.

A third of the adult population is now HIV-positive in Botswana, Lesotho, Swaziland, and Zimbabwe. In other eastern and southern African countries, between 10 and 25 percent of the adult population is HIV-positive. AIDS is spreading also to African countries outside of the "AIDS corridor," which now runs from Ethiopia to South Africa. In Africa as a whole, there are 29 million HIV-positive people. Tragedies like that of the man in southern Uganda and Constance have happened many times over the past decades, and will happen many more times in the future. More than 2 million people in Africa died from AIDS in 2002. Their places in the epidemic were taken by the 3.5 million Africans newly infected in 2002.

AIDS gets attention. Celebrities and statesmen—ranging from Bill Clinton and Nelson Mandela to Bono and Ashley Judd—call for action. The anti-globalization activists also focus on AIDS. Oxfam calls for access to life-saving drugs for AIDS patients in Africa. American activists at international AIDS conferences (such as American health secretary Tommy Thompson at a conference in Barcelona in 2002) shout down anyone not responding with sufficient alacrity, *pour encourager les autres.*

The foreign aid doyens have also woken up to the problem. The actors include the UN agency UNAIDS, the World Bank's multicountry program to fight AIDS in Africa, the World Health Organization's Commission on Macroeconomics and Health, and the Global Fund to Fight AIDS, TB, and Malaria.

In his 2003 State of the Union Address, President George W. Bush announced the release of fifteen billion dollars in foreign aid to fight AIDS. The initiative was passed by Congress, and Bush signed it into law on May 27, 2003.

It is great that public figures are publicizing the needs of AIDS victims. Many people feel compassion in the face of the death sentence of millions of HIV-positive people in Africa, and in the face of fear that the epidemic will keep spreading.

Yet behind this recent Western attention to AIDS is a tale of two decades of neglect, prevarication, incompetence, and passivity by all those same political actors and aid agencies. By the time researchers found the incoherent victim in southern Uganda in 1989, and even years before that, the West had all the information it needed to predict (and virtually every expert did predict) that AIDS would kill tens of millions of people worldwide, above all in Africa, if nothing was done.

Paradox of Evil and the White Man's Burden

Scholars of religion talk about the paradox of evil, which says you cannot have all three of the following conditions hold: (1) a benevolent God; (2) an all-knowing and all-powerful God; and (3) evil things happening to good people. If you have (1) and (2), then why would God (3) let bad things happen to good people?

Similarly, in the White Man's Burden, you cannot have all the following hold: (1) the White Man's Burden is acting in the interests of the poor in the Rest; (2) the White Man's Burden is effective at resolving poor people's problems; and (3) lots of bad things, whose prevention was affordable, are happening to poor people. If (3) happens, then either (1) or (2) must not hold. Religion is a matter of faith in an invisible Supreme Being, so the contradictions inherent in the Paradox of Evil are more easily tolerated by true believers. Foreign aid is not a faith-based area, however. It is a visible policy with visible dollars meant to help visible people.

The breakdown of the aid system on AIDS is a good test case of the paradox of evil in foreign aid. It reflects how out of touch were the Planners at the top with the tragedy at the bottom, another sign of the weak power of the intended beneficiaries. It shows how ineffective Planners are at making foreign aid work. It is hard to imagine anything more in the interest of the poor than preventing the spread of a fatal disease. Today, the Western aid community has finally woken up to AIDS. Now that community has moved from inaction to ineffective action. Aid for AIDS still appears mismatched to the choices of the poor.

Health Triumphs

The failure on AIDS is all the more striking when we consider that health is he area where foreign aid has enjoyed its most conspicuous successes.[1] Maybe the part of the White Man's Burden that addresses disease offers a more hopeful picture than the malfunctioning bureaucracy in other areas. The healers are working on an issue where the needs and wants of the poor were more obvious—they don't want to die—and so feedback is less critical. The outcomes are more observable, as deaths tend to get noticed by others.

The successes may tell us about the ability of aid agencies to be effective when they have narrow, monitorable objectives that coincide with the poor's needs and with political support in the rich countries for an uncontroversial objective like saving lives. As the previous chapters argue, areas with visible individual outcomes are more likely to put Searchers in charge—in contrast to the power of Planners in areas where nobody can be held individually accountable, such as economic growth. I also hypothesize that Searchers are more likely to succeed at their narrow goals than the Planners are to succeed at their more general goals.

A vaccination campaign in southern Africa virtually eliminated measles as a killer of children.

Routine childhood immunization combined with measles vaccination in seven southern African nations starting in 1996 virtually eliminated measles in those countries by 2000. A national campaign in Egypt to make parents aware of the use of oral rehydration therapy from 1982 to 1989 cut childhood deaths from diarrhea by 82 percent over that period. A regional program to eliminate polio in Latin America after 1985 has eliminated it as a public health threat in the Americas. The leading preventable cause of blindness, trachoma, has been cut by 90 percent in children under age ten in Morocco since 1997, thanks to a determined effort to promote surgery, antibiotics, face washing, and environmental cleanliness. Sri Lanka's commitment to preventing maternal deaths during childbirth has cut the rate of maternal mortality from 486 to 24 deaths per 100,000 births over the last four decades. A program to control tuberculosis in China cut the number of cases by 40 percent between 1990 and 2000. Donors collabourated on a program to wipe out river blindness in West Africa starting in 1974, virtually halting the transmission of the disease. Eighteen million children in the twenty-country area of the program have been kept safe from river blindness since the program began. An international effort eradicated smallpox worldwide. Another partnership among aid donors contributed to the near eradication of guinea worm in twenty African and Asian countries where it was endemic. Beginning in 1991, a program of surveillance, house spraying, and environmental vector control halted transmission of Chagas' disease in Uruguay, Chile, and large parts of Paraguay and Brazil. Worldwide, as we see in chapter 3, infant mortality in poor countries has fallen and life expectancy has increased.

Many of these programs benefited from donor funding and technical advice. In Egypt's fight against childhood diarrhea, for example, it was a grant from USAID and technical advice from the World Health Organization (WHO). In China's campaign against tuberculosis, it was a World Bank loan and WHO advice. In Morocco,

the drug company Pfizer donated antibiotics to fight trachoma. Although the aid agencies have not calculated the aid impact in a scientifically rigorous way, the broad facts support the belief that aid was effective in many of the above health interventions. Alas, instead of expanding success in the many health areas where it had triumphed, the international health community was going to get bogged down in its equivalent of Vietnam: AIDS.

The Coming Storm

The health successes make the failure on AIDS stand out even more. As with any contagious disease, early action is far more effective than later action. A bucket of water is enough to put out a campfire; it takes more to put out a forest fire.

On the plus side, it was the West that solved the scientific problem of what caused AIDS, making prevention efforts possible. Unfortunately, this knowledge did not translate into effective prevention in Africa.

The World Bank advertises that it is now the "world's single largest funder of AIDS programs" (the same claim is made by the World Health Organization and by the U.S. Agency for International Development). The World Bank doesn't mention that it did a total of one project dedicated to AIDS before 1993 (an eight-million-dollar loan to Mobutu in Zaire in 1988). The World Bank today endorses the WHO calculation that Africa needs one billion dollars a year in AIDS-prevention spending. Yet over the entire period 1988–99, the World Bank spent fifteen million dollars a year on all AIDS projects in Africa. In 1992, a World Bank study noted that the Bank "has done little to initiate prevention in countries in which the risk of spread is high."

Why did the West not act more vigorously early on in the AIDS crisis? Was it because people didn't know how bad the crisis would become, because action was ineffective, or simply because it took millions of deaths to make it a headline issue worth responding to?

The defense that the West didn't know is not credible. As long ago as 1986, AIDS in Africa was attracting international attention. On October 27, 1986, an article in the *Times* of London said: "A catastrophic epidemic of AIDS is sweeping across Africa. . . . the disease has already infected several millions of Africans, posing colossal health problems to more than 20 countries. . . . 'Aids has become a major health threat to all Africans and prevention and control of infection . . . must become an immediate public health priority for all African countries,' says report published in a leading American scientific journal."

Signs of the coming epidemic appeared even earlier. A sample of prostitutes in Butare, Rwanda, in 1983 found that 75 percent were infected. A later study by the group that reported this statistic dated the general awareness that Central Africa was at risk for the spread of AIDS back to 1983 as well.[2]

The World Bank did its first AIDS strategy report in 1988. The report said the crisis was urgent. It presciently detected "an environment highly conducive to the spread of HIV" in many African countries. It noted that the epidemic was far from reaching its full potential and that "the AIDS epidemic in Africa is an emergency situation and appropriate action must be undertaken now."[3] Yet the effort at the time was underwhelming: the World Bank made a grant of one million dollars to the World Health Organization (WHO) in the 1988/1989 fiscal year to fight AIDS.

A 1992 World Bank retrospective on the 1988 strategy damns it with faint praise: "In view of the 1988 decision to deal with AIDS using existing resource levels and the small PHN [Population, Health, and Nutrition] staff that has had to handle a steadily increasing work program, we conclude that the agenda in the 1988 Strategy Paper has been reasonably well implemented."[4]

The World Bank's 1993 World Development Report, whose theme was health, notes that "At present, most national AIDS programs are inadequate, despite international attention and the significant effort by WHO to help design and implement plans for controlling AIDS." Translation: it's the WHO's fault.

An article in 1991 in the World Bank/IMF quarterly magazine predicted that thirty million people would be infected worldwide by the year 2000 if nothing was done.[5] The actual figure would turn out to be forty million, but the point is: more than a decade ago many knew that a catastrophic epidemic was under way.

The 1992 World Bank study, while noting the lack of progress, did sound the obligatory refrain that progress was under way, not least because "countries have been informed of the Bank's increasing attention to AIDS."

The World Bank itself was directing the tiny flows of AIDS financing to "currently affected countries," while "little has been done by the Bank to prevent AIDS in less affected countries with a high potential for spread." The 1992 report closed with the curious admonition that "AIDS should not be allowed to dominate the Bank's agenda on population, health, and nutrition issues in Africa." Raising this issue early in the epidemic is strange, when an ounce of prevention *is* worth a pound of cure. Now AIDS work has crowded out treatment of other equally lethal threats to Africans because its spread was not averted. The best way to have kept AIDS from "dominating the Bank's agenda" was to have prevented its spread.

Perhaps we can better understand the aid community's difficulties on prevention if we realize that prevention was not very visible to the rich-country public. Although insiders knew that a horrific AIDS crisis was brewing in Africa in the late 1980s and early 1990s, this attracted little attention from Western media or politicians. Part of the problem was probably that aid agencies didn't know what to do to address the crisis, but the above examples show little evidence that they were searching for answers. Only *after* a truly massive number of people were infected with HIV did AIDS gain the sufficient level of visibility for action.

Not Following Your Own Advice

By 1998, the World Bank had done ten stand-alone AIDS projects. Researcher Julia Dayton was hired by the Bank to analyze its programs.[6]

Dayton found that only half of the fifty-one World Bank projects with AIDS components promoted condom use or financed condom purchases. To understand this omission, consider another Dayton finding: almost none of the fifty-one projects did any economic analysis of what an effective AIDS interventions was.

Dayton also found that World Bank country teams were missing in action on AIDS. AIDS was already reaching epidemic levels in Côte d'Ivoire, Haiti, Kenya, and Zambia in the 1990s. The World Bank's Country Assistance Strategy Documents in the 1990s for those countries did not describe HIV prevalence or transmission, recommend STD. or HIV/AIDS-prevention or care, or in fact analyze HIV/AIDS at all. Ironically for aid agencies that often are trying to do everything, "everything" sometimes leaves out some high priorities.

Day of Judgment

Shortly after Dayton's report was issued, the World Bank produced another AIDS report. The World Bank Africa vice-president wrote in the introduction to this 2000 report that "AIDS is completely preventable." He gave a prediction that "those who look back on this era will judge our institution in large measure by whether we recognized this wildfire that is raging across Africa for the development threat that it is, and did our utmost to put it out. They will be right to do so."[7] He could have spared us the use of the future tense.

The World Bank did produce a Monitoring and Evaluation Operations Manual, prepared jointly by UNAIDS and the World Bank.[8] The manual sensibly warns that "the more complex an M&E system, the more likely it is to fail." It then spends fifty-two pages laying out its ex-tremely complex M&E system. This includes the ten-step M&E program (step 3: "NAC [National AIDS Councils] and stakeholders engage in an intensive participatory process to build ownership and buy-in, particularly for the overall M&E system and programme monitoring"). There is also the list of thirty-four indicators (none of which involves monitoring "core transmitters"), the nineteen-point terms of reference for the M&E consultant to the NAC, and the "summary terms of reference for specialized programme activity monitoring entity." The accepted scientific standard for any program evaluation, the randomized controlled trial, did not make it into the manual.

The Kitty Genovese Effect

Winston Moseley killed Kitty Genovese, a twenty-eight-year-old bar manager, in Queens, New York, in 1964. Her murder is the first news story I remember from my childhood. As Moseley first stabbed Kitty, neighbors heard her screams but didn't call the police. Moseley drove away and then came back and stabbed her some more, till she died. Police later identified thirty-eight neighbors who saw or heard part of the attack. The eyewitnesses' failure to call police became a symbol of the callousness of urban America. I think my mother showed me the newspaper to illustrate the wickedness of big-city folks.

The last thing I want to do is defend such bad Samaritans, but economists point out that the callousness of each individual was not as great as their group behavior suggests. All the neighbors agreed that saving Kitty's life would have been worthwhile. Outraged commentators pointed out that only one out of those thirty-eight people had to call the police, but that was exactly the problem. Calling the police would have had some cost to the individual, who may later have had to testify and may have feared retribution from the associates of the killer. Each of the thirty-eight people might have been willing to bear this cost to save Kitty's life, but preferred that someone else make the call. With so many witnesses to the scene, each person calculated a high probability that someone else *would* make the call and save Kitty. Therefore, each person did nothing. If there had been only one witness, and if that person had known he was the only witness, he would have been more likely to call the police.

The Kitty Genovese effect is another plausible example of the problem of collective responsibility I mention in chapter 5, which leads to bureaucratic inaction. Each development agency is one among many responsible for solving crises in the poor countries. Each agency may altruistically care about the poor. Suppose that action by one agency will be enough to solve a problem, and all agencies will share in the glory of the triumph; it is difficult to tell which agency's effort made the difference. If effort is costly and diverts resources away from other organizational goals, each agency will prefer that some other agency make the effort. The more agencies that could act, the less likely that action will occur.

The Genovese effect can also operate within aid bureaucracies. Each department might wish that results happen, but would prefer that some other department achieve them, with glory for all. Departments then get into the game of shifting responsibility for difficult tasks onto other departments, which drives the leaders of even the most results-oriented agency insane.

Action does become more likely as the status quo deteriorates due to inaction. The crisis could eventually become big enough to outweigh the option of waiting for someone else to act. In the Kitty Genovese example, a neighbor did eventually call the police. Kitty was dead by then.

A story like this could help account for the long period of inaction on the AIDS crisis, until the crisis was so severe that finally aid agencies acted.

Orphans in the Storm

Mary Banda, about sixty-five, lives in Lusaka, Zambia.[9] Five of her eight children have died from AIDS. In Zambia, adult children usually care for their aged parents. AIDS reversed the equation for Mary Banda. Instead of her children caring for her, she is caring for eight orphaned grandchildren, ranging in age from six to twenty.

Mbuya (Grandmother) Banda doesn't get much help from her three surviving children. One of her children is in South Africa, and Mbuya hasn't heard from her. Her youngest daughter is unmarried and unemployed. Her remaining daughter is married, but does not work; her husband can only sporadically find work. She comes around with a bag of mealie meal (cornmeal) every now and then.

The biggest problem is finding food for the orphans. Mrs. Banda sells groundnuts by the road, and grows a little maize, sweet potato, and greens. It is never quite enough. Only two of the children are in school, where they are sometimes refused entry because they lack fees, shoes, and uniforms.

When her children became sick from AIDS, she tried traditional healers as well as the hospital. Mary Banda believes her children died from witchcraft—a sign of the need to adjust to local conditions with prevention messages. Her four deceased daughters were businesswomen buying secondhand clothes in Lusaka and exchanging them for groundnuts in the villages, and then reselling the groundnuts in Lusaka. She believes villagers jealous of their success bewitched her daughters through their feet. She blames her son's death on witchcraft from jealous-rivals after his work promoted him. She wishes her children had seen a witchdoctor to get preventive medicine to put on their feet.

Discussion of African beliefs in witchcraft is taboo in aid agencies, as nobody wants to reinforce ill-informed stereotypes. Unfortunately, political correctness gets in the way of making policy, as conventional public health approaches may not work if people *do* believe that witchcraft causes illness and turn to traditional healers. Americans and Europeans also believed in witches when they were at similar levels of income as Africa (and many Americans still do today; hence the spiritualism section at the Barnes & Noble bookstore in Greenwich Village—one of the intellectual capitals of the United States—is three times the size of the science section). Moreover, many American evangelicals believe divine intervention can cure illness.

Beliefs in invisible malign forces in Africa are not so surprising when a virus visible only to scientists is killing previously healthy young people. Princeton political scientist and ethnographer Adam Ashforth documented the widespread belief in Soweto, South Africa, that witchcraft causes many symptoms of illness, including symptoms similar to AIDS.[10] AIDS-prevention efforts would do much better to work with traditional healers on fighting HIV transmission than to ignore beliefs in witchcraft because of political sensitivities.

Mrs. Banda speaks for her generation of Mbuyas: "I'm an old woman who's suffering. When I was young, I never thought such cruel things could happen. When I think about it, I pray and cry, but I don't like to cry because it'll upset the children."

At least Mrs. Banda's grandchildren-have her to care for them. A group even more unlucky is Lusaka's growing population of street children. AIDS orphans with no one to care for them are on the street. The manager of a shelter for abandoned kids, Rodgers Mwewa, noticed the increase in orphaned children coming into Lusaka. The traditional extended-family system of caring for children is breaking down because too many of its adult members are dead. "HIV is destroying families and family bonds," says Mwewa.[11]

The street children don't live long: cars frequently hit them, they get into fights, and they resort to petty crime, drugs, or sniffing glue. They are beaten up by the police. Worst of all, the children sell themselves for sex, and thus sooner or later acquire the HIV virus that killed their parents.

Less anecdotal evidence confirms that orphans in Africa face a rough road. The less orphans can rely on family, the worse off they are. Princeton University scholars Anne Case, Chris-

tine Paxson, and Joseph Ableidinger found in a study of orphans in ten African countries that orphans who live with unrelated adults get less schooling than orphans who live with nonparental relatives, who themselves get less schooling than children living with their parents. These effects show up even as discrimination within the household. For example, an orphan living with her aunt and uncle typically gets less schooling than her cousin, the aunt and uncle's child.[12]

Africa's AIDS crisis is leaving a generation of undereducated, undernourished, underparented orphans who will soon be adults. As if Africa's development crisis weren't bad enough for the current generation, the orphans of AIDS complicate development even more.

Treating the Sick

Now that twenty-nine million people in Africa are HIV-positive, compassion would call for treating the sick, right? Yet pity is not always a reliable guide to action. By a tragic irony, compassion is driving the fight against AIDS in Africa in a direction that may cost more lives than it saves. It is political suicide in rich countries to question AIDS treatment. Too bad—what should matter is what helps the poor the most, not what sells politically in rich countries. This political pressure led Planners to fixate on the goal of treatment even when the costs were so prohibitive that it diverted money from cheaper actions that Searchers had found to save many more lives.

The Western aid community is now installing a gold-plated barn door after the horse has been stolen. Foreign aid programs are now starting to finance the "triple-drug cocktail" known as highly active antiretroviral therapy (HAART), which has dramatically lowered AIDS mortality in the West. All of the actors described earlier signed on to financing AIDS treatment. The UN General Assembly Special Session passed a resolution calling for AIDS treatment. This used to be impossible for low-income African AIDS patients, because of high drug prices (ten thousand dollars a year per patient). However, competition from a growing number of generic HIV/AIDS drugs has cut prices, which are now as low as $304 per year per patient.[13] This caused leaders of international aid agencies, such as former WHO director-general GrÖ Harlem Brundtland, to ask, "Does anyone deserve to be sentenced to certain death because she or he cannot access care that costs less than two dollars a day?" The WHO started a "3 by 5" campaign to get three million HIV-positive patients on antiretroviral therapy by the end of 2005.

Saving lives is not so simple. First of all, the focus on drug prices understates the expense and difficulty of treatment. Three hundred and four dollars is just the price of the first-line therapy drugs per year. The population first needs to be tested to see who is HIV-positive. Patients need to have their viral load tested to see if they should start taking drugs and, after taking them, if the drugs are working to decrease the viral load. The drugs are toxic, with potentially severe side effects. Health workers need to adjust the combination of drugs when side effects are too extreme. Patients need counseling and monitoring to make sure they are taking the medicine (if there is less than full adherence to treatment, the virus builds up resistance to the drugs). Patients also need treatment for the opportunistic infections that afflict AIDS sufferers. So treatment is more expensive than just the cost of the drugs. The World Health Organization is working with a figure of $1,500 per year per patient for delivering treatment to prolong the life of an AIDS patient by one year. Even if the WHO can drive down the price of the drugs further, the cost per year would still be $1,200. Other experts use similar figures.[14] But is even this number too high to justify giving a person another year of life?

The advocates for treatment stress the universal human right for HIV-positive patients to have access to life-saving health care, no matter what the cost. This is a great ideal, but a utopian one. There are also other ideals—first of all, prevention of the further spread of AIDS. And what about the universal human right for health care

for other killer diseases, freedom from starvation, and access to clean water? Who chose the human right of universal treatment of AIDS over the other human rights? A non-utopian approach would make the tough choices to spend foreign aid resources in a way that reached the most people with their most urgent needs.

Poor people have many other needs besides AIDS treatment. The total amount of foreign aid for the world's approximately three billion poor people is only about twenty dollars per person per year. Is the money for AIDS treatment going to be "new money" or will it come from these already scarce funds? President Bush's 2005 budget proposal increased funding for the American AIDS program (especially treatment), but cut money for child health and other global health priorities by nearly a hundred million dollars (later reversed after protests).[15]

Bush's cut in other health spending was particularly unfortunate when two and a half times as many Africans die from other preventable diseases as die from AIDS. These diseases include measles and other childhood illnesses, respiratory infections, malaria, tuberculosis, diarrhea, and others. Worldwide, in 2002 there were 15.6 million deaths from these causes, as opposed to 2.8 million deaths from AIDS.[16]

A well-established public health principle is that you should save lives that are cheap to save before you save lives that are more expensive to save. That way you save many more lives using the scarce funds available. Prevention and treatment of these other diseases cost far less than AIDS treatment.

Granting life through prevention of AIDS itself costs far less than AIDS treatment. A years' supply of condoms to prevent HIV infection costs about fourteen dollars. In a 2002 article in *The Lancet*, Andrew Creese from the World Health Organization and co-authors estimated that AIDS-prevention interventions such as condom distribution, blocking mother-to-child transmission, and voluntary counseling and testing could cost as little as one to twenty dollars per year of life saved, and twenty to four hundred dollars per

HIV infection averted (even though this study may overstate the confidence that these things always work). Other studies come up with similar estimates.[17]

Then there are other diseases for which Searchers have found cheap interventions (although we have seen that the Planners' domination of aid often interferes with making these things work). The medicines that cure TB cost about ten dollars per case of the illness. A package of interventions designed to prevent maternal and infant deaths costs less than three dollars per person per year. Worldwide, three million children die a year because they are not fully vaccinated, even though vaccines cost only pennies per dose. One in four people worldwide suffers from intestinal worms, though treatments cost less than a dollar per year. A full course of treatment for a child suffering even from drug-resistant malaria costs only about one dollar. In fact, Vietnam, a relatively poor country, reduced deaths from malaria by 97 percent from 1991 to 1997 with a campaign that included bed nets and antimalarial drugs.[18] A bed net program in Tanzania also reduced mortality significantly.[19] (The availability of such cheap remedies makes it all the more tragic that malaria is still so widespread—we are back to the second tragedy of the world's poor.)

Overall, the World Bank estimates the cost per year for a variety of health interventions like these to range from five to forty dollars, compared with the fifteen-hundred-dollar cost of prolonging the life of an AIDS patient by a year with antiretroviral treatment. The $4.5 billion the WHO plans to spend on antiretroviral treatment for one more year of life for three million could grant between seven and sixty years of additional life for five times that many people—fifteen million. For the HIV-positive patients themselves, you could reach many more of them to prolong their lives by treating the opportunistic infections, especially TB, that usually kill AIDS victims.

Other researchers come up with similar numbers. For example, Harvard economics professor Michael Kremer noted in an article in *The Journal of Economic Perspectives* in 2002: "for every person treated for a year with antiretroviral therapy, 25 to 110 Disability Adjusted Life Years could be saved through targeted AIDS prevention efforts or vaccination against easily preventable diseases."

A group of health experts wrote in the prestigious medical journal *The Lancet* in July 2003 about how 5.5 million child deaths could have been prevented in 2003, lamenting that "child survival has lost its focus." They blamed in part the "levels of attention and effort directed at preventing the small proportion of child deaths due to AIDS with a new, complex, and expensive intervention."[20]

The WHO expects the added years of life for AIDS patients from antiretroviral treatment to be only three to five years—not exactly a miracle cure.[21] The United Nations Population Division in 2005 similarly estimated that the added years of life from antiretroviral treatment to be a median of 4.5 years.[22] After that, resistance to the first-line treatment (the one with the cheap drugs, which is all that is on the table in Africa, outside of South Africa) builds up and full-blown AIDS sets in. Other estimates are even more pessimistic. The average length of effectiveness of the first-line treatment in Brazil, which has a large-scale treatment program, has been only fourteen months.[23]

The big question is whether poor Africans themselves would have chosen to spend scarce funds on prolonging some lives with AIDS treatment, as opposed to saving many lives with other health interventions. Would the desperately poor themselves, such as those on an income of one dollar a day, choose to spend fifteen hundred dollars on antiretroviral treatment? Should the West impose its preferences for saving AIDS victims instead of measles victims just because it makes the West feel better?

Path of Least Resistance

Getting a complex AIDS and development crisis under control just by taking a pill is irresistible to politicians, aid agencies, and activists. We see here again one bias toward observable actions by aid agencies. The activists' cause plays well in the Western media because the tragedy of AIDS victims even has a villain—the international drug companies that were reluctant to lower the price on life-saving drugs—which makes mobilization for the cause even easier.

AIDS treatment is another example of the SIBD syndrome—rich-country politicians want to convince rich-country voters that "something is being done" (SIBD) about the tragic problem of AIDS in Africa. It is easier to achieve SIBD catharsis if politicians and aid officials treat people who are already sick, than it is to persuade people with multiple sexual partners to use condoms to prevent many more people from getting the disease. Alas, the poor's interests are sacrificed to political convenience. When the U.S. Congress passed Bush's fifteen-billion-dollar AIDS program (known as the President's Emergency Plan for AIDS Relief, or PEPFAR) in May 2003, it placed a restriction that no more than 20 percent of the funds be spent on prevention, while 55 percent was allocated for treatment.[24]

In a fit of religious zealotry, Congress also required organizations receiving funds to publicly oppose prostitution. This eliminates effective organizations that take a pragmatic and compassionate approach to understanding the factors that drive women into prostitution. Programs that condemn prostitutes are unlikely to find a receptive audience when they try to persuade those prostitutes to avoid risky behavior.

To make things even worse, the religious right in America is crippling the funding of prevention programs to advocate their own imperatives: abstain from sex or have sex only with your legally married spouse. Studies in the United States find no evidence that abstinence programs have any effect on sexual behavior of young people, except to discourage them from using condoms.[25] The evangelists' message has not convinced American youth, so the evangelists want to export it to African youth. Moreover, devout women who follow the sex-within-marriage mantra are still at risk if their husbands have sex

with other partners without using condoms before or during their marriage. The religious right threatens NGOs that aggressively market condoms with a cutoff of official aid funds, on the grounds that those NGOs are promoting sexual promiscuity. Pushed by the religious right, Congress mandated that at least one third of the already paltry PEPFAR prevention budget go for abstinence-only programs.

The Vatican is also pushing its followers to oppose condom distribution in Africa because of religious doctrine that forbids the use of birth control.[26] These religious follies are one of the most extreme examples of rich peoples' preferences in the West trumping what is best for the poor in the Rest.

While prevention is tied up in religious knots, everyone seems to agree on treatment. The gay community, a group usually not identified with the religious right, is also emphasizing treatment. Activist groups such as ACT UP helped along the push for treatment—in their Web site for the 2002 Barcelona AIDS conference, they mentioned "treatment" eighteen times, but didn't mention "prevention" once.[27] Why do we have a well-publicized Treatment Access Coalition when there is no Prevention Access Coalition? Why didn't the WHO have a "3 by 5" campaign intended to *prevent* three million new cases of AIDS by the end of 2005? The activists have been only too successful in focusing attention on treatment instead of prevention. A LexisNexis search of articles on AIDS in Africa in *The Economist* over the previous two years found eighty-eight articles that mentioned "treatment" but only twenty-two that mentioned "prevention."

Instead of spending ten billion dollars on treatment over the next three years, money could be spent on preventing AIDS from spreading from the 28 million HIV-positive Africans to the 644 million HIV-negative Africans. Thailand has successfully implemented prevention campaigns targeting condom use among prostitutes, increasing condom usage from 15 percent to 90 percent and reducing new HIV infections dramatically. Senegal and Uganda have apparently also had success with vigorous prevention campaigns promoted by courageous political leaders (although the Ugandan government is now backing off from condom promotion under pressure from religious leaders).

If money spent on treatment went instead to effective prevention, between three and seventy-five new HIV infections could be averted for every extra year of life given to an AIDS patient. Spending AIDS money on treatment rather than on prevention makes the AIDS crisis *worse*, not better. If we consider that averting an HIV infection gives many extra years of life to each individual, then the case for prevention instead of treatment gets even stronger. For the same money spent giving one more year of life to an AIDS patient, you could give 75 to 1,500 years of additional life (say fifteen extra years for each of five to one hundred people) to the rest of the population through AIDS prevention.

We should ask the aid agencies why they want to put this much money now into the treatment of AIDS for twenty-nine million people when the same money spent to prevent the spread of HIV might have spared many of the twenty-nine million from infection. This past negligence is *not* an argument for or against any particular direction of action today—we must move forward from where we are now. But it does show how politicians and aid bureaucrats react passively to dramatic headlines and utopian ideals rather than according to where the small aid budget will benefit the most people. Is this what poor people themselves would choose to spend the money on?

Trade-offs

It is the job of economists to point out trade-offs; it is the job of politicians and Planners to deny that trade-offs exist. AIDS campaigners protest that AIDS treatment money is "new money" that would have been otherwise unavailable, but that just begs the question of where new money is best spent. Why are there not campaigns to

spread even further the successful campaigns against children's diarrhea, where a given amount of money—raised from the same sources—would reach many more people than money for AIDS treatment?

The utopian reaction is that the West will spend "whatever it takes" to cover *all* the health programs described above. This was the approach taken by the WHO Commission on Macroeconomics and Health in 2001. This commission recommended that rich countries spend an additional twenty-seven billion dollars on health in poor countries by 2007, which at the time was more than half of the world's foreign aid budget to poor countries. They ramp this number up to forty-seven billion dollars by 2015, of which twenty-two billion would be for AIDS. The commission's report was influential in gaining adherents for AIDS treatment in poor countries.

In an obscure footnote to the report, the commission notes that people often asked it what its priorities would be if only a lower sum were forthcoming, but it says it was "ethically and politically" unable to choose. The most charitable view is that this statement is the commission's strategy to get the money it wants. Otherwise, this refusal to make choices is inexcusable Public policy is the science of doing the best you can with limited resources—it is dereliction of duty for professional economists to shrink from confronting trade-offs. Even when you get new resources, you still have to decide where they would be best used.

If you want priorities and trade-offs, you can get them in the WHO itself. The WHO's 2002 World Health Report contains the following common sense: "Not everything can be done in all settings, so some way of setting priorities needs to be found. The next chapter identifies costs and the impact on population health of a variety of interventions, as the basis on which to develop strategies to reduce risk."[28]

The next chapter in the WHO report actually states that money spent on educating prostitutes saves between one thousand and one hundred times more lives than the same amount of money spent on antiretroviral treatment.[29]

Getting back to the WHO Commission on Macroeconomics and Health, the commission's sum, according to its own assumptions, did not eliminate all avoidable deaths in the poor countries. These sums, not to mention total foreign aid, are paltry relative to all the things that the world's three billion desperately poor people need. The commission *did* place some limit on what it thought rich countries were willing to spend to save lives in poor countries. *Everybody* places limits on what they spend on health. Even in rich countries, people could maximize their chances of catching killer diseases early enough for treatment by, say, having a daily MRI. Nobody, except possibly Woody Allen, actually does this, because it's too costly relative to the expected gain in life and relative to other things that rich people would like to spend money on. Virtually nobody was advocating AIDS treatment in Africa when the drug cocktail cost more than ten thousand dollars per year. Everybody, except political campaigners, knows that money, whether "new" or "old," is limited.

A political campaigner giving a graphic description of AIDS patients dying without life-saving drugs is hard to resist, making the trade-offs described earlier seem coldhearted. But money should not be spent according to what the West considers the most dramatic kind of suffering. Others with other diseases have their own chronicles of suffering. The journalist Daniel Bergner describes the relentless wailing of mothers in Sierra Leone who have lost a child to measles, the wailing that never stopped in a village during a measles epidemic. The high fever of measles stirs up intestinal worms, which spill out from the children's noses. Sores erupt inside their mouths. The parents in desperation pour kerosene down the children's throats. The graves of the dead children lie behind their parents' huts, mounds of dirt covered by palm branches.[30]

Take also the small baby dying in his mother's arms, tortured by diarrhea, which can be pre-vented so easily and cheaply with oral rehydration therapy. *Many* deaths can be prevented more cheaply than treating AIDS, thus reaching many more suffering people on a limited aid budget. Nobody asks the poor in Africa whether they would like to see most "new" money spent on AIDS treatment as opposed to the many other dangers they face. The questions facing Western AIDS campaigners should not be "Do they deserve to die?" but "Do we deserve to decide who dies?"

Constance, the HIV-positive mother from Soweto whom I mention at the beginning of this chapter, had an interesting perspective on priorities. When I asked her to name Soweto's biggest problem, she did not say AIDS or lack of antiretroviral treatment. She said, "No jobs." Finding a way to earn money to feed herself and her children was a more pressing concern for her than her eventual death from AIDS.

The more sophisticated way to deny that trade-offs exist is to insist that each part of the budget is necessary for everything else to work. When asked to choose between guns and butter, the canny politician insists that guns are necessary to protect the butter. In the AIDS field, strategic responses gave us the mantra "prevention is impossible without treatment." The proposition rests on the plausible reasoning that people will not come forward to be tested (most HIV-positive Africans do not know they are HIV-positive) unless there is hope of treatment. Some bits of evidence support this intuition, but the notion has not really been subjected to enough empirical scrutiny. Moreover, it is also plausible, and there is also a little evidence, to support the idea that treatment makes prevention more difficult. There is evidence that people in rich countries engaged in riskier sexual behavior *after* HAART became available.[31] Prevention campaigns did work in Senegal, Thailand, and Uganda without being based on treatment. Finally, there remains the risk that treatment with imperfect adherence will result in emergence of resistant strains of HIV, so that treatment itself will sow the seeds of its own downfall.[32]

Dysfunctional Health Systems

Admittedly, these trade-offs are oversimplified. Cost-effectiveness analysis—which compares different health interventions according to their estimated benefits (years of lives saved) and costs (drugs, medical personnel, clinics, hospitals)—gives us these numbers. This is the mainstream approach in the international public health field. Many of the advocates for treatment, such as Grö Harlem Brundtland and WHO staff, buy into this approach. They just fail to follow the logic through to the conclusion that you could save many more lives spending on other health interventions—including AIDS prevention—with what they propose to spend on AIDS treatment.

Lant Pritchett of Harvard's Kennedy School and Jeffrey Hammer and Deon Filmer of the World Bank criticize these cost-effectiveness calculations for the oversimplifications they are. Just because it costs a dollar to treat a person's illness, it doesn't follow that giving a dollar to the national health system will result in treating that person. We have already seen what a difficult time international aid planners have in getting even simple interventions to work.

Despite the health successes noted earlier, Filmer, Hammer, and Pritchett talk about "weak links in the chain" that leads from the donors dollar to the person's treatment. The second tragedy of the world's poor means that many effective interventions are not reaching the poor because of some of the follies of Planners mentioned in previous chapters.

Because of the insistence on working through governments, funds get lost in patronage-swollen national health bureaucracies (not to mention international health bureaucracies). In countries where corruption is as endemic as AIDS, health officials often sell aid-financed drugs on the black market. Studies in Cameroon, Guinea, Tanzania, and Uganda estimated that 30 to 70 percent of government drugs disappeared before reaching the patients. In one low-income country, a crusading journalist accused the ministry of health of misappropriating fifty million dollars in aid

funds. The ministry issued a rebuttal: the journalist had irresponsibly implied that the fifty million dollars had gone AWOL in a single year, whereas they had actually misappropriated the money over a *three-year* period.

I have heard from multiple sources of AIDS money disappearing before it reached any real or potential victims. In Cameroon, the World Bank lent a large amount for AIDS, which the health ministry handed out to local AIDS committees. Critics allege there was virtually no monitoring and no controls and are not quite sure what the local committees did, except for vaguely defined "AIDS sensitization." In one alleged case, a local committee chair threw a large party for his daughter's wedding under the category of "AIDS sensitization."

Many doctors, nurses, and other health workers are poorly trained and poorly paid. The AIDS treatment campaigners are oblivious to these harsh realities of medical care in poor countries. The worst part about the heartfelt plea for money for AIDS treatment is that it will save many fewer lives than campaigners promise.

Of course, similar arguments would also weaken the case for the allegedly more cost effective health interventions on illnesses such as diarrhea, malaria, and measles. They do not work everywhere as well as they should, as the rest of this book makes clear. But this complication does not strengthen the argument for funding AIDS treatment in Africa. The cheap interventions have some successes, as noted earlier. They are cheap because they are simpler for Searchers to find ways to administer—a measles vaccination has to happen only at one given point just for each child. A bed net impregnated with insecticide has to be handed out just once to each potential malaria victim, along with the information on how to use it, then impregnated again periodically.

The treatment of AIDS with drugs is vastly more complicated and depends on many more "links in the chain": refrigeration, lab tests, expert monitoring and adjusting therapy if resistance and toxic side effects emerge, and educating the patient on how to take the drug. In Europe and North America, 20 to 40 percent of AIDS patients do not take their drugs as prescribed. Resistance will emerge if there are lapses from the correct regimen. Even with good intentions, government bureaucrats currently do a poor job making sure that drug supply matches demand in each locale. Unfortunately for the patients, it is critical that AIDS treatment not be interrupted by drug shortages (critical both for effectiveness and for preventing resistant strains from developing). A 2004 article in the *Journal of the American Medical Association*, while generally positive about treatment in developing countries, sounded some concerns:

> Finally, how will the tens of thousands of health care professionals required for global implementation of HIV care strategies be trained, motivated, supervised, resourced, and adequately reimbursed to ensure the level of care required for this complex disease? To scale up antiretroviral therapy for HIV without ensuring infrastructure, including trained practitioners, a safe and reliable drug delivery system, and simple but effective models for continuity of care, would be a disaster, leading to ineffective treatment and rapid development of resistance.[33]

Even doing the huge amount of testing required to find out who is HIV-positive and eligible for treatment would likely overwhelm health budgets and infrastructure in poor countries.

The tardy response to the AIDS crisis has meant that it has built up to an unbearable tragedy—to the point that it's now too late to save many millions of lives. Spending money on a mostly futile attempt to save all the lives of this generation of AIDS victims will take money away from saving the lives of the next generation, perpetuating the tragedy. The political lobby for treatment doesn't mention that no amount of treatment will stop the crisis. The only way to stop the threat to Africans and others is *prevention*, no matter how unappealing the politics or how uncomfortable the discussion about sex. The task is to save the next generation before it is again too late.

Let's commend the campaigners wanting to spend money on AIDS treatment in Africa for their dedication and compassion. But could they redirect some of that compassion to where it will do the most good?

Feedback and Idealism Again

Why did the health system fail on AIDS when foreign aid successes are more common in public health than in other areas? The AIDS crisis was less susceptible to feedback, and the interests of the poor were not coincident with rich-country politics. The necessary actions were in the area of prevention, which doesn't involve just taking a pill or getting a shot, as in many of the other successes. The donors showed shamefully little interest in researching the sexual behavior that causes AIDS to spread or in which prevention strategies work to change that behavior. Donors should have asked, "How many people have we prevented from becoming HIV-positive?"

A patient who is already HIV-positive is a highly visible target for help—a lot more visible than someone who is going to get infected in the future but doesn't yet know it. The rich-country politicians and aid agencies get more PR credit for saving the lives of sick patients, even if the interests of the poor would call for saving them from getting sick in the first place. This again confirms the prediction that aid agencies skew their efforts toward visible outcomes, even when those outcomes have a lower payoff than less visible interventions.

The politicians and aid agencies didn't have the courage to confront the uncomfortable question of how to change human sexual behavior. The AIDS failure shows that the bureaucratic healers too often settle for simply handing out pills.

Heroes

The AIDS disaster in Africa features many ineffective bureaucrats and few energetic rescuers.

But there are a few heroes. A group called HIVSA works in Soweto, South Africa, helping people like Constance. Its energetic director, Steven Whiting, was formerly an affluent interior designer. He stumbled on the AIDS issue by chance when he got the contract to renovate the headquarters of the Perinatal HIV Research Unit at the largest hospital in Soweto. He was so moved by what he saw there that he decided to quit his job and devote his efforts full time to fighting AIDS.

HIVSA does the little things that make a difference. It provides the drug nevirapine to block transmission of the HIV virus from mothers to newborns. Doctors give just one dose during labor, an intervention that is highly cost effective compared with other AIDS treatments. To follow up, HIVSA provides infant formula to HIV-positive new mothers, since breast-feeding can also transmit the HIV virus to newborns. Less tangibly, HIVSA provides support groups meeting in health clinics throughout Soweto to help HIV-positive mothers confront the stigma of HIV and their many other problems. (One hint of such problems: the signs all over the clinics announcing that no guns are allowed inside the clinics.) When the mothers visit the clinics, they get a free meal and nutritional supplements. Mothers and HIVSA staff work in community gardens attached to each clinic to provide food. HIVSA staff are almost all from the Soweto community and are HIV-positive.

Constance has problems that are overwhelming, but her most recent baby was born HIV-negative, thanks to nevirapine. HIVSA's free meals, nutritional supplements, and emotional support make her life a little more bearable.

If only all the West's efforts at fighting AIDS were so constructive at giving the poor victims what they want and need. The West largely ignored AIDS when it was building up to a huge humanitarian crisis, only to focus now on an expensive attempt at treatment that neglects the prevention so critical to stop the disaster from getting even worse.

Snapshot: Prostitutes For Prevention

Prostitutes in Sonagachi, the red-light district of Calcutta, India, form a world unto themselves. Social norms about female sexual behavior in India are such that prostitution carries an even larger stigma in India than elsewhere. Cut off from the wider world, prostitutes have their own subculture, with an elite of madams and pimps. As in any subculture, its members strive for status. Prostitutes who aspire to greater status attain it most commonly by attracting long-term clients.

Many well-intentioned bureaucrats have tried to help the prostitutes by "rescuing" them and taking them to shelters to be trained in another profession, such as tailoring. However, sex work pays a lot better than tailoring, and former prostitutes face harassment and discrimination in the outside world. Hence, most "rescued" women returned to prostitution. But the advent of the AIDS epidemic in India and the well-known role of prostitutes in spreading AIDS caused increased concern about these failures.

Dr. Smarajit Jana, head of the All India Institute of Hygiene and Public Health, had another idea in 1992. He and his team would learn the subculture of the prostitutes and work with it to fight AIDS. They formed a mutually respectful relationship with the madams, pimps, prostitutes, and clients. They noted the class system within Sonagachi. By trial and error, and with feedback from the prostitutes, Dr. Jana and his team hit upon a strategy for fighting AIDS. The strategy was awfully simple in retrospect: they trained a group of twelve prostitutes to educate their fellow workers about the dangers of AIDS and the need to use condoms. The peer educators wore green medical coats when they were engaged in their public health work, and they attained greater status in Sonagachi. Condom use in Sonagachi increased dramatically. By 1999, HIV incidence in Sonagachi was only 6 percent, compared with 50 percent in other red-light districts in India.

The project had other, unexpected consequences. The increased confidence of the peer educators and the media attention on the success of prevention efforts led the community to aspire to greater things. The prostitutes formed a union to campaign for legalization of prostitution and a reduction in police harassment, and to organize festivals and health fairs. Dr. Jana's approach based on feedback from the intended beneficiaries succeeded when so many other AIDS prevention programs had failed.

NOTES

1. Center for Global Development, "Millions Saved: Proven Successes in Global Health," Washington, D.C., 2004.

2. Bekki J. Johnson and Robert S. Pond, "AIDS in Africa: A Review of Medical, Public Health, Social Science, and Popular Literature," MISEORE, Campaign Against Hunger and Disease in the World (Episcopal Organization for Development Cooperations), Aachen, West Germany, 1988.

3. World Bank, Africa Technical Department, "Acquired Immune Deficiency Syndrome (AIDS): The Bank's Agenda for Action in Africa," October 24, 1988.

4. Jean-Louis Lamboray and A. Edward Elmendorf, "Combatting AIDS and Other Sexually Transmitted Diseases in Africa: A Review of the World Bank's Agenda for Action," World Bank Discussion Paper no. 181, Africa Technical Department, 1992, p. 29.

5. Jill Armstrong, "Socioeconomic Implications of AIDS in Developing Countries," *Finance and Development* 28, no. 4 (December 1991): 14–17.

6. Julia Dayton, "World Bank HIV/AIDS Interventions: Ex-ante and Ex-post Evaluation," World Bank discussion paper no. 389, Washington, D.C., 1998, p. 9.

7. World Bank, Africa Region, "Intensifying Action Against HIV/AIDS in Africa: Responding to a Development Crisis," 2000.

8. http://www.worldbank.org/afr/aids/map/me_manual.pdf.

9. This story comes from Emma Guest, *Children of AIDS: Africa's Orphan Crisis*, London: Pluto Press, 2001.

10. Adam Ashforth, *Witchcraft, Violence, and Democracy in South Africa*, Chicago: University of Chicago Press, 2005, pp. 8–10.

11. Guest, *Children of AIDS*, pp. 144–47.

12. Anne Case, Christina Paxson, and Joseph Ableidinger, "The Education of African Orphans," Princeton University mimeograph, 2003, http://www.wwsprinceton.edu/%7Erpds/Downloads/case_paxson_education_orphans.pdf.

13. WHO/UNAIDS, "Report on the Methods Used to Estimate Costs of Reaching the WHO Target of '3 by 5,'" February 10, 2004, p. 6.

14. Andrew Cresse, Katherine Floyd, Anita Alban, Lorna Guiness, "Cost-effectiveness of HIV/AIDS Interventions in Africa: A Systematic Review of the Evidence," *The Lancet* 359 (2002): 1635–42; Lilani Kumaranayarake, "Cost-Effectiveness and Economic Evaluation of HIV/AIDS-Related Interventions: The State of the Art," in *International AIDS Economics Network, State of the Art: AIDS and Economics*, HIV/AIDS Policy Project, www.iaen.org/conferences/stateofepidemic.php., 2002.

15. http://www.interaction.org/advocacy/budget_request_05.html, FY2005 Foreign Operations Budget Request Summary and Analysis.

16. WHO, World Health Report 2003, Annex 2.

17. See, for example, Emiko Masaki, Russell Green, Fiona Greig, Julia Walsh, and Malcolm Potts, "Cost-Effectiveness of HIV Prevention Versus Treatment for Resource-Scarce Countries: Setting Priorities for HIV/AIDS Management," Bay Area International Group, School of Public Health, University of California at Berkeley, 2002.

18. http://www.massiveeffort.org/html/success_stories__vietnam.html, http://rbm.who.int/cmc_upload/0/000/017/025/vietnam-ettling.pdf.

19. Salim Abdulla, Joanna Armstrong Schellenberg, Rose Nathan, Oscar Mukasa, Tanya Marchant, Tom Smith, Marcel Tanner, Christian Lengeler, "Impact on Malaria Morbidity of a Programme Supplying Insectide-Treated Nets in Children Aged Under Two Years in Tanzania: Community Cross-Sectional Study," *British Medical Journal*, 322 (February 3, 2001): 270–73.

20. Gareth Jones, Richard W. Steketec, Robert E. Black, Zulfiqar A. Bhutta, Saul S. Morris, and the Beliagio Child Survival Study Group, "How Many Child Deaths Can We Prevent This Year?" *The Lancet* 362 (2003): 65–71.

21. WHO/UNAIDS, "Report on the Methods Used to Estimate Costs of Reaching the WHO Target of '3 by 5,'" February 10, 2004.

22. United Nations Population Division (UNDP), "World Population Prospects," 2004 revision, 2005, p. 22.

23. David Canning, "The Economics of HIV/AIDS Treatment and Prevention in Developing Countries," Harvard School of Public Health, mimeograph, 2005, in *Journal of Economic Perspectives*.

24. Center for Health and Gender Equity and Sexuality, Information and Education Council of the United States, "The U.S. Global AIDS Strategy: Politics, Ideology, and the Global AIDS Epidemic," May 2003.

25. Human Rights Watch, "The Less They Know, the Better: Abstinence-Only HIV/AIDS Programs in Uganda," *Human Rights Watch* 17, no. 4a (March 2005).

26. Helen Epstein, "God and the Fight Against AIDS," *New York Review of Books*, April 28, 2005.

27. Barcelona AIDS Conference Reports, "President Bush Is Killing People with AIDS by Lack of Leadership," http://www.actupny .org/reports/bcn/Bcnbush AUpr.html.

28. WHO, World Health Report 2002, "Reducing Risks, Promoting Healthy Life," Geneva, 2002, p. 92.

29. Ibid., pp. 123, 132.

30. Daniel Bergner, *In the Land of Magic Soldiers: A Story of White and Black in West Africa*, New York: Farrar, Straus, & Giroux, 2003, pp. 66–68.

31. Dr. Stan Lehman and colleagues, CDC, presentation at XIII International AIDS Conference, Durban, South Africa, 2000.

32. Warren Stevens, Steve Kaye, and Tumani Corrah, "Antiretroviral Therapy in Africa," *British Medical Journal* 328 (January 31, 2004): 280–82.

33. Merle A. Sande and Allan Ronald, "Treatment of HIV/AIDS: Do the Dilemmas Only Increase?" *Journal of the American Medical Association* 292, no. 2 (July 14, 2004): 267.

LAURIE GARRETT

THE NEXT PANDEMIC?

Probable Cause

Scientists have long forecast the appearance of an influenza virus capable of infecting 40 percent of the world's human population and killing unimaginable numbers. Recently, a new strain, H5N1 avian influenza, has shown all the earmarks of becoming that disease. Until now, it has largely been confined to certain bird species, but that may be changing.

The havoc such a disease could wreak is commonly compared to the devastation of the 1918–19 Spanish flu, which killed 50 million people in 18 months. But avian flu is far more dangerous. It kills 100 percent of the domesticated chickens it infects, and among humans the disease is also lethal: as of May 1, about 109 people were known to have contracted it, and it killed 54 percent (although this statistic does not include any milder cases that may have gone unreported). Since it first appeared in southern China in 1997, the virus has mutated, becoming heartier and deadlier and killing a wider range of species. According to the March 2005 National

From *Foreign Affairs* 84, no. 4 (July/Aug., 2005): 3–23.

Academy of Science's Institute of Medicine flu report, the "current ongoing epidemic of H5N1, avian influenza in Asia is unprecedented in its scale, in its spread, and in the economic losses it has caused."

In short, doom may loom. But note the "may." If the relentlessly evolving virus becomes capable of human-to-human transmission, develops a power of contagion typical of human influenzas, and maintains its extraordinary virulence, humanity could well face a pandemic unlike any ever witnessed. Or nothing at all could happen. Scientists cannot predict with certainty what this H5N1 influenza will do. Evolution does not function on a knowable timetable, and influenza is one of the sloppiest, most mutation-prone pathogens in nature's storehouse.

Such absolute uncertainty, coupled with the profound potential danger, is disturbing for those whose job it is to ensure the health of their community, their nation, and broader humanity. According to the Centers for Disease Control and Prevention (CDC), in a normal flu season about 200,000 Americans are hospitalized, 38,000 of whom the from the disease, with an overall mortality rate of .008 percent for those infected. Most of those deaths occur among people older than 65; on average, 98 of every 100,000 seniors with the flu die. Influenza costs the U.S. economy about $12 billion annually in direct medical costs and loss of productivity.

Yet this level of damage hardly approaches the catastrophe that the United States would face in a severe flu pandemic. The CDC predicts that a "medium-level epidemic" could kill up to 207,000 Americans, hospitalize 734,000, and sicken about a third of the U.S. population. Direct medical costs would top $166 billion, not including the costs of vaccination. An H5N1 avian influenza that is transmittable from human to human could be even more devastating: assuming a mortality rate of 20 percent and 80 million illnesses, the United States could be looking at 16 million deaths and unimaginable economic costs. This extreme outcome is a worst-case scenario; it assumes failure to produce an effective vaccine

rapidly enough to make a difference and a virus that remains impervious to some antiflu drugs. But the 207,000 reckoning is clearly a conservative guess.

The entire world would experience similar levels of viral carnage, and those areas ravaged by HIV and home to millions of immunocompromised individuals might witness even greater death tolls. In response, some countries might impose useless but highly disruptive quarantines or close borders and airports, perhaps for months. Such closures would disrupt trade, travel, and productivity. No doubt the world's stock markets would teeter and perhaps fall precipitously. Aside from economics, the disease would likely directly affect global security, reducing troop strength and capacity for all armed forces, UN peacekeeping operations, and police worldwide.

In a world where most of the wealth is concentrated in less than a dozen nations representing a distinct minority of the total population, the capacity to respond to global threats is, to put it politely, severely imbalanced. The majority of the world's governments not only lack sufficient funds to respond to a superflu; they also have no health infrastructure to handle the burdens of disease, social disruption, and panic. The international community would look to the United States, Canada, Japan, and Europe for answers, vaccines, cures, cash, and hope. How these wealthy governments responded, and how radically the death rates differed along worldwide fault lines of poverty, would resonate for years thereafter.

What Once Was Lost

Nearly half of all deaths in the United States in 1918 were flu related. Some 675,000 Americans— about six percent of the population of 105 million and the equivalent of 2 million American deaths today—perished from the Spanish flu. The average life expectancy for Americans born in 1918 was just 37 years, down from 55 in 1917.

Although doctors then lacked the technology to test people's blood for flu infections, scientists reckon that the Spanish flu had a mortality rate of just less than one percent of those who took ill in the United States. It would have been much worse had there not been milder flu epidemics in the 1850s and in 1889, caused by similar but less virulent viruses, which made most elderly Americans immune to the 1918–19 strain. The highest death tolls were among young adults, ages 20–35.

The Spanish flu got its name because Spain suffered from an early and acute outbreak, but it did not originate there. Its actual origin remains uncertain. The first strain was mild enough to prompt most World War I military forces to dismiss it as a pesky ailment. When the second strain hit North America in the summer of 1918, however, the virus caused a surge of deaths. First hit was Camp Funston, an army base in Kansas, where young soldiers were preparing for deployment to Europe. The virus then spread swiftly to other camps and on troop ships crossing the Atlantic, killing 43,000 U.S. military personnel in about three months. Despite the entreaties of the military's surgeons general, President Woodrow Wilson ordered continued shipments of troops aboard crowded naval transports, which soldiers came to call "death ships." By late September 1918, so overwhelmed was the War Department by influenza that the military could not assist in controlling civic disorder at home, including riots caused by epidemic hysteria. Worse, so many doctors, scientists, and lab technicians had been drafted into military service that civilian operations were hamstrung.

Under these conditions, influenza swept from the most populous U.S. cities to extraordinarily remote rural areas. Explorers discovered empty Inuit villages in what are now Alaska and the Yukon Territory, their entire populations having succumbed to the flu. Many deaths were never included in the pandemic's official death toll—such as the majority of victims in Africa, Latin America, Indonesia, the Pacific Islands, and Russia (then still in the throes of revolution). What is known about the toll in these regions is staggering. For example, influenza killed 5 percent of the population of Ghana in only two months, and nearly 20 percent of the people of Western Samoa died. The official estimate of 40–50 million total deaths is believed to be a conservative extrapolation of European and American records. In fact, many historians and biologists believe that nearly a third of all humans suffered from influenza in 1918–19—and that of these, 100 million died.

In the last years of the nineteenth century and the early years of the twentieth, a series of important scientific discoveries spawned a revolution in biology and medicine and led pioneers such as Hermann Biggs, a New York City doctor, to create entire legal and health systems based on the identification and control of germs. By 1917, the United States and much of Europe had become enthralled by the hygiene movement. Impressive new public health infrastructures had been built in many cities, tens of thousands of tuberculosis victims were isolated in sanatoriums, the incidences of child-killing diseases such as diphtheria and typhoid fever had plummeted, and cholera epidemics had become rare events in the industrialized world. There was great optimism that modern science held the key to perfect health.

Influenza's arrival shattered the hope; scientists still had virtually no understanding of viruses generally, and of influenza in particular. The hygienic precautions and quarantines that had proved so effective in holding back the tide of bacterial diseases in the United States proved useless, even harmful, in the face of the Spanish flu. As the epidemic spread, top physicians and scientists claimed its cause was everything from tiny plants to old dusty books to something called "cosmic influence." It was not until 1933 that a British research team finally isolated and identified the influenza virus.

Most strains of the flu do not kill people directly; rather, death is caused by bacteria, which surge into the embattled lungs of the victim. But the Spanish flu that circulated in 1918–19 was a direct killer. Victims suffered from acute cyanosis, a blue discoloration of the skin and mucous membranes. They vomited and coughed up blood, which also poured uncontrollably from their noses and, in the case of women, from their genitals. The highest death toll occurred among pregnant women: as many as 71 percent of those infected died. If the woman survived, the fetus invariably did not. Many young people suffered from encephalitis, as the virus chewed away at their brains and spinal cords. And millions experienced acute respiratory distress syndrome, an immunological condition in which disease-fighting cells so overwhelm the lungs in their battle against the invaders that the lung cells themselves become collateral damage, and the victims suffocate. Had antibiotics existed, they may not have been much help.

Oops

In January 1976, 18-year-old Private David Lewis staggered his way through a forced march during basic training in a brutal New Jersey winter. By the time his unit returned to base at Fort Dix, Lewis was dying. He collapsed and did not respond to his sergeant's attempts at mouth-to-mouth resuscitation.

In subsequent weeks, U.S. Army and CDC scientists discovered that the virus that had killed Lewis was swine flu. Although no other soldiers at Fort Dix died, health officials panicked. F. David Matthews, then secretary of health, education, and welfare, promptly declared, "There is evidence there will be a major flu epidemic this coming fall. The indication is that we will see a return of the 1918 flu virus that is the most virulent form of flu. In 1918, a half million people died [in the United States]. The projections are that this virus will kill one million Americans in 1976."

At the time, it was widely believed that influenza appeared in cycles, with especially lethal forms surfacing at relatively predictable intervals. Since 1918–19, the United States had suf-

fered through influenza pandemics in 1957–58 and 1968–69; the first caused 70,000 deaths and the second 34,000. In 1976, scientists believed the world was overdue for a more lethal cycle, and the apparent emergence of swine flu at Fort Dix seemed to signal that another wave had come. The leaders of the CDC and the Department of Health, Education, and Welfare (HEW) warned the White House that there was a reasonably high probability that a catastrophic flu pandemic was about to hit. But opinion was hardly unanimous, and many European and Australian health authorities scoffed at the Americans' concern. Unsure of how to gauge the threat, President Gerald Ford summoned the polio-fighting heroes Jonas Salk and Albert Sabin to Washington and found the long-time adversaries in remarkable accord: a flu pandemic might truly be on the way.

On March 24,1976, Ford went on national television. "I have just concluded a meeting on a subject of vast importance to all Americans," he announced. "I have been advised that there is a very real possibility that unless we take effective counteractions, there could be an epidemic of this dangerous disease next fall and winter here in the United States. . . . I am asking Congress to appropriate $135 million, prior to the April recess, for the production of sufficient vaccine to inoculate every man, woman, and child in the United States."

Vaccine producers immediately complained that they could not manufacture sufficient doses of vaccine in such haste without special liability protection. Congress responded, passing a law in April that made the government responsible for the companies' liability. When the campaign to vaccinate the U.S. population started four months later, there were almost immediate claims of side effects, including the neurologically debilitating Guillain Barré Syndrome. Most of the lawsuits—with claims totaling $3.2 billion—were settled or dismissed, but the U.S. government still ended up paying claimants around $90 million.

Swine flu, however, never appeared. The head of the CDC was asked to resign, and Congress never again considered assuming the liability of pharmaceutical companies during a potential epidemic. The experience weakened U.S. credibility in public health and helped undermine the stature of President Ford. Subsequently, an official assessment of what went wrong was performed for HEW by Dr. Harvey Fineberg, a Harvard professor who is currently president of the Institute of Medicine. Fineberg concluded:

> In this case the consequences of being wrong about an epidemic were so devastating in people's minds that it wasn't possible to focus properly on the issue of likelihood. Nobody could really estimate likelihood then, or now. The challenge in such circumstances is to be able to distinguish things so you can rationally talk about it. In 1976, some policymakers were simply overwhelmed by the consequences of being wrong. And at a higher level [in the White House] the two—likelihood and consequence—got meshed.

Fineberg's warnings are well worth remembering today, as scientists nervously consider H5N1 avian influenza in Asia. The consequences of a form of this virus that is transmittable from human to human, particularly if it retains its unprecedented virulence, would be disastrous. But what is the likelihood that such a virus will appear?

Devolution

Understanding the risks requires understanding the nature of H5N1 avian flu specifically and influenza in general. Influenza originates with aquatic birds and is normally carried by migratory ducks, geese, and herons, usually without harm to them. As the birds migrate, they can pass the viruses on to domesticated birds—chickens, for example—via feces or during competitions over food, territory, and water. Throughout history, this connection between birds and the flu has spawned epidemics in Asia, especially southern China. Aquatic flu viruses are more likely to pass into domestic animals—and then into humans—in China than anywhere else

in the world. Dense concentrations of humans and livestock have left little of China's original migratory route for birds intact. Birds that annually travel from Indonesia to Siberia and back are forced to land and search for sustenance in farms, city parks, and industrial sites. For centuries, Chinese farmers have raised chickens, ducks, and pigs together, in miniscule pens surrounding their homes, greatly increasing the chance of contamination: influenza can spread from migrating to domestic birds and then to swine, mutating and eventually infecting human beings.

Ominously, as China's GDP grows, so do the expensive appetites of the country's 1.3 billion people, more of whom can afford to eat chicken regularly. Today, China annually raises about 13 billion chickens, 60 percent of them on small farms. Chicken farming is quickly morphing into a major industry, with some commercial poultry plants rivaling those in Arkansas and Georgia in scale—but lagging behind in hygienic standards. These factors favor rapid influenza evolution. By the close of the twentieth century, at least two new types of human-to-human flu spread around the world every year.

Influenza viruses contain eight genes, composed of RNA and packaged loosely in protective proteins. Like most RNA viruses, influenza reproduces sloppily: its genes readily fall apart, and it can absorb different genetic material and get mixed up in a process called reassortment. When influenza successfully infects a new species—say, pigs—it can reassort, and may switch from being an avian virus to a mammalian one. When that occurs, a human epidemic can result. The transmission cycles and the constant evolution are key to influenza's continued survival, for were it to remain identical year after year, most animals would develop immunity, and the flu would die out. This changing form explains why influenza is a seasonal disease. Vaccines made one year are generally useless the following.

Among the eight influenza genes there are two, dubbed H and N, that provide the code for proteins recognized by the human immune system. Scientists have numbered the many types of H and N proteins and use this system to classify a virus. A different viral combination of H and N proteins will trigger a different human immune response. For example, if a strain of H2N3 influenza circulates one year, followed by a different variety of H2N3 the next year, most people will be at least partially immune to the second strain. But if an H2N3 season is followed by an outbreak of H3N5 influenza, few people will have any immunity to the second virus, and the epidemic could be enormous. But a widespread epidemic need not be a severe or particularly deadly one: a virus' virulence depends on genes other than the two that control the H and N proteins.

Scientists first started saving flu virus samples in the early twentieth century. Since that time, an H5N1 influenza has never spread among human beings. According to the World Health Organization (WHO), "No virus of the H5 subtype has probably ever circulated among humans, and certainly not within the lifetime of today's world population. Population vulnerability to an H5N1-like pandemic virus would be universal." As for virulence, within about 48 hours of infection, H5N1 avian influenza kills 100 percent of infected chickens—although the virulence of a potential human-to-human transmissible H5N1 is impossible to predict.

A team of Chinese scientists has been tracking the H5N1 virus since it first emerged in Hong Kong in 1997, killing 6 people and sickening 18 others. The strain came out of southern China's Guangdong Province, where it apparently was carried by ducks, and hit Hong Kong's chicken population hard. After authorities there killed 1.5 million chickens—almost every single one in Hong Kong—the outbreak seemed to stop. But the virus had not disappeared; rather, it had retreated to China's Guangdong, Hunan, and Yunnan provinces, spreading once again to aquatic birds.

From 1998 to 2001 the virus went through multiple reassortments and moved back to domestic birds, spreading almost unnoticed in Chinese chicken flocks. It continued to evolve at high speed: 17 more reassortments occurred, and in January 2003 the "z" virus emerged, a mutant powerhouse that had become tougher, capable of withstanding a wider range of environmental challenges. The z virus spread to Vietnam and Thailand, where it evolved further, becoming resistant to one of the two classes of antiflu drugs, known as amantadines, or M2-inhibitors.

In early 2004, it became supervirulent and capable of killing a broad range of species, including rodents and humans. That permutation of the virus was dubbed "z+." In the first three weeks of January 2004, z+ killed 11 million chickens in Vietnam and Thailand. By April 2004, 120 million chickens in Asia had died of flu or been exterminated to slow the influenza brushfire. The avian epidemic stopped for a while, but in July another 1 million chickens died from the disease. The z+ virus was causing massive internal bleeding in the birds. By the beginning of 2005, with chickens dying and customers shying away from what remained, the Asian poultry industry had lost nearly $15 billion.

By April 2005, the H5N1 virus had also moved to pigs. Scientists isolated the disease from swine in a part of Indonesia where pigs are raised underneath elevated wood-slatted platforms that house chickens. Less rigorous investigations had previously indicated that pigs in China and Vietnam may also have been infected by H5N1 influenza. The discovery in Indonesia provided disturbing evidence that the virus was infecting mammals, although it was not yet known how widely the swine disease had spread or how lethal it was for the animals.

Hard to Kill

Over the course of this brief but rapid evolution, the H5N1 virus developed in ways unprecedented in influenza research. It is not only incredibly deadly but also incredibly difficult to contain. The virus apparently now has the ability to survive in chicken feces and the meat of dead animals, despite the lack of blood flow and living cells; raw chicken meat fed to tigers in Thailand zoos resulted in the deaths of 147 out of a total of 418. The virus has also found ways to vastly increase the range of species it can infect and kill. Most strains of influenza are not lethal in lab mice, but z+ is lethal in 100 percent of them. It even kills the very types of wild migratory birds that normally host influenza strains harmlessly. Yet domestic ducks, for unknown reasons, carry the virus without a problem, which may explain where z+ hides between outbreaks among chickens.

Traditional Asian methods of buying, slaughtering, and cooking meat make it hard to track the spread of an influenza virus—and tracking it is critical to preventing the disease from spreading. In Asia, consumers prefer to buy live chickens and other live animals at the market, slaughtering them in home kitchens. Asians thus have a high level of exposure to potentially disease-carrying animals, both in their homes and as they pass through the markets that line the streets of densely packed urban centers. For someone trying to trace a disease, Asia is a nightmare: with people daily exposed to live chickens in so many different environments, how can a sleuth tell whether an ailing flu victim was infected by a chicken, a duck, a migratory heron—or another human being?

Although most of the 109 known human H5N1 infections have been ascribed to some type of contact with chickens, mysteries abound, and many cases remain unsolved. "The virus is no longer causing large and highly conspicuous outbreaks on commercial farms," a 2005 WHO summary of the human z+ cases states. "Nor have poultry workers or cullers turned out to be an important risk group that could be targeted for protection. Instead, the virus has become stealthier: human cases are now occurring with no discernible exposure to H5N1 through contact with diseased or dead birds."

If proximity to infected animals is the key, why have there been no deaths among chicken handlers, poultry workers, or live-chicken dealers? The majority of the infected have been young adults and children. And there has been one documented case of human-to-human transmission of the z+ strain of the H5N1 virus—in late 2004, in Thailand. Several more such cases are suspected but cannot be confirmed. According to the WHO, there is "no scientific explanation for the unusual disease pattern."

Assessing and understanding H5N1's virulence in humans has also proved elusive. When it first appeared in Hong Kong in 1997, the virus killed 35 percent of those it was known to have infected. (Less severe cases may not have been reported.) The z strain of the disease, which emerged in early 2003, killed 68 percent of those known to have been infected. In H5N1 cases since December 2004, however, the mortality has been 36 percent. How can the fluctuation over time be explained? One disturbing possibility is that H5N1 has begun adapting to its human hosts, becoming less deadly but easier to spread. In the spring of 2005, in fact, H5N1 infected 17 people throughout Vietnam, resulting in only three deaths. Leading flu experts argue that this sort of phenomenon has in the past been a prelude to human influenza epidemics.

The medical histories of those who have died from H5N1 influenza are disturbingly similar to accounts of sufferers of the Spanish flu in 1918–19. Otherwise healthy people are completely overcome by the virus, developing all of the classic flu symptoms: coughing, headache, muscle pain, nausea, dizziness, diarrhea, high fever, depression, and loss of appetite. But these are just some of the effects. Victims also suffer from pneumonia, encephalitis, meningitis, acute respiratory distress, and internal bleeding and hemorrhaging. An autopsy of a child who died of the disease in Thailand last year revealed that the youth's lungs had been torn apart in the all-out war between disease-fighting cells and the virus.

Bad Medicine

According to test-tube studies, z+ ought to be vulnerable to the antiflu drug oseltamivir, which the

Roche pharmaceuticals company markets in the United States under the brand name Tamiflu. Yet Tamiflu was given to many of those who ultimately succumbed to the virus; it is believed that medical complications induced by the virus, including acute respiratory distress syndrome, may have prevented the drug from helping. It is also difficult to tell whether the drug contributed to the survival of those who took it and lived, although higher doses and more prolonged treatment may have a greater impact in fighting the disease. A team of Thai clinicians recently concluded that "the optimal treatment for case-patients with suspected H5 infection is not known." Lacking any better options, the WHO has recommended that countries stockpile Tamiflu to the best of their ability. The U.S. Department of Health and Human Services is doing so, but supplies of the drug are limited and it is hard to manufacture.

What about developing a Z+ vaccine? Unfortunately, there is only more gloom in the forecast. The total number of companies willing to produce influenza vaccines has plummeted in recent years, from more than two dozen in 1980 to just a handful in 2004. There are many reasons for the decline in vaccine producers. A spate of corporate mergers in the 1990s, for example, reduced the number of major international pharmaceutical companies. The financial risk of investing in vaccines is also a key factor. In 2003, the entire market for all vaccines—from polio to measles to hepatitis to influenza—amounted to just $5.4 billion. Although that sum may seem considerable, it is less than two percent of the global pharmaceutical market of $337.3 billion. Unlike chemical compounds, vaccines and most other biological products are difficult to make and can easily become contaminated. There is also a large and litigious antivaccine constituency—some people believe that vaccines cause harmful side effects such as Alzheimer's disease and autism—adding considerable liability costs to manufacturers' bottom lines.

The production of influenza vaccines holds particular drawbacks for companies. Flu vaccines must be made rapidly, increasing the risk of contamination or other errors. Because of the seasonal nature of the flu, a new batch of influenza vaccines must be produced each year. Should sales in a given year prove disappointing, flu vaccines cannot be stockpiled for sale in a subsequent season because by then the viruses will have evolved. In addition, the manufacturing process of flu vaccines is uniquely complex: pharmaceutical companies must grow viral samples on live chicken eggs, which must be reared under rigorous hygienic conditions. Research is under way on reverse genetics and cellular-level production techniques that might prove cheaper, faster, and less contamination-prone than using eggs, but for the foreseeable future manufacturers are stuck with the current labourious method. After cultivation, samples of the viruses must be harvested, the H and N characteristics must be shown to produce antibodies in test animals and human volunteers, and tests must prove that the vaccine is not contaminated. Only then can mass production commence.

The H5N1 strain of avian flu poses an additional problem: the virus is 100 percent lethal to chickens—and that includes chicken eggs. It took researchers five years of hard work to devise a way to grow the 1997 version of the H5N1 virus on eggs without killing them; although there have been technological improvements since then, there is no guarantee that an emerging pandemic strain could be cultivated fast enough.

In the current system, all influenza vaccines must be quickly made following a WHO meeting of flu experts held every February. At that gathering, scientists scrutinize all available information on the flu strains known to be circulating in the world. They then try to predict which strains are most likely to spread across every continent in the next six to nine months. (This year the WHO committee chose three human flu strains, of types H3N2 and H1N1, to be the basis of the next vaccine.) Samples of the chosen strains are delivered to pharmaceutical companies around the world for vaccine production, and the vaccines are hopefully available to the public by September or

October—a few months after influenza typically strikes Asia, in the early summer. Europe and the Americas are usually hit shortly after, in September. Because viruses constantly change themselves, the process cannot be executed earlier in the year.

Although new technology may allow an increase in production capacity, manufacturers have never made more than 300 million doses of flu vaccine in a single year. The slow pace of production means that in the event of an H5N1 flu pandemic millions of people would likely be infected well before vaccines could be distributed.

Global Reach

The scarcity of flu vaccine, although a serious problem, is actually of little relevance to most of the world. Even if pharmaceutical companies managed to produce enough effective vaccine in time to save some privileged lives in Europe, North America, Japan, and a few other wealthy nations, more than six billion people in developing countries would go unvaccinated. Stockpiles of Tamiflu and other anti-influenza drugs would also do nothing for those six billion, at least 30 percent of whom—and possibly half—would likely get infected in such a pandemic.

Resources are so scarce that both wealthy and poor countries would be foolish to count on the generosity of their neighbors during a global outbreak. Were the United States to miraculously overcome its vaccine production problems and produce ample supplies for U.S. citizens, Washington would probably deny the vaccine to neighbors such as Mexico, since governments tend to reserve vaccine supplies for their own citizens during emergencies. Were the United States to falter, it would probably not be able to rely on Canadian or European generosity, as it did just last year. When the United Kingdom suspended the license for the Chiron Corporation's U.K. production facility for flu vaccine due to contamination problems, Canada and Germany bailed the United States out, supplying additional doses until the French company Sanofi Pasteur could manufacture more. Even with this assistance, however, the United States' vaccine needs were not fully met until February 2005—the tail end of the flu season.

In the event of a deadly influenza pandemic, it is doubtful that any of the world's wealthy nations would be able to meet the needs of their own citizenry—much less those of other countries. Domestic vaccine purchasing and distribution schemes currently assume that only the very young, the elderly, and the immunocompromised are at serious risk of dying from the flu. That assumption would have led health leaders in 1918 to vaccinate all of the wrong people. Then, the young and the old fared relatively well, while those aged 20 to 35—today typically the lowest priority for vaccination—suffered the most deaths from the Spanish flu. And so far, H5N1 influenza looks like it could have a similar effect: its human victims have all fallen into age groups that would not be on national vaccine priority lists, and because H5N1 has never circulated among humans before, it is highly conceivable that all ages could be susceptible. Every year, trusting that the flu will kill only the usual risk groups, the United States plans for 185 million vaccine doses. If that guess were wrong—if all Americans were at risk—the nation would need at least 300 million doses. That is what the entire world typically produces each year.

There would thus be a global scramble for vaccine. Some governments might well block foreign access to supplies produced on their soil and bar vaccine export. Since little vaccine is actually made in the United States, this could prove a problem for Americans in particular. Facing such limited supplies, the U.S., European, and Japanese governments might give priority to vaccinating heads of state around the world in hopes of limiting social chaos. But who among the elite would be eligible? Would their families be included? How could such a global triage be executed justly?

A similar calculus might be necessary for countries engaged in significant military operations. Troop movements would certainly help spread the disease, just as World War I aided the growth of the 1918–19 Spanish flu. Back then, the flu wreaked havoc on combatant nations. In the summer of 1918, influenza killed far more soldiers than did bombs, bullets, or mustard gas. By October, some 46 percent of the French army was off the field of battle—ailing, dying, or caring for flu victims. Influenza death tolls among the various military forces generally ranged from 5 to 10 percent, but some segments fared even worse: historian John Barry has reported that 22 percent of the Indian members of the British military died.

In the event of a modern pandemic, the U.S. Department of Defense, with the lessons of World War I in mind, would undoubtedly insist that U.S. troops in Iraq and Afghanistan be given top access to vaccines and antiflu drugs. About 170,000 U.S. forces are currently stationed in Iraq and Afghanistan, while 200,000 more are permanently based elsewhere overseas. All of them would potentially be in danger: in late March, for example, North Korea conceded it was suffering a large-scale H7N1 outbreak—taking place within miles of some 41,000 U.S. military forces. It is impossible to predict how such a pandemic influenza would affect U.S. operations in Iraq, Afghanistan, Colombia, or any other place.

Armed forces throughout the world would face similar issues. Most would no doubt pressure their governments for preferential access to vaccine and medications. In addition, more than a quarter of some African armies and police forces are HIV positive, perhaps making them especially vulnerable to influenza's lethal impact. Social instability resulting from troop and police losses there would likely be particularly acute.

Such a devastating disease would clearly have profound implications for international relations and the global economy. With death tolls rising, vaccines and drugs in short supply, and the potential for the virus to spread further, governments would feel obliged to take drastic measures that could inhibit travel, limit worldwide trade, and alienate their neighbors. In fact, the z+ virus has already demonstrated its disruptive potential on a limited scale. In July 2004, for example, when the z+ strain reemerged in Vietnam after a three-month hiatus, officials in the northern province of Bac Giang charged that Chinese smugglers were selling old and sickly birds in Vietnamese markets—where more than ten tons of chickens are smuggled daily. Chinese authorities in charge of policing their side of the porous border, more than 1,000 kilometers long, countered that it was impossible to inspect all the shipments. Such conflicts are now limited to the movement of livestock, but if a pandemic develops they could well escalate to a ban on trade and human movement.

Although there is little evidence that isolation measures have ever slowed the spread of influenza—it is just too contagious—most governments would likely resort to quarantines in a pandemic crisis. Indeed, on April 1, 2005, President George W. Bush issued an executive order authorizing the use of quarantines inside the United States and permitting the isolation of international visitors suspected of carrying influenza. If one country implements such orders, others will follow suit, bringing legal international travel to a standstill. The SARS (severe acute respiratory syndrome) virus, which was less dangerous than a pandemic flu by several orders of magnitude, virtually shut down Asian travel for three months.

As great as they would be, the economic consequences of travel restrictions, quarantines, and medical care would be well outstripped by productivity losses. In a typical flu season, productivity costs are ten times greater than all other flu-related costs combined. The decline in productivity is usually due directly to worker illness and absenteeism. During a pandemic, productivity losses would be even more disproportionate because entire workplaces—schools, theaters, and public facilities—would be shut down to limit human-to-human spread of the virus. Workers' illnesses also would likely be even more severe and last even longer than normal. Frankly, no models of social response to such a pandemic have managed to factor in fully the potential effect on human productivity. It is therefore impossible to reckon accurately the potential global economic impact.

Ailing

The potential for a pandemic comes at a time when the world's public health systems are severely taxed and have long been in decline. This is true in both rich and poor countries.

The Bush administration recognized this weakness following the anthrax scare of 2001, which underscored the poor ability of federal and local health agencies to respond to bioterrorism or epidemic threats. Since that year, Congress has approved $3.7 billion to strengthen the nation's public health infrastructure. In 2003, the White House also took several steps to improve the nation's capacity to respond to a flu pandemic: it increased funding for the CDC's flu program by 242 percent, to $41.6 million in 2004; gave the National Institutes of Health an additional 320 percent in funds for flu-related research and development, for a total of $65.9 million; increased spending on the Food and Drug Administration's licensing capacity for flu vaccines and drugs by 173 percent, to $2.6 million; and spent an additional $80 million to create new stockpiles of Tamiflu and other anti-influenza drugs. On August 4, 2004, the Department of Health and Human Services also issued its pandemic flu plan, detailing further steps that would be taken by federal and state agencies in the event of a pandemic. Several other countries have released similar plans of action.

But despite all this, a recent event underscored the United States' tremendous vulnerability. In October 2004, the American College of Pathologists mailed a collection of mystery microbes prepared by a private lab to almost 5,000 labs in 18 countries for them to test as part their recertification. The mailing should have been routine procedure; instead, in March 2005 a Canadian lab discovered that the test kits included a sample of H2N2 flu—a strain that had killed four million people worldwide in 1957. H2N2 has not been in circulation since 1968, meaning that hundreds of millions of people lack immunity to it. Had any of the samples leaked or been exposed to the environment, the results could have been devastating. On learning of the error, the WHO called for the immediate destruction of all the test kits. Miraculously, none of the virus managed to escape any of the labs.

But the snafu raises serious questions: If billions have been spent to improve laboratory capabilities since 2001, why did nobody notice the H2N2 flu until about six months after the kits had been shipped? Why did a private company possess samples of the virulent flu? Why was the sample included in the kits? In the aftermath of the September 11, 2001, attacks and the anthrax scare, many countries reclassified 1957–58 and 1968–69 influenza strains as Level 3 pathogens, requiring extreme care in their handling, distribution, and storage—why did the United States still consider H2N2 to be a mere Level 2 pathogen, a type frequently mailed and studied? Finally, around the world, what other labs—public and private—currently possess samples of such lethal influenza viruses? The official CDC answer to these questions is, "We don't know."

Even with all of these gaps, probably the greatest weakness that each nation must individually address is the inability of their hospitals to cope with a sudden surge of new patients. Medical cost cutting has resulted in a tremendous reduction in the numbers of staffed hospital beds in the wealthy world, especially in the United States. Even during a normal flu season, hospitals located in popular retirement areas have great difficulty meeting the demand. In a pandemic, it is doubtful that any nation would have adequate medical facilities and personnel to meet the extra need.

National policymakers would be wise to plan now for worst-case scenarios involving quarantines, weakened armed services, and dwindling hospital space and vaccine supplies. But at the end of the day, effectively combating influenza will require multilateral and global mechanisms. Chief among them, of course, is the WHO, which since 1947 has maintained a worldwide network that conducts influenza surveillance. The WHO system oversees laboratories all over the world, chases (and sometimes refutes) rumors of pandemics, pushes for government transparency regarding human and avian flu cases, and acts as an arbiter in negotiations over vaccine production, trade embargoes, and border disputes. Its companion UN agency, the Food and Agriculture Organization (FAO), working closely with the World Organization for Animal Health, monitors flu outbreaks in animal populations and advises governments on culling flocks and herds, cross-border animal trade, animal husbandry and slaughter, and livestock quarantine and vaccination. All of these organizations have published lengthy guidelines on how to respond to a pandemic flu, lists of answers to commonly asked questions, and descriptions of their research priorities—most of which have been posted on their Web sites.

The efforts of these agencies should be bolstered, both with expertise and dollars. The WHO, for example, has an annual core budget of just $400 million, a tiny increment of which is spent on influenza- and epidemic-response programs. (In comparison, the annual budget of New York City's health department exceeds $1.2 billion.) An unpublished internal study estimates that the agency would require at least another $600 million for its flu program were a pandemic to erupt. It is in every government's interest to give the WHO and the FAO the authority to act as impartial voices during a pandemic, able (theoretically) to assess objectively the epidemic's progress and rapidly evaluate research claims. The WHO in particular must have adequate funding and personnel to serve as an accurate clearinghouse of information about the disease, thereby preventing the spread of false rumors and global panic. No nation can erect a fortress against influenza—not even the world's wealthiest country.

Few members of the U.S. Congress or its legislative counterparts around the world were alive when the great Spanish flu swept the planet. There may be some who lost parents, aunts, or uncles to the 1918–19 pandemic, and perhaps even more have heard the horror stories that were passed down. But politics breeds shortsightedness, and for decades the threat of an influenza pandemic has been easily forgotten, and therefore ignored at budget time. Politicians and health leaders made many serious errors in 1918–19; some historians say that President Wilson sent 43,000 soldiers to their deaths by forcing them aboard crowded ships to join a war he had already won. But in those days, human beings had no understanding of their influenza foe.

In 1971, the great American public health leader Alexander Langmuir likened flu forecasting to trying to predict the weather, arguing that "as with hurricanes, pandemics can be identified and their probable course projected so that warnings can be issued. Epidemics, however, are more variable [than hurricanes], and the best that can be done is to estimate probabilities."

Since Langmuir's time a quarter of a century ago, weather forecasting has gained a stunning level of precision. And although scientists cannot tell political leaders when an influenza pandemic will occur, researchers today are able to guide policymakers with information and analysis exponentially richer than that which informed the decisions of President Ford and the 1976 Congress. Whether or not this particular H5N1 influenza mutates into a human-to-human pandemic form, the scientific evidence points to the potential that such an event will take place, perhaps soon. Those responsible for foreign policy and national security, the world over, cannot afford to ignore the warning.

AMARTYA SEN

UNIVERSAL TRUTHS: HUMAN RIGHTS AND THE WESTERNIZING ILLUSION

My students seem to be very concerned and also very divided on how to approach the difficult subject of human rights in non-Western societies. Is it right, the question is often asked, that non-Western societies should be encouraged and pressed to conform to "Western values of liberty and freedom"? Is this not cultural imperialism? The notion of human rights builds on the idea of a shared humanity. These rights are not derived from citizenship of any country, or membership of any nation, but taken as entitlements of every human being. The concept of universal human rights is, in this sense, a uniting idea. Yet the subject of human rights has ended up being a veritable battleground of political debates and ethical disputes, particularly in their application to non-Western societies. Why so?

A Clash of Cultures?

The explanation for this is sometimes sought in the cultural differences that allegedly divide the world, a theory referred to as the "clash of civilizations" or a "battle between cultures." It is often asserted that Western countries recognize many human rights, related for example to political liberty, that have no great appeal in Asian countries. Many people see a big divide here. The temptation

From *Harvard International Review* 20, no. 3 (summer 1998): 40–43. This article is a revised version of the Commencement Address given at Bard College on May 24, 1997. Related arguments were presented in Professor Sen's Morgenthau Memorial Lecture ("Human Rights and Asian Values") at the Carnegie Council on Ethics and International Affairs on May 1, 1997, and published by the Carnegie Council.

to think in these regional and cultural terms is extremely strong in the contemporary world.

Are there really such firm differences on this subject in terms of traditions and cultures across the world? It is certainly true that governmental spokesmen in several Asian countries have not only disputed the relevance and cogency of universal human rights, they have frequently done this disputing in the name of "Asian values," as a contrast with Western values. The claim is that in the system of so-called Asian values, for example in the Confucian system, there is greater emphasis on order and discipline, and less on rights and freedoms.

Many Asian spokesmen have gone on to argue that the call for universal acceptance of human rights reflects the imposition of Western values on other cultures. For example, the censorship of the press may be more acceptable, it is argued, in Asian society because of its greater emphasis on discipline and order. This position was powerfully articulated by a number of governmental spokesmen from Asia at the Vienna Conference on Human Rights in 1993. Some positive things happened at that conference, including the general acceptance of the importance of eliminating economic deprivation and some recognition of social responsibility in this area. But on the subject of political and civil rights the conference split through the middle, largely on regional lines, with several Asian governments rejecting the recognition of basic political and civil rights. In this argument, the rhetoric of "Asian values" and their differences from Western priorities played an important part.

If one influence in separating out human rights as specifically "Western" comes from the pleading of governmental spokesmen from Asia, another influence relates to the way this issue is perceived in the West itself. There is a tendency in Europe and the United States to assume, if only implicitly, that it is in the West—and only in the West—that human rights have been valued from ancient times. This allegedly unique feature of Western civilization has been, it is assumed, an alien concept elsewhere. By stressing regional and cultural specificities, these Western theories of the origin of human rights tend to reinforce, rather inadvertently, the disputation of universal human rights in non-Western societies. By arguing that the valuing of toleration, of personal liberty, and of civil rights is a particular contribution of Western civilization, Western advocates of these rights often give ammunition to the non-Western critics of human rights. The advocacy of an allegedly "alien" idea in non-Western societies can indeed look like cultural imperialism sponsored by the West.

Modernity as Tradition

How much truth is there in this grand cultural dichotomy between Western and. non-Western civilizations on the subject of liberty and rights? I believe there is rather little sense in such a grand dichotomy. Neither the claims in favor of the specialness of "Asian values" by governmental spokesmen from Asia, nor the particular claims for the uniqueness of "Western values" by spokesmen from Europe and America can survive much historical examination and critical scrutiny.

In seeing Western civilization as the natural habitat of individual freedom and political democracy, there is a tendency to extrapolate backwards from the present. Values that the European Enlightenment and other recent developments since the eighteenth century have made common and widespread are often seen, quite arbitrarily, as part of the long-run Western heritage, experienced in the West over millennia. The concept of universal human rights in the broad general sense of entitlements of every human being is really a relatively new idea, not to

be much found either in the ancient West or in ancient civilizations elsewhere.

There are, however, other ideas, such as the value of toleration, or the importance of individual freedom, which have been advocated and defended for a long time, often for the selected few. For example, Aristotle's writings on freedom and human flourishing provide good background material for the contemporary ideas of human rights. But there are other Western philosophers (Plato and St. Augustine, for example) whose preference for order and discipline over freedom was no less pronounced than Confucius' priorities. Also, even those in the West who did emphasize the value of freedom did not, typically, see this as a fight of all human beings. Aristotle's exclusion of women and slaves is a good illustration of this nonuniversality. The defenses of individual freedom in Western tradition did exist but took a limited and contingent form.

Confucius and Co.

Do we find similar pronouncements in favor of individual freedom in non-Western traditions, particularly in Asia? The answer is emphatically yes. Confucius is not the only philosopher in Asia, not even in China. There is much variety in Asian intellectual traditions, and many writers did emphasize the importance of freedom and tolerance, and some even saw this as the entitlement of every human being. The language of freedom is very important, for example, in Buddhism, which originated and first flourished in South Asia and then spread to Southeast Asia and East Asia, including China, Japan, Korea, and Thailand. In this context it is important to recognize that Buddhist philosophy not only emphasized freedom as a form of life but also gave it a political content. To give just one example, the Indian emperor Ashoka in the third century BCE presented many political inscriptions in favor of tolerance and individual freedom, both as a part of state policy and in the relation of different people to each other. The domain of toleration,

Ashoka argued, must include everybody without exception.

Even the portrayal of Confucius as an unmitigated authoritarian is far from convincing. Confucius did believe in order, but he did not recommend blind allegiance to the state. When Zilu asks him how to serve a prince, Confucius replies, "Tell him the truth even if it offends him"—a policy recommendation that may encounter some difficulty in contemporary Singapore or Beijing. Of course, Confucius was a practical man, and he did not recommend that we foolhardily oppose established power. He did emphasize practical caution and tact, but also insisted on the importance of opposition. "When the [good] Way prevails in the state, speak boldly and act boldly. When the state has lost the Way, act boldly and speak softly," he said.

The main point to note is that both Western and non-Western traditions have much variety within themselves. Both in Asia and in the West, some have emphasized order and discipline, even as others have focused on freedom and tolerance. The idea of human rights as an entitlement of every human being, with an unqualified universal scope and highly articulated structure, is really a recent development; in this demanding form it is not an ancient idea either in the West or elsewhere. But there are limited and qualified defenses of freedom and tolerance, and general arguments against censorship, that can be found both in ancient traditions in the West and in cultures of non-Western societies.

Islam and Tolerance

Special questions are often raised about the Islamic tradition. Because of the experience of contemporary political battles, especially in the Middle East, the Islamic civilization is often portrayed as being fundamentally intolerant and hostile to individual freedom. But the presence of diversity and variety within a tradition applies very much to Islam as well. The Turkish emperors were often more tolerant than their European contemporaries. The Mughal emperors in India, with one exception, were not only extremely tolerant, but some even theorized about the need for tolerating diversity. The pronouncements of Akbar, the great Mughal emperor in sixteenth century India, on tolerance can count among the classics of political pronouncements, and would have received more attention in the West had Western political historians taken as much interest in Eastern thought as they do in their own intellectual background. For comparison, I should mention that the Inquisitions were still in full bloom in Europe as Akbar was making it a state policy to tolerate and protect all religious groups.

A Jewish scholar like Maimonides in the twelfth century had to run away from an intolerant Europe and from its persecution of Jews for the security offered by a tolerant Cairo and the patronage of Sultan Saladin. Alberuni, the Iranian mathematician, who wrote the first general book on India in the early eleventh century, aside from translating Indian mathematical treatises into Arabic, was among the earliest of anthropological theorists in the world. He noted and protested against the fact that "depreciation of foreigners . . . is common to all nations towards each other." He devoted much of his life to fostering mutual understanding and tolerance in his eleventh-century world.

Authority and Dissidence

The recognition of diversity within different cultures is extremely important in the contemporary world, since we are constantly bombarded by oversimplified generalizations about "Western civilization, . . . Asian values," "African cultures," and so on. These unfounded readings of history and civilization are not only intellectually shallow, they also add to the divisiveness of the world in which we live. Boorishness begets violence.